February 24–26, 2019
Seaside, CA, USA

I0047358

Association for Computing Machinery

Advancing Computing as a Science & Profession

FPGA'19

Proceedings of the 2019 ACM/SIGDA International Symposium on
Field-Programmable Gate Arrays

Sponsored by:
ACM SIGDA

Supported by:
Trimberger Family Foundation, Xilinx, Intel, Achronix, Lattice Semiconductor, Huawei, Aldec, Two Sigma, and Microchip

Association for Computing Machinery

Advancing Computing as a Science & Profession

The Association for Computing Machinery
2 Penn Plaza, Suite 701
New York, New York 10121-0701

ISBN: 978-1-4503-6137-8 (Digital)

ISBN: 978-1-4503-6739-4 (Print)

Additional copies may be ordered prepaid from:

ACM Order Department
PO Box 30777
New York, NY 10087-0777, USA

Phone: 1-800-342-6626 (USA and Canada)
+1-212-626-0500 (Global)
Fax: +1-212-944-1318
E-mail: acmhelp@acm.org
Hours of Operation: 8:30 am – 4:30 pm ET

FPGA 2019 Chairs' Welcome

We are delighted to welcome you to the 2019 ACM International Symposium on Field-Programmable Gate Arrays (ACM FPGA 2019). ACM FPGA is the premiere forum for the presentation of new and exciting research on all aspects of FPGA technology, which include:

- Novel FPGA architectures and circuits.
- Advances in CAD tools for FPGAs, in areas such as technology mapping, placement, routing, and others.
- High-level design methodologies that permit FPGA design at higher levels of abstraction.
- New applications for FPGAs, particularly for energy efficient and high performance computation.

Aside from the technical sessions, the conference provides the opportunity for FPGA researchers and practitioners from around the world to network with long-time friends and make new connections in a beautiful setting. This year the conference venue has moved a short distance to Seaside, California, but remains close to the spectacular coastline of the Monterey Bay and the attractions in the cities of Monterey and Pacific Beach.

This year the program committee received 161 paper submissions, of which 139 papers met submission guidelines and were reviewed. This represents an increase of almost 40% from last year. As a result, we've extended the conference program to 3 full days, consisting of 24 full research papers (10 pages), 6 short research papers (6 pages), and 2 peer-reviewed tutorials (10 pages). Overall 23% of reviewed papers were accepted. 63 submissions were selected to be presented as posters and appear in these proceedings in abstract form. In addition, 3 invited tutorials will also be presented, with accompanying material published in the proceedings.

At FPGA 2019, we continue to see a huge interest in using FPGAs for Machine Learning, particularly for efficient inference of Deep Neural Networks. This year over 40% of submissions were related to Machine Learning. Invited industry keynotes and tutorials will highlight new tools and architectures for maximizing the efficiency of Deep Neural Networks. The field of deep learning continues to change rapidly and FPGAs seem well positioned for many new applications, in both data center and in embedded environments.

The other big trend for FPGAs in the past year has been towards widespread deployment in data centers, with almost all major data center providers enabling access to FPGAs-as-a-Service. At the same time, CPUs and GPUs continue to dominate Supercomputer deployments. The panel discussion, at the Monday evening banquet, will consider whether FPGAs can impact other high performance computing applications. The panel will include representatives from the FPGA and Supercomputing communities. We expect a lively exchange among the panelists!

We would like to thank the members of the Program Committee and secondary reviewers, whose names appear on the following pages, for devoting considerable time and effort evaluating the submissions and providing thoughtful feedback to the authors. We would like to thank Prof. Deming Chen from the University of Illinois for moderating the panel session. Special thanks to Lisa Tolles, Mikaela Brunstetter, Joanne Lateulere and John Lateulere for logistical support, and our sponsors for making FPGA 2019 possible.

Welcome to ACM FPGA 2019!

Stephen Neuendorffer
Program Chair
Xilinx, USA

Kia Bazargan
General Chair
University of Minnesota, USA

Table of Contents

Session 3: Computing Architectures

Poster Session 1

Tutorial 2

Panel

Tutorial 3

Session 6: Networks and NOCs

Session 7: Heterogenous Platforms

Session 8: Devices and Security

Poster Session 3

Session 9: Memory

FPGA 2019 Organization

General Chair:
Kia Bazargan,
Univ. of Minnesota,
USA

Program Chair:
Stephen
Neuendorffer, Xilinx,
USA

Finance Chair:
Jason H. Anderson,
Univ. of Toronto,
Canada

Publicity Chair:
Jing Li,
Univ. of Wisconsin,
USA

Program Committee:

Michael Adler,
Intel,
USA

Jason H. Anderson,
Univ. of Toronto,
Canada

Aydin Aysu,
North Carolina
State Univ.,
USA

Trevor Bauer,
Xilinx,
USA

Kia Bazargan,
Univ. of Minnesota,
USA

Vaughn Betz,
Univ. of Toronto,
Canada

Michaela Blott,
Xilinx,
Ireland

Eli Bozorgzadeh,
Univ. of California,
Irvine,
USA

Philip Brisk,
Univ. of California,
Riverside,
USA

Deming Chen,
UIUC,
USA

Peter Cheung,
Imperial College
London,
United Kingdom

Derek Chiou,
Microsoft/UT
Austin,
USA

Paul Chow,
Univ. of Toronto,
Canada

Eric Chung,
Microsoft Research,
USA

Jason Cong,
UCLA,
USA

George
Constantinides,
Imperial College
London,
United Kingdom

Sabya Das,
Synopsys Inc,
USA

James Davis,
Imperial College
London,
United Kingdom

Azadeh Davoodi,
Univ. of
Wisconsin -
Madison,
USA

Carl Ebeling,
Univ. of
Washington,
USA

Hadi
Esmaeilzadeh,
Univ. of
California, San
Diego,
USA

Suhaib A. Fahmy,
Univ. of Warwick,
United Kingdom

Wenyi Feng,
Microchip
Corporation,
USA

Dinesh Gaitonde,
Xilinx,
USA

Ilya Ganusov,
Intel,
USA

Jeffrey Goeders,
Brigham Young
Univ.,
USA

Jonathan Greene,
Microsemi,
USA

James C. Hoe,
Carnegie Mellon
Univ.,
USA

Brad Hutchings,
BYU,
USA

Mike Hutton,
Google,
USA

Paolo Ienne,
EPFL,
Switzerland

Mahesh Iyer,
Intel Corporation,
USA

Nachiket Kapre,
Univ. of Waterloo,
Canada

Sinan Kaptanoglu,
Microsemi Fellow,
USA

Vinod Kathail,
Xilinx,
USA

Alireza Kaviani,
Xilinx,
USA

Martin
Langhammer,
Intel,
United Kingdom

Miriam Leeser,
Northeastern
Univ.,
USA

Philip Leong,
The Univ. of
Sydney,
Australia

Jing Li,
Univ. of
Wisconsin-
Madison,
USA

Michael Wirthlin,
Brigham Young
Univ.,
USA

Grace Zgheib,
Ecole
Polytechnique
Federale de
Lausanne (EPFL),
Switzerland

Wei Zhang,
Hong Kong Univ.
of Science and
Technology,
Hong Kong
Special
Administrative
Region of China

Zhiru Zhang,
Cornell Univ.,
USA

Additional Reviewers:

Mohamed Abdelfattah
Mikhail Asiatici
Gregg Baeckler
Kalen Brunham
Jing Chen
Young-kyu Choi
Aravind Dasu
Ashutosh Dhar
Shounak Dhar
Roberto DiCecco
Anuj Dubey
Sean Fox
Hasan Nazim Genc
Cong Hao
Jenny Huang
Sitao Huang

Lana Josipovic
Li Jun
Parivallal Kannan
Yi-Hsiang Lai
Xinheng Liu
Charles Lo
Jason Luu
Pongstorn Maidee
Ian McInerney
Ben Morcos
Duncan Moss
Tan Nguyen
Alessandro Pappalardo
Lucian Petrica
Arzhang Rafii
SeyedRamin Rasoulinezhad

Daniel Rozhko
Varun Sharma
Love Singhal
Nish Sinnadurai
Mirjana Stojilovi
Hsin-yu Ting
Yaman Umuroglu
Stelios Venieris
Erwei Wang
Christopher Yarp
Mang Yu
Boyu Zhang
Jialiang Zhang
Xiaofan Zhang
Yuan Zhou
Wei Zuo

FPGA 2019 Sponsors and Corporate Patrons

Sponsors:

Logistics Support:

sig da (acm)

Trimberger Family Foundation

Gold Corporate Patrons:

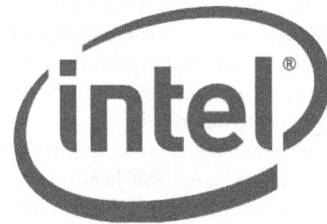

XILINX.

intel

Silver Corporate Patrons:

LATTICE SEMICONDUCTOR.

2σ TWO SIGMA

Achronix

ALDEC. THE DESIGN VERIFICATION COMPANY

MICROCHIP

HUAWEI

The P4→NetFPGA Workflow for Line-Rate Packet Processing

Stephen Ibanez
Stanford University
sibanez@stanford.edu

Gordon Brebner
Xilinx Labs
gjb@xilinx.com

Nick McKeown
Stanford University
nickm@stanford.edu

Noa Zilberman
University of Cambridge
noa.zilberman@cl.cam.ac.uk

ABSTRACT

P4 has emerged as the *de facto* standard language for describing how network packets should be processed, and is becoming widely used by network owners, systems developers, researchers and in the classroom. The goal of the work presented here is to make it easier for engineers, researchers and students to learn how to program using P4, and to build prototypes running on real hardware. Our target is the NetFPGA SUME platform, a 4×10 Gb/s PCIe card designed for use in universities for teaching and research. Until now, NetFPGA users have needed to learn an HDL such as Verilog or VHDL, making it off limits to many software developers and students. Therefore, we developed the P4→NetFPGA workflow, allowing developers to describe how packets are to be processed in the high-level P4 language, then compile their P4 programs to run at line rate on the NetFPGA SUME board. The P4→NetFPGA workflow is built upon the Xilinx P4-SDNet compiler and the NetFPGA SUME open source code base. In this paper, we provide an overview of the P4 programming language and describe the P4→NetFPGA workflow. We also describe how the workflow is being used by the P4 community to build research prototypes, and to teach how network systems are built by providing students with hands-on experience working with real hardware.

CCS CONCEPTS

• **Networks** → **Programming interfaces**; • **Hardware** → **Networking hardware**;

ACM Reference Format:
Stephen Ibanez, Gordon Brebner, Nick McKeown, and Noa Zilberman. 2019. The P4→NetFPGA Workflow for Line-Rate Packet Processing. In *The 2019 ACM/SIGDA International Symposium on Field-Programmable Gate Arrays (FPGA '19), February 24–26, 2019, Seaside, CA, USA.* ACM, New York, NY, USA, 9 pages. https://doi.org/10.1145/3289602.3293924

1 INTRODUCTION

Networking switches, routers, and network interface cards (NICs) have traditionally been dominated by ASICs that process packets using a *fixed function* pipeline. While some programmable devices are used (e.g. NPUs [23], FPGAs [38], CPUs [30]), conventional wisdom in networking states that programmable forwarding devices are slower, more expensive and consume more power. However, this is

being challenged by a new breed of programmable switches and NICs matching the performance, power and cost of fixed-function devices [7, 8, 25]. Network system designers are exploiting the programmability to add new features to the forwarding plane, including telemetry [19], layer-4 load balancing [21], encryption, and in-network caching [16].

With various programmable forwarding devices now available, what high-level language should be used to program them? This was the motivation for the creation of the P4 language [4], which in recent years has become the first *de facto* language for programming forwarding devices.

The P4 language was designed with three goals in mind:

- Protocol independence — network devices should not be hard coded to support specific protocols.
- Field reconfigurability — programmers should be able to change the fundamental packet processing behavior of network devices after they have been deployed.
- Portability — packet processing programs should not be tied to a specific device.

There are many benefits to using P4 for programming network devices. Network operators can easily add support for new features into their network devices. Programmers can remove the features that they are not using in order to reduce complexity in their networks. Oftentimes network failures are caused by interactions between protocols that network operators do not even know they are using. The memory and compute resources within network devices can be flexibly allocated amongst the desired features. Programmable data planes are also bringing about much greater visibility into the network as new diagnostic techniques start to emerge, such as In-band Network Telemetry (INT) [19]. The P4 programming model brings with it a software-style development process which enables a rapid design cycle, fast innovation, and the ability to fix data plane bugs in the field. Additionally, network operators are able to keep their own ideas because they do not need to share their P4 programs with anyone. Hence, companies are able to maintain a competitive advantage.

An FPGA-familiar reader will recognize that the benefits of P4 described above directly intersect with benefits of using programmable hardware such as FPGAs. So one question that directly follows from this observation is why FPGAs, and HDLs such as Verilog or generic high-level synthesis, are not just used to implement all network devices. One of the reasons is because of the performance gap between FPGAs and ASICs. While the performance gap has decreased in recent years, top of the line ASICs can still process packets about an order of magnitude faster than top of the line FPGAs [12]. Another reason is because the steep learning curve that is required to program FPGAs using hardware description languages hinders the ability of network programmers to implement new features rapidly. Notwithstanding this, many network devices are in fact implemented using FPGAs, especially network interface cards [12], but typically the implementation has to be done by hardware experts.

Operating at a higher level of domain-specific abstraction, the P4 language identifies the key primitives that are used to build packet processing devices. P4 programs can then be compiled onto any device that supports the language's underlying primitives, including high speed packet processing ASICs [25], NPUs [24], software switches running on CPUs [33], and FPGAs [38].

The need to enable the programming of FPGAs using P4 therefore has a twofold motivation:

- Operators want to have a standard way to configure the behavior of their network devices, in order to ease the burden of managing networks. The industry is converging on using P4 for this purpose, and hence packet processing FPGAs within such devices must become P4 programmable.
- FPGAs are a useful platform on which to prototype P4 designs at hardware line rates that may later be deployed on other network devices with more customized hardware.

The P4 community has produced an open source software emulation environment [28], which has proved to be an extremely useful tool that developers can use to prototype P4 applications. However, this software platform has some significant limitations; most notable is the limited performance which makes it impossible for developers to gauge how their application will perform in a realistic environment. Furthermore, the software target is very flexible and does not realistically capture the constraints of an actual hardware implementation. For these reasons, we believe the P4 community can embrace FPGAs as the basis of an open source hardware environment to resolve these difficulties. In particular, this paper adopts the existing open source NetFPGA family as the hardware platform for research and development of P4 programs. The NetFPGA platform is a low-cost, open-source, FPGA-based networking device, which has been specifically designed for teaching and research.

This paper provides a tutorial introduction to the P4→NetFPGA workflow:

- We provide an overview of the P4 language (Section 2), P4-SDNet (Section 3) and the NetFPGA platform (Section 4).
- We describe the main new contribution which ties these components together: the open source P4→NetFPGA workflow (Section 5), its building blocks, and its operation.
- We discuss use cases of the P4→NetFPGA workflow in research and teaching (Section 6) and its future roadmap (Section 7).
- Finally, we provide information on how to get started immediately on using the P4→NetFPGA workflow (Section 9).

2 P4 LANGUAGE OVERVIEW

This section provides a brief overview of the P4 programming language. The goal is not to provide a comprehensive description, but rather just enough detail for a reader to grasp the fundamental concepts.

Figure 1 depicts the general process of programming a P4 device. The vendor of a packet processing device provides three components to the user:

- The packet processing target device.
- A P4 architecture model to expose the programmable features of the target to the P4 programmer.
- A compiler to map the user's P4 program into a target-specific configuration binary file which is used to tell the target how it should be configured to process packets.

The user provides a P4 main program to instantiate the architecture model, by filling in its programmable components. The user also provides control software (i.e. a control plane) which is responsible for controlling the packet processing device at run time.

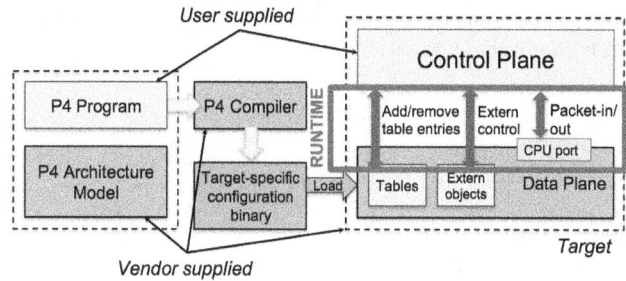

Figure 1: The process of programming a P4 target.

In order to make network devices protocol independent, i.e. without built-in implementations of specific protocols, P4 programmers define the format of all protocol headers that they want the device to handle. Here is an example that shows how a programmer might define the Ethernet and IPv4 headers. Note that typedef statements can be used to make the code more readable.

```
typedef bit<48> macAddr_t;
typedef bit<32> ip4Addr_t;
header ethernet_t {
    macAddr_t dstAddr;
    macAddr_t srcAddr;
    bit<16>   etherType;
}
header ipv4_t {
    bit<4>    version;
    bit<4>    ihl;
    bit<8>    diffserv;
    bit<16>   totalLen;
    bit<16>   identification;
    bit<3>    flags;
    bit<13>   fragOffset;
    bit<8>    ttl;
    bit<8>    protocol;
    bit<16>   hdrChecksum;
    ip4Addr_t srcAddr;
    ip4Addr_t dstAddr;
}
struct headers {
    ethernet_t  ethernet;
    ipv4_t      ipv4;
}
```

A P4 architecture model can contain P4-programmable elements of two types: parsers and control blocks. Parsers are responsible for extracting headers out of an incoming stream of bytes. They are implemented as a finite state machine with three predefined states: start, accept, and reject. An implementation may also contain other user defined states. Parsers always start in the start state, execute one or more statements, then transition to the next state until reaching either the accept or reject state.

Below is an example implementation of a P4 parser. In this simple example, the parser first uses the packet_in object's extract method to fill out the fields of the Ethernet header. It then transitions to either the parse_ipv4 state or the accept state based on the value of the Ethernet header's etherType field. Within the parse_ipv4 state, the parser simply extracts the IPv4 header and then transitions to accept.

```
parser MyParser(packet_in packet,
                out headers hdr) {
  state start {
    packet.extract(hdr.ethernet);
    transition select(hdr.ethernet.etherType) {
      0x800  : parse_ipv4;
      default: accept;
    }
  }
  state parse_ipv4 {
    packet.extract(hdr.ipv4);
    transition accept;
  }
}
```

Control blocks can be used to represent both match-action packet processing logic as well as packet deparsers. A match-action processing block uses tables, actions, and imperative code to manipulate input headers and metadata. This match-action packet processing model was originally introduced as the centerpiece of the OpenFlow model for Software Defined Networking (SDN) [20].

When a P4 programmer defines a match-action table, they declare various properties such as the header and/or metadata field(s) to match upon, the type of match to be performed, a list of all possible actions that can be invoked, the number of entries to allocate for the table, and a default action to invoke if no match is found. A table entry contains a specific key to match on, a single action to invoke when the entry produces a match, and any data to provide to the action when it is invoked. Table entries are populated at run time by the control plane software.

The following is an example p4 match-action control block implementation and Table 1 shows how the forward table might be populated. This simple example will forward all IPv4 packets that arrive on port 1 to port 2; and all IPv4 packets that arrive on port 2 to port 1. All other packets will be dropped.

Table 1: Example entries for the forward table.

Key	Action ID	Action Data
1	set_output_port ID	2
2	set_output_port ID	1

```
control MyMatchAction(inout headers hdr,
                      inout std_meta_t std_meta) {
  action set_output_port(bit<8> port) {
    std_meta.output_port = port;
  }
  action mark_to_drop() {
    std_meta.drop = 1;
  }
  table forward {
    key = { std_meta.ingress_port: exact; }
    actions = {
      set_output_port;
      mark_to_drop;
    }
    size = 1024;
    default_action = mark_to_drop();
  }
  apply {
    if (hdr.ipv4.isValid()) {
      forward.apply();
    } else {
      mark_to_drop();
    }
  }
}
```

Deparsers are special cases of control blocks that perform the inverse operation of parsers. Their job is to reassemble the packet headers onto an outgoing packet byte stream. A header is added to the packet using the packet_out object's emit method. Deparsing is implemented using the P4 control block mechanism because it only involves sequential logic as used for actions. Below is an example deparser implementation: it simply reinserts the Ethernet and IPv4 headers back into the packet.

```
control MyDeparser(packet_out packet,
                   in headers hdr) {
  apply {
    packet.emit(hdr.ethernet);
    packet.emit(hdr.ipv4);
  }
}
```

In addition to defining the interfaces of all parser and control blocks, a P4 architecture definition also defines the format of any standard metadata buses as well as the set of externs that can be invoked within P4 programs. Standard metadata buses, conveying sideband data alongside each packet, are used to allow P4-programmable elements to interact with non-programmable elements within the architecture. Externs are used to execute device specific logic; their implementation is not described in P4 and programs only see the inputs and outputs.

3 XILINX P4-SDNET OVERVIEW

The Xilinx SDNet product was originally built as a design environment centered around an internally-created packet processing language called PX [5], which pre-dated P4 by a number of years. The goals and capabilities of PX and P4 intersect in many — indeed most — ways. As the networking community has converged on using P4 as the standard language, Xilinx has embraced the change and, in the first instance, added a P4 to PX translator to the SDNet design environment. Figure 2 depicts the process of compiling P4 programs using this version of SDNet. The front end translator maps P4 programs into corresponding PX programs and also produces a JSON file with information about the design that is required by the runtime control software. The PX program is passed, along with configuration parameters, into SDNet which then produces an HDL module that implements the user's P4 program. Relative to hand-optimized RTL designs, the result produced by SDNet is generally within about 2x the logic and memory resource utilization. Additionally, SDNet generated designs can be configured to process packets at line rates between 1 and 400 Gb/s. SDNet also produces a SystemVerilog simulation testbench, C drivers to configure the PX tables, and an optional C++ model of the PX program to be used for debugging purposes. Recognizing the momentum behind P4, the next (2019) generation of SDNet provides a native P4 compiler, without the intermediate step via PX. This provides substantial improvements in packet processing pipeline latency, and in FPGA resource use.

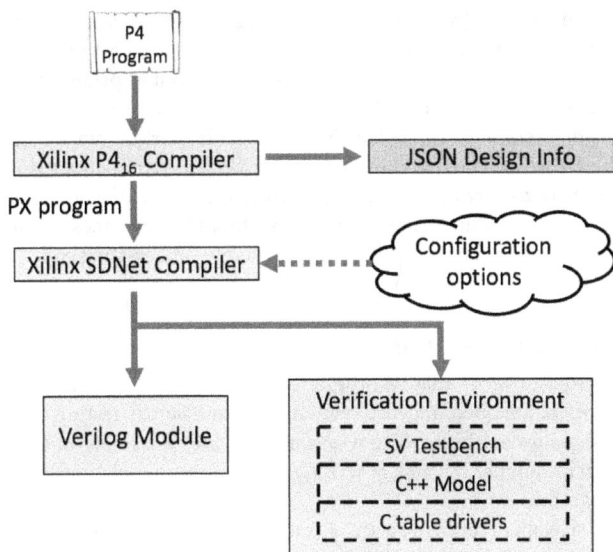

Figure 2: The Xilinx P4-SDNet compilation flow. P4 programs are first translated into a PX program, which is then compiled into a Verilog module using the SDNet flow. SDNet also produces a verification environment.

4 NETFPGA OVERVIEW

The NetFPGA project is a teaching and research tool, designed to allow packets to be processed at line-rate in programmable hardware. The NetFPGA project consists of four elements: boards, tools and reference designs, a community of developers, and contributed projects. The NetFPGA hardware family consists of three generations of FPGA-based networking boards; the latest is the SUME board [39] which has total I/O capacity of 100 Gb/s. All of the

NetFPGA boards are designed with a PCIe connector so that networking software running on a host machine is able to interact with the FPGA accelerated packet processing logic. All of the code and documentation is openly hosted on GitHub [22].

Figure 3 depicts a block diagram of the canonical NetFPGA reference design. A similar design is used for NICs, switches, and IPv4 routers. It consists of four 10G SFP+ input/output ports along with one DMA interface for the CPU path. The NetFPGA data path consists of three main components: Input Arbiter, Output Port Lookup, and Output Queues. The Input Arbiter admits packets from the ports into the data path, towards the Output Port Lookup Module, where the main packet processing occurs and an output port is selected. The Output Queues buffer packets while they wait to be sent to the outputs. The core data path uses a 256-bit wide bus and runs at 200 MHz, fast enough to support an aggregate of 40 Gb/s from all four SFP+ ports.

NetFPGA has been used in classrooms for about 15 years with over 2,000 boards deployed. However, it has always required students to program in Verilog or VHDL, placing it off limits to many. While there are many students interested in learning about networked systems, relatively few have the necessary prerequisite knowledge in both hardware design and networking. Similarly, networking researchers wishing to prototype their ideas in hardware have needed to learn Verilog or VHDL.

To bridge this gap, the P4→NetFPGA workflow was created, with the goal of making it much easier for networking students and researchers to process packets in hardware. By allowing students to program NetFPGA using P4, instructors can give their students hands-on experience working with real hardware, while allowing them to focus on learning networking concepts rather than the minutiae involved in FPGA design. Similarly, networking researchers can rapidly prototype new systems without being bogged down in hardware development.

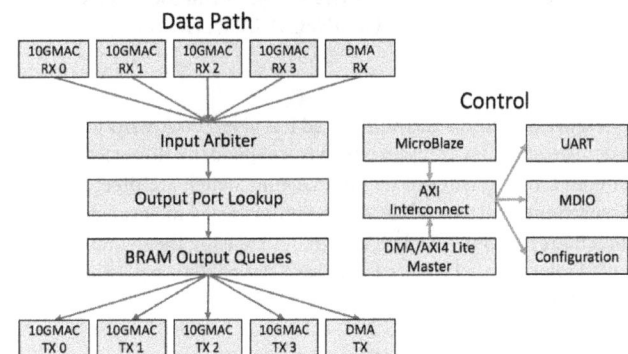

Figure 3: A block diagram of the NetFPGA reference design.

5 P4→NETFPGA WORKFLOW OVERVIEW

P4 designs for the NetFPGA SUME board are based on the Simple-SumeSwitch architecture, shown in Figure 4. The simple architecture consists of a parser, a match-action pipeline, and a deparser, and is ideal for new P4 developers to start experimenting with because, unlike the standard P4 Portable Switch Architecture (PSA) [29], it

Table 2: Description of the SimpleSumeSwitch `sume_metadata` fields.

Field Name	Size (bits)	Description
`pkt_len`	16	Size of the packet in bytes (not including the Ethernet preamble or FCS)
`src_port`	8	Port on which the packet arrived (one-hot encoded)
`dst_port`	8	Set by the P4 program - which port(s) the packet should be sent out of (one-hot encoded)
`send_dig_to_cpu`	8	Set the least significant bit of this field to send the `digest_data` to the CPU
`*_q_size`	16	Size of each output queue at P4 processing start time, measured in of 32-byte words

is simpler and easier to understand. At the same time, it is flexible enough to implement many networking protocols/algorithms. In contrast to the PSA, SimpleSumeSwitch is less comprehensive and does not include all features needed for a commodity switch Instead, its goal is to provide just enough features to be an effective experimental tool. Users can also opt to define their own architecture if need-be. Table 2 describes the format of the SimpleSumeSwitch's `sume_metadata` bus and the functionality of each field.

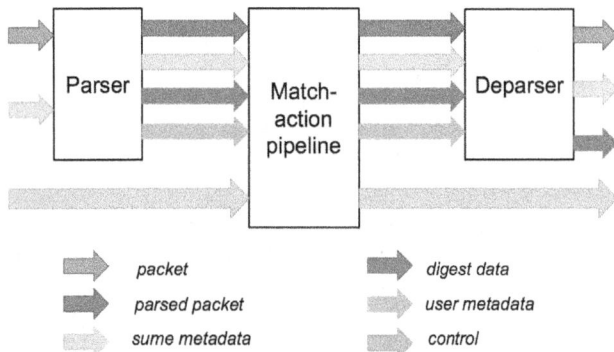

Figure 4: Block diagram of the SimpleSumeSwitch P4 architecture used within the P4→NetFPGA workflow.

Figure 5 outlines the automated P4→NetFPGA workflow. The user provides a P4 program which is compiled (by Xilinx P4-SDNet) into an HDL instance of the SimpleSumeSwitch architecture. The SimpleSumeSwitch module is then automatically integrated into the NetFPGA Reference Switch design by replacing the default output port lookup module. Here is the basic set of steps used within the workflow:

(1) Write P4 program
(2) Implement custom extern modules (optional)
(3) Write python script to generate test data for simulations
(4) Run HDL simulations
(5) Build bitstream for FPGA
(6) Test the design on hardware

The workflow was designed so that almost all user effort goes into steps 1-3, with all other steps being automated so that users can completely avoid working in terms of HDL if they wish. The remainder of this section describes various aspects of the P4→NetFPGA workflow in more detail.

5.1 Extern Function Library

The core P4 language is limited to expressing stateless packet processing. However, extern functions can be used to execute functions that cannot be described in P4, including stateful functions. Extern functions are implemented in HDL and the P4 program just sees the inputs and outputs, as parameters and results. In order to abstract away all HDL details from the programmer, P4→NetFPGA provides a library of commonly-used extern functions, as shown in Table 3.

The supported extern functions are divided into two categories: stateful and stateless. The key difference is that stateful operations cannot be pipelined between packets in order to preserve consistency guarantees. The stateful extern functions are inspired by the Domino atoms [35]. Each one performs an atomic read-modify-write operation on some state for each packet. The set of extern functions are selected such that they can be used as primitives to implement a wide variety of common algorithms.

For users who are relatively comfortable working with HDL, the P4→NetFPGA workflow makes it very easy to add support for custom extern function implementations. After implementing an extern module, users simply need to add a few lines to one configuration file and do not need to modify any existing code.

5.2 Simulation Environment

In order to verify that P4 programs are behaving as expected, developers are encouraged to run simulations before testing their designs on hardware. The workflow provides a number of tools to help simplify the task of writing and running simulations of P4 programs.

Developers can write a script consisting of a set of commands to populate match-action table entries. These entries will be automatically added to the P4 tables at the start of each simulation.

Developers may also make use of a framework built on top of the Python Scapy module [3] to write a script that generates input packets & metadata along with the corresponding expected output packets & metadata.

Once the packets and metadata have been produced, users run two stages of simulation. The first stage is to run the testbench produced by the SDNet compiler. This will apply the user defined input packets and metadata into the generated SimpleSumeSwitch HDL module and then compare the outputs with the expected outputs. After verifying that these simulations behave as expected, the user runs a command to install the SimpleSumeSwitch HDL module as a NetFPGA IP core. The second stage of simulations uses the same stimuli to verify that the SimpleSumeSwitch module was successfully integrated into the NetFPGA reference design.

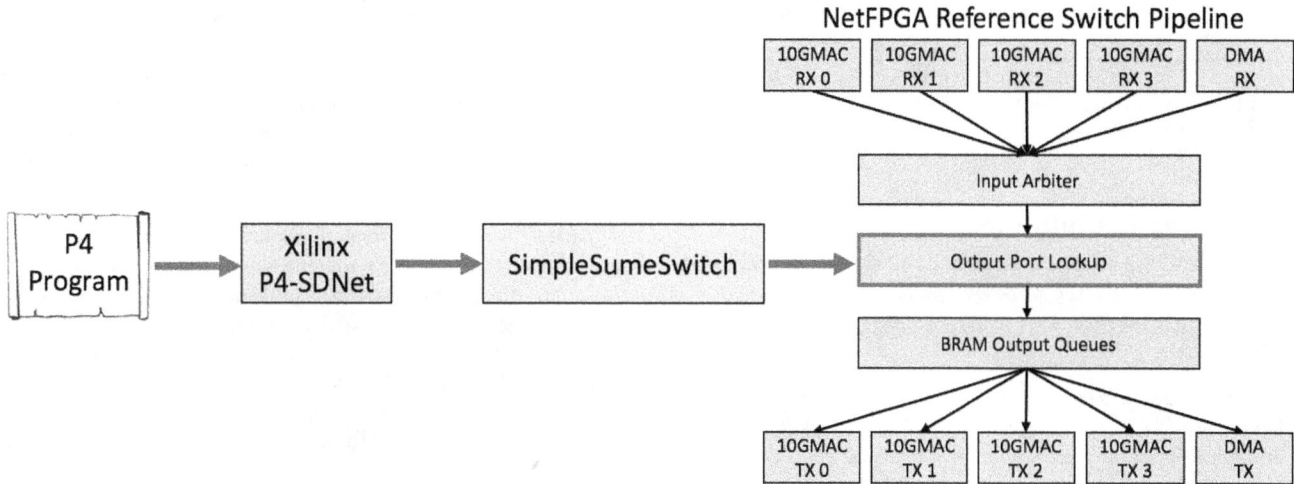

Figure 5: The automated P4→NetFPGA compilation flow. P4 programs are compiled into an HDL instance of the Simple-SumeSwitch architecture, which is then used to replace the output port lookup module in the NetFPGA Reference Switch design.

Table 3: The P4→NetFPGA extern function library.

Stateful Atomic Extern Functions	
Name	Description
RW	Read or write state
RAW	Read, add to, or overwrite state
PRAW	Either perform RAW or do not perform RAW based on predicate
ifElseRAW	Two RAWs, one each for when a predicate is true or false
Sub	IfElseRAW with support for subtraction as well
Stateless Extern Functions	
Name	Description
IP Checksum	Given an IP header, compute the IP checksum
LRC	Longitudinal redundancy check, simple hash function
timestamp	Generate timestamp (measured in clock cycles, granularity of 5ns)

After all simulations indicate that the P4 program is behaving properly, the user runs one command to build the FPGA bitstream and can then test the design on hardware.

5.3 Runtime Control

In addition to configuring the FPGA to implement the user's P4 program, the P4→NetFPGA workflow also produces a set of program specific Python API functions which enable the user to write software that controls the FPGA at runtime. In particular, the API functions allow the user to add/remove table entries and read/write stateful externs. The control software is thus able to dynamically influence how the FPGA processes packets without changing the hardware design. The Python API functions are wrappers around the C table drivers generated by SDNet.

The workflow also produces an interactive command line utility that can be used to interact with the P4 program at runtime as well as query various compile time information about the program. This utility has proved to be very useful for debugging.

6 P4→NETFPGA IN PRACTICE

For the vast majority of new FPGA developers, learning to write P4 programs is significantly easier than learning to write HDL modules. Table 4 compares the number of lines of code (LOC) required to implement an Ethernet learning switch and an IPv4 router using both Verilog and P4. P4 programs are drastically more concise, largely because P4 exposes the abstractions that are needed to implement these types of applications. If we allow program size to serve as an indicator of code complexity then P4 programs are clearly easier to reason about. As a result, the P4→NetFPGA workflow allows researchers to rapidly implement research prototypes, and instructors to quickly teach students networked-systems design using real hardware.

Table 4: P4 vs Verilog lines of code comparisons.

	Verilog LOC	P4 LOC
Ethernet Learning Switch	1213	82
IPv4 Router	3889	266

6.1　Research Applications

The P4→NetFPGA research community is already thriving and has demonstrated that the workflow can be used to develop interesting research vehicles. This section will describe some of these applications.

In-band network telemetry (INT). This has been coined as the killer application for programmable data planes. INT [19] concerns gaining more visibility into the network, as packets traversing it collect programmable information. It provides answers to questions such as: Which path did my packet take through the network? Which rules did my packet take to get where it is now? How long did my packet queue at each switch? Who did my packet share a queue with? It can answer these questions without adding any additional packets into the network. For decades, network operators have been using limited tools like ping, traceroute, and SNMP to debug their networks. The amount of visibility provided by INT is a leap forward and is of great interest to network operators. An example implementation of the INT protocol can be found in the P4→NetFPGA repository [15].

Distributed Proactive Congestion Control. Most Internet congestion control algorithms are *reactive* in the sense that they first measure congestion signals from the network, such as packet loss or queue size, and then *reactively* adjust flow rates. *Proactive* algorithms, on the other hand, use explicit information about the flows and network topology to directly compute optimal flow rates *before* congestion occurs. The P4→NetFPGA workflow was used to develop a prototype proactive algorithm based on [17] in which the network switches exchange messages with each other and compute the optimal flow rates in a distributed fashion.

Stateless load-aware load balancing. Load balancing connections across many replicated instances of the same application is a very important task in modern data centers. The challenging aspect of building one of these load balancers is that all packets belonging to a particular connection must always be passed to the *same* application instance — a property called *per connection consistency* (PCC). Typically, there are hundreds or even thousands of servers dedicated to performing this sort of load balancing in a data center. SilkRoad [21] proposed implementing stateful load balancing in modern programmable switch devices hence eliminating the need for an army of software load balancers, thus saving cost. More recently, Benoit et. al. proposed SHELL [31] — a stateless application-aware load balancer prototyped using P4→NetFPGA that is able to closely approximate PCC. By making the load balancer implementation stateless, the design becomes much more scalable and practical to implement on hardware devices with limited memory.

Programmable Data Plane Verification. As programmable network devices become more common the reality is that network design bugs will become more common as well. The need is to reliably debug and validate the functionality of programmable designs running on hardware targets. NetDebug [6] proposes a P4-based programmable architecture for testing and validating network designs, running at line rate. NetDebug has a prototype implemented on P4→NetFPGA and has demonstrated exposing functional, performance and compiler bugs.

Network Accelerated Consensus. Consensus protocols are not typically the first thing to come to mind when thinking about networking applications. However, P4xos [10] suggests that by leveraging new P4 programmable network devices, significant performance improvements can be obtained over the traditional end host only implementations. Huynh et. al. show that in-network consensus acceleration is also useful for making storage class memory (SCM) fault tolerant [11]. Both of these works used P4→NetFPGA prototypes to demonstrate the practicality of the approach.

In addition to the examples described above, there have been many other designs prototyped using the workflow. These designs range from simple network functions, through in-network computing to games. For example:

- Hardware-accelerated firewall for 5G mobile networks.
- Named data networking with programmable switches.
- Heavy hitter detection.
- Network-accelerated sorting.
- In-Network key-value cache.
- In-Network compression.
- IP packet fuzzer.
- A game of tic-tac-toe, with a switch opponent.

6.2　Teaching Contributions

P4's ease-of-use makes it a good vehicle for teaching networking concepts. The P4→NetFPGA workflow was adopted by members of the P4 Consortium's Education Workgroup [9], and is being used for teaching in world-leading universities. For example, it was used for teaching how to build a fully functioning Internet router on the NetFPGA SUME board [13], replacing a Verilog-based course. The students implemented the routing protocol in software on the Linux host and the FPGA packet forwarding logic in P4. Only 25% of the students had prior experience with Verilog and none had prior experience with P4. Within six weeks of the course, all the students were able to build, in pairs, a functioning IPv4 router. The students demonstrated interoperability with other routers, building a small topology and testing various failure conditions. By transitioning from Verilog to the P4→NetFPGA workflow, the learning curve was dramatically reduced, the pace of the class was accelerated, and it was opened up to students with a wider variety of backgrounds.

7　FUTURE WORK

We are supporting, and continuing to evolve, the P4→NetFPGA workflow. With this in mind, there are a number of aspects that can be improved including the runtime control interface and support for user-defined target architectures.

Looking forward, we plan to add support for P4Runtime [27], which is quickly becoming the standard way to control P4 programs at run time. Supporting P4Runtime will enable P4→NetFPGA developers to easily write either a local or remote control plane and will simplify the task of integrating designs into systems that already support P4Runtime, such as ONOS [2].

In contrast to P4-programmable ASICs, FPGAs are flexible enough to support arbitrary packet processing architectures. In an effort to take advantage of this flexibility we plan to add support for users to be able to define custom P4 architectures rather than being constrained to use the SimpleSumeSwitch. This will allow developers to create more expressive P4 programs as well as experiment with their own custom modules within the architecture.

8 RELATED WORK

High level languages such as Vivado HLS and OpenCL are increasingly used to compile C-style programs onto FPGAs. Despite their popularity, they are normally used as a productivity tool by hardware engineers rather than by networking or software engineers. The flow of these languages was originally intended to target compute acceleration rather than packet processing. In principle, the C language is more expressive than the domain-specific P4, and could potentially be used for networking purposes. However, at the moment, it does not expose convenient abstractions or libraries that allow network developers to rapidly prototype new designs in hardware.

There have been two published attempts to build P4 compilers that target Vivado HLS [18, 32]. Similarly, P4FPGA [37] compiles P4 programs into Bluespec [26], another high level synthesis language. Unlike P4→NetFPGA, these compilers require the user to actively go through an intermediate language, and provide a compiler only, rather than a full workflow. Furthermore, these projects lack community support or have since been deprecated.

Benacek et. al. developed a P4 parser compiler [1] that does not utilize an intermediate high level language. This compiler and workflow are completely closed source, and support only specific platforms, and hence are difficult to use for academic research and teaching.

Emu [36] is an extension to the Kiwi [34] compiler, which provides a way to compile .NET programs into RTL. Emu provides a standard library that can be used to build network systems. Unlike P4, .NET programs have not been widely adopted within the networking community as a way to express packet processing. Additionally, Emu programs are not inherently pipelined and hence do not guarantee line rate performance.

9 GETTING STARTED

The global P4→NetFPGA community consists of over 200 members from both industry and academia and it continues to grow. See the GitHub documentation [14] to find out more and learn how to get started. The documentation includes a set of on-line tutorials with step-by-step instructions that walk through the process of compiling P4 programs, running simulations, building the bitstream, and testing on hardware [15]. Community members are encouraged to contribute in any number of ways including, but not limited to:

- New P4 projects
- Extern function implementations
- Bug fixes or improvements
- Performance analysis tools and benchmarks
- Improved documentation

10 CONCLUSION

As P4 adoption continues to grow, more and more researchers seek out P4-programmable targets. Unfortunately, their choices have been mostly limited to either very low-end software emulation tools or very high-end (and expensive) P4 programmable ASICs. We developed the P4→NetFPGA workflow with the goal of bridging this gap. The community has already demonstrated that it is indeed possible to build low-cost, high-performance, P4 prototypes on real hardware using this workflow.

11 ACKNOWLEDGEMENTS

We thank the many people who have contributed to the NetFPGA project over the years. In particular, we acknowledge Andrew W. Moore and the NetFPGA development team at the University of Cambridge, whose efforts have enabled us to build the P4→NetFPGA workflow using NetFPGA SUME.

We also thank Robert Halstead and Chris Neely for their vital roles in developing the Xilinx P4-SDNet compiler, and in helping with the development of this workflow. Furthermore, we acknowledge the Xilinx University Program (XUP) for its continued support of the NetFPGA project.

This project was partially funded by the the Leverhulme Trust (ECF-2016-289) and the Isaac Newton Trust.

REFERENCES

[1] Pavel Benácek, Viktor Pu, and Hana Kubátová. 2016. P4-to-vhdl: Automatic generation of 100 gbps packet parsers. In *Field-Programmable Custom Computing Machines (FCCM), 2016 IEEE 24th Annual International Symposium on.* IEEE, 148–155.

[2] Pankaj Berde, Matteo Gerola, Jonathan Hart, Yuta Higuchi, Masayoshi Kobayashi, Toshio Koide, Bob Lantz, Brian O'Connor, Pavlin Radoslavov, William Snow, et al. 2014. ONOS: towards an open, distributed SDN OS. In *Proceedings of the third workshop on Hot topics in software defined networking.* ACM, 1–6.

[3] Philippe Biondi. 2018. Scapy. https://scapy.net/

[4] Pat Bosshart, Dan Daly, Glen Gibb, Martin Izzard, Nick McKeown, Jennifer Rexford, Cole Schlesinger, Dan Talayco, Amin Vahdat, George Varghese, et al. 2014. P4: Programming protocol-independent packet processors. *ACM SIGCOMM Computer Communication Review* 44, 3 (2014), 87–95.

[5] Gordon Brebner and Weirong Jiang. 2014. High-speed packet processing using reconfigurable computing. *IEEE Micro* 34, 1 (2014), 8–18.

[6] Pietro Bressana, Noa Zilberman, and Robert Soulé. 2018. A Programmable Framework for Validating Data Planes. In *Proceedings of the ACM SIGCOMM 2018 Conference on Posters and Demos.* ACM, 1–3.

[7] Broadcom. 2018. Jerico2 Ethernet Switch Series. https://www.broadcom.com/products/ethernet-connectivity/switching/stratadnx/bcm88690

[8] Cavium. 2018. XPliant Ethernet Switch Product Family. https://cavium.com/xpliant-ethernet-switch-xp60-and-xp70-family.html

[9] P4 Language Consortium. 2018. *Education Workgroup.* Repository, https://github.com/p4lang/education/wiki.

[10] Huynh Tu Dang, Pietro Bressana, Han Wang, Ki Suh Lee, H Weatherspoon, M Canini, N Zilberman, F Pedone, and R Soulé. 2018. *P4xos: Consensus as a Network Service.* Technical Report. Research Report 2018-01, USI.

[11] Huynh Tu Dang, Jaco Hofmann, Yang Liu, Marjan Radi, Dejan Vucinic, Robert Soulé, and Fernando Pedone. 2018. Consensus for Non-Volatile Main Memory. In *2018 IEEE 26th International Conference on Network Protocols (ICNP).* IEEE, 406–411.

[12] Daniel Firestone, Andrew Putnam, Sambhrama Mundkur, Derek Chiou, Alireza Dabagh, Mike Andrewartha, Hari Angepat, Vivek Bhanu, Adrian Caulfield, Eric Chung, et al. 2018. Azure Accelerated Networking: SmartNICs in the Public Cloud. In *15th USENIX Symposium on Networked Systems Design and Implementation (NSDI 18), Renton, WA.*

[13] Stephen Ibanez. 2018. CS344 - Build an Internet Router. https://build-a-router-instructors.github.io/

[14] Stephen Ibanez. 2018. P4->NetFPGA Workflow. https://github.com/NetFPGA/P4-NetFPGA-public/wiki

[15] Stephen Ibanez. 2018. Tutorial Assignments. https://github.com/NetFPGA/P4-NetFPGA-public/wiki/Tutorial-Assignments

[16] Xin Jin, Xiaozhou Li, Haoyu Zhang, Robert Soulé, Jeongkeun Lee, Nate Foster, Changhoon Kim, and Ion Stoica. 2017. Netcache: Balancing key-value stores with fast in-network caching. In *Proceedings of the 26th Symposium on Operating Systems Principles*. ACM, 121–136.

[17] Lavanya Jose, Lisa Yan, Mohammad Alizadeh, George Varghese, Nick McKeown, and Sachin Katti. 2015. High speed networks need proactive congestion control. In *Proceedings of the 14th ACM Workshop on Hot Topics in Networks*. ACM, 14.

[18] Jehandad Khan and Peter Athanas. 2017. Creating Custom Network Packet Processing Pipelines on HMC-Enabled FPGAs. In *Proceedings of the third workshop on Networking and Programming Languages (NetPL)*.

[19] Changhoon Kim, Anirudh Sivaraman, Naga Katta, Antonin Bas, Advait Dixit, and Lawrence J Wobker. 2015. In-band network telemetry via programmable dataplanes. In *ACM SIGCOMM*.

[20] Nick McKeown, Tom Anderson, Hari Balakrishnan, Guru Parulkar, Larry Peterson, Jennifer Rexford, Scott Shenker, and Jonathan Turner. 2008. OpenFlow: enabling innovation in campus networks. *ACM SIGCOMM Computer Communication Review* 38, 2 (2008), 69–74.

[21] Rui Miao, Hongyi Zeng, Changhoon Kim, Jeongkeun Lee, and Minlan Yu. 2017. SilkRoad: Making Stateful Layer-4 Load Balancing Fast and Cheap Using Switching ASICs. In *Proceedings of the Conference of the ACM Special Interest Group on Data Communication*. ACM, 15–28.

[22] NetFPGA.org. 2018. NetFPGA. https://netfpga.org/

[23] Netronome. 2018. About Agilio SmartNICs. https://www.netronome.com/products/smartnic/overview/

[24] Netronome. 2018. P4 Introduction. https://www.netronome.com/technology/p4/

[25] Barefoot Networks. 2018. Tofino. https://www.barefootnetworks.com/products/brief-tofino/

[26] Rishiyur Nikhil. 2004. Bluespec System Verilog: efficient, correct RTL from high level specifications. In *Formal Methods and Models for Co-Design, 2004. MEMOCODE'04. Proceedings. Second ACM and IEEE International Conference on*. IEEE, 69–70.

[27] P4.org. 2018. Announcing P4Runtime. https://p4.org/api/announcing-p4runtime-a-contribution-by-the-p4-api-working-group.html

[28] P4.org. 2018. behavioral-model. https://github.com/p4lang/behavioral-model

[29] P4.org. 2018. Portable Switch Architecture (PSA). https://p4.org/p4-spec/docs/PSA.html

[30] Ben Pfaff, Justin Pettit, Teemu Koponen, Ethan J Jackson, Andy Zhou, Jarno Rajahalme, Jesse Gross, Alex Wang, Joe Stringer, Pravin Shelar, et al. 2015. The Design and Implementation of Open vSwitch.. In *NSDI*, Vol. 15. 117–130.

[31] Benoît Pit-Claudel, Yoann Desmouceaux, Pierre Pfister, Mark Townsley, and Thomas Clausen. 2018. Stateless Load-Aware Load Balancing in P4. In *2018 IEEE 26th International Conference on Network Protocols (ICNP)*. IEEE, 418–423.

[32] Jeferson Santiago da Silva, François-Raymond Boyer, and JM Langlois. 2018. P4-compatible High-level Synthesis of Low Latency 100 Gb/s Streaming Packet Parsers in FPGAs. In *Proceedings of the 2018 ACM/SIGDA International Symposium on Field-Programmable Gate Arrays*. ACM, 147–152.

[33] Muhammad Shahbaz, Sean Choi, Ben Pfaff, Changhoon Kim, Nick Feamster, Nick McKeown, and Jennifer Rexford. 2016. Pisces: A programmable, protocol-independent software switch. In *Proceedings of the 2016 ACM SIGCOMM Conference*. ACM, 525–538.

[34] Satnam Singh and David J Greaves. 2008. Kiwi: Synthesis of FPGA circuits from parallel programs. In *Field-Programmable Custom Computing Machines, 2008. FCCM'08. 16th International Symposium on*. IEEE, 3–12.

[35] Anirudh Sivaraman, Alvin Cheung, Mihai Budiu, Changhoon Kim, Mohammad Alizadeh, Hari Balakrishnan, George Varghese, Nick McKeown, and Steve Licking. 2016. Packet transactions: High-level programming for line-rate switches. In *Proceedings of the 2016 ACM SIGCOMM Conference*. ACM, 15–28.

[36] Nik Sultana, Salvator Galea, David Greaves, Marcin Wójcik, Jonny Shipton, Richard Clegg, Luo Mai, Pietro Bressana, Robert Soulé, Richard Mortier, et al. 2017. Emu: Rapid prototyping of networking services. In *2017 USENIX Annual Technical Conference (USENIX ATC 17)*. 459–471.

[37] Han Wang, Robert Soulé, Huynh Tu Dang, Ki Suh Lee, Vishal Shrivastav, Nate Foster, and Hakim Weatherspoon. 2017. P4FPGA: A rapid prototyping framework for p4. In *Proceedings of the Symposium on SDN Research*. ACM, 122–135.

[38] Xilinx. 2018. SDNet. https://www.xilinx.com/products/design-tools/software-zone/sdnet.html

[39] Noa Zilberman, Yury Audzevich, G Adam Covington, and Andrew W Moore. 2014. NetFPGA SUME: Toward 100 Gbps as research commodity. *IEEE micro* 34, 5 (2014), 32–41.

Visual System Integrator

Invited Tutorial

Sandeep Dutta
System View Inc
sandeep@systemviewinc.com

Adnan Yunus
System View Inc
adnan@systemviewinc.com

Artem Marisov
System View Inc
artem@systemviewinc.com

Matt Menezes
System View Inc
matt@systemviewinc.com

Somayeh Rahimipour
System View Inc
somayeh@systemviewinc.com

ABSTRACT

Visual System Integrator (VSI) provides behavioural modelling and automated design of entire systems of digital and software running on heterogeneous devices and heterogeneous accelerators. VSI provides run time profiling and metric reporting the tool also provides users with everything needed for rapid design explorations, behavioural and/or RTL simulations, hardware in loop, external processors, and FPGA design creation of heterogeneous features, including embedded processors, memories and interfaces.

CCS CONCEPTS

• **Computer systems organization → Heterogeneous (hybrid) systems**; • **Software and its engineering → Visual languages; Interface definition languages; Application specific development environments**;

KEYWORDS

System Integration, Heterogeneous systems

ACM Reference Format:
Sandeep Dutta, Adnan Yunus, Artem Marisov, Matt Menezes, and Somayeh Rahimipour. 2019. Visual System Integrator: Invited Tutorial. In *The 2019 ACM/SIGDA International Symposium on Field-Programmable Gate Arrays (FPGA '19), February 24–26, 2019, Seaside, CA, USA.* ACM, New York, NY, USA, 4 pages. https://doi.org/10.1145/3289602.3293926

1 INTRODUCTION

Modern systems are increasing complex and often span across multiple chips (CPUs, FPGAs and custom hardware accelerators). Along with the accelerating complexity of these systems engineers and developers have increasing hard time integrating the systems that they have created. Visual System Integrator provides developers, engineers, and system architects with a comprehensive way to model, simulate and deploy complex systems that span across heterogenous hardware.

2 PLATFORM AND APPLICATION LAYER

A heterogeneous system can consist of an arbitrary number of CPUs, FPGAs, and other computation components. To address this the VSI design methodology is done in layers. The "platform layer" describes hardware components (contexts) of the system and the infrastructure which connects these contexts. The "platform" can consist of multiple CPUs and/or FPGAs connected via a set of predefined "transports". VSI provides a library of transports to choose from ,for example a FPGA may be connected to a CPU via "PCI/e" , a CPU maybe connected to another CPU via "TCP/IP" .

The "application layer" describes the functional processing blocks and how they are connected or interact with each other. The VSI runtime uses a "dataflow" model to communicate between the processing blocks. The user builds the system as multiple parallel dataflow graphs, the VSI runtime is inherently parallel and executes each block on its own thread by default.

The application layer has the ability to communicate with the platform layer via "system interfaces" these are defined in the platform layer. Figure 1 represents a three dimensional view of the two layers with the system interface tunneling between them.

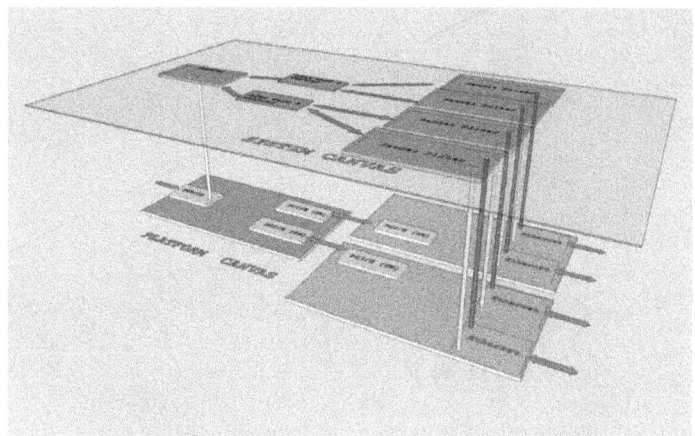

Figure 1: Conceptual 3D view of layer.

3 WORKFLOW

Figure 2 shows the typical workflow. Users starts by describing the platform layer of their heterogeneous system, they can also choose to start by importing a predefined platform. The next step is to create their application layer, there can be multiple platforms and applications in a given project, but each application layer is associated with a single platform. In a newly created application the contexts defined in the platform layer are shown as empty hierarchy boxes which map one to one to the contextes created in the platform. The user can then create their application by placing processing blocks into each context and connecting the interfaces of the processing blocks to represent the dataflow between the processing blocks.

Once all the processing blocks have been placed in their desired contexts, the user generates their system; this step will generate the projects for the contexts present in the systems. For all FPGAs contexts VSI system compiler will generate VIVADO projects for all CPU contexts the system compiler will generate CMake projects. The platform can be modified during the development life-cycle. The system compiler also generates portions of the runtime and driver configuration depending on the interfaces crossing context boundaries.

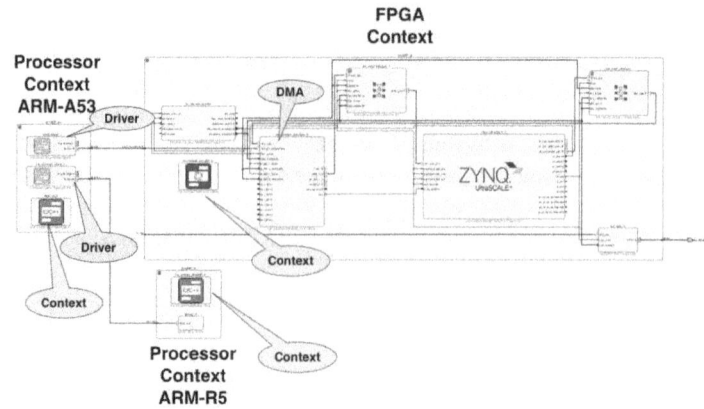

Figure 2: Workflow.

3.1 Platform Definition

Figure 3 shows an example platform definition for the Xilinx MP-SoC chip. The platform shows three separate contexts a) The ARM-A53 processor subsystem, b) The ARM-R5 processors and c) The FPGA portion of the chip. Note that the contexts are be on separate physical chips or on the same chips. The platform shows the drivers (in the software context) connected to the DMA subsystem (in the FPGA context). The blocks marked as a context describe the details of the context. For software contexts it is used to describes the processor type, compiler to be used, libraries to link and any other information that is required to generate a complete executable for this context. For hardware contexts it describes the device id, FPGA part, implementation strategy, and any other information required to generate a complete Vivado [1] project.

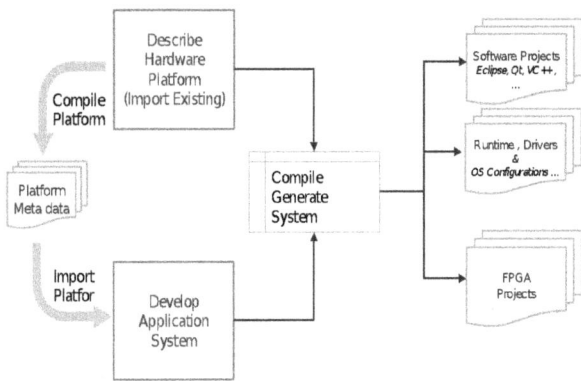

Figure 3: Platform.

3.2 Application System

Figure 4 shows a complete application using the platform described in Figure 3. The application spans across all three contexts. For software contexts the VSI system compiler will generate a multi-threaded application, the user is given a choice of thread-priority and the CPU the thread is going to execute on. For hardware contexts the system compiler will perform appropriate interface conversion and connect the clocks and resets to corresponding sources. The system compiler generates the runtime to communicate with the driver and the DMA subsystem if the connection crosses context boundaries.

During the development process the user may need to "simulate" the hardware portion of their design. VSI allows the user to "switch' the FPGA harware context to a simualtor, in this case the DMA sub-system in the platform is replaced by a transaction generator. The VSI system compiler will transfer data to & from the block running in the simulator using the "transaction generator".

A more complex system can be described by adding more than one FPGA and/or processor in the "platform". The tool enforces no restrictions to the number of FPGAs or processors that can be described in the platform. The user can partition their desing accross multiple FPGAs and processors.

3.3 Execution Model

The VSI runtime allows the user three different execution models for each block. The execution models are the same regardless of the "context" the block is placed in, they are applicable to C/C++/Java & Python blocks only. For blocks coded in other languages (Verilog/VHDL) the user determines the execution model.

(i) Run-to-Completion. In this model the block is executed when data arrives on designated "trigger" inputs. The inputs are evaluated at the start of execution, the outputs are propagated once the block finishes execution.

(ii) Blocking-reads & Writes. The block can use the "hls stream" class to control its execution explicitly. For example a block may issue a blocking "read" to wait for data on a given input. The blocking "read" will be cleared when another block issues a "write" on the channel that is connected to this particular input. Care must be taken to avoid deadlocks in this execution model.

This execition model can be used to create feedback paths in the dataflow graph, e.g. a block may delay sending data on its output if a block further in the dataflow graph can inidicate "congestion".

(iii) Run-on-Timer. The user can specify that the block will execute at certain time interval. The timer interval should be greater than the time required for the block to perform its action.

The user can mix & match the these execution models, i.e. one block may use the "Run-to-completion" model and can feed data to a block which is executing a "Blocking-read-write" scheme.

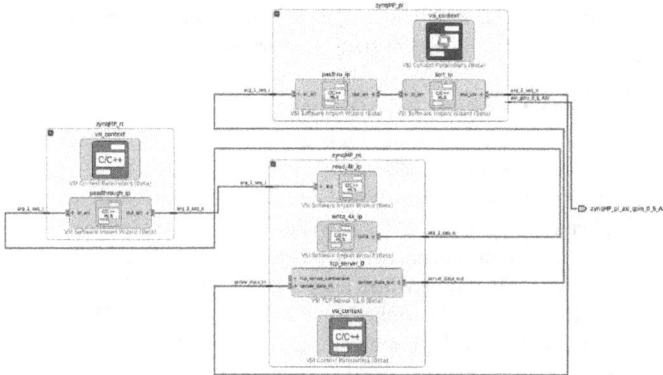

Figure 4: Application System.

4 INTERNAL TOOL-FLOW

Figure 5 shows the overall internal flow of the system compiler. The compiler operates in separate stages. This allows for incremental development. The user compiles the platform, this step generates portions of the hardware design as well as an intermediate metadata repository. The next stage the user creates an application system and imports the platform. This associates the platform to the application system. This binding needs to be updated if any changes are made to the platform layer. The changeable binding between the platform layer and the application layers allows the user to change the characteristics of the platform layer while maintaining the application layer mapping the same. For example the user may choose to replace the FPGA context with a simulator for verification purposes and switch it back to FPGA once the verification is complete. The system compiler generates structural C++ representation of the complete application before generating the Software and Hardware projects. The C++ generated can be compiled by a standard C++ compiler and is used as an execution model for portions of the Software context.

4.1 C++ Intermediate Representation

The C++ intermediate form captures all information about the heterogeneous system, this includes the "platform" layer and "system" layer. The structural C++ form represents the hierarchies in the

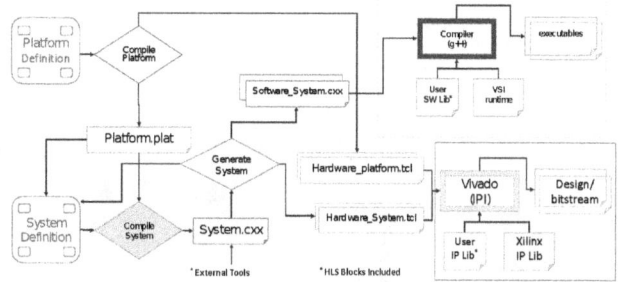

Figure 5: Tool Internal flow.

block diagram as "namespaces" and the blocks as C++ "class". The attributes of the blocks are represented as protected class variables and the interfaces as "public" class variables. The C++ uses a few special classes to describe the connectivity between the blocks.

Input, Output and Inout classes: The interfaces of a block should be one of these three classes.

Connect class: This class represents the connection between two interfaces. Listing below shows a pseudo C++ example generated by VSI during the compilation process. The figure shows two contexts in the platform layer, enclosed in the namespace vsi_platform, zynqMP_pl (hardware) and zynqMP_ps (software), the parameters (protected variables) in the context class shows the different attributes of the contexts.

The system layer is represented in the namespace "vsi_system" and contains the processing blocks for each of the contexts in the platform layer. In this case the processing block "tcp_server_2021" is the software context "zynqMP_ps" since it is enclosed in the namespace zynqMP_ps. Similarly the processing block "dilate_ip" is in the hardware context "zynqMP_pl". The parameters of each of the processing blocks are shown in the "protected" variables in the class, the interfaces are represented by the "public" variables. A Connect class is created for each output interface and is initialized at the end of the class declarations. The Connect class shows the connection between the interfaces.

```
namespace vsi_platform {
  namespace zynqMP_pl {
    class zynqMP_pl {
    protected:
      string fpga_part = "xczu3eg-sbva484-1-e";
      string fpga_board = "ultra96";
    } zynqMP_pl;
  }
  namespace zynqMP_ps {
    class zynqMP_ps {
    protected:
      string cpu_type = "ARM64";
      long num_cpus = 1;
      string OS = "Linux";
    } zynqMP_ps;
  }
}

namespace vsi_system {
```

```
namespace zynqMP_ps {
  class tcp_server {
  protected:
    long port_no = 2021;
  public:
    Input server_data_in;
    Connect Connect_server_data_in ;
    Output server_data_out;
    Input tcp_server_connection;
  } tcp_server;
};
namespace zynqMP_pl {
  class dilate_ip {
  protected:
    string Component_Name = "system_filters_vsi_gen";
  public:
    Input arg_1_seq_i;
    Connect Connect_arg_1;
    Output arg_2_seq_o;
  } dilate_ip ;
};
Connect zynqMP_pl::dilate_ip::Connect_arg_1 =
  Connect(
    vsi_system::zynqMP_pl::dilate_ip::arg_1,
    vsi_system::zynqMP_ps::tcp_server::server_data_out);
Connect zynqMP_ps::tcp_server::Connect_server_data_in =
  Connect(
    vsi_system::zynqMP_ps::tcp_server::server_data_in ,
    vsi_system::zynqMP_pl::dilate_ip::arg_2_seq_o);
}
```

5 RUNTIME LIBRARY

Visual System Integrator provides a software library written in C++ that provides a hardened multithreaded implementation of classes containing functionality such as input/output as well as a highly configurable block that can wrap arbitrary unmodified user provided code or a third-party library. Additionally, the trace class provides a channel to bring the trace data available from various hardware and software contexts and unify into a single stream. The data is passed between each class using an abstract C++ transport class that provides a consistent API regardless of the actual underlying transport that the data is passing through. Input/output classes provide connectivity to industry standard protocols such as TCP/UDP as well as posix file IO. The configurable class is provided to emulate the hardware execution behavior. This ensures portability when the code block is in a software context. Other functionality that is native to the hardware contexts, such as timer and data-driven execution is also provided. Additionally, it contains the implementation for various transports and protocols that is instantiated at system generation time.

The Runtime library is divided into two portions the fixed portion and the generated portion. The fixed portion consists of the implementation of the runtime classes. The VSI system compiler will generate a portion of the runtime depending on the location of the blocks begin connected. For example if the source block is a hardware context (zynqMP_pl) and the destination block is in the software context (zynqMP_ps) then the compiler will generate a posix fileio interface to read the data as it arrives fromt the hardware (Universal driver is described in the following section). If both blocks are in the software context then the compiler will generate an elastic buffer between the blocks.

6 RUN-TIME PROFILING (TRACE)

The VSI runtime provides a powerful trace facility which allows the user to collect transaction level trace information on any interface during system execution. Each trace event is associated with an universal timestamp this allows the user to quickly identify both functional problems as well as performance bottlenecks. The trace collection system is very light weight and designed to be retained in a deployed system and can be used to detect and debug in-field problems. The trace data from all contexts are routed to the main controlling software context. The collection is performed over the existing connections defined in the platform and no separate interfaces are required to be defined. In the hardware contexts trace is collected using a shallow FIFO, which collect the timestamp when an event occurs on a specific interface. When FIFOs overflow an overflow event is registered, this alerts the user that some event could have been lost. The user has several options to control the trace collection to prevent such an overflow.

7 UNIVERSAL FPGA DRIVER

VSI provides an open source linux driver to handle all the data communication between CPU and FPGA. With the VSI FPGA driver each peripheral within the FPGA will become a file which the user application can read data from, write data to, or poll for data or interrupts. System specific parameters are passed to the driver module at installation time which allows the driver to initialize shared infrastructure for all peripheral such as interrupts and DMAs. The information for each peripheral is given to the driver with IOCTL calls which allows the correctly communicate with the peripheral. Once initialized each file can now be accessed by the user application. Depending on how the file is setup these peripherals can be many different things, such as control registers, memory, or an axi stream. All of the parameters and the files required to install and setup the driver are generated by VSI. The flexibility of the driver allows just one driver to be used for many different use cases, this allows VSI to effectively generate many different applications while using just a single driver. Acknowledgements References

REFERENCES

[1] Xilinx, I. Introduction to fpga design with vivado high-level synthesis.

Build Your Own Domain-specific Solutions with RapidWright

Invited Tutorial

Chris Lavin and Alireza Kaviani
Xilinx Research Labs
San Jose, CA
chris.lavin@xilinx.com,alireza.kaviani@xilinx.com

ABSTRACT

As the complexity of programmable architectures increases with advances in silicon process technology, there is a growing need to extract greater productivity and performance from the tools. Due to their inherent reconfigurability, FPGAs are proving to be valuable targets for more efficient domain-specific architectures. However, FPGA implementation tools are designed for a broad set of applications.

In this paper we describe RapidWright, an open source framework that enables customized implementations for Xilinx FPGAs. RapidWright enables implementation tools that can take advantage of the great potential of domain-specific attributes—leading to greater productivity and performance. The focus of this paper is to provide an introductory reference of RapidWright and its use cases so that others may be empowered to adapt their implementations to their domain-specific applications.

CCS CONCEPTS

• **Hardware** → **Reconfigurable logic and FPGAs**; • **Computer systems organization** → *Reconfigurable computing*;

KEYWORDS

Domain-specific, Open Source, FPGA, Xilinx, Vivado

ACM Reference Format:
Chris Lavin and Alireza Kaviani. 2019. Build Your Own Domain-specific Solutions with RapidWright. In *The 2019 ACM/SIGDA International Symposium on Field-Programmable Gate Arrays (FPGA '19), February 24–26, 2019, Seaside, CA, USA.* ACM, New York, NY, USA, Article 4, 9 pages. https://doi.org/10.1145/3289602.3293928

1 INTRODUCTION

RapidWright [1] is an open source platform with a gateway to Xilinx's back-end implementation tools (Vivado) that raises the implementation abstraction while maintaining the full potential of advanced FPGA silicon. RapidWright works synergistically with Vivado through design checkpoints (DCPs, see Figure 1) to enable highly customizable implementations. Vivado can produce highly

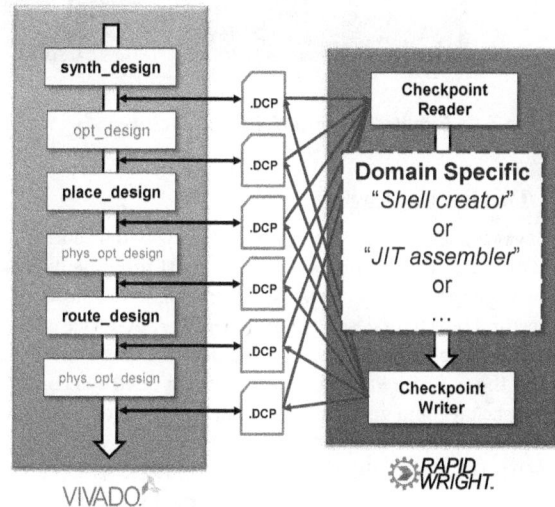

Figure 1: Vivado and RapidWright DCP Compatibility

optimized implementations for key design modules to deliver the highest performance. RapidWright can then replicate, relocate and assemble these tuned modules to compose a complete application and preserve high performance.

RapidWright's native gateway to Vivado also sets the groundwork for an ecosystem aimed at further advancing FPGA tools. It empowers academic and industry researchers by combining the commercial credibility of FPGA tools with the agility of an open source framework, leading to innovative solutions that might not be feasible otherwise.

This paper serves as a supplemental reference to the RapidWright tutorial with an aim to provide some fundamentals about the framework and introductory use cases. In the remainder of this paper we describe RapidWright and its capabilities in Section 2, some example use cases in Section 3 and conclude in Section 4. Supplementary material on Xilinx architecture is included in Appendix A to help orient the reader regarding specific RapidWright constructs.

2 RAPIDWRIGHT STRUCTURE

RapidWright is implemented in Java and distributed with a foundational API library that provides access to design checkpoint (DCP) files and Vivado-compatible device models. A high-level diagram showing the organization of the project is shown in Figure 2. There are three core Java packages (groups of classes) within RapidWight: `device`, `edif` (logical netlist) and `design` (physical netlist) and this section describes the purpose and composition of each one.

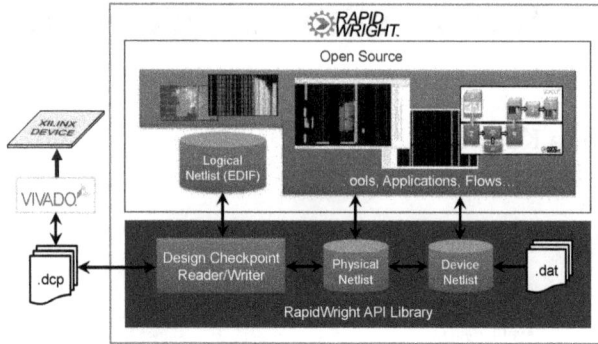

Figure 2: RapidWright Structure

2.1 Device Package

The device package contains classes and APIs that correspond to constructs in the silicon devices. The most prominent class in this package is the Device class, which makes available all of the architectural resources described in Appendix A. A device is supplemented by package, speed grade and temperature grade information through the use of a Package class. When a device is combined with its package and grade information, this uniquely identifies a Xilinx part, represented by the Part class.

The Device class is the top level object in RapidWright and has direct accessors to all other levels of hierarchy except for BELs as shown in the first row of Table 1. In contrast to the other two packages, the data provided in the device package is static. Most of the interaction between a user's design and the device occurs at the Tile, Site and BEL levels of hierarchy. The BEL class can be one of three kinds of non-routing objects in a Site: a Logic BEL, a Routing BEL and a Port (of the Site). This is designated by its class member enum of type BELClass. Most components within the device architecture are assigned an integer index. This helps to lower memory usage by eliminating the need to explicitly represent a component of the architecture with a dedicated object. It also helps by providing faster lookups. In some cases, such as TileTypeEnum and SiteTypeEnum, the index has been explicitly enumerated and an enum is used instead.

In parallel with the logical hierarchy of Xilinx devices, there are several constructs for representing routing resources. At the lowest level, pins on BELs are represented by the BELPin class. Pins on Site objects can be referenced by creating dynamic objects of type SitePin. Inside a Site, wires called "site wires" connect BELPin objects. Connectivity of a site wire is stored with each BELPin and also in the Site object. Site wires do not have an explicit object for representation, but their name, index and connectivity are available on Site and BELPin objects.

RapidWright provides the same inter-site routing resources as Vivado, namely Wire, Node and PIP objects (see second row of Table 1). These objects are generated on demand as there can be several millions of unique instances of each.

2.2 EDIF Package (Logical Netlist)

In Vivado, all designs post synthesis have a logical netlist that can be exported to the EDIF (Electronic Design Interchange Format) netlist format. Vivado also includes EDIF in the design checkpoint file format and has facilities to read and write it (read_edif and write_edif). RapidWright reads, represents and writes logical netlist information in the EDIF format and the edif package is written to accommodate this need. It was written with Vivado-generated EDIF in mind and may not support every corner case of the EDIF 2 0 0 specification.

The EDIFNetlist is the top level class that contains the netlist and cell libraries. All EDIF-related objects have EDIF as a class name prefix. The EDIFNetlist keeps a reference to the top cell which is wrapped in the EDIFDesign class. It also maintains a top cell instance reference that is generated when the file is loaded.

Although a full explanation of netlist modeling and relationships are beyond the scope of this paper, an attempt to clarify the contextual meaning of some of the classes will be made. One important distinction to make is between EDIFPort and EDIFPortInst. At one level, an EDIFPort belongs to an EDIFCell and an EDIFPortInst belongs to an EDIFCellInst. An additional distinction is that an EDIFPort can be a bussed-based object whereas an EDIFPortInst can only represent a single bit. An EDIFNet defines connectivity inside an EDIFCell by connecting EDIFPortInst objects together (port references on cell instances inside the cell or to external port

Table 1: RapidWright and Vivado Device Object Model Reference

RapidWright Class	RapidWright Java API	Vivado Class Property	Vivado Tcl API
Device	Device.getDevice(String partName)	-	-
SLR	Device.getSLR(int id)	slr	get_slrs -filter SLR_INDEX==$id
ClockRegion	Device.getClockRegion(String name)	clock_region	get_clock_regions $name
Tile	Device.getTile(String name)	tile	get_tiles $name
Site	Device.getSite(String name)	site	get_sites $name
BEL	Site.getBEL(String name)	bel	get_bels -of $site -filter NAME==$name
PIP	Device.getPIP(String name)	pip	get_pips $name
Wire	Device.getWire(String name)	wire	get_wires $name
Node	Device.getNode(String name)	node	get_nodes $name
SitePIP	Site.getSitePIP(BELPin input)	site_pip	get_site_pips $name
SitePin	Device.getSitePin(String name)	site_pin	get_site_pins $name
int (SiteWire)	Site.getSiteWireIndex(String name)	site_wire	(Vivado GUI)
BELPin	Site.getBELPin(String name)	bel_pin	get_bel_pins $name

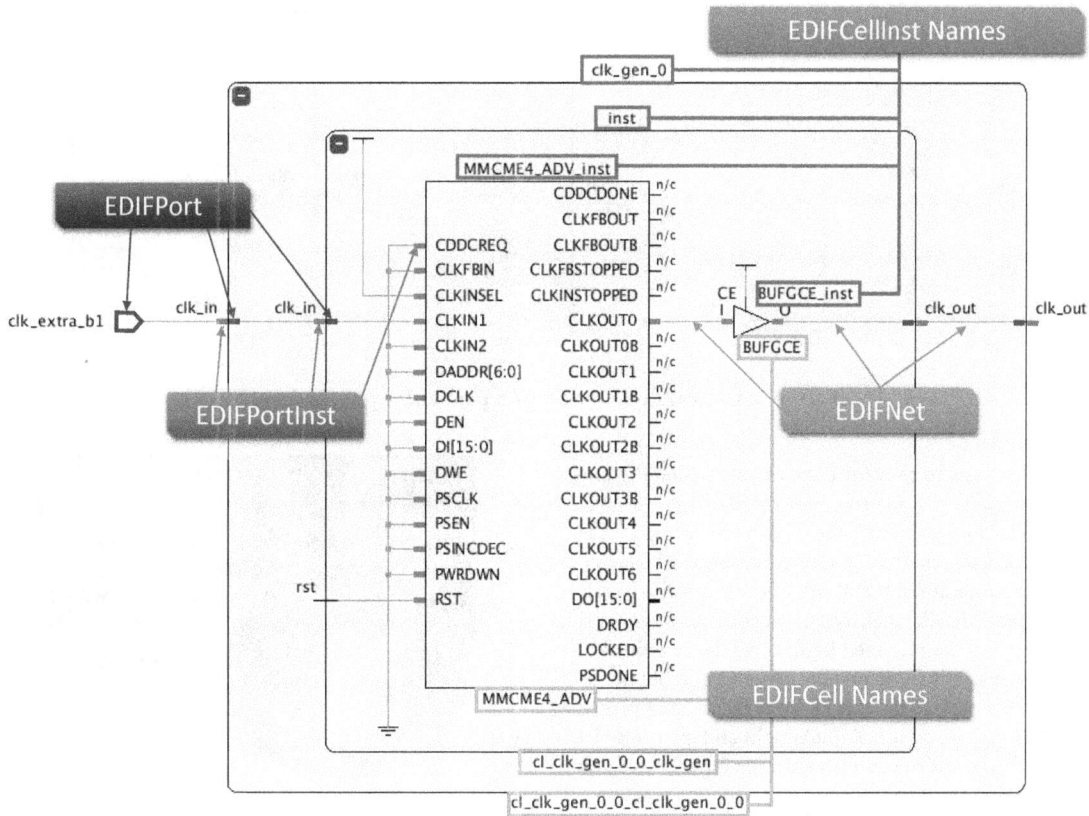

Figure 3: EDIF Data Structure Reference to Vivado Netlist View

references entering/leaving the cell). Figure 3 illustrates how Rapid-Wright EDIF-based objects map to a Vivado netlist schematic view.

2.3 Design Package (Physical Netlist)

The design package is the collection of objects used to describe how a logical netlist maps to a device netlist. A design is also referred to as a physical netlist or implementation. It contains all of the primitive logical cell mappings to hardware, specifically the cell to BEL placements and physical net mapping to programmable interconnect or routing.

The Design class in RapidWright is the central hub of information for a design. It keeps track of the logical netlist, physical netlist, constraints, the device and part references among other things. The Design class is most similar to a design checkpoint in that it contains all the information necessary to create a DCP file. The remainder of this subsection describes the major object classes found in the design package.

2.4 Cell (A BEL Instance)

At the lowest level, a RapidWright Cell maps a logical leaf cell from the EDIF netlist (EDIFCellInst) to a BEL as shown in Figure 4. The cell name is typically the full hierarchical logical name of the leaf cell to which it maps. A cell also maintains the logical cell pin mappings to the physical cell pin mappings (BELPins).

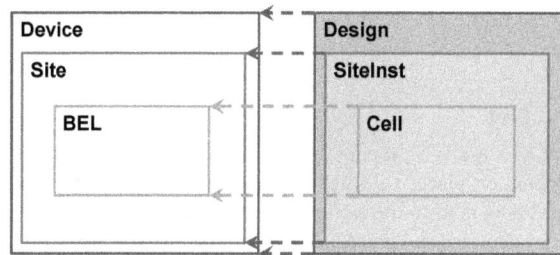

Figure 4: Shows mapping between BEL/Cell, Site/SiteInst and Device/Design.

2.5 SiteInst

Design representation and implementation in Vivado is BEL-centric (BELs and cells). The SiteInst keeps track of three major mappings/attributes:

(1) Map of all cells to BELs (placements in site)
(2) Activated Site PIPs (intra-site routing)
(3) Nets to Site Wires (intra-site routing)

Each SiteInst maps to a single, compatible site within a device. The SiteInst is configured to a type using a SiteTypeEnum that is either the primary type or an alternate site type of the host site. RapidWright also preserves the same Vivado "fixed" flag which is

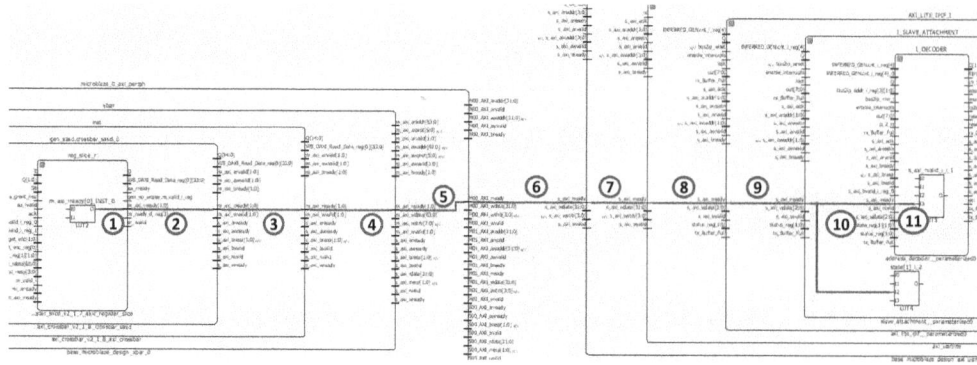

Figure 5: Logical netlist view of a particular physical net

used in certain situations to prevent components inside the site from being moved.

Routing nets inside of a site (intra-site) is different from routing outside of sites (inter-site) and the SiteInst maintains all relevant information concerning intra-site routing. Routing inside of a site must account for placed cells, their type and context. In general, when constructing placed and routed logic, it can be beneficial to compare SiteInst content from Vivado-generated implementations to ensure correctness. This can be done by loading placed and routed DCPs from Vivado into RapidWright and querying the respective SiteInst objects to establish patterns for site wire and site PIP usage.

Routing is accomplished inside a site through SitePIPs, which establish a connection through routing BELs and some logic BELs (such as LUTs). The SiteInst object in RapidWright maintains site PIP usage. By default, all site PIPs are turned off. If a SitePIP is added to the SiteInst then it is marked as being turned on or used.

2.6 Net

A Net in RapidWright contains the routing information to physically connect placed cells using device interconnect or PIPs. Many logical nets map to the same physical net, for example, consider the net depicted in Figure 5. This figure shows the logical netlist connection of three cells over one physical net. However, there are 11 separate logical nets (represented in RapidWright by a EDIFNet) in the logical netlist that must be traversed in order to make the connection. In contrast, Figure 6 shows one physical net for all logical nets.

The implementation of a physical net is stored as a collection of PIPs. PIPs connect nodes together and specify a path from a site pin source to one or more site pin sinks. These instances of site pins are represented by SitePinInst objects (instances of SiteInst objects). The rest of the physical net implementation (intra-site routing) is stored in a SiteInst where a path from site pins to BEL pins is described using annotated site wires and SitePIPs.

2.7 Module

A Module in RapidWright is a physical netlist container, which is a collection of SiteInst and Net objects that describe an abstract

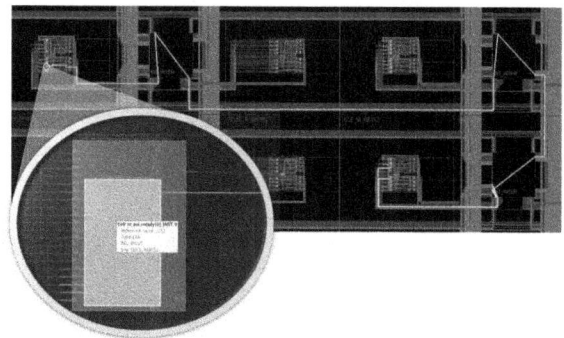

Figure 6: Physical netlist view of a particular physical net

definition of an implementation. This object is unique to Rapid-Wright and is one of its enabling constructs that allows placed and routed information to be preserved, relocated and replicated. A module contains both the logical and physical netlist elements and corresponds to a hierarchical cell within a netlist. It is similar to a placed and routed out-of-context DCP, however RapidWright enables the implementation to be replicated or relocated to multiple compatible areas of the fabric.

A RapidWright module is represented by the Module class in the design package. A module is a definition object whose SiteInst and Net objects specify a blueprint for a pre-implemented block that can potentially be 'stamped' out and relocated in valid locations around a device. The ModuleInst represents the instance object of a Module and is part of the implemented portion of a physical netlist.

2.8 Module Instance

A ModuleInst is an instance of a Module. Typically, definitions of a hierarchical cell are captured in a Module and then 'stamped out' using the module instance construct in a design. The placed and routed locations of the SiteInst and PIPs found in the Nets are relatively relocated according to the desired offset during instantiation or re-location. Modules typically pre-calculate all valid placement locations ahead of time and are stored with the module to make instantiation and placement fast.

ModuleInsts, like Modules, are a collection of SiteInst and Net objects. Each of these object names are prefixed with the name of the ModuleInst, for example, if a module had a SiteInst named "SLICE_X2Y2" and a Net named data_ready, a newly created module instance named "fred" would have counterpart SiteInst and Net objects called "fred/SLICE_X2Y2" and "fred/data_ready."

The Module and ModuleInst constructs are not available in Vivado or the DCP file format. Therefore, if these constructs are used in a RapidWright design they will be 'flattened' when written out as a DCP.

3 RAPIDWRIGHT USE CASES

RapidWright provides a unique set of capabilities not readily available using Vivado alone. Some of these capabilities include direct creation of placed and routed circuits, parameterizable circuit generators and module reuse through pre-implemented modules. This section briefly introduces these concepts as a primer of RapidWright capabilities.

3.1 Direct Synthesis of Placed and Routed Circuits

RapidWright is designed with sufficient capabilities to produce completely valid placed and routed circuits from scratch. It is not recommended to pursue this approach for large or complex designs, but it can be extremely useful in situations where a well-defined implementation is desired.

The circuit in Figure 7 is created, placed and routed using RapidWright code in Listing 1. Although this "hello, world" example is simple, it provides a small glimpse of the possibilities RapidWright has to offer. This circuit is a two-input AND gate packed into a LUT targeting the Zynq device on a PYNQ-Z1 board. It connects two button inputs to an output LED and will only illuminate if both buttons are pressed.

At runtime, the code is able to load the device model for a Zynq 7020 part, create the netlist, place the cells, route their interconnections and write out a DCP file in less than two seconds. Note that RapidWright provides APIs that both create cells in the netlist and places them on the device. For each Cell created, an EDIFCellInst is created and instantiated in the EDIFNetlist of the Design. This example also shows that intra-site routing and inter-site routing are separate APIs to allow for greater flexibility in implementation.

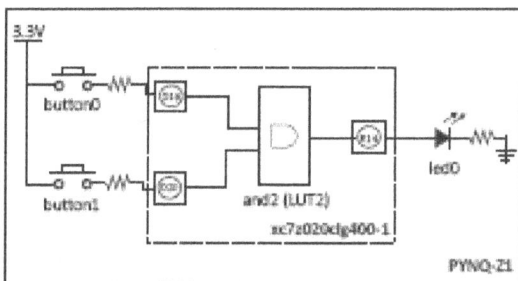

Figure 7: RapidWright "hello, world" Example

```
// Create a new empty design using the PYNQ-Z1 device part
Design d = new Design("HelloWorld",Device.PYNQ_Z1);

// Create and place all the design elements (LUT2, and 3 IOs)
String placementLoc = "SLICE_X100Y100/A6LUT";
String v = "LVCMOS33";
Cell and2    = d.createAndPlaceCell("and2", Unisim.AND2, placementLoc);
Cell button0 = d.createAndPlaceIOB("button0", PinType.IN , "D19", v);
Cell button1 = d.createAndPlaceIOB("button1", PinType.IN , "D20", v);
Cell led0    = d.createAndPlaceIOB("led0"   , PinType.OUT, "R14", v);

// Connect Button 0 to the LUT2 input I0
Net net0 = d.createNet("button0_IBUF");
net0.connect(button0, "O");
net0.connect(and2, "I0");

// Connect Button 1 to the LUT2 input I1
Net net1 = d.createNet("button1_IBUF");
net1.connect(button1, "O");
net1.connect(and2, "I1");

// Connect the LUT2 (AND2) to the LED IO
Net net2 = d.createNet("and2");
net2.connect(and2, "O");
net2.connect(led0, "I");

// Route intra-site nets (portions of net in a site)
d.routeSites();

// Route inter-site nets (between sites)
new Router(d).routeDesign();

// Save our work in a Design Checkpoint file
d.writeCheckpoint("HelloWorld.dcp");
```

Listing 1: RapidWright "hello, world" Code Example

3.2 Parameterizable Circuit Generators

RapidWright's ability to create fully placed and routed circuits from scratch enables a new class of design we call generators. Several parameterizable circuit generators are included with the RapidWright distribution. One significant example is the parameterizable SLR crossing generator which can produce a DCP solution within a few seconds. This SLR crossing generator targets UltraScale+ devices as they have the architectural capabilities that enable clocking techniques that achieve near-spec (>700MHz) performance (UltraScale and Series 7 devices, do not possess these capabilities).

The generator will create pairs of flip flops in a netlist for each crossing signal and will place them at the appropriate Laguna sites to leverage the dedicated super long line (SLL) interconnect paths. As mentioned in [1], using both dedicated RX and TX Laguna site flops will often produce hold time violations. RapidWright is able to circumvent this issue by routing the clock in such a way that all TX and RX flops are connected exclusively to the same clock arm. This enables a tuning of the clock delay at the common leaf clock buffer for each group of crossing signals in each direction respectively.

Additionally, the SLR crossing generator can potentially create a custom clock root for each SLR crossing group (crossings in the same clock region) to minimize the inter-SLR compensation timing penalty. By fabricating the netlist, placing the flops onto the dedicated RX and TX Laguna sites and custom routing the clock to tune leaf clock buffers and create clock roots, the generator is able to create a placed and routed DCP of an SLR bridge in a few seconds.

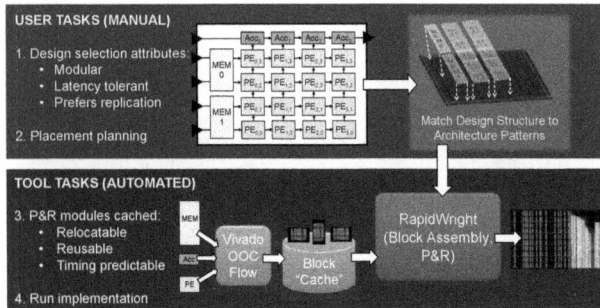

Figure 8: Pre-implemented Methodology

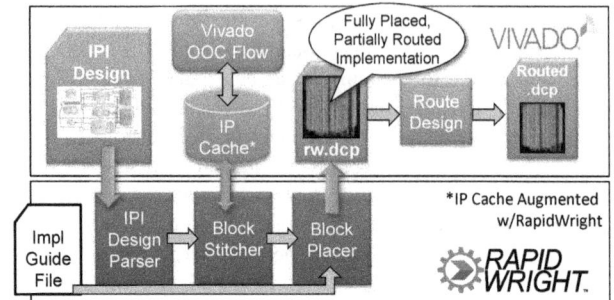

Figure 9: Pre-implemented Block Compilation Flow

3.3 A Modular Pre-implemented Methodology

One of the key attributes of RapidWright is the ability to capture optimized placement and routing solutions in a module and reuse them in multiple contexts or locations on a device. Vivado often provides good results for small implementation problems (smaller than 10k LUTs within a clock region). However, as design size grows, it is no longer practical to find near-optimal solutions within a short compile time. We show how to preserve and reuse high quality solutions in RapidWright with pre-implemented modules, and propose a methodology of how they can improve the overall system performance in a large design.

3.3.1 Pre-implemented Modules. Pre-implemented modules are self-contained netlist cells that contain relative placement and routing information (generally with a rectangular footprint) targeting a specific FPGA device. RapidWright generates pre-implemented modules by invoking Vivado to synthesize, place and route them out-of-context (OOC) of the original design. RapidWright then preserves and packages the placement and routing information from the OOC DCP as a RapidWright Module (see Section 2.7).

For a pre-implemented module to be reusable, it often needs to be area constrained with a pblock with the additional property CONTAIN_ROUTING=1. This ensures that placement and routing of the module is restricted to the respective rectangle, reducing its footprint such that it has a higher number of compatible placement locations across the device.

3.3.2 Design Strategy and Flow. RapidWright endows users with a new design vocabulary by caching, reusing and relocating pre-implemented blocks. We believe this to be an enabling concept and offer a high performance design strategy as depicted in Figure 8.

The first step requires the design architect to select and/or re-structure a proposed design such that it can take full advantage of the benefits provided by pre-implemented modules. We define restructuring as a design refactoring that reflects three favorable design characteristics: (1) modularity, (2) module replication and (3) latency tolerance. Modularity uncovers design structure so it can be strategically mapped to architectural patterns. When modules are replicated, reuse of those high quality solutions and architectural patterns can be exploited to increase the benefits. Finally, if the modules within a design tolerate additional latency, inserting pipeline elements between them improves both timing performance and relocatability.

After the design architect has successfully restructured and modularized a design, step two of Figure 8 is followed. Here, the design architect creates an implementation guide file (see Section 3.3.3) that captures how best to map the modules of a design to the architecture of the target device. Specifically, pblocks (area constraints) are chosen for those pre-implemented modules of interest and physical locations are chosen for each instance. This step provides the design architect an opportunity to navigate FPGA fabric discontinuities. These discontinuities include boundaries such as IO columns, processor subsystems, and most significantly, SLR crossings. Such architectural obstacles cause design disruptions when targeting high performance. However, by leveraging the pre-implemented methodology provided in RapidWright, custom-created implementation solutions can be identified and planned out to manage the fabric discontinuities by custom module placement. Ultimately, this process is iterative and can inform useful RTL/design changes by focusing design structure to better match architectural resources.

Step three of the design strategy is an automated flow provided with RapidWright, whose details are denoted in Figure 9. We leverage Vivado IP Integrator (IPI)[7] for design input. IPI offers an interactive block-based approach for system design by providing an IP library, IP creation flow and IP caching. RapidWright takes advantage of IPI by using leaf IP blocks as de-facto pre-implemented blocks and also by leveraging the IP caching mechanism. The Rapid-Wright pre-implemented flow extends the caching mechanism to go beyond synthesis, by performing OOC placement and routing on the block within a constrained area. The flow begins by invoking Vivado's typical IPI synthesis and creating pre-implemented blocks for each module if not already found in the cache. RapidWright has an IPI Design Parser (EDIF-based) that creates a black-box netlist where each instance of a module is empty, ready to receive the pre-implemented module. The block stitcher reads the IP cache and populates the IPI design netlist. After stitching, the blocks are placed according to the implementation guide file from the design architect. Once all the blocks are placed, RapidWright creates a DCP file that is read into Vivado that completes the final routes.

3.3.3 Implementation Guide File. An implementation guide file (extension *.igf) allows the application architect to communicate all of the specific implementation customization aspects of the packing and placement phase. An example snippet of an implementation guide file can be seen in Figure 10.

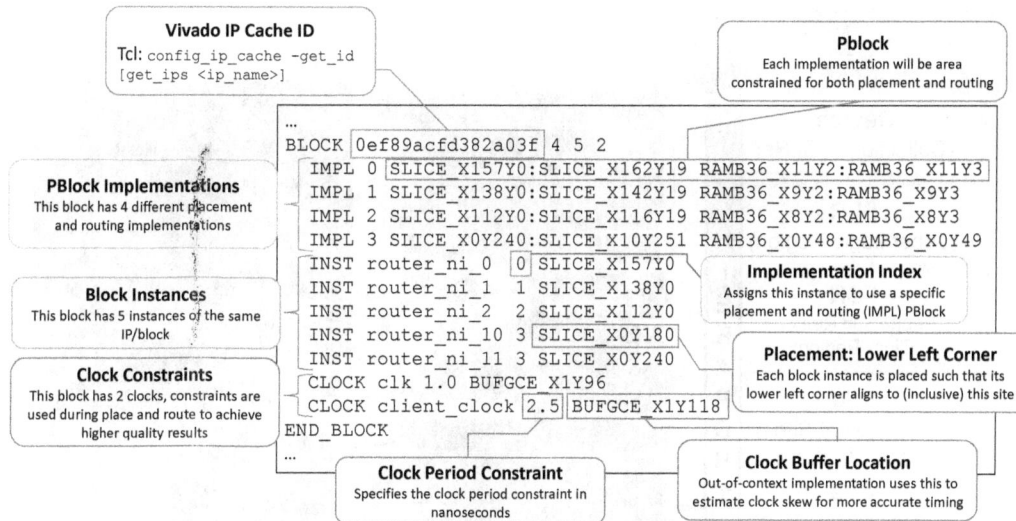

```
...
BLOCK 0ef89acfd382a03f 4 5 2
    IMPL 0 SLICE_X157Y0:SLICE_X162Y19  RAMB36_X11Y2:RAMB36_X11Y3
    IMPL 1 SLICE_X138Y0:SLICE_X142Y19  RAMB36_X9Y2:RAMB36_X9Y3
    IMPL 2 SLICE_X112Y0:SLICE_X116Y19  RAMB36_X8Y2:RAMB36_X8Y3
    IMPL 3 SLICE_X0Y240:SLICE_X10Y251  RAMB36_X0Y48:RAMB36_X0Y49
    INST router_ni_0   0 SLICE_X157Y0
    INST router_ni_1   1 SLICE_X138Y0
    INST router_ni_2   2 SLICE_X112Y0
    INST router_ni_10  3 SLICE_X0Y180
    INST router_ni_11  3 SLICE_X0Y240
    CLOCK clk 1.0 BUFGCE_X1Y96
    CLOCK client_clock 2.5 BUFGCE_X1Y118
END_BLOCK
...
```

Figure 10: Implementation Guide File (*.igf) Example

The block construct describes all of the potential implementations for a particular block/IP. For each uniquely configured IP (entry in the IP cache), there exists a block. Multiple instances of the same block/IP can exist and this construct allows the application architect to map instances by name to a specific implementation.

Each block has one or more IMPLs. Each implementation carries a pblock and potentially some SUB_IMPL which allows for sub pblocks to be applied to portions of the logic inside the block. Each IMPL is indexed so that it can be referenced and applied to specific instances of the block. The application architect takes special care in selecting implementations and their pblocks to maximize there potential performance, architectural footprint and placement packing efficiency.

The SUB_IMPL is an optional construct that allows finer-grained pblocks to be applied to a partial subset of the block/IP in an implementation. One field requires a Tcl command that returns a subset of cells that should be included in the sub implementation and associated pblock. Multiple sub implementation entries can exist for each implementation. For example, if a particular IP is tall and narrow and there are specific cells that need to be placed at the top and bottom, the SUB_IMPL construct can be used to pblock the top and bottom specific cells in sub pblock of the overall implementation.

In each design, there will be one or more instances of a block/IP. Each instance has a unique name and must be assigned to an implementation. Each instance also requires a placement which is provided by denoting a specific site onto which the lower left corner of the pblock of the respective implementation could be placed.

The clock construct describes a clock input to the block or IP and allows it to apply a clock period constraint in nanoseconds. It also requires the BUFGCE site from which the clock will be driven so that during placement and routing, the clock skew can be estimated.

4 CONCLUDING REMARKS

We have provided an introductory overview and use cases for Rapid-Wright. RapidWright enables an implementation vocabulary that lays the ground work for next generation domain-specific tools targeting FPGAs. As FPGAs present a valuable platform for domain-specific architectures, the tools' productivity and performance will become even more critical to the success of a project. We invite industry and academic researchers to help us build a new generation of domain-specific tools that will further capitalize on the potential of FPGAs.

For more examples, documentation and tutorials on RapidWright, please visit www.rapidwright.io.

A APPENDIX: XILINX ARCHITECTURE

RapidWright is an implementation-centric framework targeting Xilinx FPGAs and to use it effectively, an understanding of Xilinx FPGA architecture will be needed. RapidWright presents the same constructs and device representations found in Vivado's device model. A cross-reference between RapidWright and Vivado objects/APIs is shown in Table 1. There are there are six major levels of hierarchy used to implement logic as shown in the first row of Table 1: Device, SLR, ClockRegion, Tile, Site and BEL. These six logic hierarchy levels are also illustrated in Figure 11. There are also several wiring and interconnect constructs related to routing listed in row 2 of Table 1: PIP, Wire, Node, SitePIP, SitePin, SiteWire and BELPin. With the exception of SitePIP, these are illustrated in Figure 12. The remainder of this section will briefly describe each of the six logical hierarchy objects with routing objects described in their context.

A.1 BEL (Basic Element of Logic)

The atomic unit of Xilinx FPGAs is a basic element of logic (BEL). There are two kinds of BELs, Logic BELs and Routing BELs. A Logic BEL is a configurable logic-based site that can support the implementation of a design cell (such as a LUT or flip-flop). Each BEL can support one or more types of UNISIM cells (UNISIM cells are described in [4] for Series 7 devices and [6] for UltraScale devices). The mapping between a leaf cell in the netlist and a BEL site is

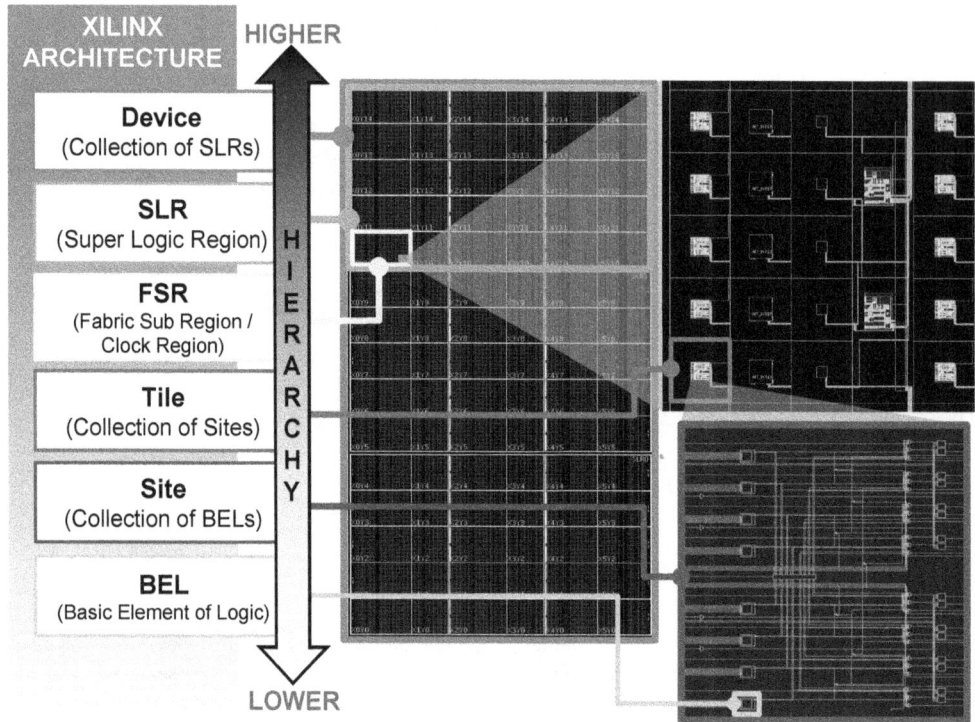

Figure 11: Xilinx FPGA Architecture Hierarchy

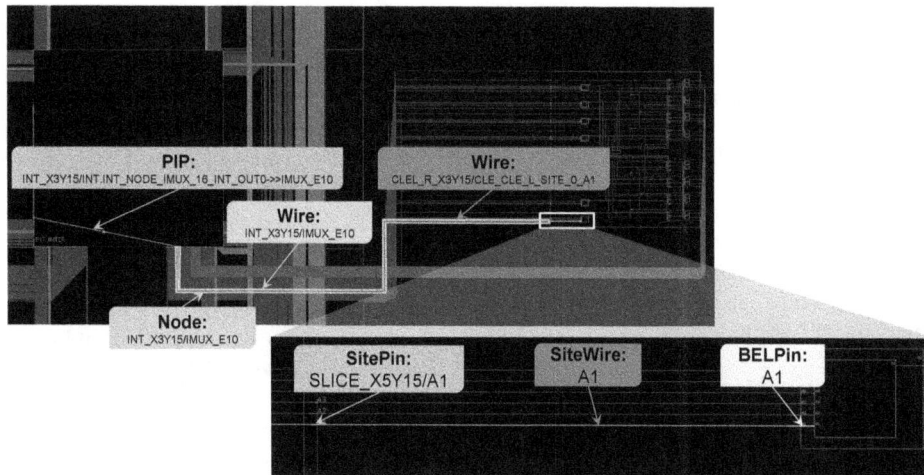

Figure 12: Intersite and Intrasite Routing Resources

referred to as the "placement" of the cell. Non-leaf cells represent hierarchy of the netlist and do not require placement. Thus, when one runs the Vivado command place_design, it is essentially mapping all leaf cells in the netlist to compatible and legal BEL sites.

Routing BELs are programmable muxes used to route signals between BELs. Routing BELs do not support any design elements (logic cells from the netlist do not occupy routing BEL sites). However, some routing BELs do have optional inversions.

BELs have input and output pins and configurable connections that connect an input pin to an output pin. These BEL-based configurable connections are called site PIPs (Programmable Interconnect Points). Both logic BELs and routing BELs can have site PIPs. However, in the case of a logic BEL, the site must be unoccupied by a cell for the site PIP to be usable. These site PIPs, when implemented in logic BELs (such as a LUT), are called "route-thrus." When routing a design, it is sometimes necessary to route through unused LUTs (or other BELs) using site PIPs to complete a route.

A.2 Site

A group of related elements and their connectivity is referred to as a site. Inside a site, one can find three major categories of objects:

(1) BELs (Logic BELs and/or Routing BELs)
(2) Site Pins (External input and output pins to the site)
(3) Site wires (connecting elements to each other and site pins)

Sites are instances of a type and each site has a unique name with an _X#Y# suffix denoting its location in the site type grid. Each site type will have its own XY coordinate grid, independent of other types. The only exception are SLICEL and SLICEM types that share the same grid space. SLICEL and SLICEM are the most common site types and are the basic configurable logic building blocks that contain LUTs and flip flops replacing the backbone of the FPGA fabric.

A.3 Tile

A collection of sites is packaged into a tile, although several tiles do not have sites. At an abstract level, Xilinx devices are created by assembling a grid of tiles. Similar to sites, each tile is an instance of a type and each tile has a unique name with an _X#Y# suffix. Tiles are designed to abut one another when laid down to construct an FPGA device.

Unlike sites and BELs, tiles do not have user visible pins. Instead, tiles contain uniquely-named wires that can connect to site pins or PIPs. In the context of a tile, PIPs connect two tile wires together. Most PIPs are present in switch box tiles (those with the "INT" prefix). Columns of switch box tiles are designed to connect to all fabric resources such as CLBs, DSPs, and BRAMs. When tiles abut, they are designed such that certain wires in the adjoining tiles line up and connect as shown in Figure 13.

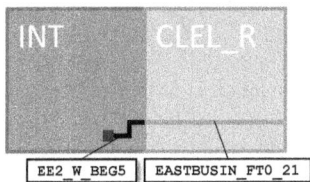

Figure 13: Two wires in abutting tiles

As there are no pins on tiles, instead cross-tile connectivity is represented by a node. A node is a collection of electrically connected wires that spans one or more tiles. Figure 14 shows how four wires in four tiles abut to form a node.

A.4 FSR (Fabric Sub Region or Clock Region)

A fabric sub region, also known as a clock region, is a replicated 2D array of tiles in the fabric. Xilinx uses a column-based architecture where each column of tiles are generally of the same type. In the UltraScale architecture, all FSRs are 60 CLBs (common logic block tiles) tall, but their width will vary depending on the mix of tile types used in its construction.

Clock routing and distribution lines are represented at the same granularity as clock regions. In UltraScale architectures, there are

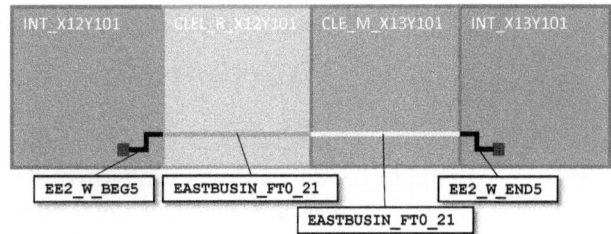

Figure 14: A node composed of four wires in tile context

24 horizontal routing tracks, 24 vertical routing tracks, 24 horizontal distribution tracks and 24 vertical distribution tracks per clock region. These routing and distribution tracks abut to tracks in neighboring clock regions to form the device clock network resource set. Additional information specific to clocking resources can be found in [2] for Series 7 devices and [3] for UltraScale devices.

A.5 SLR (Super Logic Region)

A super logic region (SLR) is a 2D grid of FSRs. This level of hierarchy is only relevant on devices that use stacked silicon interconnect technology (SSIT – also known as 2.5D), essentially a packaging of multiple die together with a silicon interposer. Each die in a multi-die device is an SLR.

In order for logic to communicate between SLRs, the UltraScale architecture employs special "Laguna" tiles in the FSRs neighboring the abutment of two SLRs. Laguna tiles have dedicated flip flop sites to aid in crossing the SLR divide.

A.6 Device

At the highest level of Xilinx architecture is the device. This encapsulates any and all SLRs present. The device object in Vivado is implicit (not directly referenced) but only one device can be loaded at a time. The core object in RapidWright is the Device class for any Xilinx device as described in Section 2.

REFERENCES

[1] C. Lavin and A. Kaviani. 2018. RapidWright: Enabling Custom Crafted Implementations for FPGAs. In *2018 IEEE 26th Annual International Symposium on Field-Programmable Custom Computing Machines (FCCM)*. IEEE, https://doi.org/10.1109/FCCM.2018.00030, 133–140.
[2] Xilinx, Inc. 2018. *UG472 (v1.14): 7 Series FPGAs Clocking Resources User Guide*. Xilinx, Inc. https://www.xilinx.com/support/documentation/user_guides/ug472_7Series_Clocking.pdf.
[3] Xilinx, Inc. 2018. *UG572 (v1.7): UltraScale Architecture Clocking Resources User Guide*. Xilinx, Inc. https://www.xilinx.com/support/documentation/user_guides/ug572-ultrascale-clocking.pdf.
[4] Xilinx, Inc. 2018. *UG953: Vivado Design Suite 7 Series FPGA and Zynq-7000 SoC Libraries Guide*. Xilinx, Inc. https://www.xilinx.com/support/documentation/sw_manuals/xilinx2018_2/ug953-vivado-7series-libraries.pdf.
[5] Xilinx, Inc. 2018. *UG973 (v2018.1): Vivado Design Suite User Guide Release Notes, Installation and Licensing*. Xilinx, Inc. https://www.xilinx.com/support/documentation/sw_manuals/xilinx2018_1/ug973-vivado-release-notes-install-license.pdf.
[6] Xilinx, Inc. 2018. *UG974: UltraScale Architecture Libraries Guide*. Xilinx, Inc. https://www.xilinx.com/support/documentation/sw_manuals/xilinx2018_2/ug974-vivado-ultrascale-libraries.pdf.
[7] Xilinx, Inc. 2018. *UG994 (v2018.2): Vivado Design Suite User Guide Designing IP Subsystems Using IP Integrator*. Xilinx, Inc. https://www.xilinx.com/support/documentation/sw_manuals/xilinx2018_2/ug994-vivado-ip-subsystems.pdf.

Synetgy: Algorithm-hardware Co-design for ConvNet Accelerators on Embedded FPGAs

Yifan Yang[1,2,*], Qijing Huang[1], Bichen Wu[1], Tianjun Zhang[1], Liang Ma[3], Giulio Gambardella[4],
Michaela Blott[4], Luciano Lavagno[3], Kees Vissers[4], John Wawrzynek[1], Kurt Keutzer[1]

[1]UC Berkeley; [2]Tsinghua University; [3]Politecnico di Torino; [4]Xilinx Research Labs

{yifan-yang,qijing.huang,bichen,tianjunz,johnw,keutzer}@berkeley.edu;
{luciano.lavagno,liang-ma}@polito.it;{giuliog,mblott,keesv}@xilinx.com

ABSTRACT

Using FPGAs to accelerate ConvNets has attracted significant attention in recent years. However, FPGA accelerator design has not leveraged the latest progress of ConvNets. As a result, the key application characteristics such as frames-per-second (FPS) are ignored in favor of simply counting GOPs, and results on accuracy, which is critical to application success, are often not even reported. In this work, we adopt an algorithm-hardware co-design approach to develop a ConvNet accelerator called Synetgy and a novel ConvNet model called DiracDeltaNet[†]. Both the accelerator and ConvNet are tailored to FPGA requirements. DiracDeltaNet, as the name suggests, is a ConvNet with only 1×1 convolutions while spatial convolutions are replaced by more efficient shift operations. DiracDeltaNet achieves competitive accuracy on ImageNet (89.0% top-5), but with 48× fewer parameters and 65× fewer OPs than VGG16. We further quantize DiracDeltaNet's weights to 1-bit and activations to 4-bits, with less than 1% accuracy loss. These quantizations exploit well the nature of FPGA hardware. In short, DiracDeltaNet's small model size, low computational OP count, ultra-low precision and simplified operators allow us to co-design a highly customized computing unit for an FPGA. We implement the computing units for DiracDeltaNet on an Ultra96 SoC system through high-level synthesis. Our accelerator's final top-5 accuracy of 88.2% on ImageNet, is higher than all the previously reported embedded FPGA accelerators. In addition, the accelerator reaches an inference speed of 96.5 FPS on the ImageNet classification task, surpassing prior works with similar accuracy by at least 16.9×.

ACM Reference Format:
Yifan Yang, Qijing Huang, Bichen Wu, Tianjun Zhang, Liang Ma, Giulio Gambardella, Michaela Blott, Luciano Lavagno, Kees Vissers, John Wawrzynek, Kurt Keutzer. 2019. Synetgy: Algorithm-hardware Co-design for ConvNet Accelerators on Embedded FPGAs. In *The 2019 ACM/SIGDA International*

---

*Work done while interning at UC Berkeley.
† Source code and pre-trained model are available at https://github.com/Yang-YiFan/DiracDeltaNet.

Symposium on Field-Programmable Gate Arrays (FPGA'19), February 24–26, 2019, Seaside, CA, USA. ACM, New York, NY, USA, 10 pages. https://doi.org/10.1145/3289602.3293902

1 INTRODUCTION

ConvNets power state-of-the-art solutions on a wide range of computer vision tasks. However, the high computational complexity of ConvNets hinders their deployment on embedded and mobile devices, where computational resources are limited. Using FPGAs to accelerate ConvNets has attracted significant research attention in recent years. FPGAs excel at low-precision computation, and their adaptability to new algorithms lends themselves to supporting rapidly changing ConvNet models.

Despite recent efforts to use FPGAs to accelerate ConvNets, as [1] points out, there still exists a wide gap between accelerator architecture design and ConvNet model design. The computer vision community has been primarily focusing on improving the accuracy of ConvNets on target benchmarks with only secondary attention to the computational cost of ConvNets. As a consequence, recent ConvNets have been trending toward more layers [2], more complex structures [3, 4], and more complicated operations [5].

On the other hand, FPGA accelerator design has not leveraged the latest progress of ConvNets. Many FPGA designs still focus on networks trained on CIFAR10 [6], a small dataset consisting of 32x32 thumbnail images. Such dataset is usually used for experimental purposes and is too small to have practical value. More recent designs aim to accelerate inefficient ConvNets such as AlexNet [7] or VGG16 [8], both of which have fallen out of use in state-of-the-art computer vision applications. In addition, we observe that in many previous designs, key application characteristics such as frames-per-second (FPS) are ignored in favor of simply counting GOPs, and accuracy, which is critical to applications, is often not even reported.

Specifically, we see a gap between ConvNet architectures and accelerator design in the following areas:

Inefficient ConvNet models: Many FPGA accelerators still target older, inefficient models such as AlexNet and VGG16, which require orders-of-magnitude greater storage and computational resources than newer, efficient models that achieve the same accuracy. With an inefficient model, an accelerator with high throughput in terms of GOPs can actually have low inference speed in terms of FPS, where FPS is the more essential metric of efficiency. To achieve AlexNet-level accuracy, SqueezeNet [9] is 50x smaller than AlexNet; SqueezeNext [10] is 112x smaller; ShiftNet-C [11], with 1.6% higher accuracy, is 77x smaller. However, not many designs target those efficient models. Additionally, techniques for accelerating older models may not generalize to newer ConvNets.

ConvNet structures: Most ConvNets are structured solely for better accuracy. Some ConvNets are structured for optimal GPU efficiency, but few, if any, are designed for optimal FPGA efficiency. For example, the commonly used additive skip connection [12] alleviates the difficulty of training deep ConvNets and significantly boosts accuracy. Despite its mathematical simplicity, the additive skip connection is difficult to efficiently implement on FPGAs. Additive skip connections involve adding the output data from a previous layer to the current layer, which requires either using on-chip memory to buffer the previous layer's output or fetching the output from off-chip memory. Both options are inefficient on FPGAs.

ConvNet operators: ConvNet models contain many different types of operators. Commonly used operators include 1×1, 3×3, 5×5 convolutions, 3×3 max-pooling, etc. More recent models also contain depth-wise, group, dilated, and factorized convolutions. Not all of these operators can be efficiently implemented on FPGAs. If a ConvNet contains many different types of operators, one must either allocate more dedicated compute units or make the compute unit more general. Either solution can potentially lead to high resource requirement, limited parallelism, and more complicated control flow. Also, hardware development will require more engineering effort.

Quantization: ConvNet quantization has been widely used to convert weights and activations from floating point to low-precision numbers to reduce the computational cost. However, many of the previous methods are not practically useful for FPGAs due to the following problems: 1) Quantization can lead to serious accuracy loss, especially if the network is quantized to ultra-low precision numbers (less than 4 bits). Accuracy is vital for many computer vision applications. Unfortunately, carefully reporting accuracy has not been the norm in the FPGA community. 2) Many of the previously presented quantization methods are only effective on large ConvNet models such as VGG16, AlexNet, ResNet, etc. Since those models are known to be redundant, quantizing those to low-precision is much easier. We are not aware of any previous work tested on efficient models such as MobileNet or ShuffleNet. 3) Many methods do not quantize weights and activations directly to fixed point numbers. Usually, quantized weights and activations are represented by fixed-point numbers multiplied by some shared floating point coefficients. Such representation requires more complicated computation than purely fixed-point operations, and are therefore more expensive.

In this work, we adopt an algorithm-hardware co-design approach to develop a ConvNet accelerator called Synetgy and a novel ConvNet model called DiracDeltaNet. Both the accelerator and the ConvNet are tailored to FPGAs and are optimized for ImageNet classification accuracy and inference speed (in terms of FPS). Our co-design approach produces a novel ConvNet architecture DiracDeltaNet that is based on ShuffleNetV2 [13], one of the state-of-the-art efficient models with small model size, low FLOP counts, hardware friendly skip connections, and competitive accuracy. We optimize the network by replacing all 3×3 convolutions with shift operations [11] and 1×1 convolution, enabling us to implement a compute unit customized for 1×1 convolutions for better efficiency. The name "DiracDeltaNet" comes from the fact that the network only convolves input feature maps with 1×1 kernels. Such kernel functions can be seen as discrete 2D Dirac Delta functions. We

further quantize the network to 1-bit (binary) weights and 4-bit activations, exploiting the strengths of FPGAs, with only a less than 1% accuracy drop. To our knowledge, our work is the first to report such high compression rate on efficient models. In short, DiracDeltaNet's small model size, low operation count, ultra-low precision and simplified operators allow us to co-design a highly customized and efficient FPGA accelerator. Furthermore, the implementation only took two people working for one month using High-Level Synthesis (HLS).

We trained DiracDeltaNet on ImageNet, implemented it on our accelerator architecture, Synetgy, and deployed on a low-cost FPGA board (Ultra96). Our inference speed reaches 96.5 FPS, surpassing previous works with similar accuracy by at least 16.9x. The DiracDeltaNet on our accelerator architecture also achieves 88.2% top-5 classification accuracy – the highest among all the previously reported embedded FPGA accelerators.

2 BACKGROUND

2.1 Efficient ConvNet Models

For the task of image classification, improving accuracy on the ImageNet [14] dataset has been the primary focus of the computer vision community. For applications that are sensitive to accuracy, even a 1% improvement in accuracy on ImageNet is worth doubling or tripling model complexity. As a concrete example, ResNet152 [12] achieves 1.36% higher ImageNet accuracy than ResNet50 at the cost of 3x more layers. In recent years, efficient ConvNet models have begun to receive more research attention. SqueezeNet [9] is one of the early models focusing on reducing the parameter size. While SqueezeNet is designed for image classification, later models, including SqueezeDet [15] and SqueezeSeg [16, 17], extend the scope to object detection and point-cloud segmentation. More recent models such as MobileNet [18, 19] and ShuffleNet [13, 20] further reduce model complexity. However, without a target computing platform in mind, most models designed for "efficiency" can only target intermediate proxies to efficiency, such as parameter size or FLOP count, instead of focusing on more salient efficiency metrics, such as speed and energy. Recent works also try to bring in hardware insight to improve the actual efficiency. SqueezeNext[10] uses a hardware simulator to adjust the macro-architecture of the network for better efficiency. ShiftNet[11] proposes a hardware-friendly shift operator to replace expensive spatial convolutions. AddressNet[21] designed three shift-based primitives to accelerate GPU inference.

2.2 ConvNet Quantization

ConvNet quantization aims to convert full-precision weights and activations of a network to low-precision representations to reduce the computation and storage cost. Early works [22, 23] mainly focus on quantizing weights while still using full-precision activations. Later works [24–27] quantize both weights and activations. Many previous works [23–25] see serious accuracy loss if the network is quantized to ultra-low precisions. Normally, an accuracy loss of more than 1% is already considered significant. Also, in many works [23, 26], quantized weights or activations are represented by low-precision numbers multiplied with some floating point coefficients. This can bring several challenges to hardware implementation. Last, but not least, most of the previous works report quantization results on inefficient models such as VGG, AlexNet, and ResNet. Given that those models are redundant, quantizing them to lower precisions is much easier. We have not yet seen any work which successfully applies quantization to efficient models.

2.3 Hardware Designs

Most existing ConvNet hardware research has focused on improving the performance of either standalone 3×3 convolution layers or a full-fledged, large ConvNet on large FPGA devices. [28] quantitatively studies the computation throughput and memory bandwidth requirement for ConvNets. [29, 30] present their own optimization for ConvNets based on analytical performance models. They achieve high throughput on VGG16 using their proposed design methodology with OpenCL. [31] designs convolution in frequency domain to reduce the compute intensity of the ConvNet. They demonstrate good power performance results on VGG16, AlexNet, and GoogLeNet. [32] implements a ternary neural network on high-end Intel FPGAs and achieves higher performance/Watt than Titan X GPU. Most of the works mentioned above and others [33–35], target inefficient ConvNets on middle to high-end FPGA devices. For compact ConvNets, [36] demonstrates a binary neural network(BNN) FPGA design that performs CIFAR10 classification at 21906 frames per second(FPS) with 283 μs latency on Xilinx ZC706 device. The BNN reports an accuracy of 80.1%. [37, 38] run the BNN on a smaller device ZC7020. Although all three works achieve promising frame rates, they have not implemented larger neural networks for the ImageNet classification. It should be noted that classification on CIFAR10 dataset is orders of magnitude simpler than ImageNet, since CIFAR10 contains 100x fewer classes, 26x fewer images, and 49x fewer pixels in each image. Networks trained on CIFAR10 dataset also have way smaller complexity compared to those trained on ImageNet. In comparison, networks for ImageNet classification are closer to real-world applicability. [39] first attempted to deploy VGG-16 for ImageNet classification on embedded device zc7020 and achieved a frame rate of 4.45 fps. Later [40] improved the frame rate to 5.7 fps. However, their frame rate was relatively low for real-time image classification tasks. [39, 41, 42] have achieved high frame rate on smaller devices, however, the accuracy of their network is not on par with [40] for ImageNet classification.

3 CONVNET DESIGN

We discuss the ConvNet design in this section. The design of our ConvNet incorporates the feedback from both the computer vision applications and hardware accelerator design. Specifically, an ideal ConvNet model for embedded FPGA acceleration should satisfy the following aspects: 1) The network should not contain too many parameters or FLOPs but should still maintain a competitive accuracy. 2) The network structure should be hardware friendly to allow efficient scheduling. 3) The network's operation set should be simplified for efficient FPGA implementation. 4) The network's weights and activations should be quantized to low-precision fixed-point numbers without much accuracy loss.

3.1 ShuffleNetV2

We select ShuffleNetV2-1.0x [13] as our starting point. ShuffleNetV2 is one of the state-of-the-art efficient models. It has a top-1 accuracy of 69.4% on ImageNet (2% lower than VGG16), but contains only 2.3M parameters (60x smaller than VGG16) and 146M FLOPs (109x smaller than VGG16).

The block-level structure of ShuffleNetV2 is illustrated in Fig. 1(a). The input feature map of the block is first split into two parts along the channel dimension. The first branch of the network does nothing to the input data and directly feeds the input to the output. The second branch performs a series of 1×1 convolutions, 3×3 depth-wise convolutions and another 1×1 convolution operations on the input. Outputs of two branches are then concatenated along the channel dimension. Channel shuffle [20] is then applied to exchange information between branches. In down-sampling blocks, depth-wise 3×3 convolutions with a stride of 2 are applied to both branches of the block to reduce the spatial resolution. 1×1 convolutions are used to double the channel size of input feature maps. These blocks are cascaded to build a deep ConvNet. We refer readers to [13] for the macro-structure description of the ShuffleNetV2.

We select ShuffleNetV2-1.0x not only because of its small model size and low FLOP count but also because it uses concatenative skip connections instead of additive skip connections. Additive skip connections, as illustrated in Fig. 2(a), were first proposed in [12]. It effectively alleviates the difficulty of training deep neural networks and therefore improves accuracy. It is widely used in many ConvNet designs. However, additive skip connections are not efficient on FPGAs. As illustrated in Fig. 2(a), both the skip and the residual branches' data need to be fetched on-chip to conduct the addition. Though addition does not cost too much computation, the data movement is expensive. Concatenative skip connections, as illustrated in Fig. 2(b), were first proposed in [3]. It has a similar positive impact to the network training and accuracy. With concatenative skip connections, data from skip branch is already in off-chip DRAMs. So we can concatenate the two branches simply by writing the residual branch data next to the skip branch data. This avoids the extra memory access in additive skip connections and alleviates the memory bandwidth pressure.

3.2 DiracDeltaNet

Based on ShuffleNetV2, we build DiracDeltaNet through the following modifications: 1) we replace all the 3×3 convolutions with shift and 1×1 convolutions; 2) we reduce the kernel size of max-pooling from 3×3 to 2×2; 3) we modify the order of channel shuffle.

We replace all of the 3×3 convolutions and 3×3 depth-wise convolutions with shift operations and 1×1 convolutions. The motivation is that smaller convolution kernel sizes require less reuse of the feature map, resulting in simpler data movement schedule, control flow, and timing constraint. As pointed out by [11], ConvNets rely on spatial convolutions (3×3 convolutions and 3×3 depth-wise convolutions) to aggregate spatial information from neighboring pixels to the center position. However, spatial convolutions can be replaced by a more efficient operator called shift. The shift operator aggregates spatial information by copying nearby pixels directly to the center position. This is equivalent to shifting one channel of feature map towards a certain direction. When we shift different

(a) ShuffleNetV2 blocks [13].

(b) Our modified DiracDeltaNet blocks. We replace depth-wise convolutions with shift operations. In the downsampling blocks, we use stride-2 max-pooling and shift operations to replace stride-2 depthwise convolutions. We also double the filter number of the 1st 1×1 convolution on the non-skip branch in each module.

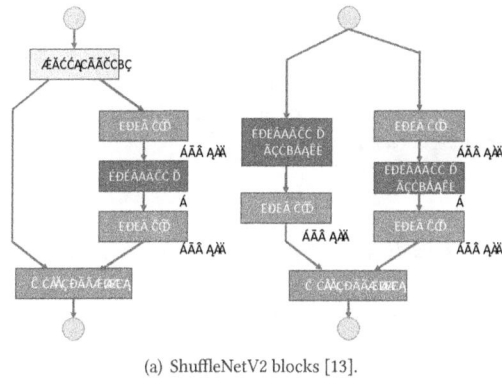

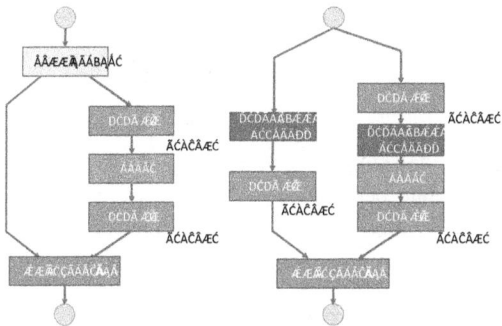

Figure 1: ShuffleNetV2 blocks vs. DiracDeltaNet blocks

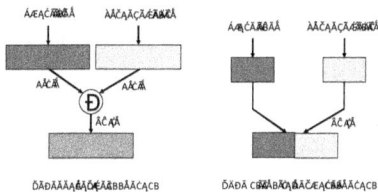

Figure 2: Additive Skip Connections vs. Concatenative Skip Connections. Rectangles represent data tensors.

(a) Transpose based channel shuffle

(b) Our channel shuffle

Figure 3: Transpose Based Shuffle (ShuffleNetV2) vs. Our HW Efficient Shuffle (DiracDeltaNet)

in addition to the identity mapping (no-shift). This simplifies our hardware implementation of the shift operation without hurting accuracy.

The first stage of ShuffleNetV2 consists of a 3×3 convolution with a stride of 2 and filter number of 24. It is then followed by a 3×3 max-pooling with a stride of 2. We replace these two layers to a module consisting of a series of 1×1 convolution, 2×2 max-pooling, and shift operations, as shown in Table 1. Compared with the original 3×3 convolutions, our proposed module has slightly fewer parameters (612 vs 648) and slightly more FLOPs (9.0M vs 8.1M). After training the network, we find that this module gives better accuracy than the original 3×3 convolution module. With our new module, we can eliminate the remaining 3×3 convolutions from our network, enabling us to allocate more computational resources to 1×1 convolutions, and thereby increasing parallelism and throughput.

In addition to replacing all 3×3 convolutions, we also reduce the max-pooling kernel size from 3×3 to 2×2. By using the same pooling kernel size as the stride, we eliminate the need to buffer extra data on the pooling kernel boundaries, thereby achieving better efficiency. Our experiments also show that reducing the max-pooling kernel size does not impact accuracy.

We also modify the channel shuffle's order to make it more hardware efficient. ShuffleNetV2 uses transpose operation to mix channels from two branches. This is illustrated in Fig. 3(a), where blue and red rectangles represent channels from different branches. The transpose based shuffling is not hardware friendly since it breaks the contiguous data layout. Performing channel shuffle in this manner will require multiple passes of memory read and write. We propose a more efficient channel shuffle showed in Fig. 3(b). We perform a circular shift to the feature map along the channel dimension. We can have the same number of channels exchanged between two branches while preserving the contiguity of the feature map and minimizing the memory accesses.

We name the modified ShuffleNetV2-1.0x model as DiracDeltaNet. The name comes from the fact that our network only contains 1×1 convolutions. With a kernel size of 1, the kernel functions can be seen as discrete 2D Dirac Delta functions. DiracDeltaNet's macrostructure is summarized in Table 1. Stage 2,3,4 consist of chained DiracDeltaNet blocks depicted in Fig. 1 with different feature map

channels in different directions, the output feature map's channel will encode all the spatial information. A comparison between 3×3 convolution and shift is illustrated in Fig. 4. A module containing a shift and 1×1 convolution is illustrated in Fig. 5.

For 3×3 depth-wise convolutions, we directly replace them with shift operations, as shown in Fig. 1(b). This direct replacement can lead to some accuracy loss. To mitigate this, we double the output filter number of the first 1×1 convolution on the non-skip branch from Fig. 1(b). Nominally, doubling the output channel size increases both FLOP count and parameter size by a factor of 2. However, getting rid of 3×3 convolutions allows us to design a computing unit customized for 1×1 convolutions with higher execution efficiency than a comparable unit for 3×3 depth-wise convolutions. In the downsample block, we directly replace the strided 3×3 depthwise convolutions with a stride-2 2×2 max-pooling. Unlike [11], our shift operation only uses 4 cardinal directions (up, down, left, right)

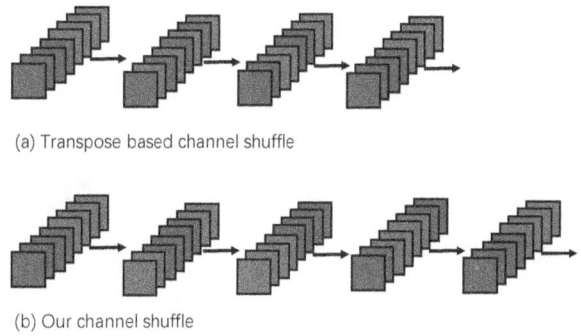

Table 1: Macro-structure of DiracDeltaNet

Layer	Output size	Kernel size	Stride	#Repeat	Output channel
Image	224				3
Conv1	224	1	1	1	
Maxpool	112	2	2	1	12
shift	112	3	1	1	
Conv2	112	1	1	1	
Maxpool	56	2	2	1	48
shift	56	3	1	1	
Stage 2	28	2	1		116
	28		1	3	
Stage 3	14	2	1		232
	14		1	7	
Stage 4	7	2	1		464
	7		1	3	
Conv5	7	1	1	1	1024
GlobalPool	1	7		1	1024
FC				1	1000

Table 2: ShuffleNetV2-1.0x vs. DiracDeltaNet

	MACs	#Params	Top-1 acc	Top-5 acc
ShuffleNetV2-1.0x	146M	2.3M	69.4%	-
DiracDeltaNet	244M	2.9M	69.7%	89.0%

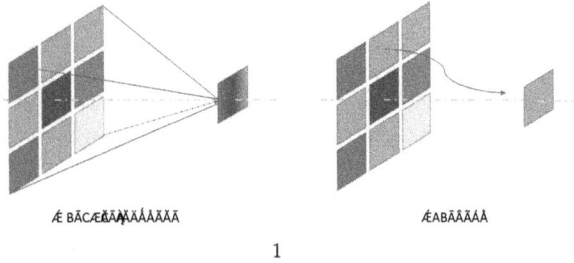

Figure 4: 3×3 Convolution vs. Shift. In 3×3 convolutions, pixels in a 3×3 region are aggregated to compute one output pixel at the center position. In the shift operation, a neighboring pixel is directly copied to the center position.

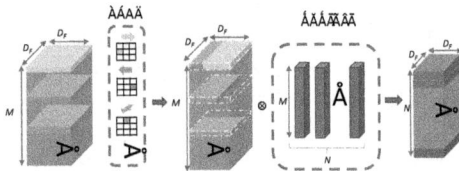

Figure 5: Using shift and 1×1 convolutions to replace 3×3 convolutions. This figure is from [11].

size, channel size and stride. We adopt the training recipe and hyperparameters described in [13]. We train DiracDeltaNet for 360 epoch with linear learning rate decay, the initial learning rate of 0.5, 1024 batch size and 4e-5 weight decay. A comparison between ShuffleNetV2-1.0x and our DiracDeltaNet is summarized in Table 2.

3.3 ConvNet Quantization

To further reduce the cost of DiracDeltaNet, we apply quantization to convert floating point weights and activations to low-precision integer values. For network weights, we follow DoReFa-Net [25] to quantize full-precision weights as

$$w_k = 2Q_k\left(\frac{\tanh(w)}{2\max(|\tanh(w)|)} + 0.5\right) - 1. \tag{1}$$

Here, w denotes the latent full-precision weight of the convolution kernel. $Q_k(\cdot)$ is a function that quantizes its input in the range of $[0, 1]$ to its nearest neighbor in $\{\frac{i}{2^k-1}|i = 0, \cdots 2^{k-1}\}$.

We follow PACT [26] to quantize each layer's activation as

$$y^l = PACT\left(x^l\right) = \frac{\left|x^l\right| - \left|x^l - \left|\alpha^l\right|\right| + \left|\alpha^l\right|}{2},$$
$$y^l = Q_k\left(y^l/\left|\alpha^l\right|\right) \cdot \left|\alpha^l\right|. \tag{2}$$

x^l is the activation of layer-l. $PACT(\cdot)$ is a function that clips the activation x^l to the range between $[0, |\alpha^l|]$. α^l is a layer-wise trainable upper bound, determined by the training of the network. It is observed that during training α^l can sometimes become a negative value, which affects the correctness of the PACT [26] function. To ensure α^l is always positive and to increase training stability, we use the absolute value of the trainable parameter α^l rather than its original value. y^l is the clipped activation from layer-l and it is further quantized to y_k^l, a k-bit activation tensor. Note that activations from the same layer share the same floating point coefficient α^l, but activations from different layers can have different coefficients. This is problematic for the concatenative skip connection, since if the coefficients α^l and α^{l-1} are different, we need to first cast y_k^{l-1} and y_k^l from fixed-point to floating point, re-calculate a coefficient for the merged activation, and quantize it again to new fixed-point numbers. This process is very inefficient.

In our experiment, we notice that most of the layers in the DiracDeltaNet have similar coefficients with values. Therefore, we rewrite equation (2) as

$$y^l = Q_k\left(y^l/\left|\alpha^l\right|\right) \cdot |s|. \tag{3}$$

where s is a coefficient shared by the entire network. This step ensures that activations from different layers of the network are quantized and normalized to the same scale of $[0, |s|]$. As a result, we can concatenate activations from different layers directly without extra computation. Moreover, by using the same coefficient s across the entire network, the convolution can be computed completely via fixed-point operations. The coefficient s can be fixed before or leave it as trainable. A general rule is that we should let s have similar values of α^l from different layers. Otherwise, if s/α^l is either too small or too large, it can cause gradient vanishing or exploding problems in training, which leads to a worse accuracy of the network.

In our network, we merge the PACT function and activation quantization into one module and name it ActQuant. The input to ActQuant is the output of 1×1 convolutions. Since the input and weight of the convolution are both quantized into fixed-point integers, the output is also integers. Then, ActQuant is implemented

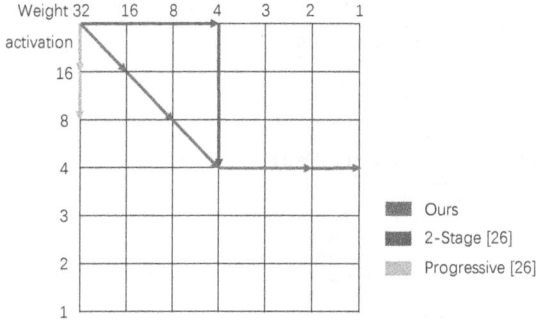

Figure 6: Quantization Grid

Table 3: Quantization Result on DiracDeltaNet

	full	w16a16	w8a8	w4a4	w2a4	w1a4
Top-1 Acc	69.7%	70.1%	70.3%	68.3%	68.5%	68.5%
Top-5 Acc	89.0%	89.2%	89.3%	88.1%	88.1%	88.2%

as a look-up-table whose parameters are determined during training and fixed during inference.

We follow [27] to quantize the network progressively from full-precision to the desired low-precision numbers. The process is illustrated in Fig. 6, where x-axis denotes bit-width of weights and y-axis denotes the bit-width of activations. We start from the full-precision network, train the network to convergence, and follow a path to progressively reduce the precision for weights or activations. At each point, we fine-tune the network for 50 epochs with step learning rate decay. Formally, we denote each point in the grid as a quantization configuration $\mathscr{C}_{w,a}(N_w)$. Here w represents the bitwidth of weight. a is the bitwidth of activation. N_w is the network containing the quantized parameters. The starting configuration would be the full precision network $\mathscr{C}_{32,32}(N_{32})$. Starting from this configuration, one can either go down to quantize the activation or go right to reduce the bitwidth of weight. More aggressive steps can be taken diagonally or even across several grids. The two-stage and progressive optimization methods proposed in [27] can be represented as two paths in Fig. 6.

In our work, we start from $\mathscr{C}_{32,32}(N_{32})$. Then we use N_{32} to initialize N_{16} and obtain $\mathscr{C}_{16,16}(N_{16})$. And we apply step lr decay fine-tuning onto N_{16} to recover the accuracy loss due to the quantization. After several epochs of fine-tuning, we get the desired low-precision configuration $\mathscr{C}_{16,16}\left(N'_{16}\right)$ with no accuracy loss. Following the same procedures, we are able to first go diagonally in the quantization grid to $\mathscr{C}_{4,4}(N_4)$. It is observed that if the bitwidth of activations are further reduced, the network will suffer from a significant accuracy loss (larger than 1%). So we change our quantization direction and walk horizontally in the grid to only quantizing weight while retaining the activation bitwidth. Finally we are able to quantize the network to $\mathscr{C}_{1,4}(N_1)$ with less than 1% top-5 accuracy loss compared to its full precision counterpart. In addition, the weights in FC layer are quantized to 8-bit. The quantization path is presented as the red curve in Fig. 6.

We use a pre-trained ResNet50 label-refinery [43] to boost the accuracy of the quantized model. Even with such radical quantization, our quantized model still preserves a very competitive top-5 accuracy of 88.2%. Most of the previous quantization works [25–27] are only effective on large models such as VGG16, AlexNet or

ResNet50. To the best of our knowledge, we are the first to quantize efficient models to such low-precisions. Our quantization result is summarized in Table 3.

4 HARDWARE DESIGN

As mentioned in section 3.2, we aggressively simplified ShuffleNetV2's operator set. Our modified network is mainly composed of the following operators:

- 1×1 convolution
- 2×2 max-pooling
- shift
- shuffle and concatenation

Our accelerator, Synetgy, is tailored to only support the operators above. This allows us to design more specialized compute units with simpler control, which enables us to further improve the hardware efficiency. The compute of the fully-connected layer can be mapped onto our convolution unit. Shuffle operation is not fully supported on FPGA. CPU-based memory copy is needed to maintain the memory layout. And the remaining average-pooling layer which is not supported on the FPGA is offloaded to the ARM processor on the SoC platform.

The benefits of simplified operator come from the algorithm-hardware co-design, which also increase the productivity of hardware implementation. The accelerator implementation only took two people working for one month using HLS.

4.1 The accelerator architecture

Fig. 7 shows the overall accelerator architecture design. Our accelerator, highlighted in light yellow, can be invoked by the CPU for computing one 1×1 Conv-Pooling-Shift-Shuffle subgraph at a time. The CPU provides supplementary support to the accelerator. Both the FPGA and the CPU are used to run the network.

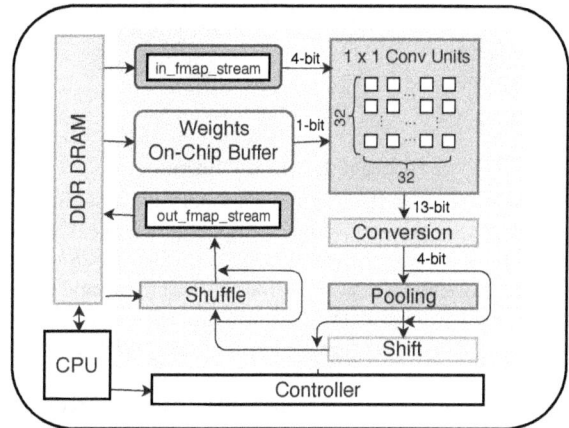

Figure 7: Accelerator Architecture

In quantized DiracDeltaNet, weights are 1-bit, input and output activations are 4-bit, and the largest partial sum is 13-bit. The width of partial sum is determined by the input feature bit width and the largest channel size. Given that the largest channel size is 464,

Table 4: Notations

Notation	Type	Description
WIDTH	variable	width of feature map
HEIGHT	variable	height of feature map
IC_TOTAL	variable	total input channel size
OC_TOTAL	variable	total output channel size
IC	constant: 32	parallelism on input channel dimension
OC	constant: 32	parallelism on output channel dimension

there are $2^4 \times 464$ possible outcomes from the convolution, which requires 13 bits to represent.

4.1.1 Dataflow Architecture. Our hardware design is based on the dataflow architecture template [44, 45]. As illustrated in Fig. 7, we first extract a few process functions from the major operations including 1×1 convolution, 2×2 max-pooling, shift, shuffle and the memory load and store. We then chain them together using FIFOs with blocking read and non-blocking write. Note that the write is blocking once the FIFO is full. All the process functions are running concurrently and the execution of each function is triggered by the arrival of the data. Therefore, more task-level parallelism can be explicitly exposed to the HLS tool in addition to the instruction-level parallelism.

4.1.2 Convolution Unit. The notations used in this section are listed in Table 4. As shown in Fig. 8, given an input feature map of size $WIDTH \times HEIGHT \times IC\_TOTAL$ and a weight kernel of size $IC\_TOTAL \times OC\_TOTAL$, the generated output feature map is of size $WIDTH \times HEIGHT \times OC\_TOTAL$ in 1×1 convolution. The 1×1 convolution is essentially a matrix-matrix multiplication.

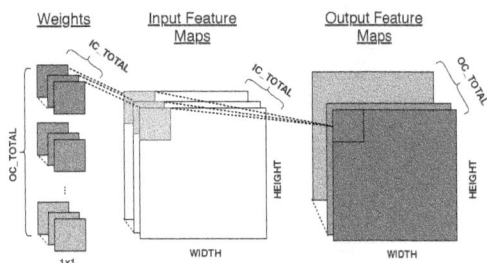

Figure 8: 1×1 Convolution

Although [1] suggests a weight stationary dataflow for 1×1 convolution dominant ConvNets, we find it not applicable to our design as the bit width of weights is much smaller than the partial sums (1 bit vs 13 bits). Transferring the partial sums on and off-chip will incur more traffic on the memory bus. Therefore, we adopt the output stationary dataflow by retaining the partial sums in the local register file until an output feature is produced.

Fig. 9 shows how we schedule the workload onto the accelerator. Note that the nested loops starting at line 17, 19 are automatically unrolled. Weights are prefetched onto on-chip BRAM *weight_buf*. We first block our inputs so $IC \times OC$ multiplications can be mapped onto the compute units at each iteration (Line 13~21). In every iteration, IC input features are fetched from the DRAM. They are convolved with OC number of weights of size IC and produce OC partial sums. Each iteration of the loop nest along the input channel dimension at line 12 takes $7 \sim 38$ cycles to finish based on

```
1 bw<4> in_fmap_dram[WIDTH*HEIGHT][IC_TOTAL/IC][IC]
2 bw<4> out_fmap_dram[WIDTH*HEIGHT][OC_TOTAL/OC][OC]
3 bw<4> weight_buf[OC_TOTAL/OC][IC_TOTAL/IC][OC][IC]
4 bw<4> in_fmap_stream [IC]
5 bw<1> weight_stream [OC][IC]
6 bw<13> partial_sum_reg [OC]
7 bw<4> out_fmap_stream [OC]
8 #pragma HLS dataflow
9 for idx in [0, WIDTH * HEIGHT):
10 | for oc_t in [0, OC_TOTAL/OC):
11 | | partial_sum_reg <- 0
12 | | for ic_t in [0, IC_TOTAL/IC):
13 | | #pragma HLS pipeline
14 | | | in_fmap_stream <- in_fmap_dram[idx][ic_t][:]
15 | | | weight_stream <- weight_buf[ic_t][oc_t][:][:]
16 | | | for ic in [0, IC):
17 | | | #pragma HLS unroll
18 | | | | for oc in [0, OC):
19 | | | | #pragma HLS unroll
20 | | | | | partial_sum_reg[oc] +=
21 | | | | | | in_fmap_stream[ic] * weight_stream[oc][ic]
22 | | out_fmap_stream <- func_convert(partial_sum_reg)
23 | | out_fmap_dram[idx][oc_t][:] <- out_fmap_stream
```

Figure 9: Pseudo Code for Kernel Compute Scheduling

the Vivado HLS report. Equivalently, it takes $7 \sim 38$ cycles to finish $IC \times OC$ 1/4 bit multiplication. The partial sums are stored in the registers, which can be simultaneously accessed in every cycle. The parameter IC and OC were tuned for the area performance tradeoff. Increasing them increases overall resource utilization but helps to reduce the total number of execution cycles.

Based on the roofline model [46], the attainable throughput is the compute-to-communication (CTC) ratio multiplied by the bandwidth when it is bandwidth bound. The CTC ratio of our compute unit for the input feature is OC_TOTAL (maximum number is 464 in DiracDeltaNet), which is a variable. Larger output channel size indicates higher CTC ratio. According to our measurement, the maximum bandwidth of the DDR channel is 6GB/s, which means 6×2 Giga input features (1 Byte contains two 4-bit features) can be loaded. The theoretical memory bound throughput should be $464 \times 6 \times 2 = 5568$GMACs $= 11136$GOPs. For compute bound problems, the attainable throughput is dependent on the compute capability. In our case, it is $IC \times OC \times freq = 32 \times 32 \times 250MHz = 256$GMACs$=512$GOPs. Based on the analysis, the convolution unit will reach the bandwidth bound before it hits the computation roofline.

4.1.3 Conversion Unit. The high bitwidth to low bitwidth conversion is performed immediately after the kernel computation. It is a step function with 16 intervals that converts 13-bit partial sum to 4-bit activation. The threshold values are different for each layer. All of the read-only threshold values are stored in on-chip BRAMs. An index number should be specified by the user function to select which set of threshold values to use for the compute of the current layer. In hardware, this unit is implemented by using 16 comparators. They are mapped onto a binary tree structure to reduce the circuit latency.

4.1.4 Pooling Unit. We adopt the line buffer design described in [37] to implement the 2×2 max-pooling layer. For every iteration, $(WIDTH + 1)$ of IC deep pixels are first fetched into the line buffers. Once the next pixel value is fetched, a 2×2 large sliding window is formed. For every 2 cycles, we compare the values in the 2×2 sliding window, output the largest one, and fetch the next 2 values. It takes IC_TOTAL/IC iterations to finish the compute.

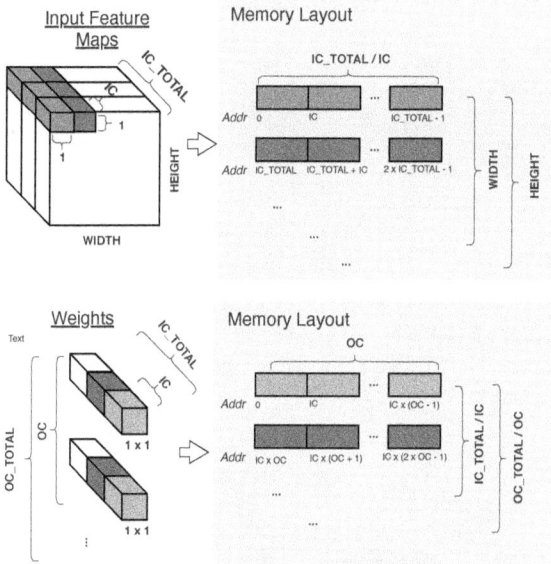

Figure 10: Input Layout in DRAM

4.1.5 Shift Unit. The line buffer design is also used for the shift operation. In the shift unit, the input images are first padded with 1 zero-value pixel at the width and height dimension. $(2 \times (WIDTH + 2) + 2)$ of pixels are then buffered and a 3×3 sliding window is formed. The shift direction is different for different input channels. It is calculated based on the input channel index. After initialization, the unit is able to produce 1 output pixel per cycle.

4.1.6 Shuffle Unit. Shuffle is implemented by changing the address offset of output features during the writeback phase. Since the shuffle operation still requires us to concatenate the outputs from the previous DiracDeltaNet block to the current DiracDeltaNet block outputs, the CPU is used to copy the output from previous DiracDeltaNet unit to the shuffled address. The memory copy operation should be done concurrently with the computation of current DiracDeltaNet unit.

4.1.7 Fully Connected Unit. We don't explicitly design a dedicated unit to compute FC layer. Instead, we map the compute of FC layer onto our existing hardware convolution unit. The feature map size is 1 for the FC layer. While the convolution unit only supports 1-bit weight, the FC layer's computation is mapped in a bit serial like manner. The convolution unit processes each bit of the FC weight iteratively and bit shift is done by configuring the step function in the conversion unit.

4.2 Software

We use the ARM processor to control the layer-based accelerator and to compute the last 7×7 average-pooling layer that is not supported by the accelerator. The host application runs on a full Linux system on the ARM CPU, which controls the memory-mapped accelerator through the UIO driver interface. The Xilinx python-based PYNQ APIs [47] are used for fast deployment of the host software code on the Ultra 96 board.

4.3 Experimental Results

We implement our accelerator, Synetgy, on the Ultra96 development board with Xilinx Zynq UltraScale+ MPSoC targeted at embedded applications. Table 5 shows the overall resource utilization of our implementation. We are able to utilize 34% of the total LUTs on the FPGA, as the bit-level 1/4bit multiplications are mapped onto LUTs. BRAMs are mainly used for implementing the FIFO channels. DSPs are used for the address calculation for the AXI protocol. Our implementation runs at 250 MHz. Power measurements are obtained via a power monitor. We measured 5.3W with no workload running on the programming logic side and 5.5W max power on the Ultra96 power supply line when running our network.

Table 5: Resource Usage

LUT	FF	BRAM	DSP
24130 (34.2%)	29867 (21.2%)	170 (78.7%)	37 (10.3%)

We compare our accelerator against previous work in Table 6. As explained before, ConvNets for ImageNet classification are usually orders of magnitude more complex than CIFAR10 classification. Therefore, we only compare accelerators targeting ConvNets for ImageNet classification with reasonable accuracy. Our work focuses on achieving competitive accuracy while improving the actual inference speed in terms of frames per second. Our experiments show that we successfully achieve those two goals. From the table, we can make the following observations: 1) Synetgy achieves the highest top-1 and top-5 accuracy on ImageNet. The only previous work that comes close to our accuracy is [40], but its frame rate is 16.9× slower than ours. 2) Among the embedded accelerators whose top-1 accuracy is higher than 60%, which is a loose constraint, our model achieves the fastest inference speed. 3) Without the accuracy constraint, the speed of [41, 42, 48] can go as fast as 864.7 frames per second. But their accuracy is rather low. 4) The peak attainable throughput of our accelerator is 418 GOPs, which is close to the theoretical compute roofline. Our average throughput (47.09 GOPs) is currently limited by the low hardware utilization. The inefficiency is mainly from the software shuffle operations and the first convolution layer whose input dimension is 3 which is much less than the hardware tiling factor *IC*. However, Synetgy still achieves competitive frame rate, demonstrating the efficacy of our co-design methodology. We see the opportunity of significant frame rate improvement through further algorithm-hardware co-design.

The reported frame rate is achieved with batch size set to 16. There is a fixed software overhead for invoking the poll-based hardware accelerator. The computation latency of the DiracDelta Block1 in Table 9 is 0.15ms when the batch size is equal to 1. The latency for a single read on the accelerator control register is 0.40ms, which is greater than the actual compute time. In order to minimize this software overhead, we increase the batch size to schedule more computation running on the accelerator per invocation. Furthermore, the weights stored in on-chip BRAM get reused more when batch size is increased. The frame rates of implementations with different batch sizes are summarized in Table 7.

We break down the runtime of the whole heterogeneous system by bypassing one component of the system and measure the runtime. The result is shown in Table 8. The whole system runs at 95.9

Table 6: Performance Comparison of Synetgy and Previous Works

	VGG-SVD[39]	AlexNet[48]	VGG16[49]	VGG16 [40]	DoReFa[42]	FINN-R [41]	Ours
Platform	Zynq XC7Z045	Stratix-V	Stratix-V	Zynq 7Z020	Zynq 7Z020	Zynq ZU3EG	Zynq ZU3EG
Frame Rate (fps)	4.5	**864.7**	3.8	5.7	106.0	200.0	96.5
Top-1 Acc	64.64%	42.90%	66.58%	67.72%	46.10%	50.3%	**68.47%**
Top-5 Acc	86.66%	66.80%	87.48%	88.06%	73.10%	N/A	**88.22%**
Precision	16b	16b	8-16b	8b	2b	1-2b	1-4b
Throughput (GOPs)	136.97	1963.96	117.80	123	410.22	400	47.09 (Overall) 418 (Peak)
Frequency(MHz)	150	150	120	214	200	220	250
Power(W)	3.0	26.2	19.1	3.0	2.3	10.2	5.5

Table 7: Frame Rate on Different Batch Size

Batch Size	1	2	4	8	10	16
Frame Rate (fps)	58.7	72.9	84.1	94.4	95.9	96.5

Table 8: Runtime Latency for Different Functional Parts of the Whole System (Batch=10)

	Runtime (ms)	Frame Rate (fps)
Overall	104.3	95.9
w/o sw avg pool	100.3	99.7
w/o fc	104.0	96.1
w/o PYNQ API call	104.2	96.0
w/o sw shuffle	70.4	142.1
hw only	65.7	152.2

Table 9: Runtime Analysis for the First and Last DiracDeltaNet Blocks in Different Operator Configurations (Batch=10)

	Runtime (ms)	
	Block1	Block2
feature map size	28	7
in&out channel	116	464
conv only	1.531	0.989
conv+pool	1.530	0.993
conv+shift	1.537	0.996
conv+shuffle	4.409	1.636
overall	4.364	1.441

FPS on ImageNet classification at a batch size of 10, including both hardware PE execution and software execution of average pooling, and shuffle. We see from the table that the CPU-based memory copy for the shuffle operation significantly degrades the performance. All other non-conv components impact the overall performance slightly.

To further understand the efficiency of various operators (1×1 conv, 2×2 max-pooling, shift, and shuffle) implemented on FPGA and CPU, we measure the runtime of the DiracDeltaNet blocks with different configurations on Synetgy. The result is summarized in Table 9. We test 2 blocks with different input feature map and channel sizes. Note that the theoretical OPs of Block1 and Block2 is the same. As shown in the table, pooling and shift incur almost no performance drop. This is because the process functions for performing these operations do not impose new bottlenecks on the dataflow pipeline. Software memory copy latency of shuffle is more significant on Block1 than Block2. This is because memory copy overhead is proportional to $HEIGHT \times WIDTH \times OC\_TOTAL$. But total OPs $HEIGHT \times WIDTH \times IC\_TOTAL \times OC\_TOTAL$ remains the same, which means that smaller feature map needs less time for memory copy. The memory copy overhead can be possibly alleviated through running bare-metal C code on the CPU.

5 CONCLUSION AND FUTURE WORKS

In this paper, we adopt an algorithm-hardware co-design approach to develop a ConvNet accelerator called Synetgy and a novel ConvNet model called DiracDeltaNet. Based on ShuffleNetV2, we optimize the network's operators by replacing all the 3×3 convolutions with shift operations and 1×1 convolutions. This allows us to build a compute unit exclusively customized for 1×1 convolutions for

better efficiency. We quantize the network's weights to binary and activations to 4-bit fixed-point numbers with less than 1% accuracy loss. These quantizations very well exploit the nature of FPGA hardware. As a result, DiracDeltaNet has a small parameter size, low computational OPs, hardware-friendly skip connections, ultra-low precision, and simplified operators. These features allow us to implement highly customized and efficient accelerators on FPGA. We implement the network on Ultra96 Soc systems. The implementation only took two people one month using HLS tools. Our accelerator, Synetgy, achieves a top-5 accuracy of 88.2% on ImageNet, the highest among all the previously published embedded FPGA accelerators. It also reaches an inference speed of 96.5 FPS, surpassing prior works with similar accuracy by at least 16.9×. While we see many more opportunities for further optimization, we believe this demonstrates the efficacy of our co-design methodology.

For the future works, we will focus on further optimization. For example, we can add more layers in the dataflow architecture to improve the compute-to-communication ratio. Correspondingly, we will need to adjust the network such that the computation subgraphs are more symmetric.

ACKNOWLEDGMENTS

We would like to thank all of the people who helped us realize this project, especially the anonymous reviewers, Kostadin Ilov, Rock Qu, Alessandro Pappalardo, Amir Gholaminejad, Peter Jin, Ravi Krishna, and Alvin Wan. The information, data, or work presented herein was funded in part by the Advanced Research Projects Agency-Energy (ARPA-E), U.S. Department of Energy, under Award Number DE-AR0000849. The Research was partially funded by ADEPT Lab industrial sponsor Intel, and ADEPT Lab affiliates

Google, Siemens, and SK Hynix. The views and opinions of authors expressed herein do not necessarily state or reflect those of the United States Government or any agency thereof.

REFERENCES

[1] Kiseok Kwon, Alon Amid, Amir Gholami, Bichen Wu, Krste Asanovic, and Kurt Keutzer. Co-design of deep neural nets and neural net accelerators for embedded vision applications. *arXiv preprint arXiv:1804.10642*, 2018.

[2] Kaiming He, Xiangyu Zhang, Shaoqing Ren, and Jian Sun. Identity mappings in deep residual networks. In *European conference on computer vision*, pages 630–645. Springer, 2016.

[3] Gao Huang, Zhuang Liu, Laurens Van Der Maaten, and Kilian Q Weinberger. Densely connected convolutional networks. In *CVPR*, volume 1, page 3, 2017.

[4] Barret Zoph, Vijay Vasudevan, Jonathon Shlens, and Quoc V Le. Learning transferable architectures for scalable image recognition. *arXiv preprint arXiv:1707.07012*, 2017.

[5] Fisher Yu and Vladlen Koltun. Multi-scale context aggregation by dilated convolutions. *arXiv preprint arXiv:1511.07122*, 2015.

[6] Alex Krizhevsky and Geoffrey Hinton. Learning multiple layers of features from tiny images. Technical report, Citeseer, 2009.

[7] Alex Krizhevsky, Ilya Sutskever, and Geoffrey E Hinton. Imagenet classification with deep convolutional neural networks. In *Advances in neural information processing systems*, pages 1097–1105, 2012.

[8] Karen Simonyan and Andrew Zisserman. Very deep convolutional networks for large-scale image recognition. *arXiv preprint arXiv:1409.1556*, 2014.

[9] Forrest N Iandola, Song Han, Matthew W Moskewicz, Khalid Ashraf, William J Dally, and Kurt Keutzer. Squeezenet: Alexnet-level accuracy with 50x fewer parameters and< 0.5 mb model size. *arXiv preprint arXiv:1602.07360*, 2016.

[10] Amir Gholami, Kiseok Kwon, Bichen Wu, Zizheng Tai, Xiangyu Yue, Peter Jin, Sicheng Zhao, and Kurt Keutzer. Squeezenext: Hardware-aware neural network design. *arXiv preprint arXiv:1803.10615*, 2018.

[11] Bichen Wu, Alvin Wan, Xiangyu Yue, Peter Jin, Sicheng Zhao, Noah Golmant, Amir Gholaminejad, Joseph Gonzalez, and Kurt Keutzer. Shift: A zero flop, zero parameter alternative to spatial convolutions. *arXiv preprint arXiv:1711.08141*, 2017.

[12] Kaiming He, Xiangyu Zhang, Shaoqing Ren, and Jian Sun. Deep residual learning for image recognition. In *Proceedings of the IEEE conference on computer vision and pattern recognition*, pages 770–778, 2016.

[13] Ningning Ma, Xiangyu Zhang, Hai-Tao Zheng, and Jian Sun. Shufflenet v2: Practical guidelines for efficient cnn architecture design. *arXiv:1807.11164*, 2018.

[14] Jia Deng, Wei Dong, Richard Socher, Li-Jia Li, Kai Li, and Li Fei-Fei. Imagenet: A large-scale hierarchical image database. In *Computer Vision and Pattern Recognition, 2009. CVPR 2009. IEEE Conference on*, pages 248–255. Ieee, 2009.

[15] Bichen Wu, Forrest N Iandola, Peter H Jin, and Kurt Keutzer. Squeezedet: Unified, small, low power fully convolutional neural networks for real-time object detection for autonomous driving. In *CVPR Workshops*, pages 446–454, 2017.

[16] Bichen Wu, Alvin Wan, Xiangyu Yue, and Kurt Keutzer. Squeezeseg: Convolutional neural nets with recurrent crf for real-time road-object segmentation from 3d lidar point cloud. *arXiv preprint arXiv:1710.07368*, 2017.

[17] Bichen Wu, Xuanyu Zhou, Sicheng Zhao, Xiangyu Yue, and Kurt Keutzer. Squeezesegv2: Improved model structure and unsupervised domain adaptation for road-object segmentation from a lidar point cloud. *arXiv preprint arXiv:1809.08495*, 2018.

[18] Andrew G Howard, Menglong Zhu, Bo Chen, Dmitry Kalenichenko, Weijun Wang, Tobias Weyand, Marco Andreetto, and Hartwig Adam. Mobilenets: Efficient convolutional neural networks for mobile vision applications. *arXiv preprint arXiv:1704.04861*, 2017.

[19] Mark Sandler, Andrew Howard, Menglong Zhu, Andrey Zhmoginov, and Liang-Chieh Chen. Mobilenetv2: Inverted residuals and linear bottlenecks. In *Proceedings of the IEEE Conference on Computer Vision and Pattern Recognition*, pages 4510–4520, 2018.

[20] X Zhang, X Zhou, M Lin, and J Sun. Shufflenet: An extremely efficient convolutional neural network for mobile devices. *arXiv:1707.01083*.

[21] H. Zhong, X. Liu, Y. He, and Y. Ma. Shift-based Primitives for Efficient Convolutional Neural Networks. *ArXiv e-prints*, September 2018.

[22] Song Han, Huizi Mao, and William J Dally. Deep compression: Compressing deep neural networks with pruning, trained quantization and huffman coding. *arXiv preprint arXiv:1510.00149*, 2015.

[23] Chenzhuo Zhu, Song Han, Huizi Mao, and William J Dally. Trained ternary quantization. *arXiv preprint arXiv:1612.01064*, 2016.

[24] Mohammad Rastegari, Vicente Ordonez, Joseph Redmon, and Ali Farhadi. Xnor-net: Imagenet classification using binary convolutional neural networks. In *European Conference on Computer Vision*, pages 525–542. Springer, 2016.

[25] Shuchang Zhou, Yuxin Wu, Zekun Ni, Xinyu Zhou, He Wen, and Yuheng Zou. Dorefa-net: Training low bitwidth convolutional neural networks with low bitwidth gradients. *arXiv preprint arXiv:1606.06160*, 2016.

[26] Jungwook Choi, Zhuo Wang, Swagath Venkataramani, Pierce I-Jen Chuang, Vijayalakshmi Srinivasan, and Kailash Gopalakrishnan. Pact: Parameterized clipping activation for quantized neural networks. *arXiv:1805.06085*, 2018.

[27] B. Zhuang, C. Shen, M. Tan, L. Liu, and I. Reid. Towards Effective Low-bitwidth Convolutional Neural Networks. *arXiv preprint arXiv:1711.00205*, 2017.

[28] Chen Zhang, Peng Li, Guangyu Sun, Yijin Guan, Bingjun Xiao, and Jason Cong. Optimizing fpga-based accelerator design for deep convolutional neural networks. In *Proceedings of the 2015 ACM/SIGDA International Symposium on Field-Programmable Gate Arrays*, pages 161–170. ACM, 2015.

[29] Jialiang Zhang and Jing Li. Improving the performance of opencl-based fpga accelerator for convolutional neural network. In *Proceedings of the 2017 International Symposium on Field-Programmable Gate Arrays*, pages 25–34, 2017.

[30] Yufei Ma, Yu Cao, Sarma Vrudhula, and Jae-sun Seo. Optimizing loop operation and dataflow in fpga acceleration of deep convolutional neural networks. In *Proceedings of the 2017 ACM/SIGDA International Symposium on Field-Programmable Gate Arrays*, pages 45–54. ACM, 2017.

[31] Chi Zhang and Viktor Prasanna. Frequency domain acceleration of convolutional neural networks on cpu-fpga shared memory system. In *Proceedings of the 2017 ACM/SIGDA International Symposium on Field-Programmable Gate Arrays*, pages 35–44. ACM, 2017.

[32] Eriko Nurvitadhi, Ganesh Venkatesh, Jaewoong Sim, Debbie Marr, Randy Huang, Jason Ong Gee Hock, Yeong Tat Liew, Krishnan Srivatsan, Duncan Moss, Suchit Subhaschandra, et al. Can fpgas beat gpus in accelerating next-generation deep neural networks? In *Proceedings of the ACM/SIGDA International Symposium on Field-Programmable Gate Arrays*, pages 5–14. ACM, 2017.

[33] Huimin Li, Xitian Fan, Li Jiao, Wei Cao, Xuegong Zhou, and Lingli Wang. A high performance fpga-based accelerator for large-scale convolutional neural networks. In *Field Programmable Logic and Applications (FPL), 2016 26th International Conference on*, pages 1–9. IEEE, 2016.

[34] Utku Aydonat, Shane O'Connell, Davor Capalija, Andrew C Ling, and Gordon R Chiu. An opencl deep learning accelerator on arria 10. In *Proceedings of the 2017 ACM/SIGDA International Symposium on Field-Programmable Gate Arrays*, pages 55–64. ACM, 2017.

[35] Xuechao Wei, Cody Hao Yu, Peng Zhang, Youxiang Chen, Yuxin Wang, Han Hu, Yun Liang, and Jason Cong. Automated systolic array architecture synthesis for high throughput cnn inference on fpgas. In *Proceedings of the 54th Annual Design Automation Conference 2017*, page 29. ACM, 2017.

[36] Yaman Umuroglu, Nicholas J Fraser, Giulio Gambardella, Michaela Blott, Philip Leong, Magnus Jahre, and Kees Vissers. Finn: A framework for fast, scalable binarized neural network inference. In *Proceedings of the ACM/SIGDA International Symposium on Field-Programmable Gate Arrays*, pages 65–74. ACM, 2017.

[37] Ritchie Zhao, Weinan Song, Wentao Zhang, Tianwei Xing, Jeng-Hau Lin, Mani Srivastava, Rajesh Gupta, and Zhiru Zhang. Accelerating binarized convolutional neural networks with software-programmable fpgas. In *Proceedings of the ACM/SIGDA International Symposium on Field-Programmable Gate Arrays*, pages 15–24. ACM, 2017.

[38] Hiroki Nakahara, Tomoya Fujii, and Shimpei Sato. A fully connected layer elimination for a binarizec convolutional neural network on an fpga. In *Field Programmable Logic and Applications (FPL), 2017 27th International Conference on*, pages 1–4. IEEE, 2017.

[39] Jiantao Qiu, Jie Wang, Song Yao, Kaiyuan Guo, Boxun Li, Erjin Zhou, Jincheng Yu, Tianqi Tang, Ningyi Xu, Sen Song, et al. Going deeper with embedded fpga platform for convolutional neural network. In *Proceedings of the 2016 ACM/SIGDA International Symposium on Field-Programmable Gate Arrays*, pages 26–35, 2016.

[40] Kaiyuan Guo, Song Han, Song Yao, Yu Wang, Yuan Xie, and Huazhong Yang. Software-hardware codesign for efficient neural network acceleration. *IEEE Micro*, 37(2):18–25, 2017.

[41] Michaela Blott, Thomas Preusser, Nicholas Fraser, Giulio Gambardella, Kenneth O'Brien, and Yaman Umuroglu. Finn-r: An end-to-end deep-learning framework for fast exploration of quantized neural networks, 2018.

[42] Li Jiao, Cheng Luo, Wei Cao, Xuegong Zhou, and Lingli Wang. Accelerating low bit-width convolutional neural networks with embedded fpga. In *Field Programmable Logic and Applications (FPL), 2017 27th International Conference on*, pages 1–4. IEEE, 2017.

[43] Hessam Bagherinezhad, Maxwell Horton, Mohammad Rastegari, and Ali Farhadi. Label refinery: Improving imagenet classification through label progression. *arXiv preprint arXiv:1805.02641*, 2018.

[44] Shaoyi Cheng and John Wawrzynek. High level synthesis with a dataflow architectural template, 2016.

[45] Xilinx. Vivado Design Suite User Guide - High-Level Synthesis (UG902), 2018.

[46] Samuel Williams, Andrew Waterman, and David Patterson. Roofline: An insightful visual performance model for floating-point programs and multicore architectures. *Communications of the Association for Computing Machinery*, 2009.

[47] Xilinx. PYNQ Introduction, 2018. https://pynq.readthedocs.io/en/v2.3/.

[48] Shuang Liang, Shouyi Yin, Leibo Liu, Wayne Luk, and Shaojun Wei. Fp-bnn: Binarized neural network on fpga. *Neurocomputing*, 275:1072–1086, 2018.

[49] Naveen Suda, Vikas Chandra, Ganesh Dasika, Abinash Mohanty, Yufei Ma, Sarma Vrudhula, Jae-sun Seo, and Yu Cao. Throughput-optimized opencl-based fpga accelerator for large-scale convolutional neural networks. In *Proceedings of the 2016 International Symposium on Field-Programmable Gate Arrays*, pages 16–25. ACM, 2016.

REQ-YOLO: A Resource-Aware, Efficient Quantization Framework for Object Detection on FPGAs

Caiwen Ding[2,+], Shuo Wang[1,+], Ning Liu[2], Kaidi Xu[2], Yanzhi Wang[2] and Yun Liang[1,3,*]

[+]These authors contributed equally.

[1]Center for Energy-Efficient Computing & Applications (CECA), School of EECS, Peking University, China

[2]Department of Electrical & Computer Engineering, Northeastern University, Boston, MA, USA

[3]Peng Cheng Laboratory, Shenzhen, China

[1]{shvowang, ericlyun}@pku.edu.cn, [2]{ding.ca, liu.ning, xu.kaid}@husky.neu.edu, [2]yanz.wang@northeastern.edu

ABSTRACT

Deep neural networks (DNNs), as the basis of object detection, will play a key role in the development of future autonomous systems with full autonomy. The autonomous systems have special requirements of real-time, energy-efficient implementations of DNNs on a power-constrained system. Two research thrusts are dedicated to performance and energy efficiency enhancement of the inference phase of DNNs. The first one is model compression techniques while the second is efficient hardware implementation. Recent works on extremely-low-bit CNNs such as the binary neural network (BNN) and XNOR-Net replace the traditional floating point operations with binary bit operations which significantly reduces the memory bandwidth and storage requirement. However, it suffers from non-negligible accuracy loss and underutilized digital signal processing (DSP) blocks of FPGAs.

To overcome these limitations, this paper proposes REQ-YOLO, a resource aware, systematic weight quantization framework for object detection, considering both algorithm and hardware resource aspects in object detection. We adopt the block-circulant matrix method and propose a heterogeneous weight quantization using *Alternative Direction Method of Multipliers* (ADMM), an effective optimization technique for general, non-convex optimization problems. To achieve real-time, highly-efficient implementations on FPGA, we present the detailed hardware implementation of block circulant matrices on CONV layers and develop an efficient processing element (PE) structure supporting the heterogeneous weight quantization, CONV dataflow and pipelining techniques, design optimization, and a template-based automatic synthesis framework to optimally exploit hardware resource. Experimental results show that our proposed REQ-YOLO framework can significantly compress the YOLO model while introducing very small accuracy degradation. The related codes are here: https://github.com/Anonymous788/heterogeneous_ADMM_YOLO.

*Corresponding author.

KEYWORDS

FPGA; YOLO; object detection; compression; ADMM

ACM Reference Format:
Caiwen Ding, Shuo Wang, Ning Liu, Kaidi Xu, Yanzhi Wang and Yun Liang. 2019. REQ-YOLO: A Resource-Aware, Efficient Quantization Framework for Object Detection on FPGAs. In *The 2019 ACM/SIGDA International Symposium on Field-Programmable Gate Arrays (FPGA '19), Feb. 24–26, 2019, Seaside, CA, USA.* ACM, NY, NY. 10 pages. DOI: https://doi.org/10.1145/3289602.3293904

1 INTRODUCTION

Autonomous systems such as unmanned aerial vehicles (UAVs), autonomous underwater vehicles (AUVs), and unmanned ground vehicles (UGVs) have been rapidly growing for performing surveillance, object detection [2], and object delivery [21] tasks in scientific, military, agricultural, and commercial applications. The full autonomy of such systems relies on the integration of artificial intelligence software with hardware.

The deployment of deep neural networks (DNNs) in autonomous systems include multiple aspects, i.e., object detection/surveillance algorithms, and advanced control (e.g., deep reinforcement learning technique). Since DNN-based advanced control is not widely in place yet, we focus on the former aspect. Object detection algorithms are different from image classification [26] in that the former need to simultaneously detect and track multiple objects with different sizes. Representative object detection algorithms include R-CNN [14] and YOLO [38]. The autonomous system applications have special requirements of real-time, energy-efficient implementations on a power-constrained system.

Two research thrusts are dedicated to performance and energy efficiency enhancement of the inference phase of DNNs. The first one is model compression techniques for DNNs [16, 29, 52, 9], including weight pruning, weight quantization, low-rank approximation, etc. S. Han et al. [16] have proposed an iterative DNN weight pruning method, which could achieve 9× weight reduction on the AlexNet model and has been applied to LSTM RNN as well [18]. However, this method results in irregularity in weight storage, and thereby degrades the parallelism degree and hardware performance, as observed in [46, 10, 51]. Recent work [10, 46] adopts block-circulant matrices for weight representation in DNNs in both image classification DNN [10] and LSTM RNN [46] tasks. This method is demonstrated to achieve higher hardware performance than iterative pruning due to the regularity in weight storage and computation. The second one is efficient hardware implementations, including FPGAs and ASICs [50, 7, 54, 36, 1, 31, 32, 49, 53]. FPGAs are gaining more popularity for striking a balance between high hardware performance and fast development round. A customized hardware solution on FPGA can offer significant improvements in energy efficiency and power consumption compared to CPU and GPU clusters.

Convolutional (CONV) layers are more computation-intensive than fully-connected (FC) layers. Recently CONV layers are becoming more important in state-of-the-art DNNs [39, 26]. Extremely-low-bit CNNs such as the binary neural network (BNN) [9] and XNOR-Net[37] have demonstrated hardware friendly ability on FPGAs [45]. Binarization not only reduces memory bandwidth and storage requirement but also replaces the traditional floating point operations with binary bit operations, which can be efficiently implemented on the look-up-tables (LUT)-based FPGA chip, whereas suffering non-negligible accuracy degradation on large datasets due to the over-quantized weight representation. More importantly, the majority of DSP resource will be wasted due to the replacement of multipliers, introducing significant overhead on LUTs. Overall, there lacks a systematic weight quantization framework considering hardware resource aspect on FPGAs. In addition, despite the research efforts devoted to the hardware implementation of image classification tasks [26, 27, 19], there lacks enough investigation on the hardware acceleration of object detection tasks.

In this paper, we propose REQ-YOLO, a resource-aware, efficient weight quantization framework for object detection by exploring both software and hardware-level optimization opportunities on FPGAs. We adopt the block-circulant matrix based compression technique and propose a heterogeneous weight quantization using ADMM on the FFT results considering hardware resource. It is necessary to note that the proposed framework is also applicable to other model compression techniques. To enable real-time, highly-efficient implementations on FPGA, we present the detailed hardware implementation of block circulant matrices on CONV layers and develop an efficient processing element (PE) structure supporting the heterogeneous weight quantization method, dataflow based pipelining, design optimization, and a template-based automatic synthesis framework.

Our specific contributions are as follows:

- We present a detailed hardware implementation and optimization of block circulant matrices on CONV layers on object detection tasks.
- We present a heterogeneous weight quantization method including both equal-distance and mixed powers-of-two methods considering hardware resource on FPGAs. We adopt ADMM to directly quantize the FFT results of weight.
- We employ an HLS design methodology for productive development and optimal hardware resource exploration of our FPGA-based YOLO accelerator.

Experimental results show that our proposed REQ-YOLO framework can significantly compress the YOLO model while introducing very small accuracy degradation. Our framework is very suitable for FPGA and the associated YOLO implementations outperform the state-of-the-art designs on FPGAs.

2 PRELIMINARIES ON OBJECT DETECTION

Deep neural networks (DNNs) have dominated the state-of-the-art techniques of object detection. There are typically two main types of object detection methods: (i) region proposal based method and (ii) proposal-free method. For the region proposal based methods,

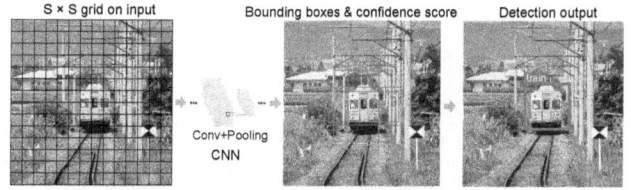

Figure 1: Example of object dection using YOLO.

R-CNN first generates potential object regions and then performs classification on the proposed regions [12]. SPPnet [20], Fast R-CNN [13], and Faster R-CNN [41] are typical in this category. As for the proposal-free methods, MS-CNN [5] proposes a unified multi-scale CNN for fast object detection. YOLO [38] simultaneously predicts multiple bounding boxes and classification class probabilities. Compared to the region proposal-based methods, YOLO does not require a second classification operation for each region and therefore it achieves significant faster speed. However, YOLO suffers from several drawbacks: (i) YOLO makes a significant number of localization errors compared to Fast R-CNN; (ii) Compared to region proposal-based methods, YOLO has a relatively low recall. To improve the localization and recall while maintaining classification accuracy, YOLO v2 [39] has been proposed. In this paper, we focus on an embedded version of YOLO - tiny YOLO [44] for hardware implementation. Compared to other versions such as YOLO v2 [39], v3 [40], and YOLO [38], it has a smaller network structure and fewer weight parameters, but with tolerable accuracy degradation.

2.1 You Only Look Once (YOLO) Network

Fig. 1 shows an overview of object detection and tiny YOLO application. It uses CONV layers to extract features from images, anchor boxes to predict bounding boxes, and regression for object detection, based on the yolov2 tiny [44] framework. The input image (frame) is separated into an $S \times S$ grid. Each grid cell detects an object and predicts B bounding boxes and the corresponding confidence scores when the grid cell and the center of object overlap each other. Typically $S = 13$ and $B = 5$. For each bounding box, there are 5 predictions made: x, y, w, h, and a confidence score. (x, y) is the coordinates of the box center located in the grid cell, and w and h are the width and height of the bounding box. The confidence score is defined as $Pr(Obj) \times IOU^{truth}_{pred}$, where $Pr(Obj)$ is the prediction probability and IOU^{truth}_{pred} is the *intersection over union (IOU)*. Here, IOU is determined by dividing the area of overlap between the predicted bounding box and its corresponding ground-truth bounding box by the area of union.

There are C *conditional class probabilities* on the grid cell containing the object, $Pr(Class_i|Obj)$, predicted by each grid cell. The *class-specific confidence scores* for each box are calculated as follows:

$$Pr(Class_i|Obj) \cdot Pr(Obj) \cdot IOU^{truth}_{pred} = Pr(Class_i) \cdot IOU^{truth}_{pred} \quad (1)$$

The scores represent how accurate the box is pertinent to the object and the probability of the object class. These predictions are encoded as an $S \times S \times (B \cdot 5 + C)$ tensor. Fig. 2 shows the architecture of tiny YOLO. It has 9 CONV layers. The input images are re-sized to 416 by 416 from the PASCAL 2007 detection dataset [12]. From the 1st to the 8th layer, a 3×3 CONV operation (stride 1 and zero padding with 1) is followed by a max pooling operation with 2×2

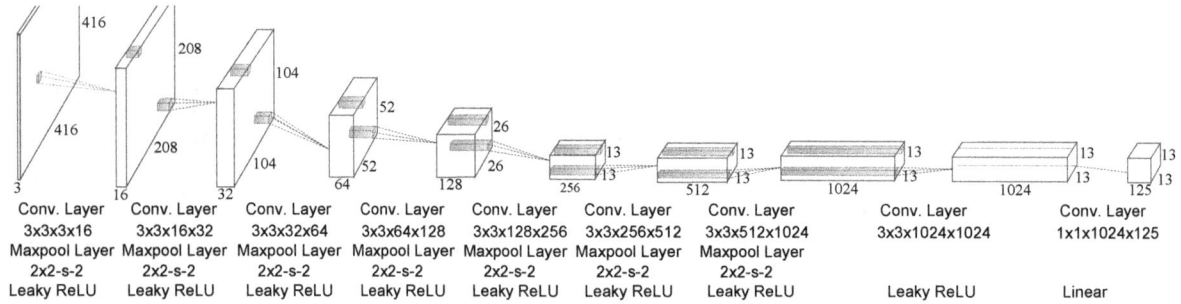

Figure 2: The tiny YOLO architecture with convolution layers.

filters and stride 2. In the last CONV layer, the 1×1 CONV operation reduces the feature space from the previous layer.

2.2 Convolutional (CONV) Layers

Convolutional (CONV) layers convolve each input feature map with an $r \times r$ weight filter. The convolutional results are then accumulated, added with a bias. After passing the intermediate result through a activation function (such as rectified linear unit (ReLU), sigmoid, or hyperbolic tangent (tanh)), we produce a single output feature map. Repeat this procedure for the rest of weight filters, we obtain the whole output feature map. Zero padding is adopted at the border to ensure the output feature maps have the same size as input. The expression of the CONV layer operation is shown in Equation (2).

$$\mathbf{y}_{c'} = f\left(\sum_{c=1}^{C} \mathbf{x}_c * \mathbf{w}_{c,c'} + \mathbf{b}_{c'}\right) \qquad (2)$$

there are C input feature maps $(\mathbf{x}_1; \mathbf{x}_2; \mathbf{x}_3; ...; \mathbf{x}_C)$ and C' output feature maps $(\mathbf{y}_1; \mathbf{y}_2; \mathbf{y}_3; ...; \mathbf{y}_{C'})$, respectively. The weight parameters of this CONV layer $\mathbf{W}$ has the shape of $[filter\_height, filter\_width, in\_channels, out\_channels]$, denoted as $\mathbf{W} \in \mathbb{R}^{r \times r \times C \times C'}$. f is the activation function and $\mathbf{b}$ is the bias as the same size as output feature maps.

2.3 Pooling layer and other types of layers

In YOLO network structure, pooling layers downsample each input feature map by passing it through a 2×2 max window (pool) with a stride of 2, resulting in no overlapped regions. Pooling layers reduce the data dimensions and mitigate overfitting issues. Max pooling is the dominant type of pooling strategy in state-of-the-art DCNNs due to its higher overall accuracy and convergence speed [7]. Batch normalization (BN) normalizes the variance and mean of the features across examples in each mini-batch [22], to avoid the gradient vanishing or explosion problems [23].

3 COMPRESSED CONVOLUTION LAYERS

3.1 Block-Circulant Matrices

We can reducing weight storage by replacing the original weight matrix with one or multiple blocks of circulant matrices, where each row/column is the cyclic reformulation of the others, as shown in Equation (3).

$$\mathbf{W}_{ij} = \begin{bmatrix} w_1 & w_{L_b} & \cdots & w_3 & w_2 \\ w_2 & w_1 & \cdots & w_4 & w_3 \\ \vdots & \vdots & \ddots & \vdots & \vdots \\ w_{L_b-1} & w_{L_b-2} & \cdots & w_1 & w_{L_b} \\ w_{L_b} & w_{L_b-1} & \cdots & w_2 & w_1 \end{bmatrix}, \qquad (3)$$

where L_b represents the row/column size of each structured matrix (or block size, FFT size).

3.2 Block-Circulant Matrices-Based CONV

CirCNN [10] and C-LSTM [46] have a detailed discussion of the inference algorithm for block circulant matrix-based DNNs. The theoretical foundation is derived in [55], which shows that the "effectiveness" of block circulant matrix-based DNNs is the same with DNNs without compression. However, CirCNN and C-LSTM do not thoroughly discuss convolutional (CONV) layers which are the major computation in state-of-the-art DNNs. In this section, we present the detailed formulation of block circulant matrix-based computation for CONV layers, which are the major computation part of the tiny YOLO algorithm.

Given an input and weight filters (tensor), in a 2-D convolution operation, we slide each filter over all spatial locations of the input, multiply the corresponding entries of the input and filter, and accumulate the intermediate product values. The result is the output of the 2-D convolution. It is well-known that the multiplication-and-accumulation (MAC) operation dominates the overall convolution computation, and will be our focus of acceleration.

Each 4-D weight tensor $\mathbf{W}$ has the shape of $\mathbf{W} \in \mathbb{R}^{r \times r \times C \times C'}$. Using block circulant matrix, we compress the input channels C and output channels C' plane of the 4-D weight tensor. According to the *circulant convolution theorem* [35, 43], instead of directly performing the matrix-vector multiplication, we could use the FFT-based fast multiplication method. In each block circulant matrix, only the first row is needed for calculation, and is termed the *index vector*. The calculation of a block circulant matrix-vector multiplication $\mathbf{W}_{ij}\mathbf{x}_j$ can be performed as follows.

$$\mathbf{a} = \mathbf{W}_{ij}\mathbf{x}_j = \mathbf{w}_{ij} \circledast \mathbf{x}_j = \text{IFFT}\left(\text{FFT}(\mathbf{w}_{ij}) \circ \text{FFT}(\mathbf{x}_j)\right) \qquad (4)$$

where '$\circledast$' denotes circular convolution, and $\circ$ represents element-wise multiplication. After the weight compression, the shape of the weight tensor becomes $r \times r \times C \times C'/L_b$. For better illustration, we stretch the compressed weight tensor from the 2-D $r \times r$ matrix to a 1-D r^2 vector. This procedure is shown in Fig. 3 (a). The outer-level brackets indicate the IDs of the output channels for weight tensor (i.e., 1, 2, ..., C'/L_b). The inner-level brackets show the IDs of index vectors for input channels (i.e., 1, 2, ..., C/L_b), where each vector with length L_b corresponds to a block circulant matrix.

Fig. 3 (b) illustrates the block circulant matrix-based CONV operation. We slide each block of FFT results of the weight kernel $\text{FFT}(\mathbf{w}_{ij})$ (marked as blue bars) over all spatial locations of the input feature maps $\text{FFT}(\mathbf{x}_j)$ of FFT results with zero padding (marked as white bars and dotted lines). We then multiply the corresponding

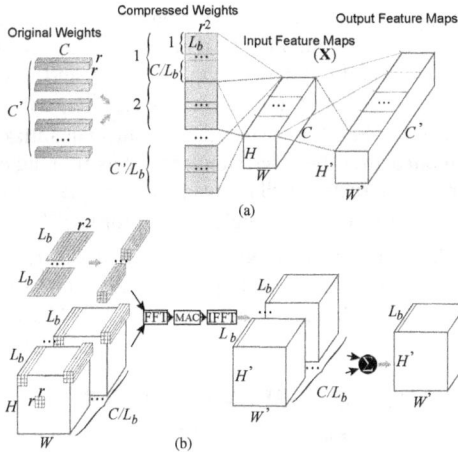

Figure 3: A block circulant matrix-based CONV layer.

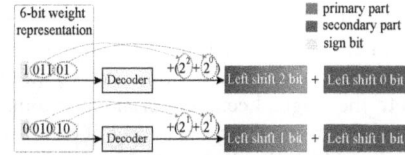

Figure 4: An illustration of the 6-bit weight representation using the mixed powers-of-two quantization.

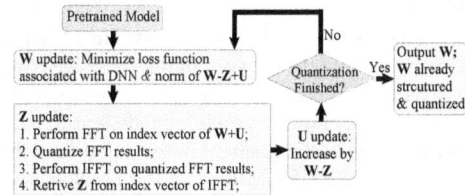

Figure 5: The overall procedure of ADMM-based weight quantization on FFT results.

FFT results of the input feature map $\text{FFT}(\mathbf{x}_j)$ and weight kernel $\text{FFT}(\mathbf{w}_{ij})$. The accumulation of the r^2 multiplication results will be sent to IFFT computing module and become the output of the block circulant matrix-based CONV operation. The forward propagation process in the CONV layer is shown in Fig. 3 (a). Please note that each weight kernel has C/L_b blocks. After finding the CONV kernel result, we sum up all the intermediate matrices and output a single matrix. This becomes one channel at the output of CONV layer. In other words, we use the first C-channel of the weight kernel to compute the first output channel of CONV layer, and so on. In addition, each output channel has its own batch normalization and bias, which will be calculated in the end.

4 THE REQ-YOLO FRAMEWORK

4.1 Heterogeneous Weight Quantization

The previous works on weight quantization [30, 52] has demonstrated the effectiveness of various quantization techniques applied to DNN models including fixed bit-length, ternary and even binary weight representations. Weight quantization can simultaneously reduce the DNN model size, computation and memory access intensity [9]. Some the other prior works have investigated the combination of equal-distance weight quantization and other mode compression techniques such as weight pruning [17, 18].

Equal-distance quantization [9], to some extent, facilitates efficient hardware implementations while maintaining accuracy requirement, whereas the power consumption and hardware resource utilization of the involved multiplications is still high. On the other hand, the powers-of-two quantization technique is extremely hardware efficient by using binary bit shift-based multiplication, however, suffering non-negligible accuracy degradation due to the highly unevenly spaced scales. To overcome the accuracy degradation problem and maintain low power consumption and resource utilization, we propose a heterogeneous weight quantization technique, i.e., we (i) adopt the equal-distance quantization for some CONV layers and (ii) we use the mixed powers-of-two-based quantization for other CONV layers. Please note that the quantization technique is identical inside each CONV layer. The mixed powers-of-two-based weight representation consists of a sign bit part and a magnitude bits part. The magnitude bits part is the combination

of a primary powers-of-two and a secondary powers-of-two part. It not only enhances the model accuracy by mitigating the uneven data scaling problem but also facilitates efficient hardware implementations. Fig. 4 illustrates a 6-bit weight representation using the mixed powers-of-two quantization method. 1 bit is for representing the sign bit, and 5-bit are for magnitude bits (in which the first 3-bit are primary; the last 2-bit are secondary). The primary and secondary part of the weight "101101" are decoded as "011" and "01", respectively. Therefore, when multiplying an input value by weight "101101", we shift the input left 2 bit and 0 bit, respectively, and sum the two products up.

4.2 ADMM for Weight Quantization

In the hardware implementation, for each block circulant matrix $\mathbf{W}_{ij}$, we actually store the FFT result $\text{FFT}(\mathbf{w}_{ij})$ instead of the index vector $\mathbf{w}_{ij}$ [10]. However, it is not straightforward to directly apply quantization on the FFT results $\text{FFT}(\mathbf{w}_{ij})$'s because of the difficulty of impact evaluations. This is a major limitation of the prior work [17, 18, 10, 46], which would be further exacerbated because both real and imaginary parts of FFT results need to be stored.

To overcome this limitation, in this section we incorporate ADMM with FFT/IFFT and use it for the heterogeneous weight quantization to directly quantize the FFT results $\text{FFT}(\mathbf{w}_{ij})$'s, which can achieve higher compression ratio and lower accuracy degradation compared with prior works. This novel method effectively leverages the flexibility in ADMM. In a nutshell, we propose to *perform quantization in the frequency (FFT) domain and perform weight mapping in the weight domain*. Details are described as follows, as also shown in Fig. 5.

Consider the quantization problem as an optimization problem $\min_{\mathbf{x}} f(\mathbf{x})$ with combinatorial constraints. This problem is difficult to solve directly using optimization tools. Through the application of ADMM [4, 24], the original quantization problem is decomposed into two subproblems, which will be iteratively solved until convergence. The first subproblem is $\min_{\mathbf{x}} f(\mathbf{x}) + q_1(\mathbf{x})$ where $q_1(\mathbf{x})$ is a differentiatede, quadratic term. This subproblem does not have combinatorial constraints and can be solved using traditional optimization method, e.g., stochastic gradient descent for DNN training. The second subproblem is: $\min_{\mathbf{x}} g(\mathbf{x}) + q_2(\mathbf{x})$, where $g(\mathbf{x})$ corresponds to the original combinatorial constraints and $q_2(\mathbf{x})$ is another quadratic term. For special types of combinatorial constraints, including block circulant matrices, quantization, etc., the second subproblem can be optimally and analytically solved, as we will see in the following discussions.

In the tiny YOLO network, the weights in the lth layer is denoted by $\mathbf{W}_l$. The loss function is represented by $f\left(\{\mathbf{W}_l\}_{l=1}^N\right)$. Assume a weight sub-matrix $(\mathbf{W}_l)_{ij} \in \mathbb{R}^{L_b \times L_b}$ is mapped to a block circulant matrix. Directly training the network in the structured format will incur a large number of equality constraints (to maintain the structure). This makes the training problem inefficient to solve using the conventional stochastic gradient descent. On the other hand, ADMM can be utilized to efficiently solve this problem, and a large number of equality constraints can be avoided.

We introduce auxiliary variables $\mathbf{Z}_l$ and $\mathbf{U}_l$, which have the same dimensionality as $\mathbf{W}_l$. Through the application of ADMM[1], the original structured training problem can be decomposed into two subproblems, which are iteratively solved until convergence. In each iteration k, the first subproblem is

$$\underset{\{\mathbf{W}_l\}}{\text{minimize}} \quad f\left(\{\mathbf{W}_l\}_{l=1}^N\right) + \sum_{l=1}^N \frac{\rho_l}{2} \|\mathbf{W}_l - \mathbf{Z}_l^k + \mathbf{U}_l^k\|_F^2, \qquad (5)$$

where $\mathbf{U}_l^k$ is the dual variable updated in each iteration, $\mathbf{U}_l^k := \mathbf{U}_l^{k-1} + \mathbf{W}_l^k - \mathbf{Z}_l^k$. In the objective function of (5), the first term is the differentiable loss function, and the second quadratic term is differentiable and convex. Thus, this subproblem can be solved by stochastic gradient descent and the complexity is the same as training the original DNN. A large number of constraints are avoided here. The result of the first subproblem is denoted by $\mathbf{W}_l^{k+1}$.

The second subproblem, on the other hand, is to quantize $\mathbf{W}_l^{k+1} + \mathbf{U}_l^k$ in the frequency domain, and the result of the second subproblem is denoted by $\mathbf{Z}_l^{k+1}$. For a matrix $(\mathbf{W}_l^{k+1} + \mathbf{U}_l^k)_{ij}$ for frequency-domain quantization, we first perform FFT on the index vector. Then we perform quantization on the FFT results. For the equal-distance quantization, we constrain them on a set of quantization levels $\alpha \times \{-(\frac{M}{2} - 1), ..., -1, 0, 1, 2, ..., \frac{M}{2} - 1\}$ associated with a layerwise coefficient α, where M is the predefined number of quantization levels; for the mixed powers-of-two quantization, we constrain them to $\alpha \times \{0, \pm 2^0, \pm 2^1, \pm 2^2, ..., \pm 2^{M_1}\} \bigcup \{0, \pm 2^0, \pm 2^1, \pm 2^2, ..., \pm 2^{M_2}\}$, where M_1 and M_2 is the total number of bits in the primary and secondary part, respectively.

This step is simply mapping each FFT value to the nearest quantization level. The quantization levels are determined by the (i) range of FFT results of index vector, and (ii) the predefined number S of quantization levels. The coefficient α may be different for different layers, which will not increase hardware implementation complexity because α will be stored along with the FFT results after quantization. Finally, as the key step, we perform IFFT on the quantized FFT results, and the restored vector becomes the index vector of $(\mathbf{Z}_l^{k+1})_{ij}$. We then retrieve block-circulant matrix $\mathbf{Z}_l^{k+1}$ from the index vector after IFFT.

We have proved that the above frequency-domain quantization procedure is the optimal, analytical solution of the second subproblem. Because of the symmetric property of quantization above and below 0, the restored index vector of $(\mathbf{Z}_l^{k+1})_{ij}$ will still be a real-valued vector. Besides, the frequency-domain quantization procedure is applied after the block circulant matrix training of DNNs, and the circulant structure will be maintained in quantization. This is because we restore a single index vector for $(\mathbf{Z}_l^{k+1})_{ij}$ and thus $(\mathbf{Z}_l^{k+1})_{ij}$ will maintain the imposed circulant structure. After the convergence of ADMM, the solution $\mathbf{W}_l$ meets the two requirements: (i) the block-circulant structure, and (ii) the FFT results are quantized.

5 HARDWARE IMPLEMENTATION

In this section, we implement the YOLO-based object detection on FPGAs. In order to achieve both low-power and high-performance, the proposed REQ-YOLO framework ensures that the limited FPGA on-chip BRAM has enough capacity to load the weight parameters from the host memory due to the following reasons: (i) the regularity of the block circulant matrices introduces no additional storage such as weight indices after compression in ESE [18]; (ii) we use the heterogeneous weight quantization using ADMM considering hardware resource, further reducing the weight storage and exploiting the hardware resource while satisfying the accuracy requirement. The extra communication overhead caused by accessing FPGA off-chip DDR for common designs [18, 34] can be eliminated.

5.1 FPGA Resource-Aware Design Flow

The resource usage model including Look-up tables (LUTs), DSP blocks, and BRAM of an FPGA implementation can be estimated using analytical models. According to our design, there are two types of PEs: DSP-based PE for equal distance quantization and shift-based PE for mixed powers-of-two quantization. In the convolution operation, suppose the DSP resource for DSP-based and shift-based PE are ΔDSP_D and ΔDSP_S, respectively, and the LUT resouce for DSP-based and shift-based PE are ΔLUT_D and ΔLUT_S, respectively. The models of # DSP, # LUT, and # BRAM are shown as follows,

$$\#DSP = \Delta DSP_D \times \#CONV_D + \Delta DSP_S \times \#CONV_D \qquad (6)$$

$$\#LUT = \Delta LUT_D \times \#CONV_L + \Delta LUT_S \times \#CONV_L \qquad (7)$$

$$\#BRAM = max\{\frac{Model\ size}{BRAM\ size}, \frac{Onchip\ bandwidth}{BRAM\ bandwidth}\} \qquad (8)$$

where $\#CONV_D$, $\#CONV_L$ are the number of CONV operations for DSP and LUT, respectively. Generally, in Xilinx Virtex-7 FPGA fabric, the BRAM size is 36kb and the BRAM bandwidth is 64b.

Indeed, replacing multiplications with bit shift operations significantly reduces the usage of DSP blocks, resulting in much less power assumption. However, the DSP resource will be wasted, causing utilization overhead on LUTs since LUT is the basic building block in implementing the logic function of bit shift operations. To fully exploit the limited FPGA resource for both LUTs and DSP blocks, we propose to adopt both the equal-distance quantization and the mixed powers-of-two-based quantization techniques for hardware implementation. More specifically, for each CONV layer, we select either equal-distance or mixed powers-of-two as the quantization method. Please note that the quantization method inside a CONV layer is identical.

---

[1]The details of the ADMM algorithm are discussed in [4]. We omit the details because of space limitation.

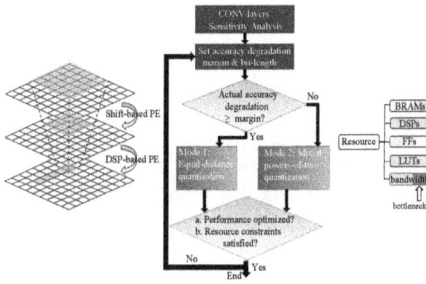

Figure 6: The mode selection rule of the resource-aware design.

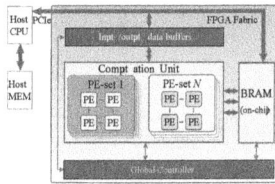

Figure 7: The overall hardware architecture on FPGA.

The selection rule is shown in Fig. 6. The design objectives are higher performance and energy efficiency satisfying the accuracy requirement. We first conduct the sensitivity analysis for each CONV layer regarding the two quantization methods (mode 1 and mode 2) and we set the initial margin for the overall degradation of the prediction accuracy and initial bit-length for weight representation. In order to reduce the accuracy degradation as much as possible, our priority choice is equal-distance quantization in those CONV layers which sensitivity are beyond the pre-set margin value since we can use DSPs for multiplication operations to enhance the accuracy. More specifically, we choose mode 2 if the actual accuracy degradation of the YOLO network is smaller than the margin value, otherwise we select mode 1. The margin value will further be refined until the performance is optimized and resource constraints (i.e., DSPs and bandwidth) are satisfied. Overall, the DSPs and LUTs usage is not the bottleneck in our design, which is different from traditional fixed-bit length weight quantization and our design is bound by bandwidth only.

5.2 Overall Hardware Architecture

Our proposed accelerator design on FPGA is composed of a computation unit, on-chip memories/BRAM, and datapath control logic. Our design does not access the FPGA off-chip memories. The FFT results of the pre-trained network model (CONV weight filters) is loaded to FPGA BRAM from the Host memory via the control of Host CPU and the PCI-express (PCIe) bus. The data buffers are used to cache input images, intermediate results and layer outputs from the previous stage slice by slice, to make preparation of the PE operation. The PEs inside of the computation unit are a collection of basic computing units that execute multiplications and additions (MACs), and other functions such as normalization, etc. The global controller orchestrates the computing flow and data flow on the FPGA fabric.

5.3 PE Design

From Eqn. (4), we observe that the FFT and IFFT operation are always executed in pairs. Therefore, we can combine and implement them as an FFT/IFFT kernel. An N-point IFFT calculation can be implemented using an N-point FFT in addition of a division operation (i.e., $\div N$) and two conjugations. There are N multipliers between FFT and IFFT, which is responsible for multiplying the intermediate results of FFT and weight values stored in BRAM. The PE is designed mainly to execute the most resource-consuming operation, i.e., matrix-vector multiplication, which will be implemented using the element-wise "FFT→MAC→IFFT" calculation according to Equation 4 (the key for the implementation with limited hardware resources). As shown in Fig. 8, the proposed PE architecture consists of a register bank, a controller, a weight decoder, a mode decoder, 2 multiplexers, and 2 FFT/IFFT kernels.

The register bank stores the FFT twiddle factors which will be loaded to the FFT operator. The weight decoder prepares the desired weight parameters format for further calculation. The mode decoder and MUX 1 work simultaneously to select the operating mode (i.e., mode 1 for equal-distance quantization and mode 2 for mixed powers-of-two quantization), under the control of the PE controller. Mux 2 is used to select the batch normalization (BN) operation depending on the layer structure. The MAC unit multiplies and accumulates the input feature maps and the pre-calculated FFT result of convolution kernel weights decoded from BRAM blocks. The two operating modes are marked in red dashed boxes, where mode 1 performs FFT/IFFT computations using multiplication-based FFT butterfly unit [8] along with a MAC unit, while mode 2 performs the FFT/IFFT computations using binary bit shifts and additions. Additionally, the MAC operation can be replaced by shift and addition in model 2.

5.4 Convolution Dataflow and Pipelining

The dataflow of input pixels from input buffers to computation unit to output bufferers is shown in Fig. 9. Taking advantage of the compressed but regular YOLO network structures, we apply inter-level and intra-level pipelining in the basic computation unit as shown in Fig. 9. In *intra-level pipelining*, there are three separate stages, i.e., load, compute, and store. This pipelining scheme generates higher level of parallelism and therefore leads to higher performance and throughput. In the *inter-level pipelining*, each pipeline stage corresponds to one level in the computation unit. There are several stages in the FFT operation depending on the input size, i.e., an

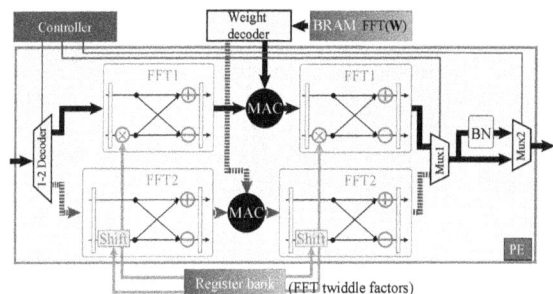

Figure 8: The PE (processing element) design.

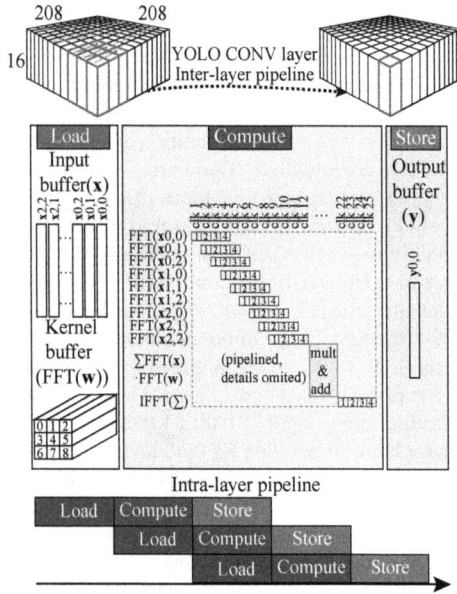

Figure 9: An illustration of the CONV operation data flow in the 2nd CONV layer.

N-point FFT uses $N/2$ butterfly units for each stage and has a total of $r = \log_2^N$ stages.

We use an input size of $208 \times 208 \times 16$ and weight kernel size $3 \times 3 \times 16$ using 16-point FFT (4 stages) as shown in Fig. 9, to demonstrate the CONV dataflow in the 2th CONV layer of the tiny YOLO network structure. Both inter-level and intra-level pipelining techniques are adopted. The input pixels are loaded to input buffers followed by a sequence corresponding to the spatial relationship with kernel window. The first input data needed for CONV operation is marked as red bars with the same input size of 16-point FFT. The PE accepts each input vector (red bar) each per clock cycle, computes the "FFT→MAC→IFFT" operation and the result is stored in the output buffer.

5.5 Design Optimization

In YOLO, the CONV operation, performed by PEs, is the most resource-intensive arithmetic. Therefore, from the perspective of computation, the hardware design optimization targets at PE size/number. Through reducing PE size/number, we can achieve less power and area consumption, leading to more available on-chip resource and more parallelism. From the communication perspective, the cost of moving data from one physical location to another on FPGAs, named communication cost, can dominate the computational energy and our design. Communication cost consists of accessing memory of weight parameters and intermediate results, and moving data bits over interconnect wires between PEs. Therefore, we can optimize the required computation and communication cost by reducing PE size/number including LUTs and DSPs, and memory access.

5.5.1 DSP Usage Optimization. Reducing the number of multiplications will be critical to the overall hardware design optimization. In the FFT operation, the multipliers of the Radix-2 FFT butterflies with twiddle factor 1 and -1 can be eliminated, and the multiplier

of those butterflies with twiddle factor j and $-j$ can be replaced with conjugation operators. In the dot product stage, the two inputs of dot product are both from FFT operators, which are conjugate symmetric. And the dot product results of such conjugate symmetric inputs are also conjugate symmetric. Therefore, in $\left(\text{FFT}(\mathbf{x}_j) \circ \text{FFT}(\mathbf{w}_{ij})\right)$ with input size of FFT N, the last $N/2 - 1$ dot product outputs can be obtained using conjugation operations from their corresponding symmetric points. And the amount of $N/2 - 1$ multipliers can be eliminated.

The DSP48E1 block in modern Xilinx FPGAs generally consists of three sub-blocks: pre-adder, multiplier, and ALU. These hard blocks directly implement commonly used functions in silicon, therefore consuming much less power and area, and operating at a higher clock frequency than the same implementations in logic. For these hard blocks with constrained resource, resource sharing could be applied. Generally, non-overlapping MAC operations are scheduled using the combination of pre-adder, multiplier blocks or ALU, multiplier blocks based on the function itself and bit-length of operands.

In order to take full advantage of the limited DSP resource and achieve more design parallelism, we further optimize the proposed design using low-bit DSP sharing. More specifically, we can divide each sub-block into smaller slices, in which the internal carry propagation between slices is segregated to guarantee independence for all slices. In other word, we can group and feed several non-overlapping operands into one of the inputs of a DSP sub-block. For example, the ALU unit in DSP48E1 block can be divided into six 8-bit smaller slices with carry out signal for 8-bit computation.

5.5.2 Reducing Weight Memory Accesses. The input feature map $\mathbf{x}_i (i \in (1, ..., C))$ is real value [12] and all the weight parameters $\mathbf{W}$ are real-valued. According to [42, 6], the FFT or IFFT result is mirrored (have the property of complex conjugated symmetry) when its inputs are real-valued. Therefore, for an FFT/IFFT with N-point inputs, we only need to store $\frac{N}{2} + 1$ of the results instead of N results into the BRAM, thereby reducing communication energy.

5.6 Design Space Exploration

To prototype and explore the hardware architecture of the proposed REQ-YOLO framework, we use Xilinx SDx 2017.1 as the commercial synthesis backend to synthesize the C/C++ based YOLO LSTM design. We feed the well-trained inference models of YOLO into the automatic synthesis backend [28, 47, 48]. A bit-length of data quantization and mode selection for each CONV layer are generated to illustrate the computation flow as shown in Algorithm 1. The operators in each graph are scheduled to compose the intra-layer or inter-layer pipeline under the design constraints, to maximally achieve full throughput and performance. At last, a code generator receives the scheduling results and generates the final C/C++ based codes, which can be fed into the commercial HLS tool for FPGA implementation.

6 EVALUATION RESULTS

6.1 Training of Tiny YOLO

We adopt the state-of-the-art object detection algorithm-tiny YOLO based on yolov2 tiny [44] as the target DNN and evaluate it on both the PASCAL VOC07+12 dataset [12] and the DataDJI detection dataset captured by the DJI UAV [11]. We set $S = 13$, $B = 5$. The DataDJI detection dataset has 12 labeled classes so $C_{DJI} = 12$, while the PASCAL VOC dataset has 20 labeled classes so $C_{VOC} = 20$. The anchor boxes sizes are pre-set by K-means clustering with $K = 5$. Our final prediction is a $13 \times 13 \times 37$ tensor for DataDJI dataset and a $13 \times 13 \times 45$ tensor for VOC dataset. After the last convolutional layer, 5 boxes for each grid cell will be obtained with their locations and scores. Then we first discard boxes that have detected a class with a score lower than the threshold, which is 0.6 in our experiment. After that, the Non-Maximum Suppression (NMS) algorithm will filter out remaining boxes that overlap with each other. The ideal output of YOLO is one bounding box for each object. Finally, for the predicted bounding box, we use IOU and mean average precision (mAP) as the metric to evaluate the object detection accuracy on DataDJI and VOC datasets, respectively.

For both datasets, we use a mini batch size of 16. The initial learning rate is set to 0.001, and divided by a factor of 10 every 20k iterations, to guarantee convergence. The ADAM [25] optimizer and standard data argumentation like random crops, color shifting, etc are used during training. The training results of the tiny YOLO using different block sizes are shown in Fig 10. Fig. 10 shows that the block circulant matrix-based training only causes a very small accuracy degradation (IOU or mAP) in general when the compression ratio is large. Among the six models, we select the YOLO-3 for the ADMM-based heterogeneous weight quantization and further hardware implementation, since it introduces small accuracy loss while maintaining the large compression ratio compared to baseline.

6.2 Accuracy after Weight Quantization

we select the YOLO-3 model with very small accuracy degradation and large weight reduction ratio for the REQ-YOLO framework and evaluate the selected model on both the PASCAL VOC dataset and the DataDJI detection dataset. For different weight (FFT results) representations from 32-bit to 6-bit, the introduced additional accuracy degradation (i.e., IOU for DataDJI and mAP for VOC) is generally very small, i.e., 0.73% for PASCAL, and 0.2% for DataDJI. Reducing the weight from 32-bit floating point to 8-bit fixed point brings

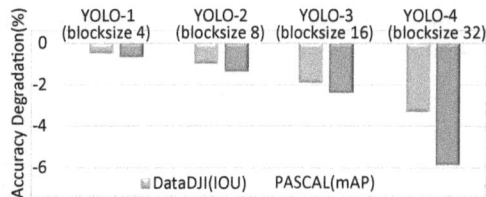

Figure 10: Test accuracy of the tiny YOLO network using different block sizes.

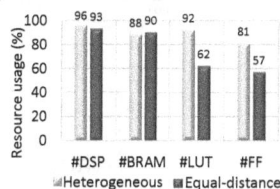

Figure 11: Resource usage comparison of two different quantization methods.

negligible additional degradation (0.07%) in IOU or mAP while the model size can further be compressed by 4×. In this way, through block circulant matrix training and ADMM-based heterogeneous quantization, we can accommodate the tiny YOLO structures to the on-chip BRAM of state-of-the-art FPGA while achieving real-time object detection, satisfying the accuracy requirement.

6.3 Performance and Energy Efficiency

6.3.1 FPGA-platform Comparison. We use the FPGA platform of Alpha Data's ADM-PCIE-7V3 for evaluating the proposed REQ-YOLO framework. The ADM-PCIE-7V3 board, comprising a Xilinx Virtex-7 (690t) FPGA and a 16GB DDR3 memory, is connected to the host machine through PCIE Gen3 × 8 I/O Interface. The host machine adopted in our experiments is a server configured with multiple Intel Core i7-4790 processors. The detailed comparison of on-chip resources of the FPGA platforms is presented in Fig. 11. We use Xilinx SDX 2017.4 as the commercial high-level synthesis backend to synthesize the high-level (C/C++) based RNN designs on the selected FPGAs. The REQ-YOLO framework of FPGA implementation is operating at 200MHz. For the tiny YOLO network, the performance of the first four layers is bound by the communication due to the large input/output feature map size. The last five layers of the YOLO network are otherwise constrained by the computation because of the increased channel size.

We conduct the comparison between the heterogeneous-based YOLO quantization method and the equal-distance-based quantization method on the selected ADM-7v3 platform. We report the resource usage (percentage) of two methods in Fig. 11. We can observe that the heterogeneous-based method better exploit the hardware resource than the equal-distance method, especially in LUT, therefore leading to higher performance and throughput. This finding also verifies our discussion in Section 5.1. The layer-wise computation, communication and latency analysis of both equal-distance quantization and heterogeneous quantization is shown in Table 1. In the communication-bound layers, the latency is the same for both methods. Overall, the heterogeneous-based method achieves 1.5× performance compared to the equal-distance method.

Table 1: Comparison of equal-distance-based quantization method and heterogeneous-based quantization method on the YOLO-3 model (block size 16).

Model	Layer	Comp. Size	Comm. In_size	Comm. Out_size	Bound Type	Equal-distance-based Latency (μs)	Equal-distance-based Model Size	Heterogeneous-based Latency (μs)	Heterogeneous-based Model Size
YOLO-3	Conv0	173,056	519,168	692,224	Comm.-bound	872.5	0.16kb	881.3	0.13kb
	Conv1	86,528	692,224	32,448	Comm.-bound	442.2	6.75kb	443.6	5.63kb
	Conv2	21,632	32,448	173,056	Comm.-bound	219.3	27.0kb	216.2	22.5kb
	Conv3	21,632	173,056	86,528	Comm.-bound	119.8	108.0kb	120.5	90.0kb
	Conv4	21,632	86,528	43,264	Comp.-bound	117.1	432.0kb	54.5	360.0kb
	Conv5	21,632	43,264	86,528	Comp.-bound	117.9	1.69Mb	69.4	1.41Mb
	Conv6	86,528	86,528	173,056	Comp.-bound	905.1	3.38Mb	430.4	2.81Mb
	Conv7	173,056	173,056	173,056	Comp.-bound	1,832.7	286.88kb	872.7	239.06kb
	Conv8	16,224	173,056	19,244	Comp.-bound	174.3	37.88kb	93.2	26.57kb
	Total	621,920	-	-	-	4,801.0	5.93Mb	3,183.6	4.95Mb

Table 2: Comparison among different tiny YOLO implementations.

Implementation	Titan X-YOLO [38]	Our GTX-YOLO	Our TX2-YOLO	Virtex-YOLO [33]	Zynq-YOLO [15]	Our FPGA-YOLO0 (Equal-distance-based)	Our FPGA-YOLO1 (Heterogeneous-based)
Device Type	Titan X	GTX 1070 GPU	TX2 embedded GPU	Xilinx Virtex-7 485t	Zynq 7020	ADM-7V3 FPGA	ADM-7V3 FPGA
Memory	12GB GDDR5	8GB GDDR5	8 GB LPDDR4	4.5 MB BRAM	0.6 MB BRAM	6.6 MB BRAM	6.6 MB BRAM
Clock Freq.	1.0 GHz	1.6 GHz	1.3 GHz	0.14 GHz	0.15 GHz (Peak)	0.2 GHz	0.2 GHz
Performance (FPS)	155	220.8	28.4	21	8	208.2	314.2
Power (W)	180	140	10.8	-	-	23	21
Energy Efficiency (FPS/W)	0.9	1.6	2.6	-	-	9.1	15.0

The results of performance and energy efficiency of our FPGA based YOLO implementations are presented in Table 2. Our FPGA-YOLO1 using heterogeneous quantization outperforms our FPGA-YOLO0 using equal-distance quantization in terms of both performance and energy efficiency, i.e., 1.5× in performance and 1.6× in energy efficiency, since the heterogeneous quantization fully exploits the hardware resource and design parallelism. Please note that since the DataDJI dataset is the latest released, we cannot find the related FPGA based implementations to compare with. For PASCAL VOC dataset, compared to other FPGA based works [15, 33], our FPGA-YOLO1 achieves at least 10× performance enhancement, while the FPGA fabric Virtex-7 690t in our platform is only slightly better than Virtex-7 485t used in [33] in resource capacity. We can not compare the energy efficiency among them since the power measurements are not provided in [15, 33].

6.3.2 Cross-platform Comparison. We implement the same YOLO network on two GPU platforms and compare with the tiny YOLO proposed in [38] using Titan X GPU. The first one is GeForce GTX 1070, which is a Nvidia GPU designed for PC. The second one is a Jetson TX2, which is the latest embedded GPU platform. The detailed specifications and comparisons among these platforms are shown in Table 2. We implement the trained model on both platforms and measure the performance using frame per second (FPS) and power consumption (W). Compared to Titan X-YOLO [38], our GTX-YOLO and our TX2-YOLO achieve 1.8× and 2.9× enhancement in energy efficiency.

Compared to GPU-based YOLO implementation (Our GTX-YOLO), our two FPGA YOLO implementations has the similar or better speed while dissipating around 6× less power, and the efficiency (performance per power) of our FPGA-YOLO0 and our FPGA-YOLO1 are 5.7× and 9.4× better, respectively. It indicates that our proposed REQ-YOLO framework is very suitable for FPGAs, since usually GPUs often perform faster than FPGAs as discussed in [3]. Compared to the GPU-based YOLO implementation with the best energy efficiency (our TX2-YOLO), our two FPGA YOLO implementations

achieve 3.5× and 5.8× improvement in energy efficiency. While our FPGA YOLO implementations are at least 7.3× faster while only dissipating at most 2.1× more power.

Overall, our proposed REQ-YOLO framework is effective on both GPUs and FPGAs. It is highly promising to deploy our proposed REQ-YOLO framework on FPGA to gain much higher energy efficiency for autonomous systems on object sections than on GPUs. More importantly, the proposed framework achieves much higher FPS over the real-time requirement.

7 CONCLUSION

In this work, we propose REQ-YOLO, a resource-aware, systematic weight quantization framework for object detection, considering both algorithm and hardware resource aspects in object detection. We adopt the block-circulant matrix method and we incorporate ADMM with FFT/IFFT and develop a heterogeneous weight quantization method including both equal-distance and heterogeneous quantization methods considering hardware resource. We implement the quantized models on the state-of-the-art FPGA taking advantage of the potential to store the whole compressed DNN models on-chip. To achieve real-time, highly-efficient implementations on FPGA, we develop an efficient PE structure supporting both equal-distance and mixed powers-of-two quantization methods, CONV dataflow and pipelining techniques, design optimization techniques focus on reducing memory access and PE size/numbers, and a template-based automatic synthesis framework to optimally exploit hardware resource. Experimental results show that our proposed framework can significantly compress the YOLO model while introducing very small accuracy degradation. Our framework is very suitable for FPGA and our FPGA implementations outperform the state-of-the-art designs.

ACKNOWLEDGMENTS

This work is supported by Beijing Natural Science Foundation (No. L172004), Municipal Science and Technology Program under Grant

Z181100008918015, and National Science Foundation under grants CNS #1704662 and CNS #1739748. We thank all the anonymous reviewers for their feedback.

REFERENCES

[1] Manoj Alwani, Han Chen, Michael Ferdman, and Peter Milder. 2016. Fused-layer CNN accelerators. In *Microarchitecture (MICRO), 2016 49th Annual IEEE/ACM International Symposium on*. IEEE, 1–12.

[2] Yakoub Bazi and Farid Melgani. 2018. Convolutional SVM Networks for Object Detection in UAV Imagery. *IEEE Transactions on Geoscience and Remote Sensing*, 56, 6, 3107–3118.

[3] Brahim Betkaoui, David B Thomas, and Wayne Luk. 2010. Comparing performance and energy efficiency of FPGAs and GPUs for high productivity computing. In *IEEE FPT'10*.

[4] Stephen Boyd, Neal Parikh, Eric Chu, Borja Peleato, Jonathan Eckstein, et al. 2011. Distributed optimization and statistical learning via the alternating direction method of multipliers. *Foundations and Trends6 in Machine learning*, 3, 1, 1–122.

[5] Zhaowei Cai, Quanfu Fan, Rogerio S Feris, and Nuno Vasconcelos. 2016. A unified multi-scale deep convolutional neural network for fast object detection. In *European conference on computer vision*. Springer, 354–370.

[6] Yun-Nan Chang and Keshab K Parhi. 2003. An efficient pipelined fft architecture. *Ieee transactions on circuits and systems ii: analog and digital signal processing*, 50, 6, 322–325.

[7] Yu-Hsin Chen, Tushar Krishna, Joel S Emer, and Vivienne Sze. 2017. Eyeriss: An energy-efficient reconfigurable accelerator for deep convolutional neural networks. *IEEE Journal of Solid-State Circuits*, 52, 1, 127–138.

[8] James W Cooley and John W Tukey. 1965. An algorithm for the machine calculation of complex fourier series. *Mathematics of computation*, 19, 90, 297–301.

[9] Matthieu Courbariaux, Yoshua Bengio, and Jean-Pierre David. 2015. Binaryconnect: training deep neural networks with binary weights during propagations. In *Advances in neural information processing systems*, 3123–3131.

[10] Caiwen Ding et al. 2017. CirCNN: Accelerating and Compressing Deep Neural Networks using Block-circulant Weight Matrices. In *Proceedings of the 50th Annual IEEE/ACM International Symposium on Microarchitecture (MICRO)*. ACM, 395–408.

[11] DJI. 2018. http://www.cse.cuhk.edu.hk/byu/2018-DAC-HDC. (2018).

[12] Mark Everingham, Luc Van Gool, Christopher KI Williams, John Winn, and Andrew Zisserman. 2010. The pascal visual object classes (voc) challenge. *International journal of computer vision*, 88, 2, 303–338.

[13] Ross Girshick. 2015. Fast R-CNN. In *Proceedings of the IEEE international conference on computer vision*, 1440–1448.

[14] Ross Girshick, Jeff Donahue, Trevor Darrell, and Jitendra Malik. 2014. Rich feature hierarchies for accurate object detection and semantic segmentation. In *Proceedings of the ieee conference on computer vision and pattern recognition*, 580–587.

[15] Kaiyuan Guo, Lingzhi Sui, Jiantao Qiu, Song Yao, Song Han, Yu Wang, and Huazhong Yang. 2016. From model to FPGA: Software-hardware Co-design for Efficient Neural Network Acceleration. In *Hot chips 28 symposium (hcs), 2016 ieee*. IEEE, 1–27.

[16] Song Han, Xingyu Liu, Huizi Mao, Jing Pu, Ardavan Pedram, Mark A Horowitz, and William J Dally. 2016. EIE: efficient inference engine on compressed deep neural network. In *Proceedings of the 43rd International Symposium on Computer Architecture*. IEEE Press, 243–254.

[17] Song Han, Huizi Mao, and William J Dally. 2015. Deep compression: compressing deep neural networks with pruning, trained quantization and huffman coding. *Arxiv preprint arxiv:1510.00149*.

[18] Song Han et al. 2017. Ese: efficient speech recognition engine with sparse lstm on fpga. In *Fpga*. ACM, 75–84.

[19] Kaiming He, Xiangyu Zhang, Shaoqing Ren, and Jian Sun. 2016. Deep residual learning for image recognition. In *Proceedings of the ieee conference on computer vision and pattern recognition*, 770–778.

[20] Kaiming He, Xiangyu Zhang, Shaoqing Ren, and Jian Sun. 2014. Spatial pyramid pooling in deep convolutional networks for visual recognition. In *European conference on computer vision*. Springer, 346–361.

[21] Donald R High and Noah Ryan Kapner. 2018. Apparatus and method for providing unmanned delivery vehicles with expressions. US Patent App. 15/638,960. (Jan. 2018).

[22] Sergey Ioffe. 2017. Batch renormalization: towards reducing minibatch dependence in batch-normalized models. In *Advances in neural information processing systems*, 1945–1953.

[23] Sergey Ioffe and Christian Szegedy. 2015. Batch normalization: accelerating deep network training by reducing internal covariate shift. *Arxiv preprint arxiv:1502.03167*.

[24] Rong Jin. 2017. Deep learning at alibaba. In *Proceedings of the 26th international joint conference on artificial intelligence*. AAAI Press, 11–16.

[25] Diederik P Kingma and Jimmy Ba. 2014. Adam: a method for stochastic optimization. *Arxiv preprint arxiv:1412.6980*.

[26] Alex Krizhevsky, Ilya Sutskever, and Geoffrey E Hinton. 2012. Imagenet classification with deep convolutional neural networks. In *Advances in neural information processing systems*.

[27] Yann LeCun. 2015. Lenet-5, convolutional neural networks. *Url: http://yann.lecun. com/exdb/lenet*.

[28] Yun Liang et al. 2012. High-level Synthesis: Productivity, Performance, and Software Constraints. *JECE'12*.

[29] Darryl Lin, Sachin Talathi, and Sreekanth Annapureddy. 2016. Fixed point quantization of deep convolutional networks. In *International conference on machine learning*, 2849–2858.

[30] Zhouhan Lin, Matthieu Courbariaux, Roland Memisevic, and Yoshua Bengio. 2015. Neural networks with few multiplications. *Arxiv preprint arxiv:1510.03009*.

[31] Liqiang Lu and Yun Liang. 2018. SpWA: An Efficient Sparse Winograd Convolutional Neural Networks Accelerator on FPGAs. In *DAC'18*.

[32] Liqiang Lu, Yun Liang, Qingcheng Xiao, and Shengen Yan. 2017. Evaluating Fast Algorithms for Convolutional Neural Networks on FPGAs. In *FCCM'17*.

[33] Jing Ma, Li Chen, and Zhiyong Gao. 2017. Hardware implementation and optimization of tiny-yolo network. In *International forum on digital tv and wireless multimedia communications*. Springer, 224–234.

[34] Hiroki Nakahara, Haruyoshi Yonekawa, Tomoya Fujii, and Shimpei Sato. 2018. A lightweight yolov2: a binarized cnn with a parallel support vector regression for an fpga. In *Proceedings of the 2018 acm/sigda international symposium on field-programmable gate arrays*. ACM, 31–40.

[35] Victor Pan. 2012. *Structured matrices and polynomials: unified superfast algorithms*. Springer Science & Business Media.

[36] Jiantao Qiu et al. 2016. Going deeper with embedded fpga platform for convolutional neural network. In *Proceedings of the 2016 acm/sigda international symposium on field-programmable gate arrays*. ACM, 26–35.

[37] Mohammad Rastegari, Vicente Ordonez, Joseph Redmon, and Ali Farhadi. 2016. Xnor-net: imagenet classification using binary convolutional neural networks. In *European conference on computer vision*. Springer, 525–542.

[38] Joseph Redmon, Santosh Divvala, Ross Girshick, and Ali Farhadi. 2016. You only look once: unified, real-time object detection. In *Proceedings of the ieee conference on computer vision and pattern recognition*, 779–788.

[39] Joseph Redmon and Ali Farhadi. 2017. Yolo9000: better, faster, stronger. *Arxiv*.

[40] Joseph Redmon and Ali Farhadi. 2018. Yolov3: an incremental improvement. *Arxiv preprint arxiv:1804.02767*.

[41] Shaoqing Ren, Kaiming He, Ross Girshick, and Jian Sun. 2015. Faster r-cnn: towards real-time object detection with region proposal networks. In *Advances in neural information processing systems*, 91–99.

[42] Sayed Ahmad Salehi, Rasoul Amirfattahi, and Keshab K Parhi. 2013. Pipelined architectures for real-valued fft and hermitian-symmetric ifft with real datapaths. *Ieee transactions on circuits and systems ii: express briefs*, 60, 8, 507–511.

[43] Julius Orion Smith. 2007. *Mathematics of the discrete fourier transform (dft): with audio applications*. Julius Smith.

[44] Trieu. 2016. https://github.com/AlexeyAB/darknet. (2016).

[45] Yaman Umuroglu, Nicholas J Fraser, Giulio Gambardella, Michaela Blott, Philip Leong, Magnus Jahre, and Kees Vissers. 2017. Finn: a framework for fast, scalable binarized neural network inference. In *Proceedings of the 2017 acm/sigda international symposium on field-programmable gate arrays*. ACM, 65–74.

[46] Shuo Wang, Zhe Li, Caiwen Ding, Bo Yuan, Qinru Qiu, Yanzhi Wang, and Yun Liang. 2018. C-LSTM: Enabling Efficient LSTM Using Structured Compression Techniques on FPGAs. In *Fpga'18*.

[47] Shuo Wang and Yun Liang. 2017. A Comprehensive Framework for Synthesizing Stencil Algorithms on FPGAs using OpenCL Model. In *DAC'17*.

[48] Shuo Wang, Yun Liang, and Wei Zhang. 2017. FlexCL: An Analytical Performance Model for OpenCL Workloads on Flexible FPGAs. In *DAC'17*.

[49] Xuechao Wei, Yun Liang, Xiuhong Li, Cody Hao Yu, Peng Zhang, and Jason Cong. 2018. TGPA: Tile-grained Pipeline Architecture for Low Latency CNN Inference. In *ICCAD'18*.

[50] Xuechao Wei, Cody Hao Yu, Peng Zhang, Youxiang Chen, Yuxin Wang, Han Hu, Yun Liang, and Jason Cong. 2017. Automated systolic array architecture synthesis for high throughput cnn inference on fpgas. In *Proceedings of the 54th annual design automation conference 2017*. ACM, 29.

[51] Wei Wen, Chunpeng Wu, Yandan Wang, Yiran Chen, and Hai Li. 2016. Learning structured sparsity in deep neural networks. In *Advances in neural information processing systems*, 2074–2082.

[52] Jiaxiang Wu, Cong Leng, Yuhang Wang, Qinghao Hu, and Jian Chen. 2016. Quantized convolutional neural networks for mobile devices. In *Computer vision and pattern recognition, 2016. cvpr 2016. ieee conference on*.

[53] Qingcheng Xiao, Yun Liang, Liqiang Lu, Shengen Yan, and Yu-Wing Tai. 2017. Exploring Heterogeneous Algorithms for Accelerating Deep Convolutional Neural Networks on FPGAs. In *DAC'17*.

[54] Chen Zhang, Peng Li, Guangyu Sun, Yijin Guan, Bingjun Xiao, and Jason Cong. 2015. Optimizing fpga-based accelerator design for deep convolutional neural networks. In *Proceedings of the 2015 acm/sigda international symposium on field-programmable gate arrays*. ACM, 161–170.

[55] Liang Zhao, Siyu Liao, Yanzhi Wang, Zhe Li, Jian Tang, and Bo Yuan. 2017. Theoretical properties for neural networks with weight matrices of low displacement rank. In *International conference on machine learning*, 4082–4090.

Reconfigurable Convolutional Kernels
for Neural Networks on FPGAs

Martin Hardieck, Martin Kumm, Konrad Möller, Peter Zipf
University of Kassel, Germany
{hardieck,kumm,konrad.moeller,zipf}@uni-kassel.de

ABSTRACT

Convolutional neural networks (CNNs) gained great success in machine learning applications and much attention was paid to their acceleration on field programmable gate arrays (FPGAs). The most demanding computational complexity of CNNs is found in the convolutional layers, which account for 90% of the total operations. The fact that parameters in convolutional layers do not change over a long time interval in weight stationary CNNs allows the use of reconfiguration to reduce the resource requirements. This work proposes several alternative reconfiguration schemes that significantly reduce the complexity of sum-of-products operations. The proposed direct configuration schemes provide the least resource requirements and fast reconfiguration times of 32 clock cycles but require additional memory for the pre-computed configurations. The proposed online reconfiguration scheme uses an online computation of the LUT contents to avoid this memory overhead. Finally, a scheme that duplicates the reconfigurable LUTs is proposed for which the reconfiguration time can be completely hidden in the computation time. Combined with a few online reconfiguration circuits, this provides the same configuration memory and configuration time as a conventional parallel kernel but offers large resource reductions of up to 80% of the LUTs.

CCS CONCEPTS

• **Computing methodologies** → **Neural networks**; • **Hardware** → *Reconfigurable logic and FPGAs*; Reconfigurable logic applications;

KEYWORDS

Convolutional Neural Networks, FPGA, runtime reconfiguration

ACM Reference Format:
Martin Hardieck, Martin Kumm, Konrad Möller, Peter Zipf. 2019. Reconfigurable Convolutional Kernels, for Neural Networks on FPGAs. In *The 2019 ACM/SIGDA International Symposium on Field-Programmable Gate Arrays (FPGA '19), February 24–26, 2019, Seaside, CA, USA*. ACM, New York, NY, USA, 10 pages. https://doi.org/10.1145/3289602.3293905

1 INTRODUCTION

Deep convolutional neural networks (CNNs) are one of the most successful machine learning approaches providing state-of-the-art classification accuracy for object detection and classification. This high accuracy is achieved by making the network *deep*, i.e., using several hidden layers. This makes CNNs computationally very demanding. Due to the inherent parallelism of CNNs, parallel computation schemes like the single-instruction-multiple-data (SIMD) architecture of graphics processing units (GPUs) are well suited to provide a high performance for training and inference. However, it was shown in recent work that field programmable gate arrays (FPGAs) are far less power demanding and achieve a similar throughput compared to GPUs when performing inference [21]. Implementing CNNs on FPGAs attracted much attention in the last years [1, 3, 11, 14, 20, 21, 23, 24, 27, 29, 31, 34]. FPGAs allow large degrees of freedom concerning data formats and widths, memory interfacing and degree of parallelism which all have to be selected carefully. Regarding the data format it was shown that fixed point formats with relatively low word sizes are sufficient compared to the hardware-demanding floating point format [12, 13, 21, 30]. Word sizes between 4 and 8 bit already reach floating point accuracy while binarized neural networks (BNNs) [6, 20, 29] and ternary CNNs [30, 35] offer further resource reduction at the price of a reduced accuracy. Regarding the complexity, the highest arithmetic complexity can be found in convolutional layers. It was reported that 90% of the total operations are required in the convolutional layers of LeNet, AlexNet and VGG16 [21].

Most of the previous FPGA-based CNN implementations [1, 3, 11, 14, 21, 23, 24, 27, 31, 34], implement the required sum-of-products (SOP) operation in a parallel fashion. Typically, previous designs heavily use the embedded multipliers or digital signal processing (DSP) blocks of the FPGAs when implementing their kernels. However, kernel sizes and the number of parallel kernels are often selected based on the limited availability of DSP blocks. It was, e. g., stated in [31] that "DSP and on-chip block RAM are the two critical resource types". In addition, for the low word-size designs discussed above DSP blocks have a poor utilization. Recent work on reconfigurable constant multipliers (RCMs) showed that 1) RCMs use considerably fewer resources compared to logic-based multipliers and 2) the reconfiguration of the coefficients is possible within very few clock cycles [15, 17, 18, 22, 32, 33]. These RCMs are based on the look-up table (LUT)-based KCM scheme proposed by Chapman [4, 5] and use either random access memory (RAM) [32, 33], shift register LUTs (SRLs) [15] or configurable look-up tables (CFG-LUTs) [17, 18, 22] as reconfigurable LUT to be able to exchange the coefficient at run-time. The most recent RCMs based on CFG-LUTs provide a reconfiguration time of 32 clock cycles, which is very fast compared to a full or partial FPGA reconfiguration. As typically large amounts of data are processed using the same coefficients (often thousands of convolutions, see Section 2) by using the weight-stationary scheme [28], this short reconfiguration time is often negligible. Hence, RCMs provide a good replacement for the DSP blocks inside the convolutional layers of CNN architectures. Either to allow the addition of more convolutional kernels implemented in logic or to replace DSP blocks which can be used to process the fully connected layers.

This work proposes different reconfigurable architectures for fixed point CNN kernels that combine and refine several advanced results from previous work. They all use a variant of Chapman's KCM technique [4, 5] combined with fast LUT-based reconfiguration [15, 17, 18, 22, 32, 33], pipelined compressor trees [2, 19] and faithful rounding [8] together with an optional online reconfiguration scheme [18, 33] which is tailored to the most recent CFGLUTs. With these different architectures, resource efficient, fast and accurate CNN kernels are possible which provide different alternatives regarding reconfiguration time and memory demands. A secondary contribution of this work is an automated and flexible tool flow. It is made available as part of the open-source code generator FloPoCo [7, 9]. This tool may be used by other researchers to generate customized hardware kernels that can be plugged into their CNN architectures. Finally, results regarding the resource utilization, performance, reconfiguration time and reconfiguration memory are presented for the proposed reconfigurable CNN kernels as well as for the straight forward convolutions used in previous work using common kernel and data word sizes. This provides a guideline to decide what performance can be expected when embedding these kernels into a given architecture. The proposed computation kernels can be directly placed into previous CNN architectures that exploit the parallelism of the convolutional kernel as a parallel SOP operation [1, 21, 27]. They can also be used as an alternative in design space exploration tools like [23]. Our work does explicitly *not* propose another CNN architecture but instead the proposed kernels can be plugged in to virtually any of the current CNN architectures for FPGAs providing reconfigurable LUTs.

In the following, some properties of popular CNNs are analyzed to motivate the use of run-time reconfiguration in the context of CNN kernels.

2 PROPERTIES OF POPULAR CONVOLUTIONAL NEURAL NETWORKS

The convolutional layers basically compute an SOP which is typically followed by an additional offset called *bias*. Often it contains a nonlinear activation function (e.g., rectified linear units, ReLU). We will focus in the following on the SOP part of the kernel. The SOP computes the convolution of the input feature map with the parameters of the kernel and produces an output feature map. There are typically several input and output feature maps which are called *channels*. Table 1 summarizes properties of the convolutional layers of popular CNNs to give an overview. The *kernel size N* describes the size of the convolutional core which is typically a square number. The column *pad* shows the number of pixels a kernel may overlap at the borders with the input feature map. *Stride* describes the distance between two consecutive computations of a kernel.

Table 1: Properties of the convolutional layers in popular CNNs, N: kernel size, P: pad, S: stride

Conv Layer	N	P	S	IF Chan.	IF Size	OF Chan.	Identical Ops (O)
AlexNet							
1	11×11	0	4	3	300	96	5,476
2	5×5	2	1	96	36	256	1,296
3	3×3	1	1	256	18	384	324
4	3×3	1	1	384	18	384	324
5	3×3	1	1	384	18	256	324
VGG16							
1	3×3	1	1	3	224	64	50,176
2	3×3	1	1	64	224	64	50,176
3	3×3	1	1	64	112	128	12,544
4	3×3	1	1	128	112	128	12,544
5	3×3	1	1	128	56	256	3,136
6–7	3×3	1	1	256	56	256	3,136
8	3×3	1	1	256	28	512	784
9–10	3×3	1	1	512	28	512	784
11–13	3×3	1	1	512	14	512	196
ResNet34							
1	7×7	0	2	3	224	64	12,100
2–7	3×3	1	1	64	56	64	3,136
8	3×3	0	2	64	56	128	784
9–15	3×3	1	1	128	28	128	784
16	3×3	0	2	128	28	256	196
17–27	3×3	1	1	256	14	256	196
28	3×3	0	2	256	14	512	49
29–33	3×3	1	1	512	7	512	49
DarkNet19							
1	3×3	0	1	3	256	32	64,516
2	3×3	2	1	32	128	64	16,900
3	3×3	4	1	64	64	128	4,900
4	1×1	5	1	128	64	64	5,476
5	3×3	6	1	64	64	128	5,476
6	3×3	8	1	128	32	256	2,116
7	1×1	9	1	256	32	128	2,500
8	3×3	10	1	128	32	256	2,500
9	3×3	12	1	256	16	512	1,444
10	1×1	13	1	512	16	256	1,764
11	3×3	14	1	256	16	512	1,764
12	1×1	15	1	512	16	256	2,116
13	3×3	16	1	256	16	512	2,116
14	3×3	18	1	512	8	1024	1,764
15	1×1	19	1	1024	8	512	2,116
16	3×3	20	1	512	8	1024	2,116
17	1×1	21	1	1024	8	512	2,500
18	3×3	22	1	512	8	1024	2,500
19	1×1	23	1	1024	8	1000	2,916

The last column of Table 1 shows the number of identical convolution operations that have to be performed for each input feature map channel, i.e., it shows the number of convolutions for which the coefficients do not change.

It can be observed from Table 1 that the number of identical convolution operations is pretty large which enables the use of run-time reconfiguration and motivates our work. In the following, the background methodologies are introduced on which the proposed reconfigurable CNN kernel is based.

3 BACKGROUND METHODOLOGIES

The proposed architectures compose advanced compressor tree techniques, LUT-based KCM and run-time reconfiguration of the LUTs. This combination is the base of our CNN core implementations and is introduced in the following.

3.1 Generic LUT-based Constant Multiplication

The main idea in the LUT-based KCM approach [4, 5] is to split the constant multiplication into several smaller ones which are bit-shifted and added to get the final product. The size of the small constant multiplications is chosen such that it directly fits the input size of an FPGA LUT tabulating all partial constant multiplier results. Consider a two's complement number x with B_i bits:

$$x = -2^{B_i-1}x_{B_i-1} + \sum_{b=0}^{B_i-2} 2^b x_b \qquad (1)$$

If this number is multiplied by a constant c_n with B_c bits, the resulting $B_c \times B_i$ multiplication can be divided into several smaller multiplications of size $B_c \times L$ (assuming that B_i is divisible by L), by rearranging the partial sums

$$\underbrace{c_n \cdot x}_{B_c \times B_i \text{ Mult.}} = c_n \left(\sum_{b=0}^{B_i-2} 2^b x_b - 2^{B_i-1}x_{B_i-1} \right)$$

$$= c_n \underbrace{\sum_{b=0}^{L-1} 2^b x_b}_{B_c \times L \text{ Mult.}} + 2^L c_n \underbrace{\sum_{b=0}^{L-1} 2^b x_{b+L}}_{B_c \times L \text{ Mult.}} + \dots$$

$$+ 2^{(K-1)L} c_n \underbrace{\left(\sum_{b=0}^{L-2} 2^b x_{b+(K-1)L} - 2^{L-1}x_{KL-1} \right)}_{B_c \times L \text{ Mult.}} . \qquad (2)$$

Now, the constant multiplication is performed by using $K = \lceil \frac{B_i}{L} \rceil$ smaller multiplications of size $B_c \times L$, each computing one partial product (PP). A K-input addition is used to add up all PPs. In case the input word size B_i is not divisible by L, the input x has to be sign extended to the next larger word size such that $B_i' = KL$ bits. Setting L to the input size of the FPGA LUT allows a direct mapping of the $B_c \times L$ constant multiplier to the FPGA LUTs. The structure of the generic constant multiplier is shown in Figure 1. For a signed multiplication, the LUT computing the most significant bits (MSBs) (rightmost sum in (2)) has to provide a signed result, while all other LUTs compute unsigned PPs.

3.2 Compressor Trees

One important part in the constant multiplication is the summation of all the bit shifted partial products (Σ block in Figure 1). This becomes even more demanding when several constant multiplications have to be performed in an SOP operation. Compressor trees offer a very efficient solution for this task. They were originally designed for multipliers but have evolved for generic arithmetic on FPGAs in the last years. While traditional compressor trees are designed of full adders and half adders, they map poorly to the LUTs and carry chains of FPGAs. It was shown by Parandeh-Afshar et al. that so called generalized parallel counters (GPCs) perform much better

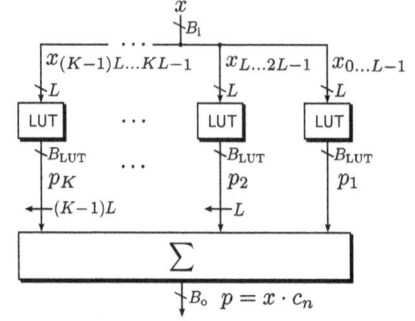

Figure 1: Generic LUT-based constant multiplier

on FPGAs [25, 26]. GPCs are multi-input compressors where each input may have a different weight which allows that the LUTs are efficiently utilized. Most recent work also utilizes the fast carry chains [16, 19, 26] which was a breakthrough in efficiency. The design of compressor trees is an optimization problem and several heuristics [2, 16, 26] as well as optimal approaches using integer linear programming [16, 19] are available. Current work shows that 40% of the LUT resources can be saved on average compared to common adder trees using 2-input adders and that the resulting circuits are 20% faster than adder trees built from ternary adders [16]. Therefore, compressor trees are used in this work for the partial product addition in KCM instead of using an adder tree.

3.3 Run-time Reconfigurable LUTs

Modern Xilinx FPGAs, namely Virtex 5/6, Spartan 6 and the whole 7 series (incl. Ultrascale and Ultrascale+), provide configurable lookup tables (CFGLUTs) whose content can be changed during run-time. They can be used as 5-input logic function with one output or as 4-input logic function with two outputs (one input less than a standard LUT) and provide a serial configuration interface consisting of the signals configuration data in (CDI), configuration data out (CDO), clock enable (CE), and configuration clock (CCLK). A change of the output function(s) can be performed by shifting 32 bit of new configuration data into CDI while CE is tied to a logical one. At the same time, the previous configuration is shifted out of CDO. This property can be used to cascade a series of CFGLUTs and to perform a serial reconfiguration of several CFGLUTs. However, each CDI input can be connected in parallel leading to a total reconfiguration time of 32 clock cycles for an arbitrary number of CFGLUTs. Alternatively to a CFGLUT, a shift-register LUT (for older Xilinx FPGA architectures) or block RAM (for other FPGAs) can be used as reconfigurable LUT. The latter is leading to some additional resources for an address counter and data multiplexers (MUXes) [33].

4 PROPOSED RUN-TIME RECONFIGURABLE CNN KERNEL ARCHITECTURE

We first introduce the generic architecture which is then further detailed in the following subsections.

4.1 Generic Architecture

The realization of a single LUT-based multiplication was shown in Section 3.1. However, a sum of products (SOP) is needed for the

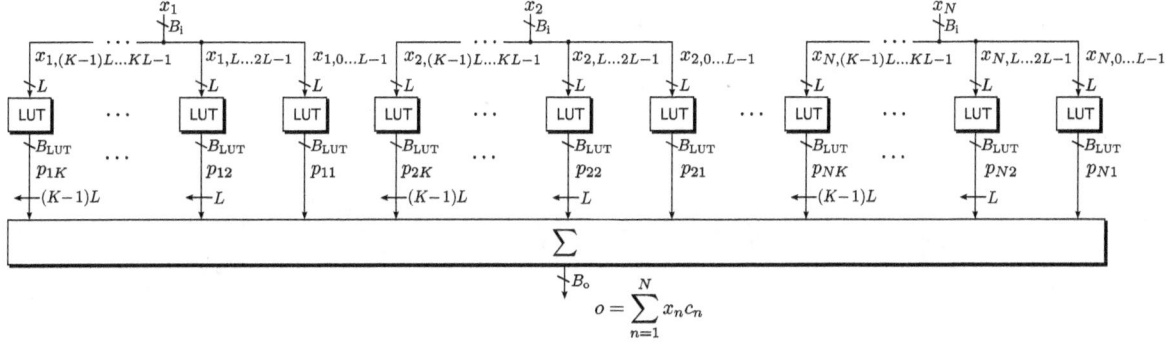

Figure 2: LUT-based SOP Architecture

convolutional kernel. Therefore, the proposed SOP architecture shown in Figure 2 is an application of the KCM approach and uses a compressor tree to sum up all partial products. The inputs $(x_1 \ldots x_N)$ in Figure 2 all have the same word length B_i. Like before, each input x_n is split into K smaller parts of word length L. The size of L is equal to the number of inputs of the used LUT. The output word size of each partial product p_{nk} is thus $B_{\text{LUT}} = L + B_c$. Finally, all partial products are added with respect to the original position of their inputs. Therefore, each p_{nk} is left shifted with its corresponding weight (left arrows) before the summation using a compressor tree (Σ). However, as the full precision output word size B_o is much larger than the input word size, a truncation or rounding has to be performed. Instead of computing bits which are thrown away afterwards, we will consider in the following which parts of the partial product LUTs and compressor tree resources are actually necessary and will provide the bit level details of the architecture.

4.2 Reconfigurable SOP based on CFGLUTs

To allow the reconfiguration of weights, the configurable CFGLUTs are used. They are used in the 4-input mode providing two outputs (O5 and O6) as a previous analytic comparison revealed that this is always advantageous compared to a single 5-input LUT [18]. For that, the input I_4 has to be tied to a logical high. The inputs $I_0 \ldots I_3$ of the CFGLUTs are connected to the N input signals which are each split into $L = 4$ bit chunks according to (2). Each block $(1 \ldots K)$ processes a different 4-bit chunk of the input values of the N different kernel inputs $(x_1 \ldots x_N)$. The resulting bits of the CFGLUT are added to the compressor tree with their corresponding shift.

The total number of different CFGLUTs contents to realize all partial products depends on the kernel size and the coefficient word size. An analytical upper bound for the number of partial product LUTs can be derived to be

$$\#\text{LUT}_{\text{PP,ub}} = 2N \left\lceil \frac{B_c + 4}{2} \right\rceil . \tag{3}$$

4.3 Faithfully Rounded SOP

The output word size B_o of the SOP operation like shown in Figure 2 is much larger than the input word size B_i and has to be reduced. There are several possibilities to perform the word size reduction, of which truncation and rounding are among the most popular

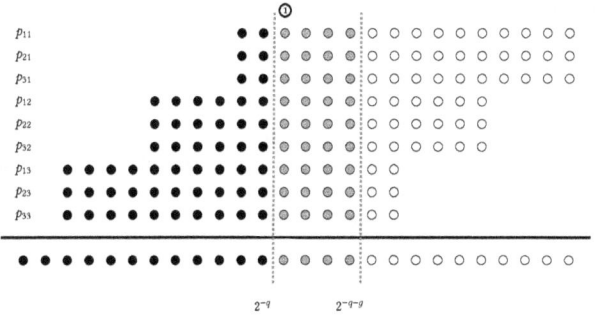

Figure 3: Example dot diagram for the proposed LUT-based SOP circuit for $N = 3$ coefficients, $B_i = B_o = B_c = 12$ bit, $L = 4$

methods. Truncation to a precision of q MSBs (excluding sign) introduces a maximum error of 2^{-q} which is called one unit in the last place (ulp). The error of correct rounding is 2^{-q-1} ($\frac{1}{2}$ ulp). However, in both methods it is required that the full precision result is available.

To illustrate this, Figure 3 shows an example dot diagram of the compressor tree for a small SOP instance of $N = 3$ coefficients using word sizes for input, output and coefficients of $B_i = B_o = B_c = 12$ bit. Each dot in the dot diagram represents one output bit of a LUT. The column of the dot (from right to left) corresponds to the weight of the bit. Adding all bits together leads to the SOP result which is indicated by the bits below the line. Even when only the upper q bits are considered in the preceding stage, all of these bits depend on results of the least significant columns due to carry propagation. This makes it necessary to compute the full result when using exact rounding or truncation.

However, the same accuracy as truncation can be achieved by using a scheme which is called *faithful rounding* [10], where the error is defined to be at most one ulp, i.e., 2^{-q}. It has the same error bound as truncation but does not necessarily lead to the same output vectors. This degree of freedom can be used to significantly reduce the hardware complexity by skipping the computation of intermediate results as long as the total error ϵ is less than or equal to one ulp, i.e., $\epsilon \leq 2^{-q}$.

A faithful rounding scheme of the SOP operation was proposed in [8] and is introduced next. First, observe that by simply removing all the dots that are located right of the dotted line at weight 2^{-q}

of Figure 3 would introduce an error of 2^{-q-1} times the column height of the bit heap (which is nine in the example of Figure 3) and is hence larger than the intended $\epsilon < 2^{-q}$. The idea from [8] is to add g additional guard bits to reduce this error. Hence, all bits to the right of the dotted line at weight 2^{-q-g} (shown in white) are discarded (and of course their corresponding LUTs). As we have N constant multipliers, each contributing

$$K = \left\lceil \frac{B_i}{L} \right\rceil \quad (4)$$

partial products from the LUTs, the total error is

$$\epsilon = KN2^{-q-g-1} . \quad (5)$$

Therefore, by selecting a sufficiently large number of guard bits g, the error can be made as small as necessary. Bounding the error to $\epsilon \le 2^{-q}$ leads to

$$KN2^{-q-g-1} \overset{!}{\le} 2^{-q} \quad (6)$$

$$g \ge \log_2(KN) - 1 . \quad (7)$$

Thus, setting $g = \lceil \log_2(KN) \rceil - 1$ guarantees that the error is faithfully rounded. However, the intermediate result has g additional guard bits and has to be rounded to the output precision q. To avoid another adder for the rounding that adds the bit at position 2^{-q-1}, the identity

$$\text{round}(x) = \left\lceil x + \frac{1}{2} \right\rceil \quad (8)$$

is used. With that, the rounding is obtained by adding a constant one bit with weight 2^{-p-1} and performing a truncation of the final result. This bit is shown at the top of column of weight 2^{-p-1} in Figure 3.

4.4 Memory Requirements

Let M_{kern} be the coefficient memory requirement of a single kernel, which is for a conventional kernel

$$M_{\text{kern,conv}} = N \times B_c . \quad (9)$$

For a reconfigurable kernel, the pre-computed LUT content has to be stored. As for each CFGLUT, 32 bit of configuration data is necessary, the memory requirements are

$$M_{\text{kern,direct}} = 32 \times \#\text{LUT}_{\text{PP}} \le 64N \left\lceil \frac{B_c + 4}{2} \right\rceil . \quad (10)$$

Note that the actual number of PP LUTs $\#\text{LUT}_{\text{PP}}$ is less than the upper bound provided in (3) due to the LUT elimination provided in Section 4.3. The memory footprint is about 32 times the memory footprint of the conventional kernel. As this may not be applicable for many applications, an online computation of LUT content is proposed in the following. Using this online configuration, only the coefficients have to be stored instead of the full configuration data, which leads to the same memory requirements as for the conventional kernel implementation.

4.5 Online Computation of LUT Contents

To reduce the large memory footprint of the reconfigurable CNN kernel, an online configuration circuit is proposed which is based on a serial multiplier [22] but extended to the required two-output LUTs. In order to perform an online configuration, the LUT content has to be computed in reverse order as the last CFGLUT entry

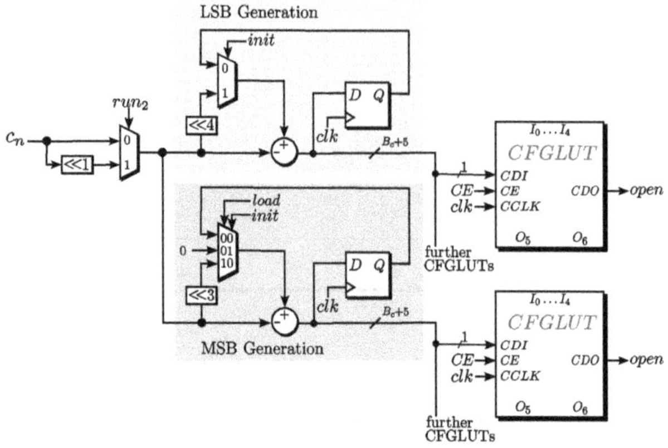

Figure 4: Proposed circuit to compute the LSB and MSB LUT content for online configuration

is shifted in first. Moreover, each CFGLUT is used as two output function and generates two bits of a partial product. Therefore, the lower part of the CFGLUT computes the bits with odd weights of the B_{LUT} bit result while the upper part of the CFGLUT computes the bits with even weight. As there is only one CDI input for lower and upper part we propose to first compute the odd bits and afterwards to compute the same but now left-shifted by one bit (which corresponds to a multiplication by two). In doing so, the lower and the upper parts of the table are computed one after the other. The proposed circuit to compute the LSB and MSB LUT contents is shown in Figure 4. The used control signals run_2 (r_2), $load$ (l) and $init$ (i), the general computation (comp.) as well as the LUT content for an example coefficient $c_n = 3$ are shown in Table 2 for each configuration step. Note that only the bits in bold face are shifted into CDI.

The inputs are the currently required coefficient c_n and the three control signals that control the MUXes. Signal run_2 is used to switch between the upper and lower part of the required CFGLUT by multiplying with two, while $init$ and $load$ are used to select the right minuend. Note that the results of the LSB generation on top and the MSB generation at the bottom provide a B_c+5 bit wide signal which is then split to provide a 1 bit wide CDI signal for several CFGLUTs. Each CFGLUT is connected to a global configuration clock and configuration enable. Thanks to the cascading possibility using CDI and CDO, the number of reconfiguration circuits R can be flexibly selected from $R = 1$ which requires a reconfiguration time of $32N$ clock cycles up to $R = N$ where only 32 cycles are required. Of course, at the cost of additional hardware resources.

4.6 Using Shadow LUTs to Hide the Reconfiguration Time

One important characteristic of the reconfiguration schemes described above is that the SOP circuit can not be used during reconfiguration. This is not a problem in the direct configuration scheme described in Section 4.2 as it only requires 32 clock cycles but may be prohibitive in the online configuration scheme above for a low number of reconfiguration circuits R. For that, a more efficient method can be used to effectively hide the reconfiguration

Table 2: Generated LUT contents for $L = 4$ and coefficient $c_n = 3$. Only the bits in bold face are shifted into CDI.

conf. step	cntrl. sig. r_2	l	i	MSB LUT comp.	CDI signal	LSB LUTs (other LUTs) comp.	CDI signal
1	0	0	1	$-1 \times c_n$	**1 1 1 1 1 1 0 1**	$15 \times c_n$	**0 0 1 0 1 1 0 1**
2	0	0	0	$-2 \times c_n$	**1 1 1 1 1 0 1 0**	$14 \times c_n$	**0 0 1 0 1 0 1 0**
3	0	0	0	$-3 \times c_n$	**1 1 1 1 0 1 1 1**	$13 \times c_n$	**0 0 1 0 0 1 1 1**
4	0	0	0	$-4 \times c_n$	**1 1 1 1 0 1 0 0**	$12 \times c_n$	**0 0 1 0 0 1 0 0**
5	0	0	0	$-5 \times c_n$	**1 1 1 1 0 0 0 1**	$11 \times c_n$	**0 0 1 0 0 0 0 1**
6	0	0	0	$-6 \times c_n$	**1 1 1 0 1 1 1 0**	$10 \times c_n$	**0 0 0 1 1 1 1 0**
7	0	0	0	$-7 \times c_n$	**1 1 1 0 1 0 1 1**	$9 \times c_n$	**0 0 0 1 1 0 1 1**
8	0	0	0	$-8 \times c_n$	**1 1 1 0 1 0 0 0**	$8 \times c_n$	**0 0 0 1 1 0 0 0**
9	0	1	0	$7 \times c_n$	**0 0 0 1 0 1 0 1**	$7 \times c_n$	**0 0 0 1 0 1 0 1**
10	0	0	0	$6 \times c_n$	**0 0 0 1 0 0 1 0**	$6 \times c_n$	**0 0 0 1 0 0 1 0**
11	0	0	0	$5 \times c_n$	**0 0 0 0 1 1 1 1**	$5 \times c_n$	**0 0 0 0 1 1 1 1**
12	0	0	0	$4 \times c_n$	**0 0 0 0 1 1 0 0**	$4 \times c_n$	**0 0 0 0 1 1 0 0**
13	0	0	0	$3 \times c_n$	**0 0 0 0 1 0 0 1**	$3 \times c_n$	**0 0 0 0 1 0 0 1**
14	0	0	0	$2 \times c_n$	**0 0 0 0 0 1 1 0**	$2 \times c_n$	**0 0 0 0 0 1 1 0**
15	0	0	0	$1 \times c_n$	**0 0 0 0 0 0 1 1**	$1 \times c_n$	**0 0 0 0 0 0 1 1**
16	0	0	0	$0 \times c_n$	**0 0 0 0 0 0 0 0**	$0 \times c_n$	**0 0 0 0 0 0 0 0**
17	1	0	1	$-2 \times c_n$	**1 1 1 1 1 0 1 0**	$30 \times c_n$	**0 1 0 1 1 0 1 0**
18	1	0	0	$-4 \times c_n$	**1 1 1 1 0 1 0 0**	$28 \times c_n$	**0 1 0 1 0 1 0 0**
19	1	0	0	$-6 \times c_n$	**1 1 1 0 1 1 1 0**	$26 \times c_n$	**0 1 0 0 1 1 1 0**
20	1	0	0	$-8 \times c_n$	**1 1 1 0 1 0 0 0**	$24 \times c_n$	**0 1 0 0 1 0 0 0**
21	1	0	0	$-10 \times c_n$	**1 1 1 0 0 0 1 0**	$22 \times c_n$	**0 1 0 0 0 0 1 0**
22	1	0	0	$-12 \times c_n$	**1 1 0 1 1 1 0 0**	$20 \times c_n$	**0 0 1 1 1 1 0 0**
23	1	0	0	$-14 \times c_n$	**1 1 0 1 0 1 1 0**	$18 \times c_n$	**0 0 1 1 0 1 1 0**
24	1	0	0	$-16 \times c_n$	**1 1 0 1 0 0 0 0**	$16 \times c_n$	**0 0 1 1 0 0 0 0**
25	1	1	0	$14 \times c_n$	**0 0 1 0 1 0 1 0**	$14 \times c_n$	**0 0 1 0 1 0 1 0**
26	1	0	0	$12 \times c_n$	**0 0 1 0 0 1 0 0**	$12 \times c_n$	**0 0 1 0 0 1 0 0**
27	1	0	0	$10 \times c_n$	**0 0 0 1 1 1 1 0**	$10 \times c_n$	**0 0 0 1 1 1 1 0**
28	1	0	0	$8 \times c_n$	**0 0 0 1 1 0 0 0**	$8 \times c_n$	**0 0 0 1 1 0 0 0**
29	1	0	0	$6 \times c_n$	**0 0 0 1 0 0 1 0**	$6 \times c_n$	**0 0 0 1 0 0 1 0**
30	1	0	0	$4 \times c_n$	**0 0 0 0 1 1 0 0**	$4 \times c_n$	**0 0 0 0 1 1 0 0**
31	1	0	0	$2 \times c_n$	**0 0 0 0 0 1 1 0**	$2 \times c_n$	**0 0 0 0 0 1 1 0**
32	1	0	0	$0 \times c_n$	**0 0 0 0 0 0 0 0**	$0 \times c_n$	**0 0 0 0 0 0 0 0**

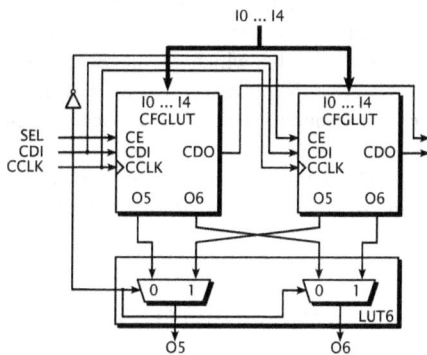

Figure 5: Reconfigurable LUT with *shadow LUT* for fast reconfiguration

time using a concept similar to *shadow registers*, where a set of registers is duplicated (typically doubled) and a control register selects the active register set. This allows to write data into the inactive (shadow) registers without immediate effects and to activate them in a single clock cycle. A similar concept is the *double buffering* scheme which is used to prevent visible artifacts in computer graphics. The same idea is used in this work by duplicating the CFGLUTs in the reconfigurable SOP circuit. We call this concept *shadow LUT* and its scheme is shown in Figure 5. The circuit in Figure 5 can replace a conventional CFGLUT. However, some control signals are different. Basically, a single CFGLUT is replaced by two CFGLUTs,

one being the active (computing) LUT and the other being reconfigured. A third 5-input, 2-output LUT (another mode of the LUT6 in current Xilinx FPGAs) is used to implement two 2:1 multiplexers to select the active LUT. As long as the reconfiguration is faster than the computing time of convolution operations with identical coefficients, this completely hides the reconfiguration time as the reconfiguration can be performed during the computation and switching the select signal from one clock cycle to the other. The number of minimum reconfiguration units $R_{\min}$ to achieve this is simply the quotient between the reconfiguration time using one reconfiguration unit ($32N$) and the number of convolutions with identical coefficients O (see Table 1)

$$R_{\min} = \left\lceil \frac{32N}{O} \right\rceil . \qquad (11)$$

Of course, the required LUTs to compute partial products are tripled (two for the CFGLUTs and one to implement the MUX) but due to the possible decrease in online reconfiguration units, this typically more than compensates the resources required for additional reconfiguration units. For the large nets, $R_{\min}$ is typically quite low as discussed in Section 5.3. Note that the conventional SOP also requires extra memory (e.g., shadow registers, distributed RAM or block RAM) to allow a reconfiguration within one clock cycle.

4.7 Properties of Different Reconfigurable Kernels

Table 3 summarizes the properties of the different architectures and their combination described above. Method "conventional SOP" corresponds to the standard implementation using N multipliers in parallel followed by an adder tree. It offers a low memory footprint for coefficient storage. Assuming that the coefficients are pre-loaded into registers (e. g., shadow registers) to allow a reconfiguration within one clock cycle, virtually no reconfiguration time ($T_{\mathrm{rec}} = 0$) is necessary as no additional cycles are spent for reconfiguration. As will be proven in the results section, the conventional SOP will lead to a high resource usage.

Method "direct conf." corresponds to the architecture proposed in Section 4.2 in which the CFGLUTs are directly configured with their pre-computed LUT contents. This method requires the least resources and a fast reconfiguration of 32 clock cycles but naturally leads to the highest memory requirement which can be bounded to 32 times the requirements of the other methods. The concrete LUT requirements for #LUT$_{\mathrm{direct}}$, #LUT$_{\mathrm{shadow}}$, #LUT$_{\mathrm{rec}}$ and #LUT$_{\mathrm{ctrl}}$ are provided in the results section.

Method "direct conf., shadow LUTs" combines the direct configuration of Section 4.2 with the shadow LUTs proposed in Section 4.6. Compared to the direct configuration scheme, the reconfiguration time of 32 clock cycles is eliminated at the cost of additional resources.

Method "online conf." combines the direct configuration scheme of Section 4.2 with R reconfiguration units as discussed in Section 4.5. By selecting R, a tradeoff point between low resource demands but slow reconfiguration of $T_{\mathrm{rec}} = 32N$ cycles by using $R = 1$ and a fast reconfiguration of $T_{\mathrm{rec}} = 32$ cycles by using $R = N$ at the cost of a medium resource usage can be selected.

Finally, method "online conf., shadow LUTs" combines the online configuration scheme with shadow LUTs and online configuration.

Table 3: Comparison between conventional and our proposed reconfigurable kernels, M_{kern} denotes the memory requirements for parameters and T_{rec} is the reconfiguration time in clock cycles

Method	M_{kern}	T_{rec}	Resource Usage
conventional SOP	NB_c	0	high
direct conf.	$64N \lceil (B_c + 4)/2 \rceil \geq 32NB_c$	32	low (#LUT$_{direct}$)
direct conf., shadow LUTs	$64N \lceil (B_c + 4)/2 \rceil \geq 32NB_c$	0	medium (#LUT$_{shadow}$)
online conf.	NB_c	$32 \lceil \frac{N}{R} \rceil$	low to medium (#LUT$_{direct}$ + $R \times$ #LUT$_{rec}$ + #LUT$_{ctrl}$)
online conf., shadow LUTs ($R = R_{min}$)	NB_c	0	medium (#LUT$_{shadow}$ + $R_{min} \times$ #LUT$_{rec}$ + #LUT$_{ctrl}$)

It is the most attractive scheme as the configuration time is completely hidden by using $R = R_{min}$ reconfiguration units, it has a low memory footprint and can be realized with very moderate LUT requirements.

5 EXPERIMENTAL RESULTS

5.1 Synthesis Results of Kernels

In order to quantify the resource usage and the maximum clock frequency, synthesis experiments have been performed for the proposed circuits. For that, an open-source VHDL code generator was implemented which is based on the FloPoCo [7, 9] library. This code generator is available in the "uni_ks" branch of the FloPoCo git repository [7]. It can be parametrized for different kernel sizes (N), different input, output and coefficient word lengths and the different reconfiguration schemes as discussed in the previous section.

For the evaluation, kernels with the most common sizes from 3×3 to 11×11 and different word lengths were generated. The word lengths of input, output and coefficients were set to be identical $B = B_i = B_c = B_o$, which was also assumed in most previous work. As lower word lengths are the most attractive, the word lengths between $B = 2 \dots 12$ were evaluated for each kernel size. As reference, a code generator for the "conventional SOP" using N pipelined multipliers and an adder tree consisting of 2-input adders was implemented which should be close to the kernels used in previous work. The generated VHDL cores were synthesized for a Virtex 6 FPGA (XC6VLX760-FF1760-2) using Xilinx ISE 14.7.

The complete synthesis results after place&route for the conventional SOPs as well as the proposed SOPs are listed in Table 4. It shows the DSP and LUT resources, the maximum frequency (f_{max}) in MHz, the memory requirements of the kernel (M_{kern}) in bit as well as the latency in clock cycles. The conventional SOP was synthesized with two different synthesis options. In the "DSP-based" setting, the usage of DSP blocks was set to 'auto' while DSPs were prevented in the "logic only" setting. Plots of the LUT resources as well as the relative LUT reduction compared to the "logic only" reference are given in Figure 6. As our goal is to provide an alternative to the limited DSP blocks, the "logic only" results are used as a reference to enable fair comparisons.

The proposed methods use the same nomenclature as introduced in Section 4.7. The direct configuration schemes ("direct conf.") do not include any online reconfiguration circuits and are given with single CFGLUTs ($R = 0$) and the shadow CFGLUT scheme (shadow $R = 0$) of Section 4.6. Their LUT results directly correspond to the #LUT$_{direct}$ and #LUT$_{shadow}$ used in the comparison in Table 3. As

the real memory M_{kern} footprint is typically less than the upper bound (10), the actual numbers are also tabulated in Table 4.

The methods using the online configuration ("online conf.") are computed by using the formulas given in Table 3. For that, the LUT results for the reconfiguration controller (#LUT$_{rec}$) are given for different coefficient word lengths in Table 5. The required LUTs for the control unit that generates the select signals were determined to be #LUT$_{ctrl} = 5$. The online configuration scheme with simple CFGLUTs was evaluated for the two extremes using $R = 1$ and $R = N$ reconfiguration units. The online configuration scheme with shadow LUTs was evaluated for the most common case $R = 1$ (see Section 5.3).

As can be observed from Figure 6, significant resource savings are possible by using the proposed reconfigurable circuits. The simplest direct configuration scheme without shadow LUTs achieves LUT reductions of 50% to 80% compared to the reference. Using the online configuration with one reconfiguration unit ($R = 1$) performs nearly identical with increasing kernel size due to the low overhead of a single reconfiguration unit. Using the other extreme of $R = N$ reconfiguration units shows the worst case where LUT reductions can be achieved for $B \geq 4$ bit, which are the most interesting word lengths for CNNs. Here, the online configuration with shadow LUTs requires much less resources and is also beneficial regarding configuration time (see Table 3). The obtained maximum frequencies are always above 100 MHz and lie often between 200 MHz and 300 MHz. Here, the kernel should not be the limiting factor in a larger CNN architecture.

5.2 Reconfiguration Time Overhead

To get an impression of the impact to CNN architectures, the relative time overhead which is defined as T_{rec}/O is provided in Table 6 for the layers having a different convolution operations count O. The direct configuration scheme and online configuration scheme with $R = N$ have both $T_{rec} = 32$ which corresponds to the fourth column while the online configuration scheme with $R = 1$ corresponds to the fifth column of Table 6. Of course, any R between 1 and N can be selected. It can be observed that the reconfiguration time overhead is low for the nets like AlexNet and VGG16 but increases towards the output layers as for those the input feature maps get smaller (see also Table 1). So, as a rule of thumb, the online configuration scheme with $R = 1$ fits best to the first layers, the R should be increased towards the output layers and an online configuration scheme with shadow LUTs should be chosen for the output layer(s) as it typically does not cause any time overhead.

Table 4: Synthesis results of conventional reference designs and several variants of the proposed design

Kernel size (N)	Word size (B)	DSP-based DSPs	LUTs	f_{max}	logic only LUTs	f_{max}	M_{kern}	Latency	direct conf. R=0 LUTs	f_{max}	shadow R=0 LUTs	f_{max}	M_{kern}	online conf. R=1 LUTs	f_{max}	R=N LUTs	f_{max}	shadow R=1 LUTs	f_{max}	M_{kern}	Latency
3 × 3	2	0	108	487	92	751	18	7	42	517	75	467	576	62	517	182	517	95	467	18	4
3 × 3	3	0	213	363	163	480	27	7	47	485	79	474	576	70	485	214	485	102	474	27	4
3 × 3	4	0	334	337	276	661	36	7	42	410	77	423	576	67	410	227	410	102	423	36	4
3 × 3	5	5	344	312	457	432	45	7	147	311	288	281	2304	175	311	359	311	316	281	45	5
3 × 3	6	5	428	298	572	437	54	7	140	306	240	249	1728	170	306	370	306	270	249	54	5
3 × 3	7	9	81	379	838	383	63	7	166	319	302	257	2304	199	319	423	319	335	257	63	5
3 × 3	8	9	91	309	864	382	72	7	142	301	250	256	1728	177	301	417	301	285	256	72	5
3 × 3	9	9	99	429	1174	373	81	7	277	271	561	262	3456	315	271	579	271	599	262	81	6
3 × 3	10	9	110	355	1360	325	90	7	284	318	477	259	2880	324	318	604	318	517	259	90	6
3 × 3	11	9	122	424	1607	372	99	7	309	301	559	253	3456	352	301	656	301	602	253	99	6
3 × 3	12	9	131	434	1844	345	108	7	281	317	489	235	2880	326	317	646	317	534	235	108	6
5 × 5	2	0	346	469	255	701	50	8	107	323	208	267	1600	127	323	487	323	228	267	50	5
5 × 5	3	0	614	347	462	474	75	8	131	327	211	282	1600	154	327	586	327	234	282	75	5
5 × 5	4	0	963	308	764	652	100	8	117	302	215	281	1600	142	302	622	302	240	281	100	5
5 × 5	5	13	1015	311	1242	434	125	8	396	284	794	243	6400	424	284	976	284	822	243	125	7
5 × 5	6	13	1256	295	1577	402	150	8	400	306	664	236	4800	430	306	1030	306	694	236	150	7
5 × 5	7	25	216	497	2291	376	175	8	438	290	831	261	6400	471	290	1143	290	864	261	175	7
5 × 5	8	25	242	409	2404	357	200	8	428	311	674	239	4800	463	311	1183	311	709	239	200	7
5 × 5	9	25	266	242	3253	364	225	8	808	238	1577	101	9600	846	238	1638	238	1615	101	225	8
5 × 5	10	25	293	342	3739	340	250	8	864	302	1609	225	9600	904	302	1744	302	1649	225	250	8
5 × 5	11	25	321	365	4420	348	275	8	909	251	1598	120	9600	952	251	1864	251	1641	120	275	8
5 × 5	12	25	346	368	5108	334	300	8	963	269	1620	228	9600	1008	269	1968	269	1665	228	300	8
7 × 7	2	0	665	441	519	671	98	9	227	323	400	267	3136	247	323	967	323	420	267	98	6
7 × 7	3	0	1205	311	904	438	147	9	241	325	435	282	3136	264	325	1128	325	458	282	147	6
7 × 7	4	0	1924	321	1503	602	196	9	220	305	435	252	3136	245	305	1205	305	460	252	196	6
7 × 7	5	25	2022	304	2459	420	245	9	775	271	1578	240	12544	803	271	1907	271	1606	240	245	7
7 × 7	6	25	2466	284	3131	419	294	9	673	279	1285	249	9408	703	279	1903	279	1315	249	294	7
7 × 7	7	49	420	435	4397	370	343	9	791	244	1609	256	12544	824	244	2168	244	1642	256	343	7
7 × 7	8	49	470	384	4647	366	392	9	791	290	1277	114	9408	826	290	2266	290	1312	114	392	7
7 × 7	9	49	518	309	6369	357	441	9	1603	294	3086	249	18816	1641	294	3225	294	3124	249	441	9
7 × 7	10	49	569	409	7365	354	490	9	1823	306	3118	229	18816	1863	306	3543	306	3158	229	490	9
7 × 7	11	49	621	308	8651	343	539	9	1754	303	3078	116	18816	1797	303	3621	303	3121	116	539	9
7 × 7	12	49	670	324	10001	334	588	9	1838	304	3133	241	18816	1883	304	3803	304	3178	241	588	9
9 × 9	2	0	1100	436	857	609	162	10	382	315	684	268	5184	402	315	1602	315	704	268	162	6
9 × 9	3	0	2025	333	1506	444	243	10	347	267	708	263	5184	370	267	1810	267	731	263	243	6
9 × 9	4	0	3198	318	2469	598	324	10	440	292	722	266	5184	465	292	2065	292	747	266	324	6
9 × 9	5	41	3363	306	4070	424	405	10	1428	290	2601	235	20736	1456	290	3296	290	2629	235	405	9
9 × 9	6	41	4157	285	5208	418	486	10	1260	295	2124	263	15552	1290	295	3290	295	2154	263	486	9
9 × 9	7	81	698	262	7367	375	567	10	1343	279	2621	262	20736	1376	279	3616	279	2654	262	567	9
9 × 9	8	81	780	308	7760	362	648	10	1369	272	2090	131	15552	1404	272	3804	272	2125	131	648	9
9 × 9	9	81	860	245	10528	307	729	10	2492	249	4879	115	31104	2530	249	5170	249	4917	115	729	10
9 × 9	10	81	943	330	12095	346	810	10	2520	287	4148	130	25920	2560	287	5360	287	4188	130	810	10
9 × 9	11	81	1031	369	14321	340	891	10	2802	303	4892	117	31104	2845	303	5885	303	4935	117	891	10
9 × 9	12	81	1112	345	16553	331	972	10	2524	273	4241	226	25920	2569	273	5769	273	4286	226	972	10
11 × 11	2	0	1487	439	1299	629	242	10	530	312	1007	262	7744	550	312	2350	312	1027	262	242	7
11 × 11	3	0	2982	328	2247	421	363	10	612	324	1050	256	7744	635	324	2795	324	1073	256	363	7
11 × 11	4	0	4699	310	3692	576	484	10	650	300	1058	240	7744	675	300	3075	300	1083	240	484	7
11 × 11	5	61	5036	305	6030	419	605	10	1942	294	3875	243	30976	1970	294	4730	294	3903	243	605	10
11 × 11	6	61	6218	288	7790	408	726	10	1920	304	3169	254	23232	1950	304	4950	304	3199	254	726	10
11 × 11	7	121	1030	343	10845	376	847	10	1999	290	3947	262	30976	2032	290	5392	290	3980	262	847	10
11 × 11	8	121	1152	309	11536	356	968	10	2036	296	3105	117	23232	2071	296	5671	296	3140	117	968	10
11 × 11	9	121	1272	260	15670	354	1089	10	3935	270	7490	116	46464	3973	270	7933	270	7528	116	1089	11
11 × 11	10	121	1395	264	18109	345	1210	10	4335	261	7595	219	46464	4375	261	8575	261	7635	219	1210	11
11 × 11	11	121	1519	275	21352	342	1331	10	4358	271	7512	128	46464	4401	271	8961	271	7555	128	1331	11
11 × 11	12	121	1640	263	24627	327	1452	10	4036	253	7648	219	46464	4081	253	8881	253	7693	219	1452	11

Table 5: Synthesis results of the online reconfiguration circuit of a single coefficient

Coefficient word length (B_c)	LUTs (#LUT$_{rec}$)	f_{max}
2	15	796.8
3	18	728.9
4	20	769.8
5	23	708.7
6	25	708.7
7	28	727.3
8	30	690.6
9	33	702.3
10	35	670.7
11	38	685.4
12	40	685.4

5.3 Resource Reduction for the Online Configuration Scheme with Shadow LUTs

As the online configuration with shadow LUTs provides the same reconfiguration speed and memory footprint as the conventional implementation, a detailed case study for real CNNs is considered in the following. First, the minimal number of reconfiguration units was evaluated using (11) for the layers having a different convolution operations count O. The result is shown in column R_{min} in Table 6. However, for the much larger and challenging nets ResNet34 and DarkNet19 taking only one or two reconfiguration units are sufficient for all the layers but the last few where the feature maps become too small.

The last three columns of Table 6 show the LUT requirements of the reference kernel, the online configuration with shadow LUTs

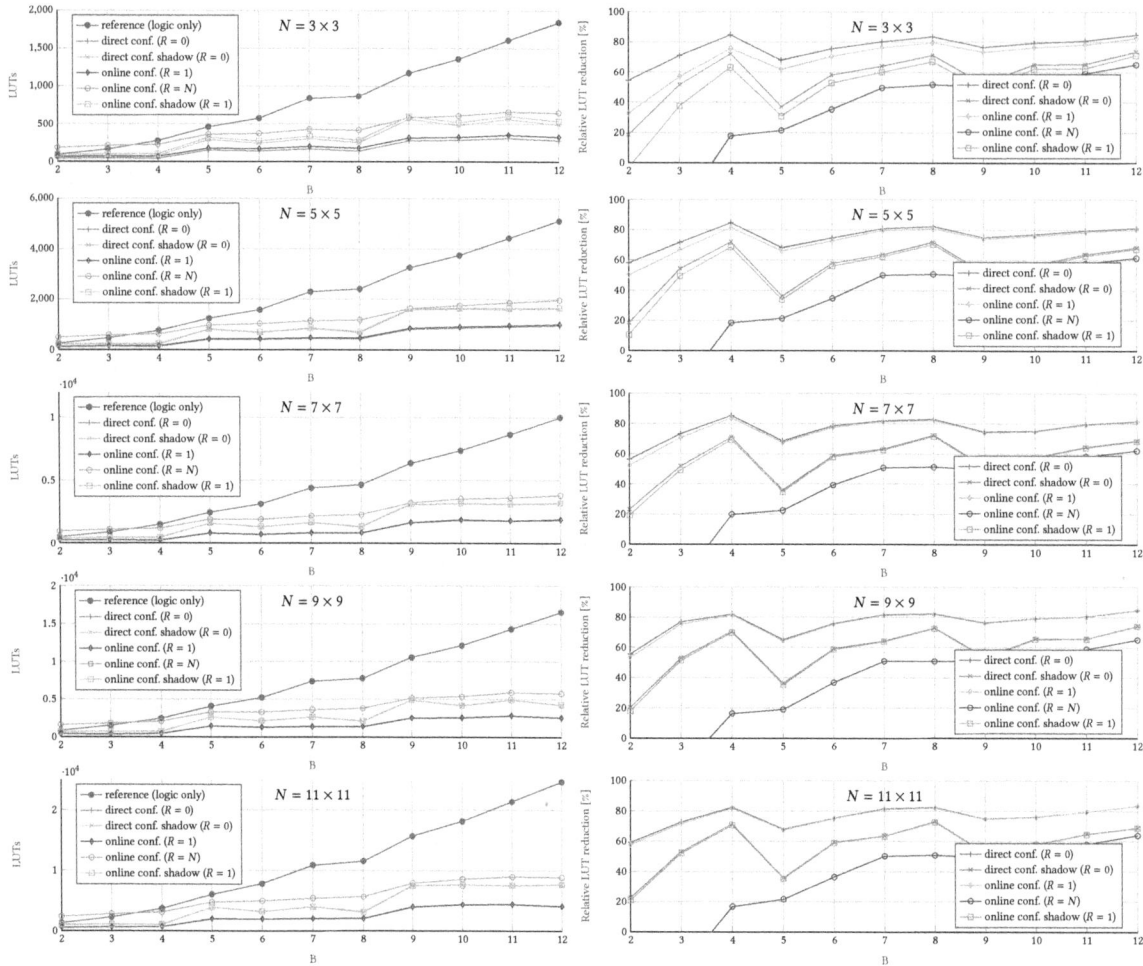

Figure 6: LUT results from synthesis (left) and the relative LUT reduction compared to the logic only reference (right) over the word size B for different kernel sizes N using the different methods

using $R_{\min}$ reconfiguration units and the corresponding LUT reduction for the common word size of $B = 8$ bit. It can be observed that 50 to 70% of the LUT requirements can be saved by using this reconfiguration scheme without any drawback concerning reconfiguration speed or memory footprint. Note that the reference in this comparison does not include the required buffers or shadow registers and corresponding multiplexers to enable this fast reconfiguration, so the actual resource reduction may be even higher.

6 CONCLUSION

Novel reconfigurable architectures were proposed to improve the sum-of-products operation used in convolutional kernels of CNNs. The alternative reconfiguration schemes were presented and analyzed regarding their memory footprint, reconfiguration time and resource usage. This analysis together with an experimental evaluation showed that the proposed architectures and schemes provide a tradeoff between these properties and offer LUT reductions of up to 80%. Even for the online configuration scheme with shadow LUTs, which offers the same memory footprint and reconfiguration time as a conventional parallel kernel implementation, LUT reductions

in the order of 50% are obtained which makes this scheme an ideal candidate for future CNN architectures and should be considered in future design space explorations.

REFERENCES

[1] Marco Bettoni, Gianvito Urgese, Yuki Kobayashi, Enrico Macii, and Andrea Acquaviva. 2017. A Convolutional Neural Network Fully Implemented on FPGA for Embedded Platforms. In *New Generation of CAS (NGCAS)*. IEEE, 49–52.

[2] Nicolas Brunie, Florent de Dinechin, Matei Istoan, Guillaume Sergent, Kinga Illyes, and Bogdan Popa. 2013. Arithmetic Core Generation Using Bit Heaps. In *IEEE International Conference on Field Programmable Logic and Application (FPL)*. 1–8.

[3] Srimat Chakradhar, Murugan Sankaradas, Venkata Jakkula, and Srihari Cadambi. 2010. A Dynamically Configurable Coprocessor for Convolutional Neural Networks. *ACM SIGARCH Computer Architecture News* 38, 3 (June 2010), 247–257.

[4] Ken Chapman. 1996. Constant Coefficient Multipliers for the XC4000E. *Xilinx Application Note* (1996), 1–8.

[5] K D Chapman. 1994. Fast Integer Multipliers Fit in FPGAs. *Electronic Design News* (1994).

[6] Matthieu Courbariaux, Itay Hubara, Daniel Soudry, Ran El-Yaniv, and Yoshua Bengio. 2016. Binarized Neural Networks: Training Deep Neural Networks with Weights and Activations Constrained to +1 or -1. *arXiv.org* (Feb. 2016), 1–11. arXiv:cs.LG/1602.02830v3

[7] Florent de Dinechin. (accessed October 1, 2018). FloPoCo Project Website. http://flopoco.gforge.inria.fr

Table 6: Time overhead for reconfiguration schemes and LUT requirements for the kernels of convolutional layers in different nets for the conventional method and the online configuration with shadow LUTs

Layer	N	Identical Ops (O)	R_{min}	Time Overhead Reconf. [%] $T_{rec} = 32$	$T_{rec} = 32N$	LUTs for B = 8 bit ref. (logic only)	online conf. shad. LUTs ($R = R_{min}$)	LUT red.
AlexNet								
1	11×11	5,476	1	0.6	70.7	11536	3140	72.8%
2	5×5	1,296	1	2.5	61.7	2404	709	70.5%
3–5	3×3	324	1	9.9	88.9	864	285	67.0%
VGG16								
1–2	3×3	50,176	1	0.1	0.6	864	285	67.0%
3–4	3×3	12,544	1	0.3	2.3	864	285	67.0%
5–7	3×3	3,136	1	1.0	9.2	864	285	67.0%
8–10	3×3	784	1	4.1	36.7	864	285	67.0%
11–13	3×3	196	2	16.3	146.9	864	315	63.5%
ResNet34								
1	7×7	12,100	1	0.3	13.0	4647	1312	71.8%
2–7	3×3	3,136	1	1.0	9.2	864	285	67.0%
8–15	3×3	784	1	4.1	36.7	864	285	67.0%
16–27	3×3	196	2	16.3	146.9	864	315	63.5%
28–33	3×3	49	6	65.3	587.8	864	435	49.7%
DarkNet19								
1	3×3	64,516	1	0.0	0.4	864	285	67.0%
2	3×3	16,384	1	0.2	1.8	864	285	67.0%
3,5	3×3	4,096	1	0.8	7.0	864	285	67.0%
4	1×1	4,096	1	0.8	0.8	77	65	15.6%
6	3×3	1,024	1	3.1	28.1	864	285	67.0%
7	1×1	1,024	1	3.1	3.1	77	65	15.6%
8	3×3	1,024	1	3.1	28.1	864	285	67.0%
9,11,13	3×3	256	2	12.5	112.5	864	315	63.5%
10,12	1×1	256	1	12.5	12.5	77	65	15.6%
14,16,18	3×3	64	5	50.0	450.0	864	405	53.1%
15,17,19	1×1	64	1	50.0	50.0	77	65	15.6%

[8] Florent de Dinechin, Matei Istoan, and Abdelbassat Massouri. 2014. Sum-of-Product Architectures Computing Just Right. *IEEE International Conference on Application-Specific Systems, Architectures and Processors (ASAP)* (2014), 41–47.

[9] F. de Dinechin and B. Pasca. 2012. Custom Arithmetic Datapath Design for FPGAs using the FloPoCo Core Generator. *IEEE Design & Test of Computers* 99 (2012), 1–6.

[10] T J Dekker. 1971. A Floating-Point Technique for Extending the Available Precision. *Numer. Math.* 18, 3 (June 1971), 224–242.

[11] Roberto DiCecco, Griffin Lacey, Jasmina Vasiljevic, Paul Chow, Graham Taylor, and Shawki Areibi. 2016. Caffeinated FPGAs: FPGA framework For Convolutional Neural Networks. In *2016 International Conference on Field-Programmable Technology (FPT)*. IEEE, 265–268.

[12] S Gupta, A Agrawal, K Gopalakrishnan Conference on Machine, and . 2015. Deep learning with limited numerical precision. *International Conference on Machine Learning* (2015), 1737–1746.

[13] Philipp Gysel. 2016. Ristretto: Hardware-Oriented Approximation of Convolutional Neural Networks. (May 2016), 1–63. arXiv:1605.06402

[14] Xushen Han, Dajiang Zhou, Shihao Wang, and Shinji Kimura. 2016. CNN-MERP: An FPGA-based memory-efficient reconfigurable processor for forward and backward propagation of convolutional neural networks. In *2016 IEEE 34th International Conference on Computer Design (ICCD*. IEEE, 320–327.

[15] Javier Hormigo, Gabriel Caffarena, Juan P Oliver, and Eduardo Boemo. 2013. Self-Reconfigurable Constant Multiplier for FPGA. *ACM Transactions on Reconfigurable Technology and Systems* 6, 3 (Oct. 2013), 1–17.

[16] Martin Kumm and Johannes Kappauf. 2018. Advanced Compressor Tree Synthesis for FPGAs. *IEEE Trans. Comput.* 67, 8 (2018), 1078–1091.

[17] M Kumm, K Möller, and P Zipf. 2013. Dynamically Reconfigurable FIR Filter Architectures with Fast Reconfiguration. *International Workshop on Reconfigurable Communication-centric Systems-on-Chip (ReCoSoC)* (2013), 1–8.

[18] Martin Kumm, Konrad Möller, and Peter Zipf. 2013. Reconfigurable FIR Filter Using Distributed Arithmetic on FPGAs. In *IEEE International Symposium on Circuits and Systems (ISCAS)*. 2058–2061.

[19] Martin Kumm and Peter Zipf. 2014. Pipelined Compressor Tree Optimization Using Integer Linear Programming. In *IEEE International Conference on Field Programmable Logic and Application (FPL)*. IEEE, 1–8.

[20] Shuang Liang, Shouyi Yin, Leibo Liu, Wayne Luk, and Shaojun Wei. 2018. FP-BNN: Binarized Neural Network on FPGA. *Neurocomputing* 275 (2018), 1072–1086.

[21] Zhiqiang Liu, Yong Dou, Jingfei Jiang, Jinwei Xu, Shijie Li, Yongmei Zhou, and Yingnan Xu. 2017. Throughput-Optimized FPGA Accelerator for Deep Convolutional Neural Networks. *ACM Transactions on Reconfigurable Technology and Systems (TRETS)* 10, 3 (July 2017), 17–23.

[22] Konrad Möller. 2017. *Run-time Reconfigurable Constant Multiplication on Field Programmable Gate Arrays*. Ph.D. Dissertation. Kassel University Press.

[23] Mohammad Motamedi, Philipp Gysel, Venkatesh Akella, and Soheil Ghiasi. 2016. Design space exploration of FPGA-based Deep Convolutional Neural Networks. In *2016 21st Asia and South Pacific Design Automation Conference (ASP-DAC*. IEEE, 575–580.

[24] Kalin Ovtcharov, Olatunji Ruwase, Joo-Young Kim, Jeremy Fowers, Karin Strauss, and Eric Chung. 2015. *Accelerating Deep Convolutional Neural Networks Using Specialized Hardware*. Technical Report. 1–4 pages.

[25] Hadi Parandeh-Afshar, Philip Brisk, and Paolo Ienne. 2008. Efficient Synthesis of Compressor Trees on FPGAs. In *Asia and South Pacific Design Automation Conference (ASPDAC)*. IEEE, 138–143.

[26] H. Parandeh-Afshar, Arkosnato Neogy, P. Brisk, and P. Ienne. 2011. Compressor Tree Synthesis on Commercial High-Performance FPGAs. *ACM Transactions on Reconfigurable Technology and Systems (TRETS)* 4, 4 (Dec. 2011), 1–19.

[27] Jiantao Qiu, Jie Wang, Song Yao, Kaiyuan Guo, Boxun Li, Erjin Zhou, Jincheng Yu, Tianqi Tang, Ningyi Xu, Sen Song, Yu Wang, and Huazhong Yang. 2016. Going Deeper with Embedded FPGA Platform for Convolutional Neural Network. In *International Symposium on Field Programmable Gate Arrays (FPGA)*. ACM, 26–35.

[28] Vivienne Sze, Yu-Hsin Chen, Tien-Ju Yang, and Joel S Emer. 2017. Efficient Processing of Deep Neural Networks: A Tutorial and Survey. *Proc. IEEE* 105, 12 (Dec. 2017), 2295–2329.

[29] Yaman Umuroglu, Nicholas J Fraser, Giulio Gambardella, Michaela Blott, Philip Leong, Magnus Jahre, and Kees Vissers. 2017. FINN: A Framework for Fast, Scalable Binarized Neural Network Inference. In *International Symposium on Field-Programmable Gate Arrays (FPGA)*. ACM, New York, New York, USA, 65–74.

[30] G Venkatesh, E Nurvitadhi, and D Marr. 2017. Accelerating deep convolutional networks using low-precision and sparsity. In *IEEE International Conference on Acoustics, Speech and Signal Processing (ICASSP)*. 2861–2865.

[31] Xuechao Wei, Cody Hao Yu, Peng Zhang, Youxiang Chen, Yuxin Wang, Han Hu, Yun Liang, and Jason Cong. 2017. Automated systolic array architecture synthesis for high throughput CNN inference on FPGAs. In *2017 54th ACM/EDAC/IEEE Design Automation Conference (DAC)*. IEEE, 1–6.

[32] Kazimierz Wiatr and Ernest Jamro. 2000. Constant coefficient multiplication in FPGA structures. In *Euromicro Workshop on Multimedia and Telecommunications*. IEEE Comput. Soc, 252–259.

[33] Kazimierz Wiatr and Ernest Jamro. 2001. Implementation of Multipliers in FPGA Structures. *International Symposium on Quality Electronic Design* (2001), 415–420.

[34] Chen Zhang, Peng Li, Guangyu Sun, Yijin Guan, Bingjun Xiao, and Jason Cong. 2015. Optimizing FPGA-based Accelerator Design for Deep Convolutional Neural Networks. In *International Symposium on Field Programmable Gate Arrays (FPGA)*. ACM, 161–170.

[35] Chenzhuo Zhu, Song Han, Huizi Mao, and William J Dally. 2016. Trained Ternary Quantization. In *International Conference on Learning Representations*. 1–10.

F5-HD: Fast Flexible FPGA-based Framework for Refreshing Hyperdimensional Computing

Sahand Salamat, Mohsen Imani, Behnam Khaleghi, and Tajana Rosing
Computer Science and Engineering Department, UC San Diego, La Jolla, CA 92093, USA
{sasalama, moimani, bkhaleghi, tajana}@ucsd.edu

ABSTRACT

Hyperdimensional (HD) computing is a novel computational paradigm that emulates the brain functionality in performing cognitive tasks. The underlying computation of HD involves a substantial number of element-wise operations (e.g., addition and multiplications) on ultra-wise hypervectors, in the granularities of as small as a single bit, which can be effectively parallelized and pipelined. In addition, though different HD applications might vary in terms of number of input features and output classes (labels), they generally follow the same computation flow. Such characteristics of HD computing inimitably matches with the intrinsic capabilities of FPGAs, making these devices a unique solution for accelerating these applications.

In this paper, we propose **F5-HD**, a fast and flexible FPGA-based framework for **refreshing** the performance of HD computing. F5-HD eliminates the arduous task of handcrafted designing of hardware accelerators by automatically generating an FPGA implementation of HD accelerator leveraging a template of optimized processing elements, according to the applications specification and user's constraint. Our evaluations using different classification benchmarks revealed that F5-HD provides 86.9× and 7.8× (11.9× and 1.7×) higher energy efficiency improvement and faster training (inference) as compared to an optimized implementation of HD on AMD R9 390 GPU, respectively.

CCS CONCEPTS

• **Hardware** → **Reconfigurable logic and FPGAs**; Electronic design automation; • **Computing methodologies** → *Machine learning approaches*.

KEYWORDS

Brain-inspired Hyperdimensional Computing; Machine Learning; FPGA-based Acceleration; Automated Template-based Hardware Generation

ACM Reference Format:
Sahand Salamat, Mohsen Imani, Behnam Khaleghi, and Tajana Rosing. 2019. F5-HD: Fast Flexible FPGA-based Framework for Refreshing Hyperdimensional Computing. In *The 2019 ACM/SIGDA International Symposium on Field-Programmable Gate Arrays (FPGA '19), February 24–26, 2019, Seaside, CA, USA*. ACM, New York, NY, USA, 10 pages. https://doi.org/10.1145/3289602.3293913

FPGA '19, February 24–26, 2019, Seaside, CA, USA
© 2019 Association for Computing Machinery.
ACM ISBN 978-1-4503-6137-8/19/02...$15.00
https://doi.org/10.1145/3289602.3293913

1 INTRODUCTION

Hyperdimensional (HD) computing is a novel computational approach that builds upon imitating the brain functionality in performing cognitive tasks [1, 2]. In fact, brain computes with patterns of neural activity, which can be realized by points in a hyperdimensional space, called hypervectors. By leveraging a non-complex and parallel set of operations on such ultra-wide vectors, HD affords promising capabilities in learning and classification applications including but not limited to language, speech, activity, and face recognition as well as classification of time-series signals [3–9]. In addition to its inclusive cognitive application space and comparatively simpler computation model than other learning paradigms[10, 11], HD computing is inherently robust against failures as the information in a hypervector is uniformly distributed over all of its comprising dimensions [1]. Moreover, HD is able to yield the accuracy of state-of-the-art while learning from only a small portion of the original training data [12, 13].

In a nutshell, HD computing is involved with constituting of and processing on hypervectors, wherein a hypervector comprises thousands of bits. For training, first, it generates a fixed set of orthogonal hypervectors each of which represents a specific feature level. Afterward, for a given input (as a preprocessed set/vector of features), it maps each feature of the input vector to the corresponding predetermined hypervector. Eventually, all the hypervectors are aggregated, which is basically performed by adding them up [3, 14]. Since the spatial or temporal location of the features does matter, the aggregation also incorporates shift operation on the representing vectors to retain the indices of the input features. After all input data are mapped to a final encoded hypervector, all encoded hypervectors belonging to the same class (label) are summed up to form the final representative hypervector of the class. Inference in HD computing is analogous; albeit the encoded hypervector passes through an associative search (a.k.a similarity check) with the representative hypervectors to identify the associated class [1].

The encoding and classifying stages of HD computing require a substantial number of bit-level addition and multiplication operations, which can be effectively parallelized [13]. These operations can also be segregated (and hence, pipelined) in the granularity of dimension level. Though they may vary in the number of input features and output classes, all HD applications follow the same computation flow, albeit with a controllable degree of parallelism and pipeline. Such characteristics of HD computing inimitably matches with the intrinsic capabilities of FPGAs [15], making these devices a unique solution for accelerating these applications; however, implementing applications on FPGAs is a time consuming process[10, 16].

In this paper, we propose F5-HD, an automated FPGA-based framework for accelerating HD computing that abstracts away the implementation complexities and long design cycles associated with hardware design from the user. F5-HD generates a synthesizable Verilog implementation of HD accelerator while taking the high-level user and target FPGA parameters into account. Essentially, F5-HD customizes upon a hand-optimized, fully-pipelined template processing element that can be parallelized according to the user-specified constraints (viz., accuracy and power). F5-HD supports both training and inference as well as model refinement through online, simultaneous, training and inference, so the model can be calibrated without interrupting the normal operation of the system. Specifically, this paper makes the following contributions:

- Proposes F5-HD, a template-based framework that generates FPGA-based synthesizable architectures for accelerating HD computing.
- Proposes a novel hardware-friendly encoding approach that reduces the required Block RAM accesses, hence, enhances resource utilization
- Provides the flexibility of customized accuracy by supporting different data-types (viz., fixed-point, binary, and power-of-two), and of customized power consumption bound by trading the parallelism.
- Enables simultaneous training and inference to refine the model without interrupting the system functionality.

Our evaluations using different classification benchmarks revealed that, in high-accuracy mode, F5-HD can provide 86.9× and 7.8× (11.9× and 1.7×) higher energy efficiency improvement and faster training (inference) as compared to an optimized implementation of HD on AMD R9 390 GPU, respectively. In the fastest mode in which each dimension is represented by a single bit (i.e., binary), F5-HD achieves 4.3× higher throughput and 2.1× throughput/Watt as compared to the baseline F5-HD using fixed-point values, while providing in average 16.5% lower classification accuracy. In addition, we observe that F5-HD framework can ensure the power consumption to be within 9.0% of the user-defined constraint, on average.

2 BACKGROUND AND RELATED WORK

In this section, we first articulate the operations behind HD computing, including encoding, training, inference, and retraining. Afterward, we review the previous work regarding the utilization and implementation of the HD computing.

2.1 Hyperdimensional Computing

HD computing builds on the fact that the cognitive tasks of the human brain can be explained by mathematical operations on ultra-wide hypervectors [1]. In other words, brain computes with patterns of neural activity, which can be better represented by hypervectors rather than scalar numbers. A hypervector comprises $\mathcal{D}_{hv}$, e.g., 10,000 bits, independent components (dimensions) whereby the enclosed information is distributed uniformly among all $\mathcal{D}_{hv}$ dimensions. This makes hypervectors robust to failure as the system remains functional under a certain number of component failings, and as degradation of information does not depend on the position of the failing components [3, 14, 17].

Encoding: As demonstrated in Figure 1, training an HD model involves a three-step procedure as follows. First, it initializes base hypervectors, each of which corresponds to a specific input feature level. Indeed, input of the HD algorithm is a feature vector $\vec{V}_{iv}$ with $\mathcal{D}_{iv}$ dimensions (elements) wherein each dimension represents a feature value $\mathcal{F}$ that has ℓ_{iv} levels:

$$\vec{V}_{iv} = \langle v_0, v_1, \cdots, v_{\mathcal{D}_{iv}} \rangle$$
$$|v_i| \in (\mathcal{F}_0, \mathcal{F}_1, \cdots \mathcal{F}_{\ell_{iv}}) \tag{1}$$

Though it is application-dependent, typical values for $\mathcal{D}_{iv}$ and ℓ_{iv} might be, respectively, 100s and four–eight for which ℓ_{iv} can be

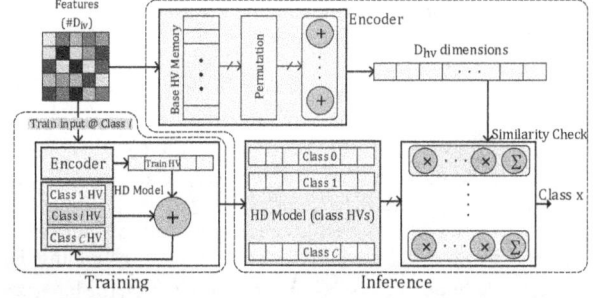

Figure 1: Overview of hyperdimensional learning and inference.

represented by two–three bits. Each of $\mathcal{D}_{iv}$ features in the feature vector needs to be mapped to a base hypervector with $\mathcal{D}_{hv}$ dimensions for subsequent processing. Therefore, to represent all possible ℓ_{iv} values of features, ℓ_{iv} different hypervectors with $\mathcal{D}_{hv}$ dimensions, namely base hypervectors, are needed. The base hypervectors are generated according to the attribute of the feature vector. In the cases that feature levels are independent and irrelevant, base hypervectors can be selected randomly, hence orthogonal. In such cases, the expected Hamming distance between two (out of ℓ_{iv}) base hypervectors is $\sim \mathcal{D}_{hv}/2$. However, for the cases that each feature level is a meaningful quantity, e.g., a continuous signal quantized to ℓ_{iv} levels, the distance between the hypervectors of two feature levels should correspond to their actual difference. For these cases, the base hypervector associated with the lowest feature level is generated randomly. Afterward, a random half ($\mathcal{D}_{hv}/2$) of its bits are flipped to produce an orthogonal base hypervector representing the other side of the horizon, i.e., the highest level of a feature. The remaining base hypervectors are generated by flipping $\frac{\mathcal{D}_{hv}/2}{\ell_{iv}-1}$ of each consecutive hypervector pair, starting from the initial base hypervector.

After specifying the base hypervectors, each element v_i of a given input feature vector is mapped to its associated base hypervector hv_{v_i} for subsequent processing. Nonetheless, as in most applications the spatial and/or temporal position of an input feature often do matter, i.e., whenever a sequence of the input features should be traced such as image and speech inputs, the encoding procedure takes the locality into account by introducing permutation operation $\mathcal{P}^{(i)}$ (which denotes i-bits cyclic left shift) on the input features before aggregation. Due to the large dimension and randomness of the base hypervectors, $\mathcal{P}^{(i)}$ keeps a hypervector and its resultant shift orthogonal. Eventually, the mapped hypervectors are aggregated according to Equation 2 to build the *query hypervector*:

$$hv(\vec{V}_{iv}) = \vec{hv}_{v_0} + (\vec{hv}_{v_1} \ll 1) + \cdots + (\vec{hv}_{v_{\mathcal{D}_{iv}}} \ll \mathcal{D}_{iv}) \tag{2}$$

Which can be reformulated as:

$$\vec{\mathcal{H}} = \vec{hv}(\vec{V}_{iv}) = \sum_{i=0}^{\mathcal{D}_{iv}} \mathcal{P}^{(i)}(\vec{hv}_{v_i}) \tag{3}$$

Training: After mapping each training input $\vec{V}_{iv}$ to hypervector $\vec{\mathcal{H}}$ as above, all hypervectors belonging to the same class (label) are simply summed to form the final representative hypervectors. Thus, assuming $\vec{\mathcal{H}}^l = \langle h_0, h_1, \cdots, h_{\mathcal{D}_{hv}} \rangle^l$ denotes a generated class hypervector for an input data with label l, the final (representative) class hypervectors are obtained as Equation 4, in which each dimension c_k is obtained through dimension-wise addition of all h_k^ls, and $\mathcal{J}$ is the number of input data with label l.

$$\vec{C}_l = \langle c_0, c_1, \cdots, c_{\mathcal{D}_{hv}} \rangle = \sum_{j=0}^{\mathcal{J}} \mathcal{H}_j^l \qquad (4)$$

All dimensions of a class hypervector $(\vec{C})$ have the same bit-width which can have various representation, e.g., binary (hence one bit), power-of-two (2^n), fixed-point (integer), etc. This makes a trade-off between accuracy, performance, and hardware complexity. The base of hypervectors are converted through thresholding. For instance, for $\mathcal{J}$ hypervectors $\vec{\mathcal{H}}_j^l$ constituting class $\vec{C}_l$, the binarized class can be obtained as follows.

$$\vec{C}_l{}' = \langle c_0', c_1', \cdots, c_{\mathcal{D}_{hv}}' \rangle, \; c_k' = \begin{cases} 0 & c_k < \frac{\mathcal{J}}{2} \\ 1 & \text{otherwise} \end{cases} \qquad (5)$$

Inference: The first steps of inference in HD computing is similar to training; an input feature vector is encoded to $\mathcal{D}_{hv}$–dimension query hypervector $\vec{\mathcal{H}}$ following Equation 3. This is followed by a similarity check between the query hypervector $\vec{\mathcal{H}}$ and all representative class hypervectors, $\vec{C}_l$. The similarity in the fixed-point and power-of-two number representations is defined as calculating the cosine similarity, which is obtained by multiplying each dimension in the query vector to the corresponding dimension of the class hypervectors, and adding up the partial products:

$$\text{similarity}(\vec{\mathcal{H}}, \vec{C}_l) = \sum_{j=0}^{\mathcal{D}_{hv}} h_k \cdot c_k \qquad (6)$$

The class with the highest similarity with the query hypervector indicates the classification result. The number of classes is application-dependent and determined by the user. This can be as simple as two classes, denoting face vs. non-face in a face-detection algorithm. Similarity checking in binarized HD model (i.e., 1-bit dimensions) simplifies to the Hamming distance between the query and class vectors, which can be carried out by a bitwise XNOR, followed by a reduction (population counter[1]) operation.

Retraining: Retraining might be used to enhance the model accuracy by calibrating it either via new training data or by multiple iterations on the same training data. Retraining is basically done by removing the mispredicted query hypervectors from the mispredicted class and adding it to the right class. Thus, for a new input feature vector $\vec{V}_{in}$ with query hypervector $\vec{\mathcal{H}}$ belonging actually to class with hypervector $\vec{C}_l$, if the current model predicts the class $C_{l'}$ where $C_{l'} \neq C_l$, the model updates itself as follows:

$$\begin{aligned} \vec{C}_l &= \vec{C}_l + \vec{\mathcal{H}} \\ \vec{C}_{l'} &= \vec{C}_{l'} - \vec{\mathcal{H}} \end{aligned} \qquad (7)$$

This, indeed, reduces the similarity between $\vec{\mathcal{H}}$ and mispredicted class $C_{l'}$, and adds $\vec{\mathcal{H}}$ to the correct class C_l to increase their similarity and the model will be able to correctly classify such query hypervectors.

2.2 Related Studies

HD computing is gaining traction as an alternative solution to perform cognitive tasks in a light-weight fashion that uses significantly simpler operations compared to conventional machine learning techniques that deal with complex learning procedures with substantial number of costly operations. So far, successful application of HD computing in varied domains has been demonstrated. language identification [18], DNA sequencing [19], physical activity prediction [5, 20], speech recognition [6, 21], and gesture recognition [12, 22], clustering [23] are just a few examples.

On par with studies investigating the HD applications, several studies have attempted to propose hardware and algorithmic solutions to enhance the efficacy of HD computing. The study in [17] proposes logical operations to generate the hypervector corresponding to each feature on the fly, in order to reduce the costly BRAM accesses. They also propose approximate majority gate to compose the binary class hypervectors without requiring to hold the summation on hypervector components in a multi-bit format in the course of training. This is, however, limited to low-accuracy binarized HD computing wherein each dimension of the query and class hypervectors is one bit. The authors of [13] propose hierarchical HD computing solution that consists of a main stage with multiple classifiers each can trade between efficiency and accuracy. There is also a decider stage that learns and selects the appropriate encoder within the main stage based on a so-called difficulty metric of the input data. The work in [21] clusters class hypervectors dimensions to reduce the number of multiplications. Additionally, by assuming the encoded input hypervector is stored in memory, they implemented the associative search of clustered HD on FPGA.

Other works leverage advances of emerging technologies in HD computing [24–26]. In [24], the authors leverage CNT-FET and Resistive RAM to fabricate an end-to-end HD computing solution. They exploit the variations in RRAM resistance and CNT-FET drives current to project the input features to query hypervectors as well as propose approximate accumulation circuit using gradual RRAM reset operation. The work in [25] demonstrates HD computing with 3D vertical RRAM in-memory kernels capable of performing multiplication, addition, and permutation by analog operations on RRAM cells.

To the best of our knowledge, F5-HD is the first automated FPGA-based framework that implements HD computing with varied model precision, capable of meeting user constraints on different FPGA platforms.

3 F5-HD FRAMEWORK OVERVIEW

F5-HD aims to abstract away the complexities behind employing FPGAs for accelerating AI applications [27]. F5-HD is an automated framework that generates synthesizable FPGA-based HD implementation in Verilog, considering the user-specified criteria, e.g., power budget, performance-accuracy trade-off, and FPGA model (available resources). F5-HD combines the advantages of hand-optimized HDL design with the bit-level yet flexible manageability of FPGA resources, which is in concordance with bitwise operations associated with HD computing, to accelerate these applications.

3.1 F5-HD Workflow

Figure 2 demonstrates F5-HD's workflow, explained as follows.

(1) Model Specification: The framework starts with specifying the application specifications, viz., the number of classes, features (i.e., input vector dimensions $\mathcal{D}_{iv}$, as well as the number of features different levels, ℓ_{iv}) and the number of training data. The user also determines the target FPGA model, hence F5-HD can get the number of available resources from a predefined library. F5-HD currently supports Xilinx 7-series FPGAs, including Virtex-7,

---

[1]A population counter basically counts the number of '1's (ones) in the given binary input.

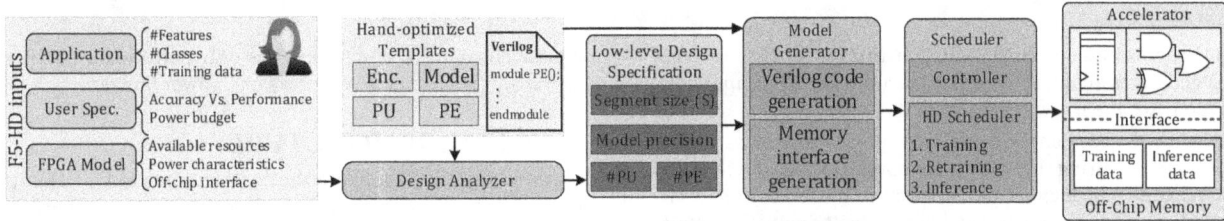

Figure 2: Overview of the proposed framework, F5-HD.

Spartan-7, and Kintex-7 families. This can be readily extended to other FPGA families. In addition, the user can dictate constraints on the power as well as performance-accuracy trading, which will be explained in the following subsections.

(2) Design Analyzer: Thereafter, F5-HD's design analyzer determines the number of resources according to the user's specification. F5-HD exploits a parameterized template architecture, mainly composed of an encoder; an associative search unit, including Processing Units and Processing Elements; as well as an HD model module that stores and updates the class hypervectors. The hardware architecture of F5-HD will be detailed in Section 4. The design analyzer determines the number of *Processing Units* (PUs), *Processing Elements* (PEs) as well as the type and number of dimension-wise functional units within each PE, according to the desired accuracy level and available resources. All the function units, e.g., encoder and PUs, utilize a specific set of building blocks with foreknown resource utilization. Thus, F5-HD design analyzer can readily figure out the parameters of the template architecture, e.g., maximum parallelization level of the encoder (see Section 4.1) and number of PEs per PU, based on their required resources (LUT, BRAM, and DSP) and the available resources.

In the case a power budget is defined by the user, the design analyzer tries to find out the maximum number of PEs that can be generated, without violating the constraints. For this regard, F5-HD estimates the power of resources, e.g., LUTs, flip-flops, DSPs, BRAMs, etc. using Xilinx Power Estimator (XPE) [28]. This requires calculating the expected activity of the resources, which is straightforward owing to the foreknown homogeneous structure of the generated architectures and the expected probability of the hypervectors at the level of the dimension. Another constraint is performance-accuracy trade-off wherein the user chooses between the highest performance with relatively lower accuracy, mediocre, and low performance with the highest accuracy. The available modes are currently fixed-point (8-bits integer representation), power-of-two in which hypervector dimensions are four-bits values that represent the exponent, and binary (i.e., each dimension is represented by one bit). It is noteworthy that the power and accuracy constraints can be applied concurrently, which provides the user with the flexibility to adapt F5-HD based on their application criteria. For instance, for real-time low-power applications, the user might specify their power budget with the binary mode of operation. The output of design analyzer is basically the number of PUs and PEs (per PU), the number of multipliers (in the case of fixed-point model) per PE, and the parallelization level of the encoder, i.e., the number of hypervector dimensions it can produce at each cycle.

(3) Model Generator: After the design analyzer specified the parameters of the template architecture, F5-HD's model generator, automatically generates the Verilog implementation of F5-HD using hand-optimized template blocks. This includes instantiating the PUs, PEs, the Block RAMs, and off-chip memory interface.

Table 1: Classification accuracy and performance of binary, power-of-two, and 8-bits fixed-point HD models running on CPU.

Application	Binary		Power-of-two		Fixed-point	
	Accuracy	Exe.time	Accuracy	Exe.time	Accuracy	Exe.time
Speech Recognition	88.1%	1.6ms	90.3%	3.4ms	95.5%	10.5ms
Activity Recognition	77.4%	0.6ms	88.0%	1.3ms	94.6%	3.4ms
Face Recognition	48.5%	0.7ms	89.6%	1.6ms	96.9%	4.6ms
Physical Monitoring	85.7%	1.1ms	90.8%	2.4ms	94.5%	7.8ms

The model generator also initializes the BRAMs with the base hypervectors. For this end, F5-HD exploits a fixed, predetermined hypervector as the seed vector, and generates the remaining $\ell_{iv} - 1$ hypervectors according to the procedure explained in Section 2.1. In the cases the user already has a trained model (i.e., base and class hypervectors), F5-HD allows direct initializing of these hypervectors.

(4) Scheduler: The next step generates the controller, which statically schedules F5-HD operations. The main scheduling tasks include loading the training or inference data from off-chip memory into local BRAMs, switching between the training, inference, and/or retraining modes. It also generates a controller to allocating and deallocating PUs for retraining, and essentially controlling the enabler of different processing units in the granularity of clock cycle. Eventually, the logic and controller are merged to realize the concrete accelerator architecture.

3.2 Accuracy-Performance Trade-off

The majority of existing HD computing methods use binarized class hypervectors to substitute the costly Cosine similarity operation in inference phase with the simpler Hamming distance operation. Although binary representation increases the throughput, in the majority of classification problems, the accuracy of the binarized HD model is not comparable to that of the HD using fixed-point dimensions [13]. In addition to the fixed-point and binary HD models, we provide power-of-two representation in the class hypervectors which replaces the costly multiplication operations with shift operations in the hardware level. Though power-of-two representation covers discrete values, it supports a larger range of numbers which helps to compensate for the accuracy drop. Table 1 compares the accuracy and execution time of HD models for four different datasets on CPU. Fixed-point model, on average, attains 5.7% and 20.5% higher accuracy compared to, respectively, power-of-two and binary models. The binary model surpasses in terms of the throughput, wherein it yields 6.5× and 2.2× performance improvement over the fixed-point and power-of-two models.

3.3 Training Modes

Similar to the training of Deep Neural Networks (DNNs), training of HD model can be enhanced by iterating over the input data, as described in Section 2.1. Note that, as in the case of DNNs, to avoid overfitting, a learned model does not necessarily predict the correct class for all data of the same training dataset, however, the accuracy can be improved by multiple iterations (equivalent to multiple *epochs* in the context of deep learning). The first epoch of F5-HD generates all query hypervectors (one per each input data) and aggregates the hypervectors with the same label l as the class hypervector $\vec{C}_l$. We denote this single-epoch learning as **model initialization**. During the subsequent optional epochs (referred to as **retraining**), which either can be specified by the user or F5-HD itself continues until the accuracy improvement diminishes, under the management of the scheduler, F5-HD enhances the model by discarding the attributes of the mispredicted query hypervector $\vec{\mathcal{H}}$ from the mispredicted class hypervector $\vec{C}'_{\mathcal{H}}$, and adding it to the correct class hypervector $\vec{C}_{\mathcal{H}}$. Retraining can be carried out immediately after model initialization, or enabled later by halting the inference phase. The principal difference between the model initialization and retraining is the latter requires prediction (i.e., inference) as well while the former simply performs aggregation. This is supported by F5-HD architecture, which is further described in Section 4.

Depending on the generality of the training data and the HD model, in certain cases, the accuracy of the classifier for real-world data might drop. To resolve this issue, F5-HD provides an **online retraining** solution which can be enabled during the runtime by user. During the online retraining, F5-HD updates the class hypervectors based on a new set of training data in real-time. Thus, F5-HD is capable of conducting model initialization, retraining, inference, and simultaneous retraining-inference (online retraining). In the inference mode, the system works normally and all the resources are assigned to calculate the similarity metric. In the online hybrid retraining mode, the system executes both inference and retraining and allocates a portion of the resources for each task. In this mode, the part of the FPGA that executes the inference task always uses the updated model during the online retraining. Therefore, in each retraining iteration, the model is updated and the inference employs the recently updated class hypervectors for prediction. Upon finishing the online retraining, all FPGA resources will be reallocated back for inference purpose.

3.4　Flow of Data

Inputs of F5-HD are vectors of extracted features, namely feature maps, which are stored in the off-chip memory. The scheduler partially loads the feature maps to the input buffer memory, distributed in FPGA local memory (Block RAMs). The encoding module generates the encoded query hypervectors of the input vector and stores them in the encoding buffer. The generated query hypervectors are then pipelined in a segregated (dimensional-wise) manner, fed to the associative search module to perform parallel similarity check with all class hypervectors, yet in a dimensional-wise manner. This requires to store the partial sums of the dimensions products. The encoding and associative search work in a synchronous manner to avoid logic starvation and maximize the physical resource utilization. Thus, in F5-HD, the encoding module outputs the same number of query hypervector dimensions that the associative search processes per cycle. Since the classification of an input vector takes multiple cycles and utilizes all the FPGA resources, the parallelization is in per-input level. That is, classification operations for a single input are pipelined and parallelized among all FPGA resources, and the subsequent input vector is loaded after the process of the current input accomplishes. Increasing F5-HD's throughput necessitates increasing the degree of parallelism in the associative search, which, in turn, demands reading higher encoded dimension per cycle. Therefore, owing to the high supported degree

of parallelism in HD computing, the only performance barriers of F5-HD are the available resources and power budget.

4　F5-HD ARCHITECTURE

In this section, we articulate the contributions of F5-HD in more details. We begin with elaborating the proposed encoding scheme that reduces the number of BRAM accesses. Afterwards, we illustrate the architecture overview and detail the functionality and structure of the building blocks in the course of training and inference. We also formulate the required resources by which the design analyzer specifies the (parametric) number of resources for the model generator.

4.1　Proposed Encoding Scheme

Both training and inference processes in HD computing need to encode the input feature hypervector, $\vec{V}_{in}$, to the query hypervector $\vec{\mathcal{H}}$, using basic permutation and addition on the base hypervectors. As previously shown by Equation 3, each element v_i of the input hypervector, based on its value $|v_i| \in (\mathcal{F}_0, \mathcal{F}_1, \cdots \mathcal{F}_{\ell_{iv}})$, selects the corresponding base hypervector $\vec{hv}_{vi}$ (out of ℓ_{iv} possible base hypervectors), rotated left by i bits, to make up the query $\vec{\mathcal{H}}$. Figure 3(a) illustrates the encoding scheme, in which the constituting bits of each dimension d_i of the query hypervector $\vec{\mathcal{H}}$ are distinguished by the same color. Accordingly, to build up e.g., dimension d_0 (d_1) from $\vec{\mathcal{H}}$, v_0 of the input hypervector chooses among b_0 (b_1) of the base hypervectors, v_1 selects from $b_{\mathcal{D}_{iv}}$ (b_0), v_2 selects from $b_{\mathcal{D}_{iv}-1}$ ($b_{\mathcal{D}_{iv}}$), etc. Recall that the dimensions of hypervectors are 1-bit wide (denoted by b_is in the figure) that aggregate in a dimension-wise scheme and form d_is, which can be in various widths and representations, e.g., fixed-point, binary, and power-of-two.

The naïve encoding scheme abstracted in Figure 3 is, however, both computationally and communicationally intractable: at each cycle it requires $\ell_{iv} \times \mathcal{D}_{hv}$ bits (multiples of 10K) of the base hypervectors to be read from the BRAMs, and $\mathcal{D}_{hv}$ population counters (PopCounters), each with input bitwidth of $\mathcal{D}_{iv}$. To resolve this, as the dimensions of the query hypervector $\vec{\mathcal{H}}$ can be calculated independently, we segregate the output query vector $\vec{\mathcal{H}}$ into the segments of $\mathcal{S}$ dimensions whereby at each clock cycle one segment is processed. Thus, processing the entire $\vec{\mathcal{H}}$ takes $\mathcal{D}_{hv}/s$ cycles. This is conceptualized in Figure 3(b), which shows the physical locations of the hypervectors bits required to build up the first $\mathcal{S}$ dimensions of $\vec{\mathcal{H}}$. Accordingly, $\ell_{iv} \times (\mathcal{S} + \mathcal{D}_{iv})$ different bits are needed to be read to create the query $\vec{\mathcal{H}}$. Notice that this approach retains the alignments of the bits; for every $\mathcal{S} + \mathcal{D}_{iv}$ consecutive bits (per base hypervector) read from the BRAM(s) at each cycle, bits 0 to $\mathcal{D}_{iv}$ are conveyed to 0th PopCounter to form d_0, bits 1 to $\mathcal{D}_{iv} + 1$ form the d_1 via the 1st PopCounter, and so on. Therefore, no logic or routing overhead is associated to align the read data.

Beside segmented processing, we further reduce the number of BRAM accesses by proposing a novel encoding scheme. The proposed encoding, first, permutes the bits of the base hypervectors *locally*, i.e., intra-segment, rather than the entire hypervector. After $\mathcal{S}$ permutations, e.g., after the first $\mathcal{S}$ features (v_is) in the input hypervector, the segments accomplish an entire permutation; hence the base hypervector for the 0th and $'\mathcal{S} + 1'^{\text{th}}$ features essentially become the same. This removes the information associated with local and/or temporal locality of the input features. In such case, we perform inter-segment permutation in which the *segments* are

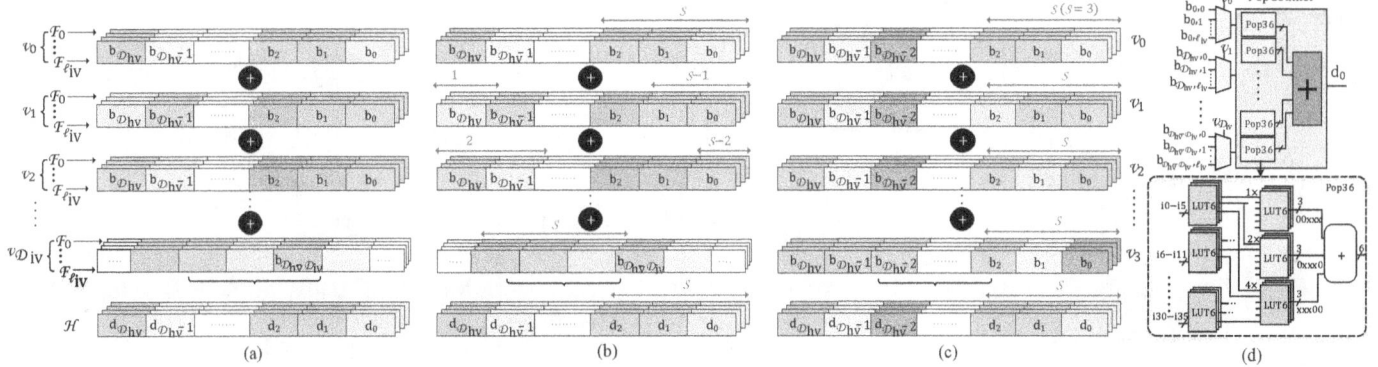

Figure 3: (a) The naïve encoding scheme (b) Baseline segmented encoding (c) The proposed encoding scheme (d) Implementation of the population counter

permuted to left *globally*, whereby bit b_k takes the place of bit b_{S+k}. In this scenario, the first S features (v_is) need S bits of the first segment, the second S input features require S bits of the right segment (which will be shifted to left by one segment), and so on. Thereby, the proposed encoding needs $\ell_{iv} \times (S \times \mathcal{D}_{iv}/S) = \ell_{iv} \times \mathcal{D}_{iv}$ bits (S bits of all ℓ_{iv} base hypervectors per every $\mathcal{D}_{iv}/S$ input features) to produce an output segment. This needs S $\mathcal{D}_{iv}$-width Pop-Counter. Figure 3(c) conceptualizes the proposed encoding scheme.

The hand-crafted hardware realization of the proposed Pop-Counter, which contributes to significant portion of the encoder and overall area footprint, is demonstrated by Figure 3(d). The main building block of the implemented PopCounter is Pop36 that produces 6-bit output for a given 36-bit input. It is made up of bunches of three LUT6 that share six inputs and output the 3-bit resultants, which are summed up together in the subsequent stage according to their bit order (position). We instantiated FPGA primitive resources, e.g., LUT6 and FDSE to build up the pipelined PopCounter, which is ∼20% area efficient than simple HDL description. The impact of PopCounter intensifies further in binary HD models wherein the associative search module is relatively small.

4.2 F5-HD Architecture

The architecture overview of F5-HD is illustrated in Figure 4, which incorporates the required modules for training, inference and online retraining of the HD computing. The main `template` architecture of F5-HD includes two levels of hierarchy: a cluster of *Processing Units* (PUs), each comprises specific number of *Processing Elements* (PEs). The assignment of PUs and PEs are selected in a way that maximizes the data reusability.

Processing Units (PUs): F5-HD contains $2 \times |C|$ PUs where $|C|$ is the number of classes (labels). In the course of inference, all C PUs perform similarity checking. Every cycle, each PU receives $S/2$ of the query hypervector's dimensions (recall that S is the segment length generated by encoder at each clock cycle, as discussed in Section 4.1). Thus, together, a pair of PUs process all S dimensions of the segment, and hence, $2 \times |C|$ PUs are able to check similarity between all $|C|$ classes in parallel. Every PU_k also contains a local buffer to prefetch (a portion of) the associated class hypervector C_k in advance to suppress the BRAM's read delay. Additionally, PU includes a pipelined accumulator to sum up and store the results of PEs, to be aggregated with the results of the next $S/2$ dimensions.

Processing Elements (PEs): Each PE contains a predetermined number of multipliers and adders (based on the FPGA size, normally eight fixed-point multipliers). However, the number of PEs in each PU which together with the PopCounters of encoder determine the level of parallelism (value of S), is specified according to the

available FPGA resources. The available resources may be restricted by the power budget, as well. PEs generally perform the similarity check through calculating the dot-product of the query and class hypervectors, though it requires different type of operations for different model precision (different representations of dimensions). Typically, PEs consist of fixed-point multipliers, which we map them to FPGA DSPs. Utilizing power-of-two HD model replaces the multiplications with shift operations in which each dimension of the query $\vec{\mathcal{H}}$ is shifted by the value specified by the corresponding element of the class hypervector. Using binary HD model further simplifies this to element-wise XNOR operations, followed by reduction or population count, in F5-HD XNOR and population count operation is combined and implemented in *XS* LUTs followed by a layer of 6-input population count logic (*P6* LUTs). Therefore, the advantage of a hand-crafted PopCounter gets further noticed in the binarized HD models. To generate HD architectures of different accuracy, F5-HD produces PEs with the specific structure, the template architecture is retained.

In the following, we explain how F5-HD architecture splits the processes during the model initialization, inference, and retraining procedures.

Model Initialization: Model initialization starts with randomly initializing of the class hypervectors as well as generating the orthogonal, base hypervectors. Since model initialization is carried out only once in the entire course of the HD computing, we try to simplify this stage and do not allocate specialized resources. Therefore, we load both the base hypervectors and initial (random) class hypervectors during initial programming of the FPGA. Thereafter, all training input data is encoded and then added to the initial class hypervector. We use the same encoding module used for generating the query hypervectors, which, at each cycle, generates S dimensions of the encoded input vector and adds it back to the corresponding class hypervector using the S-wide adder incorporated in the *model* module (see Figure 4).

Inference: Figure 4 demonstrates the structure of the inference block in F5-HD architecture. The encoded query hypervector $\vec{\mathcal{H}}$ is broadcast to all PUs, each of which shares $S/2$ corresponding dimensions of its prefetched associated class hypervector between its PEs. PUs accumulate the sum-of-the-products to be aggregated with the subsequent segments' results. After processing the entire query hypervector accomplished, i.e., after $\mathcal{D}_{hv}/S$ cycles, the final similarity resultant of each class is obtained by adding the accumulated values of each PU pair. Eventually, the comparator outputs the class index with the greatest similarity metric.

Retraining: Remember from Section 2.1 that during the retraining stage, the HD model performs inference on the same input data

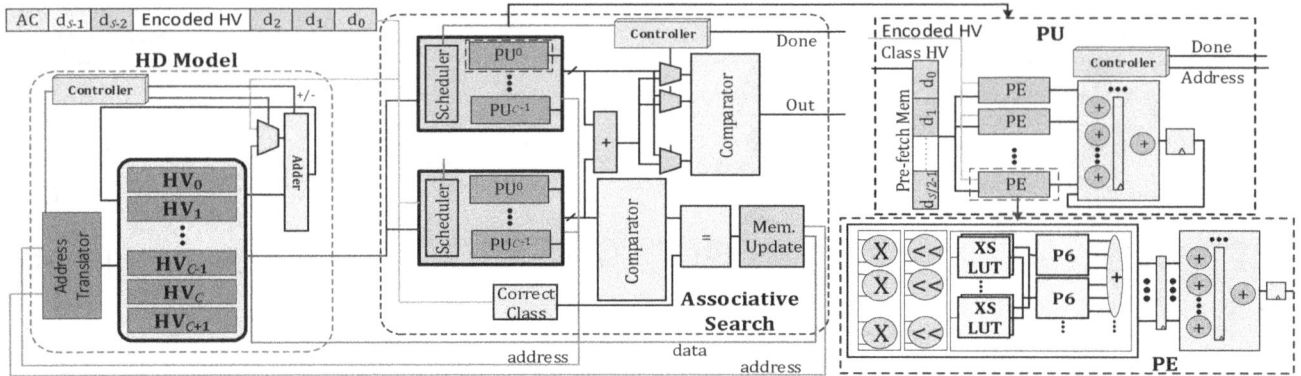

Figure 4: Overview of the HD classification, consisting of HD model, associative search, PUs and PEs structure.

and, in the case of misprediction, updates the necessary classes, i.e., the correct and mispredicted classes. In F5-HD architecture, it is performed by passing the mispredicted query hypervector to the *HD model* module, which adds (subtracts) the query to (from) the correct (mispredicted) class. The correct class index is specified by the label of input data. In summary, retraining involves with inference, followed by a potential model update.

Online Retraining/Inference: In this operating mode, the encoder generates $S/2$ dimensions for the inference, and $S/2$ for the retraining data. Using the upper pairs of PUs (see Figure 4), inference executes by $1/2$ of its typical throughput and takes $2 \times \mathcal{D}_{hv}/s$ per input. The other half of PUs perform retraining, which, as already discussed, includes an inference followed by a potential model update. In the case of a misprediction which demands a model update, the inference should be halted to update the required classes. To avoid this, we have dedicated two additional hypervectors to write the updated classes (hypervectors). Upon a misprediction, the query hypervector will be subtracted from the mispredicted class, which is already being read by the inference module segment by segment, so no additional read overhead will be imposed. Thereafter, the hypervector will be added to the correct class. After updating each of the correct and mispredicted hypervectors, the address translator modifies the physical address of the two classes to point the right hypervector. Note that till the mispredicted classes are updated, the HD model works with the previous classes.

Resource Constraints: As the number of PUs are fixed, the number and size of PEs (i.e., number of multipliers per PE) per each PU affect the level of parallelism in HD computing. This, however, is also restricted by the number and bandwidth of on-chip RAMs as well as the dictated power budget. The following equations summarize the constraint of different resources F5-HD assumes in generating F5-HD architecture.

$$\overbrace{A_{PopCounter} \times S}^{encoding} + \overbrace{2 \times |C| \times \mathcal{N}_{PE} \times A_{PE}}^{Similairty\ checker} < \text{LUT}_{max} \quad (8)$$

$$\overbrace{2 \times |C| \times \mathcal{N}_{PE} \times DSP_{PE}}^{Similairty\ checker} + \overbrace{S}^{model\ updater} < \text{DSP}_{max} \quad (9)$$

$$\frac{\overbrace{|C| \times S \times bitwidth}^{HD\ model\ read\ access} + \overbrace{\mathcal{D}_{iv} \times \ell_{iv}}^{encoding}}{36} < \text{BRAM}_{max} \quad (10)$$

In these equations, A_X denotes the area of module X in terms of number of LUTs, $\mathcal{N}_{PE}$ is the number of PEs in each PU, DSP_{PE} is the number of DSPs per PE (in the case of fixed-point models). We also map the adder of the model updater into DSP blocks, as evident

from Equation 9. Notice that, in the proposed architecture, the computation is limited by BRAM accesses (rather than BRAM memory). Thus, we have assigned the constraint on BRAM bandwidth. It is also noteworthy that our experiments revealed the design is barely routable for LUT utilization rates above ~90%. Hence, LUT$_{max}$ is set to 90% of the device LUTs.

5 EXPERIMENTAL RESULTS

F5-HD is a flexible framework for efficient implementation of different HD computing applications in FPGA hardware, respecting the application specifications and user's requirements. The entire F5-HD software support including user interface and code generation has been implemented in C++ on CPU. The software customizes template blocks to generate an optimized hardware for each application, based on the user's optimization, accuracy, and power preferences. The output of F5-HD framework is an FPGA-mapped implementation of a given HD application in Verilog HDL. We verify the timing and the functionality of the F5-HD by synthesizing it using Xilinx Vivado Design Suite[29]. The synthesized code has been implemented on Kintex-7 FPGA KC705 Evaluation Kit. We used Vivado XPower tool to estimate the device power.

We compare the performance and energy efficiency of F5-HD accelerator running on FPGA with AMD R9 390 GPU and Intel i7 7600 CPU with 16GB memory. For GPU, the HD code is implemented using OpenCL and is optimized for performance. We used Hioki 3334 and AMD CodeXL [30] for the power measurement of CPU and GPU, respectively. We implement F5-HD on three FPGA platforms including Virtex-7 (XC7VX485T), Kintex-7 (XC7k325T), and Spartan-7 (XC7S100) to evaluate the efficacy of F5-HD on various platforms with different available resources, power characteristics and power budget. We evaluate the efficiency of F5-HD on four practical workloads including **Speech Recognition (ISO-LET)** [31]: the goal is to recognize voice audio of the 26 letters of the English alphabet, **Activity Recognition (UCIHAR)** [32]: the objective is to recognize human activity based on 3-axial linear acceleration and 3-axial angular velocity, **Physical Activity Monitoring (PAMAP)** [33]: the goal is to recognize 12 different human activities such as lying, walking, etc., and **Face Detection**: the goal is to detect faces among Caltech 10,000 web faces dataset [34] from negative training images, i.e., non-face images which are selected from CIFAR-100 and Pascal VOS 2012 datasets [35].

5.1 Encoding

Encoding module is used in both training and inference. This encoder works in a pipeline stage with the initial training and associative search (similarity checking) modules. Thus, the more generated

Table 2: The maximum number of generated encoded dimensions per cycle using Kintex FPGA

#Features	64	128	256	432	512
Baseline	975	449	254	128	110
F5-HD	1505	837	481	243	211

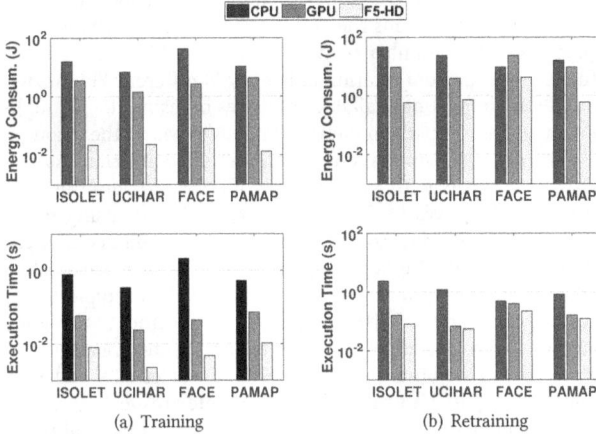

(a) Training　　　　　　　　　　(b) Retraining

Figure 5: Energy consumption and execution time of F5-HD **versus other platforms during (a) training and (b) one epoch of retraining.**

dimensions by the encoding module, the more throughput F5-HD can achieve. To evaluate the effectiveness of our proposed encoding algorithm, we compare the hardware implementation of F5-HD encoding with a baseline HD computing encoding [13].

Table 2 compares the number of generated dimensions per cycle in F5-HD and the baseline encoding modules. In the baseline segmented encoding, to generate S dimensions of the encoded hypervector, we showed that HD architecture needs to read $S + \mathcal{D}_{iv}$ dimensions of each base hypervector, where S and $\mathcal{D}_{iv}$ are the segment length and length of the input hypervector, respectively. In contrast, as we explained in Section 4.1, F5-HD encoding module is implemented using a hardware-friendly permutation as well as LUT-based XNORand PopCount modules that reduces the resource usage. Our evaluation on data points with 64 features shows that F5-HD encoder can provide 1.5× higher throughput as compared to the baseline segmented encoder. This throughput improvement increases to 1.9× for data points with 512 features. This is because the delay of the adder (population counter) dominates as the number of features (hence, the size of the population counter) increases.

5.2　Training

Initial Model Training: HD generates the initial model by a one-time passing through the training dataset. Regardless of the exploited models (viz., binary, power-of-two or fixed-point), in F5-HD we train the HD model using fixed-point operations and eventually we quantize the class hypervectors based on the defined model precision. Figure 5(a) shows the energy consumption and execution time of HD running on Intel i7 CPU, AMD R9 390 GPU, and Kintex-7 FPGA platforms during the initial training. The initial training consists of the encoding module which maps data points into high-dimensional space and hypervectors aggregation which generates a hypervector representing each class. In conventional computing systems, e.g. CPU and GPU, the majority of training time is devoted to the encoding module, since these architectures have not been customized to process binary vectors in 10K dimensions. In contrast,

F5-HD can implement the encoding module effectively using FPGA primitives. Our evaluation shows that F5-HD provides, on average, 86.9× and 7.8× (548.3× and 148.2×) higher energy efficiency and faster training as compared to GPU (CPU) platform, respectively.

Retraining: Similarity checking (a.k.a associative search) is the main contributor to HD energy consumption and execution time during both retraining and inference. In retraining, associative search checks the similarity between a fixed-point query hypervector with all stored class hypervectors using cosine metric. Since the HD encoding is expensive on conventional computing units, in CPU and GPU implementations, the retraining processes on the encoded training data which are already stored in memory. In contrast, due to the efficient F5-HD encoding functionality and in order to reduce the off-chip memory access, F5-HD encodes the training data on every iteration. Figure 5(b) compares the HD computing retraining efficiency on three CPU, GPU, and FPGA platforms. The results are reported for F5-HD retraining on a single epoch. Our evaluation shows that F5-HD provides 1.6× and 10.1× faster computation as compared to GPU and CPU platforms, respectively. Although the GPU performance is comparable to F5-HD, F5-HD provides 7.6× higher energy efficiency due to its lower power consumption.

5.3　Inference

Figure 6 compares the energy consumption and execution time of HD inference running on different platforms. All results are reported for the case of using the fixed-point model. The inference includes the encoding and associative search modules. The encoding module maps a test data into high-dimensional space, while the associative search module checks the similarity of the encoded data to pre-stored class hypervectors. The results show that the efficiency of applications changes depending on the number of features and the number of classes. For applications with a large feature size, F5-HD requires a costly encoding module, while applications with a large number of classes, e.g., ISOLET, devote the majority of the energy/execution time to perform the associative search. Our evaluation shows that F5-HD achieves 11.9× and 1.7× (616.8× and 259.9×) higher energy efficiency and faster inference as compared to GPU (CPU) platform respectively.

F5-HD can have different design choices for inference. Using fixed-point module F5-HD provides the maximum classification accuracy but relatively slower computation. Using binary and power-of-two model, the encoding dominates the F5-HD energy/execution time, while for the fixed-point model the majority of resources are devoted to the associative search. F5-HD removes the multiplications involved in cosine similarity using power-of-two model, resulting in higher computation efficiency. Finally, the binary model is the most efficient F5-HD model, where the similarity check can be performed by using Hamming distance. Figure 7 shows the F5-HD inference efficiency using power-of-two and binary models. All results are normalized to the throughput and throughput/Watt of F5-HD with fixed-point model. For applications with low feature size, e.g., PAMAP, the encoding module maps a large number of data points into high-dimensional space. This makes the associative search a dominant part of inference computation when using fixed-point model. On the other hand, in face detection with a low number of classes and high feature size, the encoding dominates the F5-HD resource and efficiency. Our evaluation shows that F5-HD using binary and power-of-two models can achieve on average 4.3× and 3.1× higher throughput than F5-HD using fixed-point model. In addition, the binary and power-of-two models provide

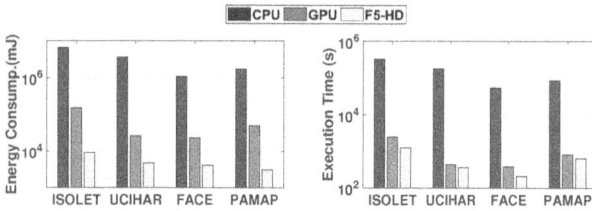

Figure 6: Energy consumption and execution time of HD during inference running on different platforms.

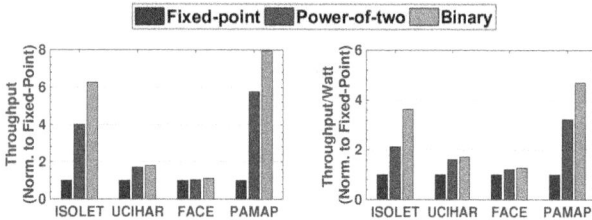

Figure 7: Throughput and throughput/Watt in F5-HD using fixed-point, power-of-two, and binary models.

Table 3: Average resource utilization and power consumption of F5-HD implemented on Kintex

		Fixed-point	Power-of-two	Binary
Resource utilization	LUT	46%	95%	82%
	BRAM	47%	46%	5%
	DSP	89%	26%	29%
Power(W)		9.8	14.8	13.9

2.1× and 1.5× higher throughput/Watt as compared to F5-HD using fixed-point model.

5.4 Resource/Power Utilization

Table 3 lists the average Kintex FPGA resource utilization implementing F5-HD using fixed-point, power-of-two, and binary models. The results are reported for F5-HD supporting both training and inference. Our evaluation shows that the fixed-point model utilizes the majority of the FPGA DSPs in order to perform the similarity check of the inference/retraining. In contrast, with binary and power-of-two models have much lower DSP utilization, as the majority of their inference computation includes bitwise operations that can be efficiently performed using LUTs and the PopCounter. In addition, F5-HD with the binary model has the lowest BRAM utilization as it can store the trained HD model using significantly lower memory size. Table 3 also provides the average power dissipation of the Kintex FPGA. The results indicate that in the fixed-point model, the number of DSPs limits the FPGA throughput, thus F5-HD consumes lower power consumption due to its overall low LUT utilization. In contrast, F5-HD using binary model highly utilizes the available LUTs on the FPGA resulting in high throughput and higher power consumption.

5.5 F5-HD on Different FPGA Platforms

To demonstrate the generality of F5-HD and further investigate its efficiency, we implement it on three different FPGA platforms, mentioned earlier in this section. Figure 8(a) compares the average throughout of F5-HD running different HD applications on these three platforms. Our evaluation shows that Virtex implementing fixed-point model provides 12.0× and 2.5× higher throughput as compared to Spartan and Kintex platforms. The efficiency of Virtex

comes from its large amount of available DSPs (2,800 DSPs with 485K LUTs), which can be used to accelerate associative search. However, F5-HD using power-of-two and binary models mostly exploit LUTs for FPGA implementation, resulting in higher throughput especially on Spartan with few numbers of DSPs. For example, Spartan using binary model can achieve on average 5.2× higher throughput than F5-HD using fixed-point model. It should be noted that in all FPGA platforms the throughput of the binary model is proportional to the number of available LUTs in FPGAs.

To compare the computation efficiency of different FPGAs, we eliminate the impact of available resources by using the throughput/Watt as the comparison metric. Figure 8(b) shows the throughput/Watt of F5-HD implemented in different platforms. As the results show, Virtex with large number of DSPs provides the maximum throughput/Watt when implementing F5-HD using fixed-point model. However, using power-of-two and binary models, Spartan provides the higher computation efficiency since most of F5-HD computation can be processed by LUTs. For example, using the fixed-point model, Virtex can provide 2.0× and 1.5× higher throughput/Watt as compared to Spartan and Kintex, respectively. However, using the binary model, Spartan provides 1.2× and 1.5× higher throughput/Watt than Virtex and Kintex respectively.

The efficiency of different FPGAs also depends on the application, i.e., number of features and classes. For applications with small feature size (e.g., PAMAP), F5-HD can encode a larger amount of data at a time, thus the associative search in inference requires higher number of DSPs and BRAM accesses to parallelize the similarity check. This makes the number of DSPs the bottleneck of computation when using a fixed-point model for PAMAP application. PAMAP using power-of-two model eliminates the majority of DSP utilization required to multiply a query and class hypervector, thus the number of BRAMs becomes the computation bottleneck. These results are more obvious on the Spartan FPGA with limited BRAM blocks.

5.6 Power Budget

As we explained in Section 3, the desired power budget is an input to F5-HD framework that can be dictated by the users before implementation of each application, which impacts the level of parallelism. When the user defines a desired power budget (P_{target}), F5-HD tries to determine the number of PEs per PU such that the implementation satisfies the power constraint. In practice, F5-HD may not precisely guarantee the desired power due to the fact that the number of PEs per PU has discrete values and the size of the application and its power consumption depend on this discrete parameter. Additionally, our initial estimation of the power consumption is according to the logical connectivity of the building blocks and may not accurately estimate the impact of signals power, which is routing-dependent[2]. Therefore, the measured power after implementation (P_{meas}) might have fluctuations around the target power level. Here we define the power fluctuation as $\Delta P = |P_{meas} - P_{target}|/P_{target}$.

Table 4 lists the average throughput (TP) and ΔP after imposing the power budget. The table also shows the normalized throughput under power constraints to the nominal throughput when no power budget is employed. The results are reported for the cases that the power budget is defined as 25% and 50% of maximum power (power of F5-HD running on the same device without power restriction) as the desired power level. Our evaluations show that our framework

---

[2]In practice, we scale the power of the signal based on the measured signal power of a base implementation

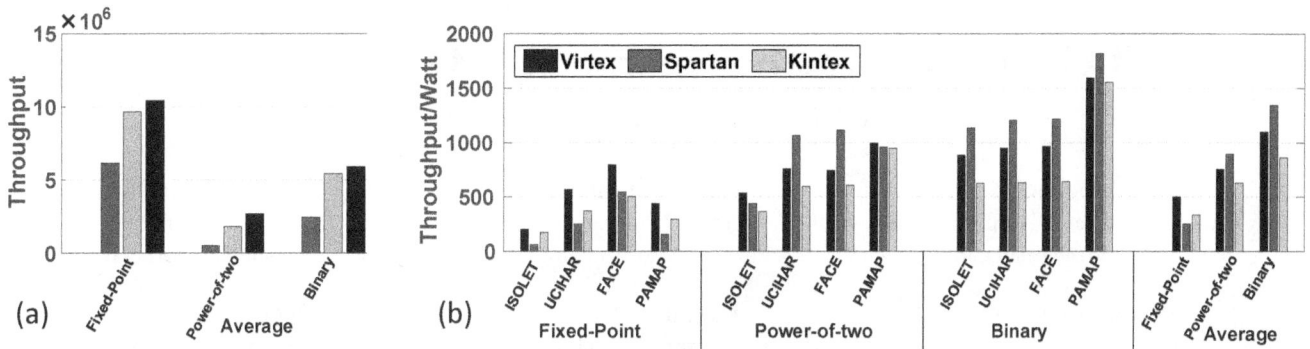

Figure 8: (a) Average throughput of different FPGAs implementing F5-HD with fixed-point, power-of-two, and binary models. (b) Throughput/Watt of F5-HD implementing different applications on FPGA platforms.

Table 4: F5-HD implementation under power constraints.

FPGA model	Power budget	Fixed-point		Power-of-two		Binary	
		TP	ΔP	TP	ΔP	TP	ΔP
Virtex	50%	2.7 (0.44×)	5.2%	5.1 (0.53×)	5.2%	6.3 (0.60×)	2.4%
	25%	1.2 (0.19×)	10.8%	1.6 (0.16×)	7.0%	2.6 (0.25×)	8.0%
Spartan	50%	0.2 (0.38×)	12.8%	0.7 (0.37×)	5.1%	1.0 (0.40×)	5.1%
	25%	0.1 (0.21×)	9.1%	0.3 (0.17×)	16%	0.6 (0.21×)	17%
Kintex	50%	1.0 (0.41×)	5.2%	2.5 (0.45×)	6.8%	4.8 (0.65×)	4.0%
	25%	0.4 (0.18×)	12.1%	1.3 (0.24×)	18%	1.7 (0.25×)	12%

can generate HD accelerator that lays within $\Delta P = 18\%$ of the target power. The power fluctuation becomes large when the targeted power is low as the magnitude of misprediction ($|P_{meas} - P_{target}|$) almost remains the same while the base power P_{target} reduces.

6 CONCLUSION

In this paper, we proposed F5-HD, an automated framework for FPGA-based acceleration of HD computing. F5-HD abstracts away the complexities behind designing hardware accelerators from the user. The proposed framework enables the user to specify the HD application specifications (e.g., the number of input features, classes and training data) as well as the desired classification quality (i.e., accuracy versus performance) and accordingly generates customized FPGA-friendly Verilog implementation. In addition to training and inference, F5-HD supports simultaneous training and inference, hence the accuracy of the HD platform can be enhanced in the field without, without interrupting its operation. We evaluated the efficiency of F5-HD extensively, whereby it showed 86.9× and 7.8× (11.9× and 1.7×) higher energy efficiency improvement and faster training (inference) as compared to an optimized implementation of HD on AMD R9 390 GPU, respectively.

ACKNOWLEDGEMENTS

This work was partially supported by CRISP, one of six centers in JUMP, an SRC program sponsored by DARPA, and also NSF grants #1730158 and #1527034.

REFERENCES

[1] P. Kanerva, "Hyperdimensional computing: An introduction to computing in distributed representation with high-dimensional random vectors," *Cognitive Computation*, vol. 1, no. 2, pp. 139–159, 2009.
[2] P. Kanerva, "Computing with 10,000-bit words," in *Communication, Control, and Computing (Allerton), 2014 52nd Annual Allerton Conference on*, pp. 304–310, IEEE, 2014.
[3] A. Rahimi, P. Kanerva, and J. M. Rabaey, "A robust and energy-efficient classifier using brain-inspired hyperdimensional computing," in *Proceedings of the 2016 International Symposium on Low Power Electronics and Design*, pp. 64–69, ACM, 2016.
[4] F. R. Najafabadi, A. Rahimi, P. Kanerva, and J. M. Rabaey, "Hyperdimensional computing for text classification," in *Design, Automation Test in Europe Conference Exhibition (DATE), University Booth*, pp. 1–1, 2016.
[5] O. J. Räsänen and J. P. Saarinen, "Sequence prediction with sparse distributed hyperdimensional coding applied to the analysis of mobile phone use patterns," *IEEE transactions on neural networks and learning systems*, vol. 27, no. 9, pp. 1878–1889, 2016.

[6] M. Imani, D. Kong, A. Rahimi, and T. Rosing, "Voicehd: Hyperdimensional computing for efficient speech recognition," in *Rebooting Computing (ICRC), 2017 IEEE International Conference on*, pp. 1–8, IEEE, 2017.
[7] F. Montagna, A. Rahimi, S. Benatti, D. Rossi, and L. Benini, "Pulp-hd: accelerating brain-inspired high-dimensional computing on a parallel ultra-low power platform," in *Proceedings of the 55th Annual Design Automation Conference*, p. 111, ACM, 2018.
[8] O. Rasanen and J. Saarinen, "Sequence prediction with sparse distributed hyperdimensional coding applied to the analysis of mobile phone use patterns," *IEEE Transactions on Neural Networks and Learning Systems*, vol. PP, no. 99, pp. 1–12, 2015.
[9] A. Joshi, J. Halseth, and P. Kanerva, "Language geometry using random indexing," *Quantum Interaction 2016 Conference Proceedings*, In press.
[10] Y. Umuroglu, N. J. Fraser, G. Gambardella, M. Blott, P. Leong, M. Jahre, and K. Vissers, "Finn: A framework for fast, scalable binarized neural network inference," in *Proceedings of the ACM/SIGDA International Symposium on Field-Programmable Gate Arrays*, pp. 65–74, ACM, 2017.
[11] S. Salamat, M. Imani, S. Gupta, and T. Rosing, "Rnsnet: In-memory neural network acceleration using residue number system," in *Rebooting Computing (ICRC), 2018 IEEE International Conference on*, pp. 1–10, IEEE, 2018.
[12] A. Rahimi, S. Benatti, P. Kanerva, L. Benini, and J. M. Rabaey, "Hyperdimensional biosignal processing: A case study for emg-based hand gesture recognition," in *Rebooting Computing (ICRC), IEEE International Conference on*, pp. 1–8, IEEE, 2016.
[13] M. Imani, C. Huang, D. Kong, and T. Rosing, "Hierarchical hyperdimensional computing for energy efficient classification," in *Proceedings of the 55th Annual Design Automation Conference*, p. 108, ACM, 2018.
[14] M. Imani, A. Rahimi, D. Kong, T. Rosing, and J. M. Rabaey, "Exploring hyperdimensional associative memory," in *2017 IEEE International Symposium on High-Performance Computer Architecture (HPCA)*, pp. 445–456, IEEE, 2017.
[15] A. DeHon, "The density advantage of configurable computing," *Computer*, vol. 33, no. 4, pp. 41–49, 2000.
[16] S. Salamat, M. R. Azarbad, and B. Alizadeh, "Improve high level synthesis for multi-dimensional nested loops using reshaping and vectorization methods for multi-level non-rectangular nested loop," in *Rebooting Computing (ICRC), 2018 IEEE International Conference on*, pp. 1–10, IEEE, 2018.
[17] M. Schmuck, L. Benini, and A. Rahimi, "Hardware optimizations of dense binary hyperdimensional computing: Rematerialization of hypervectors, binarized bundling, and combinational associative memory," *arXiv preprint arXiv:1807.08583*, 2018.
[18] M. Imani et al., "Low-power sparse hyperdimensional encoder for language recognition," *IEEE Design & Test*, vol. 34, no. 6, pp. 94–101, 2017.
[19] M. Imani et al., "Hdna: Energy-efficient dna sequencing using hyperdimensional computing," in *BHI*, pp. 271–274, IEEE, 2018.
[20] Y. Kim et al., "Efficient human activity recognition using hyperdimensional computing," in *IoT*, p. 38, ACM, 2018.
[21] M. Imani et al., "Fach: Fpga-based acceleration of hyperdimensional computing by reducing computational complexity," in *ASP-DAC*, IEEE, 2019.
[22] M. Imani et al., "A binary learning framework for hyperdimensional computing," in *DATE*, IEEE/ACM, 2019.
[23] M. Imani et al., "Hdcluster: An accurate clustering using brain-inspired high-dimensional computing," in *DATE*, IEEE/ACM, 2019.
[24] T. F. Wu, H. Li, P.-C. Huang, A. Rahimi, J. M. Rabaey, H.-S. P. Wong, M. M. Shulaker, and S. Mitra, "Brain-inspired computing exploiting carbon nanotube fets and resistive ram: Hyperdimensional computing case study," in *Solid-State Circuits Conference-(ISSCC), 2018 IEEE International*, pp. 492–494, IEEE, 2018.
[25] H. Li et al., "Hyperdimensional computing with 3d vrram in-memory kernels: Device-architecture co-design for energy-efficient, error-resilient language recognition," in *Electron Devices Meeting (IEDM), 2016 IEEE International*, pp. 16–1, IEEE, 2016.
[26] S. Gupta et al., "Felix: fast and energy-efficient logic in memory," in *ICCAD*, p. 55, ACM, 2018.
[27] B. Falsafi, B. Dally, D. Singh, D. Chiou, J. Y. Joshua, and R. Sendag, "Fpgas versus gpus in data centers," *IEEE Micro*, vol. 37, no. 1, pp. 60–72, 2017.
[28] "Xilinx power estimator user guide." User Guide, June 2017.
[29] T. Feist, "Vivado design suite," *White Paper*, vol. 5, 2012.
[30] "Amd." http://developer.amd.com/tools-and-sdks/opencl-zone/codexl/.
[31] "Uci machine learning repository." http://archive.ics.uci.edu/ml/datasets/ISOLET.
[32] "Uci machine learning repository." https://archive.ics.uci.edu/ml/datasets/Daily+and+Sports+Activities.
[33] A. Reiss and D. Stricker, "Creating and benchmarking a new dataset for physical activity monitoring," in *Proceedings of the 5th International Conference on PErvasive Technologies Related to Assistive Environments*, p. 40, ACM, 2012.
[34] G. Griffin, A. Holub, and P. Perona, "Caltech-256 object category dataset," 2007.
[35] M. Everingham, S. A. Eslami, L. Van Gool, C. K. Williams, J. Winn, and A. Zisserman, "The pascal visual object classes challenge: A retrospective," *International journal of computer vision*, vol. 111, no. 1, pp. 98–136, 2015.

Efficient and Effective Sparse LSTM on FPGA with Bank-Balanced Sparsity

Shijie Cao*
Harbin Institute of Technology
caoshijie0501@gmail.com

Chen Zhang
Microsoft Research
zhac@microsoft.com

Zhuliang Yao*
Tsinghua University
v-zhuyao@microsoft.com

Wencong Xiao*
Beihang University
v-wencxi@microsoft.com

Lanshun Nie
Harbin Institute of Technology
nls@hit.edu.cn

Dechen Zhan
Harbin Institute of Technology
dechen@hit.edu.cn

Yunxin Liu
Microsoft Research
yunxin.liu@microsoft.com

Ming Wu
Microsoft Research
miw@microsoft.com

Lintao Zhang
Microsoft Research
lintaoz@microsoft.com

ABSTRACT

Neural networks based on Long Short-Term Memory (LSTM) are widely deployed in latency-sensitive language and speech applications. To speed up LSTM inference, previous research proposes weight pruning techniques to reduce computational cost. Unfortunately, irregular computation and memory accesses in unrestricted sparse LSTM limit the realizable parallelism, especially when implemented on FPGA. To address this issue, some researchers propose block-based sparsity patterns to increase the regularity of sparse weight matrices, but these approaches suffer from deteriorated prediction accuracy.

This work presents *Bank-Balanced Sparsity* (BBS), a novel sparsity pattern that can maintain model accuracy at a high sparsity level while still enable an efficient FPGA implementation. BBS partitions each weight matrix row into banks for parallel computing, while adopts fine-grained pruning inside each bank to maintain model accuracy. We develop a 3-step software-hardware co-optimization approach to apply BBS in real FPGA hardware. First, we propose a bank-balanced pruning method to induce the BBS pattern on weight matrices. Then we introduce a decoding-free sparse matrix format, *Compressed Sparse Banks* (CSB), that transparently exposes inter-bank parallelism in BBS to hardware. Finally, we design an FPGA accelerator that takes advantage of BBS to eliminate irregular computation and memory accesses. Implemented on Intel Arria-10 FPGA, the BBS accelerator can achieve 750.9 GOPs on sparse LSTM networks with a batch size of 1. Compared to state-of-the-art FPGA accelerators for LSTM with different compression techniques, the BBS accelerator achieves 2.3 ~3.7x improvement on energy efficiency and 7.0 ~34.4x reduction on latency with negligible loss of model accuracy.

KEYWORDS

FPGA; Deep Neural Networks; LSTM; Weight Pruning; Inference; Bank-Balanced Sparsity

ACM Reference Format:
Shijie Cao, Chen Zhang, Zhuliang Yao, Wencong Xiao, Lanshun Nie, Dechen Zhan, Yunxin Liu, Ming Wu, and Lintao Zhang. 2019. Efficient and Effective Sparse LSTM on FPGA with Bank-Balanced Sparsity. In *The 2019 ACM/SIGDA International Symposium on Field-Programmable Gate Arrays (FPGA '19), February 24–26, 2019, Seaside, CA, USA*. ACM, New York, NY, USA, 10 pages. https://doi.org/10.1145/3289602.3293898

1 INTRODUCTION

Neural networks based on Long Short-Term Memory (LSTM) have been widely used in interactive and latency-sensitive applications such as machine translation, speech recognition and speech synthesis [13, 20, 24]. The size and computational cost of these LSTM models continue to grow in order to achieve better model accuracy. However, the stringent requirement on computational resources makes it challenging to achieve low inference latency for large networks. The most time-consuming part of LSTM inference is *matrix-vector multiplication* (MxV). As the size of the LSTM network grows, MxV cost grows quadratically, thus significantly increasing the inference cost.

Weight pruning is a model compression technique to reduce overall memory and computational costs. Early works [8, 10] discover that removing LSTM weights below a small threshold has negligible impact on model accuracy. By clamping a significant portion of the weights to 0, weight pruning approach converts dense weight matrices to unstructured sparse matrices, thus reducing the computation and memory required to carry out inference.

After pruning, the most significant part of LSTM inference changes from dense MxV to *sparse matrix-vector multiplication* (SpMxV). Though requiring less computation, the irregularity of SpMxV limits the maximum performance and energy efficiency achievable on hardware accelerators [17, 19, 27]. Unstructured sparse matrices cannot efficiently utilize underlying hardware resources due to three reasons: 1) the unbalanced non-zero weights distribution

*Contribution during internship at Microsoft Research.

might cause workload skew among processing elements (PEs); 2) concurrent irregular memory accesses to a dense vector lead to memory access conflicts, which could stall the parallel execution; and 3) sparse matrix representations such as *compressed sparse row* (CSR) use indexes to track non-zero values, which require decoding before computation.

To address these issues, further works [17, 19] suggest using coarser-grained weight pruning methods to induce more structured sparsity patterns for better hardware acceleration. Coarse-grained pruning methods prune weights in the granularity of blocks. From the hardware perspective, blocks of non-zero weights can enable contiguous memory accesses and better utilize parallel computation resources. Unfortunately, it becomes challenging to maintain the same model accuracy when block sparsity is applied. Block sparsity constrains the locality of the non-zero weights, and important weights could be mistakenly pruned, resulting in model accuracy loss. Furthermore, the block size (i.e., pruning granularity) is application-sensitive, making it another hyper-parameter to tune. Existing work often needs to search a range of block sizes to find a trade-off between model accuracy and hardware efficiency [13, 17].

This work presents *Bank-Balanced Sparsity* (BBS), a novel sparsity pattern for pruning LSTM. Bank-balanced pruning splits each weight matrix row into multiple equal-sized banks, and adopts fine-grained pruning to each bank independently to obtain identical sparsity among banks. BBS preserves the unstructured distribution of non-zero weights inside each bank, thus maintaining higher model accuracy than that of block sparsity. Experimental results in Section 6 demonstrate that BBS achieves almost the same model accuracy as unstructured sparsity and significantly outperforms block sparsity when pruning weights at the same sparsity level.

Importantly, BBS is also amenable to FPGA acceleration because it inherently provides a balanced matrix partitioning for parallel computing. We design an FPGA accelerator to take advantage of the benefits of BBS to eliminate the computational overheads existed in unstructured sparsity. Specifically: 1) our accelerator utilizes the intrinsic bank-balanced property in BBS to achieve high parallelism in SpMxV with guaranteed load balance; 2) our accelerator supports concurrent random access requests to vector elements without conflicts in SpMxV by adopting banked scratchpad memory to buffer vectors; 3) to avoid decoding overheads of sparse matrix formats, we introduce a novel format for BBS matrices that is decoding-free in our FPGA accelerator. Notably, the BBS accelerator is highly efficient even for inference with a batch size of 1, by exploiting fine-grained parallelism from a single sample which is challenging for unstructured sparsity.

Overall, this paper makes the following contributions:

(1) We propose Bank-Balanced Sparsity, a novel sparsity pattern that can both maintain model accuracy and enable an efficient FPGA accelerator implementation.

(2) We design an FPGA-based accelerator for BBS that eliminates load-imbalance, irregular memory accesses and decoding overheads, and achieves good efficiency for LSTM inference even at a batch size of 1.

(3) Implemented on Intel Arria-10 FPGA, the BBS accelerator achieves 750.9 GOPs on large LSTMs without batching. Compared to state-of-the-art LSTM FPGA accelerators, we achieve

2.3 ~3.7x improvement on energy efficiency and 7.0 ~34.4x reduction on latency with negligible loss of model accuracy.

2 BACKGROUND

2.1 Long Short-Term Memory.

LSTM is one of the most successful cells used in Recurrent Neural Networks (RNNs) [11]. An LSTM network computes a mapping from an input sequence $X = (x_1, ..., x_T)$ to an output sequence $Y = (y_1, ..., y_T)$ by using the following equations iteratively from $t = 1$ to T:

$$i_t = \sigma(W_{ix}x_t + W_{ir}y_{t-1} + W_{ic}c_{t-1} + b_i) \quad (1)$$

$$f_t = \sigma(W_{fx}x_t + W_{fr}y_{t-1} + W_{fc}c_{t-1} + b_f) \quad (2)$$

$$g_t = \sigma(W_{cx}x_t + W_{cr}y_{t-1} + b_c) \quad (3)$$

$$c_t = f_t \odot c_{t-1} + g_t \odot i_t \quad (4)$$

$$o_t = \sigma(W_{ox}x_t + W_{or}y_{t-1} + W_{oc}c_{t-1} + b_o) \quad (5)$$

$$m_t = o_t \odot h(c_t) \quad (6)$$

$$y_t = W_{ym}m_t \quad (7)$$

where the W terms denote weight matrices, the b terms denote bias vectors. The symbols i, f, o and c are respectively the input gate, forget gate, output gate and cell activation (long-term memory). The $\odot$ operator denotes element-wise multiplication, and the $+$ operator denotes element-wise addition. σ is the logistic activation function and h is the hyperbolic tangent (Tanh) activation function.

Among all operators in LSTM, matrix-vector multiplication (MxV) is the most memory-intensive and computation-intensive operator. The dimensions of x_t, y_t and c_t are often the same, say D. Therefore, the number of weights is $12 \times D^2$. In each step of the inference calculation, the number of operations in MxV is $24 \times D^2$, and the number of operations in element-wise operators (EWOP) is $9 \times D$. As a consequence, accelerating MxV is the key to low latency LSTM inference.

2.2 Weight Pruning

It is widely observed that Deep Neural Networks (DNNs) have a lot of redundancy in weights. Pruning away (forcing to zero) a proper number of unimportant weights won't affect model accuracy. Moreover, weight pruning can reduce the model size and computational complexity for energy efficient hardware acceleration. Deep Compression [9, 10] provides a threshold-based weight pruning technique. This method prunes away small weights whose absolute values are less than a predefined threshold and retrains the remaining weights. Pruning and retraining are iteratively applied to generate the sparse DNN model.

As mentioned in the introduction, unrestricted pruning of weight matrices is unfriendly to hardware acceleration. Further work [17, 19] proposes coarse-grained pruning methods to prune blocks of weights. They pick the maximum magnitude or the average magnitude of the weights within a block as the representative of the entire block. If the representative magnitude is less than a predefined threshold, the entire block will be pruned. However, the pruning granularity affects hardware efficiency as well as model accuracy. Deep neural network designers struggle to balance model accuracy and hardware efficiency.

3 BANK-BALANCED SPARSITY

Our proposed sparsity pattern, *Bank-Balanced Sparsity* (BBS), achieves both high model accuracy and high hardware efficiency. In this section, we first describe the pattern of BBS and the motivation for designing it. Then, we present the detailed bank-balanced pruning algorithm to induce BBS on LSTM weight matrices. Finally, we analyze the pruning effectiveness of BBS in terms of achievable accuracy and sparsity. The efficient hardware acceleration design for BBS will be introduced in the next section.

3.1 Bank-Balanced Sparsity Pattern

For matrices represented in BBS, each matrix row is split into multiple equal-sized banks (i.e., sub-rows), and each bank has the same number of non-zero values. Figure 1 illustrates BBS with an example and compares it with unstructured sparsity and block sparsity. In this example, three sparse matrices with different sparsity patterns are all pruned from the dense example weight matrix in Figure 1(a)) with a sparsity ratio of 50%. Fine-grained pruning globally sorts the weights and prunes the smallest 50% of weights, leading to an unstructured sparse matrix (Figure 1(b)); Coarse-grained pruning induces a block sparse matrix (Figure 1(c)) by setting the block size to 2x2 and the block representative with the block average; Our bank-balanced pruning induces a bank-balanced sparse matrix (Figure 1(d)) by splitting each matrix row into 2 equal-sized banks and applying fine-grained pruning inside each bank independently.

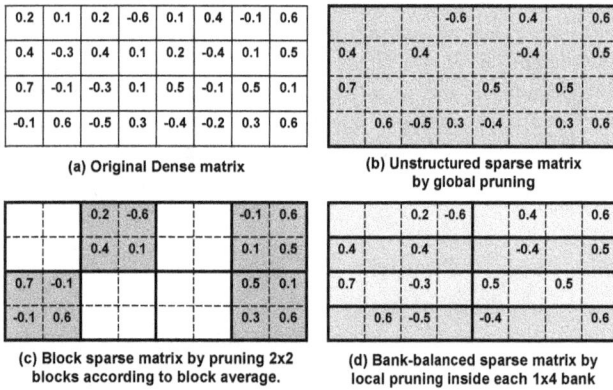

0.2	0.1	0.2	-0.6	0.1	0.4	-0.1	0.6
0.4	-0.3	0.4	0.1	0.2	-0.4	0.1	0.5
0.7	-0.1	-0.3	0.1	0.5	-0.1	0.5	0.1
-0.1	0.6	-0.5	0.3	-0.4	-0.2	0.3	0.6

(a) Original Dense matrix

			-0.6		0.4		0.6
0.4		0.4			-0.4		0.5
0.7				0.5		0.5	
	0.6	-0.5	0.3	-0.4			0.3	0.6

(b) Unstructured sparse matrix by global pruning

		0.2	-0.6			-0.1	0.6
		0.4	0.1			0.1	0.5
0.7	-0.1					0.5	0.1
-0.1	0.6					0.3	0.6

(c) Block sparse matrix by pruning 2x2 blocks according to block average.

		0.2	-0.6			0.4	0.6
0.4		0.4			-0.4		0.5
0.7		-0.3		0.5		0.5	
	0.6	-0.5		-0.4			0.6

(d) Bank-balanced sparse matrix by local pruning inside each 1x4 bank

Figure 1: Comparing BBS with unstructured sparsity and block sparsity by pruning a dense matrix with a sparsity ratio of 50%.

We design this BBS sparsity pattern with consideration of both hardware efficiency and model accuracy. In general, partitioning weight matrix into multiple sub-matrices is mandatory for parallel computing. In BBS, each matrix row is split into multiple banks with the same size and same sparsity. This bank-balanced partitioning enables an efficient SpMxV design to exploit both inter-row parallelism and intra-row parallelism (i.e., inter-bank parallelism) with guaranteed load balance and no vector access conflicts. The detailed SpMxV design for BBS will be described in Section 4.1. In addition, since BBS applies fine-grained pruning within each bank independently, the relatively large weights which contribute more to model accuracy in each bank can be preserved.

Another potential design for a sparsity pattern would be to split weight matrices into 2-D blocks like block sparsity and apply fine-grained pruning within each 2-D block. Larger weights within each block can be preserved as well in this scheme. However, after pruning, each 2-D block is still an unstructured sparse matrix. It is still challenging to design an efficient hardware accelerator architecture due to the irregularity of sparse sub-matrices. For example, parallelizing SpMxV across 2-D blocks leads to concurrent irregular vector accesses.

3.2 Bank-Balanced Pruning Algorithm

To induce BBS on LSTM weight matrices, we adopt a bank-balanced pruning method that prunes each bank independently with the same threshold percentage to obtain the same sparsity ratio among banks.

Algorithm 1 Bank-Balanced Pruning Algorithm

Input:
    The matrix to be pruned, M;
    The number of banks per row, $BankNum$;
    The expected sparsity, $Sparsity$;
Output:
    The pruned matrix, M_p;
1: **for** each $M_i \in M.rows$ **do**
2:     Divide the row M_i into $BankNum$ blocks;
3:     **for** each $bank \in M_i$ **do**
4:         Sort the elements in $bank$;
5:         Calculate the bank internal threshold T in line with $Sparsity$;
6:         **for** each $element \in bank$ **do**
7:             prune $element$ **if** $element < T$;
8:         **end for**
9:     **end for**
10: **end for**
11: **return** the pruned matrix, M_p;

Like previous pruning methods, we apply the bank-balanced pruning method iteratively to a pre-trained network, and fine-tune the network after each pruning iteration to restore the model accuracy. Algorithm 1 illustrates the detailed bank-balanced pruning method to induce BBS on LSTM weight matrices. In each pruning iteration, bank-balanced pruning first partitions each matrix row to multiple equal-sized banks and sorts the weights within each bank by their absolute values. The importance of weights is represented as their bank internal ranking of absolute values. Iteratively, a percentage of weights with the smallest absolute values are pruned. We slowly increase the pruning percentage from 0% to the target sparsity, while the rate of increase decreases with each pruning iteration. During pruning, if the model accuracy drops significantly and cannot be recovered via fine-tuning, we withdraw this pruning iteration and stop the pruning procedure.

3.3 Analysis of Our Pruning Method

Intuitively, a pruning method should remove only smaller weights and preserve larger weights that contribute more to model accuracy. Fine-grained pruning clamps weights of small magnitudes to

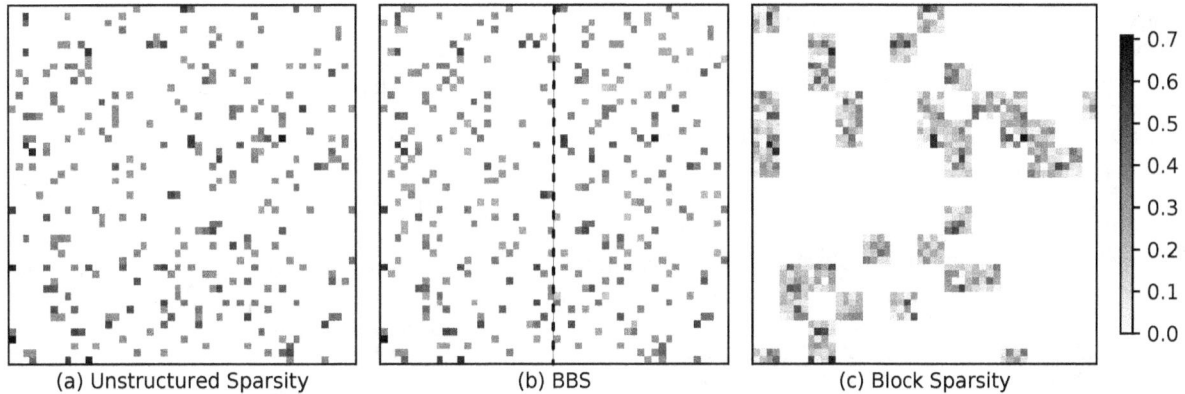

Figure 2: Weight map visualization after pruning with (a) unstructured sparsity, (b) BBS, and (c) block sparsity (sparsity ratio = 90%). These weight maps are 64 × 64 sub-matrices of the whole 1500 × 1500 matrix.

zero and preserves large weights to maintain model accuracy. For bank-balanced pruning, we adopt fine-grained pruning inside banks independently, so large weights inside each bank can be preserved. In contrast, coarse-grained pruning prunes blocks of weights, which constrains the locality of preserved non-zero weights, and therefore some important weights could be mistakenly pruned while some unimportant weights are instead preserved. For the example in Figure 1, the bank-balanced sparse matrix in (d) preserves similar larger weights as the unstructured sparse matrix in (b), but the block sparse matrix in (c) removes some large weights (e.g., 0.4 and 0.5) but preserves some small weights (e.g. 0.1 and -0.1).

Table 1: Percentages of the largest weights that are preserved in various sparsity patterns (sparsity ratio = 90%).

Weight Matrices	Unstructured Sparsity	BBS	Block Sparsity
W_{ix}	100.00%	91.30%	42.76%
W_{fx}	100.00%	81.39%	24.26%
W_{cx}	100.00%	84.45%	24.24%
W_{ox}	100.00%	85.62%	22.97%

To verify the pruning effectiveness of BBS and compare it with unstructured sparsity and block sparsity, we analyze and visualize the weight matrices after corresponding pruning methods in a real LSTM model [28]. The hidden size of this LSTM model is 1500. Table 1 shows the percentage of the largest weights that are preserved in various sparsity patterns. Here we show the results of W_{ix}, W_{fx}, W_{cx} and W_{ox}, other weight matrices have similar results. In this analysis, the sparsity ratios are all 90%, the bank size of BBS is 32 and the block size of block sparsity is 4 × 4. Unstructured sparsity by fine-grained pruning naturally preserves 100% largest weights because it globally prunes weights with smallest magnitudes. BBS preserves more than 80% of the largest weights by fine-grained pruning inside each bank, while block sparsity only preserves less than half of (or even quarter of) the largest weights. Figure 2 visualizes these three kinds of sparse weight matrices of a 64 × 64 sub-matrix which is randomly selected from the whole 1500 × 1500 W_{ix}. Grey grids indicate non-zero parameters and the grey level indicates the magnitude of the absolute value. For the second matrix

represented in BBS, each row has two banks (left and right sides of the dashed line). Each bank has 3 non-zero weights. We can see that the weight map of BBS is very similar to the weight map of unstructured sparsity, but the weight map of block sparsity is quite different because of the locality constraint.

In terms of achievable sparsity and accuracy, experimental results on two typical data sets [7, 18] demonstrate BBS has almost the same effectiveness as unstructured sparsity and outperforms block sparsity, described in Section 6.2.

4 SPARSE MATRIX COMPUTATION AND FORMAT FOR BBS

As mentioned, the irregularity of unstructured sparsity is not hardware friendly due to unbalanced computation, irregular memory accesses and decoding overheads. In contrast, the intrinsic bank-balanced property of BBS enables effective hardware designs to address these issues. For BBS, we introduce a highly parallel SpMxV design with guaranteed load balance and no vector access conflicts, and an associated decoding-free sparse matrix format for the SpMxV design.

4.1 Highly Parallel SpMxV Design

SpMxV consists of multiple dot product operations, one for each sparse matrix row and the dense vector. The standard practice of using multiple PEs to parallelize dot products across matrix rows can reduce computation time. However, irregular memory access patterns of unstructured sparse matrices restrict further parallelism within a dot product.

In addition to inter-row parallelism, BBS enables an efficient SpMxV design to exploit intra-row parallelism (i.e. inter-bank parallelism) through the bank-balance partitioning. Figure 3 illustrates how to exploit inter-bank parallelism in computing a dot product of two vectors (i.e., a BBS matrix row and the dense vector). The multiplications for the non-zero elements inside each bank are performed serially, while the multiplications in different banks are performed in parallel. In this example, the sparse matrix row is divided into 4 banks, as is shown in different colors. The size of each bank is 3 and the sparsity is 1/3. The multiplied dense vector is divided into 4 banks accordingly. Our design computes the dot product of two vectors by accumulating dot products of su vectors whose sizes are all the number of banks (N). Each bar of the sparse matrix row provides one non-zero element to for one sub-vector (e.g., (A, C, E, G)), while dense vector elements a fetched based on the indices of non-zero values to form anoth sub-vector (e.g., (v_0, v_3, v_7, v_9)). For computing a dot product sub-vectors, N pair-wise multiplications are executed in parall Multiple dot products of sub-vectors are calculated in sequent: and accumulated to obtain the dot product of complete vectors.

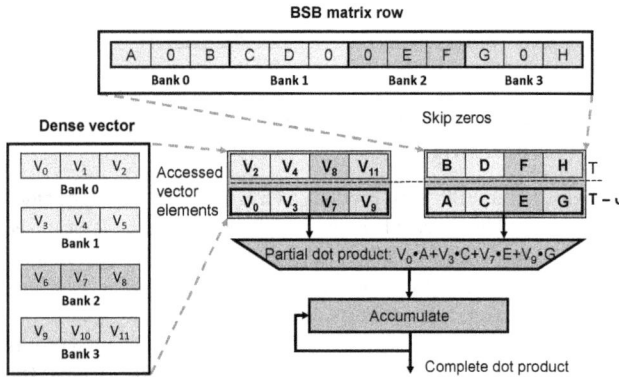

Figure 3: Exploiting inter-bank parallelism in dot product computation of one BBS matrix row and the dense vector.

The bank-balanced property in BBS eliminates load imbalance and irregular memory accesses. In BBS matrices, every row (and every bank) has the same number of elements which automatically guarantees the load balance across rows and banks in SpMxV. When calculating a partial dot product, BBS ensures one and only one element is accessed in each bank. Therefore, storing each vector bank in an independently accessible block RAM can supply vector elements simultaneously with high bandwidth and without memory access conflicts. The detailed FPGA implementation is shown in Section 5.

4.2 Decoding-Free Sparse Matrix Format

Various sparse matrix formats have been proposed to reduce the memory footprint of sparse matrices. However, existing formats introduce decoding overheads when performing sparse matrix multiplications. For FPGA implementation, decoding sparse formats consumes hardware resources and incurs latency. In order to eliminate decoding overheads, we introduce a sparse matrix format called *Compressed Sparse Banks* (CSB) that is specifically designed for BBS.

Compressed Sparse Row (CSR) is a commonly used sparse matrix format [1]. We use CSR as a representative encoding of existing formats for explanation and comparison. Figure 4(a) shows a bank-balanced sparse matrix represented in dense format. Figure 4(b) shows its corresponding CSR encoding. CSR incurs two types of overheads for SpMxV operation. First, CSR format encodes all non-zero elements in a row-major order. Thus, rearranging the non-zero elements are inevitable in order to exploit inter-bank parallelism in SpMxV. Second, CSR format stores column indices and row pointers

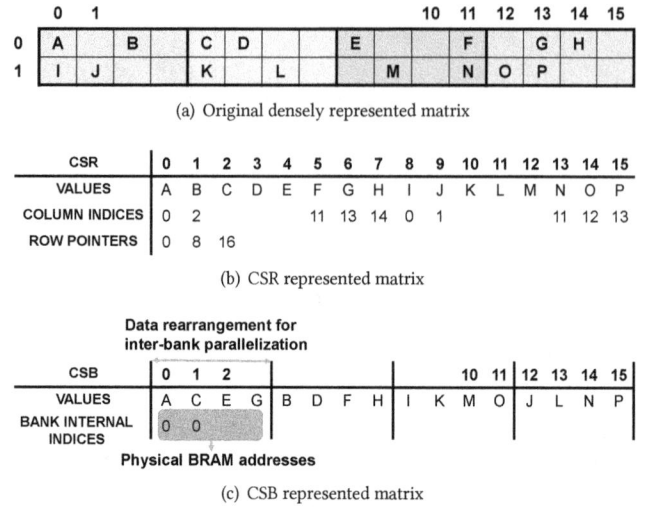

Figure 4: The comparison between CSR and CSB.

to track the location of each non-zero value. Thus, calculating memory addresses is required to fetch vector elements. Other encoding formats, such as CSC and COO have similar limitations [1].

The proposed CSB format takes advantage of the balanced property of BBS and eliminates the need for decoding. Figure 4(c) shows the CSB representation of the corresponding matrix. The CSB encoding uses two arrays to represent a bank-balanced sparse matrix. In the first array (i.e., values), all non-zero values are first arranged in row-major order. Inside each row, the first non-zero elements in each banks (e.g., (A, C, E, G)) are listed first, then the second elements, and so on. The purpose of this data rearrangement is to explicitly expose inter-bank parallelism, thus every successive N elements in CSB can be directly fetched and computed upon in parallel. The second array (i.e., indices) lists the bank internal indexes of non-zero values which are column indices modulo bank size K. When each of the N vector banks is stored in a separate BRAM block on FPGA, the bank internal indices can be directly regarded as physical addresses to fetch the N corresponding vector elements in the BRAM blocks.

5 LSTM ACCELERATOR

In this section, we introduce the BBS accelerator, an FPGA-based accelerator for LSTM networks with bank-balanced pruning. The BBS accelerator is implemented as an accelerator on the PCIe I/O bus to serve LSTM inference requests from the host server. Our design specially accelerates LSTM networks at a batch size of one to reduce inference latency by devoting the on-chip resources to exploiting as much parallelism as possible from one single sample.

5.1 Overall Architecture

Figure 5 shows the overall architecture of the BBS accelerator, which consists of a sparse matrix-vector multiplication unit (SpMxV Unit), an element-wise vector operation unit (EWOP Unit), a direct memory access module (DMA) for load/store operations, on-chip memories for matrices and vectors (Matrix Memory and Vector Memory), and a central controller. Before hardware acceleration, the host

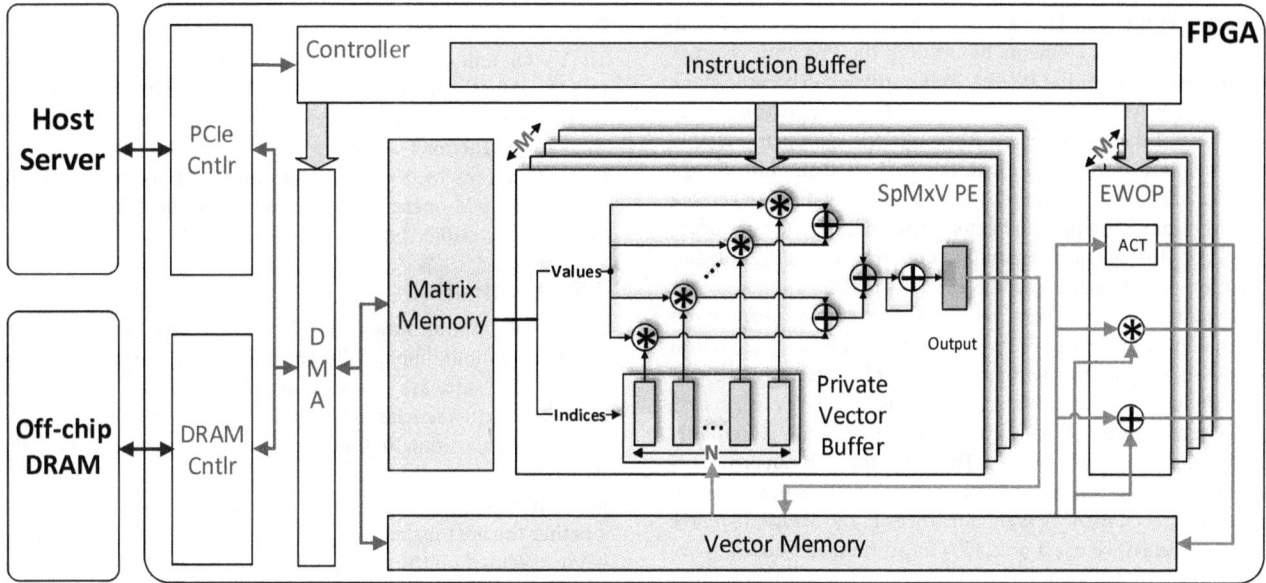

Figure 5: Overall architecture.

server uses the bank-balanced pruning method to prune weight matrices and represents sparse matrices in our proposed Compressed Sparse Banks (CSB) format, then a lightweight compiler generates instructions for the hardware accelerator to accomplish the computation of LSTM. The controller receives and stores instructions from the host server in the instruction buffer and dispatches them to their corresponding modules to execute.

The two important types of instructions are load/store instructions and computational instructions:

Load/Store Instructions. Load/Store instructions are executed in the DMA module to transfer weight matrices and input/output vectors. A load instruction reads data (model weights and inputs) from host memory/off-chip DRAM to on-chip memories. A store instruction writes data (outputs) from on-chip memories to host memory/off-chip DRAM. In practice, in many cases weight pruning can reduce model size enough to fit in on-chip memories. For serving real-time LSTM with low latency, the default mode is to completely rely on on-chip memories. For large models that can not fully fit into on-chip memories even with compression, the BBS accelerator uses load/store instructions to read/write weight matrices from/to off-chip DRAM.

Computational Instructions. As introduced in Section 2, all operations in sparse LSTM can be put into 2 categories: SpMxV and EWOP (including addition, multiplication and three kinds of activations). Therefore, we design two kinds of computational instruction: SpMxV instruction and EWOP instruction to fulfill LSTM computation. The SpMxV instruction is executed in the SpMxV unit to read the required matrix and vector from on-chip memories, then compute dot products for matrix rows, and finally write the result vector back to the vector memory. The EWOP instruction is executed in the EWOP unit to read required vector(s) from the vector memory and write the resulting vector of element-wise addition/multiplication/activations back to the vector memory.

5.2 SpMxV Unit

The SpMxV unit implements the highly parallel design described in Section 4.1. The SpMxV unit consists of M parallel processing elements (PEs) that compute dot products of distinct matrix rows and the dense vector concurrently to exploit inter-row parallelism, while each PE is designed to exploit intra-row (i.e., inter-bank) parallelism in a single dot product operation.

In the center of Figure 5, we show the detailed architecture of a PE. Each PE contains a private vector buffer (PVB) to buffer the dense vector being multiplied, because vector elements are randomly accessed multiple times for all matrix rows in SpMxV. The PE computes the dot product of two vectors by accumulating dot products of sub vectors. This computation includes 5 steps: (1) The PE reads N matrix row elements from the matrix memory and N vector elements based on the sparse indices from the private vector buffer. (2) N multipliers operate simultaneously to obtain N scalar products. (3) An N-input adder tree sums N scalar products to calculate the partial dot product. (4) One more accumulator is used to obtain the complete dot product. (5) The dot product result is written back to global vector memory. The PE is fully pipelined so that one operation can be processed per clock cycle.

With M PEs and N multipliers per PE, this PE array achieves $M \times N$ parallelism for a single SpMxV operation.

5.3 Private Vector Buffer

In each SpMxV PE, N weight elements can be simultaneously accessed in one clock cycle because non-zero values have already been rearranged by CSB encoding format and contiguously stored in matrix memory. However, to access dense vector elements, the PVB needs to support N random memory accesses concurrently. Each BRAM in FPGA provides only two read and/or write ports. Using a single BRAM to buffer dense vectors can not supply N elements from random addresses concurrently. Multi-pumping [25] and vector replication [14] are two alternative solutions. Multi-pumping supplies N elements by running the PEs with N times lower frequency than the BRAM. This approach decreases clock rate significantly. Vector replication provides more ports by creating replicas of the entire vector. Although this approach is simple to implement, it is difficult to scale due to limited on-chip storage resources in FPGA and generally large input/output/state vectors in LSTM. Since each private vector buffer has stored a replicate of the multiplied vector for parallel computing across PEs, further replicating vectors inside each PE is unacceptable.

In order to support random vector accesses at a high bandwidth without replicas inside a PE, we adopt the banking approach to buffer vectors [5]. In this approach, the multiplied vector is also split into banks according to the bank partitioning of matrix rows in BBS. As shown in Figure 6, N banks of vector elements are stored in N independently accessible BRAMs. Therefore, the PVB can provide N elements simultaneously with N bank internal indices (i.e., physical addresses for each BRAM). Weight matrices in LSTMs usually have the same size, so we use a unified N in pruning and configure N as the number of BRAMs in PVB. However, for some LSTMs that have weight matrices of different sizes, different Ns are selected in pruning to find an optimal sparsity, and the largest N is configured

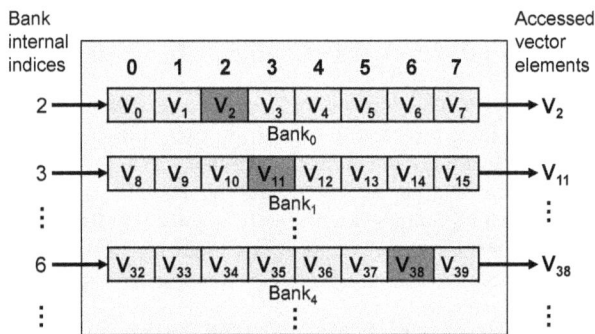

Figure 6: Banked private vector buffer.

In some studies, banking is adopted to support random memory accesses to achieve high memory bandwidth [5, 31]. However, due to the irregularity of data accesses, banked memory cannot handle imbalance workloads across banks and concurrent access requests to the same BRAM. Addressing these issues requires additional logic and clock cycles [5, 31]. The biggest difference of our banked private vector buffer is that balanced memory access requests and no memory access conflicts are automatically guaranteed because of the intrinsic bank-balanced property of BBS. The SpMxV PE accesses one and only one element in each BRAM per cycle.

Before a SpMxV operation, the vector to be multiplied requires to be duplicated in each PE's private vector memory to exploit inter-row parallelism. This brings new challenges. First, broadcasting vector elements to various PEs leads to high fan-out and thus results in a low achievable clock frequency. We use a systolic array structure to achieve high clock frequency, similar to [22]. The second is the additional access latency. We double-buffer the private vector buffer for pipelined data transfer and computation.

5.4 EWOP Unit

The EWOP unit performs various element-wise operations on vectors based on the instruction opcode. Vector addition and multiplication generate one result vector by reading two source vectors. Activation functions only read one source vector and apply nonlinear functions to it to generate one result vector. The EWOP unit contains M operators operating in parallel for each kind of operations to reduce latency.

5.5 Controller

In the computation flow of LSTM, some SpMxV operations and EWOP operations among different gates can be performed simultaneously. The software compiler analyzes the dependencies and indicates the dependencies to instructions. The controller parallelizes instructions according to their dependent instructions indicated by the software compiler. When the SpMxV unit or the EWOP unit is idle (which means an instruction is finished), the controller checks whether the next instruction has a dependency on the instruction being executed on the other unit. If not, the controller dispatches the next instruction to the idle unit, so that the SpMxV unit and EWOP unit can work simultaneously.

6 EVALUATION

Our evaluation centers around two aspects: the model accuracy of BBS and the hardware efficiency of BBS accelerator.

6.1 Experimental Setup

We implemented the BBS accelerator in System Verilog, synthesized with Quartus Prime 17.1, and evaluated on a custom FPGA PCIe card with an Intel-Arria 10 FPGA [3]. The FPGA has 4 GB DDR3-1600 DRAM external memory. The host CPU is an Intel Xeon E5 2650 processor which is only responsible for data pre-processing and result collecting. The FPGA communicates with the host CPU through a PCIe Gen 3x8 bus, which supports up to 16 GB/s bidirectional bandwidth.

We evaluate the system with an LSTM language model of the PTB dataset [18] and an LSTM speech recognition model of the TIMIT dataset [7]. PTB dataset is widely used in Natural Language Processing (NLP) research. It consists of 929k training words, 73k validation words, and 82k test words and it has 10k words in its vocabulary. We adopt the LSTM model in [28], which achieves very good quality on the PTB dataset. The small model has 200 hidden units per layer, while the medium one has 650 and the large one has 1,500. The TIMIT corpus is designed to provide speech data for acoustic-phonetic studies. It contains broadband recordings of 630 speakers of eight major dialects of American English, each reading ten phonetically rich sentences. For the LSTM speech recognition model, we set the input size to 153, the hidden size to 1024, and projection size to 512 which are consistent with previous studies [8, 21].

6.2 BBS Model Accuracy

6.2.1 Comparison with Unstructured and Block Sparsity. We first evaluate the model accuracy of BBS and compare it with unstructured sparsity and block sparsity. Figure 7 and Figure 8 show the sparsity-accuracy trade-off results of various sparsity patterns on PTB and TIMIT data sets, respectively. We use 64 banks in BBS and 4×4 blocks in block sparsity. For experiments of the LSTM language model, we use the large model with the hidden size of 1,500. Perplexity is a metric to quantify language model quality. As shown in Figure 7, the perplexity curve of our BBS is very close to the perplexity curve of unstructured sparsity. Both unstructured sparsity and BBS can preserve the perplexity until 80% of weights are pruned away. These two patterns even achieve slightly better model accuracy at around 60% sparsity compared to the dense baseline one. The perplexity of block sparsity starts to increase significantly at 40% sparsity. Experiments on the LSTM speech recognition model show similar results (shown in Figure 8). BBS and unstructured sparsity can achieve 90% sparsity without accuracy loss, while block sparsity can only achieve 70% sparsity. These experimental results demonstrate that BBS has almost the same effectiveness as random sparsity and outperforms block sparsity in terms of achievable accuracy or sparsity during pruning.

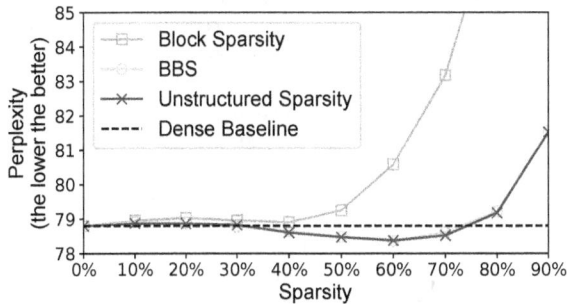

Figure 7: Sparsity-Perplexity trade-off of various sparsity patterns on PTB dataset.

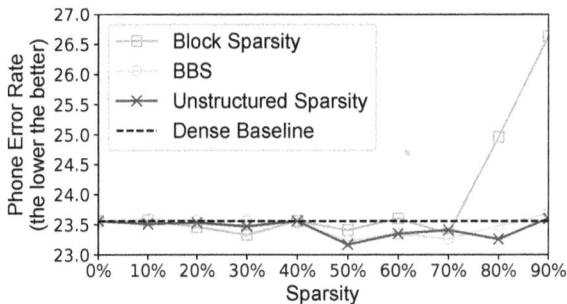

Figure 8: Sparsity - Phone Error Rate trade-off of various sparsity patterns on TIMIT dataset.

6.2.2 Sensitivity to Bank Size. We further explore the accuracy sensitivity of BBS to the bank size. As a comparison, we also explore the accuracy sensitivity of block sparsity to the block size. Table 2 shows the model accuracy at varying block/bank sizes for the large LSTM language model. As shown, BBS achieves almost the same model accuracy regardless of the change of bank size. For block sparsity, however, increasing the block size adversely affects model accuracy.

6.2.3 Quantization on Pruned Model. Quantization can achieve more compression rate and hardware efficiency for deep learning models by reducing the number of bits that represents a weight [9, 15]. In this work, we study the accuracy sensitivity of BBS to

Table 2: Perplexity sensitivity to the block size in block sparsity and the bank size in BBS.

Model		Perplexity on Sparsity		
		60%	70%	80%
Block Sparsity	block size: 4×4	80.6	83.2	88.1
	block size: 8×8	82.4	86.4	95.2
	block size: 16×16	83.7	88.3	99.5
BBS	bank size: 25	78.3	78.6	79.4
	bank size: 50	78.4	78.7	79.2
	bank size: 100	78.4	78.6	79.2

quantization bits. We apply the linear quantization method to LSTM models after bank-balanced pruning with 16-bit, 8-bit, and 4-bit fixed points. Both weights and activations are quantized. Table 3 shows the effects of quantization under different bits on the large LSTM language model after bank-balanced pruning. The perplexity is 78.8 for the original dense model and slightly increases to 79.2 after pruning away 80% weights with BBS. 16-bit quantization on the pruned model maintains the same perplexity, while more aggressive quantization deteriorates perplexity.

Table 3: Language model perplexity after quantization under different bits.

Quantization Scheme	Perplexity (%)
float-32 dense model	78.8
float-32 BBS model	79.2
fixed-16 BBS model	79.2
fixed-8 BBS model	79.8
fixed-4 BBS model	143.1

6.3 BBS Accelerator Efficiency

6.3.1 Resource Utilization, Clock Rate and Power Consumption. Table 4 shows the resource utilization, clock rate and power consumption of our BBS accelerators. The reported results are based on post-fit results from Quartus Prime 17.1. The operator bits (i.e., data precision) is 16-bit since 16-bit is accurate enough to maintain model accuracy. The BBS accelerator sets to M = 64, N = 64, and thus the accelerator contains 64 PEs in the SpMxV unit, and each PE has 64 multipliers executing in parallel. The Intel Arria 10 FPGA contains 1518 DSPs which can be implemented as 3036 multipliers. The LSTM accelerator fully utilizes DSPs for multipliers, and use additional ALMs for extra multipliers. We use M20Ks for the matrix memory, and use MLABs for the private vector buffer because it consists of relatively small memories that require independently accessible ports.

Table 4: Resource utilization, clock rate and power consumption.

ALMs (%)	M20Ks (%)	DSPs (%)
289k (68%)	2509 (92%)	1518 (100%)
Clock Rate (MHz)		Power (Watt)
200		19.1

6.3.2 Latency and Throughput. Our accelerator is highly efficient even with a batch size of 1, so we measure the latency of our BBS accelerator without batching and calculate the corresponding throughput. For small, medium and large LSTM language models on the PTB data set, we also use three different numbers of banks (16,32,64) to prune models. Pruning away 80% weights incurs no effect on model accuracy. Table 5 shows the latency of one LSTM and its corresponding throughput. The achievable performance increases as the model scale or the number of bank increases because of higher hardware utilization of the underlying PEs. In the case of the large model with 1,500 hidden units and using 64 banks in matrix partitioning, our accelerator takes 4.8us to finish a whole LSTM layer, corresponding to 750.9 GOPS at a batch size of one.

Table 5: Latency and throughput results of running LSTM language networks of various scales and various numbers of banks.

LSTM hidden size	Num of banks	Latency (us)	Throughput (GOPS)
200 (small)	16	1.7	37.3
	32	1.4	43.4
	64	1.3	47.4
650 (medium)	16	4.3	158.8
	32	2.8	238.0
	64	2.1	318.5
1500 (large)	16	13.9	257.7
	32	7.8	458.5
	64	4.8	**750.9**

6.3.3 Comparison with state-of-the-art LSTM Accelerators. We compare the performance of our BBS accelerator with three state-of-the-art LSTM accelerators on FPGA: ESE [8], C-LSTM [21] and DeltaRNN [6]. These three studies adopt different optimization techniques to reduce computation requirements. ESE [8] uses the weight pruning based compression technique and improve inference efficiency through batching multiple samples, but lacks optimization of irregular memory accesses to reduce latency for a single batch request. C-LSTM [21] represents weight matrices with block-circulant matrices and proposes an accelerator with an FFT-based computing kernel. DeltaRNN [6] uses the delta network algorithm to reduce MxV operations and corresponding weight fetches by skipping dispensable neuron activation changes below a threshold.

Table 6 shows the comparison results. We apply BBS to the same LSTM model on the TIMIT dataset as ESE and C-LSTM adopt. We use the accuracy and performance numbers of ESE, C-LSTM and GRU reported in their papers. The performance numbers of DeltaRNN are based on GRU which is an optimistic estimation because GRU is simpler than LSTM. With the same model on the same data set, BBS achieves comparable compression rate and model accuracy as ESE and C-LSTM. While our BBS accelerator achieves 2.3x and 3.7x improvement on energy efficiency, and 34.4x and 7.0x speedup on latency (or throughput at a batch size of one) compared to ESE and C-LSTM. The reason why BBS accelerator can achieve better single batch performance than ESE is that it enables the extra

dimension of parallelism and addresses the low memory bandwidth issue of irregular memory access in SpMxV.

7 RELATED WORK

Network Compression. Network compression can reduce the memory and computation requirements of a neural network, increase its inference speed and save energy [9]. Compression algorithms mainly include pruning [10], sparsity-inducing regularization [23], quantization [15]. Based on the original sparsity method, further studies propose structured sparsity methods by adding constraints on the locality of non-zero weights [17, 19, 26]. Structured sparsity is more amenable to hardware acceleration compared to unstructured sparsity.

DNN accelerators. Hardware acceleration of DNNs has received significant attention from both industry and academia [4, 12, 16, 29]. Due to the widely adopted pruning-based compression techniques, many accelerators for sparse neural networks are proposed [8, 21, 30]. These works explored specialized sparse matrix multiplication module that directly operates on sparse neural networks. Although these accelerators achieve higher performance than general processors, the irregular computation and memory accesses in sparse neural networks still restrict the maximum parallelism achievable on customized accelerators.

SpMxV accelerators. SpMxV is most computation-intensive and memory-intensive part in LSTM inference. Many FPGA and GPU accelerators for SpMxV have been proposed [2, 5]. However, SpMxV is hard to optimize due to its irregular memory access characteristics. By contrast, neural network pruning methods bring a restricted freedom to define the sparsity structure (e.g. hardware friendly sparsity) in weight matrices. BBS is a kind of structured sparsity pattern that increases hardware efficiency, while incurs negligible loss on model accuracy.

8 CONCLUSION

This paper proposes a novel sparsity pattern, BBS (bank-balanced sparsity), that achieves both high model accuracy for pruning LSTM and high hardware efficiency on FPGA. Our insight into designing BBS is partitioning weight matrix rows into banks for parallel computing and adopting fine-grained pruning inside each bank to maintain model accuracy. Evaluated on speech recognition and language model tasks, BBS achieves almost the same model accuracy as purely unstructured sparsity at various sparsity levels. Our BBS accelerator on FPGA takes advantage of the intrinsic bank-balanced property of BBS, achieving high efficiency even for a batch size of 1. Compared to state-of-the-art FPGA accelerators for LSTM with different compression techniques, BBS accelerator achieves 2.3 ~3.7x improvement on energy efficiency and 7.0 ~34.4x reduction on latency with negligible loss of model accuracy.

9 ACKNOWLEDGEMENTS

We would like to thank Ningyi Xu, Wenqiang Wang, Bojie Li and Yun Wang for all technical discussions and valuable suggestions on improving this paper. We thank the anonymous reviewers for their insightful feedbacks and comments. Shijie Cao was partly supported by National Nature Science Foundation of China (No.61772159).

Table 6: Speedup comparison with state-of-the-art LSTM accelerators

	ESE[8]	C-LSTM[21]	DeltaRNN[6]	Ours
Platform	XCKU060	Virtex-7	XC7Z100	Arria 10 GX1150
Frequency (MHz)	200	200	125	200
Sparsity (%)	88.7	87.5	-	87.5
Quantization	fixed-12	fixed-16	fixed-16	fixed-16
Accuracy Degradation	0.30%	0.32%	-	0.25%
Throughput (GOPS)	282.2	131.1	192.0	304.1
Power (W)	41.0	22.0	7.3	19.1
Energy Efficiency (GOPS/W)	6.9	6.0	26.3	15.9
Latency(us)	82.7	16.7	-	**2.4**
Throughput at batch 1 (GOPS)	8.8	43.7	192.0	**304.1**
Effective Throughput at batch 1 (GOPS)	79.2	349.6	1198.0	**2432.8**

REFERENCES

[1] 2018. Sparse Matrix Formats. https://docs.scipy.org/doc/scipy/reference/sparse.html/. (2018).

[2] Nathan Bell and Michael Garland. 2008. *Efficient sparse matrix-vector multiplication on CUDA*. Technical Report. Nvidia Technical Report NVR-2008-004, Nvidia Corporation.

[3] Adrian M Caulfield, Eric S Chung, Andrew Putnam, Hari Angepat, Jeremy Fowers, Michael Haselman, Stephen Heil, Matt Humphrey, Puneet Kaur, Joo-Young Kim, and others. 2016. A cloud-scale acceleration architecture. In *The 49th Annual IEEE/ACM International Symposium on Microarchitecture*. IEEE Press, 7.

[4] Jeremy Fowers, Kalin Ovtcharov, Michael Papamichael, Todd Massengill, Ming Liu, Daniel Lo, Shlomi Alkalay, Michael Haselman, Logan Adams, Mahdi Ghandi, and others. 2018. A Configurable Cloud-Scale DNN Processor for Real-Time AI. In *2018 ACM/IEEE 45th Annual International Symposium on Computer Architecture (ISCA)*. IEEE.

[5] Jeremy Fowers, Kalin Ovtcharov, Karin Strauss, Eric S Chung, and Greg Stitt. 2014. A high memory bandwidth fpga accelerator for sparse matrix-vector multiplication. In *Field-Programmable Custom Computing Machines (FCCM), 2014 IEEE 22nd Annual International Symposium on*. IEEE, 36–43.

[6] Chang Gao, Daniel Neil, Enea Ceolini, Shih-Chii Liu, and Tobi Delbruck. 2018. DeltaRNN: A Power-efficient Recurrent Neural Network Accelerator. In *Proceedings of the 2018 ACM/SIGDA International Symposium on Field-Programmable Gate Arrays*. ACM, 21–30.

[7] John S Garofolo, Lori F Lamel, William M Fisher, Jonathan G Fiscus, and David S Pallett. 1993. DARPA TIMIT acoustic-phonetic continous speech corpus CD-ROM. NIST speech disc 1-1.1. *NASA STI/Recon technical report n* 93 (1993).

[8] Song Han, Junlong Kang, Huizi Mao, Yiming Hu, Xin Li, Yubin Li, Dongliang Xie, Hong Luo, Song Yao, Yu Wang, and others. 2017. Ese: Efficient speech recognition engine with sparse lstm on fpga. In *Proceedings of the 2017 ACM/SIGDA International Symposium on Field-Programmable Gate Arrays*. ACM, 75–84.

[9] Song Han, Huizi Mao, and William J Dally. 2015. Deep compression: Compressing deep neural networks with pruning, trained quantization and huffman coding. *arXiv preprint arXiv:1510.00149* (2015).

[10] Song Han, Jeff Pool, John Tran, and William Dally. 2015. Learning both weights and connections for efficient neural network. In *Advances in neural information processing systems*. 1135–1143.

[11] Sepp Hochreiter and Jürgen Schmidhuber. 1997. Long short-term memory. *Neural computation* 9, 8 (1997), 1735–1780.

[12] Norman P Jouppi, Cliff Young, Nishant Patil, David Patterson, Gaurav Agrawal, Raminder Bajwa, Sarah Bates, Suresh Bhatia, Nan Boden, Al Borchers, and others. 2017. In-datacenter performance analysis of a tensor processing unit. In *Proceedings of the 44th Annual International Symposium on Computer Architecture*. ACM, 1–12.

[13] Nal Kalchbrenner, Erich Elsen, Karen Simonyan, Seb Noury, Norman Casagrande, Edward Lockhart, Florian Stimberg, Aaron van den Oord, Sander Dieleman, and Koray Kavukcuoglu. 2018. Efficient Neural Audio Synthesis. *arXiv preprint arXiv:1802.08435* (2018).

[14] Charles Eric LaForest, Ming G Liu, Emma Rae Rapati, and J Gregory Steffan. 2012. Multi-ported memories for FPGAs via XOR. In *Proceedings of the ACM/SIGDA international symposium on Field Programmable Gate Arrays*. ACM, 209–218.

[15] Darryl Lin, Sachin Talathi, and Sreekanth Annapureddy. 2016. Fixed point quantization of deep convolutional networks. In *International Conference on Machine Learning*. 2849–2858.

[16] Shaoli Liu, Zidong Du, Jinhua Tao, Dong Han, Tao Luo, Yuan Xie, Yunji Chen, and Tianshi Chen. 2016. Cambricon: An instruction set architecture for neural networks. In *ACM SIGARCH Computer Architecture News*, Vol. 44. IEEE Press, 393–405.

[17] Huizi Mao, Song Han, Jeff Pool, Wenshuo Li, Xingyu Liu, Yu Wang, and William J Dally. 2017. Exploring the regularity of sparse structure in convolutional neural networks. *arXiv preprint arXiv:1705.08922* (2017).

[18] Mitchell Marcus, Beatrice Santorini, Mary Ann Marcinkiewicz, and Ann Taylor. 1999. Treebank-3 LDC99T42. *CD-ROM. Philadelphia, Penn.: Linguistic Data Consortium* (1999).

[19] Sharan Narang, Eric Undersander, and Gregory Diamos. 2017. Block-Sparse Recurrent Neural Networks. *arXiv preprint arXiv:1711.02782* (2017).

[20] Haşim Sak, Andrew Senior, and Françoise Beaufays. 2014. Long short-term memory recurrent neural network architectures for large scale acoustic modeling. In *Fifteenth annual conference of the international speech communication association*.

[21] Shuo Wang, Zhe Li, Caiwen Ding, Bo Yuan, Qinru Qiu, Yanzhi Wang, and Yun Liang. 2018. C-LSTM: Enabling Efficient LSTM using Structured Compression Techniques on FPGAs. In *Proceedings of the 2018 ACM/SIGDA International Symposium on Field-Programmable Gate Arrays*. ACM, 11–20.

[22] Xuechao Wei, Cody Hao Yu, Peng Zhang, Youxiang Chen, Yuxin Wang, Han Hu, Yun Liang, and Jason Cong. 2017. Automated systolic array architecture synthesis for high throughput CNN inference on FPGAs. In *Design Automation Conference (DAC), 2017 54th ACM/EDAC/IEEE*. IEEE, 1–6.

[23] Wei Wen, Chunpeng Wu, Yandan Wang, Yiran Chen, and Hai Li. 2016. Learning structured sparsity in deep neural networks. In *Advances in Neural Information Processing Systems*. 2074–2082.

[24] Yonghui Wu, Mike Schuster, Zhifeng Chen, Quoc V Le, Mohammad Norouzi, Wolfgang Macherey, Maxim Krikun, Yuan Cao, Qin Gao, Klaus Macherey, and others. 2016. Google's neural machine translation system: Bridging the gap between human and machine translation. *arXiv preprint arXiv:1609.08144* (2016).

[25] Hasan Erdem Yantir, Salih Bayar, and Arda Yurdakul. 2013. Efficient implementations of multi-pumped multi-port register files in FPGAs. In *Digital System Design (DSD), 2013 Euromicro Conference on*. IEEE, 185–192.

[26] Zhuliang Yao, Shijie Cao, and Wencong Xiao. 2018. Balanced Sparsity for Efficient DNN Inference on GPU. *arXiv preprint arXiv:1811.00206* (2018).

[27] Jiecao Yu, Andrew Lukefahr, David Palframan, Ganesh Dasika, Reetuparna Das, and Scott Mahlke. 2017. Scalpel: Customizing dnn pruning to the underlying hardware parallelism. In *Proceedings of the 44th Annual International Symposium on Computer Architecture*. ACM, 548–560.

[28] Wojciech Zaremba, Ilya Sutskever, and Oriol Vinyals. 2014. Recurrent neural network regularization. *arXiv preprint arXiv:1409.2329* (2014).

[29] Chen Zhang, Peng Li, Guangyu Sun, Yijin Guan, Bingjun Xiao, and Jason Cong. 2015. Optimizing fpga-based accelerator design for deep convolutional neural networks. In *Proceedings of the 2015 ACM/SIGDA International Symposium on Field-Programmable Gate Arrays*. ACM, 161–170.

[30] Shijin Zhang, Zidong Du, Lei Zhang, Huiying Lan, Shaoli Liu, Ling Li, Qi Guo, Tianshi Chen, and Yunji Chen. 2016. Cambricon-X: An accelerator for sparse neural networks. In *Microarchitecture (MICRO), 2016 49th Annual IEEE/ACM International Symposium on*. IEEE, 1–12.

[31] Shijie Zhou, Rajgopal Kannan, Yu Min, and Viktor K Prasanna. 2018. FASTCF: FPGA-based Accelerator for STochastic-Gradient-Descent-based Collaborative Filtering. In *Proceedings of the 2018 ACM/SIGDA International Symposium on Field-Programmable Gate Arrays*. ACM, 259–268.

Cloud-DNN: An Open Framework for Mapping DNN Models to Cloud FPGAs

Yao Chen[1], Jiong He[1], Xiaofan Zhang[2], Cong Hao[2], Deming Chen[1,2]

[1]Advanced Digital Sciences Center, Singapore

[2]University of Illinois at Urbana-Champaign, IL, USA

{yao.chen, Jiong.he}@adsc-create.edu.sg, {xiaofan3, congh, dchen}@illinois.edu

ABSTRACT

The efficacy and effectiveness of Convolutional Neural Networks (CNNs) have been proven in a wide range of machine learning applications. However, the high computational complexity of CNNs presents a critical challenge towards their broader adoption in real-time and power-efficient scenarios. FPGAs are poised to take a significant role for high-performance and energy-efficient computation of CNNs for both mobile (e.g., UAVs, self-driving cars, and IoT devices) and cloud computing domains. However, implementing an effective CNN system onto FPGAs efficiently remains problematic. The current cloud-based FPGAs with unique design constraints and architectural characteristics further increase the challenges. To address these challenges, we propose a novel open-source automated tool chain called Cloud-DNN. Our tool chain takes trained CNN models specified in Caffe as input, performs a set of transformations, and maps the model to a cloud-based FPGA. Cloud-DNN can significantly improve the overall design productivity of CNNs on FPGAs while satisfying the emergent computational requirements. Our design provides an alternative solution compared to other cloud-based options (e.g., GPUs or TPUs) while offering flexible, and high performance DNN inferences. The unique features of Cloud-DNN include the optimizations with cloud-platform characteristics and the support of easier and streamlined implementation. Experimental results demonstrate up to 104.55× performance improvement when compared to CPU implementation and comparable usability, flexibility, and strong quality compared to other state-of-the-art DNN inference implementations on standalone FPGAs.

KEYWORDS

DNN Accelerator; FPGA; High-Level Synthesis; Cloud Computing

ACM Reference Format:

Yao Chen, Jiong He, Xiaofan Zhang, Cong Hao, Deming Chen. 2019. Cloud-DNN: An Open Framework for Mapping DNN Models to Cloud FPGAs. In *The 2019 ACM/SIGDA International Symposium on Field-Programmable Gate Arrays (FPGA'19), February 24–26, 2019, Seaside, CA, USA*. ACM, New York, NY, USA, 10 pages. https://doi.org/10.1145/3289602.3293915

FPGA '19, February 24–26, 2019, Seaside, CA, USA

© 2019 Association for Computing Machinery.

ACM ISBN 978-1-4503-6137-8/19/02...$15.00

https://doi.org/10.1145/3289602.3293915

1 INTRODUCTION

We have witnessed an increasingly growing interest in designing Deep Neural Networks (DNNs) that can perform highly accurate inference for extensive applications [1]. Conventionally, higher inference accuracy can be obtained by deeper and wider networks which include larger number of network layers and channels. Such features impose dramatic increase of computational complexity and memory demands which require sophisticated hardware accelerators to tackle the computing and memory accessing complexities. The state-of-the-art hardware accelerators for DNNs commonly exploit different resources such as CPUs, GPUs, FPGAs or ASICs to deliver sufficient performance under application-specific constraints. However, the energy-hungry CPU- and GPU-based accelerators will not meet the energy/power limits while the ASIC-based designs require long time-to-market period. Overall, FPGAs offer a promising alternative for DNN acceleration with improved latency, high energy efficiency and high flexibility.

The recent adoption of FPGA demonstrates its great capability for running DNN-related applications in both cloud servers and mobile devices [2–7]. This combination between programmable hardware and DNNs has enabled more possibilities to reshape the landscape of deep learning applications for real-time performance, high throughput, and high energy efficiency. Recent studies have reported great performance in image classification/detection [8–11], image/video description [12], speech recognition [13], and machine translation [14] using FPGAs. The FPGA-based designs also benefit by the increasingly popular design flow using high-level synthesis (HLS), where high-level programming languages are used for abstract descriptions of hardware functions instead of following register-transfer level (RTL) designs [15–17]. Since DNNs are composed of layers of regular structures, such as convolution and pooling, HLS is well suited to optimize these regular computations in DNNs [12, 14–16, 18–21]. Meanwhile, growing interest of using FPGA to accelerate DNN workloads drives the deployment of FPGAs on cloud services (e.g., Amazon AWS and Microsoft Azure) which are used by cloud customers in a pay-as-you-go scheme. The availability and flexibility of FPGAs in the cloud raise new challenges in the design and implementation of deep learning models on these platforms.

In real world applications, DNN workloads are usually compute-intensive due to the nature of the input data (e.g. streaming frames of data from sensors such as acoustics, high-definition (HD) videos and images, etc). In many cases, the entire network model may not fit into a single FPGA fabric due to large amount of neurons, weight data and intermediate results. These factors together incur a complex computational problem of massive data to be processed with increasing computations per input data entry. Naturally, cloud

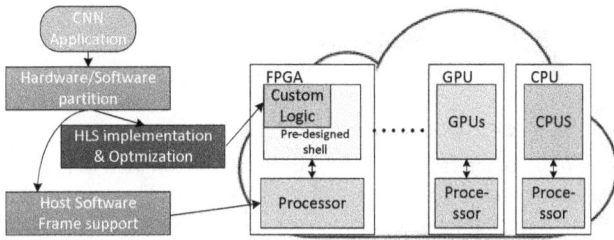

Figure 1: Mapping CNN application to cloud based FPGA.

computing platforms are poised to address this problem efficiently, as they can offer sufficient computation resources and high speed network interface to support complicated DNNs and streams of HD inputs. FPGAs offer an attractive solution operating as the backbone for such cloud platforms by providing low-latency, energy-efficient computations. Cloud FPGAs can help drive the DNN computing revolution in coming years (Figure 1). However, there are still many challenges and promising opportunities in designing an effective and efficient DNN inference accelerator on cloud FPGAs according to the following observations.

1) High performance and fast development. Cloud applications always desire fast development to support the latest DNN-based applications. Compared to conventional FPGA design flow, HLS-based design methodology provides better efficiency and design productivity, which can speed up the hardware design and verification on cloud FPGAs. However, the implementation may not be able to fully satisfy the performance requirements of the application without hardware optimization. HLS-based optimization is a practical way to improve the design quality such as specifying pipelines, unrolling loops, and handling data transfers. Therefore, a well-designed synthesizable C++ template which integrates all necessary optimizations is able to ease the development effort for users. Automatically and adaptively applying HLS optimizations for different workloads provides an easy-to-use DNN-to-Cloud implementation framework even for users who do not have domain knowledge for either FPGA or HLS tools.

2) Architectural characteristics. Contrasting with embedded platforms, resources in cloud FPGAs are usually sufficient for a large accelerator given the high capacity and capability of the FPGA chip, which is created by a manufacturing process called Stacked Silicon Interconnect (SSI) technology [22] for the Xilinx chips used in AWS. The SSI technology combines multiple Super Logic Region (SLR) components (or dies) mounted on a passive Silicon Interposer. However, this characteristic carries a trade-off between design size and operating frequency. It is very difficult to fit a design which has large amount of internal routing into such cloud FPGA without timing violations because of the long cross-die routing problem and the distributed on-chip memory. As an instance, the large convolutional accelerator shown in Figure 2 (shown with purple color) can not meet the timing due to the long crossing-die interconnections. However, the timing could easily be achieved by splitting the big accelerator into three smaller ones (shown with yellow, red and blue) with bus or FIFO connections between them. Other requirements such as bandwidth and design flexibility might be constrained by the pre-designed shell of the cloud platform. For instance, the AWS F1 platform could only provide 6.5GB/s host to FPGA memory bandwidth in the current release. Designs on

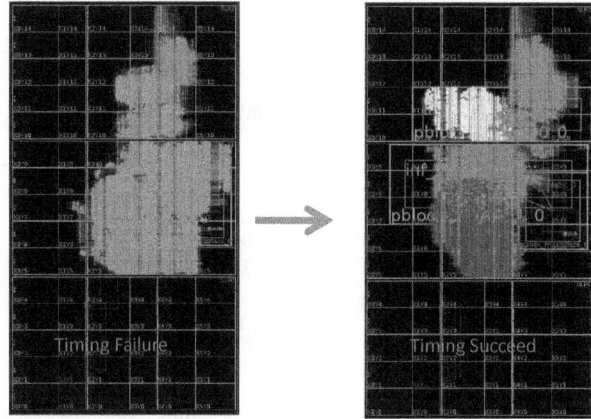

Figure 2: Cross-die routing difficulties.

AWS F1 also require the integration of the AWS Shell IP to achieve control/communication to/from host CPU. The flexibility of the system clock is also constrained by the AWS Shell IP into several limited options. Such platform constraints should be considered during DNN model implementation. In our Could-DNN flow, such platform constraints are taken into consideration during the model generation and optimization.

3) Software framework support. An efficient system in the cloud requires the scheduling of the hardware modules and the proper allocation of the tasks, and their corresponding design and optimization can be critical to the overall performance (Figure 1). Open-source software frameworks have become increasingly important for machine learning applications such as Caffe and Tensorflow. While these libraries support CPU and GPU implementations, they do not offer support for direct FPGA mapping. Our proposed framework is an open-source tool chain that can map a given trained Caffe network model to FPGA in the cloud without understanding the hardware details, while leveraging inherent FPGA advantages. With well designed hardware driver and API functions, the generated accelerators can be easily integrated into existing DNN frameworks. Our core contributions include:

- We design a fully synthesizable C++ template library with the considerations of FPGA implementation characteristics which can fit into HLS design flow.
- We propose an automated generation flow that maps DNN models in Caffe to FPGA implementations without any tedious hardware programming and verifications.
- We propose a design space exploration algorithm including task clustering and scheduling, to generate an optimized system configuration to maximize the overall performance.
- We also generate a corresponding software stack together with the DNN accelerator, to provide a complete system level solution for the users who need acceleration services.

The rest of this paper is organized as follows. Section 2 introduces the overall flow of Cloud-DNN. Section 3 presents the detailed design and model of the synthesizable library. Section 4 discusses the generated system architecture and the design methodology. Section 5 presents the details of our Cloud-DNN framework. The evaluation results and analysis are shown in Section 6. Related work is discussed in Section 7. We conclude this paper in Section 8.

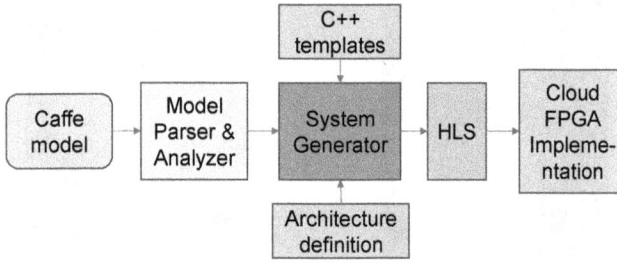

Figure 3: Cloud-DNN flow overview.

2 CLOUD-DNN OVERVIEW

Our Cloud-DNN framework takes a network model trained by Caffe as input and generates a high performance inference accelerator system as output. The overall flow is shown in Figure 3. The network model files (prototxt and caffemodel [23]) are first extracted and analyzed to obtain parameters and to reorder the weights by a model parser and analyzer. Then, the network is constructed based on a pre-designed synthesizable C++ template function library and pre-defined system architecture. The layer task allocation and the exploration of the accelerator configurations are applied during the network construction. After the C++ functions for the network model are constructed, they are passed through the HLS and design tools to generate the FPGA implementation. The corresponding host software solution is also generated automatically based on user specification and the results from model analyzer.

3 SYNTHESIZABLE LIBRARY DESIGN

Although there are various types of DNNs for a great variety of applications with entirely different topological structures, the number of basic layer types is relatively small, such as convolutional layer, fully-connected layer, pooling layer, and activation functions. With such features, DNN can be well defined based on layer types and channel numbers and eventually the required computation and memory resources can be determined before detailed implementation. HLS requires the memory allocation and interface of the targeted function to be specified statically before compilation, which is well suited to optimize DNNs. In order to satisfy this design flow, we describe two computational patterns of typical CNN operations: Tensor-to-Tensor (TT) and Element-wise (EW), as shown in Table 1.

Table 1: Two computation patterns of typical CNNs.

Tensor-to-Tensor (TT)	Conv, Pooling, FC, LRC, Unpooling, Deconv, Dropout, etc.
Element-wise (EW)	ReLU, Sigmoid, Tanh, BN, etc.

We follow the same tiling-based convolutional accelerator design strategy in existing works [20, 21], and extend their idea to support both TT and EW function template without losing flexibility. To support the emerging DNNs with constantly increasing demands on both computation and memory, we propose a highly salable and flexible solution. The proposed templates are designed to be scalable functional accelerator cores, and the neural network interfaces are considered with the memory bank design together to support multi-accelerator network construction. Before we discuss the detailed

templates, we first introduce the parameter settings within layer accelerators for various functional layers.

3.1 Layer Accelerator Template

A set of parameters are used to customize the function templates to accomplish the computation of the layers as well as to meet the performance requirements after being synthesized to hardware. The element-wise functions and tensor-to-tensor functions are designed separately due to the nature of computations.

3.1.1 Element-wise functions. Typical activation functions such as $Tanh()$, $sigmod()$, $ReLU()$ of a DNN are all element-wise functions. These functions always follow the layers that process tensor data but only compute a single input for every function call. Different from activation functions, Batch Normalization (BN) is a novel approach used in recent CNNs to enable fast training convergence. The operations of BN need four pre-trained values which are constant during the inference. The BN is described as:

$$x_{out} = (x_{in} - bn_0)/bn_1 \tag{1}$$

$$y_{out} = sc_0 \times x_{out} + sc_1 \tag{2}$$

We convert BN into an EW function that computes an output element for every corresponding input data. In order to save hardware resources on constructing new layer hierarchy, we design functional templates of activation layers with customizable data types and directly in-line them into the data output module in each layer accelerator function. In this way, hardware resources can be saved by removing the need for a dedicated activation function layer within the network.

3.1.2 Tensor-to-Tensor functions. Tensor-to-Tensor functions contain numerical parameters since both the input and output data have multiple dimensions. Hence, the data pattern and the computation processes are defined by the parameters of the data dimension and patterns accordingly.

Convolutional Accelerator. A typical convolution layer is comprised of 6 levels of for-loops. We follow the design principles described in the state-of-the-art HLS convolution layer accelerator design in [20, 21], and extend it to provide a more flexible system integration support. Based on the computational nature of a convolution layer, we illustrate the computation with a list of variables including $(M, N, R_{in}, C_{in}, R, C, K, S, P, act)$, which represent the number of output and input feature maps M and N, output and input feature size on two dimensions (R, C) and (R_{in}, C_{in}), kernel size K, stride size S, padding size P, and activation function type act, respectively. By leveraging existing convolution loop optimizations in [20, 21], layer computations are processed in multiple rounds to provide data transmission flexibility. The customizable parameters for a convolution accelerator include (T_m, T_n, T_r, T_c), where T_m and T_n represent the number of output and input feature maps, and T_r and T_c represent the width and height of output feature maps, respectively. The accelerator is designed with a 512-bit data input and output port. As shown in Figure 4 a), all the accelerator parameters are customizable so that the accelerator configuration can be tailored based on the input network model parameters.

Pooling Accelerator. The pooling layer processes the input data with a sliding window and returns the results with a selection

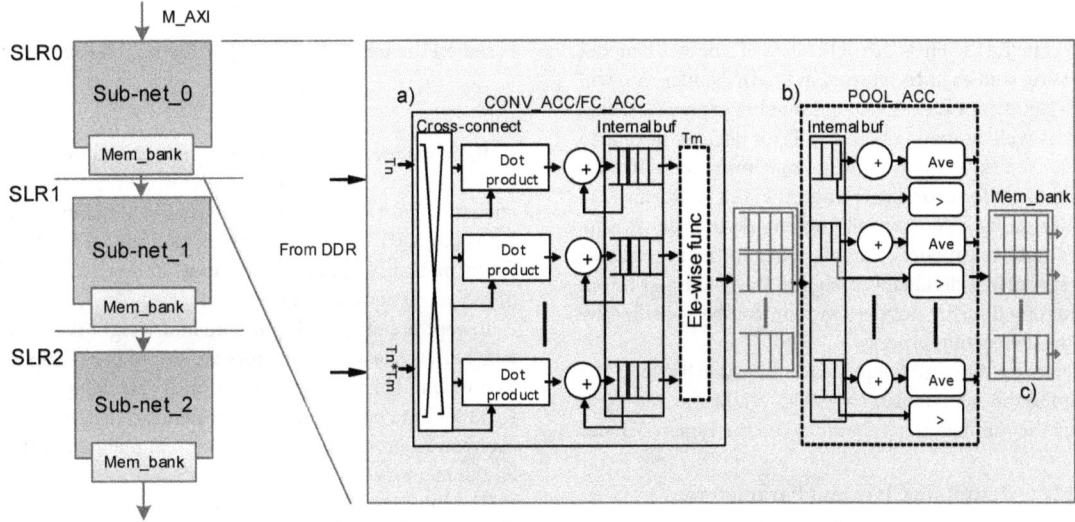

Figure 4: Sub-net, layer accelerator and memory bank templates.

method, i.e., maximum or average values. The functionality of pooling is simple, but it requires data transmission flexibility to be used in top-level application design. Therefore, we design the pooling layer as a standalone layer accelerator rather than merging it into a convolutional accelerator. Because the pooling layer does not change the input/output tensor dimension, there is only one parameter T_n for the input/output feature numbers, so the pooling accelerator parameters are denoted as (T_n, T_r, T_c), with the same definition as the convolution layer accelerator (shown in Figure 4 b)). The variables list to process a pooling layer is $(N, R_{in}, C_{in}, R, C, K, S, P, p\_act)$, correspondingly.

Fully connected Accelerator. The fully connected (FC) layer or the inner-product layer performs matrix multiplication of the input features and coefficients. Different from the convolutional accelerator, the outputs of FC accelerator are vectors, which does not contain the loops for output feature dimensions. The FC accelerator is also designed in the manner of convolutional accelerator but with the T_r and T_c equals to 1. Similarly, the FC layer parameters include (T_m, T_n) and a variable list including $(N, R_{in}, C_{in}, R, K, f\_act)$.

3.2 Sub-net Template

Large DNNs can contain many layers. Hence, in our design, the entire network is split into sub-nets based on the method introduced in Section 5.2. Since each FPGA in popular cloud platform incorporates three dies (e.g., AWS and Alicloud), in this work, we in general partition the DNN into three sub-nets. The sub-nets are mapped to different dies in an SSI-based FPGA and connected with memory banks or through external memory, so the sub-nets can execute concurrently. Each sub-net contains different numbers of layer accelerators guided by a design space exploration (DSE) engine (Section 5) aiming at optimizing the performance under platform constraints.

3.2.1 In/out memory bank. The memory banks between sub-nets are used to buffer the 3-dimensional feature data passed between them. It also provides the design flexibility to meet the timing constraints for the crossing-die routing. So the size of each bank will be determined by the data storage of the sub-nets. The on/off-chip

choice is decided by the storage size. We define the parameters of memory banks as $(on/off\_chip, bram\_num, depth, width)$, which represents the on/off-chip decision, the number of RAM banks, the depth of the RAM bank and the data width. The on-chip RAM memory bank is generated with a group of RAM interfaces and a group of AXI interfaces through AXI interconnection. The off-chip memory bank is instantiated on the external RAM with AXI interface. The AXI interface is used to provide crossing-die connection ability by taking advantage of the timing insensitivity of the data FIFO in the AXI interconnect.

3.2.2 Sub-net template. Each of the sub-nets contains a number of layer accelerators. The layer accelerators in a sub-net are connected through the memory bank to enable a pipelined execution scheme. The overall sub-net and layer accelerator template is shown in Figure 4. The number of accelerator instances and every parameter of the convolution/pooling kernels are determined by the algorithm presented in Section 5.

This algorithm uses the input and output values (including padding and stride) of the convolutional layers in a model and outputs the customized accelerator configurations based on the layer accelerator templates. The corresponding memory bank size is also calculated based on the model parameters under the platform constraints. The interface of the sub-net for feature data and weight is designed as AXI interface to ease the connection with external memory or previous memory bank. This also allows us to take advantage of the memory bank to overcome the difficulty of cross-die data transmission. The output data port is defined as BRAM or AXI bus interface based on the location of the following buffer, and could be directly connected to the following memory bank, as is shown in Figure 4. Also, the mismatch between the accelerator interface and the data width supported by the cloud shell system is resolved at the interface with ranging logic, to keep the unified memory mapping for all the components in the accelerator system.

3.2.3 Quantized network model support. Data quantization is a practical method for reducing both the memory footprint and computational complexity. This is accomplished by lowering the data precision and reducing the bit-width of the data in a network model. Numerous existing studies have shown that the DNN inference will not suffer from significant accuracy drop using lower precision data if the network is well trained [13, 24, 25]. Prior designs have also shown the resource saving and performance improvement with fixed-point arithmetic for neural networks on FPGA platforms [11]. Since we are designing a generalized framework, in order to support quantized network models, all data types in the accelerator templates are specified individually, such that the data types for all accelerators involved in the network system can be specified by users during the generation process.

The parameters for different templates are shown in Table 2. The parameters for the sub-net templates are *ACC_NUM* and *Acc_type*, which specifies the number of accelerators and the types of them.

Table 2: Template Class and Parameters.

Template class	Parameters
$CONV\_ACC$	$DataType, T_m, T_n, T_r, T_c$
$POOL\_ACC$	$DataType, T_n, T_r, T_c$
FC_ACC	$DataType, T_n, T_r, T_c$
ACT	$DataType, ActType$
Mem_bank	$on/off\_chip, bram\_num, depth, width$
$Sub\-net$	ACC_NUM, Acc_type

3.3 Accelerator Model

During network construction, three groups of parameters are required: 1) the network split method and 2) parameters of the accelerators (including accelerator number) and 3) the layer tasks allocated to the accelerators. To find the optimal parameter configuration with given resource constraints, accurate resource and performance models for each layer accelerator are necessary.

3.3.1 Hardware resource cost. Adjusting the parameters of the accelerator has varying effects on resource consumption. An accurate formulation of the resource cost and parameter settings is critical for system performance optimization. Based on our experimental results and previous literature [20, 21], the LUT and FF are not the bottleneck for accelerator system generation. The DSP and on-chip RAM are potential limiting factors, and thus are carefully evaluated in our modeling process.

DSP usage. The primary use of DSP modules in a convolutional accelerator is the unrolled $T_m \times T_n$ dot-product and accumulator modules. The DSP cost is related to the processing data type. Therefore, the DSP consumption in a convolutional accelerator can be formulated as Equation 3. The data type and corresponding number of DSPs for a single dot-product and accumulator engine is shown in Table 3.

$$N_{DSPconv} = DSP_{data\_type} \times (T_n \times T_m) \quad (3)$$

The max pooling accelerator does not consume DSP resources. However, the average pooling accelerator requires DSP modules for the computation of average value output, which can be formulated

Table 3: Data type and DSP cost.

Data Type	float	fixed32	fixed24	fixed16	fixed8
DSP Cost	5	4	2	1	0.5

based on the unroll factor (T_n) of the pooling accelerator.

$$N_{DSPpave} = 1 \times T_n + 1 \quad (4)$$

RAM usage. RAM resources are required by every layer accelerator for inter- and intra- accelerator data buffering. Although current cloud FPGAs provide alternative on-chip storage like Ultra RAM (URAM), the RAM consumption model is similar to BRAM. So we make use of the BRAM model in estimating the RAM usage of the accelerator system.

Except the original input data and weight data, output feature data between layer accelerators are stored in on-chip RAM as much as possible. The RAM consumption is calculated in two aspects: 1) RAM for data buffers in layer accelerators, 2) RAM for data buffers between layer accelerators. The system memory cost is the sum of all the memory cost listed above.

The internal BRAM used by the layer accelerator is affected by the tile size of the input and output features (T_{r_in}, T_{c_in}) and (T_r, T_c), the tiled input/output channel number (T_m, T_n) as well as the architectural information of (S, P) for stride and padding of the layers in the input DNN model. The weight buffer size depends on the maximum kernel size of layers allocated to the layer accelerator. Furthermore, the memory banks between layer accelerators and between sub-nets are other major RAM consuming components and are estimated with the value of M, R, C related to the output of the layers and the total instantiated number of them.

A single BRAM block is constrained to one read and one write port. RAMs in FPGA are organized as distributed blocks with fixed memory capacity, which is 18Kb block BRAM (288Kb block for URAM) in our target platforms. As a result, in our BRAM usage approximation, each of the partitioned buffers occupy at least one BRAM block. The approximated RAM consumption for the accelerator system is shown in Equation 5 and 6, where M_{acc} and M_{bank} stands for the RAM occupied by the layer accelerator and the memory bank between layer accelerators. The $factor$ refers to the $\left\lceil \frac{sizeof(datatype)}{18bit} \right\rceil$ and the $blocksize$ refers to the 1K depth of the RAM blocks in our platform. T_{r_in} and T_{c_in} are two parameters calculated with the (S, P) and (T_r, T_c) mentioned above. When the buffer size is small (less than 16), such as the weight buffers for most of the network models, we do not count them as BRAM since they are implemented with LUTRAM resources in the FPGA chip.

$$M_{acc} = \sum \begin{cases} 2 \times T_n \left\lceil \frac{T_{r\_in} \times T_{c\_in} \times factor}{blocksize} \right\rceil \\ 2 \times T_n \times T_m \times \left\lceil \frac{K_{max} \times K_{max} \times factor}{blocksize} \right\rceil \\ T_m \times \left\lceil \frac{T_r \times T_c \times factor}{blocksize} \right\rceil \end{cases} \quad (5)$$

$$M_{bank} = \sum M_{max} \times \left\lceil \frac{R_{max} \times C_{max} \times factor}{blocksize} \right\rceil \quad (6)$$

The on-chip memory size is used as one of the physical constraints during the design space exploration in Section 5 to ensure that the accelerator could fit into our device.

3.3.2 Accelerator performance model. Before constructing a network, a performance model of each layer accelerator is built to guide the selection of suitable accelerator parameters.

Convolutional accelerator. With the tiling-based convolutional accelerator design method, the cycles to compute a tiled convolution task is modeled as Equation 7.

$$Conv\_kernel_{cycles} = T_r \times T_c \times K^2 \tag{7}$$

The execution of a convolution layer is divided into multiple rounds of computation on tiled input data matrix. Since we keep the T_r and T_c as constant values for our convolutional accelerator, latency in terms of cycles for reading input (lat_{in}) and outputting results (lat_{out}) of each call of the tiled convolution is related to the interface capacity and data volumes.

We also use double buffering throughout the template library to improve the overall performance of the convolution layer design. We apply double buffer for inputs and weights but not outputs in order to simplify the data flow of the template function. With the consideration of input/output data transfer latency, we use Equation 8 to estimate the performance of running convolutional layer.

$$l_{lat} = \left\lceil \frac{R}{T_r} \right\rceil \times \left\lceil \frac{C}{T_c} \right\rceil \times \left\lceil \frac{M}{T_m} \right\rceil \times \left(\left\lceil \frac{N}{T_n} \right\rceil \right.$$
$$\left. \times max(lat_{in}, Conv\_kernel_{cycles}) + lat_{out} \right) \tag{8}$$

Pooling layer. The pooling layer accelerator has a similar computation pattern as the convolutional accelerator. Since the input and output channel number for the pooling layer are equal, it does not take the output loop dimension change into account. Following the same method of modeling the convolution layer, the pooling layer accelerator performance could be estimated with the same equation above by simply setting both the $\left\lceil \frac{M}{T_m} \right\rceil$ and $Conv\_kernel_{cycles}$ to 1.

FC layer. Fully connected layers in convolutional neural networks are always bounded by input data transfer due to the large amount of weight data and relatively small amount of computations. We share our convolution layer accelerator design with the fully connected layer but setting the T_r and T_c to 1 to turn it into a matrix multiplication accelerator, so the performance models are also applicable.

Our accelerators are optimized with double buffering for the feature data input, so each of the computation in a layer is running in parallel with the data load to increase total throughput. Due to the varying data requirements for different layers, in order to speed up the overall execution, we balance the sub-net computation as well as the computation of the layer accelerators in a sub-net; the optimization algorithms are presented in Section 5.

4   SYSTEM ARCHITECTURE GENERATION

The complexity and variability of CNN applications result in a difficult hardware accelerator system design process, especially when the cloud FPGA platform is equipped with the SSI technology. Our design methodology incorporates a system architecture that shares hardware resources between adjacent layers flexibly. The automated system generator also requires a targeted system architecture in order to connect to the pre-designed shell that wraps the on-cloud FPGA.

Table 4: API library overview.

Class	Function	Description
Data Transfer	ExttoSysbCpy	External to system data trans
	SysbtoExtCpy	System to external data trans
	BuftoBufCpy	Buffer to buffer data trans
Accelerator Control	AccStart	Start Accelerator execution
	AccStop	Stop Accelerator execution
	AccStatusChk	Check Accelerator status
	AccInt	Accelerator Interrupt control
	ParamTrans	Transfer accelerator params
Thread Control	Set Flag	Set thread flag
	ThreadStatus	Report thread status
Data Arrangement	3DReorder	3D data re-ordering
	2DReorder	2D data re-ordering

4.1   Hardware-software Scheme

The FPGA platform is treated as a callable accelerator within our design. The control of the accelerator status is managed by the host processor, accomplished by light weight tasks on the processor. The entire DNN inference process is wrapped as a task unit and allocated to the FPGA accelerator. The accelerator is wrapped as a PCIe device and the application call sets do not need to know the details of the hardware.

The API functions required during the runtime of the accelerator system are shown in Table 4. The input data is first transferred to the pre-allocated accelerator memory space. The start of the inference process is controlled by host software, and the runtime will also be monitored. System debugging is supported by the software for convenience.

Due to the nature of CNN data access patterns, the code that runs on the host processors need to be compatible with the accelerator system. Hence, we generate the corresponding software functions that take charge of weight arrangement as well as function calls to the individual sub-nets composing the network model.

4.2   On-cloud Integration

Cloud FPGAs are designed to provide a huge amount of logic and memory resources compared to embedded platforms. In order to fully utilize the on-chip memory of the targeted FPGA, we instantiate as many memory buffers as required by the accelerator to store data on-chip to take advantage of the data locality to improve performance. The cross-die connection of the FPGA becomes a performance bottleneck. Long routing lines prevent the design from meeting timing constraints or force a lower frequency. In order to address this issue, we allocate the sub-nets to different silicon dies in the FPGA chip with additional physical constraint during the implementation process. The sub-nets transfer data through the memory banks with the help of the timing insensitive FIFOs in the AXI interconnect. Host to accelerator system communication is carried out through the pre-designed shell of the cloud platform and the accelerator system also has access to the entire off-chip memory space. Our targeted application system consists of four major components, 1) sub-net constructed with layer accelerators and corresponding control logic, 2) pre-designed shell of the platform, 3) host CPU and memory, and 4) external memory on the FPGA side. The architecture of generated system is shown in Figure 5.

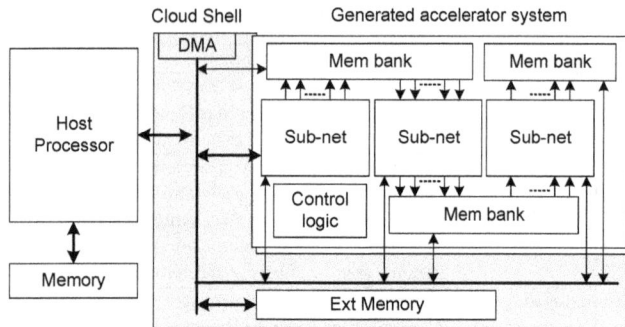

Figure 5: Targeted system architecture.

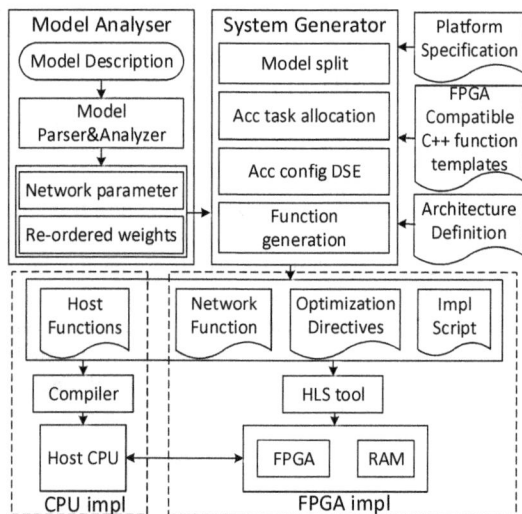

Figure 6: Cloud-DNN generation flow.

The parameters of the accelerator are customized based on the input network model during the system generation process. The detailed accelerator configuration algorithm is discussed in Section 5.

5 CLOUD-DNN FRAMEWORK IN DETAIL

The detailed functionality of our Cloud-DNN flow is presented in this section, including the detailed model analyser, the system generator, system construction and the host software generation.

5.1 Model Parser and Analyzer

By taking advantage of the flexibility of high-level programming, machine learning frameworks for CNN implementation contain detailed and accessible network parameter information, e.g. data size, intermediate result dimensions, etc. However, HLS-based hardware implementations require all the buffer sizes and dimensions to be known before compilation. In order to support existing deep neural network flows, we extract the detailed network structure description for the layers defined in the original network model. It includes all layer types and input/output feature size, stride size, padding size, etc.

5.2 Sub-net Instantiation

5.2.1 Model split. As all the multiplication and addition operations in our design are provided by the on-chip DSP resource, so the

computational capacity of the FPGA is determined by the capacity of on-chip DSP. Given a NN layer, the execution latency is proportional to the DSP resource allocated to it [12]. For our current designs targeting a single FPGA chip in the cloud, there are 3 silicon dies wrapped in one FPGA chip. Based on our design methodology for the accelerator templates, most routing resources are consumed by the long interconnect in the accelerator. Considering the large amount of computation intensive layers in the original input model, in order to satisfy the computational requirement as well as reduce the timing issue caused by the crossing die routing, we split the original model into 3 sub-nets according to the number of on-chip silicon dies based on the computation requirement of the layers in a model. Also, in order to simplify the control of the accelerator, we do not violate the order and the branches in the original network model. Thus, the input model is split into 3 sub-nets with balanced computational requirement. In this way, the critical routing part for the accelerators and between accelerators remains on the same die. The data communication between the sub-nets are through external memory or across the silicon dies that handled by the bus interface with built-in buffering logics.

5.2.2 Layer accelerator task allocation. After the original DNN model is split into sub-nets, the design space exploration for the sub-nets is processed independently. There are two tasks to be accomplished: 1) accelerator task allocation and 2) accelerator configuration design space exploration. Although the configuration of a single accelerator may affect the performance of the sub-net it belongs to, the optimization target is a balanced overall throughput. With our model split method, we need to obtain an optimal configuration for all the sub-nets. Although convolutional layers are computationally intensive, the data bandwidth is also a critical requirement for optimal accelerator performance [20]. Current cloud-based FPGAs have strict data transfer bandwidth (e.g., AWS F1 provides overall read/write at 6.5GB/s from host CPU to FPGA). These metrics have been taken into consideration in our accelerator parameter computation model. Therefore, all the parameters for the accelerators that have been discussed in Section 3 will be configured during the parameter configuration procedure with the constraint of hardware resource, on/off-chip bandwidth and the characteristic of input model.

5.2.3 Problem definition and solver. Model split and accelerator allocation are both critical processes to the overall system performance. To solve it, we formulate it as the following problem.

Given the number of DSP and RAM (BRAM and URAM) resources per die, $\{DSP_i\}$ and $\{RAM_i\}$, with a *Bandwidth* limitation, maximizing the overall throughput with the layer specifications of a DNN model, where the layers are denoted as $\{L_j\}$. The accelerators in a single die as well as the sub-nets are working in a pipelined manner, so the overall latency is dominated by the maximum latency of a single accelerator in each die. Bandwidth limitation is used to verify if the current accelerator configuration could be achieved. The parameter configuration exploration is shown as Algorithm 1. Firstly, the input network model is analyzed and split into 3 sub-nets based on the computation requirements of the layers. Then a straightforward greedy search based design space exploration algorithm is illustrated for each of the sub-nets to determine the best configuration of the ($Acc\_num, T_m, T_n, T_r, T_c$) parameters with the additional constraints for verification. At the same time, a list of the number of accelerators for each silicon die and the label of layers in the model that are allocated for the accelerators is generated accordingly, which are Acc_num_k and l_list. The GOP in the algorithm posedu code denotes the computational operations required by a certain set of layers. The DSE is the design space exploration function that searches for the best accelerator configuration with a given number of DSP for a set of layers based on Equation 7 and 8. We also consider the DSP consumption of pooling layer when necessary as well as the computation latency of both pooling and FC layers.

Algorithm 1 Accelerator configuration search

Input: $DSP_i, RAM_i, Bandwidth, L_j$
Output: k groups of $T_m, T_n, T_r, T_c, Acc\_num, l\_list$
 1: Model analysis $\leftarrow L_j$
 2: Split L_j with GOP to sub-nets $\rightarrow S_i$
 3: **for** S_i **do**
 4:     Task allocation $\rightarrow Acc\_num, l\_list$
 5:     **for** Acc_num_k **do**
 6:         DSE $\leftarrow min(max(latency of Acc\_num_k))$
 7:         Verify parameters $\leftarrow$ Bandwidth
 8:     **end for**
 9:     Choose optimal T_m, T_n, T_r, T_c with Acc_num_k, l_list
10: **end for**

The best parameter setting is generated as a configuration file, based on which the accelerator templates are customized and then the sythesizable C++ code is generated.

5.3 System Construction

The sub-net cores and the system buffers are instantiated separately to provide flexibility to the system buffer control and the implementation flow. The targeted system includes the following three major components.

5.3.1 Sub-net core synthesis. After the C++ code is generated with the customized parameters, the accelerator code is synthesized with HLS optimization pragmas. The HLS tool converts the C++ code for the sub-nets into an exportable hardware IP.

5.3.2 System buffer generation. The system buffers are generated with the hardware synthesis tool using pre-designed Tcl scripts. With our structural design, the Tcl files only requires the generation parameters to generate the buffers. During the accelerator system construction, the flow call the buffer generation scripts accordingly to the accelerators that are generated and instantiate it as a separate module. This will also ease the physical implementation by providing clear edge for the memory module, so that the large size of sub-net core accelerators could meet the timing requirements.

5.3.3 Cloud shell integration. Generally, the cloud platforms provide a unified interface as a shell for the host CPU to communicate and manage the FPGA resources through PCIe interface. In order to provide a high data transmission speed as well as control flexibility, the input of our accelerator system is defined with AXI compatible interfaces. Specifically, AXI_Lite for accelerator control and AXI bus is for data transfer. The sub-net accelerators are attached as an AXI memory mapped device within the generated system. The cloud shell is instantiated together with an AXI Interconnect component that provides enough AXI interfaces to connect with our generated accelerator.

5.4 Host Software Generation

The corresponding software for the host processor to control and communicate with the generated accelerator is also automatically generated after the accelerator parameters have been determined. All functions in the inference process of the network model are parameterized, as presented in Section 4, and the host function refers to the parameter file generated by system generator and accomplishes the data transfer and accelerator control.

All the above processes are automated. Our flow starts from the input model analysis and proceeds to the subsequent stages until finally generating the accelerator system targeting the specific cloud platform.

6 EVALUATION

Our flow aims to provide general support for CNN model implementation on cloud FPGAs, so we test multiple CNN models with their FPGA based quantized versions. We first evaluate the system performance generated with our flow. After that, we compare it to the software version as well as state-of-the-art FPGA implementations.

6.1 Experimental Setup

The generation flow is designed with a Python interface. The accelerator core IP is generated with Vivado_HLS (v2017.4) and the corresponding memory banks are generated with Vivado in the same design package, so as the implementation of the on cloud system. We use both the AWS F1 EC2 2X.large instance (Shell version 1.4.2) and our own local FPGA cloud as our target platforms, which are all equipped with one Xilinx VU9P FPGA chip. The FPGA contains 2585K logic elements and 6840 DSPs with 75.9Mb block RAMs and 270 Mb UltraRAMs. Software implementation of the network models are running on 6 core Intel Xeon E5-2430 CPU with 15MB cache and 8 core Intel Xeon E5-2609 CPU with nVidia GPU Pascal Titan X as comparison. The network models involved in our tests are AlexNet, VGG-16 and ResNet-50.

6.2 Cloud-DNN System Performance

We first evaluate the accelerator performance generated by our flow for the given network models. The overall performance is collected by measuring the processing time and throughput for running inference on our cloud FPGA platforms. The accelerator customization and system resource consumption of the benchmark models are measured and reported in Table 5. The data types for these DNN models are all fixed16. For both AWS and local cloud FPGA platforms, we use the same accelerator configuration. The selected accelerator number and parameter settings are generated by the algorithms described in Section 5. We do not consider Flip-Flop resource since FPGA is a register-rich platform.

The generated accelerator system targets a higher utilization of the on-chip resources especially for DSPs that provide the computation capacity. For all the models involved in our experiments, the utilization of the DSP resources is higher than 78%. Different DNNs

Table 5: Generated system configuration and performance.

Model	Configuration (Acc_type, Tm,Tn,Tr,Tc) (C=Conv, F=FC)			Plat.	Resource(%)				Clock (MHz)	Perf. (ms/img)	Overall GOPS
					DSP	BRAM	URAM	LUT			
AlexNet	[C,96,3,28,28]	[C,55,13,13,13]	[C,256,5,13,13]	AWS	82.05	60.16	83.02	61.38	125	3.96	335.86
	[C,128,11,27,27]	[C,64,17,13,13]	[F,512,1,1,1]	Local	82.05	54.87	83.02	57.62	214	2.32	575.00
VGG-16	[C,32,1,32,32]	[C,37,8,28,28]	[C,128,5,28,28]	AWS	78.2	80.2	84.4	64.7	125	28.96	1068.37
	[C,64,11,32,32]	[C,86,7,28,28]	[C,128,5,28,28]	Local	78.2	74.5	84.4	58.5	214	16.92	1828.61
	[C,128,8,28,28]	[C,128,7,28,28]	[F,512,1,1,1]								
Resnet-50	[C,64,6,28,28]	[C,16,7,1,1]	[C,64,7,14,14]	AWS	80.25	83	82.01	62.4	125	13.9	721.58
	[C,64,7,28,28]	[C,128,5,14,14]	[C,64,7,7,7]	Local	80.25	76	82.01	58.9	214	8.12	1235.35
	[C,128,7,28,28]	[C,256,4,14,14]	[C,128,7,1,1]								

require different accelerator system configurations to perform optimally. The architectural differences of the input DNN models also show a different utilization on memory (BRAM and URAM) and DSP resources. VGG-16 and Resnet-50 also require the DDR memory during the runtime to temporarily store the intermediate data due to the big volume of intermediate data.

The accelerators on local FPGA cloud show better performance in terms of clock frequency than those on AWS cloud, as the clock of the local FPGA is provided by the Memory Interface Generator (MIG) module. Thus, it can be more flexibly configured to different values. However, the clock of accelerators on AWS cloud is provided by AWS F1 shell IP which aims at better programmability by sacrificing flexibility in configuring the clock frequency. Though there exist solutions such as crossing clock domain design that can achieve the same goal, it inevitably complicates the system design and makes it less robust due to the incompatibility between two clock domains, even at a great cost of engineering efforts. Thus, we only present the more dependable/trustworthy results on AWS cloud in this paper, and leave a more sophisticated implementation on AWS cloud as future work of this project. Also, our local shell is lighter than the shell IP that is provided by AWS F1, therefore, the physical constraints for our local implementation are easier to achieve compared to the AWS F1 implementation.

6.3 Comparison with Software Implementation

We compare the performance of our accelerators to the pure software counterparts. The results are shown in Table 6 where the performance of CPU is taken as baseline.

For all three models, our Cloud-DNN generated design shows better performance than CPU and GPU implementations. Our proposed design shows a similar performance trend with CPU and GPU regarding the network size and the corresponding computation requirement changes. Although both FPGA and GPU platforms can deliver great performance advantages compared to CPU, our FPGA-based design can provide much better energy efficiency by taking advantage of the high computation density and the low clock frequency.

6.4 Comparison with Prior Implementations

We compare the performance of the network models generated with our flow to the state-of-the-art published results[5, 20, 26–28], including both fully-fledged frameworks and dedicated accelerators as shown in Table 7.

Our generated systems outperform previously designs in terms of per image processing latency and system throughput. We also compare the FPGA energy efficiency to the existing designs. Our

generated systems show 1.5× to 11.2× better energy efficiency in GOPS/W by taking advantage of the higher computation density on the cloud platform.

7 RELATED WORK

Among the machine learning frameworks, Caffe and Tensorflow can be considered as the most popular ones working with DNN hardware implementations since extensive number of recently published work take Caffe and Tensorflow as their front-end for DNN training [2, 3, 5, 7–9, 12, 20]. These popular frameworks support a Python/C++ interface for DNN definition and training, which can be convenient and efficient for future export to FPGA-based design flow, especially for automated tool for generating FPGA-based DNN accelerators.

The authors in [2] propose an automation tool called DNNBuilder for building DNN accelerators on FPGAs to satisfy the performance and energy efficiency demands on mobile devices and cloud severs. This tool takes Caffe and Tensorflow as front-end to define and train DNNs in software and uses pre-built RTL components as the building blocks to generate DNN accelerators. A framework called DNNWEAVER is proposed in [3] that uses hand-optimized design templates for accelerator generation with the input Caffe specifications. Same machine learning frameworks are also used in the design proposed in [27] as the front-end, but this work employs hybrid templates (RTL+HLS) to meet the tradeoff between performance and flexibility.

Previous literature also focus on building framework extensions from Caffe and Tensorflow, to support FPGA-based DNN implementation. A Caffe extension in [26] is accomplished by accelerating CNNs using a proposed uniform accelerator design. However, this universal solution also leads to low efficiency while handling different applications. Caffe framework is also modified by the author in [29] to support image classification on FPGA. They use a Winograd convolution algorithm and involve HLS as the implementation method. However, their system throughput only reaches 50 GFLOPS.

8 CONCLUSION AND FUTURE WORK

In this paper, we proposed Cloud-DNN, an open-source framework that automatically maps DNN models trained by Caffe to FPGAs in the cloud for inference acceleration. The Cloud-DNN framework provides automated structural optimizations during the FPGA implementation, and creates network description with our pre-designed C++ template library. The corresponding host code is also generated simultaneously. The DNN implementations show

Table 6: Comparison with software implementations.

Platform	CPU			CPU+GPU			Cloud-DNN-Local		
Device	E5-2430			E5-2609 + Pascal Titan X			VU118		
Model	AlexNet	VGG-16	ResNet-50	AlexNet	VGG-16	ResNet-50	AlexNet	VGG-16	ResNet-50
Data Type	float32			float16			fixed16	fixed16	fixed16
Clock(MHz)	1.9GHz			1GHz			214MHz		
Latency/Image (ms)	242.562	794.238	557.5	5.0486	25.7583	13.79	2.32	16.92	8.12
Speedup(×)	1	1	1	48.05	30.83	40.427	104.55	46.94	68.66

Table 7: Comparison with other designs.

Design	[26]	[20]	[5]	[27]	[28]	Cloud-DNN-AWS	Cloud-DNN-Local
CNN model	VGG16	AlexNet	VGG16-SVD	VGG-19	VGG-16	VGG-16	
Platform	VX690T	VX485T	XC7Z045	Str. V GSMD5	Arr. 10 GX1150	VU9P	
DSPs(used/total)	2833/3600	2240/2800	780/900	1036/1590	1518/1518	5349/6840	
Clock(MHz)	150	100	150	150	200	125	214
Data type	fixed16	float	fixed16	fixed16	fixed16	fixed16	
Power(Watt)	26	18.61	9.63	~25	-	48.62	49.25
Lat./Img.(ms)	65.13	21.61	224.60	-	42.98	28.96	16.92
Thro.(GOPS)	354	61.62	136.97	364.36	720.15	1068.37	1828.61
Eff.(GOPS/W)	13.62	3.31	14.22	14.57	-	21.97	37.13

comparable or better performance to state-of-the-art solutions on FPGAs as well as better energy efficiency compared to CPU and GPU implementations. This framework enables users to quickly create and deploy DNNs on cloud FPGAs. Thus, we provide an efficient and high-performance/energy efficiency FPGA solution for Caffe frameworks in the cloud so users have an additional choice other than always relying on CPU and GPU.

Our workflow is designed in a modular fashion which allows easy extensions for new layer types. There are some potential extensions of this work, such as supporting a wider range of DNNs. Also extending our current flow to support other frameworks like TensorFlow, MXNet and PyTorch is under exploration. We also plan to extend Cloud-DNN to utilize multiple FPGAs in the future. Our current release could be found at https://github.com/microideax/Open-Dnn.git.

ACKNOWLEDGMENTS

This work is partly supported by the National Research Foundation, Prime Minister's Office, Singapore under its Campus for Research Excellence and Technological Enterprise (CREATE) programme, and Alibaba Group through Alibaba Innovative Research (AIR) programme. It is also partly supported by the IBM-Illinois Center for Cognitive Computing System Research (C3SR) - a research collaboration as part of IBM AI Horizons Network.

REFERENCES

[1] Yann LeCun, Yoshua Bengio, and Geoffrey Hinton. Deep learning. *Nature*, 521(7553):436–444, 2015.
[2] Xiaofan Zhang et al. DNNBuilder: an automated tool for building high-performance DNN hardware accelerators for FPGAs. In *Proc. of ICCAD*, 2018.
[3] Hardik Sharma et al. From high-level deep neural models to FPGAs. In *Proc. of MICRO*, 2016.
[4] Jialiang Zhang et al. Improving the performance of OpenCL-based FPGA accelerator for convolutional neural network. In *Proc. of FPGA*, 2017.
[5] Jiantao Qiu et al. Going deeper with embedded FPGA platform for convolutional neural network. In *Proc. of FPGA*, 2016.
[6] Xiaofan Zhang et al. Machine learning on FPGAs to face the IoT revolution. In *Proc. of ICCAD*, 2017.
[7] Junsong Wang et al. Design flow of accelerating hybrid extremely low bit-width neural network in embedded FPGA. In *Proc. of FPL*, 2018.
[8] Huimin Li et al. A high performance FPGA-based accelerator for large-scale convolutional neural networks. In *Proc. of FPL*, 2016.
[9] Naveen Suda et al. Throughput-optimized OpenCL-based FPGA accelerator for large-scale convolutional neural networks. In *Proc. of FPGA*, 2016.
[10] Su Liu et al. Real-time object tracking system on FPGAs. In *Proc. of SAAHPC*, 2011.
[11] Yufei Ma et al. Optimizing loop operation and dataflow in FPGA acceleration of deep convolutional neural networks. In *Proc. of FPGA*, 2017.
[12] Xiaofan Zhang et al. High-performance video content recognition with long-term recurrent convolutional network for FPGA. In *Proc. of FPL*, 2017.
[13] Song Han et al. ESE: Efficient speech recognition engine with compressed LSTM on FPGA. 2016.
[14] Li Qin et al. Implementing neural machine translation with bi-directional GRU and attention mechanism on FPGAs using HLS. In *Proc. of ASP-DAC*, 2019.
[15] Xinheng Liu et al. High level synthesis of complex applications: An h. 264 video decoder. In *Proc. of FPGA*, 2016.
[16] Kyle Rupnow et al. High level synthesis of stereo matching: Productivity, performance, and software constraints. In *Proc. of FPT*, 2011.
[17] Deming Chen et al. Lopass: A low-power architectural synthesis system for FPGAs with interconnect estimation and optimization. *TVLSI*, 18(4):564–577, April 2010.
[18] Andrew Canis et al. LegUp: high-level synthesis for FPGA-based processor/accelerator systems. In *Proc. of FPGA*, 2011.
[19] Emanuele Del Sozzo et al. On the automation of high level synthesis of convolutional neural networks. In *Proc. of IPDPSW*, 2016.
[20] Chen Zhang et al. Optimizing FPGA-based accelerator design for deep convolutional neural networks. In *FPGA*, 2015.
[21] Yongming Shen et al. Maximizing cnn accelerator efficiency through resource partitioning. In *Proc. of ISCA*, 2017.
[22] Xilinx. Large FPGA methodology guide. 2012.
[23] Yangqing Jia et al. Caffe: Convolutional architecture for fast feature embedding. In *Proc. of ACMMM*, 2014.
[24] Song Han et al. Deep compression: Compressing deep neural networks with pruning, trained quantization and huffman coding. 2015.
[25] Philipp Gysel et al. Hardware-oriented approximation of convolutional neural networks. 2016.
[26] Chen Zhang et al. Caffeine: towards uniformed representation and acceleration for deep convolutional neural networks. In *Proc. of ICCAD*, 2016.
[27] Yijin Guan et al. FP-DNN: An automated framework for mapping deep neural networks onto FPGAs with RTL-HLS hybrid templates. In *Proc. of FCCM*, 2017.
[28] Yufei Ma et al. An automatic RTL compiler for high-throughput FPGA implementation of diverse deep convolutional neural networks. In *Prof. of FPL*, 2017.
[29] Roberto DiCecco et al. Caffeinated FPGAs: FPGA framework for convolutional neural networks. In *Proc. of FPT*, 2016.

Versal: The Xilinx Adaptive Compute Acceleration Platform (ACAP)

Kees Vissers
Xilinx
2100 All Programmable Drive, San Jose, CA 95124
kees.vissers@xilinx.com

ABSTRACT

In this presentation I will present the new Adaptive Compute Acceleration Platform. I will show the overall system architecture of the family of devices including the Arm cores (scalar engines), the programmable logic (Adaptable Engines) and the new vector processor cores (AI engines). I will focus on the new AI engines in more detail and show the architecture, the integration in the total device, the programming environment and some applications, including Machine Learning and 5G wireless applications.

Author Keywords

Versal, AI engine, VLIW processor

BIOGRAPHY

Kees Vissers graduated from Delft University in the Netherlands. He worked at Philips Research in Eindhoven, the Netherlands, for many years. The work included Digital Video system design, HW –SW co-design, VLIW processor design and dedicated video processors. He was a visiting industrial fellow at Carnegie Mellon University, where he worked on early High Level Synthesis tools. He was a visiting industrial fellow at UC Berkeley where he worked on several models of computation and dataflow computing. He was a director of architecture at Trimedia, and CTO at Chameleon Systems. For more than a decade he is heading a team of researchers at Xilinx. The research topics include next generation programming environments for processors and FPGA fabric, high-performance video systems, machine learning applications and architectures, wireless applications and datacenter applications. He has been instrumental in the High-Level Synthesis technology and one of the technical leads in the novel ACAP technology. He is now a Fellow at Xilinx.

FPGA'19, February 24–26, 2019, Seaside, CA, USA.
© 2019 Copyright is held by the owner/author(s).
ACM ISBN 978-1-4503-6137-8/19/02.
DOI: https://doi.org/10.1145/3289602.3294007

Xilinx Adaptive Compute Acceleration Platform: Versal™ Architecture

Brian Gaide, Dinesh Gaitonde, Chirag Ravishankar, Trevor Bauer

bgaide@xilinx.com, dineshg@xilinx.com, chiragr@xilinx.com, trevor@xilinx.com

Xilinx Inc.

ABSTRACT

In this paper we describe Xilinx's Versal™ Adaptive Compute Acceleration Platform (ACAP). ACAP is a hybrid compute platform that tightly integrates traditional FPGA programmable fabric, software programmable processors and software programmable accelerator engines. ACAP improves over the programmability of traditional reconfigurable platforms by introducing newer compute models in the form of software programmable accelerators and by separating out the data movement architecture from the compute architecture. The Versal architecture includes a host of new capabilities, including a chip-pervasive programmable Network-on-Chip (NoC), Imux Registers, compute shell, more advanced SSIT, adaptive deskew of global clocks, faster configuration, and other new programmable elements as well as enhancements to the CLB and interconnect. We discuss these architectural developments and highlight their key motivations and differences in relation to traditional FPGA architectures.

KEYWORDS

ACAP, Versal, FPGA, Stacked Silicon, SSIT, Adaptable Compute Acceleration Platform, Math Engine, NoC, FPGA Architecture, FPGA CAD, Xilinx

ACM Reference Format:
Brian Gaide, Dinesh Gaitonde, Chirag Ravishankar, Trevor Bauer. 2019. Xilinx Adaptive Compute Acceleration Platform: Versal™ Architecture. In *Proceedings of The 2019 ACM/SIGDA International Symposium on Field-Programmable Gate Arrays (FPGA '19)*. ACM, New York, NY, USA, 10 pages. https://doi.org/10.1145/3289602.3293906

1 INTRODUCTION

It is well known that the benefits of process technology scaling are reducing [1]. The benefits of a new technology node alone are often insufficient to justify the development costs of a next generation device, forcing more aggressive innovations at the architectural and system levels [2, 3]. With the recent explosion of data and surge of machine learning and AI applications, the needs for compute have also been increasing. Due to the high costs of sub-16nm technology nodes and the continually changing requirements of these applications, developing ASICs for these markets is challenging. By

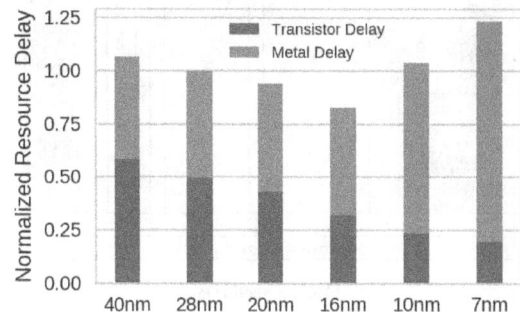

Figure 1: Metal and Transistor Delays For a Quad Routing Resource Across Different Technology Nodes (normalized to total delay at 28nm)

virtue of their configurable nature, field-programmable gate arrays excel in applications with varying workloads and requirements, circumventing the economic challenges of heterogeneous compute platforms with reconfigurable hardware [4]. FPGA platforms have recently been deployed on the cloud to democratize these systems at a larger scale [5–8].

Many compute intensive solutions today operate in a thermal envelope and are thus power limited. Although power and delay per operation drop with technology scaling, they no longer drop at a rate that satisfies exponentially increasing compute demands. Metal resistance is another critical challenge that has worsened with technology scaling [9]. Although wire distances shrink with lithography, wire cross-sectional area shrinks quadratically, resulting in a net increase in resistance each generation. Hence, even though transistor delays continue to decrease with smaller transistors, total path delays may not. In Figure 1, we show the minimum wire pitch delay of an interconnect routing resource over several technology nodes assuming that the physical distance of a given logical span also scales. Despite the physical distance shrink and transistor delay speed up, total delay actually increases with more advanced process nodes. Hence, we are forced to use thicker metal with lower resistance to reduce wire delays. As technology scales, metal resources therefore become more expensive and architectural changes need to be made to use them more efficiently.

One of the hurdles to greater adoption of traditional FPGA architectures is ease of use. Recently, there has been a drive towards software solutions to improve the user abstraction level to interact with FPGAs [10]. However, wide-spread use of re-configurable hardware without the requirement for expertise remains elusive.

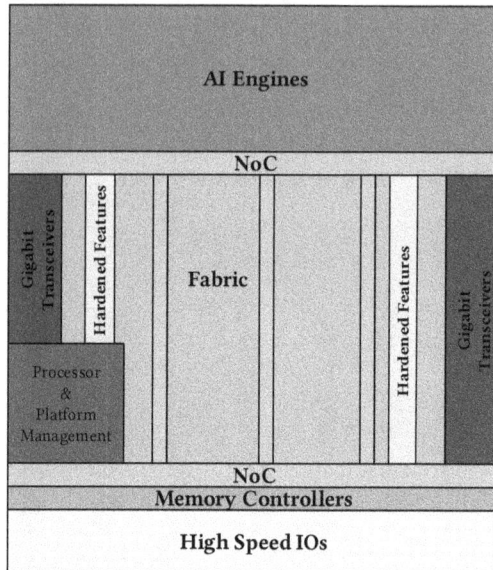

Figure 2: Versal Representative Device Floorplan

In this paper, we present a new class of re-configurable devices called the Adaptive Compute Acceleration Platform (ACAP), invented by Xilinx to provide a solution for the compute and communication needs of modern applications. We describe the 7nm based Versal™ Architecture, which is a new re-configurable platform architecture that solves the economic, technological, and ease of use challenges mentioned above. We provide a general overview of the architectural changes with some experimental results. We limit the scope of this paper to the re-configurable fabric and the related subsystems. In Section 2, we describe the features of the Versal Architecture at a high level and distinguish it from a traditional FPGA. In Section 3, we describe the programmable fabric and the various enhancements made to tackle the economic and technological challenges. Section 4 describes a 4th generation stacked silicon interposer technology with new capabilities for multi-die devices. We briefly describe the clocking structure, hardened Network-On-Chip (NoC) and the Configuration system in Section 5.

2 FLOORPLAN

In Figure 2, we show a representative device floorplan for Versal architecture based ACAP. The fabric portion of the device is similar to a traditional FPGA, including resources such as LUTs, flip-flops, DSPs, BRAMs, and the relatively recently introduced UltraRAMs [11], all arranged in a columnar topology. Changes to these blocks are described in Section 3.

What makes ACAP unique is that it hardens all the necessary platform management functions and separates them from the FPGA core logic. The processor and platform management controller occupy the lower left region of the chip. The adjacency of the Processor Subsystem (PS) to Gigabit Transceivers (GTs), memory controllers, and the NoC enables those blocks to be used together without any of the fabric being programmed.

GTs can occupy the left and right edges of the fabric regions. Note that high speed IOs in Versal now run along the bottom and, optionally, top edges of the die. Integrated with those IOs are hardened memory controllers to interface with off-chip memory such as DDR and HBM.

Across the top of this example Versal architecture based floorplan is an array of AI Engines designed to accelerate math intensive functions for applications including machine learning and wireless.

Finally, the chip pervasive hardened network-on-chip (NoC) augments the traditional fabric interconnect and enables a new class of high speed, system level communication between the various heterogeneous features, including the PS, DDR, AI Engines and FPGA fabric.

2.1 Hardened Features

A key benefit of FPGAs is adaptability provided by configurable fabric and other on-chip compute and memory blocks. One recent trend has been the use of FPGAs for accelerating various functions that were traditionally implemented on CPUs. In these environments, most of the peripherals are standardized. These standard application components like memory controllers and PCIE generally don't benefit from that adaptability enough to justify their cost in soft fabric.

A substantial portion of the FPGA fabric can be spent on this functionality as illustrated in Figure 3, which shows the placement of shell logic that performs static platform level functionality when an instance of AWS F1 FPGA [5] is invoked. Moreover, design effort is spent in ensuring that these platforms meet timing and do not interfere with the place and route of the actual accelerator cores. This logic implements memory controllers, PCIE connectivity and provides ports for rest of the compute to interface with the memory controller. Additionally, this solution requires loading a minimal state configuration prior to loading any user specific functionality.

In contrast, the memory controllers, PCIE and associated interfaces are all hardened and directly connectable in the Versal architecture. As a result, once powered up, the FPGA boots up in a state ready for use without the need to bootstrap any soft logic first. This reserves the FPGA fabric purely for user functionality

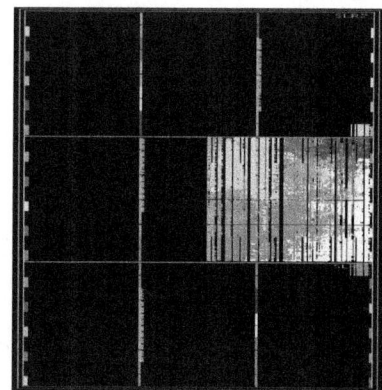

Figure 3: Static Platform Logic for AWS F1 Instance based on UltraScale™Architecture

and also helps non-traditional FPGA users productively use the ACAP without detailed device knowledge.

Some features are ubiquitous enough to include on all devices, such as hardened memory controllers and NoC infrastructure. However, other blocks are market specific and not always necessary. Therefore, Versal architecture comprises a framework that enables swapping different features in and out of different devices. For example, some devices have AIEs along their top edge. Other devices may have IO or fabric along their top edge. Similarly, some devices have HBM interfaces in place of DDR IO and controllers. A-to-D converters can replace GTs, and a variety of smaller hard IP blocks (forward error correction, MAC blocks, Interlaken, PCIE, etc.) can occupy slots within the fabric array. In this respect, the Versal architecture enables a platform that continues the trend towards enabling families of domain specific devices [12, 13].

2.2 Perimeter IO

Since Virtex-4, Xilinx FPGAs have had columnar IOs. There are several advantages to columnar IOs, including tight integration with the fabric and area efficiency. However, multiple technology trends have led to perimeter IO being more appropriate for the Versal architecture. IO cells don't tend to shrink with Moore's Law. Similarly, as noted, the cost of using long metal wires has increased. As a result, over the past generations of FPGAs, the increasing interconnect delays and clock skew incurred by metal crossing over large IO columns have led to software tools partitioning designs across these boundaries. Additionally, IO package trace breakouts from the die interior can be challenging and performance limiting. As a result, the implementation of perimeter IOs enables higher performance IOs and less fabric disruption.

2.3 Regularity

Overlays have become more powerful and popular among FPGA users [14–16]. Use of a domain specific overlay has substantial productivity benefits. Since overlays are very structured designs, using analytical techniques to implement them lets tools extract more performance from FPGAs rather than traditional generic RTL based implementation tools. One way to make overlays easier to implement is to have very regular patterns of fabric columns. However, in a traditional FPGA architecture, even perfectly repeated columns of fabric don't enable a perfect "stamp and repeat" of user IP, because communication interfaces to those blocks would not be identical. Each repeated IP would need to be uniquely configured to enable routing connections to the external environment.

Versal architecture based devices are the first class of modern devices from Xilinx that offer a high level of fabric regularity. The composition of clock regions repeats at regular intervals across each device. This permits two significant productivity improvements. It permits relocatability of IP in both the X and Y directions without having to do complete reimplementation. Moreover, if each IP communicates with the rest of the design over the NoC (discussed in Section 5.2), even global communication interfaces do not have to be reimplemented when an IP is relocated. Thus, Versal enables the possibility of importing pre-implemented placed and routed IP and replicating the same IP at different locations. Utilizing this

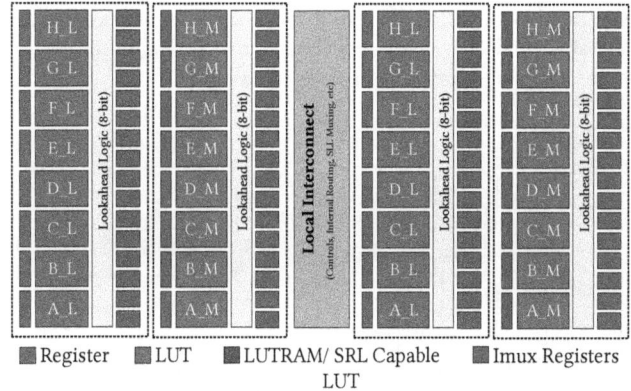

Figure 4: Versal CLB Block Diagram

regularity also can enable hierarchical place and route run times to be several times faster than flat implementation flows.

3 PROGRAMMABLE FABRIC

Compared to UltraScale™, the Versal architecture has some significant differences to its fabric (i.e. CLB, Interconnect, DSP, BRAMs, URAMs, etc.). Various design choices were made to increase device capacity and facilitate more complex designs in a technology with metal resistance and cost challenges. We briefly describe the design choices and present some experimental results in this section.

3.1 CLB

The CLB in the Versal architecture contains 4 times the number of LUTs and registers (32 LUTs and 64 registers) as the UltraScale CLB (8 LUTs and 16 registers). The components are noted in figure 4. Internals of the CLB, such as wide function muxes, carry chain, and internal connectivity were redesigned to increase total device capacity by reducing area per utilized logic function. A dedicated local interconnect structure resides within each CLB to support more versatile intra-CLB connectivity. By enlarging the CLB to include 4X the number of logical elements, we subsume a significant fraction of local nets internally, thereby reducing global track demand. Each of these enhancements are discussed in detail below.

3.1.1 Versal-based Look-Up Table. Compared to UltraScale, the look-up table (*LUT*) in Versal is enhanced to increase effective packing density and functionality. The UltraScale 6-input LUT has two outputs and it can implement either any 6-input function or two independent functions of up to 5 unique inputs. As shown in Figure 5, the 6-input LUT in Versal has an additional output, O5_2, and some circuitry on the second fastest input. This enables us to pack two independent functions of up to 6 unique inputs.

One goal of implementation tools is to maximize device utilization by packing logic into fewer logic elements. If two LUTs are placed close by, merging them into one physical LUT frees up additional resources while minimally perturbing the natural placement of the design. Figure 6a shows packing density improvements on a design suite of customer designs. It illustrates the number of legal LUT merging candidates within a given radius for Versal, normalized to UltraScale. For example, if we permit merging of LUTs separated in placement by less than or equal to a distance of 5, in Versal we find 21.5% more candidates to merge than in UltraScale, thus increasing logic per unit area accordingly.

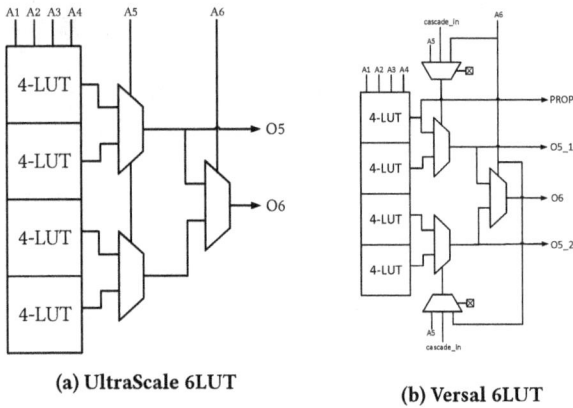

(a) UltraScale 6LUT (b) Versal 6LUT

Figure 5: 6LUT Comparison between UltraScale and Versal

Also new to Versal is a dedicated, fast LUT to LUT cascade path which improves timing for paths with multiple levels of logic. The vertical cascade path daisy chains adjacent LUTs together by muxing into the second fastest LUT pin. Synthesis, placement, and packing tools can take advantage of the cascade connectivity to create fast and efficient macros implemented with the LUT and cascade path.

An additional output named "prop", in Figure 5b is added to implement carry lookahead functionality, which we describe in section 3.1.3

3.1.2 Wide Functions. We chose to remove the dedicated wide function muxes that existed in UltraScale, in favor of targeting more versatile LUTs for this function. Although dedicated wide function muxes enable fast, efficient, and compact implementations, they lack placement and routing flexibility. For designs with many wide functions, a synthesis tool has two options. It could use the dedicated wide function logic in the CLB or synthesize the same logic using regular LUTs. Wide functions implemented using dedicated logic result in large objects which have far more pins than a typical LUT - a hard 32 input mux will have around 37 inputs and one output. Placement algorithms do not perform well when they are asked to place instances with widely varying pin counts. As a result, it was observed that using the hardened wide function often features resulted in worse overall performance, worse wirelength, and tougher to route designs. By implementing wide functions in LUTs, tools can build muxes that span multiple slices, spread the mux out if necessary, and support a greater variety of topologies (priority muxes, unbalanced or sparse trees, etc.). The global speed advantages of a more flexible architecture offset the local speed advantages of the prior hardened solution. The effect of this modification on the worst case critical path of a suite of customer designs is shown in Figure 6b. The normalized geomean on this suite of designs does not change, with some outliers showing an increase in critical path up to 14%. We find that this is an acceptable tradeoff for reduced area usage in all designs

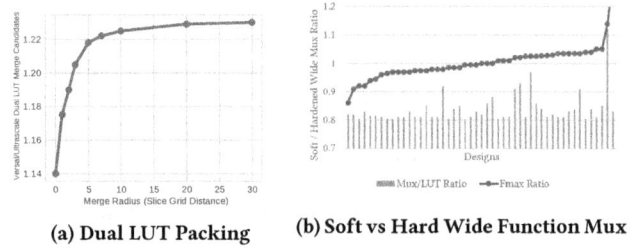

(a) Dual LUT Packing (b) Soft vs Hard Wide Function Mux

Figure 6: Comparison between UltraScale and Versal

3.1.3 Carry Chains. A significant portion of UltraScale's dedicated carry logic is removed in Versal and absorbed into the LUT using the new cascade paths (see Figure 7). Dedicated carry logic area as a result reduced by a factor of 5 while keeping long carry chain speeds constant (comparing both at 7nm). Elimination of these dedicated carry signals also led to a reduction in CLB output muxing costs, since LUT outputs double as both generic LUT function and arithmetic function outputs.

3.1.4 Other CLB Changes. The Versal-based CLB has 25% fewer outputs per LUT compared to the UltraScale CLB. We converted that into additional connectivity for each CLB output at roughly cost parity and increased routabilty.

Each register in the CLB can be individually bypassed without affecting packing density. This also provides more output pin options for internal nets in the CLB to drive the interconnect, which improves routing flexibility.

Half of the LUTs in each CLE are capable of functioning as distributed memories or shift registers. Our analysis showed that deeper LUTRAM modes (128, 256 and 512 bit) were used in less than 1% of all instances, hence hardened support for these modes were removed in favor of a soft decoder based solution.

The combination of these changes make for a more streamlined and efficient CLB in the Versal architecture. Hard functions that were rarely used or whose use could be detrimental were removed and replaced by enhanced LUT connectivity.

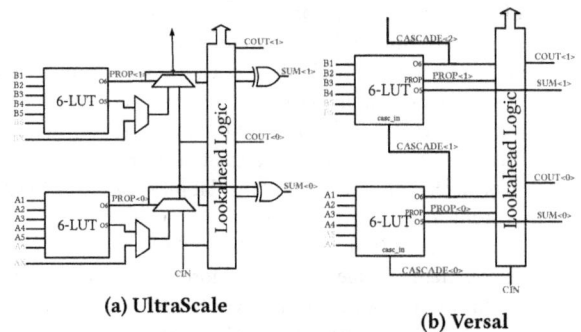

(a) UltraScale (b) Versal

Figure 7: UltraScale vs Versal Carry Logic (8-bit structure, only 2 bits shown. Grayed inputs not used in carry mode.)

3.2 Local Interconnect

3.2.1 CLB Internal Routing. A significant fraction of nets have very localized sources and destinations. An additional layer of routing muxes exists within the Versal-based CLB to achieve more success connecting local internal nets without requiring the general interconnect. Since local routes are shorter and can be squeezed with tighter pitches onto fewer, lower level metal layers, the implementation cost of local routes is substantially less than global routes. With the internal CLB routing structure in Versal, almost every CLB output pin can drive every input pin on the same CLB using local routes.

We placed and routed a set of customer designs on both the UltraScale CLB and the Versal-based CLB and report the number of pin to pin connections contained within a single CLB. On average, we found that 18% of all pin to pin connections are theoretically intra-CLB connections for a CLB in Versal, contrasted to 7% within the smaller UltraScale CLB. In Figure 8a, this is captured as "Total Internal Connections."

In practice, not all theoretical connections are achievable. However, we demonstrate that roughly 83% of those theoretical connections are actually routed in Versal, compared to only about 28% of UltraScale theoretical connections. Figure 8a illustrates this. As the "Internally Satisfied Connections" shows, only 2% of all nets in UltraScale are successfully routed within a CLB compared to 15% in Versal, increasing internal net routing by a factor of almost 8X while only modestly increasing the cost of the CLB.

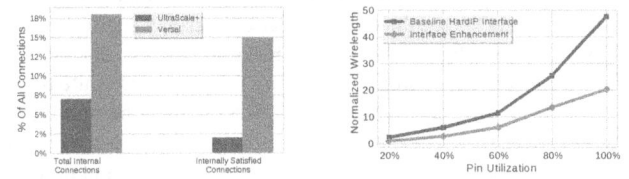

(a) Internal Routing Structure in Coarse CLB

(b) Enhanced Interface to Hard Macro Blocks

Figure 8: Benefit of Local Interconnect Enhancements

3.2.2 Interface Enhancement for Hard Macro Blocks. Similar to the Versal-based CLB, a local interconnect structure was added to the interface of every hard macro block (BRAM, DSP, PCIe, etc.) to enhance routability for highly utilized and congested designs. Every path from the general interconnect to a hard block goes through a layer of local interconnect muxing structures which reduces stress on the general interconnect.

To illustrate this, we experimented with a simple design consisting of registers driving the input pins of a hard macro block at various utilizations. We constrained the registers to be some distance away horizontally and let the placer choose their destinations within the constrained region. We routed the designs with and without the interface enhancements and report the normalized wirelength in Figure 8b. We saw decreased wirelength with the interface enhancements and the wirelength gap widens at higher pin utilizations, which indicates that the stress on global interconnect is reduced.

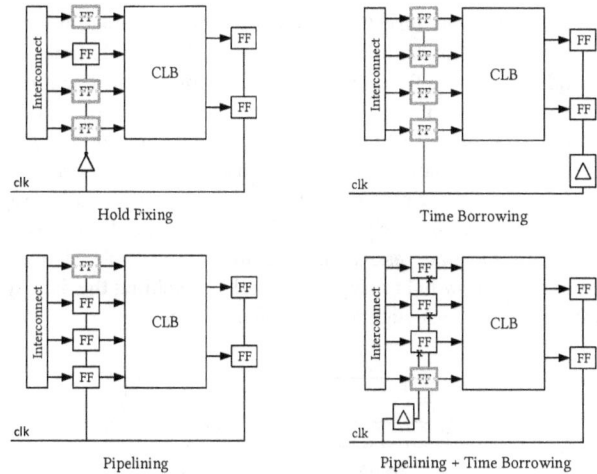

Figure 9: Imux Registers

3.3 Imux Registers

In order to facilitate easier implementation of high performance designs, we introduce a new feature to the fabric called the Imux Register Interface (IRI). Imuxes are the traditional name of input muxing to each block; Imux Registers are registers placed in-line with the Imuxes. These are flexible, bypassable registers on the input side of all blocks. Compared to an approach where registers exist on every interconnect resource [17] ("registers-everywhere approach"), Imux Registers are a more cost effective solution to increasing design speed while requiring far less design adaptation.

In the "registers-everywhere approach", there is a significant negative "up front performance tax" - a sea of interconnect registers increase the delay of every routing resource when not used in every route. Secondly, cost mandates that the resulting registers be a simple flop with no enable, reset or initialization functionality. Adding control sets increases the cost of registers themselves, plus the infrastructure necessary to connect control signals would be prohibitive. Thirdly, structural constraints such as the presence of sequential loops, pipeline balancing, and hold requirements typically constrain how aggressively one can use pipelining. Registers on every mux can simply not be used due to those constraints.

With IRI, the Versal architecture adds a substantial amount of registers but not beyond what are useable, and each register is far more capable. Each register is fully featured and supports clock enable, reset, and initialization, as well as time shifting capabilities. As with any added resource, the registers have a a cost in terms of area and delay. However, as we demonstrate, even without any user design modification, IRI delivers a performance increase (not decrease) for most designs.

The Versal architecture supports aggressive time borrowing techniques described in [18]. We support time borrowing at a much finer level than in [18]. UltraScale+™ enabled time shifting only for a clock shared by 30 CLB slices, whereas Versal has per CLB slice time shifting capabilities. The programmable delay lines per CLB can be used by itself or in concert with pipelining. Figure 9 shows the different cycle time reduction modes supported. Time borrowing enables the register to act as if it existed out in the interconnect and still effectively bisect timing paths. Figure 12 illustrates this effect and other modes and how each one reduces cycle time.

Additionally, the IRIs support a "hold fixing" mode. Each Imux Register can be optionally clocked on the opposite clock edge, stalling data for half a cycle. Time borrowing is often limited in practice by how many registers share the same delay. Borrowing time on one register may cause hold violations for the other registers within the same cluster. By selectively using "hold fixing" mode, thus, more aggressive time borrowing is available. Figure 10 demonstrates how hold fixing mode works by shifting the data eye away from the clock edge to avoid indeterminacy.

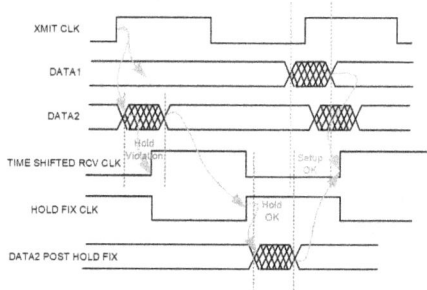

Figure 10: Hold Fixing Mode Timing Waveforms

Figure 11 illustrates the average timing impacts of the various modes across a suite of customer designs, limiting design modifications to pipeline insertion (no redesign of feedback loops). We used the same set of customer designs to also compare with our own "registers-everywhere approach". Adding Imux Registers to the architecture incurs an initial penalty of about 4% due to (a) growth of block widths, which stretches horizontal routing resources, and (b) additional delay of bypassing the new register. However, the additional benefits to time borrowing more than offset the initial penalty. Note that these benefits do not require any design modification and has improved performance. Unlike our approach, a "registers-everywhere approach" incurs a larger initial penalty that cannot be recovered without pipeline insertion or retiming. If one assumes that designs were indeed allowed to be pipelined, and pipelining was the only technique applied, then the "registers-everywhere approach" has better performance than

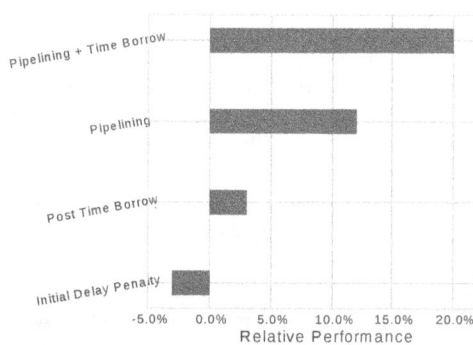

Figure 11: Imux Register Performance Gains

the IRI flops approach. However, when we use pipelining in conjunction with time-borrowing simultaneously - a feature that for all practical purposes can only exist in the IRI implementation, we are able to minimize the gap on the high end. In short, IRI register approach can deliver performance very close to that achieved by the "registers-everywhere approach" but at a fraction of the cost in area and power. Moreover, this approach also benefits traditional designs where design modification in the form of adding pipeline stages is not permitted.

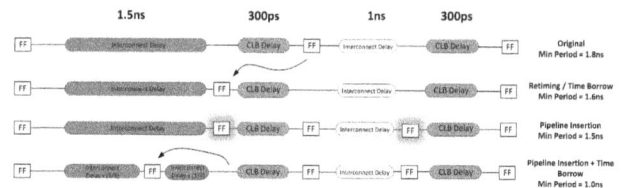

Figure 12: Cycle Time Reductions from Pipelining and Time Borrowng

4 SSIT

Versal uses a 4th generation stacked silicon interposer technology (SSIT) to construct ultra-large and heterogenous devices at reasonable costs. Multiple active silicon dice called Super Logic Regions (SLRs) are stacked on a passive interposer and connected together through microbumps and metal traces on the interposer. Prior works show that the total number of inter-SLR routing tracks (or SLLs) is about 25% of the routing tracks observed in an arbitrary horizontal cut within an SLR, therefore the place-and-route tools need to have awareness of the multi-SLR architecture and inter-die interfaces [19]. The design may be partitioned with a minimal number of connections between SLRs to reduce delays and routing congestion at the SLR boundaries.

4.1 SLL Interface Architecture

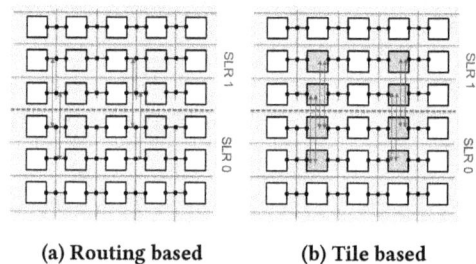

(a) Routing based   (b) Tile based

Figure 13: SLL Channel Architecture

We classify the SLL interface architectures in previous SSIT based devices as "routing based" and "logic tile based". In 28nm based 7-series Xilinx FPGAs, the interfaces were "routing based." Connections to microbumps from the FPGA fabric were made directly on the routing channels. Tri-stated wires on each individual SLR were shorted on the interposer, which allowed the router to treat the SLLs just as another routing resource with drivers and

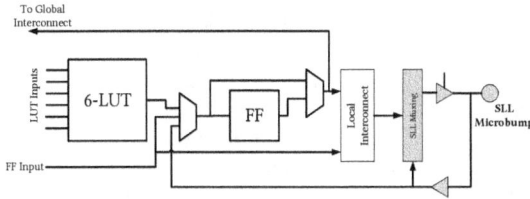

Figure 14: Access to/from FFs within the CLB from/to SLLs

loads in different SLRs. Since routing channels are ubiquitous on the FPGA fabric relative to logical tiles, this had the software effect of simply extending the existing routing infrastructure.

20/16nm based UltraScale FPGAs introduced the "Laguna" tiles, which were specialized logic tiles that displaced CLB tiles at each SLR boundary. Laguna tiles contain optional registers to create fast synchronous SLL connections across the SLR boundaries. This achieved inter-SLR frequencies of more than 500MHz in the -2 speedgrade [20]. However, to minimize total Laguna cost, each column of Laguna tiles appears relatively infrequently compared routing based approach and has much greater inter-SLR connections per channel. [19] showed that the concentration of inter-SLR connections at Laguna tile channels could result in routability hot spots.

The Versal SSIT architecture connecting SLRs includes a hybrid approach that maximizes the benefits of both routing based and logic tile based SLL interfaces. Instead of a standalone Laguna tile, we distribute and embed the SLL interface into each CLB. Costs are kept at a minimum by leveraging the CLB's interconnect and internal routing. We take advantage of the larger 4X CLB's internal routing structure as described in Section 3 to provide local access to each SLL. The internal routing structure also provides fast connectivity to and from registers within the CLB. As shown in Figure 14, the registers have optional bypass capability, which allows the SLL interface to operate synchronously or asynchronously. In addition, the same register type and control set granularity is used for intra-SLR and inter-SLR connections, giving more options on the placement of a given register. Similar to the routing based SLL interface, there are significantly more SLL channels and fewer tracks per channel.

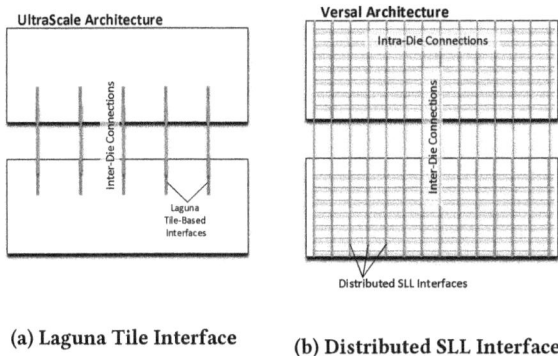

(a) Laguna Tile Interface

(b) Distributed SLL Interface

Figure 15: SLL Interface

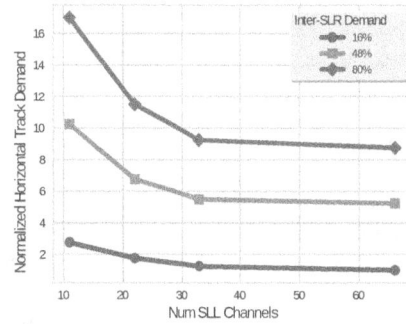

Figure 16: Horizontal Estimated Channel Demand. The sample UltraScale device contains 11 SLL channels while Versal contains 33.

Near the SLR edge, the pattern connects CLBs in one SLR to another. Towards the center of the SLR, the pattern creates a full mesh connecting CLBs within the same SLR. We discuss intra-SLR routing in the following section.

In Figure 16, we use the evaluation methodology described in [19] to implement multi-SLR synthetic designs with controlled inter-SLR connectivity. We compute the horizontal estimated channel demand as the number of SLL channels per device increases while keeping the total number of SLLs constant. We observe a decline in horizontal track demand as we increase the number of SLL channels. As the inter-SLR demand grows, the incremental benefit of adding more SLL channels is greater. When 80% of the SLLs are used, the horizontal congestion reduces by 50% in the Versal (hybrid) vs. UltraScale (tile-based) approach.

The reduction in horizontal congestion directly translates to better routability. We also observed a 40% reduction in horizontal wirelength and a 5% improvement in routability with the Versal hybrid SLL interface vs. UltraScale's tile-based Laguna interface.

4.2 Intra-SLR Routing

As shown in Figure 15, the Versal Architecture also takes advantage of the interposer to create a full mesh of long distance wires both between and within SLRs. This results in a more scalable routing architecture, since larger SSIT devices (which typically are targeted for designs of higher routing complexity) have an extra layer of routing that smaller devices do not have to pay for. This feature did not exist in any prior SSIT architectures. The long wires on the interposer are also about 30% faster than regular interconnect routes for similar logical distances. Long SLL wires on the interposer alleviate both horizontal and vertical routing congestion by freeing up local routing resources. Across our suite of designs, we observe an 8% reduction in horizontal wirelength and a 6% reduction in vertical wirelength within each SLR due to the interposer routing structure. The reduction is greater for designs that span a higher number of SLRs.

5 GLOBAL SUBSYSTEMS

5.1 Global Clocking

FPGA architectures have the unique problem of supporting many clock networks in spatially variable locations. Metal resistance is not scaling well, so as transistor delays continue to improve, clock delays associated with long wires do not. CPUs or ASICs often use thick metal layers to distribute clocks. FPGAs cannot afford this without sacrificing clocking capacity. Since clock load locations are not pre-defined, many clocks must run throughout the chip in parallel. In addition, FPGA architectures cannot afford to have per-device fully customized clocking solutions. The Versal architecture needed to be scaleable in order to support several device variants that span an order of magnitude in size. At the same time, clock frequencies continue to increase to keep up with external bandwidth demands. Clock skew as a percentage of cycle overhead thus increases too. We used a 3-prong approach to reduce clocking overhead: 1) adaptive clock deskew, 2) isolated clock supplies, and 3) local clock dividers.

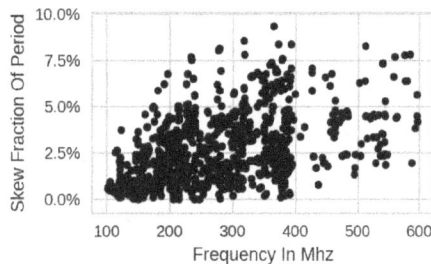

Figure 17: Skew as a fraction of clock period as a function of frequency

Even the most perfectly balanced clock tree incurs skew penalties primarily due to process mismatch along nominally matched paths. In order to reduce clock skew without sacrificing clocking capacity, we implemented an adaptive clock deskew scheme that actively modulates delays within the clock tree so that the process variation and even topological variations are tuned out. Traditionally, skew is computed based on a min/max spread of possible arrival times set by the range that the process can vary for a given speed grade, which becomes untenable for higher speed designs. Adaptive deskew tunes propagation delays so that process variation becomes a non-factor, increasing Fmax of all designs but especially the higher performance ones. Figure 17 shows a suite of UltraScale based customer designs that illustrate the trend of higher frequency designs incurring greater clock skew penalties.

Versal devices are broken into a grid of fabric regions, where each fabric region denotes clocking segmentation at its boundaries. The number of fabric regions varies based on device from less than 10 to over 100. The Versal adaptive deskew scheme has phase detectors at each fabric region boundary. These phase detectors send phase mismatch information back to a delay line and state machine within each fabric region. Based on the phase detector feedbacks, each fabric region auto-negotiates its own delay until the phase mismatch at all adjacent boundaries are minimized. Figure 18b shows one

simulation result, a relative magnitude comparison where each line represents the delay to a given fabric region over time before and after adapative deskew is enabled. Each deskew state machine is initially programmed by software to nominally equalize delay from the clock source to each fabric region. Then, the adaptive deskew system is enabled to match actual silicon delays at the fabric region boundaries. To make the process transparent to the user, the entire deskew process occurs as a step during configuration, using a configuration clock, so that user clocks need not be active and continously running.

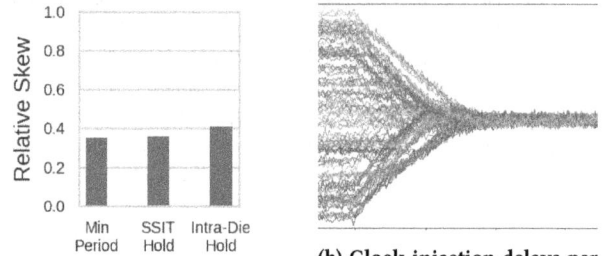

(a) Skew improvement due to adaptive deskew

(b) Clock injection delays per region as adaptive deskew is enabled

Figure 18: Impact Of Adaptive Deskew

Adaptive deskew directly minimizes region to region clock skew, but in turn also reduces global skew. The same scheme is also used across SSIT boundaries, so that the historically higher clock skew between SLRs is also critically reduced. We expect to enable registering of inter-die paths on both source and destination sides in a system synchronous environment without causing hold violations and needing special software support [20]. As shown in Figure 18a, global clock skew measured in terms of setup, hold, intra or inter die, are all expected to reduce by 60% or more.

In order to reduce clock jitter, the fabric region to region clock spines are implemented on a more isolated supply, where decoupling capacitors could be added more liberally. Although clock and data jitter are largely uncorrelated over long distances, we found at the local level that data and clock jitter are more correlated and thus kept the leaf level clocks on the local common supply.

Timing closure between related clocks generated from the same source can be challenging, since in most architectures the nearest common node from a timing perspective is at the PLL or DLL, which can be nanoseconds away from clock loads. Designs that operate different portions of the same logical design at frequencies which are divided from a master frequency is now very common. We added clock dividers to every clock leaf, which allows a single clock to be distributed through the clock network and then multiple frequencies generated locally at the leaf level. Inter clock skew reduces as a result by an order of magnitude assuming the related clock is a divided version (divide by 2,4, or 8) of the base clock. This not only improves clock skew for paths with related clock frequencies, but it also results in reduced global clock track demand. In previous architectures, every variant of the master clock had to be routed in parallel across the entire device. In Versal architecture, we route only the single master clock and derive divided frequencies as demanded by the placement.

To reduce clocking power, we enable designs to use dual-edge clocking in a way that is transparent to the user. Each clock leaf can opportunistically use its clock divider to send the clock at half rate and then each fabric block multiplies the clock back to its original frequency. Dual edge clocking introduces a duty cycle distortion timing penalty overhead, so software would enable only clock leaves that have sufficient slack to use dual-edge. Since leaf clocks are further down the clock tree than clocks spines, there are many more of them, and thus they consume the bulk of global clock power (roughly 80%). Even though the clock spines send the clock at full rate and not all clock leaves use dual-edge, total clock power can still reduce substantially. For example, if 80% of clock leaves can take advantage of this feature, global clock power reduces by 40%.

5.2 Network on Chip

FPGAs have been very successful in providing users with a bit level configurable interconnect. This interconnect emulates the routing done during the design of an ASIC in the configurable fabric of an FPGA. The semantics that each routing resource presents to the user are very similar to that of a routing track in ASIC design. Such a model provides tremendous flexibility in the way users can map their designs. But this fine level of granularity suffers from significant loss of efficiency [21]. Secondly, increasingly larger portions of the device resources are now being spent in managing this communication. As was described in Section 1 this problem is worsened by interconnect technology trends as well.

To address the issue of bit level management it makes sense to organize data movement into wide standardized bussed interfaces. ASICs and SoCs faced a similar problem of moving many high bandwidth datastreams. These were initially addressed by busses. A next step was to increase bus pipelining. This was followed by a move to point-to-point interconnects with many independent parallel paths. An addition to these was to fully packetize the data and control information to more efficiently use the wires and buffers in the network [22]. These networks are now commonly referred to as NoC. In packet switched NoCs, the same physical resource is used to route communication between multiple ports, thus increasing area efficiency.

For FPGAs, researchers have similarly proposed various techniques to improve on the efficiency of bit level interconnect. These include requiring users to reason at the word level rather than at bit level [23], to implementing NoCs as hardened interconnect resources on the FPGA [24–26]. In the Versal architecture, we implement a hardened NoC as a separate level of interconnect augmenting the traditional FPGA interconnect. The traditional FPGA interconnect continues to provide bit level flexibility, but as more and more of the system level communication occurs in a structured fashion, the NoC is able to absorb much more of the interconnect demand. This separates system level communication implementation from compute implementation. In traditional FPGA implementations, since both communication and compute were implemented on the programmable fabric, designs with demanding interconnect resulted in reduced compute and vice versa. Moreover, it is now not important to co-locate where compute occurs with where communication needs of the compute are satisfied. Consider the concrete case of a compute IP requiring access to some memory controller. In order to close timing at high frequencies (required to support high bandwidths), the compute would have to be placed close to the memory controller. Alternately, the physical implementation tools would have to be smart enough to insert on-demand pipelining. On the other hand, with NoC, it is possible for the compute to be implemented anywhere on the FPGA. All it needs to do is hook up to the nearest NoC port for communication to occur at a guaranteed bandwidth.

Figure 19 shows the topology of the NoC in relation to rest of the device resources. The NoC topology is a compromise between increased routing flexibility and minimal perturbation to the rest of the fabric. Most academic NoC topologies focus on implementing a mesh. There are several advantages of a mesh topology in terms of routing flexibility. However, a pure mesh topology is expensive and would be underutilized. In Versal, NoCs appear in the main fabric as columns. In a columnar architecture, the NoC columns integrate with the rest of the fabric just like any other block - DSP, BRAM etc would. Each column is sized sufficiently to be able to saturate the bandwidth of a DDR4/LPDDR4 memory controller operating at the maximum supported speeds. At the bottom and top of the device there are a greater number of NoC channels that interface with the processor and the memory controllers. The reason for higher bandwidth topologies at the top and bottom edges is to provide some flexibility to resources that demand memory bandwidth from more than one controller. Topologies with higher cross sectional bandwidths at the top and bottom make compute kernel placement an easier problem than it otherwise would have been.

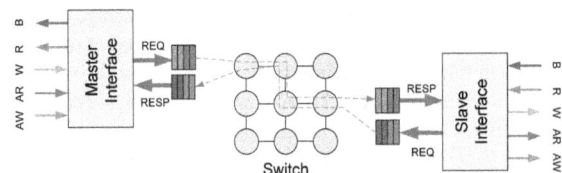

Figure 19: NoC Conceptual Diagram

Figure 19 shows the blocks that make up a NoC topology. The primary block is a four ported switch which routes traffic from any of the four ports to any of the other ports. Peripherals such as masters, slaves or memory controllers form the endpoints in this topology. Masters perform either a read or a write request addressing any of the slaves or memory controller which in turn fulfill these requests. Fabric ports can serve both as masters and slaves. The physical transport is managed by the routing tables within each switch which tell it how to route each packet. It is the task of the NoC software layer to ensure that bandwidth demands are met without deadlock. The NoC supports standard AXI4 memory mapped and streaming semantics and different classes of Quality of Service. It also supports multiple virtual channels to alleviate head of line blocking of traffic and to aid deadlock free routing.

Within the device, the NoC provides ports that permit communication from the processor to all the peripherals. There are also NoC ports at regular intervals in the fabric for soft implementations of some compute to communicate either with each other or with the peripherals. The NoC integrates the entire memory address space of the device. Any master attached anywhere in the device, whether via the fabric or the processor subsystem can address any other slave in the device whether it is a port on the NoC or whether it is a memory controller. This level of integration is extended to SSI devices as well. All masters can address any slave in any die using a uniform address space.

5.3 Configuration

The configuration system in Versal architecture has increased both in terms of capabilities as well as configuration speed. By pipelining the configuration infrastructure and increasing the config bus width, we were able to achieve an 8X speedup in terms of configuration time per bit. Any design that reconfigures frequently will have less configuration overhead and more time for computation. Readback speedups are even more pronounced at 56-300X relative to UltraScale. This is due to a combination of configuration infrastructure speedup, concentrating flop state readback memory into fewer address frames, read pipeline efficiency gains, and enabling parallel readback of multiple dice in a device. For designs with lower Fmax (50Mhz or less), it is possible to take snapshots of the design state without stopping the clock.

The platform management controller (PMC) is a dedicated processor that handles device management control functions such as power sequencing, initialization, boot, configuration, security, power management, and health monitoring. It consists of a hardened microblaze core, boot ROM, peripheral interfaces, security accelerators, and power management units. Similar to UltraScale devices, fabric blocks are configured via a distributed array of memory cells controlled by a grid of address and data lines. Relying on the same system to program peripheral blocks however is problematic, primarily because these blocks have no fixed physical relationship with the interior fabric. An additional configuration mecahnism was added to service these blocks that runs in tandem with the NoC, known as the NoC Peripheral Interface (NPI). NPI is a streamlined packet based switch network that routes in a tree structure to the peripheral blocks, and is seamlessly integrated into the configuration sequencing. The PMC can selectively write to and poll status registers on specific endpoints.

From a partial reconfiguration standpoint, reconfigurable region granularity has become finer. Most reconfiguration regions are now the size of single blocks, and blocks that share common physical space are seperated logically to minimize loss in functionality when requiring specific regions to reconfigure.

6 CONCLUSION

Xilinx addresses current semiconductor technological, economical, and scalability challenges with the new 7nm ACAP heterogeneous compute platform. The Versal™ architecture tightly integrates programmable fabric, CPUs, and software-programmable acceleration engines into a single device that enables higher levels of software abstraction, enabling more rapid development of hardware accelerators that solve next generation problems.

REFERENCES

[1] E. Track, N. Forbes, and G. Strawn, "The End of Moore's Law," *Computing in Science Engineering*, vol. 19, no. 2, pp. 4–6, Mar 2017.

[2] D. Patterson. The Past is Prologue: A New Golden Age For Computer Architecture. [Online]. Available: https://cra.org/wp-content/uploads/2018/07/2018_CRA_Snowbird_Keynote_Patterson.pdf

[3] J. Hennessy. (2018, 03) The end of road for general purpose processors & the future of computing. [Accessed: 2018-09-12]. [Online]. Available: https://web.stanford.edu/~hennessy/Future%20of%20Computing.pdf

[4] Y. Li, X. Zhao, and T. Cheng, "Heterogeneous computing platform based on cpu+fpga and working modes," in *2016 12th International Conference on Computational Intelligence and Security (CIS)*, Dec 2016, pp. 669–672.

[5] Xilinx, "Xilinx FPGAs to be deployed in new Amazon EC2 F1 Instances," *Xilinx Press Releases*, 2016.

[6] ——, "Baidu deploys Xilinx FPGAs in new public cloud acceleration services," *Xilinx Press Releases*, 2017.

[7] ——, "Xilinx selected by Alibaba cloud for next-gen FPGA cloud acceleration," *Xilinx Press Releases*, 2017.

[8] A. M. Caulfield, E. S. Chung, A. Putnam *et al.*, "A cloud-scale acceleration architecture," in *2016 49th Annual IEEE/ACM International Symposium on Microarchitecture (MICRO)*, Oct 2016, pp. 1–13.

[9] L.-C. Lu, "Physical Design Challenges and Innovations to Meet Power, Speed, and Area Scaling Trend," in *Proceedings of the 2017 ACM on ISPD*. New York, NY, USA: ACM, 2017, pp. 63–63.

[10] SDAccel development environment. [Online]. Available: https://www.xilinx.com/products/design-tools/software-zone/sdaccel.html

[11] *UltraRAM: Breakthrough Embedded Memory Integration on Ultrascale+ Devices*, Xilinx.

[12] G. Singh and S. Ahmad, "Xilinx 16nm datacenter device family with in-package HBM and CCIX interconnect," 2017, HotChips,.

[13] B. Farley, J. McGrath, and C. Erdmann, "An all-programmable 16-nm RFSoC for Digital-RF communications," *IEEE Micro*, vol. 38, no. 2, pp. 61–71, Mar 2018.

[14] R. Nimaiyar *et al.*, "Xilinx DNN Processor An Inference Engine, Network Compiler + Runtime for Xilinx FPGAs," 2018, HotChips.

[15] A. K. Jain, D. L. Maskell *et al.*, "Throughput oriented FPGA overlays using DSP blocks," in *2016 DATE Conference Exhibition*, March 2016, pp. 1628–1633.

[16] "GRVI Phalanx on Xilinx Virtex Ultrascale+: A 1,680-core, 26 mb risc-v parallel processor overlay," in *3rd International Workshop on Overlay Architectures For FPGAs*, 2016.

[17] D. Lewis, G. Chiu, J. Chromczak *et al.*, "The Stratix™10 highly pipelined FPGA architecture," in *Proceedings of the 2016 ACM/SIGDA International Symposium on Field-Programmable Gate Arrays*, ser. FPGA '16. New York, NY, USA: ACM, 2016, pp. 159–168. [Online]. Available: http://doi.acm.org/10.1145/2847263.2847267

[18] I. Ganusov and B. Devlin, "Time-borrowing platform in the Xilinx Ultrascale+ family of FPGAs and MPSoCs," in *2016 26th International Conference on Field Programmable Logic and Applications (FPL)*, Aug 2016, pp. 1–9.

[19] C. Ravishankar, D. Gaitonde, and T. Bauer, "Placement strategies for 2.5D FPGA fabric architectures," in *2018 28th International Conference on Field Programmable Logic and Applications (FPL)*, Sept 2018.

[20] C. Ravishankar, H. Fraisse, and D. Gaitonde, "SAT based Place-And-Route for High-Speed Designs on 2.5D FPGAs," in *2018 International Conference on Field-Programmable Technology*, Dec 2018.

[21] I. Kuon and J. Rose, "Measuring the gap between FPGAs and ASICs," in *Proceedings of the 2006 ACM/SIGDA 14th International Symposium on FPGAs*, ser. FPGA '06. New York, NY, USA: ACM, 2006, pp. 21–30.

[22] W. J. Dally and B. Towles. "Route packets, not wires: On-chip inteconnection networks," in *Proceedings of the 38th Annual DAC*, ser. DAC '01. New York, NY, USA: ACM, 2001, pp. 684–689.

[23] A. Ye and J. Rose, "Using Bus-based Connections to Improve Field-Programmable Gate-Array Density for Implementing Datapath Circuits," *IEEE Trans. Very Large Scale Integr. Syst.*, vol. 14, no. 5, pp. 462–473, May 2006.

[24] R. Gindin, I. Cidon, and I. Keidar, "NoC-based FPGA: Architecture and routing," in *First International Symposium on Networks-on-Chip (NOCS'07)*, May 2007, pp. 253–264.

[25] G. Schelle and D. Grunwald, "Exploring FPGA network on chip implementations across various application and network loads," in *2008 International Conference on Field Programmable Logic and Applications*, Sept 2008, pp. 41–46.

[26] M. S. Abdelfattah and V. Betz, "Design tradeoffs for hard and soft FPGA-based networks-on-chip," in *2012 International Conference on Field-Programmable Technology*, Dec 2012, pp. 95–103.

Math Doesn't Have to be Hard: Logic Block Architectures to Enhance Low-Precision Multiply-Accumulate on FPGAs

Andrew Boutros[1,2,*], Mohamed Eldafrawy[1,*], Sadegh Yazdanshenas[1] and Vaughn Betz[1,2]

[1]Department of Electrical and Computer Engineering, University of Toronto, Toronto, ON, Canada

[2]Vector Institute, Toronto, ON, Canada

{firstname.lastname}@mail.utoronto.ca,vaughn@eecg.utoronto.ca

ABSTRACT

Recent work has shown that using low-precision arithmetic in Deep Neural Network (DNN) inference acceleration can yield large efficiency gains with little or no accuracy degradation compared to half or single precision floating-point by enabling more MAC operations per unit area. The most efficient precision is a complex function of the DNN application, structure and required accuracy, which makes the variable precision capabilities of FPGAs very valuable. We propose three logic block architecture enhancements to increase the density and reduce the delay of multiply-accumulate (MAC) operations implemented in the soft fabric. Adding another level of carry chain to the ALM (extra carry chain architecture) leads to a 1.5× increase in MAC density, while ensuring a small impact on general designs as it adds only 2.6% FPGA tile area and a representative critical path delay increase of 0.8%. On the other hand, our highest impact option, which combines our 4-bit Adder architecture with a 9-bit Shadow Multiplier, increases MAC density by 6.1×, at the cost of larger tile area and representative critical path delay overheads of 16.7% and 9.8%, respectively.

KEYWORDS

Logic block architecture; Soft multipliers; Low-Precision; Deep learning;

ACM Reference Format:

Andrew Boutros, Mohamed Eldafrawy, Sadegh Yazdanshenas and Vaughn Betz. 2019. Math Doesn't Have to be Hard: Logic Block Architectures to Enhance Low-Precision Multiply-Accumulate on FPGAs. In *The 2019 ACM/SIGDA International Symposium on Field-Programmable Gate Arrays (FPGA '19), February 24–26, 2019, Seaside, CA, USA*. ACM, New York, NY, USA, 10 pages. https://doi.org/10.1145/3289602.3293912

1 INTRODUCTION

Since the demonstration of their huge potential in the 2012 ImageNet large-scale visual recognition challenge [13], deep neural networks (DNNs) have resulted in numerous breakthroughs in the machine intelligence field. They have rapidly replaced classical machine learning approaches that are based on hand-crafted domain-specific features in various areas such as computer vision and natural language processing. However, the state-of-the-art accuracy achieved by DNNs comes at the cost of increased computational complexity as DNN models become bigger and deeper to achieve higher accuracy. As a result, high-performance and energy-efficient hardware acceleration is necessary to deploy DNN models both in mobile devices and large-scale datacenter services that have tight power budget and latency constraints. From this perspective, FPGAs offer an attractive solution for accelerating DNNs due to their higher energy efficiency and lower latency compared to GPUs, as well as their flexibility and lower NRE cost compared to ASICs.

Two of the main classes of DNNs are convolutional neural networks (CNNs) and long short-term memories (LSTMs) which are considered the state-of-the-art models for visual recognition and natural language processing, respectively. CNNs are typically composed of several convolution layers in which an input feature tensor is convolved with a set of kernels to produce the output feature tensor consumed by the subsequent layer [13]. Recent CNN models consist of up to a thousand convolutional layers, followed by at least one fully-connected layer [22]. On the other hand, LSTMs consist of a series of matrix-vector multiplications followed by non-linear activation functions to compute the values of input, output and forget *gates* over several time steps [10]. Thus, the fundamental operation in both CNNs and LSTMs is multiply-accumulate (MAC) of weights and input features. With the introduction of high-bandwidth memory [24] and persistent DNNs that can store all model parameters in on-chip memory [9], off-chip communication has become less problematic and the primary bottleneck is the number of MACs that can be performed on-chip per cycle.

Recently, research efforts have shown that huge gains can be achieved by using low-precision arithmetic in DNN inference acceleration with little or no accuracy degradation compared to half or single precision floating-point [19]. The flexibility of FPGAs in implementing custom bitwidth datapaths gives them an additional advantage compared to GPUs in accelerating low-precision DNNs, particularly as there is no one precision that is always optimal. Mishra et al showed that a wide range of fixed-point precisions occur on the pareto optimal curve of CNN inference accuracy vs. hardware cost, with precisions from 2- to 8-bits all having a role to play [19]. Rybalkin et al showed similar promise for low-precision fixed point LSTM inference, with pareto-optimal points for high accuracy networks ranging from 3 to 8 bits of precision [21]. Microsoft's Project BrainWave achieves very high performance on LSTMs and gated recurrent units (GRUs) using non-standard block floating-point representations with mantissa precisions as low as

2 to 5 bits (implying 3 to 6 bit multiplies) mapped to soft logic multipliers and adders [9].

The desire for even higher performance low-precision multiply-accumulate on FPGAs motivated recent work to enhance FPGA DSP blocks to natively support low-precision 9-bit and 4-bit multiplication and MAC operations at minimal block area overhead [4]. However, DSP blocks represent only 5% of the FPGA core area in DSP-rich devices [15] which significantly dilutes the overall gains of these enhancements. Logic blocks are the most abundant resource in an FPGA, typically constituting about two thirds of its core area [6], and thus efficiently exploiting them can have more impact on the overall performance of an application than DSP block enhancements. In this work, we investigate architectural changes to the FPGA logic blocks that can significantly increase the density of on-chip low-precision MAC operations at minimal area and delay cost. Our contributions in this paper are the following:

- We propose three different architectural enhancements to the logic fabric of current commercial FPGAs to improve the density of on-chip MAC operations.
- We extend the COFFE automatic transistor sizing tool [25] to support more sophisticated logic block architectures similar to those in Intel Stratix-10 FPGAs, as well as our proposed enhancements.
- We evaluate the density and speed gains of these enhancements when implementing 4- to 9-bit multiply and MAC operations.
- We quantify the impact of our proposed changes on logic block area and on the delay of key paths that impact the speed of the FPGA logic for general use.

2 BACKGROUND

2.1 The Evolution of the FPGA Soft Logic

While various basic building blocks have been used for FPGA logic [20], current commercial FPGAs all use various forms of look-up tables (LUTs) as the basis of their logic elements [23]. A K-LUT can implement any K-input logic function by storing its truth table in SRAM cells and using the K inputs as multiplexer selection lines to choose between the stored values. Classical FPGA architecture exploration studies showed that LUTs with 4 to 6 inputs provide the best area-delay product for a wide range of benchmark circuits [2], with 6 LUTs being faster but less area-efficient than 4-LUTs.

The Stratix II architecture [16] introduced *fracturable LUTs*; these LUTs add a small amount of circuitry so that they can not only implement a single K-input function, but can alternately also implement two $K-1$-input functions by dividing the K-LUTs' truth table and output selection multiplexer. Fracturable LUTs can implement circuit critical paths with large LUTs to reduce the number of LUTs in series and help speed, while still packing two smaller logic functions into a single fracturable LUT when it is more area-efficient.

The latest FPGAs from both Xilinx and Intel use fracturable 6-LUT logic fabrics, but make different design choices on how flexible the fracturing is. The Stratix-10 Adapative Logic Module (ALM) [17] is a 6-LUT that can be fractured to implement any two 5-input functions that use no more than 8 distinct inputs, while the Virtex Ultrascale+ 6-LUT can be fractured to implement two 5-input functions with no more than 5 distinct inputs [7]. Both of

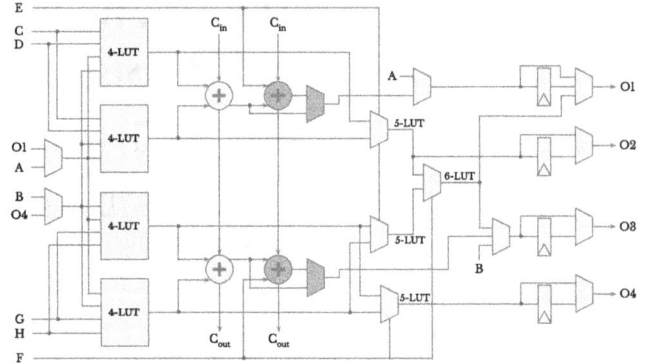

Figure 1: ALM architecture of Stratix-10 with the proposed Extra Carry Chain architecture modifications (highlighted in red).

these architectures also have dedicated structures to implement arithmetic (sum and carry) functions; in Stratix-10 a fracturable 6-LUT is paired with two bits of hard arithmetic, while Xilinx Ultrascale+ pairs each 6-LUT with one bit of arithmetic.

2.2 Stratix-10 ALM Architecture

In later portions of this paper we will show that a key factor in the efficiency of a logic block's implementation of a multiply operation is how many arithmetic functions it can perform per LUT/logic element. This leads us to choose Stratix-10, which has 2-bits of hardened arithmetic per ALM, as the baseline against which we will compare our enhancements. Fig. 1 shows the ALM architecture in Intel Stratix-10 FPGAs [11]. Each ALM is a 6-LUT that can be fractured into two 5-LUTs. It has 2 bits of arithmetic (i.e. two full adders) with dedicated routing wires for the carries, 8 distinct inputs (A-H), and 4 outputs (O1-O4). An ALM can operate in two major different modes as follows:

(1) The normal mode in which the ALM can implement either a 6-input logic function, or two 5-input or smaller functions that together use no more than 8 distinct inputs. This allows implementation of two independent 4-LUTs, or two 5-LUTs that share two inputs and so on.

(2) The arithmetic mode in which four 4-LUTs feed the four inputs of the two full adders. In this mode, the 4-LUTs can implement identity functions to simply pass inputs to the adders or they can implement simple pre-addition logic if all four 4-LUTs use six or fewer distinct inputs.

A logic array block (LAB) contains 10 ALMs along with a local routing crossbar that allows connections from ALM outputs to inputs within the LAB and connections from the general (inter-logic-block) routing wires to the ALM inputs. There are also direct-connect wires which let ALM outputs in one LAB directly drive the local interconnect in the LABs to its immediate left and right, thereby allowing high speed nearest neighbor connections without use of the general routing. Each ALM can drive four outputs to the general routing, for a total of 40 outputs per LAB. Dedicated carry chain routing wires run between the ALMs of the same LAB to form multi-bit adders, and dedicated routing between vertically adjacent LABs allows wider adders to be efficiently constructed.

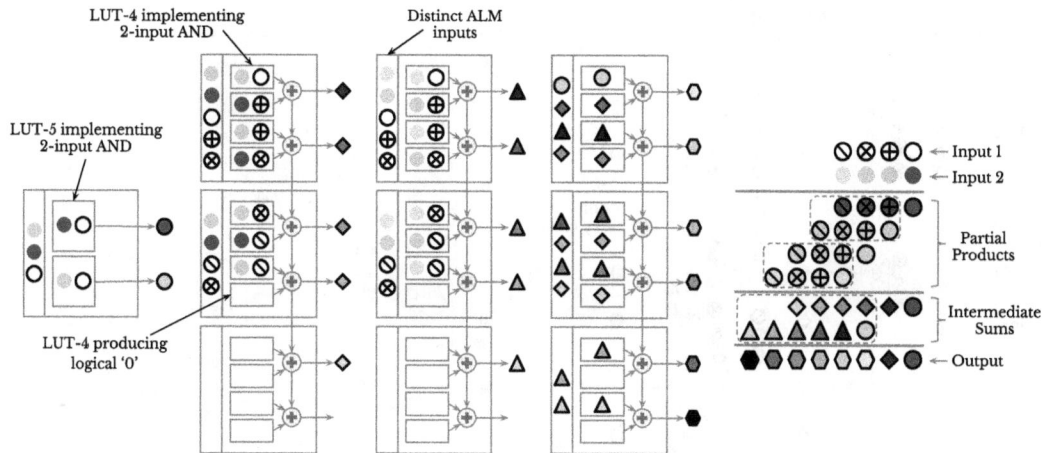

Figure 2: The mapping of a 4-bit unsigned multiplier to the current Stratix-10 ALM architecture.

2.3 Low-Precision Multipliers on FPGAs

Recent work has proposed DSP block architectural changes to support 9-bit and 4-bit multiplication and MAC operations for low-precision deep learning on FPGAs [4]. Despite doubling and quadrupling the capacity of DSP blocks in implementing 9-bit and 4-bit multipliers respectively, the overall performance of CNN inference improved by only a factor of 1.3× and 1.6×. The reason is twofold; Firstly, DSP blocks consume only 5% of the FPGA core area in current DSP-rich architectures which significantly dilutes the gain from making them capable of performing more low-precision multiplications. Secondly, as the multiplication bitwidth decreases, the multiplier array size shrinks quadratically and thus implementing small multiplications in the abundantly available logic blocks becomes a viable option. These reasons motivate the investigation of architectural changes at both the ALM and LAB levels to increase the efficiency of the FPGA's soft fabric in implementing multipliers in general, and more specifically smaller ones of size 4- to 9-bits.

In order to understand how multipliers are mapped to the Stratix-10 ALM architecture, we experimented with different sizes of multipliers ranging from 4-bit up to 9-bit on Quartus Prime Pro 17.1. For simplicity, we will explain the mapping of an unsigned 4-bit multiplier but we also found in our experiments that a signed or unsigned multiplier of any size from 4-bit to 9-bit is mapped using the same approach. In Fig. 2, the two multiplicands are represented by either patterned or coloured circles. The combination of a colour and a pattern represent an AND operation between the two corresponding bits while the reduction of two patterned coloured circles (i.e. two partial product bits) results in other shapes.

Most of the ALMs are used in the arithmetic mode such that the 4-LUTs implement the AND gates to produce the partial product bits which are then added using the hard carry chains. In a 4-bit multiplier, three and a half ALMs are needed to generate and add each of the two pairs of partial products in the first reduction stage as shown in Fig. 2. Then the second stage of reduction requires three additional ALMs to produce the final result. This results in a total of 10 ALMs for a 4-bit multiplier.

To validate our choice of the Stratix-10 ALM as a baseline, we also performed similar experiments in mapping 4- to 9-bit multiply-accumulate units to a Virtex Ultrascale+ device using Vivado 2018.1.

On average 70% more fracturable LUTs were required than when targeting Stratix-10 ALMs. For both the Virtex Ultrascale+ and Stratix-10 architectures we iteratively shrank the floorplan until compilation failed in order to ensure we had found the densest mapping possible in each device.

2.4 CAD for FPGA Circuit Design

To evaluate our proposed architectures, we must determine their impact on the logic tile (logic block plus its associated routing) area, as well as the delay of many paths within the tile. We use the COFFE FPGA transistor sizing and modeling tool for this purpose [8]. Given a description of the tile architecture, COFFE builds the relevant subcircuits for SPICE simulation, estimates layout area, adds wire loads, and iteratively optimizes the sizing of each type of transistor. By directly using SPICE for delay estimation, COFFE can accurately model delay in recent process nodes, and its full custom circuitry and transistor sizing approach matches the design style of commercial FPGA logic tiles. We use the latest release of COFFE, which more accurately models wire loads by creating and optimizing a floorplan of the logic tile, and whose area and delay estimates have been shown to correlate well with published commercial FPGA values [25]. This version of COFFE can also implement logic in standard cells for heterogeneous blocks, which allows us to incorporate standard cell logic within the logic tile for one of our architecture variants (shadow multipliers in Section 3.3).

The latest release of COFFE can model fracturable LUTs and either one or two bits of arithmetic per fracturable LUT [25]. However, it still requires considerable modifications to enable modeling more sophisticated ALM architectures similar to those of state-of-the-art commercial FPGAs as shown in Fig. 1. Our enhancements to COFFE will be discussed later in Section 4.2.

3 LOGIC ARCHITECTURE ENHANCEMENTS

In this section, we present three different architectural enhancements to FPGA logic blocks, two of which are on the ALM level while the third is on the logic cluster (i.e. LAB) level. For each architectural enhancement, we describe the circuitry added to the ALM or the LAB and show, as a simple example, how a 4-bit unsigned multiplier would map to the soft logic of the enhanced FPGA.

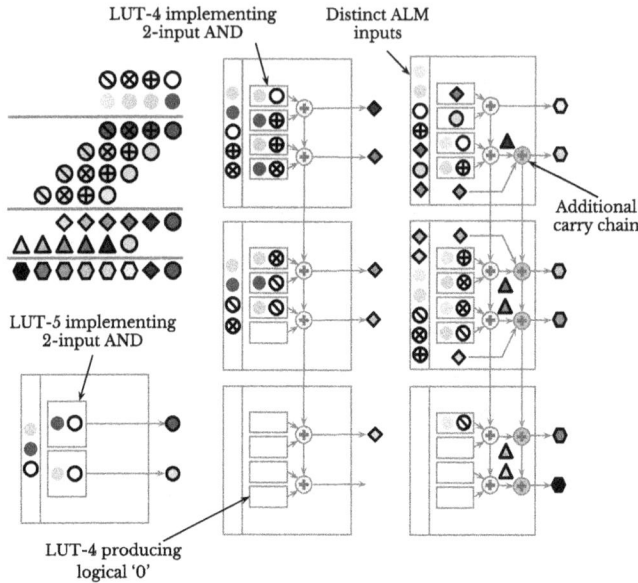

Figure 3: Mapping a 4-bit unsigned multiplier to the Extra Carry Chain architecture.

3.1 Extra Carry Chain

When examining the mapping of multipliers to the Stratix-10 soft logic as described in Section 2.3, we can observe that the LUTs inside the ALMs are used to implement the partial product generation 2-input AND gates in the first reduction stage. After that, only the carry chains are used to implement the subsequent reduction stages while the LUTs are used as identity functions to feed the hard adders with inputs as shown in the rightmost ALM column in Fig. 2. This results in an inefficient ALM utilization and emphasizes the need to implement more efficient adder reduction trees in order to increase the on-chip MAC density.

To address this, we propose adding another carry chain to the ALM such that the two new adders get their inputs from the two sum outputs of the first carry chain and the two ALM inputs (E and F) that are left unused in the arithmetic ALM mode as shown in Fig. 1. By doing this, we can use the second level of adders to perform another stage of reduction within the same ALMs instead of using the adders of another set of ALMs and leaving their LUTs unusable, as is the case in the current Stratix-10 architecture. Fig. 3 shows the mapping of a 4-bit multiplier to the proposed ALM architecture with an additional carry chain. The first pair of partial products are generated and added in 3 ALMs and then reduced with the second pair in another 3 ALMs using the added carry chain. This results in a mapping that consumes only 7 ALMs instead of the 10 ALMs required in the baseline Stratix-10 ALM architecture. This architectural enhancement does not require additional inputs or outputs to or from the ALM and thus the area overhead of the two adders and the 2:1 multiplexers allowing them to be bypassed (highlighted in red in Fig. 1) is minimal. The additional carry chain decreases the number of ALM levels not only for multipliers but also for adder reduction trees in general. For example, a 3-to-1 adder would require only one ALM level in the Extra Carry Chain architecture compared to two levels with the current Stratix-10 architecture.

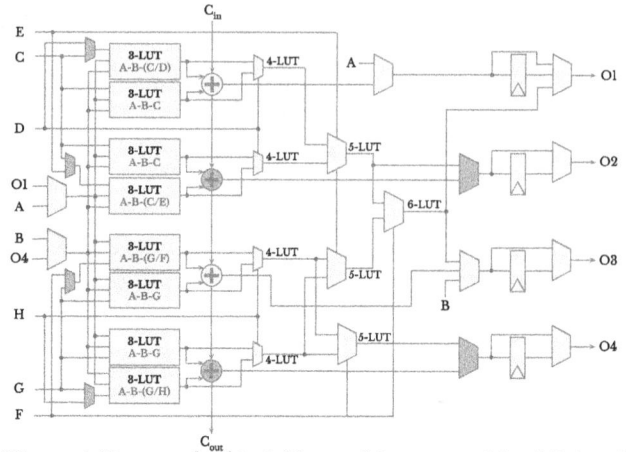

Figure 4: Proposed 4-bit Adder architecture with additional full adders and multiplexing (highlighted in red).

3.2 Deeper Fracturability: 4-bit Adder

Another approach to increase the density of MAC operations is to harden more adders per ALM to create a single but wider carry chain. Since multipliers use the 4-LUTs before adders to implement only two-input AND gates as shown in Fig. 2, the 4-LUTs are extremely underutilized. Therefore, we propose going one level deeper with ALM fracturability by splitting each 4-LUT into two 3-LUTs, followed by four bits of arithmetic instead of two as shown in Fig. 4. To compute and sum eight partial products in this ALM we must configure each of the eight 3-LUTs as a 2-input AND gate. This requires a total of 16 inputs. However, since there are many shared signals, the number of distinct inputs is only eight matching the ALM's input ports count. The reason is the input sharing nature of multiplier arrays which produce N^2 partial product bits from only $2N$ input bits for any multiplier bitwidth N. Fig. 5 shows the mapping of an unsigned 4-bit multiplier to ALMs with 4 bits of arithmetic. It shows that none of the used ALMs has more than 8 distinct inputs. This observation holds for signed and unsigned multipliers of all sizes.

Although we do not need additional input ports, we need to ensure that we can deliver the correct inputs to the 3-LUTs both to implement multiplier arrays and also to use the adders to implement a standalone 4-bit adder per ALM for general design use. For this reason, we add the small 2:1 multiplexers (highlighted in red in Fig. 4) in front of four out of the eight 3-LUTs. These multiplexers provide us with enough flexibility to deliver the 8 ALM inputs to the 3-LUTs to implement equations (1) and (2) in case of multiplier arrays and standalone adders respectively. Table 1 shows the assignment of ALM inputs (A-H in Fig. 4) as well as the function that each of the eight 3-LUTs implements for both scenarios. Also, to be able to output the result of all four adders, we add two 2:1 output select multiplexers before the FFs for outputs O2 and O4 as shown in Fig. 4.

$$
\begin{array}{cccc}
a_0b_4 & a_0b_3 & a_0b_2 & a_0b_1 \\
a_1b_3 & a_1b_2 & a_1b_1 & a_1b_0 \ +
\end{array}
\tag{1}
$$

$$
\begin{array}{cccc}
 & a_3 & a_2 & a_1 & a_0 \\
 & b_3 & b_2 & b_1 & b_0 \ +
\end{array}
\tag{2}
$$

Table 1: ALM input assignment and LUT masks for implementing multiplier arrays and standalone adders (Eq. (1) and (2), receptively) using the 4-bit Adder architecture.

Input	L1	L2	L3	L4	L5	L6	L7	L8
Mult (Eq. 1)	B&D $(a_1 b_0)$	A&C $(a_0 b_1)$	B&C $(a_1 b_1)$	A&E $(a_0 b_2)$	B&F $(a_1 b_2)$	A&G $(a_0 b_3)$	B&G $(a_1 b_3)$	A&H $(a_0 b_4)$
Add (Eq. 2)	D (a_0)	C (b_0)	A (b_1)	E (a_1)	F (a_2)	B (b_2)	G (a_3)	H (b_3)

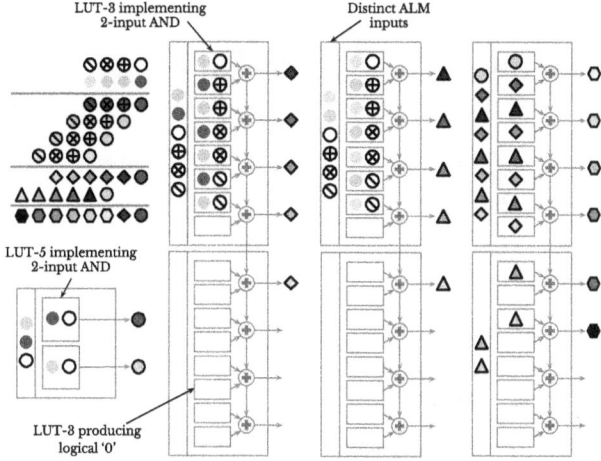

Figure 5: Mapping a 4-bit unsigned multiplier to the 4-bit Adder architecture.

3.3 Shadow Multipliers

In [12], Jamieson and Rose proposed *shadow clusters*. These are normal FPGA logic clusters added to hard blocks such as BRAMs or DSP blocks which can be used only when the hard blocks are not used. The motive was to increase the area efficiency for applications that do not fully utilize the hard blocks on an FPGA. However, for DL applications, DSP blocks are more valuable and are usually the bottleneck when implementing DL accelerators on current FPGAs [5]. Therefore, a more effective way to increase the density of on-chip MAC operations is to add a *shadow* hard multiplier within each logic cluster. In order to avoid adding any extra local or inter-tile routing area, this shadow multiplier borrows the input and output ports of some of the ALMs in the cluster; no extra ALM input muxes are built and no cluster inputs or outputs are added. As shown in Fig. 6a this makes some ALMs unusable when the shadow multiplier is in use.

We evaluate hardening various shadow multiplier sizes. As the hard multiplier bitwidth increases, the logic cluster area overhead increases and it leaves more ALMs unusable since it needs more input and output ports. On the other hand, a larger hard multiplier results in more efficient implementations of larger multiplies in the soft logic. Therefore, this design choice relies heavily on the multiplication bitwidths used by the target application. We experiment with shadow multiplier sizes ranging from 4- to 9-bits and show the trade-off between ALM savings and cluster area overhead in the results section of this paper.

FPGA applications have diverse needs for multiplication: there will be a variety of multiplication precisions, and a mix of signed and unsigned multiplication. To ensure our shadow multiplier is as flexible as possible, we design a special multiplier array, shown in Fig. 6b, that enables efficient implementation of two's complement

signed multiplications of bigger sizes. The invertible cells (Fig. 6d) and the signed/unsigned cells are added to implement a Baugh-Wooley signed multiplication [3], and are marked with crossed circles and 'S' symbols respectively. The 'S' bits are 1 for a signed multiply and 0 otherwise, and the invertible cells are controlled using three different sign control signals ($C1$, $C2$ and $C3$) in our multiplier array instead of a single control signal in conventional ones.

Fig. 6e illustrates how a 6-bit signed multiplier can be implemented using a 4-bit shadow multiplier built using a conventional multiplier array. The hard multiplier is forced to implement the lower left corner of the multiplier array to align the invertible cells in the hard multiplier with the positions where they are needed in a 6-bit multiplier. This results in 5 partial results to be reduced in the soft logic in addition to extra logic to correct the contamination of the misplaced 'S' bit from the hard multiplier.

However, when using a multiplier array with three distinct sign control signals, we can invert the corner cell, disable the inversion of the bottom boundary cells and set the green S to 0, as shown in Fig. 6f. This enables the hard multiplier to implement the top left corner of the multiplier array resulting in no contamination bits and only 3 partial results to reduce in the soft logic. Larger multiplications can also be mapped to this architecture by combining several hard multipliers. For instance, an 8-bit multiplication can be implemented using four 4-bit multipliers and one level of carry chain to combine their outputs.

4 EVALUATION

4.1 ALM Savings for Multiplies and MACs

To quantify the increase in multiply and MAC operation density achieved by each of the three architectural changes presented in Section 3, we hand-map multipliers and MAC units of sizes ranging from 4- to 9-bit to the logic blocks of a Stratix-10-like architecture as well as the three proposed ones. We verify our mapping for the baseline architecture with synthesis results from Quartus 17.1. For MAC units, Quartus does not perform any cross-boundary optimizations between the multiplier array and the accumulator and therefore we follow the same approach in our hand-mapping to maintain a fair comparison across architectures. We present results where the accumulator is the same width as the multiplier output; however any other assumption leads to the same trend in results.

Fig. 7 shows the ALMs required for 4- to 9-bit multiplier and MAC units with a baseline ALM, as well as our Extra Carry Chain and 4-bit Adder architectures. Both proposed architectures outperform the baseline across all multiplier and MAC precisions. For standalone multipliers, the Extra Carry Chain and the 4-bit Adder architectures reduce ALM usage by 29% and 36% on average across this range of multiplier sizes, respectively. For MAC operations both proposed architectures perform similarly, with the Extra Carry Chain and 4-bit Adder architectures reducing average ALMs per MAC operation

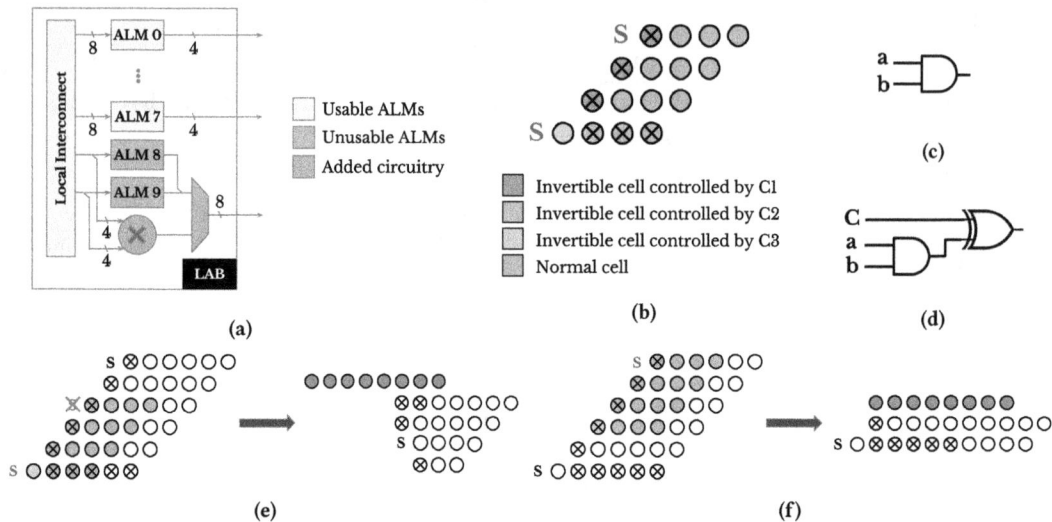

Figure 6: Shadow multiplier: (a) Hard multiplier placement in logic block, (b) Hard multiplier design, (c) Normal multiplier cell, (d) Invertible multiplier cell, and 6-bit multiplication mapped to 4-bit hard multiplier (e) using conventional multiplier array and (f) using enhanced multiplier array with three distinct sign control signals.

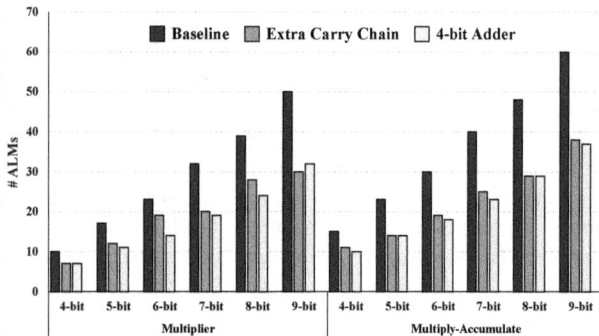

Figure 7: ALM utilization for 4- to 9-bit multipliers and MACs on Stratix-10, Extra Carry Chain and 4-bit Adder architectures.

vs. the baseline by 36% and 38%, respectively. The Extra Carry Chain architecture can implement the accumulation adder in the second carry chain of the last reduction stage of the multiplier array so its advantage over the baseline architecture is larger on MAC operations than on multiplies.

We map multipliers and MACs to the Shadow Multiplier architecture discussed in Section 3.3 to achieve the highest reduction in ALM count rather than the shortest critical path delay. The average ALM savings increase with the hard multiplier size; for instance, when implementing a 9-bit multiplier using the 9-bit Shadow Multiplier architecture only 5 ALMs are consumed since they were made unusable by selecting the output of the multiplier (see Fig. 6a). On average for 4-bit to 9-bit MAC operations, the reduction in ALMs used or unusable vs. the baseline varies from 46% for a 4-bit Shadow Multiplier to 88% for a 9-bit Shadow Multiplier architectures. These are larger reductions than those achieved by the Extra Carry Chain or 4-bit Adder architectures, but the Shadow Multiplier architecture also adds more area to the FPGA tile.

In Section 3 we ensured that our logic enhancements respect the architectural constraint that each ALM can use no more than 8 inputs. There is also a constraint on the number of inputs to a logic block – in Stratix-10 the number of LAB local routing wires is 60, and therefore the sum of the number of distinct input signals to all ALMs within a LAB must be at most 60 [17]. While our architecture enhancements increase MAC density, all the LABs produced for all 3 enhanced architectures for MAC units from 4- to 9-bits still fit comfortably within this local routing limit. The 4-bit Adder architecture has the highest LAB local routing demand, but even in this case, the MAC mappings we choose balance partial product (low-input-demand) and adder tree (higher-input-demand) operations in LABs and the worst-case LAB local routing demand is only 46 (out of 60) wires.

4.2 COFFE Flow: Extensions and Technology

Section 4.1 showed that the three proposed architectural changes will lead to considerable savings in the total number of ALMs needed to implement multipliers on the soft fabric. However, the architecture changes will also increase the size of the logic block and will impact the delay of some paths within the logic block as well; for a complete evaluation we need to compute these overheads. As mentioned previously, we extend the COFFE CAD tool in several ways so that it can model and evaluate these new architectures. First, we add flexible control over the way inputs connect to fracturable LUTs; this enables us to better capture the functionality of a Stratix-10 ALM which is our baseline architecture. Second, we add new options for carry chain architectures. COFFE could model 1-bit and 2-bits of carry chain per ALM/fracturable LUT; we added support for 4 bits of arithmetic per fracturable LUT. We also extended COFFE to support two cascaded carry chains per ALM. Next, we modified COFFE to support deeper fracturing of LUTs; this was particularly important to enable efficient use of the large number of arithmetic bits per fracturable LUT in some of our proposed architectures. COFFE previously supported fracturing a 6-LUT into two 5-LUTs; we extended COFFE so it can now also fracture a 6-LUT into four 4-LUTs or eight 3-LUTs. These deeper levels of fracturing are needed

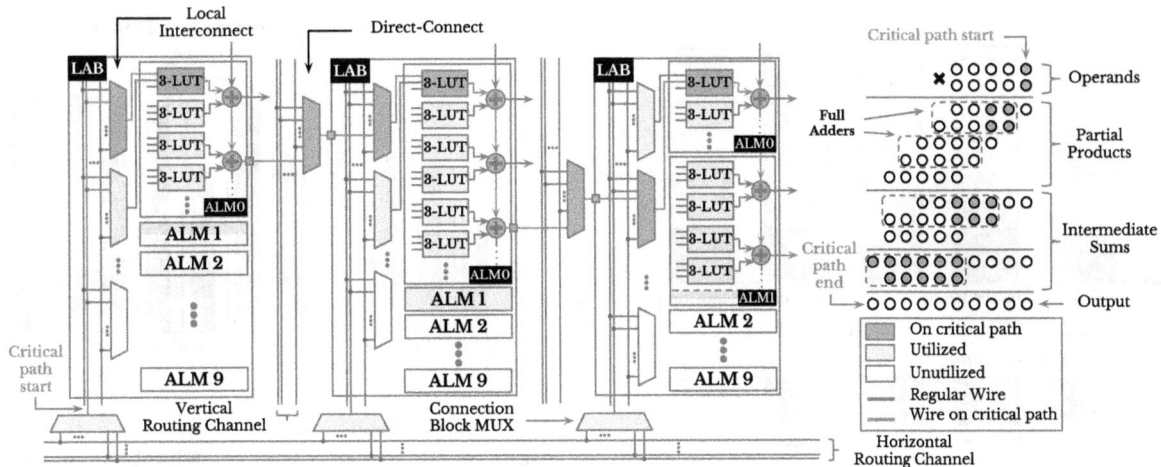

Figure 8: Critical path of a 5-bit multiplier mapped to the 4-bit Adder architecture.

Table 2: Routing and tile architecture parameters.

Parameter	Value	Parameter	Value
N (ALMs/LAB)	10	Fs	3
W (Channel width)	320	Fcin	0.2
L (Wire segment length)	4	Fcout	0.025
I (Inputs/LAB)	40	Fclocal	0.5

to model the LUTs feeding the carry chain in Stratix-10 and in one of our proposed architectures, respectively. We also added finer control over COFFE's intra-ALM routing so we could add multiplexers where necessary to make these new features as useful as possible. Since wire load affects both transistor sizing and delay significantly, we also created a floorplan for the proposed ALM that is used within COFFE to estimate all the intra-ALM wire lengths.

With these modifications, COFFE now has three additional modes of operation which allow us to perform area and delay measurements for three new architectures: the Stratix-10-like architecture, Stratix-10 with a second level of carry chain adders (both shown in Fig. 1) and finally the deeper fracturability design with 4-adders per ALM (Fig. 4). We believe these new features open up new areas for exploration and will be helpful to future FPGA logic block architecture research as well[1].

To evaluate the area and delay impact of shadow multipliers we created a structural system verilog implementation of our enhanced multiplier array with 3 distinct sign controls and parameterized precision. DSP block multiplies in FPGAs are typically implemented with standard cells, and accordingly we used a standard cell flow for the shadow multiplier: Synopsys Design Compiler 2013.03 for synthesis, Cadence Innovus for place and route, and 28 nm ST Microelectronics standard cell libraries. We used COFFE's full custom flow with 22 nm HP predictive technology model SPICE decks [1], so we scale the area of the resulting standard cell block to 22 nm and input it to COFFE, along with the area of the input drivers and output select multiplexers (see Fig. 6a). This allows COFFE to model the increased wire length due to the extra tile area, and to resize buffers where appropriate to cope with the larger loads.

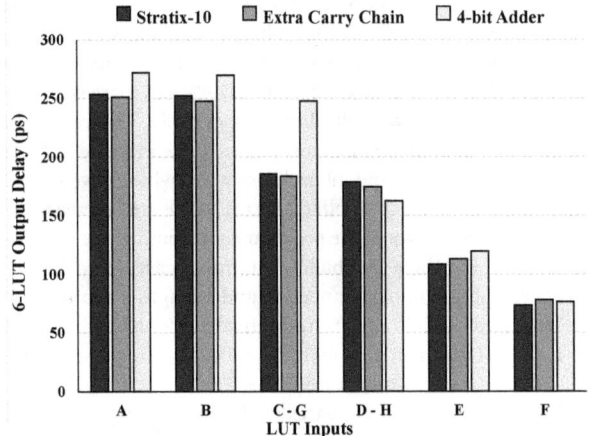

Figure 9: LUT input delays for the Stratix-10, Extra Carry Chain and 4-bit Adder architectures.

4.3 Tile Area and Delay Cost

COFFE sizes transistors to optimize a user-specified cost function of area and delay. For this study we have chosen a cost function of $area \cdot delay^2$ as it reflects the greater emphasis on delay compared to area typical in high-performance FPGAs like Stratix-10. The routing architecture and logic cluster parameters are chosen to match those in [8], as they are representative of recent Stratix series architectures; these parameters are summarized in Table 2.

Fig. 10 shows the area breakdown of the baseline, Extra Carry Chain, and 4-bit Adder architectures along with 4- and 9-bit Shadow Multiplier architectures using the baseline ALM. The Extra Carry Chain architecture and the 4-bit Adder architecture show small tile area increases over the baseline, of 2.6% and 2.9%, respectively. The major contributor to this increase is doubling the number of full adders per ALM for both architectures, which led to an approximately 2% area increase. The remainder of the area increase is primarily due to the extra multiplexing required by these architectures – as Fig. 1 and 4 show there are also two and six 2:1 multiplexers added in the Extra Carry Chain and 4-bit Adder architectures vs. the baseline, respectively.

---

[1] This enhanced version of COFFE is available at:
https://github.com/vaughnbetz/COFFE/tree/lbChanges

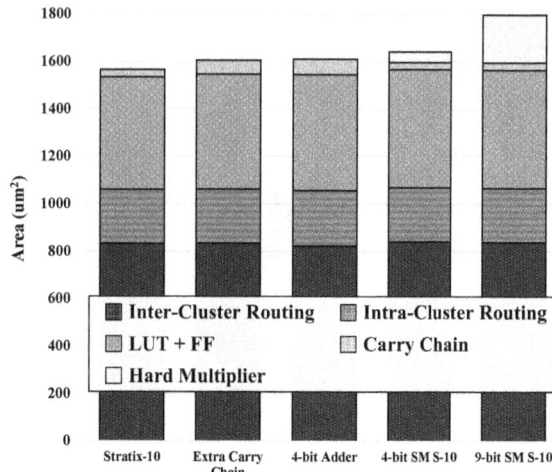

Figure 10: Tile area breakdown for various architectures.

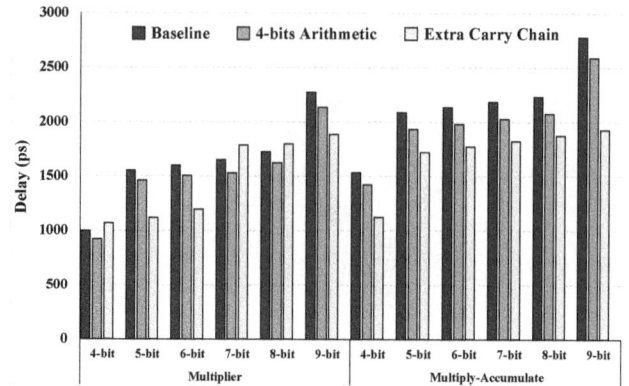

Figure 11: Multiplier and MAC critical path delays for Stratix-10, Extra Carry Chain and 4-bit Adder architectures.

As shown in Fig. 10, the 4- and 9-bit shadow multipliers increase the logic tile area more significantly, by 5.0% and 14.8% respectively. The main contributor to this increase in area is the added shadow multiplier which contributed a 2.9% and 12.8% area increase in case of 4- and 9-bit shadow multipliers, respectively. The remaining portion of the overall area increase is due to the increase in buffer sizes to drive the intra- and inter-cluster wires which have become longer due to the hard multiplier's area. The tile area increase also leads to some slowdown in the programmable routing due to longer wire-lengths. For the 4-bit shadow multiplier case, the delay of a direct (nearest neighbor) connection and a length 4 routing wire have increased by 4.4% and 1%, respectively. A 9-bit shadow multiplier increases routing delay more: by 9.5% for a direct connection and 6.5% a length 4 routing wire.

While the small area increases of the Extra Carry Chain and 4-bit Adder architectures mean that the routing wire delays are not significantly impacted, some LUT delays are. The delay of each LUT input from the local interconnect of the LAB to the 6-LUT output is shown in Fig. 9 for each ALM architecture. This figure shows the delays for the 8 inputs of the ALM; note that input C has exactly the same delay as input G and similarly inputs D and H have the same delay.

For the Extra Carry Chain architecture, inputs A, B, C, and D have a slightly lower delay compared to the baseline architecture; this is due to small variations in wire load and transistor sizing decisions made by COFFE. Inputs E and F have experienced a 10.4% and 4.2% increase in delay, respectively. In this architecture a connection is added from both these inputs to the new full adders in the ALM, increasing the capacitive loading of these inputs and hence increasing their delay. Overall the Extra Carry Chain architecture leads to very little change in the key delay paths in the tile.

The 4-bit Adder architecture has more impact on tile delay, and shows an increase in delay for all of its inputs except D and H. As Fig. 4 shows, this architecture contains eight 3-input LUTs feeding four adders. For the Stratix-10 baseline and Extra Carry Chain architectures there are instead four 4-LUTs in front of the adders, and COFFE speeds up these 4-LUTs by inserting buffers after the first two stages of pass transistors, evenly dividing the 4 cascaded pass gates in the 4-LUTs. In the 3-LUTs of the 4-bit Adder architecture

such even buffering is no longer an option, and instead COFFE implements 3 stages of pass gate with no internal buffering to realize the 3-LUTs with a buffer only at the LUT output. This leads to a 7% delay increase for inputs A and B. Input C's delay increases by 34% as it is also impacted by the extra 2:1 multiplexers (see Fig. 4) added to ensure all the necessary signals can reach the 3-LUTs when in multiplier mode.

4.4 Overall MAC Area and Delay

As mentioned in Section 4.1, we hand map multipliers and MAC units of 4-bit to 9-bit precisions for each architecture evaluated. This allows us to calculate the number of ALMs used (or rendered unusable) by the mapping and to determine the logic and routing on the critical path. By combining these ALM counts and critical paths with the tile areas, logic delays and routing component delays computed by COFFE and summarized in Section 4.3, we can determine the overall multiplier and MAC speed and density achieved by each architecture.

We implement all multipliers as AND gates (i.e a partial product using LUTs) followed by a sequence of carry chains to sum the partial products. Fig. 8 shows the critical path of a 5-bit multiplier implemented using the 4-bit Adder architecture. The right hand-side of the figure shows the partial products and how the addition reductions are performed. The solid circles show the operands and the partial products on the critical path. The rest of the figure shows how this multiplier is mapped to the soft logic. The addition operations occurring on the critical path need 6 ALMs which could fit in one LAB; however, for clarity we map them to different LABs in this figure. For the intra-ALM routing we assume that the critical path signal will use the direct-connect between (or within) LABs and have a delay of a directly-driven (no multiplexer) wire spanning one LAB, plus the delay of a connection block and the local cluster interconnect. This is not a best case placement and routing as the local cluster routing is slightly faster than direct connect, but it represents a high quality placement and routing and is applied consistently for all architectures.

Fig. 11 shows the delay of 4- to 9-bit multiply and MAC operations mapped to the baseline, Extra Carry Chain and 4-bit Adder architectures. The results show that for the multiply operations over all the multiplier sizes chosen in this study, the 4-bit Adder

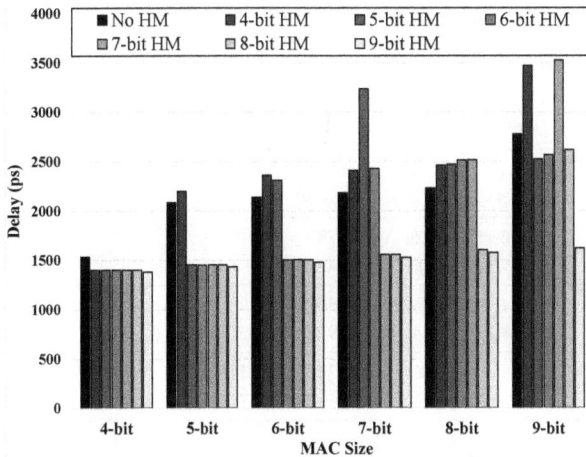

Figure 12: MAC critical path delays for Stratix-10 architectures with shadow multiplier sizes from 4- to 9-bit.

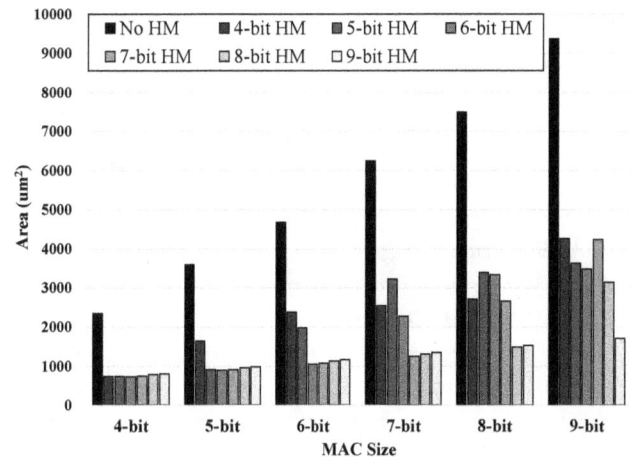

Figure 13: MAC areas for Stratix-10 architectures with shadow multiplier sizes from 4- to 9-bit.

and the Extra Carry Chain architectures show an average reduction of 3.9% and 8.4% in the critical path delay respectively over the baseline architecture. For MAC operations the delay reduction increases to 7.2% and 20% in the case of the 4-bit Adder and Extra Carry Chain architectures, respectively; the extra adders in these architecture benefit MAC even more than multiply. The speed gains are larger with the Extra Carry Chain architecture because it is able to pack two levels of an adder reduction tree in one LAB, reducing the number of (direct connect) routing hops.

For the Shadow Multiplier architecture, the way the multipliers are implemented depends on the hard multiplier size available in the logic block as well as the size of the multiplier to be synthesized. If the size of the multiplier to be synthesized is smaller than or equal to the size of the hard multiplier size, then the critical path delay will simply be the LAB input to LUT input delay, hard multiplier delay and the output select multiplexer delay. As discussed in Section 3.3 larger multiplies can be implemented either by combining a single shadow multiplier with ALM logic to complete the multiplier array, or by combining multiple shadow multipliers with ALM carry chains to sum their outputs. We evaluate both options and choose the one with smaller area (used plus unusable ALMs). The critical path delays and the areas required to implement 4- to 9-bit MACs using 4- to 9-bit Shadow Multiplier architectures are shown in Fig. 12 and Fig. 13. The critical path delay of a MAC operation increases with the multiplication size to the point were multiple hard multipliers can be combined without significantly impacting the area. For instance, Fig. 12 shows that the critical path delays of 6-bit to 8-bit MACs are almost the same when implemented on the 4-bit Shadow Multiplier architecture; this is because all 3 MAC sizes map to four 4-bit hard multipliers. For the same reason, Fig. 13 shows that there is almost no change in area for this 6- to 8-bit MAC precision range on a 4-bit Shadow Multiplier architecture.

Table 3 summarizes the performance of all the proposed architectures, along with a fifth architecture which is a combination of the Shadow Multiplier architecture and the 4-bit Adder architecture. We show multiple variations of the Shadow Multiplier architectures using three different hardened multiplier sizes (4, 6, and 9-bit). We are interested both in what gains we can achieve when the

architecture is used for MACs and what cost it entails in terms of tile area and delay for other circuits. In order to evaluate the impact of our proposed architectures on the delay of a typical design which does not exploit our new features, we used the notion of the representative critical path delay [14]. From our experience the representative critical path delay is divided into 70% routing delay, 25% logic delay and 5% carry chain delay; using these ratios we can combine the COFFE delay numbers for each architecture into the single delay metric shown in the table. The average MAC critical path delay and average MAC area numbers are geometric averages over 4-bit to 9-bit MAC operations. The bold numbers in each row in Table 3 show the best value for each category.

The Shadow Multiplier architectures achieve higher MAC area reductions compared to the Extra Carry Chain and the 4-bit Adder architectures. MAC area is further reduced by combining the 4-bit Adder architecture with the Shadow Multiplier architecture – this combination achieves an 83.6% average MAC area reduction with a 9-bit shadow multiplier. Shadow multipliers of size 6-bit and larger are faster than the Stratix-10 baseline and have MAC delay reductions comparable to the Extra Carry Chain and the 4-bit Adder architectures. The 4-bit Shadow Multiplier architecture is the slowest architecture (8% slower than the baseline) so 6-bit or larger shadow multipliers are more desirable. The high MAC area reductions of 6-bit and larger shadow multipliers unfortunately come with a considerable increase in the FPGA tile area and the representative critical path delay, and this cost grows with shadow multiplier size. Accordingly the 6-bit shadow multiplier seems like the best size: it achieves a 68% MAC area reduction at a reasonable cost of 2.3% representative critical path delay increase and 3.8% tile area growth. Combining a 6-bit shadow multiplier with the 4-bit Adder architecture reduces MAC area, but increases the area and delay penalties for general logic.

On the other hand, the Extra Carry Chain architecture shows the smallest increase in representative critical path delay (0.8%) and the smallest tile area increase (2.6%) over the Stratix-10 baseline so it is the least intrusive change in terms of its impact on general applications. Despite its small cost, the Extra Carry Chain architecture reduces the average MAC delay by 20.9% and the average MAC

Table 3: Area and Delay summaries for Stratix-10 architecture, Extra Carry Chain architecture, 4-bit Adder architecture, 4-, 6-, and 9-bit Shadow Multiplier architectures built on Stratix-10 and 4-bit Adder architectures.

Architectures	Stratix-10	Extra Carry Chain	4-bit Adder	SM on Stratix-10			SM on 4-bit Adder		
				4-bit	6-bit	9-bit	4-bit	6-bit	9-bit
Rep. Crit. Path Delay (ps)	119.2	**120.2** (+0.8%)	122.5 (+2.7%)	121.1 (+1.6%)	122.0 (+2.3%)	126.6 (+6.2%)	125.1 (+4.9%)	126.5 (+6.1%)	130.9 (+9.8%)
FPGA Tile Area (um^2)	1565	**1605** (+2.6%)	1610 (+2.9%)	1642 (+4.9%)	1624 (+3.8%)	1797 (+14.8%)	1629 (+4.1%)	1702 (+8.8%)	1826 (+16.7%)
Avg. MAC crit. Path Delay (ps)	2127	1682 (-20.9%)	1975 (-7.2%)	2304 (+8.3%)	1906 (-10.4%)	**1502** (-29.4%)	2542 (+19.5%)	2042 (-4.0%)	1528 (-28.2%)
Avg. MAC Area (um^2)	5097	3337 (-34.9%)	3205 (-36.8%)	2095 (-58.8%)	1621 (-68.1%)	1218 (-76.0%)	1166 (-77.1%)	996 (-80.4%)	**835** (-83.6%)

area by 34.9%. As this architecture benefits not only multiply and MAC operations but also any adder tree, it is also likely to result in area and delay reductions in other arithmetic applications.

Finally, the 4-bit Adder architecture achieves a slightly higher MAC area reduction (36.8%), with a slightly higher representative critical path delay increase (2.7%) and tile area increase (2.9%) than the Extra Carry Chain architecture; this makes it another fairly low-risk ALM change. This architecture will also benefit not just multiplication as it can implement all standalone adders and subtractors in half as many ALMs as in the Stratix-10 baseline. Given that arithmetic functions constitute over 20% of the logic primitives in recent benchmark sets [18] and most map to standalone adders or subtractors, this architecture is likely to yield significant ALM count reductions for a wide range of designs.

5 CONCLUSION AND FUTURE WORK

In this paper we proposed three different architectures which increase the MAC density in FPGAs, thereby improving FPGA performance on deep learning applications. The Extra Carry Chain architecture adds a second level of carry chains in the ALMs, making the reduction trees of the multiply operation more efficient. The 4-bit Adder architecture widens the carry chains in each ALM and increases the level of fracturability of their LUTs. The Shadow Multiplier architecture adds hard multipliers to the logic blocks without adding programmable routing, thereby keeping its cost lower.

We extended the COFFE transistor sizing and optimization tool to support these new architectures, and used it to generate detailed area and delay models. With a small impact on the tile area (+2.6%) and the representative critical path delay (+0.8%), the Extra Carry Chain architecture can achieve a 21% and a 35% reduction in average MAC delays and areas, respectively. The 4-bit Adder architecture achieves slightly better MAC area reductions, at the cost of slightly more tile area and representative critical path delay impact. MAC area reductions as high as 84% (representing a 6.1× increase in MAC density) can be achieved by combining the Shadow Multiplier and 4-bit Adder architectures. However, this comes with higher costs for general circuits: a tile area overhead of 16.7% and representative critical path delay increase of 9.8%.

ACKNOWLEDGMENTS

The authors would like to thank Huawei and the Vector Institute for funding support.

REFERENCES

[1] 2018. Predictive Technology Model (PTM). http://ptm.asu.edu/
[2] E. Ahmed and J. Rose. 2004. The effect of LUT and cluster size on deep-submicron FPGA performance and density. *TVLSI* 12, 3, 288–298.
[3] C. Baugh and B. Wooley. 1973. A two's complement parallel array multiplication algorithm. *TC* 100, 12.
[4] A. Boutros et al. 2018. Embracing diversity: Enhanced DSP blocks for low-precision deep learning on FPGAs. In *FPL*. 1–8.
[5] A. Boutros et al. 2018. You cannot improve what you do not measure: FPGA vs. ASIC efficiency gaps for convolutional neural network inference. *TRETS* 11, 3.
[6] M. Burich. 2012. Conference workshop: FPGAs in 2032, challenges and opportunities in the next 20 years, convergence of programmable solutions. In *FPGA*.
[7] S. Chandrakar et al. 2015. Enhancements in UltraScale CLB architecture. In *ISFPGA*. 108–116.
[8] C. Chiasson and V. Betz. 2013. COFFE: Fully-automated transistor sizing for FPGAs. In *FPT*. 34–41.
[9] J. Fowers et al. 2018. A configurable cloud-scale DNN processor for real-time AI. *ISCA*, 1–14.
[10] I. Goodfellow et al. 2016. *Deep learning*. Vol. 1. MIT press Cambridge.
[11] Intel Corporation. 2017. Intel Stratix 10 logic array blocks and adaptive logic modules user guide (UG-S10LAB).
[12] P. Jamieson and J. Rose. 2006. Enhancing the area-efficiency of FPGAs with hard circuits using shadow clusters. In *FPT*. 1–8.
[13] A. Krizhevsky et al. 2012. ImageNet classification with deep convolutional neural networks. In *NIPS*. 1097–1105.
[14] I. Kuon and J. Rose. 2011. Exploring area and delay tradeoffs in FPGAs with architecture and automated transistor design. *TVLSI* 19, 1, 71–84.
[15] M. Langhammer and B. Pasca. 2015. Floating-point DSP block architecture for FPGAs. In *ISFPGA*. ACM, 117–125.
[16] D. Lewis et al. 2005. The Stratix II logic and routing architecture. In *ISFPGA*. 14–20.
[17] D. Lewis et al. 2016. The Stratix 10 highly pipelined FPGA architecture. In *ISFPGA*. ACM, 159–168.
[18] J. Luu et al. 2014. On hard adders and carry chains in FPGAs. In *FCCM*. 52–59.
[19] A. Mishra et al. 2017. WRPN: wide reduced-precision networks. *arXiv preprint arXiv:1709.01134*.
[20] J. Rose et al. 1993. Architecture of field-programmable gate arrays. *Proc. IEEE* 81, 7, 1013–1029.
[21] V. Rybalkin et al. 2018. FINN-L: Library extensions and design trade-off analysis for variable precision LSTM networks on FPGAs. In *FPL*. 1–8.
[22] V. Sze et al. 2017. Efficient processing of deep neural networks: A tutorial and survey. *Proc. IEEE* 105, 12, 2295–2329.
[23] S. M. Trimberger. 2015. Three ages of FPGAs: A retrospective on the first thirty years of FPGA technology. *Proc. IEEE* 103, 3, 318–331.
[24] Xilinx Inc. 2017. Virtex UltraScale+ HBM FPGA: A revolutionary increase in memory performance.
[25] S. Yazdanshenas and V. Betz. 2017. Automatic circuit design and modelling for heterogeneous FPGAs. In *ICFPT*. 9–16.

LANMC: LSTM-Assisted Non-Rigid Motion Correction on FPGA for Calcium Image Stabilization

Zhe Chen
University of California, Los Angeles
Los Angeles, California
zhechen@ucla.edu

Hugh T. Blair
University of California, Los Angeles
Los Angeles, California
tadblair@ucla.edu

Jason Cong
University of California, Los Angeles
Los Angeles, California
cong@cs.ucla.edu

ABSTRACT

Calcium imaging is an emerging technique for visualizing and recording neural population activity at large scale in *vivo*. Non-rigid motion correction is a critical step in the calcium image analysis pipeline due to non-uniform deformations of the brain tissue during the data collection. Existing non-rigid motion correction algorithms are costly in computation time and energy, and it is hard to implement such algorithm in real time on an embedded device. In this paper, we propose LANMC, an LSTM-assisted non-rigid motion correction method for real-time calcium image stabilization. This method reduces the computational cost by using the LSTM inference to predict the non-rigid motion. Based on this method, we demonstrate a non-rigid motion correction implementation for real-time calcium image stabilization on FPGA. Experimental results show that the non-rigid motion correction can be accomplished within 80 μs on the Ultra96 under 300 MHz frequency, and the latency outperforms that on a 12-thread CPU by 82x.

KEYWORDS

Calcium image, long short-term memory (LSTM), motion correction

ACM Reference Format:
Zhe Chen, Hugh T. Blair, and Jason Cong. 2019. LANMC: LSTM-Assisted Non-Rigid Motion Correction on FPGA for Calcium Image Stabilization. In *The 2019 ACM/SIGDA International Symposium on Field-Programmable Gate Arrays (FPGA '19), February 24–26, 2019, Seaside, CA, USA.* ACM, New York, NY, USA, 6 pages. https://doi.org/10.1145/3289602.3293919

1 INTRODUCTION

Calcium imaging is a neural recording technique that can monitor neural population activity in *vivo* [15]. Recent progress in miniaturized fluorescent calcium imaging has enabled this technique to be realized in a light-weight head mounted miniscope sensor device for freely moving mice and rats [1, 6]. Such device can generate terabytes of data over days of recording, creating a huge computational burden for calcium imaging analysis [7].

Motion correction is a critical step in the calcium image analysis. It removes motion artifacts caused by inevitable displacement of the brain inside the skull during the image capturing. Due to the

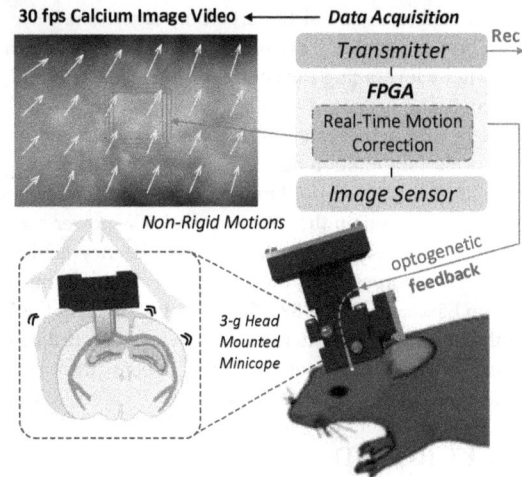

Figure 1: Real-time non-rigid motion correction for calcium image sensed by head-mounted miniscope [1].

non-uniform deformations of the brain tissue, the motion artifacts can be non-rigid, which increases the difficulty for the motion correction. An effective non-rigid motion correction algorithm has been proposed in [14], but it is costly in computation and not efficient for the real-time implementation. Real-time rigid motion correction for calcium imaging has been realized on CPU [7], but it does not account for the brain tissue deformation.

A real-time non-rigid motion correction for calcium image stabilization is in demand. Fig. 1 illustrates a flow-diagram for a closed-loop neurofeedback application in which the real-time non-rigid motion correction plays an important role in supporting the optogenetic feedback stimulation. Compared with state-of-the-art embedded CPUs and GPUs, FPGA is more appropriate for this application, because its customizable processing architecture can provide higher energy efficiency, shorter processing latency, and more flexible interface in processing data from the sensor. As the temporal and spatial resolution of the miniscope image sensor keeps increasing, it remains challenging to implement highly efficient non-rigid motion correction on FPGA due to the algorithm complexity, especially considering the limited hardware resource and energy budget on a head-mounted device.

In this paper, we propose a long short-term memory (LSTM) assisted non-rigid motion correction (LANMC) algorithm and implement it on FPGA for real-time calcium image stabilization. First, we introduce the method in saving computation and evaluate its performance by making comparison with existing non-rigid motion correction algorithm. Then we introduce our FPGA design which is orthogonal to the proposed method for a highly efficient implementation. Finally, we report experiment results and compare processing speed and energy efficiency against the CPU which is commonly used in existing miniscope data acquisition platform.

The contributions of this paper are summarized as follows:

- To the best of our knowledge, we are the first to propose using LSTM for the non-rigid motion correction and realize real-time non-rigid motion correction for calcium image stabilization in real time. Our method can reduce the computation cost by 95% while maintaining acceptable accuracy compared to a state-of-the-art offline algorithm.
- We propose a folding architecture for real-time contrast filtering by leveraging the central symmetry of a 17×17 filter kernel. The proposed architecture saves over 70% of operations, and achieves 25 cycle processing latency and 169 op/cycle computation density during the runtime.
- We implement non-rigid motion correction for calcium image stabilization on the Ultra96 with 4.5 W power consumption. Under 300 MHz, the processing latency achieves 80 μs, which outperforms the evaluation result on multi-core Xeon E5-2860 CPU by 82x. Combined with using the LSTM inference, our implementation has close to 4 orders of energy efficiency gain compared to the conventional offline non-rigid motion correction on CPU.

2 BACKGROUND

2.1 Conventional Non-Rigid Motion Correction

Motion correction is a critical processing step in a variety of calcium image analysis algorithms [7, 13, 14]. Recent work shows that piecewise rigid motion correction can effectively reduce non-rigid motion artifacts and outperform other methods for calcium image stabilization [14]. Fig. 2 illustrates the processing flow of this method[1]. For calcium image analyzed here, the first step is to enhance the image with a contrast filter that removes the bulk of the background [14]. The kernel size of the filter is determined by the diameter of the cell bodies in the source image, and 17×17 was the minimum kernel size for generating sufficiently accurate motion correction results. The second step is to divide the field of view of the image into overlapping patches $f(i,j) \in \mathbb{R}^{N_P \times N_P}, i \in [1, \lceil W/N_P \rceil]$, $j \in [1, \lceil L/N_P \rceil]$, to perform the piecewise rigid motion correction. For each patch, the algorithm calculates its cross correlation $CC(i,j) \in \mathbb{R}^{N_P \times N_P}$ against a template $g(i,j) \in \mathbb{R}^{N_P \times N_P}$ from the frequency domain through 2D FFT/IFFT operations. Finally, the motion vector for each image patch is extracted by finding the position of the maximum amplitude of the cross correlation, and the subpixel resolution is achieved through the interpolation [7].

2.2 Algorithm Complexity

For the algorithm described in Section 2.1, suppose the kernel size of the filter is $N_K \times N_K$, and the image patch size is $N_P \times N_P$. The operation count per image frame can be estimated by

$$C_{NoR} = \left(2N_K^2 - 1\right)WL + \left(8N_P^2 log_2 N_P + 2N_P^2\right)\left\lceil \frac{W}{N_P} \right\rceil \left\lceil \frac{L}{N_P} \right\rceil \quad (1)$$

---
[1]Histogram equalization is adopted on the filtered image for better visibility.

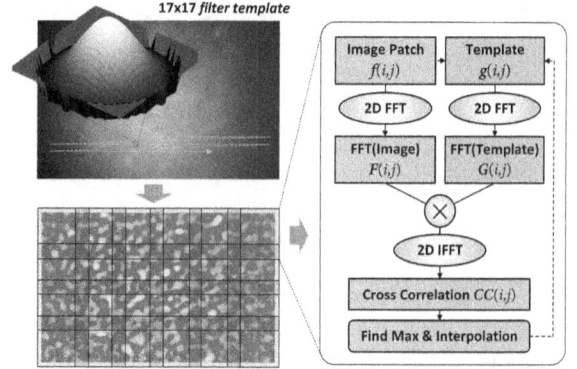

Figure 2: Conventional non-rigid motion detection flow.

in which W and L represent the width and length of the calcium image. For simplicity, we assume N_P is a power of two, and ignore the cost of the interpolation. The first addend is derived from the contrast filter with complexity $O(N_K^2)$ per pixel, while the second addend is contributed by the motion vector extraction with complexity $O(N_P^2 log_2(N_P))$ per patch. For a typical parameter set with $N_K=17$ and $N_P=128$, the contrast filter dominates the operation count. The goal of this paper is to reduce the complexity described in Eq. 1 and realize an efficient non-rigid motion correction with short latency for real-time calcium image analysis.

2.3 LSTM Inference

LSTM is a type of recurrent neural networks that has been successfully used in a variety of time-series prediction tasks [10]. For an LSTM model with one layer and N_H hidden nodes, the inference output for the current time step is based on the updates of four independent types of gates: input gate (I), forget gate (F), cell gate (G) and output gate (O) by taking advantage of the recurrent connections from the hidden nodes. Recent work shows that a compact LSTM model with a typical setting of $N_H=5$ can achieve sufficient accuracy in approximating IIR filter functions [3]. The inference complexity of N_H-node LSTM derived by

$$C_{LSTM}(N_H) = 16N_H^2 + 6N_H \quad (2)$$

shows its good potential for high efficiency on-line inferencing.

3 PROPOSED METHOD

3.1 LSTM-based Non-Rigid Motion Correction

We propose a non-rigid motion correction algorithm for miniscope captured calcium image based on LSTM inference to reduce the computation cost. As Fig. 3(a) shows, instead of performing heavy motion calculations for each divided image patch $f(i,j)$, we evaluate the motion only at a central $N_C \times N_C$ pixel region, and then we use the calculation result to predict non-rigid motions of all image patches based on LSTM inference.

Fig. 3(b) shows the motion extraction from the central region and all image patches throughout the calcium image video session. The displacement of each patch $f(i,j)$ is represented by a motion vector containing two values $\{x_{i,j}, y_{i,j}\}$. These values represent the rigid motion against the template along the horizontal and vertical axes with sub-pixel precision. For motion extraction at the central

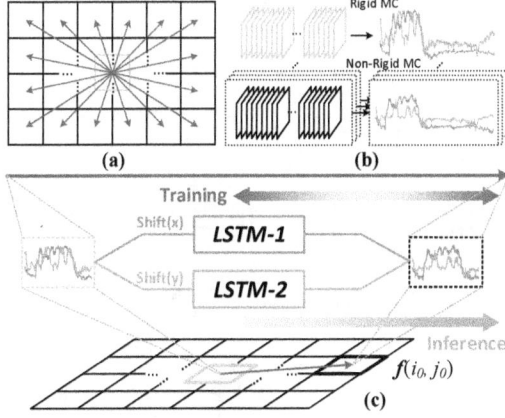

Figure 3: (a) Proposed LSTM-assisted non-rigid motion correction. (b) Motion vector extraction for the central region and all image patches. (c) LSTM inference on one patch.

region, a light-weight rigid motion correction described in Fig. 2 is performed to reduce the computation cost. For motion extraction at all image patches, a non-rigid motion correction algorithm NoRMCorre [14] is used to achieve high accuracy.

Fig. 3(c) illustrates the LSTM-assisted method in detail. Since all image patches are independent, we only show one projection from the central region to an image patch $f(i_0, j_0)$ for simplicity. The operation of the LSTM can be divided into two stages: offline training and online inference. During the training, the motion vector time series $\{x_C, y_C\}$ extracted at the central region is used as input, and the motion vector time series extracted at the patch $f(i_0, j_0)$ are used as the target. A pair of compact LSTM networks are trained to adapt the motion vector components of the central region to those of the patch $f(i_0, j_0)$ along the horizontal and vertical axes, respectively. After the LSTM networks are well trained, they are deployed to inference the offline motion correction at much shorter latency and much lower computational cost.

For the rigid motion correction at the central region, the operation count per frame can be derived by:

$$C_{Rigid} = \left(2N_K^2 - 1\right) N_C^2 + \left(8N_P^2 \log_2 N_P + 2N_P^2\right) \quad (3)$$

and the computation cost saving can be estimated by:

$$G_{eff} = C_{NoR} / \left(C_{Rigid} + C_{LSTM} (N_H) \left\lceil \frac{W}{N_P} \right\rceil \left\lceil \frac{L}{N_P} \right\rceil \right) \quad (4)$$

Considering the miniscope [1] resolution 752×480 and parameters N_C = 128 and N_H = 5, the G_{eff} results in 22.2x by keeping the default settings in Section 2.2. It indicates that 95% of operations can be saved by taking advantage of the LSTM inference for the non-rigid motion correction.

3.2 Algorithm Evaluation

We carried out an evaluation based on 26 sessions of calcium image videos, lasting for 50 seconds each. We used 25 sessions as the training set, and the remaining session as the test set. During the offline training, we derived the input based on the rigid motion correction shown in Fig. 2, and extracted non-rigid motion vectors

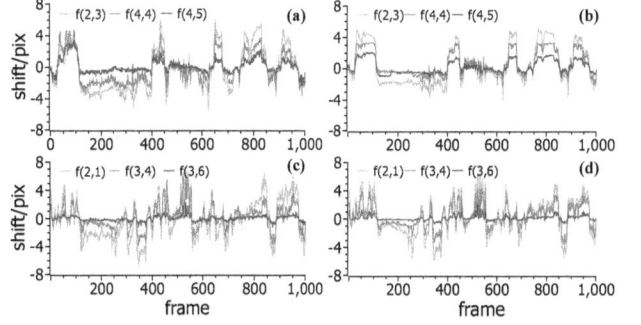

Figure 4: Extracted motion vectors in horizontal/vertical direction from three different image patches by using the NoRMCorre method (a)/(c) and the LSTM inference (b)/(d).

using the NoRMCorre [14] as the training targets. For each image patch $f(i, j)$, we trained a pair of compact 5-node LSTM networks using Caffe [11] to predict motion vectors in horizontal and vertical directions. We adopted the step learning rule, and set both the base learning rate and the gamma to be 0.1. During the inference, we fed the rigid motion vector of the central region extracted from the test video to the well-trained LSTMs, and the outputs were used as an approximation of non-rigid motion vectors for each image patch $f(i, j)$. Fig. 4 shows a comparison on non-rigid motion correction carried out by conventional method and the LSTM inference. Fig. 4(a) and (c) show vectors extracted by conventional methods from three selected image patches in horizontal and vertical directions, respectively, whereas Fig. 4(b) and (d) shows motion vectors inferenced by the LSTMs correspondingly.

We used the residual of optical flow (ROF) measurement [14] to evaluate the accuracy of the proposed method. Fig. 5 (a) and (b) show the evaluation results on No.451-453 and No.554-556 frames with obvious non-rigid motion artifacts. We first extracted the ROF of the registered frames based on optical flow [5], and then calculated the averaged ROF map for the vector plot and evaluated the ROF per pixel within the map. As the results show, the non-rigid motion correction algorithm NoRMCorre can get rid of most of the non-uniform motion artifacts, whereas the LANMC corrects significant amount of non-rigid motions by approximating the NoRMCorre. By using the LSTM inference, the ROF can be reduced by 69.2% and 50% for the selected frame periods, respectively.

Table 1 summarizes the evaluated ROF for non-rigid, rigid and LSTM-assisted methods on the test session. Evaluation results show that the LANMC on average reduces 48% ROF compared with the rigid method, and the accuracy is comparable with the NoRMCorre. We also compared the horizontal component mean absolute difference (MAD) $diff(x)$, vertical component MAD $diff(y)$ and amplitude MAD $diff(a)$ among these methods. Comparison results in Table 1 show that the LSTM-assisted method achieves higher accuracy than the rigid method in approximating the NoRMCorre method.

4 FPGA DESIGN

The FPGA design of the LANMC consists of a contrast filter accelerator, an FFT-based cross correlation module for motion vector extraction at the central region, and an LSTM inference kernel for non-rigid motion prediction at all distributed image patches.

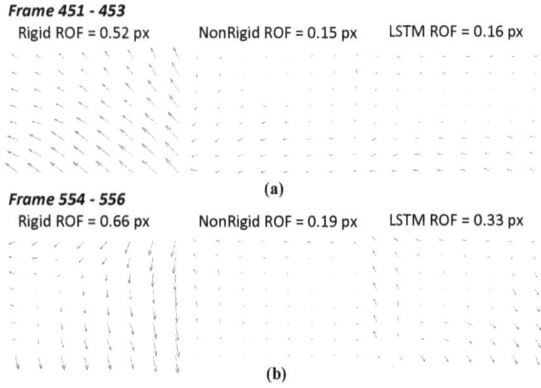

Frame 451 - 453
Rigid ROF = 0.52 px   NonRigid ROF = 0.15 px   LSTM ROF = 0.16 px

(a)

Frame 554 - 556
Rigid ROF = 0.66 px   NonRigid ROF = 0.19 px   LSTM ROF = 0.33 px

(b)

Figure 5: Mean ROF of the motion corrected (a) No.451-453 frames and (b) No.554-556 frames across time by the rigid, non-rigid and LSTM-assisted methods.

Table 1: Performance of the LSTM method compared with conventional motion correction algorithms

	ROF(pixel)	$diff(x)$	$diff(y)$	$diff(a)$
NoRMCorre [14]	0.19±0.11	0	0	0
Rigid Method	0.60±0.45	0.879	0.658	1.248
LANMC	0.31±0.22	0.621	0.362	0.804

4.1 Contrast Filter Design

A key observation at the contrast filter described in Section 2.1 is that the template of the filter is symmetric about the horizontal, vertical and diagonal axes. This provides the opportunity to reduce the computation efforts. Instead of performing multiplication for each coefficient in the filter template, we can first add up the input values corresponding to the coefficients in symmetry, and then multiply the sum with the coefficient to get the equivalent result. By leveraging this reordering, logic and memory resource costs in realizing the contrast filter can be reduced. Fig. 6 shows the proposed folding architecture for the contrast filter. The architecture features three stages of folding data flow. On the first stage, instead of feeding the N_K 8-bit pixels from the 1D column buffer directly to a $N_K \times N_K$ processing element (PE) array [4], we inserted an adder stage between the column buffer and a shift register array, as Fig. 6(a) shows. The adder stage reduced the amount of data and the corresponding array size by half with negligible latency overhead. In a similar manner, Fig. 6(b) shows the second-stage folding architecture leveraging the vertical symmetry. For each row of PE, we employed a row of 9-bit adders to fold the horizontal partial sums. Finally, in the quarter-size array, we used a last stage of 10-bit adders to sum the values having a diagonal line of symmetry as shown in Fig. 6(c). With three stages of folding, the requirement on the multiplication count is reduced to one eighth, and we in further skipped multiplication with zeros to save computation. Table 2 shows a comparison on hardware cost between the implementations with and without folding. By taking advantage of the folding, the proposed architecture saves >80% logic and registers and >60% DSPs. Evaluation on multicore CPU with OpenMP shows that the

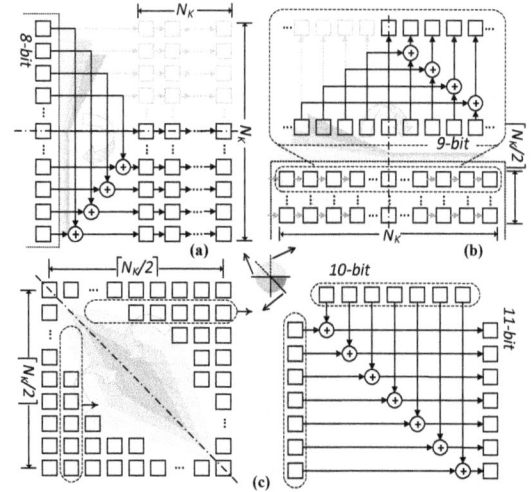

Figure 6: Proposed (a) 1st stage (b) 2nd stage and (c) 3rd stage folding architecture for the contrast filter featuring centrally symmetric coefficients.

Table 2: FPGA resource saving by the folding architecture

	W/ Folding	W/O Folding	Resource Saving
LUT	1211	6373	81.0%
FF	1972	11809	83.3%
DSP	22	56	60.7%
SRL	15	489	96.9%

Table 3: Comparison on runtime of the full frame filtering with multi-core CPU

	This work	4 thr	8 thr	12 thr	16 thr
Freq(MHz)	100	300	1200 - 1500		
Runtime(ms)	3.73	1.25	135	90	53

folding speeds up the contrast filtering by 1.8x. Table 3 shows the runtime comparison on contrast filtering with folding between the FPGA and the Xeon E5 2860 CPU. The FPGA design achieves 25 clock cycle latency, and the runtime under 300 MHz outperforms the evaluation on the CPU by over 40x speedup.

4.2 Reused Parallel FFT/IFFT

As Section 2.1 introduces, an efficient way to calculate the cross correlation is to perform dot product at the frequency domain. We implemented the 2D $N_P \times N_P$ FFT/IFFT transforms by carrying out consecutive NP horizontal and N_P vertical N_P-point FFT/IFFTs. Computation unit and BRAM buffer resource for each round of N_P-point transforms are reused. In order to achieve short processing latency, we unrolled the FFT/IFFT transformer by 4. In addition, we partitioned the BRAM into 4 blocks to cope with the computation throughput. Fig. 7 shows the proposed timing for the BRAM access and the transfer of the data to the FFT/IFFT units. We stored both the input and the result data in a row-major order. For horizontal

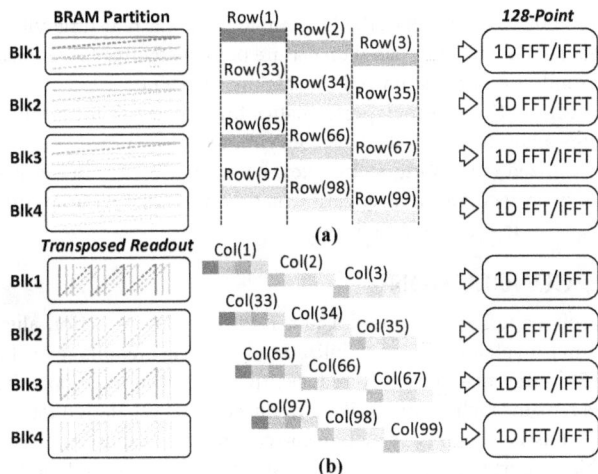

Figure 7: (a) BRAM partition and FFT/IFFT unrolling for row-wise parallel operation, and (b) transposed BRAM readout timing for column-wise parallel FFT/IFFT operations.

Table 4: Comparison on latency and FPGA resource usage

	Freq	Latency	LUT	FF	DSP
This work	300MHz	45.8 μs	8913	12624	60
	100MHz	137.4 μs	8886	12539	60
Ref. [2]	100MHz	328.2 μs	14036	14622	108

FFT/IFFT transforms, the data can be fetched independently from the BRAMs, and the FFT/IFFT units operate in parallel, as Fig. 7(a) shows. For vertical FFT/IFFT transforms, the data access from the BRAM is organized in pipeline avoiding confliction, as Fig. 7(b) shows. The initial latency between two rows is NP/4 clock cycles, and the FFT/IFFT units are in full operation. Table 4 shows the comparison on processing latency and hardware cost of 2D FFT/IFFT for motion detection. Our proposed reusable parallel FFT/IFFT implementation outperforms [2] by 2.38x in processing latency under the same 100 MHz clock frequency, and our design reduces 25% logic resource and >40% DSP.

4.3 LSTM Inference Kernel

Fig. 8 shows the proposed microarchitecture for the LSTM inference kernel [3]. The LSTM inference for all distributed image patches can be fully unrolled. However, it will cause a linear increase on hardware cost as the number of image patches increases. In order to save the computation resource and balance the processing time for each stage of the non-rigid motion correction algorithm, we shared the LSTM kernel in predicting motion vector components in each patch, and reused the same kernel for all patches. We stored weights and states for all LSTM instantiations in an affordable on-chip buffer. Inside each LSTM kernel, the arithmetic units are unrolled by a factor of 4 corresponding to the number of gate types in the LSTM model. Within each unrolled unit, the matrix vector multiplication between LSTM weights and states can be pipelined with initial interval (II) equal to 1.

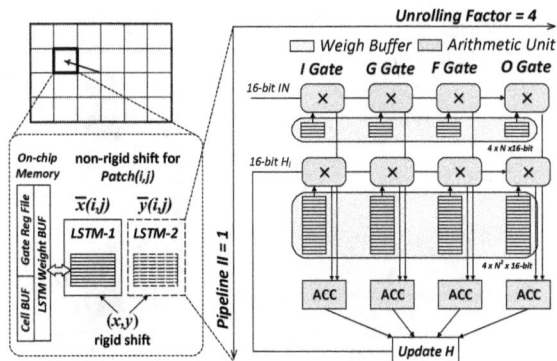

Figure 8: Microarchitecture for the LSTM inference [3].

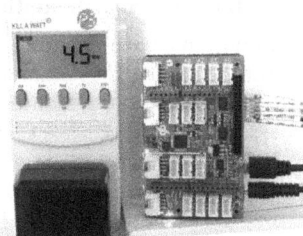

Figure 9: Power measurement of the non-rigid motion correction implementation on the Ultra96 board.

Table 5: FPGA resource utilization on the Ultra96

	LUT	FF	BRAM	DSP
Contrast Filter	1211	1972	0	22
Cross Correlation	8901	12624	34	60
Interpolation	3212	5175	0	36
LSTM	2129	1896	2	28
Overall	28338	37446	139	146
Utilization	40.16%	26.53%	64.35%	40.56%

5 EXPERIMENT RESULT

We carried out the non-rigid motion correction implementation on both the ZC706 and the Ultra96 boards. We first verified the proposed LSTM-assisted non-rigid motion correction on the ZC706 by testing it with an external miniscope image sensor connected through the FMC interface. Then we ported the same design onto the Ultra96, and test it with emulated data stream generated inside the SoC device. The operating frequency on the Ultra96 achieves 300 MHz, and the processing latency for each frame is 79.65 μs, which leaves a large margin for consecutive calcium image analysis algorithm considering the 33-ms frame interval. The power consumption of this implementation is 4.5 W, as shown in Fig. 9, and the breakdown of the hardware usage is shown in Table 5. The interpolation is realized in single precision floating point, while the rest kernels are in 16-bit fixed-point. The adopted bit quantization does not degrade the accuracy achieved in simulation in Section 3.2. Besides the listed kernels, our design also included a frame buffer, DMA controller, AXI interface and peripherals, which contribute to the overall hardware cost.

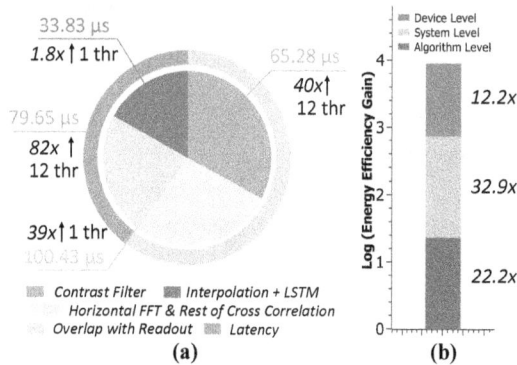

Figure 10: (a) Breakdown of runtime on FPGA and (b) energy efficiency gain over the CPU implementation.

We compared our implementation with the evaluation on the Xeon E5-2680 CPU with 12 threads. The runtime comparison results are shown in Fig. 10(a). The comparison result shows that the FPGA can achieve 82x speedup in processing latency over CPU. The main reason is that the FPGA design not only speeds up the most time consuming contrast filter by 40x, but also hides 60% runtime behind the read-out timing of the image sensor. For the cross correlation and the LSTM inference, we only evaluated the CPU performance with single thread because the data dependency limits the performance on multi threads, and the runtime is trivial compared to the filter stage. Compared with the single-thread CPU implementation, the FPGA achieves 39x speedup for the cross correlation with the 100.43 μs runtime, and 1.8x speedup for the LSTM inference stage with the 33.83 μs runtime. We can potentially achieve higher speedup for the LSTM inference by duplicating the LSTM kernels, but benefit will be very limited considering additional hardware resource cost given that the LSTM inference is not the bottleneck in performance. Fig. 10(b) summarizes the energy efficiency gain over the high performance multi-core CPU achieved by our work. First, our proposed LSTM-based method contributes 22.2x energy efficiency gain by reducing the computational complexity from the algorithm level. Secondly, our FPGA system design provides 32.9x gain by realizing consistent speedup for each kernel step. Finally, the adoption of the state-of-the-art FPGA device adds another 12.2x gain, in which we suppose the power consumption of the CPU using 12 threads is 51.4 W based on the thermal design power specification, and the power consumption of the FPGA is 4.5 W. In all, we get close to 4 orders of energy efficiency gain over a conventional non-rigid motion correction implementation on CPU.

6 RELATED WORK

Motion correction for calcium image has been sufficiently discussed in previous literatures [7, 13, 14]. A non-rigid motion correction method proposed in [14] outperforms other methods in accuracy, but it costs a long processing time due to the high computation complexity. [13] proposed another motion correction methods for calcium image, but it is only suitable for offline analysis. [7] realized a real time rigid motion correction on CPU for calcium image analysis, but it operates offline and the runtime is >60x longer than this work. [8] proposed FPGA acceleration for motion estimation based on block matching, and [2] realized motion blur removal

on FPGA based on 2D FFT. [12] implemented a real-time video stabilization on FPGA based on feature point matching. Since these methods are not customized for calcium image non-rigid motion correction, the accuracy performance limit their use for calcium image analysis. Finally, beyond conventional image processing and customized computing techniques, neural network training has also been recognized as effective method to improve computing efficiency in recent research [9].

7 CONCLUSION

In this paper, we proposed a non-rigid motion correction algorithm for calcium image stabilization by taking advantage of the LSTM inference. It largely reduces the computation complexity and remains high accuracy. We introduced the FPGA design for the LSTM-assisted non-rigid motion correction method. Our design can achieve short latency for real-time calcium image non-rigid motion correction and high energy efficiency, and it has the potential to be built into existing miniaturized head mounted miniscope device.

ACKNOWLEDGMENTS

This work is partially supported by the NSF under Grant No.: CCF-1436827 and No.:DBI-1707408. The authors would like to thank Dr. Daniel Aharoni for his help on the miniscope device.

REFERENCES

[1] Denise J. Cai, Daniel Aharoni, Tristan Shuman, and et al. 2016. A shared neural ensemble links distinct contextual memories encoded close in time. *Nature* 534 (2016), 115–118.
[2] T.N. Chandrapala, L.M.A.P. Cabral, S. Ahangama, and et al. 2012. Hardware implementation of motion blur removal. In *Int. Conf. Field Program. Log. Appl.* 243–248.
[3] Zhe Chen, Andrew Howe, Hugh T. Blair, and et al. 2018. CLINK: Compact LSTM inference kernel for energy efficient neurofeedback devices. In *Proc. Int. Symp. Low Power Electron. Des.* 2:1–2:6.
[4] Ye Han Cong Shi, Jie Yang and et al. 2014. A 1000fps vision chip based on a dynamically reconfigurable hybrid architecture comprising a PE array and self-organizing map neural network. In *IEEE Int. Solid-State Circuits Conf. Dig. Tech. Pap.* 128–129.
[5] Gunnar Farnebäck. 2003. Two-frame motion estimation based on polynomial expansion. In *Image Anal.* Springer Berlin Heidelberg, 363–370.
[6] Kunal K Ghosh, Laurie D Burns, Eric D Cocker, and et al. 2011. Miniaturized integration of a fluorescence microscope. *Nat. Methods* 8 (2011), 871.
[7] Andrea Giovannucci, Johannes Friedrich, Matthew Kaufman, and et al. 2017. OnACID: Online analysis of calcium imaging data in real time. In *Adv. Neural Inf. Process. Syst.* 2378–2388.
[8] Diego Gonzalez, Guillermo Botella, Soumak Mokheerje, and et al. 2011. FPGA-Based acceleration of block matching motion estimation techniques. In *Int. Conf. Field Program. Log. Appl.* 389–392.
[9] Xin He, Liu Ke, Wenyan Lu, and et al. 2018. AxTrain: Hardware-oriented neural network training for approximate inference. In *Proc. Int. Symp. Low Power Electron. Des.* 20:1–20:6.
[10] Sepp Hochreiter and Jürgen Schmidhuber. 1997. Long short-term memory. *Neural Comput.* 9, 8 (1997), 1735–1780.
[11] Yangqing Jia, Evan Shelhamer, Jeff Donahue, and et al. 2014. Caffe: Convolutional architecture for fast feature embedding. In *Proc. 22nd ACM Int. Conf. Multimed.* New York, NY, USA, 675–678.
[12] Jianan Li, Tingfa Xu, and Kun Zhang. 2017. Real-time feature-based video stabilization on FPGA. *IEEE Trans. Circuits Syst. Video Technol.* 27, 4 (2017), 907–919.
[13] Jinghao Lu, Chunyuan Li, Jonnathan Singh-Alvarado, and et al. 2018. MIN1PIPE: A miniscope 1-photon-based calcium imaging signal extraction pipeline. *Cell Rep.* 23, 12 (2018), 3673–3684.
[14] Eftychios A. Pnevmatikakis and Andrea Giovannucci. 2017. NoRMCorre: An online algorithm for piecewise rigid motion correction of calcium imaging data. *J. Neurosci. Methods* 291 (2017), 83–94.
[15] Christoph Stosiek, Olga Garaschuk, Knut Holthoff, and et al. 2003. In vivo two-photon calcium imaging of neuronal networks. *Proc. Natl. Acad. Sci. U. S. A.* 100, 12 (2003), 7319–7324.

On-chip FPGA Debug Instrumentation for Machine Learning Applications

Daniel Holanda Noronha[1], Ruizhe Zhao[2], Jeff Goeders[3], Wayne Luk[2] and Steven J.E. Wilton[1]

[1]University of British Columbia, [2]Imperial College London, [3]Brigham Young University

danielhn@ece.ubc.ca,ruizhe.zhao15@imperial.ac.uk,jgoeders@byu.edu,w.luk@imperial.ac.uk,stevew@ece.ubc.ca

ABSTRACT

FPGAs provide a promising implementation option for many machine learning applications. Although simulations or software models can be used to explore the design space of these applications, often the final behaviour can not be evaluated until the design is mapped to the FPGA and integrated into the target system. This may be because long run-times are required, or because the environment can not be adequately described using a software model. Once unexpected behaviour is observed, on-chip debug is notoriously difficult; typically a design is instrumented with on-chip trace buffers that record the run-time behaviour for later interrogation.

In this paper, we describe instrumentation that can accelerate the process of debugging machine learning applications implemented on an FPGA. Unlike previous work, our instrumentation is optimized to take advantage of characteristics of this application domain. Our instruments gather useful domain-specific information about the observed variables instead of recording the raw values of those elements. Results show that the proposed instruments provide at least 17.8x longer visibility in the most conservative of our experiments at a low area and latency cost.

CCS CONCEPTS

• **Hardware** → VLSI; EDA; **Design for debug**.

ACM Reference Format:
Daniel Holanda Noronha, Ruizhe Zhao, Jeff Goeders, Wayne Luk and Steven J.E. Wilton. 2019. On-chip FPGA Debug Instrumentation for Machine Learning Applications. In *The 2019 ACM/SIGDA International Symposium on Field-Programmable Gate Arrays (FPGA '19), February 24–26, 2019, Seaside, CA, USA.* ACM, New York, NY, USA, 6 pages. https://doi.org/10.1145/3289602.3293922

1 INTRODUCTION

Recent years have seen tremendous interest in machine learning algorithms and techniques. Although CPUs and GPUs are often sufficient for training and inference tasks, Field-Programmable Gate Arrays (FPGAs) may lead to implementations that are faster and/or lower power. These advantages have led many researchers to propose novel FPGA-oriented architectures and techniques, and have spurred significant commercial activity.

Designing an FPGA-based machine learning application can be done using RTL-based design, high-level synthesis (HLS), or domain-specific translation flows (eg. [7, 12]). Regardless of how these applications are implemented, debugging these designs can be extremely difficult, for at least three reasons. First, unlike many application domains, inference and training tasks normally require very long run-times (many training or inference samples) before their overall behaviour can be understood. As an example, consider an error in a training application that causes many weights to be incorrectly clamped to zero; this could not be observed or understood without running many training samples. This means that hardware-oriented simulation techniques may not be sufficient to understand the operation of the design. Second, the "correctness" of machine learning applications can often not be determined by looking at individual signals/variables in isolation. As an example, during training, there is no "correct" value for a weight; the correctness depends on the ensemble of weights acting together. This means existing debug tools, which are optimized for examining the behaviour or specific signals are variables, are less useful. Third, machine learning applications are often designed at a high level (eg. C in HLS-based flows or Python in flows such as [7]) and automated tools are used to translate these high level designs into a circuit. This means that hardware-oriented debug flows, which provide visibility in the context of the hardware design, may not provide information in a form that is useful for the designer (this is similar to the observation in [5]).

In this paper, we present a flow to accelerate the debug of machine learning applications on FPGAs. Like existing hardware debug flows, we allow the user to add instrumentation that records the behaviour of the design as it runs at speed. Unlike existing flows, our instrumentation is optimized specifically for machine learning applications. Specifically, this work provides novel histogram, spatial sparsity, and summary generating instrumentation. These instruments are designed to summarize data on-chip in a way that maximizes the utilization of trace buffer space, while providing information that is meaningful to an engineer trying to understand the behaviour of the chip.

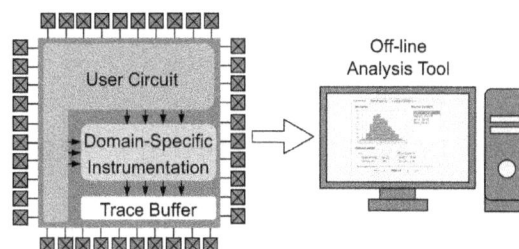

Figure 1: Domain-Specific Debug Instrumentation

Although the flow in this paper could be applied to any hardware implementation of machine learning algorithms, it is especially relevant for FPGAs for two reasons. First, FPGAs are often the first hardware implementation method for a new product (either as a prototype or before cost reduction), so this type of debugging is most likely to be performed in an FPGA. Second, this technique enables rapid debug and design, which is essential as FPGAs start to appear in cloud-based systems. We anticipate that FPGA companies are especially well-positioned to take advantage of our techniques.

This paper is organized as follows. Section 2 provides context for our work by describing recent efforts in on-chip debug instrumentation. Section 3 then describes our overall approach and instrumentation architecture. Section 4 shows how the data obtained from the instruments can be displayed to the user in a meaningful way. Section 5 evaluates our proposal in terms of trace length, area overhead, and circuit speed.

2 PREVIOUS WORK AND CONTEXT

Although software simulators are an important part of any debug ecosystem, simulation alone many not be sufficient to find the root cause of many types of bugs. Bugs that require long run-times to manifest, or those that occur due to specific input patterns may be missed by simulation. The only method to find the cause of these types of bugs is to execute the hardware in a real system, running at speed, driven by real input traffic.

Understanding the behaviour of a design running at speed is difficult due to limited I/O pins; FPGA vendors provide tools such as Intel's SignalTap II and Vivado's ILA [1, 14] to instrument a user design, at compile time, such that the behaviour of important signals can be stored on-chip during execution for later interrogation. Examining the traces of these signals can allow an engineer to understand the behavior of the design and try to track down the root cause of unexpected behaviour. Academic work has also considered adding such instrumentation at run-time [3, 11], decreasing the time between debug iterations.

Recent academic work has extended this instrumentation, optimizing it specifically for designs that are generated by high-level synthesis compilers [2, 4–6]. These works show that significant compression is possible by understanding the schedule of the design (which is available from the HLS tool) and using this information to only record signal values when they are scheduled to change. This compression allows a longer trace history to be stored on-chip, meaning fewer debug iterations are typically required to identify the root cause of a bug.

Debugging for machine learning applications is often done using software tools such as Tensorboard. Our approach is different in that Tensorboard is aimed at debugging a software model, while our approach is for debugging an application running on an FPGA.

3 DOMAIN-SPECIFIC INSTRUMENTATION

3.1 Overall Approach

Similar to previous flows, we instrument the user design at compile time to enable runtime recording of circuit behaviour (Figure 1). However, while previous work stores the raw values of variables

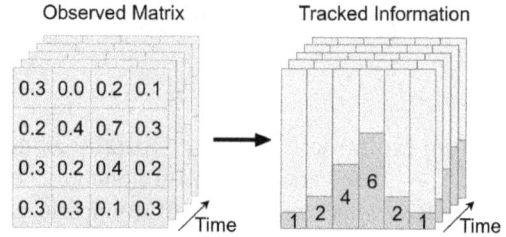

Figure 2: Distribution Instrument Overview

or signals into the on-chip trace buffers, we use on-chip domain-specific compression to store aggregated information about important variables or signals, making much more efficient use of memory. After the chip has been run, this information can be retrieved and used with our off-line analysis tool to allow the user to relate specific values to quantities in the original design, allowing them to better understand the behaviour of the circuit.

3.2 Debug Instruments

The domain-specific compression is done using one or more *instruments*, each of which monitors the behaviour of signals and summarizes the behaviour in the associated trace buffer(s). Each instrument summarizes the behaviour in a different way. The instruments we have selected are inspired by Tensorboard, which is used for debugging software implementations of machine learning applications. Below, we describe three of these instruments.

3.2.1 Distribution Instrument. Many machine learning applications consist of large arrays (eg. activations or weights). Often, during debugging, it is useful to understand the overall distribution of values in an array. This may help, for example, to determine if

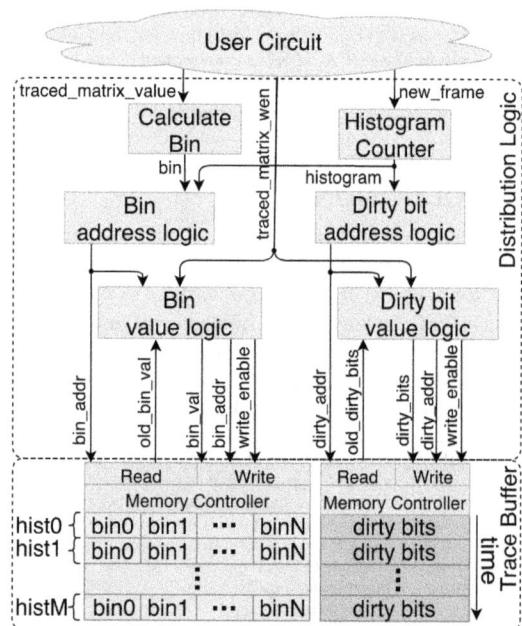

Figure 3: Distribution Instrument Architecture

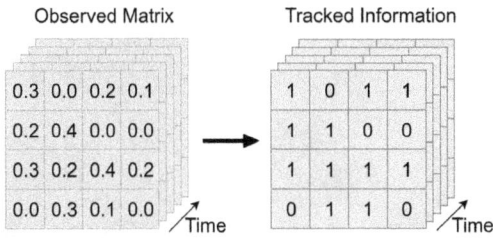

Figure 4: Spatial Sparsity Instrument Overview

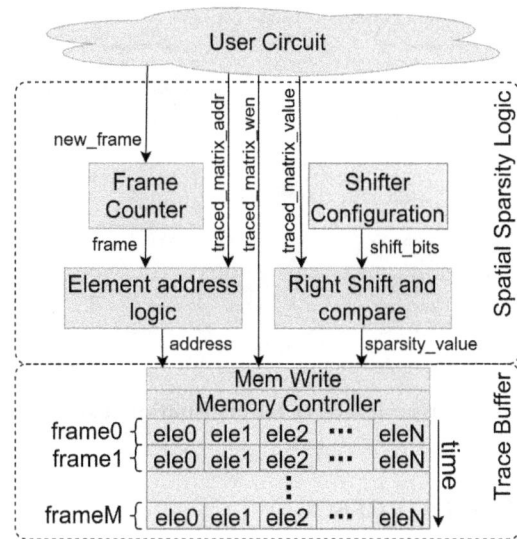

Figure 5: Spatial Sparsity Instrument Architecture

an error is causing activations to "clamp" at a minimum or maximum value, or whether, during training, weights are spanning the entire space provided by their representation's bit-width. Using techniques such as [5], that capture raw variable values, it would be possible to record all values in an array, and then perform the distribution analysis off-line. However, for large arrays, this may result in very inefficient use of trace buffer memory; every change to every element in the array would consume an entry in the trace buffer.

Instead, we provide an instrument that monitors all words in a specified array (memory) and aggregates the values into a *histogram*. This is shown conceptually in Figure 2, and an architecture is shown in Figure 3. The trace buffer contains one word per bin in each histogram. Each time an element of an identified array is updated, comparators are used to select the appropriate bin, and increment the associated word in the trace buffer. After the run is complete, the histogram can be read, and the user can use this information to understand the nature of the run-time values of the activations or weights stored in the array.

Rather than storing a single histogram, our trace buffer is divided into *frames*, each large enough to store one histogram. In a CNN, a frame may represent all calculations corresponding to a single input image; in other types of deep learning networks, a frame may represent a single training or inference sample. At the start of each frame (sample or image), a new histogram is initiated. Since we implement our trace buffers using embedded memories with limited ports, we cannot reset all entries in a histogram to zero in one cycle. Instead, we use a second memory containing dirty bits to track which bins have valid or invalid values. Each word in the dirty bits memory contains the dirty bits for all the bins of one entire histogram. Every time a new histogram is initiated (start of a new frame), all the bits in the word corresponding to this new histogram are marked as dirty. If a bin needs to be incremented and its value is marked as dirty, the value stored to this bin will be one, and the associated dirty bit will be deasserted.

The user can choose multiple variables (arrays) to observe using our proposed distribution instruments. For each of the arrays selected, a copy of the architecture shown in Figure 3 is inserted.

This association of a histogram to a frame is unique in this work. In [5], events to signals and variables are stored in order, however, there is no explicit association between those events and the context (in our case a frame) for which they occur. This association provides debug information in a manner which may be more natural for the user, possibly leading to more insight and faster debug cycles. An envisaged user interface will be described in Section 4.

3.2.2 Spatial Sparsity Instrument. Many errors in machine learning applications can manifest as arrays of weights and/or activations that are zero (or close to zero). The Spatial Sparsity instrument monitors specified activation or weight arrays, and, rather than storing all updates to these arrays, stores an indication whether the array is zero (within a predetermined threshold) or non-zero. This provides information about the sparsity of a given array. This is shown conceptually in Figure 4 and an architecture for this instrument is shown in Figure 5. The same logic could also be used to track elements close to 1, another upper bound or not a number (NaN).

Again, the trace buffer is treated as a set of frames, where each frame corresponds to a single input sample or image. Since only one bit is required to represent each element of the observed array a very long trace length can be achieved when compared to simply tracking all the changes as in [5].

3.2.3 Summary Statistics Instrument. Multiple summary statistics can also be used to represent the data we are trying to observe. Some examples of summary statistics include measure of tendency, such as arithmetic mean; measure of statistical dispersion, such as standard deviation; and measure of shape of the distribution, such as skewness. Although many of those statistics can be explored for most of applications, there are some summary statistics that can be especially useful for debugging machine learning applications.

In our instrumentation we focused on calculating the sparsity of the observed matrix to illustrate the example of gathering summary statistics to assist debugging machine learning circuits. Differently from the spatial sparsity instrument, the sparsity summary statistic instrument will not retain information regarding the location of elements that are equal to zero. Instead, a simple counter is used to track how many of the elements written into the observed matrix are zero valued.

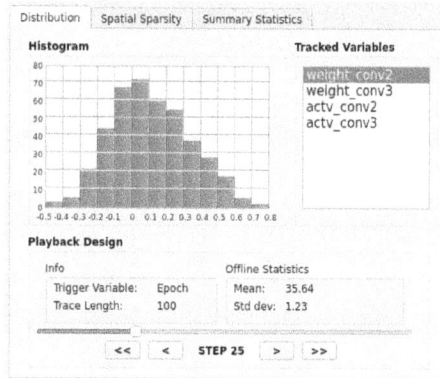

Figure 6: User interface for distribution instrument

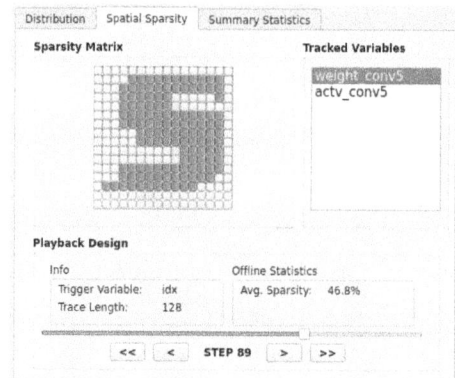

Figure 7: User interface for spatial sparsity instrument

4   USER INTERFACE

After the chip has been run, the data is obtained from the trace buffers and displayed to the user. Differently than hardware-oriented debug flows [1, 13] which display trace data using waveforms, or HLS-based debug flows [2, 5, 6] which display trace data in terms of user-visible C variables, we display data in the context of higher-level machine learning constructs. In the instrumentation architectures described in Section 3, data is associated with frames, each frame typically representing an input image in a CNN or input data item in other machine learning applications. In our user interface, we display the data in the context of frames in a form that we believe is useful for the user.

Our user interface consists of a set of tabs, as shown in Figures 6 and 7. Each tab corresponds to one type of debug instrument. Each debug instrument can be used multiple times to track different variables (arrays). For the distribution instrument, the associated tab shows a histogram. For the spatial sparsity instrument, the tab shows a graphical representation of sparsity. In both cases, the user can step through frames (rather than single-stepping lines of code) providing insight into how the traced matrix corresponds to the input image or dataset. Although it would be possible to obtain the same insight using a code-oriented debugger [5], the relationship between frame and variable value may not be clear, especially in the presence of hardware optimizations, possibly complicating the debugging process.

5   RESULTS AND DISCUSSION

In this section, we first compare our technique to the general-purpose debug instrumentation from [5]. We then present two architecture studies.

5.1   Comparison to General-Purpose Debug Instrumentation

To compare to previous work, we use kernels that are part of Convolutional Neural Networks (CNNs) generated using a tool that constructs CNNs of varying sizes and capabilities [15]. We use three kernels, one consisting of a single 28x28 convolution, one consisting of eight 28x28 convolutions and one consisting of 32 28x28 convolutions.

We compare seven different debugging configurations for each kernel. The first two configurations are from the general-purpose debug techniques in [5]. Unlike this work, these are not tailored to machine learning applications, and the debug logic is designed to simply capture raw variable values. The first configuration (1) tracks all user-visible variables, while the second (2) only tracks the elements in the array corresponding to the output of the convolutions. The remaining five configurations correspond to using the domain-specific debug instruments presented in this work to also observe the output of the convolutions. This includes configurations for the (3) distribution instrument with 32 bins, (4) the distribution instrument with 128 bins, (5) the spatial sparsity instrument, (6) the summary statistics instrument, and (7) a final configuration combining the distribution (32 bins) and spatial sparsity instruments (summary statistics sparsity is calculated off-line). As in [5, 9], 100Kb of trace memory was assumed in all configurations; in the configuration in which all instruments are included, the trace memory is partitioned among the those instruments.

For each kernel and configuration, the instrumentation is added, and the design synthesized, placed, and routed using Quartus II 16.1 (an average of 10 runs with different seeds is used). Table 1 shows the results. The fifth column shows the number of times that information about the frames can be stored in the trace memory. In the general-purpose approaches, where raw signal values are recorded, not even a single frame of convolution results can be stored in the trace buffer. However, using the data aggregation approaches presented in this paper, data for many frames can be stored in the same trace buffer space. The eighth column in the table shows the normalized trace size compared to configuration (2), which corresponds to the best general-purpose approach. When all proposed instruments are included, information about the frames can be stored for 21.8–24.1x longer.

Table 1 also shows area and F_{max} results (post place-and-route). As can be seen, the instrumentation is small, even when all three instruments are included. The impact of the instrumentation on F_{max} is similar to the previous work for large kernels; we anticipate we could reduce this impact by pipelining the instrumentation.

Although the proposed instruments significantly increase the trace size of large signals, it is not appropriate for tracing small signals. We believe that integrating those instruments with general purpose debug is an interesting venue for research.

Table 1: Resources and trace length when compared to general purpose debug

Configuration	Kernel	FMax (MHz)	LEs	Trace Size§	Normalized FMax	Normalized LEs	Normalized Trace size
Uninstrumented User Circuit	32x28x28	214.06	2483	-	1.00x	0.73x	-
	8x28x28	264.38	2439	-	1.01x	0.73x	-
	1x28x28	281.94	2308	-	0.97x	0.72x	-
(1) General Purpose [5] - Trace all signals	32x28x28	212.19	3575	0.003	0.99x	1.05x	0.024x
	8x28x28	255.02	3534	0.015	0.98x	1.06x	0.030x
	1x28x28	266.79	3397	0.132	0.92x	1.07x	0.033x
(2) General Purpose [5] - Single Matrix Trace	32x28x28	213.79	3391	0.124†	1x	1x	1x
	8x28x28	260.05	3324	0.498†	1x	1x	1x
	1x28x28	287.89	3167	3.985†	1x	1x	1x
(3) Distribution Instrument - 32 bins	32x28x28	200.48	2867	195	0.93x	0.84x	1,572.5x
	8x28x28	227.65	2834	223	0.87x	0.85x	447.7x
	1x28x28	229.87	2676	284	0.79x	0.84x	71.2x
(4) Distribution Instrument - 128 bins	32x28x28	189.62	3670	48	0.88x	1.08x	387.0x
	8x28x28	225.17	3600	55	0.86x	1.08x	110.4x
	1x28x28	228.98	3488	71	0.79x	1.10x	17.8x
(5) Spatial Sparsity Instrument	32x28x28	200.46	2547	3	0.93x	0.75x	24.1x
	8x28x28	211.13	2531	15	0.81x	0.76x	30.1x
	1x28x28	214.70	2393	127	0.74x	0.75x	31.8x
(6) Summary Statistics Instrument - Sparsity	32x28x28	213.17	2557	6666	0.99x	0.75x	53,758.0x
	8x28x28	258.75	2531	7692	0.99x	0.76x	15,445.7x
	1x28x28	285.30	2390	10000	0.99x	0.75x	2,509.4x
(7) Proposed instruments combined♯	32x28x28	189.23	2930	3	0.88x	0.86x	24.1x
	8x28x28	206.69	2927	14	0.79x	0.88x	28.1x
	1x28x28	220.51	2786	87	0.76x	0.87x	21.8x

§ Number of times information about the entire 32-bit frame could be tracked.
† All memory bits are used for dataflow trace buffer and only the values of the observed matrix are traced.
♯ Distribution (32bins) and spatial sparsity instruments; Sparsity summary statistic is calculated off-line.

5.2 Architecture Study 1: Distribution Instrument

In this experiment, we vary the number of bins used in the distribution instrument while keeping the number of histograms in the trace buffer constant, and measure the impact on the total memory bits, area, and speed. In all cases, the output of a 32-bit 32x28x28 convolution is tracked.

The results are shown in Figure 8. The horizontal axis corresponds to the number of bins used in each histogram, while different lines represent the size of the trace buffer in terms of the number of histograms that this trace buffer is able to store. The left-most point in each graph corresponds to an uninstrumented circuit (0 bins).

As shown, the frequency drops as the number of bins increases, however, the impact is less than 5% when using 64 bins and 64 frames. In terms of area, the relationship between the number of LEs and the number of bins is linear; this is because most of the area is due to the comparators required to build the histogram circuit. The number of memory bits needed by the distribution instrument also increases with the number of bins; this quantity can be calculated using:

$$mBits = nHist * nBin * (binWidth + 1), \qquad (1)$$

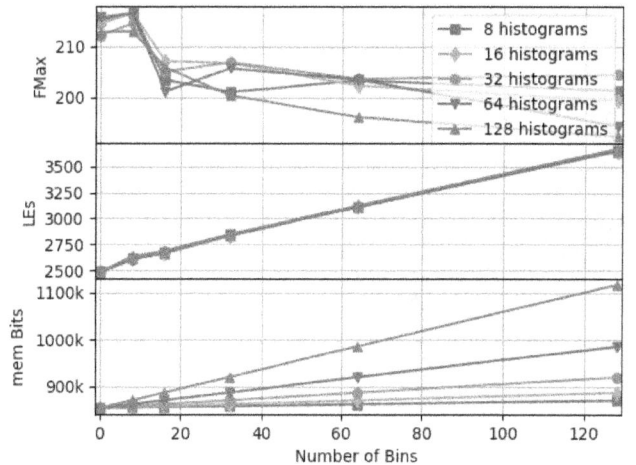

Figure 8: Maximum frequency, logic elements and memory bits used by distribution instrument when tracking 32x28x28 matrix

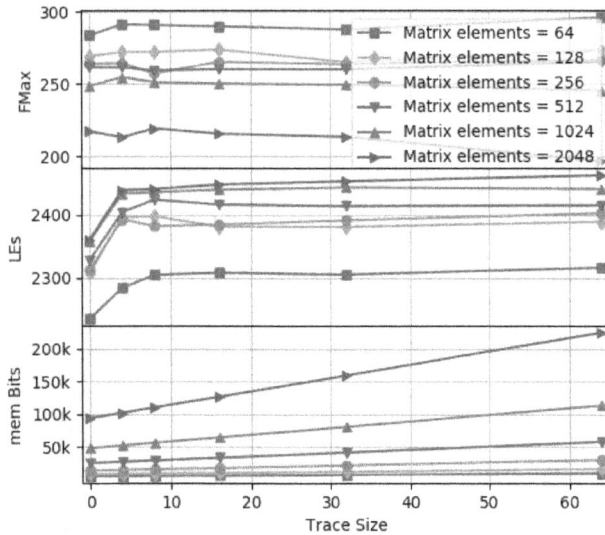

Figure 9: Maximum frequency, logic elements and memory bits used by spatial sparsity instrument

where *mBits* is the number of memory bits, *nHist* is the number of histograms tracked in the trace buffer, *nBins* is the number of bins of each histogram and *binWidth* the bit-width of each bin in the histogram. The *binWidth* is given by

$$binWidth = \lceil log2(sigLen + 1) \rceil \qquad (2)$$

in which *sigLen* corresponds to the number of elements in the matrix being traced.

5.3 Architecture Study 2: Spatial Sparsity Instrument

In this experiment, we focus on the spatial sparsity instrument. We vary the number of frames traced while keeping the size of each frame constant, for several kernels. The results are shown in Figure 9. Each line in the graph corresponds to a different kernel. The left-most point is the uninstrumented circuit (trace size = 0).

As shown in the central plot of Figure 9, the spatial sparsity instrument has an initial area overhead that does not increase with the trace size and is approximately the same for all circuits. This is different from the distribution instrument, which presents almost no initial area cost, but a growing number of logic elements when the number of bins increases.

The latency of the circuit has not shown to be sensitive to the spatial sparsity instrument for most cases. The only exception is a slight decrease in the maximum frequency when tracking 2048 elements.

Figure 9 also shows the number of memory bits required to implement this instrument. This quantity can be calculated using

$$mBits = tSize * mEle, \qquad (3)$$

where *tSize* corresponds to the trace size and *mEle* corresponds to the number of elements of the matrix being tracked.

6 CONCLUSIONS

In this paper, we have presented a debug infrastructure that can be used either as a stand-alone tool or in concert with existing debug infrastructure to enhance visibility of machine learning circuits. The proposed infrastructure allows the user to run the design at speed and record information for later interrogation. Unlike previously published debug tools, our instrumentation leverages the specific characteristics inherent in machine learning algorithms to provide an insight of the behaviour of the observed variables without tracking all changes to a variable. We show that our system is able to trace signals for a fraction of the area cost, enabling the designer to achieve a longer trace-lengths when compare to state-of-the-art debug infrastructures.

Current and future work includes evaluating and adapting the proposed approach to various deep learning networks, combining it with high-level debugging aids such as assertions [8] for edge computing and for cloud applications, exploring the possibility of extensions to cover the debugging of application-specific devices such as the TPU [10] and integrating this work with Tensorboard for a unified software/hardware debug framework.

ACKNOWLEDGEMENTS

We thank both NSERC COHESA and Intel for their FPGA Programming Optimizations ISRA (Intel Strategic Research Alliance).

REFERENCES

[1] Altera. 2015. *Quartus Prime Pro Edition Handbook*. Vol. 3. Chapter 9: Design Debugging Using the SignalTap II Logic Analyzer.
[2] N. Calagar, S.D. Brown, and J.H. Anderson. 2014. Source-level Debugging for FPGA High-Level Synthesis. In *Int'l Conf. on Field Programmable Logic and Applications*.
[3] F. Eslami and S. J. E. Wilton. 2015. An adaptive virtual overlay for fast trigger insertion for FPGA debug. In *Int'l Conf. on Field Programmable Technology (FPT)*.
[4] J. Goeders and S.J.E. Wilton. 2014. Effective FPGA debug for high-level synthesis generated circuits. In *Field Programmable Logic and Applications (FPL), 2014 24th International Conference on*. https://doi.org/10.1109/FPL.2014.6927498
[5] J. Goeders and S.J.E. Wilton. 2017. Signal-Tracing Techniques for In-System FPGA Debugging of High-Level Synthesis Circuits. *IEEE Trans. on Computer-Aided Design of Integrated Circuits and Systems* 36, 1 (Jan 2017), 83–96.
[6] K.S. Hemmert, J.L. Tripp, B.L. Hutchings, and P.A. Jackson. 2003. Source level debugger for the Sea Cucumber synthesizing compiler. In *Symposium on Field-Programmable Custom Computing Machines*. 228–237.
[7] D. Holanda Noronha, B. Salehpour, and S. J. E. Wilton. 2018. LeFlow: Enabling Flexible FPGA High-Level Synthesis of Tensorflow Deep Neural Networks. In *International Workshop on FPGAs for Software Programmers*.
[8] E. Hung, T. Todman, and W. Luk. 2017. Transparent in-circuit assertions for FPGAs. *IEEE Transactions on Computer-Aided Design of Integrated Circuits and Systems* 36, 7 (July 2017), 1193–1202.
[9] A. Jamal, J. Goeders, and S.J.E. Wilton. 2018. Architecture Exploration for HLS-Oriented FPGA Debug Overlays. In *Proceedings of the 2018 ACM/SIGDA International Symposium on Field-Programmable Gate Arrays (FPGA '18)*. ACM, New York, NY, USA, 209–218.
[10] N. Jouppi, C. Young, N. Patil, and D. Patterson. 2018. A domain-specific architecture for deep neural networks. *Commun. ACM* 61, 9 (Sept 2018), 50–59.
[11] A. Kourfali and D. Stroobandt. 2016. Efficient Hardware Debugging using Parameterized FPGA Reconfiguration. In *Int'l Parallel and Distributed Processing Symposium Workshop*. 277–282.
[12] S.I. Venieris and C. Bouganis. 2016. fpgaConvNet: A Framework for Mapping Convolutional Neural Networks on FPGAs. In *2016 Int'l Symposium on Field-Programmable Custom Computing Machines (FCCM)*. 40–47.
[13] Xilinx. 2012. *ChipScope Pro Software and Cores: User Guide*.
[14] Xilinx. 2016. Integrated Logic Analyzer v6.1: LogiCORE IP Product Guide. http://www.xilinx.com/support/documentation/ip_documentation/ila/v6_1/pg172-ila.pdf. (April 2016).
[15] R. Zhao, H. Ng, W. Luk, and X. Niu. 2018. Towards Efficient Convolutional Neural Network for Domain-Specific Applications on FPGA. *arXiv preprint arXiv:1809.03318* (Sept 2018).

Poster Session 1

Scheduling Data in Neural Network Applications

Thaddeus Koehn, Northrup Grumman Corporation
Peter Athanas,
Virginia Polytechnic Institute & State University
Contact: tkoehn@vt.edu

Neuromorphic computing is becoming common in diverse systems, including time-sensitive, real-time systems. This requires that large data sets be processed quickly with low latency. A stream processing architecture helps achieve this goal by beginning processing as soon as samples are received.

In this paper, to achieve a low-latency implementation, neurons are parsed into fine-grain operations and scheduled onto stages of the pipeline. Wide datapaths that process multiple samples in each stage of the pipeline greatly improve throughput and latency. Also, the sparsity of partially connected neural networks allows proposed schedulers to further decrease latency. These schedulers use 'greedy' heuristics based on data dependencies to develop a reduced latency schedule. The schedulers were testing against sets of

1000 partially-connected neural networks, with sets ranging in number of layers from three to fifteen. The set of heuristics developed showed reductions of up to 67% over a sequential schedule.

Keywords: Schedulers, Sparse Neural Networks, Low Latency

DOI: https://doi.org/10.1145/3289602.3293930

Fault Testing a Synthesizable Embedded Processor at Gate Level using FPGA Emulation

Tom J. Mannos, *Sandia National Laboratories*
Brian Dziki, *Department of Defense*
Moslema Sharif, *Sandia National Laboratories*
Contact: tjmanno@sandia.gov

While several applications exist to fault-test software at the abstract level, gate-level fault testing has traditionally been limited to injecting faults into small, dedicated circuits, due the computational time required for gate-level simulations and the logic resources (LUTs and registers) required for FPGA emulation. In our work, we leverage the extensive resources of the Ultrascale and Ultrascale+ platforms to systematically test faults on all gate-level inputs of an ASIC or FPGA implementation of an embedded processor running a user application. Using a configurable, synthesizable saboteur circuit connected using a scan chain and controlled with a state machine, we tested four different types of faults on each logic gate of the LEON3 CPU running an AES 256 application. The entire process took just under two hours, a 7200X speedup from

gate-level simulation. Though neither the hardware nor software employed fault mitigation techniques, we were surprised to discover multiple stuck-at-0, stuck-at-1, and delay faults that resulted in total or partial key and plaintext leakage through the communications serial port. Overall, we identified 22 unique faulty behaviors, four of which involve some form of crypto or memory leakage. These occurred in roughly the same proportions in ASIC and FPGA netlists of the LEON3, suggesting robustness of the analysis to different implementations. Of the four static fault types tested, delay faults were the most effective at uncovering behaviors of concern.

Keywords: Fault injection testing; FPGA emulation; ASIC prototyping; embedded processing; cryptography

DOI: https://doi.org/10.1145/3289602.3293931

Base64 Encoding on OpenCL FPGA Platform

Zheming Jin, *Argonne National Laboratory*
Hal Finkel, *Argonne National Laboratory*
Contact: zjin@anl.gov

Base64 encoding has many applications on the Web. Previous studies are focused on improving the efficiency of Base64 encoding on central processing units (CPUs). As field-programmable gate arrays (FPGAs) are becoming promising heterogeneous computing components in high-performance computing (HPC), and high-level synthesis (HLS) is more mature, we are motivated to optimize Base64 encoding on an FPGA using HLS. In this paper, we explain the algorithm, converts the algorithm to a kernel written in Open Computing Language (OpenCL), and optimize the kernel targeting an Intel Arria 10 FPGA. We evaluate the performance and power of the kernel implementations on the CPU, graphics processing units (GPUs), and FPGA computing platforms. The experimental results show that we can significantly improve the performance of Base64 encoding with the FPGA-specific optimizations. Compared to an Intel Xeon Platinum 8167 CPU, an Nvidia Tesla K80 GPU, and an Nvidia Tesla P100 GPU, the performance (the number of cycles per byte) of Base64 encoding on an Arria10-based FPGA platform is 3.98X higher than that on the K80 GPU, 17X higher than that on the CPU, and 1.83X lower than that on the P100 GPU for large input data sizes. The performance per watt on the FPGA is 1.1X lower than that on the P100 GPU, and 8.25X and 13.2X higher than that on the CPU and the K80 GPU, respectively.

Keywords: FPGA; OpenCL; Base64 encoding

DOI: https://doi.org/10.1145/3289602.3293932

Scalable High Performance SDN Switch Architecture on FPGA for Core Networks

Sasindu Wijeratne, *University of Moratuwa*
Ashen Ekanayake, *University of Moratuwa*
Sandaruwan Jayaweera, *University of Moratuwa*
Danuka Ravishan, *University of Moratuwa*
Ajith Pasqual, *University of Moratuwa*
Contact: 130665u@uom.lk

Due to the increasing heterogeneity in network user requirements, dynamically varying day to day network traffic patterns and delay in network service deployment, there is a huge demand for scalability and flexibility in modern networking infrastructure, which in return has paved way for the introduction of Software Defined Networking (SDN) in core networks. In this paper, we present an FPGA-based switch which is fully compliant with OpenFlow; the pioneering protocol for southbound interface of SDN. The switch architecture is completely implemented on hardware. The design consists of an OpenFlow Southbound agent which can process OpenFlow packets at a rate of 10Gbps. The architecture contains a primary pipeline which is capable of achieving core network throughputs and an auxiliary pipeline leading to the Openflow agent. Single clock cycle Content Accessible Memory (CAM) architecture supports the overall design to achieve its throughput and latency requirements. The proposed architecture speed scales up to 400Gbps while it consumes only 60% resources on a Xilinx Virtex-7 featuring XC7VX485T FPGA. Switch fabric is capable of connecting to a control plane running upon a host PC via PCIe which provides an opportunity at research level to explore SDN in core networks. Moreover, the architecture is experimented for different scaled versions using line rates of 10G, 25G and 100G. By using FPGA based embedded platforms which support sufficient number of ports and their line rates, this architecture can be deployed in core networks.

Keywords: Software Defined Networking; Core Network; FPGA; OpenFlow; Content Accessible Memory; PCIe

DOI: https://doi.org/10.1145/3289602.3293933

A Deep-Reinforcement-Learning-Based Scheduler for High-Level Synthesis

Hongzheng Chen, *Sun Yat-sen University*
Minghua Shen, *Sun Yat-sen University*
Contact: chenhzh37@mail2.sysu.edu.cn

As the most important stage in high-level synthesis (HLS), scheduling mostly relies on heuristic algorithms due to their speed, flexibility, and scalability. However, designing heuristics easily involves human bias, which makes the scheduling unpredictable in some specific cases. In this paper, we propose a deep-reinforcement-learning (Deep-RL) based scheduler for HLS. It maximumly reduces the human involvement and learns to schedule by itself. Firstly, we introduce a novel state and action

representation for constrained scheduling problems, which is the foundation of the learning task. Secondly, we use a training pipeline to train the policy network. Supervised learning is used to initialize the weight of the network, and reinforcement learning is used to improve the performance, which makes the Deep-RL based scheduler practical for HLS. Finally, we compare our scheduler with the ASAP schedule and the optimal ILP schedule. Experimental results show our scheduler can reduce up to 74% resource usage compared with the original ASAP schedule, and the gap between the optimal solution is small. Notably, this is the first work leveraging reinforcement learning in HLS and has great potential to be integrated into different HLS systems.

Keywords: High-level synthesis; Scheduling; Deep reinforcement learning; FPGA

DOI: http://dx.doi.org/10.1145/3289602.3293934

Accelerating 3D CNN-based Lung Nodule Segmentation on a Multi-FPGA System

Junzhong Shen, Deguang Wang, You Huang,
Mei Wen, Chunyuan Zhang,
National University of Defense Technology
Contact: shenjunzhong@nudt.edu.cn

Lung nodule segmentation is one of the most significant steps in many Computer Aided Detection (CAD) systems used for lung nodule identification and classification. Three-dimensional convolutional neural networks (3D CNNs) have become a promising method in lung nodule segmentation, as this method can achieve higher detection accuracy than conventional methods. It has been proven that FPGAs can provide the most energy-efficient solution for CNN acceleration. However, the high computational complexity and memory requirements of 3D CNNs make it challenging to accelerate 3D CNNs on a single FPGA, as this will further bottleneck the performance of a 3D CNN-based CAD system. Accordingly, in this work, we focus on accelerating the 3D CNN-based lung nodule segmentation on a multi-FPGA platform by proposing an efficient mapping scheme that takes advantage of the massive parallelism provided by the platform, as well as maximizing the computational efficiency of the accelerators. Experimental results show that our system is able to achieve high computational efficiency and thereby a state-of-the-art performance of 14.5 TOPS at 200 MHz. Comparisons with CPU and GPU solutions demonstrate that our system achieves a 29.4x performance gain over CPU and a 10.5x energy efficiency improvement over GPU.

Keywords: Lung nodule segmentation; 3D CNNs; multi-FPGA

DOI: http://dx.doi.org/10.1145/3289602.3293935

SparseBNN: Joint Algorithm/Hardware Optimization to Exploit Structured Sparsity in Binary Neural Network

Xin He, Liu Ke, Xuan Zhang,
Washington University of St. Louis
Contact: hex0102@gmail.com

To reduce power-hungry floating point operations and memory accesses in deep neural networks, quantized neural networks are proposed that replace floating point multiplications with simplified reduced-precision operations. To compensate for the accuracy loss due to the high degree of quantization, wider neural network layers with three or more times as many feature maps are employed. One by-product from these inflated layers is increased redundancy in the network. To further improve computational efficiency and leverage this inherent redundancy, we propose a joint optimization approach that simultaneously explores hardware-oriented training and efficient accelerator implementation of binary neural networks (BNN) in FPGAs. More specifically, our SparseBNN method consists of two parts. First, SparseBNN-SW is a training algorithm developed to enhance the structured sparsity of BNNs by 1) training for zero-valued ternary weights instead of binary that are more amenable to pruning and 2) regulating the sparsity for more efficient hardware deployment. Next, we present SparseBNN-HW, an accelerator architecture designed to directly execute the inference on the sparse-encoded format to save both memory access and computations. Experimental results on various representative datasets demonstrate that SparseBNN improves the power efficiency (GOPS/Watt) and resource efficiency (GOPS/kLUT) over the baseline BNN FPGA implementation by 1.70X and 2.22X.

Keywords: Neural Network Acceleration; Binary Neural network; Structural sparsity; Hardware-software codesign

DOI: https://doi.org/10.1145/3289602.3293937

A Deep Learning Inference Accelerator Based on Model Compression on FPGA

Lu Jing, Jun Liu, Fuhai Yu, *Inspur Corporation*
Contact: jinglu@inspur.com

Convolutional neural networks (CNN) have demonstrated state-of-the-art accuracy in image classification and object detection owing to the increase in data and computation capacity of hardware. However, this state-of-the-art achievement depends heavily on the DSP floating-point computing capability of the device, which increases the power dissipation and cost of the device. In order to solve the problem, we made the first attempt to implement a CNN computing accelerator based on shift operation on FPGA. In this accelerator, an efficient Incremental Network Quantization (INQ) method was applied to compress the CNN model from full precision to 4-bit integer, which represents values of either zero or power of two. Then the multiply and accumulate (MAC) operations for convolution layer and fully-connected layer was converted to shift and accumulation (SAC) operations, and SAC could be easily implemented by the logic elements of FPGA. Consequently, parallelism of CNN inference process can be further expanded. For the SqueezeNet model, single image processing latency was 0.673ms on Intel Arria 10 FPGA (Inspur F10A board) showing a slightly better result than on NVIDIA Tesla P4, and the compute capacity of FPGA increased by 1.77 times at least.

Keywords: CNN; FPGA; Shift and Accumulation; Model Compression; Quantization; Energy Efficiency

DOI: https://doi.org/10.1145/3289602.3293938

Sparse Winograd Convolutional Neural Networks on Small-scale Systolic Arrays

Feng Shi, Haochen Li, *University of California Los Angeles*
Yuhe Gao, *University of Hong Kong*
Benjamin Kuschner, Song-Chun Zhu,
University of California Los Angeles
Contact: shi.feng@cs.ucla.edu

The reconfigurability, energy-efficiency, and massive parallelism on FPGAs make them one of the best choices for implementing efficient deep learning accelerators. However, state-of-art implementations seldom consider the balance between high throughput of computation power and the ability of memory subsystem to support it. In this paper we implement a framework on FPGA by combining the sparse Winograd convolution, clusters of small-scale systolic arrays, and a tailored recursive Z-Morton memory layout design. We also provide an analytical model analysis for the general Winograd convolution algorithm as design reference. Experimental results on various CNN models show that it achieves very high computation resource utilization, 20x~30x energy efficiency and more than 5x speedup compared with the dense implementation.

Keywords: FPGA, Neural networks, Winograd transform, systolic arrays

DOI: https://doi.org/10.1145/3289602.3293939

HSC-FPGA: A Hybrid Spin/Charge FPGA Leveraging the Cooperating Strengths of CMOS and MTJ Devices

Ramtin Zand, *University of Central Florida*
Ronald F. DeMara, *University of Central Florida*
Contact: ramtinmz@knights.ucf.edu

The HSC-FPGA offers an intriguing feasible architecture for the next generation of configurable fabrics, which allows embracing the advantages of both CMOS and beyond-CMOS technologies without requiring significant modification to the routing structure, programming paradigms, and synthesis tool-chain of the commercial FPGAs. In the HSC-FPGA, the intrinsic characteristics of magnetic random access memory (MRAM)-look-up table (LUT) circuits are used to implement sequential logic, while combinational logic circuits are implemented by static random access memory (SRAM)-LUTs. Fabric-level simulation results for the developed HSC-FPGA show that it can achieve at least 18%, 70%, and 15% reduction in terms of area, standby power, and read power consumption, respectively, for various ISCAS-89 and ITC-99 benchmark circuits compared to conventional SRAM-based FPGAs. The power consumption values can be further decreased by the power-gating allowed by the non-volatility feature of MRAM-LUTs. Moreover, the benefits of increased heterogeneity for reconfigurable computing is extended along realizing probabilistic computing paradigms within a fabric, which is enabled by probabilistic spin logic devices. The cooperating strengths of technology-heterogeneity and heterogeneity in computing paradigm in the proposed HSC-FPGA are leveraged to develop energy-efficient and reliability-aware training and evaluation circuits for deep belief networks with memristive crossbar arrays and p-bit based probabilistic neurons.

Keywords: reconfigurable computing; FPGA; spintronics; post-CMOS architectures; hybrid device technology reconfigurable logic fabrics, MRAM; probabilistic spin logic device; p-bit.

DOI: https://doi.org/10.1145/3289602.3293940

Evaluating and Enhancing Intel® Stratix® 10 FPGAs for Persistent Real-Time AI

Eriko Nurvitadhi, Dongup Kwon, Ali Jafari,
Andrew Boutros, Jaewoong Sim, Phillip Tomson,
Huseyin Sumbul, Gregory Chen, Phil Knag,
Raghavan Kumar, Ram Krishnamurthy,
Debbie Marr, *Intel Labs*
Sergey Gribok, Bogdan Pasca, Martin Langhammar,
Aravind Dasu, *Intel Programmable Solutions Group*
Contact: eriko.nurvitadhi@intel.com

Interactive intelligent services (e.g., smart web search) are becoming essential datacenter workloads. They rely on data-intensive artificial intelligence (AI) algorithms that do not use batch computation due to their tight latency constraints. Since off-chip data accesses have higher latency and energy consumption than on-chip accesses, a persistent AI approach with the entire model stored in on-chip memory is becoming the new norm for real-time AI. This approach is the cornerstone of Microsoft's Brainwave FPGA-based AI cloud and was recently added to Nvidia's cuDNN library. In this work, we implement, optimize and evaluate a Brainwave-like neural processing unit (NPU) on a large Stratix-10 FPGA. We benchmark it against a large Nvidia Volta GPU running cuDNN persistent AI kernels. Across real-time persistent RNN, GRU, and LSTM workloads, we show that Stratix-10 offers ~3× (FP32) and ~10× (INT8) better latency than GPU (FP32), which uses only ~6% of its peak throughput. Then, we propose TensorRAM, an ASIC chiplet for persistent AI that is 2.5D integrated with an FPGA in the same package. TensorRAM enhances the on-chip memory capacity and bandwidth, with enough multi-precision INT8/4/2/1 throughput to match that bandwidth. Multiple TensorRAMs can be integrated with Stratix-10. Our evaluation shows that a small 32-mm^2 TensorRAM on 10nm offers 64MB of SRAMs with 32TB/s on-chiplet bandwidth and 64 TOP/s (INT8). A small Stratix-10 with a TensorRAM (INT8) offers 16× better latency and 34× energy efficiency compared to GPU (FP32). Overall, Stratix-10 with TensorRAM offers compelling and scalable persistent AI solutions.

Keywords: Deep learning; AI; real-time; FPGA; ASIC; GPU

DOI: https://doi.org/10.1145/3289602.3293943

Parrot: A More Effective Parallel Routing Approach to FPGAs

Minghua Shen, Nong Xiao, *Sun Yat-Sen University*
Contact: shenmh6@mail.sysu.edu.cn

In this paper, we propose Parrot, a more effective parallel routing approach that exploits angle-based space recursion partitioning for parallel FPGA routing. Parrot partitions entire routing region into two subregions such that all of the nets are assigned to three sets, where the first set consists of the nets that their terminal pins are distributed in two subregions and the other two sets consists of the nets that their terminal pins are located in their own respective subregions. Note that load balance is always used to guide the partitioning for a greater degree of parallelism. Moreover, all of the sets can be recursively partitioned in the same way to implement the scalable parallel routing and in each recursion, the first set is routed in serial before the other two sets are routed in parallel to generate the deterministic results. In addition, the synchronization overheads can be further reduced to improve the parallelism. Experimental results shows that Parrot can scale to 32 processor cores to provide about 16x speedup on average with acceptable impact on the quality of results. This is about 3x improvement over the state-of-the-art parallel router in terms of maximum average speedup.

Keywords: FPGA; FPGA CAD; Routing and Parallel Routing; Recursive Partitioning

DOI: https://doi.org/10.1145/3289602.3293944

A Reconfigurable Accelerator for Sparse Convolutional Neural Networks

Weijie You, Chang Wu, *Fudan University*
Contact: wuchang@fudan.edu.cn

Convolutional Neural Networks (CNNs) have been shown to be very useful in image recognition and other AI applications. CNNs are usually computationally intensive. To address the challenge of overwhelming calculation requirements, researchers have proposed network compression methods to reduce the number of synaptic weights and the amount of computations. In this paper, we propose an input row based sparse convolution neural network accelerator on FPGAs that performs sparse CNN computing efficiently. Similar to the DNNWEAVER architecture, our accelerator also uses two-level architecture hierarchy, with multiple Processing Units (PUs) and each PU comprises a set of basic Processing Elements (PEs). The number of PEs in a single PU and the number of PUs in a design are reconfigurable for different CNNs for best performance. Our architecture does not require the large multiplexer for data selection as needed in Cambricon-X, thus, is more suitable for larger accelerator designs for high performance. Besides, we propose a weight merging method to balance the computation load on different PUs to maximize the overall computation efficiency. For evaluation, we implement our design with 32 PUs and each with 14 PEs. When compared with the DNNWEAVER implementation for non-sparse VGG16 network, we get an overall performance of 3.6x speedup running at 100MHz on a Xilinx ZC706 board and reach the speed of 297 GOPS.

Keywords: FPGA; Sparse Convolution Neural Networks; Accelerator

DOI: https://doi.org/10.1145/3289602.3293945

Overcoming Data Transfer Bottlenecks in DNN Accelerators via Layer-Conscious Memory Managment

Xuechao Wei[1,3,*], Yun Liang[1], Peng Zhang[3],
Cody Hao Yu[2], Jason Cong[1,2,3,+]
[1]Center for Energy-Efficient Computing and Applications,
School of EECS, Peking University, China
[2]Computer Science Department, University of California,
Los Angeles, CA, USA
[3]Falcon Computing Solutions, Inc. Los Angeles, CA, USA
Contact: {xuechao.wei, ericlyun}@pku.edu.cn,
pengzhang@falcon-computing.com,
{hyu, cong}@cs.ucla.edu

Deep Neural Networks (DNNs) are rapidly evolving to satisfy the performance and accuracy requirements in many real world applications. The evolution renders DNNs more and more complex in terms of network topology, data sizes and layer types. Currently most state-of-the-art DNN accelerators adopt a uniform memory hierarchy (UMH) design methodology, which means that the data transferring of all convolutional and fully connected layers must go through the same memory levels. Unfortunately, for some layers, the performance is always bounded by off-chip memory transferring. It is caused by the saturating of data reuse happening in on-chip buffers, resulting in underutilization of on-chip memory. To address this issue, we propose a layer-conscious memory hierarchy (LCMH) methodology for DNN accelerators. LCMH could determine the memory levels of all the layers according to their requirements for off-chip memory bandwidth and on-chip buffer size for the data sources. As a result, the off-chip memory footprints of memory bounded layers could be avoided by keeping the data of them on chip. In addition, we provide architectural support for the accelerators equipped with LCMH. Experimental results show that designs with layer-conscious memory management could achieve up to 36% speedup compared with the designs wth UMH and 5% improvement over state-of-the-art designs.

Keywords: DNNs; FPGA; Accelerator; Memory management

DOI: https://doi.org/10.1145/3289602.3293947

A Pixel-Parallel Virtual-Image Architecture for High Performance and Power Efficient Graph Cuts Inference

Tianqi Gao, *University of Illinois Urbana Champaign*
Rob A. Rutenbar, *University of Pittsburgh*
Contact: gao19@illinois.edu

Graph Cuts is a popular technique for Maximum A Posteriori inference in computer vision. It transforms a Markov Random Field problem into a network flow problem, solved via the Push-Relabel algorithm. While attractively simple, the large size of a typical image and the large number of necessary pixel-level iterations render the technique computationally expensive. Prior accelerator attempts have been reported with GPUs and FPGAs. In [1], the first pixel-parallel architecture was demonstrated in FPGA, but limited to only 256-pixel images. This paper extends this pixel-parallel concept and makes following contributions: a "Virtual Image" architecture solves the size limitation: large images are decomposed into "tiles", and "stacked" on the physical processor array; appropriate addressing mechanisms handle virtual pixels and a range of tile edge effects; scaling up the processor array to 1536 pixels; a novel and hardware-friendly heuristic shortens the convergence. We demonstrate the first working virtual-image Graph Cuts accelerator, applied to standard 640x480 images. Scaling up the hardware and the new heuristic bring 6.5x and 1.65x speedups respectively compared with [1]. The design is 7-20x faster than prior FPGA designs, and roughly comparable in speed to a modern GPU benchmark. However, the architecture also offers significant performance-per-unit-power advantages. Formulating a figure of merit particularly for Graph Cuts inference – *Graph Cuts per second per Watt* - our architecture is about 4 times better than other implementations.

Keywords: FPGA; Machine learning; Hardware Acceleration; Computer Vision

DOI: https://doi.org/10.1145/3289602.3293948

Unleashing the Power of Soft Logic for Convolutional Neural Network Acceleration via Product Quantization

Jialiang Zhang, *UW-Madison*
Jing Li, *UW-Madison*
Contact: Jialiang.zhang@ece.wisc.edu

To reduce the load of taxing CNN infrastructures, both industry and academia show great interest in building specialized hardware for CNN acceleration. Numerous FPGA-based accelerators have been proposed to better utilize *hard* blocks. However, the capability of *soft* logic has not been fully explored. Prior works either fail to utilize *soft* logic for computation or inefficiently use *soft* logic to mimic the function of *hard* blocks.

In this work, to better utilize *soft* logic we propose to use the native function of *soft* logic, i.e. as distributed memory, which yields more than 20x throughput compared to implementing multiplication operations. To fully leverage this potential, we present a framework to more efficiently accelerate CNN-based inference. Firstly, we employ product quantization (PQ) to convert most of the multiplications to a reduced number of distributed memory accesses and additions. We then constructed an analytical model to reveal the complex relationship between the inference accuracy and the utilization of hard blocks and *soft* blocks. Based on the model, we select optimal PQ parameters for a balanced design. In the rest of this paper, we describe the complete system implementation and discuss the experimental results. According to our results on Xilinx VU9P FPGA, we can achieve a 140 Tops equivalent throughput and 475 Gops/W energy efficiency with less than 0.5% accuracy degradation.

Keywords: CNN; FPGA; Product Quantization

DOI: https://doi.org/10.1145/3289602.3293951

Highly Efficient Sparse Neural Network Computing: Hardware and Software Solutions

Yanjie Gu, Jian Yu, Tieli Sun,
Chen Pan, Zhenhao Feng, Liewei Xu,
*Shanghai Fudan Microelectronics Group
Company Limited*
Chang Wu, *Fudan University*
Contact: guyanjie@fmsh.com.cn

In this study, we propose a software-hardware combined solution for efficient sparse neural network computing. Much of the connections between each layers are pruned in sparse neural network. Usually the weights are in compressed format, but the corresponding feature map data need to be pared before passing to computation engine. Since the compressed weights require indirect memory access, there needs a large amount of multiplexers to locate the data position. Motivated by this, we propose a new architecture with a much smaller data selection multiplexer design. In our hardware architecture, the data are selected in a smaller range so that the scale of multiplexer can be reduced. This is paired with our software network pruning method. Compared with the structured or pattern-based pruning method, our algorithm does not impose such restriction and just ensure that there are same numbers of non-zero elements in each z-channel array of the weights. The non-zero elements can be distributed at any position in the array. We also use dual channel for better efficiency on data scheduling. Our experimental results show that our architecture can reach 3x overall speedup for 25% sparsity networks when compared with non-sparse engines with the same amount of computing resources. In the future, we plan to further improve our pruning algorithm, and tape out our hardware design.

Keywords: Sparse neural network; Network pruning; Hardware acceleration

DOI: https://doi.org/10.1145/3289602.3293952

FPGA-based Distributed Edge Training of SVM

Jyotikrishna Dass, Yashwardhan Narawane,
Rabi Mahapatra, Vivek Sarin,
Texas A&M University, College Station
Contact: dass.jyotikrishna@tamu.edu

Support Vector Machine (SVM) is a widely used supervised machine learning algorithm for classification. Training SVM is challenging due to high computational cost and memory requirements. More often such training is handled at back end servers leading to significant communication and energy overheads. This approach is unsuitable for edge analytics which is a growing trend with various IoT applications. Enabling efficient training on the edge requires a distributed computing approach that has negligible communication overhead and an energy-efficient hardware design to execute it. In this paper, we present a scalable FPGA-based design for distributed SVM training amenable for edge-based learning. Specifically, we implement a pipelined QRSVM IP logic on Xilinx Virtex UltraScale+ VU9P FPGA. Each synthesized IP core operates at 125 MHz with a power dissipation of 39 Watts. We evaluate the training time, parallel speedup, scalability, and energy efficiency of the proposed design on five SVM benchmarks on a multiple FPGA system comprising up to eight FPGA units. When compared with software implementation on the traditional embedded system edge processors like ARM Cortex-A15, the proposed FPGA implementation is around 3x to 24x faster and 2x to 8x more energy efficient on the above benchmarks.

Keywords: SVM; Machine Learning; FPGA; Distributed Computing; QR Decomposition

DOI: https://doi.org/10.1145/3289602.3293954

Transistor-Level Optimization Methodology for GRM FPGA Interconnect Circuits

Zhengjie Li, Yuanlong Xiao, Yufan Zhang, Yunbing Pang,
Jian Wang*, Jinmei Lai , *Fudan University*
Contact: wjian@fudan.edu.cn, jmlai@fudan.edu.cn

Due to its dominance in the whole chip area, power and delay, the FPGA interconnect circuits are traditionally designed by full custom design method. We present an automated transistor-level sizing optimization methodology for GRM FPGA interconnect circuits. In order to get accurate and effective predicated area, the commonly used diffusion sharing, transistor folding and inputs sharing are considered. To get the accurate and effective delay value, we avoid the inaccuracy of using linear device model, and use two schemes to build wire model: the wire within a circuit and the wire between interconnect circuits. To decrease simulation time, we propose multi-thread acceleration method and the Minimum-Final-Delay (MFD) algorithm which optimizes interconnect circuit as a whole, not separated part. For switch box optimization, MFD algorithm requires 38% less number of simulations than COFFE's algorithm. We use 65nm CMOS process technology for evaluation. For different optimization strategy, we emphasize either representative critical path delay or overall layout area. Compare to full-custom design method, the global cost can be decrease by 3% ~ 17%. For different transistor sizing combinations, 10/50 threads can be ~ 9X/15X faster than single-thread. Compared with the manual design method, our optimization methodology explores larger design space, and it decreases the circuit design optimization time from months to hours.

Keywords: Transistor-level optimization; Area model; Wire load model; Minimum-Final-Delay algorithm; Multi-thread acceleration

DOI: https://doi.org/10.1145/3289602.3293955

Multi-Commodity Flow-Based Spreading in a Commercial Analytic Placer

Nima Karimpour Darav
Microsemi Corporation
Kitchener, Ontario, Canada
nima.karimpourdarav@microchip.com

Andrew Kennings
University of Waterloo
Waterloo, Ontario, Canada
akennings@uwaterloo.ca

Kristofer Vorwerk
Microsemi Corporation
Kitchener, Ontario, Canada
kris.vorwerk@microchip.com

Arun Kundu
Microsemi Corporation
San Jose, California, USA
arun.kundu@microchip.com

ABSTRACT

Modern analytic placement tools are commonly built around the idea of iterative Lower Bound (LB) and Upper Bound (UB) placement. The LB step optimizes wirelength and timing while ignoring overlap and cell-type constraints, whereas the UB step attempts to spread cells and satisfy constraints without harming design quality. Top-down geometric partitioning techniques have traditionally been used to spread cells during UB placement. We propose a new, network flow-based approach for UB placement which does a better job of preserving quality by optimizing the *displacement* of cells from their LB positions. Our approach not only addresses cell overlap, but also accommodates complex region constraints and simultaneously spreads unit-sized logic, carry chains, and blocks like RAMs and DSPs. Our technique is scalable, does not require geometric partitioning, and is suitable for both flat and clustered placement flows. We deployed our algorithm in a commercial FPGA CAD flow, and show that it reduces HPWL by 6.4% on average (up to 22.8% in the best case) while improving worst-slack timing in over 90% of designs, compared to a state-of-the-art alternative.

CCS CONCEPTS

• **Mathematics of computing** → **Network flows**; • **Hardware** → **Reconfigurable logic and FPGAs**; **Placement**.

KEYWORDS

FPGA placement; network flows; analytic placement

ACM Reference Format:
Nima Karimpour Darav, Andrew Kennings, Kristofer Vorwerk, and Arun Kundu. 2019. Multi-Commodity Flow-Based Spreading in a Commercial Analytic Placer. In *The 2019 ACM/SIGDA International Symposium on Field-Programmable Gate Arrays (FPGA '19), February 24–26, 2019, Seaside, CA, USA.* ACM, New York, NY, USA, 10 pages. https://doi.org/10.1145/3289602.3293896

1 INTRODUCTION

Placement is a key component in the Computer-Aided Design (CAD) flow in that it accounts for a majority of the runtime while being largely responsible for overall design quality. Traditional placement algorithms based on simulated annealing [2] or min-cut partitioning [14] generally do not scale well, and this has led to a significant increase in interest for analytic placement techniques.

Many analytic placers are built upon the idea of iterative LB and UB placement. This strategy has been shown to produce competitive solutions in both the Application Specific Integrated Circuit (ASIC) [6, 11, 13] and Field Programmable Gate Array (FPGA) [9, 12, 15, 16] domains. Within the LB step, several objectives—such as wirelength and timing—are optimized while ignoring overlap constraints and other placement restrictions. The UB step seeks to produce a fairly non-overlapping placement with the goal of preserving the relative positions provided by the LB placement. To spread movable objects subject to defined constraints, the UB step in many modern ASIC and FPGA placement tools [6, 9, 11–13, 15, 16] exploits the idea of *rough legalization*. Full legalization and detailed improvement are applied to further enhance the quality and satisfy all remaining constraints.

For FPGA placement, the UB step must not only preserve the quality and information inherent in the LB placement, but it must also account for the presence of heterogeneous cells—Look-Up Tables (LUTs), Flip-Flops (FFs), different types of Random Access Memory (RAM), Digital Signal Processors (DSPs), and so forth—which are subject to varying placement constraints. To this end, we propose a new approach to UB placement which preserves the quality of the LB solution and accounts for the constraints imposed by modern FPGA architectures.[1]

The main contributions of this paper are as follows:

(1) Our technique empirically outperforms existing UB spreading heuristics [11, 13] in terms of quality while *maintaining comparable runtime.*

(2) The proposed algorithm is suitable for spreading both flat and clustered FPGA netlists.

[1] As an aside, our proposed UB placer was developed for FPGA placement within a commercial tool, but the idea of using flow for UB placement is equally applicable to ASIC placement in which heterogeneity is not as much of a concern.

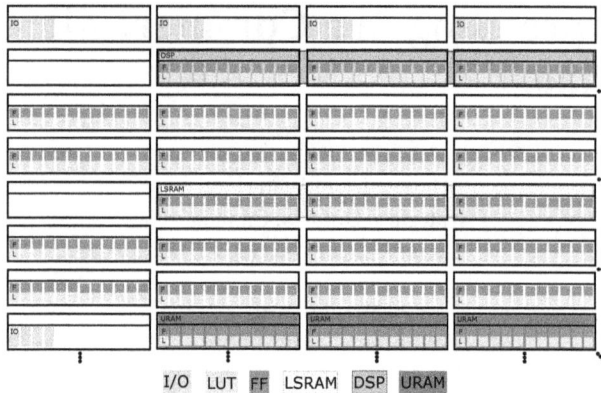

Figure 1: Logical view of the north-west corner of a Microsemi PolarFire FPGA. A similar pattern repeats throughout the die.

(3) Our technique optimizes maximum and average cell displacement and preserves the relative ordering of cells from the LB solution.

(4) All placeable objects are accounted for, during spreading, *at the same time*, even when those objects compete for the same resources.[2] Moreover, the technique considers the availability of FPGA resources and the impact to placement legality imposed by overlapping region constraints—a constraint not described by previous works.

The rest of this paper is organized as follows. Section 2 describes our target FPGA architecture and analytic placement flow, along with related work. Our proposed network flow-based spreading algorithm is elaborated in Section 3. Numerical results are presented in Section 4, where we demonstrate the superiority of flow-based spreading versus prior methods. Section 5 summarizes our work and provides directions for future investigations.

2 PRELIMINARIES
2.1 FPGA Architecture

We developed our tool for the Microsemi PolarFire[TM] FPGA architecture, a depiction of which is presented in Figure 1 [4]. It is a row-oriented FPGA consisting of I/Os along the periphery, 4-input LUTs, FFs, DSPs, URAMs, and LSRAMs blocks. Each 4-input LUT and FF are paired into *modules*. Groups of 12 modules are considered a *cluster*. Clusters have architectural constraints which must be observed when inserting modules into clusters (e.g., limits on control signals, clocks, and regular input and output signals). LUTs support *carry chains* for the efficient implementation of certain operations (e.g., counters and adders). LUTs involved in a carry chain *must* be placed adjacent to each other in the same row.

The URAM and LSRAM blocks support different RAM applications. Additionally, the architecture supports the use of *math chains*, consisting of multiple DSP blocks, to create wide multipliers. DSP

---
[2]Traditional flow-based methods such as bipartite matching handle neither mixed-sized movable objects nor large designs without dividing the design into smaller sub-problems [12]. In contrast, our proposed method handles mixed sized-objects such as *carry chains* and *math chains* seamlessly as part of the formulation.

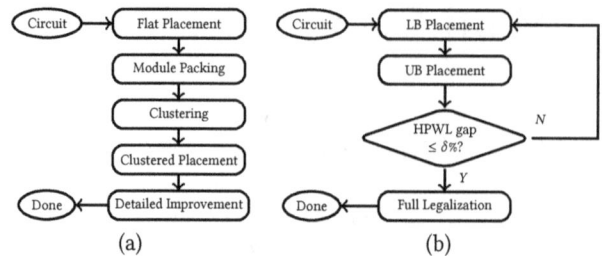

Figure 2: Typical CAD flow for FPGA placement in which different placements are obtained via analytic placement.

blocks involved in chains must be placed next to each other in the same row. In the absence of a DSP or RAM block, *LUTs and FFs can be placed in the interface logic sites normally occupied by the DSP and RAM to improve utilization, so long as those LUTs do not employ carry chains.* Further FPGA details are described in [4].

Different blocks can be different widths. If the width of a cluster is Ω, then DSP blocks have width 3Ω, URAM blocks have width Ω, and LSRAM blocks have width 3Ω. Carry chains and math chains which span multiple clusters and are an integer multiple of Ω. Objects smaller that a cluster (e.g., modules) have widths of $k\Omega$ where k is a fraction < 1. The placement of a circuit into this FPGA requires the placement of unequally-sized, heterogeneous cells onto discrete physical locations. The architectural features of this FPGA are typical of all modern FPGAs.

2.2 CAD Flow

Microsemi's Libero® software implements a CAD flow similar to that illustrated in Figure 2 for placing PolarFire designs. In Figure 2(a), given a mapped design, LUTs and FFs are packed into modules which, in turn, are packed into clusters. Packing and clustering satisfy architectural constraints of the FPGA and ensure that the design will fit into the device while maximizing signal absorption in individual clusters [8]; it may be performed with or without an initial placement. An initial flat placement is not typically required to be a feasible placement—its purpose is to provide physical information to help the packing and clustering make better decisions about wirelength, timing and routability optimization. Subsequent to packing and clustering, clustered placement is performed to place all clusters as well as IP blocks (RAMs and DSPs) in the netlist. Detailed placement further optimizes the design by moving individual modules and instances between clusters.

Both flat and clustered placement can be performed via analytic placement as illustrated in Figure 2(b). LB placement is performed via quadratic programming using the Bound-to-Bound (B2B) model [19]. Weighted edges to target locations are included, along with additional weighted edges for timing optimization. UB placement performs a *rough legalization* to spread objects and find target locations for the subsequent LB placement. The Libero software has historically employed a variant of top-down geometric partitioning to spread cells in over-capacitated areas of the device while preserving the relative order of the movable objects from the LB solution. This geometric partitioning accounts for the heterogeneous nature of the FPGA netlists and device architectures.

Iterations continue until the HPWL of the LB and UB placements differ by $\leq \delta\%$. Legalization is applied to remove final overlap, to ensure that cells are placed onto suitable sites (depending on their type), and to verify that placement constraints are satisfied. Timing analysis and routability estimation (not shown in Figure 2) can be performed throughout analytic placement.

Unlike full legalization, which must ensure that all placement constraints are satisfied, the rough legalization performed during UB placement is not required to guarantee legality, in exchange for more efficient runtime. That said, it is desirable for the UB placer to produce a placement which is "as legal as possible" since the accuracy of the timing and routability estimation are improved when the spread-out placement closely matches the final placement.

2.3 Related work

We review several recent works with CAD flows similar to Figure 2. In [9], the HeAP wirelength-driven analytic placer is described for heterogeneous FPGA placement; it is a direct adaptation of the ASIC placer SimPL [11]. The HeAP placer is designed for clustered placement, with packing and clustering performed using a commercial tool. HeAP uses geometric partitioning and non-linear shifting [11] to spread movable objects in overfilled areas of the FPGA. Cut lines are placed during geometric partitioning to account for the architecture, and the placement of heterogeneous blocks is accomplished by spreading different block types separately.

Several analytic placers for FPGAs were introduced in [12, 15, 16] after the International Symposium on Physical Design (ISPD) placement contests of 2016 and 2017 [17, 18]. In [15], the GPlace-pack and GPlace-flat placers are described, wherein UB placement is performed using top-down geometric partitioning. The tool RippleFPGA was introduced in [16]—based on the work of [10]—in which top-down geometric partitioning and FPGA constraints are taken into account during the legalization. UTPlacerF [12] performs both flat and clustered placement and closely follows the flow in Figure 2, with its UB placement based on SimPL. During flat placement, both a wirelength-driven and routability-driven phase are employed, but both phases use analytic placement as shown in Figure 2(b). RAM and DSP blocks are legalized using bipartite matching. As stated in [12], solving a complete matching problem is impractical for larger designs and, consequently, the placement region is divided into a set of uniform rectangles and matching is applied to each rectangle separately. After flat placement, packing and clustering are performed using physical information, and clustered placement is computed with an analytic method.

For rough legalization, the aforementioned approaches mainly rely on heuristics and top-down geometric partitioning (augmented with other heuristics to handle heterogeneity). These methods may not be able to preserve the quality of the LB placement since the minimum perturbation during the process is not guaranteed.

The spreading problem was identified as an important step worthy of its own investigation in [20], where the use of top-down geometric partitioning was questioned. The approach presented in [20] does not rely on partitioning, but rather on creating a force map akin to that used in ASIC placement tools (e.g., [7]). The flow-based strategy which we describe in this work spreads all block types simultaneously whereas [20] only spreads logic blocks and

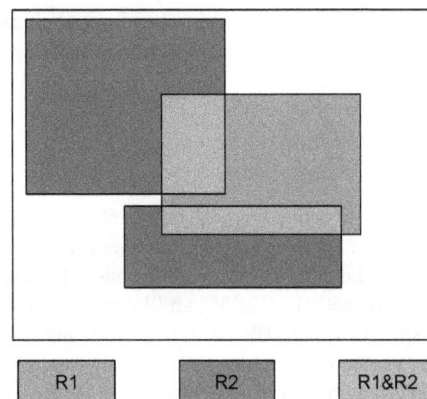

Figure 3: Two overlapping region constraints R1 (in pink) and R2 (in blue). The overlapping area is highlighted in gray.

requires that RAM and DSP blocks be spread separately. Our technique is runtime-efficient and scalable, and accounts for both maximum and average cell displacement, which preserves the quality of the LB placement while maintaining the ordering of movable objects. Finally, our flow-based algorithm handles overlapping region constraints which can restrict the placement of objects within the FPGA—a constraint not considered in previous works.

2.4 Region Constraints

Region constraints may be specified in the Libero software flow as part of a user-initiated floorplanning strategy [3]. Several overlapping region constraints can be defined for a design, as shown in Figure 3. If a cell is assigned to a region R, the cell must be placed inside the region; however, other clusters not assigned to any region can be placed either inside or outside of R. In contrast to the constraints considered in [6], the region constraints in Libero may be *overlapping*—this poses a *significant* challenge because cells may compete for the same locations, so all regions must be accounted for simultaneously.

3 PROPOSED SPREADING ALGORITHM

Our proposed spreading algorithm is inspired by [5] which is a legalization tool for ASICs. However, there are key differences for FPGA placement and for spreading. We begin by defining some nomenclature. Let D represent the set of logical (placeable) clusters in a design, comprising 5 subsets: D_a, D_m, D_u, D_s, and D_l, corresponding to the carry chains, DSP, URAM, LSRAM, and general logic clusters (i.e., no carry chains), respectively.[3] Let n be a positive integer and $\Omega = 12$ which is the maximum number of modules in a physical cluster (cf. Section 2). We define the width (W) for each logical cluster in each subset as:[4]

- $\forall d_{a,i} \in D_a$, $W(d_{a,i}) = n\Omega$. Thus, logical cluster $d_{a,i}$ (a carry chain) may horizontally span several physical clusters.

---

[3]I/Os in commercial FPGAs can be subject to special placement and timing considerations, and the details of their automatic placement are beyond this paper.
[4]Although we present this work for a clustered placement flow, we note that our proposed method can be directly used for a flat placement flow by setting Ω to an appropriate value and defining, for example, an additional set D for modules.

- $\forall d_{m,i} \in D_m$, $W(d_{m,i}) = 3n\Omega$. Thus, logical cluster $d_{m,i}$ (a single DSP or a math chain) will horizontally span several physical clusters.
- $\forall d_{u,i} \in D_u$, $W(d_{u,i}) = \Omega$.
- $\forall d_{l,i} \in D_l$, $W(d_{l,i}) = \Omega$.
- $\forall d_{s,i} \in D_s$, $W(d_{s,i}) = 3\Omega$.

Similar to [6], any defined region constraint is tagged by a number (color) $r > 0$ and the die area is tagged (colorized) by $r = 0$ as the *default region*. Let bins V represent the nodes of a flow network, composed of 4 subsets: V_a, V_m, V_u, and V_s, corresponding to the carry chain sites, DSP sites, URAM sites, LSRAM sites of the FPGA architecture, respectively, which are vertically aligned with the sites of the FPGA architecture. Each bin $v_i \in V$ has the same height as an FPGA site but with width equal to Ω. Therefore, each DSP or LSRAM site is represented by three bins because the width of a DSP or LSRAM site is equal to 3Ω. Each bin v_i keeps a color vector of regions overlapping with bin v_i. Let objects Γ represent part of the logical cluster set D in our flow network, where each object $\gamma_i \in \Gamma$ has the same size as a bin $v_i \in V$. (For flat placement, the size of an object would be smaller than a bin.) Objects representing a cluster have the same color as the region the cluster is assigned to. Let the width of an object γ_i be $W(\gamma_i)$. The total width of objects $\Gamma(v_i)$ in a bin v_i is computed as $W(\Gamma(v_i)) = \sum_{\gamma_i \in \Gamma(v_i)} W(\gamma_i)$. Let $supply(v_i) = max\{0, W(\Gamma(v_i)) - \Omega\}$. A bin v_i is an overflowed (supply) bin if $supply(v_i) > 0$; or, put differently, if the total width of objects $\Gamma(v_i)$ assigned to bin v_i is greater than the width of bin v_i, bin v_i is considered to be overflowed because each bin cannot include more than one object without overlap.

Let $demand(v_i) = max\{0, \Omega - W(\Gamma(v_i))\}$. A bin v_i is a sink bin if $demand(v_i) > 0$. (Sink bins do not include any objects.) Resolving all overflowed bins is the main objective of our algorithm subject to several constraints that are described further in this paper. The problem is considered a *multi-commodity* flow problem [1] for two key reasons. First, the set Γ is composed of five subsets Γ_a, Γ_m, Γ_u, Γ_s, and Γ_l which in turn represent logical clusters D_a, D_m, D_u, D_s, and D_l. The first four subsets of objects can be transferred only between two bins in the same subset while the objects of set Γ_l can be transferred between any two bins. For example, if bin $v_{a,i} \in V_a$ includes two objects $\gamma_{a,1} \in \Gamma_a$ and $\gamma_{l,1} \in \Gamma_l$, $\gamma_{a,1}$ may be transferred only to a bin in subset V_a while $\gamma_{l,1}$ can be transferred to any given bin. Second, there may be several objects which together represent a wide logical cluster, subject to the constraint that those objects should be placed at bins that are on the same row and horizontally-adjacent. A bin v_i is *compatible* with an object γ_j if and only if either the color of object γ_j is zero (representing *default region*) or the color of object γ_j is included in the color vector of bin v_i and either $\gamma_j \in \Gamma_l$ or $\gamma_j \in \Gamma_x$ and $v_i \in V_x$ where $x \in a, m, u, s$. In our approach, heterogeneous clusters are handled seamlessly by using a single network flow problem.[5] A summary of terms used in this paper is presented in Table 1.

---

[5]Our proposed algorithm can be easily adapted to address routability based on cell bloating or target density. For example, a cell bloating technique [12] is accomplished by changing object widths. For target density adjustment [16], bin capacities can be adjusted.

Table 1: Nomenclature used in this paper.

Term	Description
n	A positive integer.
Ω	The maximum number of modules in a physical cluster.
A	The given FPGA architecture.
N	The given circuit.
D	The set of placeable clusters in the design.
D_x	The set of clusters with the same type. D_a, D_m, D_u, D_s, and D_l in turn indicate the set of carry chains, DSP, URAM, SRAM, and general logic clusters.
$d_{x,i}$	Cluster i in set D_x.
V	The set of nodes (bins) of the network flow constructed for the design.
$|V|$	The size of set V.
V_x	The set of bins with the same type. V_a, V_m, V_u, and V_s, and V_l in turn indicate the set of carry chain sites, DSP sites, URAM sites, SRAM sites.
$v_{x,i}$	Bin i in set V_x.
Γ	The set of network flow objects representing clusters D.
$|\Gamma|$	The size of set Γ.
Γ_x	The set of network flow objects with the same type. $\Gamma_a, \Gamma_m, \Gamma_u, \Gamma_s$, and Γ_l represent D_a, D_m, D_u, D_s, and D_l, respectively.
$\gamma_{x,i}$	Object i in set Γ_x.
$\Gamma(v_i)$	The set of objects inside bin v_i.
$\hat{\Gamma}(d_i)$	The set of objects representing cluster d_i.
$W(d_i)$	The width of cluster d_i.
$W(\gamma_i)$	The width of an object γ_i.
$W(\Gamma(v_i))$	The total width of objects assigned to bin v_i.
$demand(v_i)$	The demand value of a bin v_i.
$supply(v_i)$	The supply value of a bin v_i.
r	The region tagged with r. $r = 0$ is used for the default region (the die area).
Λ	The set of overfilled bins at iteration *iter*.
$|\Lambda|$	The size of set Λ.
λ_i	An overfilled bin ($supply(\lambda_i) > 0$).
iter	The current iteration of the algorithm.
Ψ	The upper-bound for maximum object movement at the current iteration of the algorithm.
$P(\lambda_i)$	The set of augmenting paths identified by Algorithm 2 for overflowed bin λ_i.
$|P|_{avg}$	The average number of the identified paths at each iteration.
p_k	An augmenting path in $P(\lambda_i)$
$demand_T$	The total demand provided by augmenting paths $P(\lambda_i)$ identified by Algorithm 2.
$\psi(\gamma_j, v_i)$	The quadratic displacement of moving object γ_j to bin v_i.
$wt(\gamma_i)$	The weight of object γ_i.

Algorithm 1: Network-Flow Based Spreading Algorithm

Require: For the given FPGA architecure A, the circuit N has been packed into a set of clusters D.

```
 1:  Γ = createObjectsFromClusters(D)
 2:  V = extractBins(A)
 3:  E = connectBins(V)
 4:  assignObjectsToBins(Γ, V)
 5:  iter = 0
 6:  repeat
 7:      Ψ = computeMaxMovement(iter)
 8:      Λ = identifyOverflowedBins(V)
 9:      Sort bins Λ in order of ascending supply values
10:      for each bin λᵢ ∈ Λ do
11:          P(λᵢ) = identify candidate paths using Algorithm 2
12:          Sort paths P(λᵢ) in order of ascending path costs
13:          for each pₖ ∈ P(λᵢ) do
14:              if supply(λᵢ) > 0 then
15:                  Move cells over path pₖ (see Section 3.3)
16:              end if
17:          end for
18:      end for
19:      iter = iter + 1
20:  until Λ is empty
21:  updateClusterPositions(D, Γ, A, V)
```

3.1 Algorithm Outline

The outline of our algorithm is presented in Algorithm 1. First, a set Γ of objects is created based on the given set D of clusters (line 1). For a given logical cluster d_i, if $W(d_i) = n\Omega$ (where n is a positive integer number), a set $\hat{\Gamma}(d_i)$ including n objects will be created such that the width of each object is equal to Ω. The color of objects representing a cluster is determined based on the color of the region the cluster is assigned to. In line 2, a set V of bins are extracted for the given FPGA device A such that each bin v_i includes a color vector of all regions (including *default region*) overlapping with bin v_i. Then, bins V are connected to each other in four directions for each region a bin is overlapping with: left, right, top, and bottom. In contrast to [5], each bin v_i is vertically connected to multiple bins in different subsets to allow objects from different subsets to be easily transformed to *compatible* bins. For example, if a given bin $v_{a,1} \in V_a$ includes two objects $\gamma_{l,1} \in \Gamma_l$ and $\gamma_{a,1} \in \Gamma_a$, additional edges allow object $\gamma_{a,1}$ to be transferred to the closest bin $v_{a,2} \in V_a$ on top or the closest bin $v_{a,3} \in V_a$ on bottom. Similarly, there are extra edges added to allow $\gamma_{l,1}$ to be vertically transferred to any closest bin in set V.

Figure 4a shows how a typical bin is connected. Since all bins at the same row are in the same subset, a bin v_i is horizontally-connected to only the two closest bins on the left and right sides. If v_i was overlapping with any defined region constraint $r > 0$, extra edges would be added to connect bins (with different types for four directions) overlapping with region constraint r.

This method for connecting bins prevents deadlocks which may be caused by blockages, overlapping regions, or a highly-utilized subset of bins. More importantly, both this method and the definition of *compatible bin* are *key* to the ability of our proposed method to: (1) spread all types of logic in all defined region constraints simultaneously; and, (2) resolve the placement of different types

of objects onto spots in the FPGA device which can accommodate different types of blocks.

In line 4, each object γ_i representing a cluster d_i is assigned to a *compatible* bin v_i with the closest quadratic distance from cluster d_i. In lines 6-20, an iterative process is applied to compute the maximum displacement and to resolve all overflowed bins. In line 7, the upper bound for maximum object movement is relaxed at each iteration based on the quadratic equation: $\Psi = \big((iter + 1) \cdot \Omega\big)^2$, where *iter* indicates the number of the current iteration.[6] In practice, the quality of the final solution is mostly independent of the order of resolving overflowed bins because cell movements are limited by Ψ; however, sorting overflowed bins Λ in order of ascending supply values has been shown to reduce runtime. This is because resolving slightly-overflowed bins first provides more candidate paths for highly-overflowed bins later—see Figure 4b and Figure 4c.

In lines 10-18, for each overflowed bin λ_i, a set $P(\lambda_i)$ of augmenting paths are identified, set $P(\lambda_i)$ is sorted in order of ascending cost to ensure that cells are moved with the minimum cost, and objects are moved along each path $p_k \in P(\lambda_i)$. Finally, the location of each logical cluster $d_i \in D$ is updated based on the location (central gravity) of its representing object (objects). Hence, the solution provided by Algorithm 1 is well-spread as clusters represented by single objects are fully-legalized while minor overlaps are permitted for clusters represented by multiple objects.

3.2 Augmenting Path Algorithm

We propose a variant of Breadth-First Search (BFS) to identify multiple candidate paths satisfying the following three constraints: (1) the quadratic displacement of any object movement along the identified paths is $\leq \Psi$; (2) there is at least one object in each bin that can be moved to the next bin along the identified paths while satisfying the first constraint; and, (3) the last bin in a candidate path is empty (i.e., a sink bin). The first constraint prevents unnecessarily long displacement. The second constraint avoids paths leading to a deadlock. The third constraint guarantees that a portion of the supply of the overflowed bin can be sunk along the identified paths.

Algorithm 2 begins by initializing the total capacity of all identified paths, $demand_T$, to zero, and initializing the "visited" status of each bin; each bin cannot be traversed more than once. The overflowed bin λ_i is inserted to an empty path p in line 6. Each path is a queue of bins whose first element is the overflowed bin λ_i. While traversing bins using our variant of BFS, any partial path is saved into a queue Q. Lines 8-28 are repeated until queue Q is empty or the total demand ($demand_T$) provided by the identified paths can sink supply λ_i. The last bin v_{src} of path p on the head of queue Q is determined; then, for each bin v_i connected to bin v_{src}, a partial path p_i is created if there is at least one *compatible* object in v_{src} that can be moved to bin v_i (lines 11-27).

The minimum cost of moving objects from v_{src} to v_i is computed using the equation: $cost = wt(\gamma^*) \cdot \psi(\gamma^*, v_i)$, where γ^* is an object in v_{src} with the minimum $cost$ such that the object is *compatible* with v_i and the quadratic movement $\psi(\gamma^*, v_i)$ of object γ^* is less than the upper bound maximum movement Ψ at the current iteration of Algorithm 1. If there is no such object in v_{src}, $cost$ is set to ∞.

---

[6]In [5], a linear equation is used for maximum movement, but we have empirically found that a quadratic approach is better for *spreading*.

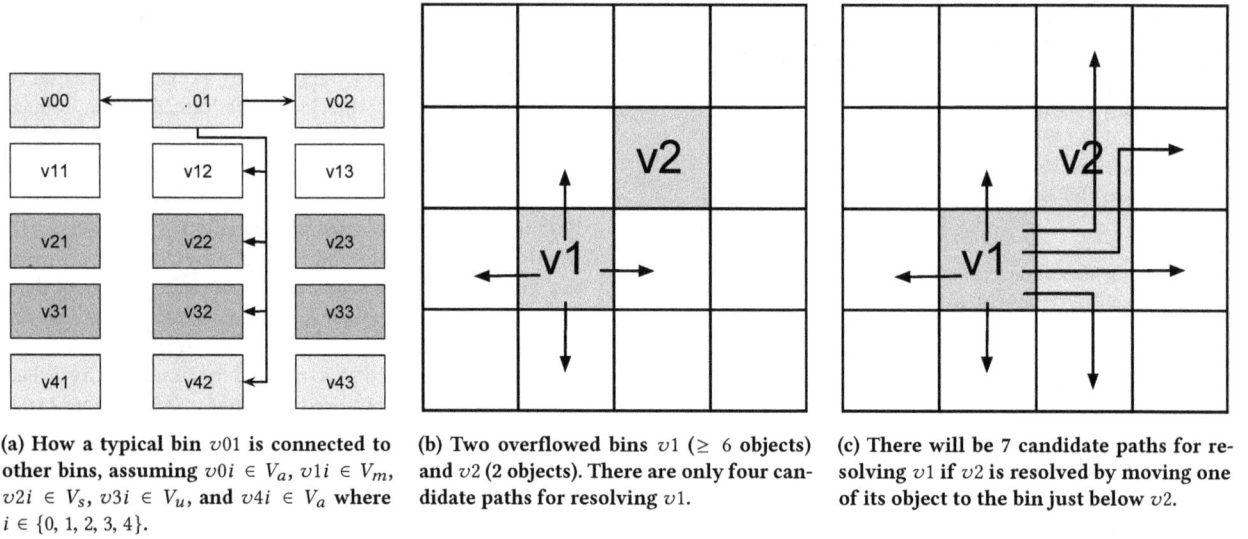

(a) How a typical bin $v01$ is connected to other bins, assuming $v0i \in V_a$, $v1i \in V_m$, $v2i \in V_s$, $v3i \in V_u$, and $v4i \in V_a$ where $i \in \{0, 1, 2, 3, 4\}$.

(b) Two overflowed bins $v1$ (≥ 6 objects) and $v2$ (2 objects). There are only four candidate paths for resolving $v1$.

(c) There will be 7 candidate paths for resolving $v1$ if $v2$ is resolved by moving one of its object to the bin just below $v2$.

Figure 4: Illustrative examples of (a) connections between bins, (b) two overflowed bins, and (c) the increase in the number of candidate paths.

Algorithm 2: Multiple Augmenting Paths

Require: Set V of all bins, set E of all network flow edges, overflowed bin λ_i, and maximum movement Ψ are given.

1: $demand_T = 0$
2: **for** each $v_i \in V$ **do**
3:    visited(v_i) = false
4: **end for**
5: visited(λ_i) = true
6: Insert λ_i into an empty path p
7: Insert path p into an empty queue Q
8: **repeat**
9:    Dequeue path p from queue Q
10:   v_{src} = the tail of path p
11:   **for** each bin v_i connected to bin v_{src} **do**
12:     **if** visited(v_i) $\neq$ true **then**
13:       $cost$ = computeCost(v_{src}, v_i, Ψ)
14:       **if** $cost \neq \infty$ **then**
15:         Create a copy p_i of path p
16:         $cost_T(p_i) = cost_T(p) + cost$
17:         Insert bin v_i into path p_i
18:         visited(v_i) = true
19:         **if** $|\Gamma(v_i)| == 0$ **then**
20:           Insert p_i into set $P(\lambda_i)$
21:           $demand_T = demand_T + \Omega$
22:         **else**
23:           Insert path p_i into queue Q
24:         **end if**
25:       **end if**
26:     **end if**
27:   **end for**
28: **until** Q is empty or supply(λ_i) $\leq demand_T$

The function $wt(\gamma^*)$ computes a weight based on the size of set $\hat{\Gamma}(d_i)$ representing logical cluster d_i where $\gamma^* \in \hat{\Gamma}(d_i)$. The term $wt(\gamma^*)$ plays an important role in our multi-commodity flow model

because it maintains the objects representing a single cluster close to each other. In lines 19-24, if the computed cost is a valid number, the new path p_i either will be considered a candidate path if v_i is empty or will be inserted into Q for further investigation.

3.3 Object Movement

Objects are moved along a path p using Algorithm 3. Before moving objects along a candidate path p, the cost of movement is recomputed as it might have been changed by moving objects along other candidate paths sharing some partial paths with path p. In addition, the order of traversing the path is reversed using a stack to avoid moving an object along path p several times. To achieve the minimum total movement, before moving an object between two subsequent bins v_{src} and v_{sink}, objects in v_{src} are sorted in order of distance to v_{sink}. Figure 5 shows an example of how objects may move along a candidate path. In this figure, $v1$ and $v2$ are overflowed bins with 2 objects each, while $v3$ is a sink bin. Bins $v1$ and $v3$ are overlapping with region $R2$ in Figure 3 while $v2$ is overlapping with both regions $R1$ and $R2$. First, the closest object to bin $v3$ is moved to sink bin $v3$ (Figure 5a) such that the object must be *compatible* with the target bin $v3$. $c3$ is not *compatible* with bin $v3$ because $c3$ is assigned to region $R1$ while $v3$ is overlapping with only region $R2$. Then, the closest *compatible* object to bin $v2$ is moved to $v2$. As shown in Figure 5c, no new overflowed bin is introduced and the source bin ($v1$) in the augmentation path is no longer overflowed.

4 EXPERIMENTAL RESULTS

Our flow-based spreading algorithm was implemented in Microsemi's Libero tool. The quality of our technique was compared to Microsemi's previous UB heuristic which employed top-down geometric partitioning and bipartite matching [9, 12]. Since the detailed

---

Algorithm 3: Cell Move

Require: Set V of all bins, set E of all network flow edges, path p and the maximum movement Ψ are given.

1: Dequeue bin v_{src} from path p
2: Insert bin v_{src} into a stack S
3: **while** p is not empty **do**
4:     Dequeue bin v_{sink} from path p
5:     cost = computeCost(v_{src}, v_{sink}, Ψ)
6:     **if** cost == ∞ **then**
7:         **return**
8:     **end if**
9:     $v_{src} = v_{sink}$
10:    Insert bin v_{sink} into stack S
11: **end while**
12: Pop bin v_{sink} from stack S
13: **while** S is not empty **do**
14:    Pop bin v_{src} from stack S
15:    Sort cells $\Gamma(v_{src})$ in bin v_{src} in order of the closest to bin v_{sink}
16:    Move the first *compatible* object from set $\Gamma(v_{src})$ to v_{sink}
17:    $v_{sink} = v_{src}$
18: **end while**

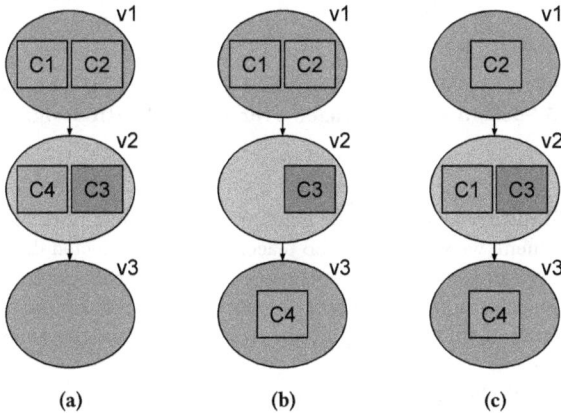

Figure 5: An example of how objects are moved along a path.

improvement step—cf. Figure 2(a)—can make additional improvements to the solution, the results in this paper are reported for the legalized placements *just after* the analytic placement step (without applying detailed improvement).

A benchmark suite of 557 designs targeting the PolarFire family was employed. The designs originate from both industry as well as Microsemi's internal development, and contain a broad mixture of logic, RAM, DSP, high-speed I/O interfaces, complex local and global clocking regimes, complicated region constraints, timing constraints, carry chains, and varying logic depths. All designs used in this work contain at least 5000 placeable logic cells, with some designs containing over 700k. The timing constraints are adjusted so that there are no critical clock-to-input or clock-to-output timing constraints (which would render the timing of each design largely dependent on I/O placement, as opposed to internal logic). Each design is placed into the smallest available PolarFire die which could contain it, as this ensures that the utilization presents

a sufficient challenge. The layout tools are configured to optimize as best as possible and not stop early if timing is met. Since the initial random seed can alter the "starting point" for the packing and clustering algorithms implemented in the commercial tool, each design is executed with 5 different random seeds and the average value of each numerical result is reported in this paper.

4.1 HPWL and Worst Slack Evaluation

Figure 6 shows the per-design improvement in Half Perimeter Wire Length (HPWL) which was achieved by switching from the original UB algorithm to our proposed flow-based algorithm, across the suite of 557 designs. Designs are sorted on the x-axis based on the achieved improvement in HPWL. The right y-axis and the left y-axis respectively show the size of a design and the percentage of HPWL improvement achieved by switching from the original UB algorithm to our proposed flow-based algorithm.

The improvement in HPWL due to flow-based spreading is 6.4% on average, with very few degradations. In some cases, the HPWL of the placement was improved by up to 22.8%. The approximate size of each design (in terms of the number of logic cells) is plotted as a line graph along the secondary axis—this shows that the improvement is not confined to any particular design size.

We examined the worst-slack estimates at the end of analytic placement as a means of evaluating our proposed algorithm's impact on design timing. Across the design suite, over 90% of the designs showed either equivalent or better critical path slack.[7] The average improvement in estimated worst slack was 389 ps per design which, in the PolarFire architecture, is approximately the same as the delay through six LUT ($A \rightarrow Y$) arcs. It is important to note that the flow-based spreading does not attempt to explicitly optimize HPWL or slack, but rather, achieves these improvements due to its superior ability in minimally perturbing the placement and object ordering.

4.2 Time Complexity and Runtime Analysis

Determining the time complexity of the proposed algorithm is challenging since the complexity is not only dependent on the number of bins and overfilled bins, but also the average number of paths identified at each iteration, which is itself a function of the number of sink bins.

The number of iterations in Algorithm 1 is bounded by $O(|v|^{0.5})$ as when $iter = O(|V|^{0.5})$, Ψ is set to a value such that any object displacement inside the die area is not greater than Ψ, and the remaining overfilled bins are completely resolved. Given the fact that the design utilization cannot be more than 100%, the number of objects cannot be greater than the number of bins ($|\Gamma| \leq |V|$). For each overfilled bin, the search space in Algorithm 2 is bounded from above and the upper-bound is $O(|V|)$ as the number of connections between a bin to other bins is limited and constant (see Figure 4a); however, the time complexity of lines 13-17 of Algorithm 1 will be on the order of $O(|V| \cdot |P|_{avg})$, ignoring the sort function in Algorithm 3.[8] Therefore, the upper-bound of the time complexity

---

[7]The improvement in timing is presented in terms of placement-based timing estimation since the results were collected prior to routing.

[8]It is fair to ignore the sort function in Algorithm 3 if $|\Lambda|$ is large enough since the average number of objects in overfilled bins would be limited by a constant number.

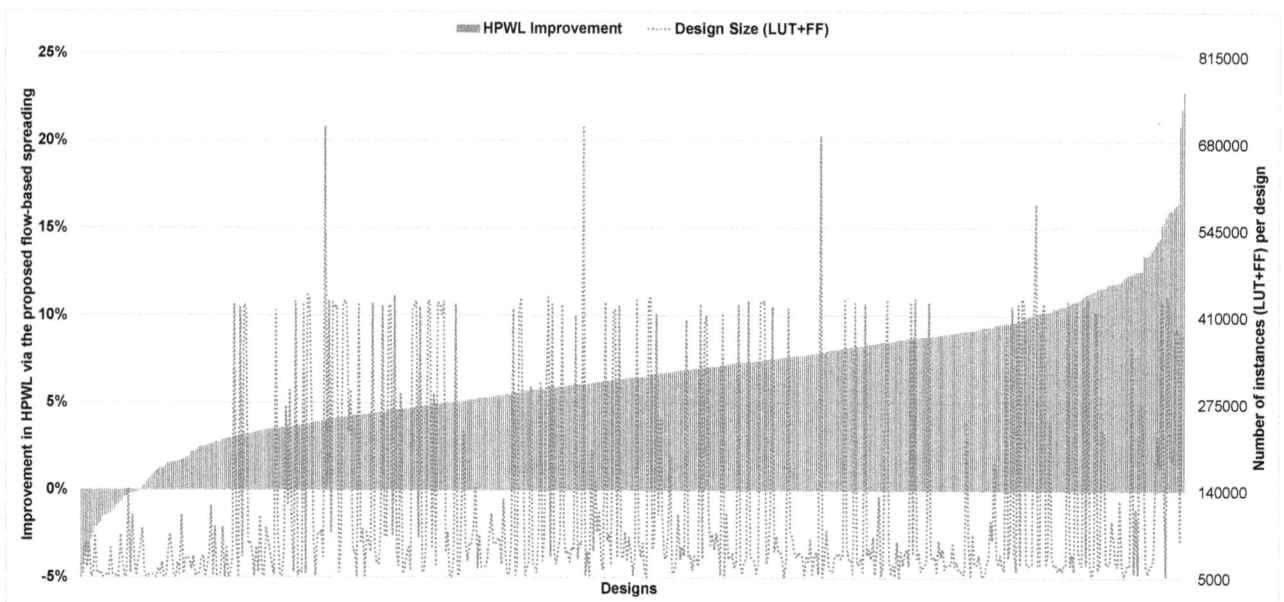

Figure 6: Improvement in HPWL due to flow-based UB spreading relative to Microsemi's original UB placer. Each blue bar represents the improvement in legalized HPWL for a design in the 557-design suite (averaged over 5 seeds), with design size plotted in red against the secondary axis.

of the entire algorithm will be $T = O(|V| \cdot min(|V|^{0.5}, |\Lambda|) \cdot |P|_{avg})$ as several bins are resolved at each iteration. Since $|\Lambda| \leq \frac{|V|}{2}$, $|V|^{0.5} < \frac{|V|}{2}$ for $|V| > 4$, and $|P|_{avg} = |V|$ for the worst case, $T = O(|V|^{2.5})$.

In practice, the flow-based spreading is very fast, particularly in the latter phases of placement when there is less overlap. Furthermore, given the higher quality of solution produced by an analytic placer with our flow technique, less time is required in latter steps of the CAD flow, such as detailed improvement and routing.

For illustrative purposes, we elaborate on the runtime of a subset of our design suite in Table 2. This subset consists of 20 designs chosen from among the suite of 557 designs based primarily on utilization. Within this sub-suite of designs, our proposed method achieved an average improvement of 6.57% in HPWL, and an improvement of 448 ps in worst slack. These results are achieved with just a 1.13% increase in runtime to the analytic placement. In our experience, this runtime increase was easily recovered from the reduced effort in subsequent phases of the CAD flow.

4.3 Displacement Investigation

The improvement in quality which was achieved by flow-based spreading can be explained predominantly by the reduction in average and maximum displacements at each iteration of the analytic placement. Figure 7 presents the improvement in average and maximum displacements at each iteration of analytic placement for a medium-sized, industrial design in the benchmark suite. Similar improvement has been observed across most other designs.

To further investigate the amount of displacement during UB placement, we selected two LB placements and subjected them to both our proposed flow-based and the original partitioning-based UB placement steps. Figure 8 illustrates the results for an early iteration of the analytic placement and the end of the analytic placement.

The displacement histograms in Figure 8 show that, regardless of the placement iteration (equivalently, the amount of overlap in the LB placement), our proposed flow-based spreading is capable of spreading more cells with less displacement compared to the original algorithm. Moreover, spreading is achieved with significantly less maximum displacement. The reduction in movement from our proposed flow-based spreading is more pronounced in early placement iterations where significantly more effort (movement) is required to purge overlap from the LB placement. It is remarkable that such improvement is possible near the end of placement when displacements are expected to be small. Although Figure 8 is for only one medium-sized design, the same trends appear across most designs.

5 CONCLUSIONS

We presented a novel network flow-based spreading algorithm for use in analytic placement, with several advantages compared to traditional methods such as [11, 13]. Our spreading algorithm is capable of handling heterogeneous blocks and device resources simultaneously. Additionally, it can handle complicated, overlapping region constraints which are not addressed in published academic works, but which must be considered for commercial deployment.

Table 2: Comparison of HPWL and slacks on 14 designs chosen from the design suite.

Design	Number of Blocks				Utilization (%)				Current Analytic Placer			Flow-Based Spreading		
	LUT+FF	URAM	LSRAM	DSP	LUT+FF	URAM	LSRAM	DSP	HPWL 10^5	WS (ns)	Runtime (min)	HPWL 10^5	WS (ns)	Runtime (min)
Test1	704912	3442	1296	780	73.2	77.5	85.3	52.7	69.69	−17.868	42.0	67.66	−13.369	46.0
Test2	433865	400	934	0	72.4	14.4	98.1	0.0	17.20	−3.264	18.5	16.31	−4.815	18.7
Test3	692105	3358	1293	775	71.9	75.6	85.1	52.4	54.90	−12.340	41.1	51.18	−11.089	44.4
Test4	103896	280	12	0	17.3	10.0	3.4	0.0	3.32	−0.666	3.8	3.12	−0.493	3.8
Test5	435750	1460	808	785	72.7	52.7	84.9	85.0	43.45	4.891	21.8	42.50	5.117	24.3
Test6	82415	96	0	0	13.8	3.5	0.0	0.0	4.59	−2.191	3.7	4.50	−2.903	3.6
Test7	232099	256	112	0	38.7	9.2	11.8	0.0	7.67	−1.035	10.8	7.14	−0.691	10.3
Test8	102179	0	0.0	924	17.1	0.0	0.0	100.0	3.36	−3.590	5.2	3.36	−3.387	5.4
Test9	434927	1484	806	784	72.6	53.5	84.7	84.9	28.48	4.371	22.2	25.46	5.039	22.2
Test10	122589	2772	0	0	20.5	100.0	0.0	0.0	6.57	−14.798	6.3	6.49	−15.098	6.3
Test11	195778	341	861	3	32.7	12.3	90.4	0.3	8.98	−1.647	6.3	8.56	−0.894	6.5
Test12	274064	304	640	0	45.7	11.0	67.2	0.0	12.74	−1.566	11.0	11.78	−0.912	10.7
Test13	49291	0	0	0	22.7	0.0	0.0	0.0	1.46	2.701	2.1	1.37	2.771	2.1
Test14	424168	1475	783	777	70.8	53.2	82.3	84.1	34.91	5.141	21.3	32.53	2.039	21.9
Test15	93539	0	0	0	43.1	0.0	0.0	0.0	1.82	−1.985	4.2	1.65	−1.201	3.9
Test16	183402	0	0	100	47.7	0.0	0.0	17.0	7.94	−9.135	11.0	6.63	−6.296	10.7
Test17	430012	1428	806	784	71.8	51.5	84.7	84.9	39.64	4.835	22.4	37.67	4.837	25.2
Test18	393376	0	0	0	65.7	0.0	0.0	0.0	19.92	−2.298	19.4	17.73	−0.737	17.6
Test19	431926	1474	809	769	72.1	53.2	85.0	83.2	32.91	5.077	22.5	30.31	4.720	23.6
Test20	70550	9	68	7	32.5	0.9	19.3	2.1	3.27	−6.756	4.5	3.20	−5.799	4.7
Average Improvement												6.57%	+448 ps	−1.13%

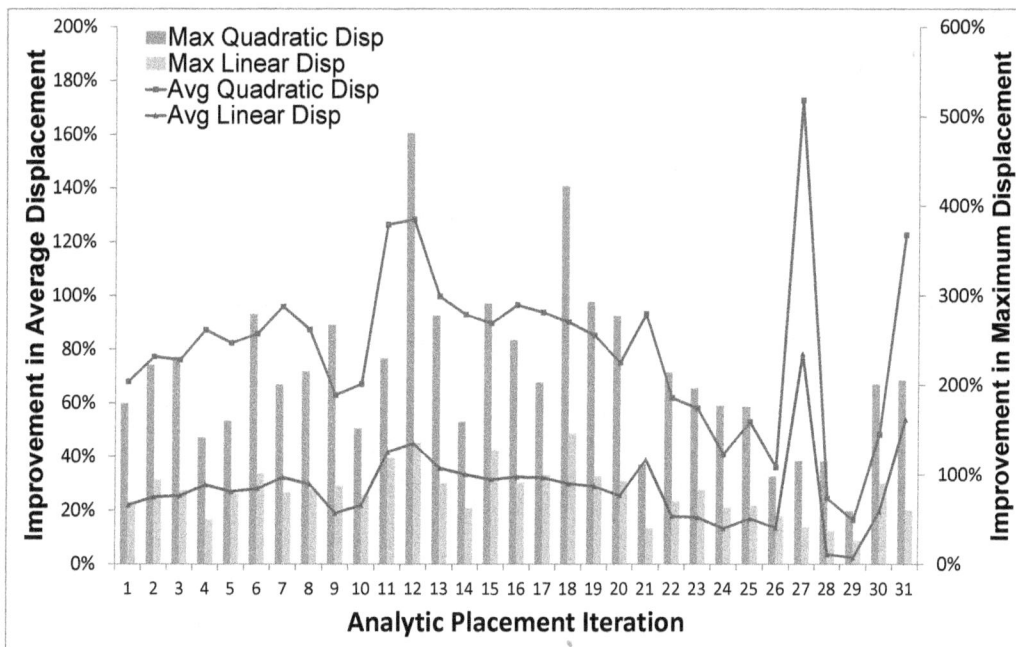

Figure 7: Improvement in displacement at each iteration of analytic placement due to our flow-based UB spreading, compared to Microsemi's original UB spreading, for a medium-sized industrial design.

By incorporating our algorithm into a commercial CAD flow, we showed an average improvement of 6.4% in HPWL and 389 ps in estimated worst-case path timing, after analytic placement, across a large set of industrial designs. Our improvements were achieved with comparable runtime and without changing any other steps of the CAD flow. We attribute the success of our strategy to its ability to optimize the perturbation from a LB placement.

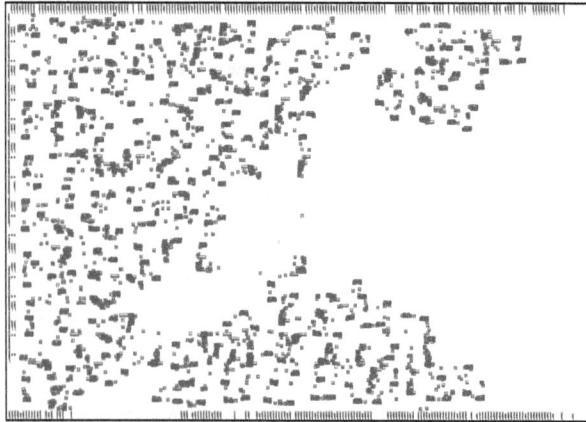

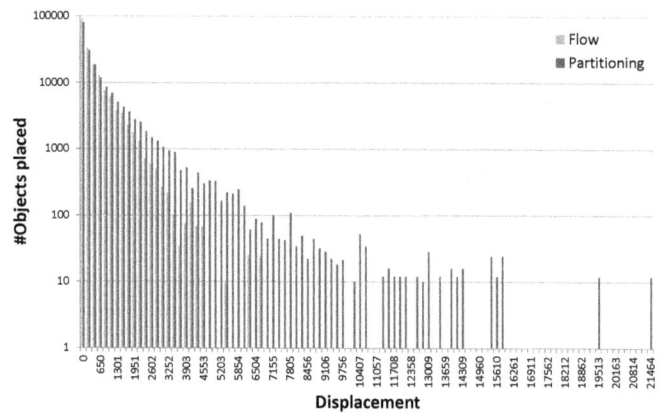

(a) LB placement and its displacement histograms near the start of analytic placement.

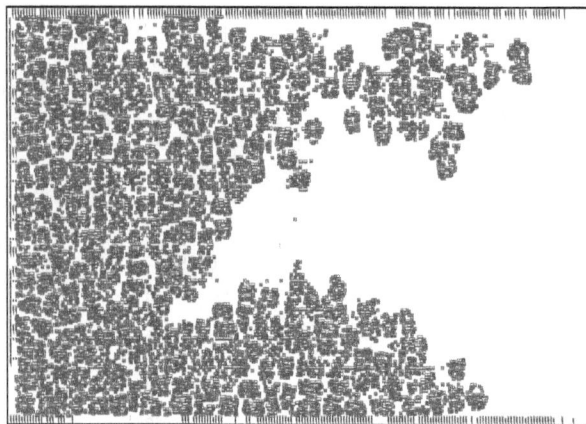

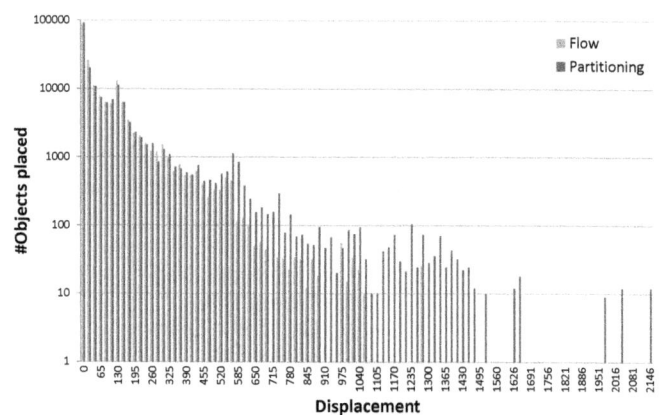

(b) LB placement and its displacement histograms near the end of analytic placement. Note that the scale of the displacement axis is much smaller, near the end of placement, because cells do not need to move as far in order to be "well-spread".

Figure 8: The average and maximum displacements are significantly reduced when using flow-based spreading compared to Microsemi's original UB spreading technique, at all stages of the analytic placement process.

REFERENCES

[1] R. K. Ahuja, T. L. Magnanti, and J. B. Orlin. 1993. *Network Flows: Theory, Algorithms, and Applications.* Prentice-Hall, Inc., Upper Saddle River, NJ, USA.

[2] V. Betz and J. Rose. 1997. VPR: A new packing, placement and routing tool for FPGA research. In *Proc. FPL.* 213–222.

[3] R.C. Cofer and B.F. Harding. 2006. *Rapid System Prototyping with FPGAs: Accelerating the Design Process.* Elsevier Science. 146–147 pages.

[4] Microsemi Corporation. 2017. *PO0137 Product Overview PolarFire FPGA.* Microsemi Corp., San Jose, CA.

[5] N. K. Darav, I. S. Bustany, A. Kennings, D. Westwick, and L. Behjat. 2018. Eh?Legalizer: A High Performance Standard-Cell Legalizer Observing Technology Constraints. *TODAES* 23, 4 (2018), 43:1–43:25.

[6] N. K. Darav, A. Kennings, A. F. Tabrizi, D Westwick, and L. Behjat. 2016. Eh?Placer: A high-performance modern technology-driven Placer. *TODAES* 21, 3 (April 2016), 37:1–37:27.

[7] Hans Eisenmann and Frank M. Johannes. 1998. Generic Global Placement and Floorplanning. In *Proc. DAC.* 269–274.

[8] W. Feng, J. Greene, K. Vorwerk, V. Pevzner, and A. Kundu. 2014. Rent's rule based FPGA packing for routability optimization. In *Proc. FPGA.* 31–34.

[9] M. Gort and J. H. Anderson. 2012. Analytic placement for heterogeneous FPGAs. In *Proc. FPL.* 143–150.

[10] X. He, T. Huang, L. Xiao, H. Tian, and E. F. Y. Young. 2013. Ripple: A robust and effective routability-driven placer. *TCAD* 32, 10 (October 2013), 1546–1556.

[11] M. C. Kim, D. J. Lee, and I. L. Markov. 2012. SimPL: An effective placement algorithm. *TCAD* 31, 1 (Jan 2012), 50–60.

[12] W. Li, S. Dhar, and D. Z. Pan. 2018. UTPlaceF: A routability-driven FPGA placer with physical and congestion aware packing. *TCAD* 37, 4 (April 2018), 869–882.

[13] T. Lin, C. Chu, J. R. Shinnerl, I. Bustany, and I. Nedelchev. 2015. POLAR: A high performance mixed-size wirelengh-driven placer with density constraints. *TCAD* 34, 3 (March 2015), 447–459.

[14] P. Maidee, C. Ababei, and B. Bazargan. 2005. Timing-driven partitioning-based placement for island style FPGAs. *TCAD* 24, 3 (2005), 395–406.

[15] R. Pattison, Z. Abuowaimer, S. Areibi, G. Grewal, and A. Vannelli. 2016. GPlace: A congestion-aware placement tool for UltraScale FPGAs. In *Proc. ICCAD.* 1–7.

[16] C-W Pui, G. Chen, W-K. Chow, K-C. Lam, J. Kuang, P. Tu, H. Zhang, E. F. Y. Young, and B. Yu. 2016. RippleFPGA: A Routability-driven Placement for Large-scale Heterogeneous FPGAs. In *Proc. ICCAD.* 1–8.

[17] Yang S., A. Gayasen, C. Mulpuri, S. Reddy, and R. Aggarwal. 2016. Routability-driven FPGA placement contest. In *Proc. ISPD.* 139–143.

[18] Yang S., C. Mulpuri, S. Reddy, M. Kalase, S. Dasasathyan, M. E. Dehkordi, M. Tom, and R. Aggarwal. 2017. Clock-aware FPGA placement contest. In *Proc. ISPD.* 159–164.

[19] P. Spindler and F. M. Schlichtmann, U. Johannes. 2008. Kraftwerk2: A fast force-directed quadratic placement approach using an accurate net model. *TCAD* 27, 8 (Aug 2008), 1398–1411.

[20] D. Vercruyce, E. Vansteenkiste, and D. Stroobandt. 2018. Hierarchical force-based block spreading for analytic FPGA placement. In *Proc. FPL.*

Simultaneous Placement and Clock Tree Construction for Modern FPGAs

Wuxi Li
Univ. of Texas at Austin
wuxi.li@utexas.edu

Mehrdad E. Dehkordi
Xilinx Inc.
mehrdad@xilinx.com

Stephen Yang
Xilinx Inc.
stepheny@xilinx.com

David Z. Pan
Univ. of Texas at Austin
dpan@ece.utexas.edu

ABSTRACT

Modern field-programmable gate array (FPGA) devices often contain complex clocking architectures to achieve high-performance and flexible clock networks. The physical structure of these clock networks, however, are pre-manufactured, unadjustable, and with only limited routing resources. Most conventional FPGA placement algorithms rarely consider clock feasibility, and therefore lead to clock routing failures. Some recent works adopt simplified clock routing models (e.g., the bounding box model) to force clock legality during placement, which, however, can often overestimate clock routing demands and results in unnecessary placement quality degradation. To address these limitations, in this paper, we propose a generic FPGA placement framework that can simultaneously optimize placement quality and ensure clock feasibility by explicit clock tree construction. We demonstrate the effectiveness and efficiency of the proposed approach using the ISPD 2017 Clock-Aware Placement Contest benchmark suite. Compared with other state-of-the-art clock legalization algorithms, the proposed approach can achieve the best routed wirelength with competitive runtime.

ACM Reference Format:
Wuxi Li, Mehrdad E. Dehkordi, Stephen Yang, and David Z. Pan. 2019. Simultaneous Placement and Clock Tree Construction for Modern FPGAs. In *The 2019 ACM/SIGDA International Symposium on Field-Programmable Gate Arrays (FPGA '19), February 24–26, 2019, Seaside, CA, USA.* ACM, New York, NY, USA, 10 pages. https://doi.org/10.1145/3289602.3293897

1 INTRODUCTION

In recent years, the drastically enhanced architecture and capacity of *Field Programmable Gate Array* (FPGA) devices have led to the rapid growth of customized hardware acceleration for modern applications, such as machine learning, cryptocurrency mining, and high-frequency trading. However, this growing capability of FPGA devices brings ever more challenges to FPGA CAD tools, especially placement engines.

Figure 1 illustrates a representative column-based FPGA architecture that has been widely adopted by many state-of-the-art commercial FPGA devices [7] (e.g., Xilinx *Virtex UltraScale* and *UltraScale+* series). In this specific architecture, each column provides one type of logic resource among *digital signal processor* (DSP), *random access memory* (RAM), I/O, and *configurable logic block* (CLB), where each CLB site further consists of multiple *lookup table* (LUT) and *flip-flop* (FF) slots. In a modern FPGA CAD flow, a design is first translated

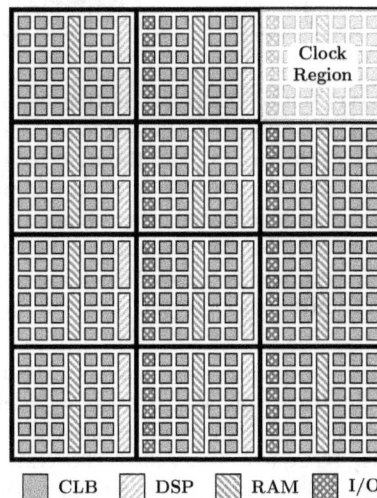

Figure 1: A representative column-based FPGA architecture adopted in state-of-the-art Xilinx UltraScale and UltraScale+ series. This device is composed of 3×4 clock regions.

into a netlist composed of LUTs, FFs, and other heterogeneous blocks (e.g., DSPs, RAMs, and I/Os) by logic synthesis and technology mapping. Then, a placement engine determines the physical locations of all the cells in an FPGA layout shown in Fig. 1. Finally, routing is conducted to realize the interconnects among these placed cells.

Given the significance of FPGA placement in determining the overall implementation quality and efficiency, lots of research efforts have been previously devoted to optimizing conventional metrics like wirelength, routability, timing, and power [2, 3, 12, 13, 16, 18–20, 22–24, 26]. However, there are still limited works in the literature considering clock feasibility during placement. With the recent increase in design complexity, there can be tens to even hundreds of global clocks in a single FPGA design. Given the limited clock routing resources on today's FPGA devices, placement without careful clock network planning can easily fail the whole implementation flow.

The clocking architecture of an FPGA device, as shown in Fig. 1, typically consists of a grid of *clock regions*. One of the most important clocking constraints in such an architecture is that only a limited number of clock networks can route through each clock region. This constraint is imposed by the pre-determined number of pre-manufactured clock routing tracks in each clock region. Considering the clock loads (e.g., FFs, DSPs, and RAMs) of a clock network can often scatter over a considerable portion of the FPGA device, it is common for a clock network to span multiple clock regions. Therefore, for clock-intensive designs, clock routing congestions can be a headache, and techniques that are capable of ensuring clock feasibility during placement becomes extremely imperative.

Several previous works have tentatively explored placement techniques with the awareness of clock feasibility for FPGAs. In [10], a cost function that penalizes high-clock-usage placements is proposed

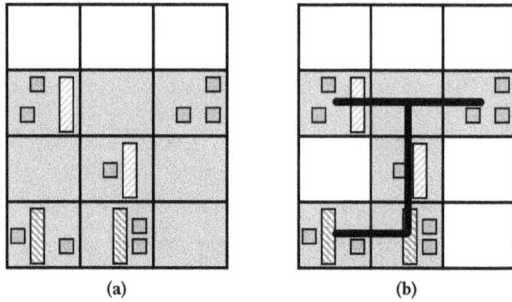

Figure 2: Illustration of the clock routing demand calculation using (a) the bounding box of clock loads (adopted in UT-PlaceF 2.0 [14], NTUfplace [3], and RippleFPGA [21]) and (b) the actual clock tree. Both figures show the same clock network with the same load distribution. Shaded areas denote the occupied clock regions. By using bounding box modeling in (a), the clock networks occupies 9 clock regions, while the actual clock tree only spans 6 clock regions in (b).

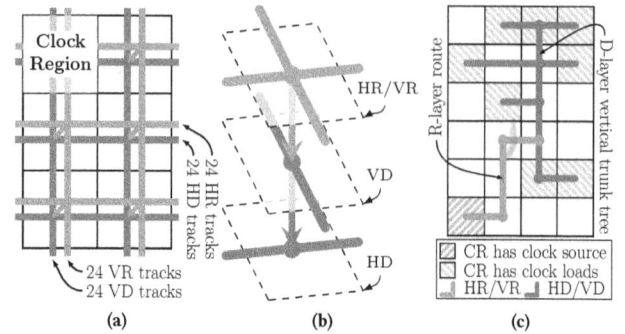

Figure 3: Illustration of the targeting clocking architecture. (a) A global view of 2 × 3 clock regions with R-layer (red) and D-layer (blue). (b) A detailed view of HR/VR/HD/VD within a single clock region. (c) The required routing pattern of a clock net.

and integrated into the simulated annealing-based *VPR* framework [2] to produce clock-friendly solutions. In the more recent *ISPD 2017 Clock-Aware Placement Contest* [28] hold by Xilinx, the top-3 winners UTPlaceF 2.0 [14], NTUfplace [3], and RippleFPGA [21] adopt a more realistic commercial FPGA clocking architecture (similar to Fig. 1). In these three works, to simplify the clock legalization problem, clock routing of clock networks is approximated by the bounding boxes of their clock loads. Figure 2(a) gives an example of this approximated modeling. It shows the distribution of all the clock loads, including CLBs, DSPs, and RAMs, in a clock network. By using the bounding box modeling method, this clock network consumes clock routing resources in all the clock regions overlapped with its bounding box (shaded regions). However, we observe that this modeling method often overestimates the actual clock routing demands. This can be illustrated by Fig. 2(b). It shows the same clock loads distribution as that in Fig. 2(a), but here, a clock tree (the bold black lines) is constructed to reveal the actual clock routing demands. Compared with the bounding box estimation in Fig. 2(a), which consumes 9 clock regions, the same clock network only spans 6 clock regions with tree construction in Fig. 2(b). Apart from the clock routing modeling inaccuracy, all these three works resolve clock routing congestions in a greedy and iterative manner. Specifically, they repeatedly push clock loads away from overflowed clock regions while greedily minimizing the placement disturbance in each step. Such a method, however, can only explore a very narrow solution space and always follows the decisions made previously, which can lead to very suboptimal or even infeasible solutions.

To remedy the aforementioned deficiencies in previous works, this paper presents a generic framework that simultaneously optimizes placement and ensures clock feasibility by explicit clock tree construction. Inspired by the branch-and-bound idea [11], we generalize the clock legalization as a tree-space exploration process. By doing so, our framework can explore a larger solution space and potentially produce better solutions compared with conventional greedy approaches. Besides, a Lagrangian relaxation [4]-based clock tree construction technique is also proposed to accurately reflect actual clock routing demands. The major contributions of this paper are highlighted as follows:

(1) Inspired by the branch-and-bound method, we interpret the solution space of clock routing as a tree, and then generalize the clock legalization as a tree exploration process of finding legal solutions.

(2) We propose a novel Lagrangian relaxation-based clock tree construction technique to accurately model the clock routing demands during FPGA placement.

(3) We tentatively study different ways of constructing and exploring the solution-space tree, and evaluate their impact on the overall quality of results and efficiency.

(4) We perform experiments on the *ISPD 2017 Clock-Aware Placement Contest* [28] benchmark suite. Compared with other state-of-the-art methods in the literature, the proposed approach achieves the best overall routed wirelength with competitive runtime.

The rest of this paper is organized as follows. Section 2 reviews the targeting FPGA clocking architecture and gives the problem definition. Section 3 overviews our overall flow and details the proposed algorithms. Section 4 shows the experimental results, followed by the conclusion and future work in Section 5.

2 PRELIMINARIES

2.1 Clocking Architecture

Our targeting FPGA device is Xilinx *UltraScale VU095*, which was also adopted in both ISPD 2016 and ISPD 2017 FPGA placement contests [27, 28]. Its clocking architecture is illustrated in Fig. 3(a) – (c). The global clocking architecture, as shown in Fig. 3(a), is physically a two-level network composed of a clock routing layer (R-layer) and a clock distribution layer (D-layer). To simplify the notations, in the rest of this paper, we will denote the horizontal/vertical routing layer as HR/VR, and the horizontal/vertical distribution layer as HD/VD. In the targeting architecture, all of HR, VR, HD, and VD layers have 24 tracks running through each of the 5 × 8 clock regions. Figure 3(b) gives a closer look within a single clock region. The connection between HR and VR layers are bidirectional, while there are only unidirectional connections from HR/VR to VD, and from VD to HD. Given this architecture, a clock tree needs to follow the pattern shown in Fig. 3(c). Specifically, it consists of two parts, a D-layer vertical trunk tree connecting all the clock regions containing clock loads, and an R-layer route connecting the clock source and the D-layer trunk tree. More detailed clocking architecture can be found in [5].

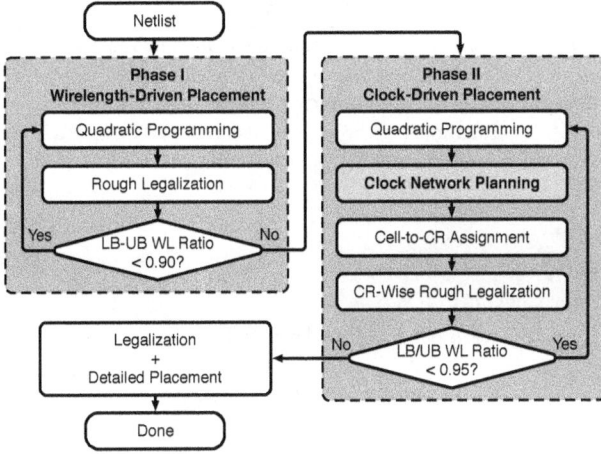

Figure 4: The proposed overall flow.

2.2 Problem Definition

In placement problem, routed wirelength is treated as one of the most important quality metrics, since it is a good first-order approximation of overall performance (frequency) and power. Therefore, in this work, our objective is to minimize the routed wirelength. Given the clocking architecture (Section 2.1) and the optimization objective, we now define our *simultaneous FPGA placement and clock tree construction* problem as follows.

PROBLEM 1 (SIMULTANEOUS FPGA PLACEMENT AND CLOCK TREE CONSTRUCTION). *Given an FPGA netlist, produce a placement with minimized routed wirelength and a corresponding clock routing solution that satisfies the targeting clocking architecture.*

3 PROPOSED ALGORITHMS

3.1 Overview of the Proposed Flow

The proposed overall flow is shown in Fig. 4. Our framework is built on top of a state-of-the-art academic FPGA placer presented in [15], and it consists of three major phases: (1) wirelength-driven placement, (2) clock-driven placement, and (3) legalization and detailed placement.

The wirelength-driven placement adopts the methodology of *SimPL* [8]. In each iteration of this phase, a quadratic program is solved to minimize the wirelength, and the rough legalization [8] technique is conducted to eliminate cell overlapping. This loop is repeated until the lower-bound wirelength and upper-bound wirelength ratio [8] (LB-UB WL Ratio) converges to 0.9. In the clock-driven placement phase, an extra *clock network planning* step is performed right after the conventional quadratic placement. It seeks to construct a legal clock routing solution with minimized placement perturbation (Section 3). After that, we assign cells to their feasible clock regions induced from the resulting clock routing and conduct rough legalization only within each clock region to preserve the clock legality. This clock region-wise rough legalization updates the anchor forces [8] of cells to point to their feasible locations found in the current placement iteration and pull them to form a more clock-feasible solution in the next iteration. The clock-driven placement phase stops when the wirelength fully converges. Finally, legalization and detailed placement are performed to further optimize the placement result while honoring the previously achieved clock routing.

As the centerpiece of the proposed flow (Fig. 4), the *clock network planning* step will be elaborated later in this paper. We first define the *clock network planning* problem and give its mathematical formulation in Section 3.2. Then, in Section 3.3, we give an intuitive explanation of a general mathematical method, the branch-and-bound method, to solve a class of problems like this. We will show that our proposed algorithms share a similar underlying idea with the branch-and-bound method. The details of them are given in Section 3.4 – 3.8.

3.2 The Clock Network Planning Problem

A well-optimized placement (in terms of conventional metrics, like wirelength, power, and timing) can often fail the clock routing. For such a case, the goal of our *clock network planning* is to find a clock-feasible solution that greatly preserves the given optimized placement. Therefore, our objective here is to minimize the total cell movement. Meanwhile, the following two constraints also need to be satisfied: (1) there should exist a legal clock routing solution, and (2) there should not exist any logic resource overflows, that is, we should be able to legalize all the cells with relatively small displacement. Given the objective and constraints, we formally define the *clock network planning problem* as follows.

PROBLEM 2 (CLOCK NETWORK PLANNING). *Given an optimized FPGA placement, find a movement-minimized cell-to-clock region assignment without logic resource overflow and a corresponding clock routing solution satisfying the targeting clocking architecture.*

Table 1: Notations Used in Clock Network Planning

$\mathcal{V}$	The set of cells.
$\S$	The set of resource types, e.g., {LUT, FF, DSP, RAM}.
$\mathcal{V}^{(s)}$	The set of cells of resource type $s \in \S$.
$A_v^{(s)}$	The cell v's demand for resource type $s \in \S$.
$\mathcal{R}$	The set of clock regions.
$C_r^{(s)}$	The clock region r's capacity for resource type $s \in \S$.
$D_{v,r}$	The physical distance between cell v and clock region r.
$\mathcal{E}$	The set of clock nets.

Given the notations defined in Table 1, Problem 2 can be written as a binary optimization problem shown in Formulation (1). It is optimized over binary variables $x_{v,r}$ to minimize the objective (1a) of total cell movement. If cell v is assigned to clock region r, then $x_{v,r} = 1$, otherwise, $x_{v,r} = 0$. Constraint (1c) guarantees that each cell is assigned to exactly one clock region. Constraint (1d) ensures that the total demand of each resource type is no more than the corresponding capacity in each clock region. Constraint (1e) requires the existence of legal clock routing solutions with respect to the assignment x. Here we do not list the closed-form expression of this constraint, since it can be extremely complicated and impossible to be tackled in practice.

$$\text{minimize}_{x} \quad \sum_{v \in \mathcal{V}} \sum_{r \in \mathcal{R}} D_{v,r} \cdot x_{v,r}, \tag{1a}$$

$$\text{subject to} \quad x_{v,r} \in \{0,1\}, \forall v \in \mathcal{V}, \forall r \in \mathcal{R}, \tag{1b}$$

$$\sum_{r \in \mathcal{R}} x_{v,r} = 1, \forall v \in \mathcal{V}, \tag{1c}$$

$$\sum_{v \in \mathcal{V}} A_v^{(s)} \cdot x_{v,r} \le C_r^{(s)}, \forall r \in \mathcal{R}, \forall s \in \S, \tag{1d}$$

$$\text{Exist a legal clock routing w.r.t } x. \tag{1e}$$

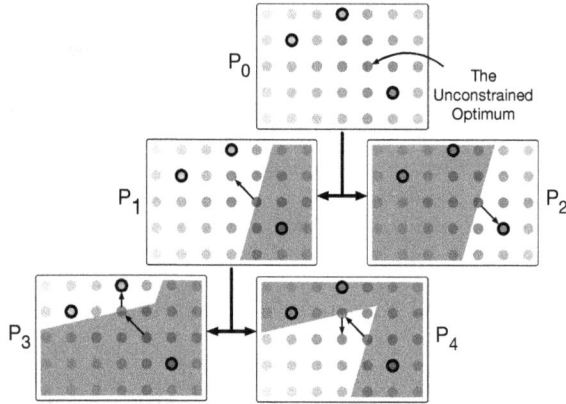

Figure 5: Illustration of the branch-and-bound method. Each circle denotes a solution and color intensity indicates its optimality. Feasible solutions are denoted by stroked circles.

3.3 Branch-and-Bound Method

A general algorithm to solve binary optimization problems, like Formulation (1), is call *branch-and-bound method* [11]. It is a tree traversal-based heuristic to search the very large solution space of possible variable assignments. Its basic idea can be illustrated by Fig. 5. In this example, we are trying to find the optimal solution of a constrained minimization problem over a discrete (e.g., binary and integral) space. Each circle here denotes a solution and the color intensity indicates its optimality (in terms of minimizing the cost without considering feasibility). Three feasible solutions are denoted by stroked circles.

A general branch-and-bound algorithm starts with solving the unconstrained problem P_0, and its optimal solution typically is not feasible, as in this example. In this case, by imposing different constraints, a branching procedure divides the solution space into several sub-spaces (P_1 and P_2), and we continue to find the unconstrained optimal solution in each of these sub-spaces. The same branching procedure is progressively performed to each sub-problem until a feasible solution is found (e.g., the solution of P_3). Once a feasible solution is reached, we can treat its cost as an upper-bound objective value of the target minimization problem, and then, all the branches with lower-bound objective values larger than it can be safely pruned in the later exploration. Using Fig. 5 as an example, if we found the first feasible solution in P_3 with the objective value of Φ, then (1) there is no need to further branch P_3, since the optimal solution of P_3 is guaranteed to be no worse than any sub-problem of P_3, and (2) there is no need to explore branches (sub-spaces) with lower-bound objective values larger than Φ, since solutions in them are guaranteed to be sub-optimal.

The branch-and-bound method can explore a sufficiently large solution space and find near-optimal solutions for various optimization problems within a limited amount of time. Our proposed clock network planning algorithm precisely borrows this idea. In the rest of this paper, we will frequently link our proposed techniques to the concepts introduced in this section for better explanation.

3.4 The Clock Network Planning Algorithm

Algorithm 1 gives our proposed clock network planning algorithm to solve Formulation (1). Besides the inputs/outputs and notations described in Problem 2 and Table 1, an extra input parameter N is

---

Algorithm 1: CLOCK NETWORK PLANNING

Input : A placement with notations defined in Table 1. The maximum number of legal solutions N.

Output: A movement-minimized cell-to-clock region assignment without logic resource overflow, and a corresponding legal clock routing solution.

1 $(\text{cost}^*, \boldsymbol{x}^*, \gamma^*) \leftarrow (+\infty, \text{none}, \text{none})$;

2 $n \leftarrow 0$;

3 $\kappa_{e,r}^{(0)} \leftarrow 1, \forall e \in \mathcal{E}, \forall r \in \mathcal{R}$;

4 $\text{stack.push}(\kappa^{(0)})$;

5 **while** stack *is not empty* **and** n < N **do**

6      $\kappa \leftarrow \text{stack.pop}()$;

7   *Get the optimal cell-to-clock region assignment* $\boldsymbol{x}^{(\kappa)}$ *and its cost* $\text{cost}^{(\kappa)}$ *under constraint* κ *(Section 3.5)*;

8   **if** *no feasible* $\boldsymbol{x}^{(\kappa)}$ *exists* **then continue**;

9   *Get the clock routing solution* $\gamma^{(\kappa)}$ *corresponding to* $\boldsymbol{x}^{(\kappa)}$ *(Section 3.6)*;

10   **if** $\gamma^{(\kappa)}$ *is overflow-free* **then**

11          $n \leftarrow n + 1$;

12   **if** $\text{cost}^{(\kappa)} < \text{cost}^*$ **then**

13              $(\text{cost}^*, \boldsymbol{x}^*, \gamma^*) \leftarrow (\text{cost}^{(\kappa)}, \boldsymbol{x}^{(\kappa)}, \gamma^{(\kappa)})$;

14   **end**

15   **end**

16   **else if** $\gamma^{(\kappa)}$ *has routing overflow* **then**

17   *Derive a set of more strict constraints* K' *from* κ *(Section 3.7)*;

18   *Remove* $\kappa' \in K'$ *that has lower-bound cost larger than* cost^* *(Section 3.8)*;

19   *Push* $\kappa' \in K'$ *into stack by their lower-bound costs from high to low*;

20   **end**

21 **end**

22 **return** $(\text{cost}^*, \boldsymbol{x}^*, \gamma^*)$;

---

required for controlling the maximum number of feasible solutions to explore. We set N to 10 in our framework.

In line 1 – 2, we initialize the best cell-to-clock region assignment ($\boldsymbol{x}^*$), its cost (cost^*), and the corresponding clock routing solution (γ^*) as invalid, and reset the number of feasible solutions n to 0. In line 3, we construct an initial clock-assignment constraint $\kappa^{(0)}$. For a clock-assignment constraint κ, each $\kappa_{e,r}$ is a binary value that indicates whether cells in clock net e can be assigned to clock region r. Similar to the branch-and-bound method starting with an unconstrained problem (Section 3.3), we also do not consider clock feasibility at the beginning and allow any cell-to-clock region assignment. Therefore, all the entries in the initial clock-assignment constraint $\kappa^{(0)}$ are set to 1 (line 3). To perform a tree traversal-based exploration like the branch-and-bound method, we maintain a stack to search the solution space in a depth-first order (DFS). The DFS starts with the constraint $\kappa^{(0)}$ (line 4) and repeated in line 5 – 21 until the stack becomes empty or enough number of feasible solutions are found (n = N). During the DFS, various clock-assignment constraints κ are branched from the constraint tree rooted at $\kappa^{(0)}$, just like the branching procedure illustrated in Fig. 5. The best solution found during this DFS exploration is returned in line 22 as the final result.

In each execution of line 5 – 21, we first fetch the clock-assignment constraint κ on the top of the stack (line 6), then get the movement-minimized cell-to-clock region assignment constrained by logic resources and κ (line 7). This step can be interpreted as, within the sub-space κ, finding the optimal solution $\mathbf{x}^{(\kappa)}$ of Formulation (1) without considering the clock constraint (1e). If no such $\mathbf{x}^{(\kappa)}$ exists, this branch will be discarded (line 8). Otherwise, we continue to evaluate the clock feasibility of $\mathbf{x}^{(\kappa)}$ by constructing a clock routing solution $\gamma^{(\kappa)}$ (line 9). If $\gamma^{(\kappa)}$ is routing overflow-free, $(\text{cost}^{(\kappa)}, \mathbf{x}^{(\kappa)}, \gamma^{(\kappa)})$ then forms a feasible solution, and we will update the best solution $(\text{cost}^*, \mathbf{x}^*, \gamma^*)$ if needed (line 10 – 15). If $\gamma^{(\kappa)}$ still has routing overflows, we will branch new clock-assignment constraints from κ to encourage more clock-friendly solutions (line 17). These new constraints $\kappa' \in K'$ can be interpreted as sub-spaces of κ, and some previously allowed clock assignments in κ can be blocked in $\kappa' \in K'$. Among these newly derived constraints, we prune those that can only lead to sub-optimal solutions (line 18), and push the remaining into the stack in the descending order of their lower-bound costs (line 19). By doing so, we always first explore the branch with the minimum lower-bound cost at each constraint tree node.

The details of each core building block in Algorithm 1 will be further elaborated in the later sections. Section 3.5 describes the cell-to-clock region assignment in line 7. Section 3.6 presents the clock routing in line 9. The clock-assignment constraint derivation in line 17 and the lower-bound cost calculation in line 18 – 19 are detailed in Section 3.7 and Section 3.8, respectively.

3.5 Minimum Cost Flow-Based Cell-to-Clock Region Assignment

The cell-to-clock region assignment (line 7 in Algorithm 1) essentially is solving the clock-unconstrained version of Formulation (1) within the sub-space of a given clock-assignment constraint κ. It can be written as a binary optimization problem shown in Formulation (2), where $\mathcal{E}(v)$ denotes the set of clocks in cell v, binary value $\kappa_{e,r}$ indicates whether cells in clock net e can be assigned to clock region r, and other notations are inherited from Table 1. Note that Formulation (1) and Formulation (2) only differ by the clock constraints (1e) and (2e).

$$\underset{\mathbf{x}}{\text{minimize}} \quad \sum_{v \in \mathcal{V}} \sum_{r \in \mathcal{R}} D_{v,r} \cdot \mathbf{x}_{v,r}, \tag{2a}$$

$$\text{subject to} \quad \mathbf{x}_{v,r} \in \{0,1\}, \forall v \in \mathcal{V}, \forall r \in \mathcal{R}, \tag{2b}$$

$$\sum_{r \in \mathcal{R}} \mathbf{x}_{v,r} = 1, \forall v \in \mathcal{V}, \tag{2c}$$

$$\sum_{v \in \mathcal{V}} A_v^{(s)} \cdot \mathbf{x}_{v,r} \le C_r^{(s)}, \forall r \in \mathcal{R}, \forall s \in \S, \tag{2d}$$

$$\mathbf{x}_{v,r} = 0, \forall (v,r) \in \{v \in \mathcal{V}, r \in \mathcal{R} \mid$$
$$\exists e \in \mathcal{E}(v) \text{ s.t. } \kappa_{e,r} = 0\}. \tag{2e}$$

The motivation of formulating Formulation (2) in this way is that it can be approximately transformed into a set of minimum-cost flow problems, each of which corresponds to a resource type (e.g., LUT, FF, DSP, and RAM). Since the minimum-cost flow is a well-studied problem, it can be efficiently solved by many mature algorithms [1]. Figure 6 gives a graph representation of the minimum-cost flow corresponding to Formulation (2) with a single resource type. It is a bipartite graph (regardless of the super source S and the super target

T) with vertices for cells $(v_1, v_2, \ldots, v_{|\mathcal{V}|})$ on the left and vertices for clock regions $(r_1, r_2, \ldots, r_{|\mathcal{V}|})$ on the right. We introduce an edge between each pair of cell and clock region, but set its capacity to 0 if the assignment is forbidden by the given constraint κ. With the edge cost and capacity settings shown in Fig. 6, computing the minimum-cost flow of amount $\Sigma_{v \in \mathcal{V}} A_v^{(s)}$ on the graph can approximate the optimal solution of Formulation (2).

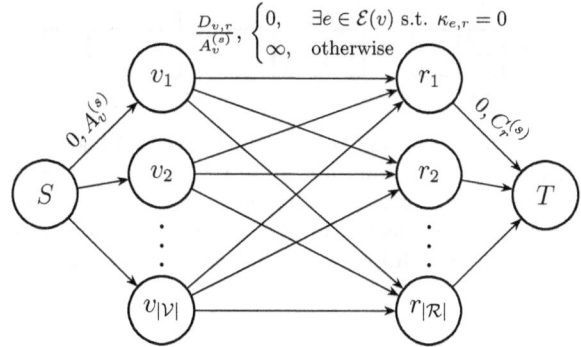

Figure 6: A graph representation of the minimum-cost flow for Formulation (2) with a single resource type. The pair of numbers on each edge denotes the unit flow cost and the flow capacity, respectively. For example, the edge between S and v_1 has a unit flow cost of 0 and a flow capacity of $A_{v_1}^{(s)}$.

The sub-optimality comes from the fact that, in a minimum-cost flow solution, a cell can be split and assigned to multiple clock regions. In such a case, we move all the "fragments" to the clock region containing the largest one among them to realize an actual cell-to-clock region assignment. In practice, the splitting only occurs in a negligibly small portion of cells, thus the global optimality can still be largely retained[1]. It is worthwhile to mention that, if the logic resource demands of all cells for a given resource type s are the same (i.e., $A_i^{(s)} = A_j^{(s)}, \forall i, j \in \mathcal{V}$), the solution given by the minimum-cost flow is also optimal for Formulation (2). This case is applicable to resource types that only have one single cell type (e.g., DSP and CLB).

A minimum-cost flow solution, however, cannot always be realized as a complete cell-to-clock region assignment, even without cell splitting. If the resulting flow amount is less than the amount of flow being pushed ($\Sigma_{v \in \mathcal{V}} A_v^{(s)}$), then not all the cells can be assigned without logic resource overflow. This can happen in scenarios where clock nets are over-constrained in too-small regions. In such a case, it is guaranteed that no feasible solutions exist in the sub-space defined by the given clock-assignment constraint κ, and thus we can safely prune this branch as described in line 8 of Algorithm 1.

3.6 Clock Tree Construction

In this section, we will present the algorithm to construct a clock tree solution for a given cell-to-clock region assignment. As introduced in Section 2.1, a clock tree consists of a D-layer vertical trunk tree that connects all clock loads and an R-layer route that connects the D-layer trunk tree to the clock source. Since the routing patterns on these two layers are very different, the routings on these two layers are conducted separately in our framework. Since R-layer routing

---

[1]This post step might produce some negligible logic resource overflows. If the logic resource constraint needs to be rigorously honored, slightly tighter logic resource capacities can be applied to leave some margin for it.

relies on the D-layer trunk location, we perform D-layer routing first, then followed by R-layer routing.

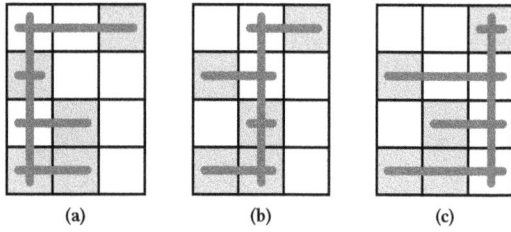

Figure 7: Three different D-layer clock tree topologies of the same clock load distribution on a 3×4 clock region grid. Each of them is a vertical trunk tree with horizontal branches connecting all the clock loads. Yellow shaded regions denote clock regions containing clock loads of the given clock net.

3.6.1 Lagrangian Relaxation-Based D-Layer Clock Tree Construction. As shown in Fig. 7, given a cell-to-clock region assignment on a clock region grid with m columns ($m = 3$ in Fig. 7), we can generate m D-layer clock tree topologies for each clock by placing the vertical trunk in different columns. Our goal here is to select exactly one clock tree topology from the m candidates for each clock such that there are no VD and HD overflows. Meanwhile, a topology-dependent objective (e.g., resource usage, clock skew, insertion delay, etc.) also needs to be optimized.

If we denote the set of m clock tree candidates of clock e (Fig. 7) by $\mathcal{T}(e)$, denote the set of all clock tree candidates by $\mathcal{T}$ (i.e., $\mathcal{T} = \bigcup_{e \in \mathcal{E}} \mathcal{T}(e)$), denote the topology cost of clock tree candidate t by ϕ_t, and use binary values $H_{t,r}/V_{t,r}$ to represent whether clock tree candidate t occupies an HD/VD track in clock region r, then the D-layer clock tree construction problem can be mathematically written as a binary optimization problem shown in Formulation (3).

$$\underset{x}{\text{minimize}} \quad \sum_{t \in \mathcal{T}} \phi_t \cdot z_t, \tag{3a}$$

$$\text{subject to} \quad z_t \in \{0, 1\}, \forall t \in \mathcal{T}, \tag{3b}$$

$$\sum_{t \in \mathcal{T}(e)} z_t = 1, \forall e \in \mathcal{E}, \tag{3c}$$

$$\sum_{t \in \mathcal{T}} H_{t,r} \cdot z_t \leq 24, \forall r \in \mathcal{R}, \tag{3d}$$

$$\sum_{t \in \mathcal{T}} V_{t,r} \cdot z_t \leq 24, \forall r \in \mathcal{R}. \tag{3e}$$

Formulation (3) is optimized over binary variables z_t to minimize the objective of topology cost (3a). If the clock tree candidate t is selected in the routing solution, then $z_t = 1$, otherwise, $z_t = 0$. Constraint (3c) ensures that exactly one candidate is selected for each clock net. Constraints (3d) and (3e) bound the HD/VD clock routing usage in each clock region (24 is the number of available HD/VD tracks in each clock region of our targeting device as described in Section 2.1). In this work, since feasibility is the only consideration for clock networks, we simply set the topology cost ϕ_t as the total HD and VD demand of t. However, other metrics (e.g., clock skew) can also be integrated in practice.

Although Formulation (3) can be optimally solved using integer linear programming techniques, they are too computationally expensive and unaffordable in our application. Therefore, we relax Formulation (3) to a much easier problem, as shown in Formulation (4). Here, we remove the two clock resource constraints (3d) and (3e), and add a set of Lagrangian multipliers [4] λ_t in the objective (4a). Each λ_t can be interpreted as the routing-overflow penalty applied to the clock tree candidate t, and we assign a larger value to it if t is likely to run through congested regions. Then, by properly updating these λ_t and iteratively solving Formulation (4), overflow-free or overflow-minimized clock routing solutions can be achieved.

$$\underset{x}{\text{minimize}} \quad \sum_{t \in \mathcal{T}} (\phi_t + \lambda_t) \cdot z_t, \tag{4a}$$

$$\text{subject to} \quad z_t \in \{0, 1\}, \forall t \in \mathcal{T}, \tag{4b}$$

$$\sum_{t \in \mathcal{T}(e)} z_t = 1, \forall e \in \mathcal{E}. \tag{4c}$$

Algorithm 2 summarizes our Lagrangian relaxation-based D-layer clock tree construction. In line 1 – 2, we create all the clock tree candidates $\mathcal{T}$ and initialize their penalties $\lambda^{(0)}$ to 0. In each Lagrangian iteration (line 4 – 8), we first get the optimal solution $z^{(i)}$ of Formulation (4) with $\lambda^{(i)}$ (line 5). Then, $\lambda^{(i+1)}$ can be derived from $\lambda^{(i)}$ by penalizing clock tree candidates that run through overflowed clock regions in the routing solution given by $z^{(i)}$ (line 6). This iteration is repeated until one of the following holds: (1) a routing overflow-free solution is found; (2) λ does not change anymore; (3) the maximum iteration count $I_{\max}$ is reached; Finally, in line 9 – 10, we backtrace all the explored solutions and return the one with the minimum routing overflow as the final result.

The optimal solution of Formulation (4), as given in function solveLR (line 11 – 18), can be efficiently obtained by picking the candidate with the minimum $\phi_t + \lambda_t$ from each candidate pool $\mathcal{T}(e)$. Function updateLR (line 19 – 37) presents our λ updating scheme. In line 20 – 26, we first calculate the base penalty $\Delta\lambda_t$ for each candidate t. As shown in line 24 – 25, for an overflowed clock region, we treat its overflow value (O_H/O_V) as the total amount of penalty and evenly distribute the penalty to all the candidates running through it. After that, in line 27 – 33, we calculate the minimum scaling factor α that can change the optimal solution of Formulation (4) with $\alpha \cdot \Delta\lambda$ being added to current λ. If such an α does not exist, λ are kept unchanged (line 34). Otherwise, we add the extra penalty $(1 + \delta) \cdot \alpha \cdot \Delta\lambda$ to $\lambda^{(i)}$ ($\delta \ll 1$ is for tie-breaking) and return the result as $\lambda^{(i+1)}$ (line 35 – 36).

3.6.2 A* Search-Based R-Layer Clock Tree Routing. The R-layer routing is responsible for connecting the clock source to the D-layer trunk tree. Given a D-layer clock routing solution, the R-layer routing is very similar to the conventional 2-pin net global routing problem. The only difference is that, in each of these 2-pin nets, one of the two "pins" is a vertical trunk (Section 2.1) instead of a single terminal. Therefore, we extend the conventional A* search [6]-based routing algorithm to treat all the clock regions occupied by the D-layer trunk as legal endpoints. Besides, a rip-up and reroute technique similar to [17] is also applied to iteratively resolve routing overflows.

3.7 Clock-Assignment Constraint Derivation

Recall that, in line 17 of Algorithm 1, for a given clock-assignment constraint κ, if an overflow-free clock routing solution cannot be found, we will derive a set of new constraints from κ to encourage

---

Algorithm 2: LAGRANGIAN RELAXATION-BASED D-LAYER CLOCK TREE CONSTRUCTION

Input : A cell-to-clock region assignment x. The maximum number of Lagrangian iterations I_{max} (default is 20).

Output: A D-layer routing solution with minimized routing overflow and topology cost.

1 *Create all clock tree candidates $\mathcal{T}$ for x (Fig. 7);*
2 $\lambda_t^{(0)} \leftarrow 0, \forall t \in \mathcal{T}$;
3 $i \leftarrow 0$;
4 **do**
5     $z^{(i)} \leftarrow \text{solveLR}(\lambda^{(i)})$ // solve Formulation (4)
6     $\lambda^{(i+1)} \leftarrow \text{updateLR}(z^{(i)}, \lambda^{(i)})$ // update λ
7     $i \leftarrow i + 1$;
8 **while** $z^{(i)}$ *has overflow* **and** $\lambda^{(i)} \neq \lambda^{(i-1)}$ *and* $i < I_{max}$;
9 $z^* \leftarrow$ *the $z^{(i)}$ with the minimum overflow;*
10 **return** $\{t \in \mathcal{T} \mid z_t^* = 1\}$;

11 **Function** solveLR(λ):
12    $z_t \leftarrow 0, \forall t \in \mathcal{T}$;
13   **foreach** $e \in \mathcal{E}$ **do**
14       $t^* \leftarrow$ *the $t \in \mathcal{T}(e)$ with the minimum $\phi_t + \lambda_t$;*
15       $z_{t^*} \leftarrow 1$;
16   **end**
17   **return** z;
18 **end**

19 **Function** updateLR($z^{(i)}, \lambda^{(i)}$):
20    $\Delta\lambda_t \leftarrow 0, \forall t \in \mathcal{T}$;
21   **foreach** $r \in \mathcal{R}$ *with HD/VD overflows of O_H/O_V* **do**
22       $\mathcal{T}_H(r) \leftarrow \{t \in \mathcal{T} \mid H_{t,r} = 1\}$;
23       $\mathcal{T}_V(r) \leftarrow \{t \in \mathcal{T} \mid V_{t,r} = 1\}$;
24   **foreach** $t \in \mathcal{T}_H(r)$ **do** $\Delta\lambda_t \leftarrow \Delta\lambda_t + \frac{O_H}{|\mathcal{T}_H(r)|}$;
25   **foreach** $t \in \mathcal{T}_V(r)$ **do** $\Delta\lambda_t \leftarrow \Delta\lambda_t + \frac{O_V}{|\mathcal{T}_V(r)|}$;
26   **end**
27    $\alpha \leftarrow \infty$;
28   **foreach** $e \in \mathcal{E}$ **do**
29       $t^* \leftarrow$ *the $t \in \mathcal{T}(e)$ being selected in iteration i;*
30   **foreach** $t \in \mathcal{T}(e)$ *that has $\Delta\lambda_t < \Delta\lambda_{t^*}$* **do**
31          $\alpha \leftarrow \min(\alpha, \frac{(\phi_t + \lambda_t) - (\phi_{t^*} + \lambda_{t^*})}{\Delta\lambda_{t^*} - \Delta\lambda_t})$;
32   **end**
33   **end**
34   **if** $\alpha = \infty$ **then return** $\lambda^{(i)}$;
35    $\lambda_t^{(i+1)} \leftarrow \lambda_t^{(i)} + (1 + \delta) \cdot \alpha \cdot \Delta\lambda_t, \forall t \in \mathcal{T}$;
36   **return** $\lambda^{(i+1)}$;
37 **end**

Algorithm 3: CLOCK-ASSIGNMENT CONSTRAINT DERIVATION FOR VD OVERFLOWS

Input : A clock-assignment constraint κ and its clock routing solution γ.

Output: A set of new clock-assignment constraints K' derived from κ that can potentially alleviate the VD-overflow.

1 $r \leftarrow$ the clock region with the most VD overflow in γ;
2 $K' \leftarrow \varnothing$;
3 **foreach** $e \in \mathcal{E}$ *that occupies VD resource in r* **do**
4   **foreach** *blockage B in Fig. 8* **do**
5        $\kappa' \leftarrow \kappa$;
6        $\kappa'_{e,b} \leftarrow 0, \forall b \in B$;
7        $K' \leftarrow K' \cup \kappa'$;
8   **end**
9 **end**
10 **return** K';

We first get the clock region r with the most VD overflow (line 1). Then, for each clock that occupies VD resource in r, we generate placement blockages in four directions, as shown in Fig 8, that can potentially alleviate the congestion in r. Finally, we impose each of these blockages on top of the current clock-assignment constraint κ to form a set of new constraints K' (line 3 – 9). If there are q clock nets occupying VD resource in r, there will be $4q$ new constraints in K', and each $\kappa' \in K'$ represent a sub-space of κ as described in Section 3.4.

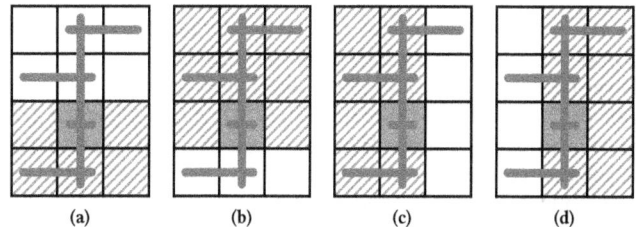

Figure 8: Four half-plane-based clock-assignment blockages (hatched/solid red regions) that are in the (a) south, (b) north, (c) west, and (d) east of a VD-overflowed clock region (solid red region).

3.7.2 Constraint Derivation for HD Overflows. Our constraint derivation for HD overflow is similar to that for VD, as described in Section 3.7.1 and Algorithm 3. However, given the fact that HD branches affect the tree topology much more locally than VD trunks, blockages of granularities finer than Fig. 8 might be able to achieve even better results. For example, the corner-based (Fig. 9) and the row-based (Fig. 10) blockages can potentially resolve the overflow with less cell movement compared with the blockages shown in Fig. 8. Surprisingly, as will be shown in Section 4.3, the blockage schemes in Fig. 9 and Fig. 10 cannot outperform that in Fig. 8 within a limited amount of time in our experiments. This might be because the blockages in Fig. 9 and Fig. 10 tend to cut the placeable region of each clock into non-convex and unconnected fragments, which significantly slow down the convergence of Algorithm 1. While using the blockages in Fig. 8, the placeable region of each clock is guaranteed to be a rectangle.

more clock-friendly solutions. In this section, we will detail this clock-assignment constraint derivation process. Since, in practice, R-layer routing is much less congested than D-layer routing and rarely fails, we will only discuss constraint derivation methods for resolving D-layer congestions. However, similar ideas are also applicable to R-layer routing.

3.7.1 Constraint Derivation for VD Overflows. Algorithm 3 summarizes our constraint deviation scheme for resolving VD overflows.

Table 3: Routed Wirelength (×10³) and Runtime (Seconds) Comparison with Other State-of-the-Art Placers (CC = 24)

Designs	UTPlaceF 2.0 [14]				NTUfplace [9]				RippleFPGA [21]				[15]				Proposed			
	WL	RT	WLR	RTR	WL	RT†	WLR	RTR†	WL	RT	WLR	RTR	WL	RT	WLR	RTR	WL	RT	WLR	RTR
CLK-FPGA01	2208	422	1.056	2.34	2098	3524	1.003	19.58	2011	288	0.962	1.60	2101	476	1.004	2.64	2092	180	1.000	1.00
CLK-FPGA02	2279	407	1.039	2.27	2173	3351	0.991	18.72	2168	266	0.988	1.49	2263	454	1.032	2.54	2194	179	1.000	1.00
CLK-FPGA03	5353	824	1.048	2.40	5049	6722	0.988	19.60	5265	583	1.031	1.70	5181	930	1.014	2.71	5109	343	1.000	1.00
CLK-FPGA04	3698	564	1.027	2.33	3710	5101	1.030	21.08	3607	380	1.002	1.57	3654	656	1.015	2.71	3600	242	1.000	1.00
CLK-FPGA05	4692	744	1.030	2.30	4523	6336	0.993	19.62	4660	569	1.023	1.76	4589	846	1.007	2.62	4556	323	1.000	1.00
CLK-FPGA06	5589	845	1.029	2.44	5169	7932	0.952	22.93	5737	591	1.056	1.71	5375	963	0.989	2.78	5432	346	1.000	1.00
CLK-FPGA07	2445	670	1.052	3.33	2380	4071	1.024	20.25	2326	304	1.001	1.51	2448	515	1.053	2.56	2324	201	1.000	1.00
CLK-FPGA08	1886	419	1.044	2.48	1843	3109	1.020	18.40	1778	247	0.984	1.46	1829	436	1.012	2.58	1807	169	1.000	1.00
CLK-FPGA09	2597	668	1.036	3.39	2499	4423	0.997	22.45	2530	327	1.009	1.66	2556	523	1.019	2.66	2507	197	1.000	1.00
CLK-FPGA10	4464	772	1.056	2.70	4294	6569	1.015	22.97	4496	512	1.063	1.79	4255	801	1.006	2.80	4229	286	1.000	1.00
CLK-FPGA11	4184	847	1.063	3.20	4031	6538	1.024	24.67	4190	455	1.064	1.72	4014	679	1.020	2.56	3936	265	1.000	1.00
CLK-FPGA12	3369	614	1.041	2.49	3244	5300	1.002	21.46	3388	409	1.047	1.66	3253	647	1.005	2.62	3236	247	1.000	1.00
CLK-FPGA13	3848	929	1.033	3.44	3818	5639	1.025	20.89	3833	441	1.029	1.63	3731	743	1.002	2.75	3723	270	1.000	1.00
Norm.	-	-	1.043	2.70	-	-	1.005	20.97	-	-	1.020	1.64	-	-	1.014	2.66	-	-	1.000	1.00

†: [9] only reports the total runtime of placement and routing, so the RT and RTR here are just for reference.

Table 4: Normalized Wirelength and Runtime Comparison with [14]-Impl Under Different Clock Capacities (CC)

Designs	CC = 24 [14]-Impl		Proposed		CC = 12 [14]-Impl		Proposed		CC = 8 [14]-Impl		Proposed		CC = 7 [14]-Impl		Proposed		CC = 6 [14]-Impl		Proposed		CC = 5 [14]-Impl		Proposed	
	WLR	RTR	WLR	RTR	WLR	RTR	WLR	RTR	WLR	RTR	WLR	RTR	WLR	RTR	WLR	RTR	WLR	RTR	WLR	RTR	WLR	RTR	WLR	RTR
CLK-FPGA01	1.002	0.99	1.000	1.00	1.003	1.01	1.003	1.03	1.013	1.28	1.011	1.09	1.011	1.40	1.019	1.13	1.024	1.45	1.029	1.19	1.066	1.67	1.031	1.18
CLK-FPGA02	1.000	0.99	1.000	1.00	1.000	1.01	1.000	0.99	1.005	1.05	1.004	1.03	1.015	1.26	1.012	1.06	1.211	1.49	1.024	1.13	1.299	2.25	1.061	1.14
CLK-FPGA03	1.001	1.00	1.000	1.00	1.002	1.06	1.001	1.04	1.022	1.18	1.008	1.12	1.043	1.59	1.013	1.10	1.444	2.22	1.023	1.23	*	-	*	-
CLK-FPGA04	0.999	0.99	1.000	1.00	1.001	1.02	1.000	1.03	1.013	1.15	1.005	1.07	1.014	1.17	1.009	1.12	1.056	1.74	1.013	1.13	1.563	3.33	1.175	1.24
CLK-FPGA05	1.000	0.99	1.000	1.00	1.000	1.05	1.001	1.04	1.007	1.33	1.004	1.10	1.021	1.52	1.009	1.13	1.059	1.70	1.032	1.24	*	-	*	-
CLK-FPGA06	1.000	1.02	1.000	1.00	1.004	1.09	1.000	1.07	1.026	1.62	1.009	1.15	1.031	1.67	1.016	1.17	1.181	2.02	1.024	1.27	*	-	*	-
CLK-FPGA07	1.001	1.00	1.000	1.00	0.999	1.03	0.999	1.04	1.014	1.28	1.009	1.07	1.058	1.43	1.015	1.14	1.354	1.70	1.046	1.20	1.417	2.56	*	-
CLK-FPGA08	1.000	0.96	1.000	1.00	1.001	0.98	1.001	1.02	1.016	1.17	1.010	1.05	1.024	1.33	1.017	1.07	1.086	1.50	1.021	1.13	1.121	1.69	1.052	1.14
CLK-FPGA09	0.998	0.99	1.000	1.00	1.000	1.03	1.000	1.01	1.002	1.07	1.003	1.02	1.011	1.24	1.008	1.06	1.013	1.42	1.011	1.11	1.358	1.62	1.045	1.19
CLK-FPGA10	0.999	0.99	1.000	1.00	1.000	1.05	0.999	1.04	1.012	1.42	1.005	1.05	1.015	1.58	1.009	1.11	1.040	1.46	1.019	1.17	*	-	1.323	1.25
CLK-FPGA11	0.999	0.99	1.000	1.00	0.999	1.02	1.000	1.03	1.006	1.05	1.003	1.05	1.017	1.46	1.011	1.08	1.030	1.73	1.017	1.13	*	-	1.511	1.56
CLK-FPGA12	0.999	0.99	1.000	1.00	0.999	1.00	1.000	1.01	1.007	1.07	1.003	1.02	1.014	1.14	1.009	1.08	1.019	1.68	1.017	1.11	*	-	1.321	1.19
CLK-FPGA13	1.000	0.99	1.000	1.00	1.000	1.00	1.001	1.02	1.006	1.12	1.004	1.02	1.028	1.37	1.013	1.05	1.192	1.65	1.026	1.12	*	-	1.070	1.20
Norm.	1.000	0.99	1.000	1.00	1.001	1.03	1.000	1.03	1.011	1.21	1.006	1.07	1.023	1.40	1.012	1.10	1.131	1.67	1.023	1.17	1.304	2.19	1.176	1.24

*: Fail to find feasible placement solutions within 1800 seconds.

Table 5: Normalized Wirelength and Runtime Comparison of Different Clock-Assignment Blockage Schemes

Designs	CC = 24 Half-Plane		Corner		Row		CC = 12 Half-Plane		Corner		Row		CC = 8 Half-Plane		Corner		Row		CC = 6 Half-Plane		Corner		Row	
	WLR	RTR	WLR	RTR	WLR	RTR	WLR	RTR	WLR	RTR	WLR	RTR	WLR	RTR	WLR	RTR	WLR	RTR	WLR	RTR	WLR	RTR	WLR	RTR
CLK-FPGA01	1.000	1.00	1.000	0.99	1.000	1.00	1.003	1.03	1.002	1.07	1.003	1.05	1.011	1.09	1.009	1.14	1.019	1.18	1.029	1.19	1.020	1.18	1.205	1.31
CLK-FPGA02	1.000	1.00	1.000	1.01	1.000	1.00	1.000	0.99	1.001	1.01	1.001	1.00	1.004	1.03	1.002	1.05	1.002	1.04	1.024	1.13	1.261	1.28	1.162	1.26
CLK-FPGA03	1.000	1.00	1.000	1.03	1.000	1.01	1.001	1.04	1.001	1.14	1.000	1.20	1.008	1.12	1.004	1.18	1.007	1.30	1.023	1.23	1.090	1.41	*	-
CLK-FPGA04	1.000	1.00	1.000	1.00	1.000	1.00	1.000	1.03	1.000	1.06	1.000	1.07	1.005	1.07	1.004	1.10	1.006	1.13	1.013	1.13	1.047	1.15	1.271	1.52
CLK-FPGA05	1.000	1.00	1.000	1.00	1.000	1.00	1.001	1.04	1.000	1.08	1.000	1.14	1.004	1.10	1.003	1.15	1.006	1.18	1.032	1.24	1.134	1.34	*	-
CLK-FPGA06	1.000	1.00	1.000	1.02	1.000	1.01	1.000	1.07	1.000	1.12	1.001	1.29	1.009	1.15	1.006	1.20	1.033	1.50	1.024	1.27	*	-	*	-
CLK-FPGA07	1.000	1.00	1.000	1.00	1.000	1.00	0.999	1.04	0.999	1.03	1.000	1.03	1.009	1.07	1.018	1.14	1.019	1.16	1.046	1.20	1.260	1.24	1.380	1.70
CLK-FPGA08	1.000	1.00	1.000	0.99	1.000	1.00	1.001	1.02	1.001	0.99	1.000	1.03	1.010	1.05	1.014	1.05	1.025	1.10	1.021	1.13	1.028	1.18	1.101	1.27
CLK-FPGA09	1.000	1.00	1.000	1.00	1.000	1.01	1.000	1.01	1.000	1.03	1.000	1.03	1.003	1.00	1.006	1.06	1.002	1.08	1.011	1.11	1.044	1.20	1.066	1.26
CLK-FPGA10	1.000	1.00	1.000	1.01	1.000	1.00	0.999	1.04	1.002	1.08	1.000	1.09	1.005	1.05	1.025	1.23	1.038	1.35	1.019	1.17	1.080	1.40	1.749	2.68
CLK-FPGA11	1.000	1.00	1.000	1.00	1.000	1.00	1.000	1.03	1.000	1.06	1.000	1.04	1.003	1.05	1.001	1.10	1.001	1.13	1.017	1.13	1.041	1.21	1.333	1.77
CLK-FPGA12	1.000	1.00	1.000	0.99	1.000	1.00	1.000	1.01	1.001	1.00	1.000	1.00	1.003	1.02	1.013	1.14	1.014	1.14	1.017	1.11	1.213	1.28	1.138	1.28
CLK-FPGA13	1.000	1.00	1.000	1.00	1.000	0.99	1.001	1.02	1.001	1.03	1.000	1.04	1.004	1.02	1.013	1.11	1.013	1.07	1.026	1.12	1.146	1.28	*	-
Norm.	1.000	1.00	1.000	1.00	1.000	1.00	1.000	1.03	1.000	1.05	1.000	1.08	1.006	1.07	1.009	1.13	1.014	1.18	1.023	1.17	1.113	1.26	1.267	1.56

*: Fail to find feasible placement solutions within 1800 seconds.

[18] Alexander S. Marquardt, Vaughn Betz, and Jonathan Rose. 1999. Using cluster-based logic blocks and timing-driven packing to improve FPGA speed and density. In *FPGA*. 37–46.

[19] Ryan Pattison, Ziad Abuowaimer, Shawki Areibi, Gary Gréwal, and Anthony Vannelli. 2016. GPlace: A congestion-aware placement tool for ultrascale FPGAs. In *ICCAD*. 68:1–68:7.

[20] Chak-Wa Pui, Gengjie Chen, Wing-Kai Chow, Ka-Chun Lam, Jian Kuang, Peishan Tu, Hang Zhang, Evangeline F.Y. Young, and Bei Yu. 2016. RippleFPGA: A routability-driven placement for large-scale heterogeneous FPGAs. In *ICCAD*. 67:1–67:8.

[21] Chak-Wa Pui, Gengjie Chen, Yuzhe Ma, Evangeline F. Y. Young, and Bei Yu. 2017. Clock-aware ultraScale FPGA placement with machine learning routability prediction. In *ICCAD*. 915–922.

[22] Senthilkumar Thoravi Rajavel and Ali Akoglu. 2011. MO-Pack: Many-objective clustering for FPGA CAD. In *DAC*. 818–823.

[23] Amit Singh, Ganapathy Parthasarathy, and Malgorzata Marek-Sadowska. 2002. Efficient circuit clustering for area and power reduction in FPGAs. *ACM TODAES*

7, 4 (2002), 643–663.

[24] Love Singhal, Mahesh A. Iyer, and Saurabh Adya. 2017. LSC: A large-scale consensus-based clustering algorithm for high-performance FPGAs. In *DAC*. 30:1–30:6.

[25] Xilinx Vivado Design Suite. 2018. https://www.xilinx.com/products/design-tools/vivado.html.

[26] M Xu, Gary Gréwal, and Shawki Areibi. 2011. StarPlace: A new analytic method for FPGA placement. *Integration, the VLSI Journal* 44, 3 (2011), 192–204.

[27] Stephen Yang, Aman Gayasen, Chandra Mulpuri, Sainath Reddy, and Rajat Aggarwal. 2016. Routability-driven FPGA placement contest. In *ISPD*. 139–143.

[28] Stephen Yang, Chandra Mulpuri, Sainath Reddy, Meghraj Kalase, Srinivasan Dasasthyan, Mehrdad E. Dehkordi, Marvin Tom, and Rajat Aggarwal. 2017. Clock-aware FPGA placement contest. In *ISPD*. 159–164.

EASY: Efficient Arbiter SYnthesis from Multi-threaded Code

Jianyi Cheng
Imperial College London
London, UK
jianyi.cheng17@imperial.ac.uk

Shane T. Fleming
Imperial College London
London, UK
s.fleming06@imperial.ac.uk

Yu Ting Chen
University of Toronto
Toronto, Ontario
joyuting.chen@mail.utoronto.ca

Jason H. Anderson
University of Toronto
Toronto, Ontario
janders@ece.toronto.edu

George A. Constantinides
Imperial College London
London, UK
g.constantinides@imperial.ac.uk

ABSTRACT

High-Level Synthesis (HLS) tools automatically transform a high-level specification of a circuit into a low-level RTL description. Traditionally, HLS tools have operated on sequential code, however in recent years there has been a drive to synthesize multi-threaded code. A major challenge facing HLS tools in this context is how to automatically partition memory amongst parallel threads to fully exploit the bandwidth available on an FPGA device and avoid memory contention. Current automatic memory partitioning techniques have inefficient arbitration due to conservative assumptions regarding which threads may access a given memory bank. In this paper, we address this problem through formal verification techniques, permitting a less conservative, yet provably correct circuit to be generated. We perform a static analysis on the code to determine which memory banks are shared by which threads. This analysis enables us to optimize the arbitration efficiency of the generated circuit. We apply our approach to the LegUp HLS tool and show that for a set of typical application benchmarks we can achieve up to 87% area savings, and 39% execution time improvement, with little additional compilation time.

CCS CONCEPTS

• **Hardware → High-level and register-transfer level synthesis**; **Logic synthesis**; **Modeling and parameter extraction**;

KEYWORDS

High-Level Synthesis; Memory optimization; Formal methods

ACM Reference Format:
Jianyi Cheng, Shane T. Fleming, Yu Ting Chen, Jason H. Anderson, and George A. Constantinides. 2019. EASY: Efficient Arbiter SYnthesis from Multi-threaded Code. In *The 2019 ACM/SIGDA International Symposium on Field-Programmable Gate Arrays (FPGA '19), February 24–26, 2019, Seaside, CA, USA.* ACM, New York, NY, USA, 10 pages. https://doi.org/10.1145/3289602.3293899

1 INTRODUCTION

FPGAs are beginning to achieve mainstream adoption for custom computing, particularly as FPGAs are deployed in datacentres, through, for example, the Microsoft Project Catapult [14] and the Amazon EC2 F1 instances [3]. However, to use such FPGA devices, familiarity with detailed digital design at a low abstraction level is required, hindering their use by engineers without a hardware background. High-level synthesis (HLS) aims to bring the benefits of custom hardware to software engineers by translating a language they are familiar with, such as C, into a hardware description. This process can significantly reduce the design time compared to manual RTL implementations. Various HLS tools have been developed by both academia and industry, such as LegUp from University of Toronto [1], Bambu from Politecnico di Milano [17], Xilinx Vivado HLS [19] and Intel's HLS Compiler [8].

The input to HLS for parallel hardware synthesis can be either single-threaded sequential code or multi-threaded concurrent code. Our work relates to multi-threaded input, which commonly involves three challenges in HLS design. Firstly, while FPGA devices provide large amounts of compute, its effective utilization is often limited by the *memory bandwidth*. Additionally, to increase the memory bandwidth, partitioning schemes can be used to split memory into smaller distributed memories or banks. This allows for parallel accesses to data items, but to ensure *correctness*, arbitration logic needs to be used to serialize accesses to each individual partition. Finally, as the number of memory partitions or compute threads increases, so do the overheads of arbitration resulting in challenge of the *system scalability*.

HLS tools, such as LegUp, often address the memory bandwidth and correctness challenges by performing automated memory partitioning and using a crossbar arbiter to ensure global accessibility. However, this approach has scalability challenges, as the fully connected arbitration logic imposes excessive routing overheads and lengthy critical paths. One solution to this problem is for users to manually edit the software code to specify disjoint regions of memory, which would enable the optimization of arbitration logic. If a user specifies that a region of memory is only accessed by one thread, then no arbitration logic is required. However, for complex code it can often be challenging and error prone for the user to manually determine memory bank exclusivity, and such an approach is counter to the fully automated design philosophy of HLS tools.

In this paper, we propose an approach called Efficient Arbiter SYnthesis (EASY) based on automated translation of a multi-threaded program into a related sequential program in the formal verification

```
1  void *assign(void *threadarg) {
2    int arg = *threadarg;
3
4    // assign element values
5    for (i = arg; i < arg+1024; i++)
6      A[i] = B[f(i)];
7
8    pthread_exit(NULL);
9  }
10
11 int main() {
12   ...
13
14   // initialize arguments to pass into threads
15   for (i = 0; i < 2; i++)
16     data[i] = i*1024;
17
18   // create the threads
19   for (i = 0; i < 2; i++)
20     pthread_create(&threads[i], NULL, assign, data[i]);
21
22   ...
23 }
```

Figure 1: Example of a simple multi-threaded C source using pthreads.

language Boogie [12], together with assertions. We then apply the Boogie tool-flow to automatically generate satisfiability modulo theory (SMT) queries, the results of which our tool interprets as directions to simplify arbitration logic in the original multi-threaded program. Our work is able to address the scalability challenge by extending the current LegUp tool flow with a fully automated static analysis flow that supports arbitrary input code.

The main contributions of this work are as follows:

1) A general technique that uses formal methods to prove memory bank exclusivity for arbitrary multi-threaded input code.

2) A technique for translating generic LLVM intermediate representation (IR) code for multi-threaded programs into the Microsoft Boogie (single threaded) verification language, suitable for proving the absence of memory bank contention.

3) A fully automated HLS pass that calls the Boogie verifier to formally prove that arbitration is not required between certain combinations of memory banks and program threads, enabling the removal or radical simplification of arbitration logic in an automated fashion.

4) Analysis and results showing that the proposed approach can achieve up to 87% area saving (geo. mean 48%) and 39% wall-clock time improvement (geo. mean 21%) over a number of benchmarks.

2 MOTIVATION

Fig. 1 gives an example of multi-threaded C code using pthreads. In each thread, a loop assigns elements of array A from data stored in array B. The element of B that is selected for each assignment uses the loop iterator, i, and the pure function int f(int i).

Each thread will use the function to decide which portions of the shared memory they are going to access. If this function is sufficiently complicated, it may be non-trivial for a developer to know how the memory should be partitioned for parallel access.

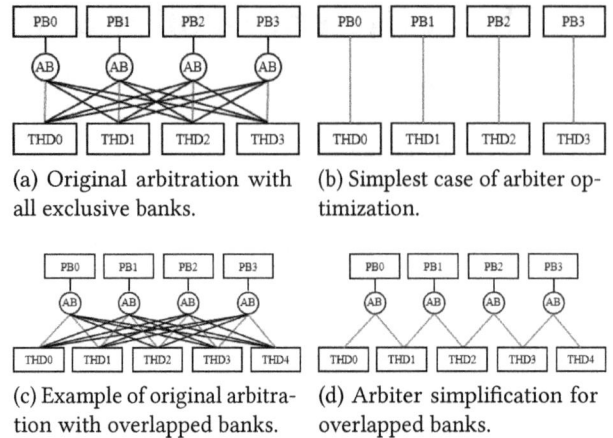

(a) Original arbitration with all exclusive banks.

(b) Simplest case of arbiter optimization.

(c) Example of original arbitration with overlapped banks.

(d) Arbiter simplification for overlapped banks.

PB: partitioned bank; THD: thread; AB: arbiter.

Figure 2: Examples of arbiter simplifications by the proposed work.

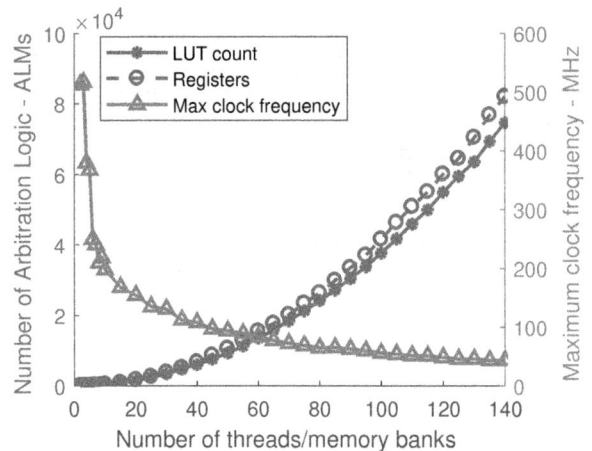

Figure 3: Evaluation on performance and chip area of original arbiters.

For example, the simplest case is f(i) = i. In this case, it is clear that the array indices accessed in each thread never overlap with the other threads, by combining knowledge of f with Line 16. For instance, thread 0 only ever accesses data at addresses 0 to 1023 of array B; while thread 1 only touches elements with addresses from 1024 to 2047. As these threads are both accessing mutually exclusive regions of B, a block partitioning strategy can be applied, where the array B of size 2048 can be divided into two sub-arrays of size 1024. Each thread accesses a unique partitioned memory bank during execution, so that the bank selection representing memory bank arbitration in hardware can be avoided.

In the architecture shown in Fig. 2(a), the LegUp HLS tool implements arbiters for each partitioned memory bank connecting to *all* threads. With many threads and banks, the size and delay of the arbitration logic becomes quite considerable. Fig. 3 shows how the arbitration logic hardware utilization and maximum clock

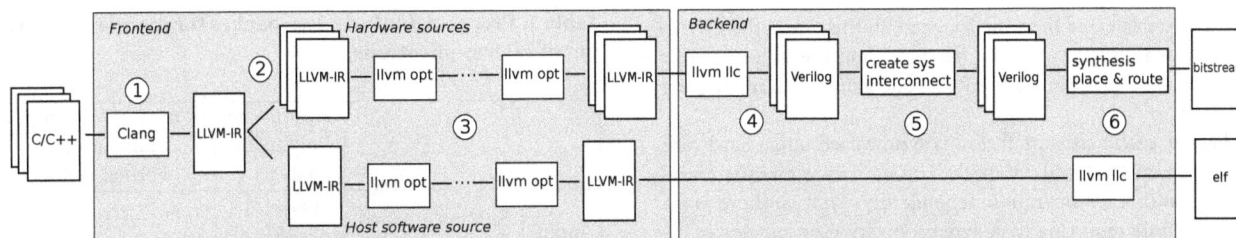

Figure 4: A coarse overview of the LegUp multi-threaded tool-flow.

frequency scales as the number of memory banks and threads are increased, where the number of threads is equal to the number of banks. As expected, increasing the number of threads causes a decrease in maximum clock frequency and increases hardware utilization. Observe that the maximum clock frequency of the arbiter drops sharply for a relatively small number of threads, eventually approaching a low sub-50MHz frequency. The figure also shows that both the logic utilization and number of registers used by the arbiters increases dramatically with the number of threads, leading to significant portion of total available resources. As the LegUp HLS tool conservatively assumes that any thread can access any bank, an arbiter port is needed for each thread. As the number of threads increases, so do the number of arbiter ports in the arbitration logic, resulting in a long propagation delay between memory banks and threads, decreasing the maximum achievable frequency.

The main objective of this work is to simplify the memory arbitration by statically proving (using the semantics of the input) that some threads are incapable of accessing some memory partitions, and optimizing the arbitration logic accordingly. With our approach, we are able to analyze the input source and through the use of formal methods, prove which thread never accesses a memory bank. Often, only the red wires shown in Fig. 2(a) are ever used during the whole execution, while the black wires are never used, demonstrating the source of conservatism and the potential benefits of arbiter simplification. After applying our approach, we achieve the connectivity in Fig 2(b), where all arbitration logic can be safely removed. A more general case is shown in Fig. 2(c), where a memory bank may be accessed by more than one thread. In this case the arbiters cannot be completely stripped out, but can still be simplified resulting in a more area-efficient arbitration architecture in Fig. 2(d).

In the context of the existing simulation-based approach [22], let T be the set of threads, and S be the subset of those observed to be accessing a given bank in simulation. Let F be the set of threads that have been formally proven by our tool to not be accessing a given block of memory. The original arbitration method for partitioned memory using S observed by [22] is to build an arbiter with $|T|$ connections conservatively, while our work builds an arbiter with $|T-F|$ connections. We know that every simulation-observed access pattern is possible, so $S \subseteq T - F \subseteq T$. Most of the time, we find $S = T - F$, which can be interpreted as 'it is safe to consider only those banks touched in simulation' (as in Fig. 2(c)). The 'best case' is $|S| = |T - F| = 1$ such as Fig. 2(a). The objective of our work is to find F for each bank.

3 BACKGROUND

3.1 The LegUp HLS tool

For this work, we have chosen to use the LegUp HLS tool, as it is the only tool that supports multi-threaded inputs, in the form of C style pthreads, with all other HLS tools only supporting single-threaded inputs [10, 19]. It is also a well known and open-source HLS tool under active development. Support for multi-threading is essential since our technique uses formal methods to optimize the generated memory interface for concurrently executing hardware threads, which is realized through the synthesis of multi-threaded code. LegUp HLS allows spatial parallelism in hardware to be exploited by software engineers, through the synthesis of concurrent threads into parallel hardware modules.

LegUp is built upon the LLVM [4] compiler framework. LLVM consists of a frontend, optimization stage, and backend. The frontend converts the input program into LLVM-IR, which can then be optimized using a collection of preexisting optimization passes, and the backend receives the final optimized LLVM-IR and generates architecture-specific machine code. In the case of LegUp, the backend performs HLS and produces a Verilog RTL circuit implementation. We now summarize the key stages in LegUp's multi-threaded synthesis flow.

1) The input C is transformed into LLVM-IR via Clang [6].

2) Each thread function destined for hardware is extracted from the rest of the source, creating a hardware LLVM-IR source for each function, and a software (host-code) LLVM-IR source.

3) The split LLVM-IR sources are transformed multiple times by a series of optimization passes: some LegUp specific, such as bitwidth minimization, and others generic, such as dead-code elimination. For the LLVM-IR host source, an additional transformation is made to convert all the pthread_create calls into the appropriate hardware function calls.

4) Each transformed LLVM-IR source is then turned into a Verilog description of a circuit using the traditional scheduling, allocation, and binding steps [15].

5) Interconnect logic and memory interfaces are generated to connect each of the circuits to the host system and instantiate them the appropriate number of times.

6) The software host code is compiled, and an FPGA hardware bitstream is generated by synthesizing the Verilog using FPGA vendor tools.

Fig. 4 shows a labeled tool-flow diagram of the stages outlined above, where stages 1–3 are often referred to as the frontend and stages 4–6 are referred to as the backend. In this work, the LLVM-IR is analyzed directly after the frontend, and the output of our analysis is used to optimize the RTL code generation in stages 4 and 5.

In LegUp, each hardware thread is synthesized into a hardware circuit with an FSM and datapath. The hardware circuits corresponding to threads operate independently. That is, there is no global schedule requiring data-synchronization on memories between threads (which can instead be achieved by using locks and synchronization barriers common in other HLS tools [18]).

One advantage of FPGA devices is the high-internal memory bandwidth, as the numerous small distributed memories (BRAMs) can be accessed concurrently. For any data shared between multiple hardware threads, LegUp constructs a shared memory out of BRAMs to provide fast local access to the data. LegUp also provides an optimization pass to partition shared arrays automatically into multiple smaller BRAM-based memories, enabling more data to be accessed concurrently [22] (c.f. Section 3.2).

As mentioned above, LegUp is unable to determine conclusively which thread will access which of the shared memories, forcing it to take a conservative approach, where it assumes any thread can access any shared memory. This assumption requires the construction of expensive crossbar-based interconnects and arbitration logic between all threads and every shared memory as illustrated in Fig. 2(a). In the current generated hardware, whenever multiple threads compete for a shared memory, only one can be granted access. The rest of the threads are stalled, unable to make progress.

3.2 Memory Partitioning Schemes

To exploit the high internal memory bandwidth available on FPGA devices, LegUp includes a partitioning optimization that can split a shared memory into multiple smaller memories [22]. Memory partitioning allows for multiple simultaneous accesses to a "shared" memory between concurrently executing threads. With an appropriately chosen partitioning scheme, simultaneous memory port accesses, which would have previously resulted in contention (i.e. stalled cycles) can now occur. By splitting memories into smaller blocks, each of the constituent smaller memories can service disjoint regions of the overall address space independently. Provided multiple threads are requesting access to portions of the address space serviced by different memories, they can access them simultaneously. The capability to partition memories thereby increases access parallelism, improving application performance.

Memory partitioning cannot be performed blindly and requires care. If partitioning is well balanced, with threads accessing disjoint regions of the address space concurrently, then performance is improved. However, if some of the partitions are very "hot" with frequent accesses and others are very "cold" with infrequent accesses, then the overheads of the partitioning logic may outweigh the benefit seen by the increased throughput. To carefully select appropriate partitioning strategies, LegUp adopts an automated simulation-trace-based approach using a light-weight memory simulator. Different partitioning schemes, complete, block, cyclic and block-cyclic, are applied and simulated on the initial memory trace to experimentally identify the partitioning strategy with the smallest memory contention frequency.

Table 1: Program analysis approaches for memory partitioning of HLS applications.

		Approaches for memory partitioning	
		Polyhedral analysis	Simulations + Formal methods
Input code	Single-threaded	[20], [2], [9]	[21]
	Multi-threaded		[22]+our work

While this approach greatly improves the throughput for multi-threaded shared memory applications, it cannot guarantee that multiple threads never access the same partition. This exacerbates the scalability challenge discussed in Section 3.1 and highlighted in Fig. 3, as now the complexity of the arbitration logic scales not just with the number of shared memories and threads, but also with the number of partitions per shared memory. Our analysis alleviates this scalability challenge, as it is able to prove which threads can access which partitions of a shared memory through a static analysis of the code. This enables us to safely optimize the arbitration logic connecting memory partitions to threads, reducing its complexity and increasing performance.

3.3 Program Analysis Tools

Program analysis has been an active research area for optimizing circuit generation with HLS tools. Table 1 shows a comparison between our work and the following related works. Polyhedral techniques have been used in HLS since the work of Liu et al. [11]. Recent work such as Wang et al. [20] on polyhedral analysis for memory partitioning has shown promising performance through performing cyclic-like partitioning, exploring the translation between accesses to an original multi-dimensional array and to the newly partitioned arrays. However, this approach is incompatible with bank switching, where the data in one bank is shared by multiple hardware units, prompting Gallo et al.'s lattice-based banking algorithm [2]. Winterstein et al. [7] propose a tool named MATCHUP to identify the private and shared memory region for a certain range of heap-manipulating programs using separation logic, targeting off-chip memory, while we perform analysis arbitrary code but currently only work with on-chip memory. The most recent work by Escobedo and Lin [9] propose a graph-based approach based on formal methods to compute minimally required memory banks for any given pattern to avoid memory contention for stencil-based computing kernels. In summary, these works are not built based on multi-threaded input, but are rather directed towards partitioning of arrays with multiple accesses in a loop body. These techniques are not applicable in multi-threaded cases, and often require code to have a particular structure (e.g. polyhedral loop nests).

Satisfiability Modulo Theories (SMT) solver-based approaches are relatively new to the HLS community, but have shown potential strengths in hardware optimization. The closest piece of work to this paper is by Zhou et al. [21], which proposes an SMT-based checker for verification of memory access conflicts based on parallel execution with banked memory, resulting in a highly area-efficient memory architecture. We both use simulation traces as a starting point for formal analysis, an approach referred to as 'mining' in [21]. However, they optimize a banking function with a model of area, while our work proves the absence of conflict for a banking function derived by [22]. Moreover, [21] does not take the whole program, with its control structures into account and instead formulates an SMT query on the banking functions themselves. Hence, it does not support input-dependent memory traces, which can be analyzed by our work.

Finally, [21] proves the existence of bank conflicts, allowing each parallel hardware unit to access different memory banks concurrently. For instance, they allow that at clock cycle 0, instance 0 accesses bank 0 and instance 1 accesses bank 1, while at clock cycle 1, parallel instance 0 accesses bank 1 and parallel instance 1 accesses bank 0. Conversely, we identify the memory banks *never* accessed by certain threads over the whole execution, because we target arbiter removal. For example, we can improve the arbitration logic in an instance where thread 0 never accesses bank 0 and bank 1 at any point, while thread 1 never accesses bank 2 and bank 3.

3.4 Microsoft Boogie

Boogie is an automatic program verifier from Microsoft Research, built on top of SMT solvers [12]. Boogie uses its own intermediate verification language (IVL) to represent the behavior of the program being verified. Instead of executing the verification code, an SMT solver is applied to reason about program behavior, including the values that variables may take. Encoding of verifications as SMT queries is automatically performed by Boogie 'behind the scenes', hidden from the user. Other works have proposed the automated translation of an original program to Boogie IVL, such as Smack [13], a automated translator of LLVM-IR code into equivalent Boogie code.

In addition to all the commands one would expect in a standard programming language, Boogie contains a number of verification-specific language constructs, which we use in our work, as detailed below:

1) `havoc x`: The `havoc` command assigns an arbitrary value to the variable x. This can be used to prove an assertion that is true for *any* values of the variable, unlike simulation-based testing which will only check assertions for particular test vectors.

2) `assume c`: The `assume` command adds tells the verifier that the condition c can be assumed to be true when trying to prove subsequent assertions. For example `{havoc x; assume (x>0);}` together encode that the variable x can be any positive value.

3) `if (*) {A} else {B}`: The special `(*)` condition tells the verifier that either branch might be taken. This construct is called non-deterministic choice.

4) `assert c`: This instructs the verifier to try to prove the condition c. For example `{havoc x; assume (x>1); assert (x>0);}` should pass, because every variable greater than one is also greater than zero.

4 METHODOLOGY

We convert the multi-threaded HLS input code into single-threaded Boogie code to verify the number of arbiter ports needed for the each partitioned bank. The Boogie code represents only those expressions from the original code that could impact on the memory bank partition index accessed by each thread. Formal techniques are applied to prove that certain arbiter ports are unnecessary. The subsections below highlight the main steps in the process, including how we translate the multi-threaded C into a Boogie program with a proper specification of program states, the construction of assertions that check whether arbitration is needed, and how we handle loops.

4.1 Multi-Threaded C and Boogie Program

Using the Boogie primitive operations outlined in Section 3.4, we can generate a single-threaded boogie program that can be used to verify bank exclusivity in our multi-threaded input code. Our approach is fully automated – an input LegUp multi-threaded source is automatically transformed into a single-threaded Boogie program as part of the compiler pass. This source translation consists of three main steps:

Step 1 : We use non-deterministic choice to exhaustively explore the state-space of all possible memory accesses.

Step 2 : For each hardware accelerated thread call in the `main` function we call a separate instance of the single-threaded Boogie code with the same inputs.

Step 3 : Within each Boogie thread instance we generate Boogie `assert` statements that are used to test for memory bank exclusivity.

First, a procedure named `thread_func` represents the memory behavior of the original thread function (named `assign` in the example code). From the example, it is intuitive that one thread accesses the array index range from `data[i]` to `data[i]+1023` in a `for` loop when `f(i) = i`. In the equivalent loop in `thread_func`, the partition index - determined using [22] - is required for verification instead of the exact data value or array index. For simplicity of demonstration, we assume here that the partition index is bit 10 of the 11-bit array index under the block partitioning scheme, but the expression can be arbitrary in general. A non-deterministic choice `if(*)` is used to model the fact that we need to capture the partition index accessed by *any* loop iteration; taking the if branch causes the verifier to flag that a read has happened with index `index` - if the branch is not taken, this corresponds to skipping this particular memory access in the original code. For this example, thread 0 can only return 0 as the set of all possible partition index is {0} with accessed array index ranging from 0 to 1023. Similarly thread 1 only returns 1.

The arbitrary partition index returning in Boogie is transformed from the extracted multi-threaded memory behavior, which consists of a number of *sliced* partitioned memory accesses. A sliced partitioned memory access is defined as a list of LLVM-IR instructions relating to the partition index, disregarding all other irrelevant instructions in the thread function [16]. We must translate these instructions for analysis of the partition index of accessed memory bank. When the data in an array is accessed such as `A[i]` in Fig. 1, the corresponding instruction in LLVM-IR code is represented as "`index = partition_index; if (*) {read = true; return;}`" in Boogie.

```
1  void *assign(void *threadarg) {            1  procedure {:inline 1} thread_func(arg: bv32)
2  // Thread function of the input            2  returns (read: bool, index: bv32) { // Summarized partition index expression
3                                              3  ... // transformed for loop:
4    int arg = *threadarg;                     4  assert i >= arg && i <= arg+1024;
5                          Loop Interpretation 5  havoc i;
6    // assign element values                  6  assume i >= arg && i <= arg+1024;
7    for (i = arg; i < arg+1024; i++)          7    // inside the equivalent for loop in Boogie code
8      A[i] = B[f(i)];                         8    index = i >> 10;  // for the case f(i) = i
9                          Step 1              9    if(*){ // non-deterministic bank address returning
10   pthread_exit(NULL);                       10     read = true;
11 }                                           11     return;
12                                             12   }
13 int main() {                                13  assert i >= arg && i <= arg+1024;
14   ...                                       14  assume false; // end of for loop
15                                             15  read = false;
16   // initialize arguments                   16  return;   // if no global memory accessed, read = false
17   // to pass into threads                   17 }
18   for (i = 0; i < 2; i++)                    18
19     data[i] = i*1024;                       19 procedure main() {// Memory bank exclusivity assertions in main function
20                                             20  call t0_read, t0_index = thread_func(0);
21   // create the threads       Step 2        21  call t1_read, t1_index = thread_func(1024);
22   for (i = 0; i < 2; i++)                    22                                          Step 3
23     pthread_create(&threads[i],             23  assert !t0_read || t0_index != 0; // Thread 0 never access bank 0 - x
24       NULL, assign, data[i]);               24  assert !t0_read || t0_index != 1; // Thread 0 never access bank 1 - ✓
25                                             25  assert !t1_read || t1_index != 0; // Thread 1 never access bank 0 - ✓
26   ...                                       26  assert !t1_read || t1_index != 1; // Thread 1 never access bank 1 - x
27 }                                           27 }
```

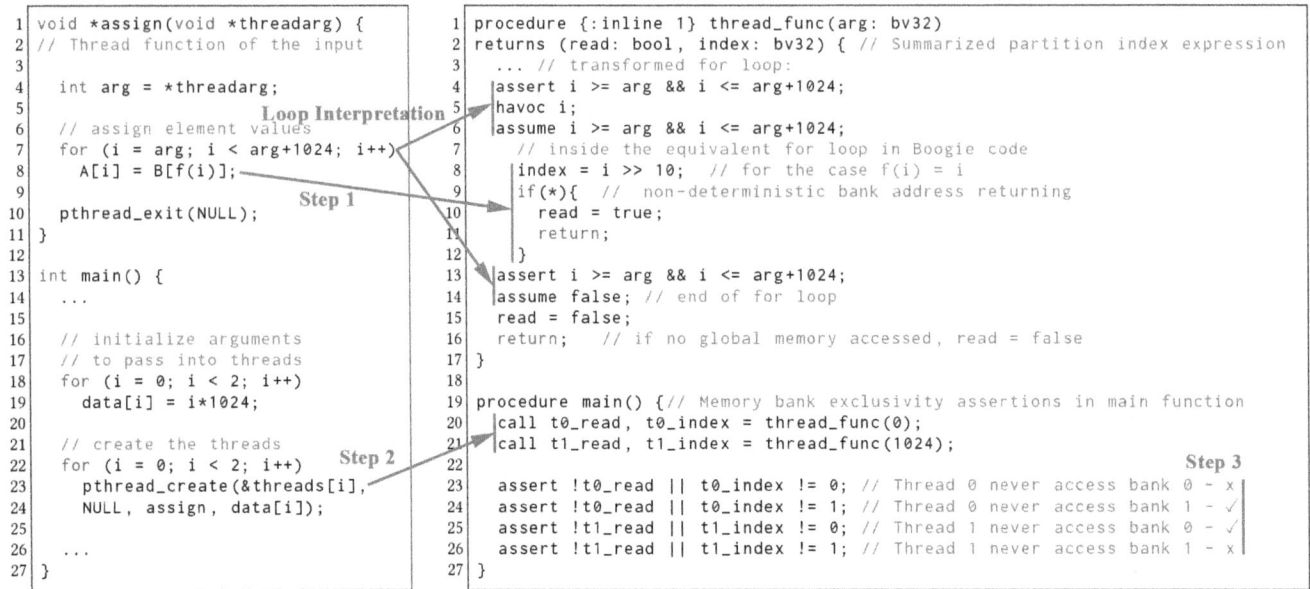

(a) Input multi-threaded C code.   (b) Output Boogie program.

Figure 5: Example of a 4-partition 4-thread case for bank exclusivity verifications.

Two further parts of the Boogie model appear in the main procedure. Instead of executing threads concurrently, the generated Boogie program calls each thread procedure in a sequential manner. These call instructions are considered as separate and independent modules for memory access analysis. Each call instruction returns a read state and an arbitrary partition index among accessed banks. Thus, the called procedure has either accessed the partitioned memory with a valid partition index, or does not access any partitioned memory, i.e. all none of the if(*) blocks have been executed.

The last part of the verification code is the list of final assertions. The final assertions are automatically generated by enumerating connections between each partitioned banks and each threads. Each single assertion states that a specific thread does not touch a specific partitioned bank. If the assertion holds, the corresponding arbitration logic can be removed in the hardware, otherwise, it is necessary to maintain this arbiter port in hardware. With Boogie code containing a list of final assertions, the Boogie verifier is automatically called to filter all failed assertions. Based on the successful assertions left in Boogie code, it formally proves that arbitration is not required between certain combinations of memory banks and program threads, stripping out or radically simplifying the arbiters as a result. This approach supports any memory access pattern, and the verification results can correctly identify where arbitration is required in the HLS-generated hardware.

4.2 Loop Interpretation

Memory accesses in loops are a primary source of memory bottlenecks, as they often correspond to the overwhelming majority of accesses. In our analysis, we aim to support loops without having to unroll them in the Boogie code, in order to be able to support general while loops and also to keep the size of the verification

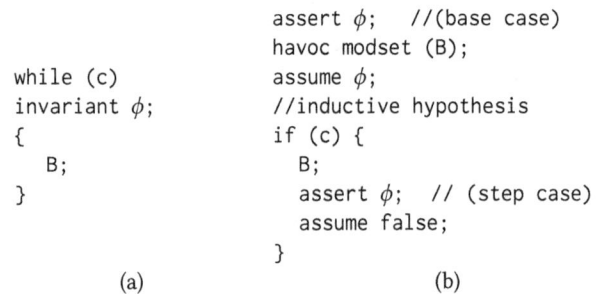

```
                                  assert φ;   //(base case)
                                  havoc modset (B);
while (c)                         assume φ;
invariant φ;                      //inductive hypothesis
{                                 if (c) {
  B;                                B;
}                                   assert φ;  // (step case)
                                    assume false;
                                  }
      (a)                                 (b)
```

Figure 6: Loop summary in verification language using loop-cutting transformation [5].

code small. A loop in Boogie code typically requires the programmer to specify a *loop invariant* to formally abstract the program state. An invariant is a property describing the program state that always holds on entry to the loop and after every iteration of the loop. Automated generation of loop invariants is an active research area in program verification. Here we adopt the approach described by Chong [5].

Fig. 6 shows the general case of our loop transformation process: in Fig. 6(a) a general structure of a while loop is described, while Fig. 6(b) shows the equivalent transformed loop in Boogie. In Fig. 6(a), a while loop contains a conditional check on variable c and a loop body B. Additionally, φ represents the loop invariant. In Fig. 6(b), the invariants for the loop are established inductively. At the entry point of loop, also known as the base case, the first assertion asks Boogie to verify that the loop invariant holds. The next few lines skip through an arbitrary number of loop iterations,

Table 2: Reference table for invariants of *for* loops of the form `for( i=start; cond; st )`

		st	
		i++	i--
cond	i < end or i > end	start <= i i < end	start >= i i > end
	i <= end or i >= end	start <= i i <= end	start >= i i >= end

```
for(i=0;i<N;i++)
{

  b = i*2;

}

assert b==2*(N-1);
```

(a) Original C source.

```
i = 0;
assert i <= N-1 && i >= 0;
havoc i, b;
assume i <= N-1 && i >= 0;
if (i<N-1) {
    b = i*2;
    i++;
    assert i<=N-1 && i>=0;
    assume false;
}
i = N-1;
if(i < N) {
    b = i*2;
    i++;
}
assert b==2*(N-1);
```

(b) Loop peeling to maintain information of b.

Figure 7: Example of loop peeling in Boogie.

havocing the variables that might be changed by the loop body (`modset(B)`), and only assuming the induction hypothesis of the loop invariant in order to prove that the invariant still holds. We note that using this transformation, we can *guess* any loop invariant ϕ without being concerned about the correctness of the resulting memory structure, because we place an obligation on Boogie to verify that a guessed invariant actually does hold.

The selection of an appropriate invariant ϕ is key to verification success. However, for the HLS benchmarks we have considered, the loops have a simple structure of increasing or decreasing single-strided for loops with strict or non-strict inequalities as loop exit conditions. We therefore implement a simple table lookup of proposed loop invariant, following Table 2. For instance, if the loop index is incrementing with an exit condition of the index being equal to the end bound, the loop invariant would be that the loop index is greater or equal to start index value, and also less than the exit bound value. For the case of an inequality check as the exit condition, the loop index is less or equal to end-bound value. Similar results can be found with inversed signs in the cases where the loop index shows decrementing behaviors.

On the other hand, for loops with dependencies, more specific invariants are required to precisely describe the loop behavior to achieve precise results. For instance, the loop bounds can be dynamic, or the code following the loop could make use of knowledge of program variables at loop exit not captured in by the loop exit condition alone. We solve this by loop peeling typically for `for` loops, which is fully automated in our tool-flow; inferring invariants for general `while` loops still needs human guidance. Fig. 7 shows an example of code transformation applied by loop peeling typically to perform a `for` loop with exit condition of i < N. Different from Fig. 6(b), this code performs two iterations for one loop. The iterations except final iteration are represented using identical arbitrary *teleporting* method, which also results in invalidation of loop body summary. After that, loop iterator is set to N-1 representing end of (N-1)th iteration following by the final iteration of the loop. The final iteration is presented as the second iteration which simulates the loop behavior of last iteration maintaining the loop body information in the last iteration valid for further assertions after the loop. Therefore, this can solve the case when the information in the loop body is required for further verification. However, it is only compatible for `for` loops at current stage. Since the number of the iterations in more general loop is unknown,

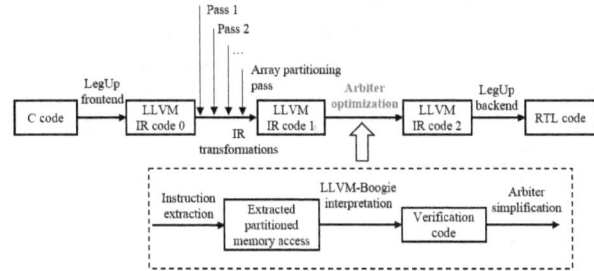

Figure 8: LegUp tool flow with proposed work integrated.

the generation of modified set configurations of loops before final iteration is challenging and to be solved.

5 INTEGRATION INTO LLVM FRAMEWORK

The automated arbitration optimization process is implemented as a series of LLVM passes. Fig. 8 shows the LegUp HLS design flow with the work of arbiter optimization integrated. One of the LegUp frontend passes performs memory partitioning [22]. This pass divides selected arrays into a number of sub-arrays, where each array is also assigned with a unique partition index. Our work is carried out after the execution of this pass. Our work can be divided into three parts. Firstly, the multi-threaded memory behavior is extracted and formulated into a mathematical expression for bank mapping. Secondly, code transformation is carried out resulting in Boogie code for memory conflict verification. Finally, we remove the unused memory ports of arbiters in all threads based on the verification results given by the Boogie code. This results in a newly optimized LLVM-IR code with efficient memory arbitration.

5.1 Partitioned Memory Access Extraction

The slicing tool [16] allows us to extract only those pieces of the code that could affect the memory banks accessed by each thread. It radically simplifies the code, so that only those operations affecting memory access patterns are retained. For example, in the motivational example of Fig. 1, all instructions that may modify the value of f(i) are retained, while other instructions in the thread function are removed. This avoids wasted runtime in analysis of instructions that are not relevant to memory access behavior.

5.2 Compilation into Boogie

In this step, the sliced LLVM-IR code is mapped into a Boogie program. The translation of individual instructions from LLVM-IR code to Boogie code is straightforward. Since the original integer type in C is 32-bit, the equivalent data type in Boogie is a 32-bit bit-vector (Boogie integers are unbounded). First, we iterate through the LLVM-IR instructions to extract variable names, which are declared at the beginning of the Boogie function. Then, the variables assigned arbitrary values are configured with havoc commands after the variable declarations. Then, LLVM-IR instructions can be directly replaced by available operators in Boogie or translated into a small number of equivalent instructions. The non-deterministic choice if(*) returning the partition index is inserted at the location where the pointer to the element in partition array is obtained. In other words, instead of accessing the requested data, the Boogie code returns the partition index of the requested bank. During interpretation, the assertions and assumptions for the transformed loops are inserted in Boogie code locations that correspond to the beginning of the entry block and the exit block of the loops in LLVM-IR code. The summarization of invariants for complex loops is achieved by recognizing phi instructions in the LLVM-IR code that are used for data reuse, where the necessary modified set for the current loop can be sliced and transformed.

In the main procedure, after listing the separate function calls in the form of procedures in Boogie, the final assertions are constructed based on the partition indices and thread indices. If N is the number of threads, and M is the number of memory partitions, the Boogie program has $N \times M$ assertions corresponding to the individual interconnections between the threads and banks. Since the thread function calls are inlined in the main procedure, recursive function calls are not possible, however, recursion is also generally not supported by HLS tools.

5.3 Arbiter Optimization Process

Based on which Boogie assertions hold, memory arbiters are simplified without affecting execution correctness. This step is carried out in the LLVM-IR code level frontend. In each thread, the bank multiplexer used to access the partitioned memory is simplified by removing ports to banks that are never accessed. An example is shown in Fig. 9, for the case of thread 0 being proven to not access sub-arrays 1 and 2. The red 'x's show hardware that is safely removed in the final circuit.

6 EXPERIMENTAL RESULTS

The FPGA family we used for results measurements is Cyclone V (5CSEMA5F31C6) in Quartus II 15.0.0. The reason is that this FPGA

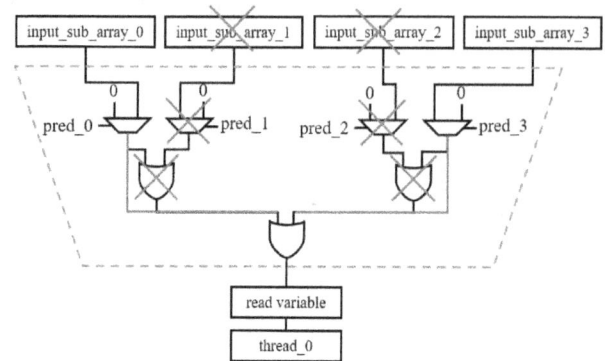

ik - local address of array *subX_ga*. bk - partition index.

Figure 9: LLVM-IR modification for efficient bank selection.

is one of the devices supported by LegUp HLS tool. We evaluate the arbitration simplification process on a set of benchmarks, assessing its impact on both circuit area and speed: F_{max}, cycle latency, and wall-clock time (cycle latency $\times 1/F_{max}$). We also discuss its impact on CAD tool run-time.

6.1 Benchmark Descriptions

We apply our approach to the eight multi-threaded benchmarks from [22]: *matrixadd, histogram, matrixmult, matrixmult (cyclic), matrixtrans, matrixtrans (block cyclic), substring* and *los*. In *matrixadd*, two integer matrices of size 128 × 128 are summed by blocking matrix operations into groups of row summations, each performed by a different thread. *Histogram* reads an input integer array of size 32768 and counts the number of elements in five distinct ranges, storing the final element distribution in a result array. Matrix multiplication is implemented with two matrices of size 32 × 32 in *matrixmult*. Similarly, the element operations are divided into groups of row summations for parallelism. In *matrixmult (cyclic)*, the matrix row allocation has been rearranged in a cyclic scheme, grouping rows with matching LSBs to be operated on by a single thread. *Matrixtrans* computes the transpose of an input matrix of size 128 × 128 following the cyclic scheme. In *matrixtrans (block cyclic)*, the row allocation to different threads is based on both MSBs and LSBs of the index in a block-cyclic partitioning scheme, where a thread transposes rows at addresses of 0-3, 32-35, 64-67 and 96-99, for instance.

Benchmark *substring* searches for a string pattern of size 3 within an input string of size 16384, counting the number of occurrences of this pattern. The input string has been divided into several continuous substrings for multi-threaded execution. The arbitration complexity is relatively high due to there being multiple expressions for partitioned bank access within a single thread. The line of sight example in *los* analyzes the presence of an obstacle between the elements in a predefined obstacle map of size 64 × 64 and center of the map, wherein an element with value 1 indicates an obstacle, while an element with value 0 represents free space. The analysis of the elements is distributed to several threads for parallelism and the resultant output is a map, where elements having value 0 represent the presence of obstacles between the test coordinates and center

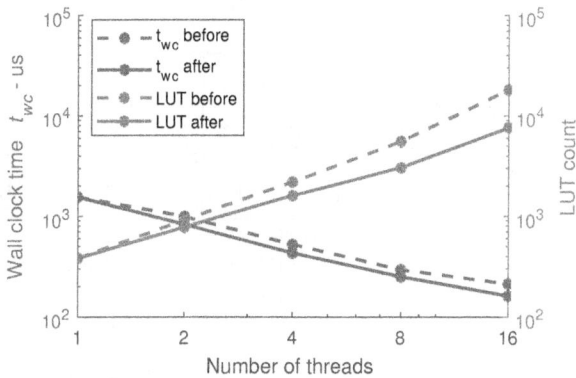

Figure 10: Evaluation of absolute parameters on *histogram* hardware with equal numbers of threads and banks.

point, while 1s are verified line-of-sight cases. This benchmark has a loop-carried dependency at the thread level, and an infinite `while` loop is used with two conditional breaks, leading to more complex partition index expressions.

6.2 Case Study: Histogram

Overall computational performance is maximized when the degree of computational parallelism matches the degree of parallelism provided by the memory system. In the simplest cases, this is often achieved when there is an equal number of partitioned banks and threads, with each thread operating on a private portion of the data. Fig. 10 shows the wall-clock time and LUT utilization of the optimized design (with efficient memory arbitration) as compared to the original architecture, for the *histogram* benchmark. Observe that the wall-clock time appears to have a linear relationship with number of threads, where more threads with sufficient memory bandwidth and no memory contention results in faster hardware execution. However, due to the increased number of parallel hardware units, hardware utilization increases quadratically, which appears to have doubled increasing rate compared to the wall-clock time. After arbiter simplification, both performance and chip area are generally improved with an increasing gap as the number of threads increases. Although the total number of clock cycles is not noticeably reduced, the critical path is optimized, improving wall clock time by up to 27%. The chip area also decreases compared to the original design by up to 58%. Since this work modifies the arbitration hardware alone, memory block usage is unchanged. However, the hardware resources for the arbitration circuit, namely LUTs and registers, are reduced appreciably. More importantly, with more threads, the improvements in performance and chip area are more effective as more arbiter ports may be removed.

6.3 Results for All Benchmarks

The post P&R results for all benchmarks are given Table 3 for the case of 16 threads and memory banks[1]. The table shows LUT and register count, F_{max}, cycle latency, and wall-clock time of the whole benchmarks. We observe that all benchmarks are improved

---
[1]Full dataset DOI: 10.5281/zenodo.1523170.

in area and performance, however, the extent of the improvement varies, depending on benchmark-specific memory-access behavior. Significant improvements in benchmarks such as *matrixmult* and *substring* are due to multiple accesses to partitioned arrays in one iteration, or to partitioning of multiple arrays, where the original arbitration circuits are larger leading to greater improvements. We also observe that the same benchmark with different memory partitioning schemes can have dramatically different results. For *matrixtrans* benchmark, the *cyclic* partitioning scheme has been applied by default, which has significantly benefited from the proposed work reaching improved clock period by 50.5% and logic by 87.4%. However, when applying *block – cyclic* scheme, it appears to have the worst improvements. This attributed to the fact that each bank is touched by all threads during execution, the arbiters cannot be simplified. Hence appropriate memory partitioning is required to perform the most efficient arbitration solution. Across all benchmarks, LUT count was reduced by up to 87%, and wall-clock time was improved by up to 39%. Greater improvements are expected for devices with more threads. On average, wall-clock time is improved by 21%, and LUT count is reduced by 58%.

6.4 Runtime analysis

While the theoretical worst-case runtime of the approach we present is exponential in program size, in practice, the runtime of the verification process is reasonably short. In addition, the increase in the number of threads also leads to more assertions, as well as duplicated thread procedure calls. The average runtime for all the benchmarks was 13 seconds. This is directly related to the number of constructed assertions, which in turn is related to two issues: the complexity of partition memory accesses and the number of threads. The longest verification time was 70s for *substring*, which has multiple memory accesses in one iteration using different partition index values resulting in multiple assertions for each access. Such verifications times are insignificant compared to Synthesis/P&R time.

7 CONCLUSIONS

In this work, we propose an automated process to simplify and/or remove memory arbiters in HLS-generated circuits for multi-threaded software code. Our flow uses previously-proposed simulation trace-based proposals for memory banking, using them as formal specifications for memory exclusivity which, if verified, guarantee that arbiters can be removed or simplified without impacting on program correctness. Across a range of benchmarks, the execution time of the circuits has been improved by up to 39% (avg. 21%) combined with an area saving of up to 87% (avg. 58%). The performances of hardware with more memory architecture are also promising from our measurements.

The novelty of this work is in the automated procedure for optimization of the arbitration circuits. We have shown that the behavior of typical concurrent multi-threaded code can be over-approximated using non-deterministic choice in sequential Boogie code, allowing existing verification tools to represent and check the verification conditions required. The runtime of the proposed compiler pass is 13 seconds, on average, across a set of 8 multi-threaded benchmarks.

Table 3: Arbitration simplification evaluation for 16 memory partitions and 16 threads.

benchmark	LUT count			Register count			Max clock frequency (MHz)			Total clock cycles			Wall clock time (μs)		
	before	after	%	before	after	%	before	after	%	before	after	%	before	after	%
histogram	18081	7639	58%	22331	13552	39%	71.79	94.54	32%	15269	14660	4%	212.7	155.1	27%
matrixadd	14286	2261	84%	14594	4176	71%	73.73	107.01	45%	2125	2122	0%	28.8	19.8	31%
matrixmult	21005	3641	83%	15872	5184	67%	74.02	85.88	16%	2130200	2130199	0%	28778.7	24804.4	14%
matrixmult(cyclic)	20880	11227	46%	15872	10479	34%	73.84	83.08	13%	2130200	2130199	0%	28848.9	25640.3	11%
matrixtrans	18653	2358	87%	14352	3548	75%	61.31	92.30	51%	37194	36167	3%	606.7	391.8	35%
matrixtrans(blockcyclic)	10606	9100	14%	8996	7402	18%	75.48	75.55	0%	62900	61715	2%	833.3	816.9	2%
substring	11029	2558	77%	11959	4718	61%	77.39	125.58	62%	443	439	1%	5.7	3.5	39%
los	23785	20610	13%	31283	25122	20%	73.81	81.46	10%	46514	45384	2%	630.2	557.1	12%
geom. mean	-	-	58%	-	-	48%	-	-	29%	-	-	2%	-	-	21%

One of the key advantages we have retained over more structured approaches, such as polyhedral methods, is the ability to deal with arbitrary code. That being said, although our tool can accept arbitrary code as input, we can certainly contrive examples where it fails to prove the necessary properties without human guidance, due either to the over approximation of multi-threaded behavior induced, or execution time. Our future work will explore the fundamental limits of this approach, both theoretically and practically.

8 ACKNOWLEDGEMENTS

The authors wish to thank Jingming Hu for his assistance with result measurements. This work is supported by EPSRC (EP/P010040/1), the Royal Academy of Engineering and Imagination Technologies.

REFERENCES

[1] A. Canis et al. 2013. LegUp: An Open-source High-Level Synthesis Tool for FPGA-based Processor/Accelerator Systems. *TECS* 13, 2 (2013).
[2] A. Cilardo and L. Gallo. 2015. Improving Multibank Memory Access Parallelism with Lattice-Based Partitioning. *TACO* 11, 4 (2015).
[3] Amazon EC2 F1 instances. 2018. (2018). https://aws.amazon.com/
[4] C. Lattner and V. Adve. 2004. LLVM: a compilation framework for lifelong program analysis & transformation. In *CGO*. IEEE, San Jose, CA.
[5] N. Y. S. Chong. 2014. *Scalable Verification Techniques for Data-Parallel Programs.* Doctoral Thesis. Imperial College London, London, UK.
[6] Clang. 2018. (2018). https://clang.llvm.org/
[7] F. Winterstein, K. Fleming, H.J. Yang, S. Bayliss and G. Constantinides. 2015. MATCHUP: Memory Abstractions for Heap Manipulating Programs. In *FPGA*. ACM, Monterey, CA.
[8] Intel HLS Compiler. 2017. (2017). https://www.altera.com/
[9] J. Escobedo and M. Lin. 2018. Graph-Theoretically Optimal Memory Banking for Stencil-Based Computing Kernels. In *FPGA*. ACM, Monterey, CA.
[10] J. Villarreal, A. Park, W. Najjar and R. Halstead. 2010. Designing modular hardware accelerators in C with ROCCC 2.0. In *FPGA*. IEEE, Charlotte, NC.
[11] Q. Liu, G.A. Constantinides, K. Masselos, and P.Y.K. Cheung. 2007. Automatic On-chip Memory Minimization for Data Reuse. In *FCCM*.
[12] M. Barnett et al. 2005. Boogie: a modular reusable verifier for object-oriented programs. In *FMCO*. ACM, Amsterdam, The Netherlands.
[13] M. Carter, S. He, J. Whitaker, Z. Rakamarić and M. Emmi. 2016. SMACK Software Verification Toolchain. In *ICSE-C*. ACM, Austin, Texas.
[14] Microsoft Project Catapult. 2018. (2018). https://www.microsoft.com/
[15] P. Coussy, M. Meredith, D.D. Gajski and A. Takach. 2009. An Introduction to High-Level Synthesis. *DTC* 26, 4 (2009).
[16] S. T. Fleming and D. B. Thomas. 2017. Using Runahead Execution to Hide Memory Latency in High Level Synthesis. In *FCCM*. IEEE, Napa, CA, USA.
[17] V.G. Castellana, A. Tumeo and F. Ferrandi. 2014. High-level Synthesis of Memory Bound and Irregular Parallel Applications with Bambu. In *HCS*. IEEE, Cupertino, CA, USA.
[18] Xilinx. 2016. SDAccel Development Environment - User Guide (v206.2). (2016).
[19] Xilinx Vivado HLS. 2017. (2017). https://www.xilinx.com/
[20] Y. Wang, P. Li and J. Cong. 2014. Theory and algorithm for generalized memory partitioning in high-level synthesis. In *FPGA*. ACM, Monterey, CA.
[21] Y. Zhou, K.M. Al-Hawaj and Z. Zhang. 2017. A New Approach to Automatic Memory Banking using Trace-Based Address Mining. In *FPGA*. IEEE, Monterey, CA.
[22] Y.T. Chen and J.H. Anderson. 2017. Automated Generation of Banked Memory Architectures in the High-Level Synthesis of Multi-Threaded Software. In *FPL*. IEEE, Ghent, Belgium.

Substream-Centric Maximum Matchings on FPGA

Maciej Besta, Marc Fischer, Tal Ben-Nun, Johannes De Fine Licht, Torsten Hoefler
Department of Computer Science, ETH Zurich

ABSTRACT

Developing high-performance and energy-efficient algorithms for maximum matchings is becoming increasingly important in social network analysis, computational sciences, scheduling, and others. In this work, we propose the first maximum matching algorithm designed for FPGAs; it is energy-efficient and has provable guarantees on accuracy, performance, and storage utilization. To achieve this, we forego popular graph processing paradigms, such as vertex-centric programming, that often entail large communication costs. Instead, we propose a *substream-centric* approach, in which the input stream of data is divided into substreams processed independently to enable more parallelism while lowering communication costs. We base our work on the *theory of streaming graph algorithms* and analyze 14 models and 28 algorithms. We use this analysis to provide theoretical underpinning that matches the physical constraints of FPGA platforms. Our algorithm delivers high performance (more than $4\times$ speedup over tuned parallel CPU variants), low memory, high accuracy, and effective usage of FPGA resources. The substream-centric approach could easily be extended to other algorithms to offer low-power and high-performance graph processing on FPGAs.

ACM Reference Format:
Maciej Besta, Marc Fischer, Tal Ben-Nun, Johannes De Fine Licht, Torsten Hoefler, Department of Computer Science, ETH Zurich . 2019. Substream-Centric Maximum Matchings on FPGA. In *The 2019 ACM/SIGDA International Symposium on Field-Programmable Gate Arrays (FPGA '19), February 24–26, 2019, Seaside, CA, USA*. ACM, New York, NY, USA, 10 pages. https://doi.org/10.1145/3289602.3293916

1 INTRODUCTION

Analyzing large graphs has become an important task. Example applications include investigating the structure of Internet links, analyzing relationships in social media, or capturing the behavior of proteins [2, 43]. There are various challenges related to the efficient processing of such graphs. One of the most prominent ones is the size of the graph datasets, reaching trillions of edges [13]. Another one is the fact that processing such graphs can be very power-hungry [4].

Deriving and approximating *maximum matchings* (MM) [9] are important and well-known graph problems. A matching in a graph is a set of edges that have no common vertices. Maximum matchings are used in computational sciences, image processing, VLSI design, or scheduling [9, 59]. For example, a matching of the carbon skeleton of an aromatic compound can be used to show the locations of double bonds in the chemical structure [59]. As deriving the exact MM is usually computationally expensive, significant focus has been placed on developing fast approximate solutions [17].

To enable high-performance graph processing, various schemes were proposed, such as vertex-centric approaches [24], streaming [54], and others [58]. These approaches have the advantage of being easily deployable in combination with the existing processing infrastructure such as Spark [62]. However, they were shown to be often inefficient [46] and they are not explicitly optimized for power-efficiency.

To enable power-efficient graph processing, several graph algorithms and paradigms for FPGAs were proposed [8, 18, 19, 23, 37, 48, 50, 61, 64–67]. Unfortunately, *none of them targets maximum matchings*. In addition, the established paradigms for designing graph algorithms that were ported to FPGAs, for example the vertex-centric paradigm, *are not straightforwardly applicable to the MM problem* [55].

In this work, we propose *the **first** design and implementation of approximating maximum matchings on FPGAs*. Our design is power-efficient *and* high-performance. For this, we forego the established vertex-centric paradigm that may result in complex MM codes [55]. Instead, basing on *streaming theory* [26], we propose a *substream-centric* FPGA design for deriving MM. In this approach, we ❶ divide the incoming stream of edges into *substreams*, ❷ process each substream independently, and ❸ merge these results to form the final algorithm outcome.

For highest power-efficiency, we execute phases ❶–❷ on the FPGA; both phases work in the streaming fashion and offer much parallelism, and we identify the FPGA as the best environment for these phases. Conversely, the final gathering phase, that usually takes < 1% of the total processing time as well as consumed power and exhibits little parallelism, is conducted on the CPU for highest performance.

To provide formal underpinning of our design and thus enable guarantees of correctness, memory usage, or performance, we base our work on the family of *streaming models* that were developed to tackle large graph sizes. A special case is the *semi-streaming model* [26], created specifically for graph processing. It assumes that the input is a sequence of edges (pairs of vertices), which can be accessed only sequentially in one direction, as a stream. The main memory (can be randomly accessed) is assumed to be of size $O(n\,\mathrm{polylog}(n))$[1] ($n$ is the number of vertices in the graph). Usually, only one pass over the input stream is allowed, but some algorithms assume a small (usually constant or logarithmic) number of passes. We investigate *a total of 14 streaming models* and *a total of 28 MM algorithms* created in these models, and use the insights from this investigation to develop our MM FPGA algorithm, ensuring both empirical speedups and provable guarantees on runtime, used memory, and correctness.

---

[1] $O(\mathrm{polylog}(n)) = O(\log^c(n))$ for some constant $c \in \mathbb{N}$

Towards these goals, we contribute:

- the first design and implementation of the maximum matching algorithm on FPGAs,
- an in-depth analysis of the potential of using streaming theory (14 models and 28 algorithms) for accelerating graph processing on FPGAs,
- a substream-centric paradigm that combines the advantages of semi-streaming theory and FPGA capabilities,
- detailed evaluation and high speedups over state-of-the-art baselines on both CPUs and FPGAs.

2 BACKGROUND AND NOTATION

We first present the necessary concepts.

2.1 Graph-Related Concepts

Graph Model We model an undirected graph G as a tuple (V, E); $V = \{v_1, ..., v_n\}$ is a set of vertices and $E \subseteq V \times V$ is a set of edges; $|V| = n$ and $|E| = m$. Vertex labels are $\{1, 2, ..., n\}$. If G is weighted, it is modeled by a tuple (V, E, w); $w(e)$ or $w(u, v)$ denote the weight of an edge $e = (u, v) \in E$. The maximum and minimum edge weight in G are denoted with w_{max} and w_{min}. G's adjacency matrix is denoted by A.

Compressed Sparse Row (CSR) In the well-known CSR format, A is represented with three arrays: *val*, *col*, and *row*. *val* contains all A's non-zeros (that correspond to G's edges) in the row major order. *col* contains the column index for each corresponding value in *val*. Finally, *row* contains starting indices in *val* (and *col*) of the beginning of each row in A. CSR is widely adopted for its simplicity and low memory footprint for sparse matrices.

Graph Matching A *matching* $M \subseteq E$ in a graph G is a set of edges that share no vertices. M is called *maximal* if it is no longer a matching once any edge not in M is added to it. M is *maximum* if there is no matching with more edges in it. Maximum matchings (MM) in unweighted graphs are called *maximum cardinality* matchings (MCM). Maximum matchings in weighted graphs are called *maximum weighted* matchings (MWM). Example matchings are illustrated in Figure 1.

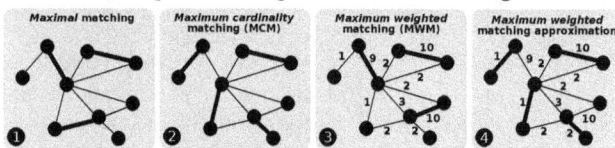

Figure 1: **Example matchings**. The edges in matchings are represented by bold lines, edge weights are represented with numbers.

Maximum Weighted Matching Given a weighted graph $G = (V, E, w)$, a maximum weighted matching is a matching M^*, such that its weight $w(M^*) = \sum_{e \in M^*} w(e)$ is maximized. An algorithm provides an ε-approximation of M^*, if – for any derived matching M – it holds that $w(M^*)/w(M) \leq \varepsilon$.

2.2 Architecture-Related Concepts

FPGAs FPGAs aim to combine the advantages of Application Specific Integrated Circuits (ASICs) and CPUs: they offer ASIC's high performance and low power usage, and they can be reconfigured to enable execution of arbitrary circuits. Usually, the FPGA clock frequency is $\approx$200MHz, dependent on the algorithm and the FPGA platform. This is an order of magnitude less compared to high-end CPUs (up to 4.7GHz [33])

and below GPUs (up to 1.5GHz [49]). However, due to the custom design deployed directly in hardware, multiple advantages such as low power consumption arise.

FPGA Components Configurable Logical Blocks (CLBs) [57], also known as Adaptive Logic Modules (ALMs) [60], implement the FPGA custom logic. To improve locality and reduce wiring overhead, CLBs are grouped together into clusters (called fabrics [57] or LABs [60]). Next, Block Random Access Memory (BRAM) allows to store small amounts of data (up to 20 kbits per BRAM [31]) and provides fast data access, acting similarly to a CPU cache. Usually, hundreds of BRAM units are distributed over a single FPGA.

FPGA+CPU Hybrid computation systems consist of a host CPU and an attached FPGA. First ❶, an FPGA can be added to the system as an accelerator; the host main memory is separated from the FPGA private DRAM memory and data must be transferred over PCIe. Often, the FPGA is configured as a PCIe endpoint with a direct memory access (DMA) controller, allowing to move data between the host and the FPGA without the need of CPU resources. PCIe is high-bandwidth oriented, but exhibits high overhead and latency for small packets [15]. This drawback is overcome by storing often accessed data in the private DRAM using the memory controller, or storing the data on chip in the FPGA's BRAM. Second ❷, the CPU and the FPGA can be directly linked by an interconnect, such as Intel's QuickPath Interconnect (QPI), providing a coherent view to a single shared main memory. Examples of these systems include Intel HARP [51] and the Xilinx Extensible Processing Platform [56]. The direct main memory access allows to share data without the need to copy it to the FPGA. To prevent direct physical main memory accesses, HARP provides a translation layer, allowing the FPGA to operate on virtual addresses. It is implemented in both hardware as a System Protocol Layer (SPL) and in software, for example as a part of the Centaur framework [52]. Moreover, a cache is available to reduce access time. According to Choi et al. [15], systems with direct interconnect exhibit lower latency and higher throughput than PCIe connected FPGAs. *In our substream-centric FPGA design for deriving MM, we use a hybrid CPU+FPGA system to take advantage of both the CPU and the FPGA in the context of graph processing.*

3 FROM SEMI-STREAMING TO FPGAS

We first summarize the analysis into the theory of streaming models and algorithms. We conducted the analysis to provide formal underpinning of our work and thus *ensure provable properties, for example correctness, approximation, or performance*. Towards this goal, *we analyzed 14 different models of streaming* (simple streaming [30], semi-streaming [26], insert-only [26], dynamic [5], vertex-arrival [16], adjacency-list [45], cash-register [47], Turnstile [47], sliding window [20], annotated streaming [11], StreamSort [3], W-Stream [22], on-line [38], and MapReduce [21]) and *28 different MM algorithms*. We present the full analysis in a separate report[2]. Here, we only provide the final outcome: the best candidates for adoption in the FPGA setting are ❶ **semi-streaming** graph algorithms that ❷ **expose parallelism by decomposing the**

---

[2]https://spcl.inf.ethz.ch/Parallel_Programming/Matchings-FPGA

Reference	Approx.	Space	#Passes	Wgh[1]	Gen[2]	Par[3]
[26]	1/2	$O(n)$	1	👎	⟳	👍
[41, Theorem 6]	$1/2 + 0.0071$	$O(n\,\mathrm{polylog}(n))$	2	👎	⟳	👍
[41, Theorem 2]	$1/2 + 0.003^{*}$	$O(n\,\mathrm{polylog}(n))$	1	👎	⟳	👍
[36, Theorem 1.1]	$O(\mathrm{polylog}(n))$	$O(\mathrm{polylog}(n))$	1	👎	⟳	⟳
[26, Theorem 1]	$2/3 - \varepsilon$	$O(n\log n)$	$O(\log(1/\varepsilon)/\varepsilon)$	👎	👎	👍
[6, Theorem 19]	$1 - \varepsilon$	$O\left(n\,\mathrm{polylog}(n)/\varepsilon^2\right)$	$O\left(\log\log(1/\varepsilon)/\varepsilon^2\right)$	👎	👎	👍
[41, Theorem 5]	$1/2 + 0.019$	$O(n\,\mathrm{polylog}(n))$	2	👎	👎	👍
[41, Theorem 1]	$1/2 + 0.005^{*}$	$O(n\log n)$	1	👎	👎	👍
[41, Theorem 4]	$1/2 + 0.0071^{*}$	$O(n\,\mathrm{polylog}(n))$	2	👎	👎	👍
[39]	$1 - 1/e$	$O(n\,\mathrm{polylog}(n))$	1	👎	👎	👍
[28, Theorem 20]	$1 - 1/e$	$O(n)$	1	👎	👎	👍
[35, Theorem 2]	$1 - \frac{e^{-k}k^{k-1}}{(k-1)!}$	$O(n)$	k	👎	👎	👍
[14]	1	$\tilde{O}\left(k^2\right)$	1	👎	⟳	⟳
[14]	$1/\varepsilon$	$\tilde{O}\left(n^2/\varepsilon^3\right)$	1	👎	⟳	⟳
[7, Theorem 1]	n^{ε}	$\tilde{O}\left(n^{2-3\varepsilon} + n^{1-\varepsilon}\right)$	1	👎	👎	⟳
[26, Theorem 2]	6	$O(n\log n)$	1	⟳	⟳	◌
[44, Theorem 3]	$2 + \varepsilon$	$O(n\,\mathrm{polylog}(n))$	$O(1)$	⟳	⟳	◌
[44, Theorem 3]	5.82	$O(n\,\mathrm{polylog}(n))$	1	⟳	⟳	◌
[63]	5.58	$O(n\,\mathrm{polylog}(n))$	1	⟳	⟳	◌
[25]	$4.911 + \varepsilon$	$O(n\,\mathrm{polylog}(n))$	1	⟳	⟳	◌
[29]	$3.5 + \varepsilon$	$O(n\,\mathrm{polylog}(n))$	1	⟳	⟳	◌
[53]	$2 + \varepsilon$	$O\left(n\log^2 n\right)$	1	⟳	⟳	◌
[27]	$2 + \varepsilon$	$O(n\log n)$	1	⟳	⟳	◌
[26, Section 3.2]	$2 + \varepsilon$	$O(n\log n)$	$O\left(\log_{1+\varepsilon/3} n\right)$	⟳	⟳	◌
[6, Theorem 28]	$\frac{1}{1-\varepsilon}$	$O\left(n\log(n)/\varepsilon^4\right)$	$O\left(\varepsilon^{-4}\log n\right)$	⟳	⟳	👍
[6, Theorem 22]	$\frac{1}{\frac{2}{3}(1-\varepsilon)}$	$O\left(n\left(\frac{\varepsilon\log n - \log\varepsilon}{\varepsilon^2}\right)\right)$	$O\left(\varepsilon^{-2}\log\left(\varepsilon^{-1}\right)\right)$	⟳	⟳	👍
[6, Theorem 22]	$\frac{1}{1-\varepsilon}$	$O\left(n\left(\frac{\varepsilon\log n - \log\varepsilon}{\varepsilon^2}\right)\right)$	$O\left(\varepsilon^{-2}\log\left(\varepsilon^{-1}\right)\right)$	⟳	👎	👍
[17]	$4 + \varepsilon$	$O(n\,\mathrm{polylog}(n))$	1	⟳	⟳	⟳

Table 1: (§ 3) **Comparison of algorithms for maximum matching.** *Approximation in expectation, [1]**Wgh**: accepted weighted graphs, [2]**Gen**: accepted general (non-bipartite) graphs, [3]**Par**: Potential for parallelization; k is the size of a given maximum matching. ⟳: A given feature is offered. 👎: A given feature is not offered. In the context of parallelization: ⟳: a given algorithm is based on a method that is easily parallelizable (e.g., sampling), 👍: a given algorithm uses a method that may be complex to parallelize (e.g., augmenting paths), ◌: it is unclear how to parallelize a given algorithm (e.g., it is based on a greedy approach).

incoming stream of edges for independent processing, for example the MM algorithm by Crouch and Stubbs [17].

3.1 Why Semi-Streaming?

The *semi-streaming model* [26] was created specifically for graph processing. It assumes that processing the incoming stream of edges can utilize at most $O(n\,\mathrm{polylog}(n))$ random memory. *Thus, algorithms under this model may address the limited FPGA BRAM capacity better than algorithms in models with weaker memory-related constraints.*

3.2 Which Semi-Streaming MM Algorithm?

Table 1 compares the considered semi-streaming and related MM algorithms. We identify those with properties suggesting an effective and versatile FPGA design: low space consumption, one pass, and applicability to general graphs. Finally, virtually all designed algorithms are approximate. Yet, as we show later (§ 5), in practice they deliver near-accurate results.

We conjecture that the majority of the considered MM algorithms deliver limited performance on FPGA because *their design is strictly sequential*: every edge in the incoming stream can only be processed after processing the previous edge in the stream is completed. However, we identify some algorithms that introduce a certain amount of parallelism. Here, we focus on the algorithm by Crouch and Stubbs [17], used as a basis for our FPGA design (last row of Table 1). We first outline this algorithm and then justify our selection.

Algorithm Intuition The MWM algorithm by Crouch and Stubbs [17] delivers a $(4 + \varepsilon)$-approximation of MWM. It

consists of two parts. In Part 1, one selects L subsets of the incoming (streamed) edges and computes a *maximum cardinality* matching for each such subset. In Part 2, the derived maximum matchings are combined into the final *maximum weighted matching*. The approach is visualized in Figure 2.

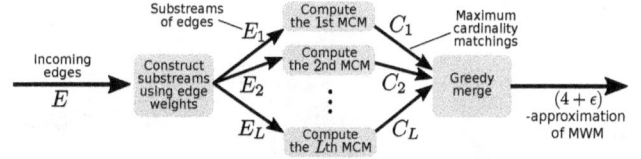

Figure 2: **The design of the MWM algorithm** of Crouch and Stubbs [17].

Algorithm Details The algorithm of Crouch and Stubbs [17] provides a $(4 + \varepsilon)$-approximation to the MWM problem assuming an unordered stream of incoming edges with possible graph updates (edge insertions). The basic idea is to reduce the MWM problem to $L \equiv O(\mathrm{polylog}(n))$ instances of the MCM problem. Given the input stream of incoming edges E, $O\left(\frac{1}{\varepsilon}\log n\right)$ many substreams are generated. Each substream E_i is created by filtering the edges according to their weight. Specifically, we have $E_i = \{e \in E \mid w(e) \geq (1+\varepsilon)^i\}$. Since an edge that belongs to substream $i + 1$ also belongs to substream i, it holds that $E_{i+1} \subseteq E_i$. Next, for each substream, an MCM C_i is constructed. The final $(4 + \varepsilon)$-approximation to MWM is greedily constructed by considering the edges of every C_i, in the descending order of i.

We select this algorithm as the basis of our substream-centric FPGA design because it ❶ can be straightforwardly parallelized, ❷ ensures only $O(n\,\mathrm{polylog}n)$ memory footprint as it belongs to the semi-streaming model, ❸ targets general weighted graphs, ❹ its structure matches well the design of a hybrid FPGA+CPU system: while substreams can be processed in parallel on the FPGA, the greedy sequential merging of substreams into the final MWM can be done on the CPU, and ❺ it requires only one pass over the streamed dataset of size $O(m + n)$, limiting expensive data transfers between the FPGA and DRAM. Now, we could not find other algorithms that would clearly satisfy all the above criteria simultaneously. However, we do not conclude that other algorithms are unsuitable for an efficient FPGA implementation, and leave developing such designs as future work.

3.3 How To Adapt Semi-Streaming to FPGAs?

In § 4, we describe the FPGA adaptation, design, and implementation of the selected semi-streaming MM algorithm. We stream the edges as stored in the CSR representation. Our substream-centric design implements a staged pipeline with throughput of up to one edge per cycle.

4 MAXIMUM MATCHING ON FPGA

We now describe the design and implementation of the substream-centric maximum matching for FPGAs.

4.1 Overview of the Algorithm

We start with a high-level overview of the MWM algorithm. A pseudo code is shown in Listing 1. For each edge, we iterate in the descending order of i over the L substreams, identifying them by their respective weights (Line 11). The

```
1  //Input: ε, E, L. Output: T (a (4+ε)-approximation of MWM).  I/O
2
3  //PART 1 (Stream processing): compute L maximum matchings
4  C: List of Lists; //L lists to store edges in L substreams
5  MB: Matrix; //The matching bits matrix of size L×n
6  substream_weights: List; //The list of substream weights;
7  //substream_weights[i] = (1+ε)^i.
8  has_added: bool; //Controlling adding an edge to only one MCM
9  foreach(WeightedEdge e : E) {
10   has_added = false;
11   for(i = L−1; i >= 0; i−−) {
12     if(e.weight >= substream_weights[i]) {
13       if(!MB[e.u][i] && !MB[e.v][i]) {
14         MB[e.u][i] = 1; MB[e.v][i] = 1;
15         if(!has_added) {//Add e only once to the matchings
16           C[i].add(e); has_added = true;
17  } } } }                                                    FPGA
18
19  //PART 2 (Post processing): combine L matchings into a MWM
20  T: List; //A list with the edges of the final MWM
21  tbits: List; //An array containing the matching bits of T
22  for(i = L−1; i >= 0; i−−) {
23    foreach(WeightedEdge e : C[i]) {
24      if(!tbits[e.u] && !tbits[e.v]) {
25        tbits[e.u] = 1; tbits[e.v] = 1;
26        T.add(e);
27  } } }
28  return T;                                                   CPU
```

Listing 1: (§ 4.1) **The high-level overview of the substream-centric MWM,** based on the scheme by Crouch and Stubbs [17]

```
1  //Input and Output: as in Listing 1.                         I/O
2
3  //PART 1 (Stream processing): compute L maximum matchings
4  for(Epoch k = 1; k <= ⌈n/K⌉; k++) {
5    Load u-matching bits from DRAM into double-buffered BRAM
6    Merge the K rows of edges (loaded from DRAM into one stream S)
7      with a merging network (Figure 4), apply lexicographic order
8    //Process each edge
9    foreach(WeightedEdge e : S) {
10     Matching bits requester loads matching bits (e.v) from DRAM
11     //Apply the 8 stage pipeline for each edge
12     Stage 1: extract v-matching bits from a data chunk,
13       determine BRAM address
14     Stage 2: load the matching bits for e.u from BRAM
15     Stage 3: wait for one cycle due to the latency of the BRAM
16     Stage 4: store the arriving BRAM data in a register, select
17       the correct matching bits, compute el[i] = e.w = (1+ε)^i
18     Stage 5: compute the matching
19     Stage 6: write u-matching bits to BRAM, write
20       v-matching bits to double-buffered BRAM if required
21     Stage 7: determine the least significant bit in te,
22       store them in variable i
23     Stage 8: write the edge to DRAM at C[i]
24       (if part of a matching), write v-matching bits to DRAM
25   }
26   Wait till all writes to DRAM are committed}                 FPGA
27
28  //PART 2 (Post processing): As in Listing 1.                 CPU
```

Listing 2: (§ 4.1–§ 4.4) The pseudocode of the substream-centric MWM algorithm, **enhanced with the blocking optimization and a lexicographic ordering.**

i-th substream weight is given by $(1+\varepsilon)^i$. For each maximum matching C_i, we use a bit matrix MB to track if a vertex has an incident edge to *ensure that C_i remains a matching* (i.e., that no two vertices share an edge). Bits included in MB are called *matching bits*. Bits in MB associated with a vertex u, *the source vertex of a processed edge*, (u-matching bits) determine if u has an incident edge included in some matching; they are included in column mb_u of matrix MB. Matching bits associated with vertex v, *the destination vertex of a processed edge*, (v-matching bits) track the incident edges of v; they are included in column mb_v of matrix MB. Since there are L matchings and n vertices, the bit matrix MB is a matrix of size $L \times n$. Furthermore, every matching stores its edges in a list. If an edge is added, a flag is set to true to prevent that the edge is added to multiple lists (Line 16). This reduces the runtime of the post-processing part, in which we iterate in the descending order over the L lists of edges to generate the $(4+\varepsilon)$-approximation to the maximum weighted matching.

Time & Space Complexity The space complexity is $O(nL)$ to track the matching bits, and $O(\min(m, n/2)L\log(n))$ to store the edges of L maximum matchings. The time complexity is $O(mL)$ for substream processing on the FPGA and $O(nL)$ for substream merging on the CPU, giving $O(mL + nL)$.

Reducing Data Transfer with Matching Bits Storage We assume that the input is streamed according to the CSR order corresponding to the input adjacency matrix. If we process a matrix row, we load the edges from DRAM to the FPGA. Further, we can store the matching bits mb_u of vertex u in BRAM on the FPGA, *since they are reused multiple times*. The matching bits of v are streamed in from DRAM. Since the matching bits for v are not used afterwards for the same matrix row, we write them back to DRAM. Using this approach, we can process the whole graph row by row and need to store only the u-matching bits in BRAM.

4.2 Blocking Design for More Performance

Problem of Data Dependency We cannot start processing the next row of the adjacency matrix until the last matching bits of the previous row have been written to DRAM, because we might require accessing the same v-matching bits again (read after write dependency). In such a design, the waiting time required after each row could grow, decreasing performance.

Solution with Blocking Rows We alleviate the data dependency by applying *blocking*. We merge K adjacent rows to become one stream; we call the merged stream of K rows an *epoch*, and denote the k-th epoch (starting counting from 1) as k. There are $\lceil n/K \rceil$ epochs in total. To enable merging the rows, we define a *lexicographic ordering* over all edges.

Lexicographic Ordering Let a tuple (u, v, w, k) denote an edge with vertices u, v, weight w, and associated epoch $k = \lfloor (u-1)/K \rfloor + 1$. Then, the lexicographic ordering is given by: $(u_a, v_a, w_a, k_a) < (u_b, v_b, w_b, k_b)$ iff $k_a < k_b \vee (k_a = k_b \wedge v_a < v_b) \vee (k_a = k_b \wedge v_a = v_b \wedge u_a < u_b)$; the edge weight is ignored. An example is in Figure 3 (top). The lexicographic ordering is implemented by a simple merging network.

Advantages of Blocking At the end of each epoch, v-matching bits are written to DRAM. This reduces the number of such transfers from n to n/K. Moreover, if edges in different rows share the same v-matching bits, only one load from DRAM is required. Finally, u-matching bits can be kept in BRAM, since they are reused multiple times.

Further Optimizations To achieve a performance of *up to one processed edge per cycle*, we pipeline the processed edges, we distribute the u-matching bits over multiple BRAMs (to facilitate reading data from different addresses), and we double buffer u-matching bits to reduce latencies.

4.3 Input and Output Format

The input to the FPGA algorithm is a custom variant of the Compressed Sparse Row (CSR) format. An example is given in Figure 3 (bottom). The format has two parts: The pointer_data and the graph_data. First, the pointer_data stores information about the start and end of each row of the adjacency matrix. An entry contains three parts: the ID of the *data chunk* with information about where the first edge is stored, the data chunk offset denoting the offset of the first edge from the start of the data chunk, and the number of associated edges (a data chunk refers to data of a given size at an aligned memory address). Each entry uses 32 bits, making an entry of the pointer_data 96 bits. We fit five entries (480 bits) in a data chunk. Second, the graph_data is a stream of edges. One entry consists of the column index and the edge weight. The row identifier is given by the corresponding entry in the pointer_data. One graph_data entry requires 64 bits, allowing to store eight edges in a data chunk.

Our custom data layout has different advantages over the usual CSR format. First, a single entry of the pointer_data already gives all required information about the start and length of the row of the adjacency matrix. This entails some redundancy compared to the traditional CSR, but only requires one load from DRAM to resolve a given edge. Further, CSR splits the column indices and values. We merge them together in one stream, reducing the number of random accesses.

The output of the FPGA consists of L substreams of edges. The i-th stream contains edges of the maximum matching C_i. We use 128 bits for each edge: 32 bits each for the vertex IDs, the edge weight, and the assigned index i of the maximum matching (which could be omitted). A single data chunk therefore contains four output edges.

4.4 Details of Processing Substreams on FPGA

We explain the interaction of the FPGA modules dedicated to generating the lexicographic ordering (Part 1) and computing the maximum matchings (Part 2); see Figure 4 and Listing 2.

4.4.1 Generating Lexicographic Ordering. As input to the FPGA, we get the address pointing to the start of pointer_data, the number of vertices n, the number of edges m, a pointer p_{out} where we write the output to, and an offset value o to distinguish the L output streams (start of output stream i is at $p_{out} + i \cdot o$). The **pointer requester** is responsible for requesting the data chunks holding the pointer_data. The requested pointers arrive at the **pointer receiver**. Given a data chunk, the pointer receiver unwraps the five pointers, and passes them to the **edge requester**. The pointer_data from the pointer receiver is passed to four different queues Q_0, Q_1, Q_2, Q_3, where

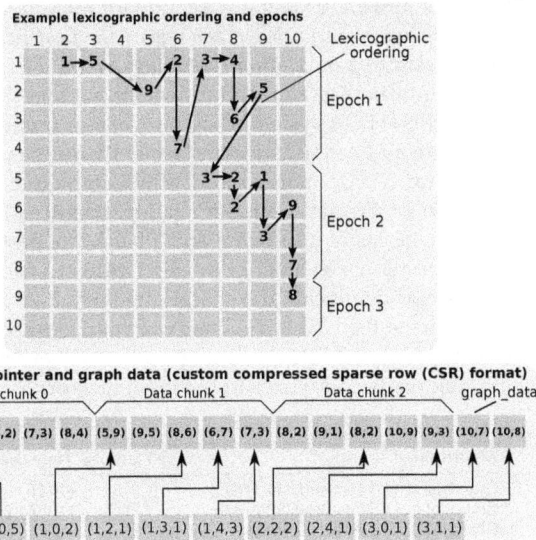

Example lexicographic ordering and epochs

Example pointer and graph data (custom compressed sparse row (CSR) format)

Figure 3: An example input adjacency matrix, its annotated lexicographic ordering illustrated by arrows ($K = 4$), and and its custom compressed sparse row (CSR) format. The entries of the adjacency matrix denote the weight of an edge.

every queue gets a subset of the pointers dependent on K. Assume for simplicity that the vertex IDs start at 0 and (K mod 4) = 0. Then, to be precise, given a pointer $p(u)$ pointing to row u, we assign $p(u)$ to Q_i if (u mod K) $\geq K/4 \cdot i \wedge (u$ mod K) $< K/4 \cdot (i+1)$. For example, with $K = 16$, Q_0 stores $p(u)$ with $u = 0, 1, 2, 3, 16, 17, 18, 19, 31 \ldots$, and Q_1 stores $p(u)$ with $u = 4, 5, 6, 7, 20, \ldots$. The pointer_data is loaded from the queues into a BRAM array BP of size K, where every entry holds two pointers ($2K$ pointers are therefore stored in total). If an entry i of BP has pointers $p(u')$ and $p(u'')$, it holds that $i = (u' \mod K) = (u'' \mod K)$ and $p(u'')$ requests edges for an epoch after $p(u')$. Therefore, only the first pointer in an entry is valid to use and we have random access to K valid pointers in total. To describe the mechanism that determines the selection of the next pointer to request new edges, we first inspect further processing steps.

The **edge receiver** gets data chunks containing graph_data from the framework and unwraps them (we use the Centaur framework [52] to access main memory independently of the CPU). Information regarding the offset and number of edges which are valid for a data chunk request is also passed from the edge requester to the edge receiver. Next, an edge $e = (u, v, w)$ is passed from the edge receiver to the **merger**. There, the edge is inserted in a *starting queue* (with ID (u mod K)). The merger merges the K streams in lexicographic ordering. It consists of a series of merging elements, where each element has two input queues and an output port. The element compares edges in its queues and outputs the edges according to the lexicographic ordering. The merging elements form a binary tree, such that for a given K, there are $K/2$ starting elements with K starting queues in total.

The edge requester can observe the size of the starting queues of the merger. It operates in two modes to determine a pointer to new edges. In mode 1, one selects a pointer $p(u)$ from queue Q_i as the next candidate if the corresponding starting (merger) queue (u mod K) does not overflow, and store the pointer in BRAM BP at position (u mod K). If mode 1 fails (for example, if there is no empty space at the appropriate position in BP), then mode 2 selects the pointer according to the merger starting queue which has the least amount of edges. Note that the edge requester also takes the requests which are in flight into account to predict the future size of the starting queue. This approach ensures that the merger queues do not overflow and their load is balanced.

For a row u which has no edges, a special information is passed from the edge requester to the edge receiver. It then inserts an artificial edge in the merger. This allows to overcome problems, where a merging element waits for new input, but does not receive any, since the adjacency matrix row is empty. The merging network filters these edges at the output port (they are not passed on).

4.4.2 Deriving L Maximum Matchings. The stream in lexicographic ordering is passed to the **matching bits requester**. This module requests the v-matching bits from DRAM. It can only operate when the bits of the epoch before have been acknowledged. Also, it only processes edges belonging to the current epoch which is defined by the **state controller**. The requested data is received in the **matching bits receiver**.

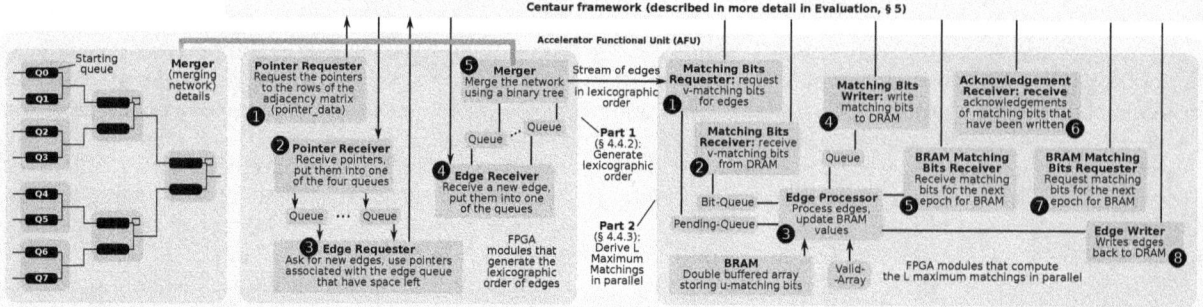

Figure 4: (§ 4.4) The **interaction of the FPGA modules** to approximate MWM. For clarity, the State Controller and the Read/Write Interface modules are omitted.

It passes the full data chunk to the **edge processor**. Using the matching bits and the ordered stream of edges, the edge processor computes the L maximum matchings in parallel in an 8-stage pipeline (Listing 2, Lines 10–24). In Stage 1, v-matching bits for a given edge are extracted from a data chunk. Further, the address of the u-matching bits in BRAM is computed. Since the more up-to-date v-matching bits might also be stored in BRAM, this address is also determined. In Stage 2, read requests to fetch the matching bits from BRAM are issued. Stage 3 only waits one clock cycle for BRAM to return the data. In Stage 4, the BRAM data arrives and is stored in a register. The stage also decides if v-matching bits are taken from the data chunk or from BRAM. Further, the stage computes the matching value te indicating if an edge $e = (u, v, w)$ belongs to substream E_i; $te[i] = w \geq (1 + \varepsilon)^i$ for $i \in \{0, \ldots, L - 1\}$. In Stage 5, the actual matching is computed. As the BRAM data from Stage 4 may already be obsolete, the computed values are also stored in registers for instant access in the next cycle. The result is passed to Stage 6, in which the updated u-matching bits (and if required also the v-matching bits) are written back to BRAM. In Stage 7, the maximum matching with the highest index, to which the edge is assigned, is determined. Finally, Stage 8 passes the edge to the **edge writer** to write it back to DRAM (if the edge is used in a matching) and also passes the updated v-matching bits to the **matching bits writer** for writing back to DRAM.

The BRAM storing the u-matching bits is double buffered. While the first BRAM buffer is used in the edge processor, the matching bits for the next epoch are loaded from DRAM to the second BRAM buffer. Since an epoch can alter the u-matching bits required for the next epoch, we write the according updates also in the double buffered BRAM if required. To prevent that stale data from DRAM overwrites the more up-to-date data, we use a register (the valid-array) as flag. After an epoch, the access is redirected to the BRAM containing the loaded data. The **BRAM matching bits requester** requests the according data from DRAM, and the **BRAM matching bits receiver** unwraps the data chunks. It passes the data to the edge processor. There, Stage 6 checks for data from the BRAM matching bits receiver and updates the according entry in the BRAM.

The **acknowledgement receiver** tracks the number of write acknowledgements from the framework and determines if all v-matching bits have been committed to DRAM when an epoch ends. When all edges from the epoch are processed, the state controller indicates the start of the next epoch.

4.5 Substream Merging on the CPU

After the L MCMs are written to DRAM, the CPU inspects them in the decreasing order to compute the final maximum matching $(4 + \varepsilon)$-approximation.

5 EVALUATION

We now illustrate the advantages of our hybrid (CPU+FPGA) MWM design and inspect resource and energy consumption. *For every benchmark, each tested algorithm was synthesized, routed, and executed on the hybrid FPGA platform specified below.*

Compared Algorithms Since to our best knowledge *no MWM algorithms for FPGAs are available*, we compare our design to three state-of-the-art CPU implementations. In total, we evaluate three CPU and two CPU+FPGA algorithms; see Table 2. First ❶, we implement a sequential CPU-only version of the substream-centric MWM, based on the scheme by Crouch and Stubbs [17], as presented in Listing 1 (CS-SEQ). Second ❷, we parallelize the algorithm with OpenMP's `parallel-for` statement to compute different maximum matchings in parallel (CS-PAR). Third ❸, we implement the algorithm by Ghaffari [27] (G-SEQ) that provides a $(2 + \varepsilon)$-approximation to MWM with time complexity of $O(m)$ and space complexity of $O(n \log(n))$ bits. Thus, this algorithm is optimal in the asymptotic time and space complexity. We compare these three algorithms to our optimized FPGA+CPU implementation, SC-OPT ❹ (SC-SIMPLE ❺ is consistently outperformed by SC-OPT and we thus usually exclude it for clarity of presentation). *To our best knowledge, we report the first performance data for deriving maximum matchings on the FPGA.*

Implementation Details We implement our algorithms on a hybrid CPU+FPGA system using the Centaur framework [52], which provides a standard interface to the Accelerator Functional Unit (AFU), the custom FPGA implementation, allowing to access main memory independently of the CPU. Centaur consists of a software and a hardware part. The software part allows to start and stop hardware functions, to allocate and deallocate the shared memory, and pass input parameters to the FPGA. The hardware part is responsible for bootstrapping the FPGA, setting up the QPI endpoint, and handling reads and writes to the main memory.

Algorithm	Platform	Time complexity
Crouch et al. [17] Sequential (CS-SEQ)	CPU	$O(mL + nL)$
Crouch et al. [17] Parallel (CS-PAR)	CPU	$O(mL/T + nL)$
Ghaffari [27] Sequential (G-SEQ)	CPU	$O(m)$
Substream-Centric, no blocking (SC-SIMPLE)	Hybrid	$O(m + nL^2)$
Substream-Centric, with blocking (SC-OPT)	Hybrid	$O(m + n/K + nL)$

Table 2: (§ 5) Overview of **the evaluated MWM algorithm implementations.**

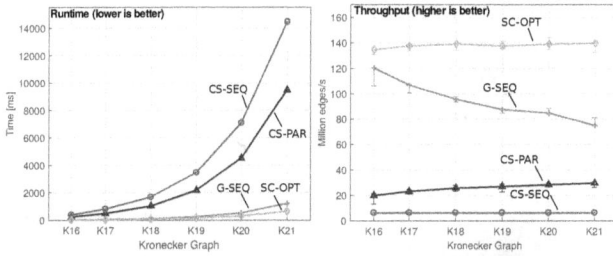

Figure 5: (§ 5.1) **Influence of graph size** n **on performance** (synthetic power-law graphs). $K = 32, L = 64, T = 4, \varepsilon = 0.1$.

Setup We use Intel HARP 2 [51], a hybrid CPU+FPGA system. It is a dual socket platform where one socket is occupied by an Intel Broadwell Xeon E5-2680 v4 CPU [32] with 14 cores (28 threads) with up to 3.3 GHz clock frequency. Each core has 32 KByte L1 cache and there is 35 MByte L3 cache in total. An Arria-10 FPGA is in the other socket. The used FPGA has speed grade 2 [34]. It provides 55 Mbit in 2,713 BRAM units and 427,200 ALMs. The FPGA is connected to the CPU by one QPI and two PCIe links. The system runs Ubuntu 16.04.3 LTS with kernel 4.4.0-96 as the operating system. All host code is compiled with gcc 5.4.0 and the -O3 compile flag.

Datasets The input graphs are shown in Table 3. We use both synthetic (Kronecker) power-law graphs of size up to $n = 2^{21}, m = 48n$ from the 10th DIMACS challenge [1] and real world KONECT [40] and SNAP [42] graphs. For unweighted graphs, we assigned weights uniformly at random with a fixed seed. The value range is given by $[1, (1 + \varepsilon)^{L-1} + 1]$.

Graph	Type	Reference	m	n
Kronecker	Synthetic power-law	DIMACS 10 [1]	$\approx 48n$	$2^k; k = 16, \ldots, 21$
Gowalla	Social network	KONECT [40]	950,327	196,591
Flickr	Social network	KONECT [40]	33,140,017	2,302,925
LiveJournal1	Social network	SNAP [42]	68,993,773	4,847,571
Orkut	Social network	KONECT [40]	117,184,899	3,072,441
Stanford	Hyperlink graph	KONECT [40]	2,312,497	281,903
Berkeley	Hyperlink graph	KONECT [40]	7,600,595	685,230
arXiv hep-th	Citation graph	KONECT [40]	352,807	27,770

Table 3: Selected used graph datasets. Kx denotes a Kronecker graph with 2^x vertices.

Measurements The runtime is measured by `clock_gettime` with parameter `CLOCK_MONOTONIC_RAW`, allowing the nanosecond resolution. The runtime of the FPGA implementations is determined by the Centaur framework. We execute each benchmark ten times to gather statistics and we use box plot entries to visualize data distributions.

5.1 Scaling Size of Synthetic Graphs

We first evaluate the impact from varying graph sizes (synthetic power-law Kronecker graphs), for the fixed amount of parallelism (the *weak scaling* experiment). The results are illustrated in Figure 5. The throughput for CS-SEQ and CS-PAR stays approximately constant below $\approx$12M edges/s. G-SEQ decreases in performance as the graph size increases. We conjecture that this is due to the increasing size of the hash map used to track pointers. This increases the time for inserts and deletes, and might also require re-allocations to increase the space. The performance for SC-OPT increases from $\approx$135M to $\approx$140M edges/s. This is because the initial (constant) overhead (due to reading from DRAM) becomes less significant with larger graphs. **We conclude that the substream-centric SC-OPT outperforms comparison targets for all consider sizes of power-law Kronecker graphs.**

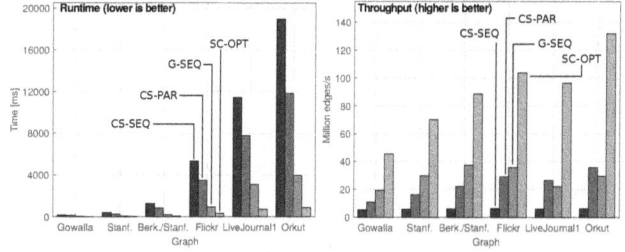

Figure 6: (§ 5.2) **Influence of graph dataset** G **on performance** (real-world graphs). $K = 32, L = 64, T = 4, \varepsilon = 0.1$.

5.2 Processing Different Real-World Graphs

We next analyze the performance of the considered designs for different real-world graphs; the results are illustrated in Figure 6. CS-SEQ and CS-PAR achieve sustained $\approx$3M edges/s and $\approx$10M edges/s, respectively. The performance of SC-OPT is $\approx$45M edges/s for small graphs due to the initial overhead of reading data from DRAM. Compared to the experiment with Kronecker graphs, the performance of both SC-OPT and G-SEQ is lower for all graphs except Orkut. The reason is the average vertex degree: it equals $\approx$48 in Kronecker graphs compared to $\approx$14 in Flickr and LiveJournal1. If the ratio is high, G-SEQ can drop many edges without further processing in an early phase. This reduces expensive updates to the hash map and lists. For SC-OPT, the waiting time (of data dependencies) lowers the performance. Still, **substream-centric SC-OPT ensures highest performance for all considered real-world graphs.**

5.3 Scaling Number of Threads T

In the CPU versions, one can compute in parallel different maximum matchings in SC-PAR using T threads. In the following, we run a *strong scaling* experiment (fixed graph size, varying T) for a power-law Kronecker graph. Figure 7 illustrates the results. Since G-SEQ and CS-SEQ are not multi-threaded, they do not scale with T. The parallelized CS-PAR reaches up to $\approx$40M edges/s, a $\approx 6\times$ improvement over the sequential version, and an $\approx 14\times$ improvement over the parallel version with one thread. Therefore, the algorithm is still $\approx 3\times$ slower than SC-OPT which achieves up to $\approx$140M edges/s on the K20 Kronecker graph. Scaling is limited since the parallel version takes L passes over the stream, whereas the other CPU algorithms process the input in one pass. The bandwidth usage of the parallel version with $T = 64$ threads is $\approx$32 GB/s ($\approx$44M edges and 64 passes in one second), assuming no data sharing. Note that we only parallelize the stream-processing part which computes the $L = 64$ maximum matchings. However, as our analysis shows that the post-processing part takes <1% of the computation time of the maximum matching, parallelization of post-processing would provide hardly any benefit. We conjecture that the scaling of SC-PAR stops due to bandwidth limitations and the limited computational resources of 14 cores. Finally, **SC-OPT is the fastest regardless of T used by other schemes.**

5.4 Approximation Analysis

We briefly analyze how well in practice SC-OPT approximates the exact MWM. The results are in Figure 8 (SC-OPT, SC-SIMPLE, CS-SEQ, and CS-PAR produce the same results).

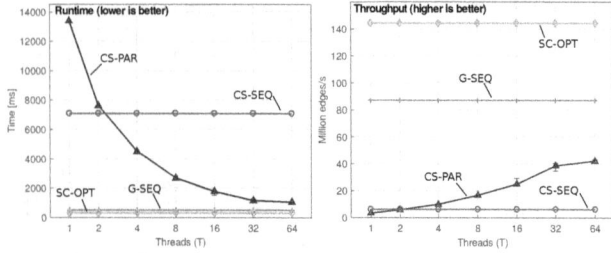

Figure 7: (§ 5.3) **Influence of the number of threads** T **on performance.** The input graph is Kronecker with $n = 2^{20}$, $K = 32$, $L = 64$, $\varepsilon = 0.1$.

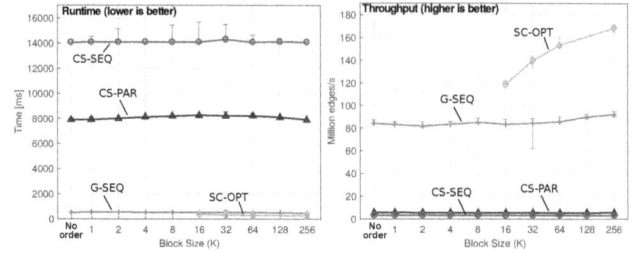

Figure 9: (§ 5.5) **Influence of epoch size** K **on the performance.** The input graph is Kronecker with $n = 2^{20}$, $L = 128$, $T = 4$, and $\varepsilon = 0.1$.

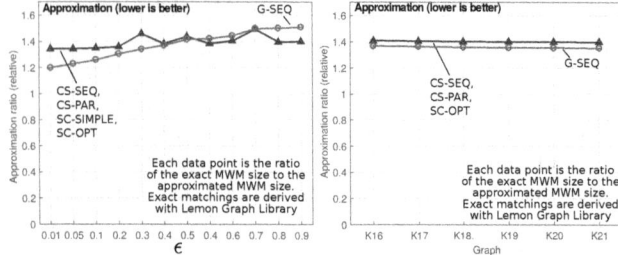

Figure 8: (§ 5.4) **Approximation analysis.** The input graph is Kronecker with $n = 2^{19}$ (left). $L = 128$, $T = 4$, and $\varepsilon = 0.1$ (right).

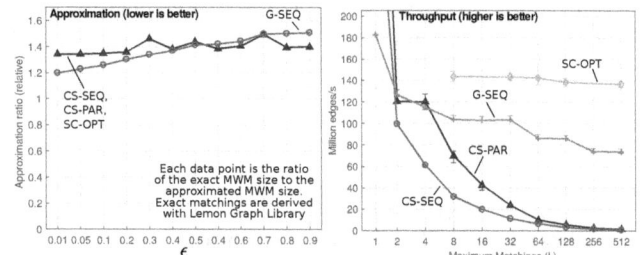

Figure 10: (§ 5.6) **Influence of** L **on performance.** The input graph is Kronecker ($n = 2^{20}$, $K = 32$, $T = 4$). As L changes, ε changes as follows: for $1 \leq L \leq 32$, we select $\varepsilon = 0.6$, for $64 \leq L \leq 128$ we select $\varepsilon = 0.1$, and for $256 \leq L \leq 512$ we select $\varepsilon = 0.03$; w_{max} is given by $w_{max} = (1 + \varepsilon)^L$. We restricted the range of L for SC-OPT due to the significant runtime required to generate different bitstreams for evaluation.

The accuracy is negligibly ($\approx 3\%$) lower than that of G-SEQ for a fixed ε and varying n (Kronecker graphs). The higher ε becomes, the more advantage over G-SEQ SC-OPT has. As higher ε entails less circuit complexity (fewer substreams are processed independently, assuming a fixed L [17]), **we conclude that the substream-centric MWM SC-OPT scheme provides better approximation than G-SEQ when physical resources become more constrained.**

5.5 Influence of Blocking Parameter K

We also analyze the performance impact from K, a parameter that determines how many rows in the streamed-in adjacency matrix are merged together using a lexicographic ordering. Figure 9 illustrates the results. On one hand, the CPU schemes cannot take significant advantage when K increases, showing that no cache locality is exploited. On the other hand, FPGA-based SC-OPT accelerates from ≈ 125M to ≈ 175M edges/s. This is up to $2\times$ faster than the work-optimal G-SEQ and up to $55\times$ faster than CS-SEQ. This is expected as the amount of stalling is reduced by a factor of n/K. Moreover, increasing K allows to share more matching bits between edges. The performance impact is reduced when K reaches 256. We conjecture this is because of the random access to the matching bits, approaching the peak random bandwidth. Furthermore, G-SEQ outperforms all other CPU implementations with up to ≈ 90M edges/s. Compared to CS-SEQ (≈ 3.15M edges/s) and CS-PAR (≈ 5.6M edges/s), this is $> 15\times$. Finally, parallelization comes with high overhead, such that the four threads in CS-PAR achieve less than $2\times$ speedup compared to CS-SEQ. **We conclude that our blocking scheme enables SC-OPT to achieve even higher speedups.**

5.6 Influence of Maximum Matching Count L

Finally, we analyze the impact of L on performance. L is the number of substreams and thus maximum matchings computed independently. CS-SEQ and CS-PAR achieve high performance with up to ≈ 400M edges/s for $L = 1$. The

performance drops linearly with L (X-axis has a logarithmic scale) to ≈ 800k edges/s for CS-SEQ and ≈ 1.3M edges/s for CS-PAR. G-SEQ also drops in performance as L increases due to ε and w_{max}. Since L increases, we also increase the range of the weight (L influences the approximation by $\varepsilon = \sqrt[L]{w_{max}} - 1$). Thus, for $L = 1$ the maximum edge weight is given by $w_{max} = 1$, allowing G-SEQ to drop many edges in an early phase. The drop of performance between $L = 32$ and $L = 64$ are due to a change in ε, requiring G-SEQ to store more data. Similarly, we change ε between $L = 128$ and $L = 256$. **SC-OPT keeps its performance at ≈ 140M edges/s (≈ 330ms) and outperforms other schemes.**

5.7 FPGA Resource Utilization

Table 4 shows the usage of FPGA resources. As maximum matchings are computed on the FPGA in one clock cycle, the number of computed matchings L influences the amount of used logic. Moreover, for SC-OPT, K and L determine the FPGA layout. Specifically, K influences the BRAM usage, since every element in the merging network requires two queues which are each mapped to one BRAM unit. We also consider the amount B [bits] of BRAM allocated to storing the matching bits. SC-OPT requires only 21% of Arria-10's BRAM and 32% out of all ALMs for a design that outperforms other targets by at least $\approx 2\times$ (Figures 9–10); these speedups can be increased even further by maximizing circuitry utilization.

FPGA Algorithm	Parameters	Used BRAM	Used ALMs
SC-SIMPLE	$\log B = 12$, $L = 8$	5.6 MBit (10%)	89,388 (21%)
SC-SIMPLE	$\log B = 18$, $L = 6$	21 MBit (38%)	88,920 (21%)
SC-OPT	$K = 32$, $L = 512$	11.5 MBit (21%)	151,998 (32%)
SC-OPT	$K = 256$, $L = 128$	24.8 MBit (45%)	350,556 (82%)

Table 4: (§ 5.7) **FPGA resource usage** for different parameters.

5.8 Energy Consumption

We estimate the energy consumption of SC-SIMPLE and SC-OPT using the Altera PowerPlay Power Analyzer Tool; see

Table 5. Furthermore, the host CPU (Broadwell Xeon E5-2680 v4) has TDP of 120 Watt [32] when all cores are in use. This is an upper bound for CS-PAR at $T = 64$. **FPGA designs reduce consumed energy by *at least* ≈88% compared to the CPU.**

Algorithm	Parameters	Energy Consumption [W]
SC-SIMPLE	$\log B = 18, L = 6$	14.714
SC-SIMPLE	$\log B = 12, L = 8$	14.598
SC-OPT	$K = 32, L = 512$	14.789
SC-OPT	$K = 256, L = 128$	14.789
SC-OPT	$K = 32, L = 64$	14.657
CS-PAR	$T = 64$	120

Table 5: (§ 5.8) **Estimated energy consumption for different parameters.**

5.9 Design Space Exploration

We now briefly analyze the interaction between the performance of our FPGA design and the limitations due to the clock frequency. The resource usage, determined by L and B, influences the frequency upper bound due to wiring and logic complexity. We applied a grid search to derive feasible frequencies for SC-SIMPLE; see Figure 11. Dark grey indicates 400MHz, light grey indicates 200MHz. Two factors have shown to limit the performance. First ❶, while computing the matching, we use an addition with a variable that uses L bits. Thus, the addition complexity grows linearly with L. More importantly ❷, the BRAM signal propagation limits the frequency. For example, for SC-SIMPLE and $\log B = 13$, the place and route report shows that the reset signal to set all BRAM units to zero becomes the critical path.

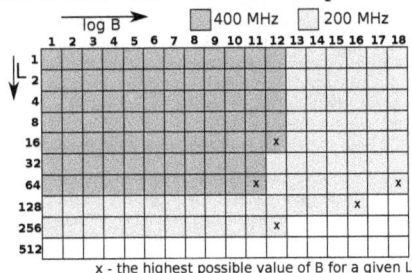

Figure 11: (§ 5.9) **Design space exploration: the used (available) frequencies.**

5.10 Optimality Analysis

We also discuss how far the obtained results are from the maximum achievable performance numbers; we focus on the most optimized SC-OPT. SC-OPT can process up to ≈175M edges/s. This is close to the optimum due to different reasons: Firstly, the implementation can process up to 1 edge per cycle (200M edges/s). Thus, the achieved performance is optimal within only ≈12%. Second, assuming that edges are read aligned from memory, it allows to read 8 edges per read request. Further, if every edge requires its own data chunk with matching bits, it needs 1 request per edge. Overall, this results in 1.25 read requests per edge. Under this assumption, the performance is limited to 160M edges/s. SC-OPT results are *higher* than this bound, which is possible because *the matching bits can be shared between edges.*

6 BEYOND SUBSTREAM-CENTRIC MM

We now briefly discuss how to apply our substream-centric FPGA design to other streaming graph algorithms. First, we identify some MM schemes that also divide the streamed dataset into substreams and can straightforwardly be adopted

to the hybrid CPU+FPGA system. The **MWM algorithm by Grigorescu et al. [29]** reduces the MWM problem to $O(\varepsilon^{-1} \log(n))$ instances of maximum matchings, which could be processed on the FPGA analogously to our design; its merging phase could also be executed on the CPU. All our optimizations, such as blocking, are applicable in this case. Moreover, the **MWM algorithm by Feigenbaum et al. [26, Algorithm 4]** does not divide the stream of edges into substreams, but its design would potentially allow for applying our blocking scheme. A key part of this algorithm is maintaining a certain value q_e associated with each edge e. Given an edge $e = (u, v, w)$, q_e depends on values q_u and q_v associated with vertices u and v. We can apply the blocking pattern by storing q_u for u in BRAM, and streaming in q_v for v. Next, the **MWM algorithm by Ghaffari [27]** provides a $(2 + \varepsilon)$-approximation. The algorithm compares the weights of incoming edges to values φ, indexed by u or v. Therefore, it can be computed on the FPGA using the blocking pattern by storing the values φ_u in BRAM, and streaming φ_v from DRAM, similarly to matching bits in our design. Further, as the algorithm requires postprocessing to derive the final result, it could be also delegated to the CPU.

We also identify algorithms unrelated to matching that could be enhanced with our design. The random **triangle counting algorithm by Buriol et al. [10]** is also a suitable candidate for the presented blocking pattern. The algorithm requires three passes. In pass 1, the number of paths of length two in the input graph is computed. In pass 2, a random path of length two is selected. In pass 3, the stream is searched for a certain edge, dependent on the randomly selected path. To reduce variance, passes 2–3 are run in parallel using a pre-determined number of random variables (up to a million). This also implies that in pass 3 every edge in the stream must be checked against a million edges. To reduce the workload, a hash map used. The map is filled with edges which are expected to occur. We propose the following approach to exploit the blocking pattern: the CPU fills a hash map for each epoch with edges expected to arrive. The map is passed to the FPGA. The edges for this epoch are streamed in and compared to the pre-filled hash map. If the epoch changes, the next hash map is passed over.

7 RELATED WORK

Our work touches on various areas. We now discuss related works, briefly summarizing the ones covered in previous sections (streaming models in § 3 and streaming maximum matching algorithms in § 3.2, Table 1, and § 6).

Graph Processing on FPGAs The FPGA community has recently gained interest in processing graphs on FPGAs. First, some established CPU-related schemes were ported to the FPGA setting, for example vertex-centric [23, 24], GAS [65], edge-centric [67], BSP [37], and MapReduce [64]. There are also efforts independent of the above, such as FPGP [18], ForeGraph [19], and others [8, 37, 48, 50, 61, 66]. These works target popular graph algorithms such as BFS or PageRank. *None of them proposes any scheme for the important problem of finding graph matchings, targeted in this work.*

Graph Matchings and FPGAs The only work related to matchings and FPGAs that we are aware of merely uses matchings to enhance FPGA segmentation design [12], *which is unrelated to deriving matchings and graph processing in general.*

Streaming Models and Algorithms We investigate the rich theory of streaming models [3, 5, 11, 16, 20–22, 26, 30, 38, 45, 47] and identify the semi-streaming model [26] as the best candidate for using together with FPGAs to deliver algorithms with provable properties that match FPGA characteristics such as limited memory. We then investigate semi-streaming algorithms for maximum matchings [6, 7, 14, 17, 25–29, 35, 36, 39, 41, 44, 53, 63] and identify the scheme by Crouch and Stubbs [17] that we use as the basis for our substream-centric design *that ensures low-power, high-performance, and high-accuracy general maximum weighted matchings on FPGAs.*

Hybrid FPGA+CPU Platforms Finally, our work is related to the study of hybrid CPU+FPGA platforms [52, 64]. We illustrate a case study with maximum matchings and show that *hybrid platforms can outperform state-of-the-art parallel CPU designs in both performance and power consumption.*

8 CONCLUSION

An important problem in today's graph processing is developing high-performance and energy-efficient algorithms for approximating maximum matchings. Towards this goal, we propose the first maximum matching algorithm for FPGAs. Our algorithm is *substream-centric*: the input stream is divided into substreams that are processed independently on the FPGA and merged into the final outcome on the CPU. This exposes parallelism while keeping communication costs low: only $O(m)$ data must be streamed from DRAM to the FPGA. Our algorithm is energy-efficient (88% less consumed energy over a tuned CPU variant) and provably accurate, fast (speedups of >4× over parallel CPU baselines), and memory-efficient ($O(n\log^c n)$ required storage).

The underlying FPGA design uses several novel optimizations, such as merging rows of the graph adjacency matrix and ordering resulting blocks lexicographically. This enables low utilization of FPGA resources (only 21% of Arria-10's BRAM and 32% out of all ALMs) while outperforming CPU baselines by at least ≈2×. Both the FPGA implementation and the substream-centric approach could be extended to other graph problems.

Finally, to the best of our knowledge, the proposed design is the first to combine the theory of streaming with the FPGA setting. Our insights coming from the analysis of 14 streaming models and 28 streaming matching algorithms can be used to develop more efficient FPGA designs.

Acknowledgements We thank Mohsen Ghaffari for inspiring discussions that helped us better understand graph streaming theory. We also thank David Sidler for his help with the FPGA infrastructure. Funded by the European Research Council (ERC) under the European Union's Horizon 2020 programme grant No. 678880. TBN is supported by the ETH Zurich Postdoctoral Fellowship and Marie Curie Actions for People COFUND program.

REFERENCES

[1] 10th DIMACS Challenge. Kronecker Generator Graphs, 2011.
[2] C. Aggarwal et al. Evolutionary network analysis: A survey. *CSUR*, 2014.
[3] G. Aggarwal et al. On the streaming model augmented with a sorting primitive. In *FOCS*, 2004.
[4] J. Ahn, S. Hong, S. Yoo, O. Mutlu, and K. Choi. A scalable processing-in-memory accelerator for parallel graph processing. *Computer Architecture News*, 2016.
[5] K. J. Ahn et al. Graph sketches: sparsification, spanners, and subgraphs. In *PODS*, 2012.
[6] K. J. Ahn and S. Guha. Linear programming in the semi-streaming model with application to the maximum matching problem. In *ICALP*, 2011.
[7] S. Assadi et al. Maximum matchings in dynamic graph streams and the simultaneous communication model. In *SODA*, 2016.
[8] B. Betkaoui et al. A framework for FPGA acceleration of large graph problems: Graphlet counting case study. In *FPT*, 2011.
[9] J. A. Bondy et al. *Graph theory with applications*. 1976.
[10] L. S. Buriol et al. Counting triangles in data streams. In *PODS*, 2006.
[11] A. Chakrabarti et al. Annotations in data streams. In *ICALP*, 2009.
[12] Y.-W. Chang et al. Graph matching-based algorithms for FPGA segmentation design. In *ICCAD*, 1998.
[13] A. Ching et al. One trillion edges: Graph processing at Facebook-scale. *VLDB*, 2015.
[14] R. Chitnis et al. Kernelization via sampling with applications to finding matchings and related problems in dynamic graph streams. In *SODA*, 2016.
[15] Y.-k. Choi, J. Cong, Z. Fang, Y. Hao, G. Reinman, and P. Wei. A quantitative analysis on microarchitectures of modern CPU-FPGA platforms. In *DAC*, 2016.
[16] G. Cormode et al. Independent sets in vertex-arrival streams. *arXiv:1807.08331*, 2018.
[17] M. Crouch and D. M. Stubbs. Improved streaming algorithms for weighted matching, via unweighted matching. In *LIPIcs-Leibniz Inf.*, 2014.
[18] G. Dai et al. FPGP: Graph Processing Framework on FPGA. In *FPGA*, 2016.
[19] G. Dai et al. ForeGraph: Exploring large-scale graph processing on multi-FPGA architecture. In *FPGA*, 2017.
[20] M. Datar et al. Maintaining stream statistics over sliding windows. *SIAM J. on Comp.*, 2002.
[21] J. Dean et al. MapReduce: simplified data processing on large clusters. *CACM*, 2008.
[22] C. Demetrescu et al. Trading off space for passes in graph streaming problems. *TALG*, 2009.
[23] N. Engelhardt and H. K.-H. So. Gravf: A vertex-centric distributed graph processing framework on FPGAs. In *FPL*, 2016.
[24] N. Engelhardt and H. K.-H. So. Vertex-centric Graph Processing on FPGA. In *FCCM*, 2016.
[25] L. Epstein et al. Improved approximation guarantees for weighted matching in the semi-streaming model. *J. on Discrete Mathematics*, 2011.
[26] J. Feigenbaum et al. On graph problems in a semi-streaming model. *Theoretical CS*, 2005.
[27] M. Ghaffari. Space-optimal semi-streaming for $(2 + \varepsilon)$-approximate matching. *arXiv:1701.03730*, 2017.
[28] A. Goel et al. On the communication and streaming complexity of maximum bipartite matching. In *SODA*, 2012.
[29] E. Grigorescu et al. Streaming weighted matchings: Optimal meets greedy. *arXiv:1608.01487*, 2016.
[30] M. R. Henzinger et al. Computing on data streams. *External Mem. Alg.*, 1998.
[31] Intel. Intel Core i7-8700K Processor, 2017.
[32] Intel. Intel Xeon Processor E5-2680 v4, 2017.
[33] Intel. Stratix 10 GX/SX Device Overview, 2017.
[34] Intel Arria. Intel Arria 10 Device Overview, 2017.
[35] M. Kapralov. Better bounds for matchings in the streaming model. In *SODA*, 2013.
[36] M. Kapralov. Approximating matching size from random streams. In *SODA*, 2014.
[37] N. Kapre. Custom FPGA-based soft-processors for sparse graph acceleration. In *ASAP*, 2015.
[38] C. Karande et al. Online bipartite matching with unknown distributions. In *STOC*, 2011.
[39] R. M. Karp et al. An optimal algorithm for on-line bipartite matching. In *STOC*, 1990.
[40] KONECT. Konect network dataset, 2017.
[41] C. Konrad et al. Maximum matching in semi-streaming with few passes. *APPROX-RANDOM*, 2012.
[42] J. Leskovec and A. Krevl. SNAP Datasets: Stanford large network dataset collection, 2014.
[43] A. Lumsdaine et al. Challenges in Parallel Graph Processing. *Par. Proc. Let.*, 2007.
[44] A. McGregor. Finding graph matchings in data streams. In *APPROX-RANDOM*, 2005.
[45] A. McGregor et al. Better algorithms for counting triangles in data streams. In *PODS*, 2016.
[46] F. McSherry et al. Scalability! but at what COST? In *HotOS*, 2015.
[47] S. Muthukrishnan et al. Data streams: Algorithms and applications. *Foundations and Trends® in Theoretical Computer Science*, 2005.
[48] E. Nurvitadhi et al. Graphgen: An FPGA framework for vertex-centric graph computation. In *FCCM*, 2014.
[49] NVidia. GEFORCE GTX 1080 Ti, 2017.
[50] T. Oguntebi et al. Graphops: A dataflow library for graph analytics acceleration. In *FPGA*, 2016.
[51] N. Oliver et al. A reconfigurable computing system based on a cache-coherent fabric. In *ReConFig*, 2011.
[52] M. Owaida et al. Centaur: A framework for hybrid CPU-FPGA databases. In *FCCM*, 2017.
[53] A. Paz and G. Schwartzman. A (2+epsilon)-approximation for maximum weight matching in the semi-streaming model. In *SODA*, 2017.
[54] A. Roy et al. X-stream: Edge-centric graph processing using streaming partitions. In *SOSP*, 2013.
[55] S. Salihoglu et al. Optimizing graph algorithms on Pregel-like systems. *VLDB*, 2014.
[56] M. Santarini. Zynq-7000 EPP sets stage for new era of innovations. *Xcell*, 2011.
[57] L. Shang et al. Dynamic power consumption in Virtex™-II FPGA family. In *FPGA*, 2002.
[58] Y. Simmhan et al. Goffish: A sub-graph centric framework for large-scale graph analytics. In *EuroPar*, 2014.
[59] N. Trinajstić et al. On some solved and unsolved problems of chemical graph theory. *International Journal of Quantum Chemistry*, 1986.
[60] J. Tyhach et al. Arria™ 10 device architecture. In *CICC*, 2015.
[61] G. Weisz et al. Graphgen for coram: Graph computation on FPGAs. In *CARL*, 2013.
[62] M. Zaharia et al. Apache Spark: a unified engine for big data processing. *CACM*, 2016.
[63] M. Zelke. Weighted matching in the semi-streaming model. *Algorithmica*, 62(1-2):1–20, 2012.
[64] J. Zhang et al. Boosting the performance of FPGA-based graph processor using hybrid memory cube: A case for breadth first search. In *FPGA*, 2017.
[65] J. Zhou et al. Tunao: A high-performance and energy-efficient reconfigurable accelerator for graph processing. In *CCGRID*, 2017.
[66] S. Zhou et al. High-throughput and energy-efficient graph processing on FPGA. *FCCM*, 2016.
[67] S. Zhou et al. Accelerating Graph Analytics on CPU-FPGA Heterogeneous Platform. *SBAC-PAD*, 2017.

Speculative Dataflow Circuits

Lana Josipović, Andrea Guerrieri, and Paolo Ienne
Ecole Polytechnique Fédérale de Lausanne (EPFL)
School of Computer and Communication Sciences
CH–1015 Lausanne, Switzerland

ABSTRACT

With FPGAs facing broader application domains, the conversion of imperative languages into dataflow circuits has been recently revamped as a way to overcome the conservatism of statically scheduled high-level synthesis. Apart from the ability to extract parallelism in irregular and control-dominated applications, dynamic scheduling opens a door to speculative execution, one of the most powerful ideas in computer architecture. Speculation allows executing certain operations before it is known whether they are correct or required: it can significantly increase fine-grain parallelism in loops where the condition takes many cycles to compute; it can also increase the performance of circuits limited by potential dependencies by assuming independence early on and by reverting to the correct execution if the prediction was wrong. In this work, we detail our methodology to enable tentative and reversible execution in dynamically scheduled dataflow circuits. We create a generic framework for handling speculation in dataflow circuits and show that our approach can achieve significant performance improvements over traditional circuit generation techniques.

ACM Reference Format:
Lana Josipović, Andrea Guerrieri, and Paolo Ienne. 2019. Speculative Dataflow Circuits. In *The 2019 ACM/SIGDA International Symposium on Field-Programmable Gate Arrays (FPGA '19), February 24–26, 2019, Seaside, CA, USA.* ACM, New York, NY, USA, 10 pages. https://doi.org/10.1145/3289602.3293914

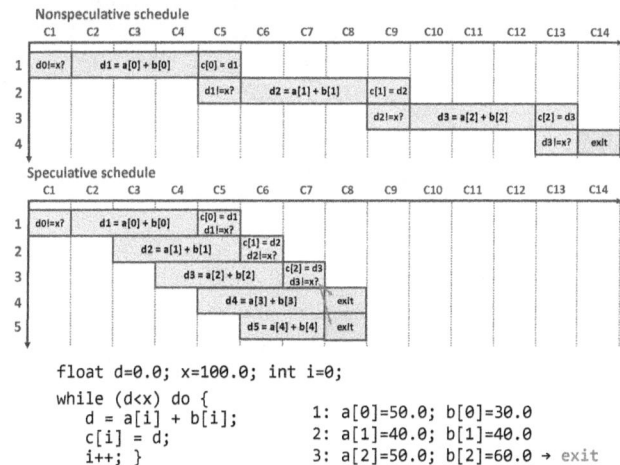

Figure 1: A nonspeculative schedule, compared to a schedule produced by a system supporting speculative behavior. The code below the schedules takes multiple clock cycles to compute the condition for executing another loop iteration. A nonspeculative circuit needs to wait for the condition, whereas the speculative circuit tentatively starts another iteration and then discards the newly computed values if they are later on determined unneeded.

1 INTRODUCTION

In the realm of processors, statically scheduled processors (usually referred to as *very long instruction word* or VLIW processors) have most suffered from the inability to accommodate arbitrary forms of speculative execution: Predicated execution (committing an instruction only if a specific condition is true) can be seen as a form of speculation when used to implement *if*-conversion (two branches of an *if-then-else* statement are both executed until the value of the condition is known). Yet, even aggressive predication is not applicable to every performance-critical control decision and Intel, as part of a failed attempt to develop a competitive general-purpose VLIW architecture, had to introduce a few dedicated speculative instructions (e.g., *advanced* and *speculative* loads [13]), de facto squeezing back into a statically scheduled processor some essential dynamic

behaviour. We believe that, analogously, statically scheduled circuits, such as those generated by common *high-level synthesis* (HLS) tools, cannot be competitive in some applications because of their inability to exploit broad classes of speculative execution.

On the other hand, part of the success of speculative execution in dynamically scheduled processors is the fact that a fairly limited set of universal techniques (i.e., register renaming, reordering buffers, and commit mechanisms) is sufficient to support speculation of virtually any critical decision worth predicting. Dataflow circuits are the spatial-computing equivalent of dynamically scheduled processors and can be generated by particular HLS tools; in this paper, we explore whether similarly broad classes of speculation can be easily supported in such circuits. We demonstrate that this indeed is possible, that it also needs a fairly small number of generic components and techniques, and that the advantage can be significant when waiting for a key execution decision is particularly time-consuming.

2 WHY HLS NEEDS SPECULATIVE BEHAVIOR

To illustrate the need to accommodate speculative behavior in circuits produced from imperative languages such as C, consider the code in Figure 1. A standard, nonspeculative HLS tool would not allow a new loop iteration to start until the condition to exit the loop has been checked—this condition is available only after performing almost the entire loop body, which largely prevents pipelining

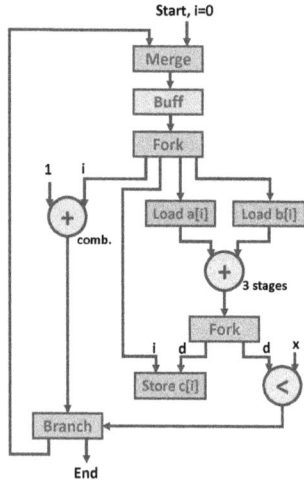

Figure 2: A dynamically scheduled circuit executing the code of Figure 1. All connections between components carry data with the corresponding bidirectional handshake signals. The Branch unit requires both the a value and a binary condition before it can issue the value it has received to the Merge unit and thus start a new iteration. Therefore, a condition which takes a long time to compute may significantly hinder performance.

of the loop. In contrast, speculation would make possible a high-throughput pipeline which tentatively starts another loop iteration on every clock cycle and, later on, discards the speculatively computed values if the loop was supposed to terminate prior to their execution (in the case of Figure 1, the addition results from the fourth and the fifth iteration are unneeded and will be discarded once this is decided by the termination check in cycle $C7$).

3 BACKGROUND ON DATAFLOW CIRCUITS

Dynamic scheduling is crucial to enable generic speculative behavior because the schedule needs to be adapted on the fly to any combination of prediction outcomes. Many dataflow or latency-insensitive protocols implement dynamically scheduled circuits, either using asynchronous or synchronous protocols; some have been used to produce circuits from imperative languages (e.g., Budiu et al. [2] and Josipović et al. [14]). In this work, without loss of generality, we choose the same handshake protocol used by Josipović et al. [14] because it leads to designs which can readily be implemented as synchronous circuits and thus directly compared to commercial tools for FPGAs. Our dataflow components communicate with their predecessors and successors using a pair of handshake signals and transfer data whenever the successor is available (passing a piece of data with the correct handshaking is colloquially referred to as exchanging a *token*). In this section, we provide an overview of the structure and properties of our circuits and describe the dataflow components that are most relevant for this work.

To produce our circuits, we follow pretty literally the methodology described by Josipović et al. [14]—and, in many respects, the exact topology is not critical for the modifications we will introduce. What matters is that our circuits are composed of subcircuits corresponding to *basic blocks* (BBs)—i.e., straight pieces of code with a single entry and single exit point. The body of each BB is a direct

translation of the dataflow graph into an interconnect of dataflow components. The control flow (i.e., the interconnections between BBs) is implemented using the following components: (1) A Merge unit propagates a token received on any of its inputs to its single output and is equivalent to *phi* nodes in the static single assignment form [19]. We allocate a Merge for every variable entering a BB. (2) A Branch unit propagates a token received at its single input to one of its multiple outputs based on a condition; it is used for implementing control flow statements. We place a Branch for every value exiting a BB and used by any successor BB.

The execution of our dataflow circuits is triggered by a start token that enters the initial BB. The token propagates through the BBs, following the control flow of the program, until it eventually arrives at the final BB, representing program completion. Although individual operations inside BBs are executed out of order, BBs are triggered in exactly the same order as the software execution of the unmodified original program. This way of building dataflow circuits implies three properties essential for the correctness of our speculative circuits: (1) **One token per loop.** On a cyclic path, there can be only a single token at a time (a token enters a BB on a cycle through a Merge; as this BB determines the next control flow decision, it is the only block that can send the token backwards into the Merge—i.e., there is no other active predecessor BB that could inject another token into this path). (2) **Strict token ordering on a path.** If there are multiple tokens on an acyclic path, they could only be injected into it by repeatedly forking at every passage the single token of a cycle and the propagation of this token in the cycle is determined by the in-order control flow decision. This means that tokens are inserted into the acyclic path in a deterministic order and nothing on this path can affect their ordering. (3) **Determinism.** Although our circuits contain nondeterministic components (e.g., Merge), the strict ordering of BBs guarantees that the execution is race-free: as tokens can enter the BB only from the single active predecessor, and no other source can inject tokens into the BB, there is nothing that can interfere with the token ordering at the BB input.

Figure 2 shows the dataflow circuit corresponding to the example in Figure 1; this simple program needs a single Branch and a single Merge node for the loop iterator i. The token carrying the iterator value is propagated to the next loop iteration whenever this is decided by the Branch condition (i.e., the comparison of the value d with x). Despite the flexibility of dynamic scheduling, if the condition takes a long time to compute (as it is the case here), the Branch unit will hold the token representing $i + 1$ until the token with the condition arrives, and the start of a new loop iteration will be delayed—speculative execution (in this case branch prediction and speculation) is needed to achieve an efficient pipeline.

4 SPECULATION IN DATAFLOW CIRCUITS

Our goal is to create a generic framework for handling speculation in dataflow circuits. The idea is that some components might be allowed to issue *speculative tokens*—that is, pieces of data which might or might not prove correct and which will combine with other (nonspeculative) tokens, resulting in more speculative tokens travelling through the circuit. In other words, speculative tokens trigger some computations which might have to be squashed and possibly repeated with the correct nonspeculative tokens. Figure 3

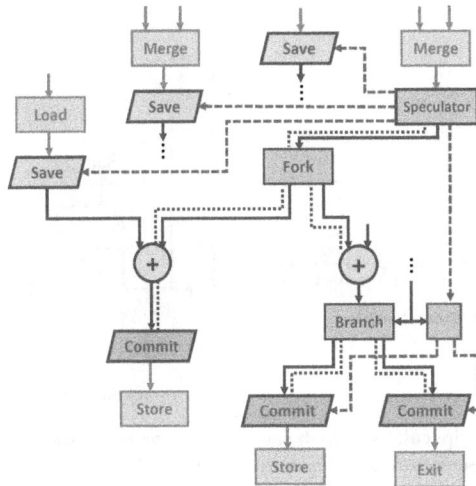

Figure 3: A region of a dataflow circuit implementing our speculative execution paradigm. The Speculator initiates the speculative execution by injecting tokens tentatively, Save units capture required inputs to the region to enable a correct replay in case of misspeculation, and Commit units prevent speculative tokens from affecting irreversibly the architectural state, such as memory. Speculative tokens are marked explicitly using an additional bit (represented by the dotted line). A dataflow control circuit (in red, dashed line) between the Speculator and the Save and Commit units carries information about speculative events (start, commit, squash, etc.).

gives a sense of our strategy: speculative tokens will be contained in a region of the circuit delimited by special components.

The first component is a *Speculator*. A Speculator is a special version of a regular dataflow component which, besides its standard functionality also has the liberty of injecting tokens before receiving any at its input(s). The most natural example is that of a Branch node which receives the value to dispatch but not the condition; a Branch Speculator could predict the missing condition and send tentatively the value through one of its outputs. If, after issuing a speculative token, the Speculator eventually receives the same data which it assumed speculatively (e.g., the condition it predicted), all is fine and execution was probably sped up; if, on the other hand, the data it eventually receives does not match the prediction, we have a case of misspeculation: the Speculator should now perform its function correctly (e.g., resend the value on the other output), but must first make sure that the speculative work done is discarded.

The reason for the output boundary of the speculative region of Figure 3 is fairly evident: clearly, speculative tokens cannot be allowed to propagate indefinitely and must not affect the architectural state of the circuit, that is the part of the state which is known and visible to the user. Therefore, the speculative region must be limited at least before components which store values in memory or before the end of the circuit. The components at the output end of the speculative region are called *Commit* units. These units simply let propagate further speculative results which turn out to be correct; much as it happens in speculative software processors, results due to misspeculation are simply squashed. Because Commit units must differentiate speculative from nonspeculative tokens (the former ones need explicit commit information before propagating,

while the latter ones can always go ahead), as Figure 3 suggests, all channels between the Speculator and the Commit units must be enriched with a control signal which indicates the speculativeness of the token being passed.

Finally, we need to bound the speculative region on the input side in order to save a copy of all regular tokens which may combine with a speculative token so as to be able to reissue them if the previous computation is squashed. We call these components *Save* units.

Section 5 details these new dataflow components and Section 6 describes how to correctly place them in the circuit. An important aspect of a speculative region, i.e., the communication between the speculative components, is only sketched in Figure 3: the Speculator should communicate with the Commit and Save units whenever it starts and stops a speculative event. We have elected to implement this communication through an additional dataflow circuit connecting all the new speculative units; while this communication is relatively straightforward (essentially, binary tokens indicating whether a speculation was successful or not), there are a few peculiarities to take into account when speculative tokens traverse Merge and Branch units. We will detail the construction of this control circuitry in Section 7. A critical situation, not represented in the qualitative example of Figure 3, occurs when the Speculator is placed on a loop: we will use an intuitive but too conservative approach in Section 6, likely to result in speculative circuits with little performance advantage, and then fully tackle this fundamental problem in Section 8.

5 COMPONENTS FOR SPECULATION

This section details the components needed to delimit a speculative region in a dataflow circuit: a Speculator to initiate the process, Save units on the inputs of the region, and Commit units on its outputs. The components are, in general, built out of standard dataflow components and they communicate with the rest of the design using the handshake protocol mentioned in Section 3.

5.1 Speculators

Speculative execution starts when a *Speculator* triggers the execution of a part of the circuit before it is certain that it needs to execute or that the execution is correct. Any dataflow component can operate as a Speculator by issuing *speculative tokens* before all of the component's input information is available (i.e., when only a subset of the input tokens is available at the inputs of the component). For instance, a Speculator Branch can speculate on the condition, causing the Branch to output the data token to one of its successors before the condition token arrives; a Speculator within a load-store queue can perform a speculative load and eagerly output a speculative data token as soon as the load address is available and before all memory dependencies are resolved.

Apart from issuing speculative tokens, the Speculator's role is to determine the correctness of a speculation and trigger actions accordingly. It therefore saves the prediction and assesses the situation once the missing input arrives. As the tokens propagate through the circuit strictly in order, the first token arriving at the particular input whose value was speculated will hold the value which resolves the first speculation. After deciding if the prediction was successful, the Speculator informs the appropriate units in the

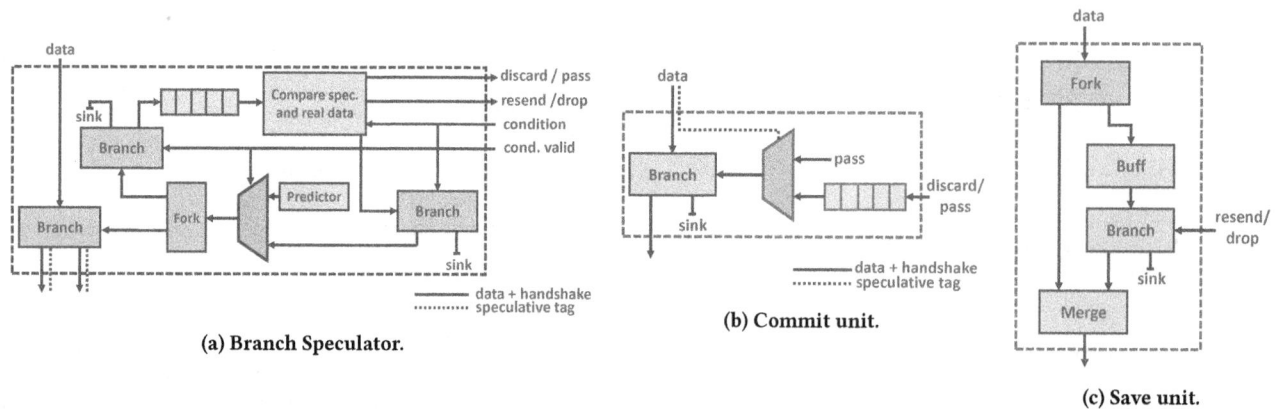

(a) Branch Speculator.

(b) Commit unit.

(c) Save unit.

Figure 4: Components for speculation. Figure 4a outlines the structure of a Branch Speculator, which can speculate on the branch condition and output a speculative data token. It later on determines the correctness of a speculation and communicates this information to the Save and Commit units. The Commit unit (Figure 4b) stalls speculative tokens until the correctness of the speculation has been determined. The Save unit of Figure 4c saves tokens that might interact with speculative ones to be able to replay the computations in case of a misspeculation.

circuit of the comparison result, allowing them to commit the speculative results or to discard the misspeculated tokens and recompute with the correct values. In the second case, the Speculator needs to insert the token holding the correct value into the circuit in order for the computations to execute anew.

The structure of one of the most natural Speculators, i.e. the Branch Speculator, is given in Figure 4a. Unlike a standard Branch, which waits for both the data and the condition to arrive before producing an output, the Branch Speculator can output a data token even when the condition is not yet present, together with a bit indicating whether the token is speculative. Eventually, it will receive a regular condition token, which it will compare with the previously speculated value (all speculatively issued values are stored in a queue within the Speculator) and send a confirmation or cancellation token to the other units. It will then either discard the real token (using the Branch subcomponent on the right of Figure 4a) or resend it into the circuit. The Speculator can issue a token only when its basic block is active, otherwise, there is no guarantee that the real token will eventually arrive to confirm or cancel the speculation (this is easy for a Branch Speculator because the arrival of a data token is a guarantee that the condition will also arrive).

Initially, we will discuss the case where only one speculative token at a time is issued into the circuit—i.e., a new speculation cannot start before the previous one has been resolved. While this is not a problem for pieces of code that do not need to repeat (i.e., speculating on a branch of an *if-else* statement), it could easily result in suboptimal performance if the Speculator is placed on a cyclic path (i.e., speculating on a loop termination condition). We will make necessary modifications to support multiple speculations from a single Speculator in Section 8.

5.2 Commit Unit

All dataflow components, apart from the Speculator, use a conservative firing rule—i.e., they produce tokens only once all of the required input operands become available. However, if one of the inputs to a dataflow component is a speculative token, the produced output token will become speculative as well—there is no guarantee

that the computed value or the decision made by the component is correct until the speculation is resolved by the Speculator. In case the speculation is incorrect, the component will output incorrect data or send a token in the wrong control flow direction: at some point, this misspeculated data will need to be discarded.

To this end, we use *Commit* units that stall speculative tokens until they receive the corresponding decision from the Speculator: in case the speculation is determined correct, the speculative tokens are converted into regular tokens and passed on to the rest of the circuit; otherwise, they are discarded by this unit. Any regular token that reaches the unit is unaffected and simply propagated through.

Figure 4b outlines the structure of the Commit unit. Data enters the unit through an internal Branch; depending on the value of the speculative bit, it is either directly passed on to the successor components (in case the data is nonspeculative), or stalled until the unit receives a decision from the Speculator. Assuming that the data path from the Speculator to this unit is long, the Speculator might issue and resolve multiple speculations before the data tokens arrive at the Commit unit. Hence, the unit contains a queue to save the decisions from the Speculator if they arrive before the data. As the tokens arrive in order on both paths, the timing relations of the two paths cannot influence correctness: the Commit unit will keep the first speculative piece of data on one path until the first confirmation or cancellation on the other path becomes available, and all tokens will be correctly matched. The output of the Commit unit is always a regular nonspeculative token.

5.3 Save Unit

In case a speculation is determined incorrect, speculative tokens are discarded and speculated computations need to reexecute with the correct values. This means that each nonspeculative token which at some point interacts with a speculative token needs to be appropriately saved until the speculation is confirmed or canceled. To this end, we use *Save* units which store the last token that passed through it until the Speculator determines the correctness of the speculation. In case the Speculator indicates that the speculation was correct or that it did not speculate on the saved values, the saved tokens are not needed and can be discarded—these values

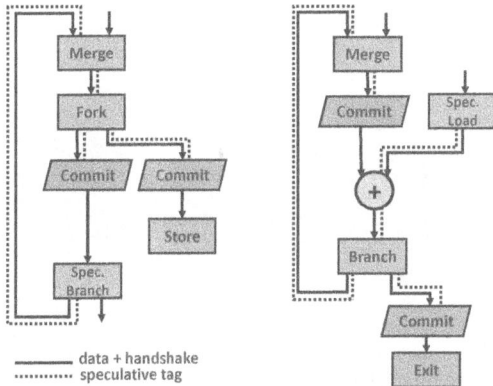

Figure 5: Placing Commit units. Our placement strategy ensures that memory is never modified by a speculative token, the program never terminates before speculation is resolved, and only nonspeculative values interact with components that might carry a speculative value.

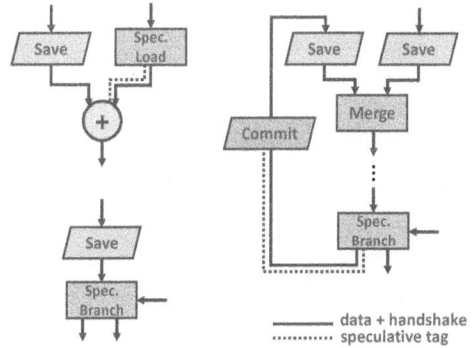

Figure 6: Placing Save units. Each token that interacts with a speculative token must be saved until the speculation is confirmed or canceled.

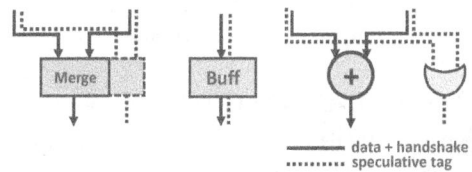

Figure 7: Extending dataflow components with a speculative tag. In most cases (e.g., Merge, Buffer, Fork), the tag is simply an additional bit propagated with the data. Components that combine multiple inputs into an output (e.g., arithmetic operations) require an OR to make the output speculative when any of the inputs is speculative.

have already been correctly propagated through the circuit and their interactions with any token issued by the Speculator produced correct results. On the other hand, if the speculation was incorrect, all Save units need to reinsert their saved token into the circuit to repeat the previously miscalculated computations.

The Save unit in Figure 4c takes a nonspeculative token as input and outputs a nonspeculative token. It requires only a single register for storing a token: for another token to arrive at the input (possible only if the unit is on a loop), the previous speculation must have been resolved and the old value inside the register has either already been reinserted into the circuit or determined unneeded and discarded through the Branch.

Note that the *discard* and *resend* outputs of the Speculator, connected to the Commit and Save units, respectively, are not equivalent: If a speculation does not occur, the Save unit still kept a token which needs to be thrown away—the Speculator must inform the unit when issuing a nonspeculative token. Commit units do not require any confirmation from the Speculator to let the nonspeculative tokens pass.

6 PLACING THE COMPONENTS

Every speculative region needs to be delimited with its own set of Commit and Save units: they ensure that misspeculated computations are appropriately squashed and replayed. This section shows where to place Commit and Save units into dataflow designs.

Every speculation needs to be resolved before terminating the program—that is, before a token reaches the Exit node. Furthermore, only regular tokens can be used for modifying memory (assuming that writes cannot be reverted) or as inputs to the Speculator (we will relax this constraint in Section 8). Therefore, we place a Commit unit on each path of the graph of dataflow components which starts at the Speculator and ends with the first of any of the following components encountered on the path: (1) an exit point of the graph; (2) the Speculator or a component carrying a speculative value; (3) a store unit. Figure 5 gives examples of correct placements of the Commit unit. Placing more than one Commit unit on a single path does not bring any benefit, as the first unit will always

resolve the speculation. The Commit units should be placed as far as possible from the Speculator, as this allows speculating on more computations and therefore increases performance in case the speculation was correct.

A Save unit is required whenever a regular token can interact with a speculative one, so the operations can reexecute in the case of a misspeculation. The following paths must contain a Save unit: (1) Each path from the start of the graph of dataflow components to any component that could combine the token with a speculative value. (2) Each cyclic path containing a Speculator or any component that could combine the token with speculative values. Since these cycles contain a Commit unit (as described in the previous section), the Save unit must be placed after it—this ensures that only regular tokens enter the Save unit, as any speculation will be previously resolved. Figure 6 shows examples of placing the Save units. To maximize performance (i.e., smaller number of correct computations to reexecute in case of a misspeculation) and minimize resource requirements (i.e., smaller number of Save units required), we place the Save units as close as possible to the end of these paths (i.e., as close as possible to the paths carrying speculative tokens).

As already suggested, the dataflow circuit between a Speculator and its Commit units needs to carry data with a speculative tag. This modification requires only a minor change to standard dataflow components: it is simply one more bit of payload which is propagated or OR'ed from all inputs to make the output is speculative when any of the inputs is speculative, as depicted in Figure 7.

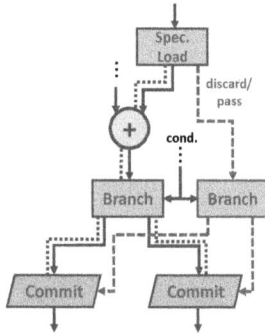

Figure 8: Connecting the Speculator to the Commit units. The cancellation or confirmation from the Speculator must be directed only to the Commit unit which is on the path of the misspeculated token. Otherwise, another token could be discarded incorrectly: if both Commit units in the figure were to receive a cancellation signal and the misspeculated token took the left branch, a correct token coming down the right branch would be eventually discarded.

7 CONNECTING THE COMPONENTS

When the Speculator determines the correctness of a speculation, it needs to inform the appropriate Save and Commit units. We add a specialized handshake network for this purpose.

7.1 Connecting the Speculator to the Commit Unit

The Speculator connects to the Commit units through a specialized network and informs them whether to discard or propagate speculative tokens. However, sending the decision to all Commit units would result in incorrect behavior. Consider the example in Figure 8: If a decision to discard the token due to a misspeculation is sent to both Commit units, and the misspeculated token takes the left output of the Branch, another token taking the right Branch output later on would be incorrectly discarded. Therefore, the information from the Speculator needs to be sent only to the units that were on the actual path taken by the speculative tokens. In such cases, we place Branches on the path connecting the Speculator and the Commit unit which receive the same conditions as the regular Branches of the dataflow circuit. Whenever a speculative token passes, the Branch in the specialized network will mimic the control flow decision took by the data token and thus correctly direct the information from the Speculator to one of the Commit units.

7.2 Connecting the Speculator to the Save Unit

The complementary problem arises when connecting the Save units—only some of them hold tokens that need to be resent to the circuit. Consider the example in Figure 9, where the Save units are placed before a Merge node. If the speculation is determined incorrect, only one of the Save units should reissue a token—however, there is nothing that can determine which of the two Save units holds the direct predecessor (i.e., which token needs to be reissued). Therefore, Merges that are on the path from the Save units to the Speculator need to remember which side a token came from. The Speculator uses this information to correctly direct the confirmation/cancellation to the proper Save unit. The dispatching is

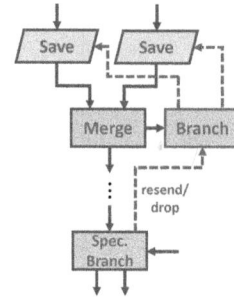

Figure 9: Connecting the Speculator to the Save units. Any Merge that is on the path from the Save units to the Speculator should memorize where tokens came from so that the Speculator can send the correct resend or discard message to the appropriate Save unit.

implemented in the specialized network as a Branch which takes the Speculator decision as data and the information from the original Merge as the condition and forwards the decision accordingly.

8 MULTIPLE SPECULATIONS FROM A SINGLE SPECULATOR

The approach described so far does not bring significant performance benefit when speculation occurs in a loop, as it requires us to conservatively wait for one speculation to end to be able to trigger a new one. This section discusses the modifications needed to increase loop parallelism.

8.1 Merging the Save and Commit Unit

In points where Save and Commit units meet, the approach taken so far allowed a new token to enter the Save unit only after the Commit unit sent out a confirmed token. Thus, all speculations through cyclic paths are sequentialized, which prevents us from achieving a high-throughput pipeline. Figure 10a shows the circuit from Figure 2 modified with the speculative components and the strategies described in the previous sections (note that the speculative tags are omitted for graphical simplicity). A nonspeculative token enters the Merge through the starting point (labeled as point 1 in the figure), passes through the Commit and Save unit (as it is nonspeculative) and reaches the Speculator (point 2). The Speculator issues a speculative value back through the Merge and into the Commit unit (point 3), which stalls the token until the condition reaches the Speculator and it informs the Commit unit of the correctness of the speculation—only then does the token pass through to the Speculator again, triggering the start of a new speculation.

Whenever a Save and Commit unit meet on a cyclic path, we can merge them into a single unit which allows issuing a speculative token even before the previous speculation has been resolved. The *Save-Commit unit* (Figure 10c) performs the combined functionality of both units: as a Save unit, it issues regular tokens to restart computations or discards them when they are no longer needed; as a Commit unit, it turns speculative tokens into regular ones or discards speculative tokens. However, unlike a regular Commit unit, this unit will also let speculative tokens pass to the successors; it will save all the tokens, corresponding to regular or speculated data from multiple loop iterations, until they are no longer needed. We

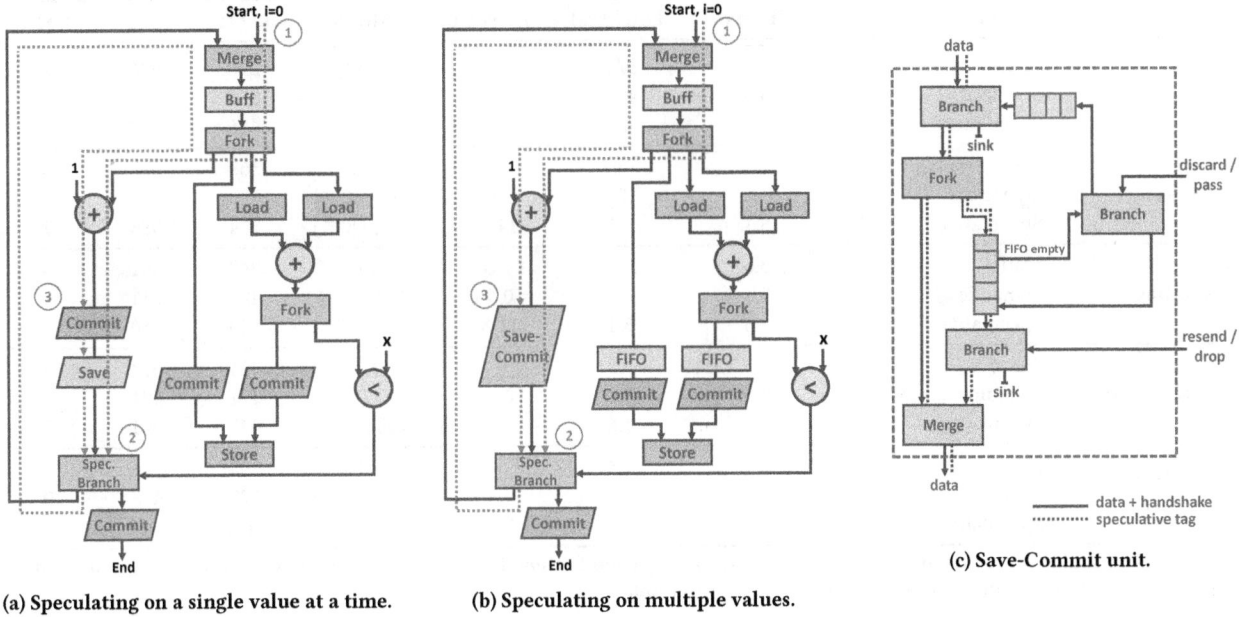

(a) Speculating on a single value at a time.   (b) Speculating on multiple values.   (c) Save-Commit unit.

Figure 10: Enabling multiple speculations from a single Speculator in the example from Figure 2. Our strategy from Section 5 results in suboptimal behavior when the speculation occurs in a loop: as Figure 10a shows, a token that is speculatively inserted into the loop will be stalled in the Commit unit (point 3 in the figure) until the speculation is resolved, preventing the triggering of a new speculation. Merging the Save and Commit units on the loop into a single unit (Figure 10b) allows issuing a new speculative token before the previous speculation has been resolved. The structure of the Save-Commit unit is illustrated in Figure 10c.

exploit the fact that the tokens are stored in the unit in order, as well as that the decisions arrive in order from the Speculator—this allows us to easily match every decision to a token queued in this unit. The action of reissuing or discarding token (usually performed by a Save unit) will be applied on the oldest stored token, which will then be discarded or reissued and, in both cases, removed from the unit as it is no longer required. If the Speculator informs the unit that a speculation was correct, the oldest token will be removed from the unit and its speculative successor will be transformed into a regular token. If the Speculator sends a decision to discard a misspeculated token, the oldest speculative token will be discarded. The Speculator will issue cancellations for each speculative token produced after the first misspeculation and each will discard one of the queued tokens. If the data tokens to cancel are not yet available, the cancellations are queued in a dedicated FIFO and the data is discarded as soon as it enters the unit.

Figure 10b shows the circuit of Figure 10a where the Save and Commit unit on the loop has been replaced with a combined Save-Commit unit. As before, the token enters through the Merge (point 1 in the figure) and is sent to the Speculator. The Speculator issues a speculative token (point 2), which is stored in the Save-Commit unit (point 3), but also immediately propagated to the Speculator to trigger another speculation, hence finally resulting in the high-throughput pipeline achieving the lower schedule of Figure 1.

8.2 Connecting the Speculator to the Save-Commit Unit

There are two paths connecting the Save-Commit unit and the Speculator, and both could contain control flow decisions: the one from

the Save-Commit output to the Speculator could contain Merges (exactly like the path from the Save unit to the Speculator in Figure 9), and the one from the Speculator to the Save-Commit input could contain Branches (same as the paths to the Commit units depicted in Figure 8). Therefore, as in the previous cases, our network dedicated for sending decisions to this unit will have to collect the control flow information from the original circuit to ensure that decision tokens are distributed the correct way. The principle is exactly the same as for connecting the Speculator to the Save and Commit units; however, each control flow point will now have to hold multiple control flow decisions (as many as the Save-Commit unit can accommodate tokens). Whenever the Speculator sends a decision, the oldest queued condition will be used and discarded. This ensures that every unit is correctly informed of the speculation.

9 SPECULATIONS FROM MULTIPLE SPECULATORS

The methodology discussed in the previous section describes a circuit with only one Speculator issuing speculative tokens. Our approach can easily be extended to support multiple Speculators in the design. The Save and Commit units and their placement strategy would be exactly the same; the only difference is that each speculative token needs to be tagged to keep track of the speculation origin—this enables each Commit unit to properly handle speculative tokens (i.e., each Commit unit should consider as speculative only the tokens from the Speculator it is connected to; all speculative tokens of a different origin should be treated as nonspeculative).

Benchmark	Design	II	CP (ns)	Time (μs)	Speedup	Slices	LUTs	FFs	DSPs
While loop	Static	11	3.7	37.4		130	270	436	2
	Dynamic	12	4.4	48.8	0.8×	129 (-1%)	353	511	2
	Speculative	~ 1	4.8	4.5	8.3×	186 (+43%)	486	582	2
Backtrack	Static	21	3.7	76.2		175	353	625	5
	Dynamic	22	3.5	75.6	1.0×	251 (+43%)	555	859	7
	Speculative	~ 1	5.1	5.1	14.9×	320 (+82%)	774	956	7
Subdiagonal	Static	17	3.6	60.0		164	342	591	5
	Dynamic	18	3.6	64.0	0.9×	179 (+9%)	424	611	5
	Speculative	~ 1	4.6	5.1	11.8×	233 (+42%)	559	650	5
Fixed point	Static	15	3.3	3.3		187	354	573	5
	Dynamic	17	3.3	3.8	0.9×	177 (-5%)	371	581	5
	Speculative	~ 6	3.8	1.6	2.1×	198 (+6%)	477	601	5
Newton-Raphson	Static	8	5.4	4.3		201	585	636	9
	Dynamic	10	5.0	5.1	0.8×	234 (+16%)	775	498	9
	Speculative	~ 1	5.5	0.6	7.2×	348 (+73%)	1181	603	9

Table 1: Timing and resource requirements for the benchmarks from Section 10.1: static scheduling (Vivado HLS), dynamic scheduling (Josipović et al. [14]), and dynamic scheduling featuring speculation.

10 EVALUATION

We compare static and dynamic implementations of various realistic kernels. The statically-scheduled baselines (indicated as *static*) are obtained using a commercial tool (Vivado HLS [20]). We compare them with dynamic designs automatically produced from C code using the methodology described by Josipović et al. [14], which results in nonspeculative circuits like that of Figure 2; we indicate the dynamically-scheduled references as *dynamic*. Finally, we manually modify these circuits with the speculative components presented in this work to obtain circuits as in Figure 10b, which are the main result of this work and are indicated as *speculative*. Although our speculative methodology is perfectly general, in our examples we speculate on a single control flow decision using Branch Speculators from Figure 4a. The Speculators contain a static predictor that assumes the branch always taken whenever the input data becomes available. Each design contains as many Speculators as there are variables which need to be speculatively issued to the successor basic block. All designs use identical floating point and integer arithmetic units and connect to the exact same RAM interface as the baseline designs from Vivado HLS. We use simulations in ModelSim [16] for functional verification and for measuring the loop initiation intervals (*II*). We synthesize the designs with Vivado to obtain the clock period from the post-routing timing analysis and the resource usage from placing and routing the designs.

10.1 Benchmarks

The designs that we consider in this section represent typical cases which can profit by branch prediction and where speculative execution should bring significant performance benefits over conservative, static scheduling. The benchmark loops are derived from real applications which can be found in literature [18].

- *While loop* is the kernel from Figure 1. The dynamic design results in the circuit of Figure 2 which we extend with speculative components to obtain the circuit of Figure 10b.

- *Backtrack* is the inner loop of the backtracking pass of the Bellman-Dijkstra-Viterbi algorithm. After labeling each state with the minimum cost to reach it, the backtracking pass looks for a unique set of edges that produce the global minimum. The states are traversed in a *for* loop which breaks when the predecessor state with the minimum cost is found. The *break* statement prevents loop pipelining, as the static tool starts a new loop iteration only after the break condition from the previous iteration has been determined false.

- *Subdiagonal* is an inner loop of a QL algorithm for determining the eigenvalues of a tridiagonal matrix. The loop looks for a single small subdiagonal element to split the matrix and contains a conditional *break* inside the loop body to return the correct subdiagonal index. As the condition for the return takes a long time to compute, it prevents static scheduling from efficiently pipelining the loop.

- *Fixed point* is an iteration method for finding the real roots of a function. It consists of a *while* loop which iterates through a sequence of improving approximate solutions until the desired degree of accuracy is achieved. Static scheduling postpones the start of a new iteration until the error computation from the previous iteration has been completed.

- *Newton-Raphson* is a hybrid algorithm of bisection and the Newton-Raphson method for finding the roots of a function. The hybrid algorithm takes a bisection step whenever Newton-Raphson would take the solution out of bounds and therefore improves the convergence properties of the algorithm over the standard Newton-Raphson method. The algorithm contains a *for* loop with an *if-else* statement to determine which of the two methods to use for a particular data point. Static predication is limited by the complex *if* condition and, as the next loop iteration requires the data computed in the current one, it must be scheduled for after the condition has been determined.

```
int i = 0;
int s = 1;

for (i = 0; i < 12; i++){
    if (x[i]*s >= 1000)
        s+=1;
}
```

Figure 11: Code used for the analysis of Section 10.3, qualitatively similar to the Newton-Raphson benchmark.

Design	II	CP (ns)	Time (μs)	Slice	LUT	FF	DSP
Static	1	5.7	0.1	1281	2088	5311	24
Dyn.	6	4.3	0.3	65	163	156	3
Spec.	2.3	5.3	0.2	154	481	301	3

Table 2: Timing and resource requirements for the static (Vivado HLS), dynamic (Josipović et al. [14]), and speculative implementation of the loop from Figure 11. The code given to the static tool was restructured to produce an aggressively-predicated schedule.

10.2 Results

Table 1 reports the timing and resource requirements of our experiments. The static scheduler constructs a conservative schedule which prevents almost any pipelining of these loops because it waits for the condition to be determined before starting a new loop iteration. In spite of the flexibility of dynamic circuits, dynamic scheduling alone does not suffice to achieve high parallelism for the exact same reason as the static schedule does not: a new loop iteration is delayed until the previous decision has been determined—i.e., the Branch waits for the condition token to arrive before propagating a data token backwards into the loop body. In contrast, the Speculator in the final design issues speculative tokens into the loop as soon as the input data becomes available and enables achieving the ideal loop initiation interval. Note that the speculative initiation interval II_{spec} is, in fact, a weighted average of the value in case of good prediction and of that for a misprediction. For all circuits but *Newton-Raphson*, there is a single misprediction when the loop is exited and therefore the average II is for all practical purposes exactly the one in Table 1. Note that $II_{spec} \approx 1$ for all benchmarks but *Fixed point*: in this case, the input data to the Branch takes 6 cycles to compute, therefore limiting the maximum issue rate of speculative tokens. The resource increase and the longer critical path (CP) are due to the additional components for speculation and the FIFOs that we added to achieve maximum parallelism.

Although the table indicates $II_{spec} \approx 1$ for *Newton-Raphson*, the situation is slightly different than in the other benchmarks: in this case, the misprediction is not an event happening only once per loop execution, but every time a bisection step is taken. The actual II is therefore data dependent but still close to 1, as the bisection step is meant to be a relatively rare event. It is worth noting that our circuits do not have any additional penalty for misprediction other than incurring the longer latency of the corresponding dynamic nonspeculative circuit. Therefore, in general and to a first-order approximation (because we ignore the difference in critical path), our circuits would perform better than a static circuit whenever the prediction accuracy $p_{correct}$ is such that $p_{correct} \cdot II_{spec\_opt} + (1 - p_{correct}) \cdot II_{nonspec} < II_{static}$. To put this in perspective using this example and again ignoring the CP difference, our circuit needs here only $p_{correct} > 22\%$ to perform better, and this branch prediction accuracy is massively below typical achievable rates.

10.3 Analysis

It is clear from Table 1 that the use of a dynamically scheduled paradigm has a nonnegligible cost in resources (already pointed out by Josipović et al. [14]); the situation is only aggravated by the support for speculation. Although all our designs are Pareto optimal (and significantly faster than the baseline designs), it is worth looking a bit closer at such results. As suggested in Section 1, predication is the way purely static scheduling methods can implement speculation (that is, by executing in parallel every possibility and selecting the right outcome later). It is usually viable when the number of predicated branches is small; thus, it is customarily used in the textbook case of *if*-conversion where only two short branches need to be followed for a very short period and are soon resolved. If resources are not strongly limited (that is in the world of spatial computing as opposed to traditional VLIW compilation), one could explore an aggressive use of *if*-conversion where many branches are predicated at once—for example, with predication spanning multiple iterations of a loop body, as it would be required in some of our benchmarks. In this section, we want to explore how competitive our technique is against highly-speculative statically-scheduled circuits beyond what our commercial tool produces.

We study here the code of Figure 11, which is qualitatively similar to our Newton-Raphson benchmark but stripped for clarity of everything except key operations. The naive version by Vivado HLS has $II = 4$ because of the loop-carried dependence on s and the multiplication (latency 4) in the condition which determines the new s (the conditional addition is predicated and executed in parallel). It is perfectly possible to restructure the code to perform aggressive *if*-conversion across basic blocks: every iteration spawns two branches corresponding to the new *if* condition, and this for each of the existing predicated branches; on the other hand, four cycles later, the computed condition resolves pairwise all open branches and halves them, leading to a steady state of in-flight branches. Assuming that the critical latencies are 1 for the addition and 4 for the multiplication, as it is the case for the components used by Vivado HLS, achieving $II = 1$ requires 16 parallel branches which compute s for every combination of the *if* conditions in the last four iterations and 8 branches computing the new conditions, also in turn depending on the conditions of the last three iterations. Essentially, the needed computational resources to achieve $II = 1$ with a purely static schedule are 8 multipliers, 8 adders and 8 comparators to execute all predicated branches in parallel. Table 2 shows the comparison of the static, manually restructured code (to achieve a static schedule with $II = 1$), dynamic, and speculative design using a dataset which predicts correctly the condition in 75% of the cases. These results suggest that, although more speculation than what common HLS tools implement is possible, the cost can be very high (notice that the cost is exponential in II_{static}, which is *only* 4 in this case). Clearly, our speculative circuit is Pareto-optimal compared to the aggressively-predicated static design. The area cost is due to the fundamental inability of statically scheduled circuits to revert some arbitrary computation and recompute it from scratch; a statically scheduled solution can only evaluate all possibilities at once and this only when the number of possible outcomes is tractable (which is not the case in a situation we have not demonstrated here but is perfectly covered by our technique—the prediction of independence trough memory of a load from all previous pending stores). On the contrary, a dynamically scheduled, speculative circuit can simply execute the single most likely path and squash and recompute mistakenly predicted outcomes. In all fairness, this also implies a worsening of the execution time when almost-perfect predictions cannot be made, like in the present example, whereas the static solution has *exactly II = 1* irrespective of predictability.

11 RELATED WORK

Much as compilers for VLIW processors do, in order to extract parallelism, many HLS approaches exploit aggressive code motion techniques to anticipate the execution of some operations before it is certain [12, 15, 17]. However, the conservatism of static scheduling hinders such optimizations in the presence of complex control flow or memory accesses. The importance of speculation has not escaped HLS researchers and some have shown partial forms of speculation; albeit remarkable, their approach lacks generality in the ability to revert arbitrarily the state after failed predictions and suffers from being applied to otherwise static schedules [7].

Latency-insensitive protocols [3, 6, 9] have been explored as a way to overcome the limitations of static scheduling and offer the flexibility needed for true speculation [11]. Several latency-insensitive approaches [4, 5, 10] describe early evaluation—predicated execution based on special tokens which discard mispredicted data. However, these techniques are applicable only for standard *if*-conversion, which static HLS can handle as well, and do not cover the more general cases of speculation that we discuss in this work. Budiu et al. went further in implementing features similar to those existing in superscalar processors in their asynchronous dataflow circuits, yet they also failed to implement a generic framework for speculation due to "the difficulty of building a mechanism for squashing the computation on the wrong paths" [1]. Our scheme for discarding and replaying computations does exactly this.

Desikan et al. [8] describe a mechanism for load-store dependence speculation in the context of dataflow processors, but have also faced challenges in building a suitable speculation resolution network: their approach is based on sending the commit/discard decisions through the dataflow graph, so the traversal of these decisions delays the commits and therefore impedes performance. In contrast, we use a dedicated, fast network which enables speculative components to communicate directly and efficiently. Moreover, their speculation scheme requires version numbering and token tagging to handle out-of-order speculative bits—our circuit design strategy ensures that tokens traverse the graph in order, which simplifies our speculation mechanism.

12 CONCLUSIONS

In this work, we present a generic methodology to enable speculative execution in dataflow circuits and show that it can reap significant benefits in appropriate situations. Our simple and methodical approach to bring arbitrary forms of speculation to dataflow circuits mirrors out-of-order processors, where the same commit-or-squash-and-replay approach is at the heart of their very successful speculative mechanisms. Others have shown that dependencies through

memory are an important case where dynamic schedules are highly profitable: the next logical step will be to build a speculative load-store queue which executes speculatively loads before pending and unresolved stores, as in common processors; the generality of our speculation scheme will simply work unmodified for this important situation. We believe all this to be key for FPGAs and HLS to be successful in new contexts such as datacenters, where applications will be more irregular, control-dominated, and software oriented than most FPGA applications are today.

ACKNOWLEDGMENTS
Lana Josipović is supported by a Google PhD Fellowship in Systems and Networking.

REFERENCES

[1] M. Budiu, P. V. Artigas, and S. C. Goldstein. Dataflow: A complement to superscalar. In *Proceedings of the IEEE International Symposium on Performance Analysis of Systems and Software*, pages 177–86, Austin, Tex., Mar. 2005.
[2] M. Budiu and S. C. Goldstein. Pegasus: An efficient intermediate representation. Technical Report CMU-CS-02-107, Carnegie Mellon University, May 2002.
[3] L. P. Carloni, K. L. McMillan, and A. L. Sangiovanni-Vincentelli. Theory of latency-insensitive design. *IEEE Transactions on Computer-Aided Design of Integrated Circuits and Systems*, CAD-20(9):1059–76, Sept. 2001.
[4] M. R. Casu and L. Macchiarulo. Adaptive latency insensitive protocols and elastic circuits with early evaluation: A comparative analysis. *Electronic Notes in Theoretical Computer Science*, 245:35–50, Aug. 2009.
[5] J. Cortadella and M. Kishinevsky. Synchronous elastic circuits with early evaluation and token counterflow. In *Proceedings of the 44th Design Automation Conference*, pages 416–19, San Diego, Calif., June 2007.
[6] J. Cortadella, M. Kishinevsky, and B. Grundmann. Synthesis of synchronous elastic architectures. In *Proceedings of the 43rd Design Automation Conference*, pages 657–62, San Francisco, Calif., July 2006.
[7] S. Dai, R. Zhao, G. Liu, S. Srinath, U. Gupta, C. Batten, and Z. Zhang. Dynamic hazard resolution for pipelining irregular loops in high-level synthesis. In *Proceedings of the 25th ACM/SIGDA International Symposium on Field Programmable Gate Arrays*, pages 189–194, Monterey, Calif., Feb. 2017.
[8] R. Desikan, S. Sethumadhavan, D. Burger, and S. W. Keckler. Scalable selective re-execution for EDGE architectures. In *Proceedings of the 11th International Conference on Architectural Support for Programming Languages and Operating Systems*, pages 120–132, Boston, MA, Oct. 2004.
[9] S. A. Edwards, R. Townsend, and M. A. Kim. Compositional dataflow circuits. In *Proceedings of the 15th ACM-IEEE International Conference on Formal Methods and Models for System Design*, pages 175–184, Vienna, Sept. 2017.
[10] H. Gädke and A. Koch. Accelerating speculative execution in high-level synthesis with cancel tokens. In *International Workshop on Applied Reconfigurable Computing*, pages 185–195, Berlin, Mar. 2008. Springer.
[11] M. Galceran-Oms, J. Cortadella, and M. Kishinevsky. Speculation in elastic systems. In *Proceedings of the 46th Design Automation Conference*, pages 292–95, San Francisco, Calif., July 2009.
[12] S. Gupta, N. Savoiu, N. Dutt, R. Gupta, and A. Nicolau. Conditional speculation and its effects on performance and area for high-level synthesis. In *Proceedings of the 14th international symposium on Systems synthesis*, pages 171–176, Oct. 2001.
[13] J. Huck, D. Morris, J. Ross, A. Knies, H. Mulder, and R. Zahir. Introducing the IA-64 architecture. *IEEE Micro*, 20(5):12–23, Sept.–Oct. 2000.
[14] L. Josipović, R. Ghosal, and P. Ienne. Dynamically scheduled high-level synthesis. In *Proceedings of the 26th ACM/SIGDA International Symposium on Field Programmable Gate Arrays*, pages 127–36, Monterey, Calif., Feb. 2018.
[15] V. Lapotre, P. Coussy, C. Chavet, H. Wouafo, and R. Danilo. Dynamic branch prediction for high-level synthesis. In *Proceedings of the 23rd International Conference on Field-Programmable Logic and Applications*, pages 1–6, Porto, Sept. 2013.
[16] Mentor Graphics. ModelSim, 2016.
[17] R. Nane, V.-M. Sima, C. Pilato, J. Choi, B. Fort, A. Canis, Y. T. Chen, H. Hsiao, S. Brown, F. Ferrandi, et al. A survey and evaluation of FPGA high-level synthesis tools. *IEEE Transactions on Computer-Aided Design of Integrated Circuits and Systems*, 35(10):1591–1604, Oct. 2016.
[18] W. H. Press, S. A. Teukolsky, W. T. Vetterling, and B. P. Flannery. *Numerical Recipes: The Art of Scientific Computing*. Cambridge University Press, Cambridge, third edition, 2007.
[19] L. Torczon and K. Cooper. *Engineering a Compiler*. Morgan Kaufmann, second edition, 2011.
[20] Xilinx Inc. *Vivado High-Level Synthesis*.

Constructing Concurrent Data Structures on FPGA with Channels

Hui Yan
Tsinghua University
Beijing, China
yan-h16@mails.tsinghua.edu.cn

Zhaoshi Li
Tsinghua University
Beijing, China
lizhaoshi@tsinghua.edu.cn

Leibo Liu
Tsinghua University
Beijing, China
liulb@tsinghua.edu.cn

Shouyi Yin
Tsinghua University
Beijing, China
yinsy@tsinghua.edu.cn

Shaojun Wei
Tsinghua University
Beijing, China
wsj@mail.tsinghua.edu.cn

ABSTRACT

The performance of High-Level Synthesis (HLS) applications with irregular data structures is limited by its imperative programming paradigm like C/C++. In this paper, we show that constructing concurrent data structures with channels, a programming construct derived from CSP (communicating sequential processes) paradigm, is an effective approach to improve the performance of these applications. We evaluate concurrent data structure for FPGA by synthesizing a K-means clustering algorithm on the Intel HARP2 platform. A fully pipelined KMC processing element can be synthesized from OpenCL with the help of a SPSC (single-producer-single-consumer) queue and stack built from channels, achieving 15.2x speedup over a sequential baseline. The number of processing element can be scaled up by leveraging a MPMC (multiple-producer-multiple-consumer) stack with work distribution for dynamic load balance. Evaluation shows that an additional 3.5x speedup can be achieved when 4 processing element is instantiated. These results show that the concurrent data structure built with channels has great potential for improving the parallelism of HLS applications. We hope that our study will stimulate further research into the potential of channel-based HLS.

CCS CONCEPTS

• **Computer systems organization** → **Reconfigurable computing**; • **Computing methodologies** → *Parallel programming languages*.

KEYWORDS

High-Level Synthesis, Concurrent Data Structures, Communicating Sequential Processes, K-means clustering, Parallelism

ACM Reference Format:
Hui Yan, Zhaoshi Li, Leibo Liu, Shouyi Yin, and Shaojun Wei. 2019. Constructing Concurrent Data Structures on FPGA with Channels. In *The 2019*

FPGA '19, February 24–26, 2019, Seaside, CA, USA
© 2019 Association for Computing Machinery.
ACM ISBN 978-1-4503-6137-8/19/02...$15.00
https://doi.org/10.1145/3289602.3293921

ACM/SIGDA International Symposium on Field-Programmable Gate Arrays (FPGA '19), February 24–26, 2019, Seaside, CA, USA. ACM, New York, NY, USA, 6 pages. https://doi.org/10.1145/3289602.3293921

1 INTRODUCTION

High-Level Synthesis (HLS) is widely used for a variety of emerging applications, and irregular data structures are widely used in most emerging applications such as the following.

- Machine-learning algorithms like the Multiscale Classifier (MSC) [11] and the K-Nearest Neighbours (KNN) [16] are based on non-binary tree and kd-tree, respectively.
- Data-mining algorithms like k-means and agglomerative clustering operate on sets and multisets [17].
- In network analysis, vertex centrality to graph clustering and the evolution of scale-free networks are widely used [3].

Unfortunately, HLS language has poor support for irregular data structure. The mainstream HLS tools are based on an imperative programming model such as C/C++. In this model, the parallelism of the irregular data structures need to be expressed explicitly. For example, a concurrent queue needs to be implemented using mutex or atomic operation in C/C++. These synchronization primitives that rely on explicit expression of parallelism are extremely costly to implement in HLS.

In this paper, we construct concurrent data structures (CDS) on FPGA with OpenCL Channels in order to fully explore intrinsic parallelism of applications based on irregular data structures. The channel syntax is originated from communicating sequential processes (CSP) programming paradigm. CSP was first proposed by A.W. Roscoe in 1977 [15], which describes a concurrency model in which multiple processes communicate using channels. Adopting channels in HLS provides a new dimension for expressing CDS, and avoids the use of synchronization primitive such as mutex or atomic from the original imperative programming paradigm. CSP is not a new idea to HLS. Both impulse C [13] and handel-C [1] incorporate CSP-based channel syntaxes. However, existing endeavours [19] only view the channel as a simple FIFO to integrate hardware modules, while neglecting its potential for exploiting intrinsic parallelism of applications.

In this paper, we apply OpenCL channels to construct concurrent data structures for filtering algorithm [8] of the K-means clustering

---

*Corresponding author: Leibo Liu (liulb@tsinghua.edu.cn)

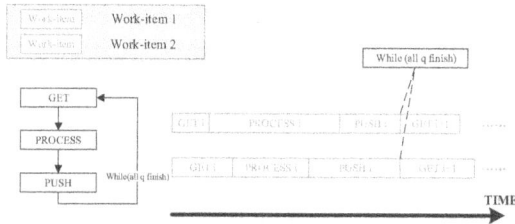

Figure 1: Simplified dataflow graph and schedule diagram of algorithm 1.

(KMC) problem with few internal dependency and fully-pipelined parallelism. Our algorithm is implemented in OpenCL (an open royalty-free standard for general purpose parallel programming [9]), and automatically compiled to hardware using Intel FPGA development kit for OpenCL [6]. On Intel HARP2 platform, We show that our algorithm yields a 10.1 × overall speedup over an earlier implementation by Ramanathan et al., which was already an optimized for FPGA based on OpenCL atomics over the previous implementation by Winterstein et al.[14, 18].

This paper is organized as follows. Section 2 introduces the K-means clustering algorithm and the OpenCL channel. Section 3 details the principles and methods of constructing concurrent data structures with channels. Hardware execution and evaluation results are presented in section 4. Section 5 concludes with a summary and discussion about future research directions.

2 BACKGROUNDS AND MOTIVATIONS

2.1 K-means Clustering Algorithm

K-means clustering (KMC) [12] is a method commonly used to automatically partition a data set into k groups. This method is based on a simple iterative scheme for finding a locally minimal solution, which is often called the k-means algorithm. There are a number of variants to this algorithm, one is called Lloyd's algorithm [10], which is based on the simple observation that the optimal placement of a center is at the centroid of the associated cluster [4]. Another one is the filtering algorithm [8], begins by storing the data points in a kd-tree [2], which reduce the amount of work by avoiding iterating all the data set.

Various researches have been conducted for synthesizing the KMC with HLS [8, 14, 18]. The most relevant to our research is the research of Ramanathan et al. [14]. They provided a case study of work-stealing, a popular method for run-time load balancing, on FPGA. Their research demonstrates for the first time the effectiveness of dynamic load balancing on FPGA with OpenCL atomics, which contributes to the research of fine-grained lock-free concurrent programs in high-level synthesis.

However, limited by the imperative programming model of HLS, although they have greatly improved the parallelism of the algorithm, it was not able to make full use of the hardware resources to dig more parallelism. Algorithm 1 is their implementation, whose hotspot is in the while loop of line 10. Fig. 1 is a simplified data flow graph (including 3 parts of operation: GET (line 11), PROCESS (line 14) and PUSH (line 15-16)) and schedule diagram of the while

---

Algorithm 1 Work-stealing KMC algorithm

1: **attribute**(reqd work group size(P,1,1))
2: **kernel** KMC(**global** tree *t[P], **local** centerset *M)
3:   **local** deque[P] q
4:   **global** heap[P] h
5:   **local** centerset[P] Ms
6:   i ← get local id(0)
7:   sid ← (i + 1) mod P
8:   Ms[i] ← M
9:   q[i].push(t[i], h[i])
10: **while** ⌐(q[0].finish && ... && q[P-1].finish) **do**
11:    success ← GET(&t[i], &h[i], q, i, &sid)
12:    q[i].finish ← ⌐success
13:    **if** success **then**
14:      **if** PROCESS(t[i], &h[i], &Ms[i]) **then**
15:        q[i].PUSH(t[i]->r, h[i])
16:        q[i].PUSH(t[i]->l, h[i])
17:      **end if**
18:    **end if**
19: **end while**
20: **barrier**
21: **if** i = 0 **then** M ← reduce(Ms)
22: **end kernel**

---

loop in Algorithm 1, assuming P = 2. It is shown in Fig. 1 that the exploitation of parallelism is subject to two restrictions. First, due to the backward dependency induced by accessing the task queue (the GET operation of the next loop needs to wait for the last PUSH operation to complete), the pipeline parallelism of the while loop body cannot be exploited. Therefore, only the task-level parallelism of multiple work-items has been expressed. Second, when there are multiple work-items, in order to implement Load balance, a work-item must be able to access N task queues simultaneously. This results in an N × N crossbar between N task queues and N work-items in the synthesis process. And because of the atomic operation requirements, this crossbar must be single-cycle. When N is large, this crossbar will seriously affect the frequency, thus affecting the overall performance.

Compared to Ramanathan et al., our implementation not only exploits pipeline parallelism among tasks, but also obviates the need for a huge crossbar on FPGA.

2.2 OpenCL Channel

The Intel FPGA SDK for OpenCL (AOCL) channel extension [7] provides a mechanism for passing data between kernels and synchronizing kernels with high efficiency and low latency, which allows kernels to communicate directly with each other through FIFO buffers. The pattern of channel-based communication between the kernels through FIFOs is very friendly to the hardware. Thus, inter-module synchronization does not need to be based on expensive locks and atomics. Instead, it can be built up from concurrent processes read and write around channel.

AOCL provides two types of APIs for channel operations. First, the blocking accesses, i.e. the `write_channel` and the `read_channel` API calls, allow the producer/consumer to send/receive data across

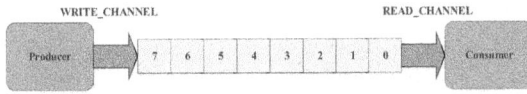

Figure 2: Channel Data FIFO Ordering.

a channel, and busy wait if vacancy/data is not available, respectively. For example, read_channel(c, &t) reads a task from channel c and assigns it to task t. Fig. 2 shows the FIFO ordering of the channel, with the data sending into the channel first and being received first. Second, there are non-blocking channel APIs. AOCL provides write_channel_nb and read_channel_nb to facilitate applications where writes/read to a FIFO buffer should not cause the kernel to stall even though the FIFO in the channel is full/empty. A nonblocking API call returns a boolean value that indicates whether a datum is successfully read/written successfully from/to the channel, i.e. the channel is not full/empty.

Since channel-based kernels (modules) are usually fuelled by tokens from channels rather than instructions from the host CPU, AOCL provides advanced attributes to reduce the overhead on hardware usage and simplify the coding efforts. The keyword autorun on a kernel without and argument indicates this kernel starts executing automatically before any kernel that the host launches explicitly. The keyword num_compute_units instructs the compiler to generate multiple copies the module.

3 CHANNEL-BASED CONCURRENT CONTAINERS

The semantics of channel offer a new perspective for synchronization unavailable in the traditional imperative programming paradigm. In this section, three CDS' are constructed with channel to act as concurrent containers for task scheduling in KMC. First, a SPSC (single-producer-single-consumer) queue is derived directly from channel to solve the inter-loop dependency of Fig. 1 so that the loop body can be fully pipelined. Second, a SPSC stack is designed to avoid the potential of deadlock due to a bounded SPSC queue during the traversal of KD-tree. Third, a MPMC stack with dynamic load balance is proposed so that multiple pipelines of KD-tree traversal can operates concurrently. All OpenCL kernels described in this section are single workitem kernels in which loops are pipelined, corresponding to one module on FPGA.

3.1 SPSC Queue

The inter-loop dependency in Fig. 1 is induced by read/write accesses to task queues since a read may depends on a prior write. If reads and writes to the task queue can be executed concurrently, and reads/writes block until the queue is not empty/full, this inter-loop dependency no longer exists. This idea is identical to using a dual-port FIFO with separate read and write port in hardware design.

However, imperative programming paradigm lacks necessary tools for describing the concurrency of a dual-port FIFO. In case of algorithm 1, in order to enable the blocking read and write in the loop body, two nested while loops for polling the dual-port FIFO are required. With current HLS techniques, this loop body is unable

---

Algorithm 2 Pseudo code of the KMC with SPSC queue

1: **channel** Task task_c;
2: **channel** Update update_c;
kernel PROCESS(**global** Tree *tree, **global** Centerset *m)
3: **while** true **do**
4:     Task t = READ_CHANNEL(task_c);
5:     **if** Update u = FILTER(t, tree, m) **then**
6:         WRITE_CHANNEL(update_c, u);
7:     **else**
8:         WRITE_CHANNEL(task_c, t.left);
9:         WRITE_CHANNEL(task_c, t.right);
10:     **end if**
11: **end while**
kernel UPDATE(**global** Centerset *m)
12: bool terminated = false; // flag for finishing traversal
13: **while not** terminated **do**
14:     Update u = READ_CHANNEL(update_c);
15:     terminated = UPDATE_CENTER(m, u);
16: **end while**

---

to be pipelined because the exact initialization interval (II) can not be determined for pipelining.

Fortunately, concurrently polling of a SPSC queue can be trivially implemented with channels. In fact, a OpenCL channel with designated depth is implemented as a dual-port FIFO on FPGA. Algorithm 2 presents the pseudo code for KMC with non-blocking channels. This algorithm is consists of two kernels. The PROCESS[†] kernel traverse the tree; whereas the UPDATE kernel updates the centroid set when certain condition is met during PROCESS. Two channels are instantiated: the update_chan transmit ready updates from PROCESS to UPDATE, and the task_chan serves as the SPSC task queue for PROCESS. Each task either creates two new tasks (line 8), or delivers an update to UPDATE (line 6).

Thanks to the independence of read/write accesses to the same channel, all inter-loop dependencies are eliminated in algorithm 2. These loops can be fully pipelined to boost hardware utilization for FPGA, as shown in Figure 3.

3.2 SPSC Stack

The above design has a fatal defect. Traversing with a queue is equivalent to the breadth-first traversal of the tree. As a result, this queue should have the capacity to store half tree nodes to ensure deadlock-freedom, which place a rigorous resource constraint. Otherwise, the queue could have been jammed, leaving the PROCESS kernel in deadlock. To relax this constraint, a pre-order traversal with the help of a stack rather than a queue could be attempted. In this way, the size of the stack only needs to exceed the depth of the tree, dubbed as h.

To enable the pre-order traversal for KMC, the task_chan as the SPSC queue is substituted with a dedicated kernel named as SPSC_STACK, which is shown in Algorithm 3. Here, the autorun attribute is used to declare that the SPSC_STACK will start executing automatically (line 3). In this way, the SPSC_STACK performs

---

[†]We omit the detail of searching for left child and right child of current node in the FILTER function of PROCESS kernel

---

Algorithm 3 Pseudo code of SPSC stack

1: **channel** Task push_c;
2: **channel** Task pop_c;
3: __attribute__((autorun))
kernel SPSC_STACK()
4:   **local** Stack stack;
5:   **while** true **do**
6:     Task t;
7:     **if** READ_CHANNEL_NB(push_c, &t) **then**
8:       pushStack(&stack, t);
9:     **end if**
10:    **if** t = peekStack(&stack) **then**
11:      **if** WRITE_CHANNEL_NB(pop_c, t) **then**
12:        popStack(&stack);
13:      **end if**
14:    **end if**
15: **end while**

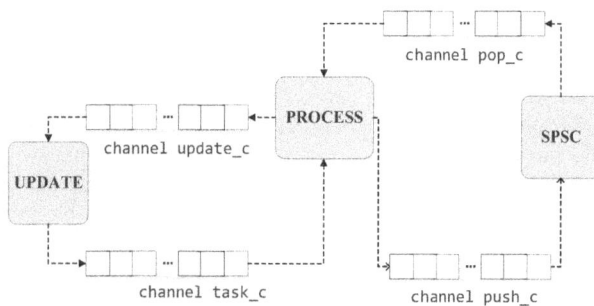

Figure 3: Representation of the implementation of KMC algorithm with SPSC Stack.

as a standalone service. A stack data type maintained as dual-port BRAM (declared in OpenCL `local` memory) is instantiated to facilitate the implementation (line 4). Two channels are utilized as interfaces to the SPSC_STACK kernel. Each cycle, the SPSC_STACK kernel polls the push channel (line 7) and writes the stack[‡]. Meanwhile if the stack is not empty it attempts to read the stack and pop a task though the pop channel (line 11). Thanks to the non-blocking channel, the interface to the SPSC_STACK kernel is much cleaner than that of imperative paradigm. The PROCESS kernel only has to actively poll the push/pop channel for task insertion/extraction.

Fig. 3 shows the overview of the KMC system with SPSC_STACK. With tasks storing in the `local` depth-h Stack of the SPSC_STACK kernel in LIFO (last-in-first-out) order, both the push and pop channels are instantiated with depth of 1 so as to guarantee the LIFO semantic of the SPSC_STACK kernel. In this case, these channels act as rendezvous point between the SPSC_STACK kernel and the PROCESS kernel.

[‡] We slightly modify the syntax of read_channel_nb of Intel FPGA OpenCL for better readability.

3.3 MPMC Stack

Since the system of Figure 3 may not exhaust all resources, we need a way to scale up our design to fully exploit the potential of FPGA. The simplest approach is to instantiate multiple copies of this system. However, due to the dynamic nature of tree traversal, the execution time of each copy is hard to be balanced at compile time. As a result, dynamic load-balance is required for scaling up the KMC application.

To this end, we build up a MPMC (multiple-producer-multiple-consumer) stack from the SPSC stack, with a uniform work distribution strategy for dynamic load balancing. Work distribution is a proactive (from the perspective of task creator) synchronous strategy where new tasks are distributed to idle processing elements uniformly, whereas work stealing is a reactive asynchronous strategy where idle processing elements asynchronously try to steal tasks from the others. We choose work distribution over work stealing because of the restriction of Intel FPGA OpenCL syntax where multiple read/write to one channel is unfavourable for pipelined designs.

Algorithm 4 shows the pseudo code for the MPMC stack. The SPSC stack from Algorithm 4 is replicated by the OpenCL attribute `num_compute_units` (line 24). A standalone kernel DISTRIBUTOR is instantiated for work distribution. It reads the pop channels (line 12) and distribute valid tasks to empty distribution channels (line 18)[§] in a round-robin way. In this way we could exempt the use of crossbar in work stealing for simplified routing.

It should be noted that algorithm 4 does not strictly adhere to the LIFO semantic of stack. Nevertheless in practice we find that KMC is robust to a small amount of priority inversion. Strict MPMC stack would require a large amount of resources, e.g. a comparator array, to implement on FPGA.

4 EVALUATION

We evaluate Channel-based Concurrent Container by comparing it with the implementation of Ramanathan et al.[14] in terms of execution time and resource utilization. Due to the utilization of atomic operation, the implementation of Ramanathan et al. does not support multi-channels access to global memory, which is the trend of the current heterogeneous system.

Fig. 4 shows the schematic of HARP2 memory system [5], a heterogeneous CPU-FPGA platform. The CCI-P interface abstracts the physical links to the processor and provides simple load/store semantics to the AFU for accessing system memory. The physical links are presented as virtual channels on the CCI-P interface. Each request can select the virtual channel, which are called VL0, VH0, and VH1. With multi-channels on the harp2 platform, the work-stealing version of Ramanathan et al. cannot run on the harp2 platform. Hence, we can only compare our implementations with their baseline, indirectly getting speedup in execution time over their optimized work-stealing version.

Following Ramanathan et al., we set the input to a tree built from 2^{20} data-points and a 128-element center-set, and run it for 16 iterations when the number of work-item $P = 1$. The execution

---

[§] Currently Intel FPGA OpenCL does not allow indexing into arrays of channels dynamically, even if is our case the index can be inferred statically. As a result, in current implementation we unroll these loops by hand.

Algorithm 4 Pseudo code of MPMC stack

```
 1: #define NUM 4 // number of processing elements
 2: channel Task push_c[NUM];
 3: channel Task dist_c[NUM];
 4: channel Task pop_c[NUM];
 5: __attribute__((autorun))
kernel DISTRIBUTOR()
 6: int phase = 0;
 7: while true do
 8:    Task temp[NUM];
 9:    #pragma unroll
10:    for i = 0, ... , NUM-1 do
11:       if not temp[(i+count)%NUM] then
12:          READ_CHANNEL_NB(push_c[i],
                 &temp[(i+count)%NUM]);
13:       end if
14:    end for
15:    #pragma unroll
16:    for i = 0, ... , NUM-1 do
17:       if temp[i] then
18:          WRITE_CHANNEL_NB(dist_c[i], &temp[i]);
19:       end if
20:    end for
21: end while
22:
23: __attribute__((autorun))
24: __attribute__((num_compute_units(NUM)))
kernel SPSC_STACK()
25: unsigned cid = get_compute_id(0);
26: ...
27: READ_CHANNEL_NB(push_c[cid], &t);
28: ...
```

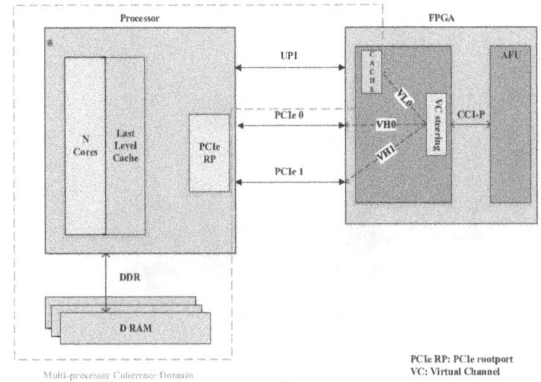

Figure 4: Intel FPGA IP System Memory Hierarchy, 1 Processor Topology.

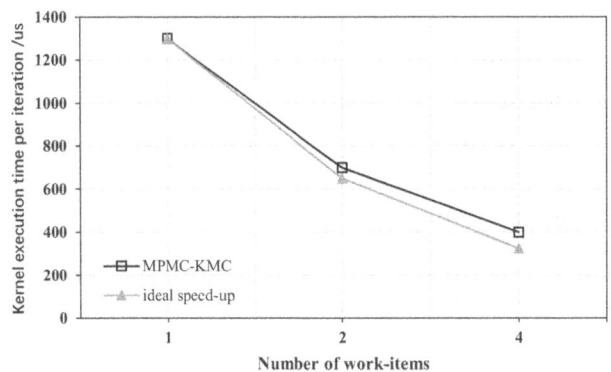

Figure 5: Kernel execution time for the MPMC-KMC algorithm.

time of this input on HARP2 is 7.4 seconds, which is similar to the execution time of 5 seconds in experiment of Ramanathan et al. [14], indicating that the execution of baseline on harp2 platform is valid. Excessive execution time on harp2 platform may be caused by insufficient page size[¶] under large data size, which is not the focus of this paper.

In the following experiments, the input to the SPSC-KMC algorithm and MPMC-KMC algorithm is a tree built from 10000 datapoints in float and a 32-element center-set in float. The center-set is updated for 64 iterations. It is worth noting that the data type for the input to sequential baseline is integer. Our design exploits the inter-task pipeline parallelism to hide the latency of floating-point operations.

4.1 Execution Time

The purpose of constructing CDS is to avoid situation where the backward dependency induced by accessing a shared task container hampers parallelism. With these concurrent containers, hardware pipelines are generated on FPGA. We compare the sequential baseline to the pipelined implementation with the SPSC stack. Their

performance on the harp2 platform are 0.0198 seconds per iteration and 0.0013 seconds per iteration, respectively. The result shows that the SPSC-KMC has a 15.2 × speedup over baseline.

In addition to using the pipeline to improve parallelism, we can also achieve task-level parallelism through MPMC stack at the same time to further improve the parallelism. Fig. 5 shows the kernel execution time (excluding host preprocessing) per iteration for MPMC-KMC algorithm with respect to number of work-items. Our MPMC-KMC performs closely to the linear scale-up (3.5x with 4 work-items). This shows that the parallel processing elements of KMC constructed with MPMC stack scales well. In addition, we extract the profile of replicated kernels, and observe the number of tasks distributed to each PROCESS kernel to be well-balanced. This observation shows that work-distribution in the MPMC stack could achieve similar load-balancing to work-stealing.

4.2 Resources

The acceleration gained from SPSC stack and MPMC stack comes at the cost of additional FPGA resources. Fig. 6 shows resource utilization for different implementations. First, we compare the

---

[¶]The HARP2 host CPU only supports 2MB huge page in the shared main memory with FPGA.

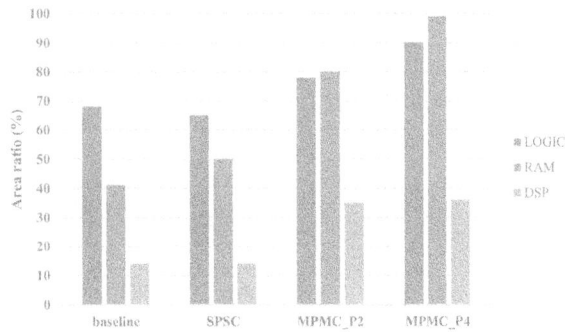

Figure 6: Comparison of resource utilization.

Table 1: Resource consumption of CCI-P

CCI-P	LOGIC	RAM	DSP
Quantity	/	637	183
Percentage	39%	23%	12%

resource utilization of baseline and SPSC. From the figure we can see that the baseline occupies less RAM resources, but uses more logic resources. And the DSP usages of both are similar. Not that the resources reported here do not exclude the CCI-P module of HARP2, whose resource consumption is shown in Table 1.

Next, we compare the resource utilization of SPSC and MPMC. From the figure we can see that with the increase of work-item, the use of various resources is increasing. When the number of work-items reaches 4, the use of RAM is close to 100%. It is worth noting that the resource consumptions related to each concurrent containers are fairly low, and do not scale up with the number of work-items. In this way, more work-items can be instantiated for future FPGAs with better support for pipelines.

5 CONCLUSIONS

In this paper we present an effective approach to improve the performance of irregular applications with high-level synthesis. By constructing a concurrent data structure with channels, we can build pipeline for the KMC algorithm without backward dependency. Meanwhile the implementation can scale up well to exploit task-level parallelism, thanks to dynamic load-balanced concurrent data structures.

Explicit parallelism in high-level synthesis have been studied extensively in past researches. However, most researches focus on using imperative programming paradigm for expressing parallelism. Our work shows that there are great potential in other paradigms such as communicating sequential processes. We hope this paper will stir more discussions on paradigms for concurrent programming constructs in high-level synthesis. After all, the plurality of parallelism in applications should lead to the plurality of parallelism in programming tools.

6 ACKNOWLEDGEMENT

This work was supported in part by National Natural Science Foundation of China (No. 61672317) and National Science Technology Major Project (No. 2016ZX01012101). We appreciate the insightful comments and feedback from the anonymous reviewers. We thank Intel for the donation of the development tool and hardware. The presented HARP-2 results were obtained on resources hosted at the Paderborn Center for Parallel Computing (PC²) in the Intel Hardware Accelerator Research Program (HARP2).

REFERENCES

[1] Matthew Aubury, Ian Page, Geoff Randall, Jonathan Saul, and Robin Watts. 1996. Handel-C language reference guide. *Computing Laboratory. Oxford University, UK* (1996).
[2] Jon Louis Bentley. 1975. Multidimensional Binary Search Trees Used for Associative Searching. *Commun. ACM* 18, 9 (Sept. 1975), 509–517. https://doi.org/10.1145/361002.361007
[3] Ulrik Brandes and Thomas Erlebach. 2005. *Network Analysis: Methodological Foundations (Lecture Notes in Computer Science)*. Springer-Verlag, Berlin, Heidelberg.
[4] Vance Faber. 1994. Clustering and the continuous k-means algorithm. *Los Alamos Science* 22, 138144.21 (1994).
[5] Intel Corporation. 2017. Intel® FPGA IP Core Cache Interface (CCI-P) Specification.
[6] Intel Corporation. 2018. Intel® FPGA SDK for OpenCL™ Pro Edition Best Practices Guide.
[7] Intel Corporation. 2018. Intel® FPGA SDK for OpenCL™ Pro Edition Programming Guide.
[8] T. Kanungo, D. M. Mount, N. S. Netanyahu, C. D. Piatko, R. Silverman, and A. Y. Wu. 2002. An Efficient k-Means Clustering Algorithm: Analysis and Implementation. *IEEE Transactions on Pattern Analysis & Machine Intelligence* 24 (07 2002), 881–892. https://doi.org/10.1109/TPAMI.2002.1017616
[9] Khronos OpenCL Working Group. 2009. The OpenCL specification. https://www.khronos.org/registry/OpenCL/specs/opencl-1.0.pdf
[10] S. Lloyd. 1982. Least squares quantization in PCM. *IEEE Transactions on Information Theory* 28, 2 (March 1982), 129–137. https://doi.org/10.1109/TIT.1982.1056489
[11] B. C. Lovell and A. P. Bradley. 1996. The multiscale classifier. *IEEE Transactions on Pattern Analysis and Machine Intelligence* 18, 2 (Feb 1996), 124–137. https://doi.org/10.1109/34.481538
[12] J. MacQueen. 1967. Some methods for classification and analysis of multivariate observations. In *Proceedings of the Fifth Berkeley Symposium on Mathematical Statistics and Probability, Volume 1: Statistics*. University of California Press, Berkeley, Calif., 281–297. https://projecteuclid.org/euclid.bsmsp/1200512992
[13] David Pellerin and Scott Thibault. 2005. *Practical Fpga Programming in C* (first ed.). Prentice Hall Press, Upper Saddle River, NJ, USA.
[14] Nadesh Ramanathan, John Wickerson, Felix Winterstein, and George A. Constantinides. 2016. A Case for Work-stealing on FPGAs with OpenCL Atomics. In *Proceedings of the 2016 ACM/SIGDA International Symposium on Field-Programmable Gate Arrays (FPGA '16)*. ACM, New York, NY, USA, 48–53. https://doi.org/10.1145/2847263.2847343
[15] A. W. Roscoe. 1997. *The Theory and Practice of Concurrency*. Prentice Hall PTR, Upper Saddle River, NJ, USA.
[16] Kwang Won Sok, Manmyung Kim, and Jehee Lee. 2007. Simulating Biped Behaviors from Human Motion Data. *ACM Trans. Graph.* 26, 3, Article 107 (July 2007). https://doi.org/10.1145/1276377.1276511
[17] Pang-Ning Tan, Michael Steinbach, and Vipin Kumar. 2005. *Introduction to Data Mining, (First Edition)*. Addison-Wesley Longman Publishing Co., Inc., Boston, MA, USA.
[18] F. Winterstein, S. Bayliss, and G. A. Constantinides. 2013. High-level synthesis of dynamic data structures: A case study using Vivado HLS. In *2013 International Conference on Field-Programmable Technology (FPT)*. 362–365. https://doi.org/10.1109/FPT.2013.6718388
[19] Jimmy Xu, Nikhil Subramanian, Adam Alessio, and Scott Hauck. 2010. Impulse C vs. VHDL for accelerating tomographic reconstruction. In *Field-Programmable Custom Computing Machines (FCCM), 2010 18th IEEE Annual International Symposium on*. IEEE, 171–174.

Rapid Cycle-Accurate Simulator for High-Level Synthesis

Yuze Chi, Young-kyu Choi,* Jason Cong, and Jie Wang
Computer Science Department, University of California, Los Angeles
{chiyuze,ykchoi,cong,jiewang}@cs.ucla.edu

ABSTRACT

A large semantic gap between the high-level synthesis (HLS) design and the low-level (on-board or RTL) simulation environment often creates a barrier for those who are not FPGA experts. Moreover, such low-level simulation takes a long time to complete. Software-based HLS simulators can help bridge this gap and accelerate the simulation process; however, we found that the current FPGA HLS commercial software simulators sometimes produce incorrect results. In order to solve this correctness issue while maintaining the high speed of a software-based simulator, this paper proposes a new HLS simulation flow named FLASH. The main idea behind the proposed flow is to extract the scheduling information from the HLS tool and automatically construct an equivalent cycle-accurate simulation model while preserving C semantics. Experimental results show that FLASH runs three orders of magnitude faster than the RTL simulation.

ACM Reference Format:
Yuze Chi, Young-kyu Choi, Jason Cong, and Jie Wang. 2019. Rapid Cycle-Accurate Simulator for High-Level Synthesis. In *The 2019 ACM/SIGDA International Symposium on Field-Programmable Gate Arrays (FPGA '19), February 24–26, 2019, Seaside, CA, USA*. ACM, New York, NY, USA, 6 pages. https://doi.org/10.1145/3289602.3293918

1 INTRODUCTION

Although FPGA has many promising features including power-efficiency and reconfigurability, the low-level programming environment makes it difficult for programmers to use the platform. In order to solve this problem, many high-level synthesis (HLS) tools such as Xilinx Vivado HLS [9] and Intel OpenCL HLS [14] have been released. These tools allow programmers to design FPGA applications with high-level languages such as C or OpenCL. This trend is reinforced by recent efforts on FPGA programming with languages of higher abstraction—such as Spark or Halide [21, 25].

Even though such progress has been made on the design automation side, a large semantic gap still exists on the simulation side. Programmers often need to use low-level register-transfer level (RTL) simulators and try to map the result back to HLS. The result is often incomprehensible to those who are not FPGA experts. Moreover, such low-level simulation takes a very long time. Some work has been done to automate hardware probe insertion from the HLS source file [4, 12, 18, 22]; however, this work requires regeneration of FPGA bitstream if there is a change in the debugging point, and the turnaround time is often in hours.

These problems can be partially solved by the software-based simulators provided by HLS tools. It takes little time to reconfigure

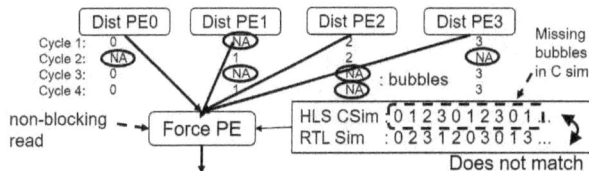

Figure 1: Molecular dynamics simulation PEs [7]

the debugging points, and no semantic gap exists between the simulation and the design. However, a well-known shortcoming of these simulators is that most of them do not provide performance estimation. In addition, we found a critical deficiency—they sometimes provide *incorrect* results.

An example can be found in the molecular dynamics simulation [7] (Fig. 1). Multiple distance processing elements (Dist PEs) filter out faraway molecules above threshold and send them to Force PE. The pruned molecules will create a bubble (empty data) in the FIFO, and Force PE will process only the valid data (after non-blocking read) in the order they are received from any of the FIFOs. However, if the modules are instantiated in the order of (Dist PE1, PE2, ... Force PE) in the source file, Vivado HLS will finish the simulation of Dist PE1 first, followed by Dist PE2, and so on. As a result, by the time Force PE is simulated, the bubbles in the FIFOs are completely removed, and the Force PE output ordering can be entirely different from the actual result. If one was analyzing the DRAM access behavior from the HLS simulation output, the person would likely draw a wrong conclusion.

Another problematic example can be found in the artificial deadlock situation [11], which occurs when the depth of the FIFO is smaller than the latency difference among modules (details in Section 3.2). The first issue is that the HLS software simulator cannot detect the deadlock situation and proceeds as if there is no problem with the design. The second issue is that after we apply a transformation to remove the deadlock, the HLS tool cannot also simulate the amount of performance degradation (Section 7.3) from the artificial stall (Section 3.2). We also found a problem in the simulation of feedback loops where the feedback data is ignored by the HLS tool (Section 3.3).

The primary reason for the incorrect simulation result is that HLS software simulators do not guarantee cycle accuracy. The comparison between the software simulator of the two most popular ([17]) commercial FPGA HLS tools, Xilinx Vivado HLS and Intel OpenCL HLS, is presented in Table 1. Vivado HLS assumes unlimited FIFO depth which makes it difficult to accurately model FIFO fullness/emptiness. Also, their sequential simulation execution model prevents correctly simulating designs with feedback

Table 1: Comparison of the software-based simulation of Xilinx Vivado HLS [24] and Intel OpenCL HLS [14]. Undesirable characteristics are in bold.

	Xilinx Viv HLS C Sim	Intel OpenCL HLS Sim
FIFO depth	**Unlimited**	Exact
Exec model	**Sequential**	Concurrent
Feedback	**Not supported**	Supported
Sim speed	~5 Mcycle/s	**~1 Mcycle/s**
Sim order	Deterministic	**Non-deterministic**
Cycle-acc	**Not cycle-accurate**	**Not cycle-accurate**

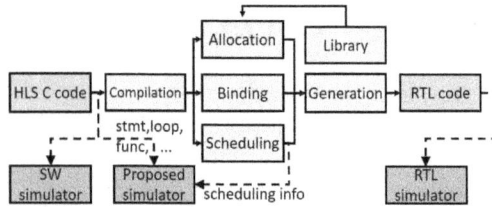

Figure 2: HLS design steps [10] and simulation flows

Figure 3: Structure and code for motivating example `toy_mpath`

loops (Section 3.3). Intel OpenCL HLS simulates about 5X slower than Vivado HLS, but it correctly simulates the FIFO depth. The tool assigns a thread to each module for concurrent simulation; however, the execution order of the threads is not deterministic and may produce different results in different simulation runs for cases in Section 3.

HLS design steps and conventional simulation flows are shown in Fig. 2. A software simulator runs fast but provides no cycle estimation and may have the correctness problem. An RTL simulator is accurate but runs slow since it incorporates low-level implementation details. Our solution to these problems is based on the idea that it may be possible to tackle both problems by simulating based on the scheduling information. It would be faster than the RTL simulation without the allocation / binding information and the component libraries; and it would solve the correctness problem of the software simulation and provide accurate performance estimation with its cycle-accuracy.

Although simulating solely based on the scheduler output (LLVM IR + scheduling information) is a possible option, we have instead decided to simulate in C syntax and augment it with scheduling information. The reason is that we wanted to raise the simulation abstraction level to further accelerate the simulation process and also make it easier for programmers to understand what is being simulated. To our knowledge, this is the first HLS-based simulation flow that takes such an approach.

By taking such an approach, however, several challenges were encountered (will be elaborated in Section 4). One problem is how to model high-level semantics such as functions and loops—as well as FIFO transactions and FIFO stalls—in a cycle-accurate fashion. Moreover, correctly simulating the task-level and pipelined parallelism that is inherent in hardware (and the corresponding RTL simulation) in sequential C semantics is a significant challenge.

In this paper we propose FLASH[1][2]—an HLS-based software simulation flow that addresses these challenges. We describe transformations that allow cycle-accurate simulation of communication and computation stages (will be explained in Section 4). Also, a method will be explained to simulate multiple levels of parallelism with C semantics. These steps will be described in Section 5.

We obtain the scheduling information from the HLS synthesis report and automatically generate a new simulation code based on the information. The new simulation code was made compatible with the conventional HLS software simulator for easy integration with the existing tool. The overall flow is described in Section 6.

Our current initial version is based on Vivado HLS, but we hope to extend our work to Intel HLS if the tool provides detailed internal scheduling information in the future.

2 RELATED WORK

Work in [4, 12, 18, 22] describe frameworks that allow users to specify debugging points in high-level language and synthesize hardware probes into the FPGA for analysis. They can be categorized

into work that has more focus on verifying functional correctness [12, 18] and work that has more focus on extracting performance-related parameters [4, 22]. Compared to the software-based flows, however, these hardware-based debuggers typically requires hours of initial overhead for bitstream generation.

There are several SystemC simulators [6, 20] that can achieve cycle-accuracy for the source code that has explicit scheduling information specified by the programmer, but this may be too difficult for non-experts. Our flow, on the other hand, achieves cycle-accuracy for a HLS C source code that does not have such user-defined scheduling information.

There are also other HLS-based software simulators. The LegUp HLS [2] simulator provides speedup prediction based on the profiling of the source code and the execution cycle from its synthesis result. HLScope+ [5] describes a method to extract cycle information that is hidden by HLS abstraction and uses Vivado HLS C simulation to predict the performance for applications with dynamic behavior. These works, however, do not guarantee cycle-accuracy.

3 PROBLEM DESCRIPTION AND MOTIVATING EXAMPLES

In this section we describe three classes of problems that cause current HLS tools to produce incorrect software simulation result. The problems are demonstrated with motivating examples in the literature.

3.1 Incorrect Data Ordering with Multiple Paths

Suppose a PE is reading data in a non-blocking fashion from multiple PEs through FIFOs as in the molecular dynamics simulation example (Fig. 1 [7]) in the introduction. If a bubble exists in a FIFO, the data consumer PE will skip the FIFO and proceed to read from the next FIFO. In software simulation, however, if the data producer PEs are instantiated in the source file before the consumer PE, Vivado HLS will simulate the data producer PEs completely before moving on the next one. This effectively removes all bubbles in the FIFO, and the order of output from the data consumers in the software simulation result will be different from the actual execution. In the Intel HLS, the simulation order of the data producers is undetermined, and thus there is no guarantee that the bubbles in the simulated result will exactly match the actual execution.

3.2 Artificial Deadlock and Stall

Consider an example in Figure 3 where the module M2 has a latency of 5 and M3 has a latency of 15. All FIFOs have a depth of 2. After M2 has produced two output elements, M4 cannot consume any of them because `fifo4` is still empty due to the long latency of M3. Due to the back-pressure from M2 and `fifo3`, `fifo1` becomes full. Then

---

[1]FLASH: Fast, ParalleL, and Accurate Simulator for HLS

[2]An extended version of this paper is available at: https://arxiv.org/abs/1812.07012

```
for(i = 0; i < N; i++){
#pragma HLS pipeline II=1
    int temp = f_in.read();
    f_out.write(...temp*3);
}
```

```
01 i = 0;
02 while (i < N){
03 #pragma HLS pipeline II=1
04     if(f_in.empty()==false){
05         int temp = f_in.read();
06         f_out.write(...temp*3);
07         i++;
08 } }
```

Figure 4: Source-to-source code transformation to avoid artificial deadlock for M3 in Fig. 3

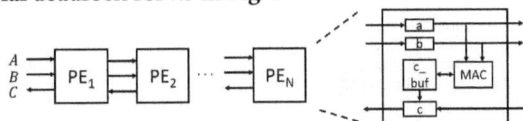

Figure 5: Matrix multiplication with linear systolic array architecture

M1 will stop producing output to fifo2 because fifo1 and fifo2 have to be written in the same cycle. fifo2 will eventually become empty, which blocks the pipeline of M3. Then none of the modules can do any further useful work, and the circuit deadlocks. This is called an artificial deadlock [11]. The deadlock is caused by the mismatching latency of multiple paths and the small FIFO depth. This can be observed in real applications, such as the dataflow-based architecture for stencil computations in [3] that contains various modules and FIFOs with different latencies and depths.

The problem is that software-based HLS simulators ignores the latency of a module. It will simulate each iteration of a loop as if the data is instantaneously passed from input to output. Thus Vivado HLS will proceed with the simulation as if the deadlock has not happened. Intel HLS compiler avoids the deadlock problem by automatically increasing the FIFO depth; however, this creates a new problem of mismatch between what is simulated and synthesized.

The second problem was found after we applied code transformation to avoid the deadlock. Figure 4 shows the transformation for M3 in Figure 3. If the input FIFO is empty, a bubble is inserted into the pipeline (line 4)—this allows the pipeline to keep processing the already-read data even if there is no additional input. The deadlock situation is removed since M4 can now receive the output from M3.

Even though the deadlock was avoided, however, the modules still have to wait for the data to be flushed. This causes a delay that we call *artificial stall*. Since HLS tools do not consider the delay due to the latency of a module, such performance degradation cannot be simulated.

3.3 Missing Data from Feedback Path

As mentioned previously, Vivado HLS simulates the functions in the order they are instantiated in the source code. This causes a problem if a feedback path exists that passes data from later instantiated functions to earlier ones. At the time earlier functions are simulated, the data would not be available. As a result, Vivado HLS simulates the program as if the feedback FIFOs are always empty. Intel HLS can simulate the feedback data from blocking read correctly, because a thread simulating each module can wait for others to pass the data—although it is not guaranteed that the feedback data from non-blocking read will arrive at the right timing.

We demonstrate this problem with matrix multiplication example ($C = A \times B$) in linear systolic array architecture [8, 16]. As shown in Fig. 5, each PE computes one column of the matrix C (C_{ij} += $A_{ik} * B_{kj}$). Data from the matrix A and B are fed into the array in the forward direction, while the results of matrix C are collected in the backward direction. If the modules are instantiated in the order of PE_1, PE_2, ..., and PE_N, Vivado HLS will simulate PE_1 assuming the FIFO for C is always empty, and this will cause the tool to produce incorrect results.

4 PROBLEM STATEMENT AND CHALLENGES

The data ordering problem (Section 3.1) can be solved if the simulator models the FIFO data transaction (read/write) and the FIFO stall (empty/full) in a cycle-accurate fashion. The artificial deadlock problem (Section 3.2) requires modules to initiate FIFO read and write at the timing that reflects the computation latency. In other words, it requires cycle-accurate modeling of *computation stages*, which we define as the computation latency between pairs of FIFO read and FIFO write. The feedback problem (Section 3.3) does not occur if the FIFO read in the feedback path is simulated after the FIFO write.

Thus, the problem is stated as follows: given a source code and its scheduling information, we need a simulator that models the communication and the computation stages in a cycle-accurate manner. The simulator also must produce correct output data.

In addition to this main requirement, the simulator should be able to provide the execution cycles of each module to help programmers apply performance optimization. Also, if the modules deadlock, the simulator should provide the content of the internal registers for debugging purpose. Moreover, the simulation code should be semantically similar to the source code as much as possible (as opposed to being a low-level code such as RTL), so that users can easily understand what is being simulated.

With such complicated requirements, several challenges arise:

- **Challenge 1 : Cycle-accurate simulation**
  It is difficult to discover the exact cycle when statements are executed since the information given by the HLS tool is very limited. Intel OpenCL HLS only provides loop initiation interval (II). Vivado HLS provides slightly more information—such as the module's finite-state machine (FSM) state when FIFO read or write is performed. However, for computation statements, it is difficult to find the exact cycle, because Vivado HLS only provides lists of LLVM IR and the corresponding FSM states. Mapping such low-level representation back to the original C code is a difficult task.
  Also, even if the schedule of all operations are known, the simulator has to *selectively* execute statements that correspond to a particular FSM state at each cycle. Moreover, the content of the variables in the previous state has to be available, and the updated variables have to be stored for the next state simulation.
- **Challenge 2 : Simulation of parallelism**
  RTL is an inherently parallel language—it has multiple levels of parallelism including task-level parallelism and pipelined parallelism. On the other hand, pure C is written in a sequential form. The challenge is in transforming C into a form that can simulate the concurrency.
- **Challenge 3 : FIFO communication and pipeline stall**
  In RTL simulation, a full or empty signal from FIFO can halt an FSM. An equivalent software simulator would also need to mimic this behavior based on the status of the FIFOs. Also, a deadlock would need to be detected if all pipelines can no longer make any progress.
- **Challenge 4 : Loop and function simulation**
  We would need to construct an equivalent model of high-level semantics, such as loops and functions.

5 AUTOMATED CODE GENERATION FOR RAPID CYCLE-ACCURATE SIMULATION

In this section, we provide a solution to each challenge in Section 4 and describe our proposed automated simulation code generation flow. For illustration, we will use the toy_mpath example (Fig. 3)

```
01 void M2_SIM(){                          //simulation function for M2
02   static int M2_state = 1;//use "static" var for the next cycle
03   ...
04   if(M2_state == 1){        //state conditional block for state 1
05     ...          //computation stmt & communication for state 1
06   }
07   else if(M2_state == 2){ //state conditional block for state 2
08     ...          //computation stmt & communication for state 2
09   }
10 }                  //exit sim function after simulating one cycle
```

Figure 6: Simulation function structure for cycle-accurate simulation

after applying the deadlock avoidance transformation discussed in Section 3.2.

5.1 Cycle-Accurate Simulation

For cycle-accurate simulation, we declare an FSM state variable for each module and copy statements to the conditional block that correspond to its simulated state. An example can be found for M2 module in lines 4–9 of Fig. 6. Only the statements for a single cycle are simulated and then the simulation function exits. The contents of the variables are restored and saved regardless of simulation function entrance or exit by using static variables (line 2).

Regardless of the exact cycle a computation statement is simulated, we exploit the fact that the behavior observed from outside the module (including the module's computation stage) would be the same as long as the inter-module FIFO communication is simulated at the correct cycle. Thus, even if the schedule of a module's computation statement is unknown, we can assign an arbitrary state that does not violate the timing causality with the cycle-known FIFO communication that has dependency with the computation statement. We assign states to the computation statements based on as-soon-as-possible scheduling policy to reduce the number of pipelined shift registers (Section 5.2.1). The simulation of computation statements and FIFO communication will be further explained in Section 5.2.1 and Section 5.3, respectively.

5.2 Simulation of Parallelism

5.2.1 Pipelined Parallelism.
In a pipelined loop, different iterations are executed in parallel in a single FSM state. The parallel factor is same as the loop iteration latency (IL, also called pipeline depth). To simulate such parallelism, we need to keep multiple copies of the same variable for each pipelined stage. For example, the "temp" variable in M2 (Fig. 3) is copied through the pipeline like shift registers (line 15 of Fig. 7). Then, instead of placing the computation for each pipeline stage in a corresponding M2_state conditional block as in Fig. 6, we place all computation in a single M2_state conditional block as shown in lines 4–23 of Fig. 7. This transformation allows us to effectively simulate the pipelined parallelism. If II is larger than 1, the computation at state i is placed at the state conditional block of $i\%II$.

It is important to note that the order of each pipeline stage has been *reversed* (st6, ... st3, st2). This limits the content of shift register to be copied to the immediate next state only in a single cycle. Also, in order to invalidate a pipeline bubble (from the artificial deadlock avoidance transformation in Section 3.2), we propagate the enable signal through the pipeline stages (line 14 and 19).

5.2.2 Task-Level Parallelism.
The task-level parallelism is simulated by processing one cycle of all modules and FIFOs in a round-robin fashion. This is processed in the scheduler loop in line 6-14 of Fig. 8. It is composed of module (line 8-9) and FIFO (line 10-11) simulation loop.

It is possible that different order of the module and FIFO simulation loop leads to different output—for example, depending on if

```
01 static bool p1_en_st3, ... p1_en_st6 = false; //enable signals
02 static int temp_st3, ... temp_st6;            //shift registers
03 ...
04 else if(M2_state == 2){ //starting state for the pipelined loop
05   ...
06   if( p1_en_st6 == true ){   //enabled 4 cycles after FIFO read
07     p1_en_st6 = false;       //disables enable signal after use
08     fifo3_arr[fifo3_wptr++] = temp_st6*711;   //FIFO data write
09     fifo3_wnum--;                             //(see Sect 5.3.1)
10   }
11   ...
12   if( p1_en_st3 == true ){    //enabled 1 cycle after FIFO read
13     p1_en_st3 = false;       //disables enable signal after use
14     p1_en_st4 = true;             //enable signal propagation
15     temp_st4 = temp_st3;    //shift register for "temp" variable
16   }
17   if( i_st2 < N ){             //loop exit condition (see Sect 5.4)
18     if( fifo1_rnum != 0 ){ //if FIFO not empty (see Sect 5.3.1)
19       p1_en_st3 = true; //enables if path for later pipe stages
20       temp_st3 = fifo1_arr[fifo1_rptr++];    //FIFO data read
21       fifo1_rnum--;                          //(see Sect 5.3.1)
22       i_st2++; ...           // loop iterator update (see Sect 5.4)
23 } } }
```

Figure 7: Code transformation to model cycle-accurate, pipelined parallelism (M2 in Fig. 3)

```
01 void (*MList[M])();                   /module func ptr list
02 void (*FList[F])();                   //FIFO func ptr list
03 Mlist[0] = M1_SIM;      .... Mlist[3] = M4_SIM;  //init
04 Flist[0] = fifo1;       .... Flist[3] = fifo4;
05
06 while(1){  //scheduler loop:
07   ...    // loop until deadlock or all modules finish
08   for(i = 0; i < M; i++)             //simulate all modules
09     Mlist[i]();
10   for(i = 0; i < F; i++)             //simulate all FIFOs
11     Flist[i]();
12   ...
13   cycle++;
14 }
```

Figure 8: Module/FIFO simulation scheduler to model task-level parallelism

the data producer PE is simulated before or after the consumer PE. A way to avoid this problem will be discussed in Section 5.3.1.

5.3 FIFO Simulation

5.3.1 FIFO Communication.
The FIFO is implemented as a circular buffer with read/write pointers (fifo_rptr and fifo_wptr) and an array (fifo_arr) of FIFO buffer size. Also, we declare fifo_rnum and fifo_wnum variables to denote the number of data and buffer space available in the FIFO. FIFO reads and writes in the source code are transformed based on Table 2. For example, the FIFO write in M2 (fifth line of M2 in Fig. 3) would be transformed to: $(fifo3\_arr[fifo3\_wptr ++] = temp\_st6 * 711; fifo3\_wnum --;)$ (line 8-9 of Fig. 7).

In addition to decreasing the number of buffer space $(fifo3\_wnum --;)$ for FIFO write, we would need to increase the number of available data $(fifo3\_rnum ++;)$. However, this process is delayed until the FIFO simulation loop (line 10-11 of Fig. 8). The reason is to ensure that simulating data producer PE earlier than the consumer PE (in the module simulation loop in line 8-9 of Fig. 8) does not allow transfer of data through the FIFO in the same cycle (1 cycle latency is needed). More details on the FIFO simulation can be found in the extended paper (see footnote[2] on page 2).

Table 2: Code transformation for FIFO communication

HLS source code	Transformed simulation code
fifo.empty()	fifo_rnum == 0
fifo.full()	fifo_wnum == 0
data = fifo.read()	data = fifo_arr[fifo_rptr++]; fifo_rnum--;
fifo.write(data)	fifo_arr[fifo_wptr++] = data; fifo_wnum--;

```
j++;                //inner loop update
if( !(j<16) ){      //inner loop cond
  i++;              //outer loop update
  j=0;              //inner loop init
  if( !(i<N/16) ){  //outer loop cond
    M1_state = 0;   //loop exit
} }
```

Figure 9: Loop condition and update for flattened loop in M1 of Fig. 3

5.3.2 Pipeline Stall Modeling. If a pipeline stall condition is met, none of the statements should be simulated at the current state. Thus, the stall condition should be placed at the beginning of a state conditional block. This will make the simulation function to exit without changing any variables. After applying the artificial deadlock avoidance transformation, FIFO read no longer causes the stall, but FIFO write will. The stall condition is met when the FIFO is full and when the state for the FIFO write statement has been enabled. For example, the pipeline stall condition that corresponds to FIFO write in line 8 of Fig. 7 would be: $if(p1\_en\_st6 \&\& fifo3\_wnum == 0)$. This condition will be added to line 5 of Fig. 7.

Note that our tool can detect a deadlock by checking if no state transition occurs (stalled) in any modules and no data transaction occurs in any FIFOs. This may happen if the user decides not to incorporate the artificial deadlock avoidance method (Section 3.2).

5.4 Loop and Function Simulation

Simulation of statements inside a pipelined loop has been discussed in Section 5.2.1. For the loop initialization statement, it is simulated upon entering the first state of a loop. The loop update expression is simulated at each iteration of a loop. If the loop condition is met after the update, state transition for loop exit occurs. For a flattened loop (e.g., M1 in Fig. 3), the update and the loop condition check is performed starting from the innermost nested loop, as illustrated in Fig. 9.

A function call is simulated by sending a module enable signal to the scheduler loop (Fig. 8). Next, the function argument values are copied into the newly called module.

6 OVERALL FLOW

The overall simulation framework of FLASH is shown in Fig. 10. Given an input Vivado HLS C code, we apply an optional pre-processing step of transforming pipelined loops to avoid artificial deadlock (Section 3.2). Also, some labels are added to easily identify loops and functions. The transformation step uses the APIs in the ROSE compiler infrastructure [19]. The transformed code is fed into the Vivado HLS for synthesis. Based on the scheduling report given by the HLS tool, the input code is automatically transformed for rapid software simulation (Section 5). The simulation code has been made compatible with the Vivado HLS software simulator for easy integration with the existing tool. As a final output, our flow currently provides the number of cycles consumed in each module. As a future effort it will be enhanced to provide both functional debugging support (e.g., data dump, triggers), and performance debugging support (e.g., module stall analysis).

7 EXPERIMENTAL RESULTS

7.1 Experimental Setup

For HLS tool, we use Vivado HLS 2018.2 [24]. For platform, we target the ADM-PCIE-KU3 board [1] with Xilinx's Ultrascale KU060 FPGA [23]. The target clock frequency is 250MHz. The simulation is conducted with a server node that has Intel Xeon Processor E5-2680 [13] and 64GB of DRAM. The simulation files were compiled with –O3 flag.

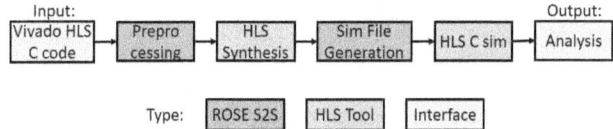

Figure 10: Overall simulation framework of FLASH

The experiment is performed on toy_mpath (Fig. 3) and three dataflow benchmarks: stencil [3], molecular dynamics simulation [7] (Fig. 1), and matrix multiplication [8] (Fig. 5).

7.2 Execution Time

As mentioned in Section 6, preprocessing, HLS synthesis, and simulation file generation steps are needed to prepare the files for the proposed simulation. The time breakdown of the steps is presented in Table 3.

Table 3: Simulation preparation time breakdown (preprocessing, HLS synthesis, and simulation file generation: Fig. 10)

Benchmark	Preproc	HLS Synth	SimFile Gen	Total
Toy_mpath	7.1s	24s	7.5s	39s
Stencil	15s	60s	22s	97s
MD_sim	8.0s	35s	11s	54s
Mat_mul	8.1s	31s	10s	49s

The simulation time comparison among Vivado HLS C simulation, Vivado HLS RTL simulation, Intel OpenCL HLS simulation (using Quartus 18.0 [15]), and our FLASH simulation flow is presented in Table 4. FLASH is about 1,390X (=1,570/1.13) faster than the RTL simulation. This confirms our initial speculation that simulating based on the scheduling information will result in much faster speed, since the simulation is not slowed by the resource allocation / binding information or the component library that exist in RTL simulation.

Table 4: Simulation time comparison among Vivado HLS C simulation, Vivado HLS RTL simulation, Intel OpenCL HLS simulation, and FLASH simulation

Benchmark	V C Sim	V RTL Sim	I OCL Sim	FLASH
Toy_mpath	0.602s	492s	4.60s	0.570s
	(1.00X)	(817X)	(7.64X)	(0.947X)
Stencil	1.46s	113s	2.63s	1.25s
	(1.00X)	(77.4X)	(1.80X)	(0.856X)
MD_sim	0.0547s	100s	0.0921s	0.0677s
	(1.00X)	(1,830X)	(1.68X)	(1.24X)
Mat_mul	0.0539s	192s	0.201s	0.0810s
	(1.00X)	(3,560X)	(3.73X)	(1.50X)
AVG	(1.00X)	(1,570X)	(3.71X)	(1.13X)

Since our flow reflects the scheduling information, we can expect some slowdown compared to the Vivado HLS C simulation. This is noticeable in Mat_mul, where the frequent FIFO stall (Table 5) lengthens the simulation process. MD_sim has a long simulation time due to the deep pipeline (55)—the overhead of copying shift registers and enable signals (Section 5.2.1) for pipeline stages becomes relatively large. However, it is interesting to note that for Toy_mpath and Stencil, FLASH was even faster than the Vivado HLS C simulation. This suggests that there was an unexpected factor which has negated the simulation speed overhead of the proposed flow. We found that this is largely attributed to the fact that Vivado HLS can allocate unlimited FIFO buffer for C simulation (Table 1). To model FIFO, the Vivado HLS C simulator uses the C++ Standard Template Library (queue.h), which incurs the overhead of dynamically allocating buffer and copying its content. For example, the C simulation time of Toy_mpath reduces from 0.602s to 0.076s if we replace FIFO library calls with fixed-size arrays (array size is set to the number of total FIFO elements written). FLASH simulation flow does not have this problem, because the FIFO library calls have been replaced with array-based communication (Section 5.3). The average slowdown of FLASH compared to the Vivado HLS C simulation is 1.13X.

Please note that in our initial research stage, we also evaluated a similar flow with SystemC. However, the overhead in SystemC simulation environment was causing a 2-3X slowdown compared to the proposed C-based flow, which motivated us to follow the current approach.

7.3 Accuracy

As explained in Section 4, the correctness problem can be solved by simulating in a cycle-accurate manner. The data value and the data ordering has been verified by comparing the output of FLASH simulator with that of the RTL simulator.

In Table 5, we compare the cycle estimation accuracy with Vivado HLS synthesis report after we specify the maximum loop bound for each loop. We were not able to provide comparison with Intel HLS since the tool does not provide cycle estimate. The estimation error rate is small for Stencil, because [3] has built-in mechanism to allocate adequate buffers. For the rest of the benchmarks, we have applied a small (1–2) FIFO depth (an example was shown in Fig. 3). This causes FIFO buffer to be frequently full and empty and leads to worse performance than what HLS tool has predicted. Our flow, on the other hand, simulates in a cycle-accurate fashion and accurately estimates such performance degradation.

Table 5: Total execution cycle predicted by Vivado HLS synthesis report and FLASH, and its error rate compared to the RTL-simulated result

Benchmark	RTL sim	Vivado HLS	FLASH
Toy_mpath	4,500,010	2,000,016	4,500,010
	-	(-56%)	(0%)
Stencil	524,309	524,299	524,309
	-	(~0%)	(0%)
MD_sim	12,089	10,498	12,089
	-	(-13%)	(0%)
Mat_mul	330,006	131,075	330,006
	-	(-60%)	(0%)
AVG	-	(-32%)	(0%)

8 CONCLUDING REMARKS

By simulating based on the scheduling information, we were able to solve the correctness issue of the software simulators and also provide accurate performance estimation. Also, simulating without allocation / binding information and component libraries allowed us to achieve three orders of magnitude faster speed compared to the RTL simulators. We have described an automated code generation flow that enables this new simulation flow.

We hope that the promising result presented in this work will motivate HLS commercial tool industry to provide additional routine that simulates based on the scheduling information only. This will substantially decrease the validation time of the customers who wish to rapidly estimate cycle-accurate performance, obtain correct output data, or detect possible deadlock situations.

As a future work, we will continue to widen the range of benchmarks so that the transformation flow will be robust enough to accommodate any Vivado HLS input code. We hope to include the Intel HLS flow if their tool's synthesis report provides detailed

schedule information in the future. Also, we will enhance the output analysis stage to provide better functional and performance debugging support. In addition, we plan to add parallelization using Pthread/OpenMP so that large-scale simulation can be performed by exploiting multicore architecture.

ACKNOWLEDGMENTS

This research is partially supported by Intel and NSF Joint Research Center on Computer Assisted Programming for Heterogeneous Architectures (CAPA) (CCF-1723773). We are grateful to Xilinx for the software and the hardware donation. We thank Professor Miryung Kim (UCLA), Chaosheng Shi (Xilinx), and Professor Zhiru Zhang (Cornell Univ.) for the helpful discussions and the suggestions. We also thank Janice Wheeler for proofreading this paper.

REFERENCES

[1] AlphaData. 2017. Alpha Data ADM-PCIE-KU3 Datasheet. (2017). http://www.alpha-data.com/pdfs/adm-pcie-ku3.pdf
[2] A. Canis, et al. 2013. From software to accelerators with LegUp high-level synthesis,. In *Proc. Int. Conf. Compilers, Architectures and Synthesis for Embedded Systems (CASES'13)*. 18–26.
[3] Y. Chi, J. Cong, P. Wei, and P. Zhou. 2018. SODA : stencil with optimized dataflow architecture. In *Proc. IEEE/ACM Int. Conf. Computer-Aided Design (ICCAD'18)*.
[4] Y. Choi and J. Cong. 2017. HLScope: High-level performance debugging for FPGA designs,. In *IEEE Ann. Int. Symp. Field-Programmable Custom Computing Machines (FCCM'17)*. 125–128.
[5] Y. Choi, P. Zhang, P. Li, and J. Cong. 2017. HLScope+: Fast and accurate performance estimation for FPGA HLS. In *Proc. IEEE/ACM Int. Conf. Computer-Aided Design (ICCAD'17)*. 691–698.
[6] M. Chung, J. Kim, and S. Ryu. 2014. SimParallel: A high performance parallel SystemC simulator using hierarchical multi-threading. In *IEEE Int. Symp. Circuits and Systems (ISCAS'14)*. 1472–1475.
[7] J. Cong, Z. Fang, H. Kianinejad, and P. Wei. 2016. Revisiting FPGA acceleration of molecular dynamics simulation with dynamic data flow behavior in high-level synthesis. *ArXiv Preprint* (2016). http://https://arxiv.org/pdf/1611.04474.pdf
[8] J. Cong and J. Wang. 2018. PolySA: polyhedral-based systolic array auto compilation. In *Proc. IEEE/ACM Int. Conf. Computer-Aided Design (ICCAD'18)*.
[9] J. Cong, et al. 2011. High-level synthesis for FPGAs: From prototyping to deployment. *IEEE Trans. Computer-Aided Design of Integrated Circuits and Systems* 30, 4 (2011), 473–491.
[10] P. Coussy, et al. 2009. An introduction to high-level synthesis. *IEEE Design & Test of Comput.* 26, 4 (2009), 8–17.
[11] S. Dai, M. Tan, K. Hao, and Z. Zhang. 2014. Flushing-enabled loop pipelining for high-level synthesis. In *Proc. Ann. Design Automation Conf. (DAC'14)*.
[12] J. Goeders and S. Wilton. 2015. Using dynamic signal-tracing to debug compiler-optimized HLS circuits on FPGAs,. In *IEEE Ann. Int. Symp. Field-Programmable Custom Computing Machines (FCCM'15)*. 127–134.
[13] Intel. 2018. Intel Xeon Processor E5-2680 v4. (2018). www.intel.com/
[14] Intel. 2018. Intel FPGA SDK for OpenCL Pro Edition. (2018). https://www.altera.com/en_US/pdfs/literature/hb/opencl-sdk/aocl-best-practices-guide.pdf
[15] Intel. 2018. Quartus Prime Pro Edition Handbook. (2018). www.intel.com/
[16] J. Jang, S. Choi, and V. Prasanna. 2005. Energy-and time-efficient matrix multiplication on FPGAs. *IEEE Trans. Very Large Scale Integration* 13, 11 (2005), 1305–1319.
[17] S. Lahti, P. Sjövall, and J. Vanne. 2018. Are we there yet? A study on the state of high-level synthesis. *IEEE Trans. Computer-Aided Design of Integrated Circuits and Systems* (2018).
[18] J. Monson and B. Hutchings. 2014. New approaches for in-system debug of behaviorally-synthesized FPGA circuits,. In *IEEE Int. Conf. Field Programmable Logic and Appl. (FPL'14)*.
[19] ROSE. 2018. ROSE compiler infrastructure. (2018). http://rosecompiler.org/
[20] T. Schmidt, G. Liu, and R. Dömer. 2017. Exploiting thread and data level parallelism for ultimate parallel SystemC simulation. In *Proc. Ann. Design Automation Conf. (DAC'17)*.
[21] E. Sozzo, et al. 2017. A common backend for hardware acceleration on FPGA. In *IEEE Int. Conf. Comput. Design (ICCD'17)*. 427–430.
[22] A. Verma, et al. 2017. Developing dynamic profiling and debugging support in OpenCL for FPGAs. In *Proc. Ann. Design Automation Conf. (DAC'17)*. 56–61.
[23] Xilinx. 2018. UltraScale architecture and product data sheet: overview (DS890). (2018). https://www.xilinx.com/support/documentation/data_sheets/ds890-ultrascale-overview.pdf
[24] Xilinx. 2018. Vivado High-level Synthesis (UG902). (2018). https://www.xilinx.com/support/documentation/sw_manuals/xilinx2018_2/ug902-vivado-high-level-synthesis.pdf
[25] C. Yu, et al. 2018. S2FA: an accelerator automation framework for heterogeneous computing in datacenters. In *Proc. Ann. Design Automation Conf. (DAC'18)*.

Poster Session 2

PAI-FCNN: FPGA Based CNN Inference System

Lansong Diao, Zhao Jiang, Hao Liang, Chang'an Ye,
Kai Chen, Li Ding, Shunli Dou, Meng Sun, Lixue Xia,
Jiansong Zhang, Wei Lin, *Alibaba Group*
Contact: muduan.zjs@alibaba-inc.com

We describe the FPGA subsystem of the Platform of Artificial Intelligence (PAI) in Alibaba Group, called PAI-FCNN. PAI-FCNN plays the role of a heterogeneous back-end for CNN inference, together with other CPU, GPU and ASIC subsystems in PAI. Driven by various business needs, we built PAI-FCNN from scratch since two years ago. We present our experience from FPGA/compiler design and implementation, to system evaluation and deployment. In particular, in order to address three practical challenges: (1) Efficient processing for diverse operators and model structure such as Deconv, Dilated Conv, Up-sampling, PReLu and Concatenation. (2) Serving multiple highly-different models on single FPGA hardware. (3) Competitive performance with alternative GPU or ASIC solutions, we extensively perform joint software & hardware design to optimize system efficiency across multiple CNN models, which includes model reconstruction in compiler software and flexible data access in data-flow CNN processor. We also incorporate reduced precision and model retraining to boost system capacity. Using U-net as an example, on Xilinx KU115 chip, with the help of 74.9% efficiency on Int16-precision hardware (with 3.226TOPS capacity) and 72.9% efficiency on mixed-int8/int3-precision hardware (with 14.746TOPS capacity), we achieve slightly better throughput and 2X higher power efficiency than P4.

Keywords: CNN; Inference; System; Compiler; Joint Software & Hardware Design; Reduced Precision

DOI: https://doi.org/10.1145/3289602.3293957

JuxtaPiton: Enabling Heterogeneous-ISA Research with RISC-V and SPARC FPGA Soft-cores

Katie Lim, *University of Washington*
Jonathan Balkind, David Wentzlaff, *Princeton University*
Contact: katielim@cs.washington.edu
Energy efficiency has become an increasingly important concern in computer architecture due to the end of Dennard scaling. Heterogeneity has been explored as a way to achieve better energy efficiency and heterogeneous microarchitecture chips have become common in the mobile setting.

Recent research has explored using heterogeneous-ISA, heterogeneous microarchitecture, general-purpose cores to

achieve further energy efficiency gains. However, there is no open-source hardware implementation of a heterogeneous-ISA processor available for research, and effective research on heterogeneous-ISA processors necessitates the emulation speed provided by FPGA prototyping.

This work describes our experiences creating JuxtaPiton by integrating a small RISC-V core into the OpenPiton framework, which uses a modified OpenSPARC T1 core. This is the first time a new core has been integrated with the OpenPiton framework, and JuxtaPiton is the first open-source, general-purpose, heterogeneous-ISA processor. JuxtaPiton inherits all the capabilities of OpenPiton, including vital FPGA emulation infrastructure which can boot full-stack Debian Linux. Using this infrastructure, we investigate area and timing effects of using the new RISC-V core on FPGA and the performance of the new core running microbenchmarks.

Keywords: heterogeneous multicore; heterogeneous ISA; heterogeneous microarchitecture; energy efficiency; manycore; shared memory

DOI: https://doi.org/10.1145/3289602.3293958

MODA-PSO: Towards Fast Hard Block Legalization for Analytical FPGA Placement

Yun Zhou, Dries Vercruyce, Dirk Stroobandt,
Ghent University
Contact: Yun.Zhou@ugent.be

Placement is a crucial step in the FPGA design tool flow, as it determines the overall performance of the circuits. Unfortunately, it is a time-consuming task. Analytical placers have been shown to be the most time-efficient while retaining good quality. One way of implementing analytical placement is to use an iterative technique that consists of optimization and look-ahead legalization, followed by an optional refinement step. In this work, with the aim towards fast hard block legalization for further accelerating analytical placement, a novel optimizer is proposed based on the modified discrete adaptive particle swarm optimization. The proposed optimizer is embedded into the publicly available analytical placer Liquid. When compared to its version using simulated annealing for hard block legalization, this approach results in a 30% reduction in hard block legalization time and a consequent 5% runtime reduction for the analytical placement, at the cost of only a 1% increase in post-routed wirelength and critical path delay. The results indicate that the nature-inspired particle swarm optimization is promising for tackling such a problem with new learning strategies and adaptation.

Keywords: Analytical FPGA Placement; Fast Legalization; Nature-inspired; Discrete Particle Swarm Optimization; Adaptive Parameters

DOI: https://doi.org/10.1145/3289602.3293959

A PYNQ-compliant Online Platform
for Zynq-based DNN Developers

Chen Chen, Jun Xia, *Jiangnan University*
Wenmin Yang, *OpenHEC Lab*
Kang Li, Zhilei Chai, *Jiangnan University*
Contact: zlchai@jiangnan.edu.cn

The Zynq heterogeneous SoC from Xilinx is able to supporting software/hardware co-designing in one single chip, making it possible to take advantage of software flexibility and hardware acceleration at the same time. PYNQ project from Xilinx is trying to take advantage of high performance and low power consumption of Zynq while improve its programmability. In order to improve the ecosystem of PYNQ and help more embedded AI applications use the Zynq-based high-efficiency computational engine, this paper proposes a PYNQ-compliant online platform (OpenHEC-PYNQ) that integrates all necessary factors for the Zynq-based DNN developer. This platform makes HDL/HLS designers able to access all resources they needed via the Internet and finish all jobs one-stop. To show effectiveness of this platform, a YOLOv2 FPGA acceleration library is implemented based on OpenHEC-PYNQ.

Keywords: FPGA; DNN; Ecosystem; Pynq; Cloud Platform

DOI: https://doi.org/10.1145/3289602.3293961

SwitchAgg: A Further Step Towards
In-Network Computation

Fan Yang, ZhanWang, Xiaoxiao Ma, Guojun Yuan,
Xuejun An, *Institute of Computing Technology,
Chinese Academy of Sciences*
Contact: yangfan@ncic.ac.cn

Many distributed applieations adopt a partition- aggregation pattern to achieve high performance and scalability. The aggregation process, which usually takes a large portion of the overall execution time, incurs large amount of network traffic and bottlenecks the system performance. To reduce network traffic, some researches take advantage of network devices to commit innetwork aggregation. However, these approaches use either special topology or middle-boxes, which cannot be easily deployed in current datacenters.

The emerging programmable RMT switch brings us new opportunities to implement in-network computation task. However, we argue that the architecture of RMT switch is not suitable for in-network aggregation since it is designed primarily for implementing traditional network functions.

In this paper, we first give a detailed analysis of in-network aggregation, and point out the key factor that affects the data reduction ratio. We then propose SwitchAgg, which is an innetwork aggregation system that is compatible with current datacenter infrastructures. We also evaluate the performance improvement we have gained from SwitchAgg. Our results show

that, SwitchAgg can process data aggregation tasks at line rate and gives a high data reduction rate, which helps us to cut down network traffic and alleviate pressure on server CPU. In the system performance test, the job-completion-time can be reduced as much as 50%.

Keywords: In-network Computation; Data Aggregation; Switch Design

DOI: https://doi.org/10.1145/3289602.329396

A Fine-Grained Sparse Accelerator
for Multi-Precision DNN

Shulin Zeng, *Tsinghua University*
Yujun Lin, *MIT*
Shuang Liang, *Tsinghua University*
Junlong Kang, Dongliang Xie, Yi Shan, *Xilinx*
Song Han, *MIT*
Yu Wang, Huazhong Yang, *Tsinghua University*
Contact: zengsl18@mails.tsinghua.edu.cn

Neural Networks (NNs) have made a significant breakthrough in many fields, while they also pose a great challenge to hardware platforms since the state-of-the-art neural networks are both communicational- and computational-intensive. Researchers proposed model compression algorithms using sparsification and quantization, along with specific hardware architecture designs, to accelerate various applications. However, the irregularity of memory access caused by the sparsity severely damages the regularity of intensive computation loops. Therefore, the architecture design for sparse neural networks is crucial to better software and hardware co-design for neural network applications.

To face these challenges, this paper first analyzes the computation patterns of different NN structures and unify them into the form of sparse matrix-vector multiplication, sparse matrix-matrix multiplication, and element-wise multiplication. On the basis of the EIE which supports only the fully-connected network and recurrent neural network (RNN), we expand it to support the convolution neural network (CNN) using the input vector transform unit. This paper designs a multi-precision multiplier with supporting datapath, which makes the proposed architecture have a better acceleration effect in the low-bit quantization with the same hardware architecture. The proposed accelerator architecture can achieve the equivalent performance and energy efficiency up to 574.2 GOPS, 42.8 GOPS/W for CNN and 110.4 GOPS, 8.24 GOPS/W for RNN under 4-bit quantization on Xilinx XCKU115 FPGA running at 200MHz. And it is the state-of-the-art accelerator supporting CNN-RNN-based models like the long-term recurrent convolutional network with 571.1 GOPS performance and 42.6 GOPS/W energy efficiency under 4-bit data format.

Keywords: sparse neural network; multiple precisions; hardware computation; accelerator architecture

DOI: https://doi.org/10.1145/3289602.3293964

Building FPGA State Machines from Sequential Code

Carl-Johannes Johnsen, Kenneth Skovhede,
University of Copenhagen
Contact: cjjohnsen@nbi.ku.dk

State machines are commonly used and well understood for hardware. However, in some cases they can introduce complexity as the program can no longer be read sequentially. We propose an extension to the SME model, which retains the sequential program structure, by using a barrier-like 'await' construct to divide a program into states. This is done by awaiting a predicate, ensuring that the sequential program does not progress until the predicate is satisfied. This initial implementation enables the clock signal as a predicate, allowing for easy partitioning of the sequential program, which is a common approach when either pipelining or sequencing a problem. Future implementations will also enable functions or signal values as predicates. The signal values will be a simple to use barrier when waiting for external input. As for the functions, it handles all the communication regarding input/output for and synchronization with the function. As always with the SME model, the problems implemented in the model can be transpiled into VHDL along with a VHDL test bench, which verifies that the generated VHDL matches the SME simulation. Our preliminary results shows that Xilinx Vivado recognises the state machines and that the SME simulation is clock cycle accurate to the simulation of the generated VHDL. Furthermore, we see reduced resource consumption and higher clock rates, as we should by leveraging state machines, without increasing the complexity and readability of the original program.

Keywords: SME; state machine; FPGA; VHDL; async; await; code complexity; HLS

DOI: https://doi.org/10.1145/3289602.3293965

Design and Implementation of a Deterministic FPGA Router on a CPU+FPGA Acceleration Platform

Dario Korolija, Mirjana Stojilović,
École Polytechnique Fédérale de Lausanne
Contact: mirjana.stojilovic@epfl.ch

FPGA routing is one the longest steps in FPGA compilation, often preventing fast edit-compile-test cycles in prototyping and development. There have been attempts to accelerate FPGA routing using algorithmic improvements, multi-core or multi-CPU platforms. Instead, we propose porting FPGA routing to a CPU+FPGA platform. Motivated by the approaches in FPGA-accelerated graph processing, we propose and implement three acceleration strategies: (1) reducing the number of expensive random memory accesses, (2) parallel and pipelined computation, and (3) efficient hardware priority queues. To reduce irregular memory accesses we first allow wire-to-pin wavefront expansion *only* when a net is reaching one of its destination pins and, second,

we group in *sets* all the wires starting at the same (x, y) coordinate of the FPGA grid and going in the same direction. Consequently, it becomes possible to design an FPGA accelerator that performs streaming memory accesses and parallel wavefront expansion on all wires in two connected sets. To test and evaluate our FPGA-accelerated PathFinder-based router, we implement it on DE1-SoC, Intel's ARM+FPGA platform and run a set of benchmarks from the VTR suite. The results show that our implementation produces deterministic and good quality output. It is also successful in accelerating a purely software version on the same CPU+FPGA platform, but not against VPR running on a powerful Intel Core-i5 CPU, due to the limitations of the chosen mid-end DE1-SoC platform. Yet, our performance prediction model suggests that higher memory bandwidth and faster FP units would render our router superior to the software alternative.

Keywords: FPGA routing; hardware acceleration; parallel maze expansion; ARM; HW/SW co-design; PathFinder

DOI: https://doi.org/10.1145/3289602.3293966

An FPGA-based Fine Tuning Accelerator for a Sparse CNN

Hiroki Nakahara, Akira Jinguji, Masayuki Shimoda,
Shimpei Sato
Tokyo Institute of Technology
Contact: nakahara.h.ad@m.titech.ac.j

Fine-tuning learns abundant feature expression for a wide range of natural images by using a pre-trained CNN model. It can be applied to a wide range of the neural network (NN)based computer vision problems. This paper proposes an FPGA-based fine-tuning accelerator for a sparse convolutional neural network (CNN). The proposed architecture consists of sparse convolutional units and pooling units with distributed stacks those are suitable for a sparse CNN. Additionally, this paper presents a fine-tuning scheme, which loads a pre-trained sparse CNN to reduce the memory size for the training step. Thus, our fine-tuning scheme stores all parameters on BRAMs and Ultra RAMs in the case of the Xilinx Virtex UltraScale+ FPGA to accelerate the training computation and reduce power consumption by eliminating energy-costly DRAM accesses. We implemented on a Xilinx Virtex UltraScale+ VC1525 acceleration development kit. Experimental results show that the proposed sparse finetuning accelerator on the FPGA can achieve four times faster, 2.9 times lower power consumption, and 11.6 times better performance per power, compared to the existing NVidia GTX1080Ti GPU.

Keywords: FPGA routing; hardware acceleration; parallel maze expansion; ARM; HW/SW co-design; PathFinder

DOI: https://doi.org/10.1145/3289602.3293967

Embracing Systolic: Super Systolization of Large-Scale Circulant Matrix-vector Multiplication on FPGA with Subquadratic Space Complexity

Jiafeng Xie, *Villanova University*
Chiou-Yng Lee, *Lunghwa University of Science & Technology*
Contact: jiafeng.xie@villanova.edu

The recent advance in artificial intelligence (AI) technology has led to a new round of systolic structure innovation. Many AI accelerators have employed systolic structure to realize the core large-scale matrix-vector multiplication for high-performance processing, which has a complexity of $o(n^2)$ for matrix size of $n \times n$ (difficult to be implemented on the field-programmable gate array (FPGA) platform). To overcome this drawback, in this paper, we propose a super systolization strategy to implement the core circulant matrix-vector multiplication into a systolic structure with subquadratic space complexity. The proposed effort is carried out through two stages of coherent interdependent efforts: (i) a novel matrix-vector multiplication algorithm based on Toeplitz matrix-vector product (TMVP) approach is proposed to obtain subquadratic space complexity; (ii) a series of optimization techniques are introduced to map the proposed algorithm into desired systolic structure. Finally, detailed complexity analysis and comparison have been conducted to prove the efficiency of the proposed strategy. The proposed strategy is highly efficient and can be extended in many neural network based hardware implementation platforms.

Keywords: Circulant matrix-vector multiplication; field-programmable gate array; large-scale; systolic structure; subquadratic space complexity; Toeplitz matrix vector product

DOI: https://doi.org/10.1145/3289602.3293968

Dataflow Systolic Array Implementations of Matrix Decomposition Using High Level Synthesis

Jie Liu, *Tsinghua University*
Jason Cong, *University of California, Los Angeles*
Contact: sibylau@outlook.com

Matrix decomposition is a fundamental topic in numerical algebra, with its applications frequently seen in a wide range of engineering fields. Many specific systolic array structures of matrix decomposition algorithms have been proposed previously to maintain high performance as the problem size scales up. In this paper, we broadly explore different mappings of most frequently used Cholesky, LU and QR decomposition algorithms to systolic arrays. We follow the canonical mapping method to define the systolic array design space. By selecting different linear projection vectors on the dependency graph of each algorithm, multiple one-dimensional and two-dimensional systolic arrays are generated. To obtain better performance, we also introduce streaming dataflow on the top module which enables heterogeneous PEs to work in

data-driven manners. All designs are implemented using the Xilinx Vivado High-Level Synthesis tools. We show in our experimental results the differences in performance and resource consumption of each mapping. We also demonstrate up to 50.13x and 4.58x better throughput of our implementations compared with the Xilinx HLS linear algebra library and the LAPACK library on CPUs.

Keywords: Systolic Array; Matrix Decomposition; Dataflow; High-Level Synthesis; Throughput

DOI: https://doi.org/10.1145/3289602.3293969

Speedy: An Accelerator for Sparse Convolutional Neural Networks on FPGAs

Liqiang Lu[1], Yun Liang[1]
Ruirui Huang[2], Wei Lin[2], Xiaoyuan Cui[2], Jiansong Zhang[2]
[1]*Peking University*   [2]*Alibaba group*
Contact: liqianglu@pku.edu.cn

Compressing CNNs to sparse have emerged as the most attractive approach to reduce the amount of computation and memory requirement. This compression is achieved by pruning the redundant connection in networks. Although existing FPGA architectures are able to excellently process dense CNN models, they cannot benefit from the computation reduction when accelerating the sparse CNN models. Because most of the arithmetic operations involve addition and multiplication with zero operands, meanwhile accelerating sparse CNN models incurs significant data encoding and decoding overhead. In this paper, we propose a FPGA accelerator Speedy that can efficiently exploit sparsity in CNN models. We first investigate the dataflow design space to explore the available performance with different parallelization strategies. The result of exploration is Speedy dataflow which provides enough parallel multiplications and maximizes the weight reuse. Finally, we propose Speedy FPGA architecture in which we apply line buffer design and high-throughput PE. Overall, Speedy achieves 11.3x-20.8x and 1.5x-6.8x speed up for Alexnet and VGGnet with 90% weight sparsity.

Keywords: CNN; FPGA; Sparse

DOI: https://doi.org/10.1145/3289602.3293970

DNNVM : End-to-End Compiler Leveraging Operation Fusion on FPGA-based CNN Accelerators

Yu Xing, Xilinx, *Tsinghua University*
Shuang Liang, *Tsinghua University*
Lingzhi Sui, Zhen Zhang, *Xilinx*
Jiantao Qiu, *Tsinghua University*
Xijie Jia, Xin Liu, Yushun Wang, Yi Shan, Xilinx
Yu Wang, *Tsinghua University*
Contact: xingy16@mails.tsinghua.edu.cn

In recent years, Convolutional Neural Network(CNN) is becoming the state-of-the-art method in a wide range of Artificial Intelligence(AI) domains. The increasingly large and complex CNN models are both computation bound and I/O bound. FPGA-based accelerators driven by custom Instruction Set Architecture(ISA) achieve a balance between generality and efficiency, and leave much room for optimization. Operation fusion which fuses adjacent operations without saving intermediate results back to off-chip DDR can greatly alleviate bandwidth pressure, operations can be executed by different computation engines concurrently for latency hiding. To leverage optimizations, especially operation fusion on custom instruction-based accelerators, we propose a full-stack compiler DNNVM(Deep Neural Network Virtual Machine). DNNVM is an integration of optimizers for framework-independent computing graph, loops and data layouts, an assembler, a runtime supporter and a validation environment. DNNVM works in the context of deep learning frameworks and transforms CNN models into a directed acyclic graph, XGraph. After analyzing the interaction among fusion depth, tiling across multiple stages and on-chip memory capacity, DNNVM enumerates all potentially profitable fusion opportunities according to custom fusion templates upon XGraph, by a subgraph isomorphism algorithm. In addition, DNNVM searches for the optimal execution strategies by a heuristic shortest-path algorithm. On Xilinx ZU2@330MHz, we achieve up to 1.26x speedup than naïve implementations without fusion on GoogLeNet. On Xilinx ZU9@330MHz, we achieve the throughput of 2.82 TOPs/s for VGG, 1.38 TOPs/s for ResNet50 – the fastest ever reported on comparable FPGAs.

Keywords: CNN; FPGA-based Accelerator; Compiler; Operation Fusion

DOI: https://doi.org/10.1145/3289602.3293972

A Hybrid Data-Consistent Framework for Link-Aware AccessManagement in Emerging CPU-FPGA Platforms

Liang Feng, Jieru Zhao, Tingyuan Liang, *HKUST*
Sharad Sinha, *IIT Goa*
Wei Zhang, *HKUST*
Contact: lfengad@connect.ust.hk

To satisfy the increasing demands of modern computing tasks, heterogeneous computing is gaining attention. The CPU-FPGA platform is especially promising since the FPGA enables customization for diverse computing tasks to be offloaded from the CPU to boost the performance and energy efficiency. Nowadays, tightly coupled CPU-FPGA platforms with shared coherent caches (such as the Intel HARP and IBM POWER with CAPI) have been proposed for enhanced CPU-FPGA data communication efficiency and a simplified programming model. In Intel's recently released CPU-FPGA platform HARP2, there are three links between the XEON multi-core CPU and the Arria 10 FPGA, two PCIes and one QPI, with a coherent FPGA cache attached before the QPI for the quick memory access and data locality benefit. The link choice for the FPGA memory accesses will heavily influence the performance in such platforms and the race among links may violate the data consistency. In order to enhance the performance and maintain the data consistency, we propose COODA, a static and dynamic hybrid framework for memory access management in HARP2-like

emerging CPU-FPGA platforms. COODA adaptively arranges the memory accesses to the preferred link to boost the FPGA cache benefit and enhance the utilization of all links. An automatic data consistency maintenance mechanism based on the static analysis is also applied by COODA to keep the whole data consistency. Based on implementation results on the real Intel HARP2 platform for diverse applications, COODA is shown to improve the performance a lot compared with the state-of-the-art methods.

Keywords: Heterogeneous Computing; FPGA; Memory; Data Consistency; Cache

DOI: https://doi.org/10.1145/3289602.3293973

On Feasibility of FPGAs Without Dedicated Programmable Interconnect Structure

Anastasiia Kucherenko, Stefan Nikolić, Paolo Ienne,
École Polytechnique Fédérale de Lausanne (EPFL)
Contact: stefan.nikolic@epfl.ch

It is a well known fact that a great majority of FPGA chip area goes into the programmable interconnect structure. Since area consumption is mostly proportional to the level of flexibility the interconnect structure offers, how much of this flexibility is really needed for the implementation of any design of interest is a logical question to pose. Going one step further, one may wonder if a dedicated programmable interconnect structure is even necessary. This work answers exactly this second question by providing constructive capability proofs, for a broad class of FPGA architectures composed solely of look-up tables (LUTs) connected in a fixed manner, to implement any circuit graph. Our proposed architectures consist of identical cells of LUTs with fixed connections, arranged on a 2D grid. Direct wires between cell input and output pins are also allowed, enabling long uninterrupted connections. We begin by formalizing the above architecture class, and then describe an algorithm capable of mapping any circuit on one specific member of it, in which each cell consists of a single 4-LUT. We derive area and runtime bounds for the algorithm, and finally extend it to be applicable to any architecture in which no LUT receives more than K – 4 inputs from within the cell (K is LUT size) and the number of sink LUTs of the cell does not exceed the number of source LUTs. Presented algorithms serve to answer the posed question, but, due to area-inefficiency, do not have much practical value at this point.

Keywords: fixed interconnect; hard-wired FPGAs; periodic graphs; universality proofs; routing algorithms

DOI: https://doi.org/10.1145/3289602.3293974

Fast Confidence Detection: One Hot Way to Detect Adversarial Attacks via Sensor Pattern Noise Fingerprinting

Yazhu Lan, *Duke University;*
Qingli Guo, *University of Chinese Academy of Sciences*
Guohe Zhang, *Xi'an Jiaotong University*
Yuanchao Xu, *Capital Normal University*
Kent W Nixon, Hai Helen Li, Yiran Chen, *Duke University*
Contact: yazhu.lan@duke.edu

Deep Neural Networks (DNNs) have shown phenomenal success in a wide range of real-world applications. However, a concerning weakness of DNNs is that they are vulnerable to adversarial attacks. Although there exist methods to detect adversarial attacks, they often suffer constraints on specific attack types and provide limited information to downstream systems. We specifically note that existing adversarial detectors are often binary classifiers, which differentiate clean or adversarial examples. However, detection of adversarial examples is much more complicated than such a scenario. Our key insight is that the confidence probability of detecting an input sample as an adversarial example will be more useful for the system to properly take action to resist potential attacks. In this work, we propose an innovative method for fast confidence detection of adversarial attacks based on integrity of sensor pattern noise embedded in input examples. Experimental results show that our proposed method is capable of providing a confidence distribution model of most of popular adversarial attacks. Furthermore, our presented method can provide early attack warning with even the attack types based on different properties of the confidence distribution models. Since fast confidence detection is a computationally heavy task, we propose an FPGA-Based hardware architecture based on a series of optimization techniques, such as incremental multi-level quantization and etc. We realize our proposed method on an FPGA platform and achieve a high efficiency of 29.740 IPS/W with a power consumption of only 0.7626W.

Keywords: DNNs; Confidence Detection; Adversarial Attacks; FPGA-Based Hardware Architecture; Sensor Pattern Noise

DOI: https://doi.org/10.1145/3289602.3293975

FTConv: FPGA Acceleration for Transposed Convolution Layers in Deep Neural Networks

Zhucheng Tang, *Peking University*
Guojie Luo, *Peking University*
Ming Jiang, *Peking University*
Contact: zhucheng.tang@pku.edu.cn

Transposed convolution, which is often used to scale up feature maps in various computer vision tasks, is a structural inverse process of convolution. Both convolution and transposed convolution, if any, account for the majority of computation in the inferences of deep neural networks. While convolution has been studied extensively, there are few investigations on accelerating transposed convolution. In this paper, we propose a fast algorithm, FTConv, to reduce the computation of transposed convolution using the Winograd algorithm, which has also been used for convolution with small kernels. Specifically, a transposed convolution can be converted into multiple convolutions after dividing the kernel into several congruence classes. Thus, we can accelerate the multiple convolutions using a modified Winograd algorithm. The transposed convolution can be obtained by interleaving output feature elements of each congruence class. We also design a Winograd ALU in four

pipeline stages to further accelerate the computation on FPGA. By carefully designing a sliding window for on-chip buffer reuse according to the memory access pattern of transposed convolution, we save the memory bandwidth by 88.2% compared with a straightforward method. We evaluate FTConv using FSRCNN-s, a neural network for super-resolution. The number of multiplications in the transposed convolution layer can be reduced by 69% over the direct computation of FSRCNN-s.

Keywords: Transposed Convolution; FPGA Acceleration; Winograd Algorithm;

DOI: https://doi.org/10.1145/3289602.3293976

Compressed CNN Training with FPGA-based Accelerator

Kaiyuan Guo, Shuang Liang, Jincheng Yu, Xuefei Ning, Wenshuo Li, Yu Wang, Huazhong Yang,
Tsinghua University
Contact: gky15@mails.tsinghua.edu.cn

Training convolutional neural network (CNN) usually requires large amount of computation resource, time and power. Researchers and cloud service providers in this region needs fast and efficient training system. GPU is currently the best candidate for CNN training. But FPGAs have already shown good performance and energy efficiency as CNN inference accelerators. In this work, we design a compressed training process together with an FPGA-based accelerator for energy efficient CNN training. We adopt two of the widely used model compression methods, quantization and pruning, to accelerate CNN training process.

The difference between inference and training brought challenges to apply the two methods in training. First, training requires higher data precision. We use the gradient accumulation buffer to achieve low operation complexity while keeping gradient descent precision. Second, sparse network results in different types of functions in forward and back-propagation phases. We design a novel architecture to utilize both inference and back-propagation sparsity. Experimental results show that the proposed training process achieves similar accuracy compared with traditional training process with floating point data. The proposed accelerator achieves 641GOP/s equivalent performance and 2.86x better energy efficiency compared with GPU.

Keywords: FPGA; Convolutional Neural Network; Training

DOI: https://doi.org/10.1145/3289602.3293977

Optimizing Order-Associative Kernel Computation with Joint Memory Banking and Data Reuse

Juan Escobedo, *University of Central Florida*
Mingjie Lin, *University of Central Florida*
Contact: johne1312@knights.ucf.edu

In this paper, we develop a joint strategy of memory banking and data reuse to specifically optimize the memory performance of any given order-associative and stencil-based computing kernel i.e., its iteration order can be reordered freely without compromising its correctness. Given any shape of stencil kernel, our methodology can achieve throughput of 1 kernel per clock cycle with only two memory banks and two data reuse buffers of constant small buffer sizes provided order-associativeness is given. This is a huge leap over all existing results for general stencil-based computing, where, depending the specific data reuse method, either a number of data reuse buffers proportional to the stencil size are required or a potentially problem-dependent reuse buffer size is needed. Furthermore, the optimal memory partition factor of existing methods is typically proportional to the actual stencil size of a given kernel, whereas in our method, the number of memory banks remains to be 2 irrespective of the stencil shape and size. On average, when compared with the mainstream methods, our approach achieves approximately 30-70\% reduction in hardware usage, while improving performance by about 15\%. Moreover, the number of independent memory banks required to accomplish conflict-free data accesses have dropped by more than 30\%.

Keywords: Data Reuse; Memory Partition; FPGA; HLS

DOI: https://doi.org/10.1145/3289602.3293980

PVT-Aware Sensing and Voltage Scaling for Energy Efficient FPGAs

Konstantinos Maragos, George Lentaris,
Dimitrios Soudris, *National Technical University of Athens,*
Vasilis F. Pavlidis, *The University of Manchester*
Contact:komaragos@microlab.ntua.gr

In this work we introduce a method to improve the energy efficiency of the FPGA devices by reducing the pessimistic operation guardbands posed by the commercial EDA tools. The proposed method bases on a voltage scaling scheme that reliably decreases the supply voltage. We deploy a uniform network of delay-based sensors across the fabric of the FPGA to sense all process, voltage and temperature variation (PVT) effects. The delay of all the sensors is calibrated to match the worst critical path delay of the target application. In that respect, the monitoring of the sensor network enables the indirect assessment of the functional integrity of the target application. The distributed placement of the sensors provides the desired sensitivity with appropriate granularity across the fabric and allows us to consider the worst-case scenario. The sensor network is integrated during the development cycle as ready-to-use software IP with negligible resource overhead, for example, 1-2% of a Zynq XC7Z020 FPGA for 10 sensors. The sensitivity of the sensors to all PVT variations and the correlation with the application operation is verified through extensive testing by using multiple FPGAs and realistic benchmarks. The aforementioned approach facilitates a closed-loop voltage scaling scheme to regulate the supply voltage and reduce the power of the system. In our experiments on a set of 28nm Xilinx XC7Z020 SoC FPGAs and realistic digital signal processing (DSP) benchmarks, we demonstrate up to 27.2% decrease in power for 13% decrease in voltage, while retaining the nominal timing performance.

Keywords: FPGA; Voltage Scaling; Process Variation; Voltage Variation; Temperature Variation

DOI: https://doi.org/10.1145/3289602.3293981

Software Hardware Co-Optimized BFS on FPGAs

Zach Sherer, Eric Finnerty, Yan Luo, Hang Liu,
University of Massachusetts Lowell
Contact: Hang_Liu@uml.edu

The configurable architectures of Field Programmable Gate Arrays (FPGAs) have lent themselves to an array of high-performance computing applications. Among those applications, Breadth-First Search (BFS), due to its significance, draws particular attention. Unfortunately, recent endeavors that offload BFS on FPGAs either simply extend the existing CPU- or GPU- based mechanisms that fail to unleash the potential of FPGAs or suffer from scalability when attempt to take advantage of the flexible hardware.

To this end, we propose a software and hardware co-optimized BFS on FPGAs to exploit the potentials of FPGAs with the following two indispensable techniques: 1). At the software optimization side, we introduce a 1-D vertical graph partition method together with an incoherent cache design to effectively eliminate the scalability issue suffered from the state-of-the-art efforts; 2). At the hardware optimization side, we advocate the three-pronged hardware design that efficiently uses caches, rapidly generates frontiers and enormously avoids expensive buffer maintaining overhead to maximize the benefits from the innate configurable hardware of FPGAs. Taken together, our evaluation demonstrates that the proposed design achieves up to 4.6× speedup over the state-of-the-art FPGA-based graph traversal project across a collection of graph datasets.

Keywords: graph computing; BFS; SoC; graph partition; hardware-software codesign; FPGA

DOI: https://doi.org/10.1145/3289602.3293982

Compute-Efficient Neural-Network Acceleration

Ephrem Wu, Xiaoqian Zhang, David Berman, Inkeun Cho, John Thendean
Silicon Architecture
Xilinx, Inc.
San Jose, USA

ABSTRACT

To enhance the performance of FPGA-based neural-network accelerators, maximizing both operating clock rates and compute efficiency is paramount. Streamlining data movement between memory and compute holds the key to boosting these metrics. To unleash latent performance in FPGA-based inference processors, we outline a convolutional neural network accelerator that operates at 92.9% of the peak FPGA clock rate. First, we map neural-network operators to a minimalist hardware architecture to simplify data movement between memory and compute. Doing so enables the design to close timing at high clock rates. Second, we describe a schedule that keeps compute utilization high. We apply this architecture to classify MNIST, CIFAR-10, and ImageNet datasets. This design achieves 95.5% compute efficiency with GoogLeNet, whose nested topology makes creating an efficient design especially challenging.

KEYWORDS

Convolutional neural networks; compute efficiency; FPGA; GoogLeNet; image classification; reduced precision; tensor processing; accelerator; deep learning; reconfigurable architecture

ACM Reference format:

Ephrem Wu, Xiaoqian Zhang, David Berman, Inkeun Cho, and John Thendean. 2019. Compute-Efficient Neural-Network Acceleration. In *Proceedings of the 2019 ACM/SIGDA International Symposium on Field-Programmable Gate Arrays, Seaside, CA, USA, Feb. 24–26, 2019 (FPGA '19)*. ACM NY, NY, USA, 10 pages. DOI:10.1145/3289602.3293925

1 DESIGN OVERVIEW

1.1 Accelerator Card

We implemented a convolutional neural network (CNN) accelerator for image classification on a VCU1525 card that houses a Xilinx VU9P FPGA (Figure 1). Our goal is to demonstrate a reconfigurable and compute-efficient architecture for CNNs, specifically those with nested structures such as GoogLeNet [17]. We define compute efficiency as the fraction of multiply-add cycles consumed in a matrix multiplier to produce results. To maximize compute efficiency and to reduce energy consumption, the design does not use any DRAM on the accelerator card. The on-chip SRAM resources in the VU9P FPGA, namely UltraRAM

FPGA '19, February 24–26, 2019, Seaside, CA, USA
© 2019 Association for Computing Machinery.
ACM ISBN 978-1-4503-6137-8/19/02...$15.00
https://doi.org/10.1145/3289602.3293925

and BRAM, have sufficient capacity and bandwidth for both activations and weights to keep the compute units busy. On initialization, this accelerator accepts commands, weights and biases from the CPU through a PCIe interface. Then the CPU streams images into the FPGA, which in turn streams results back to the CPU. We implemented one FPGA bitstream that can take different weights and commands to implement different CNNs to classify MNIST, CIFAR-10, and ImageNet datasets.

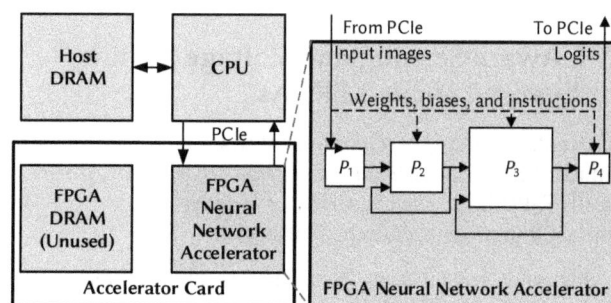

Figure 1: Neural-network accelerator. © Ephrem Wu.

1.2 Accelerator Processor Chain

The accelerator is a pipeline of four processors, labeled P_1 to P_4 in Figure 1. P_1, P_2, and P_3 are convolution processors, whereas P_4 computes only fully-connected layers. These processors compute both convolution and fully-connected layers using matrix multiplications. P_4 is simpler than the convolution processors in that it lacks a pointer generator to read convolution input patches from memory. Although one processor is sufficient to implement an entire CNN, and one processor per layer in principle achieves the highest compute efficiency, we implemented four processors to balance throughput and generality.

1.3 Processor Architecture

Figure 2a shows the general structure of the four processors in Figure 1. Each processor consists of a controller that executes neural-network commands, weight- and activation-tensor memories, a block-floating-point matrix-vector multiplier that computes convolution and fully-connected layers, a non-linear unit that implements activation and pooling functions, and an activation-tensor network that organizes activation tensors in SRAMs.

1.3.1 Matrix-Vector Multiplier. The matrix-vector multiplier is a multiply-add systolic array with N_1 input broadcast lanes and N_2 output reduction lanes. In one cycle, it computes

$$z \leftarrow Pq + r, P \in \mathbb{R}^{N_2 \times N_1}, q \in \mathbb{R}^{N_1}. \qquad (1)$$

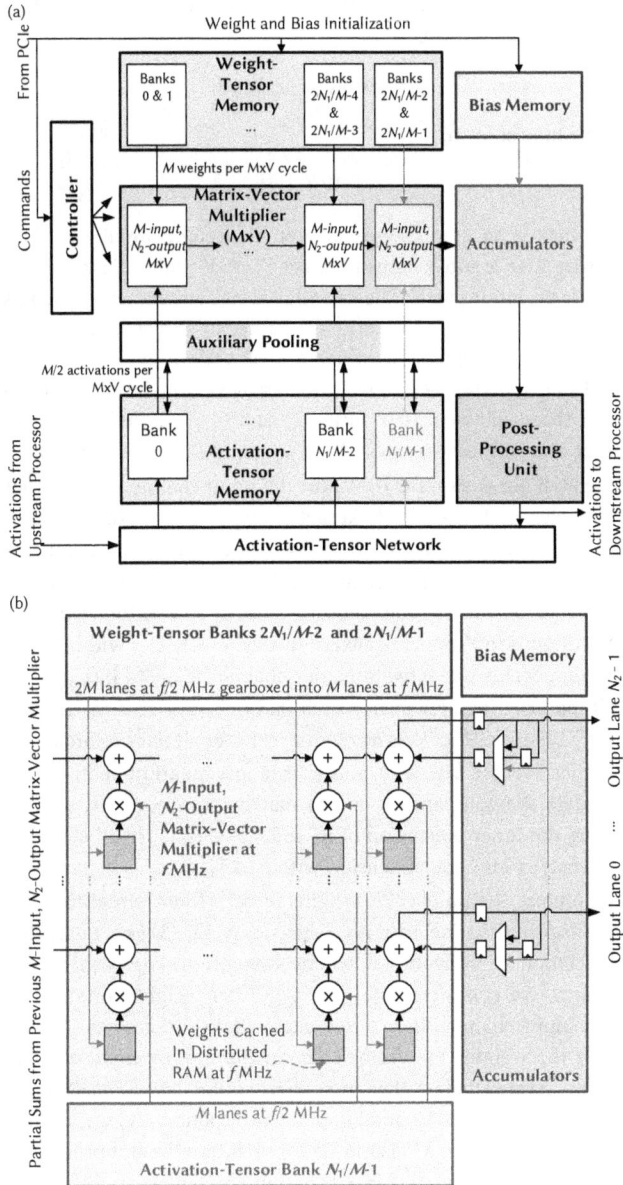

Figure 2: (a) Neural-network processor (b) The last M input lanes of the matrix-vector multiplier. M divides N_1. © Ephrem Wu.

Physically, the matrix-vector multiplier is an $N_1 \times N_2$ crossbar array of processing elements, segmented into $M \times N_2$ array slices that are aligned to the weight- and activation-tensor memories for hierarchical place-and-route (Figure 2a). Each processing element has a 128-byte distributed weight cache and a multiplier-add unit

with a full-precision adder (Figure 2b). The weight cache at output lane i and input lane j caches the matrix element $p_{ij} \in P$, feeding the corresponding multiplier one weight per cycle. It is double-buffered to accept new weights in one buffer while the matrix-vector multiplier reads from the other buffer. The weight cache is updated once per input batch. Even with a batch size of one, the weight cache update bandwidth is far below the read bandwidth. Therefore, along each input lane, every weight cache shares a cache-write bus. (See the vertical red lines in Figure 2b.)

1.3.2 Numerical Formats and Activation Rescaling. We encode tensor elements as block-floating-point numbers [21]. A block-floating-point number t in a block of numbers T is $t = 2^{E_T} D_t$, where E_T is the block exponent and D_t is an integer. Exponent storage and bandwidth are therefore amortized over an entire block of numbers. Our design rescales activations between layers with arithmetic shifting. We obtained block-floating-point weights and activations with Ristretto [6]. For GoogLeNet, we encode weights as signed 8-bit integers (int8) sharing the block exponent -7. We encode elements after input mean subtraction as signed 16-bit integers (int16) sharing also the exponent -7. We encode output activations (after ReLU) as unsigned 8-bit integers (uint8) with per-layer block exponents in the range [-2, 5]. Except for the first layer, which multiplies int16 numbers by int8 weights, all other layers multiply uint8 activations by int8 weights. The matrix-vector multiplier accepts fixed-point numbers and accumulates dot products in full-precision (int48). The post-processing unit converts these dot products into uint8 activations.

1.3.3 Weight- and Activation-Tensor Memories. The weight- and activation-tensor memories have sufficient bandwidth to keep the matrix-vector multiplier busy. In contrast to the spatial lane mapping in [3], our convolution schedule maps spatial axes to compute cycles and maps channels to lanes. This mapping generalizes convolution to any number of spatial dimensions while keeping compute efficiency high. We therefore channelize the tensor memory by dividing it into *banks*, each covering M of the N_1 input lanes (Figure 2a). For instance, consider using 64-bit SRAMs to build a tensor memory that feeds a matrix-vector multiplier with 8-bit lanes. A bank that is one SRAM wide feeds $M = 64/8 = 8$ input lanes in parallel. We partition the weight-tensor memory into banks similarly. Within each bank, each tensor memory lane in Figure 2b serves exactly one matrix-vector multiplier lane. Such channelization enables tiling of memory and compute, facilitating timing closure under tight constraints. Because the number of channels is typically a multiple of eight, we make N_1 also a multiple of eight to maximize compute efficiency. We also make N_1 a multiple of M to maximize memory capacity and bandwidth utilization.

The VU9P FPGA has 38.4 MiB of SRAM, enough to hold weights, biases, and activations for three concurrent GoogLeNets. (GoogLeNet has 7 million 8-bit weights and biases and the largest activation tensor is 196 KiB.) We stack SRAMs depth-wise within a bank to provide enough storage. The weight-tensor memory typically has more bandwidth than the activation-tensor memory. For instance, each activation bank of processor P_3 outputs eight activations every two DSP cycles (32 bits per cycle) but each weight-tensor bank has twice the bandwidth.

1.3.4 Multi-Channel Accumulators. Each output lane in the matrix-vector multiplier writes to two or three accumulators. (See the block labeled "Accumulators" in Figure 2b.) In each output lane, each accumulator stores a partial sum for a unique output channel time-interleaved in that output lane. Section 2.3 describes how this approach reduces activation read bandwidth.

1.3.5 Fused Post-Processing Unit. Post-processing functions such as activation, max-pooling, average pooling, rescaling, rounding, and saturation do not consume tensor memory read bandwidth. Fused with the matrix-vector multiplier output, the post-processing unit has its own buffer and can be reconfigured to adapt to new algorithms. For instance, the list of activation functions has been growing over the years. There are 10 activation functions in TensorFlow [1] and 21 in PyTorch [12] as of this writing. We can insert new post-processing functions or remove obsolete ones by updating the FPGA bitstream.

1.3.6 Auxiliary Pooling. Aside from pooling in post-processing, the accelerator supports auxiliary pooling in parallel with matrix multiplication. Auxiliary pooling is optional, useful for the pooling layer inside the GoogLeNet Inception module, as opposed to pooling between these modules.

1.3.7 Activation-Tensor Network. The activation-tensor network is collision-free and delivers activations from the post-processing unit to the activation-tensor memory. This network is usually inter-processor but sometimes also intra-processor, for instance in P_2 and P_3 because they process more than one layer. Because we only build $N_1 \times N_2$ matrix-vector multipliers such that $N_1 \geq N_2$, we can schedule computation such that any output in the $N_2 \times N_1$ activation-tensor network connects to at most one input. The network therefore requires no arbitration.

1.3.8 Controller. Each processor has a controller that executes a program to evaluate layers in a neural network. These layers are nodes in a computation graph in frameworks such as TensorFlow [1], PyTorch [12], and Caffe [10]. A controller program is a sequence of commands, each of which evaluates a computation subgraph with at most four layers: a convolution or dense layer, a fused activation layer, a fused pooling layer, and an auxiliary pooling layer.

2 CONVOLUTION

2.1 Multi-Dimensional Convolution

We generalize the formulation of 2D convolution as matrix multiplication in [2] to any number of dimensions. There are $N + 2$ axes in an N-dimensional CNN: N spatial axes, an output channel axis, and an input channel axis. Much of the literature focuses on 2D convolution, and rightly so, presenting it as a nested loop with six levels (Listing 1 in [15] and the code fragment in [9]). In this way, N-dimensional convolution becomes a nested loop with $2N + 2$ levels. Rather than working with the pyramid

of doom, we reason about convolution with only three axes by flattening all spatial axes and leaving the two channel axes unchanged.

Consider two views of convolution—tensor and matrix—the former for neural-network frameworks and the latter for hardware accelerators. We translate N-dimensional convolution from the tensor form,

$$y = \mathrm{conv}_N(w, x, b; \phi), \qquad (2)$$

to the matrix form,

$$Y = WX + B. \qquad (3)$$

Our task is to map the pre-activation, weight, input, and bias tensors y, w, x and b to the matrices $Y, W, X,$ and B. Each column in X is an input patch. The set ϕ holds hyperparameters such as padding, stride, dilation, etc., to define, in the spatial domain, which input patch creates which pre-activation.

Table 1 juxtaposes convolution variables in the tensor form with those in the matrix form. C_{in} and C_{out} are the number of input and output channels. $D_{\mathrm{in},i}, D_{\mathrm{out},i},$ and $D_{\mathrm{weight},i}$ are the sizes of spatial dimension $i \in [0, N)$ for the input channels, the output channels, and the filter kernels, respectively. Note that ϕ determines $D_{\mathrm{out},i}$ based on $D_{\mathrm{in},i}$. By convention, row i of Y holds pre-activations in output channel i. The row ordering of W and B therefore follows this convention. Again, by convention, we order the columns in Y by spatial axis 0 to axis $N - 1$. The width of Y is the number of pre-activations per channel, $N_{\mathrm{out}} \equiv \prod_i D_{\mathrm{out},i}$. The column ordering of X must match that of Y. The bias matrix B is Cbe^T, where $e \in \mathbb{R}^{N_{\mathrm{out}}}$ is a column vector of all ones to broadcast the bias vector $b \in \mathbb{R}^{C_{\mathrm{out}}}$ and C is a permutation matrix that reorders the components in b to match the row ordering of Y. Along the inner dimension of W and X, we collapse all N spatial dimensions into one dimension with $F \equiv \prod_i D_{\mathrm{weight},i}$ elements. F is therefore the number of weights in each filter kernel for each input-output channel pair. As F encodes N, Eq. (3) generalizes the description of convolution to any dimension. For each output channel, we concatenate C_{in} sets of F filter weights, one set for each input channel, into a row vector in W. By convention, we order the weight row-vector components first by input channel (input-channel major), then by spatial axis 0, 1, and so on. (See the example in Section 2.2 and Eq. (5).) Correspondingly, we arrange each input patch in X (also in $\mathbb{R}^{C_{\mathrm{in}}F}$) such that the dot product of row i in W and column j in X is output pre-activation j in output channel i.

Table 1: Dimensionality of convolution variables

Tensor Form	Matrix Form
$y \in \mathbb{R}^{D_{\mathrm{out},0} \times \dots \times D_{\mathrm{out},N-1} \times C_{\mathrm{out}}}$	$Y \in \mathbb{R}^{C_{\mathrm{out}} \times N_{\mathrm{out}}}$
$w \in \mathbb{R}^{D_{\mathrm{weight},0} \times \dots \times D_{\mathrm{weight},N-1} \times C_{\mathrm{out}} \times C_{\mathrm{in}}}$	$W \in \mathbb{R}^{C_{\mathrm{out}} \times C_{\mathrm{in}}F}$
$x \in \mathbb{R}^{D_{\mathrm{in},0} \times \dots \times D_{\mathrm{in},N-1} \times C_{\mathrm{in}}}$	$X \in \mathbb{R}^{C_{\mathrm{in}}F \times N_{\mathrm{out}}}$
$b \in \mathbb{R}^{C_{\mathrm{out}}}$	$B \in \mathbb{R}^{C_{\mathrm{out}} \times N_{\mathrm{out}}}$

2.2 An Example

Consider the 2D convolution example in Table 2. There are $C_{out} = 4$ output channels, so the output matrix Y in Eq. (4), the weight matrix W in Eq. (5), and the bias matrix in Eq. (7) have four rows. We write the pre-activation in Y in output channel c_{out} at spatial coordinates (r, c) as $y_{[r,c]^T, c_{out}}$. Each output channel has $N_{out} = \prod_i D_{out,i} = 2 \times 3 = 6$ elements, so both the output matrix Y and the input matrix X (in (6)) have six columns each. Similarly, each element in X at spatial coordinates (r, c) in input channel c_{in} is $x_{[r,c]^T, c_{in}}$. The weight in W at spatial coordinates (r, c) in the kernel where output channel c_{out} and input channel c_{in} intersect is $w_{[r,c]^T, c_{out}, c_{in}}$. The inner dimension of W and X is $C_{in}F = C_{in} \prod_i D_{weight,i} = 8$.

Table 2: 2D convolution example

Layer Hyperparameter	Symbol	Example Value
Convolution Spatial Axes	N	2
Kernel Shape	$F = D_{weight,0} \times D_{weight,1}$	2×2
Number of Input Channels	C_{in}	2
Number of Output Channels	C_{out}	4
Input Channel Spatial Shape	$D_{in,0} \times D_{in,1}$	2×3
Output Channel Spatial Shape	$N_{out} = D_{out,0} \times D_{out,1}$	2×3
Zero Padding	Part of ϕ	Left, top: 1 Right, bottom: 0
Stride	Part of ϕ	1 in both dimensions

$$Y = \begin{bmatrix} y_{[0\atop 0],0} & y_{[1\atop 0],0} & y_{[0\atop 1],0} & y_{[1\atop 1],0} & y_{[0\atop 2],0} & y_{[1\atop 2],0} \\ y_{[0\atop 0],1} & y_{[1\atop 0],1} & y_{[0\atop 1],1} & y_{[1\atop 1],1} & y_{[0\atop 2],1} & y_{[1\atop 2],1} \\ y_{[0\atop 0],2} & y_{[1\atop 0],2} & y_{[0\atop 1],2} & y_{[1\atop 1],2} & y_{[0\atop 2],2} & y_{[1\atop 2],2} \\ y_{[0\atop 0],3} & y_{[1\atop 0],3} & y_{[0\atop 1],3} & y_{[1\atop 1],3} & y_{[0\atop 2],3} & y_{[1\atop 2],3} \end{bmatrix} \quad (4)$$

$$W = \begin{bmatrix} w_{[0\atop 0],0,0} & w_{[0\atop 0],0,1} & w_{[1\atop 0],0,0} & w_{[1\atop 0],0,1} & w_{[0\atop 1],0,0} & w_{[0\atop 1],0,1} & w_{[1\atop 1],0,0} & w_{[1\atop 1],0,1} \\ w_{[0\atop 0],1,0} & w_{[0\atop 0],1,1} & w_{[1\atop 0],1,0} & w_{[1\atop 0],1,1} & w_{[0\atop 1],1,0} & w_{[0\atop 1],1,1} & w_{[1\atop 1],1,0} & w_{[1\atop 1],1,1} \\ w_{[0\atop 0],2,0} & w_{[0\atop 0],2,1} & w_{[1\atop 0],2,0} & w_{[1\atop 0],2,1} & w_{[0\atop 1],2,0} & w_{[0\atop 1],2,1} & w_{[1\atop 1],2,0} & w_{[1\atop 1],2,1} \\ w_{[0\atop 0],3,0} & w_{[0\atop 0],3,1} & w_{[1\atop 0],3,0} & w_{[1\atop 0],3,1} & w_{[0\atop 1],3,0} & w_{[0\atop 1],3,1} & w_{[1\atop 1],3,0} & w_{[1\atop 1],3,1} \end{bmatrix} \quad (5)$$

$$X = \begin{bmatrix} 0 & 0 & 0 & x_{[0\atop 0],0} & 0 & x_{[0\atop 1],0} \\ 0 & 0 & 0 & x_{[0\atop 0],1} & 0 & x_{[0\atop 1],1} \\ 0 & 0 & x_{[0\atop 0],0} & x_{[1\atop 0],0} & x_{[0\atop 1],0} & x_{[1\atop 1],0} \\ 0 & 0 & x_{[0\atop 0],1} & x_{[1\atop 0],1} & x_{[0\atop 1],1} & x_{[1\atop 1],1} \\ 0 & x_{[0\atop 0],0} & 0 & x_{[0\atop 1],0} & 0 & x_{[0\atop 2],0} \\ 0 & x_{[0\atop 0],1} & 0 & x_{[0\atop 1],1} & 0 & x_{[0\atop 2],1} \\ x_{[0\atop 0],0} & x_{[1\atop 0],0} & x_{[0\atop 1],0} & x_{[1\atop 1],0} & x_{[0\atop 2],0} & x_{[1\atop 2],0} \\ x_{[0\atop 0],1} & x_{[1\atop 0],1} & x_{[0\atop 1],1} & x_{[1\atop 1],1} & x_{[0\atop 2],1} & x_{[1\atop 2],1} \end{bmatrix}. \quad (6)$$

$$B = [b_0, b_1, b_2, b_3]^T e^T \quad (7)$$

2.3 Scheduling

We multiply large matrices using the block-matrix multiplication algorithm. Our matrix-vector multiplier (Section 1.3.1) is a DSP supertile array from [22], executing Eq. (1) each cycle. This array caches a sub-matrix that includes all weights from a subset of the output channels. With this sub-matrix, the array computes all corresponding pre-activations in one *output pass*. Our architecture is *weight-stationary* [16]: a weight stays with the same multiplier. This approach simplifies memory networks for physical design.

Algorithm 1. Multi-Dimensional Convolution

Compute multi-dimensional convolution as the matrix operation $Y \leftarrow WX + B$. The array slice $x[a:b]$ references the array x using indices from a to $b - 1$, inclusive. Arrays are multi-dimensional. Array indices and index ranges are comma-separated.

1 Initialize $P_{standby}$ to all zeros
2 $P_{standby} \leftarrow W[0 : \Phi_{out}(0)N_2, 0 : C_{in}F]$ // caching
3 **for** $h \in [0, H)$ // output pass
4    $P_{active} \leftarrow P_{standby}$
5    $k \leftarrow \sum_{i=0}^{h-1} \Phi_{out}(h)$
6   **if** $h < H$ // cache weights for next pass
7      $P_{standby} \leftarrow W[kN_2 : (k + \Phi_{out}(h))N_2, 0 : C_{in}F]$
8   **for** $j \in [0, N_{out})$ // pre-activation
9   **for** $\phi_{in} \in [0, \Phi_{in})$ // $\Phi_{in} = \lceil C_{in}/N_1 \rceil$ input phases
10   **for** $f \in [0, F)$
11         $q \leftarrow X[(\phi_{in}F + f)N_1 : (\phi_{in}F + f + 1)N_1, j]$
12   **for** $\phi_{out} \in [0, \Phi_{out}(h))$ // output phase
13           $P \leftarrow P_{active}\left[\begin{array}{c} \phi_{out}N_2 : (\phi_{out} + 1)N_2, \\ (\phi_{in}F + f)N_1 : (\phi_{in}F + f + 1)N_1 \end{array} \right]$
14   **if** $\phi_{in} = 0$ // initialize accumulators to biases
15             $z_{\phi_{out}} \leftarrow [b_{(k+\phi_{out})N_2}, \cdots, b_{(k+\phi_{out}+1)N_2-1}]^T + Pq$
16   **else**
17             $z_{\phi_{out}} \leftarrow z_{\phi_{out}} + Pq$
18   $Y[kN_2 : (k + \Phi_{out}(h))N_2, j] \leftarrow \begin{bmatrix} z_0 \\ z_1 \\ \vdots \\ z_{\Phi_{out}(h)-1} \end{bmatrix}$ // $z_i \in \mathbb{R}^{N_2}$

Algorithm 1 computes Eq. (3) one output pass at a time. Given the matrix $W \in \mathbb{R}^{C_{out} \times C_{in}F}$ in Eq. (3), Algorithm 1 caches $\Phi_{out}(h)N_2$ rows of W in output pass h, where $\Phi_{out}(h)$, a small integer, is the number of *output phases* in the output pass (lines 2 and 7). Therefore, the number of output passes, H, relates to the number of output channels as $C_{out} \leq N_2 \sum_{h=0}^{H-1} \Phi_{out}(h)$. The weight sub-matrix in each output phase is $N_2 \times C_{in}F$, which the array consumes over $\Phi_{in} = \lceil C_{in}/N_1 \rceil$ input phases, each taking F (non-consecutive) cycles (line 10). In output pass h, Algorithm 1 consumes the $\Phi_{out}(h)N_2 \times C_{in}F$ weight sub-matrix. It does so in output-phase-major order, therefore reusing each input activation vector on the input broadcast bus $\Phi_{out}(h)$ times (line 12). One output pass therefore takes $N_{out}\Phi_{in}F\Phi_{out}(h)$ cycles to create a $\Phi_{out}(h) \times N_{out}$ output sub-matrix (line 18).

We constrain $\Phi_{out}(h)$ to be either two or three, so the activation vector changes at most once every two DSP cycles, allowing the activation-tensor memory to operate at half the DSP clock rate. In practice, output channels out-number reduction lanes, i.e. $C_{out}/N_2 \geq 2$, so there is always at least one output pass with two or more output phases. When $\lceil C_{out}/N_2 \rceil$ is greater than two—and odd—the output pass sequence is a string of two-phase passes followed by a three-phase pass. (Without the three-phase pass, there is a two-phase pass that is at most 50% utilized.) For instance, to distribute $C_{out} = 80$ output channels across $N_2 = 16$ output lanes, we use $H = 2$ passes in which $\Phi_{out}(0) = 2$ and $\Phi_{out}(1) = 3$ to satisfy $C_{out} = N_2 \sum_{h=0}^{H-1} \Phi_{out}(h)$.

Summing within dot product operations occurs in the DSP48 internal adder cascade, which can operate at the maximum clock rate of the DSP tiles. [22] reports timing closure at the maximum clock rate on a VU3P FPGA. With the VU9P FPGA, which is three times as large as the VU3P, we anticipated timing degradation. Despite clock skews in the larger VU9P device, all our matrix multipliers operate at 92.9% of the peak DSP clock rate.

Continuing with the example in Table 2, consider a matrix multiplier with two input lanes and two output lanes ($N_1 = N_2 = 2$). We need only $H = 1$ output pass with $\Phi_{out}(0) = 2$ output phases to halve the input vector read bandwidth. There is $\Phi_{in} = C_{in}/N_1 = 1$ input phase. Therefore, each supertile caches $\Phi_{in}\Phi_{out}(0) = 2$ kernels in its distributed memory. The schedule computes $\Phi_{out}(0)N_2 = 4$ output rows at a time by reusing the four rows of weights cached in the matrix multiplier. Our matrix multiplier skips zero padding. The first column in X has six padded zeros and only two non-zero entries. As a result, the matrix-vector multiplier completes the first column of Y by computing in the first cycle

$$\begin{bmatrix} y_{[0]},0 \\ y_{[0]},1 \end{bmatrix} \leftarrow \begin{bmatrix} w_{[1]},0,0 & w_{[1]},0,1 \\ w_{[1]},1,0 & w_{[1]},1,1 \end{bmatrix} \begin{bmatrix} x_{[0]},0 \\ x_{[0]},1 \end{bmatrix} + \begin{bmatrix} b_0 \\ b_1 \end{bmatrix}$$

and reusing the input vector in the second cycle to compute

$$\begin{bmatrix} y_{[0]},2 \\ y_{[0]},3 \end{bmatrix} \leftarrow \begin{bmatrix} w_{[1]},2,0 & w_{[1]},2,1 \\ w_{[1]},3,0 & w_{[1]},3,1 \end{bmatrix} \begin{bmatrix} x_{[0]},0 \\ x_{[0]},1 \end{bmatrix} + \begin{bmatrix} b_2 \\ b_3 \end{bmatrix}.$$

Specifically, the biases initialize the accumulators. The matrix multiplier then takes the next four cycles to compute the second column in Y:

1. $$\begin{bmatrix} y_{[0]},0 \\ y_{[0]},1 \end{bmatrix} \leftarrow \begin{bmatrix} w_{[0]},0,0 & w_{[0]},0,1 \\ w_{[0]},1,0 & w_{[0]},1,1 \end{bmatrix} \begin{bmatrix} x_{[0]},0 \\ x_{[0]},1 \end{bmatrix} + \begin{bmatrix} b_0 \\ b_1 \end{bmatrix}$$

2. $$\begin{bmatrix} y_{[0]},2 \\ y_{[0]},3 \end{bmatrix} \leftarrow \begin{bmatrix} w_{[0]},2,0 & w_{[0]},2,1 \\ w_{[0]},3,0 & w_{[0]},3,1 \end{bmatrix} \begin{bmatrix} x_{[0]},0 \\ x_{[0]},1 \end{bmatrix} + \begin{bmatrix} b_2 \\ b_3 \end{bmatrix}$$

3. $$\begin{bmatrix} y_{[0]},0 \\ y_{[0]},1 \end{bmatrix} \leftarrow \begin{bmatrix} y_{[0]},0 \\ y_{[0]},1 \end{bmatrix} + \begin{bmatrix} w_{[1]},0,0 & w_{[1]},0,1 \\ w_{[1]},1,0 & w_{[1]},1,1 \end{bmatrix} \begin{bmatrix} x_{[1]},0 \\ x_{[1]},1 \end{bmatrix}$$

4. $$\begin{bmatrix} y_{[0]},2 \\ y_{[0]},3 \end{bmatrix} \leftarrow \begin{bmatrix} y_{[0]},2 \\ y_{[0]},3 \end{bmatrix} + \begin{bmatrix} w_{[1]},2,0 & w_{[1]},2,1 \\ w_{[1]},3,0 & w_{[1]},3,1 \end{bmatrix} \begin{bmatrix} x_{[1]},0 \\ x_{[1]},1 \end{bmatrix}$$

So far, we have described the first six cycles that create the first two output columns in Y. The matrix multiplier reads the rest of the input matrix in the next 24 cycles to complete the output matrix (Figure 3). Note that the N_1 elements read from the input matrix in the same cycle share the same spatial coordinates. This

row ordering simplifies read pointer generation since the controller can compute just one pointer every $\Phi_{out}(h)$ cycles.

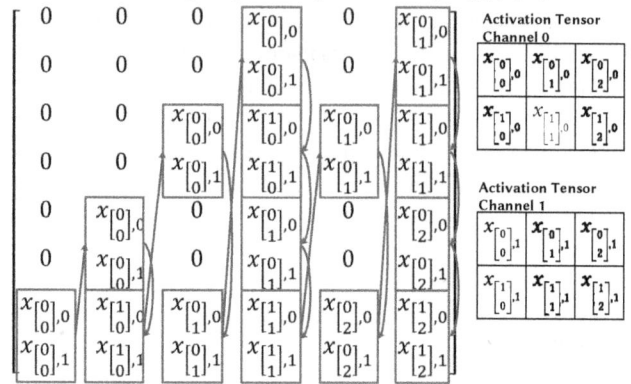

Figure 3: Activation read ordering. © Ephrem Wu

3 RESULTS

3.1 Neural Networks

To evaluate the inference processor architecture and implementation, we mapped three neural networks, each for one dataset, to the Xilinx VU9P FPGA. We implemented what we call M-Net for the MNIST dataset and C-Net for the CIFAR-10 dataset (Table 3). For the ImageNet dataset [13], we implemented GoogLeNet. We do not provide its configuration here as it is documented in [17]. M-Net and C-Net are miniature versions of GoogLeNet, with these two networks differing only in the number of input channels in the first layer. Specifically, M-Net accepts monochrome images whereas C-Net accepts color images. We optimized the processing pipeline for GoogLeNet. As such, we expected less compute efficiency from C-Net and M-Net.

Table 3. M-Net and C-Net for MNIST and CIFAR-10

Layer	Kernel	Stride	Input	
			Feature Map	Channels
Conv1_ReLU	7x7	1	28x28	1 for MNIST 3 for CIFAR-10
MaxPool1	3x3	2	28x28	64
Conv2r_ReLU	1x1	1	14x14	64
Conv2_ReLU	3x3	1	14x14	64
MaxPool2	3x3	2	7x7	192
Conv3_ReLU	3x3	1	7x7	192
AvgPool	7x7	1	7x7	1024
FC			1x1	1024
Softmax			1x1	10

3.2 Inference Processor Implementation

To illustrate the versatility of the processing pipeline, we mapped M-Net, C-Net, and GoogLeNet to the same FPGA bitstream. Because the underlying design is the same, three different programs can implement these networks without reconfiguration. We initially prototyped one inference pipeline on a Xilinx VU3P FPGA, the smallest FPGA in the Xilinx UltraScale+ Virtex family.

As the Xilinx VCU1525 card became available, we instantiated three copies of the VU3P design on the VU9P FPGA on this card. The VU9P consists of three identical super-logic regions (SLRs), each essentially a VU3P. For ease of porting, we placed one processing pipeline in each SLR, each running with a batch size of one. To simplify timing closure, every SLR operates in its own mesochronous clock domain. Inter-SLR communication is minimal since we only use it only for low-bandwidth tasks such as job dispatch and result collection. To speed up place-and-route, we pre-placed DSP supertiles, UltraRAMs, and BRAMs. The cards in our lab run the matrix multiplier array at 720 MHz, the rest of the processing pipeline (control, SRAMs, etc.) at 360 MHz, and the PCIe interface at 250 MHz.

Table 4. Number of linear layers in each processor

Processor	Input Lanes N_1	Output Lanes N_2	Number of Linear Layers		
			MNIST (M-Net)	CIFAR-10 (C-Net)	ImageNet (GoogLeNet)
P_1	21	8	1	1	1
P_2	32	16	2	2	2
P_3	96	16	1	1	54
P_4	8	1	1	1	1

To balance design complexity and compute efficiency, we picked the number of processors and sized each processor primarily for GoogLeNet, as it is the most compute- and memory-intensive among the three networks. A one-size-fits-all single-processor inference pipeline is the simplest to design but may lack compute efficiency. A one-processor-per-layer design is tailor-made to be compute-efficient but is inflexible and complicates inter-layer activation-tensor management.

The number of convolutional channels is the principal factor that influences when we add a processor to an inference-processing pipeline. We decided to implement four processors, namely P_1 to P_4. See Table 4 for the number of linear layers processed for each network. Each processor works on its own subset of layers from the overall compute graph. For instance, among the 58 linear layers in GoogLeNet, P_1 evaluates just the first convolutional layer. Whereas all other layers have the number of channels being multiples of eight, the first layer of an image-classification network has only three input channels. Specifically, we sized P_1 to take in 21 lanes and output eight lanes (a.k.a. a 21×8 processor). Because the first layer uses 7×7 filters, seven cycles suffice to produce an output element with 100% compute efficiency. We made P_2 compute the next two convolutional layers and P_3 the next 54 (nine Inception modules each with six convolutional layers). We did not pack these 56 layers into one processor because the number of channels in P_2 is still relatively low: both layers in P_2 have only 64 input channels and the last layer has 192 output channels, whereas the next 54 layers have up to 1024 channels. To keep compute efficiency high, we needed a medium-size P_2 and a big P_3. We subsequently made P_2 a 32 × 16 processor and P_3 a 96 × 16 processor. As we will discuss in the next subsections, the first three processors have similar initial cycle times (Table 5), which means that when they

form a processing pipeline, no significant performance bottleneck develops. Because contemporary image-classification networks use just one lightweight fully-connected layer at the end of the network, we dedicated P_4 to computing this final layer. The challenge in designing this layer is not compute but weight memory. Fortunately, the UltraRAM on the VU9P provides sufficient storage and bandwidth.

On-chip UltraRAM and BRAM implement weight- and activation-tensor memories. We use these SRAM resources as two-port (1R1W) memory blocks, protecting both activations and weights with SECDED ECC. To ensure design uniformity, we use both the UltraRAM and the BRAM as 64-bit wide memory before ECC. Specifically, the UltraRAM is a 4096 × 64-bit SRAM and the BRAM is a 512 × 64-bit SRAM.

We divide the activation-tensor memory into inter-processor vs. intra-processor memory. The inter-processor memory is a two-port, double-buffered memory that implements flow control between adjacent processors. We divide the intra-processor memory into multiple pages to store temporary tensors to avoid hardware hazards. Different pages are in different memory blocks, so they get dedicated bandwidth. In GoogLeNet, for instance, we store intermediate tensors along branches within the Inception module in a different page from the concatenated tensors between Inception modules. We stagger in time the activations from each lane of the activation-tensor memory to match what the matrix multiplier systolic array requires—input lane $i + n$ receives its activation n DSP cycles after lane i. This design enables the matrix multiplier to process two consecutive layers without pipeline bubbles.

The weight-tensor memory has a write port for the host to download weights and a read port for the neural-network processor to retrieve weights. The host and the neural-network processor see different aspect ratios of the same weight-tensor memory. The host sees the weight-tensor memory as a narrow and deep memory since it writes the weight-tensor memory only during network initialization. The neural-network processor sees the weight-tensor memory as a wide and shallow memory because it needs sufficient weight update bandwidth.

We scale the bandwidth of the weight- and activation-tensor memories to keep the matrix multiplier busy. For instance, layers that use block floating-point activations and weights with eight bits of precision pack eight activations or weights to fill the 64-bit memory width. Eight activations or eight weights enter the matrix multiplier in parallel. Because we set the number of matrix multiplier output phases (Section 2.3) to either two or three, each input lane needs at most one new input activation every two or three DSP clock cycles. The activation-tensor memory therefore operates at half the DSP clock rate to reduce dynamic power and to ease timing convergence. The weight-tensor memory also operates at the same clock rate but uses a wider output bus to ensure sufficient bandwidth to keep the matrix multiplier busy.

3.3 Initial Cycle Time
The *initial cycle time* of each processor measures the intrinsic performance of a processor. The inverse of the initial cycle time of a processor is the throughput of that processor in the absence

of backpressure—when all downstream inter-processor activation-tensor buffers are empty. Table 5 captures the initial cycle time for each processor from our cycle-accurate analytical model. We validated this model in simulations and in the lab by measuring the time between the first two input tensors arriving at the same node in the design. (Double buffering of activation tensors between processors guarantees that no backpressure occurs for the first two tensors.) With flow control, the entire processor pipeline operates at a single rate in the steady state and the slowest processor dictates the overall throughput. To minimize stalls, we size the processors to minimize *variation* in initial cycle times across the processing pipeline. The initial cycles times of the first three processors, P_1 to P_3, have a relative range of only 3.2% for GoogLeNet (between 686432 and 708671 cycles). The last processor, P_4, although significantly faster than the other three, has little impact on the pipeline compute efficiency since it consumes relatively few compute resources.

Table 5. Array shapes vs. initial cycle times

Processor	Input Lanes	Output Lanes	Cycles per Job		
			MNIST (M-Net)	CIFAR-10 (C-Net)	ImageNet (GoogLeNet)
P_1	21	8	38848	38848	691792
P_2	32	16	39968	39968	686432
P_3	96	16	46208	46208	708671
P_4	8	1	1280	1280	128000
Steady-State Pipeline Cycle Time			46208	46208	708671
Throughput (Jobs/s) with One Pipeline (VU3P, 720 MHz)			15582	15582	1016
Throughput (Jobs/s) with Three Parallel Pipelines (VU9P, 720 MHz)			46745	46745	3046

3.4   Quantifying Efficiency

We strive to keep every multiply-add unit as busy as possible by countering two sources of inefficiency—one temporal and one spatial. First, imbalance in initial cycle times stalls processors (in time). Second, failure to distribute computation across every matrix-vector multiplier lane idles away lanes (in space).

We quantify temporal efficiency with *balance factors*. Given K processors in a pipeline, in which processor $P_k, k \in [1, K]$, has initial cycle time t_k, the balance factor for processor P_k is $t_k / \max_k t_k$. The balance factor of a processing pipeline is the average processor balance factors weighted by processor compute resources. In this way, Table 6 re-expresses Table 5 in relative terms. During design space exploration, we size matrix-vector multipliers to maximize the pipeline balance factors.

We define *distribution efficiency* as, given some load distribution algorithm, the number of multiply-add cycles that contribute to a result as a fraction of such available cycles to create the result. Idle lanes in the matrix multiplier reduce distribution efficiency. In our design, this occurs when (1) the inner dimension of the matrix multiplication is not a multiple of the number of input lanes ($N_1 \nmid C_{in}F$), (2) when the number of output channels is not at least twice the number of output lanes ($C_{out} < 2N_2$), or

(3) the number of output channels is not a multiple of the number of output lanes ($N_2 \nmid C_{out}$). For instance, P_3 has 96 input lanes and 16 output lanes. Given 128 input and output channels, the distribution efficiency of a 3×3 layer is $\frac{128 \times 3 \times 3}{\lceil 128 \times 3 \times 3/96 \rceil 96} \times \frac{128}{\lceil 128/16 \rceil 16} = 1$; if this layer uses 1×1 filters, the distribution efficiency is $\frac{2}{3}$.

Compute efficiency is the product of balance factor and distribution efficiency. Table 7 captures the distribution efficiency of all Inception modules in GoogLeNet. Inception 3b consumes the most cycles and therefore impacts the pipeline compute efficiency the most. This module achieves 95.6% distribution efficiency. Within this module, the 3×3 layer requires 3.4 times the operations compared to the average. Its distribution efficiency weighs heavily because, just as with the balance factor of a processing pipeline, the distribution efficiency of a layer sequence is the average of the distribution efficiency weighted by the initial cycle time of each layer. In Table 8, although the other layers in Inception 3b have distribution efficiency from 89% to 92%, the 3×3 layer is 100% efficient, raising the Inception-3b distribution efficiency to 95.6%. Table 9 summarizes the compute and distribution efficiencies for each processor and for the entire pipeline under three datasets. The pipeline compute efficiency of each network is close to 100%, which confirms that there are no significant bottlenecks in the pipeline.

Table 6. Balance factors

Processor	Processor Share of Resources	Balance Factor		
		MNIST (M-Net)	CIFAR-10 (C-Net)	ImageNet (GoogLeNet)
P_1	7.6%	84.1%	84.1%	97.6%
P_2	23.0%	86.5%	86.5%	96.9%
P_3	69.1%	100.0%	100.0%	100.0%
P_4	0.4%	2.8%	2.8%	18.1%
Pipeline	100.0%	95.3%	95.3%	98.8%

Table 7. Inception module distribution efficiency

Inception Module	Dist. Efficiency	Inception Module	Dist. Efficiency	Inception Module	Dist. Efficiency
3a	96.3%	4b	91.5%	4e	95.7%
3b	95.6%	4c	94.0%	5a	96.8%
4a	96.6%	4d	93.9%	5b	96.3%

Table 8. Per-Layer distribution efficiency in Inception 3b

Inception 3b Layer	Input Channels	Output Channels	Number of Cycles	Dist. Efficiency
1x1	256	128	18816	89%
3x3_reduce	256	128	18816	89%
3x3	128	192	107616	100%
5x5_reduce	256	32	4704	89%
5x5	32	96	38928	92%
pool_proj	256	64	9408	89%
Inception 3b			198288	95.6%

Table 9. Processor compute and distribution efficiencies

Processor	MNIST (M-Net)		CIFAR-10 (C-Net)		ImageNet (GoogLeNet)	
	Comp.	Dist.	Comp.	Dist.	Comp.	Dist.
P_1	27.9%	33.2%	83.7%	99.6%	97.6%	100.0%
P_2	86.5%	100.0%	86.5%	100.0%	96.9%	100.0%
P_3	100.0%	100.0%	100.0%	100.0%	95.2%	95.2%
P_4	2.8%	100.0%	2.8%	100.0%	18.1%	100.0%
Pipeline	91.1%	95.2%	95.3%	99.7%	95.5%	96.7%

3.5 Steady-State Latency

We measure the latency of a processing pipeline at the steady state when the inter-processor double buffers are filled. The latency is the time difference from (1) when an input tensor for a job is ready for the pipeline to consume to (2) when the pipeline completes the output tensor for that job. In our implementation, P_1 does not begin processing an input tensor until all elements are ready, and softmax does not begin until P_4 has produced all logits. We can compute the pipeline latency from the initial cycle time of each processor, i.e. t_k for processor P_k. First, we look for the slowest processor, say, P_{m_1}, which slows down all its upstream counterparts so that they all operate with the same cycle time t_{m_1} in the steady state. The latency through the pipeline segment P_1 to P_{m_1} is therefore $m_1 t_{m_1}$. Then we look for the slowest processor P_{m_2} downstream of P_{m_1}. P_{m_2} in turn slows down its upstream neighbors until P_{m_1+1} to the cycle time t_{m_2}, so the latency through this new pipeline segment is $(m_2 - m_1)t_{m_2}$. We repeat this calculation until the last processor P_K is the slowest in the iteration. The total latency is the sum of the latencies of all pipeline segments. Formally, given $K > 1$ processors in the pipeline $\langle P_1, P_2, ..., P_K \rangle$, the steady-state latency is $L(K) = \sum_{i=1}(m_i - m_{i-1})t_{m_i}$, where

$$m_i = \begin{cases} 0, & i = 0 \\ \underset{k \in [m_{i-1}+1, K]}{\arg\max} t_k, & m_{i-1} < K \\ \text{undefined}, & m_{i-1} = K \end{cases}.$$

Note that if the initial cycle time never goes up from one processor to the next along a pipeline, then the pipeline latency is the sum of these initial cycle times. For our four-processor pipeline, we have $m_1 = 3$ and $m_2 = 4$. Therefore, the latency is $L(4) = 3 \times 708671 + 128000 = 2254013$ cycles. At 720 MHz, this latency is 3.13 ms. Since this pipeline is stable and non-preemptive, Little's Law serves as a sanity check. For instance, with the GoogLeNet use case, the average number of jobs in flight based on Little's Law is the product of throughput and latency, i.e. $1016 \times 3.13 \times 10^{-3} = 3.2$. This value is less than four (the number of processors) because the last processor is significantly faster than the rest.

3.6 Resource Utilization

The current version of this design implements three identical processing pipelines and can operate with independent weight tensors. It does not use any off-chip DRAM, although a DRAM interface can be added to the tensor SRAMs in future versions. The host initializes the FPGA weight, bias, and firmware SRAMs once via the PCIe interface. This interface is then used only for downloading jobs to the FPGA and collecting results from it. As shown in Table 10, the design is heavy on memory and compute and light on logic: logic consumes 24.4% of the LUTs (just 10.4% for the controllers), 100% of UltraRAM and 40.4% BRAM principally as tensor buffers, and 55.8% of the available DSP slices as matrix multipliers. The balance of the DSP slices can be used for pre- or post-processing in future versions. The computation uses block floating-point arithmetic with five exponent bits. Processor P_1 uses 16 significant bits for activations and input biases. The other processors use just eight bits. All weights and biases are quantized to 8 bits (again with 5-bit exponents). For processors P_2 and P_3, we use the techniques in [4] to pack two 8-bit multiply-adds into one DSP slice. To reduce the one-for-every-eight DSP48 overhead for overflow avoidance, we implement this function in LUTs instead. LUTs also implement other functions such as max pooling, ReLU, block floating-point management, interconnections, and, of course, the controllers. The design consumes 21.8% of the distributed RAMs, most as part of the supertile array weight cache. Because the PCIe interface is only used for downloading jobs and collecting results, a Gen2 x4 interface provides enough bandwidth.

Table 10. VU9P resource utilization

Resource	Used	Available	Utilization (%)
URAM	960	960	100.0
DSP48E2	3817	6840	55.8
RAMB36E2	791.5	2160	40.4
LUT Memory	129019	591840	21.8
LUT as Logic	288463	1182240	24.4
Serdes	4	76	5.3
PCIE40E4	1	6	16.7

3.7 Verification

We built a GoogLeNet reference design using TensorFlow [1]. This design emulates the 48-bit full-precision addition in the matrix multiplier RTL and allows us to compare all internal tensors, not just classification results. We compared this reference design against the RTL and the FPGA bitstream. The former gave us high observability but low throughput; the latter let us compare only classification results but at 3046 images per second.

4 RELATED WORK

Table 11 compares compute efficiency, normalized operating clock rates, and overall efficiency of FPGA-based neural-network designs for three datasets: MNIST, CIFAR-10, and ImageNet. This table does not report throughput explicitly. Comparing designs directly with throughput does not immediately reveal characteristics intrinsic to the architecture or the implementation. For instance, [5] uses 256 DSP48 slices on a Xilinx Zynq XC7Z045 FPGA at 250 MHz with 16-bit precision, achieving a throughput of 34.6 frames per second, whereas our design uses 3817 DSP48 slices at 720 MHz with 8-bit precision and classifies 3046 images per second on a Xilinx VU9P FPGA. Normalization sheds light on the link between architecture and implementation to establish apples-to-apples comparisons. To compare operating clock rates from different FPGAs, we divide them by their respective peak DSP clock rates. For instance, our design operates at 720 MHz and the peak DSP clock rate is 775 MHz [27]. The normalized clock rate is therefore 92.9%. Compared to using throughput directly as a metric, which varies by FPGA, compute efficiency and normalized clock rates better evaluate hardware architecture and ease of physical design. Only the ImageNet results are based on the same neural network, namely GoogLeNet [17], as different researchers use different networks to classify the MNIST and the CIFAR-10 datasets.

Our design scores the highest compute efficiency and normalized clock rates across all three datasets. It therefore also achieves the highest overall efficiency, the product of the first two metrics. Despite consuming all available UltraRAMs and 40.4% of the BRAMs, our design still operates at a normalized clock rate of 92.9%. Normalized clock rates from other designs in Table 11 range from 15.3% to 38.4%, consistent with what [22] observes. Our compute efficiency is above 91% for all three datasets. Specifically, our design operates at 95.5% compute efficiency running GoogLeNet on the ImageNet dataset.

There is a large gap in overall efficiency between our design (88.7%) and the next highest (34.9%) from a design named Snowflake [5]. Although Snowflake achieves 91% compute efficiency, timing closure at only 38.4% of the peak device clock rate dramatically reduces its overall efficiency. We see three architectural differences that impact timing closure: clock domains, global interconnection networks, and compute units.

First, only the compute path operates in the fast-clock domain (the DSP48 clock); the rest of the design operates at half of this clock rate (that is, in the slow-clock domain). Specifically, only the matrix-vector multiplier, the accumulator, and the post-processing unit are in the fast-clock domain. These blocks do not include BRAM and UltraRAM resources, which, on the VU9P in the -2 grade, can operate up to 737 MHz (BRAM) and 600 MHz (UltraRAM), lower than the DSP48 slices at 775 MHz [27]. Like most designs, Snowflake runs control, memory, and compute at the same clock rate, so the slowest resource dictates the maximum clock rate possible for the entire design. Owing to output-lane time multiplexing in the matrix-vector multiplier ($\Phi_{out}(h) > 1$ in Algorithm 1), our activation-tensor memory has a read bandwidth of less than one activation per lane (specifically, in our design ½ or 1/3 activation per lane because we constrain the number of output phases to either two or three). Accordingly, we halve the clock rate for the path from the output of the post-processing unit, through the activation-tensor network, and back to the activation memory's write port. In our design, the weight-tensor memory delivers twice the bandwidth that the activation-tensor memory does to keep the matrix-vector multiplier busy. Weight cache read and write addresses can change every fast-clock cycle, but, in the slow-clock domain, the controller generates these addresses ahead of time. Tensor memory addresses only change once every two or three fast-clock cycles, so (again) the controller can issue them using the slow clock.

Second, lane matching among our matrix-vector multiplier, fused post-processing unit, and tensor memories simplifies global routing, another reason why our design meets tight timing constraints. The output of each tensor memory lane serves only one matrix-vector multiplier input lane (Figure 2b). An internal pipeline delivers weights and activations to the destined multiplier. Similarly, each matrix-vector multiplier output lane connects to just one post-processing input lane. Since any-to-any connectivity between the post-processing unit output and the activation-tensor memory input is unnecessary, the activation-tensor network is simpler than a crossbar switch. For example, even for the largest processor, P_3, which has 96 input lanes and 16 output lanes, none of the 96 multiplexers in the activation-tensor network has more than five inputs. A crossbar switch, on the other hand, would require 16 inputs for each multiplexer. In contrast, Snowflake draws activations from memory through a crossbar switch, which feeds different ports such as vector MAC

Table 11. Clock rate and compute efficiency comparison

Reference	Dataset	Realized Clock Rate (% of Peak)	Compute Efficiency	Overall Efficiency
[7]	MNIST	27.7%	5.2%	1.4%
[23]	MNIST	15.4%	13.8%	2.1%
[14]	MNIST	27.2%	29.4%	8.0%
[20]	MNIST	15.3%	55.4%	8.5%
[25]	MNIST	23.1%	47.7%	11.0%
[24]	MNIST	18.1%	89.6%	16.3%
[18]	MNIST	30.8%	70.0%	21.6%
This work	MNIST	**92.9%**	**91.1%**	**84.6%**
[7]	CIFAR-10	27.7%	4.1%	1.1%
[14]	CIFAR-10	27.2%	4.9%	1.3%
[20]	CIFAR-10	15.3%	51.2%	7.9%
[24]	CIFAR-10	18.1%	69.6%	12.6%
[18]	CIFAR-10	30.8%	90.0%	27.7%
This work	CIFAR-10	**92.9%**	**95.3%**	**88.5%**
[11]	ImageNet	15.4%	15.0%	2.3%
[19]	ImageNet	19.2%	66.6%	12.8%
[15]	ImageNet	26.1%	93.8%	24.5%
[8]	ImageNet	30.8%	81.4%	25.1%
[5]	ImageNet	38.4%	91.0%	34.9%
This work	ImageNet	**92.9%**	**95.5%**	**88.7%**

multiplier inputs, vector MAC adder inputs, max-pooling units, and other memory. Without a fused post-processing unit like the one in our design, Snowflake relies on a crossbar switch to interconnect memory and different functional units, creating not only more global routing but also more memory round trips.

Third, our matrix-vector multiplier operates close to the maximum DSP48 clock rate owing to a 2D systolic array structure. This is an extension to the 1D systolic array structure found in many FPGA signal-processing applications. Within the matrix-vector multiplier, known as the DSP supertile array in [22], input activations and partial sums flow orthogonally in a systolic array, which is simple to pipeline globally. Specifically, the fabric implements the narrow, 8-bit input activation pipeline, whereas the DSP48 output cascade implements the wide, 48-bit partial sum chain. (See "Adder Cascade" in [26].) The DSP48 slice comes with a 48-bit summing cascade to be connected by abutment without any fabric resources. The FPGA vendor guarantees its operation at the maximum DSP48 frequency. In contrast to using DSP slices as multiply-add (MADD) units in a systolic array, Snowflake uses DSP slices as multiply-accumulate (MAC) units. A MAC creates one wide output per DSP slice. The many MAC outputs in Snowflake coalesce within the fabric, taking up precious resources and complicating timing closure. When MAC units create partial sums in the Snowflake cooperative mode, a shift register in the fabric transports them to yet another MAC to create the final sum. Except for the few partial sums in the accumulators, partial sums in our matrix-vector multiplier are distributed along the DSP supertile array summing cascade. These partial sums are hidden from the fabric and therefore do not create critical timing paths.

5   CONCLUSION AND FUTURE WORK

High-throughput neural network accelerators require both high compute efficiency and high clock rates. While a few architectures achieve high compute efficiency, we have not seen high normalized clock rates for an entire FPGA accelerator reported in the literature. (The DSP arrays in [22] attain 100% normalized clock rates but are not entire accelerators.) In this paper, we presented a CNN accelerator architecture that achieves 95.5% compute efficiency running GoogLeNet. This architecture is favorable to timing closure at high clock rates. Our FPGA design runs at 720 MHz or 92.9% of the peak 775 MHz clock rate. The overall efficiency is 88.7%. As far as we know, the closest overall efficiency to ours from the literature is 34.9%, suggesting that both compute efficiency and clock rates are critical to realizing performance inherent in FPGAs.

We implemented our design on a Xilinx VU9P FPGA, which consists of three super logic regions (SLRs) connected through a silicon interposer. Each SLR is essentially the smaller VU3P FPGA. We first experimented with our accelerator on a VU3P FPGA, and then instantiated three copies of it on a VU9P FPGA, one on each SLR. In the future, we would like to implement our design on large, multi-die FPGAs as if they were monolithic devices. Successfully doing so reduces latency even further and yields more scheduling flexibility.

Acknowledgements

We would like to thank Sairam Menon, Anil Martha, Kumar Vemuri, and Arun Kumar Patil for quantizing GoogLeNet for us.

REFERENCES

[1]   Abadi, M. et al. 2016. TensorFlow: A System for Large-Scale Machine Learning. In 12th USENIX Symposium on Operating Systems Design and Implementation (OSDI '16). 265–283.
[2]   Chellapilla, K., Puri, S. and Simard, P. 2006. High Performance Convolutional Neural Networks for Document Processing. In Tenth International Workshop on Frontiers in Handwriting Recognition.
[3]   Chen, Y.H., Krishna, T., Emer, J.S. and Sze, V. 2017. Eyeriss: An Energy-Efficient Reconfigurable Accelerator for Deep Convolutional Neural Networks. IEEE J. Solid-State Circuits. 52, 1 (2017), 127–138. DOI:https://doi.org/10.1109/JSSC.2016.2616357.
[4]   Fu, Y., Wu, E. and Sirasao, A. 2017. 8-Bit Dot-Product Acceleration. https://www.xilinx.com/support/documentation/white_papers/wp487-int8-acceleration.pdf.
[5]   Gokhale, V., Zaidy, A., Chang, A.X.M. and Culurciello, E. 2017. Snowflake: An efficient hardware accelerator for convolutional neural networks. In 2017 IEEE International Symposium on Circuits and Systems (ISCAS). 1–4.
[6]   Gysel, P., Pimentel, J., Motamedi, M. and Ghiasi, S. 2018. Ristretto: A Framework for Empirical Study of Resource-Efficient Inference in Convolutional Neural Networks. IEEE Trans. Neural Networks Learn. Syst. 29, 11 (2018), 5784–5789.
[7]   Hegde, G., Siddhartha, Ramasamy, N. and Kapre, N. 2016. CaffePresso. In Proceedings of the International Conference on Compilers, Architectures and Synthesis for Embedded Systems (CASES '16). 1–10.
[8]   Huang, Y., Shen, J., Qiao, Y., Wen, M. and Zhang, C. 2018. MALMM: A multi-array architecture for large-scale matrix multiplication on FPGA. IEICE Electron. Express. 15, 10 (2018), 1–12. DOI:https://doi.org/10.1587/elex.15.20180286.
[9]   Jia, Y. and Shelhamer, E. Convolution in Caffe: A Memo. https://github.com/Yangqing/caffe/wiki/Convolution-in-Caffe:-a-memo.
[10] Jia, Y., Shelhamer, E., Donahue, J., Karayev, S., Long, J., Girshick, R., Guadarrama, S. and Darrell, T. 2014. Caffe. Proc. ACM Int. Conf. Multimed. - MM '14. (2014). DOI:https://doi.org/10.1145/2647868.2654889.
[11] Ngo, K. 2016. FPGA Hardware Acceleration of Inception Style Parameter Reduced Convolution Neural Networks. Master's Thesis, School of Inform. and Commun. Technol. (ICT), KTH Royal Institute of Technology, Stockholm, Sweden.
[12] Paszke, A., Chanan, G., Lin, Z., Gross, S., Yang, E., Antiga, L. and Devito, Z. 2017. Automatic differentiation in PyTorch. In Advances in Neural Information Processing Systems 30.
[13] Russakovsky, O., Deng, J., Su, H., Krause, J., Satheesh, S., Ma, S., Huang, Z., Karpathy, A., Khosla, A., Bernstein, M., Berg, A.C. and Li, F.-F. 2015. ImageNet Large Scale Visual Recognition Challenge. Int. J. Comput. Vis. 115, 3 (2015), 211–252. DOI:https://doi.org/10.1007/s11263-015-0816-y.
[14] Sharma, H., Park, J., Mahajan, D., Amaro, E., Kim, J.K., Shao, C., Mishra, A. and Esmaeilzadeh, H. 2016. From high-level deep neural models to FPGAs. In Proceedings of the Annual International Symposium on Microarchitecture (MICRO). 17:1–17:12.
[15] Shen, Y., Ferdman, M. and Milder, P. 2017. Maximizing CNN Accelerator Efficiency Through Resource Partitioning. In Proc. 44th Annu. Int. Symp. Comput. Architecture (ISCA). 535–547.
[16] Sze, V., Chen, Y.H., Yang, T.J. and Emer, J.S. 2017. Efficient Processing of Deep Neural Networks: A Tutorial and Survey. In Proceedings of the IEEE. 2295–2329.
[17] Szegedy, C., Liu, W., Jia, Y., Sermanet, P., Reed, S., Anguelov, D., Erhan, D., Vanhoucke, V. and Rabinovich, A. 2015. Going deeper with convolutions. In Proceedings of the IEEE Computer Society Conference on Computer Vision and Pattern Recognition (CVPR '15). 1–9.
[18] Umuroglu, Y., Fraser, N.J., Gambardella, G., Blott, M., Leong, P., Jahre, M. and Vissers, K. 2017. FINN: A Framework for Fast, Scalable Binarized Neural Network Inference. In Proceedings of the 2017 ACM/SIGDA International Symposium on Field-Programmable Gate Arrays. 65–74.
[19] Venieris, S.I. and Bouganis, C.-S. 2017. fpgaConvNet: A Toolflow for Mapping Diverse Convolutional Neural Networks on Embedded FPGAs. http://arxiv.org/abs/1711.08740.
[20] Wang, Y., Xu, J., Han, Y., Li, H. and Li, X. 2016. DeepBurning: Automatic generation of FPGA-based learning accelerators for the Neural Network family. In 2016 53rd ACM/EDAC/IEEE Design Automation Conference (DAC). 110:1–110:6.
[21] Wilkinson, J.H. 1963. Rounding Errors in Algebraic Processes. Natl. Phys. Lab. Notes Appl. Sci. Her Majesty's Station. Off. (HMSO), London. (1963).
[22] Wu, E., Zhang, X., Berman, D. and Cho, I. 2017. A high-throughput reconfigurable processing array for neural networks. In 2017 27th International Conference on Field Programmable Logic and Applications. 1–4.
[23] Zhang, C., Li, P., Sun, G., Guan, Y., Xiao, B. and Cong, J. 2015. Optimizing FPGA-based Accelerator Design for Deep Convolutional Neural Networks. In Proceedings of the 2015 ACM/SIGDA International Symposium on Field-Programmable Gate Arrays. 161–170.
[24] Zhong, G., Dubey, A., Cheng, T. and Mitra, T. 2018. Synergy: A HW/SW Framework for High Throughput CNNs on Embedded Heterogeneous SoC. http://arxiv.org/abs/1804.00706.
[25] Zhou, Y. and Jiang, J. 2016. An FPGA-based accelerator implementation for deep convolutional neural networks. In Proceedings of 2015 4th International Conference on Computer Science and Network Technology, ICCSNT 2015. 829–832.
[26] 2018. UltraScale Architecture DSP Slice User Guide (UG579), v1.7. Xilinx, Inc.
[27] 2018. Virtex UltraScale+ FPGA Data Sheet: DC and AC Switching Characteristics (DS923), v1.8. Xilinx, Inc.

FPGAs in Supercomputers: Opportunity or Folly?

Deming Chen
Department of Electrical and Computer Engineering
University of Illinois of Urbana-Champaign
Illinois, United States of America
dchen@illinois.edu

ABSTRACT

Supercomputers play an important role in the field of computational science, and are used for a wide range of computationally intensive tasks in various fields. So far, the building blocks for supercomputers have been dominated by CPUs and GPUs. Although FPGAs start to play an important role for cloud computing such as those used in AWS and Microsoft Azure, FPGAs haven't been adopted to build top supercomputers yet. In this evening panel, panelists from industry, research institute, and academia will attempt to answer the following questions, propose actions, and present their point of view through lively discussions and debates.

1) Is there a need to bring FPGAs into supercomputers? Why or why not?

2) Are there unique applications that are specifically suitable for FPGAs for supercomputing fields?

3) What are the challenges and/or major issues facing FPGAs for supporting supercomputing?

4) What and where are the opportunities? Who are the stakeholders?

5) Name one thing that the FPGA industry should (or should not) do in the near term to facilitate FPGA's induction into supercomputers.

CCS CONCEPTS

• Computer systems organization

KEYWORDS

FPGAs; Reconfigurable Computing; Supercomputer

FPGA '19, February 24–26, 2019, Seaside, CA, USA
© 2019 Copyright is held by the owner/author(s).
ACM ISBN 978-1-4503-6137-8/19/02.
https://doi.org/10.1145/3289602.3293929

Fractal Synthesis

- Invited Tutorial -

Martin Langhammer	Gregg Baeckler	Sergey Gribok
Intel PSG	Intel PSG	Intel PSG
Martin.Langhammer@intel.com	Gregg.Baeckler@intel.com	Sergey.Gribok@intel.com

ABSTRACT

This paper will describe Fractal Synthesis, which is a new set of synthesis, clustering, and packing algorithms for FPGA devices, which dramatically increases the utilization and effective performance for arithmetic rich designs. The emergence of AI inferencing as a significant new FPGA application has brought some of the shortcomings of the FPGA and current design flows into focus. We describe new results where near 100% logic utilization of the FPGA is not only possible, but deterministic, with consistent high clock rates. Alternately, smaller datapaths can be synthesized, and combined to make chip filling designs. In one benchmark consisting of purely arithmetic datapath for a large Stratix®10 FPGA (E-2 speedgrade), we will show 92% logic utilization at 460 MHz for an automatically placed arithmetic datapath, and 410MHz with 97% logic utilization. Furthermore, we describe new results, where these performance and density level can be applied to non-arithmetic designs, by extending these techniques to placement.

CCS CONCEPTS

• **Hardware** → **Reconfigurable logic and FPGAs**; **Logic synthesis**; **Technology-mapping**; **Physical synthesis**; **Placement**; • **Software and its engineering** → **Compilers**.

KEYWORDS

FPGA, Fractal Synthesis, Fractal Packing

ACM Reference Format:
Martin Langhammer, Gregg Baeckler, and Sergey Gribok. 2019. Fractal Synthesis: - Invited Tutorial -. In *The 2019 ACM/SIGDA International Symposium on Field-Programmable Gate Arrays (FPGA '19), February 24–26, 2019, Seaside, CA, USA.* ACM, New York, NY, USA, 10 pages. https://doi.org/10.1145/3289602.3293927

1 INTRODUCTION

Traditionally, FPGAs have been a restricted platform, with two significant shortcomings: full utilization of the logic and other resources was essentially impossible, and performance could not be defined in advance. A skilled designer could reasonably expect to achieve around 85% utilization for a typical design. Closing timing

was design dependent, and would often have required a combination of design optimization, tools effort, and manual floorplanning. A project that largely consisted of soft arithmetic, and therefore used a large number of carry chains, would suffer a lower utilization, usually around 70%. As utilization increased, performance (Fmax) generally decreased - often dramatically, as the logic use neared the maximum achievable for that design. Furthermore, compilation time often increased significantly, and non-linearly, as the device became fuller.

Recently AI inferencing has become perhaps the most high profile application area for FPGA [3, 19, 23]. Inferencing usually requires many low precision arithmetic operations. High density arithmetic capability is critical for FPGA success, as there are many other existing and emerging technologies, such as GPU, and ASSP [15, 22]. Benchmarking is normally in TFLOPs, with TFLOPs/W becoming increasingly important as a differentiator against traditional GPU competitors. One advantage of FPGAs is that the routing flexibility allows data to appear where you want, when you want, potentially increasing sustained to peak performance, while at the same time reducing latency. The Microsoft Project Brainwave design [14], offers up to 75% sustained to peak performance on LSTM type inferencing on single batch workloads, making it the highest performance implementation for this type of solution on current devices.

In this paper, we introduce an enhanced flow for FPGA clustering and packing, which incorporates arithmetic mapping, synthesis and re-synthesis, with emphasis on LAB level optimization. While clustering and packing are often used interchangeably in the literature, we will make a distinction here. We define clustering as the combination of likely related elements, and packing as achieving full utilization of the logic.

Fractal Synthesis (Fractal) can effectively double FPGA performance density compared to normal methods. This increase in capability consists of three elements. First, regularization of multipliers [16] will decrease logic cost for low precision multipliers by around 30% over previously reported numbers. Logic utilization in the device (especially for arithmetic datapaths) is increased by 40% over current algorithms. Lastly, the combination of arithmetic and packing regularization maintains datapath performance as logic utilization increases, with 90% of the performance of a small reference circuit with 90% of the device full, and 75% performance for an entirely full FPGA, even for the largest member of a device family. The effect of these three improvements is cumulative. Additionally, the compile times (including place and route) are relatively linear, from low utilization to full chip utilization, even for very large (1M LUT) designs.

We will use the term regularization interchangeably in this paper, referring to the mapping level, packing and clustering level, and the impact of these algorithms on the full chip level. We will refer to these collectively as Fractal Synthesis - at every level, and within each level, the optimization applied looks like a subset - either logically or physically - like the level above it or below it. We make the following contributions:

(1) Based on earlier work on multiplier regularization, we describe improved logic mapping of arithmetic functions to current and proxy FPGA architectures.

(2) We describe a new clustering and packing algorithm, that not only creates a more densely packed (i.e. functionality per LUT) cluster, but often utilizes 100% of the cluster.

(3) We manage to reliably fill large (1M LUT+) devices to near 100% of the device with arithmetic datapaths, with a predictable and repeatable Fmax. We can also implement complex systems with well over 90% of FPGA logic and feature utilization.

(4) We describe how the Fractal methods can be extended to regularize an entire FPGA with heterogeneous components and subdesigns.

Our goal is to make the FPGA deterministic, where the area and performance of designs are known at the time of design entry, even when coded behaviorally. We will start with complex datapath designs, such as used for AI inferencing.

This paper is organized as follows. First, background information will be examined in two ways: known clustering and packing algorithms for FPGAs, and an initial comparison with the elements of Fractal. Next, we will look at the mapping of previous and current AI designs, including the initial near full datapath mapping during the development phase of Fractal. The problem statement for high density, low precision arithmetic will then be defined, with some worked examples to illustrate the FPGA packing issues for datapath. Multiplier regularization, which was recently introduced to balance FPGA routing and logic resources for arithmetic will be reviewed. Fractal Synthesis will then be introduced, which clusters and packs a (optionally regularized) datapath into FPGA resources efficiently. Results for multiplier regularization and Fractal will be then presented separately. We will then list and briefly preview new placement results which arise from extending Fractal to the whole device level.

2 BACKGROUND

2.1 Previous Packing Algorithms

Over the last two decades, there has been a large body of literature on FPGA clustering, or packing as it is alternately known, and often reported in conjuction with placement algorithms. There are a number of different types of FPGA clustering algorithms. Perhaps the most common are seed-based methods, such as VPACK [4], T-VPack [18], and RPack [7]. There are also partioning based methods, such as PPack [13], as well as placement guided methods, such as DPack and HDPack [8]. In this section, we will examine various aspects of some of these approaches, and in the second half of this section, we will comment on how our new methods are different or similar to published methods, as applicable.

Seed-based methods start with a basic logic element (BLE), and keep adding new BLEs into a configurable logic block (CLB) based on metrics such as an attraction function. Partitioning methods

use a k-way partitioning to generate a set of potential CLBs, and the adjust the CLB set to obtain a legal packing. Placement guide methods first generate a potential global placement, followed by regrouping clusters.

A common theme through many of the published approaches is depopulation of the CLBs to improve routability. Uniform depopulation uses Rent's rule to balance wires and logic, while non-uniform depopulation first attempts to route the design, and then depopulates congested regions.

In [17], a routability driven packing uses physical information derived from an analytic global placement. A 'congestion aware depopulation technique' is used, followed by 'congestion aware placement'. The authors claim that other published seed-based and partitioning-based techniques only use logical packing, which may cluster cells that are far apart, and that placement based packers have poor quality location information. They also state that depopulation is important to reduce congestion.

VPACK [4] is one of the first seed-based cluster methods, and uses a greedy algorithm to add BLEs to a cluster. The attraction function is based on the number of inputs and outputs that the considered BLE has in common with the existing ones in the cluster; this is meant to minimize routing stress to the CLB by using shared connections where possible. The cluster is considered full when the number of inputs exceeds the maximum allowed for the CLB. Experimental results showed that the optimal number of inputs for a cluster of 4 input BLEs was 2N+2 wires, where N is the maximum number of BLEs in the cluster.

The RippleFPGA [9] approach combines an iterative packing and placement algorithm, combining FPGA and ASIC (analytic placement) methods. One of the motivations stated is that the seed-based packing methods such as VPACK pack too tightly to make efficient use of the CLB. Instead, the presented method uses an initial global analytic placement (GP) of a flat netlist to minimize wire cost. BLE mapping is soft, meaning that BLEs can be reassigned or merged in later stages. BLEs are then packed into a CLB implicitly, using a Tetris style legality checker (LG).

Although [12] is written from the perspective of FPGA architecture - specifically embedded ripple carry adders and their effect on benchmark efficiency, in terms of both design performance and tools performance - packing using VPR was examined in detail. A proxy for modern FPGA architecture was given, using a partially depopulated crossbar, which can be used as a basis to examine different clustering approaches.

Tessier [21] starts with the assumption that using 100% of an FPGA is infeasible, largely because providing routing resources needed to support this level of utilization is not possible. A figure of 85% utilization is given as more reasonable. Uniform depopulation is used to ensure routability.

The VTR project [20] introduces a modified version of VT-Pack with a modified attraction function, which adds logic depth as a parameter. This timing driven methodology improved performance by approximately 5% over earlier area driven flows.

2.2 Fractal Synthesis Packing Algorithm

At this point we will make some comments about the differences in the Fractal Synthesis packing and clustering algorithms, compared to all previously published methods. We will split the comparison into four different elements, and more detail on each of these will be given later in Section 6.

2.2.1 Seed Based Clustering. The seed-based clustering methods use attraction functions based on shared inputs and outputs, which may be enhanced with logic complexity analysis for timing driven compilation flows. Fractal does not use shared inputs and outputs, but rather associated I/O, i.e. adjacent bits in a number or vector. Sometimes this is enforced by a carry chain, but this can also apply to combinatorial logic. In later stages of Fractal packing, the attraction function will be based on the logical distance of a candidate function to the already packed functions in a cluster, assuming that the clustering can be completed after legality checking.

2.2.2 Partitioning or Analytic Placement. Aspects of this are naturally part of the Fractal Synthesis clustering approach. A synthesized netlist, especially if pre-processed through the multiplier regularization flow (see Section 5) will likely already be grouped in a hierarchical manner. The Fractal clustering algorithm will perform multiple sweeps across the portion of the database with the Fractal compilation flow enabled; this will examine a large number of clustering and packing possibilities, while maintaining the natural structure of the datapaths.

2.2.3 Depopulation. Existing clustering methods expect that 100% packing is not possible, and implement various depopulation strategies to improve the chance of fitting. Fractal Synthesis will attempt a 100% packing if possible. Because of the way the packing locations are fixed within each cluster, physical dummy cells may need to be inserted, in other words, a hard depopulation strategy. On average, Fractal achieves 97% packing efficiency, which means our hard depopulation typically takes 3% of the cluster area. In some cases, we achieve 100% utilization.

2.2.4 Logic Synthesis and Re-synthesis. All other clustering methods use post synthesis information. Some then iterate with the placement step. In contrast, Fractal iteratively re-synthesizes the datapaths during packing. Additional combinatorial functions may be created during this re-synthesis process, which may or may not be packed back with the originating function, at the end of the process.

3 PREVIOUS RESULTS

A large number of papers have been published recently on AI implementations on FPGA. We will first look at some recent results using standard design methods, and then an example built with a Fractal Synthesis prototype flow.

In [6], two expected performance levels are given for FPGA inferencing applications on Xilinx VU9P devices: the first assumes 80% device utilization, and a 250MHz clock frequency. Later in the paper, an expected performance of 400MHz is given. The reported results, however, are only 109MHz. The authors state that a higher performance is achievable with careful floorplanning and attention to timing closure. In a more recent paper [5], the estimates are updated to a clock frequency of 400 MHz, with 90% DSP and 70% LUT utilization. Actual clock frequencies achieved and reported

in the paper range from 100 MHz to 300MHz, but only with small activation and weight precisions, typically from 1 to 3 bits.

The Microsoft Project Brainwave accelerator [11] was introduced in 2017, with a single batch peak performance of 48 TFLOPs at 300MHz for an RNN type of algorithm on an Intel Stratix®10 280 FPGA. A low precision floating point format, MS-FP9, was used. A device utilization of 92% ALM and 100% DSP resources was reported.

We generated the datapaths for this project using the development algorithms for Fractal Synthesis. The low precision mantissa multipliers in the custom floating point format did not benefit from the multiplier regularization at that time, but the clustering and packing algorithms resulted in datapaths that were 97% efficient; the 92% ALM use can be explained by the 80% of the device that contained datapaths being Fractal packed and the remaining 20% of the design packed with a normal design flow.

In addition [10], the full design synthesis time dropped by almost 80% and the full device compile time (including place and route) by approximately 60%. An added benefit was in the tools server memory footprint, which was reduced by 40%.

4 PROBLEM STATEMENT

We will use the proxy for a modern FPGA soft logic structure described in [12] for the target to illustrate the problem of efficiently packing a large AI design. A number of LUTs, optionally connected with a hardened carry chain, have 6 inputs and one output each. The group of LUTs are fed by a partially (50%) populated cross bar switch. First, we will define a proxy for a large current FPGA, with 1M 6LUTs (and therefore 1M bits of arithmetic). The LUTs will be grouped together in blocks of 16 (with an unbroken carry chain), so we will have approximately 62,500 groups. Carry chains can be continued between blocks, but at a reduced speed compared to inside the block. This architecture is not meant to represent any existing FPGA, and may be thought of having a mix of characteristics of Intel and Xilinx devices.

Now assume we will build an AI inferencing accelerator, consisting of 32 element dot products (DOTs), with 5x5 multipliers. Signed magnitude representation will be used, with unsigned multipliers and a signed adder tree. One mapping of the 5x5 multiplier to these LUTs may consist of four carry chains (where possible, two pencil and paper partial product bit positions are computed, and added per LUT), of lengths 6,7,7, and 8. We will ignore the requirements for register balancing in this structure and assume that additional registers are available where and when required at no cost. The DOT32 will require 31 adders: 16 of length 12, 8 of length 13, 4 of length 14, 2 of length 15, and a final one of length 16. All adders individually will therefore fit into a single LUT block. A single DOT requires 1318 LUTs: 896 LUTs for the multipliers and 422 LUTs for the adder tree. We will target an FPGA with around 80% DOT utilization, leaving 20% of the logic available for the application management. A 600 DOT32 design (79% logic utilization) will contain the carry chain combinations shown in Table 1.

There are therefore 776,400 arithmetic bits contained in 95,400 carry chains. Our place and route tool is now required to map these 95,400 carry chains into 50,000 (80% of the device) blocks.

The logic synthesis of this DOT is trivial, as the partial product generation maps directly to the LUTs associated with the carry

Table 1: Example Design Resources

Carry Chain Length	Number	Number Bits	Weight Chains	Weight Bits
6	19200	115200	0.201	0.148
7	38400	268800	0.402	0.346
8	19200	153600	0.201	0.196
12	9600	115200	0.101	0.148
13	4800	62400	0.050	0.080
14	2400	33600	0.0252	0.043
15	1200	18000	0.0125	0.023
16	600	9600	0.0063	0.0012

Table 2: 3×3 **Multiplier** $\{a_2, a_1, a_0\} \times \{b_2, b_1, b_0\}$

Column	5	4	3	2	1	0
PP0	0	0	0	$p_{0,2}$	$p_{0,1}$	$p_{0,0}$
PP1	0	0	$p_{1,2}$	$p_{1,1}$	$p_{1,0}$	0
PP2	0	$p_{2,2}$	$p_{2,1}$	$p_{2,0}$	0	0

Table 3: 3×3 **Multiplier in Two Levels with Auxiliary Functions**

Column	5	4	3	2	1	0
PP0	0	$p_{2,2}$	$p_{2,1}$	$p_{2,0}$	$p_{0,1}$	$p_{0,0}$
PP1	0	$AUX_2 \oplus p_{1,2}$	AUX_2	AUX_1	$p_{1,0}$	0

chains, and the routing density can be easily supported by the partially populated crossbar without local congestion. The fitting of the DOTs in our relatively simple example is therefore dependent on the mapping of the carry chains into the logic blocks. We can start with a cutting algorithm approach, and fit the adder tree first. All of the carry chains in the adder tree will fit into a block, with 75% to 100% utilization, although the carry chain weighting will give an average of 81% utilization for this portion of the DOT product (the adder tree is 31% of the total DOT area). A number of cut patterns are possible for the multipliers. Two each of the multiplier carry chains fit into each 16 bit block, with the maximum packing at 88% utilization, although this depends on a logical separation between two of the 8 bit blocks. This may not be supported in the LUTs, for example as a hardware separation (such as the blocks being decomposable into two half blocks). A more likely scenario is that each 8 bit chain would occupy a single block, reducing the multiplier packing to 74%. Alternately, the 6 and 8 bit carries could be combined, increasing the packing back up to 88%. Our simple, synthetic example will likely fall into the utilization range of 76% to 86% - but several caveats need to be considered. We still need to account for the balancing registers - and additional routing congestion this introduces - as well as the ability of current placement algorithms to understand relationships between arithmetic components in the context of a group of functions, such as found in a dot product.

We use this same proxy FPGA again, but with a DOT40 of 6x6 multipliers. One construction of the multiplier may contain four 8 bit carries and a 10 bit carry, again without accounting for balancing registers and logic. In the case of our proxy group being decomposable into two 8 bit subgroups, this multiplier could pack to 88%, but only to 53% if decomposition was not supported. Recent Intel Arria®and Stratix®devices have 20 bit groups that are decomposable; in this case utilization would be 70% for a single multiplier, but there is a possibility that one of the 10 bit carry chains from another multiplier would be able to use the half LAB left over, and increase packing to 87%. But in either our proxy or the Intel case, the adder tree utilization would be relatively poor. In summary, the packing efficiency of the 6x6 DOT products would range between 50% to 80%, again not accounting for real world issues such as balancing logic.

The naive mapping of multipliers by the pencil and paper method (where a pair of partial products is mapped to a single LUT layer with it's associated carry chain) has been previously reported. We will now improve this by looking for optimizations across multiple logic levels using multiplier regularization, mapping arithmetic more effectively to both logic and routing.

Note that this problem statement has only highlighted the issues with packing: clustering, which can introduce additional complexities, has not been considered. The new algorithms in the following sections will work on both.

5 MULTIPLIER REGULARIZATION

Multiplier regularization has been described in detail in [16]. The algorithms have been updated since, with current multiplier numbers provided in the results section later in this paper. We will largely repeat the description of a simple example, the regularization of a 3x3 unsigned multiplier, to illustrate the concept of re-synthesis into a combination of carry based and combinatorial based arithmetic. These methods allow us to restructure a longer carry chain into a combination of smaller carry chains, which can be packed into the target bins more tightly. The combinatorial functions can then be potentially packed into remaining space around the carry chains. The combinatorial functions are typically connected to the carry chain based functions by a single wire, which is an easy route, whether packed closely or further away.

In [16] the combinatorial functions generated by the decomposition methods described herein are known as auxiliary functions. We will also use the auxiliary function name to distinguish the pre-Fractal decompositions from the iterative re-synthesis results, which we will name combinatorial functions.

We will take the figures 1 and 2 and tables 2 and 3 from [16]. In both the figures and tables, a partial product bit is denoted as $p_{x,y}$, where bit y from the multiplicand is ANDed with bit x from the multiplier.

We define a regular arithmetic structure as one that is balanced across routing, logic, and datapath construction. A 4x4 multiplier is a good example of this - two pairs of partial products can be mapped to (and subsequently added by) two respective single levels of logic, and summed with an adder in a third level of logic. A 8x8 multiplier can be constructed in a similar way, with two levels of adder tree to add the sums of four pairs of partial products. The 3x3 multiplier used for our regularization example is highly irregular; one of the three partial products in table 2 will occupy a level of of logic by itself, and the adder tree is also unbalanced. The partial product bits can be reordered as shown in fig. 1. Although this makes the level of logic processing the first pair of partial products more efficient, the

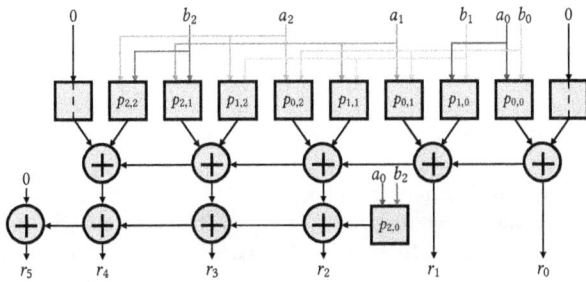

Figure 1: Known 3x3 Mapping

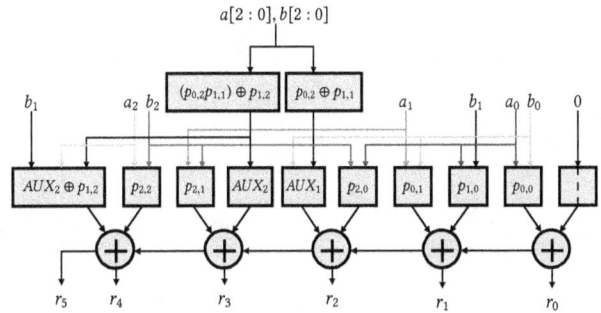

Figure 2: New 3x3 Mapping

final adder is used only to add the LSB of the third partial product. This is a poor result, from both logic and latency perspectives.

Ternary addition is supported in some modern FPGAs, but often not pervasively, because of routing congestion. The regularization IP will balance binary and ternary addition to ensure the LAB is intially routable, but the re-synthesis steps in the later Fractal iterations may change both logic and routing, and are therefore legality checked.

If we can remove, or at least restate the LSB of the last row (ideally merging into the first two rows), then the multiplier will only need a single level of logic. We will start by calculating the redundant form compression of the two partial product bits above the LSB. The sum ($p_{0,2} \oplus p_{1,1}$) will replace these two bits (leaving a space where the $p_{2,0}$ bit can be moved into, but the redundant carry ($a_2 \cdot b_0 \cdot a_1 \cdot b_1$) needs to be moved to the next column. This in turn creates another 3 high column, but we can create another redundant form compression of this column as well. The $p_{1,2}$ bit shares its two bits with the redundant carry input.

A single ALM (the auxilary function in this case) is used to create the redundant sum for the first sum, and a combination of a redundant carry of the first column, and the redundant sum of the second column. The 6 needed inputs do not overstress the local routing, as these are shared with the total of 4 ALMs needed for the regularized 3x3 multiplier, in other words, only 1.5 bits per ALM are needed here.

The one remaining issue is that another redundant carry is required into the next column. If implemented in another auxiliary function, this would negate any area savings. The redundant carry is $(a_2 \cdot b_0) \cdot (a_1 \cdot b_1) \cdot (a_2 \cdot b_1)$, which can be simplified to $(a_2 \cdot b_0) \cdot (a_1 \cdot b_1)$. By inspection, we can create this function from the auxilary redundant carry function, XORed with $p_{1,2}$.

This mapping is shown in Figure 2. Although the local wiring pattern appears to be busier than that unregularized function, the number of independent nets is approximately the same (two more local ones are required for the auxilary function connections to the main logic chain), and the overall structure of the multiplier is much simplified.

Multiplier regularization can be applied to an already regular multiplier structure (such as a 4x4 unsigned multiplier), by first de-regularizing the multiplier, and then regularizing the irregular components. Fig. 3 shows a pencil and paper partial product arrangement of the subject 4x4 unsigned multiplier. Pairs of partial products can be calculated, and then added, in a single layer of

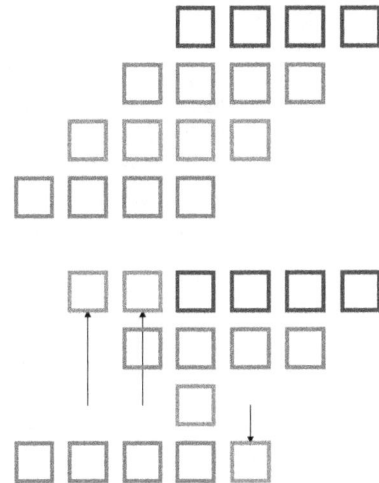

Figure 3: Multiplier De-regularization and Re-regularization

logic, which also contains an embedded carry chain. The two sums can then be added by a third carry chain, in a separate group of logic. This is a very efficient structure in modern FPGAs, but can be further improved by first de-regularizing, and then re-regularizing the multiplier.

Partial product bits are moved from the third partial product to the first, second, and last partial products, respectively, as shown in the second segment in Fig. 3. The most significant four bits of the new arrangement of the first three partial products is analogous to the 3x3 unsigned multiplier case. There is an additional column of two partial products to the column of three partial products, but this does not affect the regularization steps.

The first three partial products are now implemented in a single level of logic and carry chain, plus an auxiliary function (not shown in Figure 4). The output of this carry chain (the two LSBs are output directly) is then added to the fourth partial product to complete the multiplication. This structure only contains two carry chains instead of three - it is both smaller and has lower latency.

Many other types of arithmetic restructuring are possible using the techniques in [16].

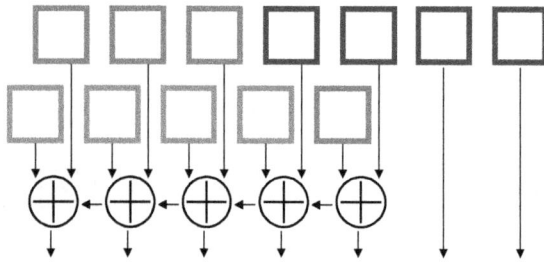

Figure 4: Re-assembling the 4x4 Multiplier

6 FRACTAL SYNTHESIS

The Fractal Synthesis feature has been added to Quartus 18.1, where it acts as an intermediate step between IP generation and synthesis. As previously described, an iterative loop of clustering, packing, and re-synthesis is performed in order to attempt a near 100% logic utilization for arithmetic datapaths in the FPGA. The output is a structured netlist that maps directly to the LUTs and carry chains in the logic array blocks (LABs) of the Intel FPGA. The synthesis step of the tools is therefore greatly simplified - a pre-computed set of full LAB mappings (with legality checking for local routing density) that cannot be materially improved by current methods.

At the core of Fractal is a variation of a bin packing algorithm. Normally, for most bin packing algorithms, there are a number of bins, each with fixed sizes. There is also a list of elements to be fit into the bins, usually of different, but fixed sizes. In Fractal, both the bin sizes and element sizes are variable, and can be adjusted to improve the packing density. The bins are logic clusters (logic array blocks, or LABs in Intel FPGAs), which can be combined with other LABs to make larger virtual bins. The elements are usually the output of multiplier regularization, which is a list of single LUT depth functions terminating in carry chains, with an associated set of auxiliary functions. The user can also define their own arithmetic datapath constructs, such as a tree of ripple carry adders, or their own multiplier architectures. The carry chain based functions are continually combined or decomposed (into smaller carry chains and combinatorial logic functions) in the algorithm loops to find the best fit.

There is only implied placement in the LABs. This is enforced with mapping the packed functions to an unbroken carry chain, whether or not the placed function is arithmetic or combinatorial. Separation is ensured by either arithmetic identity or kill bits, the latter of which can be logical or physical. Logical kills are synthesized, and do not affect the utilization or routing density.

The Fractal pass is very fast, and works by an exhaustive search, sweeping across a set of virtual bin sizes, and varying indexes of the database containing the carry chain elements. Often, even large designs will use a relatively small number of similar datapath structures. As Fractal packing only produces an implied relative placement, the optimized datapaths can be readily morphed anywhere across the device. We will show some examples of this in the results section.

Algorithm 1 gives pseudocode for the algorithm. We will now give some detail and explanation on some of the steps. The outer loop (line 1) slowly varies the bin size, by combining LABs into larger virtual LABs. Carry chains are allowed to span the physical LAB boundaries. The inner loop (line 2) searches through the list of input elements, with differing sweep patterns.

If an element does not fit into a location within the local search space, the space will be spanned again and a fit attempted with re-synthesis. Re-synthesis will start with the element to be placed, and continued with every other element in that bin, until a fit is either made or determined to be impossible. The combinatorial functions extracted from re-synthesis are placed in a database, to be placed near the end of Fractal. New bins are added when a bin is entirely full, or a placement attempt fails anywhere in the local search space.

Once the elements have been placed, the combinatorial functions are placed in empty locations (LUTs) in the local search space. This step is then repeated for the auxiliary functions from the original database. Combinatorial functions are placed first, as they are more likely to have a high level of connectivity to the element they were removed from. In contrast, auxiliary functions by definition have a single bit connectively to a single LUT input. Some combinatorial functions - from re-synthesis, the auxiliary function list, or both - may be unplaced in a bin. This is not an issue - they will be handled in the Quartus placement stage.

Finally, all LUTs in a bin that do not have a function mapped to them - here referred to as unreachable LUTs - will have a dummy function inserted, which acts as a hard depopulation. Re-synthesis by Quartus into these LUTs is not allowed. There may be some unreachable LUTs even when there are unplaced combinatorial functions from re-synthesis or auxiliary functions - this is likely if the distance is too far (routing stress) or a kill cannot be inserted at that location for separation.

The result metrics (area, utilization, predicted routing patterns) are measured, and stored along with the bin size and sweep pattern. Unreachable LUTs and physical kills will reduce the effective utilization number. The best pass (defined by outer and inner loop specifications) is then repeated on the original input database, and passed to the synthesis step. Legality checking (local routing stress) is applied multiple times, and is not shown here.

Many details have been omitted here, such as re-synthesis methods, insertion and management of kill function - either virtual or physical, and the cost functions to manage search spaces.

7 RESULTS

To give a context on the DOT areas, we first report on the small precision multiplier resources using multiplier regularization. We then describe the results of two experiments which were run using Fractal Synthesis.

7.1 Small Precision Multiplier Resources

Although both devices use a similar ALM logic structure, the Intel Arria®10 has a more richly featured ALM for arithmetic; we show that this will typically reduce multiplier sizes by 10%-30%. Comprehensive results for small bitwidth multipliers are given for comparison in tables 4 and 5. For example, the Arria®10 6x6 unsigned multiplier is 13 ALMs, while the Stratix®10 6x6 unsigned multiplier requires 19 ALMs.

Algorithm 1: Fractal Synthesis Algorithm

    Input : first pass synthesized datapath, create database of carry chains and auxiliary functions.
    Output: arithmetic constructs mapped to individual BLEs in LABs

```
1  loop
      //sweep across a set of virtual bin sizes
2     loop
         //sweep order of grouping inside local groups of database
3        if indexed element placed then
4           advance to next index;
5        else
            //try to place
6           while (bin list) do
7              if this element fits into the current bin then
8                 place here;
9                 exit while;

10          if not fit then
11             while (bin list) do
12                calculate overhang past end of bin;
13                while (elements pointing to this bin) do
14                   if current element can be resynthesized into carry + combinatorial element then
15                      while (combinatorial bits can be removed from element) do
16                         place combinatorial element in separate database;
17                         index back to element it was taken from;
18                         adjust endpoint indexes of all other elements in this bin;
19                         if element fits then
20                            exit while;

21                if last element did not fit then
22                   back out all re-synthesis for entire bin;
23                if end of list then
24                   add new bin to list;

25             if fit bin full then
26                create new bin;


27  while (all elements in database) do
28     check placed in a bin;

29  while (all combinatorial functions) do
30     while (bins within threshold distance of element) do
31        place if space is available on carry chain (including physical kill);

32  while (all auxiliary functions) do
33     while (bins within threshold distance of element) do
34        place if space is available on carry chain (including physical kill);

35  forall bins do
36     forall BLEs do
37        fill empty BLE with hard depopulation;
```

7.2 Increasing Arithmetic Density

A signed-magnitude 5x6 DOT32 structure was defined, and instantiated in a Stratix®10 280 ES-2 device, using increasingly dense arrays. Speed was relatively flat across a wide range of utilizations. Table 6 summarizes the fitting results.

Perhaps more interesting are the floorplans of the compiled designs, which give a good indication on the effectiveness of the Fractal Synthesis algorithm. Figures 5a through 5d show how Quartus handles the Fractal packed DOTs.

In Fig. 5a, 512 DOTs were instantiated, and Quartus evenly distributed them across the die. Notice that that the shape of the DOTs is very similar everywhere on the device, although only relative packing is implied in the DOT.

Table 4: Arria®10 Unsigned Multiplier ALM Count

Arria 10	2	3	4	5	6	7	8
2	2	2.5	3	3.5	4	4.5	5
3		3	4.5	5.5	6.5	7.5	8.5
4			6	7	8.5	10	11.5
5				9	10.5	12.5	14.5
6					13	15.5	17.5
7						18	20
8							23.5

Table 5: Stratix®10 Unsigned Multiplier ALM Count

Stratix 10	2	3	4	5	6	7
2	2	2.5	3	3.5	4	4.5
3		4	5	6	7	8
4			7	8.5	10	11.5
5				11	15	18
6					19	22
7						24.5

Table 6: Performance vs. Density

DOTs	Utilization	FMax (MHz)
512	38%	579
768	57%	560
1024	75%	536
1280	92%	460

Table 7: Normal Quartus Flow - DOT Fitting

DOTs	LABs	ALMs	FMax (MHz)	Compile Time
1120	96%	73%	542	13h33m
1140	97%	73%	no-fit	no-fit
1150	97%	73%	no-fit	no-fit

Table 8: Fractal Synthesis Flow - DOT Fitting

DOTs	LABs	ALMs	FMax (MHz)	Compile Time
1024	74%	74%	536	10h42m
1280	91%	83%	463	14h18m
1400	94%	91%	451	16h57m
1500	96%	97%	409	19h40m

In Fig. 5b, the DOT density was increased by 50%. The shape of the DOTs has hardly changed. The DOTs are more tightly packed, but still evenly distributed.

In Fig. 5c, the DOT density has increased to 75% of the available logic. The shape of the DOTs is changing to improve the packing, but the datapaths are still uniformly distributed.

In Fig. 5d the DOT density is now 92%, with almost all of the logic used. The Fractal packed DOTs, which are mapped to full LABs, can easily be morphed to create a completely regular structure. There is virtually no whitespace left in the device.

We analyzed the performance of the 1280 DOT design on a DOT by DOT basis. There was only a 3% variation from average speed across the entire device. Fractal Synthesis is smoothing out the variation from placement and routing to be just slightly more that the inherent variation in FPGA resource delay, which is typically 1%-2%.

Finally, Fig. 6 shows the floorplan of an individual DOT. Every ALM in every LAB is used - one or more of ALM components such as logic, logic plus carry chain, or just carry chain - although purely chain usage is low. (To interpret this figure, LABs are shown as horizontal bars without a different color border. Dark blue denotes that a structure is used, and there are multiple structures in each ALM. Note that in every LAB, there is a continuous use of at least one structure in every ALM). For this DOT, 97% packing efficiency is achieved, which means that there is a 3% hard depopulation

included. This utilization pattern is repeated throughout the device. One difference between this method and normal FPGA design flows is that the unused portions of the device (usually as whole LABs) are essentially untouched in terms of logic or routing, and can be filled with other circuitry.

7.3 Maximum Arithmetic Density

Next, we attempted to find the maximum FPGA utilization for both datapaths using a normal FPGA flow, and ones via Fractal Synthesis. For these experiments we used the production release of Quartus 18.1, targeting a Stratix®10 280 E-2 device. Other FPGA devices and tools flows may give different results.

Our methodology for the normal FPGA flow was to run many DOT combinations, bracketing fit and no-fit regions, and converging to the point of failure. Table 7 shows the final three runs.

This is in line with our expectation of normal tools capability for arithmetic fitting. Essentially all of the logic (LABs) are at least partially used, but with only 73% efficiency. Our earlier problem statement examines why this packing ratio can be explained for traditional clustering algorithm. Performance is still quite high at 542MHz just before the no fit point. We then tried the same experiments with the Fractal Synthesis directive in Quartus turned on. Quartus managed to pack the device almost completely full, with results detailed in Table 8.

Fractal Synthesis can create placements that are somewhat slower than normal synthesis for some designs; this can be explained because of the local fitting constraints that are imposed on logic structures, while in the normal tools flow, there can still be significant freedom in BLE clustering. Notice that the compile times are close to linear - a geometric increase in place and route times would normally be expected for very full designs. The regular cluster pattern created by Fractal greatly simplifies the placement solution space for full chip designs.

8 FUTURE WORK

The current Fractal algorithms focus on clustering and packing regularization. We are now extending these concepts to placement, moving from implied placement in a LAB with a flexible location,

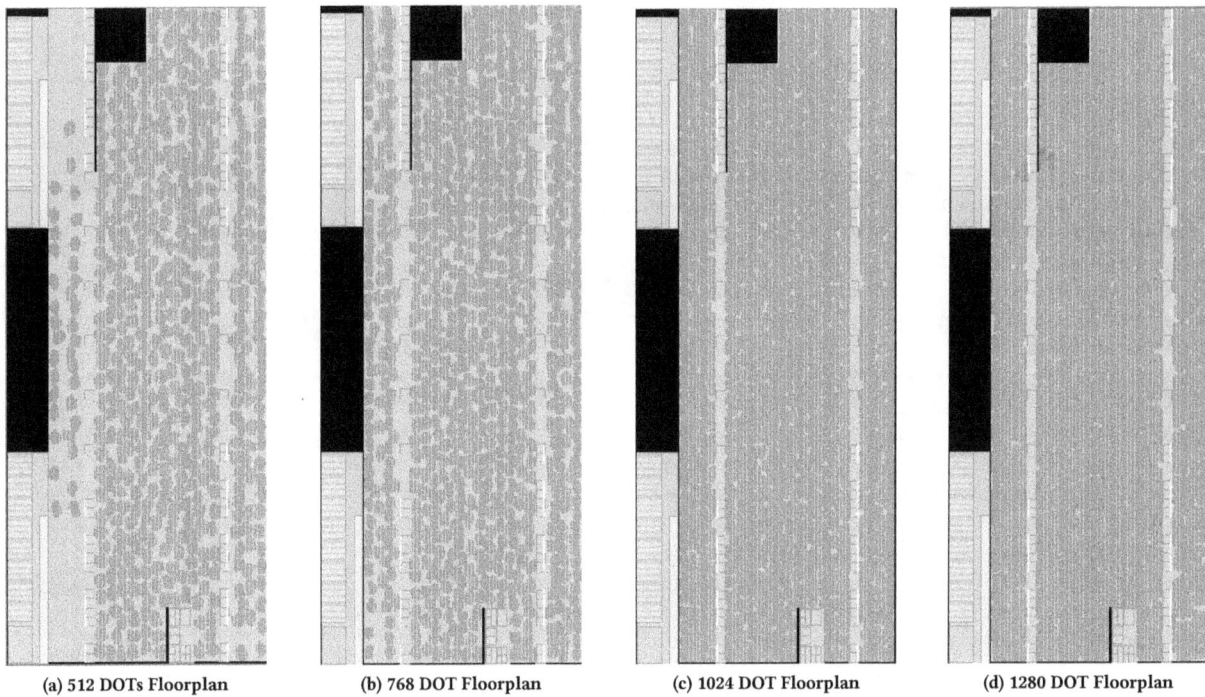

(a) 512 DOTs Floorplan   (b) 768 DOT Floorplan   (c) 1024 DOT Floorplan   (d) 1280 DOT Floorplan

Figure 5: Floorplan of various size DOT product densities

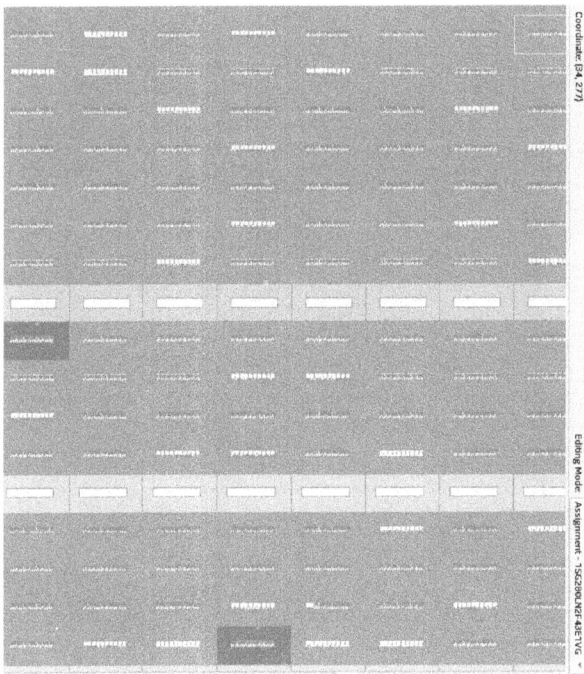

Figure 6: Individual DOT Floorplan

to fixing complete LABs or groups of LABs to specific points on the

device. This can be used for partitioning large designs, where either most or all LABs are placed, or where a number of anchor points are defined, and the rest of the design placed using the normal placement flow.

We will be reporting on results such as memory aggregation, and processor arrays, where we map hundreds of processors into a packed regular structure.

NoCs and datapipes can be challenging to map effectively onto an FPGA. Although there is a large body of work in this area, these are usually for smaller word widths (such as 32b). Regularization makes it possible to guarantee both performance and utilization - fat data pipe distribution on current FPGAs, with end to end connectively of 300 Gbps is now possible. In addition, control distribution and narrow pipes can be spread across the device with short latencies. Although we can currently confidently use Fractal Synthesis to achieve 500MHz device speeds with greater than 90% datapath utilization from a behavioral description, full system design (which also requires data and control distribution) still requires careful design floorplanning. We expect to shortly report entirely behaviorally described synthesized systems at the current datapath speeds.

The Fractal Synthesis algorithms are improving as well. We have shown results here where we can map to 100% ALM use and 100% LAB use - and extend this to the entire device level - but not every component of every ALM is used. A combination of improved synthesis (next generation multiplier regularization) and clustering will extend the current algorithms to use both combinatorial logic and carry chains for every ALM, while maintaining a legal wiring pattern. This reduces overall logic utilization by 10%-15%, while maintaining 100% ALM use in the LABs.

9 CONCLUSIONS

In this paper we introduce the Fractal Synthesis clustering and packing algorithm, which uses an iterative arithmetic re-synthesis step to approach 100% logic utilization for arithmetic datapaths. These types of designs have traditionally been the most problematic for FPGAs, often with poor fitting and performance results. In contrast, the FPGA is now almost deterministic for applications such as AI, with a high confidence of area and speed available immediately after the Fractal Synthesis step, which only takes seconds.

We also reviewed the many current FPGA clustering and packing approaches in order to understand why they may be relatively poor at packing large arithmetic designs. This is reinforced by an illustration of some example inferencing datapaths onto a proxy of a modern FPGA device. Fractal Synthesis uses a very different approach than previously reported methods - the bin packing algorithm uses both dynamic bin sizes and dynamic element sizes, the latter of which are adjusted by arithmetic re-synthesis methods. The result is a netlist that is already mapped to FPGA resources, and is compatible with the standard tools flow placement and routing steps that follow.

We show results for increasing dense datapath mappings, with up to 97% device full. Compile times remain roughly linear as device utilization increases. Finally, we describe how the regularization concepts can be extended to placement, which can be used to map systems to FPGAs with known area and performance. Our goal is to extend our algorithms to the behavioral description of complex systems with deterministic results in the near future.

REFERENCES

[1] 2018. *Intel Arria® 10 Device Overview.* https://www.intel.com/content/dam/altera-www/global/en_US/pdfs/literature/hb/arria-10/a10_overview.pdf.

[2] 2018. *Intel Stratix® 10 GX/SX Device Overview.* https://www.intel.com/dam/www/programmable/us/en/pdfs/literature/hb/stratix-10/s10-overview.pdf.

[3] Mohamed S Abdelfattah, David Han, Andrew Bitar, Roberto DiCecco, Shane OConnell, Nitika Shanker, Joseph Chu, Ian Prins, Joshua Fender, Andrew C Ling, et al. 2018. DLA: Compiler and FPGA Overlay for Neural Network Inference Acceleration. *arXiv preprint arXiv:1807.06434* (2018).

[4] V. Betz and J. Rose. 1997. Cluster-based logic blocks for FPGAs: area-efficiency vs. input sharing and size. In *Proceedings of CICC 97 - Custom Integrated Circuits Conference.* 551–554. https://doi.org/10.1109/CICC.1997.606687

[5] M. Blott, T. Preusser, N. Fraser, G. Gambardella, K. O'Brien, and Y. Umuroglu. 2018. FINN-R: An End-to-End Deep-Learning Framework for Fast Exploration of Quantized Neural Networks. *ArXiv e-prints* (Sept. 2018). arXiv:1809.04570

[6] Michaela Blott, Thomas Preusser, Nicholas Fraser, Giulio Gambardella, Kenneth O'Brien, Yaman Umuroglu, and Miriam Leeser. 2017. Scaling Neural Network Performance through Customized Hardware Architectures on Reconfigurable Logic. 419–422. https://doi.org/10.1109/ICCD.2017.73

[7] E. Bozorgzadeh, S. Ogrenci Memik, and M. Sarrafzadeh. 2001. RPack: Routability-Driven packing for cluster-based FPGAs. In *Asia South Pacific Design Automation Conference.* 629–634.

[8] D. T. Chen, K. Vorwerk, and A. Kennings. 2007. Improving Timing-Driven FPGA Packing with Physical Information. In *2007 International Conference on Field Programmable Logic and Applications.* 117–123. https://doi.org/10.1109/FPL.2007.4380635

[9] G. Chen, C. Pui, W. Chow, K. Lam, J. Kuang, E. F. Y. Young, and B. Yu. 2018. RippleFPGA: Routability-Driven Simultaneous Packing and Placement for Modern FPGAs. *IEEE Transactions on Computer-Aided Design of Integrated Circuits and Systems* 37, 10 (Oct 2018), 2022–2035. https://doi.org/10.1109/TCAD.2017.2778058

[10] Eric Chung. 2018. Microsoft. Personal Communication.

[11] Eric Chung, Jeremy Fowers, Kalin Ovtcharov, Michael Papamichael, Adrian Caulfield, Todd Massengil, Ming Liu, Daniel Lo, Shlomi Alkalay, Michael Haselman, et al. 2017. Accelerating persistent neural networks at datacenter scale. In *Hot Chips*, Vol. 27.

[12] Kevin E. Murray, Scott Whitty, Suya Liu, Jason Luu, and Vaughn Betz. 2015. Timing-Driven Titan: Enabling Large Benchmarks and Exploring the Gap between Academic and Commercial CAD. *ACM Transactions on Reconfigurable Technology and Systems* 8 (04 2015), 1–18. https://doi.org/10.1145/2629579

[13] Wenyi Feng. 2012. K-way partitioning based packing for FPGA logic blocks without input bandwidth constraint. 8–15. https://doi.org/10.1109/FPT.2012.6412103

[14] J. Fowers, K. Ovtcharov, M. Papamichael, T. Massengill, M. Liu, D. Lo, S. Alkalay, M. Haselman, L. Adams, M. Ghandi, S. Heil, P. Patel, A. Sapek, G. Weisz, L. Woods, S. Lanka, S. K. Reinhardt, A. M. Caulfield, E. S. Chung, and D. Burger. 2018. A Configurable Cloud-Scale DNN Processor for Real-Time AI. In *2018 ACM/IEEE 45th Annual International Symposium on Computer Architecture (ISCA).* 1–14. https://doi.org/10.1109/ISCA.2018.00012

[15] Norman P. Jouppi, Cliff Young, Nishant Patil, David Patterson, Gaurav Agrawal, Raminder Bajwa, Sarah Bates, Suresh Bhatia, Nan Boden, Al Borchers, Rick Boyle, Pierre-luc Cantin, Clifford Chao, Chris Clark, Jeremy Coriell, Mike Daley, Matt Dau, Jeffrey Dean, Ben Gelb, Tara Vazir Ghaemmaghami, Rajendra Gottipati, William Gulland, Robert Hagmann, C. Richard Ho, Doug Hogberg, John Hu, Robert Hundt, Dan Hurt, Julian Ibarz, Aaron Jaffey, Alek Jaworski, Alexander Kaplan, Harshit Khaitan, Daniel Killebrew, Andy Koch, Naveen Kumar, Steve Lacy, James Laudon, James Law, Diemthu Le, Chris Leary, Zhuyuan Liu, Kyle Lucke, Alan Lundin, Gordon MacKean, Adriana Maggiore, Maire Mahony, Kieran Miller, Rahul Nagarajan, Ravi Narayanaswami, Ray Ni, Kathy Nix, Thomas Norrie, Mark Omernick, Narayana Penukonda, Andy Phelps, Jonathan Ross, Matt Ross, Amir Salek, Emad Samadiani, Chris Severn, Gregory Sizikov, Matthew Snelham, Jed Souter, Dan Steinberg, Andy Swing, Mercedes Tan, Gregory Thorson, Bo Tian, Horia Toma, Erick Tuttle, Vijay Vasudevan, Richard Walter, Walter Wang, Eric Wilcox, and Doe Hyun Yoon. 2017. In-Datacenter Performance Analysis of a Tensor Processing Unit. In *Proceedings of the 44th Annual International Symposium on Computer Architecture (ISCA '17).* ACM, New York, NY, USA, 1–12. https://doi.org/10.1145/3079856.3080246

[16] Martin Langhammer and Gregg Baeckler. 2018. High Density and Performance Multiplication for FPGA. In *25th IEEE Symposium on Computer Arithmetic, ARITH 2018, Amherst, MA, USA, June 25-27, 2018.* 5–12. https://doi.org/10.1109/ARITH.2018.8464695

[17] Wuxi Li, Shounak Dhar, and David Z. Pan. 2016. UTPlaceF: A Routability-driven FPGA Placer with Physical and Congestion Aware Packing. In *Proceedings of the 35th International Conference on Computer-Aided Design (ICCAD '16).* ACM, New York, NY, USA, Article 66, 7 pages. https://doi.org/10.1145/2966986.2980083

[18] Alexander (Sandy) Marquardt, Vaughn Betz, and Jonathan Rose. 1999. Using Cluster-based Logic Blocks and Timing-driven Packing to Improve FPGA Speed and Density. In *Proceedings of the 1999 ACM/SIGDA Seventh International Symposium on Field Programmable Gate Arrays (FPGA '99).* ACM, New York, NY, USA, 37–46. https://doi.org/10.1145/296399.296426

[19] Duncan J.M Moss, Srivatsan Krishnan, Eriko Nurvitadhi, Piotr Ratuszniak, Chris Johnson, Jaewoong Sim, Asit Mishra, Debbie Marr, Suchit Subhaschandra, and Philip H.W. Leong. 2018. A Customizable Matrix Multiplication Framework for the Intel HARPv2 Xeon+FPGA Platform: A Deep Learning Case Study. In *Proceedings of the 2018 ACM/SIGDA International Symposium on Field-Programmable Gate Arrays (FPGA '18).* ACM, New York, NY, USA, 107–116. https://doi.org/10.1145/3174243.3174258

[20] Jonathan Rose, Jason Luu, ChiWai Yu, Opal Densmore, Jeffrey Goeders, Andrew Somerville, Kenneth Kent, Peter Jamieson, and Jason Anderson. 2012. The VTR project: architecture and CAD for FPGAs from verilog to routing. 77–86. https://doi.org/10.1145/2145694.2145708

[21] Russell Tessier and Heather Giza. 2000. Balancing Logic Utilization and Area Efficiency in FPGAs. In *Field-Programmable Logic and Applications: The Roadmap to Reconfigurable Computing*, Reiner W. Hartenstein and Herbert Grünbacher (Eds.). Springer Berlin Heidelberg, Berlin, Heidelberg, 535–544.

[22] N Toon and S Knowles. 2017. Graphcore. https://www.graphcore.ai

[23] Hanqing Zeng, Ren Chen, Chi Zhang, and Viktor Prasanna. 2018. A Framework for Generating High Throughput CNN Implementations on FPGAs. In *Proceedings of the 2018 ACM/SIGDA International Symposium on Field-Programmable Gate Arrays (FPGA '18).* ACM, New York, NY, USA, 117–126. https://doi.org/10.1145/3174243.3174265

Network-on-Chip Programmable Platform in Versal™ ACAP Architecture

Ian Swarbrick
Xilinx Inc.
San Jose, California
iswarbri@xilinx.com

Dinesh Gaitonde
Xilinx Inc.
San Jose, California
dineshg@xilinx.com

Sagheer Ahmad
Xilinx Inc.
San Jose, California
sagheer@xilinx.com

Brian Gaide
Xilinx Inc.
San Jose, California
brian.gaide@xilinx.com

Ygal Arbel
Xilinx Inc.
San Jose, California
ygala@xilinx.com

ABSTRACT

This paper outlines the Network-on-Chip (NoC) on Xilinx's next generation Versal™ architecture. It is a hardened NoC that is present in Xilinx's next-generation 7nm architecture devices. These devices include many other new hardened features that make up the Adaptable Computing Acceleration Platform (ACAP) devices. There is a trend in FPGA devices of hardening many commonly used components such as processors, memory controllers and other IO controllers. The next generation of Xilinx devices take this a step further by providing a device-global memory mapped NoC which connects these components and the fabric in an integrated fashion. The NoC unifies communication between the processor system, FPGA fabric, memory subsystem and other hardened accelerator functions. This paper gives an overview of the Versal architecture NoC. It also motivates some of the specific characteristics of the architecture. We show how hardening the NoC lets users quickly implement high performance system level interconnect.

KEYWORDS

ACAP, Versal, FPGA, Stacked Silicon, SSIT, Adaptable Compute Acceleration Platform, NoC, FPGA Architecture, FPGA CAD, Xilinx

ACM Reference Format:
Ian Swarbrick, Dinesh Gaitonde, Sagheer Ahmad, Brian Gaide, and Ygal Arbel. 2019. Network-on-Chip Programmable Platform in Versal™ ACAP Architecture. In *Proceedings of The 2019 ACM/SIGDA International Symposium on Field-Programmable Gate Arrays (FPGA '19)*. ACM, New York, NY, USA, 10 pages. https://doi.org/10.1145/3289602.3293908

1 INTRODUCTION

A few major trends require a rethinking of how data movement is implemented on FPGAs. Firstly, FPGAs are becoming platforms on which significantly more complex designs are being implemented than just a few years ago. Memory and IO interfaces have also

increased their bandwidths by several factors. Newer memory interfaces, such as HBM for example [1] require FPGAs to be able to manage the movement of 16 to 32 times the memory bandwidth than just a couple of generations ago. Finally, FPGAs are now an attractive platform for a different class of designs - compute acceleration [2]. For users looking to FPGAs to accelerate diverse compute applications, the expertise of the designers lies in individual domain specific architectures and not the details of FPGA interconnect architecture.

In the face of these trends, the micro-architecture of FPGA interconnects has not changed over several generations. Within the framework of a bit level programmable interconnect that FPGAs have traditionally provided, architects have tried to address the above mentioned concerns [3]. Tuning the micro-architecture in response, though still very important, is not sufficient to address the scale of these trends.

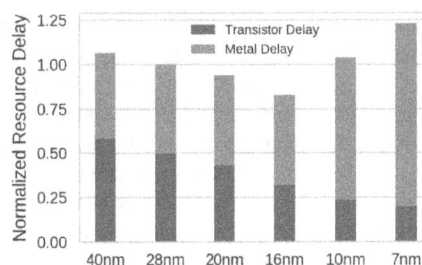

Figure 1: Metal and Transistor Delays For the Same Logical Resource Across Different Technology Nodes (normalized to total delay at 28nm)

The recent slowdown of Moore's law scaling further exacerbates these problems. Although transistor performance has been scaling with technology, metal parasitics have not [4]. Figure 1 shows this quite starkly. Over generations, if one had simply scaled both metal and transistors with technology, the delay for a typical resource would have increased over the last two technology nodes even though each resource now has to travel a shorter distance given scaling of lithography. Metal resistance is threatening to overwhelm any performance benefits one expects from scaling. In the context of a traditional FPGA this is even more concerning because interconnect delays form an increasing portion of the total delays of critical paths. Even more disconcertingly, as designs scale, the amount of interconnect that needs to be provisioned per unit of logic increases. Failing to do so increases the probability that any given design would fail to route, take too long to implement, or suffer from serious degradation in performance. Techniques such as pipelining interconnect [5] have been introduced to manage the problem of performance degradation in the face of larger interconnect delays.

One major problem with traditional FPGA interconnects has been the semantics of routing. FPGA interconnects present to the user an emulated version of metal tracks that ASIC designers have. The semantics of using a metal track and using an interconnect mux are very similar. There are two major forms of inefficiency in these semantics as they apply to global data movement. The first major inefficiency is the fact that each logical communication channel lays claim to some unique physical resource irrespective of how often it really needs to communicate. That is, one designs a system level interconnect under the assumption that the logical entity laying claim to the resource needs to use it at every clock cycle. Secondly, since one does not know apriori how much delay each wire will suffer, the frequency of the design and thus the achieved interconnect bandwidth is defined by the slowest path in the entire implementation - something that is only known after one implements a design.

Since this problem is not unique to FPGAs, it is instructive to see how ASICs and SOCs have managed it. In the early 2000s many ASICs and SoCs were transitioning from on-chip busses to pipelined busses, and then to fully packetized networks [6, 7]. The primary motivation was to support ever-increasing bandwidth of intra- chip data movement. Since NoCs share the same physical resource across several endpoints, it resulted in more efficient use of wires. Packetized interfaces typically have simple flow control structures that are designed to be heavily pipelined. Since all interfaces in packetized networks are point-to-point, pipelining such interfaces was far simpler helping one achieve higher frequency. Packetization provides narrower data-paths that run faster due to lower fanout. It also reduced the width off all the data-path buffers allowing the solutions to scale upwards with some degree of area efficiency. As NoC solutions became commonplace, commercial vendors offered configurable IP solutions that were widely adopted [8, 9] in ASICs and SoCs. In order to get a simplified high performance system level interconnect, communicating blocks had to sacrifice two features of traditional FPGA communication. First, it was no longer possible to guarantee the latency of communication between two communicating blocks at exact cycle granularity. Although one could for specific flow patterns be able to bound the latency, in general one cannot be certain some traffic will reach its destination in a fixed number of clock cycles, no later and no earlier. Secondly, since the ingress and egress ports of a NoC follow some protocol, it was now required that all communicating blocks that utilize the NoC conform to that protocol. Note that in traditional FPGA communication synthesis, one was free to customize a protocol for each problem instance. This flexibility, while attractive in principle, is not worth a lot when modern systems are designed by composing communicating blocks that may already have been designed

without knowledge of who they will communicate with. Standard interfaces are increasingly becoming the norm [10, 11].

2   NETWORK ON CHIP

There are excellent surveys of NoC microarchitectures and algorithms elsewhere [12–14]. In this paper for the sake of completeness and to motivate some of the terms we use subsequently, we briefly discuss NoCs.

Although there are non-packetized form of NoCs, in this paper when we refer to a NoC we mean a packetized on-chip interconnect that is used to pass transactions around a chip. Most on-die interconnects support some industry standard interface to various IPs such as OCP [11] or AXI [10]. Internally the datapaths are packetized and often (but not always) run at higher clock frequency than the external interfaces.

Standard protocols such as OCP and AXI need to cater to device communication requirements. This involves much more than carrying just address and data of transactions. There is typically more information that needs to be transported. The following are examples of the "sideband" information that needs to be communicated as well.

- Ordering ID - indicates the relative order of transactions. Transactions with the same ordering ID return in order with respect to one another.
- Memory protection attributes - indicates the protection privilege attributes of the transaction.
- Cache attributes - The cache allocation policy.
- Write response attributes - indicate if write response needs to come from the slave or can be generated early.
- Packing attributes - indicates if the data can be packed/unpacked at a width conversion point.
- Byte strobes - Qualifiers for write data.
- Size and alignment - The transaction may not start on an aligned boundary and/or may be narrower than the datapath.
- Transaction type - For example, incrementing or wrapping burst.
- Burst length - the number of data beats in a burst.
- QoS - Priority attributes.
- User - Application specific information bits.

Topology is a key consideration for any NoC. The network topology can be a regular structure such as a mesh, torus or hypercube or an ad-hoc topology tailored to the SoC data-path requirements. The internal data transport of the NoC arranges data into a train of packets, made up of *flits* (flow-control digits). Although the size of a packet could vary depending on the communication pattern, the size of a flit is fixed. The flit is the basic unit of transfer. Each data buffer in the network is flit sized. The first flit is normally a header flit. It contains packet control, address information and route information to indicate where the packet is going. Subsequent flits contain data and possibly some other auxillary information. The final flit in a packet is the tail, normally indicated by setting a *last* bit in the flit.

The network is made up of flit buffers and packets flow through the network like carriages of a train: it is possible for the header flit to arrive at the destination before the last flit has left the source. This type of flow control is referred to as *wormhole routing* [15].

This type of flow control manages buffers at the flit level. To send part of the packet onwards from one node to the next, *virtual cut-through* [16] is used. This only requires reservation of a single flit buffer rather than resources for the entire packet. A packet can be back-pressured, in which case it will be temporarily stalled in place. This may block other packets from progressing. This situation where unrelated packets cannot make forward progress because some other flow is backpressured is called *head-of-line* blocking. This can be addressed by using *virtual channels* or VCs [17, 18].

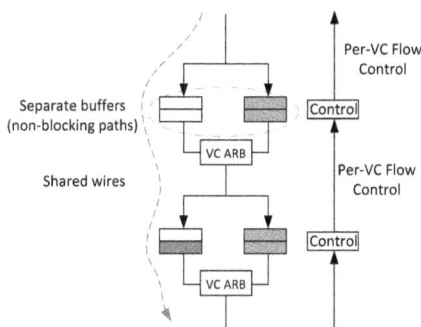

Figure 2: Virtual Channel Flow Control with high priority VC

VC flow control involves multiple groups of flit buffers multiplexing onto a shared set of wires. The intent is to use the wires efficiently. Packet flits are the unit of arbitration and transmission across the shared wires. One VC may be blocked by backpressure at the destination. This does not prevent another VC from making forward progress. Consider the example shown in Figure 2. The blue flits are writes going to DDR. The DDR controller is servicing reads while writes are queued waiting for a DDR bus turnaround. A high priority read flit is transmitted on the other VC. The flit continues to progress to the destination even though the other VC is temporarily blocked. Virtual channels are commonly used to provide independent flow control. Another use of VCs is to avoid routing deadlocks (which is beyond scope of this paper). Another use for VCs is to provide differential Quality-of-Service (QoS). Dataflows are separated into some number of traffic classes. One example set of traffic classes (which is the set used by the Versal™ NoC) is Low Latency (LL), Isochronous (ISOC) and best-effort (BE). An example of LL traffic are cache line refills from a CPU. Such traffic is very bursty with variable bandwidth requirements. LL traffic is treated with high priority at any arbitration point in the network. An example of ISOC traffic is video frame data. Such traffic is regular and the bandwidth is predictable. ISOC traffic has a deadline after which the data is no longer useful and some system constraint will be violated. ISOC traffic is treated with the same high priority as LL traffic. BE traffic gets whatever service is available. The only requirement is that it does not starve.

NoCs have different options for routing algorithms. This determines how the packets are steered from source to destination. Most commercial NoCs that are implemented on chips employ deterministic routing. Unlike adaptive routing which responds to the condition of the network, deterministic routing employs a fixed route between each source and destination pair. Deterministic routing helps simplify both the routing algorithm and the implementation of individual switches. Deterministic routing lets one statically compute the achieved bandwith given a topology and a traffic pattern. It also simplifies proving that the network will not deadlock and will preserve certain ordering guarantees versus adaptive routing.

3 VERSAL NETWORK-ON-CHIP

3.1 Versal Family Of Devices

Figure 3 shows the floorplan of a representative Versal device along with a view of how the NoC integrates with the rest of the device. Several other devices with widely varying capacities and capabilities will be built using the same general floorplan philosophy. Understanding how the device scales and how the NoC scales along with it is important to understand the various tradeoffs we made when architecting the NoC.

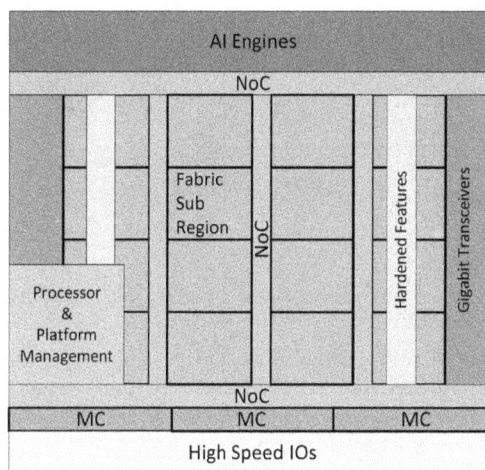

Figure 3: Example Versal Floorplan

There are four main portions of the device

- The bottom of the device is occupied by general purpose high speed IOs and memory controllers. Note that one way in which one adds more memory controllers to the device is by increasing the width of the device.
- The top of the device is occupied by AI-specific compute engines [19]. From the point of view of the NoC they are just another source or destination for traffic flows. Not all markets that Versal is targeted for benefit from AI compute engines. In that case, that region is replaced with other blocks targetted for other markets. Specifically, the top portion of the device could also be similar to the bottom portion in that it could contain memory controllers and IOs as well.
- The left and right sides of the device are occupied mostly by high performance transceivers which provide very high bandwidth serial communication to and from the device. There is a processor subsystem and a platform management system at the lower left.
- The rest of the device is occupied by traditional FPGA fabric.

The NoC appears as a skeleton running through all the major components in the device. It integrates communication between each of the major subsystems: IOs, AI compute engines, processor and fabric. The Versal adaptive compute acceleration platform implements a hardened packet switched network as an integral part of the fabric. It implements a deterministic routing flow with wormhole routing. It supports multiple VCs to help avoid deadlock and head-of-line blocking. It also supports multiple Quality-of-Service (QoS) classes, the details of which are described in a later section. The Versal NoC is not simply a replacement for fabric interconnect. It has two roles. Firstly, it provides a persistent addressable interconnect that unifies all the resources on the platform. Versal NoC operates even in the absence of any configured fabric. Secondly, switching and routing functions that would previously have consumed fabric resources can now be mapped on the programmable Versal NoC.

3.2   Packet Transport

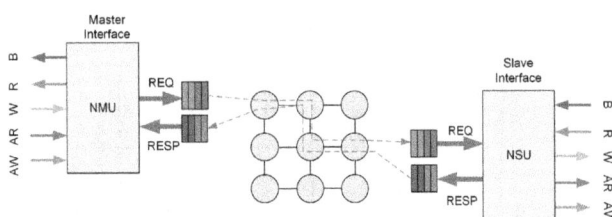

Figure 4: End-To-End Axi Conversion Topology

The Versal NoC provides standard AXI interfaces for external hard/soft masters/slaves to connect with. We begin with a high level end-to-end description to illustrate the packetization/depacketization process. This is shown in Figure 4. The ingress logic to the NoC is referred to as NoC Master Unit (NMU) and the egress logic is referred to as NoC Slave Unit (NSU). The interfaces conform to the AXI4 [10] protocol with five separate channels - Read Address, Write Address, Write Data, Read Data and Write Response (B in Figure 4). Besides a memory mapped interface, the NoC also supports AXI4 streaming as well. In the native AXI protocol, the write address channel is physically separate from the write data channel. This separation allows a slave to begin processing of a write transaction before the write data arrives. Since very few slaves use this flexibility in practice, we combine the write address and write data channels when in the packet domain. This combined write channel and the remaining three channels are packetized and merged onto four separate virtual channels (two request path and two response path). The packets are transported through the high-speed packet domain and at the destination the conversion process is reversed to present the AXI transaction to the slave. The same process is followed in the response path to get response from the slave back to the master. The packet domain is optimized for efficient physical transport. The protocol for packet transport was designed so that it would be possible to run it at high frequency with low wire count. Designing the entire physical transport to be natively AXI would have resulted in a much lower performance NoC. The benefits of standard AXI interfaces is maintained by converting the native format to AXI at the endpoints. The ingress and egress blocks have clock frequencies decoupled from the packet

domain clock frequency. This permits the NoC to run at a high frequency independently of the attached masters and slaves. Each link, whether it be between switches, or between NMU, NSU and switches are full-duplex links. In short, the Versal NoC has a proprietary physical transport protocol that provides AXI compatible ports at the endpoints.

3.3   NoC Topology

Having shown the end-to-end packet transport concept we now provide more details of the Versal NOC topology and how it fits in to the device architecture. The Versal NoC is architected to work across a family of devices each of which have very different requirements in terms of size, power and performance. The NoC is implemented as a set of building blocks that scale up or down to meet the requirements of each device.

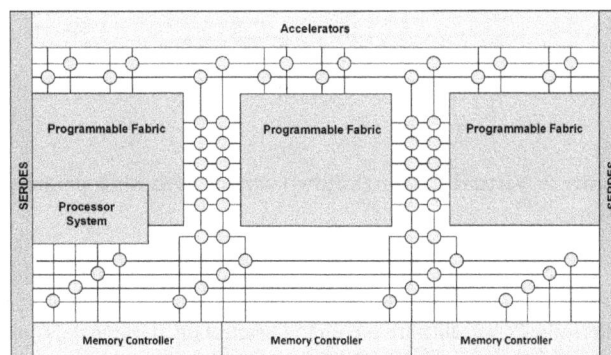

Figure 5: Example NoC Topology

Figure 5 shows an example device. We do not show the details of the programmable fabric, the processor subsystem, nor the other peripherals to focus on the NoC topology. Each yellow circle in the picture represents a NoC switch. The topology terminates in either NMU or NSU ports on the programmable fabric, processor subsystem, memory controllers or other hardened accelerators. The drawing exaggerates the size of the NoC in relation to the fabric for illustration purposes. There are Horizontal NoC (HNoC) sections at the top and bottom of the device. The HNoCs connect up and down to hardened components. In this example the processor system connects downwards to the NoC. The bottom HNoC with 4 horizontal physical lanes connects down to multiple DDR memory controllers. When the top HNoC does not drive DDR controllers, but instead connects to the AI compute engines, it has only 2 horizontal lanes. The reason for this asymmetry is because one of the primary reasons for a NoC is to present a unified memory space for all NMUs on the device. As a result it helps to permit more cross sectional bandwidth for the NoC topology when it attaches to memory than when it attaches to the compute engines. Tools can optimize the scheduling of operations in the AI compute engines to use the NoC optimally. The NoC connects to the FPGA fabric through vertical NoC components (VNoCs). The VNoCs have a simple repeating slice structure. The slices are stacked to form a VNoC column. The device height determines how many VNoC slices make up a column - typically 3-8 per die. Depending on the horizontal dimensions of a device there can be up to 5 VNoCs. This provides scalability: as the VNoC height grows, it has more fabric connections. As the device gets wider, more VNoCs are added to provide more vertical bandwidth. As the device width grows, the total bandwidth supplied by peripheral devices grows as well. Since the number of VNoC columns also grows with width, the horizontal cross sectional bandwidth of the device matches the peripheral bandwidth. VNoC columns are integrated within the fabric just like any other block - DSPs for example. The VNoC does not appear as a break in the interconnect fabric. Interconnect signals that were supposed to route over blocks continue to route over VNoC.

It is common for NoCs with a regular topology to use a mesh. That is not necessary or useful in our case. There are multiple VNoCs in the fabric and each master or slave simply connects to the nearest one. Adding more horizontal connections would not significantly improve access to the NoC. Horizontal connections would also disrupt the fabric more than is permissible. Columnar integration with the fabric is natural in the context of FPGAs that are integrated in columns. VNoCs then appear as just any other columnar compute block that is integrated within an FPGA. An additional constraint is that the VNoCs must be narrow and only use lower metal layers in order to not disrupt the usability of the surrounding fabric. Horizontal connectivity using HNoCs is provided either at the top or bottom of the device. HNoCs are sized to have more physical channels than the VNoCs. This provides enough horizontal bandwidth for fabric clients attached to a particular VNoC to access memory controllers at all horizontal locations in the device - a key feature enabling a uniform view of memory across the entire device for all clients.

One key driver of the NoC requirements is to effectively manage access to DDR. To have the correct scaling characteristics, there is approximately one VNoC column containing two physical channels for every 64-bit hardened DDR/LPDDR memory controller. The datapath width and frequency of each VNoC is matched to the memory controller bandwidth [1]. It would be too restrictive if masters could only access the nearest memory controller. The HNoC has sufficient bandwidth to effectively support access from any VNoC master to any memory controller. Simply presenting 2 to 4 memory controllers as separate pools of memory is cumbersome to manage for any application. To alleviate this, the NoC supports programmable memory interleaving. This feature treats a set of memory controllers as one pool of memory. The interleaving can be fine grained - as little as 128 bytes or upto 4K. The underlying hardware manages the chopping of transactions and ordering to make the interleaving transparent from outside the NoC.

The NoC bandwidth and resources scale both in terms of the device memory bandwidth and fabric size. The number of fabric ports on each VNoC scales with the height of the device and the number of VNoC columns scales with device memory bandwidth. This enables the NoC to support the entire memory bandwidth and at the same time allow for enough fabric access to consume it.

Each horizontal and vertical line in Figure 5 between nodes represents a full-duplex link. Each link is 128 bits wide and operates at default frequencies from 900MHz to over 1GHz. The raw throughput of each unidirectional link (without considering packet overheads) is over 16 GB/sec in each direction. The NoC provides unified physically addressed access to all of the hard and soft components on the device. The NoC has programmable routing tables. These must be initially programmed at boot time. A separate tree-structured peripheral bus is implemented inside the NoC just for this purpose. This provides a deterministic programming path before the NoC itself is configured. Each device has a platform management subsystem that contains a dedicated processor that can independently perform programming at boot time.

In traditionally designed interconnects using fabric, access to DDR memory controllers is often via full crossbars implemented in fabric using LUTs and flops. This guarantees that the crossbar itself does not have any variable structural latency although the memory controller will. Using a NoC, both the packet transport and memory controller will have variable latency. A NoC compiler handles the provisioning of routes. It is the task of the compiler to ensure that system wide latency and bandwidth constraints are met given user inputs. This is a shift in design methodology that raises the level of abstraction. Users now reason in terms of traffic flows and their requirements rather than how they get mapped on fabric. A hardened NoC decouples the compute portion of a system level design from the system level interconnect. Traditionally, since both compute and interconnect competed for the same physical resource, they had to be co-designed. This flow decouples those concerns from one another. Timing closure of the transport is now guaranteed. It does not depend on the implementation tools nor on how large a compute is instantiated in the fabric.

3.4 Inter-die Connectivity

Xilinx has built devices larger than what is economically possible on a single die using SSI technology [20]. An interposer extends the interconnect of each die and permits signals in one die to communicate with instances in another. We extend this metaphor for NoC topology as well. The entire NoC for multi die devices is also logically unified via interposers. For most devices, the full bandwidth of each VNoC can be transferred from one SLR to the next. Logically, this means that the VNoC columns just continue as they cross SLRs. The latency to cross the SLRs is single digit NoC clock cycles plus a clock domain crossing.

Figure 6 shows a 2-die NoC topology. The inter-die-bridge (IDB) extends the NoC from one die to the other. Transmission is single data-rate and source synchronous clocking is employed. Each VNoC on each die is extended to the other VNoC on the destination die. Each bridge supports the entire VNoC bandwidth. In short, this permits the tools to think of the entire device's NoC topology as being made up of homogenous VNoC columns whose height spans multiple dies.

3.5 Designing With Versal Architecture NoCs

In order to implement designs on the NoC, the user needs to specify some flows. These flows are expressed in terms of expected bandwidth between masters and slaves. For example, Table 1 shows one

---

[1]For example, a device with 64 bit DDR4 3200 has 25.6GBps bandwidth. A VNoC running at 1GHz has two physical channels supporting upto 16GBps each per direction.

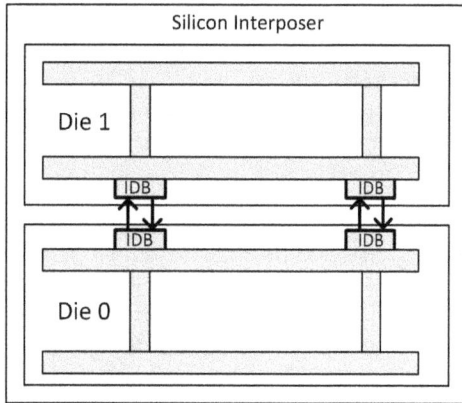

Figure 6: NoC Topology Across Multiple Die SSI Integration

such problem where three masters each share bandwidth from one controller. In this problem we specify three traffic classes - LL, ISoC and BE.

Master	Slave	Traffic Class	Traffic Type	Request BW (Gbps)
M0	DDR	LL	Read	2
M0	DDR	BE	Write	2
M1	DDR	ISoC	Read	4
M1	DDR	ISoC	Write	4
M2	DDR	BE	Read	8
M2	DDR	BE	Write	8

Table 1: Example Interconnect Demand Problem

Besides just describing the flows, the user can optionally also restrict the placement of the masters and slaves to those available on the device. Note that this problem may not be satisfiable given the limitations of the topology or the controller. In this case, the expectation is that the problem will be solved so that LL and ISoC traffic get what they have asked for and the BE traffic will get serviced based on what is left.

In order to implement these flows on the device we use a flow called the NoC compiler. The NoC compiler can be thought of as the NoC equivalent of traditional fabric based place and route tools. The Noc compiler implements each flow on the device by assigning the master and slaves to the appropriate ports. Each master is bound to some NMU and each slave (DDR in this case) to some memory controller. The compiler also realizes all the routes from each master to each slave and back using the the topology of the network and the capacity of each switch.

Since the topology is not a mesh, it is not possible to use simple routing algorithms like dimension-ordered routing [18] for deadlock avoidance. The number of objects that the NoC router has to deal with is several orders of magnitude less than what a traditional fabric router deals with. As a result, it is tractable to deploy exact algorithms that provide the globally optimum solution for a wide range of NoC routing problems. Besides ensuring that no switch or link is over subscribed, the implementation tools have to guarantee

that VC separation across various QoS classes is managed. The NoC compiler also establishes routes that are deadlock free.

This notion of mapping a problem definition to masters, slaves and routes is similar to the problem of placing and routing a regular design on FPGA fabric. There are a few key differences however. Routing on a NoC has different semantics than regular FPGA routing. Multiple flows can share the same physical resource provided the total link capacity is not oversubscribed. Moreover, the structure of the routing table in each switch limits routing to only those routes that satisfy some predicate. The exact details of those restrictions is beyond the scope of this paper. It is important to note that computing the placement and routing of flows or detecting their infeasibility is something that takes a fraction of the time it takes to compute this in soft implementations - seconds instead of hours. The NoC compiler is thus able to give almost interactive feedback on the system level interconnect design feasibility.

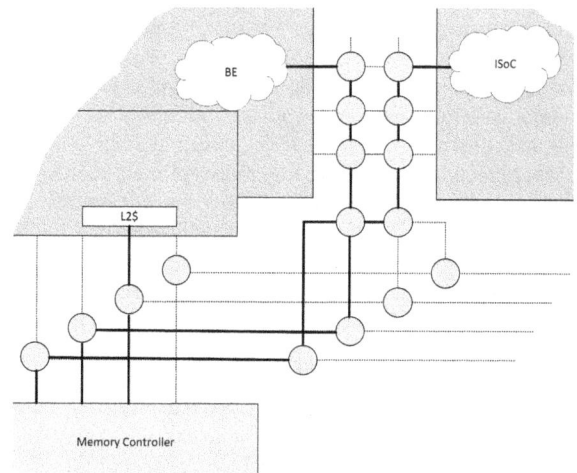

Figure 7: Example routing for problem in Table 1

Figure 7 shows the placement of the masters and the slaves and the routes established by the compiler to implement the routes. We will talk more about the properties of the solution to this problem in Section 5.

3.6 Differences from SoC NoCs

SoCs and ASICs have been using NoCs for many years. The requirement for such devices are different to those for a programmable device. In a fixed-function device the NoC topology, bandwidth and QoS requirements are known in advance. One can then design both the topology and the size of the datapath and other NoC architecture features to optimize for that application. In a programmable device however, these depend on a mixture of fixed and programmable functions whose behavior varies substantially based on the application being mapped. This requires a high degree of programmability from the NoC. Specifically, the Versal NoC architecture has to permit all possible point to point communication. Each egress port must be reachable from every ingress port. In a traditional NoC based system, one could have multiple instances of NoCs optimized for different needs. Within a programmable NoC platform, the compilers have to manage all the flows within the constraints of the hardened NoC architecture. This requires some level of over provisioning of the NoC resources and a high degree of programmability. For example, in the Versal NoC we provision for more VCs (8) and QoS classes (3) than would be required for typical applications. The entire topology of the NoC also needs to be designed using repeatable blocks. This permits easy integration and lets one design a family of devices with different communication and compute needs using the same blocks.

This requirement of block based design has significant implications for the switch microarchitecture. Consider, for example, the sizing of routing tables within each switch. For custom NoC topologies, one can size the routing table of each switch to be whatever best serves the flows one intends to use the NoC for. For a programmable platform however, since the same switch is used throughout the entire device and also across devices in the Versal platform, the sizing of the routing table and the semantics associated with routing has to be invariant across the entire platform. The same routing table size needs to scale from small to large devices. This problem is akin to the problem of interconnect design for traditional LUT level fabrics. The interconnect tile for regular FPGAs needs to be similarly sized to permit devices with widely varying capacities to be built. It is not possible for design cost reasons to customize an interconnect architecture per device.

- The architecture has to support enough VCs to permit easy route assignment to alleviate both head-of-line blocking and prevent deadlocks
- Given diverse communication styles, the architecture has to support enough QoS types to cover the entire space.
- The topology has to be made of blocks that can be repeated and tiled across the entire platform. Specifically, one is not allowed to change the size of the routing table for switches that exist in large devices compared to those that exist in smaller devices.
- The architecture has to allow for programmable datawidth at NMU/NSU. The interface needs to match the the datawidth of the attached fabric logic components. The NoC takes care of datawidth adaptation removing the need for the fabric to perform this function.
- The switches have to support programmable routing tables. The routes need to be customized both depending on which device from the product family is used and the specific application running on the device.
- The address map needs to be configurable as it has a device dependency. One may have 4 DDR on top and 4 on bottom or any other combo. The user may want to control the address map and we provide one by default to simplify user design.
- The NoC needs to support partial reconfigurability. At the route level we can tear down a connection and establish new routes while some unrelated packets are in flight. Details of this capability are outside the scope of this paper.
- The network topology has to adjust to device size and bandwidth in a predictable way.

4 RELATED WORK

There is a long history of researchers defining structured ways of communicating within FPGAs. Several researchers [21–24] have proposed implementing soft NoCs on FPGAs. In this work, they exploit the fact that the NoC is implemented on an FPGA to customize the features and topology of the NoC to the specific problem. FPGA specific optimizations are also introduced to demonstrate how one would tune the microarchitecture, topology and routing algorithms to use FPGA resources as sparingly as possible while designing a high performance NoC. In the Versal architecture, since the fabric capabilities remain the same, soft NoCs can continue to be implemented. That is, the user can implement soft extensions to the core NoC for local communication. In practice, given the frequency with which fabric ports appear in the Versal architecture, the need to do this would be infrequent.

Other researchers tried to optimize by hardening only some of the blocks that make up a NoC platform [25, 26]. More recently [27] researchers have proposed hardening NoCs in an FPGA. These works motivate the need for a hardened NoC given current communication needs. This work is similar in the sense that this paper also describes a hardened NoC. Unlike previous work however, we show what tradeoffs and optimizations one has to do in defining the microarchitecture and topology in order for the platform to scale in the right way. We also identify several other design decisions which ensure that the platform integrates with the PL fabric and other peripherals in a seamless manner.

5 RESULTS

For traditional architectures, Xilinx SmartConnect IP [28] is the standard way of designing system level interconnect. This IP is then implemented using the traditional fabric resources. This IP and the implementation algorithms, Vivado [29] in our case, have been designed to stress the FPGA as little as possible while delivering as high performance as possible. From now on, when we talk about a fabric implementation of some communication, unless stated otherwise, it is implemented using these set of tools - Xilinx SmartConnect IP and Vivado. We also implement all the fabric designs using the UltraScale+™ platform. Although the Versal platform provides significant improvements to the fabric architecture, for the purposes of this work, implementing them on a Versal or UltraScale+ fabric would not materially change the results.

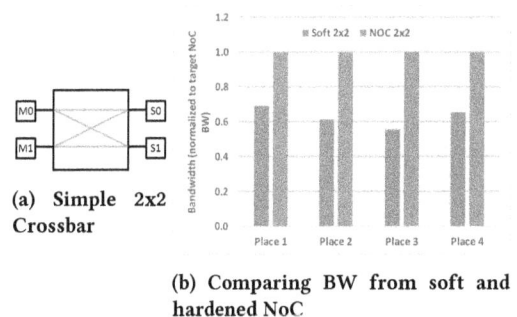

(a) Simple 2x2 Crossbar

(b) Comparing BW from soft and hardened NoC

Figure 8: Implementing simple crossbar

We will first demonstrate how with the hardened NoC it is possible for clients that use it to be placed anywhere on the die and still be able to use the NoC bandwidth effectively. We do this by demonstrating that bandwidth is sensitive to client placement in soft implementations while immune to it in hardened NoC. We also demonstrate that computing the achievable bandwidth for any configuration is far simpler in the case of hardened NoC than it is for soft implementations. Consider the implementation of a simple 2x2 crossbar as shown in Figure 8a. It consists of two masters communicating with two slaves. The datapath width is fixed at 128 bits. It is assumed that the bandwidth demand of each master with respect to each slave is identical. We implemented this crossbar structure by restricting the placement of the masters and the slaves at various places. As the Figure 8b shows, the resulting bandwidth achieved by the topology thus depends on where the masters and slaves are placed and how much effort is spent on optimizing them. On the other hand, bandwidth achieved by the NoC does not depend on the placement of the masters and slaves. It bears mentioning that placement of masters and slaves does need to be optimized for communication patterns that are extremely complex. A random placement of the masters and slaves would not provide optimal bandwidth for such situations. Having said that, in the case of NoC, placing masters and slaves and then computing the bandwidth achieved is a task that takes seconds rather than several hours in case of fabric implementations.

Let us now consider scaling up the simple crossbar from Figure 8a. We will compare the bandwidth achieved using a soft implementation of the crossbar using fabric resources. Computing the precise way in which larger crossbars should be built is not easy to figure out. There are a few competing concerns. In order to increase the supported bandwidth, one wants to implement the design at as high a frequency as possible. But as one builds larger crossbars, the amount of fabric resources required and the complexity of the netlist makes closing timing at demanding frequencies very hard to do. Traditionally, this has been managed by increasing the width of the data busses so that the frequency at which one needs to close the timing reduces for the same bandwidth.

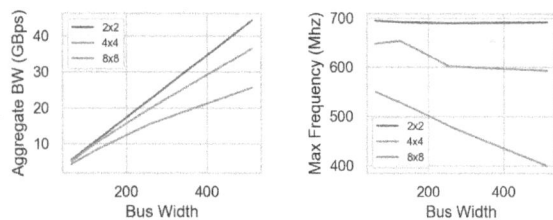

Figure 9: FMax and BW Scaling with Crossbar Size

Figure 9 shows the performance of various crossbar sizes at various data widths. Naively, one would expect the bandwidth supported by larger data widths to be larger (or the same if we are hitting the limits of what the fabric can do) since the frequency requirements of the crossbar designs is looser. But as the figure shows that even though aggregate bandwidth for large crossbars increases with increasing data widths, the increase is quite small. This is because crossbars involve netlists which are very tightly coupled. Increasing the data width of tightly coupled netlists causes the performance to degrade to such an extent that increased data widths is not able to compensate as much. In short, it is not easy for

the system designer to figure out apriori what the optimum data width and frequencies they should target to satisfy the communication requirements. This is especially true if the crossbar size is large. On the other hand, although Figure 9 does not show it, the bandwidth achieved by the NoC is not such a strong function of crossbar configurations. The actual achievable bandwidth is also very easy to figure out apriori.

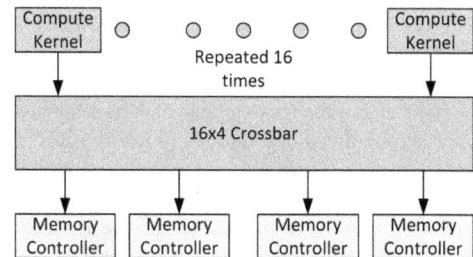

Figure 10: Interconnect topology for an FPGA acceleration design

Next we consider the system level interconnect design for an FPGA acceleration workload. FPGAs are able to accelerate diverse workloads because one can use the reconfigurable fabric to implement domain specific designs. Runtime intensive workloads are partitioned into mostly independent "kernels" which then serve as parallel threads on which compute can be accelerated. The number of kernels one can fit on an FPGA depends on the capacity of the FPGA and the complexity of each kernel. In such cases, each kernel either reads or writes from one or more memory controllers. As a result, system level interconnect for such designs involves building a crossbar with the number of masters equalling the number of kernels and slaves equalling the number of memory controllers. Figure 10 shows a typical configuration for acceleration on FPGAs. In this case, 16 kernels read and write from 4 memory controllers - so we need a 16x4 crossbar. We assumed that the crossbar would need to be sized so that each of the kernels could saturate about a quarter of the bandwidth of one DDR4 memory controller.

The system level interconnect and the memory controllers were implemented on an UltraScale+ device using standard Vivado [29] tools. We assumed that running the crossbar design with 512 bit busses at 333Mhz would saturate all the memory controllers. For this implementation we did not include much in the way of kernel complexity. We replaced kernels with some generic low performance traffic generators. We wanted to let the fabric implementation have as much flexibility as possible and not be constrained by kernel placement. In practice, however, kernel timing closure and placement has to be solved simultaneously with interconnect placement. We could also have sized each master's data width to align with its bandwidth requirement and introduced width converters in the crossbar. For this experiment, we chose to do the simplest design. For this design, given the extra flexibility, we were able to meet all the bandwidth requirements. Figure 11 shows the placement of the memory controllers and the crossbar design. Besides using a significant amount of the fabric resources, ensuring that this closes timing requires user intervention in the form of detailed placement and routing directives.

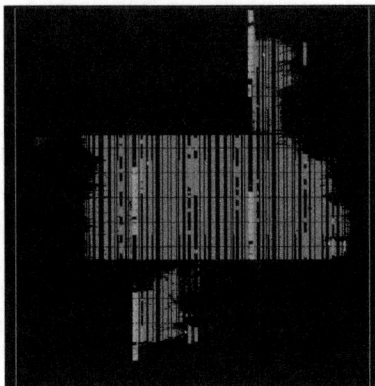

Figure 11: Fabric Implementation of Design in Figure 10

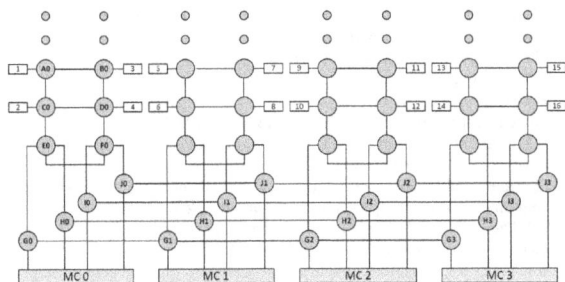

Figure 12: NoC Mapping of Design in Figure 10

In constrast, when the same structure is mapped on the Versal architecture none of the usual fabric resources are consumed. The logical mapping of the problem in Fig 10 on Versal architecture NoC is shown in Figure 12. The 16 masters are placed in NMUs connecting to four VNoC columns. Each master generates one quarter of the DDR4 bandwidth and the tool chain (NoC compiler) ensures that the bandwidth is available. The memory controllers have four ports and the horizontal NoC has four lanes. This gives the tool chain a great deal of flexibility in routing the flows. Notice that the compiler assumed that the interleaving from each master to each memory controller was uniform. This may not be the case in practice for some problems. In those cases, the user by simply redefining the characteristics of the flows, have the compiler generate a solution more optimized to the modified problem. Alternately, since the number of objects involved are only a handful, the user can selectively (or by constraints) spread out the routes so that the maximum utilization of a link is as small as possible. This makes the solution resilient towards dynamic changes in traffic characteristics. There could be a period of time, for example, when each master does not interleave perfectly across all four memory controllers, but only across a couple of them. Note that placement of the memory controllers and the NMUs to ensure bandwidth requirements are met is a far simpler problem in the case of NoC than in the case of fabric implementation.

We now demonstrate how the QoS features of NoC can tailor the specifics of communication besides just the bandwidth. Not all masters require equal claim over the NoC resources at all times.

System performance often benefits greatly from providing preferential access to some masters. For example, processor performance is heavily dependent on latency to DDR. Since in Versal, the NoC is a shared resource, it is important for the user to be able to preserve low latency access to memory. In this section we describe a simple performance test and show the effect of the QoS controls. As a motivating example, we use the same testcase described in Table 1. In this simple usecase there are multiple masters going to a single slave, in this case a DDR4 memory controller. The mapping of the four masters is shown in Figure 7.

As the figure shows, there are three masters each requesting bandwidth from the same memory controller. We now show performance data for this configuration for a specific QoS scenario. All reported performance data are from SystemC simulation of the NoC and DDR with traffic models providing the stimulus.

There are three sets of read and write data flows. The low latency (LL) traffic comes from the ARM multi-core CPU cluster in the processor system. The traffic is modeled using a traffic generator at the NoC boundary. All LL accesses are 64 byte (cache line size). The address pattern starts with a random address and then performs four sequential accesses before jumping to a new random address. The isochronous (ISOC) traffic is representative of a video/display application. The traffic is uniform 256 byte accesses with a linear address sequence. The best effort traffic is also 256 byte, uniform and linear. The ISOC and LL requestors in this simulation request only the required bandwidth. The best-effort (BE) requestors generate more traffic than is expected to be serviced - that is, they are oversubscribing the memory bandwidth.

Figure 13 shows the results of the simulation. It can be seen that for the LL and ISOC traffic the requested bandwidth is met. It can also be seen that the average latency remains close the minimum latency, showing that the traffic is treated with higher priority relative to the best effort traffic. The best effort traffic receives less bandwidth than it is requesting, as expected. Also since the memory controller is oversubscribed, the average latency of the best effort traffic is high compared with the minimum latency. Note that the latency number in the plot are normalized to LL read latency. The LL read latency is normalized to 1.0 and all other latency numbers are relative to that.

6 CONCLUSION

This paper outlined the Versal NoC that is part of Xilinx 7nm ACAP solutions. The NoC addresses many longstanding difficulties moving data in programmable devices in an efficient, scalable manner. Having a hardened high bandwidth network-on-chip has numerous benefits. Significant fabric area can be saved in designs that move large amounts of data and/or involve switching. The user design flow can be simplified by pushing timing closure from a global concern to one at the module level. Differential QoS ensures that chip-wide traffic can be appropriately classified and managed. Inter-chip connectivity provides a uniform memory mapped view across devices. A compiler tool raises the level of user abstraction to the traffic flow level. The compiler manages competing traffic constraints given by the user and provides reporting on the achievable solution. Data was shown illustrating the benefits for timing closure and the methodology improvements enabled by the NoC were

(a) Bandwidth Per Flow

(b) Latency Per Flow

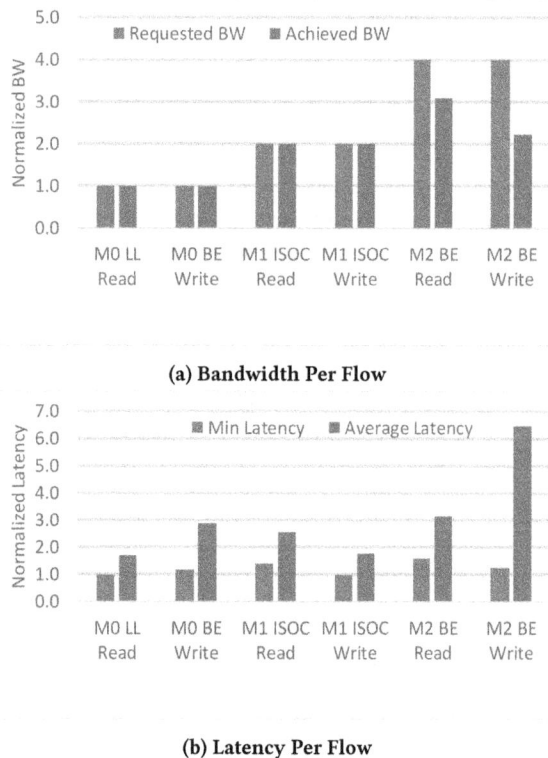

Figure 13: Bandwidth and Latency After NoC Routing For Flows in Table 1

described. Differential QoS is a necessary feature to support a wide range of markets and use cases. A simple example of NoC/DDR dataflows using differential QoS was described. The Versal NoC is a new feature of Xilinx FPGAs in the 7nm generation. It raises the level of design abstraction for users. It fits within the ACAP concept by decoupling acceleration kernels from the various hardened pieces of the surrounding platform.

ACKNOWLEDGEMENTS

The authors would like to thank the reviewers for their feedback. Also thanks to Brad Danofsky, Ramakrishna Kishore Tanikella, Vijay Kumar Reddy and Nikhil Dhume for experimental data. We also wish to thank the many Xilinx teams that contributed to the Versal NoC development.

REFERENCES

[1] H. Jun, J. Cho, K. Lee, H. Son, K. Kim, H. Jin, and K. Kim, "HBM (high bandwidth memory) DRAM Technology and Architecture," in *2017 IEEE International Memory Workshop (IMW)*, May 2017, pp. 1–4.
[2] A. M. Caulfield, E. S. Chung, A. Putnam, H. Angepat, J. Fowers, M. Haselman, S. Heil, M. Humphrey, P. Kaur, J. Kim, D. Lo, T. Massengill, K. Ovtcharov, M. Papamichael, L. Woods, S. Lanka, D. Chiou, and D. Burger, "A cloud-scale acceleration architecture," in *2016 49th Annual IEEE/ACM International Symposium on Microarchitecture (MICRO)*, Oct 2016, pp. 1–13.
[3] S. Chandrakar, D. Gaitonde, and T. Bauer, "Enhancements in Ultrascale CLB Architecture," in *Proceedings of the 2015 ACM/SIGDA International Symposium on Field-Programmable Gate Arrays*, ser. FPGA '15. New York, NY, USA: ACM, 2015, pp. 108–116. [Online]. Available: http://doi.acm.org/10.1145/2684746.2689077
[4] M. T. Bohr, "Interconnect scaling - the real limiter to high performance ULSI," in *Proceedings of International Electron Devices Meeting*, Dec 1995, pp. 241–244.
[5] D. Lewis, G. Chiu, J. Chromczak, D. Galloway, B. Gamsa, V. Manohararajah, I. Milton, T. Vanderhoek, and J. Van Dyken, "The Stratix™10 Highly Pipelined FPGA Architecture," in *Proceedings of the 2016 ACM/SIGDA International Symposium on Field-Programmable Gate Arrays*, ser. FPGA '16. New York, NY, USA: ACM, 2016, pp. 159–168. [Online]. Available: http://doi.acm.org/10.1145/2847263.2847267
[6] W. J. Dally and B. Towles, "Route packets, not wires: on-chip interconnection networks," in *Proceedings of the 38th Design Automation Conference (IEEE Cat. No.01CH37232)*, June 2001, pp. 684–689.
[7] L. Benini and G. De Micheli, "Networks on Chips: A new SoC paradigm," vol. 35, pp. 70–78, 02 2002.
[8] Sonics inc. [Online]. Available: https://sonicsinc.com
[9] J.-J. Lecler and G. Baillieu, "Application Driven Network-on-chip Architecture Exploration & Refinement for a Complex SoC," *Des. Autom. Embedded Syst.*, vol. 15, no. 2, pp. 133–158, Jun. 2011. [Online]. Available: http://dx.doi.org/10.1007/s10617-011-9075-5
[10] AMBA AXI and ACE Protocol Specification AXI3, AXI4, and AXI4-Lite, ACE and ACE-Lite. [Online]. Available: https://developer.arm.com/docs/ihi0022/d
[11] Open Core Protocol 3.0 Specification. [Online]. Available: http://www.accellera.org/images/downloads/standards/ocp/OCP_3.0_Specification.zip
[12] D. Becker, "Efficient microarchitecture for network-on-chip routers," Ph.D. dissertation, Stanford University, 2012.
[13] L. Benini and G. De Micheli, *Networks on Chips*, 2006.
[14] T. Bjerregaard and S. Mahadevan, "A survey of research and practices of network-on-chip," *ACM Comput. Surv.*, vol. 38, no. 1, Jun. 2006. [Online]. Available: http://doi.acm.org/10.1145/1132952.1132953
[15] L. M. Ni and P. K. McKinley, "A survey of wormhole routing techniques in direct networks," *Computer*, vol. 26, no. 2, pp. 62–76, Feb 1993.
[16] P. Kermani and L. Kleinrock, "Reprint of 'virtual cut-through: A new computer communication switching technique'," *Computer Networks*, vol. 66, pp. 4–17, 2014.
[17] W. J. Dally, "Virtual-channel flow control," *IEEE Transactions on Parallel and Distributed Systems*, vol. 3, no. 2, pp. 194–205, March 1992.
[18] Dally and Seitz, "Deadlock-free message routing in multiprocessor interconnection networks," *IEEE Transactions on Computers*, vol. C-36, no. 5, pp. 547–553, May 1987.
[19] J. e. a. Noguera, "Xilinx Project Everest: "HW/SW Programmable Engine"," 2018, hotChips.
[20] R. Chaware, K. Nagarajan, and S. Ramalingam, "Assembly and Reliability Challenges in 3D Integration of 28nm FPGA Die on a Large High Density 65nm Passive Interposer," in *2012 IEEE 62nd Electronic Components and Technology Conference*, May 2012, pp. 279–283.
[21] B. Sethuraman, P. Bhattacharya, J. Khan, and R. Vemuri, "LiPaR: A Lightweight Parallel Router for FPGA-based Networks-on-chip," in *Proceedings of the 15th ACM Great Lakes Symposium on VLSI*, ser. GLSVLSI '05. New York, NY, USA: ACM, 2005, pp. 452–457. [Online]. Available: http://doi.acm.org/10.1145/1057661.1057769
[22] M. K. Papamichael and J. C. Hoe, "CONNECT: Re-examining conventional wisdom for designing nocs in the context of FPGAs," in *Proceedings of the ACM/SIGDA International Symposium on Field Programmable Gate Arrays*, ser. FPGA '12. New York, NY, USA: ACM, 2012, pp. 37–46. [Online]. Available: http://doi.acm.org/10.1145/2145694.2145703
[23] N. Kapre and J. Gray, "Hoplite: Building austere overlay NoCs for FPGAs," in *2015 25th International Conference on Field Programmable Logic and Applications (FPL)*, Sept 2015, pp. 1–8.
[24] Y. Huan and A. DeHon, "FPGA optimized packet-switched NoC using split and merge primitives," in *2012 International Conference on Field-Programmable Technology*, Dec 2012, pp. 47–52.
[25] R. Gindin, I. Cidon, and I. Keidar, "NoC-Based FPGA: Architecture and Routing," in *First International Symposium on Networks-on-Chip (NOCS'07)*, May 2007, pp. 253–264.
[26] R. Francis and S. Moore, "Exploring hard and soft networks-on-chip for FPGAs," in *2008 International Conference on Field-Programmable Technology*, Dec 2008, pp. 261–264.
[27] M. S. Abdelfattah and V. Betz, "The Case for Embedded Networks on Chip on Field-Programmable Gate Arrays," *IEEE Micro*, vol. 34, no. 1, pp. 80–89, Jan 2014.
[28] AXI SmartConnect. [Online]. Available: https://www.xilinx.com/products/intellectual-property/smartconnect.html
[29] *Vivado Design Suite User Guide*, Xilinx.

HopliteBuf: FPGA NoCs with Provably Stall-Free FIFOs

Tushar Garg, Saud Wasly, Rodolfo Pellizzoni, Nachiket Kapre
{t3garg,swasly,rpellizz,nachiket}@uwaterloo.ca
University of Waterloo
Ontario, Canada

ABSTRACT

Deflection-routed NoCs like Hoplite and HopliteRT take advantage of FPGA-specific features to deliver low-cost, high-frequency, FPGA-friendly communication networks. However, they suffer from long packet deflection penalties, low sustained throughputs, and feature limitations such as out-of-order delivery of packets. In this paper, we introduce the HopliteBuf NoC, and an associated static analysis tool, that eliminates deflections entirely while simultaneously adding in-order delivery feature using (1) small, stall-free FIFOs with provable occupancy bounds, and (2) linearization of vertical rings of the torus Hoplite topology to improve provable link utilization. We implement these FIFOs using cheap LUT SRAMs (Xilinx SRL32s, and Intel MLABs) to absorb packet contention. We evaluate conditions for stall-free behavior using static analysis that compute upper bounds on FIFO occupancy based on the communication pattern. Our static analysis deliver bounds that are not only better (in latency) than HopliteRT but also tighter by 2–3×. Across 100 randomly-generated flowsets mapped to a 5×5 system size, HopliteBuf is able to route a larger fraction of these flowsets with <128-deep FIFOs, boost worst-case routing latency by ≈2× for mutually feasible flowsets. At 20% injection rates, HopliteRT is only able to route 1–2% of the flowsets while HopliteBuf can deliver 40–50% sustainability.

ACM Reference Format:
Tushar Garg, Saud Wasly, Rodolfo Pellizzoni, Nachiket Kapre. 2019. Hoplite-Buf: FPGA NoCs with Provably Stall-Free FIFOs. In *The 2019 ACM/SIGDA International Symposium on Field-Programmable Gate Arrays (FPGA '19), February 24–26, 2019, Seaside, CA, USA*. ACM, New York, NY, USA, 10 pages. https://doi.org/10.1145/3289602.3293917

1 INTRODUCTION

A well-regulated Network-on-Chip (NoC), being necessary to the safe operation of a real-time system, the right of the NoC packets to travel without unpredictable backpressure, shall not be infringed.

High-performance communication networks are vital for supporting connectivity requirements of modern FPGA designs. FPGA logic can be configured to implement packet-switched NoCs to allow IP blocks to interact with each other at the cost of stealing logic and routing resources away from the developer. In contrast, the system-level interface bandwidth requirements are driving FPGA

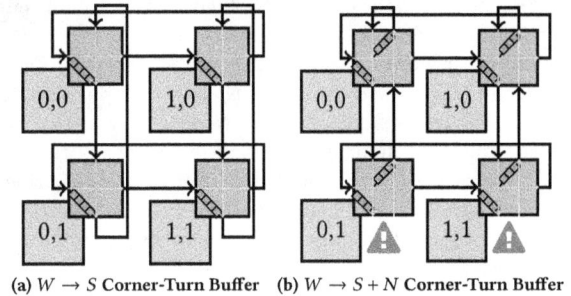

(a) $W \rightarrow S$ Corner-Turn Buffer (b) $W \rightarrow S + N$ Corner-Turn Buffer

Figure 1: 2×2 HopliteBuf NoC Topology with Stall-Free Corner-Turn buffers (▭▭▭). Stall-Free buffers are sized to never go full avoiding the need for backward flow control. The $W \rightarrow S + N$ topology disconnects vertical rings (⚠) and introduces an extra uphill multiplexer in each router.

vendors to embrace hardened NoC resources that bake in the network functionality without using any soft logic. Regardless of the choice of soft or hard NoC technology, real-time system developers wishing to use FPGAs need tool support to analyze the timing properties of their FPGA mappings to ensure they are able to meet relevant scheduling deadlines. Real time systems are characterized by a need to rigorously prove timing requirements of various computing and communicating blocks. For instance, the ISO 26262 standard [4] requires performance isolation between communicating components on a chip and livelocks in NoCs violate this requirement. While timing analysis of statically-scheduled FPGA datapaths is simple, the analysis of communicating components using a shared dynamically-scheduled resource like a NoC is not so. NoC performance analysis is notoriously hard; it is often pessimistic and leads to over-provisioning of resources. In this paper, we aim to build analysis-friendly, low-cost FPGA NoCs and develop accompanying analysis tools to prove worst-case NoC packet routing latencies.

Resource-efficient NoCs like Hoplite and HopliteRT provide a scalable, low-cost fabric for designing FPGA communication networks using soft logic. Both these NoCs are built on the idea of deflection routing that avoids the cost of packet buffering. The routers for these NoCs can be as small as 86–89 6-LUTs for 64-bit payloads operating at 1.2–1.3 ns clock period on a Virtex-7 485T FPGA. However, packets may suffer long deflection penalties in the fabric (Hoplite, and HopliteRT) and packets may even suffer livelocks where packets deflect endlessly (Hoplite). This behavior is a problem for real-time FPGA applications in mission-critical environments like self-driving cars and automotive systems, unmanned drones, avionics, and biomedical devices. Such application domains need strict timing guarantees for bounding worst-case behavior and allowing certification of the products for use in the field.

A conventional, buffered, packet-switched NoC might be a tempting alternative. However, deeply buffered NoCs with classic flow control are too expensive to implement on the FPGA, and are hard to analyze for static analysis of buffer bounds due to the complexity of packet interactions. Contemporary buffered FPGA NoCs like CMU CONNECT [12] and Penn Split-Merge [3] NoCs are very expensive and occupy 1000s of LUTs/router for 32-bit routers. Furthermore, the state-of-the-art analysis of NoC buffer bounds [6, 7] is pessimistic due to the complexity of modeling pipelining effects and mixing of various flows in the network.

In this paper, we propose the HopliteBuf NoC, shown in Figure 1, derived from the low-cost Hoplite NoC. HopliteBuf introduces (1) small stall-free buffers for certain router functions to simplify flow control, to (2) eliminate deflections with any associated livelocks, (3) provides optional linearization of vertical NoC rings to enhance analysis that, (4) bounds buffer sizes to distributed-RAM friendly implementation sizes. The key contributions of our work is the microarchitecture of analysis-friendly HopliteBuf NoC routers, topology modifications coupled with a buffer sizing algorithm that is able to determine the worst-case occupancies for all the FIFOs in the NoC. In particular, the proposed topology in Figure 1b with two corner-turn buffers and no vertical loopback simplifies static analysis of buffer sizes. This also improves provable wire utilization while preserving wiring cost and requiring a modest increase in LUT count over Figure 1a. For our workloads we observe that these occupancies are small enough to be realizable in LUT-based FIFOs (Xilinx SRL32s, and Intel MLABs). The HopliteBuf NoC is more expensive that Hoplite or HopliteRT by 3–4× due to buffering, but still cheaper than full-blown conventional buffered NoCs.

We summarize the main contributions of our work here:

- Design of an FPGA NoC torus topology to enhance static analysis for computing buffer bounds and NoC router microarchitecture redesign with stall-free FIFOs to eliminate deflections and provide in-order packet delivery. Optimization and customization of the NoC router RTL to match Xilinx and Intel FPGAs.

- Development of a buffer sizing algorithm to compute the worst-case bounds on FIFO occupancies. Use of vertical NoC link linearization to improve provable link utilization. Static analysis tools compute upper bounds on size of FIFOs required for stall-free operation, source queueing delay, in-flight routing latency under various conditions.

- Engineering of a robust simulation infrastructure to compute cycle counts of packet traversals in the NoC. Resource and performance analysis of the NoC under various synthetic workloads.

2   BACKGROUND

We now review existing literature on deflection-routed FPGA overlay NoCs: Hoplite and HopliteRT to highlight the underlying resource-performance tradeoffs, features and limitations of these NoCs.

Hoplite is an FPGA-friendly NoC router that uses torus topology and eliminates buffering and flow control to provide a low-cost implementation on modern FPGAs. Packets traverse using DOR (dimension-ordered routing) policy in the X-dimension (horizontally, W→E) first before turning (W→S) and routing in the Y-dimension (vertically, N→S). This simple design requires a pair of 2:1 muxes as shown in Figure 2a. The DOR control logic is very

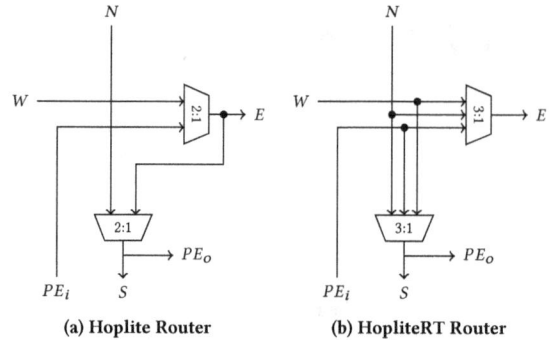

(a) Hoplite Router   (b) HopliteRT Router

Figure 2: High-level design sketches of Hoplite (can livelock) and HopliteRT (no livelock) FPGA NoC Routers. HopliteRT adds a N→E turn to Hoplite to eliminate livelock. Both designs fit one bit of crossbar in one Xilinx 6-LUT.

simple and consumes very few LUTs as it can be constructed directly on valid signals of the incoming packets alone. Packets exiting the NoC must do so over the S port to allow the mux and wires to be shared by both south-bound and exiting packets. A separate output valid signal helps determine the nature of the packet. The NoC client is provided the lowest priority and cannot inject a packet is the router has packets on both ports. A key limitation of Hoplite is the inability of the NoC to avoid livelock. This is possible as a W packet continues to get deflected to the E port as long as a packet on N port wants to travel S. Furthermore, a series of packets sent from a source client to a destination client may take different paths through the network and need not deflect in identical manner.

HopliteRT is a refinement over Hoplite that inverts the priorities and deflects N packet to the E (hence the new N→E turn in Figure 2b). Thus, HopliteRT requires two 3:1 muxes but still requires the same number of LUTs as Hoplite due to common multiplexer selection inputs to both muxes. HopliteRT overcomes the livelock limitation by forcing the N packet to deflect E and reappear as a W packet with higher priority. This simple modification means that a packet will only suffer a single deflection at a given switch as it descends down the NoC. The adaptation not only avoids livelock but puts an upper bound on in-flight NoC latency to $\Delta X + \Delta Y \times m + 2$ for an $m \times m$ NoC. This indicates that, in the worst-case, the torus NoC could reduce down to a ring $O(m^2)$.

While HopliteRT costs the same as Hoplite and removes livelocks, it still suffers from an unusually high worst-case deflection bound while doing nothing to eliminate out-of-order delivery. Reducing a bandwidth-rich torus to a ring is neither an efficient nor scalable use of FPGA resources. Reordering of packets now becomes the responsibility of the NoC client and can add extra memory resources at the endpoints. In this paper, we propose develop a new NoC that not only preserve livelock-free behavior, but also provides improved latency bounds along with in-order packet delivery.

3   HOPLITE WITH STALL-FREE BUFFERS

In this section, we describe the design of an FPGA NoC router with stall-free buffering. We explain the core switch microarchitecture, associated routing policy and discuss FPGA mapping.

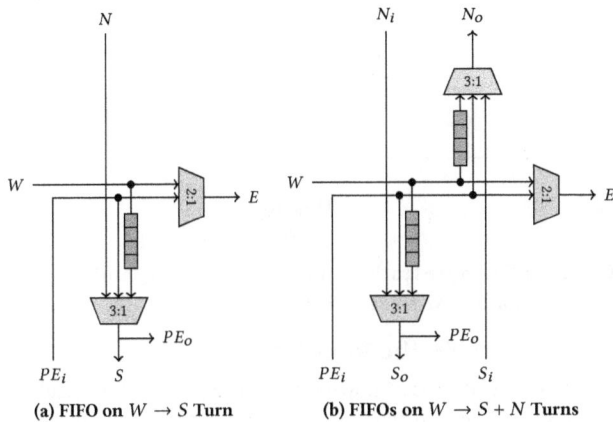

(a) FIFO on $W \rightarrow S$ Turn

(b) FIFOs on $W \rightarrow S + N$ Turns

Figure 3: Two design alternatives for adding buffers to the Hoplite NoC router. $W \rightarrow S$ adds a buffer on the corner turn, while $W \rightarrow S + N$ adds an extra uphill buffer.

3.1 The Idea

Earlier in Figure 1, we sketched two variants of the proposed HopliteBuf topologies with buffers for turning packets. In Figure 3, we show the switch microarchitectures of these variants. The basic multiplexing functionality implements turns to support DOR routing scheme. What this means is that, unlike the HopliteRT design, our proposed microarchitecture does not support the $N \rightarrow E$ turn. Now, recall that contention in Hoplite arises from packets wanting the same S resource either for turns ($W \rightarrow S$) or for vertical descent ($N \rightarrow S$). We can choose to make either or both of these conflicting parties wait in buffers, but the $W \rightarrow S$ option is preferred as it limits buffering penalty for a given flow to a **single** buffer. Buffering the $N \rightarrow S$ path will force packets descending vertically to wait at each hop prolonging their stay in the network. This would make both end-to-end routing latency as well as FIFO size larger than needed. Hence, we focus only on W packets for buffering. We now elaborate on the two design options that only buffer W packets in two ways:

- $W \rightarrow S$ **buffer**: In this scenario, packets turning from W port to S will be buffered if a $N \rightarrow S$ packet arrives at that router in the same cycle. The routing policy now prioritizes N packets over W packets as there is no longer the option of deflecting to E like in HopliteRT. The East mux now sees W, and PE as input, and South mux sees W' (FIFO output), N, and PE as inputs. The multiplexer select lines also need to be distinct as the routing combinations prevent sharing. We discuss how this may fit on the FPGA fracturable LUT organization in the Section 3.2 and the restrictions of the routing combinations in Section 3.3. From the perspective of the NoC, the packet will have to wait in a buffer **only** at the point of turn. The PE_o exit shares the same wires as the S just like in the original Hoplite and HopliteRT routers to avoid paying the extra cost of exit multiplexers. Empirical evaluation has shown negligible performance hit from this cost-saving transformation.
- $W \rightarrow S + N$ **buffer**: In this second scheme, the routing policy introduces a $S \rightarrow N$ link and allows a new $W \rightarrow N$ turn. At first glance, this may seem like an unlikely design choice as

inserting an entirely new routing path will increase LUT resource costs. While this is true, this scheme does **not** increase wiring requirements as seen in Figure 1b. The vertical wrap-around link in the original Hoplite ring is now forced to traverse through the switch on the way uphill. Thus total wirelength stays unchanged. Furthermore, as well will see later, this organization enhances the static analysis pass by removing the loopback and allows a higher provable link utilization on the vertical ring. You may notice we retain the shared single exit to the client PE_o that shares wires with the S port. As the vertical ring is disconnected, traffic is delivered to destination PEs only on the downhill traversal. This is another cost-saving measure that eliminates introducing an exit multiplexer along with an accompanying FIFO for packets on the uphill $S_i \rightarrow N_o$ that may wish to exit sooner.

3.2 FPGA Implementation

A Xilinx 6-LUT is fracturable into two 5-LUTs with five common inputs across both LUTs. This allows you to implement one function of 5-inputs (any function) and one function of 6-inputs (if it overlaps with the 5-input function) in the same LUT. An Intel ALUT is organized differently and has 8-inputs shared across two 6-LUTs. The two 6-LUTs have four common inputs, and two distinct inputs each. They can implement two functions of 6-inputs as long as they share four inputs. Apart from logic, certain Xilinx LUTs can be programmed as 32-deep memories or shift registers. Intel offers a similar functionality with their MLAB (Memory Logic Array Block) resources. The stall-free buffer component of our new designs are implemented using these cheap resources.

Original Hoplite Mapping: When implementing the original Hoplite router shown in Figure 2a on a Xilinx FPGA, we can easily fit the two 2:1 muxes in two Xilinx 5-LUTs to allow a compact 1 6-LUT mapping per bit of switching. This is possible as the East 2:1 mux can use a 5-LUT (requiring 3 inputs), while the South 2:1 mux can be mapped to the embedded 2:1 mux that drives the O6 output (needing two more inputs, only one of which needs to be unique). When implementing the original Hoplite router on an Intel FPGA, it is trivially possible to fit this in a single ALM with two 6-LUTs without even forcing the East mux serialization. This is because we can the 3:1 mux (South mux if implemented fully) needs 5 inputs while the 2:1 mux only needs 3. Two of these inputs are shared by both muxes (W and PE_i), while the distinct mux select inputs can be supplied to the two 6-LUTs independently without violating the common input restriction.

Mapping $W \rightarrow S$ FIFO Design This design requires the switching crossbar to consume four packet inputs: N, W, W' (FIFO output) and PE_i inputs along with 3 mux-select inputs. This already exceeds the 6-input LUT capacity of the Xilinx FPGA and cannot use fracturing. On the Intel FPGA, we require four common inputs to each 6-LUT; this constraint is satisfied by our design thereby enabling a compact fit. Additionally, we can supply two unique inputs to each 6-LUT which is adequate to support the mux-select signals.

Mapping $W \rightarrow S + N$ FIFO Design This design requires the switching crossbar to consume six packet inputs: N_i, W, W' ($W \rightarrow S$ FIFO), W'' ($W \rightarrow N$ FIFO) and PE_i and 5 mux-select inputs. We choose to split the turning packets into separate FIFOs to prevent

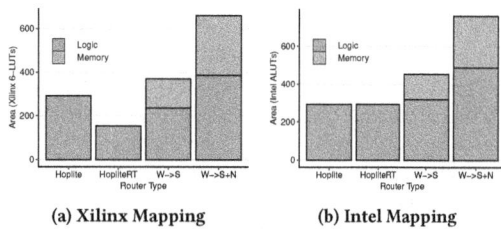

(a) Xilinx Mapping (b) Intel Mapping

Figure 4: LUT utilization for logic and memory across various Hoplite routers on Xilinx and Intel FPGAs with Payload=128b and FIFO=32 deep.

mutual interference between traversing flows. The total distributed RAM capacity stays same as it just split into two SRL32 or MLAB instantiations instead of a longer single distributed RAM block. Here, with limited opportunity for input sharing, the resulting design is larger in LUT cost, but as we will see later, this allows efficient use of the NoC links.

We quantify the LUT utilization of the various Hoplite routers in Figure 4. The design size scales linearly with the product of Datawidth of the NoC × Depth of the FIFO on both vendor parts. With 32-deep FIFOs mapped to distributed RAMs, the storage fraction ▨ increases design size by 1.2–1.5×. For the dual-FIFO design, the extra multiplexing also increases cost of the switching logic ▨.

3.3 Routing Policy

The original Hoplite and HopliteRT routers implemented bufferless deflection routing rooted in Dimension-Ordered Routing (DOR) policy. The policy ensured that arriving packets from W and N ports were sent to E and S ports respectively. For turning packets, Hoplite prioritizes N port over the W port thereby introducing the possibility of livelock, while HopliteRT prioritizes W over N to ensure bounded NoC routing delays. Thus, HopliteRT deviates from DOR by allowing a $N \rightarrow E$ deflection that is not permitted under standard DOR implementation.

For HopliteBuf, we restore DOR routing policy but introduce extra decision logic for servicing FIFO packets. With buffering, W packets are forced to wait in the buffer thereby transferring priority to N port for $W \rightarrow S$ variant, and to N_i and S_i packets for $W \rightarrow S + N$ variant. All routers still accept PE packets with the least priority.

4 LATENCY AND BUFFER SIZE ANALYSIS

We now turn our attention to static analysis of the NoC traffic to bound buffer sizes and worst-case injection and in-flight traversal latencies. This is important to establish whether we can realize them in distributed FPGA RAMs (SRLs and MLABs). We first introduce our regulation and traffic model. We then develop a network calculus approach to FIFO size and worst-case latency analysis for HopliteBuf. The presence of cycles in the torus topology make this analysis susceptible to instability, but we are able to provide an analytic solution that employs a topology linearization alternative (Figure 1b) to eliminate cycles.

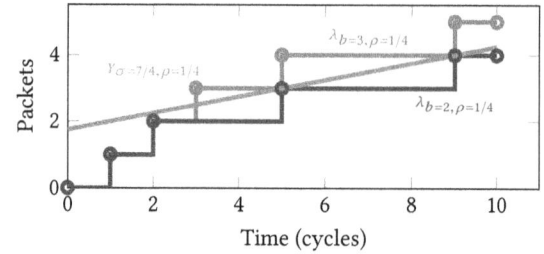

Figure 5: Example traffic curves for $\lambda_{b=3,\rho=1/4}$ and $\lambda_{b=2,\rho=1/4}$ along with an arrival curve for $\gamma_{\sigma=7/4,\rho=1/4}$.

4.1 Client Traffic Regulation

Injection regulation is a known technique from network calculus to establish well-defined behavior of network traffic at runtime for off-chip internet-scale systems. We adapt token bucket regulation [14] for use in an on-chip context at the NoC clients to enforce traffic discipline on the NoC. This is done transparently and the datapath design just needs to obey the standard NoC valid-ready interface (AXI-stream). We can implement this regulation on the FPGA using two simple counters per NoC client and require **no** buffers at the client-NoC interface. The regulator is programmed with a rate ρ and burst b that reflects the communication requirements of the application. At run-time, the regulator maintains a token counter. A packet can only be injected if the NoC is ready (no other packet is blocking the client) and there is at least one token in the counter; the token is consumed upon sending the packet. New tokens are generated and added to the counter at a rate ρ, provided that the counter has not saturated to its maximum value of b tokens.

4.2 Traffic Model

DEFINITION 1. **Traffic curve:** *To analyze the traffic characteristics, we introduce a traffic curve $\lambda_{b,\rho}(t)$ to denote the maximum number of packets sent on a NoC link in any interval of t cycles. By definition, a token bucket regulator with parameters b, ρ provides a traffic curve:*

$$\lambda_{b,\rho}(t) = \min\left(t, b + \lfloor \rho \cdot (t-1) \rfloor\right). \tag{1}$$

Example: Traffic curves for two regulators with $b = 2$, $\rho = 1/4$ and $b = 3$, $\rho = 1/4$ are depicted in Figure 5 (the arrival curve γ will be introduced in Section 4.4). Consider the regulator with $b = 3$. The traffic curve derivation assumes that the bucket is initially full. Hence, $b = 3$ packets can be sent consecutively at times $t = 1, 2, 3$. After the first packet is sent at time $t = 1$, the regulator starts generating a new packet, which is then added to the bucket at time $1 + 1/\rho = 5$; this corresponds to the fourth transmitted packet. Afterwards, new packets are sent every $1/\rho$ cycles.

In this analysis, we consider an $(m \times m)$ matrix of clients (x, y). Each client sends packets as part of one or more flows; all packets within the same flow have the same destination and use the same token bucket regulator. Hence, we use $F = \{f_1, \ldots, f_i, \ldots\}$ to denote the set of flows in the system, where for each flow f: $(f.xs, f.ys)$ represents the source client of the flow; $(f.xd, f.yd)$ represents the destination client; and $f.b, f.\rho$ represent the regulator parameters. Note that two different flows f_i and f_j might share the same source, or the same destination.

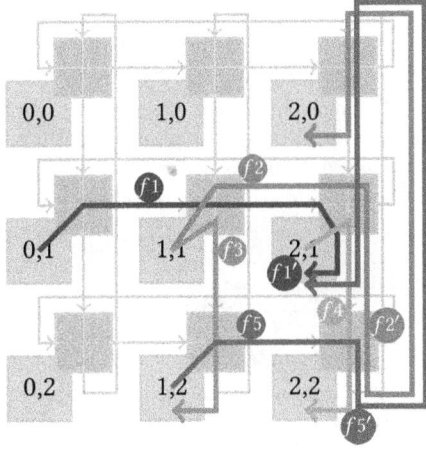

Figure 6: Example $W \to S$ NoC design with five flows $f_{1...5}$.

Table 1: Flow parameters for the example NoC. Γ^C are the conflicting flows used in Section 4.3; $f_{W \to S}$ and $f_{N \to S}$ are the $W \to S$ and $N \to S$ interfering flows used in Section 4.4. '-' denotes not applicable.

flow	source	dest	Γ^C	$f_{W \to S}$	$f_{N \to S}$
f_1	(0,1)	(2,1)	none	f_2	f_5'
f_2	(1,1)	(2,0)	f_3, f_1	f_1	f_5'
f_3	(1,1)	(1,2)	f_2	-	-
f_4	(2,1)	(2,2)	f_1', f_2', f_5'	-	-
f_5	(1,2)	(2,1)	none	none	$f_2' + f_4$

Example: We present a running example of a NoC with five flows $f_{1...5}$ using the $W \to S$ buffer design in Figure 6. Note that we use f_i' to denote a flow after it leaves a buffer, as buffering can increase the burstiness of the flow (packets queued up in a buffer can be flushed directly back-to-back). Relevant flow parameters are tabulated in Table 1. We discuss how to apply the analysis to the $W \to S + N$ design in Section 4.5 as the flows have been linearized and have no loops. For the $W \to S$ design, the analysis is harder due to the loopback of the vertical ring. The instability created by loopbacks is a notoriously challenging problem in network calculus [9] and results in lower provable bounds on link utilization. We analyze the unique problem formulation presented by the HopliteBuf torus network and propose a technique for deriving these bounds and improving link utilization through linearization of the vertical ring.

Our analysis derives three sets of parameters:

- Injection latency $Injection(f)$ for each flow $f \in F$; this is the maximum time that the source client $(f.xs, f.ys)$ can be stalled waiting to send a packet of f.
- Maximum queuing delay $Delay(f)$ for each turning flow f.
- Backlog for each router; this is the maximum number of packets that are queued waiting to be transmitted (excluding the packet that might be transmitted in the current clock cycle).

4.3 Injection Latency

We first determine the set Γ^C of conflicting flows for f, that is, the set of flows that can block injection of a packet of f. It comprises:

- all other flows injected by the same source client, since a client can only inject a single packet per clock cycle;
- all flows originating from other clients that traverse the same mux used by f at its source router $(f.xs, f.ys)$.

Example: For flow f_2 in Figure 6, the conflicting set comprises flow f_3 (same client) and flow f_1 (E mux). For f_4, the set comprises flows f_1', f_2' and f_5' (S mux).

Assume that each flow in Γ^C is bounded by a traffic curve $\lambda_{b,\rho}(t)$; we define $b(\Gamma^C)$ as the sum of the burstiness parameters b of traffic curves for flows in Γ^C, and $\rho(\Gamma^C)$ as the sum of their rate parameters. Based on the token bucket regulator analysis provided in [14], we then obtain:

$$Injection(f) = \lceil 1/f.\rho \rceil - 1 + \left\lceil \frac{\sigma(\Gamma^C)}{1 - \rho(\Gamma^C)} \right\rceil. \qquad (2)$$

Note that the condition $\rho(\Gamma^C) < 1$ implies that the cumulative rate of conflicting flows is less than 1 packet/cycle; this guarantees that packets of flow f are not permanently blocked at the source. Furthermore, if the client wishes to inject a sequence of $k > 1$ packets, it is possible to obtain an improved bound on the injection latency for the whole sequence as long as $k \le f.b$. For simplicity we consider single-packet injection with $f.b = 1$.

It remains to determine the traffic curve $\lambda_{b,\rho}(t)$ for each interfering flow. For a flow f_i that has not yet traversed a buffer, the curve is simply $\lambda_{f.b, f.\rho}(t)$. We show how to derive the traffic curve for a flow f_i' that leaves a $W \to S$ buffer in the next section.

4.4 Vertical Ring Analysis $W \to S$ Design

We now analyze the behaviour of flows turning on a vertical ring through a $W \to S$ buffer. We employ the theory of network calculus [9] for FIFO-arbitrated flows to derive deterministic bounds on queuing delay and backlog. In particular, we show that the delay and backlog depend on the burstiness and rate of flows entering the FIFO buffer, as well as the burstiness and rate of flows routed $N \to S$. To apply the theory, we need to introduce a new type of curves.

DEFINITION 2. *Leaky bucket arrival curve*: *A flow f is said to the bounded by a leaky bucket arrival curve $\gamma_{\sigma, \rho}(t)$ if the number of packets transmitted by the flow in any time interval t is bounded by:*

$$\gamma_{\sigma, \rho}(t) = \sigma + \rho \cdot t.$$

In this case, $f.\sigma$ and $f.\rho$ are arrival curve parameters for the flow.

Luckily, we can convert between traffic curves of the form $\lambda_{b,\rho}(t)$ and arrival curves $\gamma_{\sigma, \rho}(t)$ according to the following lemma (a formal proof is provided in Lemma 1 in Appendix):

- to convert $\lambda_{b,\rho}(t)$ into $\gamma_{\sigma, \rho}(t)$, we set $\sigma = b - \rho$;
- to convert $\gamma_{\sigma, \rho}(t)$ into $\lambda_{b,\rho}(t)$, we set $b = \lceil \sigma + \rho + 1 \rceil$.

Example: Refer again to Figure 5. The traffic curve $\lambda_{b=2, \rho=1/4}(t)$ is upper bounded by $\gamma_{\sigma=7/4, \rho=1/4}(t)$. Similarly, arrival curve $\gamma_{\sigma=7/4, \rho=1/4}(t)$ is upper bounded by $\lambda_{b=\lceil 7/4+1/4+1 \rceil, \rho=1/4}(t) = \lambda_{b=3, \rho=1/4}(t)$; $\gamma_{\sigma=7/4, \rho=1/4}(t) > \lambda_{b=3, \rho=1/4}(t)$ for $t = 1, 2$, but since the NoC link cannot send more than one packet per cycle, $\lambda_{b=3, \rho=1/4}(t)$ is still a valid traffic bound. In essence, Lemma 1 allows us to "convert" a flow with a traffic curve $\lambda_{b,\rho}(t)$ into an arrival curve $\gamma_{\sigma,\rho}(t)$ and vice-versa, albeit at some loss of precision.

Finally, there are situations where we need to aggregate (combine) flows transmitted on the same link; for example, flows f_2' and f_4 entering router $(2,2)$ from N. Note that for two arrival curves $\gamma_{\sigma',\rho'}(t)$ and $\gamma_{\sigma'',\rho''}(t)$, it immediately holds that $\gamma_{\sigma',\rho'}(t) + \gamma_{\sigma'',\rho''}(t) = \gamma_{\sigma'+\sigma'',\rho'+\rho''}(t)$: hence, the arrival curve for the aggregate of flows traversing the same link can be expressed by summing the σ and ρ parameters of the arrival curves for the individual flows.

Figure 7 illustrates the flows required for analysis at one NoC router. Here, f and f' represent a flow under analysis before and after leaving the $W \rightarrow S$ buffer; $f_{W \rightarrow S}$ represents the aggregate of all other interfering flows traversing the buffer; $f_{N \rightarrow S}$ represents the aggregate of all interfering flows traversing the router in the $N \rightarrow S$ direction; and $f_{PE \rightarrow S}$ represents the aggregate of all flows injected by the client at that router directly S. As discussed in Section 3.3, the S mux arbitration gives lowest priority to the client; hence, we do not have to consider flow $f_{PE \rightarrow S}$ when analyzing flow f, but it will interfere in the $N \rightarrow S$ direction on the next router. Regarding the other flows, $f_{N \rightarrow S}$ has higher priority than f, while $f_{W \rightarrow S}$ and f are FIFO scheduled as they traverse the same buffer.

Assuming that each flow is described by an arrival curve, we then obtain the following relations involving the curve parameters [1]:

$$f'.\rho = f.\rho; \tag{3}$$

$$f'.\sigma = f.\sigma + f.\rho \cdot \frac{f_{N \rightarrow S}.\sigma + f_{W \rightarrow S}.\sigma}{1 - f_{N \rightarrow S}.\rho}; \tag{4}$$

$$Backlog = f.\sigma + f_{W \rightarrow S}.\sigma + (f.\rho + f_{W \rightarrow S}.\rho) \cdot \frac{f_{N \rightarrow S}.\sigma}{1 - f_{N \rightarrow S}.\rho} \tag{5}$$

$$Delay(f) = \frac{f.\sigma}{1 - f_{N \rightarrow S}.\rho - f_{W \rightarrow S}.\rho} + \frac{f_{N \rightarrow S}.\sigma + f_{W \rightarrow S}.\sigma}{1 - f_{N \rightarrow S}.\rho} \tag{6}$$

under the condition that $f.\rho + f_{N \rightarrow S}.\rho + f_{W \rightarrow S}.\rho < 1$ (that is, the link is not saturated).

Based on Equation 3, buffering does not increase the rate of flows. Furthermore, based on Lemma 1, for any flow f_i that has not been buffered, including flow f, we have $f_i.\sigma = f_i.b - f_i.\rho$. Hence, the only unknowns in Equation 4 are the values $f_i'.\sigma$ for flows that have crossed a buffer. To analyze the system, we thus apply the so-called Time Stopping Method in network calculus [9]: we treat the values $f_i'.\sigma$ as variables, and write a system of linear equations

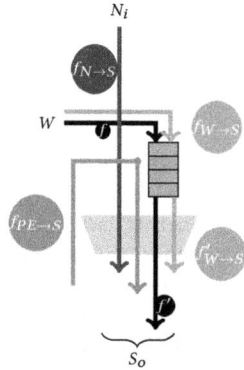

Figure 7: Flows through a $W \rightarrow S$ router.

by applying Equation 4 to each flow that enters a given vertical ring. If the values of $f_i'.\sigma$ obtained by solving the system of equations are valid (that is, bounded and positive), then $\gamma_{f_i'.\sigma, f_i'.\rho}(t)$ upper bounds flow f_i'. Otherwise, the network cannot be analyzed.

Example: Assume $f_1.\rho + f_2.\rho + f_5.\rho < 1$. For flow f_1, $f_{W \rightarrow S}$ comprises flow f_2, while $f_{N \rightarrow S}$ comprises flow f_5'. Since for any flow $f_i.\sigma = f_i'.\sigma$ and $f_i.\sigma = f_1.b - f.\rho$, we obtain:

$$f_1'.\sigma = f_1.b - f_1.\rho + f_1.\rho \cdot (f_5'.\sigma + f_2.b - f_2.\rho)/(1 - f_5.\rho).$$

Similarly, applying Equation 4 to flows f_2, f_5 under the added assumption $f_2.\rho + f_4.\rho + f_5.\rho < 1$ yields:

$$f_2'.\sigma = f_2.b - f_2.\rho + f_2.\rho \cdot (f_5'.\sigma + f_1.b - f_1.\rho)/(1 - f_5.\rho),$$
$$f_5'.\sigma = f_5.b - f_5.\rho + f_5.\rho \cdot (f_2'.\sigma + f_4.b - f_4.\rho)/(1 - f_2.\rho - f_4.\rho).$$

Hence, we solve a linear system of three equations to determine the value of variables $f_1'.\sigma, f_2'.\sigma, f_5'.\sigma$, which can then be used to determine the backlog at each router and delay for each flow according to Equations 5, 6. Furthermore, by applying Lemma 1, we derive equivalent traffic curves $\lambda_{\lceil f_i'.\sigma + f_i'.\rho + 1 \rceil, f_i'.\rho}(t)$ for f_1', f_2' and f_5', which we use to bound the injection latency of f_4. As an example, if we set $b = 1, \rho = 1/4$ for all regulators, we obtain $f_1'.\sigma = f_2'.\sigma = 33/20$, and $f_5'.\sigma = 39/20$, which result in backlogs of $14/5$ at $(2,1)$ and $39/20$ at $(2,2)$. Hence, we need a minimum $W \rightarrow S$ buffer size of $\lfloor 14/5 \rfloor + 1 = 3$ at $(2,1)$ and $\lfloor 39/20 \rfloor + 1 = 2$ at $(2,2)$; note we add 1 to the buffer size to account for a packet being read from the buffer and transmitted in the current clock cycle.

Despite this, it is known [1, 9] that the circular dependencies introduced by a ring design can reduce the sustainable (provable) per-link utilization of the network by up to 50%. We now present the linearization alternative that overcomes this low peak utilization.

4.5 Linearized Analysis: $W \rightarrow S + N$ Design

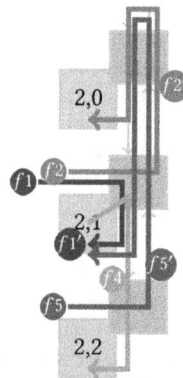

Figure 8: $W \rightarrow S + N$ design example: rightmost column.

The analysis for the $W \rightarrow S + N$ design proceeds in a similar manner, but is much simpler as no vertical loopback exists. The same injection latency computation is performed, albeit the set Γ_f^C can be different compared to the $W \rightarrow S$ design since a flow that was conflicting on the S mux could now turn N instead. Similarly, the same conditions in Equations 3-6 can be applied after decoupling each router in two parts: a south component containing the $W \rightarrow S$ buffer and S mux, and a north component containing the $W \rightarrow N$ buffer and N mux. Since packets are transmitted in different directions for the two components, when writing the equation for the north components we use flows $f_{S \rightarrow N}$ and $f_{W \rightarrow N}$ in place of $f_{N \rightarrow S}$ and $f_{W \rightarrow S}$.

Example: Figure 8 shows the resulting decomposition for the rightmost column of the flow set depicted in Figure 6. Note that the

[1]In details, Proposition 1.3.4 in [9] is first used to determine a service curve for the aggregate of flows f, $f_{W \rightarrow S}$. Corollary 6.2.3 is then used to derive $f'.\rho, f'.\sigma$, as well as the service curve for f. Backlog and delay bounds follow from Theorems 1.4.1, 1.4.2.

Table 2: Conflicting and interfering flows for the $W \rightarrow S + N$ design. '-' denotes not applicable, as the flow is not buffered in that direction.

flow	Γ^C	$f_{W \rightarrow S}$	$f_{N \rightarrow S}$	$f_{W \rightarrow N}$	$f_{S \rightarrow N}$
f_1	none	none	f_5'	-	-
f_2	f_1, f_3	-	-	none	f_5'
f_4	f_1', f_5'	-	-	-	-
f_5	none	-	-	none	none

topmost router $(2, 0)$ only implements the south component, as no flow can be injected north at $(2, 0)$. The sets of conflicting flows Γ^C_f and interfering flows $f_{N \rightarrow S}, f_{W \rightarrow S}, f_{S \rightarrow N}, f_{W \rightarrow N}$ are provided in Table 2. Compared to the $W \rightarrow S$ design, the number of conflicting and interfering flows is reduced.

When compared to the $W \rightarrow S$ design, we do not need to solve a system of equations to compute the $f_i'.\sigma$ values: since the $W \rightarrow S + N$ design disconnects vertical rings, we can apply Equation 4 to flows with destinations on a column x by ordering the flows based on the router at which they turn, in the order of packet propagation: from $(x, m - 1)$ to $(x, 1)$ for flows turning N, and then from $(x, 0)$ back to $(x, m - 1)$ for flows turning S. As long as no link is saturated, this guarantees that the analysis computes bounded delay and backlog.

4.6 Scaling regulation

For multiple flows starting from a client, we can design traffic regulators in two primary ways:

- We can implement a new token regulator for each outgoing flow by replicating counters per flow to deliver good analysis outcomes at increasing cost. For each outgoing flow per client, we need two counters to implement token regulation. This cost may be acceptable for a handful of outgoing flows.
- Alternatively, we can compute cumulative ρ and b parameters across all flows and program a single regulator. The rates and bursts are computed by summing the individual flow properties. This optimization will need a single regulator and single set of counters keeping costs low. However, this will result in pessimistic injection latency analysis due to interference.

5 EVALUATION

We present the performance measurement results for our FPGA optimized NoC and associated results from static analysis. We are interested in understanding the worst case NoC routing latency properties, its breakdown, buffer depth bounds, as well as routing coverage. We also want to confirm the properties of static analysis bounds and understand their impact of distributed FPGA RAM mapping costs. We show results for 5×5 NoCs to retain narrative consistency, but can generate other RTL networks and bounds for other sizes as well. We use two synthetic workloads which are commonly used in the real-time systems community:

- We use ALL-TO-ONE pattern that gets all NoC clients to target a same NoC address: a shared resource like an external DRAM, PCIe, or Network port.
- We also use synthetic uniform RANDOM traffic pattern that is expressed a set of flows, *i.e.* flowsets. We evaluate the NoCs using

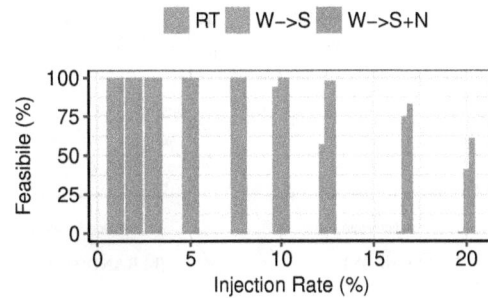

Figure 9: Feasible flowsets for RANDOM traffic with b=1 at 5×5 system size with 128-deep FIFOs in the NoC routers.

100 separately-generated synthetic flowsets. Each flowset is a collection of m^2 distinct streaming flows. Each flow captures data communication between a source-destination pair of clients. All flows have the same burstiness and rate which is increased until the links saturate.

5.1 RTL Simulation Results

We first examine the results (feasibility, latency, FIFO sizing) of cycle-accurate RTL simulations of the different NoCs.

5.1.1 Flowset Feasibility. For our designs, we cap the maximum FIFO occupancy at 128 to enable low-cost realizations. As a result some combination of flowset communication pattern and injection rate ρ will likely be infeasible. If any FIFO ever goes full, we classify that configuration as not feasible. We want to know what fraction of our 100 randomly-generated flowsets were able to route without any of the NoC FIFOs every going full at a given rate.

In Figure 9, we plot the number of feasible flowsets for RANDOM traffic pattern on the different NoCs. For HopliteRT, there are no FIFOs, but we know that flowsets are not feasible when the interfering flows on any link exceed the link bandwidth, *i.e.* you cannot use more than 100% of any link capacity. The deflection pattern for HopliteRT forces traffic to travel through longer paths through the NoC thereby interfering with a lot of other traffic flows. Hence, the feasibility trends for HopliteRT fall drastically above 16% injection rates. The HopliteBuf NoCs are more resilient and support a larger fraction of the flowsets for larger injection rates. At the peak supported injection rate of 20%, HopliteBuf supports up to 50–60% of the flowsets, while HopliteRT only routes 1–2% of the flowsets. As predicted from the linearization analysis in Section 4.5, the $W \rightarrow S + N$ topology allows the system to support more traffic and a slightly greater fraction of the synthetic combinations are feasible at even 20% injection rates. Higher feasibility translates into more FPGA developer freedom in being able to support their communication requirements.

5.1.2 Worst-Case Latency Trends. We expect the use of buffering will help reduce worst-case routing latencies as we eliminate deflections. However, the improvements will be balanced by the penalty of waiting in the FIFOs. In Figure 10 we show this effect for two traffic patterns with burst b=1. The common odd trend here is the *decrease* in injection latency as a function of injection rate. This is not an illusion, and is a result of the fact that the client

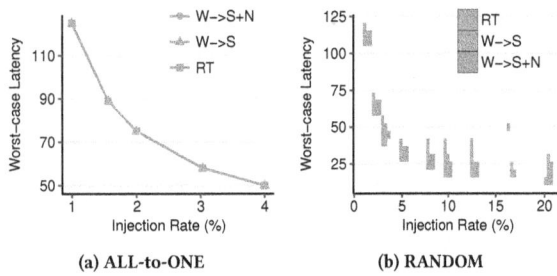

(a) ALL-to-ONE　　　**(b) RANDOM**

Figure 10: Worst-case latency trends for the different NoCs with 5×5 system sizes and b=1. HopliteBuf performs better for RANDOM pattern, and offers no improvements for ALL-TO-ONE traffic.

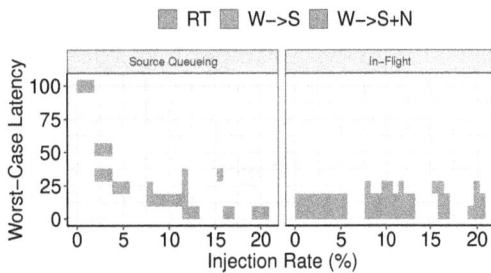

Figure 11: Breakdown of Source-Queueing and In-Flight NoC latencies for RANDOM workload with b=1 at 5×5 system size. Both metrics improved due to buffering.

is regulated and may miss the token cycle which scales with the injection rate ρ of the regulator. At large enough injection rates we eventually start to see an increase due to network congestion but this is marginal. For the ALL-TO-ONE traffic pattern, the waiting time in the FIFOs lines up with the penalty of deflections resulting in no observable difference between the different designs. For RANDOM traffic, we show a distribution of measured cycle counts across the 100 flowsets. There is a clear benefit to using buffers to avoid deflections as bufferless HopliteRT shows a wider spread of achieved worst-case latencies. The buffer waiting time is lower than the penalty of deflections resulting in tighter latency spreads for HopliteBuf NoCs. Furthermore, $W \rightarrow S$ designs suffer a buffer wait only at a single turn, it exhibits slightly worse performance that the two-FIFO $W \rightarrow S + N$ design. Overall HopliteBuf is 1.2–2× better than HopliteRT in terms of worse-case routing latencies. We also see that HopliteRT is poorly unable to support the highest injection rate of 20% that is well-supported by the HopliteBuf NoCs. Thus, the presence of buffers not only improves (reduces) worst-case latencies, but also supports higher data rates. This is expected as HopliteRT steals unnecessary bandwidth in the X-ring due to deflection.

5.1.3 Worst-Case Latency Breakdown. In Figure 11 we show a breakdown of worst-case latency into its source queueing (waiting time at PEs) and in-flight latency (actual routing time in the NoC). The improvements due to elimination of deflections does show up in better in-flight routing latencies, but larger wins are visible during source queueing. This is because the NoC is blocking the PE

injection ports less often by keeping packets in the buffers instead of wasting injection slots due to deflection. For HopliteRT routing scheme, the $N \rightarrow E$ deflection potentially sends packets along the *scenic route* around each X-ring (at most once) generating traffic conflicts where none would exist for conventional DOR routing. HopliteBuf chooses FIFO waiting on conflicts thereby reducing contention in other X-rings and a drop in source queueing delays. As we see, the NoC traversal time is mostly unaffected even in presence of FIFOs.

5.1.4 Latency Distribution. In Figure 12, we show the histogram of worst-case packet latencies for the different NoCs for RANDOM traffic with burst b=1, and injection rate ρ=7.5% at 5×5 system size. We note that the HopliteRT NoC has a much wider spread than the FIFO designs. This is because deflections create unpredictable trips through the NoC X-rings. In contrast, a victimized packet just sits in a buffer and the waiting time in the buffer is much lower than round-trips around the ring. As expected, the $W \rightarrow S$ design has a marginally wider distribution than the $W \rightarrow S + N$ design as the packets have an extra choice during the turn.

5.1.5 FIFO Sizing. Ultimately, the NoC with improved worst-case latencies is useful to us only if the buffer sizes are reasonable to realize on modern FPGAs. For a single LUT we can get 16–32 storage bits for our FIFOs making it possible to build LUTs using these low-cost components. We cap our experiments at 128-deep FIFO

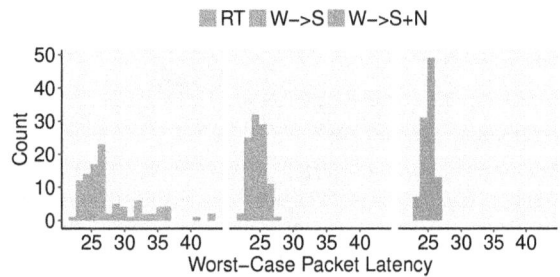

Figure 12: Distribution of worst-case packet latencies for RANDOM workload with b=1, ρ=7.5% at 5×5 system size. HopliteRT has a wider spread due to the unpredictable nature of the deflections. HopliteBuf has narrower spreads.

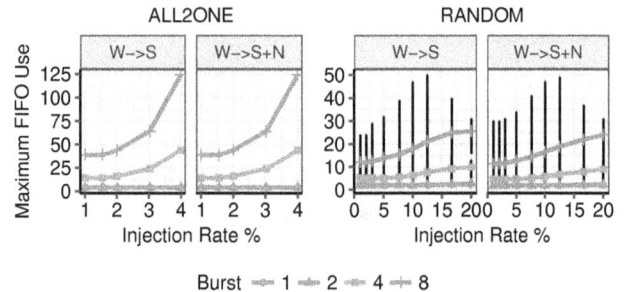

Figure 13: Maximum FIFO usage trends from RTL simulations of NoCs with 5×5 system sizes. For RANDOM traffic, we observe a spread of maximum FIFO use as per pattern in the flowset, but lower than ALL-TO-ONE pattern.

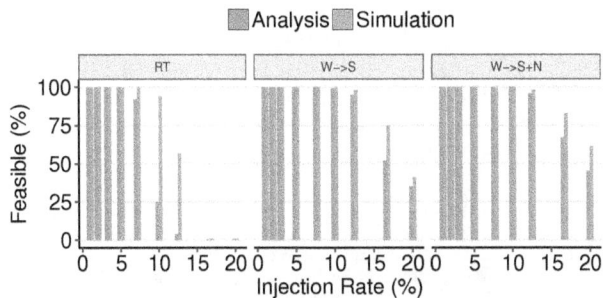

Figure 14: Feasible flowsets predicted by static analysis. Analysis is more conservative than simulation for HopliteRT, but much tighter for HopliteBuf.

sizes to keep NoC LUT cost at 4 LUTs/bit. For ALL-TO-ONE traffic pattern shown in Figure 13, we will observe high FIFO usage in the column containing the destination client. As burst length increases, the FIFO usage also scales linearly with very low utilization with a burst length of 1–2. RANDOM traffic shown in Figure 13 exhibits slightly lower FIFO usage and demonstrates a spread of occupancies depending on connectivity pattern. While no experiment occupies more than 50 entries in the FIFO, on average, we only need ≈20–25 entries. We note an odd reduction in FIFO occupancy above 10% injection rate. This is because an increasing subset of flowsets are not feasible with 128-deep FIFO limit *i.e.* FIFOs start going full.

5.2 Analysis

We now examine the quality of our static analysis predictions and compare them to simulated data.

5.2.1 Feasible Flowsets. Our analysis tools take the communication pattern of a flowset, its injection rate ρ and burst b to determine if it is can route successfully without making a FIFO ever go full. Analysis is more conservative, and you will note that Figure 14 is different from the simulation data in Figure 9. Our simulation results are for 1K packets per client, and there may be longer simulation conditions that ultimately go infeasible. Hence, we trust our analysis data as it is backed by the formal proofs explained in Section 4. Here, we see HopliteRT dropping dramatically above 8% while HopliteBuf clones closely track simulation results. At 11% rates, we see analysis predict feasibility of only 2–3% of HopliteRT and ≈90% for HopliteBuf. Back in Figure 9, simulation results showed 50% of HopliteRT were feasible and ≈90% for HopliteBuf. This suggests tighter analysis bounds for HopliteBuf resulting in better provable utilization of resources.

5.2.2 Worst-Case Latency: Analysis vs. Simulation. In Figure 15, we show the predicted worst-case latency count as a result of our static analysis vs. actual observed latencies through simulation. As expected, the predicted bounds are worse with analysis due to pessimistic assumptions regarding interference of traffic flows. HopliteRT predictions are as much as 1.5× worse than the $W \rightarrow S + N$ predictions due to pessimism inherent in the HopliteRT routing algorithm. It is interesting to see that a few flowsets mapped to HopliteRT at 16–20% injection rates actually simulate fine, but are discarded by analysis as infeasible, yet again due to analytic pessimism. Furthermore, we see that the $W \rightarrow S+N$ predictions are

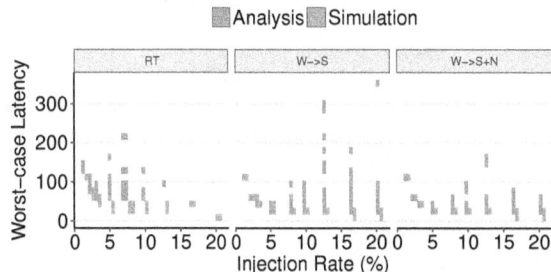

Figure 15: Worst-Case Latency Prediction-vs-Simulation, RANDOM traffic, b=1, 5×5 system size, 128-deep FIFOs.

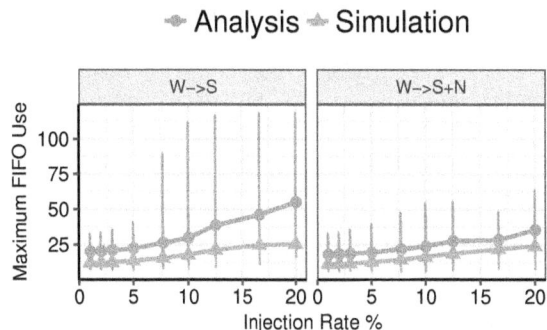

Figure 16: Worst-Case FIFO size Prediction-vs-Simulation for RANDOM traffic at 5×5 system size with 128-deep FIFOs and burstiness of 8.

significantly tighter than the $W \rightarrow S$ predictions. This is primarily due to the challenges associated with analyzing loopy flows in the vertical ring. When comparing the wider $W \rightarrow S$ spread to HopliteRT, it is important to note that a significant chunk of flowsets were infeasible when mapped to HopliteRT (See Figure 14). Thus, the larger latencies are due to $W \rightarrow S$ being able to feasibly route flowsets and doing so with high latencies than not being able to do so at all. The $W \rightarrow S + N$ analysis is significantly better than $W \rightarrow S$ and has a larger feasibility to compound the matter.

5.2.3 FIFO Sizing: Analysis vs. Simulation. In Figure 16, we compare the result of static analysis with simulated data for FIFO usage for a 5×5 NoC with RANDOM traffic and a worst-case burstiness of 8. For the $W \rightarrow S$ topology, we cap the maximum FIFO size to 128 to stay within reasonable 4 LUTs/bit FIFO cost. In this case, the FIFOs go full for a few flowsets only above a healthy 15% injection rate. For the $W \rightarrow S + N$ topology, the FIFO sizes are capped at 64 (for a sum of 128) and only go full at a higher 20$ injection rate. For both cases, we observe that simulated data shows lower occupancies than the prediction by as much as 2.5× (on average 1.5×). This is expected due the pessimism in the analysis but the LUT cost impact is limited due to SRL32 packing quantization.

For FPGA implementation, we can choose to size all FIFOs in the NoC to the largest size, or customize each FIFO independently as per the static analysis. We observe that the largest size of 128 is rarely observed, and roughly 50% of our occupancies are below the 32 threshold. Thus, we can customize the right SRL depth to further save resources by as much as 2×.

6 DISCUSSION AND RELATED WORK

Real-time NoC design has mostly focused in two directions:

- **Time-division multiplexed (TDM) NoCs** [2, 5, 11]: These NoCs require complete knowledge of the communication flows to build static TDM scheduling tables used for both packet injection and routing. However, this approach tends to be unsuitable for NoCs that need to support both real-time flows requiring worst case guarantees and best effort flows where average case delay matters.

- **Prioritized NoCs** [7, 13]: Here, packets are arbitrated based on the relative priority of the constituent flow instead of requiring complete knowledge. While this approach more effectively supports clients of different criticality, it requires expensive virtual channels: at each port, every priority flow needs a different buffer.

In this paper, we rely on a standard network calculus framework [9] to bound queuing delay and backlog so that we can guarantee the stall-free property of the buffers. The use of regulators to bound the maximum network latency is well-known in the context of network calculus. In particular, introducing a regulator at each router port can solve the dependencies issue in the $W \to S$ cyclic design, ensuring that the network remains stable up to full link utilization. Instead of expensive per-flow, per-router regulation popularly used in off-chip networks where cost of wiring is dominant, our work uses a cheaper per-flow regulator at injection.

PaterNoster NoC [10] is similar to Hoplite and uses a torus topology along with deflection routing. However, it is not optimized for FPGAs and uses many multiplexers and corner buffer. The use of corner buffer does help improve throughput but the NoC falls back to deflection routing when the buffers go full. In contrast, our NoC analysis guarantees stall-free behavior without resorting to deflections or affecting delivery order.

The **Kim NoC** router [8], uses separate X and Y rings like Hoplite, introduces an intermediate buffer for X→Y traversal, again like HopliteBuf, but uses backpressure flow control to manage full buffers. This topology uses multiplexers abundantly as it is targeted as ASICs, and would not match the LUT fabric of the FPGA as well as Hoplite or HopliteBuf. Furthermore, HopliteBuf does not require backpressure flow control either as FIFOs are not allowed to go full.

We anticipate our static analysis tools to help compute latency bounds on the newly-announced **Xilinx Versal NoC** with hardened FIFOs of known sizes. Unlike LUT-based HopliteBuf NoC used in this study, the Versal hard-NoC FIFOs do not need to be designed with LUT-FIFO capacity constraints.

7 CONCLUSIONS

We present HopliteBuf, an FPGA-based NoC with lightweight buffering and associated static analysis tools to better support NoC communication requirements of real-time FPGA applications. HopliteBuf introduces LUT-based stall-free FIFOs to the NoC router to absorb deflections and provide in-order routing of packets. We develop static analysis tools that can compute worst-case buffer occupancy bounds, along with latency bounds for communication patterns with rate, and burst information known up-front. In our experiments with 100 randomly-generated flowsets, we show that HopliteBuf is able to deliver 40–50% feasibility at 20% injection rates

while the competing state-of-the-art HopliteRT NoC only supports 25% feasibility at 10% injection rates at 2× worse latency bounds..

REFERENCES

[1] Ahmed Amari and Ahlem Mifdaoui. 2017. Worst-case timing analysis of ring networks with cyclic dependencies using network calculus. In *Proceedings of the IEEE International Conference on Embedded and Real-Time Computing Systems and Applications (RTCSA)*. IEEE.

[2] Kees Goossens and Andreas Hansson. 2010. The aethereal network on chip after ten years: Goals, evolution, lessons, and future. In *47th DAC*. IEEE, 306–311.

[3] Yutian Huan and A DeHon. 2012. FPGA optimized packet-switched NoC using split and merge primitives. In *Field-Programmable Technology*. 47–52.

[4] S. Jeon, J. Cho, Y. Jung, S. Park, and T. Han. 2011. Automotive hardware development according to ISO 26262. In *13th International Conference on Advanced Communication Technology (ICACT2011)*. 588–592.

[5] N. Kapre. 2016. Marathon: Statically-Scheduled Conflict-Free Routing on FPGA Overlay NoCs. In *2016 IEEE 24th Annual International Symposium on Field-Programmable Custom Computing Machines (FCCM)*. 156–163. https://doi.org/10.1109/FCCM.2016.47

[6] H. Kashif and H. Patel. 2014. Bounding buffer space requirements for real-time priority-aware networks. In *2014 19th Asia and South Pacific Design Automation Conference (ASP-DAC)*. 113–118.

[7] Hany Kashif and Hiren Patel. 2016. Buffer Space Allocation for Real-Time Priority-Aware Networks. In *proceedings of the IEEE Real-Time and Embedded Technology and Applications Symposium (RTAS)*. IEEE, 1–12.

[8] John Kim. 2009. Low-cost router microarchitecture for on-chip networks. In *42st Annual IEEE/ACM International Symposium on Microarchitecture (MICRO-42 2009), December 12-16, 2009, New York, New York, USA*, David H. Albonesi, Margaret Martonosi, David I. August, and José F. Martínez (Eds.). ACM, 255–266. https://doi.org/10.1145/1669112.1669145

[9] Jean-Yves Le Boudec and Patrick Thiran. 2001. *Network Calculus: A Theory of Deterministic Queuing Systems for the Internet*. Springer-Verlag.

[10] Jörg Mische and Theo Ungerer. 2012. Low Power Flitwise Routing in an Unidirectional Torus with Minimal Buffering. In *Proceedings of the Fifth International Workshop on Network on Chip Architectures (NoCArc '12)*. ACM, New York, NY, USA, 63–68. https://doi.org/10.1145/2401716.2401730

[11] Jörg Mische and Theo Ungerer. 2014. Guaranteed Service Independent of the Task Placement in NoCs with Torus Topology. In *Proc. 22Nd RTNS. (RTNS '14)*. ACM, 151:160. https://doi.org/10.1145/2659787.2659804

[12] Michael K Papamichael and James C Hoe. 2012. CONNECT: re-examining conventional wisdom for designing nocs in the context of FPGAs. In *Proceedings of the ACM/SIGDA international symposium on Field Programmable Gate Arrays*. ACM, 37–46.

[13] Zheng Shi and Alan Burns. 2008. Real-Time Communication Analysis for On-Chip Networks with Wormhole Switching. In *Second ACM/IEEE NOCS (nocs 2008) (NOCS '08)*. IEEE, 161–170. https://doi.org/10.1109/NOCS.2008.4492735

[14] Saud Wasly, Rodolfo Pellizzoni, and Nachiket Kapre. 2017. HopliteRT: An efficient FPGA NoC for real-time applications. In *F. Program. Technol. (ICFPT), 2017 Int. Conf.* IEEE, 64–71.

A APPENDIX

LEMMA 1. *(1) A flow bounded by traffic curve $\lambda_{b,\rho}(t)$ is also bounded by arrival curve $\gamma_{b-\rho,\rho}(t)$. (2) Similarly, a flow bounded by arrival curve $\gamma_{\sigma,\rho}(t)$ on any NoC link is also bounded by traffic curve $\lambda_{\lceil \sigma+\rho+1 \rceil,\rho}(t)$.*

PROOF. Part (1). Based on the curve definitions, we have:

$$\lambda_{b,\rho}(t) = \min\left(t, b + \lfloor \rho \cdot (t-1) \rfloor\right)$$
$$\leq b + \rho \cdot (t-1) = b - \rho + \rho \cdot t = \gamma_{b-\rho,\rho}(t).$$

Part (2). Again by definition:

$$\gamma_{\sigma,\rho}(t) = \sigma + \rho \cdot t = \sigma + \rho + \rho \cdot (t-1) \leq \sigma + \rho + \lfloor \rho \cdot (t-1) \rfloor + 1$$
$$\leq \lceil \sigma + \rho + 1 \rceil + \lfloor \rho \cdot (t-1) \rfloor.$$

Since furthermore a NoC link cannot transmit more than one packet every clock cycle, the flow is bounded by:

$$\min(t, \lceil \sigma + \rho + 1 \rceil + \lfloor \rho \cdot (t-1) \rfloor) = \lambda_{\lceil \sigma+\rho+1 \rceil,\rho}(t).$$

$\square$

The Network Management Unit (NMU): Securing Network Access for Direct-Connected FPGAs

Daniel Rozhko
University of Toronto
Toronto, Ontario
rozhkoda@eecg.toronto.edu

Paul Chow
University of Toronto
Toronto, Ontario
pc@eecg.toronto.edu

ABSTRACT

Reconfigurable compute devices, namely Field Programmable Gate Arrays (FPGA), have increasingly been deployed in datacenters and cloud infrastructures. Such devices have proven effective at performing certain types of compute tasks, often performing these tasks faster, with lower latency, at a higher throughput, and/or at lower power than traditional compute devices (e.g. CPUs). Some recent works have demonstrated the benefits of deploying such devices as direct-connected nodes, i.e., the FPGAs are connected directly to the datacenters' network infrastructure. In this work, we introduce the concept of the Network Management Unit (NMU), which secures the network from potentially unwarranted access from malicious or malfunctioning FPGA applications; specifically, the NMU targets network traffic originating from (or targeted towards) an application resident solely on the FPGA itself. We argue that this is a necessary feature of direct-connected reconfigurable compute devices. We present the design of several NMUs, introduce a taxonomy for describing these different designs, and analyze the trade-offs of each design. The NMUs discussed range from those that employ hairpin routing techniques to push management to the next level switch, to those that perform routing and access control directly.

CCS CONCEPTS

• **Networks** → **Network management**; *Routers*; *Firewalls*; • **Hardware** → **Reconfigurable logic applications**; *Networking hardware*; *Hardware accelerators*.

KEYWORDS

FPGA, Reconfigurable Computing, Networking, Management, Access Control, Routing, Encapsulation

ACM Reference Format:
Daniel Rozhko and Paul Chow. 2019. The Network Management Unit (NMU): Securing Network Access for Direct-Connected FPGAs. In *The 2019 ACM/SIGDA International Symposium on Field-Programmable Gate Arrays (FPGA '19), February 24–26, 2019, Seaside, CA, USA.* ACM, New York, NY, USA, 10 pages. https://doi.org/10.1145/3289602.3293903

1 INTRODUCTION

There have been many high-profile works demonstrating the potential of heterogeneous compute environments, i.e., datacenters and clouds with multiple types of compute devices. One area of particular focus has been the deployment of reconfigurable hardware compute devices, such as Field Programmable Gate Arrays (FPGAs). The Catapult work [19], presented by Microsoft, is perhaps one of the best known industry works to demonstrate the benefits of using FPGAs to accelerate contemporary compute tasks, specifically Bing search in that work. Many other works have followed, including a deployment of FPGAs by IBM [13], Amazon [1], and various academic works [10][21][15].

How these FPGAs are provisioned within the datacenter or cloud environment varies by implementation. Traditionally, these devices have been connected to existing servers as add-in cards, with all communication performed through the host server. For example, the OpenCL [20] programming paradigm, implemented for Xilinx FPGAs through the SDAccel platform [5], assumes such a host-centric compute model. Some more recent works, including the work by Byma et al. [10], and the later Catapult v2 work from Microsoft [11], instead connect the FPGAs directly to the datacenters' network infrastructure. These later works enable paradigms where the reconfigurable compute devices are peers to the traditional CPU-based servers, a more flexible deployment model [14].

Many FPGA deployments and works focus on FPGAs as offload engines; software applications offload a compute-intensive portion of their computation to an optimized hardware implementation, though communication and memory management is still handled by the originating software application. Direct-connected deployment models highlight a different possible use-case: FPGAs as application-hosts in and of themselves. In this latter case, the application running on the FPGA could retrieve data from the network, perform some processing, store some results, and send data out to the network in response. For the work presented in this paper, we target this added network functionality; network traffic originating from the FPGA must be secured to protect the common datacenter networking infrastructure.

When it comes to network traffic originating from an FPGA application, those deployments that target a host-centric model must send all network traffic through the software stack of the attached CPU-based system and can thus be secured in the software domain. In contrast, the *direct-connected* deployment model exposes the datacenters' networks to communication from the reconfigurable compute device directly. If such devices are provisioned to multiple users/customers in some cloud-like fashion, malicious users could compromise the network or snoop the private data of other nodes. In addition, even with trusted-developer-only deployments,

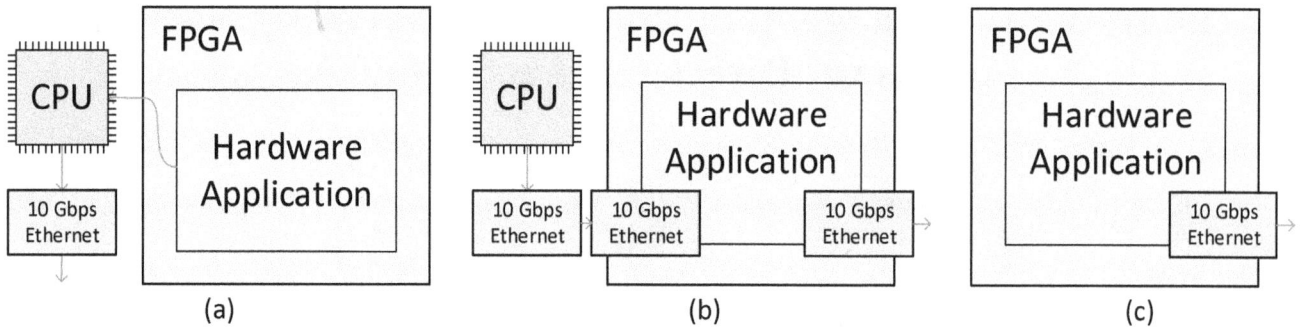

Figure 1: Network Access Modes (a) Host-Centric, (b) Bump-in-the-Wire, (c) Direct-Network-Connected

malfunctioning or errant hardware applications may raise some of these same issues. Some security layer must be provided between hardware applications and the network interfaces. We present the Network Management Unit (NMU) in this paper, as our primary contribution, to address this security layer need.

The remainder of this paper is organized as follows. Section 2 presents previous works that deploy FPGAs in the datacenter and describes any network security features those works use. Section 3 introduces the concept of the NMU, and presents the design of various types of NMUs. Details of the hardware implementations of the described NMUs are presented in Section 4, with an evaluation of the area and latency implications of those designs shown in Section 5. Finally, Section 6 concludes the work and presents avenues for future work.

2 BACKGROUND

Network security has been considered in other virtualization works before, both in a limited capacity in previous FPGA-based works and extensively in the software domain. Those previous considerations, and their applicability to the work presented here, are discussed in this section.

2.1 Targeted Deployment

A depiction of some popular FPGA deployment models is shown in Figure 1. Each of these models has different security concerns with regards to network traffic. Figure 1 (a) shows a host-centric model, which as mentioned in the introduction, does not need explicit network security enforced in the hardware. Figure 1 (b) shows a bump-in-the-wire model, like the one included in the Catapult v2 system [11]. In this case, the network security instantiated in the FPGA might include the securitization of traffic originated from the FPGA and the host system. Finally, Figure 1 (c) shows a direct-network-connected configuration, which simply has a network connection. In this last case, only FPGA-originating network traffic is secured.

For the purposes of this work, only FPGA-originating network traffic is considered for securitization; i.e., only Figure 1 (c) of Figure 1 is explicitly considered. The software complexities of the host-centric model in Figure 1 (a) and the extended use-case of Figure 1 (b) are not considered in this work. However, the configuration of Figure 1 (b) could certainly be used in the mode of Figure 1 (c),

though we focus specifically on FPGA-originating traffic and do not explicitly consider processing CPU traffic.

The NMU, and the context in which it is to be deployed, is shown in the system diagram of Figure 2. This system diagram considers a solely direct network connected FPGA, so no CPU host connection is included. As shown in the figure, the NMU sits between the applications that generate the traffic (on the FPGA) and the Ethernet controller. The NMU can be shared between multiple applications on the same FPGA, though no slowdown from contention is introduced if the NMU can operate at the full line-rate of the Ethernet controller (the NMUs presented in this work all operate at line-rate). An interconnect is included to arbitrate access to the NMU if multiple applications are present on the FPGA. The NMU inspects all outgoing traffic and disallows packets that violate the access permissions of the sender from being transmitted. In addition, it routes incoming traffic to the correct application or interface.

2.2 Related Work

Microsoft's initial datacenter FPGA deployment, Catapult v1, used host-connected FPGAs with an FPGA-only network interconnecting the devices [19]; without a connection to the main datacenter network, the FPGAs can only interface with each other and not regular network traffic. Catapult v2 [11] introduced FPGAs with an Ethernet network connection to the main datacenter network. Security for FPGA-originating network traffic is ensured using a router that encapsulates datum packets from the hardware application in a custom Transport Layer protocol, called the Lightweight Transport Layer (LTL) protocol. This methodology limits all hardware applications to operate above the Transport Layer for secure operation.

The work presented by the IBM Research group considers a multi-tenant device. Multiple hardware applications on a single FPGA are provisioned through a Partial Reconfiguration (PR) tool flow to allow for separate regions of the FPGA to be programmed individually [13]. Multiple users on a single FPGA motivates the need for security between the users, which the work discusses in the context of shared memory. The FPGAs in the IBM deployment are configured in a host-centric design and have no network connections, therefore no network security need be considered for FPGA-originating network traffic.

Amazon's deployment of FPGAs in their AWS cloud offering is unique in that Amazon has made the FPGAs available to program

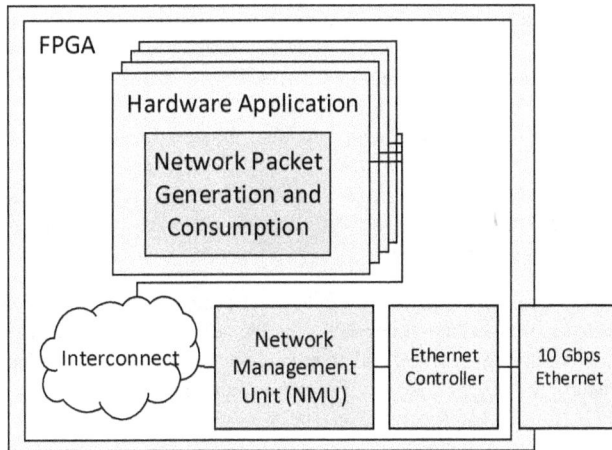

Figure 2: System Architecture with NMU

directly by its AWS customers [1]. This would obviously open up the FPGA devices to potentially malicious users, and is an important provisioning model that motivates the need for security further. The FPGA cards are connected to a host server and a dedicated FPGA only interconnection network, similar to the Catapult v1 work. As the FPGAs are not connected to the datacenter's network infrastructure, network security for FPGA-originating network traffic is not required in the FPGA hardware.

The work presented by Byma et al. does not include any host connection. The FPGAs are connected directly to the network [10]. The FPGAs are also provisioned as multi-tenant devices, similar to the IBM work. Network security for FPGA-originating network traffic is considered explicitly; outgoing traffic is policed by replacing the source Media Access Control (MAC) address supplied by the user with an assigned address, preventing MAC address spoofing. This solution ensures security between hardware applications on the same FPGA only by excluding the ability to route between the hardware applications and does not prevent unauthorized destination MAC addressing, both of which are limitations addressed by our work.

Complete switch solutions have also been implemented on FP-GAs [17] [22], and they can provide the same level of security afforded to software systems, such as Access Control Lists (ACLs), adherence to routing protocols and stateful inspection. However, they consume significant resources on the order of 15-36% LUTs and 45-62% of BRAMs for the devices used. Alternative solutions must be sought that minimizes the area overhead.

2.3 Software Analogues

In the software domain, the National Institute of Standards and Technology (NIST) details some common methodologies used to secure access to a shared network by Virtual Machines (VMs) in a virtualized environment [12]. The main methodology presented is the virtual switch, a fully functional switch implemented in software that switches traffic from the virtual network connections to the physical network interface and the next-level physical switch. The hardware switch solutions of [17] and [22] could be considered

hardware analogues to these software virtual switches. Distributed virtual switches extend the virtual switch concept by provisioning and managing virtual switches on multiple physical nodes simultaneously, an avenue that could be explored for hardware NMU solutions in future work.

Another common network security methodology, according to NIST, is the firewall: devices and/or security layers within switches or software that filter traffic such that only allowed connections are left to pass-through to the network. The set of allowed connections is often specified in what are termed Access Control Lists (ACLs), or alternatively Network Access Control Lists (NACLs). Firewall functionality can be provisioned using physical appliances installed in the network, through ACLs implemented in the physical switches of the network, or through firewalls implemented in the virtual switch solutions mentioned earlier.

For multi-tenant environments, the pushing of ACLs to a physical firewall appliance or the next-level physical switch is often termed *hairpinning*, since traffic from the VM is first routed to the physical appliance and then to its final destination. Note, for such a firewall implementation to work, some level of source semantics enforcement must be done before routing to the firewall appliance such that the traffic is uniquely identifiable. Such hairpinning techniques are considered here for analogous hardware solutions.

A final consideration, virtual networking subdivides the physical network into virtual networks that can be provisioned to different users and isolated from each other. The simplest form of virtual networking is the Virtual LAN (VLAN) tag, IEEE 802.1Q [2]. The VLAN tag includes a 12-bit virtual ID that allows switches to identify, and isolate packets between, devices on the same virtual network. Such tagging can often be done by the switches themselves at ingress to the network. Additionally, network virtualization can be provided using encapsulation-based methods, VXLAN [18] or NVGRE [16]; Virtual Tunnel Endpointss (VTEPs), often implemented within virtual switches, perform the encapsulation and de-encapsulation.

3 THE NETWORK MANAGEMENT UNIT

The related work brings to light two specific motivations for further network security. First, deployments wherein users can directly program the FPGAs with a custom bitstream opens the datacenter to potentially malicious or malfunctioning user applications. Second, virtualization trends are pushing deployments towards multi-tenancy, with hardware applications sharing a single device and, by extension, a single network interface. Even in the case that there is only one hardware application, this hardware application may have multiple logical network interfaces that need to be secured separately. The software analogues demonstrate some of the needs of such network security, namely the enforcement of access control (either directly or by hairpinning such functionality to the next-level physical switch or some hardware appliance), and the ability to route traffic between logical interfaces on the same FPGA.

In traditional software virtual environments, VMs share memory and I/O connections. The memory sharing is generally provisioned by hardware means, specifically, data isolation is provided through the employment of a Memory Management Unit (MMU) [9]. As an analogy to the MMU, which provides memory data isolation, we propose the creation of an NMU, which provides network domain

Table 1: NMU Taxonomy Summary

Type (A|B|C|E) [R] [v] - [L2|L3|L4]	
Type A	No access controls provided within the FPGA, some tagging such that ACLs can be applied at the next-level physical switch (hairpinning)
Type B	Source semantics enforcement for all outgoing traffic from hardware applications, allowing ACLs at the next-level switch with no spoofing
Type C	Source semantics enforcement and some simple dest. based access controls (e.g. restrict to a single dest, or restrict multicast/broadcast)
Type E	Encapsulation: hardware applications send payload without generating packet headers, network packet generation done in the NMU itself
Type *R	Routing between hardware applications on the same FPGA done inside of the NMU (no hairpinning)
Type *v	Virtualized networking environment supported
[L2|L3|L4]	Network protocol stack layer at which the NMU operates (L2 = MAC, L3 = IP, L4 = Transport)
E.g. Type A-vepa, Type A-etag, Type Av, Type ARv, Type B-L2, Type B-L3, Type B-L4, Type BR-L2, Type BR-L3, Type BR-L4, Type C-L2, Type C-L3, Type C-L4, Type CR-L2, Type CR-L3, Type CR-L4, Type E-L2, Type E-L3, Type E-L4, Type ER-L2, Type ER-L3, Type ER-L4, Type ERv-vxlan, Type ERv-nvgre, Type Ev-vxlan, Type Ev-nvgre, Universal	

isolation. Based on the related work, and the trends we identified, we contend that the NMU is required to enable the secure deployment of direct-connected FPGAs in multi-user or multi-tenant datacenters and cloud deployments.

In the remainder of this section, we present several potential NMU designs and a taxonomy for describing NMUs: a summary of this taxonomy is shown in Table 1.

3.1 Access Control

Access control functionality can be done within the NMU, or hairpinned to the next level switch. All the traffic that is processed by the NMU is normal network traffic (conformant to all relevant networking standards), and as such it is completely interoperable with standard network equipment. Thus, no special consideration must be made when implementing some ACLs on the NMU and some ACLs on the next level switch. The first criteria by which we categorize potential NMU designs is the level of access control done within the NMU rather than pushed to the next level switch.

3.1.1 Type A NMUs. At the lowest level, we have NMUs that do not inspect outgoing packets at all and push all access control functionality to the next-level switch (and potentially a further firewall appliance); we term these Type A NMUs. Of course, for the next-level switch to be able to uniquely identify separate logical interfaces, some methodology must be employed to mark outgoing packets as originating from a particular logical interface. Two recent different IEEE standards could be used to this end.

The Edge Virtual Bridging standard (802.1Qbg) [3] allows for a single physical port of a switch to be treated as multiple logical ports by associating each logical connection with a specific Service VLAN

tag. Similarly, the Bridge Port Extension standard (802.1pr) [4] allows for a single physical port on a switch to be expanded into multiple individually managed connections using a custom tag structure. Thus, a Type A NMU should employ such tagging to push both routing and access control to the next-level switch.

The simplicity of Type A NMUs lend themselves to simple hardware realizations, but they require all ACLs to be implemented at the next-level switch, tightly coupling the hardware application to the switch configuration.

3.1.2 Type B NMUs. The next level of access control is source semantics enforcement, i.e., ACLs that ensure the sender addresses in the packets are correct and no other device addresses are spoofed; we term these Type B NMUs. If source semantics are enforced on the FPGA, further access controls can be applied at the next-level switch without the configuration complexity of the Type A NMUs. Also, the Type B NMU does not rely on relatively new IEEE standards that may have limited adoption. While the configuration complexity is reduced, most access controls must still be implemented on the next-level switch; Type B NMU solutions remain tightly coupled to the switch configuration.

3.1.3 Type C NMUs. We define Type C NMUs as those that perform both sender and destination-based access controls on the FPGA. The full scope of what might constitute access control could be quite wide, and in fact might include the full implementation of a switch on the FPGA. As discussed in Section 2, such an implementation is likely infeasible or carries too high an overhead. We must narrow the specific access controls available.

Some previous works have shown FPGA datacenter deployments that rely solely on static point-to-point links between the FPGAs. Limiting the NMU's access control to a single destination field per logical network interface would allow for some access control to be implemented in the Type C NMU at a relatively lower cost. Moreover, multiple logical network interfaces can be provided to each hardware application to implement point-to-multipoint connectivity. Other simple destination-based rules can also be included, such as limiting the ability to send multicast packets, and limiting IP traffic to a specific subnet. We contend that these simple access controls are powerful enough for many tasks.

The Type C NMU adds complexity in the hardware implementation, and as such area overhead, however it removes the tight coupling between the hardware application and the network infrastructure, which should greatly ease deployment. Of course, this is limited: if the point-to-point access controls are not sufficient enough to isolate the network accesses, more powerful ACLs in the next-level switch would be needed.

3.1.4 Type E NMUs . Finally, Type E NMUs eliminate the need for access controls by moving packet encapsulation into the NMU itself; instead of users performing network packetization within their own hardware applications, they simply send the payload to the NMU, which encapsulates it within the appropriate network packet. This is the methodology imposed in the implementation by Tarafdar et al. [21], and implied as an option in the Catapult v2 work with the introduction of the LTL protocol [11].

Type E NMU solutions can be quite simple in terms of the hardware required to implement them, and there is no tight coupling between the hardware application deployment and the network configuration. Type E NMUs are however the least flexible, as they impose point-to-point only connectivity. Type E NMUs also share network encapsulation hardware between the hardware applications, reducing area utilization, but thus also requiring hardware applications to be rewritten to target the encapsulation-based NMU scheme.

3.2 Type C NMU Implementation Specifics

As mentioned in Section 3.1.3, a full set of sender and destination based ACLs would result in an unwieldy and untenable NMU to be implemented alongside the reconfigurable hardware applications. We broadly outlined that, motivated by many existing FPGA applications that rely solely on static point-to-point network connectivity, our Type C NMUs implement a limited set of ACLs. The specific destination-based ACLs included in our NMU implementations are summarized in this section.

At Layer 2 (MAC), destination ACLs can limit packets to a single specific destination address or limit the ability to send multicast/broadcast packets. At Layer 3 (IP), destination ACLs can limit packets to a single specific destination address, limit packets to a specific IP subnet, allow/deny traffic sent to public IP addresses, or limit the ability to send multicast/broadcast packets. And at Layer 4 (TCP/UDP), destination ACLs can limit packets to a specific destination port. Any destination ACLs not explicitly supported in the above list of restrictions would need to be implemented in the next level switch with our implementation.

3.3 Routing

Another functionality that might be required is the routability of traffic between logical network interfaces located on the same FPGA. In general, hairpin routing to the next-level switch and back is not possible since the IEEE switch specifications explicitly forbid the re-routing of packets to the interface on which the packet was received. The Edge Virtual Bridging [3] and the Bridge Port Extensions [4] protocols are exceptions, so the Type A NMUs based on these standards enable routability by default.

*3.3.1 Type *R NMUs.* For other NMU types, routability between the logical network interfaces can only be provided by including routing functionality directly in the NMU; we term such NMUs as Type *R NMUs (where the wildcard is replaced by the appropriate access control type). Note, routability does not necessarily need to be provided, though this would impose on the cloud management framework the limitation that two applications that need to communicate with each other must be provisioned on different FPGAs; this might be an onerous limitation. This is the methodology employed by Byma et al. [10] for example.

Another consideration that might eliminate the need for routability built into the NMU is whether or not intra-FPGA traffic can be routed before it is prepared as a network packet (i.e., without the overhead of a network protocol). However, routability would still be needed in the NMU to support deployments where the applications are blind to the location of the destination nodes; a destination node could be included on the same FPGA or on a different FPGA, and the sender's outgoing packet would be the same.

3.4 Virtualization

From the NIST publication, another common way to ensure network security is by encapsulating packets within a virtual network, such as a VLAN or a VXLAN.

*3.4.1 Type *v NMUs.* A VLAN-based NMU would tag each logical network interface with the appropriate VLAN tag without having to parse the packet itself, and as such we classify it as a Type A NMU (Types Av and ARv). A VXLAN-based NMU would encapsulate the whole packet within a VXLAN delivery packet, and as such we classify it as a Type E NMU (Types Ev and ERv). We term these NMUs as Type *v (where the wildcard is replaced with the appropriate access control type and whether routability is supported).

3.5 Network Layer

Routing functionality and access control can be implemented at various levels of the network protocol stack, depending on the desired abstraction to present to the hardware application. For example, the hardware applications might have their own MAC addresses, or they might share a MAC/IP address and differ only on the Layer 4 port number. NMUs can be designed to process packets at a specific layer of the network protocol stack: MAC-only NMU, MAC/IP NMU, and MAC/IP/Layer4 NMU.

Note, all of the components designed for the NMUs described in this work conform completely with the IEEE network standards and the IETF internet standards. The NMU is designed such that the FPGA deployment is completely network interoperable with traditional networking equipment and software compute nodes.

4 HARDWARE DESIGN

To simplify the design of these NMUs, and to effectively measure the trade-offs between the NMU varieties, the design was split into two stages: the design of repeatable packet processing elements, and the overall system architecture.

4.1 Principle Sub-Components

To implement the functionality required of the NMUs, as described in Section 3, we need packet processing components that can examine the packets and pull out the relevant header information, as well as modify the packets by inserting and removing headers/fields.

4.1.1 Packet Parser. Packet parsers are used to pull out header information from a packet. This header information is then generally compared to some ACLs or a routing table. Previous works doing packet processing on FPGAs range from complex programmable parser designs [7], to simpler parsers generated from domain specific languages [8]. A focus point of our solution is to minimize the hardware overhead of network security for virtualized FPGAs, so we focus on the simpler designs.

The simple parser architectures include parsers for each part of the network protocol stack, cascading the parsers and accumulating the parsed information. For example, parsers could be created and connected in a cascade for MAC-parsing, IPv4-parsing, ARP-parsing, etc. The parsers themselves are generally simple, including a counter that counts the current position within the packet stream, and specialized field extractors that look for particular offsets within the packet for the field to be extracted. Note, the position that the

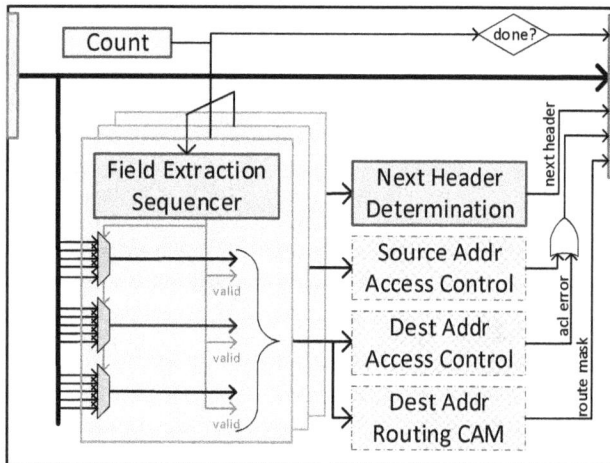

Figure 3: Packet Parser Architecture

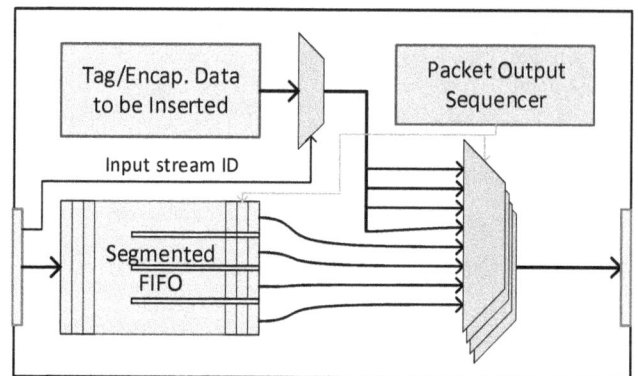

Figure 4: Tagger & Encapsulation Architecture

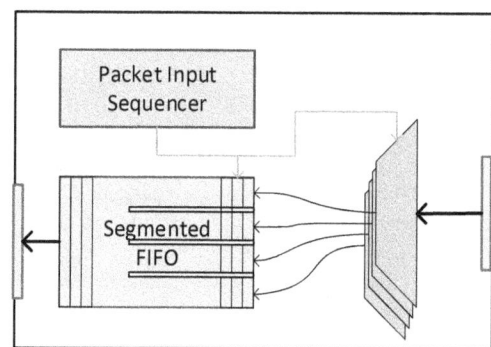

Figure 5: De-Tagger & De-Encapsulation Architecture

field extractor must look for to find the field can change based on previous packet fields extracted, and so cannot necessarily be hard-coded.

We employed a similar parser design in our work. Figure 3 shows a number of *Field Extraction Sequencers* that each extract a particular field in the packet. The extracted fields are then compared against ACLs and routing tables to determine whether or not an ACL has been violated and whether the packet matches a routing destination. The *Source Addr Access Control* from Figure 3 implements source-semantics ACLs and would be used in Type B and Type C NMUs. The *Dest Addr Access Control* from Figure 3 implements destination-semantics ACLs and would be used in Type C NMUs. The *Dest Addr Routing CAM* from Figure 3 implements the routing table and would be used in Type *R NMUs. The outputs of these ACL and routing CAM components, the current ACL status and the current CAM match vector, are forwarded to the next parser such that the cumulative ACL status and routing destination can be determined after the final parser in the parsing chain.

Traditional packet parsing systems pull out all the fields of interest, through some series of packet parsers, and then pass those fields en masse to some routing table or flow table structure to be analyzed and processed. A key difference in our design is the inclusion of the access control and routing CAM logic for a particular field directly within the parser responsible for extracting that field. This design allows for the cascaded parsers to simply pass along the cumulative routing and ACL status instead of the entire field (which might contribute to high register utilization in highly pipelined designs). Access control and routing CAM components can be excluded if not needed for a particular NMU type.

4.1.2 Tagger/Encapsulation. The tagger and encapsulation components are used to insert bytes at the beginning or in the middle of a packet, to support the Type A and Type E NMUs respectively. To insert bytes into a packet, the incoming packet stream must first be divided into segments, which can be read and pushed to the output individually. This is accomplished using a segmented FIFO, where the segments form multiple FIFO outputs. The segmentation

is done on a 16-bit basis, since all network headers at Layer 4 and below are aligned to 16-bit boundaries.

Figure 4 shows the implemented tagger/encapsulation core, with the input driving a segmented FIFO. The output stream is generated by using multiplexers to select from the segments of the input FIFO, and the tag/encapsulation data to be inserted into the packet. A *Packet Output Sequencer*, implemented as a Finite State Machine, sequences the input and the bytes of the data to construct the output packet. The stream ID from the input is used to determine which logical network interface sent the packet that is currently being processed. This ID is used to index into the *Tag/Encap Data* register file to access the tag data to be inserted into packets specifically from that logical interface.

Note, since the encapsulator can run at the 10Gbps Ethernet line-rate, the depth of the FIFO does not impact performance. The FIFO only serves the functional role of buffering incoming data beats to be read out in a segmented fashion. For that reason, the FIFOs are left to a minimum depth for all of the evaluations presented in this paper. Other FIFOs, not specifically included inside the encapsulator, are included elsewhere in the NMU to buffer packets and avoid dropped packets.

4.1.3 De-Tagger/De-Encapsulation. The de-tagger and de-encap components do the opposite task as the tagger and encapsulator. For packets coming in from the network, these components can be

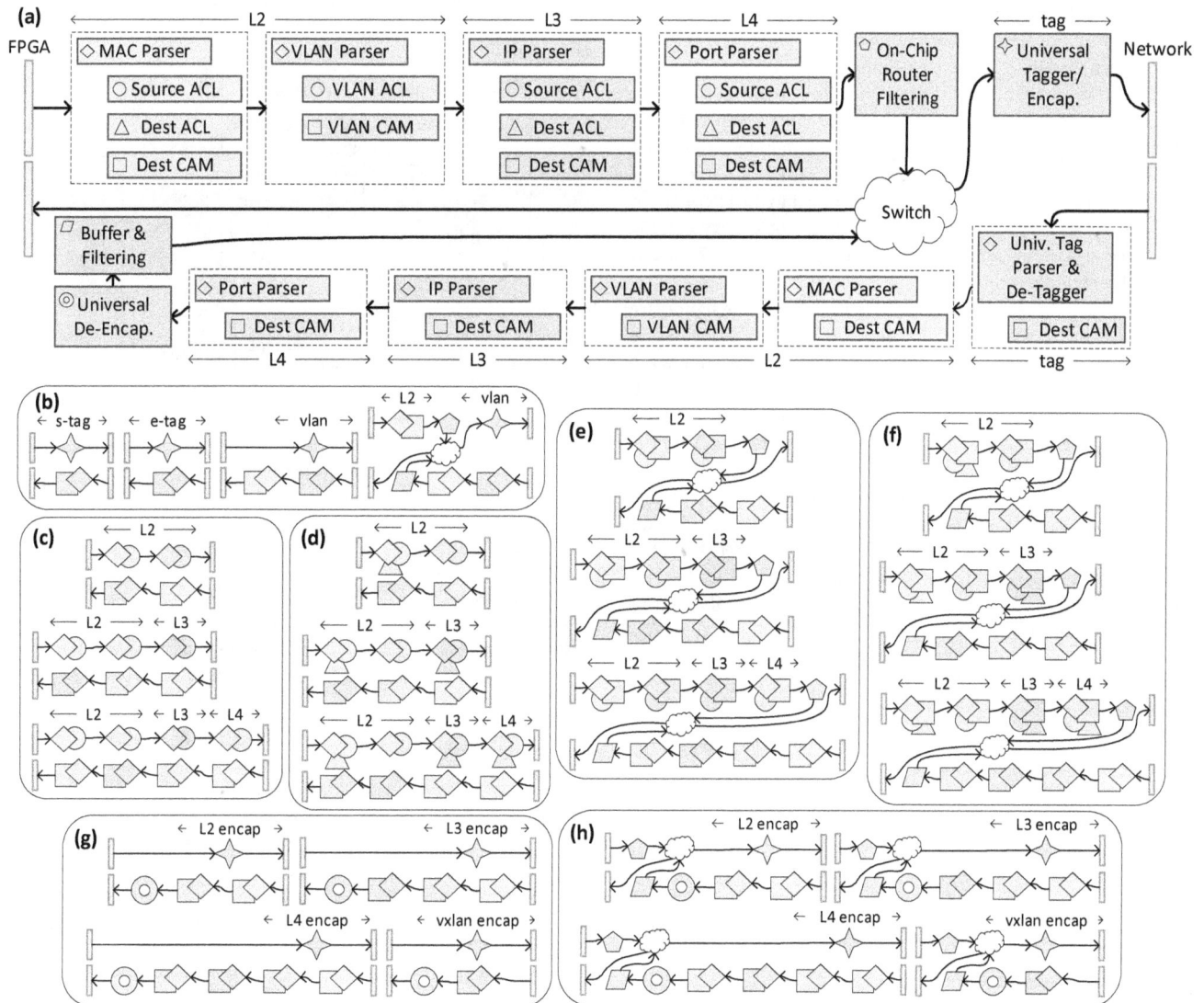

Figure 6: Network Management Unit System Architecture (a) Universal NMU, with components labeled and marked with symbols to be used as the legend for sub-figures (b) Type A NMUs (c) Type B NMUs (d) Type C NMUs (e) Type BR NMUs (f) Type CR NMUs (g) Type E NMUs (h) Type ER NMUs

used to strip some bytes from the packet that are not needed in the downstream hardware applications, like various tag information or whole network headers in the case of Type E NMUs. The design is similar to the tagger and encapsulator of Figure 4, except the direction of packet flow is reversed. The implementation is shown in Figure 5. The 16-bit segments of the input from the network drive multiplexers that in turn drive the FIFO. The input side of the FIFO is segmented, and the output side is full-width. The *Packet Output Sequencer* drives the selects of the multiplexers and the enables of the FIFOs to discard the appropriate bytes. Again, the depth of the FIFO is left to the minimum operational depth since it has no impact on performance.

4.2 System Architecture

Figure 6 shows the design of various NMUs, including a Universal NMU that can implement any of the deployment modes discussed with each of the NMU variants. Specifically, the Universal NMU is depicted in Figure 6 (a). As stated in Section 4.1.1, the parser components are cascaded, with routing CAMs and ACL components integrated within the parsers rather than in some later packet processing stage.

Packets flowing from the FPGA to the network (left to right in the figure) pass through parsing stages for MAC, VLAN, IP, and the Transport layer. In addition, not shown in the figure, an ARP stage is included that is processed in parallel with the IP Parser. CAMs in the parsers are included to determine whether egress packets should be routed back to another logical interface in the FPGA, in effect implementing a routing table for all logical network interfaces on the FPGA. The parser chain is followed by an *On-Chip Router Filtering* component, to implement a fully described ACL for on-chip routing. A bitmask, which contains a bit for each logical network connection, is used to mask out any communications that are not permissible according to this ACL. This is followed by a switch that allows for packets to be routed back into the FPGA or out to the network. The switch used is a Xilinx AXI Stream switch [6], configured as a partial crossbar. Finally, a tagger/encapsulator can be used to implement the tagging or encapsulation modes.

Packets arriving from the network (right to left in the figure) are first de-tagged (if a tagging mode happens to be enabled) before being passed to the ingress path parsers. While these parsers are logically separate from the egress path parsers, the CAMs used in all the parsers are register-based and the registers are shared between both versions of the parsers, reducing the area utilization. After the parsers, a de-encapsulation stage is included to support any of the encapsulation modes. Finally, a buffering stage that can hold at least one maximum transmission sized packet must be included since the ingress port to the FPGA is shared with the packets rerouted inward from the egress path; packets must be buffered so they are not lost or dropped. The Universal NMU in Figure 6 (a) also acts as a legend for the remaining pictorially depicted NMUs in (b)–(h).

5 TRADEOFF EVALUATION

In this section we evaluate the area, performance and functionality trade-offs of the different types of NMUs.

5.1 Test Platform

The NMU designs were tested on an Alpha Data 8k5 FPGA add-in board with a 10Gbps Ethernet connection; the FPGA on that Board is a Xilinx Kintex Ultrascale XCKU115. All tests were done using the Xilinx Vivado 2018.1 software, and the associated versions of the PCIe Subsystem and Ethernet Subsystem cores.

The NMU was placed in a system with four hardware applications, each connected to the ingress and egress ports of the Ethernet controller through an AXI Stream switch. Each application is provided eight logical network connections, so the NMUs evaluated support 32 total logical connections. The number of *logical connections* refers to the total number of unique managed network interfaces (i.e., AXI-Stream interfaces) that can be handled by the NMU. The overhead of the NMU scales with this number of logical connections.

The Ethernet controller has a datapath width of 64-bits and operates at 156.25 MHz, which is the clock used for the whole test platform (except for the PCIe controller). All of the NMUs, and all of their sub-components, are clocked at this 156.25 MHz clock speed. The applications themselves simply include a Block RAM that stores packet data, a DMA device to send that packet data out to the network, and a DMA engine that receives data from the network to store to Block RAM. Each of the *Apps* is controlled through PCIe by a host PC that manages the test setup. The Host is also responsible for configuring the NMU. In our implementation, the NMU's ACLs and routing table are configured over the PCIe

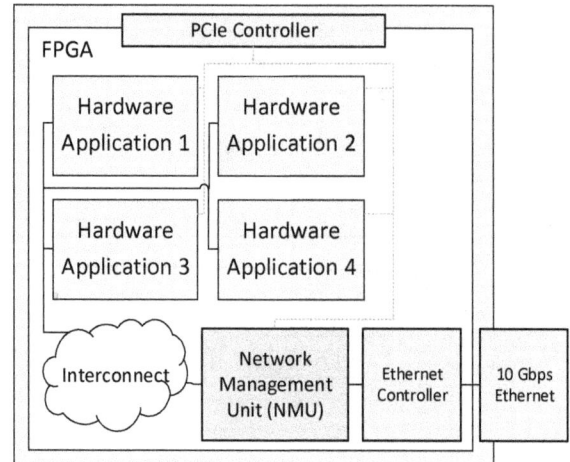

Figure 7: Multi-Application Test Setup

connection, using the AXI-Lite register interface. Figure 7 shows the architecture of the test platform.

To place a more realistic stress on the place-and-route tools, a floor planning methodology is used to spread the applications spatially across the FPGA, though for simplicity the SLR boundary (boundary between the two silicon dies in the XCKU115 FPGA) is not crossed.

5.2 Evaluation

To evaluate the various NMUs based on the descriptions in Section 3, each of those design decisions is compared on an area utilization and unloaded latency basis. Note, such designs would generally be evaluated in terms of throughput as well, but all of the packet processing components used in this work operate at the 10Gbps line-rate of the Ethernet controller (i.e., the throughput of all NMUs is 10Gbps); by extension, the maximum design frequency is also an irrelevant value since the frequency is determined by the frequency required by the Ethernet controller to operate at its target line-rate (the frequency used is 156.25MHz). All of the results are shown in Table 2.

5.2.1 Access Control. Part (b) of Table 2 shows the area and latency results of the four different types of NMUs. The Type A NMU, as expected, has the lowest area and latency, though this is likely because the Type A NMU does not need on-FPGA switching to allow the hardware applications to communicate (The Bridge Port Extensions E-tag standard allows for hairpin routing). The encapsulation based NMU has a slightly lower utilization, indicating that Type E NMUs might be preferable to reduce area utilization, though this is at the cost of slightly increased latency caused by the included segmented FIFOs in the packet path. Finally, we note that the added overhead of implementing some destination-based access controls (i.e. Type C NMUs) is fairly minimal.

5.2.2 Virtualization. The results of the evaluation for the two virtualized networking NMUs are shown in Part (c) of Table 2. The VLAN based virtualization solution uses about the same amount of resources as the Type B and Type C NMUs from Part (b), though

Table 2: NMU Area and Latency Comparisons

	CLB LUTs	Flip-Flops	Latency (cyc.) out/in
(a) Universal	23,014 (3.47%)	16,336 (1.23%)	13–18 / 19–25
(b) Access Control Evaluation			
Type A-etag	4049 (0.61%)	5010 (0.38%)	1 / 4–6
Type BR-L2	7199 (1.09%)	4311 (0.32%)	5–10 / 6–8
Type CR-L2	7424 (1.12%)	4378 (0.33%)	5–10 / 6–8
Type ER-L2	6133 (0.92%)	4316 (0.33%)	6–7 / 8–10
(c) Virtualization Evaluation			
Type ARv	7218 (1.09%)	5827 (0.44%)	6–8 / 8–10
Type ERv	9606 (1.45%)	5628 (0.42%)	6–7 / 9–15
(d) Routability Evaluation			
Type Av	3753 (0.57%)	4582 (0.35%)	1 / 4–6
Type B-L2	3516 (0.53%)	2883 (0.22%)	1–6 / 2–4
Type C-L2	3687 (0.56%)	2867 (0.22%)	1–6 / 2–4
Type E-L2	3392 (0.51%)	3113 (0.23%)	1 / 4–6
(e) Network Layer Evaluation			
Type CR-L2	7424 (1.12%)	4378 (0.33%)	5–10 / 6–8
Type CR-L3	11,645 (1.76%)	6372 (0.48%)	6–11 / 7–12
Type CR-L4	12,550 (1.89%)	7053 (0.53%)	6–11 / 7–12

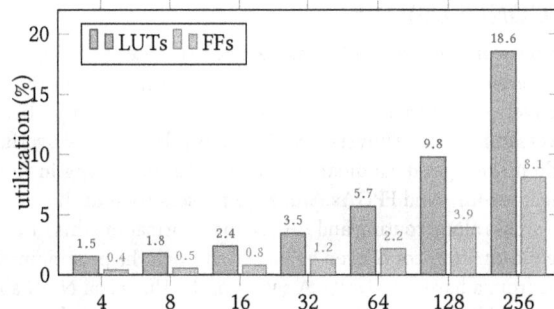

Figure 8: Universal NMU utilization vs number of logical connections

there is added latency from the tagging functionality. The VXLAN virtualized solution has a much higher utilization because it must parse a full Layer 4 packet first before identifying the virtual ID and routing the packet. The modest area overhead relative to the other NMUs might be worth it considering the ease of deployment, and ubiquity, of virtual network solutions.

5.2.3 Routability. Dropping the requirement that there be routability between co-resident hardware applications cuts the area utilization in half for the Type B and Type C NMUs, and nearly in half for the other NMUs, as shown in Part (d) of Table 2. There is also a drop in latency from removing the switching. Note, while there are area and latency benefits to dropping the routability, it likely will lead to a more difficult system to manage, as described in Section 3.3.1.

5.2.4 Network Layer. From Part (e) of Table 2, we note that the biggest increase in area utilization yet in this evaluation is a result of elevating functionality to Layer 3 (IP4) and Layer 4 (Transport) of the Network stack. There is a 57% increase in LUT utilization from Layer 2 to Layer 3, suggesting that much of the area utilization is in parsing and controlling the IPv4 network packets. Previous FPGA works have built on top of Layer 2 network Packets (e.g. Byma et. al. [10]), but higher layer protocols may be needed if FPGAs span broadcast domains.

5.2.5 Universal NMU. The Universal NMU's latency and area results are shown in Part (a) of Table 2. There is a considerable, though not unreasonable, increase in latency over other NMU solutions. This is expected, as more pipeline stages were required to meet timing and all packets must pass through both tagging and encapsulation stages. The latency numbers shown assume no UDP

checksum calculation; if a checksum is to be calculated in UDP-Encap mode (i.e. Type ER-L4), the entire packet would need to be buffered during the computation. This adds an additional 190 cycles for a maximally-sized packet of 1522 bytes.

The total area utilization is just under 3.5% of the LUTs available on the FPGA, which includes LUTs configured as logic as well as LUTs configured as LUTRAMs and Shift Registers. In terms of flip-flops, the Universal NMU's utilization is just 1.23%, so overall the area overhead of the NMU is quite modest. Figure 8 shows how the Universal NMU scales with number of logical connections, reaching to just over 18% LUTs and 8% of FFs at 256 connections. This low utilization can be attributed to the modified parser design discussed in Section 4.1.1, and the pairing-down of network security functionality from a fully functional switching capability to the minimally necessary access controls of the NMU. Our Universal NMU design did not scale well beyond 256 logical connections (failed to route); this may limit future applications, especially those secured at Layer 4 since using more than 256 ports (TCP/UDP) is fairly common in the software domain.

The Universal NMU is fairly small compared to the Kintex Ultrascale XCKU115 FPGA. When the Universal NMU was run through place and route for a Virtex Unltrascale+ XCKVU13P, it required only 1.32% of the LUTs and 0.44% of the FFs. As FPGAs increase in size, the resource needs of the NMU solution approach nearly negligible quantities. This small size also suggests that hardening the NMU would not need a significant allocation of die area.

Finally, the Universal NMU can be compared to a full switch solution implemented on an FPGA. The solution presented in [22] is a relatively low utilization OpenFlow switch implemented on a Xilinx Virtex-7 VX485T FPGA. That solution uses 15.93% of the LUTs and 7.84% of the FFs. When the Universal NMU (with 32 logical connections) was run through place and route for this FPGA, it required 7.36% of the LUTs and 2.48% of the FFs. This is less than half the LUTs and less than a third of the FFs compared to the full switch solution. Note, this OpenFlow switch we compare to is actually quite a simplified OpenFlow implementation that includes only a single (banked) OpenFlow Table. While it does enable ACLs that are not possible with the Universal NMU, this comparison shows that the NMU solution exhibits much lower overhead than even the simplest of OpenFlow switches.

6 CONCLUSIONS

As a network security solution, particularly one targeting virtualized environments, the NMU is a low overhead solution that effectively covers many FPGA deployment use-cases. In particular, the versatility of the Universal NMU and its relatively low overhead would make a good candidate component for hardening in future datacenter-targeted FPGAs. Since the parsers used in this design simply pass along routing and ACL status information, this intermediate information could even be passed through the programmable fabric from a hardened NMU. A subset of the Universal NMU's features could be hardened (e.g. Type B-L2), leaving optional features, or even custom protocols, to be implemented in the fabric using this intermediate interface.

While the solution presented does provide a great deal of flexibility in implementing FPGA network security, there are some shortcomings that could be investigated in future work. More complex network management features, such as stateful connection tracking or Network Address Translation (NAT), might be useful. In addition, many FPGAs are moving to 100 Gbps or faster network speeds; future NMUs could target these network speeds. The work presented here only considered a single network interface, though multiple network interfaces could also be considered, which would likely increase the total overhead of the system in a trade-off for total system bandwidth. Finally, determining exactly which types and features of NMUs to implement/harden will always be a function of the tenable restrictions that can be applied to FPGA-targeted hardware applications; further and ongoing investigation of this is always necessary.

The evaluation presented in this work shows the hardware overhead of the NMU solution, though future work should also evaluate the software overhead of NMU management. As mentioned in Section 3.1, the level of ACLs provisioned within the NMU, and by consequence the level of ACLs that must be implemented in the next level switch, greatly impact the management complexity of the solution. Much of this management complexity is realized in the software of the cloud management framework. The impact of using different types of NMUs on this software should be studied, especially in the context of ACL update and migration operations. In addition, the NMU should be tested with real applications within a functional cloud deployment in future work, to evaluate the impact on such datacenter-scale FPGA deployments of the NMU solution.

Securing network access for direct-connected FPGAs is a vital part in enabling FPGA deployments in cloud and datacenter settings. To facilitate this security, we contend that the NMU should be as ubiquitous for network-connected FPGAs as the MMU is for modern-day CPUs.

7 ACKNOWLEDGMENTS

We would like to thank and acknowledge Xilinx, Huawei, and NSERC for the funding and material provided for this project.

REFERENCES

[1] [n. d.]. Amazon EC2 F1 Instances. aws.amazon.com/ec2/instance-types/f1/ [Accessed: 8-April-2018].
[2] 2006. IEEE Standard for Local and Metropolitan Area Networks—Virtual Bridged Local Area Networks. *IEEE Std 802.1Q-2005 (Incorporates IEEE Std 802.1Q1998, IEEE Std 802.1u-2001, IEEE Std 802.1v-2001, and IEEE Std 802.1s-2002)* (May 2006), 1–300.
[3] 2012. IEEE Standard for Local and metropolitan area networks–Media Access Control (MAC) Bridges and Virtual Bridged Local Area Networks–Amendment 21: Edge Virtual Bridging. *IEEE Std 802.1Qbg-2012 (Amendment to IEEE Std 802.1Q-2011 as amended by IEEE Std 802.1Qbe-2011, IEEE Std 802.1Qbc-2011, IEEE Std 802.1Qbb-2011, IEEE Std 802.1Qaz-2011, IEEE Std 802.1Qbf-2011, and IEEE Std 802.aq-2012)* (July 2012).
[4] 2012. IEEE Standard for Local and metropolitan area networks–Virtual Bridged Local Area Networks–Bridge Port Extension. *IEEE Std 802.1BR-2012* (July 2012).
[5] 2016. *SDAccel Environment*. Technical Report UG1164 v2016.3. Xilinx.
[6] 2018. *AXI4-Stream Infrastructure IP Suite*. Technical Report PG085 v2.2. Xilinx.
[7] M. Attig and G. Brebner. 2011. 400 Gb/s Programmable Packet Parsing on a Single FPGA. In *2011 ACM/IEEE Seventh Symposium on Architectures for Networking and Communications Systems*. 12–23. https://doi.org/10.1109/ANCS.2011.12
[8] P. BenÁącek, V. Pu, and H. KubÁątovÁą. 2016. P4-to-VHDL: Automatic Generation of 100 Gbps Packet Parsers. In *2016 IEEE 24th Annual International Symposium on Field-Programmable Custom Computing Machines (FCCM)*. 148–155. https://doi.org/10.1109/FCCM.2016.46
[9] Abhishek Bhattacharjee and Daniel Lustig. 2017. Architectural and Operating System Support for Virtual Memory. *Synthesis Lectures on Computer Architecture* 12, 5 (2017), 1–175. https://doi.org/10.2200/S00795ED1V01Y201708CAC042
[10] S. Byma, J. G. Steffan, H. Bannazadeh, A. L. Garcia, and P. Chow. 2014. FPGAs in the Cloud: Booting Virtualized Hardware Accelerators with OpenStack. In *IEEE 22nd Annual International Symposium on Field-Programmable Custom Computing Machines*. 109–116. https://doi.org/10.1109/FCCM.2014.42
[11] A. M. Caulfield, E. S. Chung, A. Putnam, H. Angepat, J. Fowers, M. Haselman, et al. 2016. A Cloud-Scale Acceleration Architecture. In *2016 49th Annual IEEE/ACM International Symposium on Microarchitecture (MICRO)*. 1–13. https://doi.org/10.1109/MICRO.2016.7783710
[12] Ramaswamy Chandramouli. 2016. *Secure Virtual Network Configuration for Virtual Machine (VM) Protection*. National Institute of Standards and Technology.
[13] Fei Chen, Yi Shan, Yu Zhang, Yu Wang, Hubertus Franke, Xiaotao Chang, and Kun Wang. 2014. Enabling FPGAs in the Cloud. In *Proceedings of the 11th ACM Conference on Computing Frontiers (CF '14)*. ACM, New York, NY, USA, Article 3, 10 pages. https://doi.org/10.1145/2597917.2597929
[14] P. Chow. 2016. An Open Ecosystem for Software Programmers to Compute on FPGAs. In *FSP 2016; Third International Workshop on FPGAs for Software Programmers*. 1–11.
[15] S. A. Fahmy, K. Vipin, and S. Shreejith. 2015. Virtualized FPGA Accelerators for Efficient Cloud Computing. In *2015 IEEE 7th International Conference on Cloud Computing Technology and Science (CloudCom)*. 430–435. https://doi.org/10.1109/CloudCom.2015.60
[16] P. Garg and Y. Wang. 2015. NVGRE: Network Virtualization Using Generic Routing Encapsulation. *IETF RFC 7637* (September 2015).
[17] B. Ho, C. Pham-Quoc, T. N. Thinh, and N. Thoai. 2016. A Secured OpenFlow-Based Switch Architecture. In *2016 International Conference on Advanced Computing and Applications (ACOMP)*. 83–89. https://doi.org/10.1109/ACOMP.2016.021
[18] M.Mahalingam, D. Dutt, K. Duda, P. Agarwal, L. Kreeger, T. Sridhar, M. Bursell, and C. Wright. 2014. Virtual eXtensible Local Area Network (VXLAN): A Framework for Overlaying Virtualized Layer 2 Networks over Layer 3 Networks. *IETF RFC 7348* (August 2014).
[19] Andrew Putnam, Adrian Caulfield, Eric Chung, Derek Chiou, Kypros Constantinides, John Demme, et al. 2014. A Reconfigurable Fabric for Accelerating Large-Scale Datacenter Services. In *Proceeding of the 41st Annual International Symposium on Computer Architecuture (ISCA)*. IEEE Press, 13–24.
[20] John E. Stone, David Gohara, and Guochun Shi. 2010. OpenCL: A Parallel Programming Standard for Heterogeneous Computing Systems. *IEEE Des. Test 12*, 3 (May 2010), 66–73. https://doi.org/10.1109/MCSE.2010.69
[21] Naif Tarafdar, Thomas Lin, Eric Fukuda, Hadi Bannazadeh, Alberto Leon-Garcia, and Paul Chow. 2017. Enabling Flexible Network FPGA Clusters in a Heterogeneous Cloud Data Center. In *Proceedings of the 2017 ACM/SIGDA International Symposium on Field-Programmable Gate Arrays (FPGA '17)*. ACM, New York, NY, USA, 237–246. https://doi.org/10.1145/3020078.3021742
[22] V. B. Wijekoon, T. M. Dananjaya, P. H. Kariyawasam, S. Iddamalgoda, and A. Pasqual. 2016. High performance flow matching architecture for OpenFlow data plane. In *2016 IEEE Conference on Network Function Virtualization and Software Defined Networks (NFV-SDN)*. 186–191. https://doi.org/10.1109/NFV-SDN.2016.7919496

HeteroCL: A Multi-Paradigm Programming Infrastructure for Software-Defined Reconfigurable Computing

Yi-Hsiang Lai[1]*, Yuze Chi[2], Yuwei Hu[1], Jie Wang[2], Cody Hao Yu[2, 3], Yuan Zhou[1], Jason Cong[2], Zhiru Zhang[1]*

[1] School of Electrical and Computer Engineering, Cornell University, USA
[2] Computer Science Department, University of California, Los Angeles, USA
[3] Falcon Computing Solutions, Inc., USA
*{yl2666,zhiruz}@cornell.edu

ABSTRACT

With the pursuit of improving compute performance under strict power constraints, there is an increasing need for deploying applications to heterogeneous hardware architectures with accelerators, such as GPUs and FPGAs. However, although these heterogeneous computing platforms are becoming widely available, they are very difficult to program especially with FPGAs. As a result, the use of such platforms has been limited to a small subset of programmers with specialized hardware knowledge.

To tackle this challenge, we introduce HeteroCL, a programming infrastructure composed of a Python-based domain-specific language (DSL) and an FPGA-targeted compilation flow. The HeteroCL DSL provides a clean programming abstraction that decouples algorithm specification from three important types of hardware customization in compute, data types, and memory architectures. HeteroCL further captures the interdependence among these different customization techniques, allowing programmers to explore various performance/area/accuracy trade-offs in a systematic and productive manner. In addition, our framework produces highly efficient hardware implementations for a variety of popular workloads by targeting spatial architecture templates such as systolic arrays and stencil with dataflow architectures. Experimental results show that HeteroCL allows programmers to explore the design space efficiently in both performance and accuracy by combining different types of hardware customization and targeting spatial architectures, while keeping the algorithm code intact.

ACM Reference Format:
Yi-Hsiang Lai, Yuze Chi, Yuwei Hu, Jie Wang, Cody Hao Yu, Yuan Zhou, Jason Cong, Zhiru Zhang. 2019. HeteroCL: A Multi-Paradigm Programming Infrastructure for Software-Defined Reconfigurable Computing. In *The 2019 ACM/SIGDA International Symposiumon Field-Programmable Gate Arrays (FPGA '19), February 24–26, 2019, Seaside, CA, USA*. ACM, New York, NY, USA, 10 pages. https://doi.org/10.1145/3289602.3293910

1 INTRODUCTION

Recent trends in technology scaling have led to a growing interest in non-traditional architectures that incorporate heterogeneity and specialization as a means to improve performance under strict power and energy constraints [4, 8–10, 16]. Heterogeneous architectures with extensive use of accelerators, such as GPUs and FPGAs, have shown significant potential in this role to bring in orders-of-magnitude improvement in computing efficiency for a wide range of applications. Along this line, the latest advances in the industry have produced highly integrated heterogeneous hardware platforms, such as the CPU+FPGA multi-chip packages by Intel [19] and the GPU/FPGA-enhanced AWS cloud by Amazon [29]. Although these heterogeneous computing platforms are becoming commercially available to a wide user base, they are challenging to program, especially with FPGAs. As a result, the use of such platforms has been limited to a small subset of programmers with specialized knowledge on low-level hardware details.

To address this deficiency, recent years have seen promising development on high-level synthesis (HLS) for FPGAs [12]. This is evidenced by the availability of commercial C++/OpenCL-to-FPGA solutions (e.g., Altera/Intel SDK for OpenCL [19] and Xilinx Vivado HLS [40]) and a rapidly growing number of FPGA designs synthesized by these tools [2, 18, 35, 42]. However, programming high-performance FPGA applications with HLS tools requires a deep understanding of hardware details and is entirely different from traditional software programming. In particular, current programming models for HLS entangle algorithm specifications with hardware customization techniques. This approach has several drawbacks: (1) In order to achieve good quality-of-results (QoRs), programmers are required to use various vendor-specific data types and pragmas/directives [43], rendering FPGA-targeted applications even less flexible and portable; (2) Existing HLS programming models cannot cleanly capture the interdependence among different hardware optimization techniques, thus weakening the support of user-guided or automatic design space exploration. For example, there is no easy way to inform the HLS tool that the shape of an on-chip buffer (e.g., depth and number of banks) directly depends on the degree of parallelization; (3) HLS users need to extensively restructure the source program to guide the tool to realize specialized architectures such as data reuse buffers and systolic arrays, which are nontrivial to describe with imperative code in C/C++.

There exists an active body of work attempting to further democratize accelerator programming by using domain-specific languages (DSLs) to simplify the development and optimization of applications in certain fields. For example, Halide [32] and Spark [41] are widely used in image processing and big data analytics, respectively. Another relevant example is TVM, which is a Python-based DSL for high-performance deep learning applications [6]. Similar to Halide, TVM separates the algorithm from temporal schedule optimization (e.g., loop tiling and reordering), which significantly improves code portability across different CPU and GPU architectures.

Along this direction, we propose HeteroCL — a multi-paradigm programming infrastructure for software-defined heterogeneous computing, currently targeting CPU+FPGA platforms. HeteroCL builds on the TVM framework and extends it by explicitly exposing heterogeneity in two dimensions: (1) in programming model with mixed declarative and imperative code, and (2) in optimization with decoupled algorithm and compute/data customization. HeteroCL is designed to retain the distinct strengths of each programming paradigm/customization technique, but eliminates the complexity in using them together in a single application. More concretely, our main technical contributions are as follows:

- The HeteroCL DSL provides a clean programming abstraction that decouples algorithm specification from three important types of hardware customization in compute, data types, and memory architectures. It further captures the interdependence among different types of hardware customization, enabling productive and systematic design space exploration.

- Unlike existing DSLs which primarily focus on separating algorithm specifications from temporal compute schedule, HeteroCL further supports bit-accurate types and enables decoupling between algorithms and data quantization schemes. This allows the programmer to productively express and explore the rich design trade-offs between performance/area and accuracy.

- HeteroCL nicely blends declarative symbolic expressions with imperative code. It also provides a unified interface to specify customization schemes for both declarative and imperative programs. This allows our framework to support a broad range of applications.

- The HeteroCL framework produces highly efficient spatial architectures by incorporating state-of-the-art HLS optimizations such as PolySA [13] for systolic arrays and SODA [7] for stencil with dataflow architectures. This allows productive and effective acceleration of many popular workloads from image processing and machine learning domains.

- We have developed a fully automated compilation flow from a HeteroCL program to heterogeneous compute platforms integrating CPUs and FPGAs. Our compiler generates LLVM code on CPUs and HLS code for FPGA targets (currently using the Merlin compiler [11]).

The remainder of this paper is organized as follows — In Section 2, we introduce HeteroCL with a motivating example and then describe each of its features in detail; Section 3 presents the HeteroCL compilation flow; We report the evaluation results in Section 4 and compare with related work in Section 5; Section 6 concludes this work and outlines future research directions.

2 THE PROGRAMMING MODEL

Figure 1 shows the overview of the proposed framework, where the input is a HeteroCL program composed of an algorithm specification and decoupled hardware customization schemes. We then lower it to an intermediate representation (IR) extended from Halide [32]. After that, we compile it to the back end specified by the users.

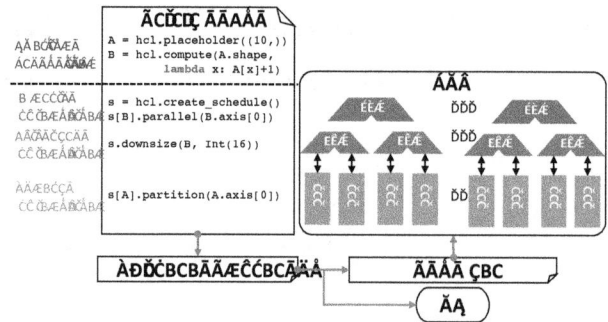

Figure 1: Overview of the HeteroCL framework.

HeteroCL is a Python-based DSL extended from TVM [6][1]. We choose TVM for the following reasons: (1) Python-based DSL provides programmers with a rich set of productive language features such as introspection and dynamic type system. (2) TVM is a tensor-oriented declarative DSL. Its declarative style is similar to TensorFlow [1], which compiles and executes the computation graph constructed by a programmer. This approach is beneficial for uncovering more high-level optimization opportunities in extracting parallelism and maximizing data reuse. (3) TVM inherits the idea of decoupling the algorithm specification from the temporal schedule, which is first proposed by Halide [32].

In addition to the features offered by TVM, HeteroCL further exposes heterogeneity in two dimensions: in hardware optimization techniques and programming paradigms. Figure 1 shows the key strength of HeteroCL, where HeteroCL programs can exploit various hardware optimization techniques efficiently by decoupling the algorithm specification from three classes of common hardware customization for FPGAs, which are compute, data type, and memory customization. HeteroCL further provides a clean abstraction to capture the interdependence among different optimization techniques. Moreover, HeteroCL integrates imperative programming with an embedded tensor-oriented programming model for the applications with regular parallelism. Users can choose the programming model that fits best to express a given component.

In the rest of the section, we first use a motivating example to show how HeteroCL abstracts different types of hardware customization and captures their interdependence. We then describe each customization in more detail. Finally, we present the imperative DSL in HeteroCL.

2.1 A Motivating Example

We use dot product operation as a motivating example that utilizes all three types of hardware customization. Figure 2a shows the host program, where we compute the dot product between vectors A and B. We offload function dot_product (L14) to FPGA for acceleration. Note that we need to batch the inputs due to FPGA on-chip resource limitation (L9). Before sending the batched inputs to the accelerator via DMA, we pack them to fully utilize the off-chip memory bandwidth (L12-13).

Figure 2b shows the optimized dot_product program implemented in HLS C++ code, where we apply all three types of hardware customization. First, we utilize data type customization by quantizing the data type of local buffers local_A and local_B from floating to fixed-point type DType (L4). By reducing the bitwidth DW, we increase the number of elements per memory I/O access, which shortens the

---

[1]Section 5 discusses the major differences between TVM and HeteroCL in more detail.

```
1 #define N = 1024
2 #define BATCH = 32
3 #define MB = 64  /* off-chip memory bandwidth */
4 #define DW = 32  /* bitwidth of the data element */
5 #define PAR = 8  /* parallelization factor */
6
7 typedef MType ap_uint<MB>;
8 void host_sw(float A[N], float B[N], float& sum){
9   for(int i = 0; i < N; i += BATCH) {
10    MType* vec_A;
11    MType* vec_B;
12    pack(A + i, vec_A);
13    pack(B + i, vec_B);
14    sum += dot_product(vec_A, vec_B);
15  }
16 }
```

(a) Host program

```
1 typedef DType fixed<DW, 2>;
2
3 DType dot_prodcut(MType* vec_A, MType* vec_B) {
4   DType local_A[BATCH], local_B[BATCH];
5   #pragma HLS partition variable=local_A factor=PAR
6   #pragma HLS partition variable=local_B factor=PAR
7   unpack(vec_A, local_A); unpack(vec_B, local_B);
8
9   DType psum = 0;
10  for (int i = 0; i < BATCH/PAR; i++)
11    #pragma HLS pipeline II=1
12    for (int j = 0; j < PAR; j++)
13      #pragma HLS unroll
14      psum += local_A[i*PAR+j] * local_B[i*PAR+j];
15  return psum;
16 }
```

(b) Optimized HLS code

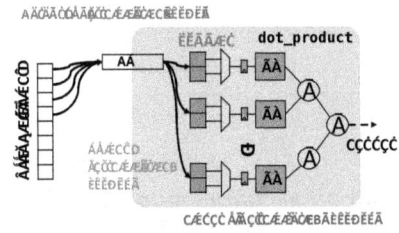

(c) Hardware diagram

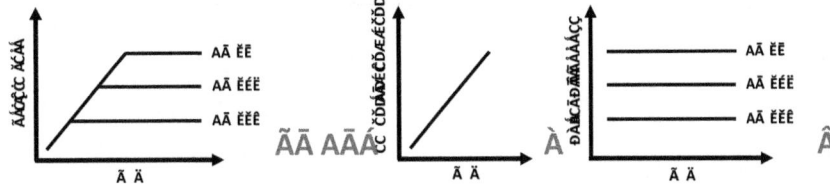

(d) Roofline diagram

Figure 2: Motivating example: dot product — This example demonstrates the interdependence between the parallelization factor PAR and the data bitwidth DW. By tuning them with different values, the performance of the whole design can be bounded by either the compute throughput (if PAR is too small) or the number of elements per I/O access (if DW is too large).

```
1 import heterocl as hcl
2 # algorithm
3 i = hcl.reduce_axis(0, BATCH)
4 psum = hcl.compute((1,), lambda x:
5   hcl.sum(A[i]*B[i], axis=i))
6 # customization primitives
7 s = hcl.create_schedule()
8 i, j = s[psum].split(i, PAR)
9 s[psum].pipeline(i)
10 s[psum].unroll(j)
```

(a) HeteroCL program

```
1 // algorithm only
2 for(int i = 0; i < BATCH; i++)
3   psum += A[i] * B[i];
4
5 // primitives applied
6 for(int i = 0; i < BATCH/PAR; i++)
7   #pragma HLS pipeline II=1
8   for(int j = 0; j < PAR; j++)
9     #pragma HLS unroll
10    psum += A[i*PAR+j] * B[i*PAR+j];
```

(b) Equivalent HLS code

Figure 3: Example of compute customization in HeteroCL.

```
1 # algorithm
2 vec_A = hcl.placeholder((128,), UInt(64))
3 local_A = hcl.unpack(vec_A)
4
5 # quantization scheme 1
6 s1 = hcl.create_scheme()
7 s1.quantize(local_A, Fixed(32, 30))
8
9 # quantization scheme 2
10 s2 = hcl.create_scheme()
11 s2.quantize(local_A, Fixed(8, 6))
```

(a) HeteroCL program

(b) Results after unpack

Figure 4: Example of data type customization in HeteroCL — Here we unpack the data sent from DMA vec_A to a local buffer local_A. The shape of the local buffer varies according to the quantization schemes. If we quantize local_A to a 32-bit/8-bit fixed-point buffer, each element of vec_A will be unpacked to two/eight elements in local_A.

data transfer latency but introduces the trade-off between throughput and accuracy. Second, we apply memory customization by using partition pragmas to bank the buffers (L5-6). Finally, we apply compute customization to improve the performance by tiling the loop (L10, 12) and using parallelization pragmas (L11, 13). This results in PAR processing elements (PEs) computing the multiplication and accumulation in parallel. With larger PAR, we achieve higher compute throughput with the trade-off of more on-chip resource. Moreover, there exists an interdependence between compute and memory customization, where we need to match the number of PEs with the memory banking factor. In this specific example, we set both parameters to PAR. Finally, we show the hardware diagram in Figure 2c, where we illustrate each type of hardware customization.

In addition, it is important to balance the computation time and the data communication time to maximize the hardware efficiency. Specifically, we need to carefully balance the two components by tuning the data bitwidth DW and the number of PEs PAR. We increase the compute throughput by increasing PAR. We also increase the number of elements per I/O access by lowering DW. However, the final performance is bounded by the minimum of the two. We use the Roofline [39] diagram in Figure 2d to show the relation between DW and PAR.

Figure 3 shows how we apply compute customization in HeteroCL. First, we define the algorithm in Figure 3a, where we first import the

HeteroCL module (L1), define the range to be sum up (L3), and use a vector/tensor-oriented *compute operation* hcl.compute to describe the multiplication and accumulation operation that sums across i and returns a scalar (L4-5). The equivalent HLS code is shown in Figure 3b (L1-3). After that, we apply *compute customization primitives*, which are called scheduling functions in Halide/TVM, to a customization scheme created in separation of the algorithm (L7). The first primitive is a loop transformation primitive which splits loop i into a two-level nested loop i and j by a factor PAR (L8). We further apply two parallelization primitives that pipeline the outer loop i (L9) and unroll the inner loop j (L10). The equivalent code after applying customization primitives is in Figure 3b (L5-10). We can see that after applying primitives, we need to restructure the HLS code, while in HeteroCL, the algorithm specification stays unchanged.

Unlike existing DSLs, we further decouple the algorithm from data type customization. Figure 4 shows the results of applying decoupled quantization schemes in HeteroCL. In the algorithm specification, we unpack data transmitted from the 64-bit DMA vec_A to a local

```
1  # memory customization primitives
2  s = hcl.create_schedule()
3  s[local_A].partition(dim=1, factor=PAR)
```

(a) HeteroCL program

```
1  DType local_A[BATCH];
2  #pragma HLS partition variable=local_A factor=PAR
```

(b) Equivalent HLS code

Figure 5: Example of memory customization in HeteroCL.

```
1   # algorithm specification
2   def dot_product(vec_A, vec_B):
3     local_A = hcl.unpack(vec_A, name="local_A")
4     local_B = hcl.unpack(vec_B, name="local_B")
5     i = hcl.reduce_axis(0, BATCH, "i")
6     return hcl.compute((1,),
7       lambda x: hcl.sum(local_A[i] * local_B[i], axis=i),
8       name="psum")
9
10  # exploring a range of DW and PAR
11  for DW in [4, 8, 16, 32]:
12    for PAR in [4, 8, 16, 32]:
13      # key parameters that depend on data bitwidth (DW)
14      DType = hcl.Fixed(DW, DW-2)
15      MType = hcl.UInt(MB)
16      NPACK = BATCH*DW/MB
17
18      vec_A = hcl.placeholder((NPACK,), dtype=MType)
19      vec_B = hcl.placeholder((NPACK,), dtype=MType)
20      psum = hcl.placeholder((1,), dtype=DType)
21      # data type customization
22      sm = hcl.create_scheme([vec_A, vec_B, psum], dot_product)
23      sm.quantize([dot_product.vec_A,
24                   dot_product.vec_B], DType)
25      # compute customization
26      sl = hcl.create_schedule_from_scheme(sm)
27      i, j = sl[dot_product.psum].split(dot_product.i, PAR)
28      sl[dot_product.psum].pipeline(i)
29      sl[dot_product.psum].unroll(j)
30      # memory customization
31      sl[dot_product.local_A].partition(dim=1, factor=PAR)
32      sl[dot_product.local_B].partition(dim=1, factor=PAR)
33
34      f = hcl.build(sl)
35      # evaluate f and pick the best customization scheme
36      if QoR(f) > best_QoR:
37        best_QoR = QoR(f)
38        best_scheme = sl
```

Figure 6: Complete dot product example in HeteroCL — This example demonstrates how HeteroCL explores the interdependence between the data bitwidth DW and parallelization factor PAR.

Table 1: Compute customization primitives currently supported by HeteroCL.

Primitive	Description
Loop transformation	
C.split(i, v)	Split loop i of operation C into a two-level nest loop with v as the factor of the inner loop.
C.fuse(i, j)	Fuse two sub-loops i and j of operation C in the same nest loop into one.
C.reorder(i, j)	Switch the order of sub-loops i and j of operation C in the same nest loop.
P.compute_at(C, i)	Merge loop i of the operation P to the corresponding loop level in operation C.
Parallelization	
C.unroll(i, v)	Unroll loop i of operation C by factor v.
C.parallel(i)	Schedule loop i of operation C in parallel.
C.pipeline(i, v)	Schedule loop i of operation C in pipeline manner with a target initiation interval v.

```
1   def knn(test_img, train_img):
2     diff = hcl.compute((10, 1800),
3       lambda x, y: train_img[x][y] ^ test_img, "diff")
4     dist = hcl.compute(diff.shape,
5       lambda x, y: popcount(diff[x][y]), "dist")
6     knn_mat = hcl.compute((10, 3), lambda x, y: 50, "init")
7     hcl.mutate(dist.shape,
8       lambda x, y: update_knn(dist, knn_mat, x, y), "update")
9     return knn_mat
10
11  s = hcl.create_schedule([test_img, train_img], knn)
12  # loop transformation primitives
13  s[knn.diff].compute_at(s[knn.update], knn.update.axis[0])
14  s[knn.dist].compute_at(s[knn.update], knn.update.axis[0])
15  s[knn.update].reorder(knn.update.axis[1], knn.update.axis[0])
16  # parallelization primitives
17  s[knn.update].parallel(knn.update.axis[1])
18  s[knn.update].pipeline(knn.update.axis[0])
```

Figure 7: Example of combining different compute customization primitives in HeteroCL.

buffer local_A without specifying the implementation (Figure 4a L3). Then, we create a quantization scheme (L6) and quantize local_A to a 32-bit fixed-point buffer using a *quantization primitive* (L7). The result of unpacking is illustrated in Figure 4b. We can get a buffer with a different shape by quantizing to another bitwidth with a separate scheme (L10-11), while the algorithm stays the same.

Similar to decoupled compute and data type customization, we further decouple the algorithm from memory customization. In Figure 5a, we first create a customization scheme (L2). We then specify the *memory customization primitive* (L3). Equivalent HLS code is shown in Figure 5b.

Finally, Figure 6 shows the complete dot product kernel in HeteroCL, where we cleanly separate the algorithm specification (L1-8) from the hardware optimization specification (L14-32). We first apply

data type customization to quantize the local buffers for better utilization of the off-chip memory bandwidth (L22-24). We then specify compute customization to tile and parallel the main computation for higher compute throughput (L26-29). Finally, we apply memory customization that banks the buffers to match the on-chip memory bandwidth with compute throughput (L31-32). Moreover, we use a two-level loop to explore the interdependence between DW and PAR (L11-12). We then evaluate the built kernel f generated by our back end for each pair of DW and PAR (L34) and pick the best scheme for final FPGA synthesis (L36-38).

In the following sections, we describe the syntax and semantics of HeteroCL for each type of customization in more detail.

2.2 Compute Customization

Compute customization improves the performance of a design by performing loop transformations and executing the computation in parallel. Similar to TVM [6], we decouple the algorithm specification from compute customization schemes. Table 1 lists compute customization primitives currently supported by HeteroCL. The primitives prevent programmers from using vendor-specific pragmas, which makes HeteroCL programs portable to different back ends.

Table 2: Data types currently supported by HeteroCL.

Data Type	Description
Int(bw)	Bit-accurate signed integer with bw bits.
UInt(bw)	Bit-accurate unsigned integer with bw bits.
Fixed(bw, fr)	Signed fixed-point type with bw bits, where there are fr fractional bits.
UFixed(bw, fr)	Unsigned fixed-point type with bw bits, where there are fr fractional bits.
Float(bw)	Floating-point type with bw bits, where bw could be 64 or 32.

Table 3: Quantization primitives currently supported by HeteroCL.

Primitive	Description
quantize(t, d)	Quantize a list of tensors t from floating to fixed point type d in the format defined in Table 2.
downsize(t, d)	Downsize a list of tensors t from integers with larger bitwidth to integers d with smaller bitwidth in the format defined in Table 2.

Figure 7 shows an example of combining different types of compute customization primitives, where we implement KNN-based digit recognition in HeteroCL. The knn algorithm contains four operations, which are diff, dist, init, and update, respectively (L1-9). By merging different operations (L13-14), changing the loop order (L15), and applying parallelization schemes (L17-18), we can finally achieve more than 10× speedup on FPGA comparing with single-core single-thread CPU execution. We further show the step-by-step speedup results in Section 4.

2.3 Data Type Customization

Quantized computation using low-bitwidth integers and/or fixed-point types is an essential technique to achieve efficient execution on FPGAs. To represent bit-accurate data types, traditional C-based HLS tools use templates such as ap_int<> and ap_fixed<>. Although this approach allows programmers to parameterize the bitwidths, they need to run a separate script to iterate through different quantization schemes. HeteroCL addresses this challenge by utilizing Python classes to represent the data types, which allows users to try out different quantization schemes within the same program. Table 2 lists the data types currently supported by HeteroCL.

Even with the bit-accurate data type support, it remains a challenge for most application developers to determine the right data types with the right bitwidth to achieve the best trade-off between accuracy and efficiency. To solve this, HeteroCL further decouples the algorithm specification from quantization schemes. HeteroCL provides two quantization primitives in Table 3, where quantize(t, d) quantizes a list of floating-point variables t to a fixed-point type d whose format is defined in Table 2. In addition, downsize(t, d) reduces the precision of a list of integer variables t to an arbitrary-bit integer type d. With quantize and downsize, programmers can explore the trade-off between performance/area and accuracy by tuning the bitwidths of variables in the algorithm. Note that this decoupled approach is well-suited for automated bitwidth-tuning frameworks based on autotuning or rule-based heuristics. Users can further provide domain-specific knowledge such as the numerical range or the distribution of a variable to quantization primitives to guide the bitwidth searching process.

```
1  def lenet(img, w_cn1, w_cn2, w_fc1, w_fc2):
2      conv1 = conv2d_nchw(img, w_cn1, "conv1")
3      pool1 = max_pool(conv1, kernel=(2,2), stride=(2,2))
4      conv2 = conv2d_nchw(pool1, w_cn2, "conv2")
5      pool2 = max_pool(conv2, kernel=(2,2), stride=(2,2))
6      flat = flatten(pool2)
7      fc1 = dense(flat, w_fc1, "fc1")
8      fc2 = dense(fc1, w_fc2, "fc2")
9      return softmax(lenet, fc2)
10
11 for i in range(2, 33):
12     s = hcl.create_scheme([img, w_cn1, w_cn2, w_fc1, w_fc2], lenet)
13     s.quantize([lenet.conv1, lenet.conv2, lenet.fc1], Fixed(i, i-2))
14     f = hcl.build(s)
15     # run the inference and compute the accuracy
```

Figure 8: Example of exploring different quantization schemes in HeteroCL.

Table 4: Memory customization primitives currently supported by HeteroCL.

Primitive	Description
C.partition(i, v)	Partition dimension i of tensor C with a factor v.
C.reshape(i, v)	Pack dimension i of tensor C into words with a factor v.
memmap(t, m)	Map a list of tensors t with mode m to new tensors. The mode m can be either vertical or horizontal.
P.reuse_at(C, i)	Create a reuse buffer storing the values of tensor P, where the values are reused at dimension i of operation C.

Figure 8 shows an example of exploring different quantization schemes in HeteroCL, where we implement LeNet [26], a convolutional neural network (CNN) for digit recognition. The pre-trained model is in floating point. To explore different quantization schemes, we simply use a for loop to iterate through different bitwidths (L11). Since we know the output values of activation are between 1 and −1, we set the integer bitwidth to two (i.e., $i - (i - 2)$) (L13). We further present the evaluation results in Section 4.

2.4 Memory Customization

Accelerating applications on FPGAs usually requires a high on-chip memory bandwidth to match the throughput of massively parallel compute units. Without customized memory architectures such as reuse buffers, the memory bandwidth could become the main hindrance preventing designs from achieving better performance. We decouple the algorithm from the memory customization and provide a set of primitives (Table 4). Moreover, programmers can apply several customization primitives in a user-defined sequence, which is not possible using pragmas supported by existing HLS tools.

Figure 9 shows an example of specifying a sequence of memory customization primitives in HeteroCL and how we define custom memory hierarchy. Figure 9a shows the implementation of 3 × 3 convolution in HeteroCL (L1-7). To increase the on-chip memory bandwidth, we introduce two custom reuse buffers, which are lb (linebuffer) and wb (window buffer), respectively (L10-11). We introduce data reuse between tensors/buffers via the reuse_at primitive. Specifically, Lines 10 and 11 specify that lb reads values from i_img and wb reads values from lb, respectively. Figure 9b illustrates how the reuse buffers operate, with the arrows indicating the data movement in each cycle. The HeteroCL compiler automatically infers the shapes of the buffers and the data to be stored based the reuse axis specified in the primitive. In this example, since wb reuses at

```
1   # algorithm specification
2   def conv(i_img, kernel):
3       ri = hcl.reduce_axis(0, 3, 'ri')
4       rj = hcl.reduce_axis(0, 3, 'rj')
5       return hcl.compute((N-2, N-2), lambda i, j: hcl.sum(
6                   i_img[i+ri, j+rj] * kernel[ri, rj],
7                   axis=[ri, rj]), name='o_img')
8   # memory customization - custom reuse buffers
9   s = hcl.create_scheme([i_img, kernel], conv)
10  lb = s[i_img].reuse_at(conv.o_img, conv.i)
11  wb = s[lb].reuse_at(conv.o_img, conv.j)
```

(a) HeteroCL code

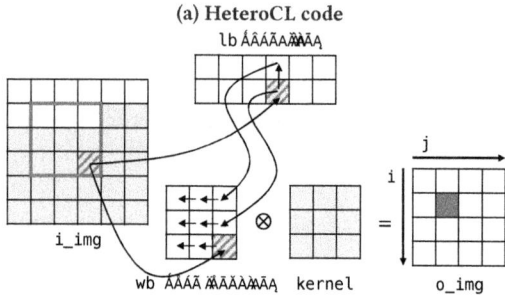

(b) Illustration of how reuse buffers operate in each cycle

Figure 9: Example of defining custom reuse buffers and their hierarchy in HeteroCL.

Table 5: Spatial architecture macros currently supported by HeteroCL.

Primitive	Description
C.stencil()	Specify operation C to be implemented with stencil with dataflow architectures using the SODA framework.
C.systolic()	Specify operation C to be implemented with systolic arrays using the PolySA framework.

loop j of operation o_img (L11), it contains data that are read in a single iteration of loop j, which corresponds to the red box in i_img. Similarly, the compiler infers the shape of lb, which stores the values of the yellow pixels in i_img.

2.5 Mapping to Spatial Architecture Templates

Many popular workloads from image/video processing and machine learning domains can be realized in a highly efficient manner on FPGAs using spatial architectures such as systolic arrays [33, 38]. However, with the traditional C-based HLS methodology, it typically requires extensive code restructuring and the insertion of a right combination of pragmas to guide the tool to generate a high-performance spatial architecture. This tedious and error-prone process is one of the major barriers for the mainstream adoption of HLS for FPGA designs. HeteroCL addresses this deficiency by introducing a set of optimization macros that synthesize the code into highly efficient spatial architecture templates. Each of these macros consists of a combination of compute and memory customization primitives. As indicated in Table 5, we currently support stencil with dataflow architectures and systolic arrays, each of which is described in more detail as follows.

Stencil with Dataflow Architecture – Stencil computation is commonly seen in many areas including image processing and numerical computing, where data elements are updated over a multidimensional grid according to some fixed, local patterns. HeteroCL incorporates the SODA framework [7], which synthesizes stencil

```
1   # algorithm specification
2   def jacobi(in_):
3     return hcl.compute(in_.shape, lambda y, x:
4         (in_[y, x-1] + in_[y-1, x] + in_[y, x] +
5         in_[y, x+1] + in_[y+1, x])/5), "out")
6   # apply compute customization and stencil macro
7   s = hcl.create_schedule([in_], jacobi)
8   s[jacobi.out].unroll(jacobi.out.axis[1], factor=3)
9   s[jacobi.out].stencil()
```

Figure 10: Example of mapping computations to stencil with dataflow architectures in HeteroCL.

patterns to a highly efficient dataflow architecture composed of reuse buffers and data streams. Figure 10 shows an example of mapping a Jacobi kernel to the stencil with dataflow architecture by using the macro s[jacobi.out].stencil() specified in Line 9. Given this macro, the HeteroCL back-end compiler will automatically identify the stencil pattern within the computation of out (L3-5) and synthesize the corresponding spatial architecture with the stencil back end (elaborated in Section 3).

```
1   # algorithm specification
2   def mmult(A, B):
3     k = hcl.reduce_axis(N)
4     return hcl.compute(A.shape,
5       lambda x, y: hcl.sum(A[x, k] * B[k, y], axis=k), "C")
6   # map to systolic arrays
7   s = hcl.create_schedule([A, B], mmult)
8   s[mmult.C].systolic()
```

Figure 11: Example of mapping a computation to systolic arrays in HeteroCL.

Systolic Array – HeteroCL further provides efficient support for mapping to systolic arrays, which are widely used spatial architectures that consist a group of processing elements locally connected to each other [25]. Featuring local interconnects and modular designs, the systolic array architecture is highly scalable and can take advantage of the enormous amount of computation resources on modern FPGAs. It is particularly suitable for applications having perfectly nested loops with uniform dependency, such as matrix-matrix multiplication. However, it is a complex task to manually create systolic array designs on FPGAs. Recent research from Intel reports that it takes several to tens of months of human effort to implement a high-performance systolic array design, even with an HLS design entry like OpenCL [33].

Similar to stencil optimization, we introduce a systolic macro in the HeteroCL DSL to allow convenient mapping from tensor code to systolic array architectures. Figure 11 shows an example of using the systolic macro for matrix-matrix multiplication. Here we specify the computation of C (L8) to be synthesized with a specialized back end, which incorporates the PolySA framework [13] for automatic systolic array generation (discussed in Section 3).

2.6 Mixed Declarative and Imperative Programming

HeteroCL blends imperative programming with an embedded declarative, symbolic style for expressing tensor-based code. The idea is to combine the advantages of both styles — Imperative programming is general and flexible, while symbolic tensorized code exposes higher-level optimization opportunities when the code allows. The flexibility offered by imperative programming enables designers to implement algorithms with less-regular parallelism that cannot be

```
1 BinOp    := + | - | * | / | % | & | ^ | >> | <<
2 BinEqOp := += | -= | *= | /=
3 CompOp   := > | >= | == | <= | = | < | !=
4 Expr     := Var | Tensor[Expr] | Number
5             | not Expr | Expr BinOp Expr
6             | Expr[Expr] # get bit
7             | Expr[Expr:Expr] # get slice of bits
8 Cond     := Expr Comp Epxr | hcl.and_(*Cond) | hcl.or_(*Cond)
9 CondStmt:= hcl.if_(Cond) | hcl.elif_(Cond) | hcl.else_()
10 Stmt    := Tensor[Expr] = Expr | Tensor[Expr] BinEqOp Expr
11            | Expr[Expr] = Expr # set bit
12            | Expr[Expr:Expr] = Expr # set slice of bits
13            | with CondStmt:
14                Stmt
15            | with hcl.for_(Expr, Expr, Expr) as Var:
16                Stmt
17            | # HeteroCL compute operations (e.g., compute)
18            | # And more
```

Figure 12: Imperative DSL in HeteroCL — We provide equivalent semantics for commonly used expressions and statements in normal Python. We also support bit-level operations for bit-accurate data types. The imperative DSL highly resembles normal Python in that they use same indentations, same rules for variable scope, and similar keywords. This relieves new users from learning a whole new set of syntax and semantics.

```
1 A = hcl.compute((10,), lambda x: x)
2 def popcount(num):
3   out = hcl.compute((1,), lambda x: 0, "out")
4   with hcl.for_(0, A.type.bits, 1, "loop1") as i:
5     out[0] += num[i] # bit selection operation
6   return out[0]
7 # extended TVM compute operation
8 B = hcl.compute(A.shape, lambda x: popcount(A[x]))
9 # decoupled data type customization
10 sm = hcl.create_scheme()
11 sm.downsize(B.out, h.UInt(4))
12 # decoupled compute customization
13 sl = hcl.create_schedule_from_scheme(sm)
14 sl[B].unroll(B.loop1)
```

Figure 13: Example of applying hardware customization to imperative DSL — We extend existing compute operations (e.g., compute) and customization primitives (e.g., unroll) in declarative code to further support imperative programming.

efficiently represented with declarative programming (e.g., sorting algorithms). It also gives full control to programmers for specifying the algorithmic details.

Some of the existing Python-based DSLs use normal Python to support imperative programming, such as TVM [6] and Hot&Spicy [34]. This approach, however, has some drawbacks: (1) The normal Python semantic is too flexible to be FPGA synthesizable. (2) A designated parser/compiler must be built, which could be error-prone. Instead of using normal Python to support imperative programming, HeteroCL provides an imperative DSL listed in Figure 12. HeteroCL further extends existing compute operations (e.g., compute) and develops new operations for mixed-paradigm programming. We show examples of supported compute operations in Table 6.

Programmers can also apply hardware customization to the imperative DSL. For instance, Figure 13 shows the popcount algorithm implemented using the imperative DSL, where we apply both compute and data type customization. Programmers access the vectors and loops declared within a HeteroCL compute operation by their names. For example, B.out in Line 11 refers to the vector out declared in Line 3; B.loop1 in Line 14 refers to the for loop loop1 in

Table 6: Compute operations currently supported by HeteroCL.

Operation	Description
compute(s, f)	Compute a new tensor of shape s. The value of each element in the new tensor is calculated according to lambda function f.
update(t, f)	Update each element of tensor t according to lambda function f.
mutate(s, f)	Write a for loop of shape s in vector code, where f is a lambda function describing the for loop body.

Line 4. Note that the algorithm behaves differently with different quantization schemes, where the bound of loop1 is determined by the bitwidth of A (Line 4).

3 BACK-END CODE GENERATION AND OPTIMIZATION

The HeteroCL framework has multiple back end supports including CPU and HLS flows targeting FPGA. Specifically, we extend the Halide IR used by TVM [6, 32] for our multi-paradigm programming model and customization primitives. The extended Halide IR serves as a unified representation for all back-end flows. In this section, we briefly summarize our FPGA back-end code generation flow.

General Back End – The HeteroCL compiler can generate a corresponding accelerator kernel in many languages, including HLS C/C++, OpenCL, and Merlin C. Merlin C is an OpenMP-like programming model used by the Merlin compiler [11] from Falcon Computing Solutions. We choose the Merlin compiler as one of our back-end tools for two reasons. First, it leverages a small set of OpenMP-like pragmas to apply certain architecture structures by source-to-source C code transformation. Since Merlin pragmas share lots of similarity with HeteroCL customization primitives, it is relatively straightforward to integrate with HeteroCL. Second, the Merlin compiler generates both HLS C kernels and OpenCL kernels for FPGAs from the unified Merlin C source code.

Table 8 shows the correspondence between HeteroCL primitives and Merlin C pragmas. The primitive unroll implies fine-grained parallelism, which indicates all loop body logic to be scheduled in the same hardware module. As a result, all sub-loops in the target loop is flattened if a user applies unroll to a non-innermost loop. On the other hand, the primitive parallel indicates coarse-grained parallelism (e.g., a PE array). In addition, if a pipeline primitive is assigned to a non-innermost loop, we map it to a coarse-grained pipeline architecture.

Since HeteroCL primitives and Merlin C pragmas mainly specify loop scheduling or memory organization, the implied architecture can be represented as a composable, parallel, and pipeline (CPP) architecture [14]. The authors in [14] have demonstrated that the CPP architecture can be applied to broad classes of applications with a good performance.

Stencil Back End – We incorporate the SODA framework proposed in [7] to implement stencil patterns with optimized dataflow architecture that minimizes the on-chip reuse buffer size. SODA takes in a lightweight DSL that describes the stencil compute patterns and design parameters. After the HeteroCL compiler identifies stencil patterns according to user-specified macros, it generates the proper DSL code to the SODA framework for hardware generation. In addition, hardware customization primitives such as loop unrolling and data quantization are also reflected in the SODA DSL as design parameters, which in turn guide the SODA framework for further optimization.

Table 7: Evaluation results of benchmarks in HeteroCL — The speedup is over a single-core single-thread CPU execution.

Benchmark	Data Sizes & Type	# LUTs	# FFs	# BRAMs	# DSPs	Freqency (MHz)	Speedup	Back End
KNN Digit Recognition [43] Image classification	K=3 #images=1800 uint49	4009	5835	88	0	250	12.5	General
K-Means Clustering	K=16 #elem=320 × 32 int32	212708	235011	32	1536	190.6	16.0	General
Smith-Waterman [36] Genomic sequencing	string len=128 uint2	110841	88369	1409	0	152.2	20.9	General
Seidel [30] Image processing / linear algebra	2160 pixel × 3840 pixel fixed16	21719	31663	46	96	250	5.9	Stencil
Gaussian [30] Image processing	2160 pixel × 3840 pixel fixed16	70833	131160	46	688	250	13.2	Stencil
Jacobi [30] Linear algebra	2160 pixel × 3840 pixel fixed16	14883	22485	46	48	250	5.0	Stencil
GEMM Matrix-matrix multiplication	1024 × 1024 × 1024 fixed16	454492	800283	932	2507	236.8	8.9	Systolic Array
LeNet Inference [26] Convolutional neural network	MNIST [15] fixed16	362291	660186	739.5	1368	250	10.6	Systolic Array

Table 8: Correspondence between HeteroCL primitives and Merlin C pragmas.

```
unroll(i, v) → #pragma ACCEL parallel flatten factor=v
```
Partial unroll the target loop by factor i and fully unroll all its sub-loops.

```
parallel(i) → #pragma ACCEL parallel
```
Wrap the body of loop i to a function and form a PE array.

```
pipeline(i, v) → #pragma ACCEL pipeline
```
Wrap the body of loop i to a function and form a load-compute-store coarse-grained pipeline.

Systolic Array Back End – Similar to the stencil back end, our compiler analyzes the user-specified systolic macros and generates annotated HLS C++ code as an input to the PolySA framework [13], which further performs automated design space exploration that optimizes the systolic array architecture including the shape of it and the interconnection between PEs.

4 EVALUATION

In this section, we evaluate the accelerators generated by HeteroCL. The platform we target is the AWS EC2 f1.2xlarge instance, which has 8 vCPU cores, 122GiB main memory, and a Xilinx Virtex Ultra-Scale+™ VU9P FPGA. The default target frequency for this platform is 250 MHz.

We select several common FPGA benchmarks from a broad range of applications that are applied with either general, stencil, or systolic array back ends. For the general back end, we have (1) KNN-based digit recognition, which is simplified from that of Rosetta [43], (2) K-means algorithm, and (3) Smith-Waterman [36]. For the stencil back end, we have (1) Gaussian, (2) Jacobi, and (3) Seidel. All of them are from Polybench [30]. For the systolic back end, we use (1) general matrix multiplication (GEMM) and (2) deep learning inference with LeNet model [26]. Among these benchmarks, KNN-based digit recognition, K-means, and Smith-Waterman need to be implemented with the HeteroCL imperative DSL.

Table 7 shows the benchmarks and the overall evaluation results. We run the baseline designs on one CPU core with a single thread. For the two systolic benchmarks, we are comparing our FPGA implementations with the GEMM function provided in Intel MKL [20] and a LeNet model optimized with TVM [6], respectively. We include memory transfer time (i.e., between DDR4 and FPGA) as part of the

Table 9: Speedup over CPU with customization primitives.

Benchmark	No Primitive	+Parallel	+Loop Transform
KNN Digit Recognition	1.2	1.6	12.5
K-Means	1.9	2.8	16.0
Smith-Waterman	0.7	20.9	20.9

Table 10: Speedup over CPU for the stencil back end – To achieve a higher speedup, we apply both compute and data type customizations on top of stencil macro. The ideal speedup is determined by the maximum off-chip memory bandwidth.

Benchmark	+stencil	+unroll	+quantize	Ideal
Seidel	0.5	2.9	5.9	6.8
Gaussian	1.1	6.7	13.2	15.6
Jacobi	0.4	2.3	5.0	5.4

total run time. After applying proper customization primitives, we achieve up to 20.9× speedup for the benchmarks with the general back end. Moreover, we can achieve up to 13.2× and 10.6× speedup for benchmarks applied with stencil and systolic array back end, respectively. In the rest of this section, we show the detailed evaluation of each back end.

General Back End – We first evaluate the impact of HeteroCL customization primitives on performance with the general back end. Table 9 shows the speedup of generated accelerator kernels after step-by-step applications of customization primitives. We first show the speedup without applying any customization primitive and that after applying parallelization primitives such as unroll and parallel. However, without applying appropriate loop transformation primitives such as split and reorder, the performance improvement could be limited. Thus, we also show the results after applying those primitives to the benchmarks. Table 9 demonstrates the permutability of HeteroCL, where programmers can easily explore the design space just by adding or removing primitives without changing the algorithm code.

Stencil Back End – Table 10 shows the speedup of the benchmarks after applying the stencil macro, customization primitives, and the ideal speedup. If we only apply the macro, we are only up to 1.1× faster because of the limited parallelism. To improve the performance, we apply parallelization primitives (i.e., unroll), which

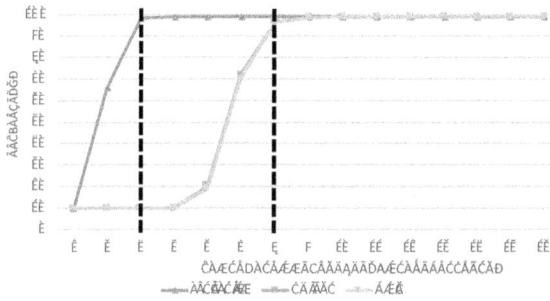

Figure 14: Accuracy of LeNet with different quantization schemes.

Table 11: Performance results of systolic array benchmarks – The performance is in terms of Giga operations per second (GOPs).

Benchmark	Backend	Data Type	Performance (GOPs)	Speedup
LeNet Inference	CPU [6]	float32	15.4	1.0
	FPGA	float32	79.8	5.2
		fixed16	137.8	8.9
GEMM	CPU [20]	float32	76.0	1.0
	FPGA	float32	245.9	3.2
		fixed16	807.6	10.6

results in up to 6.7× speedup. At this stage, since the performance bottleneck of all benchmarks is the off-chip memory bandwidth (about 13.8GB/s), we cannot get higher throughput by further increasing the unrolling factor. To address this, we quantize the single-precision floating-point numbers to 16-bit fixed-point numbers. As a result, the required external memory bandwidth could be reduced and we can achieve an additional 2× speedup. As a reference, the last column shows the ideal speedup assuming the memory bandwidth is perfectly utilized. In summary, Table 10 shows that by combining spatial architecture macros with other types of hardware customization, we can further improve the performance.

Systolic Array Back End – We finally evaluate the benchmarks applied with systolic macros. For both applications, we evaluate the impact of data type customization on performance, which we present in Table 11. By using both spatial architecture macros and data type customization primitives, we can improve the performance of both designs.

We further show the accuracy results after applying different quantization schemes to LeNet benchmark in Figure 14, where the X-axis shows the number of total bitwidth and the Y-axis shows the accuracy. We demonstrate three different scenarios, which are quantizing the activation, weights, and both, respectively. We observe that with 8-bit fixed-point type, the accuracy degradation is marginal. Moreover, if we choose to quantize the activation only, 4-bit fixed-point type is the best choice.

5 RELATED WORK

There exists a large body of work on HLS and domain-specific programming. In this section, we survey a small subset of representative efforts on C-based HLS, DSLs for hardware accelerator designs, and those that support decoupled algorithm and optimizations.

C-based HLS – HLS tools such as LegUp [5], Intel FPGA SDK [21], and Xilinx Vivado HLS [40] allow developers to write FPGA designs in C/C++ and OpenCL, delivering higher productivity than traditional register-transfer-level (RTL) designs. The recently introduced Merlin compiler greatly simplifies the HLS design by applying source-to-source transformation to automatically generate optimized HLS-C or OpenCL programs [11]. However, to achieve good QoRs, developers are required to use various vendor-specific data types and pragmas/directives, rendering FPGA design with HLS less flexible and portable.

HeteroCL lifts the abstraction level of FPGA programming and provides developers with a systematic way to efficiently explore various trade-offs, making FPGA design more portable and productive.

DSLs for Hardware Accelerator Design – There is a growing interest in compiling programs written in high-level languages (e.g., Python, Scala) into reconfigurable hardware accelerators. Hot & Spicy compiles annotated Python code into HLS C/C++, where the annotations are translated into pragmas [34]. DHDL introduces a representation of hardware using parameterized templates in Scala that captures locality and parallelism information and compiles the representation into FPGAs and CGRAs [24]. Spatial extends DHDL by adding a set of low-level abstractions for control and memory [23]. However, in these DSLs the algorithm specification is tightly entangled with hardware optimizations, making design space exploration less productive.

HeteroCL decouples algorithm specification from hardware customization, and abstracts three important types of hardware customization into a set of customization primitives, enabling productive and systematic design space exploration. HeteroCL further offers additional macros in stencil and systolic for efficient mapping to highly optimized spatial architecture templates.

DSLs with Decoupled Algorithm and Optimization – Most computing patterns in image processing and deep learning can be concisely described as nested loops in a declarative programming paradigm, as illustrated in a lot of DSLs [17, 22, 27, 37]. Halide first proposes to decouple the algorithm specification from the temporal schedule [32]. Tiramisu extends Halide by adding explicit communication, synchronization, and mapping buffers to different memory hierarchies [3, 33]. Jing Pu, et al. also extend Halide to support custom reuse buffers and support FPGAs and CGRAs as back end [31]. T2S extends Halide by decoupling the spatial schedule from the algorithm specification, which allows programmers to define systolic-array-like architectures [33]. TVM builds a deep learning compiler stack on top of Halide IR, supporting both CPUs and GPUs [6]. While the declarative programming paradigm in these DSLs is powerful, it cannot express applications beyond image processing and deep learning.

HeteroCL, as a multi-paradigm programming infrastructure, nicely blends declarative symbolic expressions with imperative code, and provides a unified interface to specify customization schemes for both declarative and imperative programs. This allows HeteroCL to support a broader range of applications.

More specifically, we list the major differences between TVM and HeteroCL as follows: (1) TVM extensively uses declarative programming to target deep learning applications, while HeteroCL supports mixed imperative and declarative programming to target general applications. (2) TVM tries to solve the optimization challenges mainly for CPUs and GPUs, while HeteroCL focuses on hardware customization for FPGA and incorporates advanced spatial architecture templates. (3) TVM programs can target FPGAs as back end by using VTA, a programmable accelerator that uses a RISC-like programming abstraction to describe tensor operations [28]. On the other hand, HeteroCL programs are not limited to tensor operations.

In addition, programmers can apply various hardware customization techniques with provided primitives while the hardware generated by VTA is pre-defined. (4) HeteroCL supports bit-accurate data types, which are not available in TVM. Furthermore, HeteroCL proposes to decouple the quantization scheme from algorithm specification.

6 CONCLUSIONS AND FUTURE WORK

We have presented HeteroCL, a multi-paradigm programming infrastructure for heterogeneous platforms integrating CPUs and FPGAs. HeteroCL not only provides a clean abstraction that decouples the algorithm from compute/data customization, but it also captures the interdependence among them. Moreover, HeteroCL incorporates spatial architecture templates including systolic arrays and stencil with dataflow architectures. We believe HeteroCL can help developers to focus more on designing efficient algorithms rather than being distracted by low-level implementation details.

We are releasing the proposed framework in an open-source format. The programming infrastructure as well as the associated documents and example designs are publicly available on the authors' website. Additionally, we plan to introduce primitives for data and device placement, and also data streaming interfaces. We will also integrate HeteroCL with more spatial architecture templates, distributed autotuning capabilities, and accurate QoR estimation boosted by machine learning techniques.

ACKNOWLEDGEMENTS

This research was supported in part by CRISP, one of six centers in JUMP, a Semiconductor Research Corporation (SRC) program sponsored by DARPA, NSF/Intel CAPA Award #1723773, DARPA Young Faculty Award D15AP00096, NSF Awards #1453378, #1436827, and #1707408, and research gifts from Intel and Xilinx. We thank Amazon for providing AWS EC2 credits. We thank Prof. Adrian Sampson (Cornell), Dr. Hongbo Rong (Intel), and Dr. Justin Gottschlich (Intel) for providing helpful feedback on the HeteroCL framework. We also thank Ritchie Zhao, Ziyan Feng, Shaojie Xiang, Yichi Zhang, Patrick Clobridge, and Qing Yu for their contributions to the HeteroCL benchmarks.

REFERENCES

[1] M. Abadi, A. Agarwal, P. Barham, E. Brevdo, Z. Chen, C. Citro, G. S. Corrado, A. Davis, J. Dean, M. Devin, et al. TensorFlow: Large-Scale Machine Learning on Heterogeneous Distributed Systems. *arXiv preprint arXiv:1603.04467*, 2016.

[2] A. Althoff and R. Kastner. A Scalable FPGA Architecture for Nonnegative Least Squares Problems. *Int'l Conf. on Field Programmable Logic and Applications (FPL)*, 2015.

[3] R. Baghdadi, J. Ray, M. B. Romdhane, E. Del Sozzo, P. Suriana, S. Kamil, and S. Amarasinghe. Tiramisu: A Code Optimization Framework for High Performance Systems. *arXiv preprint arXiv:1804.10694*, 2018.

[4] S. Borkar and A. A. Chien. The Future of Microprocessors. *Communications of the ACM*, 2011.

[5] A. Canis, J. Choi, M. Aldham, V. Zhang, A. Kammoona, J. H. Anderson, S. Brown, and T. Czajkowski. LegUp: High-level Synthesis for FPGA-Based Processor/Accelerator Systems. *Int'l Symp. on Field-Programmable Gate Arrays (FPGA)*, 2011.

[6] T. Chen, T. Moreau, Z. Jiang, H. Shen, E. Yan, L. Wang, Y. Hu, L. Ceze, C. Guestrin, and A. Krishnamurthy. TVM: End-to-End Optimization Stack for Deep Learning. *arXiv preprint arXiv:1802.04799*, 2018.

[7] Y. Chi, J. Cong, P. Wei, and P. Zhou. SODA: Stencil with Optimized Dataflow Architecture. *Int'l Conf. on Computer-Aided Design (ICCAD)*, 2018.

[8] A. A. Chien, A. Snavely, and M. Gahagan. 10x10: A General-Purpose Architectural Approach to Heterogeneity and Energy Efficiency. *Procedia Computer Science*, 2011.

[9] E. S. Chung, P. A. Milder, J. C. Hoe, and K. Mai. Single-Chip Heterogeneous Computing: Does the Future Include Custom Logic, FPGAs, and GPGPUs? *Int'l Symp. on Microarchitecture (MICRO)*, 2010.

[10] J. Cong, M. A. Ghodrat, M. Gill, B. Grigorian, K. Gururaj, and G. Reinman. Accelerator-Rich Architectures: Opportunities and Progresses. *Design Automation Conf. (DAC)*, 2014.

[11] J. Cong, M. Huang, P. Pan, D. Wu, and P. Zhang. Software Infrastructure for Enabling FPGA-Based Accelerations in Data Centers. *Int'l Symp. on Low Power Electronics and Design (ISLPED)*, 2016.

[12] J. Cong, B. Liu, S. Neuendorffer, J. Noguera, K. Vissers, and Z. Zhang. High-Level Synthesis for FPGAs: From Prototyping to Deployment. *IEEE Trans. on Computer-Aided Design of Integrated Circuits and Systems (TCAD)*, 2011.

[13] J. Cong and J. Wang. PolySA: Polyhedral-Based Systolic Array Auto Compilation. *Int'l Conf. on Computer-Aided Design (ICCAD)*, 2018.

[14] J. Cong, P. Wei, C. H. Yu, and P. Zhang. Automated Accelerator Generation and Optimization with Composable, Parallel and Pipeline Architecture. *Design Automation Conf. (DAC)*, 2018.

[15] L. Deng. The MNIST Database of Handwritten Digit Images for Machine Learning Research. *IEEE Signal Processing Magazine*, 2012.

[16] H. Esmaeilzadeh, E. Blem, R. S. Amant, K. Sankaralingam, and D. Burger. Dark Silicon and the End of Multicore Scaling. *Int'l Symp. on Computer Architecture (ISCA)*, 2011.

[17] J. Hegarty, J. Brunhaver, Z. DeVito, J. Ragan-Kelley, N. Cohen, S. Bell, A. Vasilyev, M. Horowitz, and P. Hanrahan. Darkroom: Compiling High-Level Image Processing Code into Hardware Pipelines. *ACM Trans. Graph.*, 2014.

[18] G. Inggs, S. Fleming, D. Thomas, and W. Luk. Is High Level Synthesis Ready for Business? A Computational Finance Case Study. *Int'l Conf. on Field Programmable Technology (FPT)*, 2014.

[19] Intel. Xeon+FPGA Platform for the Data Center. https://www.ece.cmu.edu/ calcm/carl/lib/exe/fetch.php? media=carl15-gupta.pdf.

[20] Intel. Intel Math Kernel Library. 2007.

[21] Intel. Intel High Level Synthesis Compiler User Guide. 2017.

[22] F. Kjolstad, S. Kamil, S. Chou, D. Lugato, and S. Amarasinghe. The Tensor Algebra Compiler. *Int'l Conf. on Object-Oriented Programming, Systems, Languages, and Applications*, 2017.

[23] D. Koeplinger, M. Feldman, R. Prabhakar, Y. Zhang, S. Hadjis, R. Fiszel, T. Zhao, L. Nardi, A. Pedram, C. Kozyrakis, et al. Spatial: A Language and Compiler for Application Accelerators. *ACM SIGPLAN Conf. on Programming Language Design and Implementation (PLDI)*, 2018.

[24] D. Koeplinger, R. Prabhakar, Y. Zhang, C. Delimitrou, C. Kozyrakis, and K. Olukotun. Automatic Generation of Efficient Accelerators for Reconfigurable Hardware. *Int'l Symp. on Computer Architecture (ISCA)*, 2016.

[25] H. Kung and C. E. Leiserson. Systolic Arrays (for VLSI). *Sparse Matrix Proceedings*, 1979.

[26] Y. LeCun, L. Bottou, Y. Bengio, and P. Haffner. Gradient-Based Learning Applied to Document Recognition. *Proceedings of the IEEE*, 1998.

[27] R. Membarth, O. Reiche, F. Hannig, J. Teich, M. Körner, and W. Eckert. Hipa^{cc}: A Domain-Specific Language and Compiler for Image Processing. *IEEE Transactions on Parallel and Distributed Systems*, 2016.

[28] T. Moreau, T. Chen, Z. Jiang, L. Ceze, C. Guestrin, and A. Krishnamurthy. VTA: An Open Hardware-Software Stack for Deep Learning. *arXiv preprint arXiv:1807.04188*, 2018.

[29] D. Pellerin. Fpga accelerated computing using aws f1 instances. *AWS Public Sector Summit*, 2017.

[30] L.-N. Pouchet. Polybench: The Polyhedral Benchmark Suite. *URL: http://www. cs. ucla. edu/pouchet/software/polybench*, 2012.

[31] J. Pu, S. Bell, X. Yang, J. Setter, S. Richardson, J. Ragan-Kelley, and M. Horowitz. Programming Heterogeneous Systems from an Image Processing DSL. *ACM Trans. on Architecture and Code Optimization (TACO)*, 2017.

[32] J. Ragan-Kelley, C. Barnes, A. Adams, S. Paris, F. Durand, and S. Amarasinghe. Halide: A Language and Compiler for Optimizing Parallelism, Locality, and Recomputation in Image Processing Pipelines. *ACM SIGPLAN Notices*, 2013.

[33] H. Rong. Programmatic Control of a Compiler for Generating High-Performance Spatial Hardware. *arXiv preprint arXiv:1711.07606*, 2017.

[34] S. Skalicky, J. Monson, A. Schmidt, and M. French. Hot & Spicy: Improving Productivity with Python and HLS for FPGAs. *IEEE Symp. on Field Programmable Custom Computing Machines (FCCM)*, 2018.

[35] Z. Wang, B. He, and W. Zhang. A Study of Data Partitioning on OpenCL-Based FPGAs. *Int'l Conf. on Field Programmable Logic and Applications (FPL)*, 2015.

[36] M. Waterman. Identification of Common Molecular Subsequence. *Mol. Biol*, 1981.

[37] R. Wei, V. Adve, and L. Schwartz. DLVM: A Modern Compiler Infrastructure for Deep Learning. *arXiv preprint arXiv:1711.03016*, 2017.

[38] X. Wei, C. H. Yu, P. Zhang, Y. Chen, Y. Wang, H. Hu, Y. Liang, and J. Cong. Automated Systolic Array Architecture Synthesis for High Throughput CNN Inference on FPGAs. *Design Automation Conf. (DAC)*, 2017.

[39] S. Williams, A. Waterman, and D. Patterson. Roofline: An Insightful Visual Performance Model for Multicore Architectures. *Communications of the ACM*, 2009.

[40] Xilinx Inc. Vivado Design Suite User Guide: High-Level Synthesis. 2012.

[41] M. Zaharia, M. Chowdhury, M. J. Franklin, S. Shenker, and I. Stoica. Spark: Cluster Computing with Working Sets. *HotCloud*, 2010.

[42] R. Zhao, W. Song, W. Zhang, T. Xing, J.-H. Lin, M. Srivastava, R. Gupta, and Z. Zhang. Accelerating Binarized Convolutional Neural Networks with Software-Programmable FPGAs. *Int'l Symp. on Field-Programmable Gate Arrays (FPGA)*, 2017.

[43] Y. Zhou, U. Gupta, S. Dai, R. Zhao, N. Srivastava, H. Jin, J. Featherston, Y.-H. Lai, G. Liu, G. A. Velasquez, W. Wang, and Z. Zhang. Rosetta: A Realistic High-Level Synthesis Benchmark Suite for Software Programmable FPGAs. *Int'l Symp. on Field-Programmable Gate Arrays (FPGA)*, 2018.

AFFIX: Automatic Acceleration Framework for FPGA Implementation of OpenVX Vision Algorithms

Sajjad Taheri
University of California, Irvine
Irvine, CA
sajjadt@uci.edu

Payman Behnam
University of Utah
Salt Lake City, UT
behnam@cs.utah.edu

Eli Bozorgzadeh
University of California, Irvine
Irvine, CA
eli@ics.uci.edu

Alexander Veidenbaum
University of California, Irvine
Irvine, CA
alexv@uci.edu

Alexandru Nicolau
University of California, Irvine
Irvine, CA
anicolau@uci.edu

ABSTRACT

Computer vision algorithms are computationally expensive and difficult to implement efficiently. Field Programmable Gate Arrays (FPGA)s offer a promising direction to reduce the computation cost by exploiting hardware parallelism. However, it is difficult to translate vision algorithms to FPGA bitstream efficiently. OpenVX is an industry standard for graph-based representation of vision algorithms. It defines a set of widely used vision kernels and data structures that can be used to form a Directed Acyclic Graph (DAG) to represent a vision algorithm. This paper proposes a framework for automatic FPGA acceleration of computer vision algorithms based on OpenVX specification, called AFFIX. AFFIX receives a vision algorithm formed using the OpenVX and generates a heterogeneous CPU-FPGA implementation. AFFIX incorporates several high level and low-level optimization methods to improve the efficiency of the FPGA implementation. It provides a configurable and extensible framework that enables vision algorithm developers to quickly develop, verify and test FPGA implementations of vision algorithms. We demonstrate the effectiveness of the proposed framework via development and evaluations of multiple vision algorithms.

CCS CONCEPTS

• **Hardware** → *Hardware accelerators*; *Hardware-software codesign*; • **Computing methodologies** → *Computer vision*; • **Software and its engineering** → *Domain specific languages*.

KEYWORDS

Acceleration; Computer vision; FPGA; OpenVX; OpenCL

ACM Reference Format:
Sajjad Taheri, Payman Behnam, Eli Bozorgzadeh, Alexander Veidenbaum, and Alexandru Nicolau. 2019. AFFIX: Automatic Acceleration Framework for FPGA Implementation of OpenVX Vision Algorithms. In *The 2019 ACM/SIGDA International Symposium on Field-Programmable Gate Arrays (FPGA '19), February 24–26, 2019, Seaside, CA, USA*. ACM, New York, NY, USA, 10 pages. https://doi.org/10.1145/3289602.3293907

1 INTRODUCTION

The ever-growing usage of vision algorithms in our daily lives[1] requires developing fast, area-efficient and low-cost implementations. Computer vision algorithms are computationally expensive as they perform complex operations on a large number of frames and pixels. They exhibit an inherent parallelism such that a same set of operations is applied to each pixel. FPGAs have been shown to be very effective in accelerating various vision processing algorithms [2–5].Unfortunately, developers may not be familiar with FPGA design, let alone efficient implementation. Even a CPU implementation of vision algorithms using programming languages such as C/C++ is time consuming and error-prone. Moreover, despite advances in High Level Synthesis (HLS) tools, they are still not able to provide efficient hardware implementation for vision algorithms developed in general purpose programming languages, such as C++[6, 7]. The main reason is that HLS tools do not incorporate specific optimization methods of vision algorithms, which are critical to the efficient implementation of such algorithms.

To overcome the problems of general HLS tools, prior works provide HLS frameworks for image processing pipelines. PolyMage [8, 9] and Halide [10, 11] for both GPUs and FPGAs, and Rigel [12] for FPGAs are examples of such works. These frameworks provide a Domain Specific Language (DSL) that can be translated into a specific architecture by modifying compilation, scheduling, and binding phases during high-level synthesis.

Halide generates image processing pipeline from a custom DSL. However, it supports only simple kernels[1]. For instance, it cannot support geometric and statistical kernels, which are common in vision algorithms. It also leaves finding the proper scheduling to the user.

Rigel [13] extends Halide by supporting more advanced kernels, including multi-rate kernels and image pyramids while supporting both static and dynamic scheduling. However, it still does not support statistical and geometric kernels. In addition, it cannot handle CPU-targeted image processing algorithms.

---

[1]Definition of the kernels is provided in Table 1

PolyMage [8, 14] converts an image processing algorithm developed using a specific DSL into a parallel implementation. It makes use of a polyhedral compiler to optimize image processing applications using tiling, and fusion of image processing stages and memory allocation. Data-dependent operations, such as statistical and table lookup operations, and also computations that have a considerable input data reuse (e.g., matrix multiplication) are out of the PolyMages scope of polyhedral overlapped tiling analysis.

All these frameworks may require manual optimizations to exploit locality and parallelism, which require much time, efforts, and expertise [15]. Besides, the user is expected to know an additional programming language to describe the application at the high level of abstraction. Finally, popular vision libraries, such as OpenCV[16], only provide efficient implementations for CPUs and GPUs.

OpenVX [17] is an open standard for cross-platform acceleration of computer vision applications. It was created to address the challenges of efficient, portable and easy to use vision processing algorithms by separating algorithm specifications and implementation. OpenVX offers a set of basic and widely used vision kernels that accelerator vendors are supposed to support. Accelerator vendors such as Nvidia and AMD support OpenVX kernel implementations(NVidia VisionWorks [18] and AMD AmdoVX[19]). OpenVX graph-based abstraction makes developing vision algorithms easier and allows global optimizations to be applied the whole graph.

To address the problems of prior works, [20–22] develop solutions for FPGA implementation of OpenVX graphs. However, these solutions support only a limited set of OpenVX kernels and are not able to provide efficient implementations of those kernels. In addition, their methods are not able to support complex algorithms with many vision kernels. They also suffer from lack of automation, configurability, and hardware/software co-optimizations. In essence, none of the previous works were able to provide a general, portable and easy to use framework to convert a high-level algorithms to CPU-FPGA heterogeneous acceleration platforms.

This paper proposes an automatic framework called AFFIX to accelerate a wide variety of vision algorithms. The AFFIX's input is an algorithm representative DAG in a textual format developed by a user. The output is a heterogeneous implementation of the vision algorithm. AFFIX develops OpenVX elements using efficient and customizable OpenCL components. It applies several high- and low- level optimization methods yo the vision graph and employs the developed OpenCL library to generate an efficient implementation. AFFIX makes use of a fast OpenCL emulator provided by Intel OpenCL SDK that allows us to emulate the whole algorithm on CPU for verification purpose. AFFIX also supports compiling OpenCL-based vision kernels with profiling enabled that measures and reports performance of kernel execution on the FPGA.

In summary, AFFIX makes the following contributions:

- It develops a scalable OpenCL library of OpenVX kernels such that they can be configured using various input parameters. This library can be used in any OpenCL program independent of the AFFIX framework to provide efficient vision kernels implementation.
- Unlike previous work, AFFIX provides a heterogeneous framework that supports a wide variety of vision kernels on both

FPGAs and CPUs. Accordingly, AFFIX is able to support many complex vision algorithms.
- AFFIX transforms OpenVX graph-based algorithms to FPGA implementation by employing several high-level and low-level optimization techniques. This framework enables vision developers to develop, verify and test FPGA implementation of a vision algorithm quickly without the need to know a DSL or any software/hardware languages.

2 VISION ALGORITHM ELEMENTS

This section describes the graph elements that are available to developers through AFFIX framework. Developers are supposed to instantiate these elements and form an algorithm in a DAG format, where the DAG nodes represent data processing kernels while the edges represent data dependencies between kernels. Such a DAG is the input to AFFIX framework.[2]

2.1 Vision Function Nodes

OpenVX provides a set of widely used vision functions that can be used as basic blocks of more complex algorithms. We have thoroughly analyzed all the vision functions provided by OpenVX v1.2 and classified them based on their data access pattern. Table 1 lists various categories of vision functions supported by AFFIX framework. These categories comprise primitive functions such as *Pixel-wise, Fixed-rate Stencil, Multi-rate Stencil, Statistical, Geometric, and Table-lookup* and non-primitive functions that can be represented by a set of primitive functions. Fig. 1 demonstrates the behavior of each category. Such classification is useful for two reasons: (1) It allows AFFIX to only implement a generic form for each category. Generic implementations are highly optimized and can be customized at compile time to represent specific vision functions. This categorization also facilitates extending AFFIX with additional vision functions that are not part of the OpenVX specification. (2) Data access patterns provide guidance for AFFIX for graph optimization, graph pipelining and scheduling.

2.2 Data Object Nodes: Images, Scalars, Arrays

Different data objects such as images, scalars, and arrays with different types are available as inputs and outputs of vision function nodes. Data object types and sizes must be set during the DAG construction time by the vision developer.

2.3 Select Nodes

Select nodes are pixel-wise nodes with two input images and one output image, all with the same data type. A Boolean input value is used to select one of the inputs and set it as the output. They are used to implement predication in vision algorithms.

2.4 Delay Object Nodes

In video processing algorithms, the input DAG is invoked for each input frame. Several video processing algorithms require information from computations of previous frames. Delay objects are nodes that provide access to arbitrary data objects (image, array, scalar)

---

[2]The current implementation provides an API to describe the DAG in Python, but other methods such as a visual designer can be incorporated.

Category	Formal Definition	Vision Functions
Pixel-wise	out(x, y) = f(in(x, y))	absolute difference, accumulate, accumulate squared, accumulate weighted, addition/subtraction, bitwise operations, channel combine, channel extract, color convert, convert bit depth, magnitude, phase, pixel-wise multiplication, threshold, min, max
Fixed-rate Stencil	$out(x, y) = \sum_{i=-k}^{i=k} \sum_{j=-k}^{j=k} f(in(x + i, y + j))$	Box filter, Sobel filter, non-maxima suppression, custom convolution, erode, dilate, Gaussian blur, nonlinear filter, integral image, Median filter
Multi-rate Stencil	$out(x, y) = \sum_{i=-k}^{i=k} \sum_{j=-k}^{j=k} f(in(Nx + i, Ny + j))$	down-sample, scale image
Statistical	$out = \sum_{i=0}^{i=Width} \sum_{j=0}^{j=Height} f(in(i, j))$	histogram, mean, standard deviation, Min,max location
Geometric	out(x, y) = in(h(x, y), h'(x, y))	remap, warp affine, warp perspective
Table lookup	out(x, y) = table[in(x,y)]	table lookup
Non-primitive	N/A	equalize histogram, fast corners, Harris corners, Gaussian image pyramid, optical flow pyramids, Canny edges, LBP, HOG, HoughLinsP

Table 1: Categorization of supported OpenVX vision functions

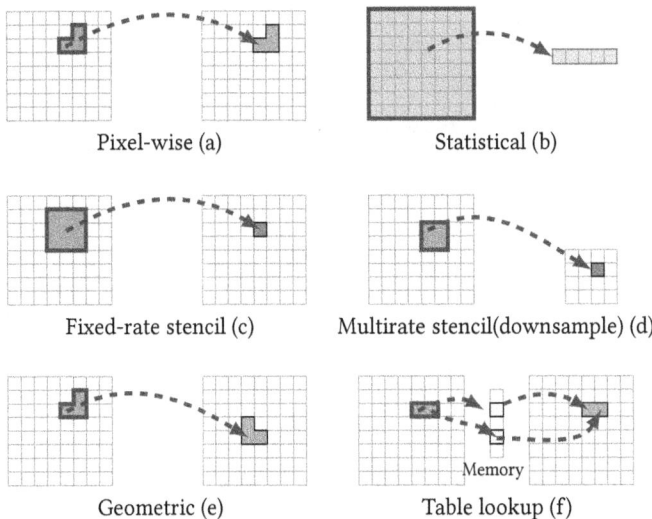

Pixel-wise (a)

Statistical (b)

Fixed-rate stencil (c)

Multirate stencil(downsample) (d)

Geometric (e)

Table lookup (f)

Figure 1: Vision function data access patterns.

from the "Nth"(N is a parameter provided by the developer) previous DAG invocation. AFFIX implements delay object nodes using circular arrays either on DRAM or BRAM (based on data size) and provides an interface to access them.

2.5 Case Study: Lane Detection (LD) Algorithm

One of the fundamental vision algorithms in autonomous driving cars is Lane Detection (LD). Many LD algorithms have been proposed over time[23, 24]. Testing proposed algorithms and implementing them on FPGAs are not straightforward. Fortunately, the AFFIX framework provides an easy to use platform to generate hardware accelerator of these algorithms. Throughout the paper, we will explain the steps that AFFIX takes to accelerate a simple LD algorithm shown in Fig. 2. Fig. 4 shows the output of different stages of the algorithm on a sample input frame. Color input frame captured by a camera in front of a vehicle (Fig. 4(a)) will be converted to a gray-scale image (Fig. 4(b)). Then, using a

perspective transform, a certain area of interest is considered for further processing (Fig. 4(c)). The image will be enhanced using a filter and threshold operation to highlight the lanes better (Fig. 4(d,e)). Finally, lane segments will be detected using probabilistic *Hough* transform (Fig. 4(f)).[3]

```
1    Inputs : Image in_img , Matrix transoform_mat , Matrix filter ,
2             Integer thresh_val
3    Output : Array line_segments
4    begin
5        y_img ← convert_to_grayscale (in_img)
6        b_img ← warp_perspective (y_img , transoform_mat)
7        f_img ← filter (b_img , filter)
8        t_img ← threshold (f_img , thresh_val)
9        line_segments ← houghlinsp (t_img)
10       return line_segments
11   end
```

Figure 2: Lane detection algorithm example

,

A vision developer can describe this algorithm quickly using AFFIX as illustrated in Fig. 3 where purple nodes represent vision functions and green nodes manifest data objects. AFFIX framework goal is to transform vision algorithms similar to the LD algorithm to FPGA-CPU implementation. Throughout the paper, we will use this example to demonstrate different steps of the framework.

---

[3]Hough transform algorithm detects curves (line, circle, etc) in an image [16]

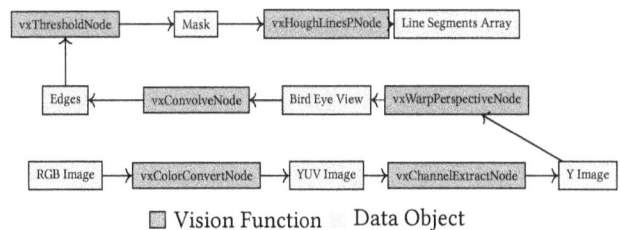

☐ Vision Function   Data Object

Figure 3: OpenVX DAG of lane detection example

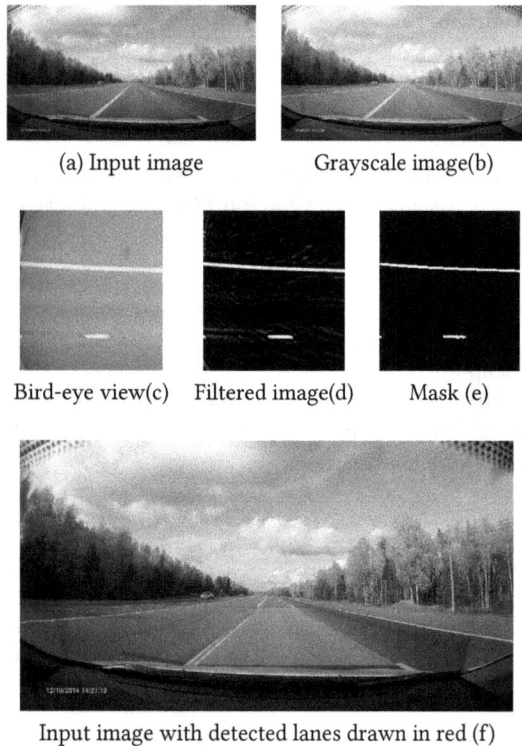

(a) Input image

Grayscale image(b)

Bird-eye view(c)   Filtered image(d)   Mask (e)

Input image with detected lanes drawn in red (f)

Figure 4: Demonstration of lane detection algorithm, (video obtained from intel.com)

3 AFFIX FLOW

This section describes the framework flow for transforming high-level vision algorithms described by a DAG to FPGA/CPU implementation. As depicted in Fig. 5 it consists of three phases to verify, analyze and generate the FPGA and CPU implementation. We describe each phase in more details in the Section 4. Users must describe the vision algorithm in a DAG format using the AFFIX provided API. Additionally, users can specify the SIMD-size as a parallelism parameter, which is helpful for design space exploration.

3.1 Verification

The first phase checks whether the input DAG follows the OpenVX specification rules. For instance, having loops in the graph is prohibited, and parameters passed to functions and images/arrays must have values within the valid range.

3.2 Analysis and Optimization

The Second phase starts with lowering the input DAG. The output of this step is a graph that only consists of primitive vision functions that are easier to analyze and optimize. Then, AFFIX applies high-level optimizations on the primitive graph resulting in a more efficient algorithm representation. Next, AFFIX splits the graph into CPU and FPGA partitions based on node availability and data dependency constraints. AFFIX aims to find the largest FPGA partitions that can be implemented as a single pipeline on the FPGA. Finally, FPGA-specific (low level) optimization techniques

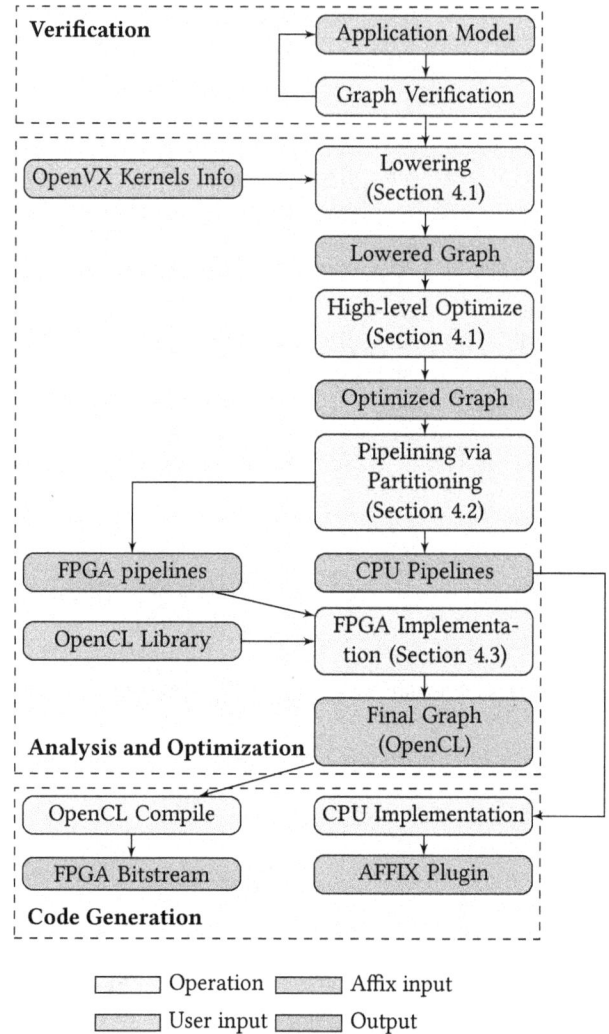

Figure 5: AFFIX framework flow

will be applied across FPGA partitions to obtain final optimized OpenCL code. In cases which there are multiple partitions, partitions are sorted based on the topological ordering and executed consecutively.[4]

3.3 Code Generation

The third phase generates both FPGA hardware and CPU software components of the system. FPGA components are implemented by specializing the constructs provided via an OpenCL library. OpenCL compiler is used to translate the generated OpenCL program into FPGA bitstream. In addition to a computational pipeline, the final hardware incorporates a standard PCI interface to the host, OpenCL controller logic, and an optional FPGA DRAM interface.

We have developed a host program that exploits OpenCL run-time API to allocate data on FPGA DRAM, pass kernel arguments, and coordinate execution of OpenCL kernels on FPGA. Software

---

[4]More optimized scheduling and execution are left for future work.

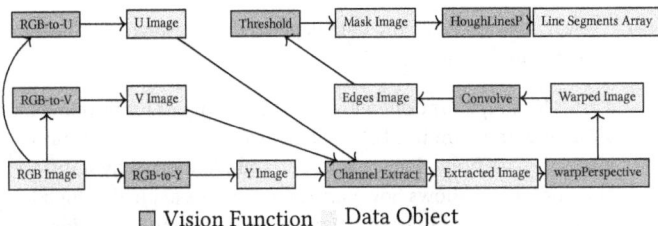

Figure 6: Lowered lane detection algorithm DAG

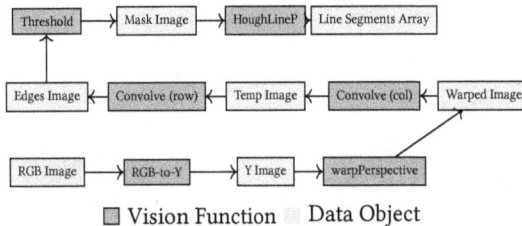

Figure 7: Optimized lane detection algorithm DAG

components are compiled separately as plugins (e.g., plugin.so) and are loaded at run-time by the host program. They implement an interface that allows the host program to invoke their vision functions.

4 AFFIX PRINCIPLES

This section describes the design principles of the AFFIX framework and how it deals with different implementation challenges.

4.1 High Level Optimizations

High-level optimizations prune and simplify the input DAG with the goal of achieving a more area- and latency-efficient hardware implementation. To enable these optimizations, vision functions nodes are already annotated with information such as data access pattern, input/output type, and their implementation using primitive kernels. These techniques are hardware-agnostic and do not need any information about the specific target FPGAs. Currently, AFFIX includes the following optimizations:

- Lowering: AFFIX lowers the DAG by replacing algorithm's non-primitive kernels (if any) with primitive kernels. Moreover, it replaces primitive kernels that have multiple outputs with multiple single output nodes. Graph lowering makes the analysis for applying optimizations simpler for AFFIX. Fig. 6 shows the transformed LD algorithm after applying the lowering step. For instance, in the case of LD algorithm, the non-primitive *vxColorConvertNode* kernel is replaced with three primitive kernels *RGBtoY,RGBtoU,RGBtoV*.
- Dead Node Elimination: This step eliminates graph nodes that are not connected to an output node. Fig. 7 demonstrates applying this step to the lowered LD algorithm. Since *ChannelExtract* node, only extracts Y Image, there will be no path from *RGB-to-U* and RGB-to-V nodes to the output. Therefore, AFFIX recognizes them as dead nodes and eliminates them from the graph.
- Separable and Symmetric Filter Implementation: Several vision functions have matrix convolution kernels. In these cases, if the coefficient matrices are separable, they can be implemented using two simpler convolutions where coefficients are two row and column matrices[25]. For instance, kernels such as *Gaussian Blur* have N*N matrix convulsions that can be represented as multiplication of two 1*N and N*1 matrices.

4.2 Pipelining using Graph Partitioning

Pipelining the input DAG on FPGA is the main technique to increase throughput. However, realizing all graph nodes on a single pipeline is not always feasible. First, all vision kernels cannot be implemented efficiently on FPGA. We have identified kernels that cannot run efficiently on FPGA in the current version of the framework.[5] If the input DAG contains one (or more) of the kernels, AFFIX will map them to the CPU for execution. For instance, AFFIX already knows *HoughLinesP* kernel in LD algorithm should be run on CPU (Fig. 3). Second, not all functions that are mapped to FPGA, can be part of the same pipeline. While, graphs that only consist of *pixel-wise, stencil, and table look-up* kernels can be implemented in a single pipeline, *statistical and geometric* kernels have data access dependencies that limit the pipelining opportunities. In such cases, AFFIX will split the graph into multiple partitions. Each partition is implemented as a separate pipeline. For instance, statistical nodes cannot be mapped to the same pipeline with their successors. The reason is that these kernels have to process the whole input before generating a valid output(e.g., mean() function). Hence, all of their downstream kernels must be implemented in different pipelines. Geometric nodes cannot be in the same pipeline as their predecessors. The reason is that inputs of geometric kernels cannot be streamed directly from the upstream kernel. This is due to fact that geometric kernels must access data in an order that is specified by a transformation matrix which is most likely different than the input stream order. Thus, the input stream must be entirely saved in memory first. Geometric nodes then can load the saved data and hence they must be the entry points of a new partition. Fig. 8 demonstrates partitioning of sample DAGs with various kernel types. DAG in the case (a) only consists of pixel-wise, stencil, and table look-up kernels. Thus, the whole DAG can be in a pipeline. Case (b) uses two statistical nodes (h and f). Hence, their successor nods (e,i) must be implemented as a separate pipeline. Case (c) uses two geometric transformation nodes (h,f). Therefore, they cannot be in the same partition as their predecessors. Case (d) uses two CPU nodes. CPU nodes cannot be part of any FPGA pipeline and for this reason, we need to have different partitions for CPU nodes, their successor, and their predecessors. Data communication between two FPGA partitions is done by using FPGA memory while FPGA and CPU partitions communicate through streaming channels. Given the mentioned partitioning constraints for a graph, there may be several valid partitioning schemes. Since we have

---

[5]Each kernel has special features and can be implemented on FPGA using several specific heuristics; however, it makes AFFIX very complex to implement all complex kernels on FPGA.

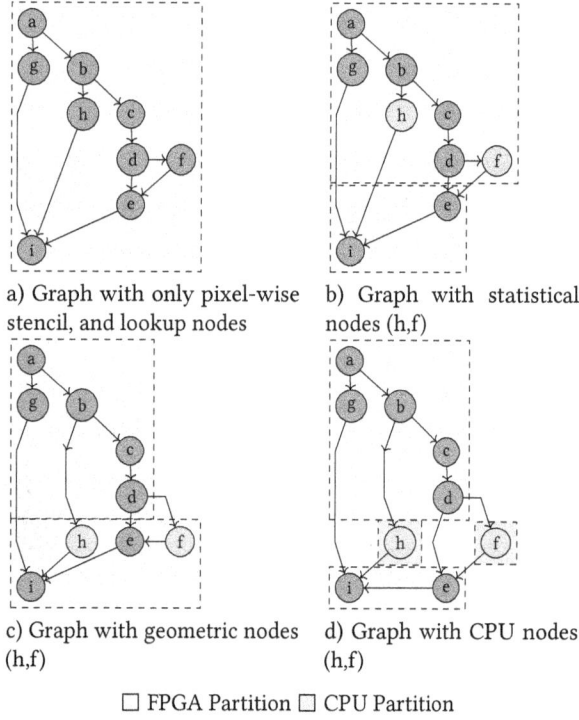

a) Graph with only pixel-wise stencil, and lookup nodes

b) Graph with statistical nodes (h,f)

c) Graph with geometric nodes (h,f)

d) Graph with CPU nodes (h,f)

☐ FPGA Partition ☐ CPU Partition

Figure 8: Partitioning of a sample algorithm graph with different vision node types composition

found the communication to be the major performance bottleneck, we formulated the partitioning problem as a Mixed Integer Linear Program (MILP) and aimed to find a partitioning that minimizes data communication across partitions described by Eq. 1. In this formulation, V is the set of DAG nodes and $E(u,v)$ specifies data transfer size between two nodes u and v. $conflict[u][v]$ is a table of Boolean values that specifies whether each pair of vertices in V cannot be mapped to the same partition (True case). The objective is to minimize equation 1 subjects to mapping and partitioning constraints. P_v in (2) is a variable that represents the partition number (a positive integer) that node v is mapped to. Y_{uv} is a Boolean variable which its true value indicates if two nodes u and v are mapped to different partitions. Constraint (4) sets the value of Y_{uv} to be 1 if $P_u! = P_v$ and constraint (5) enforces mapping of incompatible nodes to different partitions. To formulate constraint (4) in canonical MILP form, we used the well-known Big-M method[26]. In this method, M is an integer that must be larger than $|P_u - P_v|$. We picked M to be equal to the number of nodes in the graph.

$$Minimize \sum_{v \in V} \sum_{u \in V} E(u, v) \times y_{uv} \qquad (1)$$

subject to:

$$\forall v \in V : |V| > P_v > 0 \qquad (2)$$

$$\forall u, v \in V : Y_{u,v} \in \{0, 1\} \qquad (3)$$

$$\forall v, u \in V : Y_{uv} = 1 \; if \; P_u! = P_v \; else \; 0 \qquad (4)$$

$$\forall v, u \in V : Y_{uv} == conflict[u][v] \qquad (5)$$

Next, we describe how data dependency between partitions are implemented.

4.2.1 Inter Pipeline Communication. The pipeline partitioning module divides the primitive DAG obtained after high-level optimization into sub-partitions. Each partition is implemented by a different pipeline. Fig. 11 shows how partitioning can be applied to high level optimized DAG of LD algorithm. Algorithm graph is divided into three partitions: *HoughLinesP* function is implemented in a CPU partition. The rest of the graph is mapped to the FPGA. However, since *WarpPerspecitve* is a geometric function, graph is segmented into one more partitions.

4.2.2 Data Streaming Patterns. AFFIX instantiates vision functions and channels to form pipelines on the FPGA. Since the data will be streamed through the pipeline, all the vision functions on the pipeline must be able to process the input in the order that input data is being streamed. While pixel-wise, memory lookup, and statistical nodes can process images with any streaming order (i.e., cases a Fig.9), other vision functions can only operate on specific streaming patterns. For instance, stencil nodes which implement a sliding window can process data streamed in raster order. However, the sliding window implementation requires storing multiple rows of the input image around the current pixel. When processing large input data sets, this leads to over utilization of on-chip memory resources. To save on-chip memory resources, input data can be partitioned into sub- images with smaller width size (i.e., cases b Fig.9). This way, the sliding window size can be shrunk accordingly. Nevertheless, since pixels at sub-image boundaries are missing, sub-image processing must overlap with each other to cover the missing pixels, which leads to re-computation. Hence a balance between area-usage and re-computation must be considered. While both case b and c can work on stencil kernel and they have equal memory requirement, case b requires less re-computation since boundary area is smaller. In algorithms with up-sampling and down-sampling nodes, the window size of kernels that operates on down/up sampled images must be adjusted accordingly. For example, if the input data has a resolution of W*H, after going through down-sampling, it will be W/2*H/2. For case a, like multiple consecutive down-samples, at some points, the image becomes small and the width becomes very small, and cost of re-computation will be significant. In those cases, it is better to buffer data from multiple tiles first and then process them once enough data for processing the tile is gathered. Consequently, we need to employ a tile-based reordering. All data reordering is either done by the host or load/store units at partition boundaries if the streaming ordering required by partitions are not compatible.

4.3 OpenCL-based FPGA Implementation of Pipelines

This section describes the implementation of FPGA pipelines using OpenCL constructs provided by the library described in Section 2. Each vision element is instantiated and configured using a C-style macro in the OpenCL program. Vision function nodes operate on data streams specified by FPGA channels. They can be connected to form deep pipelines on the FPGA. Fig. 10 demonstrates general hardware realization of different categories of vision function nodes.

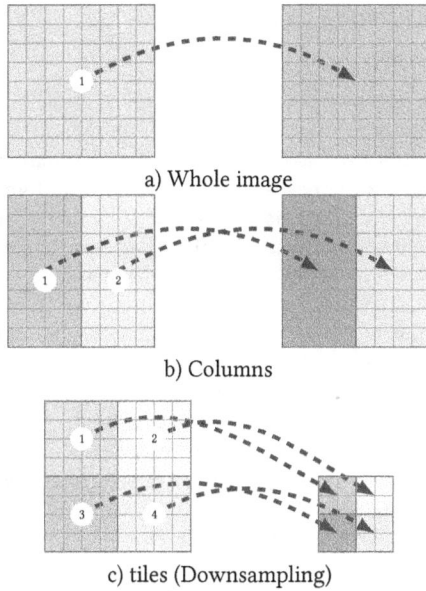

a) Whole image

b) Columns

c) tiles (Downsampling)

Figure 9: Different ways to partition and stream the images. Cases b and c assume sliding window implementation for images with 4 columns.(For all cases raster ordering is used.)

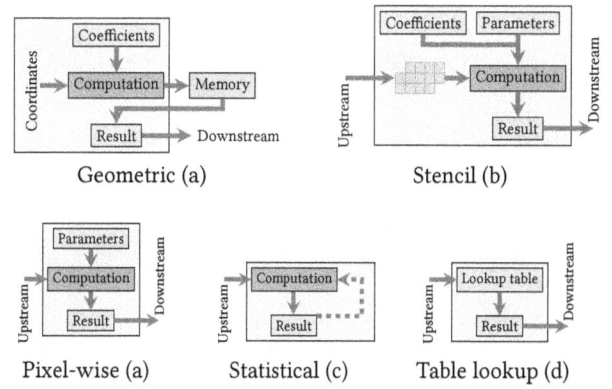

Geometric (a)   Stencil (b)

Pixel-wise (a)   Statistical (c)   Table lookup (d)

Figure 10: General implementation of different kernel categories

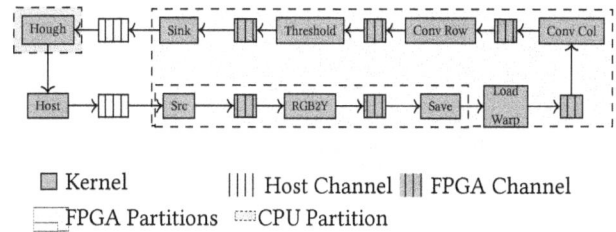

☐ Kernel |||| Host Channel |||| FPGA Channel
⌐ FPGA Partitions ⌐⌐⌐CPU Partition

Figure 11: Graph partitioning of the lane detection algorithm

Parameters that can configure the behavior of kernels at compile time include input/output data types (e.g., uchar, short, float), SIMD width to set the parallelism, numerical precision, and internal buffer size. Each kernel template also accepts an OpenCL function as the vision operator. Such functions can be developed by users to extend OpenVX list of vision functions. Most of the kernel parameters are either inferred from the provided DAG (e.g., input dimension, vision operator, matrix coefficients) or determined automatically using high level and low level optimization techniques (e.g. buffer size). The only parameter that has to be set by a user is SIMD width to adjust the favorite performance. Vision functions can be configured to operate on different values of SIMD width ranging from 1 to 32 (limited by hardware constraints such as communication bandwidth). By increasing SIMD width, kernels operate on superpixels, which are a collection of neighboring pixels. Fig. 12 shows the OpenCL program of LD vision algorithm using AFFIX provided components.

4.3.1 Inter Kernel Communication thorough Channels. Kernels communicate through channels in AFFIX framework. Channels are on-chip FIFOs that can be customized by their width (i.e., data size) and depth (i.e., number of elements). Channels are also used for storing scalar values and small arrays for future references of the vision algorithm. However, they can only be realized between two kernels(i.e., a producer and a consumer). To transfer data from one kernel to multiple kernels a special kernel is provided that reads data from the input channel and replicates it to multiple output channels.

4.3.2 Global Memory (DRAM) Access. In some cases, vision algorithms require a large amount of data storage: (1) algorithms that need to maintain a large state/model and (2) algorithms that are

divided into multiple FPGA partitions where partitions need large intermediate data from the previous partition(s). In these cases, data need to be stored/loaded into the FPGA global memory. AFFIX defines two special kernels that can load to and store data from FPGA memory. Address of allocated memory will be obtained at run-time and will be passed to these kernels as a kernel argument by the host program.

4.3.3 Low-Level Optimizations. AFFIX applies several low-level optimizations on OpenCL implementation of the primitive kernels through HLS pragmas. OpenCL compilers usually support pragma directives to guide optimization and hardware generation such as loop unrolling, kernel optimization, interface generation, and memory optimization. The primary goals of low level optimization techniques are to ameliorate overall performance(FMAX), achieve "ideal pipelines" (i.e., pipelines with Initiation Interval (II) of 1") for loops with large number of iterations, and save FPGA resource usages without significant performance degradation. These optimization methods include deciding on loop unrolling factors, SIMD-width, local memory configuration (i.e., port numbers), channel depth and width, and sliding window size.

- FPGA Channel Depth Optimization: To prevent deadlock and also save on FPGA resources, channel depth must be

```
#define SIMD_SZ 8
#define WIN_SZ 320

// Partition 1
CHANNEL(ch_in, uint, SIMD_SZ)
CHANNEL(ch_y, uchar, SIMD_SZ)
SRC(ch_in)
RGBTOY(SIMD_SZ, ch_in, ch_y)
SAVE(ch_y)

// Partition 2
CHANNEL(ch_warped, uchar, SIMD_SZ)
CHANNEL(ch_conv_row, uchar, SIMD_SZ)
CHANNEL(ch_con_col, uchar, SIMD_SZ)
CHANNEL(ch_thresh, uchar, SIMD_SZ)
float[9] conv_col = {...};
float[3] conv_row = {...};
WARP_LOAD(ch_warped, SIMD_SZ)
CONV_ROW(ch_warped, ch_conv_row, 9, conv_row, ...)
CONV_COL(ch_conv1, ch_con_col, 3, conv_col, ...)
THRESH(ch_conv_col, SIMD_SZ, thresh_val, ch_thresh)
SINK(ch_thresh)
```

Figure 12: Simplified OpenCL code of the lane detection algorithm example

optimized. AFFIX calculates optimal channel depth by matching latency of input ports of all nodes in the DAG. Latency is a function of kernel type (e.g., pixel-wise functions have a latency of zero, while stencil functions need to fill up the sliding window first and have variable latency that depends on the window size) and also the generated hardware (i.e., how deep the pipelining for each kernel will be). AFFIX adjusts the optimal channel depth by examining RTL implementation of the design generated by the OpenCL compiler. After extracting it, the design will be recompiled with proper channels' depth set.

- Critical Path Breaking: To avoid FMax degradation by increasing the parallelism, kernels' critical paths are identified and broken into multiple stages by inserting additional registers[27].
- Sliding Window Size Optimization: Stencil kernels use sliding window implementation to support data streaming. Sliding windows must be large enough to store "K" rows of the input image (for a (2k by 2K) convolution). However, very large window size incurs a performance/area overhead. Input image will be partitioned according to the calculated window size.

4.4 User-Defined Kernels

AFFIX supports user-defined kernels. However, users must provide CPU and FPGA implementation for the new vision functions. Since AFFIX is already integrated with open source computer vision library (i.e., OpenCV), access to a wide variety of functions for developing user-defined kernels is available.

5 EXPERIMENTAL SETUP

5.1 workloads

We have developed several vision algorithms using AFFIX framework and measured execution time and FPGA resource usage of the generated hardware. The characterization of algorithms are demonstrated in Table 2. For developing some of the algorithms, we have to extend the OpenVX vision functions list by implementing new functions. These algorithms are either process a single grayscale (one channel) or an RGBX image (four channels).

Canny's algorithm finds the edges in the input grayscale by enhancing the Sobel based edge detection with a novel hysteresis threshold method. Thresholding step is the final step in the algorithm and is implemented as a CPU function. Hence, this algorithm is partitioned into an FPGA and a CPU partition.

Automatic Contrast adjusts the contrast of the input color (RGBX) image based on the histogram of pixel intensity values. In FPGA implementation of this algorithm, hardened floating-point DSPs are used for accurate color conversion. Since this algorithm uses histogram information (has one statistical node), its graph is partitioned into two pipelines on the FPGA.

Lane detection Algorithm finds lane segments in the input color image. It uses perspective transformation to focus on "bird-eye-view" of the grayscale image and searches for line segments using probabilistic Hough transformation. This algorithm is described in details throughout the paper.

Color Copy prepares and enhances the input color image for color printing. It involves color conversion between different color spaces such as LAB and CMYK, several image processing operations, and half-toning algorithm based on error diffusion. Color conversions are done using large 3-D lookup tables. FPGA hardened floating-point DSPs are used to implement tetrahedral interpolation [28] of color spaces. Error diffusion algorithm[29] has a non-supported data access pattern and is implemented on the CPU. The rest of the graph is implemented in two partitions (pipeline stages) on the FPGA.

Census Transform calculates visual descriptors based on census transform for an input grayscale image and is implemented as a single pipeline on the FPGA. We extended OpenVX with census transform vision function.

SIFT Keypoints searches for image's representative keypoints in multiple scales of the Gaussian image pyramid (We set pyramid levels to five). The candidate keypoints then can be associated with descriptor vectors, which are useful for image recognition, but are excluded in our implementation. This algorithm is implemented in a single pipeline on the FPGA. Output of this algorithm will be a list of detected keypoints (coordinates, detection scale).

5.2 Methodology

The CPU used in experiments was Intel Core i7-4770 processor with 8 logical cores. Arria10 GX FPGA reference board with 1150K logic units, 1500 DSPs, and 2GB DDR4 attached external memory with Gen3x8 PCIe interface is used as the accelerator. PCIe communication is full duplex (i.e., simultaneous read/write). By streaming the data between host and the FPGA, it is possible to overlap communication and computation on the FPGA.

Benchmark	Domain	No Function Nodes	No sion Functions	Exten- vision	No CPU nodes	No Geo Nodes	No Stats Nodes	No Graph Partitions
Canny Edges	Image Processing	1	0		1	0	0	2
Automatic Contrast	Image Processing	6	0		0	0	1	2
Lane Detection	Image Processing	6	0		0	1	0	3
Color Copy	Color Printing	42	4		1	0	0	3
Census Transform	Visual Descriptors	4	1		0	0	0	1
SIFT keypoints	Visual Descriptors	116	2		0	0	0	1

Table 2: Workload characterization

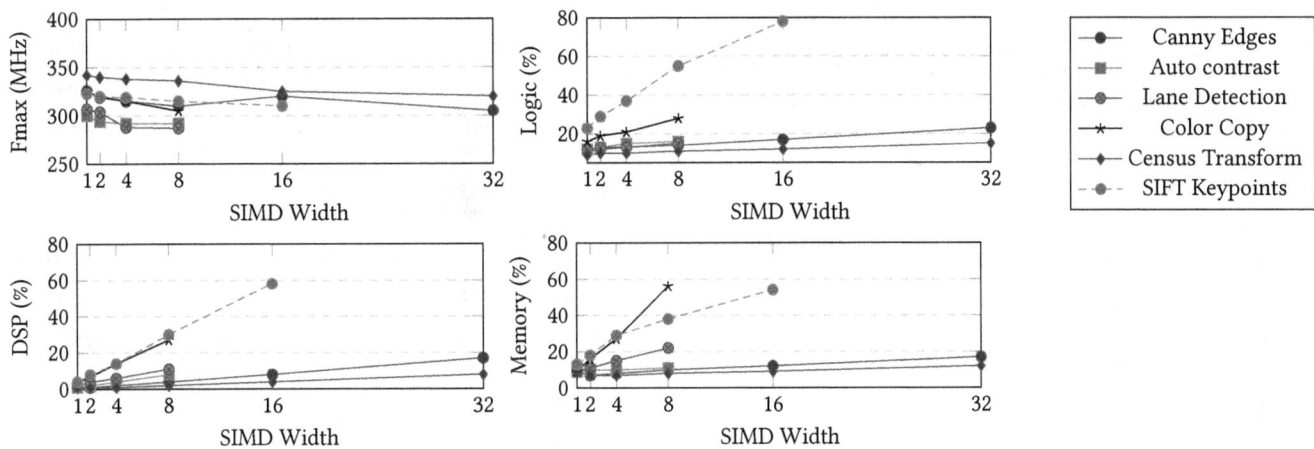

Figure 13: Arria 10 resource utilization and maximum working frequency of algorithms with different SIMD width

We have optimized the input algorithms with our framework and synthesized the output OpenCL code using Intel OpenCL SDK 18.1. We have tested different values for parallelism (i.e., SIMD_width) in the range of 1 to the maximum possible parallelism for each algorithm. FPGA board has a PCIe interface of 32 bytes which limits the maximum parallelism. Hence maximum SIMD_SIZE is 8 for algorithms that operate on color images (RGBX) and 32 for those working with grayscale images are used. We use Gurobi [30] optimizer software to solve partitioning problem.

6 EVALUATION

Table 3 reports average total execution time of the optimized CPU version (using 8 cores and vectorized with AVX intrinsics), and heterogeneous implementations of the algorithms produced via the framework with varying degree of parallelism. Reported execution time includes both communication and computation. As it is shown, Execution time scales proportionally to the inverse of parallelism until communication between CPU/FPGA reaches maximum PCIe bandwidth.

Fig. 13 demonstrates FPGA resource utilization and maximum working frequency of the benchmarks by varying SIMD width. Reported resource usage includes overhead for OpenCL control

and board interface components such as PCIe and external memory(about 9% Logic and 10% Memory). The results indicate that by increasing parallelism the maximum frequency will not drop significantly. Furthermore, resource usage is increased linearly when the amount of parallelism is increased.

Table 4 shows logic resource savings percentage by using separable filter implementation of Gaussian filter in compassion to non-separable baseline. As it can be observed by increasing the filter size the amount of saving will be increased.The reason is that separable filter involves $2 \times n$ MAC operations while non-separable baseline version demands n^2 MAC operations. This technique was applicable to filters used in Canny edges, lane detection, census transform, and SIFT keypoints algorithms.

7 CONCLUSION

This paper proposes a general purpose, configurable, and easy to use framework called AFFIX for acceleration of OpenVX vision algorithms on heterogeneous CPU-FPGA platforms. AFFIX partitions the input algorithms into CPU and FPGA partitions and implements FPGA partitions using a parametric OpenCL library. It employs several optimization methods to generate efficient hardware on FPGA. AFFIX source code is available on GitHub[6] under BSD license and

---

[6]https://github.com/sajjadt/affix

Benchmark	Input size	CPU (AVX+8 Cores)	FPGA SIMD=1	FPGA SIMD=2	FPGA SIMD=4	FPGA SIMD=8	FPGA SIMD=16	FPGA SIMD=32
Canny Edges	3840x2160x1	15 ms	28 ms	15 ms	8 ms	5 ms	4 ms	4 ms
Automatic Contrast	3840x2160x4	21 ms	84 ms	45 ms	22 ms	13 ms	N/A	N/A
Lane Detection	3840x2160x4	46 ms	57 ms	27 ms	14 ms	12 ms	N/A	N/A
Color Copy	3840x2160x4	83 ms	45 ms	32 ms	23 ms	19 ms	N/A	N/A
Census Transform	3840x2160x1	12 ms	27 ms	14 ms	7 ms	4 ms	3 ms	3 ms
SIFT keypoints	3840x2160x1	223 ms	56 ms	27 ms	14 ms	10 ms	10 ms	N/A

Table 3: Average total execution time of CPU only vs Arria10 accelerated algorithms with different SIMD width

Filter Size	5x5	7x7	9x9	11x11	13x13
Logic Saving (%)	5	16	26	36	44

Table 4: Logic saving of separable implementation of 2D filters on Arria10 compared to non-separable baseline implementation

we believe it will be a useful asset for vision researcher to develop, test, verify and accelerate their proposed algorithm.

8 ACKNOWLEDGEMENTS

This work is supported by the Intel corporation.

REFERENCES

[1] Computer vision technology permeates our daily lives. https://www.iotforall.com/computer-vision-applications-in-daily-life/. Accessed: 2018-09-01.
[2] W James MacLean. An evaluation of the suitability of fpgas for embedded vision systems. In *null*, page 131. IEEE, 2005.
[3] Chen Zhang, Peng Li, Guangyu Sun, Yijin Guan, Bingjun Xiao, and Jason Cong. Optimizing fpga-based accelerator design for deep convolutional neural networks. In *Proceedings of the 2015 ACM/SIGDA International Symposium on Field-Programmable Gate Arrays*, pages 161–170. ACM, 2015.
[4] Dominik Honegger, Helen Oleynikova, and Marc Pollefeys. Real-time and low latency embedded computer vision hardware based on a combination of fpga and mobile cpu. In *Intelligent Robots and Systems (IROS 2014), 2014 IEEE/RSJ International Conference on*, pages 4930–4935. IEEE, 2014.
[5] Eesa Nikahd, Payman Behnam, and Reza Sameni. High-speed hardware implementation of fixed and runtime variable window length 1-d median filters. *IEEE Transactions on Circuits and Systems II: Express Briefs*, 63(5):478–482, 2016.
[6] Andrew Canis, Jongsok Choi, Mark Aldham, Victor Zhang, Ahmed Kammoona, Jason H Anderson, Stephen Brown, and Tomasz Czajkowski. Legup: high-level synthesis for fpga-based processor/accelerator systems. In *Proceedings of the 19th ACM/SIGDA international symposium on Field programmable gate arrays*, pages 33–36. ACM, 2011.
[7] Felix Winterstein, Samuel Bayliss, and George A Constantinides. High-level synthesis of dynamic data structures: A case study using vivado hls. In *Field-Programmable Technology (FPT), 2013 International Conference on*, pages 362–365. IEEE, 2013.
[8] Ravi Teja Mullapudi, Vinay Vasista, and Uday Bondhugula. Polymage: Automatic optimization for image processing pipelines. In *ACM SIGARCH Computer Architecture News*, volume 43, pages 429–443. ACM, 2015.
[9] Nitin Chugh, Vinay Vasista, Suresh Purini, and Uday Bondhugula. A dsl compiler for accelerating image processing pipelines on fpgas. In *Parallel Architecture and Compilation Techniques (PACT), 2016 International Conference on*, pages 327–338. IEEE, 2016.
[10] Jonathan Ragan-Kelley, Connelly Barnes, Andrew Adams, Sylvain Paris, Frédo Durand, and Saman Amarasinghe. Halide: a language and compiler for optimizing parallelism, locality, and recomputation in image processing pipelines. *ACM SIGPLAN Notices*, 48(6):519–530, 2013.

[11] Jing Pu, Steven Bell, Xuan Yang, Jeff Setter, Stephen Richardson, Jonathan Ragan-Kelley, and Mark Horowitz. Programming heterogeneous systems from an image processing dsl. *ACM Trans. Archit. Code Optim.*, 14(3):26:1–26:25, August 2017.
[12] James Hegarty, Ross Daly, Zachary DeVito, Jonathan Ragan-Kelley, Mark Horowitz, and Pat Hanrahan. Rigel: Flexible multi-rate image processing hardware. *ACM Transactions on Graphics (TOG)*, 35(4):85, 2016.
[13] Jing Pu, Steven Bell, Xuan Yang, Jeff Setter, Stephen Richardson, Jonathan Ragan-Kelley, and Mark Horowitz. Programming heterogeneous systems from an image processing dsl. *ACM Trans. Archit. Code Optim.*, 14(3):26:1–26:25, August 2017.
[14] Prashant Singh Rawat et al. Resource conscious reuse-driven tiling for gpus. In *IEEE International Conference on Parallel Architecture and Compilation Techniques*, pages 99–111, 2016.
[15] Frederik Grull, Manfred Kirchgessner, Rainer Kaufmann, Michael Hausmann, and Udo Kebschull. Accelerating image analysis for localization microscopy with fpgas. In *Field Programmable Logic and Applications (FPL), 2011 International Conference on*, pages 1–5. IEEE, 2011.
[16] Gary Bradski. The opencv library. *Dr. Dobb's Journal: Software Tools for the Professional Programmer*, 25(11):120–123, 2000.
[17] Erik Rainey, Jesse Villarreal, Goksel Dedeoglu, Kari Pulli, Thierry Lepley, and Frank Brill. Addressing system-level optimization with openvx graphs. In *Proceedings of the IEEE Conference on Computer Vision and Pattern Recognition Workshops*, pages 644–649, 2014.
[18] Cuda accelerated computer vision library. https://developer.nvidia.com/embedded/visionworks. Accessed: 2018-09-01.
[19] Amd openvx open-source on github. https://github.com/GPUOpen-ProfessionalCompute-Libraries/amdovx-core. Accessed: 2018-09-01.
[20] Hossein Omidian and Guy GF Lemieux. Exploring automated space/time tradeoffs for openvx compute graphs. In *Field Programmable Technology (ICFPT), 2017 International Conference on*, pages 152–159. IEEE, 2017.
[21] Hossein Omidian and Guy GF Lemieux. Janus: A compilation system for balancing parallelism and performance in openvx. In *Journal of Physics: Conference Series*, volume 1004, page 012011. IOP Publishing, 2018.
[22] Sajjad Taheri, Jin Heo, Payman Behnam, Jeffrey Chen, Alexander Veidenbaum, and Alexandru Nicolau. Acceleration framework for fpga implementation of openvx graph pipelines. In *2018 IEEE 26th Annual International Symposium on Field-Programmable Custom Computing Machines (FCCM)*, pages 227–227. IEEE, 2018.
[23] Young Uk Yim and Se-Young Oh. Three-feature based automatic lane detection algorithm (tfalda) for autonomous driving. *IEEE Transactions on Intelligent Transportation Systems*, 4(4):219–225, 2003.
[24] Aharon Bar Hillel, Ronen Lerner, Dan Levi, and Guy Raz. Recent progress in road and lane detection: a survey. *Machine vision and applications*, 25(3):727–745, 2014.
[25] Cornelius Lanczos. *Linear differential operators*, volume 18. SIAM, 1997.
[26] Wayne L Winston, Munirpallam Venkataramanan, and Jeffrey B Goldberg. *Introduction to mathematical programming*, volume 1. Thomson/Brooks/Cole Duxbury; Pacific Grove, CA, 2003.
[27] Donald V Steward. The design structure system: A method for managing the design of complex systems. *IEEE transactions on Engineering Management*, (3):71–74, 1981.
[28] James M Kasson, Wil Plouffe, and Sigfredo I Nin. Tetrahedral interpolation technique for color space conversion. In *Device-Independent Color Imaging and Imaging Systems Integration*, volume 1909, pages 127–139. International Society for Optics and Photonics, 1993.
[29] RW Steinberg and L Floyd. An adaptive algorithm for spatial greyscale. *Proc. Soc. Inf. Disp.*, 17:75–77, 1976.
[30] Gurobi Optimization. Inc.,gurobi optimizer reference manual, 2015. *URL: http://www. gurobi. com*, 2014.

A Modular Heterogeneous Stack for Deploying FPGAs and CPUs in the Data Center

Nariman Eskandari
University of Toronto
Toronto, Ontario
nariman.eskandari@mail.utoronto.ca

Naif Tarafdar
University of Toronto
Toronto, Ontario
naif.tarafdar@mail.utoronto.ca

Daniel Ly-Ma
University of Toronto
Toronto, Ontario
d.lyma@mail.utoronto.ca

Paul Chow
University of Toronto
Toronto, Ontario
pc@eecg.toronto.edu

ABSTRACT

In this work we present a heterogeneous deployment stack, called *Galapagos*, that includes the abstraction of individual nodes (FPGAs and CPUs), the communication protocols between nodes and the orchestration and connection of these nodes into clusters. The stack we create is also highly modular, allowing users to explore a design space in the implementation of their cluster such as different network protocols or communication layers. The communication layer we have currently implemented within our hardware stack, called *HUMboldt*, handles heterogeneous communication between multiple FPGAs and CPUs. We implement *HUMboldt* using High-Level Synthesis (HLS) to ensure functional portability of communicating kernels, allowing us to prototype hardware kernels in software. Our results have shown that our modular approach to this heterogeneous deployment stack has introduced very little area and latency overhead in the FPGAs and can still perform at line-rate, bottlenecked solely by the network links connecting the nodes. Our results also highlight the scalability of our design as our performance remains limited by the network links when the cluster size increases.

KEYWORDS

Abstraction layers, reconfigurable computing, deployment stack, heterogeneous computing, FPGAs, communication Layer, orchestration, high-performance computing, cloud computing

ACM Reference Format:
Nariman Eskandari, Naif Tarafdar, Daniel Ly-Ma, and Paul Chow. 2019. A Modular Heterogeneous Stack for Deploying FPGAs and CPUs in the Data Center. In *The 2019 ACM/SIGDA International Symposium on Field-Programmable Gate Arrays (FPGA '19), February 24–26, 2019, Seaside, CA, USA.* ACM, New York, NY, USA, Article 4, 10 pages. https://doi.org/10.1145/3289602.3293909

1 INTRODUCTION

The integration of accelerators in the data center has been shown to be beneficial [1, 2] but using heterogeneity can be difficult for data center application developers and system administrators. This heterogeneity is especially difficult for application developers when integrating FPGAs as this usually requires the user to design the application and management circuitry, including the network stack and memory management. This difficulty increases substantially at scale not only for the management of the individual FPGAs but the connection and communication between them. In this work we approach the challenge of integrating FPGAs at scale through the use of a hardware stack shown in Figure 1. A hardware stack, analogous to software stacks, represents different layers of abstraction, giving users the flexibility for the amount of abstraction they require and allows them to have different implementations of individual layers of the stack. The flexibility provided by a modular implementation of a stack allows researchers to explore a design space with respect to different implementations of heterogeneous clusters easily, as the layers can be changed independent of each other as long as the interfaces between the layers remain the same. Some example explorations could be the research of the integration of future internet network protocols such as Content Centric Networks or IPV6, or using different transport layers such as TCP or UDP, or building application-specific layers.

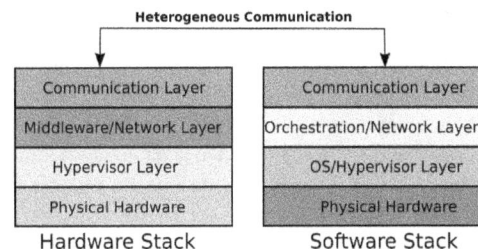

Figure 1: Our definition of a hardware deployment stack with traditional software deployment stack [3].

For both application developers and system administrators, the lack of a common communication standard among clusters of accelerators and CPUs raises challenges in creating communication links between different devices, and supporting the network connections between these devices. This communication layer is a bridge between the hardware deployment stack we made in this paper with traditional software deployment stacks. Another desirable attribute for application developers is functional portability of a distributed application across different devices, which usually requires a developer to tailor an application specifically for each device and manage its communication. Both heterogeneity and functional portability become even more daunting at the data center scale where we can have potentially thousands of nodes interacting. We believe the challenges can be addressed with a portable communication layer across both CPUs and FPGAs, which we address in this paper.

The main contributions of this paper are as follows. First, we create our heterogeneous deployment stack by building on top of an open source FPGA orchestration tool [4]. The original tool maps streaming FPGA kernels onto FPGA abstractions and connects the multiple FPGAs together. This tool handles the abstraction of individual FPGAs and FPGA clusters. However, due to specific implementation issues, there are some scalability limitations that we first address. We also change the tool from a monolithic FPGA clustering tool to a heterogeneous deployment stack by introducing modularity at different layers such as the Communication layer and Middleware/Network layer. We demonstrate the modularity by having the same application communicate over different network protocols, such as Ethernet and TCP, without changing the application. In this paper Ethernet refers to Layer 2 Ethernet protocol within the OSI Network stack. We call our entire heterogeneous deployment stack *Galapagos*. As an example communication layer within *Galapagos* we build *HUMboldt*, which is a heterogeneous message passing communication layer, allowing messages to be sent amongst and across different FPGA kernels and CPU kernels. This is implemented as a high-level synthesisizable (HLS) and software library allowing an application developed with this library to be functionally portable across both CPUs and FPGAs. The functional portability is important because it enables application development in a pure software environment. Once correct functionality has been achieved, parts of the code can be ported to run as hardware without modifying the code.

The remainder of the paper is organized as follows. Section 2 provides background about our definition of a heterogeneous stack, different communication models and the infrastructure we build on. Section 3 explores related works in traditional software deployment stacks, other communication layers specifically on multi-FPGA clusters. Section 4 explores our modular rebuild of an FPGA cluster generator, the implementation details of our communication layer, and provides details on how to interface with our system and tool flow. Section 6 shows our results with microbenchmarks measuring the performance of our communication layer and infrastructure between FPGAs and CPUs. Lastly, we conclude our paper in Section 7 and give future work in Section 8.

2 BACKGROUND

In this section, we introduce our Hardware Stack for deploying heterogeneous applications in FPGA and CPU clusters. This stack can be seen in Figure 1. We elaborate in detail on the Communication Layer as this layer is used to bridge FPGA and CPU nodes within a cluster. We also highlight other layers that are used at the lower levels for various levels of abstraction.

Each layer of the stack represents a different view of usability for the user. Each of these layers provides a standard API to the layer above. This allows a user to have different implementations of a particular layer of the stack without a complete redesign of their system, as long as they maintain the API between these layers. The modularity of the stack allows researchers to explore a design space of different implementations of heterogeneous clusters. The bottom layer of both stacks, which is the Physical Hardware layer, represents the actual physical hardware with no abstraction. The next layer, which is the Hypervisor layer in Hardware and the OS-/Hypervisor layer in Software, represents a single node abstraction. In both hardware and software, the user is provided a set of abstractions for the I/O on the individual node. In our hardware stack there is no virtualization on the I/O as the user gets full access to the I/O, whereas software virtualization allows multiple users to share the I/O with the view that they each have the full I/O port. The layer above the Hypervisor refers to the orchestration and connection of individually abstracted nodes, which we refer to as Middleware/Networking in Hardware and Orchestration/Networking in Software. Lastly, we bridge the hardware and software stack through the use of a Communication layer. The Communication layer is highly dependent on the communication model of a given application. In this work we implement an example Communication layer but due to the modular design of our system other communication layers can be built.

2.1 Hypervisor and Middleware/Network Layer

In this section, we describe the open source framework that provides us with the Hypervisor and Middleware/Network Layer of the hardware stack. We rebuild the original Middleware/Network layer to increase its scalability and modularity. This framework is described in [4] and further extended in [5]. In these works, Tarafdar et al. introduce a multi-FPGA abstraction layer that maps a graph of streaming IP blocks connected by a large logical switch onto a multi-FPGA network-connected cluster that is provisioned from an elastic pool of cloud resources. From a high-level, the user provides a collection of kernels, a logical file describing the entire cluster and a mapping file of kernels to physical FPGAs. The high-level view of this framework is shown in Figure 2. The user is returned a network handle for their FPGA cluster.

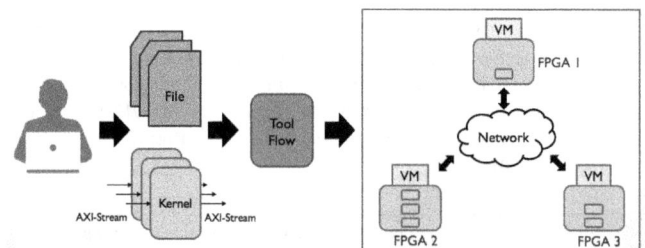

Figure 2: High-level view of original open-source framework

Each FPGA in the cluster has its physical resources abstracted with a Hypervisor. The Hypervisor exposes a control interface through PCIe and a data interface through the 10G Ethernet port, connecting to an application region. The high-level view of the Hypervisor is shown in Figure 3. Within the application region, the framework places an interconnect on each FPGA to interface with all kernels within the cluster (either directly connects to kernels that are locally connected or encapsulates the packet with network information to make a network hop). This direct connection to all packets has an inherent limitation as the interconnect has at most 16 ports, thus limiting the total number of kernels within the entire cluster to 16. Furthermore, the modularity of this implementation is limited as the user is forced to use Ethernet packets between FPGAs, making the communication unreliable. More details about the data center infrastructure, and network architecture can be found in [4], and more details on the FPGA Hypervisor can be found in [5].

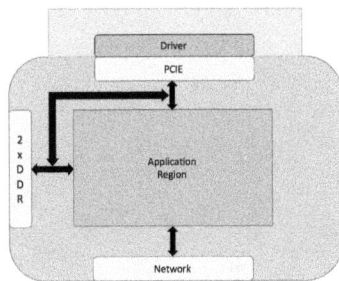

Figure 3: Hypervisor

2.2 Communication Layer

The communication layer is very application-specific as different applications exhibit different communication traffic patterns. Two popular communication models are streaming and message passing. In a streaming model, data is being sent continuously through a point-to-point channel. Some implementations of streaming communication layers include the Real-time streaming protocol (RTSP) [6] and MPEG-DASH [7]. These layers are typically built on top of network protocols like UDP, or even Ethernet as these protocols have better latency but lack reliability by default.

In a message passing model, data can be transferred between arbitrary nodes. Generally, shorter packets provide lower latency while longer packets provide better throughput because message overheads are minimized. Users must partition data into messages and include a destination address when sending, unlike a stream where it is a continuous flow of data to one or more preconfigured receivers. The most common implementation of a message passing model is the Message Passing Interface (MPI) [8]. We have decided to implement our first communication layer as a subset of MPI because there has been prior work in implementing MPI on an FPGA cluster. MPI is also a well-known standard API that is widely used in various types of HPC applications. This helps us with our goals of heterogeneity, functional portability and scalability.

Another messaging protocol that has a significant user community is ZeroMQ (0MQ) [9]. ZeroMQ uses a socket-like interface that supports multiple message patterns such as request-reply and publish-subscribe. By using a socket-like interface, it would also be easier to use it like a FIFO, or streaming interface.

3 RELATED WORK

The work we present in this paper is a heterogeneous multi-FPGA and CPU deployment stack. In this section, we explore other deployment stacks used in a homogeneous CPU environment as well as other FPGA cluster implementations and heterogeneous communication layers.

3.1 Software Deployment Stacks

Distributed and big data computing often requires the use of many compute nodes, traditionally software nodes. Figure 1 on the right shows an example of a software stack. Clusters of software nodes are grouped and connected with orchestration software such as Heat, which is part of OpenStack [10]. Orchestration software usually provisions a group of individual software nodes, and connects the software nodes between them. These nodes are often connected with popular network protocols such as IP. However on top of these interconnected software nodes, depending on the application, a user can deploy a communication layer to easily communicate between these nodes. For example, if the application describes streaming kernels then the user would want to use a communication layer amenable to streaming such as ZeroMQ [9].

3.2 FPGA Cluster Implementations for the Data Center

The flagship implementation of FPGAs in the data center is Microsoft's first version of Catapult, which includes FPGA clusters connected to a CPU as an offload engine [1]. This has limited flexibility as the FPGAs are connected to the network through the CPU. Microsoft addressed this lack of flexibility in their second iteration of Catapult [2], in which all FPGAs are connected to the network directly. To keep the network switch requirements constant, CPU network connections are made through the FPGA, as opposed to having both CPUs and FPGAs connected to the network. The work presented in this paper has a physical infrastructure similar to that of the second iteration of Catapult with network-connected FPGAs, however we also connect the CPUs directly to the network, avoiding the complexity of bypassing CPU network packets through the FPGA. We approach the challenge of heterogeneity by creating a uniform communication layer between CPUs and FPGAs to virtualize a heterogeneous network connection to look the same to both hardware and software functions. Our work also builds on top of [4], which is an orchestration layer on top of a heterogeneous network fabric, abstracting away the difficulties of configuring a multi-FPGA cluster. This is a higher level of abstraction than used in Catapult based on what is presented in the available publications.

There has been some work at a smaller scale to provide multi-FPGA orchestration. One example is the Maxeler MPC-X project [11]. A ring of eight FPGAs is connected to a network that can receive job requests as data-flow graphs. This data-flow graph is then mapped onto a set of the FPGAs available in the ring, abstracting the mapping and representation of a multi-FPGA application onto a physical multi-FPGA topology. Our work in this paper looks at a similar level of abstraction in a flexible network topology such as the one in Catapult.

3.3 Heterogeneous Communication Layers

In this section, we explore other implementations of heterogeneous communication layers. We look at two in particular: the first being TMD-MPI [12] and the second being Novo-G# [13].

3.3.1 TMD-MPI.
The work presented in [12] explores an implementation of MPI within a multi-FPGA environment called TMD-MPI. TMD-MPI implements a subset of the MPI protocol to allow hardware or software processing engines on the FPGA to communicate amongst each other on the same FPGA and across multiple FPGAs. The hardware versions of the MPI functions are implemented in VHDL. In this paper, a subset of these functions are described in HLS-synthesizable C code.

TMD-MPI was created to be portable across multiple physical platforms so it was implemented in several layers, including layers that correspond to the physical setup of the network connected FPGAs. In this paper, we avoid the need to create equivalent layers as our communication layer modularly builds on an improved cluster generator tool that handles the communication of blocks within an FPGA and across multiple FPGAs in a data center.

3.3.2 Novo-G#.
The work presented in [13] is a heterogeneous environment with 24 CPU servers that are connected via PCIe to FPGA boards with 4 Stratix V FPGAs. There are direct connects between the FPGAs on an individual board forming a 3D torus with a custom hardware network stack to support these direct connections. If needed, communication between host nodes can use MPI. The Novo-G# is a system that shows both the use of a custom hardware network stack for FPGA-to-FPGA communication as well as a model where accelerators are connected to host nodes and the host nodes can communicate using a standard software MPI library. In this paper, hardware and software components of the same application can communicate with the same communication layer as peers, which makes it much easier to use hardware or software interchangeably for any computing kernel.

4 IMPLEMENTATION

We rebuilt the open source framework described in [4] to improve modularity, reliability, and scalability. This improved framework provides the *Galapagos* stack with the Hypervisor and Middleware/Network Layer. These improvements allow the user to implement designs with different network protocols (e.g Ethernet or TCP) and communication layers by changing a configuration file describing the heterogeneous cluster. The user can target any number of available devices (FPGA and/or CPU) with a limit of 16 kernels per FPGA due to the number of ports on the Xilinx switch IP core. Once we addressed a few limitations of the original open-source framework, we built *HUMboldt* as a Communication Layer. Due to the modularity of the system, *HUMboldt* can fit on top of both TCP and Ethernet without changing the user application and its interfaces. *HUMboldt* maintains functional portability between hardware and software nodes. The heterogeneous connection between FPGAs and CPUs is easy to scale up as the user only needs to change two configuration files.

4.1 Galapagos Middleware/Networking Layer

The application region that can be built by the original open-source framework Middleware/Network Layer and the *Galapagos* Middleware/Network Layer can be seen in Figures 4 and 5. Both iterations of this framework take a description of a cluster composed of streaming kernels with a unique ID and maps it to multiple FPGAs. Each streaming kernel uses the AXI-stream protocol [14] with a dest field to specify which kernel the packet is destined for. A logical view of this infrastructure is a large switch connecting all the kernels within the cluster. The framework transforms this logical switch into two physical switches, with the first being an AXI-stream switch on the FPGA and the second being a top-of-rack network switch.

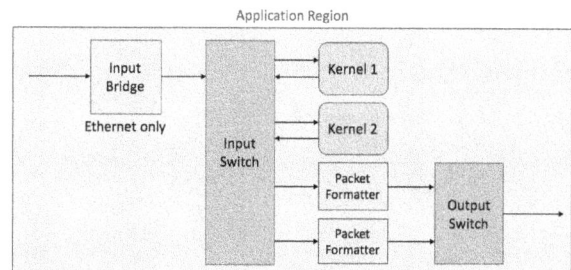

Figure 4: The original open-source framework from [4].

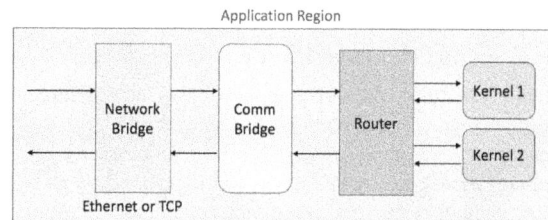

Figure 5: A high-level overview of *Galapagos*.

In the framework, described in [4] Ethernet packets are transformed into AXI-stream packets through the use of an Input Bridge. This then connects to an AXI-stream switch on the FPGA. This switch is connected to all kernels within the cluster, either directly if on the same FPGA, or through a Packet-Formatter module that encapsulates the AXI-stream packet with the appropriate Ethernet headers, and places the AXI-stream dest field in the Ethernet payload (one packet formatter for each kernel outside the FPGA). These direct connections limit scalability as the number of kernels in the cluster is limited by the 16 ports of the AXI-stream switch.

In the Middleware/Network Layer of *Galapagos*, we first addressed scalability by creating an AXI-stream router. The AXI-stream protocol is independent of higher layer protocols. The block diagram of the router is shown in Figure 6. The router on each FPGA includes a routing table indexed by the unique ID of each kernel in the entire cluster (including kernels not on this FPGA) and the network address (Ethernet or IP) of the FPGA that has each kernel. All kernels output their packets to the router that reads the AXI-stream dest field of the packet and then looks up the network destination in the routing table. Then, the packet is either routed back to the AXI-stream switch or routed out to the network. The number of ports on this router is equal to the number of kernels only on this FPGA, as all packets leaving the FPGA share one channel. This limits us to have up to 16 kernels on a particular FPGA as opposed to the entire cluster as per the original design. The routing table is automatically generated by our modifications to the cluster generator.

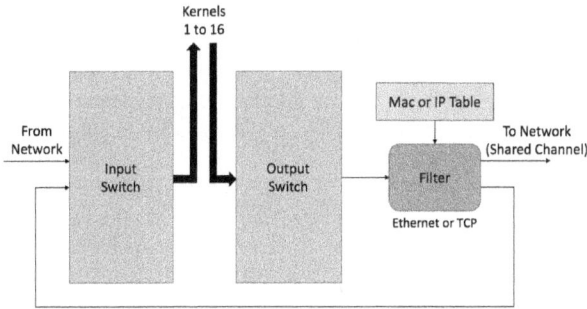

Figure 6: Router

The network bridge that is shown in Figure 5 is responsible for converting network packets into AXI-stream format and vice versa. For the Ethernet Network Bridge of Figure 5, this paper combines the Input Bridge and a modified version of the Packet Formatter of Figure 4 into a single module. The block diagram of this module is shown in Figure 7. The modified packet formatter is equipped with a look up table that has the MAC addresses for each destination kernel. Using the MAC address lookup table in the packet formatter decreases resource utilization as it only uses one packet formatter logic with a small memory instead of multiple packet formatters for each kernel outside the FPGA, and it helps the *Galapagos* to be more scalable.

In [4] the multi-FPGA communication uses the Ethernet protocol, which is not reliable. In the Middleware/Network Layer of *Galapagos*, to address reliability, an optional TCP core [15] is integrated into the framework. In this paper an additional Network Bridge is created for TCP, allowing us to standardize the interface between the Hypervisor and the Application Region. The standardization of the interface allows us to use both TCP and Ethernet interchangeably, thus addressing modularity. The block diagram of the TCP Network Bridge is illustrated in Figure 8. Observe that the interfaces are the same as for the Ethernet Network Bridge in Figure 7.

A user may wish to create a communication layer (e.g. MPI) on top of standard network layers. A communication bridge is used to transform network packets to communication layer compliant packets. In the Middleware/Network Layer of *Galapagos*, we have implemented a Comm Bridge that translates the AXI-stream packets of the Network Bridge to conform to the underlying MPI packet protocol used by HUMboldt. If we wanted to support ZeroMQ we would implement an appropriate Comm Bridge to support that protocol. Separating the functions of the Network Bridge and the Comm Bridge makes it possible to change the network protocol

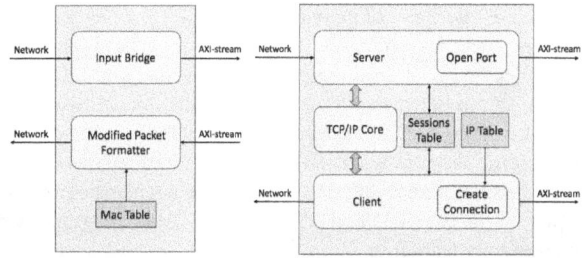

Figure 7: Ethernet Net- Figure 8: TCP Network Bridge. work Bridge

independent of the communication layer, and vice versa. We further address modularity by allowing the user to configure the network protocol (Ethernet or TCP) and communication bridge via the mapping configuration file. Details of the mapping file can be found in Section 4.3.

4.2 HUMboldt Communication Layer

Due to the layered design of *Galapagos*, the implementation of the communication layer can be any communication model as long as it adheres to the AXI-stream interface, and the appropriate communication bridge to convert AXI-stream packets into communication layer specific packets is provided. The communication layer we present here implements *HUMBoldt*, a minimal subset of MPI that is sufficient to enable basic message passing between kernels. MPI is a standard API that defines signatures for functions such as sending and receiving messages. These signatures must remain the same for all implementations of MPI. Even though the implementation for these functions vary according to platform (e.g FPGA or CPU), the standardization of the protocol for *HUMBoldt* allows for communication between heterogeneous platforms.

4.2.1 MPI Communication Layer. Here, we provide a brief explanation of MPI and the subset of the MPI library that we support, which we call Heterogeneous Uniform Messaging (*HUMboldt*). Using MPI, many parallel processes (ranks) communicating via messages can be run on multi-node platforms. We will refer to ranks as kernels to be consistent with our previous use of the term *kernels*. In MPI software implementations, such as MPICH [16] and OpenMPI [17], functions are provided to transmit data among different kernels in various ways. The minimum subset of MPI functions needed for communication and currently implemented in HUMboldt:

(1) *MPI_Init*: This function initializes the MPI environment, and does the basic setup such as network interface initialization.
(2) *MPI_Send and MPI_Recv*: These two functions are building blocks of the MPI programming model that enable data transmission among kernels. For every Send to a kernel, there must be a matching Receive on that kernel to get the data from the sender.
(3) *MPI_Finalize*: Makes sure that all kernels are done with their processes.

Other MPI functions can be added to the HUMboldt library by writing additional HLS-synthesizable functions. These functions will fit into the same HUMboldt flow.

There are two types of networks in our *HUMBoldt* communication layer. The Intra-FPGA AXI-stream network is used for kernels that are located in the same physical FPGA, and the Inter-node communication between FPGAs and CPUs uses the network. The network communication currently supports TCP or Ethernet but any network protocol with an AXI-stream interface can be used. We use the same underlying *HUMBoldt* protocol for kernels communicating within the same node (FPGA or CPU) and between nodes, as our communication bridge encapsulates a *HUMBoldt* compliant packet with the appropriate network header (e.g TCP or Ethernet) to handle the inter-node communication.

Figure 9 shows the Envelope that carries the *HUMBoldt* messages between kernels. The first two bytes correspond to the destination and source kernels. The Packet Types are *send request, clear to send, data,* or *done*, where the different packet types are used to implement the message passing protocol underlying *HUMBoldt*. The next three bytes specify the size of the message being sent. In the standard implementation of MPI, the Tag is an option for the user to tag optional metadata to transactions, and for compatibility purposes we keep this as a field in the Envelope used for *HUMBoldt*. The Data Type field helps to process the different data types properly.

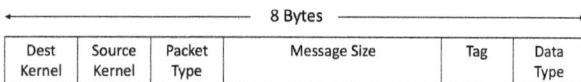

←	8 Bytes					→
Dest Kernel	Source Kernel	Packet Type	Message Size		Tag	Data Type

Figure 9: Envelope Packet

4.3 System Interface

This subsection specifies how the user would interface with the *Galapagos* hardware stack. A user provides application files as well as the cluster description files. The tool flow of the heterogeneous stack takes these files, and makes a cluster that all the hardware and software kernels can communicate.

In Listing 1, we illustrate an example of a common model for HPC applications in which one kernel is responsible for distributing data to several other kernels, and gathers processed data, when all kernels are done.

```
1  #include "HUMboldt.h"
2  #define MAX_ITR 10
3  #define DATA_SIZE 1000
4  #define TAG 0
5
6  int main(int argc, char* argv[])
7  {
8      HUM_Init(&argc,&argv);
9      int data_array[DATA_SIZE];
10     int size = atoi(argv[1]);
11     int rank = atoi(argv[2]);
12
13     for(int i = 0 ; i < MAX_ITR ; i++){
14         if(rank == 0){
15             for(int r = 1; r < size ; r++)
16                 HUM_Send(data_array,DATA_SIZE,
                            MPI_FLOAT,r,TAG,MPI_COMM_WORLD);
17         }
18         else{
19             HUM_Recv(data_array,DATA_SIZE,MPI_FLOAT
                        ,0,TAG,MPI_COMM_WORLD);
20         }
21         /* process data*/
22         if(rank == 0){
```

```
23             for(int r = 1 ; r < size ; r++)
24                 HUM_Recv(data_array,DATA_SIZE,
                            MPI_FLOAT,r,TAG,MPI_COMM_WORLD);
25         }
26         else
27             HUM_Send(data_array,DATA_SIZE,MPI_FLOAT
                        ,0,TAG,MPI_COMM_WORLD);
28     }
29     HUM_Finalize();
30     return 0;
31 }
```

Listing 1: HUMboldt sample code

The code in Listing 1 needs a few minor modifications to be synthesizable by Vivado HLS. For example in line 6, instead of argc and argv to input the size and kernel number (rank) we use two constant ports. These values are assigned automatically in the tool flow using the logical description file of the kernels, so there is no need for lines 10 and 11. Furthermore, some HLS pragmas should be added just for interfaces that are always the same. These changes are shown in Listing 2. These modifications can be done using a very simple script, but essentially, the same code can be run as software or implemented as hardware in an FPGA. This code demonstrates that *HUMBoldt* is heterogeneous and functionally portable for different processing nodes in a cluster.

```
1  int main(const int size, const int rank)
2  {
3  #pragma HLS INTERFACE ap_ctrl_none port=return
4  #pragma HLS resource core=AXI4Stream variable=
          stream_out
5  #pragma HLS resource core=AXI4Stream variable=
          stream_in
6  #pragma HLS DATA_PACK variable  = stream_out
7  #pragma HLS DATA_PACK variable  = stream_in
```

Listing 2: HUMboldt synthesizable sample code

In addition to the code in Listing 1, cluster description files are required for *Galapagos*. Listing 3 is a sample logical file, and Listing 4 is a sample mapping file. Line 5 in Listing 3 shows an example of the *rep* field to determine the number of replications of each kernel within the entire cluster. This shows that how easy it is to have multiple replications a kernel. The *num* is an unique identifier of each kernel that can be used in mapping file.

The logical file in Listing 3 is mostly the same as the original open-source framework logical file in [4]. However, there are some small changes that are as follows. There are different naming conventions for the reset and the clock ports in the Vivado environment. In the modified logical file the user can specify the clock and reset port names (Line 6 and 7). One feature that makes this complex heterogeneous system easy to use is that a user is able to debug it by monitoring some signals. A debug capability has been added to the system, by which the signals that are marked as debug (Lines 12 and 17 of Listing 3) will be connected to a Xilinx ILA core. The Xilinx Integrated Logic Analyzer (ILA) IP core[18] is a logic analyzer that can be used to monitor the internal signals of a design, running on an FPGA. Another capability that is added to the system interface of *Galapagos* is defining a constant port that can be assigned automatically by the tool flow (Lines 19 to 23).

Listing 4 shows how the kernels, which are defined in the logical file, can be mapped into one or more FPGAs. In lines 20 to 24 it can be seen that the kernels 1-16 are mapped to a single FPGA. This shows how easy it is to scale the system by changing some lines in the configuration files. The mapping file of the original open-source framework [4] has the same capability that *Galapagos* inherited. However, as mentioned in Section 4.1, the original framework has the limitation of 16 kernels within the entire cluster, but, *Galapagos* has no limitation for the total number of kernels. It has only the limitation of 16 kernels per FPGA.

Some additional features are added to the mapping file to support heterogeneity and modularity. For example, in Listing 4 lines 4 and 18 show two different types of nodes (software and hardware), which addresses heterogeneity and how easy it is to change a kernel from hardware to software, or vice versa. Furthermore to address modularity, the user can specify a bridge for their communication layer as shown in lines 10 to 16. If the user does not specify a bridge, then it is assumed the kernels will communicate directly via AXI-stream. Modularity within the network layer can be observed in line 19, where the user can specify the network protocol (e.g TCP or Ethernet), and network addresses as demonstrated in lines 6-7 and 25-26. The network addresses would be supplied by the manager of the data center.

```
1   <?xml version="1.0" encoding="UTF-8"?>
2   <cluster>
3       <kernel> hardware_core_name
4           <num> 1 </num>
5           <rep> 96 </rep>
6           <clk> aclk </clk>
7           <aresetn> aresetn </aresetn>
8           <id_port> kernel_id </id_port>
9           <interface>
10              <direction> in </direction>
11              <name> stream_in_V </name>
12              <debug/>
13          </interface>
14          <interface>
15              <direction> out </direction>
16              <name> stream_out_V </name>
17              <debug/>
18          </interface>
19          <const>
20              <name> size </name>
21              <val> 4 </val>
22              <width> 16 </width>
23          </const>
24      </kernel>
25      <kernel> cpu
26          <num> 0 </num>
27          <rep> 1 </rep>
28      </kernel>
29  </cluster>
```

Listing 3: Sample Logical File

```
1   <?xml version="1.0" encoding="UTF-8"?>
2   <cluster>
3       <node>
4           <type> sw </type>
5           <kernel> 0 </kernel>
6           <mac_addr> ac:c4:7a:88:c0:47 </mac_addr>
7           <ip_addr> 10.1.2.152 </ip_addr>
8       </node>
9       <node>
10          <appBridge>
11              <name> communication_bridge_eth_mpi </
                      name>
12              <to_app> to_app_V </to_app>
13              <from_app> from_app_V </from_app>
14              <to_net> to_net_V </to_net>
15              <from_net> from_net_V </from_net>
16          </appBridge>
```

```
17              <board> adm-8k5-debug </board>
18              <type> hw </type>
19              <comm> eth </comm>
20              <kernel> 1 </kernel>
21              .
22              .
23              .
24              <kernel> 16 </kernel>
25              <mac_addr>  fa:16:3e:55:ca:02 </mac_addr>
26              <ip_addr> 10.1.2.101 </ip_addr>
27      </node>
28  </cluster>
29  ~
```

Listing 4: Sample Map File

5 TOOL FLOW

To make the *Galapagos* stack work transparently and conveniently across a heterogeneous platform, a tool flow is required that takes the cluster description files (Listing 3 and Listing 4) and *HUMboldt* code (Listing 1), and creates the whole cluster automatically. Recall that one of the goals is to use identical code whether it is to run as a software kernel or as a hardware kernel. This means that the tool flow will have two paths, one to create software executables and the other to build FPGA bitstreams in a user-defined platform. Figure 10 shows the flows for hardware and software kernels.

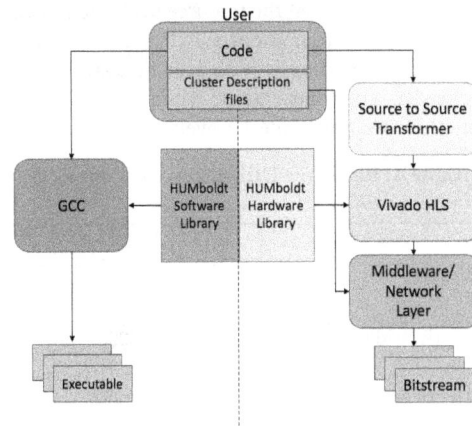

Figure 10: Software and Hardware Tool Flow

5.1 Software Kernels

Building software kernels is essentially the same as what is currently done for standard MPI software distributions. The first step is to link in the *HUMboldt* software library to the user code.

5.2 Hardware Kernels

The building of the hardware kernels requires transforming the original source code into a form that can be used with high-level synthesis (HLS). HLS essentially creates a block of hardware using software code. The hardware path of the tool flow gives these hardware blocks as well as cluster description files to the middleware/Network Layer, and it creates the bitstreams for the FPGAs in the cluster.

6 EVALUATION

In this section, the evaluation of our current platform is presented. We consider the resource utilization, latency and throughput, and scaling and heterogeneity of our platform.

The testbed that we use to run our test scenarios is a cluster of servers with Intel Xeon E5-2650 CPUs running at 2.20 GHz, each with 12 physical cores, so via hyper-threading 24 software threads can be running. The FPGAs that are located in the same network of this cluster are Xilinx Kintex UltraScale XCKU115-2-FLVA1517E devices on Alpha data ADM-PCIE-8K5 boards [19]. All network connections are 10G ethernet connected to a Dell Networking S4048-ON 10G switch. Our *HUMBoldt* implementation is used for any configurations that include a hardware node. To test the best software to software implementation, we just use MPICH, which is a mature open-source MPI implementation.

6.1 Resource Utilization of Infrastructure and Communication Layer

The resource utilization of the different layers of *Galapagos* including the Hypervisor that we got from [4] plus other parts of the Middleware/Network Layer, including off-chip memory support that we added, network bridges, communication layer bridges, and the router within the application region are shown in Table 1. The percentages, which are shown in brackets, are relative to the KU115 FPGAs. Observe that the resource utilization of *Galapagos* is about 20% when the user chooses TCP, and it is 15% when the user chooses Ethernet. The resources used here are not necessarily extra overhead as a developer would require resources to create a custom multi-FPGA interconnect as well.

Table 1: Resource Utilization of Galapagos

Galapagos Layer	LUTs	Flip-Flops	BRAMs
I) Hypervisor	95332 (14.4%)	120367 (9.1%)	255 (11.8%)
II) Network Bridge TCP	29146 (4.39%)	32582 (2.4%)	86 (4.0%)
III) Network Bridge Ethernet	582 (0.09%)	1087 (0.08%)	2 (0.09%)
IV) Communication Bridge TCP to *HUMboldt*	1039 (0.1%)	1585 (0.1%)	1 (0.046%)
V) Communication Bridge Ethernet to *HUMboldt*	729 (0.1%)	1332 (0.1%)	1 (0.046%)
VI) Router with 16 ports	5067 (0.8%)	6310 (0.5%)	1 (0.046%)
Total TCP (I + II + IV + VI)	130584 (19.7%)	160847 (12.1%)	343 (15.9 %)
Total Ethernet (I + III + V + VI)	101710 (15.3%)	129096 (9.7%)	259 (12.0%)

The other resource utilization to consider is related to the *HUMboldt* kernels. Each kernel can use any of the functions that are defined in the *HUMboldt* communication layer library. Once a *HUMboldt* function is called in the user code, the module for that function will be added to the hardware of that kernel. Multiple calls to the

same function do not increase the instantiations of the hardware module. The resource utilization of each function is presented in Table 2. It can be seen that the current Send and Receive functions require minimal additional hardware resources.

Table 2: Resource Overhead of HUMBoldt Communication Layer API Functions

HUMboldt Function	LUTs	Flip-Flops	BRAMs
HUM_Send	389 (0.06%)	372 (0.03%)	0 (0%)
HUM_Recv	1180 (0.18%)	1072 (0.08%)	0 (0%)

6.2 Latency and Throughput

We have created a microbenchmark to test the send and receive functionality of our system, with one kernel sending and another kernel receiving. We change the implementation of the kernel from hardware to software and test several configurations. The configurations are as follows: software to hardware, hardware to hardware (on the same FPGA), hardware to hardware (on different FPGAs), and hardware to software. These configurations are tested with both TCP and Ethernet. Furthermore, we test the following software configurations with MPICH: software to software (on the same CPU), and software to software (on different CPUs). MPICH uses TCP for network communication. We test these using MPICH to compare the best software implementation of MPI to our *HUMboldt* communication layer. The measurements reported were averaged over many runs until results converged. For MPICH, convergence required close to a million runs due to OS and other processes effects whereas our hardware results required about 10 runs.

Figures 11 and 12 show the throughput of our benchmark. Our *HUMboldt* communication layer and the respective bridge transforming *HUMboldt* packets into network packets performs at line-rate and the effective data throughput is limited by the 10G Ethernet Core in the Hypervisor along with the respective packet headers required for TCP and Ethernet (hence the higher throughput in Ethernet than TCP). For simplicity all our kernels are connected to the same 156.25 MHz clock, which is the output of the Ethernet core running at 10G. This limits our internal FPGA throughput to 10G, however in theory this can be modified for a faster clock. Furthermore for homogeneity all kernels on the same and different nodes use the same communication protocol, however this could be further optimized by simplifying the protocol of kernels on the same node. Between hardware and software in Figure 11, we cannot scale past a 128 KB payload after which we notice packet drops using Ethernet because of the lack of reliability. This is because the software kernel cannot receive data as fast as the hardware can send it. Between two hardware kernels, we achieved close to the maximum TCP core bandwidth that is mentioned in [15]. The curves show the expected shape where the bandwidth improves as the payload size, and hardware to hardware works best when compared to links involving a software node. Note that the curve for hardware to hardware in the same FPGA is the same in both Ethernet and TCP cases because the routing is done internal to the FPGA without needing to add the Ethernet or TCP headers. The hardware to software TCP is about half that of software to hardware. This is because the software node cannot process packets as fast as the packets received from the hardware node, thus dropping packets and initiating retransmissions.

We do not plot the latency and bandwidth between two software nodes on the same CPU because they would be difficult to show on the same graph as the others due to the scaling required and there is no additional information gained by plotting them on the same graph. We present these numbers only to illustrate the challenge of competing with MPI implemented in a shared-memory processor running at over 2 GHz. MPICH uses shared memory for the communication, much of which can fit in the cache so the bandwidth can be very high and the latency very low. The observed bandwidth for a 512 KB payload is approximately 60 GB/s with a latency of 0.21 μs. It can also be seen that MPICH shows a very high throughput for small packets and then drops off. We do not understand the inner workings of MPICH to explain this behavior, but we suspect optimizations for small packets or possibly cache effects.

The latency is shown in Table 3. We define latency as the time for sending a zero-payload size transaction, including sending an *envelope*, receiving a *clear to send*, sending a zero-payload packet, and receiving a *done*. We measure the cycle counts with a probe (Xilinx Integrated Logic Analyzer) running on the hardware with a 156.25 Mhz clock. The latency for two kernels sending and receiving an entire transaction (all four packets) on the same FPGA is deterministic and takes 29 cycles. When the receiving kernel is on another node (different FPGA or CPU) we incur an additional latency required to transform *HUMboldt* packets into network packets. Each packet would be processed through a communication bridge and a network bridge. These latencies are shown in Table 4.

Table 3: Latency of zero-payload packets

Microbenchmarks	Ethernet (μs)	TCP (μs)
Hardware to Hardware (same node)	0.2	0.2
Hardware to Hardware (different node)	5.7	15.2
Software to Hardware	27.5	48.8
Hardware to Software	34.7	81.2

Table 4: Per Packet Additional Latency

Component and Protocol	Send (cycles)	Receive (cycles)
TCP Communication Bridge	9	5
Ethernet Communication Bridge	6	5
TCP Network Bridge	177	199
Ethernet Network Bridge	7	12

On top of the internal FPGA latencies that are mentioned above there is a non-deterministic latency of the network depending on the network topology. It can be seen that whenever any communication uses a network link, the additional cycles for the bridges is very small except when TCP is used. Also, whenever there is a software node involved, it is clear that handling protocols in software is much slower than in hardware.

As a sanity check of our numbers we can make an approximate comparison to the latency number measured for Microsoft Catapult [2] where they report an FPGA to FPGA round-trip latency of 2.88μs when using their LTL communication layer over a 40G Ethernet link through a single top-of-rack switch. Table 3 shows that the FPGA to FPGA latency when using the Ethernet network link (hw to hw diff) on our platform is about 6 μs, which is the sending and receiving of four packets of 8 bytes according to the *HUMboldt* protocol. A single round-trip latency is therefore about 3 μs. On top of Ethernet, Catapult uses UDP frame encapsulation, IP routing, and adds their LTL protocol [2], which we do not have with a raw Ethernet link. Catapult is also running at 40G versus our 10G, so they are sending more bytes at a higher rate. While the round trip numbers are similar, it can be seen that they are not directly comparable. However, we argue that our implementation is within reason compared to Catapult.

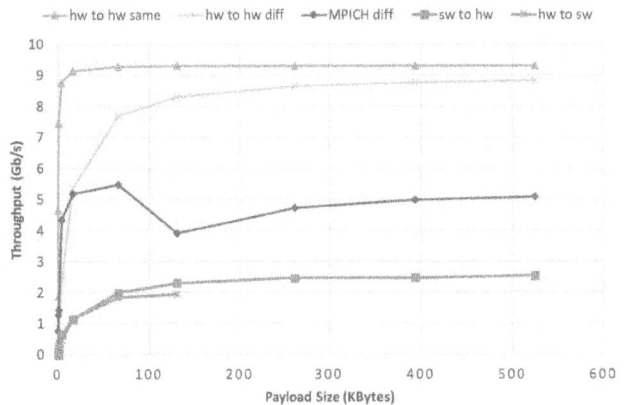

Figure 11: Ethernet Throughput.

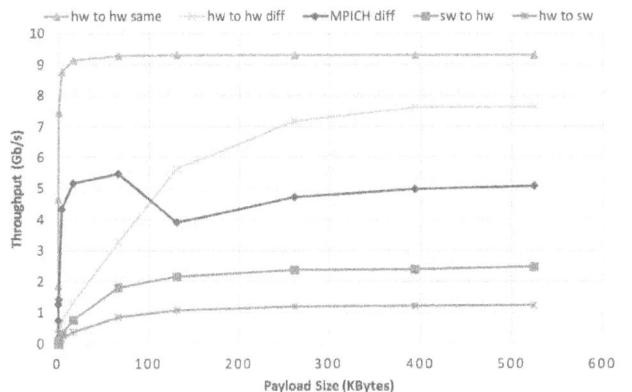

Figure 12: TCP Throughput.

6.3 Scalability, Heterogeneity and Performance

To test scalability and heterogeneity, we built a simple application proxy shown in Listing 1 that is representative of a common

270

computing pattern. It has a central node forking tasks to many processes and gathering the results. The goal of this application is to exercise our platform and show how easy it is to scale the application to run with different numbers of nodes. The number of nodes within our system can scale to the depth of the routing table, which is currently set to 256 but can be updated as required. Furthermore, we have a limitation of 16 kernels per FPGA. Within our experiment we easily implemented several working configurations up to 96 kernels across 6 FPGAs (limited by the number of FPGAs available in our cluster) by just making a few changes in the configuration files as described in Section 5. Our experiments have shown that scaling to 96 kernels is still limited by the network link and not by our infrastructure. We have scaled our microbenchmark experiments with 96 kernels across 6 FPGAs and have observed the same performance between two kernels. Within our experiment, we also tested heterogeneity by implementing multiple kernels in hardware and software and demonstrated functional correctness across a distributed heterogeneous application.

Our experiments have shown that with limited latency overhead (on the order of up to 200 cycles when TCP is used) and no throughput overhead we can provide scalability and heterogeneity. Furthermore, some latency overhead will be incurred by any multi-FPGA communication link as some protocol must be in place to connect the FPGAs together. The small performance overhead of our abstraction layers means that the upper bound performance of a multi-FPGA application will not be significantly affected by our abstractions. The true performance of any distributed application will be dependent mainly on the scalability of the application itself, and how well the application can map to hardware and not be impacted by our abstraction layers. Therefore, we limit our experiments to our microbenchmarking, which strictly tests the underlying communications and our ability to scale without any affects that are application dependent.

7   CONCLUSION

A heterogeneous deployment stack is necessary to give users flexible heterogeneous clusters at scale. The modularity in our stack, *Galapagos* is realized and demonstrated with the creation of the *HUMboldt* communication layer on top of multiple implementations of a networking protocol. This modularity will allow researchers to be able to experiment with different implementations of heterogeneous clusters. These layers of abstraction work at linerate, allowing users to focus on their application. We show that we can target both heterogeneity and scalability quite easily, as we can use multiple configurations that we can easily scale by changing two configuration files. We have also shown that heterogeneity can be achieved by combining a software and hardware deployment stack through a common layer, which in our case is the use of a communication layer such as *HUMboldt*. This work is open-source and can be downloaded at https://github.com/tarafdar/galapagos and https://github.com/eskandarinariman/HUMboldt.

8   FUTURE WORK

We have built *Galapagos* and *HUMboldt* to make it easier to build multi-FPGA and heterogeneous systems. To show the true power

of this infrastructure, we will build some showcase applications that can leverage such a platform.

The *HUMboldt* layer currently supports message passing using a minimal subset of the MPI standard. To more fully support MPI, more functions need to be implemented, which just adds to the current library. A fully heterogeneous MPI should leverage existing software implementations, such as MPICH [16] to achieve the most efficient implementation of MPI on the software side. This could be achieved by bridging *HUMboldt* to MPICH.

To support more types of applications it would be good to add the streaming communication model to *HUMboldt*. Because of the modularity that we added to *Galapagos*, and the HLS implementation of *HUMboldt*, it will not be difficult to add streaming. Just as we have done by using MPI for message passing, it would be good to use a popular programming model such as ZeroMQ [9] to define the interfaces.

In general, since communication is often a bottleneck in multi-node applications, more work needs to be done to implement efficient heterogeneous communications. The *Galapagos* platform makes it possible to do this exploration without changing the application layers so it will be easy to see the impact of different communication protocols on any applications we build.

REFERENCES

[1] Andrew Putnam et al. A Reconfigurable Fabric for Accelerating Large-Scale Datacenter Services. *ACM SIGARCH Computer Architecture News*, 42(3):13–24, 2014.
[2] Adrian Caulfield et al. Configurable Clouds. *IEEE Micro*, 37(3):52–61, 2017.
[3] Naif Tarafdar et al. Galapagos: A Full Stack Approach to FPGA Integration in the Cloud. *IEEE Micro*, 38(6):18–24, Nov 2018.
[4] Naif Tarafdar et al. Enabling Flexible Network FPGA Clusters in a Heterogeneous Cloud Data Center. In *Proceedings of the 2017 ACM/SIGDA International Symposium on Field-Programmable Gate Arrays*, pages 237–246. ACM, 2017.
[5] Naif Tarafdar et al. Heterogeneous Virtualized Network Function Framework for the Data Center. In *Field Programmable Logic and Applications (FPL), 2017 27th International Conference on*, pages 1–8. IEEE, 2017.
[6] Henning Schulzrinne et al. Real Time Streaming Protocol (RTSP). Technical report, 1998.
[7] Iraj Sodagar. The MPEG-Dash standard for multimedia streaming over the internet. *IEEE MultiMedia*, (4):62–67, 2011.
[8] Marc Snir. *MPI–the Complete Reference: the MPI Core*, volume 1. MIT press, 1998.
[9] Pieter Hintjens. *ZeroMQ: Messaging for Many Applications*. " O'Reilly Media, Inc.", 2013.
[10] Kumar Rakesh et al. Open source solution for cloud computing platform using OpenStack. *International Journal of Computer Science and Mobile Computing*, 3(5):89–98, 2014.
[11] Maxeler Technologies. MPC-X Series. https://www.maxeler.com/products/mpc-xseries, 2015.
[12] Manuel Saldaña et al. MPI as a programming model for high-performance reconfigurable computers. *ACM Transactions on Reconfigurable Technology and Systems (TRETS)*, 3(4):22, 2010.
[13] Alan D George et al. Novo-G#: Large-scale reconfigurable computing with direct and programmable interconnects. In *High Performance Extreme Computing Conference (HPEC), 2016 IEEE*, pages 1–7. IEEE, 2016.
[14] AXI Xilinx. Reference Guide, UG761 (v13. 1). *URL http://www. xilinx. com/support/documentation/ip documentation/ug761 axi reference guide. pdf*, 2011.
[15] D. Sidler et al. Scalable 10Gbps TCP/IP Stack Architecture for Reconfigurable Hardware. In *2015 IEEE 23rd Annual International Symposium on Field-Programmable Custom Computing Machines*, pages 36–43, May 2015.
[16] William Gropp et al. A High-Performance, Portable Implementation of the MPI Message Passing Interface Standard. *Parallel Computing, volume=22, number=6, pages=789–828, year=1996, publisher=Elsevier*.
[17] Edgar Gabriel et al. Open MPI: Goals, Concept, and Design of a Next Generation MPI Implementation. In *European Parallel Virtual Machine/Message Passing Interface Users' Group Meeting*, pages 97–104. Springer, 2004.
[18] Product Guide. LogiCORE IP Soft Error Mitigation Controller v3. 3. *Xilinx Inc*, 2016.
[19] Alpha Data. Alpha Data 8k5 boards. https://www.alpha-data.com/dcp/products.php?product=adm-pcie-8k5, 2017.

Impact of Soft Errors on Large-Scale FPGA Cloud Computing

Andrew M. Keller and Michael J. Wirthlin
NSF Center for Space, High-Performance, and Resilient Computing (SHREC)
Deptartment of Electrical and Computer Engineering
Brigham Young University
Provo, Utah
andrewmkeller@byu.edu,wirthlin@byu.edu

ABSTRACT

FPGAs are being used in large numbers within cloud computing to provide high-performance, low-power alternatives to more traditional computing structures. While FPGAs provide a number of important benefits to cloud computing environments, they are susceptible to radiation-induced soft errors, which can lead to silent data corruption or system instability. Although soft errors within a single FPGA occur infrequently, soft errors in large-scale FPGAs systems can occur at a relatively high rate. This paper investigates the failure rate of several FPGA applications running within an FPGA cloud computing node by performing fault injection experiments to determine the susceptibility of these applications to soft-errors. The results from these experiments suggest that silent data corruption will occur every few hours within a 100,000 node FPGA system and that such a system can only maintain high-levels of reliability for short periods of operation. These results suggest that soft-error detection and mitigation techniques may be needed in large-scale FPGA systems.

CCS CONCEPTS

• **Computer systems organization → Reliability**; *Availability*; • **Hardware → Fault models and test metrics; System-level fault tolerance**; *Board- and system-level test*; *Error detection and error correction*; *Failure prediction*; *Failure recovery, maintenance and self-repair*; *Redundancy*.

KEYWORDS

FPGA cloud computing; FPGA data centers; soft error rate, SER; single event upset, SEU; architectural vulnerability factor, AVF; fault injection; critical bit; reliability; recovery; Intel FPGA; mission time

ACM Reference Format:
Andrew M. Keller and Michael J. Wirthlin. 2019. Impact of Soft Errors on Large-Scale FPGA Cloud Computing. In *The 2019 ACM/SIGDA International Symposium on Field-Programmable Gate Arrays (FPGA '19), February 24–26, 2019, Seaside, CA, USA*. ACM, New York, NY, USA, 10 pages. https://doi.org/10.1145/3289602.3293911

1 INTRODUCTION

Field programmable gate arrays (FPGAs) are increasingly being used in cloud computing environments to perform application-specific computation. FPGAs offer a configurable fabric that can be used to accelerate a variety of important applications. In some applications, FPGAs provide higher performance and power efficiency than super-scalar CPUs [27] or GPUs [15]. The large number of nodes found within modern cloud computing suggests that many FPGAs will be needed in FPGA-based cloud computing systems.

With large-scale deployment of any technology, there is increased risk of a single node failing, which can jeopardized the integrity or stability of the overall system. Although the failure rate for a single node may be very small, the failure rate of large-scale systems increases linearly with the number of devices. This scaling has been seen in DRAM [22], microprocessors [14], and FPGAs [19]. An important failure mechanism for FPGAs is caused by radiation-induced soft errors. These errors do not cause permanent damage to the device, but they can modify the internal state or memory of the system [1]. Since FPGAs contain a large amount of memory to configure routing, logic, and other aspects of a design, upsets within the memory of an FPGA can corrupt more than just the data stored in sequential logic elements – such upsets can change the behavior of the circuit configured on the device. The effects of soft errors on single FPGA systems are well understood [7] and methods for addressing these effects have been developed for FPGAs operating in harsh radiation environments such as space.

This paper studies the impact that soft errors have on large-scale FPGA systems within cloud computing. Fault injection is performed on an FPGA system that is tightly coupled with a CPU host. The evaluated device is an Intel Stratix V FPGA, which has been used in cloud-scale accelerated architectures [6]. Through fault injection, the soft error rates of several data-center-like FPGA designs are estimated. Collected data is used to appropriately scale soft error rates to a realistic large-scale FPGA system. Silent data corruption (SDC) is identified as the dominant failure mechanism. SEU detection and recovery approaches are discussed. The most vulnerable design, Mandelbrot, demonstrated a 11.3% vulnerability to soft errors. Running this application, a hundred-thousand node system operating at a high altitude in Denver, Colorado, would experience an SDC every 3.75 hours. Without any methods to detect and address soft errors, such a system could only operate for two minutes with a 99% probability of no SDC.

2 FPGAS IN THE CLOUD

FPGAs are being used in cloud computing because of their flexibility, performance, and energy efficiency. Unlike CPUs and GPUs, FPGA resources can be custom configured for a specific target application. As a result, applications running on an FPGA can make better use of resources to exploit more parallelism, yielding higher performance and better energy efficiency. In [15], the Intel Stratix 10 FPGA is shown to provide 60% higher performance at 2.3× better energy efficiency (i.e., performance per watt) than the Titan X Pascal GPU for a deep neural network application. Using FPGAs in data centers makes these benefits available to a wide variety of applications.

FPGAs can accelerate many high performance computing (HPC) applications. In science, business, and everyday living, applications exist that require HPC. In [3], several Intel Stratix V FPGAs are used to accelerate DNA sequencing – an application in Genomics [21]. In [25], financial applications are accelerated using FPGAs. In [8], Microsoft accelerated the serving of deep neural networks for real-time artificial intelligence on Intel Stratix 10 FPGAs. Many other cloud-computing applications are being accelerated using FPGAs.

Several companies are actively deploying large-scale FPGA systems. Microsoft entered the FPGAs-in-data-center scene early with their launch of Catapult in 2014. They revamped their architecture in 2016, at which point they had 50,000 Stratix V GS D5 FPGAs deployed in their test system [6]. As of August 2017, Microsoft has deployed hundreds of thousands of FPGAs in their data centers [11]. Amazon Web Services (AWS) followed suit with their announcement of FPGA cloud instances in November 2016, which became generally available in April of 2017. As of June 2018, FPGA instances are now available from four different ASW regions–US East (N. Virginia), US West (Oregon), EU (Ireland), and AWS Gov-Cloud (US). They offer instances with up to eight Xilinx Virtex UltraScale Plus FPGAs and currently partner with sixteen companies to provide cutting edge FPGA applications and services. Other companies, such as Baidu, Nimbix, and Micron, are also involved in using FPGAs for cloud computing. It is likely that FPGAs will continue to be used in data centers for cloud computing and that the number of deployed FPGAs will continue to increase [10].

FPGAs in data centers are typically reprogrammable SRAM-based FPGAs closely coupled with a CPU host as depicted in Figure 1. SRAM-based FPGAs use static volatile memory to store device configuration, making it possible to reprogram the device an unlimited number of times. The FPGA and host are usually connected with a high bandwidth interface such as PCIe. Large memory storage with DRAM is often available for acceleration tasks and is shared between the FPGA and processor to facilitate communication between the FPGA and processor. Multiple FPGAs can be connected to the same host or be networked together as part of an advanced acceleration architecture [6]. Some FPGA resources are dedicated to external interfaces, but most are made available to the main acceleration task, often referred to as the kernel or role.

To gather soft error sensitivity data, a single node FPGA system, similar to that shown in Figure 1, will be used for the experiments in this paper. The example node consists of a single host and a single FPGA accelerator board. The host is a Dell Precision T7510 server, equipt with two Intel Xeon E5-2609 processors and 16 GB of ECC-protected RAM, operating Window 10 Professional. A Terrasic DE5-net FPGA accelerator board with the Intel Stratix V GX A7 FPGA and 4 GB of RAM is connected to the host via a PCIe 8× connection. FPGA application designs are implemented on this node using OpenCL and a Terrasic provided board support package.

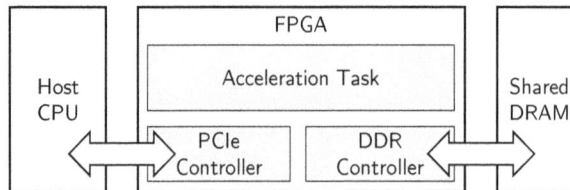

Figure 1: Typical FPGA Data Center Node

Table 1: Neutron SER for 28-nm FPGAs

Device	Stratix V GX A7	Kintex 7 325T
CRAM FIT/Mbit	63	74 ± 18%
CRAM Bits	~99,000,000	~73,000,000
CRAM FIT/Device	6,200	5,400
CRAM MTTU NYC	18.3 years	21.2 years

3 SOFT ERRORS IN FPGAS

Any observable change in a microelectronic device caused by a single energetic particle strike is known as a single event effect or SEE [1]. SEEs in terrestrial environments are primarily caused by high-energy neutrons, thermal neutrons, and alpha particles [5]. The most common SEE in FPGAs are single event upsets (SEUs) that cause flip-flops and other state elements to change their value. Although non-destructive, SEUs can have a significant effect on the operation of an FPGA design and the data it produces [28].

3.1 Soft Error Rates

The soft error rate, or the rate at which soft errors occur, is often measured in terms of failures in time (FIT) and mean time to failure (MTTF). FIT is defined as the average number of failures that occur within a billion hours of operation [1]. MTTF is the inverse of FIT scaled to a unit of time such as years; 1000 FIT roughly corresponds to a 100 year MTTF. Soft error rates for large memory components are often reported in terms of FIT per megabit, (i.e., 10^6), or FIT/Mbit. Neutron FIT rates are typically normalized to the amount of radiation present outdoors in New York City (NYC) at sea level during average solar activity. In these conditions, approximately 13 high-energy, (i.e., greater than 10 MeV), neutrons pass through a square centimeter of area every hour (13 $cm^{-2}h^{-1}$).

The raw terrestrial neutron FIT rates for two different 28-nm SRAM-based FPGAs are shown in Table 1. These devices contain large amounts of configuration memory or CRAM. For each device, the raw CRAM FIT rate per megabit is shown. CRAM FIT rate estimates for the Intel Stratix V and the Xilinx Kintex 7 come from [13] and [29] respectively; the number of CRAM bits are taken from vendor tool reports. Since both FPGAs are based on 28-nm technology, their estimated FIT rates are similar. The mean time between a single SEU occurring in a single Stratix V is 18 years.

The mean time to upset of a CRAM bit in a multiple FPGA system can be computed by dividing the mean time to upset (MTTU) of a single FPGA by the number of FPGAs in the system. The MTTU of a CRAM for different sized systems using the Intel Stratix V GX A7 FPGA is shown in Table 2. With one-hundred thousand FPGAs deployed, an upset occurs on average once every one and a half

Table 2: Stratix V GX A7 Mean Time to Upset at NYC SER

FPGAs	Years	Days	Hours	Min.	Sec.	Total (Sec.)
1	18	127	15	28	27	6E+8
10	1	304	23	8	50	6E+7
100		67	0	30	53	6E+6
1,000		6	16	51	5	6E+5
10,000			16	5	6	6E+4
100,000			1	36	30	6E+3
1,000,000				9	39	6E+2
10,000,000					57	6E+1

Table 3: Neutron flux at various locations

Location	Elevation	Relative Neutron Flux
Seattle, WA	160 ft	1.05
Moscow, Russia	490 ft	1.14
Chicago, IL	590 ft	1.19
Denver, CO	5280 ft	3.76
Los Alamos Natl. Lab.	7380 ft	5.60
Leadville, CO	10170 ft	10.79
White Mtn. Res. Sta.	12500 ft	15.07

hours. This example shows that as the number of deployed FPGAs reach cloud-scale, the rate of upsets occurring in the entire system increases linearly with the size of the system.

Location also plays an important role in the rate of upsets. Higher altitudes experience higher upset rates than New York City sea level. For example, systems deployed at White Mountain Research Center in the USA receive 15× the reference amount or a neutron flux of approximately 195 $cm^{-2}h^{-1}$ [1]. Several factors influence neutron flux including geomagnetic cutoff, solar activity, and atmospheric depth or elevation. Elevation is the most important parameter for determining terrestrial neutron flux. Table 3 shows the neutron flux measured at various locations.

An example of SER scaling based on location is found in the SEU data mentioned in [6], which reports one SEU in FPGA configuration logic every 1025 machine days, (i.e., for a single FPGA instance). The Stratix V GS D5 FPGA used in [6] has approximately 79 million CRAM bits based on the critical bits report generated by vendor tools. Using the 63 FIT/Mbit CRAM upset rate from [13] scaled to the number of CRAM bits in the device gives an entire device SEU rate of 5000 FIT at NYC sea level. This translates to 1 upset every 8333 machine days, suggesting that the location of their data center is somewhere with a neutron flux that is approximately 8× greater than NYC, (i.e., 8333 divided by 1025). As seen in Table 3, this level of neutron flux scaling is feasible based on location. Thus, location deployment can have considerable impact on the upset rate of deployed FPGAs.

3.2 Effect of SEUs on FPGA Designs

SEUs in SRAM-based FPGAs corrupt values of memory associated with device configuration and active design state. CRAM bits enable routes, set look-up table (LUT) equations, and adjust the behavior

Table 4: Breakdown of State in a Stratix V GX A7 FPGA

Type	Bits	Percentage
CRAM	91,170,156	60%
BRAM (M20K)	52,428,800	34%
LUTRAM (MLAB)	7,511,040	5%
Flip-Flop	938,880	1%

of circuit components. Some CRAM bit may be associated with device wide behavior. Active design state and user-memory values are stored in non-CRAM bits. These bits include registers, (i.e., flip-flops), distributed memories, (i.e., LUTRAMs), block memories, (i.e., BRAMs), and control registers for specialized IP, like digital signal processing blocks (DSPs) or high-speed transceivers. Values stored in non-CRAM bits can be altered during run time whereas CRAM bits do not typically change once initialized.

Corrupting CRAM bits within an FPGA can cause an operating design to operate differently than expected causing a variety of design failures [28]. Upsets in CRAM can disconnect routes, short routes together, change timing characteristics, invalidate LUT equations, and disturb general circuit operation. They can also indirectly corrupt values in user-memory by causing incorrect values to be stored or by preventing correct values from being saved in memory (e.g., stuck clock enable signal). When SEUs occur in user-memory, bits, counters, state machines, pipelines and other sequential logic elements take on incorrect values, which can be detrimental.

The state elements within an SRAM-based FPGA are dominated by CRAM bits making CRAM bits the primary concern for soft errors. The composition of known internal state subject to radiation-induced upsets in an Intel Stratix V GX A7 FPGA is shown in Table 4. CRAM bits make up 60% of all known internal state in this device. Although block memories make up an additional 34% of the known internal state, they can be protected from radiation induced single-event effects with error correction codes (ECC). Upsets in CRAM bits, however, immediately affect the operation of the underlying circuit. Even if such upsets are repaired at a later time, they introduce operational behaviors that may affect computations performed in the FPGA.

The number of CRAM bits listed in Table 4 exceeds that of LU-TRAM and flip-flop bits by a factor of ten, making upsets in the smaller population much less likely. When a LUTRAM is used for read-only logic, its bits are counted as a CRAM bits. Although upsets in non-CRAM bits, (e.g., bits in flip-flops, M20Ks, MLABs), are less likely, they should not be disregarded; these bits play an important role and can cause disruptive behavior if upset.

3.3 Architectural Vulnerability Factor

Not all upsets in CRAM will affect the functionality of a design. Upsets in bits that are unassociated with the resources used by an active design should not disrupt the design behavior, (e.g., a bit in a LUT that is not used by an active design). Upsets in bits that are associated with resources used by a design may alter the underlying circuit, but the effects of the upset on the design may be hidden by error masking. Masking occurs when timing, logic, or design functionality prevent SEUs from causing failure. Different FPGA designs operating on the same device have different soft

Table 5: Benchmark Design Resource Utilization

Design	Total ALMs		Routing
FD3D	190,612	(81.21%)	30.50%
Mandelbrot	173,755	(74.03%)	29.40%
Channelizer	145,180	(61.85%)	23.40%
Matrix Multiply	135,405	(57.69%)	28.40%
FFT1D	129,767	(55.29%)	20.80%
FFT2D	121,015	(51.56%)	22.20%
JPEG Decoder	95,250	(40.58%)	17.70%
Compute Score	94,575	(40.29%)	22.10%
Boardtest	57,547	(24.52%)	11.90%
Video Downscaling	50,914	(21.69%)	10.80%
Vector Op	49,503	(21.09%)	9.90%
Vector Add	49,039	(20.89%)	9.70%
Sobel	48,573	(20.69%)	9.20%
Hello World	46,329	(19.74%)	8.60%

Table 6: Critical Bits

Design	Injectable	Total Critical	
FD3D	98,502,636	69,740,486	(70.8%)
Mandelbrot	98,029,036	66,122,603	(67.5%)
Channelizer	98,534,636	62,673,556	(63.6%)
Matrix Multiply	98,573,036	58,774,590	(59.6%)
FFT1D	98,514,796	57,182,508	(58.0%)
FFT2D	98,439,276	56,797,420	(57.7%)
JPEG Decoder	98,386,796	41,360,019	(42.0%)
Compute Score	98,394,476	44,450,948	(45.2%)
Boardtest	98,578,156	24,009,160	(24.4%)
Video Downscaling	98,587,116	20,934,957	(21.2%)
Vector Op	98,549,996	19,589,044	(19.9%)
Vector Add	98,587,116	19,838,814	(20.1%)
Sobel Filter	98,597,996	19,067,514	(19.3%)
Hello World	98,603,107	18,132,374	(18.4%)

error sensitivities with varying responses to soft errors. Generally speaking, designs that use more resources tend to be more sensitive to soft errors than designs that use fewer resources.

The benchmark designs used in this paper all utilize a different amount of FPGA resources and we expect the SEU sensitivity of each design to vary based on their utilization. The resource utilization of these designs are listed in Table 5. Design are listed in order of highest utilization to lowest utilization based on the number of adaptive logic modules (ALMs) that are used by the design. There are 234,720 ALMs in the Stratix V GX A7 and the device utilization ranges from 20% for the Hello World design to 81% for the FD3D design. Routing influences the overall resource utilization but does not directly contribute to total ALM utilization.

Vendors provide tools to classify bits as associated or unassociated with resources used by the active design. Intel Quartus Prime calls associated bits *critical bits* and allows the users to tag specific hierarchical modules as separate regions, meaning users could exclude portions of the design from tagging if so desired. The number of critical bits estimated by the tools for each of the benchmark designs is summarized in Table 6. Two numbers are given for each design: the injectable bits and the total critical bits. The number of injectable bits represents the number of CRAM bits that can be artificially upset through fault injection. This number varies from design to design since some LUTs are used as user-memories and cannot have faults injected into them. The critical bits percentage is also shown in parentheses. As expected, the percent of the CRAM bits that are critical varies significantly from design to design and corresponds to the resource utilization of the design.

Many critical bits that are used by a design will not cause functional failure if upset. The effect of some CRAM upsets may be masked by the timing, logic, and the current state of the design [24]. A soft error occurring too late in a clock cycle to be latched into memory, or an upset in a register whose value will be over written before it is used are examples of temporal masking. Downstream logic that prevents the errors induced by an upset from propagating is an example of logical masking. An upset in a portion of the design that is unused, like test logic, is an example of functional masking.

Because some upsets in CRAM have no effect on the overall functionality of a design, the raw SEU FIT rate of an FPGA device overestimates the soft error rate of an actual FPGA application. The *architectural vulnerability factor* or AVF [14] is a parameter that is often used to scale the raw soft error rate by an application-specific sensitivity. The AVF is defined as the probability that a CRAM fault will cause a failure in the application design. The overall failure rate is the product of the AVF and the raw SEU soft error rate.

To determine the overall failure rate of specific FPGA accelerator designs, the AVF for the FPGA circuit needs to be estimated. The AVF can be estimated through fault simulation, fault injection, or radiation testing. Fault injection emulates the occurrence of an SEU by altering values in CRAM bits during runtime [18] and is a common approach for estimating overall failure rate. AVF is estimated in fault injection by taking the ratio of the number of faults that cause design failures with the total number of faults injected into the design. Radiation testing accelerates the occurrence of SEUs by exposing the device to greatly increased levels of radiation [17].

3.4 System Failure Modes

SEUs that cause failure can trigger a variety of system failure modes. Broadly classified, failures observed during fault injection experiments of this paper fall into one of three main categories: host unresponsive, FPGA unavailable, and silent data corruption. These are likely the failure modes that would be seen in an FPGA cloud computing platform. All failure modes observed in the experiments of this paper could be resolved by repairing the fault, reprogramming the FPGA, or power cycling the system. No permanent damage was observed during the fault injection experiments of this paper.

3.4.1 Host Unresponsive. Host unresponsive failures occur when an SEU in the FPGA causes system instability in the host. Instability includes lack of network response from the host, host unresponsiveness to keyboard and mouse input, and crashes including abrupt power failure. This instability may stem from issues in the driver or hardware, but the underlying causes are unknown. In the experiments of this paper, host unresponsive failures were primarily observed as a loss of remote connection from the test operator to the host (see Figure 2). This failure mode is relatively easy to detect and can be resolved by rebooting the system.

3.4.2 FPGA Unavailable. Any SEU that makes it so that the host can not connect to or initialize the FPGA is considered an FPGA unavailable failure. This failure mode manifested itself in many different forms during the fault injection experiments performed during this work. These behaviors include the host not being able to find any FPGAs on the system, not being able to open the target FPGA, PCIe link errors, reading the incorrect kernel or hardware ID, and not being able to initialize the clock, etc. Any behavior that prevents the host-application from initializing the kernel without reprogramming the FPGA is considered an FPGA unavailable failure. Like host unavailable, this failure mode is easy to detect. Recovering from this behavior mainly involves reprogramming the FPGA, but recovering may sometimes require a power cycle.

3.4.3 Silent data corruption (SDC). The most challenging behavior is when an upset causes the FPGA to return incorrect data. In most cases, this data corruption is not detectable by the application and passes as correct data. This event is called silent data corruption or SDC and is the most common failure mode. The severity of SDCs vary from application to application. For some applications, SDCs are not a problem because the returned data is transient and can afford being incorrect, (e.g., web-search results); in other applications, SDC caries severe consequences, (e.g., SQL database commit). SDC can originate from soft errors in several places throughout a design. Errors in the interfaces between the FPGA and host or DRAM could instill SDC during read and write operations. This was observed in the Boardtest application when 4 GB of randomly generated data was transfered to and from DRAM through the FPGA. SDC could also occur from upsets deep inside the logic of a target application. SDC failure modes were caught in the fault injection experiments by comparing the FPGA results against golden result test vectors stored on the host. In practice, SDCs are not detectable by the system.

4 FAULT INJECTION EXPERIMENTS

Fault injection is a common way of emulating soft errors to observe soft error system response [18]. In the experiments of this paper, a random fault injection campaign is used. Faults to inject are selected at random for two purposes. First, this mode of injecting faults better models the behavior of SEUs in deployed environments or at an accelerated radiation test. Second, collecting random samples models population sampling and makes it possible to statistically estimate the overall SEU sensitivity of a design under test. Using random faults to estimate overall sensitivity is known as statistical fault injection (SFI) [20]. SFI provides a good estimate of the overall sensitivity of a target device given sufficient samples. The more samples that are collected, the tighter confidence intervals will be.

Confidence intervals in these experiments are calculated using the Clopper-Pearson binomial proportions confidence interval [9]. Data collected in these fault injection experiments are presented as percentages of sensitivity, or AVF, bounded by a proper confidence interval. The data claims no absolutes but rather a 95% confidence bound within a certain interval, meaning that the true sensitivity lies within the interval with a 95% confidence. To achieve reasonably

tight confidence intervals, many thousands of faults were injected into each design. Confidence intervals are such that the overall confidence interval, (i.e., upper bound minus the lower bound), of each experiment falls with 10% of the estimated value.

The goals of the fault injection experiments summarized in this paper are to record system response behavior to configuration upsets, quantify the sensitivity of a design to upset-induced failure, and discuss the benefits and drawbacks of various SEU response approaches. This information is then used to better understand the impact of SEUs on a much broader scale for large-scale FPGA deployments. As such, several benchmarks running on an example node are tested using a fault injection framework. The framework is designed to iteratively inject a fault, execute a test application and record system response. This flow is applied to all benchmark designs until sufficient data is collect. The following sections detail the benchmark designs, and fault injection framework used to collect the data needed to accomplish the goals of this paper.

4.1 Benchmark Designs

To gain a better understanding of soft-error induced failure modes and how frequent such failure modes occurs, it is necessary to sample a diverse set of designs. As such, 15 different applications are included in the experiments of this paper ranging from a simple "Hello World" design to complex signal processing and computation. As expected, AVF failure rates vary among the designs, but common trends are found among the results.

All of the benchmark designs used in this work originated from example designs posted on the Intel FPGA SDK for OpenCL – Developer Zone [12] and from the Terrasic OpenCL board support package for the DE5-net Stratix V GX A7 FPGA developer board [26]. Some designs were excluded from this experiment because they did not fit on the target device. All of the included designs and their respective resource utilizations are listed in Table 5.

All designs listed in Table 5 were compiled by the Intel Quartus Prime 18.0 Standard edition OpenCL compiler using the Terrasic DE5-net BSP. They each use a wide range of resource. The smallest design, Hello World, has the simplest kernel and is dominated by the overhead of OpenCL supporting hardware. OpenCL hardware includes a PCIe controller, a DDR3 controller, and other interface components used by the framework. In addition to the OpenCL hardware, a fault injection and SEU detection IP core were added to each design, with very little overhead, to support fault injection.

4.2 Fault Injection Setup

To collect enough data for this experiment, it was necessary to develop an automated test flow and accompanying equipment setup. The behavior of the host, FPGA, and application under an imposed configuration upset is the object of interest in these experiments. The test setup and accompanying flow are geared towards capturing strange behavior and overcoming adverse effects to restore the environment to a working state for subsequent sampling.

Figure 2 displays the test setup and components used by the experiments in this work. The host is the Dell Precision T7610 described in Section 2. The Stratix V GX A7 FPGA is part of the Terrasic DE5-Net accelerator board. The test operator is an Intel NUC. It orchestrates the entire flow of the experiments. The test

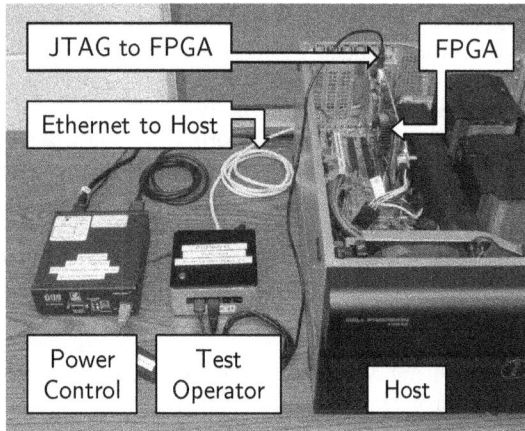

Figure 2: Experiment Setup for Fault Injection Testing

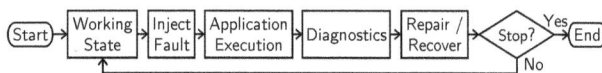

Figure 3: Fault Injection Flow

operator interacts with the FPGA via JTAG to inject faults and configure the device. Interaction with the host by the test operator is conducted via Ethernet. This allows the test operator to execute host applications and observe behavior. When injected faults cause experiment instability, the remote power control allows the test operator to power cycle the host and FPGA concurrently.

4.3 Fault Injection Flow

Several fault injection flows have been developed to capture system response behavior to upsets and estimate sensitivity [18]. Experiments in this paper follow the flow shown in Figure 3. To begin, the system must be brought into a working state. At this point, a fault is introduced and the host application is executed to stress the system while the fault is present. After a period of delay, which allows any errors to propagate, a series of diagnostics are run to observe the health of the system. These diagnostics check the output of the application correctness and check the status of the host and FPGA. If abnormal behavior occurs, the event is recorded and a series of recovery procedures are conducted. If there is no abnormal behavior, the injected fault is repaired. With the system back in a working state, the test is repeated until sufficient data is collected for the target application.

An important part of the described flow is the ability to diagnose incorrect system behavior. Detecting host unresponsiveness and unavailability of the FPGA is straight forward: if the test operator can not communication with the host, the host is unresponsive; if the host can not initialize the kernel, the FPGA is unavailable. Detecting SDC is less strait forward. In these experiments, SDC is detected by comparing the output of the kernel against co-computation by the CPU on the host, or by comparing the output against a golden copy stored on the host.

When a failure is detected, recovery is necessary. After recover actions are taken, (see Section 6), the system is assumed to be in

a working state. This is not a perfect assumption. The injected fault can cause non-CRAM bits to become corrupt, (e.g. bits in an M20K). This kind of corruption can persist between runs of the target application. Several runs of the host application may complete successfully before corruption of non-CRAM bits causes a failure. It is assumed that subsequent runs will catch failures caused by non-CRAM bit corruption and that eventually the FPGA will be reprogrammed to remove this corruption. Once the system has been recovered, the test proceeds.

Each injected fault took a minute to test on average. This includes time spent reprogramming the FPGA, injecting faults, waiting for host application and diagnostic tests to complete, and recovering from failure. The data presented in the next section represents approximately 100 days of continuous testing distributed among all of the included benchmark designs. Faults were injected and externally scrubbed using the Quartus fault injection debugger (FID) and associated IP cores. These operations took an average of 4 to 6 seconds to complete. Programming via JTAG takes 12 seconds with an additional overhead of 20 seconds to start the FID software. When reprogramming via JTAG, a system reboot is necessary so that the host can recognize the FPGA, which takes three minutes to complete. The same overhead is needed to perform a complete power cycle.

4.4 Results

The results from the fault injection experiments are shown in Table 7. This table lists all of the tested benchmark designs, the ALM utilization, the number of faults injected for each design, and the percent of injections that caused SDC, FPGA unavailable, and host unresponsive failure. Designs are listed in descending order by the overall AVF of the design for *any* failure. The percentage within parentheses represents the percent of injections that caused failure normalized to the ALM utilization. This metric is included to give a sense of the relative sensitivity of each design to soft errors. Some designs are much larger than others, but by using a normalized AVF, it can be seen that smaller designs, like video downscaling, are more sensitive to soft errors per utilized ALM than larger designs, like Mandelbrot. The ratio between the percentage of critical bits and the AVF for any failure is also included.

Even some of the most highly utilized designs have a small AVF based on the results from Table 7. For example, Mandelbrot utilizes 74% of the available ALMs, yet only 11.6% of randomly upset bits will cause a failure in the system. ALM utilization is closely related to the percentage of critical bits. Comparing the percentage of critical bits to the AVF for any failure, most designs have an AVF that is 6× smaller their percentage of critical bits. The AVF for any failure, of all designs, is at least 5× smaller than their respective ALM utilizations, suggesting that the AVF for any failure of any FPGA design is likely much less than the ALM utilization or the percentage of bits that are critical in the design.

Due to all of the masking effects present in a design, (see Section 3.3), and variations in routing utilization, it is possible for a design with lower utilization to have a higher overall AVF than another design with higher device utilization. For example, FD3D uses 7% more of the device than Mandelbrot yet it is 2.8% less sensitive (i.e., its AVF is 2.8% less than that of Mandelbrot). Another example

Table 7: Fault Injection Results, AVF for specific behaviors (normalized to ALM utilization)

Design	ALM Utilization	Critical Bits	Faults Injected	Silent Data Corruption		FPGA Unavailable		Host Unresponsive		Any Failure AVF		Critical Bits to AVF Ratio
Mandelbrot	74%	67%	9,301	11.3%	(15.3%)	0.3%	(0.4%)	0.02%	(0.03%)	11.6%	(15.7%)	5.8×
Matrix Multiply	58%	60%	17,094	9.0%	(15.5%)	0.5%	(0.9%)	0.03%	(0.05%)	9.6%	(16.6%)	6.2×
FFT2D	52%	58%	5,223	8.5%	(16.4%)	0.5%	(0.9%)	0.00%	(0.00%)	9.0%	(17.4%)	6.4×
FFT1D	55%	58%	7,389	8.2%	(14.8%)	0.4%	(0.7%)	0.18%	(0.32%)	8.8%	(15.9%)	6.6×
FD3D	81%	71%	8,094	8.2%	(10.1%)	0.5%	(0.6%)	0.00%	(0.00%)	8.8%	(10.8%)	8.0×
JPEG Decoder	41%	42%	7,948	3.4%	(8.5%)	3.3%	(8.2%)	0.14%	(0.34%)	7.0%	(17.2%)	6.0×
Compute Score	40%	45%	7,310	5.3%	(13.2%)	1.2%	(3.0%)	0.00%	(0.00%)	6.6%	(16.3%)	6.8×
Channelizer	62%	64%	10,709	5.1%	(8.2%)	0.4%	(0.6%)	0.03%	(0.05%)	5.5%	(8.9%)	11.6×
Boardtest	25%	24%	12,247	3.4%	(13.7%)	0.6%	(2.6%)	0.03%	(0.13%)	4.1%	(16.6%)	5.9×
Video Downscaling	22%	21%	11,641	3.0%	(13.7%)	0.6%	(2.9%)	0.04%	(0.20%)	3.7%	(17.1%)	5.7×
Vector Op	21%	20%	6,790	2.6%	(12.2%)	0.4%	(1.7%)	0.04%	(0.21%)	3.0%	(14.3%)	6.6×
Vector Add	21%	20%	11,623	2.0%	(9.6%)	0.4%	(1.8%)	0.04%	(0.21%)	2.5%	(11.7%)	8.0×
Sobel Filter	21%	19%	6,638	1.3%	(6.2%)	0.5%	(2.5%)	0.03%	(0.15%)	1.9%	(9.0%)	10.2×
Hello World	20%	18%	15,442	0.1%	(0.4%)	0.2%	(0.9%)	0.01%	(0.03%)	0.3%	(1.5%)	61.3×

of this is Channelizer and JPEG decoder. Generally speaking, the fewer resources a design uses, the smaller its overall AVF will be.

When the AVF for any failure within a design is scaled by the ALM utilization of a design, the normalized AVF among all designs is quite similar. Excluding Hello World, the normalized AVF for any failure among all of the designs resides between 9% and 17% with a mean of 14%. This suggests a strong relationship between device utilization and actual AVF. There is greater relative variation in the normalized AVF for FPGA unavailable and host unresponsive failure modes. This suggests that these failure modes are more closely tied to shared overhead among the designs such as bits associated with device interfaces and device wide status registers.

Silent data corruption is the dominating failure behavior. It accompanied up to 11.3% of all randomly injected faults depending on application resource utilization and other factors. For most of the designs, this failure modes represents the great majority of all failure occurrences. The other two failure modes, FPGA unavailable and host unresponsive, are fairly small in comparison. With the exception of the JPEG Decoder and Compute Score applications, the AVF for the FPGA unavailable failure behavior was fairly consistent across applications. It accompanied about 0.6%, (i.e., one in 168), of all random faults. The host unresponsive behavior did not occur very frequently. It accompanied about 0.04%, (i.e., one in 2,500), of all random faults. This failure mode has a similar AVF among all designs suggesting that it is likely related to SEUs in shared overhead rather than SEUs in the logic of specific applications.

5 FAILURE RATE FOR LARGE-SCALE SYSTEMS

In very large-scale FPGA systems, a design with a small AVF can still fail frequently. For the purpose of studying the impact of soft errors on large-scale FPGA cloud-computing, a 100,000 node system deployed in Denver, Colorado, (3.8× NYC neutron flux) made up of Stratix V GX A7 FPGAs is considered. An AVF of 1% in this situation equates to 23.6 million FIT or a MTTF of one-and-a-half days.

Unlike the other failure modes, SDC is not detectable and will occur with up to 11.3% of all random upsets in the data set collected,

Table 8: SDC MTTF on a 100,000 node system in Denver, CO

Design	FIT	MTTF
Mandelbrot	266,000,000	3.8 Hours
Matrix Multiply	212,000,000	4.8 Hours
FFT2D	200,000,000	5.0 Hours
FFT1D	193,000,000	5.2 Hours
FD3D	193,000,000	5.2 Hours
JPEG Decoder	80,000,000	12.5 Hours
Compute Score	125,000,000	8.0 Hours
Channelizer	120,000,000	8.3 Hours
Boardtest	80,000,000	12.5 Hours
Video Downscaling	71,000,000	14.2 Hours
Vector Op	61,000,000	16.3 Hours
Vector Add	47,000,000	21.2 Hours
Sobel Filter	31,000,000	1.3 Days
Hello World	2,000,000	2.5 Weeks

(i.e., Mandelbrot). An AVF of 11.3% in the considered 100,000 node system equates to 266 million FIT or an MTTF of 3.75 hours. Table 8 lists the FIT and corresponding MTTF for each design as if deployed on the considered 100,000 node system.

Other failure modes would occur less frequently and would be easier to detect and address. In the considered system, FPGA unavailable events would range from 5 M to 78 M FIT with a 14 M FIT average among designs, (i.e., 3 day MTTF); host unresponsive events would have a FIT up to 4 M averaging 1 M, (i.e., 1.5 month MTTF). Because these failure modes occur much less frequently and are more easily detected and addressed, they pose a much smaller threat to system integrity and stability than SDC.

5.1 Reliable Computing and Mission Time

Although the metric "Mean-Time to Failure" (MTTF) provides a useful measure for understanding the overall rate at which failures in the system will occur, it does not adequately represent the fact that many failures in the system will occur in sooner than the

Table 9: Mission Time for Different Reliabilty Constraints

r	0.5	0.9	0.99	0.999	0.9999	0.99999
$MT(r)$ (sec)	9,446	1,436	137	13.6	1.36	.14

MTTF estimate. In fact, 63% of the failures expected in the system will occur within a time that is less than the MTTF (with some of these failures occurring in a much shorter time than the MTTF). The MTTF metric can give a false sense of security in suggesting that the system will operate without failure for the amount of time specified by the MTTF estimate.

A better measure for evaluating the rate of SDC failure for a computing system is to estimate the time in which the system can operate above a pre-specified level of reliability, r. This measure is called the "mission time" (MT) and is a function of a minimum reliability constraint, r. For example, the mission time of a system that must operate with a reliability of r=0.99 (i.e., MT(0.99)) indicates the amount of time that the system can operate with a probability of success of 99% or higher. The mission time can be computed from the continuous time reliability function, $R(t)$. The reliability function for failure due to soft errors can be modeled by an exponential function used for modeling constant failure rate systems [23]:

$$R(t) = e^{-\lambda t}, \tag{1}$$

where λ is the constant failure rate (failures/time). The mission time can be determined by assigning $R(T)$ the reliability constraint, r, and solving for t,

$$MT(r) = \frac{-ln(r)}{\lambda}. \tag{2}$$

The constant failure rate can be determined by taking the reciprocal of the mean-time to SEU upset (MTTU) estimate and scaling it by the AVF for SDC events, or $\lambda = \text{AVF}_{SDC}/\text{MTTU}$.

For the 100,000 node system in Denver running the Mandelbrot benchmark, the MTTU = 5790/3.76 = 1540 sec and λ = .113/1540 = 7.3×10^{-5} failures/second. With a reliability constraint of r = .99, the mission time for this system is only 137 seconds (about 6 minutes). This result suggests that the system can only operate for about two minutes with a 99% confidence that no SDC events have corrupted the data. This time is far less than the estimated mean-time to SDC failure of 13,628 seconds. The mission time for other reliability constraints on this platform is summarized in Table 9.

Examining mission time in relation to reliable computing shows that a high confidence in the computational correctness comes in short bursts of operation. Even designs with a low SDC AVF have short-lived mission-times for high-reliability. For example, on a 100,000 node Stratix V GX A7 FPGA system at NYC flux, a design with a 1% AVF for SDCs only maintains a reliability higher than five-nines (i.e., 0.99999) for six seconds. Such short periods of time at high reliability may not be long enough for application tasks to complete and still meet reliability requirements.

6 SEU DETECTION AND RECOVERY

Because SRAM-based FPGAs are sensitive to single-event effects, FPGA vendors provided methods for detecting SEUs within the CRAM and and repairing the CRAM state. The technique for detecting and repairing CRAM state is called Configuration Scrubbing.

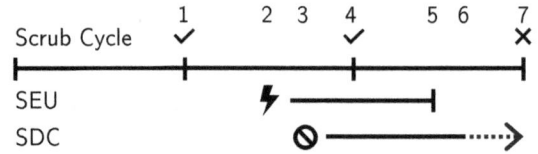

Figure 4: Scrub cycles, SEU occurrence, and SDC

Configuration scrubbing is the continuous process of reading the configuration memory, determining if there are errors, and correcting these errors if found. Configuration scrubbing is asynchronous to the operation of the active design and is performed silently in the background. The data in the configuration memory can be repaired by the use of error correction coding (ECC) that is included in the configuration memory frames. Single-error correction, double-error detection (SECDED) codes are used to allow all single-bit errors within a frame to be corrected and all double-errors to be detected. In addition to SECDEC encoding, a checksum is computed for the entire configuration memory to detect complex errors that are not detected or corrected with SECDED encoding [2].

Although configuration scrubbing is able to detect and correct SEU-induced CRAM errors, this process is not instantaneous and takes a considerable amount of time. For the Stratix V device used in paper, the time it takes to perform a whole device CRAM scrub cycle varies from 47 milliseconds to 24.20 seconds depending on the internal clock frequency and the clock divisor. No matter how long the scrub cycle takes, SEUs in CRAM will be present for millions of clock cycles before they are detected and possibly corrected. For example, consider a device with a 100 ms scrub period and a global clock operating on a 100 MHz clock. On average, an upset in CRAM will be present for 50 ms or five million clock cycles in this device before it is detected and corrected by scrubbing. This temporary CRAM upset may cause undesirable behavior in the design that may or may not go away with the scrubbing.

Figure 4 diagrams scrubbing along side an SEU event and occurrence of an SDC. At position 1 in the diagram, a scrub cycle completes. No SEUs are detected or corrected during the scrub cycle as denoted by a check mark. At position 2, an SEU occurs in the CRAM. This upset remains in the CRAM until it is detected and corrected by the scrubbing engine. At position 3, an SDC appears on the outputs of the design. This occurs after the upset has been present in the device for several clock cycles. Errors introduced by the upset take time to propagate through the design. At position 4, a subsequent scrub cycle completes. This scrub cycle reports that no SEUs were detected or corrected even though an SEU occurred since the last completion of a scrub cycle. If an SEU occurs in a CRAM frame after the frame is evaluated as part of the current scrub cycle, then the SEU may remain present and undetected until the next scrub cycle. At position 5, the scrubbing engine detects the SEU and corrects it. At position 6, the SDC induced by the upset either flushes out of the design or remains present as denoted by the dotted continuation of the SDC. At position 7, the final scrub cycle shown completes and reports that an SEU was detected and corrected as denoted by an X.

Enabling internal CRAM scrubbing does not eliminate erroneous behavior caused by SEUs in CRAM. Scrubbing only limits the periods of time during which SEU induced errors can propagate. If an upset corrupts state that persists for long periods of time, (e.g., counters, state-machines, status registers, infrequently written block memories), then this corruption will remain even after the upset is removed. In some cases, the corrupted data will naturally flush out of the system during normal use or through a design reset. Other situations will require the device to be reprogrammed or power cycled to remove the corruption [16].

In the fault injection experiments of this paper, every time a failure is detected, a series of successively more drastic recovery actions are conducted in succession to bring the system back into a working state. This procedure makes it possible to determine the least invasive recovery option necessary for each occurrence of a failure. The first action taken is scrubbing. Scrubbing is performed by repairing the injected fault or removing it from CRAM. Success of the recovery action is determined by a subsequent execution of the host application and diagnostic results. If no issue is encountered, (i.e., the application completes without any failure), the system is considered to be a working state and fault injection continues. If failure behavior remains after scrubbing, a reprogramming of the FPGA is attempted to resolve the issue. After this recovery action, the host application is run again. If the application finishes cleanly, fault injection continues with the next random fault; otherwise, the host is gracefully shutdown and a power cycle is performed on the host and FPGA concurrently.

Table 10 lists each benchmark design, the number of SDC events observed, and the distribution of successful recovery actions taken. SDC occurred in these benchmarks because of an upset present in the CRAM of the device, (i.e. injected fault). Repairing the upset does not undo the SDC that has already occurred, but it can restore the system to a working state so that subsequent computations are be processed correctly. Table 10 shows that configuration scrubbing can restore the proper functionality of a design a high percentage of the time when an SEU occurs. For many of the designs, configuration scrubbing is able to restore functionality 98% of the time. That being said, some situations still required the FPGA to be reprogrammed or the host computer and FPGA to be power cycled before proper functionality is restored. This is likely do the corruption of user memory, (e.g., non-CRAM bits, block memory, flip-flops), or other persistent state [16]. This data shows that scrubbing is effective in restoring design functionality and that, although the rate is small, some situations still require reprogramming the FPGA or power cycling the node.

6.1 Response Options

Knowing that SEUs can cause disruptive behavior, an appropriate SEU detection and recovery mechanism should be implement to address this concern. Depending on the application, some failure behavior may be tolerable and users may only want to respond to the most severe failure behavior caused by SEUs. There are a number of different recovery approaches a user could take:

(1) Disable scrubbing, respond when a failure is detected,
(2) Enable scrubbing, respond when a failure is detected,
(3) Respond every time an SEU is detected, or

Table 10: SDC System Restoration

Design	Events	Scrub	Reprogram	Power Cycle
Mandelbrot	1,050	99.5%	0.5%	0.0%
Matrix Multiply	1,530	99.2%	0.8%	0.0%
FFT2D	442	99.1%	0.9%	0.0%
FFT1D	606	99.2%	0.8%	0.0%
FD3D	667	98.7%	1.3%	0.0%
JPEG Decoder	273	98.2%	1.1%	0.7%
Compute Score	390	97.2%	2.8%	0.0%
Channelizer	541	98.0%	2.0%	0.0%
Boardtest	412	97.1%	2.9%	0.0%
Video Downscaling	345	94.2%	5.8%,	0.0%
Vector Op	174	95.4%	4.6%	0.0%
Vector Add	233	98.3%	1.3%	0.4%
Sobel Filter	85	90.6%	8.2%	1.2%
Hello World	12	66.7%	8.3%	25.0%

(4) Respond only to upsets in the most critical regions.

A user could take a minimal approach by disabling scrubbing and only responding to detectable failure modes: FPGA unavailable and host unresponsive. In the system referenced in Section 5, these events are infrequent. FPGA unavailable would occur once every 3 days on average and host unreachable would occur once every 1.5 month on average. Using this approach, users should at least consider periodically checking for SEUs and recording their occurrence for use in failure analysis when unexpected behavior occurs. This mode misses out on the protection from continual SDCs that scrubbing provides. Going without this protection may not be a great concern, especially if the FPGA is frequently reprogrammed.

Enabling scrubbing and only responding to detectable failures is a good option for preventing continual SDC. In most cases, scrubbing is a very effective means for restoring the system to a working state, but scrubbing alone will not completely prevent SDCs from ever happening. User concerned about SDCs should consider responding to SEUs as they are detected. Responding only to upsets in critical regions reduces how frequently action must be taken but adds complexity recovery implementation. In the system referenced in Section 5, CRAM SEU events have a 25 minute MTTF, and SEU in critical CRAM bit events have a 38 minute MTTF. Depending on the system and operating design, responding only to upsets in critical bits may or may not be worth the additional effort required. In the referenced system, SDC events have a 3.8 hour MTTF. This shows that only 1 in 9 SEU responses would actually prevent an SDC if the user responded to every SEU and only 1 in 6 responses would be necessary if the user responded only to upsets in critical bits within the reference system. The other responses are effectively overhead for the selected recovery approach.

Response to an SEU can range from a simple reset to discarding previously generated data and power cycling the system. In order to respond to an SEU, the user must be given access to the appropriate SEU detection signals. With these signals, the user can then decide how to respond when an SEU occurs. To tolerate a large number of SEU-induced failures at a software level, at a minimum, hardware must be able to detect and report any SEUs in a timely enough manner so that the software level can isolate resulting errors and take appropriate recovery actions [4]. Assuming computation between nodes is independent, overhead of response would be minimal, as only effected nodes would need to be recovered. Additional software or design level fault-tolerance techniques could also be used to detect and correct errors. As more large-scale FPGA accelerator platforms come online, the number of nodes and risk of SEU-induced SDC necessitate the implementation of an appropriate SEU response mechanism.

7   CONCLUSION

Industry is making use of hundreds of thousands of FPGAs to accelerate cloud computing applications. The FPGAs being used are susceptible to radiation-induced soft errors. Individual nodes have a relatively low soft error rate, (e.g., 1 upset every 18 years on average for a Stratix V GX A7 FPGA in NYC neutron flux); but when numerous nodes are deployed, the soft error rate increases dramatically. This paper looks at the impact of SEUs on large-scale FPGA cloud-computing systems. A hypothetical, but realistic hundred-thousand node Stratix V GS A7 FPGA system deployed in Denver is considered where upsets occur on average every half-hour.

Not all SEUs adversely affect the functionality of an FPGA cloud computing application, but some compromise system integrity and stability. Fault injection testing of 15 designs estimates their overall AVF to be between 0.3% and 11.6% depending on resource utilization and error masking. Estimated AVF was found to be at least 5× smaller than the percentage of utilized ALMs or percentage of bits tagged as critical. Most observed failures were SDC events. Within a 100,000 node system deployed in Denver, the design with the highest AVF, (i.e., Mandelbrot), would have a 3.8 hour MTTF for SDC, a 3 day MTTF for FPGA unavailable, and a 1.5 month MTTF for host unresponsive. FPGA unavailable and host unresponsive behaviors are easy to detect; responding to these events carries negligible overhead.

SDC is difficult to detect and can have broad impact on the system. Applications that require high-reliability must have short mission-times or implement appropriate SEU response techniques. In the considered 100,000 node environment mission-time for a reliability specification of 0.99 is less than two minutes. Scrubbing can be used to address SDC by responding to SEUs as they occur. One less the AVF is the percentage of SEU responses that are unnecessary. System wide response to each SEU can significantly lower availability and will not necessarily address all SDC events. One in 10 upsets occurs in non-CRAM bits based on the ratios between the populations and approximately one in every hundred SEU would occur in non-CRAM design state of the Mandelbrot design. To avoid SDC from upsets in non-CRAM bits, additional mitigation-techniques need to be applied to the target design.

ACKNOWLEDGMENTS

This work was supported by the Utah Space Grant Consortium and by the I/UCRC Program of the National Science Foundation under Grant No. 1738550.

REFERENCES

[1] 2006. Measurement and reporting of alpha particle and terrestrial cosmic ray-induced soft errors in semiconductor devices. Retrieved December 12, 2018 from https://www.jedec.org/sites/default/files/docs/JESD89A.pdf

[2] P. Adell et al. 2008. Assessing and mitigating radiation effects in Xilinx SRAM FPGAs. In 2008 European Conference on Radiation and Its Effects on Components and Systems. 418–424.

[3] J. Arram et al. 2015. RAMETHY: Reconfigurable acceleration of bisulfite sequence alignment. In Proceedings of the 2015 ACM/SIGDA International Symposium on Field-Programmable Gate Arrays. ACM, New York, NY, USA, 250–259.

[4] L. Barroso et al. 2018. The Datacenter as a Computer: An Introduction to the Design of Warehouse-Scale Machines, Third edition. Synthesis Lectures on Computer Architecture 13, 3 (2018), 1–189. https://doi.org/10.2200/S00874ED3V01Y201809CAC046

[5] R. Baumann. 2001. Soft errors in advanced semiconductor devices – Part I: The three radiation sources. IEEE Transactions on Device and Materials Reliability 1, 1 (2001), 17–22.

[6] A. Caulfield et al. 2016. A cloud-scale acceleration architecture. In 2016 49th Annual IEEE/ACM International Symposium on Microarchitecture. IEEE, 1–13. https://doi.org/10.1109/MICRO.2016.7783710

[7] M. Ceschia et al. 2003. Identification and classification of single-event upsets in the configuration memory of SRAM-based FPGAs. IEEE Trans. Nucl. Sci. 50, 6 (2003), 2088–2094.

[8] E. Chung et al. 2018. Serving DNNs in real time at datacenter scale with Project Brainwave. IEEE Micro 38, 2 (2018), 8–20.

[9] C. Clopper and E. Pearson. 1934. The use of confidence or fiducial limits illustrated in the case of the binomial. Biometrika 26, 4 (1934), 404–413.

[10] Deloitte. 2017. Hitting the accelerator: the next generation of machine-learning chips. Retrieved December 12, 2018 from https://www2.deloitte.com/content/dam/Deloitte/global/Images/infographics/technologymediatelecommunications/gx-deloitte-tmt-2018-nextgen-machine-learning-report.pdf

[11] B. Frank. 2017. Microsoft unveils Brainwave, a system for running super-fast AI. Retrieved December 12, 2018 from https://venturebeat.com/2017/08/22/microsoft-unveils-brainwave-a-system-for-running-super-fast-ai/

[12] Intel. 2018. Intel FPGA SDK for OpenCL – Developer Zone. Retrieved December 12, 2018 from https://www.intel.com/content/www/us/en/programmable/products/design-software/embedded-software-developers/opencl/developer-zone.html

[13] A. Keller et al. 2018. Dynamic SEU Sensitivity of Designs on Two 28-nm SRAM-Based FPGA Architectures. IEEE Trans. Nucl. Sci. 65, 1 (2018), 280–287.

[14] S. Mukherjee et al. 2003. A systematic methodology to compute the architectural vulnerability factors for a high-performance microprocessor. In Proceedings. 36th Annual IEEE/ACM International Symposium on Microarchitecture, 2003. MICRO-36. 29–40.

[15] E. Nurvitadhi et al. 2017. Can FPGAs beat GPUs in accelerating next-generation deep neural networks?. In Proceedings of the 2017 ACM/SIGDA International Symposium on Field-Programmable Gate Arrays. ACM, New York, NY, USA, 5–14.

[16] B. Pratt et al. 2006. Improving FPGA Design Robustness with Partial TMR. In 2006 IEEE International Reliability Physics Symposium Proceedings. IEEE, 226–232.

[17] H. Quinn. 2014. Challenges in Testing Complex Systems. IEEE Trans. Nucl. Sci. 61, 2 (2014), 766–786. https://doi.org/10.1109/TNS.2014.2302432

[18] H. Quinn et al. 2013. Fault Simulation and Emulation Tools to Augment Radiation-Hardness Assurance Testing. IEEE Trans. Nucl. Sci. 60, 3 (2013), 2119–2142.

[19] H. Quinn and P. Graham. 2005. Terrestrial-based radiation upsets: a cautionary tale. In 13th Annual IEEE Symposium on Field-Programmable Custom Computing Machines. 193–202.

[20] P. Ramachandran et al. 2008. Statistical Fault Injection. In 2008 IEEE International Conference on Dependable Systems and Networks With FTCS and DCC (DSN). IEEE, 122–127.

[21] E. Schadt et al. 2010. Computational solutions to large-scale data management and analysis. Nature Reviews Genetics 11, 9 (2010), 647–657.

[22] B. Schroeder. 2011. DRAM errors in the wild: A large-scale field study. Commun. ACM 54, 2 (2011), 100–107.

[23] D. Siewiorek and R. Swarz. 1998. Reliable computer systems (third ed.). A. K. Peters, Natick, MA.

[24] A. Silburt et al. 2008. Specification and Verification of Soft Error Performance in Reliable Internet Core Routers. IEEE Trans. Nucl. Sci. 55, 4 (2008), 2389–2398.

[25] I. Stamoulias et al. 2017. Hardware accelerators for financial applications in HDL and High Level Synthesis. In 2017 International Conference on Embedded Computer Systems: Architectures, Modeling, and Simulation. 278–285.

[26] Terasic. 2018. Stratix V - DE5-Net FPGA Development Kit. Retrieved December 12, 2018 from https://www.terasic.com.tw/cgi-bin/page/archive.pl?Language=English&No=526

[27] D. Thomas et al. 2009. A comparison of CPUs, GPUs, FPGAs, and massively parallel processor arrays for random number generation. In Proceedings of the ACM/SIGDA International Symposium on Field Programmable Gate Arrays. ACM, New York, NY, USA, 63–72.

[28] M. Wirthlin. 2015. High-reliability FPGA-Based systems: Space, high-energy physics, and beyond. Proc. IEEE 103, 3 (2015), 379–389.

[29] Xilinx Inc. 2018. Device Reliability Report. Xilinx Inc. Retrieved December 12, 2018 from https://www.xilinx.com/support/documentation/user_guides/ug116.pdf

Breaking the Trust Dependence on Third Party Processes for Reconfigurable Secure Hardware

Aimee Coughlin, Greg Cusack, Jack Wampler, Eric Keller, Eric Wustrow
University of Colorado Boulder

ABSTRACT

Modern CPU designs are beginning to incorporate secure hardware features, but leave developers with little control over both the set of features and when and whether updates are available. Reconfigurable logic (e.g., FPGAs) has been proposed as an alternative as it is both hardware, so can have similar capabilities at a reasonable performance degradation, and programmable, allowing customization of the secure hardware. This programmability, however, opens new attack vectors that allow an adversary to re-program the FPGA. Past attempts to solve this rely on a party maintaining a shared key with the FPGA, but these business processes to keep that key secret have been shown to be quite vulnerable.

In this paper, we propose a new mechanism which eliminates the trust dependence on third party processes. This new mechanism consists of a self-provisioning stage, where keys are generated internal to the FPGA and never exposed externally, coupled with a secure update mechanism which allows updates to be governed by a policy defined by the secure hardware application. To demonstrate, we fully implemented these mechanisms on a Xilinx Zynq UltraScale+ FPGA along with an example secure co-processor with remote attestation with a flexible root of trust (in contrast to Intel SGX which fixes the root of trust to be Intel). Our performance evaluation of two applications, a password manager and a contact matching application, illustrates using FPGAs is practical.

CCS CONCEPTS

• **Security and privacy → Key management**; **Tamper-proof and tamper-resistant designs**; • **Hardware → Reconfigurable logic and FPGAs**.

KEYWORDS

Secure Hardware; FPGA; Trusted Execution Environment; SGX

ACM Reference Format:
Aimee Coughlin, Greg Cusack, Jack Wampler, Eric Keller, Eric Wustrow. 2019. Breaking the Trust Dependence on Third Party Processes for Reconfigurable Secure Hardware. In *The 2019 ACM/SIGDA International Symposium on Field-Programmable Gate Arrays (FPGA '19), February 24–26, 2019, Seaside, CA, USA*. ACM, New York, NY, USA, 10 pages. https://doi.org/10.1145/3289602.3293895

Feature	TPM	TZ	SGX
Flexible Root of Trust	●	●	○
TEE	○	●	●
Remote Attestation	●	○	●
Peripheral Access	○	●	○
Trusted Input	○	◐	○
Hardware RNG	●	○	●
Hardware Crypto	●	◐	◐
Secure Storage	●	○	●
Shared Architecture	◐	●	●
Oblivious Memory	○	○	●
Cache SC Defense	●	○	○
TLB SC Defense	○	●	○

Table 1: Comparing the features supported by Trusted Platform Modules (TPMs), ARM TrustZone (TZ), and Intel SGX. ● represents support, ◐ represents partial support or support that depends on how the design is instantiated, and ○ represents no support.

1 INTRODUCTION

Secure hardware provides many benefits for securing computing systems. It enables encrypting sensitive data where physical access to the device is required to decrypt it [7], authenticating data feed systems [41], scaling blockchain transactions [26], and has the promise to address many of the security challenges with cloud computing [15]. However, despite the potential benefits, we are stuck with a constrained ecosystem of secure hardware providers.

Due to the cost, time, and complexity of designing and manufacturing processor hardware [4, 5], the design choices and trade-offs are decided unilaterally by the small set of chip manufacturers. This results in scattered support of a wide range of features, and ultimately limited selection for users of secure hardware. Table 1 presents a summary of several secure hardware systems and the features they choose to support. Even in this modest set of features, there is no existing system that offers every feature, despite each system implementing features the other does not.

Furthermore, updates to secure hardware systems in response to discovered vulnerabilities [11, 13, 14, 17, 33, 36, 37, 40] or demand for new features are at worst impossible, and at best gated by the chip manufacturers, leaving system designers that use secure hardware at the mercy of a few companies.

In this paper, we seek to empower the individuals that ultimately use secure hardware to make decisions that are right for their needs, rather than the hardware manufacturers making choices for them.

Prior research has proposed that programmable hardware, such as field-programmable gate arrays (FPGAs), are suitable for implementing security functions [19–23, 28, 29, 32, 35]. FPGAs are programmable, providing flexibility to define the exact features that are needed, while allowing updates and retaining the performance benefits of hardware [20, 23]. Importantly, FPGAs are no longer special purpose devices, but becoming pervasive in computing platforms such as cloud computing (*e.g.*, Amazon [1] and Microsoft data centers [10, 18, 31]), and in embedded systems for which secure hardware can provide great benefits, such as self-driving cars [2].

The programmable nature of FPGAs, however, raises a significant concern with regards to using them as a basis for realizing secure hardware – an attacker can read or modify the contents of the FPGA. This is in contrast to secure hardware systems built into silicon, which are "fixed", and cannot have their functionality changed after manufacture. Modern FPGAs include hardware that supports encrypted bitstreams [9, 39]. While an improvement, we argue that this doesn't completely solve the problem, but this only reduces the control of reprogrammability to a single party. This party is responsible for generating and maintaining the keys that protect access and functionality of the device. In other words, it depends on human / business processes, which, as history has shown with the frequent password and other data leaks [38] (including secure boot keys [11]), cannot be counted on.

In this paper, we introduce a novel mechanism to address this problem where we build on the capabilities provided by modern FPGAs and *put the device itself in control over the programmability*, thus removing the trust dependence on a third party's processes and providing developers with control over how the secure hardware is protected. This consists of two key aspects. The first is a self-provisioning mechanism where a device is initially brought up in a provisioning configuration, and then internally generates keys, and reprograms itself using these keys. In this way, the keys which control the configuration of the FPGA are only accessible internal to the device. The second is a policy driven update mechanism, where the hardware running in the FPGA is programmed with a policy which determines under what conditions to allow an update. In this way, we empower the secure hardware developer with the choice for how updates can occur (which could include a policy to block all updates). This allows the developer to choose (and commit to) how updates are (or aren't) performed on the device, allowing them to decide between a locked-down design similar to silicon-based secure hardware, or leaving systems flexible once deployed.

We demonstrate that this new mechanism is practical today with off-the-shelf FPGAs. Our implementation uses the Xilinx Zynq UltraScale+ MPSoC FPGA on the ZCU102 board. The application of this is broad, but as a single running example, we implement a secure coprocessor with an Intel SGX-like remote attestation feature. Unlike SGX's attestation, our remote attestation is designed to allow the device provisioner to choose who the root of trust is (rather than Intel's fixed root of trust being Intel), allowing for a wider range of trusted third parties to enable verified remote execution. We further use this running example to enable updates, which are motivated in this case to enable a response to newly discovered vulnerabilities, such as Spectre [25]. We provide an SDK to compile programs to execute in this secure co-processor environment. Unique to this FPGA environment, we can compile the developer's C code to either hardware using high-level synthesis, or to software to run on a soft processor (a CPU implemented using the FPGA logic). We built two applications on top of this customized secure co-processor – a password manager (similar to the example in the Intel SGX tutorial),

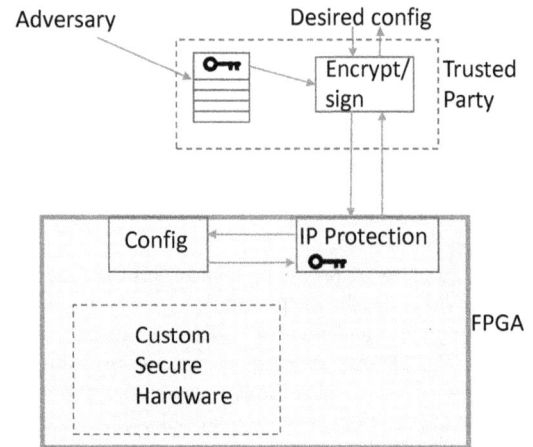

Figure 1: Custom secure hardware on an FPGA with IP protection. A designated party shares a cryptographic key with the FPGA which is used to ensure only FPGA configuration signed/encrypted with this key can re-program the FPGA. The designated party uses processes to protect the storage of the key, but an adversary can attack those processes and gain access to the shared key.

and a contact matching application (emulating the SGX-enabled private contact discovery service operated by Signal [27]).

In the remainder of the paper we first discuss the past efforts of secure hardware on FPGAs (Section 2). We then provide an overview of the system architecture, threat model, and motivating example in Section 3. We describe the the architecture in Sections 4 and 5. We then describe the implementation of the self-provisioning and secure update mechanism (Section 6) and the secure co-processor with remote attestation (Section 7). We wrap up with evaluation (Section 8), and conclusions and future work (Section 9).

2 PAST ATTEMPTS (AND WHY PROCESS TRUST MATTERS)

In this paper we propose using FPGAs as a platform to build secure hardware. Here, we discuss past works, and identify the key unmet challenge in reaching this goal.

2.1 Security Functions on an FPGA

The idea of implementing security functions on an FPGA is not new. In fact, it has been proposed for decades. Research has been published on everything from network security applications (*e.g.*, firewalls [28] and intrusion detection [35]) to cryptographic algorithms [21]. More recently, and highly related to our motivating examples, the SAFES architecture demonstrated the use of FPGA components to provide security primitives and guarantee invariants in program execution [23], and Sanctum is a RISC ISA extension realized on an FPGA that mitigates software side-channels and protects DRAM access [20].

Although these examples demonstrate the ability to implement security functions on an FPGA, they do not address the somewhat obvious threat of an adversary who reprograms the FPGA, changing the device configuration and functionality. We argue that for many secure hardware applications, this is a particularly important threat to address. For instance, if a device manufacturer wishes to offer remote attestation features (such as in Intel SGX) or hardware-protected keys for hardware security modules (HSMs), their design must protect against an adversary with physical (or remote) control over the device after its initial configuration.

By default FPGA's provide no protection to their configuration, allowing an adversary to read or reprogram whatever functionality is placed in it, allowing them to read out sensitive keys or change the device's behavior.

2.2 Security Functions with Bitstream Encryption

In response to this, FPGA manufacturers introduced bitstream protection technology, whether for intellectual property (IP) protection or specifically to support secure hardware [9, 39]. As illustrated in Figure 1, a third party programs a key into the FPGA and then maintains that key (external to the FPGA) so that it can be used to create an FPGA configuration that is encrypted and/or signed. In this way, knowledge of that key is needed to program the FPGA or read its configuration.

While an improvement, it fundamentally depends on a human-driven / business process to protect the key that is programmed into the FPGA. Unfortunately, this has proven to be a challenging problem and particularly fragile means for security. We have seen countless data leaks, including passwords [38] and even secure boot keys [11] (things that we *should* be able to assume won't be leaked). In addition, governments can compel key-holders to divulge their secrets in order to attack individuals, such as in the FBI vs. Apple [3], ultimately undermining end-user trust in the systems. In short, IP protections only serve to focus an adversary's efforts on the process, and once successful would still be able to read or modify any FPGA that was under the 'protection' of that party.

3 SYSTEM ARCHITECTURE

3.1 High-level Overview

We present our high-level design which eliminates the human / business processes from the trust chain. We do this by designing the FPGA to have control over its own reprogrammability, and allowing it to determine when (or if) to allow updates to itself. This design eliminates the need for a trusted party to maintain keys through a business processes, which we argue has historically been shown to be problematic.

The self-provisioning system is designed to allow the device to be initially provisioned once by a system manufacturer into a secure state, and thereafter prevent any future updates externally. To do this, we leverage existing secure hardware systems used for IP protection (*e.g.,* secure boot) that controls the boot process of the device. We configure the secure boot to only allow a single configuration to be loaded into the FPGA. This configuration effectively locks out external access, preventing an adversary with physical access from changing the hardware loaded into the FPGA. Once in this state, **not even the original manufacturer can directly change the configuration**. The private keys used to sign this configuration are generated on the FPGA during provisioning, and stored in a secure storage that is only accessible to the FPGA itself once booted. Because secure boot prevents loading arbitrary

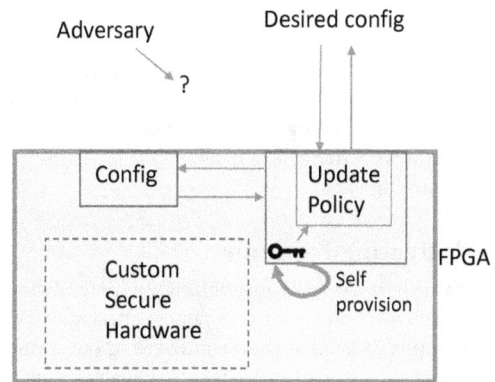

Figure 2: Secure Hardware on an FPGA with Self-Provisioning and Secure Updates. As the keys are only held within the FPGA, and updates are governed by hardware that implements an update policy, an adversary cannot gain access to the key or re-program the FPGA.

bitstreams into the FPGA, nothing except the FPGA itself has access to the secret keys needed to sign new bitstreams.

This self-provisioning process prevents any future updates from being applied from an external source, but still allows the device itself to authorize and apply updates. We note that a developer could decide to disallow updates entirely by programming a configuration that simply discarded its own key, and gain the benefits of silicon-based secure hardware. However, should the developer wish to leverage the reprogrammability of the FPGA, they can choose to do so. If they do, the FPGA is configured with a subsystem for authorizing and applying updates to itself. This subsystem can implement security policies that are more powerful than simply giving up a remote key to the manufacturer. For example, in addition to a signed update from the manufacturer, the subsystem could determine if it is currently in a certain unlocked or safe state, or could require the user to authorize an update explicitly before it signs the new hardware and reprogramms itself. This architecture allows a manufacturer to commit to a security policy, and force themselves (and would-be adversaries) to follow these.

3.2 Threat Model Overview

The adversary in our model is someone who desires to modify the secure hardware implemented in the FPGA or to read back state of the secure hardware implemented in the FPGA. Our work seeks to solve the problem of trusting an external party with maintaining keys that protect the FPGA configuration/state from this adversary. This requires a distinction between trust in operational processes and trust in functionality. In particular, we assume that the FPGA manufacturer is trustworthy at the time the device is created and provisioned, but that the manufacturer may become untrustworthy at a later time, either by being compromised, legally compelled, or having shifting business priorities. Thus, we assume that the original functionality of the FPGA as initially provisioned contains no backdoors or other malicious components, but that any long-term keys maintained by the manufacturer can be compromised.

We ignore the threat of implementation bugs in the secure hardware application, and side-channels on the FPGA that may inadvertently compromise the security of the system [24]. Though likely to exist, we stress two points: first, existing secure hardware also suffers implementation bugs and side channel attacks, and second, our architecture is better able to handle these problems by allowing comprehensive updates.

3.3 Motivating Example

As a motivating example of customized secure hardware, we will focus on a secure co-processor with remote attestation. While there are other applications that can be built using our design, secure co-processors are a powerful example that enables a wide range of security applications.

Intel Software Guard Extensions (SGX) [4, 5] is an extension introduced by Intel to their CPUs which provides a *Trusted Execution Environment* (TEE), allowing developers to write software that executes in a context isolated from the rest of the system, including the operating system. SGX also supports remote attestation of the software running in this TEE, but is designed to only allow Intel to verify remote attestations. Others that use SGX for remote attestation must trust Intel to verify that a remote system is running the code it claims to be running.

In our motivating example, say a company needs SGX-like capabilities, but wishes to use a different party (or even itself) as the trusted source which provides the proof and verification needed in the remote attestation process. This is not possible with Intel (or any existing systems today), so this company would use or design a secure co-processor targeted at an FPGA that provides a TEE with remote attestation. When combined with our self-provisioning system with updates, they can trust that an adversary will not be able to alter their design and, by extension, trust that their TEE will behave as they designed.

This company also wishes to be able to respond to vulnerabilities and deploy patches to their secure co-processor. This comes from experience, as there are numerous examples of vulnerabilities discovered in secure hardware after its release [11, 13, 14, 17, 33, 36, 37, 40]. With the ability to update, the company protects itself from being locked into a vulnerable system or needing to recall physical hardware. Updates, they determine, should be signed by them and should also be verified by their users through the use of a PIN provided in a separate (assumed secure) channel to the user.

In Section 7 we will discuss our implementation of this specific co-processor system.

4 SELF-PROVISIONING

The goal of this work is to ensure that we can program an FPGA with a configuration implementing some custom secure hardware and trust that a malicious party cannot modify it. On the surface, secure boot would appear suitable for this. A secure boot system operates by verifying a signature over a booted configuration against a public key programmed into the system's configuration, such as a secure storage device. The trusted developer has the corresponding secret key and is theoretically the only party that can generate a correctly signed configuration. However, if this secret key is leaked to another party, then this party can put any configuration into the device.

Our solution still makes use of the IP protection hardware used by prior work [30, 39], but changes how the secure boot keys are managed. The problems with the use of secure boot are not related to how the hardware is implemented – the IP protection hardware was never compromised. It is the business processes that are used to protect the keys that we eliminate. Our self-provisioning system achieves this by generating the secure boot key pair on the device and storing the secret key in the device's storage. The system uses this key to sign a single initial configuration, which then becomes the only configuration that can exist in the FPGA.

The self-provisioning system is simply a trusted piece of software that is run on the device itself to generate keys which will be stored on the device and never exposed.

First, the FPGA is empty with no secure boot set up. The *self-provisioner* configuration is loaded and executes a series of steps, as summarized below:

(1) Generate a keypair for the secure boot system.
(2) Sign the *initial* FPGA configuration with the generated secret key.
(3) Store the secret key in secure storage.
(4) Program the public key to the secure boot system on the device.

At this point, the FPGA's secure boot has been set up and the keys are stored in secure storage on the device. Only the single configuration, determined at provisioning time is allowed to be loaded as it is the only one which has been signed by the secure boot keys. A power cycle of the device will then cause this *initial* configuration to be loaded onto the FPGA. In order for a different configuration to be loaded, it must be signed by the secret that only exists on the device and must be authorized by the security policy of the update mechanism (discussed in the next subsection) of this initial configuration.

The *initial* configuration could be the desired secure hardware application itself (*e.g.,* the secure co-processor with remote attestation), if known at provisioning time. If unknown, or if more flexibility is desired, an option would be to load an initial configuration that does not have any secure hardware application, but can have an update policy that suits the protection desired until loaded with the initial application (*e.g.,* a one-time use key). The update system would then be used to load the actual secure hardware application onto the FPGA. Note that this will result in overwriting the update system's policy with that of the secure hardware application's policy.

5 POLICY CONTROLLED SECURE UPDATES

The secure update system provides the second component of our platform that allows for applications to make use of the FPGA's reprogrammability. As described in the previous section, once self-provisioning is complete, only a single configuration can exist in the FPGA. However, since the generated secret is accessible to the FPGA, the FPGA can authorize a new configuration. Therefore, to allow for updates, a subsystem needs to be implemented by developers that will implement a security policy. This subsystem will receive updates and will verify that they conform to the selected security policy before using the secret key to authorize an update.

The update subsystem will enforce a security policy, but this policy must be selected and implemented by the developer of the application. Examples of security policies are:

- Update signed by a trusted developer.
- Correct PIN input by user at update time.
- User PIN and trusted signature required.
- No updates allowed.

This list of policies is not exhaustive, but is representative of potential policies. What this enables is choice for the secure hardware developer. They could trust their own processes (to safeguard keys), or, better yet, safeguard against leaks by utilizing a policy which requires signing *and* a PIN, and perhaps extend the policy to allow a new key for signing updates to be regenerated through some local action.

To support this, we require the developer to implement the enforcement of the chosen policy as part their application. This is because these implementations depend heavily on the capabilities of the device and developers will have their own requirements, such as signature algorithms or input devices, that cannot be prescribed for all use cases. We give an example implementation that is not portable outside of our device used for implementation in the next section, but can be used as an example to build other update systems off of, even when implementing a different security policy.

In general, the secure update system is responsible for performing two tasks, irrespective of the implementation or chosen policy. The first task is to receive updates and enforce that these updates adhere to the security policy before allowing them to be authorized (such as verifying a signature or user PIN). The second task is to use the device-only secret key to sign updates that pass verification and program the signed update to the device. Therefore, an update subsystem must perform these steps:

(1) Receive an update.
(2) Verify that the update conforms to the update security policy.
(3) Use the secret key to sign the update.
(4) Overwrite the existing FPGA configuration such that the update will execute in future power cycles of the device.

As the update system is implemented as part of the initial configuration of the FPGA that is authorized by the self-provisioning system, there is no other way to change the configuration. Therefore, the configuration is secure from being overwritten except by another update that conforms to the chosen policy. This requires that the developer implements the update policy correctly, as there are several attacks, such as man-in-the-middle, downgrade and rollback attacks, that can compromise a security policy that performs only simple authentication. Therefore, update best-practices should be followed, such as the use of sequence numbers and signatures, when implementing a security policy. This is further discussed in the next section, where we discuss which attacks that the update policy we implemented defends against and which it is still vulnerable to.

6 IMPLEMENTATION

To demonstrate our platform, we implemented a self-provisioning system and an example application that includes an update subsystem. Our example application is a secure coprocessor that offers similar features to SGX, and is described further in the next section. In this section, we present how we implemented the self-provisioning system and the update subsystem, which any implementation of our platform will need to provide. We also describe the implementation of a secure storage capability in our device, as both the self-provisioning system and the update system require a secure storage system. We implemented our demonstration application using the Xilinx ZCU102 Evaluation Kit. This system combines a quad-core ARM CPU and a Xilinx FPGA and includes all of the needed IP protection hardware that is required for our platform.

6.1 Self-Provisioning

In an ideal system, the FPGA would have direct internal control over the IP protection hardware, with all other peripherals restricted from accessing these systems. However, we were limited by the device we used for our implementation, in that the FPGA does not have direct access to most peripherals in the device's interconnect design. Instead, the coupled ARM CPU is the master of the system, meaning that our provisioning system needed to be run as a software program rather than as a system in the FPGA. This imposes some increased risk of exposure of generated keys, as the ARM system memory is more accessible than the FPGA, but since the self-provisioning system is expected to execute in a trusted facility, this increased risk can be mitigated.

The self-provisioning system that we implemented performs the tasks outlined in the previous section. The provisioner (*e.g.,* the device manufacturer or distributor) will load the self-provisioner onto the device's persistent storage (in our case, an SD card) along with the initial FPGA configuration to be signed. We, acting as the provisioner, have generated the self-provisioning operating system using Xilinx's proprietary tools such that when the device is powered on, the provisioner is executed.

Once booted, the provisioner loads a simple Ubuntu filesystem that executes a single script. This script generates an RSA-4096 keypair for the secure boot system (the ZCU102 secure boot hardware uses 4096-bit RSA keys) and stores it securely. As the only persistent storage available on our device is the SD card, we also leverage additional IP protection hardware that is used for FPGA encryption. This hardware utilizes a small amount of secure storage (battery-backed RAM (BBRAM)) that cannot be read once it is programmed. The self-provisioning system generates an encryption key, programs the encryption key to the BBRAM, and uses the encryption key to encrypt the generated secure boot keypair. On each future boot, the encryption hardware can decrypt the secret key if needed without it being decryptable outside of the device.

Once the keypair has been generated and the secure storage initialized with the encryption hardware, the self-provisioner uses the keypair and Xilinx's tools to generate a signed boot image containing the initial FPGA configuration that is in the proprietary format used by our device. The output file is then placed onto the SD card so that it will be loaded on the next power cycle of the device. Finally, the self-provisioner will program the generated public key into the IP protection secure boot system of the device, locking the device to only being able to run the boot image that was generated, which contains the initial FPGA configuration.

At this point, the self-provisioner is finished and reboots the device. On the next boot, the signed FPGA configuration will be running and will be the only hardware that can be loaded into the FPGA, as the secure boot system will not let any other configurations that are not signed by the key into the FPGA, and no other such configurations can exist, since the secure boot key only exists on the device itself.

6.2 Update System

As required by our platform's architecture, the self-provisioning system locks down our device so that only a single FPGA configuration can exist in the FPGA. To support updates, our platform requires that developers include an update subsystem that will implement a security policy, but we require that the developers provide their own implementations. This is because developers need to make application-specific and device-specific decisions about how to implement the system. In this section, we describe the implementation we used for our application that demonstrates what these application-specific and device-specific can be.

The update system that we provided implements the required functionality of our platform. We selected a security policy that requires a trusted signature over the update and the input of a user's PIN before the update will be accepted. The verification of the security policy is performed by the FPGA, but because the FPGA does not have direct access to the SD card on our device, and because the boot image format that the update must be converted to is also proprietary, the actual generation of the boot image cannot be done in the FPGA. Instead, when the FPGA authorizes an update, the device will reboot into a simple update operating system that is similar to the self-provisioning system previously described. This means that our update operating system is implemented partially in the authorized FPGA configuration, but also in the update operating system and a trusted bootloader.

When an update is authorized, the update subsystem will store a flag into the secure storage that is only accessible to the FPGA. Upon reboot, the bootloader will check for the existence of this flag and boot into a different operating system. This update system in the FPGA will then release the private key to the operating system after the trusted bootloader indicates that it has booted. The update operating system's only task is to use the secret key and Xilinx's tools to generate a compatible boot image that contains the updated FPGA configuration. Once it has generated this boot image and placed it into persistent storage, the operating system will reboot the device into normal operation.

As can be seen, our device has several limitations that require special implementation considerations, specifically the fact that the FPGA does not have direct access to most system peripherals. In addition, for the enforcement of our security policy, we require user PINs to be six digits in length and we require all updates to be signed using the ED25519 signature algorithm. Other update systems may choose to use different requirements. We also make use of the MicroBlaze soft CPU to implement the update system, whereas other implementations may choose to use other methods, such as pure Verilog or a different CPU. Because of these considerations, we do not provide a single implementation, as any implementation depends upon the capabilities of the device, the requirements of the application, and the exact update security policy that is chosen.

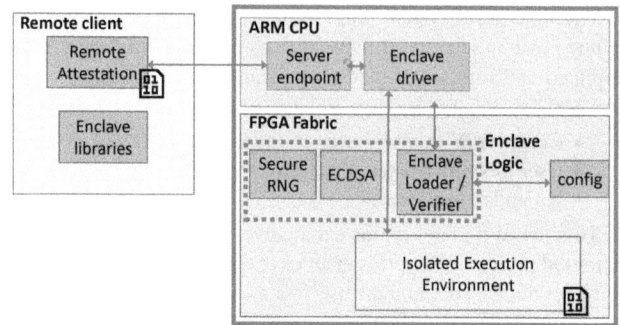

Figure 3: Secure Coprocessor and Remote Attestation Design. Here we run the FPGA as a coprocessor and are able to enforce isolation and perform remote attestation. A remote attestation client uploads a program to an untrusted server. The program is launched in a Isolated Execution Environment in the FPGA by enclave logic, which also signs the program code and performs a key exchange. The driver communicates with the program in the enclave over a shared buffer and relays data to the client.

6.3 Secure Storage

As mentioned in the previous two sections, the self-provisioning system and the update system both need to store secrets that are only accessible to the FPGA. However, our device does not provide such a capability directly, nor does it allow for the FPGA to directly write to the SD card. To solve this problem, we leverage the built-in encryption hardware, as mentioned previously, in the form of an AES accelerator that is backed by a secure encryption key storage in BBRAM. The self-provisioning system initializes this accelerator with a random key that never is stored except in the BBRAM and uses the accelerator to encrypt data. Using the accelerator, we can achieve a secure storage that prevents data from decrypted outside of the device.

However, the FPGA cannot directly pass data to the AES accelerator. Instead, we require that a proxy be run in the CPU of our device that passes data between the FPGA and the AES accelerator, and stores the encrypted data onto the SD card. To further protect the data, we have also implemented a corresponding subsystem in our application that interacts with this agent, which encrypts any arbitrary data generated by our application using an FPGA-only key that is stored in a dedicated eFuse array only accessible to the FPGA. This ensures that when passing data to the CPU agent after boot that no cleartext data is available in the CPU's memory.

7 A CUSTOMIZED SECURE COPROCESSOR WITH REMOTE ATTESTATION

In Section 3 we described a motivating example where a company wishes to have a secure co-processor with remote attestation where the root of trust is flexible (i.e., not the manufacturer, as in SGX). In this section we elaborate on the hardware design, the software development kit to develop software applications, and two example software applications (password manager and contact matching) that were built with our software development kit.

7.1 Hardware Design

7.1.1 Isolated Execution Environment. The code that can be provided to the secure co-processor to run in an isolated manner is in the form of a partial configuration bitstream. There are two options we support for the internal architecture of this hardware. The surrounding logic is identical in both cases, but it is the contents of the configuration bitstream which differ.

Option 1: Software Enclave.

To provide a software environment for software isolation and remote attestation, we implemented a MicroBlaze [8] soft CPU inside the FPGA as part of the secure hardware application. Any code that executes in this CPU is isolated from the untrusted operating system and can be trusted to execute once loaded. Developers provide their code to the SDK, which will then generate the needed logic to execute this code in a MicroBlaze CPU.

Option 2: Hardware Enclave.

Alternatively, developers can directly provide hardware, so long as it is able to perform the interaction with the untrusted software. This does not imply the developer has to develop hardware. They can develop logic directly for the FPGA in any manner that they choose, including by synthesizing the developer's software (C code) into a compatible bitstream using high-level synthesis, as is described in Section 7.2.

The developer can make the decision between having their enclave's code (provided as C code) synthesized to hardware or executed on a soft CPU based on the complexity of the application – more complex applications are more difficult to synthesize to hardware, but an application synthesized to hardware will have better performance. The SDK will generate a resulting partial bitstream based on the developer's choice and the synthesis results that either includes the application directly implemented as FPGA logic, or a soft CPU in the FPGA logic that executes their application's code. The SDK also generates an untrusted program (*i.e.,* the "Enclave driver") that runs on the device's (untrusted) CPU to interact with the enclave program via a memory buffer in the FPGA.

7.1.2 Enclave Code Loader. In order to securely program this co-processor, we utilize custom logic that ensures that when any trusted code (*i.e.,* a trusted "enclave" program, similar to SGX) is loaded, a hash of this program is taken and a signature verification are performed. As illustrated in Figure 3, the code of the application is provided to the logic in the form of a partial bitstream, which specifies a configuration which will reprogram only part of the FPGA. The enclave logic will use the internal configuration access port (ICAP) to program the partial bitstream (the enclave program) into the area of the FPGA reserved for executing the secure enclave, leaving the rest of the FPGA (*e.g.,* enclave logic) untouched.

In addition, the enclave logic reads an ECDSA private key from the secure storage, and uses it to sign the hash of the bitstream and a message from the enclave during the remote attestation process. As shown in Figure 3, a remote client can upload a program to services running in the untrusted operating system, which will then pass the program to the enclave logic.

7.1.3 Remote Attestation. The attestation protocol implemented by our secure hardware and companion software is shown in Figure 4. In this protocol, a remote verifier uploads a program (in the form

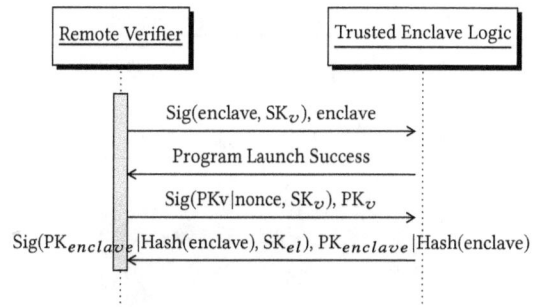

Figure 4: Remote Attestation Sequence: In the remote attestation protocol, the remote verifier uploads a program (enclave) signed by its private key (SK_v). The enclave launches the program and notifies the verifier, which then requests an attestation by sending its signed public key (PK_v). The enclave logic uses this key to derive a shared secret for the enclave and responds with a signature of an ephemeral public key for the enclave ($PK_{enclave}$) and the hash of the enclave, signed by a long-term key for the enclave logic (SK_{el}).

of a partial bitsream) signed by its Ed25519 private key (SK_v) [16]). The program will be launched by the enclave logic, and the verifier will be notified upon completion. The verifier will then request an attestation by uploading its signed public key (PK_v). The enclave logic then generates an ephemeral key pair for this attestation to establish a shared secret for the enclave ($PK_{enclave}$, $SK_{enclave}$), and signs $PK_{enclave}$ and the hash of the enclave program with its long-term attestation key (PK_{el}, SK_{el}). The enclave sends these to the verifier, along with a certificate chain configured at provision time by the root of trust for this device. Using this certificate, the verifier then verifies the signature and checks that the hash matches the expected hash of the uploaded enclave program. If so, the verifier can calculate a shared secret using $PK_{enclave}$ and SK_v, just as the enclave logic calculates a shared secret using PK_v and $SK_{enclave}$. Using this shared secret known only to the verifier and the isolated enclave, a secure channel can be established.

To generate secure ephemeral keys during this process, we have included a cryptographic random number generator within the trusted hardware of the FPGA, as implemented by the Cryptech OpenHSM project [34]. The module draws randomness from both the LSB of A/D conversion noise as well as a ring of digital oscillators implemented as a set of adders with the carry out inverted and fed back as carry in. This entropy is collected and hashed using SHA512 to whiten it. The resulting digest is used to seed a ChaCha stream cipher's key and IV which is used as a PRNG to provide random numbers to the enclave logic to securely generate keypairs.

7.2 SDK

In addition to designing the hardware of our software isolation system, we have also designed a software development kit to make it easier to develop software applications that run in the system. Figure 5 shows the major components of the SDK. A developer creates untrusted code that runs on the ARM CPU of our system in the untrusted operating system (arm.c), code that implements the trusted functions that are run in the isolated enclave (enclave.c),

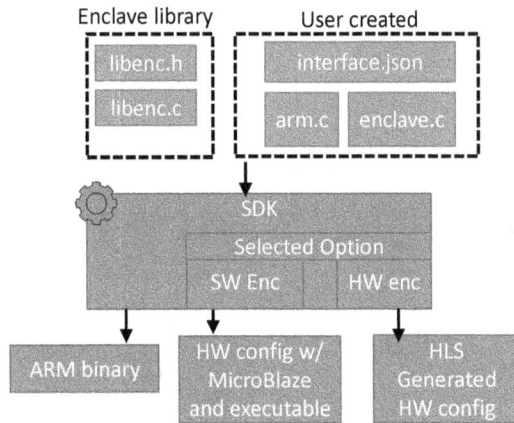

Figure 5: SDK Development Flow

and a description of the API the application wishes to use to communicate between the trusted and untrusted code (interface.json). This interface describes the inputs and outputs of the trusted code as well as the function signatures of the specific methods. The developer also has access to the enclave library (libenc.h, libenc.c) that provides functions to launch an enclave, which is done by interacting with the enclave logic.

The developer provides their code to the SDK. For a software enclave, the SDK will output a partial configuration bitstream (which was pre-built) that contains a MicroBlaze [8] soft CPU (i.e., a processor implemented in the FPGA logic). The SDK will cross-compile the enclave code and add the memory to the configuration bitstream. For a hardware enclave, the SDK will utilize the Vivado [12] high-level sythesis tool, which generates Verilog from C code. Then it will synthesize that design and generate a partial configuration bitstream.

In both cases, the SDK will use the API interface definition to generate communication code between the enclave and the ARM CPU using the dedicated shared buffer. Also, in both cases, the SDK will cross-compile the application code for the ARM instruction set. The (untrusted) ARM binary's will load the trusted code into the enclave using the enclave library.

7.3 Password Manager Application

As an illustration of running isolated software in this secure hardware module, we implemented a password manager that encrypts stored credentials under a master password. Passwords are encrypted and decrypted in an enclave with only the encrypted data being stored in persistent storage. To access a password, the enclave must be provided the encrypted data and a master password. The enclave then derives a decryption key using this password and a device-only key that can only be accessed from the enclave.

To use the manager, a user provides their master password to a client program which interacts with the enclave. The user then has the option to enter information for passwords, usernames and identifiers (e.g., a website). This information is given to the enclave to encrypt, and passed back to the client application to store in persistent storage. Retrieving data is achieved by interacting with the client program and requesting data by its identifier, which will

cause the enclave to decrypt it and return it to the client. This password manager is similar in design to an example application SGX provided by Intel [6].

Our implementation cannot remove all possible attack vectors, as the password manager must still function to provide data in plaintext in order for it to be useful for users to interact with unmodified programs. However, we can force any attacks to be *online*, in the sense that the adversary must query the password manager in the trusted enclave, rather than simply be able to make copies and reveal the entire database. This is because the encrypted password database can only be decrypted using the user's master password and the FPGA's device-only key. Even if the database is exported and the user's password is compromised, the data cannot be decrypted without interacting with the enclave running on the device on which it was first encrypted. We present a performance analysis of user interaction with the password manager in Section 8.

7.4 Contact Matching Application

As a second example to show how our isolated environment can execute code that has been synthesized into FPGA logic using high-level synthesis, we have developed a second application. This application emulates the SGX-enabled contact discovery service operated by Signal [27], except implemented using C++ and synthesized into hardware using our SDK. This application's purpose is to receive an encrypted list of contacts (i.e., phone numbers) from a user and determine the intersection of this with a database of all registered users of the service. The solution used by Signal is designed to prevent the operators of the service from learning the contacts in the uploaded list while still allowing for users to determine the intersection with the total database. By executing in an SGX enclave, Signal is able to conceal which contacts are found to match, and return an encrypted result to the user. Our contact matching application provides similar functionality, but executes its code in FPGA logic that has been synthesized using our SDK. We present the performance of this application in Section 8.

8 EVALUATION

As an example secure hardware application, we built a secure co-processor with remote attestations. Here, we we evaluate the performance of example applications for this secure co-processor along with associated metrics about how long it takes to load and perform a remote attestation. For all of our applications we continue to use the ZCU102 Evaluation Kit running Ubuntu 15.10.

8.1 Software Enclave Performance Benchmarks

To test the performance impact of executing code on a Microblaze CPU, we designed several microbenchmarks to test memory and computation performance, along with end-to-end performance.

Software Enclave SHA512 Performance. We created a program that hashes a buffer of random data using SHA512 in both an enclave and directly on the main CPU. As the enclave executes on the embedded Microblaze CPU, we expect the performance to be much worse, and this experiment is intended to determine if using our SDK to create enclave programs imposes additional overhead.

The performance of the Microblaze enclave is approximately 20x worse than the reference implementation on the ARM CPU. However, both implementations scale linearly with the size of the data being hashed. There does not appear to be any overhead caused by using our SDK to develop a program for the enclave, and it appears that the execution performance of the Microblaze CPU is the main performance bottleneck, as expected. We stress that while our system has significantly less performance than that of pure hardware implementations, very few secure applications require the full performance of the main processor, but instead emphasize security, isolation, and ease of implementation over raw throughput.

Password Manager Performance. Illustrating the point that the performance impact of our implementation commonly would impact a relatively small fraction of the overall perceived performance, we measured the time to add and retrieve passwords from the password manager application described in Section 7.3, for passwords of up to 100 characters in length. As seen in Figure 7, both with and without running in an enclave results in an average 202ms latency (with less than 0.3 difference in the worst case). Likewise, for reasonable passwords up to 100 characters, the latency for decrypting a password from the manager is roughly 120ms for both implementations, well within the realm of usability (for passwords much larger than that, the impact of the performance difference does become noticeable as more time is spent in the enclave).

Enclave Memory Access Performance. To measure the memory access performance of an enclave, the enclave is simply tasked with copying an input buffer to an output buffer, and the performance is compared to the ARM CPU's performance at the same task. We measured an overhead for Microblaze access times ranging linearly from 100x for small chunks of data (0-250 bytes) to 12x for larger chunks (2 Kbytes and larger).

8.2 Hardware Enclave Performance

To show that our SDK can also achieve acceptable performance for large scale processing, particularly through high-level synthesis (compiling C code directly to hardware), we developed a second application that performs a similar service as the contact discovery service operated by Signal. As discussed previously, the purpose of our application is to receive a list of phone numbers from a user and determine the intersection with a larger database, and then return the result to the user. We compared the performance of this application to a software-only implementation that used the same contact list and database. As shown in Figure 6, the synthesized hardware version achieves a throughout of up to 3x compared to the software solution. We used contact list sizes of 128 contacts, represented as SHA512 hashses, and database sizes ranging from 800 contacts to 819,200 contacts, also represented as SHA512 hashes.

8.3 Enclave Logic Microbenchmarks

Enclave Loading Performance. Our final benchmark measures the throughput of loading enclave program binaries of various sizes. After testing using binaries ranging in size from 20 KB to 1 MB, the throughput remained constant at 35 KB/s.

Remote Attestation Performance. To measure the end-to-end performance of performing a remote attestation, we implemented a

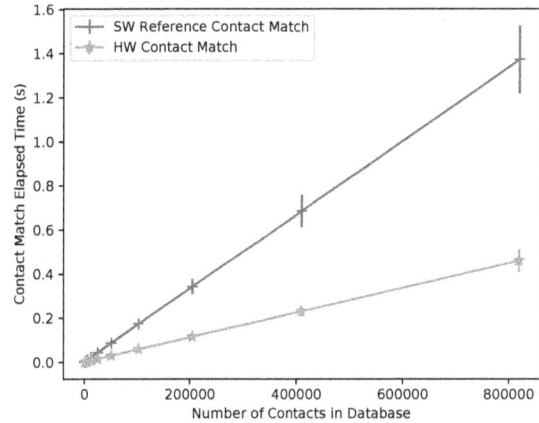

Figure 6: Contact Matcher Performance Performance of matching a contact list against a larger database in a software-only implementation and an HLS-synthesized version. The hardware version achieves an average of approximately 3x compared to the software version.

private set intersection calculation program that calculates the intersection of two sets of integers in an enclave, with one set being uploaded in encrypted form using the shared secret negotiated by the remote attestation protocol, and the other provided to the enclave by the local host, similar the contact discovery feature used by Signal [27]. In each attestation, a fixed amount of data is passed in each message, which is the public key of the verifier in one message, and then the signed public key and hash of the enclave in the response. This experiment measures the average time to pass these messages, for the enclave logic to generate the keys and sign the message, and the time for the client to verify the response and calculate the shared secret. After performing 1000 trials in ideal laboratory network conditions between a verifier and the device running the trusted enclave logic, the average remote attestation time was 107.2 ms with a standard deviation of 8.604 ms.

9 CONCLUSIONS AND FUTURE WORK

In this paper we introduced a new mechanism which allows FPGAs to be used to implement customized secure hardware without depending on human / business processes to maintain the secrecy of keys used to protect the FPGAs configuration process. We introduced the concept of self-provisioning and a secure update process which allows for policies which govern whether an update is allowed or not. As a proof of concept, we implemented the framework on the Xilinx Zynq Ultrascale+ FPGA and built a secure co-processor with remote attestation that has a flexible root of trust. Going forward, a key direction we intend to pursue is to further strengthen the threat model and seek to more completely decouple the underlying mechanisms from the secure hardware applications – that is, modify the design such that the framework can provide run-time support for loading secure hardware applications, rather than the current boot-time support.

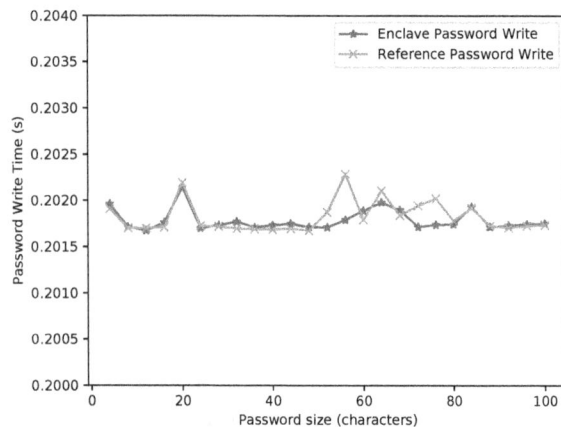

Figure 7: Password Manager Write Performance Time spent adding passwords to the password manager when protected by an enclave and when using a reference implementation running completely on the ARM CPU without an enclave.

Acknowledgements. We thank the anonymous reviewers for their input on this paper. This research was supported in part by the National Science Foundation under grants 1406192 (SaTC) and 1700527 (SDI-CSCS).

REFERENCES

[1] Amazon EC2 F1 Instances: Run Customizable FPGAs in the AWS Cloud. https://aws.amazon.com/ec2/instance-types/f1/.

[2] Ces: Intel goes for self-driving cars. https://www.electronicsweekly.com/news/design/ces-intel-goes-self-driving-cars-2017-01/.

[3] FBI Apple encryption dispute. https://en.wikipedia.org/wiki/FBI\T1\textendashApple_encryption_dispute.

[4] Intel Software Guard Extensions. https://software.intel.com/en-us/sgx.

[5] Intel Software Guard Extensions (SGX): A Researcher's Primer. https://www.nccgroup.trust/uk/about-us/newsroom-and-events/blogs/2015/january/intel-software-guard-extensions-sgx-a-researchers-primer/.

[6] Introducing the Intel Software Guard Extensions Tutorial Series. https://software.intel.com/en-us/articles/introducing-the-intel-software-guard-extensions-tutorial-series.

[7] iOS Security - iOS 11. https://www.apple.com/business/docs/iOS_Security_Guide.pdf.

[8] MicroBlaze Soft Procesor Core. https://www.xilinx.com/products/design-tools/microblaze.html.

[9] Microsemi: Security. https://www.microsemi.com/product-directory/fpga-soc/1738-security.

[10] Project catapult. https://www.microsoft.com/en-us/research/project/project-catapult/.

[11] Secure Golden Key Boot. https://rol.im/securegoldenkeyboot/.

[12] Vivado user guide. http://www.xilinx.com/support/documentation/sw_manuals/xilinx2014_1/ug902-vivado-high-level-synthesis.pdf.

[13] CVE-2016-3287. Available from MITRE, CVE-ID CVE-2016-3287, July 2016.

[14] CVE-2016-3320. Available from MITRE, CVE-ID CVE-2016-3320, Aug. 2016.

[15] A. Baumann, M. Peinado, and G. Hunt. Shielding applications from an untrusted cloud with haven. *ACM Trans. Comput. Syst.*, 33(3), Aug 2015.

[16] D. J. Bernstein, N. Duif, T. Lange, P. Schwabe, and B.-Y. Yang. High-speed high-security signatures. *Journal of Cryptographic Engineering*, pages 1–13, 2012.

[17] F. Brasser, U. Müller, A. Dmitrienko, K. Kostiainen, S. Capkun, and A.-R. Sadeghi. Software grand exposure: SGX cache attacks are practical. In *11th USENIX Workshop on Offensive Technologies (WOOT 17)*, Vancouver, BC, 2017. USENIX

Association.

[18] A. M. Caulfield et al. A cloud-scale acceleration architecture. In *IEEE/ACM International Symposium on Microarchitecture (MICRO)*, Oct 2016.

[19] P. Chodowiec and K. Gaj. Implementation of the twofish cipher using FPGA devices. Technical report, Electrical and Computer Engineering, George Mason University, 1999.

[20] V. Costan, I. A. Lebedev, and S. Devadas. Sanctum: Minimal risc extensions for isolated execution. *IACR Cryptology ePrint Archive*, 2015:564, 2015.

[21] A. Dandalis, V. K. Prasanna, and J. D. Rolim. A Comparative Study of Performance of AES Final Candidates Using FPGAs. In *Cryptographic Hardware and Embedded Systems (CHES)*, 2000.

[22] A. J. Elbirt and C. Paar. An FPGA Implementation and Performance Evaluation of the Serpent Block Cipher. In *Proc ACM/SIGDA International Symposium on Field Programmable Gate Arrays (FPGA)*, 2000.

[23] G. Gogniat, T. Wolf, W. Burleson, J.-P. Diguet, L. Bossuet, and R. Vaslin. Reconfigurable hardware for high-security/high-performance embedded systems: the safes perspective. *IEEE Transactions on Very Large Scale Integration (VLSI) Systems*, 16(2):144–155, 2008.

[24] T. Huffmire, B. Brotherton, G. Wang, T. Sherwood, R. Kastner, T. Levin, T. Nguyen, and C. Irvine. Moats and drawbridges: An isolation primitive for reconfigurable hardware based systems. In *IEEE Security and Privacy*, 2007.

[25] P. Kocher, D. Genkin, D. Gruss, W. Haas, M. Hamburg, M. Lipp, S. Mangard, T. Prescher, M. Schwarz, and Y. Yarom. Spectre attacks: Exploiting speculative execution. *CoRR*, abs/1801.01203, 2018.

[26] J. Lind, I. Eyal, F. Kelbert, O. Naor, P. R. Pietzuch, and E. G. Sirer. Teechain: Scalable blockchain payments using trusted execution environments. *CoRR*, abs/1707.05454, 2017.

[27] M. Marlinspike. Technology preview: Private contact discovery for signal. https://signal.org/blog/private-contact-discovery/, 2017.

[28] J. T. McHenry, P. W. Dowd, F. A. Pellegrino, T. M. Carrozzi, and W. B. Cocks. An FPGA-based coprocessor for ATM firewalls. In *Proc IEEE Symposium on Field-Programmable Custom Computing Machines (FCCM)*, 1997.

[29] S. McMillan and C. Patterson. Jbits implementations of the advanced encryption standard (rijndael). In *International Conference on Field Programmable Logic and Applications*, pages 162–171. Springer, 2001.

[30] E. Peterson. XAPP 1323: Developing Tamper-Resistant Designs with Zynq UltraScale+ Devices. https://www.xilinx.com/support/documentation/application_notes/xapp1323-zynq-usp-tamper-resistant-designs.pdf, Aug 2018.

[31] A. Putnam et al. A reconfigurable fabric for accelerating large-scale datacenter services. In *Proc. Annual International Symposium on Computer Architecuture (ISCA)*, 2014.

[32] M. Riaz and H. M. Heys. The fpga implementation of the rc6 and cast-256 encryption algorithms. In *Electrical and Computer Engineering, 1999 IEEE Canadian Conference on*, volume 1, pages 367–372. IEEE, 1999.

[33] M. Schwarz, S. Weiser, D. Gruss, C. Maurice, and S. Mangard. Malware guard extension: Using SGX to conceal cache attacks. *CoRR*, abs/1702.08719, 2017.

[34] P. Selkirk and J. Strömbergson. https://trac.cryptech.is/browser/core/rng/trng.

[35] I. Sourdis and D. Pnevmatikatos. Fast, large-scale string match for a 10gbps fpga-based network intrusion detection system. In *Field Programmable Logic and Application*, 2003.

[36] N. Weichbrodt, A. Kurmus, P. Pietzuch, and R. Kapitza. AsyncShock: Exploiting synchronisation bugs in Intel SGX enclaves. In *European Symposium on Research in Computer Security*, pages 440–457. Springer, 2016.

[37] S. Weiser and M. Werner. Sgxio: Generic trusted i/o path for intel sgx. In *Proceedings of the Seventh ACM on Conference on Data and Application Security and Privacy*, CODASPY '17, pages 261–268, New York, NY, USA, 2017. ACM.

[38] Wikipedia. List of data breaches. https://en.wikipedia.org/wiki/List_of_data_breaches.

[39] K. Wilkinson. XAPP 1267: Using Encryption and Authentication to Secure an UltraScale/UltraScale+ FPGA Bitstream. https://www.xilinx.com/support/documentation/application_notes/xapp1267-encryp-efuse-program.pdf, Aug 2018.

[40] Y. Xu, W. Cui, and M. Peinado. Controlled-channel attacks: Deterministic side channels for untrusted operating systems. In *Security and Privacy (SP), 2015 IEEE Symposium on*, pages 640–656. IEEE, 2015.

[41] F. Zhang, E. Cecchetti, K. Croman, A. Juels, and E. Shi. Town crier: An authenticated data feed for smart contracts. In *Proc. ACM SIGSAC Conference on Computer and Communications Security (CCS)*, 2016.

Characterization of Long Wire Data Leakage in Deep Submicron FPGAs

George Provelengios
UMass Amherst
Amherst, MA
gprovelengio@umass.edu

Chethan Ramesh
UMass Amherst
Amherst, MA
cramesh@umass.edu

Shivukumar B. Patil
UMass Amherst
Amherst, MA
spatil@umass.edu

Ken Eguro
Microsoft Research
Redmond, WA
eguro@microsoft.com

Russell Tessier
UMass Amherst
Amherst, MA
tessier@umass.edu

Daniel Holcomb
UMass Amherst
Amherst, MA
dholcomb@umass.edu

ABSTRACT

The simultaneous use of FPGAs by multiple tenants has recently been shown to potentially expose sensitive information without the victim's knowledge. For example, neighboring long wires in SRAM-based FPGAs have been shown to allow for clandestine data exfiltration. In this work, we explore distinct characteristics of this signal crosstalk that could be used to enhance or prevent information leakage. First, we develop a mechanism to characterize the crosstalk coupling that exists between neighboring wires at the femtosecond scale. Second, we show that it is possible to reverse engineer channel layouts by determining which pairs of routing resources/links in the channel exhibit coupling to each other even if this information is not provided by the FPGA vendor. To fully characterize these effects, we examine long wire coupling on different types of wires across three devices implemented in different technology nodes from 65 to 20 nm. We experimentally demonstrate that information leakage is apparent for all three FPGA families.

CCS CONCEPTS

• **Computer systems organization** → **Security**;

KEYWORDS

FPGA, side channel, crosstalk

ACM Reference Format:
George Provelengios, Chethan Ramesh, Shivukumar B. Patil, Ken Eguro, Russell Tessier, and Daniel Holcomb. 2019. Characterization of Long Wire Data Leakage in Deep Submicron FPGAs. In *The 2019 ACM/SIGDA International Symposium on Field-Programmable Gate Arrays (FPGA '19), February 24–26, 2019, Seaside, CA, USA*. ACM, New York, NY, USA, 6 pages. https://doi.org/10.1145/3289602.3293923

1 INTRODUCTION

As the use of FPGAs for computing becomes ubiquitious, the platforms and compute models supported by FPGAs become more diverse. While most FPGA deployments continue to support the use of the entire FPGA with circuits created by a single entity, the emergence of *multi-tenant* FPGA scenarios with circuits created and used by multiple users has grown in interest. Recent work has recognized embedded computing with cores from multiple sources [1] and cloud computing with multiple users sharing FPGA hardware [4] as contemporary multi-tenant scenarios with many more virtualization opportunities on the horizon [6].

While the multi-tenant use of FPGAs provides a mechanism for maximizing the utilization of FPGA resources, it does also present unique security challenges. Several recent research studies have shown that multi-tenant scenarios can lead to side channel attacks where the attacker does not have physical access to the FPGA [1, 4, 5, 8]. One class of these attacks [1, 4] uses information obtained using a single "attacker" wire that is adjacent to a victim wire in an FPGA routing channel. Although initial work has shown these types of attacks to be robust, the full nature of the threat is unclear, as the level of accuracy in quantifying data transmission between neighboring wires has not been comprehensively explored.

In this work, we address three important issues related to crosstalk-based attacks in SRAM-based FPGAs. Our contributions include:

- We present a precise characterization of the effect of a neighboring wire on a channel wire's delay. This new model is shown to be robust across a range of hardware implementations of attack circuitry.
- In some cases, FPGA companies do not publicly disclose wiring adjacency for FPGA routing channels, limiting a user's ability to ensure that wires adjacent to critical routes are unused. In this work, we show that it is straightforward to determine routing adjacency for all channel wires using crosstalk effects as a guide in building an adjacency map.

The remainder of the paper is organized as follows. Section 2 provides perspective on the delay and adjacency characterizations performed in this paper. The methodology used in our work is detailed in Section 3. In Section 4 we explain our approach for determining channel adjacency. The sensitivity of each wire to coupling is addressed in Section 5. Section 6 concludes the paper and offers directions for future work.

2 BACKGROUND

2.1 FPGA Long Wire Attacks

The presence of a communication channel between adjacent FPGA long wires ("long lines") has previously been confirmed for both Xilinx [1] and Intel [4] FPGAs. In both studies it was shown that the logic value carried on a wire changes the delay of its immediate neighbor in a significant and measurable way. A logic 1 value *transmitted* by the victim effectively reduces the delay on the adjacent wire and a logic 0 has the opposite effect. Effectively, the delay change allows a wire to *receive* information about its neighbor, potentially allowing the information to be used in a clandestine attack. Giechaskiel *et al.* [1] examined the effects of transmitter switching rate and wire length, among other parameters. Ramesh *et al.* [4] showed that crosstalk-based leakage could be used as a side channel to successfully obtain a 128-bit key from an FPGA implementation of the AES block cipher. The wire leakage is well suited for use in side channel attacks, which are inherently robust to noise and able to exploit small correlations between the side channel measurements and secret data.

Both studies noted above relied on the use of a ring oscillator (RO) to receive information from the victim (transmitter). One RO wire is adjacent to the victim wire, and the frequency of oscillation is obtained by a binary counter triggered by the RO. The difference in RO frequency for two trials is determined by using a relative count metric [4] determined over two measurement periods. The count difference ΔRC when first a logic 0 (first trial) and then a logic 1 (second trial) are transmitted can be represented as:

$$\Delta RC = \frac{C^1 - C^0}{C^1} \qquad (1)$$

where C^1 and C^0 are the measured counts for transmitted logic 1 and 0, respectively. Although useful, the results of this approach depend on the delay of the entire RO rather than just the delay of the wire adjacent to the victim. In this work we more precisely quantify the delay effects caused by wire adjacency to make the characterization of transmitter values clearer.

The precise delay characterization of FPGA wires has been explored in several contexts unrelated to signal adjacency. Yu *et al.* [7] used ROs to measure the delay of a number of FPGA resources, including channel wires in isolation. Gojman *et al.* [3] employed a path-based approach to consider delays of all channel wires in an FPGA. Fine-grained FPGA timing measurement using time-to-digital converters (TDCs) was used by Gnad *et al.* [2] to assess process variations. None of these studies considered the differentiation of same-wire delays due to the behavior of surrounding wires.

2.2 Determining FPGA Channel Wire Adjacency

FPGA vendors differ in terms of providing customers with easy access to channel adjacency information for their FPGA devices.

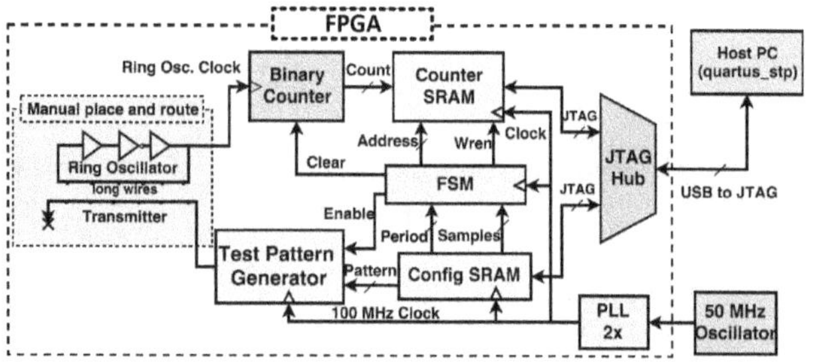

Figure 1: Experimental framework for evaluating long wire delay effects on SRAM FPGAs [4].

Adjacency information for Xilinx SRAM FPGA devices can be visually determined from Vivado floorplanning tools, version 2018.2. However, the corresponding view in Intel's visual editor does not allow a user to infer adjacency (Quartus Prime v18.1). Knowledge of adjacency is necessary if a user wishes to deploy fine-grained isolation by ensuring that sensitive wires have no neighbors that could snoop on their values using crosstalk.

3 METHODOLOGY

We perform experiments on three different classes of FPGAs that are fabricated in different technology nodes. Our experiments are performed on two Cyclone IV GX (EP4CGX150DF31) FPGA Development Kits, one Stratix V (5SGXEA7K2F40C2N) GX Development Kit, and one DE5a-Net Arria 10 GX (10AX115N2F45E1SG) FPGA Development Kit. The Cyclone IV, Stratix V, and Arria 10 devices are implemented in 60nm, 28nm, and 20nm CMOS technologies, respectively.

Fig. 1 shows the block diagram of the test setup used to assess the long wire covert channels in these system types. In each experiment, the *transmitter* and *receiver* are implemented in the FPGA in one or more vertical long wires. A test pattern generator assigns either a logic 1 or a logic 0 to the transmitter in each trial and the effect on the frequency of the receiver is measured by counting its oscillations during 1024 trials of 21ms each unless noted otherwise. Half of the 1024 trials use a transmitted value of 1, and the other half use a transmitted value of 0. The ring oscillator, transmitter and receiver are placed and routed using place and route constraints.

3.1 Metric

We introduce a new metric Δt that captures the amount by which the value of the transmitter affects the propagation delay of transitions on the receiver wire. This metric is designed to eliminate the RO-based variability introduced by the ΔRC metric in Eq. 1. The changes in propagation delay on the receiver wire are on the order of 100s of femtoseconds, and cannot be measured directly. However, they can be inferred from frequency measurements collected by on-chip circuitry counting ring oscillator cycles.

During each period of a ring oscillator, every circuit node in the ring makes exactly one rising and one falling transition. The period of a ring oscillator that contains a particular receiver wire of interest can be described as the sum of four terms: $d_{rx\uparrow}$ represents the propagation delay of a rising transition on the receiver, $d_{n\uparrow}$ represents the summed propagation delays of one rising transition on all other ring nodes, and $d_{rx\downarrow}$ and $d_{n\downarrow}$ represent the receiver and summed ring node delays for the corresponding falling transitions. Using superscripts to denote the value of the transmitter during a measurement, the frequency of the ring when the transmitter holds a value of 1 can therefore be written as $f^{(1)}$ shown in Eq. 2. Term $f^{(0)}$ is defined analogously for the case of a 0-valued transmitter. Measuring the frequency of the same ring oscillator with a transmitted 0-value and 1-value allows for calculating Δt as shown in Eq. 3. The delay terms ($d_{n\uparrow}$ and $d_{n\downarrow}$) that are unrelated to the receiver wire cancel out from the two frequency measurements, leaving only the delay changes in the receiver wire. The value Δt represents the change in propagation delay on the receiver wire that is caused by the change on the value of the transmitter. More precisely, as shown by the second line of Eq. 3, Δt is the average propagation delay change over rising ($d_{rx\uparrow}$) and falling transitions ($d_{rx\downarrow}$) of the receiver. We make no claim as to whether the change in receiver delay is occurring predominantly on one transition or equally on both.

$$f^{(1)} = \frac{1}{d_{n\uparrow} + d_{rx\uparrow}^{(1)} + d_{n\downarrow} + d_{rx\downarrow}^{(1)}} \qquad (2)$$

$$f^{(0)} = \frac{1}{d_{n\uparrow} + d_{rx\uparrow}^{(0)} + d_{n\downarrow} + d_{rx\downarrow}^{(0)}}$$

$$\Delta t = \left(\frac{1}{f^{(0)}} - \frac{1}{f^{(1)}} \right) / 2$$
$$= \left(\left(d_{rx\uparrow}^{(0)} - d_{rx\uparrow}^{(1)} \right) + \left(d_{rx\downarrow}^{(0)} - d_{rx\downarrow}^{(1)} \right) \right) / 2 \qquad (3)$$

The Δt metric is different from the metric of fractional change in oscillator counts that is used in prior work [1, 4] and also shown in Eq. 1, and we use Fig. 2 to demonstrate the motivation for using the new metric. The two cases shown in Fig. 2 use the same neighboring transmitter and receiver wires on the same Cyclone IV chip, with the transmitter and receiver wires running parallel to each other for a length of 10 C4 wire segments running upward from position X113Y2. The only difference between the two scenarios is that the ring oscillator circuit used for measurement in the figure at left has extra wiring delay added to the ring intentionally, such that its period is roughly 50% higher than the circuit used for the figure at right. The added delay is on a part of the ring away from the transmitter and receiver wires, and therefore does not impact their coupling. A good metric should indicate the same amount of coupling in both cases. In each case, we measure the oscillator frequencies as shown and compute the value of Δt using Eq. 3, obtaining values of 3.28 ps in the first case and 3.32 ps in the second. The good agreement between the two experiments demonstrates that Δt captures the change of the receiver delay while being insensitive to the overall ring delay. The prior metric of ΔRC is sensitive to the overall ring delay and yields a fractional change in oscillator frequency of 2.66E-4 and 4.05E-4 in the two experiments (a 52% discrepancy), despite no changes to the part of the circuit in which

the coupling occurs. Removing the dependence of the characterization metric on oscillator frequency is important for accurately characterizing the leakage, because the ring oscillator frequency will inevitably change across experiments that vary parameters such as technology node, or the length or type of wires used for transmitter and receiver.

4 RECOVERING CHANNEL LAYOUT THROUGH MEASUREMENT

In this section we show that characterizing the coupling between wires makes it possible to infer channel layout, which could enable design isolation techniques to reduce the risk of leakage between adjacent wires. Layout/adjacency information of a channel is inferred by testing all possible transmitter-receiver pairs in the channel, and measuring the value of Δt to check for evidence of coupling for each pair. Wires that impact each other are reasonably assumed to be neighbors in the channel.

The C4 channel in a Cyclone IV device has 96 wires, of which 48 travel in the upward direction. We explore these 48 wires to determine which are neighbors. Each LAB can connect to 12 of the 48 wires, and it takes a vertical span of 4 logic array blocks (LABs) to fill the channel. Each of these 48 wires can be the receiver or transmitter, so 2,304 pairs of wires are considered to exhaustively characterize the channel. Fig. 3 demonstrates the coupling that exists between all pairs of the 48 wires. The measurements are collected using transmitter and receiver wires that are 10 C4 wires long, and then normalizing the value of Δt to the length of a single C4. In particular, the 48 wires in the channel being characterized are driven from LABs X12Y2, X12Y3, X12Y4, and X12Y5. The correspondence between the indices $0 - 47$ and the physical resources of Cyclone IV are given in Tab. 1. Looking carefully at Fig. 3 we can see for example that transmitters at the 16th and 40th indices induce significant values of Δt on a receiver in the 4th index. This implies that wires X12Y4S0I4 (16th index) and X12Y6S0I4 (40th index) are likely the neighbors of X12Y3S0I4 (4th index). For most of the 48 wires, when used as receivers, we are able to identify two other wires that as transmitters cause significant values of Δt. These are hypothesized to be the left and right neighbors in the channel. Some wires in the channel do not have two clear neighbors, and this will be investigated in future experiments. The coupling is observed to be bidirectional; if there is a significant effect when the transmitter is index i and the receiver is index j, then a similar value of Δt will occur when the receiver is index i and the transmitter is index j.

5 CHARACTERIZATION

5.1 Susceptibility of Each Wire to Leakage

We are able to identify neighbors for all C4 wires in the channel of the Cyclone IV device using the technique from the previous section (see Fig. 3). Based on finding the same adjacency information for six different channels on the device, we assume that all channels are similar, and collect results from experiments performed across multiple channels. Fig 4 shows for each wire in the channel, the range of Δt values indicating how much the wire delay can be changed by the value of its neighbor. There is a range of values

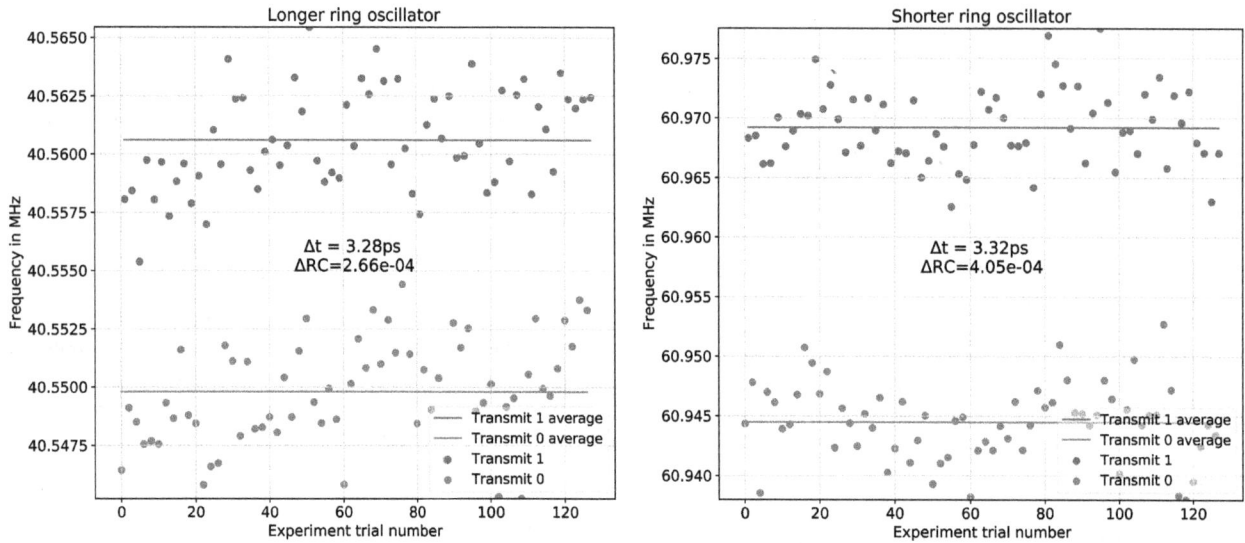

Figure 2: Figure shows measured receiver frequency for the same transmitter and receiver wires when measured with two different length ring oscillators. The two cases yield a similar value of Δt but different values of the prior metric of fractional count difference (ΔRC). This result demonstrates that Δt is invariant to ring frequency but ΔRC is not. Receiver frequency in each trial is measured by counting the number of oscillations in one second.

Index	Logic Element	Wire in Channel
0	LCCOMB_X12_Y2_N0	X12Y3S0I0
1	LCCOMB_X12_Y2_N2	X12Y3S0I1
2	LCCOMB_X12_Y2_N4	X12Y3S0I2
3	LCCOMB_X12_Y2_N6	X12Y3S0I3
4	LCCOMB_X12_Y2_N10	X12Y3S0I4
5	LCCOMB_X12_Y2_N14	X12Y3S0I5
6	LCCOMB_X12_Y2_N16	X12Y3S0I6
7	LCCOMB_X12_Y2_N18	X12Y3S0I7
8	LCCOMB_X12_Y2_N20	X12Y3S0I8
9	LCCOMB_X12_Y2_N22	X12Y3S0I9
10	LCCOMB_X12_Y2_N24	X12Y3S0I10
11	LCCOMB_X12_Y2_N28	X12Y3S0I11

Table 1: Correspondence between indices of Fig. 3 and physical resources on the target Cyclone IV device. This list includes only the first LAB. The next 12 indices use the same resources at position X12Y3, and so forth for the remaining 24 indices at positions X12Y4 and X12Y5.

for each index because the same measurements are taken using 6 different channels at different columns in the chip and 5 trials for each. This result shows that, regardless of which wire is used for routing a sensitive signal, there exists another wire in the channel with the potential to exfiltrate that sensitive data if used as a covert receiver.

5.2 Comparing Different Long Wire Types

Fig. 5a shows the value of Δt for chains of C4 wires that are combined to create different length transmitter and receiver wires in

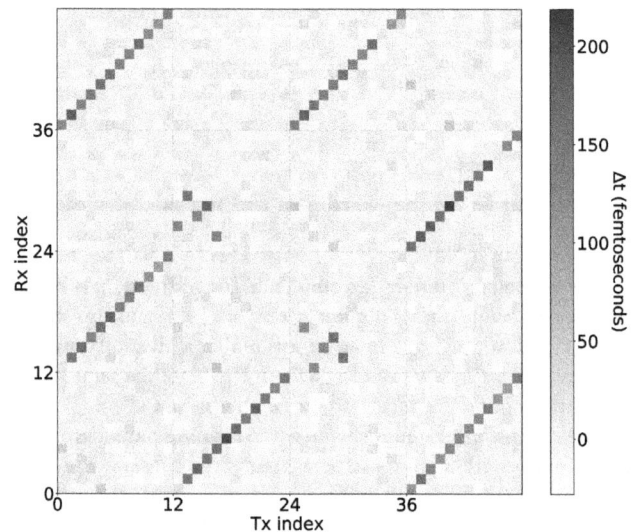

Figure 3: Figure shows the measured value of Δt per C4 wire segment for all pairs of wires in a C4 channel on a Cyclone IV device. See Tab. 1 for explanation of how the indices correspond to physical resources.

the three devices. These specific neighboring wires were chosen arbitrarily, but are representative of the typical coupling between neighbors (see Fig. 4). Each line in the plot represents an experiment performed in a single column, and the points on the line correspond to measurements made within that column using different lengths of adjacent transmitter and receiver wires. The experiment is repeated at different columns in the chip to produce the multiple lines.

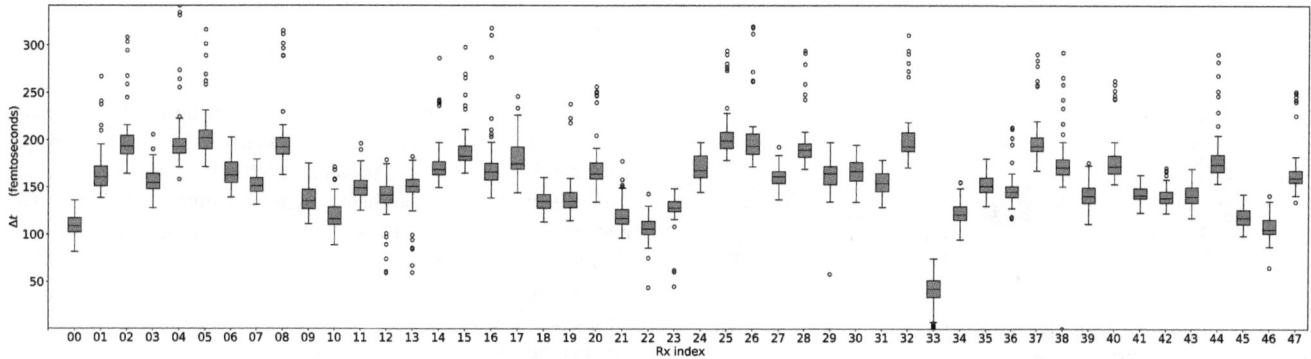

Figure 4: The distribution of observed Δt for each wire in the channel when the wire is used as a receiver and its neighbor is used as a transmitter. In this context, neighbor is defined as the single wire that has the largest impact on the receiver. There is a range of values for each index because the same measurements are taken on 6 different channels at different columns in the chip.

Cyclone IV is measured at locations X12, X36, X60, X84, X100, and X113. Stratix V is measured at locations X12, X50, X108, X171 and X204. Arria 10 is measured at locations X14, X60, X108, X160 and X208. Because the three devices have different numbers of rows, the longest wire that can be created within a column is different for each device. The lengths of wires are given in terms of the number of LABs spanned vertically by the receiver and transmitter. The change in propagation delay on the receiver wire is observed to be linear in the length of the adjacency, so we consider for comparison a single value of Δt/LAB which reflects the slope of the lines in Fig. 5a. We observe values of 47.8fs/LAB, 14.0fs/LAB, and 8.2fs/LAB in Cyclone IV, Stratix V, and Arria 10.

Fig 5b shows an analogous plot to Fig. 5a but using the longer C14, C16, and C27 wires on the devices. Cyclone IV is measured at locations X12, X27, X59, X107 to create the different lines. Stratix V is measured at locations X12, X50, X108, X171 and X204. Arria 10 is measured at locations X14, X60, X108, X160 and X208. The values we observe for Δt/LAB in these cases are 14.6fs/LAB in Cyclone IV, 3.9fs/LAB in Stratix V, and 16.5fs/LAB in Arria 10. The unknown layout strategies that may be employed for each wire type prevents a carefully controlled comparison, yet our results do show that the coupling exists across wires and designs, and that its effect is linear in the length of the adjacent wires.

5.3 Technology Comparison

Fig. 6 compares the coupling of different long wire types on Cyclone IV, Stratix V, and Arria 10 devices. It should be noted that these devices differ not only in their process technology, but also may have different layout strategies tailored to their technology node and intended market segment. The coupling is given in terms of Δt/LAB as in the previous section, meaning that the given number represents the additional increment by which the receiver is slowed down by the transmitter value for every LAB spanned vertically by the two adjacent wires. If any application requires routing sensitive signals on long wires in which the other wires in the channel are untrusted, this analysis can guide a designer in deciding whether to

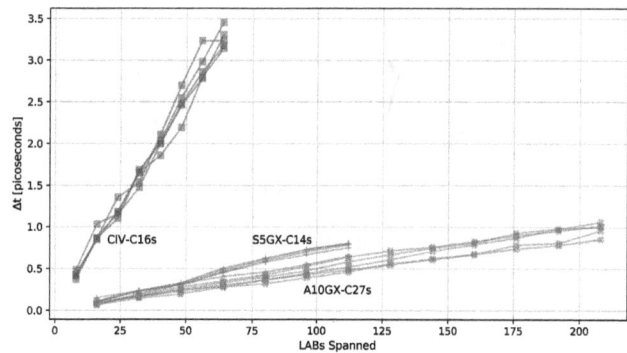

(a) C4 wires

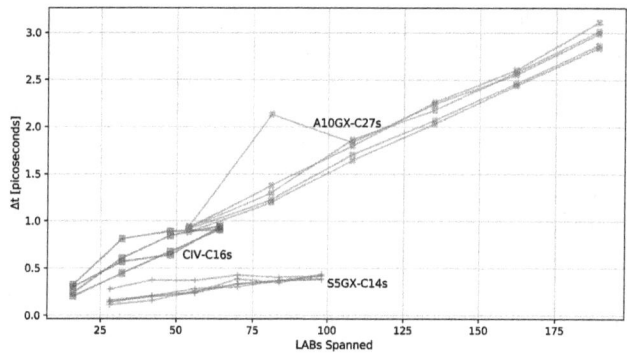

(b) C14/C16/C27 wires

Figure 5: Measured values of Δt versus length of wire for three different devices. Different lines represent the same wire when measured in different columns across the chip. Each measurement is repeated three times and results are averaged to minimize noise.

use a long sequence of C4 wires, or a reduced number of the longer wire types.

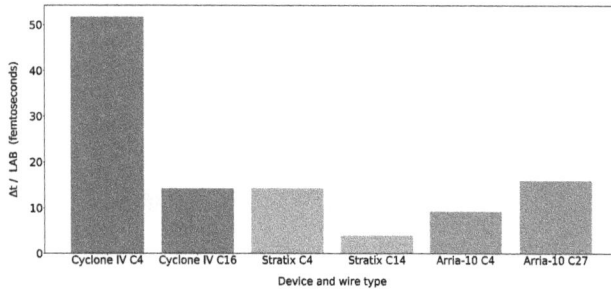

Figure 6: Values of Δt/LAB observed using two different wire types on three different devices. Significant leakage is observed in all devices, and there is not a clear trend across technology nodes.

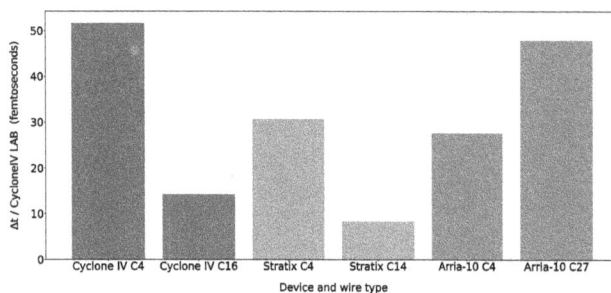

Figure 7: Values of Δt/LAB when normalized to a wire length that matches the height of a LAB on a 60nm technology Cyclone IV device.

The physical size of each LAB changes with technology node. Therefore, a comparison of coupling per-LAB-span on devices implemented in different technologies is not a fair comparison of coupling per-unit-length. To consider coupling per wirelength in absolute terms, one must adjust for technology scaling. We do this by trying to estimate the amount of coupling on a wire span that is equivalent in length to the LAB height in the Cyclone IV's 60nm technology. Assuming that LAB height scales proportional to minimum feature size of the technology node, then the height of one LAB in the Cyclone IV's 60nm technology is equivalent in height to 2.14 LABs in Stratix V (28nm) and 3 LABs in Arria 10 (20nm). Adjusting by these factors yields the data shown in Fig. 7.

6 CONCLUSION

Previous work shows the existence of coupling between neighboring long wires on both Xilinx and Intel SRAM FPGAs. In this paper we have presented an accurate method for quantifying the amount of coupling that exists between neighboring long wires. Our approach can detect and quantify delay changes on the order of femtoseconds that are caused by the logic value of neighboring wires. We use the method to characterize coupling on FPGAs in three different technology nodes including 20nm technology. We show that coupling between long wires can be used to recover adjacency information from channels if the information is not freely

available from the device vendor. Our findings show that the leakage exists and is significant across all the FPGAs tested.

The experimentally measured delay in the examined wires verifies that length is not the only factor contributing to Δt values. Physical design and layout strategies may determine the propagation delay of the wires as well. Nevertheless, the experimental methods in this paper can help designers to quantify the data leakage susceptibility of sensitive signals in their design in order to decide whether mitigation is needed. Leakage can be avoided by disallowing multiple tenants to share use of a single channel, and future work in this direction can analyze how to share channels and maximize utilization while still ensuring that all wires carrying sensitive data are protected from snooping by neighbors.

Acknowledgement

This research was funded by NSF/SRC grant CNS-1619558 and a grant from Intel's Corporate Research Council.

REFERENCES

[1] I. Giechaskiel, K. B. Rasmussen, and K. Eguro. 2018. Leaky Wires: Information Leakage and Covert Communication Between FPGA Long Wires. In *Proceedings of the 2018 on Asia Conference on Computer and Communications Security (ASIACCS '18)*. ACM, New York, NY, USA, 15–27.

[2] D. R. E. Gnad, F. Oboril, S. Kiamehr, and M. B. Tahoori. 2018. An Experimental Evaluation and Analysis of Transient Voltage Fluctuations in FPGAs. *IEEE Transactions on Very Large Scale Integration (VLSI) Systems* 26, 10 (Oct 2018), 1817–1830.

[3] B. Gojman, S. Nalmela, N. Mehta, N. Howarth, and A. DeHon. 2015. GROK-LAB: Generating real on-chip knowledge for intra-cluster delays using timing extraction. *ACM Transactions on Reconfigurable Technology and Systems (TRETS)* 7, 4 (2015), 32.

[4] C. Ramesh, S. B. Patil, S. N. Dhanuskodi, G. Provelengios, S. Pillement, D. Holcomb, and R. Tessier. 2018. FPGA side channel attacks without physical access. In *IEEE International Symposium on Field-Programmable Custom Computing Machines*. 45–52.

[5] F. Schellenberg, D. R. E. Gnad, A. Moradi, and M. B. Tahoori. 2018. An inside job: Remote power analysis attacks on FPGAs. In *Design, Automation & Test in Europe Conference & Exhibition, DATE 2018*.

[6] S. Yazdanshenas and V. Betz. 2018. Interconnect Solutions for Virtualized Field-Programmable Gate Arrays. *IEEE Access* 6 (Feb. 2018), 10497–10507.

[7] H. Yu, Q. Xu, and P. H. W. Leong. 2010. Fine-grained characterization of process variation in FPGAs. In *2010 International Conference on Field-Programmable Technology*. 138–145.

[8] M. Zhao and G. E. Suh. 2018. FPGA-based remote power side-channel attacks. In *2018 IEEE Symposium on Security and Privacy (SP)*. IEEE, 229–244.

Temporal Thermal Covert Channels in Cloud FPGAs

Shanquan Tian and Jakub Szefer
Yale University
{shanquan.tian,jakub.szefer}@yale.edu

ABSTRACT

With increasing interest in Cloud FPGAs, such as Amazon's EC2 F1 instances or Microsoft's Azure with Catapult servers, FPGAs in cloud computing infrastructures can become targets for information leakages via convert channel communication. Cloud FPGAs leverage temporal sharing of the FPGA resources between users. This paper shows that heat generated by one user can be observed by another user who later uses the same FPGA. The covert data transfer can be achieved through simple on-off keying (OOK) and use of multiple FPGA boards in parallel significantly improves data throughput. The new temporal thermal covert channel is demonstrated on Microsoft's Catapult servers with FPGAs running remotely in the Texas Advanced Computing Center (TACC). A number of defenses against the new temporal thermal covert channel are presented at the end of the paper.

CCS CONCEPTS

• **Security and privacy** → **Side-channel analysis and counter-measures**; *Malicious design modifications*;

KEYWORDS

Covert Channels, Cloud FPGA, Ring Oscillator, FPGA Security

ACM Reference Format:
Shanquan Tian and Jakub Szefer. 2019. Temporal Thermal Covert Channels in Cloud FPGAs. In *The 2019 ACM/SIGDA International Symposium on Field-Programmable Gate Arrays (FPGA '19), February 24–26, 2019, Seaside, CA, USA.* ACM, New York, NY, USA, 7 pages. https://doi.org/10.1145/3289602.3293920

1 INTRODUCTION

FPGAs are increasingly being used in cloud computing infrastructures to allow users to accelerate their computation through use of custom hardware logic. Many cloud providers now support Cloud FPGAs, including Amazon's EC2 F1 instances [6] (for generic use), Microsoft's Azure with Catapult [7] servers (for AI), or Alibaba Cloud's F3 instances [4] (currently "available for testing by invited users"). Cloud FPGAs are also available for remote sharing by academics through deployments such as at the Texas Advanced Computing Center (TACC) [14] (for generic research use).

The business model of Cloud FPGAs focuses on temporal sharing of the hardware between users. When one user is not using

the FPGA, it can be assigned to other users. Cloud providers such as Amazon now charge by the minute or even by the second for certain instance types [2], and an FPGA can be almost instantly rededicated to other users once one user is finished using it. In addition to temporal sharing, there is also possibility of spatial sharing. One FPGA can be assigned to multiple users at the same time – this has been explored in academia but so far is not deployed in real Cloud FPGA infrastructures as far as the authors are aware. Interestingly, most researchers have focused on exploring spatial side and covert channels in FPGAs. For example, they have explored cross-talk based channels, e.g., [12]. Meanwhile, channels not requiring spatial proximity or sharing of FPGA have not been widely explored. We present one such new channel, the Temporal Thermal Covert Channel, in this work.

To realize the covert channel, a ring oscillator (RO) heater and RO sensor modules are used. An RO is a temperature-to-frequency transducer suitable for thermal monitoring on FPGAs [3]. With proper calibration, ROs can be used as temperature sensors; comparing oscillation counts of an RO at a fixed location on an FPGA board at different times allows one to observe relative changes in the temperature of the FPGA board over time. Meanwhile, for controlling temperature, a free running RO can be used to generate heat, by constantly toggling transistors and maximizing dynamic power [1]. Use of a sensor diode for measuring temperature is also possible, and potentially more accurate. However, cloud providers can easily disable the access to the diode, or physically remove it to prevent temperature sensing. Use of RO sensors eliminates the need to depend on access to the sensor diode.

In the temporal thermal channel, to transmit information, the sender can either enable RO heater (to generate heat and send 1) or not enable it (to keep FPGA temperature low and send 0). Once the sender vacates the FPGA, a receiver may load their design with RO sensors on the same FPGA to read the current FPGA temperature.

RO based heater and sensor modules were developed for this project and tested both in lab setting and on Texas Advanced Computing Center (TACC) with Microsoft's Catapult servers. With TACC, users can remotely access Altera Stratix V FPGAs which are in the Catapult servers [14], and load their custom logic into the FPGAs. This work shows that without endangering the FPGAs (as first tested on local Stratix V FPGAs) a heater module is able to sufficiently raise the temperature of FPGA that the change can be observed up to 2 minutes later without use of error correcting codes (ECC) for the transmission, and about 3 minutes later when error rates in transmission of the data are less than 30% and can be corrected with use of ECC. This already includes effects of data center cooling which constantly cools the servers and the FPGAs, which cannot be controlled by the attacker as the FPGAs are accessed remotely by the cloud users.

Furthermore, due to abundance of FPGAs in TACC (and likewise in other deployments such as Amazon F1 or Microsoft Azure), the

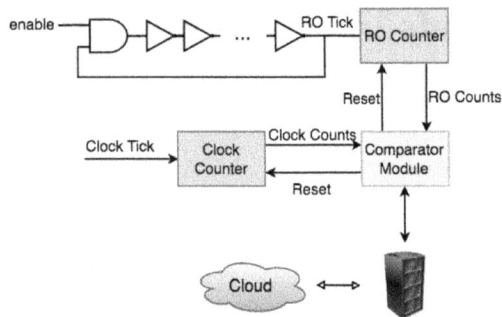

Figure 1: Block diagram of an RO sensor: a free running RO (top-left) drives RO Counter, meanwhile a clock from FPGA's crystal oscillator is used to drive Clock Counter; the outputs from two counters are compared to measure the RO loop's frequency and deduce the temperature; software running on the server attached to the FPGA is used to start and stop the sensor and obtain the RO counts.

heaters and sensors can be run on multiple FPGAs in parallel. The OOK scheme can be used to encode data into heat, and use of multiple FPGAs in parallel linearly increases the bandwidth.

1.1 Contributions to Cloud FPGA Security

This paper makes a number of new contributions:

- Development of the new temporal thermal covert channel based on ring oscillator heaters and sensors.
- Deployment and evaluation of the temporal thermal covert channel on real Cloud FPGA using Catapult servers in TACC.
- Design of defense strategies to mitigate temporal thermal covert channels.

2 BACKGROUND

This section provides background on ring oscillator (RO) circuits on FPGAs. It also gives brief overview of Cloud FPGA deployments that allow for remote access to FPGAs.

2.1 RO Temperature Sensor

A ring oscillator temperature sensor can be built by using an odd number of inverters which are connected in a loop, as shown in Figure 1. The RO sensor further includes an *AND* gate to enable or disable the oscillation of the loop. The sensor works by counting number of oscillations of the loop, compared to some reference counter. The delay through the inverters and wires of the RO depends on the temperature, while the crystal oscillator used for the reference counter is not significantly affected by temperature.

More gates, higher the accuracy, but the lower sensitivity of the sensor to the temperature (T). As T increases, the average inverter gate delay (d) increases, and frequency (f) of the RO oscillations is reduced, the relationship is shown in Equation 1.

$$T \nearrow \Longrightarrow d \nearrow \Longrightarrow f \searrow \qquad (1)$$

Specifically, frequency is linearly proportional to temperature. Furthermore, the frequency is inversely proportional to number N of inverter gates in the RO. These relationships are shown in Equation 2 below.

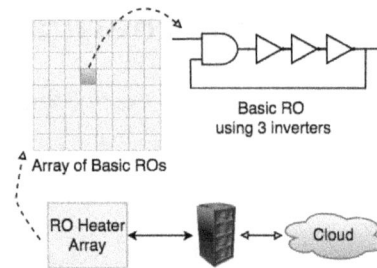

Figure 2: Block diagram of an RO heater: an array of RO loops with 3 inverters each is used; software running on the server attached to the FPGA is used to start and stop the heater.

$$f \propto T \quad and \quad f \propto N^{-1} \qquad (2)$$

Based on the design shown in Figure 1, number of RO counts can be used as relative frequency if clock counting time is fixed. Frequency (f) can be replaced by RO counts in Equation 1 and 2.

The RO sensor should be manually placed on the FPGA (via constraints directives in the design tools) so that it is always at same location on the FPGA fabric. Note that the sensor's operation itself will generate heat, thus the sensor should be turned on for as short time as possible so as not to influence the temperature.

The same logical 3-inverter RO placed in different parts of the FPGA, or in same location but on different FPGAs, will give different RO counts for the same temperature. This is due to manufacturing variations as well as different wire lengths that connect different logic blocks on the FPGAs. However, RO placed in the same location on the same FPGA, even after the FPGA is reprogrammed, will have same behavior. And, regardless of the placement, the frequency and temperature keep their relationship, shown in Equations 1 and 2. By reprogramming the FPGA with the same RO in the same location, and measuring the frequency changes, the relative temperature changes can be observed.

2.2 RO Heater

The RO heater is designed as an array of free-running ROs with an odd number of inverters each. An RO heater diagram is shown in Figure 2. Recall from Equation 2 that the frequency (f) is inversely proportional to the size N the RO. Meanwhile, dynamic power (P) is proportional to frequency and number of switching elements. Smaller ROs have higher frequency, but also have smaller number of inverters in the RO. Consequently, an RO with 3 inverters gives the highest power density by allowing most number of ROs to fit in an unit area. The relationship is shown in Equation 3.

$$N \searrow \Longrightarrow \left(\frac{P}{area}\right) \nearrow \qquad (3)$$

The RO heater should typically also be manually placed on the FPGA to control the location of the inverters. Especially, the whole RO heater array can be constrained to a pre-specified region of the FPGA to maximize heat density.

2.3 Cloud FPGA Platforms

Increasing number of cloud computing providers are adding FPGAs to their deployments, the so-called Cloud FPGAs. Cloud FPGAs allow users to deploy custom logic into the FPGAs and use them along with other servers and compute resources maintained by the cloud provider. Benefits of Cloud FPGA include on-demand access, and all the tools and licenses are maintained by the cloud provider.

Many existing Cloud FPGA deployments are available today. Amazon's EC2 F1 instances [6] allow access to servers with Xilinx UltraScale+ FPGAs. Microsoft's Azure also includes access to FPGAs and their Catapult servers [7] which Intel (previously Altera) Stratix V FPGAs. Meanwhile, Alibaba Cloud's F3 instances [4] give access to Xilinx VirtexUltraScale+ FPGAs. The Texas Advanced Computing Center (TACC) includes option to access Microsoft's Catapult servers [14] which are the same Catapult servers (and FPGAs) as deployed by Microsoft in their data centers.

The Cloud FPGA deployments typically involve FPGA connected to the server via PCIe bus, and users are able to write software that communicates with the FPGAs via memory mapped registers or through direct memory access (DMA). Users can load their designs on the FPGA, and today each user is dedicated whole FPGA for their use. Spatial sharing does not seem to be deployed in practice, while temporal sharing, explored in this paper, is widely used.

3 DEVELOPING TEMPORAL THERMAL COVERT CHANNEL ON FPGAS

The temporal thermal covert channel on FPGAs is motivated by the fact that Cloud FPGAs are shared in time by different cloud users. While the logical state of the FPGA is erased (or overwritten) when a new bitstream is loaded, the physical state may not be "erased" between when different users use the FPGA. In particular, this work shows that thermal energy of the FPGA takes time to dissipate. In the performed experiments on real Cloud FPGA deployment, the time for the heat to dissipate is on the order of minutes, allowing a user to observe the physical thermal state left over when prior user finished using the FPGA.

3.1 Covert Channel Overview

The timeline of the operation of the new covert channel is shown in Figure 3. It assumes that the sender and receiver share or can access the same set of FPGA boards; and that the sender and receiver are able to load custom logic designs onto the FPGAs. We assume the design will comply with Cloud FPGA provider's design rules and does not violate any Cloud FPGA restrictions[1]. Since multiple FPGAs are used, the sender, Alice, and receiver, Bob, need to pre-agree on which FPGA will be used to send which bit of data.

To transmit information, simple on-off keying (OOK) is used in this project. OOK is a simple form of amplitude modulation, where a logical 1 corresponds to presence of a signal and logical 0 corresponds to absence of a signal. In this work, presence of signal corresponds to high temperature of the FPGA chip, while absence of a signal corresponds to low temperature of FPGA chip. Heating is achieved by use of RO heater. Temperature sensing is achieved by use of RO sensor. Neither operation requires special permissions

---

[1]Section 5 discusses defenses cloud providers can deploy, such as special design rules, and how some design checking rules fail to prevent this attack.

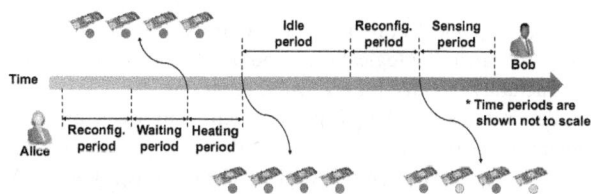

Figure 3: Cloud FPGAs are shared by different users. The timeline shows the six time periods relevant to the Temporal Thermal Covert Channel with 4 FPGAs. Blue dots indicate FPGA is a steady state idle temperature. Red dots indicate the FPGA is at elevated heated temperature. Orange dots indicate the FPGA is still heated above the idle temperature, but heat has dissipated somewhat and it is not as hight as just after heating (red dots). In this example Alice sends 0101 and Bob is able to receive 0101.

or hardware, and can be readily executed on today's Cloud FPGA deployments, such as Catapult servers in TACC.

3.2 Threat Model and Assumptions

Our covert channel assumes that the sender, Alice, is in possession of some secret information, such as encryption keys, that she wants to leak to Bob. Further, Alice and Bob can obtain access to the same set of FPGAs in a cloud computing setting and identify each FPGA so they know which FPGA is sending which bit (using unique serial numbers or hardware fingerprinting [13]). The details of how the FPGAs are identified are beyond the scope of this paper. Especially, we assume the *idle period*, discussed shortly, is sufficiently long to identify the FPGAs. Our evaluation shows this is true in TACC.

3.3 Data Transmission with One FPGA

This section first explains how the transmission works with one FPGA, and later section expands on how multiple FPGAs can be used in parallel.

The *reconfiguration periods* (see Figure 3) are needed to account for the time the sender or the receiver take to load their design onto the FPGA. During *reconfiguration period* for Alice she loads the design with the RO heater, while during *reconfiguration period* for Bob he loads the design with the RO sensor.

To begin transmission, the *waiting period* may be needed so the sender, Alice, can ensure that the FPGA is at a steady state temperature corresponding to the FPGA having been unused for a long time. The FPGA is unused at this time to allow to fully cool off, e.g. by loading the RO heater design but not enabling it yet. If Cloud FPGA allows for operations such as explicitly resetting the FPGA, that can be used instead to reset the FPGA and let it stay idle.

Next, the sender enables their actual bitstream (which contains RO heater module), and starts the heating process during the *heating period*. If the sender wants to transmit a logical 1, the FPGA is heated; if the sender wants to transmit a logical 0, the FPGA is not heated and remains at the steady state temperature from the first step. Once the FPGA has been heating for desired amount of time, the sender can log out from the remote machine.

If the required *heating period* is similar to the *waiting period*, i.e. cooling period, the two can actually be overlapped, setting *heating period* to zero. This is because while some FPGAs that are needed to transmit a logical 1 are being heated, the other FPGAs that are needed to transmit a logical 0 are cooling. Our evaluation shows this is actually possible for the TACC scenario.

Following, there is the *idle period* when no user is using the remote machine. The *idle period* assumes the cloud provider enforces that no design is loaded into FPGA between users, e.g., the FPGA is reset after user logs out of the remote machine. During *idle period*, no heating of the FPGA occurs. It is possible that a *zombie period* occurs instead of the *idle period*. Zombie period occurs if the cloud provider allows the FPGA to keep running with existing configuration, even when user logs out. If *zombie period* occurs, then the duration of the *idle period* is effectively zero as the sender's design keeps running and heating the chip up to until the receiver loads their design.

Finally, the receiver loads a new bitstream with the RO sensor during the *sensing period*. After the RO sensor runs and the receiver observes the frequency, the receiver can compute the current temperature of the FPGA chip, and can deduce if a logical 1 (high heat) or logical 0 (low heat) were transmitted by the sender[2].

3.4 Data Transmission with Multiple FPGAs

Using multiple FPGAs in parallel can be used to linearly increase the transmission bandwidth. With Cloud FPGAs, sender can use almost arbitrary number of FPGAs, only limited by their financial cost. Most cloud providers already provide 1 FPGA and 8 FPGA setups by default [6], thus use of multiple of 8 FPGAs seems natural fit for covert transmission.

To transmit the data in parallel, the sender can synchronize the servers with FPGAs, e.g. using network time protocol, and begin transmission at the same time. The sender and receiver need to pre-agree which FPGA will transmit which data bit. Once agreed, the sender starts the transmission by heating selected FPGAs. When *idle period* begins, the receiver needs to locate each FPGA through unique serial numbers, or by use of hardware fingerprinting methods [13]. Once located, the receiver does not have to wait to read all data bits in parallel at same time, but can read each bit individually as soon as each FPGA's temperature is measured with the RO sensor.

3.5 Limits of RO Sensor and Transmission of Multiple Bits per FPGA

Existing work has shown that it is possible to heat up different regions of the FPGA [1]. However, observing the differences in temperature of different parts of the FPGA over time is not trivial. The existing work [1] used high-resolution thermal cameras and observed the FPGA at what is equivalent to 0s of the *idle period*, i.e. at the moment when the FPGA is being heated, and not afterwards.

For this work, we have explored heating up different regions of the FPGA, and indeed, 2 or 4 regions can be possibly distinguished

---

[2]If the receiver has not previously used the RO on this particular FPGA, he will not know what frequency corresponds to the steady state or the heated FPGA. However, he can simply measure the RO frequency, and then wait for the duration equivalent to the sender's *waiting period*, and measure the RO frequency again, knowing the second measurement corresponds to the steady state idle temperature. Comparing the two reveals if the FPGA was in steady state or not during the first measurement. Next time the FPGA is used to transmit a bit of data, the second measurement is no longer needed as the receiver remembers the steady state frequency for the RO on this FPGA.

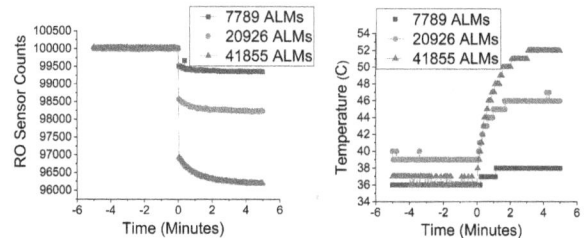

Figure 4: Left figure shows the frequency of the RO sensor as three different sized heaters are turned on at time 0. It can be seen that the heater size determines the maximum temperature reached at different times. Right figure shows the actual temperatures collected with built-in temperature sensor diodes.

when RO sensor is active at the same time as the heater. However, with non-zero *idle period*, the heat from one region of the FPGA spreads quickly to the whole FPGA and transmission of 2 or more bits per FPGA in the temporal thermal covert channel is not possible in devices we evaluated. As described before, however, multiple bits can trivially be transmitted using multiple FPGAs which are leased from the cloud provider in parallel.

4 EVALUATION

The evaluation was performed on Cloud FPGA instances from TACC. The servers in TACC are the same as Microsoft's Catapult servers, and use Altera Stratix V 5SGSMD5H2F35I3L FPGAs. The experiments were performed using heaters of three different sizes, 7789, 20926, and 41855 ALMs[3], corresponding to 4.5%, 12.1% and 24.2% logic utilization out of whole FPGA in the Catapult servers.

4.1 Heating Time Evaluation

Figure 4 (left side) shows the heating time it takes to achieve steady state temperature for the three different heater sizes. The temperature is measured by an RO sensor. Recall, number of RO counts (or RO sensor frequency) decreases as temperature increases, and same RO placed at same location but on different FPGAs will give different RO counts for the same temperature. Thus this graph shows the normalized numbers of RO counts for comparison. Based on the evaluation of the Stratix V FPGAs, for the heaters with 7789, 20926, and 41855 ALMs, it took about 60, 120, and 240 seconds to achieve steady state frequency respectively.

Figure 4 (right side) also shows reference temperature obtained from a built-in temperature sensor which is included in Stratix V. It can be seen the temperature rises much more slowly than the RO frequency. This can be explained by the fact that in Figure 4 (left side) the heater and RO sensor are running at the same time. Therefore, the initial sharp drop of the RO sensor counts is due to FPGA supply voltage change as the large heater array turns on at 0s. The remaining, more gradual frequency reduction after that is due to the thermal processes.

---

[3]ALMs (Adaptive Logic Modules) are basic logic cell units in Intel (previously Altra) FPGAs, they are equivalent to Slices in Xilinx FPGAs.

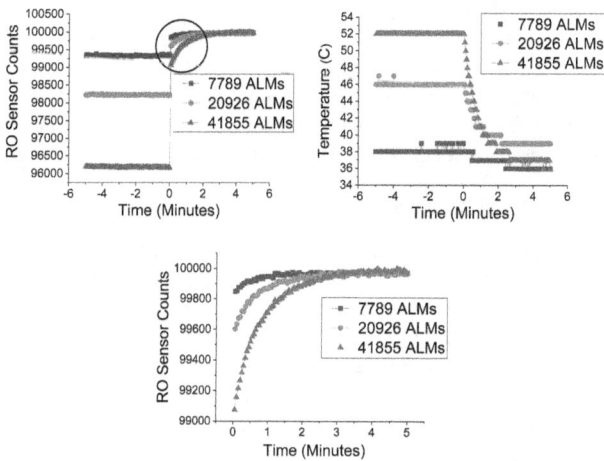

Figure 5: Top-left figure shows the frequency of the RO sensor as three different sized heaters are turned off at time 0. It can be seen that heater size determines the cooling speed and time. Top-right figure shows the actual temperatures collected with built-in temperature sensor diodes. Bottom figure shows the RO sensor frequency after heater is turned off – this is a zoom-in of the top-left figure.

4.2 Cooling Time Evaluation

Figure 5 shows the time it takes for the FPGA to dissipate all the heat generated by the heater. The RO counts (frequency) increase as temperature decreases as the FPGA cools off. Based on the evaluation of the Stratix V FPGAs, for the heaters with 7789, 20926, and 41855 ALMs, it took about 40, 90, and 180 seconds for FPGA to return to idle state temperature. The large initial increase in frequency (Figure 5, top-left, at 0s) is due to FPGA voltage changes as the large heater array turns off. Figure 5 (bottom) shows the zoom-in of the frequency changes after the heater is turned off, showing more gradual increase due to cooling off of the FPGA.

4.3 Bandwidth Evaluation

First, the bandwidth for one FPGA to transmit one bit can be computed using the formula shown in Equation 4.

$$bandwidth = \frac{H(1/2 + e/2) - (1/2) \times H(e)}{((t_r + t_w + t_h) + t_i + (t_r + t_s))} \quad bits/s \quad (4)$$

where t_w is the waiting time required for sender to wait for the FPGA to cool off, t_h is the heating time, t_i is the idle time between when the sender and receiver are using the FPGAs, t_s is the sensing time, t_r is the reconfiguration time for every new project on FPGA, and e is the error rate. H is binary entropy function where $H(x) = -x \log_2 x - (1 - x) \log_2 (1 - x)$ [5].

Expected bandwidths are computed based on below values. The t_w can be set to 0s as the cooling time and waiting time are about the same (based on data such as from Figures 5 and 4). The t_h can be 240s (based on using heater with 41855 ALMs, from Figure 4). The t_i is variable and depends on the cloud provider setting. The t_r is approximately 4.12 seconds on TACC. The t_s is 30s (time to run a software program on the server and read the RO counts from FPGA on TACC).

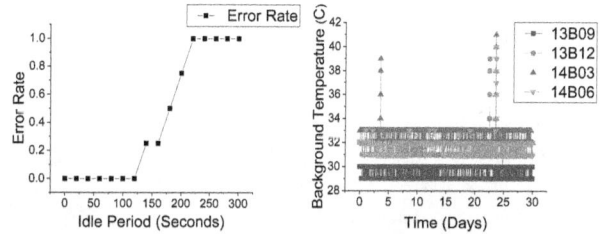

Figure 6: Left figure shows the error rate in the transmission of data using heater of size 41855 ALMs. As the measurement time approaches the cooling period time, the error rate approaches 100%. Right figure shows the ambient TACC temperature as measured using built-in temperature sensor diodes over a period of 30 days, showing steady data center temperature around the FPGAs. 13B09, 13B12, 14B03 and 14B06 are server names.

Bandwidths for using a set of N FPGAs running in parallel to transmit N bits for different idle time periods t_i, are shown in Figure 7, computed using Equation 4 multiplied by N, where $N \in \{1, 8, 16, 32, 64, 128, 256\}$.

4.4 Noise and Error Evaluation

To evaluate the errors in transmission, 8 FPGAs in TACC were used in parallel. Figure 6 (left) shows the data transmission error rate as a function of the length of the idle time between sender and receiver. As expected from the evaluation of the heating and cooling time shown in Figures 4 and 5 data can be successfully transmitted with 100% success rate when the idle time is up to 120s (2 minutes). Many error correction algorithms are able to support error rates up to 30%. If such error correction is deployed, the idle time can be extended to 160s or more.

Noise in the measurements can be influenced by temperature changes in the environment of the FPGA. Figure 6 (right) shows 30-day measurement of the temperature in the TACC FPGAs that were used in this project. The figure shows very steady data center temperature around FPGAs. Thus the noise due to temperature changes in the environment is not factored into this evaluation.

4.5 Total Channel Bandwidth and Cost

Figure 7 shows the possible bandwidth for idle times of 0, 1, 2, 3 and 4 minutes and for 1, 8, 16, 32, 64, 128 and 256 FPGAs used in parallel. The bandwidth is linear in relation to the number of FPGAs used; and the number of FPGAs is only limited by the available FPGAs in cloud provider or the cost that attacker can incur.

To better quantify the cost of leaking a key, an example of leaking 128-bit AES encryption key using 128 FPGAs on Amazon EC2 is shown in Table 1. The cost is surprisingly small and can be used to assign monetary value to the covert channel.

5 DEFENSE STRATEGIES

A number of defense strategies can be deployed by the Cloud FPGA providers to defend against the new covert channel.

Enforce Minimum Idle Period: The best strategy is to enforce a minimum idle period between users, so the FPGA is allowed to cool off to a steady state temperature. Some cloud providers charge by the minute, or even by the second, for use of their resources [2],

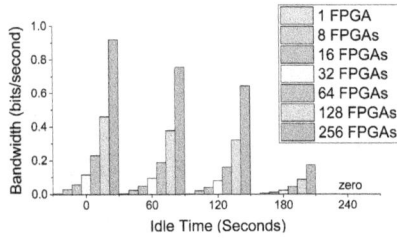

Figure 7: The figure shows the possible bandwidths for different idle times and number of FPGAs used parallel. The bandwidths account for the error rate. Bandwidths are computed using Equation 4 multiplied by the number of FPGAs used in parallel.

Table 1: Estimated cost to leak 128-bit AES key on Amazon EC2. As of September 2018, F1 instances cost \$1.65 per hour or \$0.0275 per minute. Thus cost for 128-bit key is computed by: 128 instances × time to leak 1 bit per FPGA × \$0.0275 per minute. Time is computed using t_r = 4.12s plus t_w = 0s plus t_h = 240s plus t_i (variable and listed in table) plus t_r = 4.12s plus t_s = 30s.

AES Key	Idle Period (t_i)	Time to Leak Key	Cost
128 bits	0 s	4.64 min.	16 \$
128 bits	30 s	5.13 min.	18 \$
128 bits	60 s	5.64 min.	20 \$
128 bits	120 s	6.64 min.	23 \$

so each idle minute is lost income, but a few minutes of idle period seems reasonable trade-off for eliminating the temporal thermal cover channels. Based on our evaluation, a period of about 10 minutes can fully ensure that FPGA has dissipated all excess heat.

Aggressive Heating or Cooling: A potential alternative is to heat or cool the FPGA to a known temperature before next user is able to use the FPGA. This is a trade-off in shorter idle time, but higher energy cost for the cloud provider to do the heating or cooling. If FPGA is always at a constant known temperature before a user uses it, there is no means for thermal data transfer.

Enact Design Rules to Check Bitstreams: Another defense strategy is to enact design rules that check the FPGA design or bitstream before it is allowed to be loaded onto the FPGA. Already some cloud providers, notably Amazon F1, perform checks on the designs they allow to load. Limitation of the approach is that it is a cat-and-mouse game. For example, the designs could be checked to prevent combinatorial loops from existing in the design, which would prevent RO from being able to be loaded on the FPGA. However, heater or sensor does not have to be based on RO design.

6 RELATED WORK

When two users' designs are loaded onto the same FPGA at the same time, for example, cross-talk between wires on the FPGA chip can be used to steal secrets [12]. Researchers have also explored how partial reconfiguration can be abused when multiple users share the same FPGA to steal another user's IP [9], or reconfigure the FPGA with a malicious bitstream [10].

Non-FPGA research which focuses on temperature includes work on multi-core platforms, where temperature can be used as a covert communication channel [11]. In addition, temperature can also be used to build side channels [8] in smart cards.

To best of our knowledge, this is the first work that explores security issues of temporal sharing of FPGAs and the new temporal covert channel in FPGAs. Furthermore, none of the listed related works have actually evaluated their designs on FPGAs in real cloud computing data centers as we have, rather evaluation is almost always done on local FPGAs "simulating" cloud deployments.

7 CONCLUSION

This paper presented a new temporal thermal covert channel in Cloud FPGAs for covert transmission of sensitive data between users of FPGAs shared in a cloud environment. This work showed cooling of FPGAs in a real cloud deployment such as TACC is slow enough to allow for data transmission through the thermal state of the FPGA chips, and the evaluation showed that even with up to a few minutes of *idle period* it is possible to transmit data. All software and hardware code used in this paper will be made available under open-source license and can be downloaded from http://caslab.csl.yale.edu/code/temporalthermalcc.

ACKNOWLEDGEMENT

The authors would like to thank TACC for the access to their Catapult infrastructure. The authors would also like to thank Dan Holcomb, Rob Moon, Remy Scott, Russell Tessier, and Wenjie Xiong, for their help and/or feedback. This work was made possible by NSF grant 1651945 and FPGA donations from Altera (now Intel).

REFERENCES

[1] Andreas Agne, Hendrik Hangmann, Markus Happe, Marco Platzner, and Christian Plessl. 2014. Seven recipes for setting your FPGA on fire–a cookbook on heat generators. *Microprocessors and Microsystems* 38, 8 (2014), 911–919.
[2] AWS News Blog. 2018. AWS News Blog – Per-Second Billing for EC2 Instances and EBS Volumes. https://aws.amazon.com/blogs/aws/new-per-second-billing-for-ec2-instances-and-ebs-volumes/.
[3] Eduardo Boemo and Sergio López-Buedo. 1997. Thermal monitoring on FPGAs using ring-oscillators. In *International Workshop on Field Programmable Logic and Applications*. Springer, 69–78.
[4] Alibaba Cloud. 2018. Alibaba Cloud – Create an f3 instance. https://www.alibabacloud.com/help/doc-detail/71545.htm.
[5] Thomas M Cover and Joy A Thomas. 2006. Elements of information theory 2nd edition. *Willey-Interscience: NJ* (2006), 187–188.
[6] Amazon F1. 2018. Amazon EC2 F1 Instances. https://aws.amazon.com/ec2/instance-types/f1/.
[7] Microsoft Azure FPGA. 2018. Microsoft Launches FPGA-Powered Machine Learning for Azure Customers. https://www.top500.org/news/microsoft-launches-fpga-powered-machine-learning-for-azure-customers/.
[8] Michael Hutter and Jörn-Marc Schmidt. 2013. The temperature side channel and heating fault attacks. In *International Conference on Smart Card Research and Advanced Applications (2013)*. Springer, 219–235.
[9] Daehee Jang, Hojoon Lee, Minsu Kim, Daehyeok Kim, Daegyeong Kim, and Brent Byunghoon Kang. 2014. Atra: Address translation redirection attack against hardware-based external monitors. In *Proceedings of the Conference on Computer and Communications Security*. ACM, 167–178.
[10] Markus Kucera and Michael Vetter. 2007. FPGA-Rootkits Hiding Malicious Code inside the Hardware. In *Proceedings of the Fifth International Workshop on Intelligent Solutions in Embedded Systems*. IEEE, 262–272.
[11] Ramya Jayaram Masti, Devendra Rai, Aanjhan Ranganathan, Christian Müller, Lothar Thiele, and Srdjan Capkun. 2015. Thermal Covert Channels on Multi-core Platforms. In *USENIX Security Symposium (2015)*. 865–880.
[12] Chethan Ramesh, Shivukumar B Patil, Siva Nishok Dhanuskodi, George Provelengios, Sebastien Pillement, Daniel Holcomb, and Russell Tessier. 2018. FPGA side channel attacks without physical access. In *International Symposium on Field-Programmable Custom Computing Machines*. 45–52.
[13] G Edward Suh and Srinivas Devadas. 2007. Physical unclonable functions for device authentication and secret key generation. In *Design Automation Conference*. IEEE, 9–14.
[14] TACC. 2018. Catapult - Texas Advanced Computing Center. https://www.tacc.utexas.edu/systems/catapult.

Poster Session 3

How to Accelerate FPGA Application in an Asynchronous Way?

Anping He, *Lanzhou University*
Jilin Zhang, *Lanzhou University*
Lvying Yu, *Lanzhou University*
Pengfei Li, *Lanzhou University*
Lian Li, *Lanzhou University*
Contact: yuly16@lzu.edu.cn

FPGA with massive customizable parallel computation capacity, is potentially good for fast time-to-market applications. However, its complex placing and routing lead to a relatively large latency and low frequency. Besides, the clock problems might make a design hard and slow, especially the one with complex control or variant computations. All of those defects seem to be from the essence of the synchronous design methodology and there does not exist an easy way to solve by clocks. Although the FPGA vendors do not supply an asynchronous design routine, flow or tool, it is still possible to implement a clockless design with a concrete FPGA chip and then harness lots of benefits that synchronous one misses, which is shown in this paper. We adopt link-joint as the asynchronous communication mechanism that discards clock limitation, but equips high throughput due to the fast handshake among neighbor clicks. The simplest link-joint circuit is click that conforms to Bundled Bound Data (BBD) protocol for local communication. Multiple clicks can be constructed and trimmed to types of micro-pipeline structures, feasibly and flexibly. With above considerations, we propose an innovative asynchronous design method for Xilinx FPGA applications, as well as the asynchronous control framework by dedicated micro-pipeline structures. Furthermore, we introduce delay maching technologies as well as whole design flow and tool-chain. All of these supply an applicable way of accelerating an asynchronous design for a FPGA. The case-studies show that communication between neighbor clicks is less than 1.1ns and the asynchronous method accelerates FPGA latency extremely.

Keywords: FPGA, Asynchronous Circuit, Click Circuit

DOI: https://doi.org/10.1145/3289602.3293953

Nuclear Reactor Simulations on OpenCL FPGA Platform

Zheming Jin, Hal Finkel,
Argonne National Laboratory
Contact: zjin@anl.gov

Field-programmable gate arrays (FPGAs) are becoming a promising choice as a heterogeneous computing component for scientific computing when floating-point optimized architectures

are added to the current FPGAs. The maturing high-level synthesis (HLS) tools, such as Intel FPGA SDK for OpenCL, provide a streamlined design flow to facilitate parallel application on FPGAs. In this paper, we evaluate and optimize the OpenCL implementations of three nuclear reactor simulation applications (XSBench, RSBench, and SimpleMOC kernel) on a heterogeneous computing platform that consists of a general-purpose CPU and an FPGA. We introduce the applications, and describe their OpenCL implementations and optimization methods on an Arria10-based FPGA platform. Compared with the baseline kernel implementations, our optimizations increase the performance of the three kernels by a factor of 35, 295, and 102, respectively. We compare the performance, power, and performance per watt of the three applications on an Intel Xeon 16-core CPU, an Nvidia Tesla K80 GPU, and an Intel Arria10 GX1150 FPGA. The performance per watt on the FPGA is competitive. For XSBench, the performance per watt on the FPGA is 1.43X higher than that on the CPU, and 2.58X lower than that on the GPU. For RSBench, the performance per watt on the FPGA is 3.6X higher than that on the CPU, and 5.8X lower than that on the GPU. For SimpleMOC kernel, the performance per watt on the FPGA is 1.74X higher than that on the CPU, and 1.65X lower than that on the GPU.

Keywords: FPGA; OpenCL; Nuclear reactor simulations

DOI: https://doi.org/10.1145/3289602.3293983

Storage Mirroring for Bare-Metal Systems on FPGA Devices

Dan Cristian Turicu,
Bitdefender, Technical University of Cluj-Napoca
Octavian Creţ, Lucia Văcariu,
Technical University of Cluj-Napoca
Contact: cturicu@bitdefender.com

Malicious applications, malware, continue to be a major security threat for computer systems. Due to the fast growing number and increasing complexity of malware, manual analysis became impractical and automated methods are preferred by security analysts. The automated dynamic analysis of malware executes the samples in controlled environments and monitors the execution for potentially malicious behavior. The vulnerability of this method is that modern malware detect these emulated or virtualized environments and suspend their malicious activities to foil the analysis. However, the malware exhibit a semantically different behavior when running directly on computer system hardware, *i.e.* bare-metal systems. Consequently, the ultimate technique for analyzing the behavior of malware is through execution of the samples in bare-metal analysis environments. Nevertheless, restoring the system to a clean state after each sample analysis is challenging.

In order to restore the storage device state of a bare-metal system to a clean state, in this paper we propose an FPGA-implemented storage mirroring technique for instantaneous restoration of the storage device and, optionally, the retrieval of the files having been modified during the sample execution. The FPGA-based system can be integrated in commodity computer systems with Serial

ATA storage devices. The retrieval of modified files is supported for systems running Windows operating systems with NTFS filesystem. The experimental results demonstrate the viability of the solution.

Keywords: Storage Mirroring; Storage Restore; Bare-Metal Malware Analysis; Serial ATA Devices; FPGA

DOI: https://doi.org/10.1145/3289602.3293985

Fast Inference of Deep Neural Networks for Real-time Particle Physics Applications

Javier Duarte, *Fermilab*
Song Han, *Massachusetts Institute of Technology*
Philip Harris, *Massachusetts Institute of Technology*
Sergo Jindariani, *Fermilab,*
Edward Kreinar, *Hawkeye 360*
Benjamin Kreis, *Fermilab*
Vladimir Loncar, *CERN*
Jennifer Ngadiuba, *CERN*
Maurizio Piedini, *CERN*
Dylan Rankin, *Massachusetts Institute of Technology*
Ryan Rivera, *Fermilab*
Sioni Summers, *Imperial College*
Nhan Tran, *Fermilab*
Zhenbin Wu, *UIC*
Contact: pcharris@mit.edu

Machine learning methods are ubiquitous and have proven to be very powerful in LHC physics, and particle physics as a whole. However, exploration of such techniques in low-latency, low-power FPGA (Field Programmable Gate Array) hardware has only just begun.FPGA-based trigger and data acquisition systems have extremely low, sub-microsecond latency requirements that are unique to particle physics. We present a case study for neural network inference in FPGAs focusing on a classifier for jet substructure which would enable many new physics measurements. While we focus on a specific example, the lessons are far-reaching. A compiler package is developed based on High-Level Synthesis (HLS) called *HLS4ML* to build machine learning models in FPGAs. The use of HLS increases accessibility across a broad user community and allows for a drastic decrease in firmware development time. We map out FPGA resource usage and latency versus neural network hyperparameters to allow for directed resource tuning in the low latency environment and assess the impact on our benchmark Physics performance scenario For our example jet substructure model, we fit well within the available resources of modern FPGAs with a latency on the scale of 100~ns.

Keywords: Fast-Inference; High Level Synthesis; Machine Learning; Physics; HLS4ML

DOI: https://doi.org/10.1145/3289602.3293986

XFER: A Novel Design to Achieve Super-Linear Performance on Multiple FPGAs for Real-Time AI

Weiwen Jiang, *Univ. of Pittsburgh & Chongqing Univ.*
Xinyi Zhang, *Univ. of Pittsburgh*
Edwin H.-M. Sha, *East China Normal Univ.*
Qingfeng Zhuge, *East China Normal Univ.*
Lei Yang, *Chongqing Univ. & Univ. of California, Irvine*
Yiyu Shi, *Univ. of Notre Dame*
Jingtong Hu, *Univ. of Pittsburgh*
Contact: jiang.wwen@pitt.edu

Real-time inference with low latency requirement has become increasingly important for numerous applications in both cloud computing and edge computing. The FPGA-based Deep Neural Network (DNN) accelerators have demonstrated the superior performance and energy efficiency over CPUs and GPUs; in addition, for real-time AI with low batch size, FPGA is expected to achieve further performance improvement over the general purpose computing platform. However, the performance gain of the single-FPGA design is hindered by the limited on-chip resource. In this paper, we leverage a cluster of FPGAs to fully exploit the parallelism in DNNs with the objective of obtaining super-linear performance. To achieve this goal, a novel design, "XFER", is proposed to deploy DNNs to FPGA cluster by splitting the DNN layer to multiple FPGAs and moving traffics from memory bus to inter-FPGA links. The resultant system can achieve both workload balance and traffic balance. As a case study, we implement Convolutional Neural Networks (CNNs) on ZCU102 FPGA boards. Evaluation results demonstrate that XFER on two FPGAs can achieve 3.48x speedup compared with state-of-the-art FPGA designs, achieving super-linear speedup.

Keywords: Multi-FPGA cluster; super-linear performance; real-time inference

DOI: https://doi.org/10.1145/3289602.3293988

An Energy-Efficient FPGA Implementation of an LSTM Network Using Approximate Computing

Elham Azari, Aykut Dengi, Sarma Vrudhula
Arizona State University
Contact: eazari@asu.edu

Long Short-Term Memory (LSTM) Recurrent Neural network (RNN) is known for its capability in modeling temporal aspects of data and has been shown to produce promising results in sequence learning tasks such as language modeling. However, due to the large number of model parameters and compute-intensive operations, existing FPGA implementations of LSTM cells are not sufficiently energy-efficient as they require large area and exhibit high power consumption. This work describes a substantially different hardware implementation of an LSTM which includes several architectural innovations to achieve high throughput and energy-efficiency. This paper includes extensive exploration of the design trade-offs and demonstrates the advantages for one common application – language modeling. Implementation of the design on a Xilinx Zynq XC7Z030 FPGA for language modeling shows significant improvements in throughput and energy-efficiency as compared to the state-of-the-art designs. It is worth mentioning that the proposed LSTM hardware architecture is also applicable to other applications that use LSTM as part of the neural network model (e.g., CNN-RNN models) or in whole (e.g., RNN models).

Keywords: Long Short-Term Memory; FPGA; Hardware Acceleration; Recurrent Neural Network

DOI: https://doi.org/10.1145/3289602.3293989

Towards Fast and Energy-Efficient Binarized Neural Network Inference on FPGA

Cheng Fu, *Iluvatar CoreX, University of California San Diego*
Shilin Zhu, *University of California San Diego*
Hao Su, *University of California San Diego*
Ching-En Lee, *Iluvatar CoreX*
Jishen Zhao, *University of California San Diego*
Contact: cfu@ucsd.edu, jzhao@ucsd.edu

Binarized Neural Network (BNN) removes bitwidth redundancy in classical CNN by using a single bit (-1/+1) for network parameters and intermediate representations, which has greatly reduced the off-chip data transfer and storage overhead. However, a large amount of computation redundancy still exists in BNN inference. By analyzing local properties of images and the learned BNN kernel weights, we observe an average of ~78% input similarity and ~59% weight similarity among weight kernels, measured by our proposed metric in common network architectures. Thus there does exist redundancy that can be exploited to further reduce the amount of on-chip computations.

Motivated by the observation, in this paper, we proposed two types of fast and energy-efficient architectures for BNN inference. We also provide analysis and insights to pick the better strategy of these two for different datasets and network models. By reusing the results from previous computation, much cycles for data buffer access and computations can be skipped. By experiments, we demonstrate that 80% of the computation and 40% of the buffer access can be skipped by exploiting BNN similarity. Thus, our design can achieve 17% reduction in total power consumption, 54% reduction in on-chip power consumption and 2.4× maximum speedup, compared to the baseline without applying our reuse technique. Our design also shows 1.9× more area-efficiency compared to state-of-the-art BNN inference design. We believe our deployment of BNN on FPGA leads to a promising future of running deep learning models on mobile devices.

Keywords: Binarized Neural Networks; Acceleration; Energy Efficiency; Input Reuse; Weight Reuse; FPGA

DOI: https://doi.org/10.1145/3289602.3293990

BRISC-V: An Open-Source Architecture Design Space Exploration Toolbox

Sahan Bandara, Alan Ehret, Donato Kava, Michel Kinsy,
Boston University
Contact: {sahanb, ehretaj, dkava, mkinsy}@bu.edu

In this work, we introduce the BRISC-V Toolbox, a register-transfer level (RTL) tool for architecture design space exploration. The BRISC-V Toolbox is an open-source, parameterized, synthesizable set of RTL modules for designing RISC-V based single and multi-core architecture systems. The toolbox is designed with a high degree of modularity. It provides highly parameterized, composable RTL modules for fast and accurate exploration of different RISC-V based core complexities, multi-level caching and memory organizations, system topologies, router architectures and routing schemes. BRISC-V can be used for both RTL simulation and FPGA based emulation. The hardware modules are implemented in synthesizable Verilog using no vendor-specific blocks. The toolbox includes a GCC RISC-V compiler tool-chain to assist in developing software for the cores and a web based system configuration graphical user interface (GUI). The BRISC-V Toolbox supports a myriad of RISC-V architectures, ranging from a simple single cycle processor to a multi-core SoC with a complex memory hierarchy and a network-on-chip. The modules are designed to support incremental additions and modifications. The module interfaces are carefully designed to enable an arbitrary pipeline depth and changes to a single module without impacting the rest of the system. The BRISC-V platform allows researchers to quickly instantiate complete working RISC-V multicore systems with synthesizable RTL correctness and make targeted modifications to fit their needs.

Keywords: Computer Architecture; RISC-V; Open-Source; Verilog; Compiler

DOI: https://doi.org/10.1145/3289602.3293991

Maverick: A Stand-alone CAD Flow for Xilinx 7-Series FPGAs

Dallon Glick, Jesse Grigg, Brent Nelson, Michael Wirthlin
NSF Center for Space, High-Performance, and Resilient Computing (SHREC), Brigham Young University
Contact: dallon.glick@byu.edu

Traditionally, an FPGA vendor's own set of computer-aided design (CAD) tools are used to generate circuits for a given vendor's FPGAs. However, numerous non-vendor CAD tools have been introduced to supplement the vendor-provided tools, allowing novel ideas to be explored and a variety of technical challenges to be addressed. This poster presents Maverick, a stand-alone CAD flow for compiling Verilog to bitstreams for Xilinx 7-Series devices. After an initial configuration design is created with Xilinx's Vivado partial reconfiguration (PR) flow to define a static design and a PR region, the Maverick flow can then compile and map Verilog design into that PR region — *without* the use of vendor tools. The Maverick flow combines two existing open source projects (Yosys and Project X-Ray) with our own RapidSmith2 tools to form an end-to-end compilation flow. It uses Yosys (synthesis), RapidSmith2 (pack, place, route), and the Project X-Ray tools (bitstream generation), taking Verilog designs as input and generating partial bitstreams as output. Several modifications were made to these existing tools and completely new tools were created, including a new RapidSmith2-based router, as a part of this work. This poster details these CAD steps and shows the results of the CAD flow running on a PYNQ-Z1 SoC's ARM processor to compile a set of HDL designs to partial bitstreams. The resulting bitstreams were configured onto the PYNQ-Z1's FPGA fabric, demonstrating the feasibility of a single-chip system which can both compile HDL designs to bitstreams and then configure them onto its own fabric.

Keywords: reconfigurable computing; design techniques, flows, methods; place & route algorithm; 3rd party FPGA CAD

DOI: https://doi.org/10.1145/3289602.3293997

Hierarchical FPGA Fabrics using 2D-Benes-BFT-Pyramid Network Layouts with Optimizations

Venkat Konda, *Konda Technologies Inc.*
Contact: Venkat@kondatech.com

Even though Benes/BFT multi-stage networks offer O(N*Log N) crosspoint complexity compared to 2D-Mesh Networks with O(N^2) crosspoint complexity, lack of known 2D-Mesh-like 2D layouts for multi-stage networks is the first main hurdle to exploit them as an FPGA fabric and consequently 2D-Mesh based fabrics have become prevalent. First, we present a fundamental layout for Benes/BFT networks making them implementable as simple as 2D-Mesh Networks, with all the wires between different logic blocks as either horizontal wires or vertical wires only, so we named them 2D-Benes or 2D-BFT Networks or 2D-Multi-stage networks in general. We apply several isomorphic transformations, and adapt Pyramid network properties. We also provide locality or nearest neighborhood connectivity, so that each logic block is directly connected its four neighbors and each logic block is connected to all its neighbors with the same path length or delay by bringing nearest neighbor connections to lower stages. Since fully connected Benes/BFT Networks is an over-kill as an FPGA fabric, we adapt several ways of crossbar depopulation and wire segmentation. We implemented various hierarchical multi-stage networks based FPGA fabric architectures, replicable at tile level, in a commercial FPGA and achieved ~2X area savings with significant power and performance improvements over 2D-Mesh based fabrics. We conclude with a summary of the benefits and drawbacks of these multi-stage networks based Hierarchical FPGA fabrics compared to prevailing 2D-Mesh network based fabrics. The foregoing Hierarchical FPGA Fabric technology was patent protected since May 25, 2007 in US8269523, US8898611, US9374322, US9509634 and their continuation patents.

Keywords: FPGA Fabrics; Multi-stage FPGA fabrics; 2D-Benes Networks; 2D-BFT Networks; 2D-BFT-Pyramid Networks; 2D-Multi-Stage Networks; Hierarchical FPGA fabrics; Flat FPGA fabrics

DOI: https://doi.org/10.1145/3289602.3293998

Flat FPGA Fabrics Derived from 2D-Benes-BFT-Pyramid Networks with Optimizations and Enhancements

Venkat Konda, *Konda Technologies Inc.*
Contact: Venkat@kondatech.com

Hierarchical FPGA fabrics based on 2D-BFT-Pyramid networks with transformations and optimizations even though offer significant area, power and performance savings still have several drawbacks compared to 2D-Mesh based FPGA fabrics. For example, hierarchical multi-stage fabrics are replicated at tile level of certain tile size do not offer consistent results regardless of the placement of the benchmarks emulated and certain precious routing resources are usable only if the signal traverses that particular hierarchy. We present several enhancements, techniques, and optimizations to transform hierarchical multi-stage networks into flat multi-stage networks i.e., make them replicable for each logic block in both multiplexers and wires. We also propose techniques to provide cascadable wires of arbitrary length with single multiplexer delay to traverse several wires of signal path or same stage connections, to enable multiple signal U-turns as opposed to only one U-turn inherent in a multi-stage network. We achieved the goal of making multi-stage network based FPGA fabric to seamlessly replace any existing 2D-Mesh based fabric, yet keeping everything else intact including placement, routing and all CAD Tools. We implemented the flat multi-stage networks based FPGA fabrics in a few commercial FPGAs with ~3X area savings and significant improvements in other dimensions and also the routing runtime in parity. We conclude with illustration of the benefits and absolutely no drawbacks for multi-stage network based Flat FPGA fabrics compared to prevailing 2D-Mesh network based fabrics. The foregoing Flat FPGA Fabric technology was patent protected since September 7, 2011 in US9374322, US9509634 and their continuation patents.

Keywords: FPGA Fabrics; Multi-stage FPGA fabrics; 2D-Benes Networks; 2D-BFT Networks; 2D-BFT-Pyramid Networks; 2D-Multi-Stage Networks; Hierarchical FPGA fabrics; Flat FPGA fabrics

DOI: https://doi.org/10.1145/3289602.3293999

HOTMeTaL: Hardware Optimization Tool for Memory Table and Logic Conversion

Michael Kapralos, *University of Connecticut*
John Chandy, *University of Connecticut*
Contact: mikepk@engineer.uconn.edu

FPGA designs are typically optimized for speed and accuracy, with the amount of available hardware considered after the fact. Balancing speed, accuracy, and hardware utilization is a difficult proposition. In this paper, we demonstrate the Hardware Optimization Tool for Memory Table and Logic Conversion

(HOTMeTaL) which helps with this tradeoff by modifying part or the majority of an existing FPGA design to use additional logic resources when memory is at a premium, or force the use of memory when logic is highly utilized; without significantly changing the overall functionality of the design. Using established minimization methods, traditionally used for programmable logic devices (PLDs), we also allow the conversion of groups or individual output bits into minimal logic circuits, which then allows the creation of several functionally identical designs, but allowing more control over the resources used in a design. After introducing the basics of the algorithm, we demonstrate the utility of this process with direct comparisons to examples from previous works. It is demonstrated that in some cases, our system will reduce the amount of logic (slices) while simultaneously removing the need to use ROMs, as the designs were originally constructed.

Keywords: FPGA; logic; minimization; PLD; BRAM; LUT

DOI: https://doi.org/10.1145/3289602.3294000

Engaging Heterogeneous FPGAs in the Cloud

Ke Zhang, Yisong Chang, Mingyu Chen, Yungang Bao, Zhiwei Xu, *State Key Laboratory of Computer Architecture, Institute of Computing Technology, Chinese Academy of Sciences; University of Chinese Academy of Sciences* Contact: {zhangke, changyisong}@ict.ac.cn

FPGA has become an essential infrastructural component in commercial cloud and datacenter for improving system performance and efficiency. Meanwhile, a heterogeneous FPGA chip (Hetero-FPGA) in which a multi-core System-on-Chip (SoC) is tightly integrated with an FPGA fabric has been successfully pioneered. Given its hardware-software co-programmability, Hetero-FPGA is supposed to become an independent and first-class cloud computing resource with networking capabilities in order to avoid involving brawny commodity x86 servers as carriers for FPGA fabrics which are usually the cases in current commercial FPGA clouds from several web vendors. Following this design paradigm, we present HeFA, a self-contained Hetero-FPGA Array architecture in cloud. We construct a high-level hardware template as well as a software stack for the Hetero-FPGA node, enabling the SoC as a primary engine to manage, coordinate and incorporate with the dominant FPGA fabric. We also propose a fully scripted design flow to make HeFA as an easy-to-use cloud infrastructure. Based on these techniques, we implement an academia prototype chassis of HeFA that includes 32 Hetero-FPGA nodes with Xilinx's Zynq MPSoC chips. By a customized cloud resource manager, the prototype is flexibly provisioned as either 32 individual FPGA nodes or multiple scalable sub-clusters to abstract arbitrary volume of reconfigurable fabrics as on-demand cloud services. In this manner, a versatile research and educational platform is delivered for agile hardware-software co-design in scenarios such as domain-specific accelerator development, open instruction set architecture-based chip design, computer system-related experimental project, and so on.

Keywords: FPGA array; Cloud computing; Hardware template; Software stack; Scripted design flow

DOI: http://dx.doi.org/10.1145/3289602.3294001

Enhancing Butterfly Fat Tree NoCs for FPGAs with Lightweight Flow Control

Gurshaant Singh Malik, *University of Waterloo*
Nachiket Kapre, *University of Waterloo*
Contact: nachiket@gmail.com

1.1.1 FPGA overlay networks-on-chip based on Butterfly Fat Tree (BFT) topology and lightweight flow control can outperform state-of-the-art FPGA NoCs, such as Hoplite and others, on metrics such as throughput, latency, cost and power efficiency, and features such as in-order delivery and bounded packet delivery times. Lightweight FPGA NoCs built on the principle of bufferless deflection routing, deliver low-LUT-cost implementations but sacrifice features such as in-order delivery, livelock freedom, and bounded delivery times. Conventional NoCs like CONNECT provide these features but are expensive in LUT cost. BFTs with flow control can deliver these features at medium cost while providing bandwidth configuration flexibility. We design FPGA-friendly routers with latency-insensitive interfaces, deterministic routing, and round-robin scheduling to develop switches that take 311-375 LUTs. We evaluate our NoC under synthetic and real-world workloads to deliver resource-proportional throughput and latency wins over competing NoCs, while significantly improving dynamic power consumption when compared to deflection-routed NoCs. We also explore bandwidth customizability of the BFT to identify best configurations for resource/application constrained scenarios. We evaluate hard implementations of these routers using TSMC 65nm cell technology and observe that 128b BFT t and pi switches fit in 123x122μ and 147x147μ tile sizes while operating at 1GHz.

2. Keywords: Network-on-chip; Butterfly Fat Trees; Hard NoCs

DOI: https://doi.org/10.1145/3289602.3294002

Efficient FPGA Implementation of Conjugate Gradient Methods for Laplacian System using HLS

Sahithi Rampalli, Natasha Sehgal, Ishita Bindlish, Tanya Tyagi, Pawan Kumar
International Institute of Information Technology
Contact: pawan.kumar@iiit.ac.in

In this paper, we study FPGA based pipelined and superscalar design of two variants of conjugate gradient methods for solving Laplacian equation on a discrete grid; the first version corresponds to the original conjugate gradient algorithm, and the second version corresponds to a recently proposed slightly modified version. In conjugate gradient method to solve partial differential equations, matrix vector operations are required in each iteration; these operations can be implemented as 5 point finite difference stencil operations on the grid without explicitly constructing the matrix. We show that a pipelined and superscalar design using high level synthesis (HLS) written in well known C language leads to a significant reduction in latencies for both variants of conjugate gradient methods. When comparing these two, we show that the later has roughly two times lower latency than the former given the same degree of superscalarity. These reductions in latencies for the newer variant of CG is due to parallel implementations of stencil operation on subdomains of the grid, and due to overlap of these stencil operations with dot product operations. In a superscalar design for the stencil operation, the computational domain needs to be partitioned, and boundary data needs to be copied, which requires padding. In a 1D partition, the padding latency increases as the number of partitions increase. For a streaming data flow model, we propose a novel traversal of the grid for 2D domain decomposition that leads to 2 times reduction in latency cost involved with padding compared to 1D partitions. The FPGA implementation of CG is roughly 7 times faster than state-of-the-art sequential implementation, and roughly 4 times faster than state-of-the-art CUDA library parallel implementation for the linear system of dimension 10000 x 10000

Keywords: FPGA, High Level Synthesis; Conjugate Gradient; Laplace System; Pipelining; Superscalarity

DOI: https://doi.org/10.1145/3289602.3294004

A FPGA Implementation of Farneback Optical Flow by High-Level Synthesis

Chia-Wei Chang, Zi-Qi Zhong, Jing-Jia Liou,
National Tsing Hua University
Contact: s101061539@m101.nthu.edu.tw

Optical flow algorithm, which estimates the motion detection of consequent video frames, is widely used in surveillance system, Advanced Driver Assistance Systems (ADAS) and object movement estimation in scene analysis. Among different optical flow algorithms, Farneback version provides a better accuracy and brightness-change-resistant displacements by estimating the flow from polynomial domain rather than intensive maps. However, high computation complexity and inconsistent data access patterns make it difficult to be implemented on a hardware platform. In this work, we present a micro-architecture design of Farneback optical flow, which is flexible for optimization with high level Synthesis (HLS) tools. The original software-based implementation was decomposed into functional blocks to balance latency of different stages and flows of data were rearranged to accommodate better memory access patterns. The data flow arrangement is based on a proposed backtrace mechanism, where DRAM accesses of polynomial coefficients in current frame makes consistent traffic patterns, and therefore make it possible to integrate more functional blocks into a deeper pipeline. For several micro-architecture design versions, we demonstrate options of fixed and floating points, optimization techniques such as multiple DMAs and different levels of pipeline integration. We implemented our design on Zedboard Mini-ITX 7045. The results show a 17x end-to-end speedup against a naive HLS version with an image size of 160x120. Considering only the hardware-

accelerated part, our FPGA implementation is 40x faster than the naive HLS version with only 50% of the FPGA hardware resources.

Keywords: Hardware Accelerators; Optical Flow; High-Level Synthesis; FPGA

DOI: https://dx.doi.org/10.1145/3289602.3294005

Efficient Acceleration of CNNs for Semantic Segmentation on FPGAs

Sebastian Vogel[1], Jannik Springer[1,2],
Andre Guntoro[1], Gerd Ascheid[2],
[1]*Robert Bosch GmbH*, [2]*RWTH Aachen University*
Contact: sebastian.vogel@bosch.com

We present a Vector Processing Engine (VPE) designed for the acceleration of Convolutional Neural Networks (CNNs) for semantic segmentation. Most CNN accelerators focus on classification. However, CNNs for semantic segmentation incorporate special layer types. Our accelerator supports not only regular convolutional layers, but also dilated convolutions and convolutions in combination with down- or up-sampling. These features are implemented in dedicated address generators which load the corresponding input vector from an input line buffer. The VPE is designed as a 64x64-array where up to 64 output features and 64 input features of a convolutional layer can be unrolled in parallel. The array has a peak performance of 4.12 TOp/s and achieves 3.85 TOp/s on a CNN for semantic segmentation – resulting in an average utilization of 93 %. The design is prototypically implemented on a Virtex UltraScale+ device with a clock rate of 250 MHz. In addition to the overall architecture, we present the two-hot quantization scheme. A value in two-hot quantization can be regarded as a combination of two power-of-two values. Hence, instead of bulky multipliers, two small bit-shifts are implemented. We design and implement dedicated arithmetic engines for this quantization scheme. Additionally, we evaluate this quantization scheme on the rather complex task of semantic segmentation. We show that the performance of an 8 bit two-hot quantization scheme is marginally lower in comparison to a regular 8 bit fixed-point variant.

Keywords: Convolutional Neural Networks; Semantic Segmentation; Multiplier-less Acceleration; Quantization

DOI: https://doi.org/10.1145/3289602.3294006

Stop Crying Over Your Cache Miss Rate:
Handling Efficiently Thousands of Outstanding Misses in FPGAs

Mikhail Asiatici and Paolo Ienne
Ecole Polytechnique Fédérale de Lausanne (EPFL)
School of Computer and Communication Sciences
CH–1015 Lausanne, Switzerland

ABSTRACT

FPGAs rely on massive datapath parallelism to accelerate applications even with a low clock frequency. However, applications such as sparse linear algebra and graph analytics have their throughput limited by irregular accesses to external memory for which typical caches provides little benefit because of very frequent misses. Non-blocking caches are widely used on CPUs to reduce the negative impact of misses and thus increase performance of applications with low cache hit rate; however, they rely on associative lookup for handling multiple outstanding misses, which limits their scalability, especially on FPGAs. This results in frequent stalls whenever the application has a very low hit rate. In this paper, we show that by handling thousands of outstanding misses without stalling we can achieve a massive increase of memory-level parallelism, which can significantly speed up irregular memory-bound latency-insensitive applications. By storing miss information in cuckoo hash tables in block RAM instead of associative memory, we show how a non-blocking cache can be modified to support up to three orders of magnitude more misses. The resulting miss-optimized architecture provides new Pareto-optimal and even Pareto-dominant design points in the area-delay space for twelve large sparse matrix-vector multiplication benchmarks, providing up to 25% speedup with 24× area reduction or to 2× speedup with similar area compared to traditional hit-optimized architectures.

ACM Reference Format:
Mikhail Asiatici and Paolo Ienne. 2019. Stop Crying Over Your Cache Miss Rate:, Handling Efficiently Thousands of Outstanding Misses in FPGAs. In *The 2019 ACM/SIGDA International Symposium on Field-Programmable Gate Arrays (FPGA '19), February 24–26, 2019, Seaside, CA, USA.* ACM, New York, NY, USA, 10 pages. https://doi.org/10.1145/3289602.3293901

1 INTRODUCTION

FPGAs can accelerate compute-intensive applications by implementing massively parallel datapaths. FPGAs also provide spatially distributed SRAM memories with low latency and large aggregate bandwidth, which can store small datasets or implement custom memory hierarchies backing the external DRAM. However, important application classes such as sparse linear algebra and graph

analytics are embarrassingly parallel and yet their memory access pattern is such that, with caches that can be realistically implemented on FPGA, most of the accesses are cache misses. In this paper, we will radically rethink the balancing between cache and miss handling logic to optimize the throughput of *read* operations when a large fraction of cache misses is inevitable. We introduce a generic approach, orthogonal to application-specific optimizations, that can provide significant speedup with little design effort. Thanks to its generality, it might be particularly valuable for solutions generated by high-level synthesis tools.

1.1 The Curse of Sparse Narrow Data

Custom memory hierarchy design and automatic generation usually rely on access patterns that have temporal and spatial locality (caches), are regular (scratchpads) or are at least known at compile-time (memory banking and address scrambling) [1, 4, 12, 30]. When access patterns have poor locality and are irregular and data-dependent, one can at best maximize memory-level parallelism (MLP) by emitting enough outstanding memory operations to fully exploit the DRAM latency; however, the throughput of the memory system is still limited to one operation per cycle per DRAM channel, at most. This imposes severe limitations on the amount of datapath parallelism that is worth implementing, limiting the advantage of using an FPGA.

The effective bandwidth gets even more limited if the operands are narrow, such as in sparse linear algebra and graph applications, which often involve irregular accesses to 32- or 64-bit scalars. This relates to the architecture of DRAM memory controllers on FPGA, which expose the memory through wide data interfaces in order to give access to the full DRAM bandwidth despite the slow FPGA clock. For example, exploiting the full 12.8 GB/s DDR3 bandwidth at 200 MHz requires transferring 512 bits per cycle. In this case, an accelerator that operates on 64-bit inputs could at best exploit one eighth of the peak DDR3 bandwidth, and most of the 512 bits returned by the DRAM controller would be discarded. Multiple accelerators whose requests are mutually uncorrelated can only be served by time-multiplexing the memory channel, canceling out any benefits due to parallelization. The only way to improve bandwidth utilization, and thus performance, would be to use larger portions of each block returned from memory.

1.2 Misses Are a Fact of Life

Figure 1 shows the histogram of the number of reuses of 512-bit blocks for an application with poor locality—accesses to the dense vector of 32-bit integers during sparse matrix-vector multiplication (SpMV) with the CSR-encoded pds-80 matrix from SuiteSparse [8]—and if the same number of read operations were performed

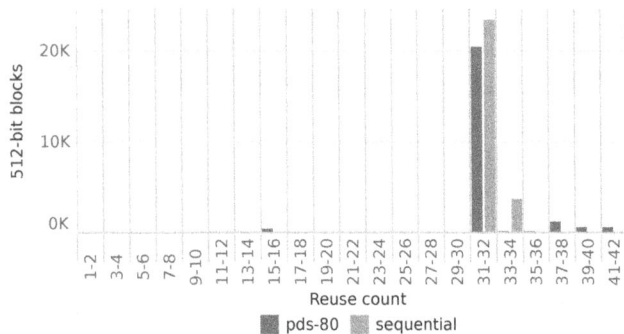

Figure 1: Spatial locality. The histogram shows the reuse count for each 512-bit block of data, for SpMV of pds-80 and for the same number of read operations scanning sequentially the same memory space. Despite showing very different cache hit rates, both memory traces have similar amounts of data reuse across the entire application execution.

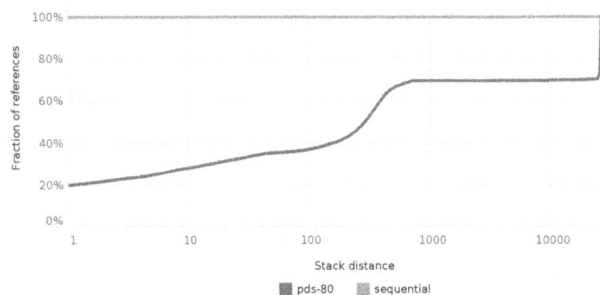

Figure 2: Temporal locality. The graph shows the fraction of 512-bit block references that have stack distance $\leq x$, for SpMV of pds-80 and a sequential memory trace. A large fraction of the reuses that occur in pds-80 are interleaved with references to many different blocks. Blocks can be stored in a cache hoping for future reuse; however, because large stack distances are common, cache lines are likely to be evicted before the next reuse, unless a large cache is used.

sequentially over the same address span. Both access patterns offer very similar opportunities for reuse; however, while the sequential access pattern achieves a $\frac{15}{16}$ = 94% hit rate on any cache with 512-bit cache lines, the hit rate of SpMV on a 128 kB direct-mapped blocking cache is only 57%. In fact, in a cache, eviction limits the time window where data reuse could occur. For the same two applications, Figure 2 shows the cumulative frequency of *stack distances*, i.e., the number of different 512-bit blocks that have been referenced between two consecutive references to the same blocks [6]. For example, for the memory trace: {746, 1947, 293, 5130, 293, 746}, the stack distances for the last access to blocks 293 and 746 are 1 and 3 respectively. While the stack distance of the sequential pattern is always zero, the SpMV cumulative histogram grows very slowly, meaning that a large fraction of reuses have large stack distance. With an ideal fully associative cache with N lines and LRU replacement, reaccessing a cache line with stack distances larger than N will always be a miss;

on a realistic cache, even reuses with stack distance lower than N could be misses.

1.3 More MSHRs or More Cache?

The previous example showed that even applications with poor temporal locality may still have some spatial locality, which caches struggle to harness due to large stack distances between reuses. Even worst, a blocking cache actually hampers performance if the hit rate is too low to compensate for the stall cycles due to the misses. Non-blocking caches reduce stall penalties by handling one or more misses without stalling. On the first miss of a cache line (a *primary* miss), the address of the cache line is sent to memory and stored in a *miss status holding register* (MSHR); the offset of the requested word within the cache line, together with the request source/tag, is stored in a *subentry* for that MSHR. Subsequent misses to the same cache line (*secondary* misses), only require the allocation of a subentry on the same MSHR with no additional memory requests. When the missing cache line is received, it is both stored in the cache and used to serve all of its pending misses [10]. In practice, the time window where a cache line could be reused now includes the time between the first miss and the arrival of the data. For the purpose of widening the reuse window, adding an MSHR with its subentries is equivalent to adding one cache line to a fully associative cache; however, storing the miss metadata may require less bits than storing the entire cache line if the number of reuses is small. Moreover, each request to memory serves multiple requests from the accelerators, effectively increasing bandwidth utilization and pushing maximum MLP beyond the DRAM latency as long as there are available MSHRs and subentries [23]. Furthermore, unlike caches, MSHRs can serve primary misses without stalling the entire system, which is crucial for throughput maximization.

1.4 Exploring MSHR-Rich Caches

Non-blocking caches are extensively used in processors; however, to minimize latency, MSHRs are usually searched associatively, which limits their number to a few tens. In practice, on realistic CPUs, there is often little benefit in dramatically increasing the number of MSHRs beyond this limit [21, 25]. On FPGAs, associative searches are even less scalable than in ASICs; yet, massively parallel, high throughput FPGA accelerators that emit a vast number of outstanding reads to hide memory latency [7, 22] could potentially benefit from an MSHR-rich architecture even more than a general-purpose processor.

In this paper, we propose a novel miss handling architecture (MHA) optimized for bandwidth-bound FPGA accelerators that perform irregular accesses to external memory. By using the abundant on-chip RAM, we show how we can efficiently implement and access thousands of MSHRs and sub-entries on FPGA. Without loss of generality, we evaluate our MHA on a simple parallel SpMV accelerator operating on a set of SuiteSparse matrices [8], which we use as representative of latency-tolerant and bandwidth-bound applications with various degrees of locality. Our architecture extends the space of possible custom memory hierarchies on FPGA, providing additional Pareto-optimal and even Pareto-dominant points in the area-performance space compared to only using blocking caches or non-blocking caches with associative MSHR lookup. Furthermore,

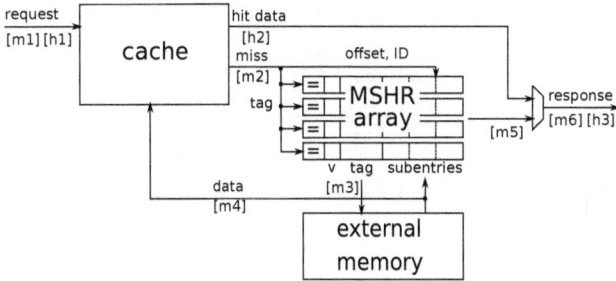

Figure 3: Structure of a non-blocking cache. On a hit (steps [h1]-[h3]), it behaves just like any cache. On a miss (steps [mi] to [m6]), the miss address and data is stored in an MSHR [m2]. If it is the first miss to a particular cache line, a memory request is sent [m3]. When the data returns from memory [m4], it is stored in the cache and used to respond to all the pending misses to this cache line [m5], [m6].

we will show that the benefit of repurposing some FPGA memory from cache to MSHRs increases as the memory access pattern gets irregular.

2 BACKGROUND

2.1 Non-Blocking Caches

Figure 3 shows the organization of a typical non-blocking cache. A non-blocking cache contains a miss handling architecture (MHA), based on an array of miss status holding registers (MSHRs), which keeps track of the in-flight misses. Each MSHR refers to one missing cache line and contains a valid bit, the tag of the cache line and one or more subentries to handle multiple misses to the same cache line.

2.2 FPGA On-Chip Memory

Modern FPGAs have at least three types of on-chip memory: flip flops, LUTRAM, and block RAM. Each bit of flip flop-based memory is exposed to the FPGA fabric, providing the highest flexibility in terms of number, type, and width of memory ports and the largest bandwidth. However, flip flop bits are the least abundant and some LUTs must be consumed to implement their access logic. LUTRAMs use LUTs to realize single-, dual-, or quad-port memories with medium depth (32-64 entries). However, they compete with combinational logic for LUTs. Block RAMs are dedicated memory resources implemented as hard logic. They provide the highest memory density and do not require any soft logic; however, they generally provide only two ports and are optimized for narrow and deep memory arrays (at least 512 entries). Therefore, the challenge is to use block RAM as much as possible, followed by LUTRAM and flip flops.

3 KEY IDEAS

3.1 Scalable MSHR Lookup and Storage

For each additional MSHR, the memory system can handle one more primary miss without stalling; similarly, each additional subentry allows servicing an extra secondary miss with no additional traffic

to the external memory. Each MSHR has modest storage requirements: ~20-30 bits for the cache line tag and its valid bit, plus ~10-20 bits for offset and request ID for each of the ~4-8 subentries. This is significantly smaller than a 512-bit cache line with its tag. Therefore, within a given on-chip memory budget, bandwidth-bound applications with irregular memory access patterns could benefit more from an increase of the number of MSHRs or subentries, which increase MLP, rather than from an expansion of the cache. In practice, however, scaling up the fully associative MSHR array (Figure 4a) also requires additional comparators and a wider multiplexer, which increase area and hurt the critical path. Moreover, on FPGA, associative MSHRs can only be mapped to flip flops, whereas an n-way set associative cache can be implemented with n block RAM modules.

A set-associative MSHR memory (Figure 4b), indexed by the lowest significant bits of the tag, can be easily mapped to block RAM and, as long as there are no collisions, lookups, insertions, and deletions can be performed in a single step. Stalling is the simplest collision handling mechanism; however, we will show in Section 6.3 that this strongly limits the maximum load factor. Using linear probing would result in *expected* constant time lookup, insertion, and deletion and, whenever any operation cannot be completed in a single step, incoming misses must be stalled.

To overcome these limitations, we propose to store MSHRs using cuckoo hashing (Figure 4c). Cuckoo hashing uses d hash tables and d hash functions $h_0, \ldots, h_{d-1}$; each key x can be stored in any hash table in bucket $H_i[h_i(x)]$. Lookups and deletions require *worst case* constant time: both involve one lookup per hash table, plus one update for deletions. For insertions, key x can be inserted in any hash table whose bucket $h_i(x)$ is empty. If all possible locations $H_i[h_i(x)]$ are occupied, a *collision* occurs: the new key x displaces an existing entry to one of its alternative locations. If all possible buckets of the displaced entry are also occupied, the process is repeated recursively until an entry can be inserted into an empty bucket. This means that insertions can still require more than one operation, during which no other misses can be handled. Expected amortized insertion time is constant as long as the load factor is bounded; the bound is 50% for $d = 2$ and grows very quickly with d [11]. To de-amortize insertion, Kirsch et al. proposed to temporarily store displaced entries in a small content-searchable queue (*stash*) [18] (Figure 4d). As soon as the input interface is idle, the MHA tries to insert the oldest entry from the stash; if this results in a collision, another entry from a different hash table is moved to the stash. By doing so, entry reinsertion effectively happens in the background without slowing down incoming requests; incoming allocations are stalled only when the stash gets full.

3.2 Flexible Subentry Storage

For their explicitly addressed MSHR architecture, Farkas and Jouppi propose to use a fixed number of subentry slots per MSHR (Figure 5a) and to stall the MHA whenever all slots of an MSHR are used. However, waiting for the specific MSHR that is full to be deallocated may take a long time, during which the MHA may miss opportunities for merging requests to in-flight cache lines, which is particularly bad in out context. Increasing the number of slots per MSHR would reduce the probability of stall at the expense of

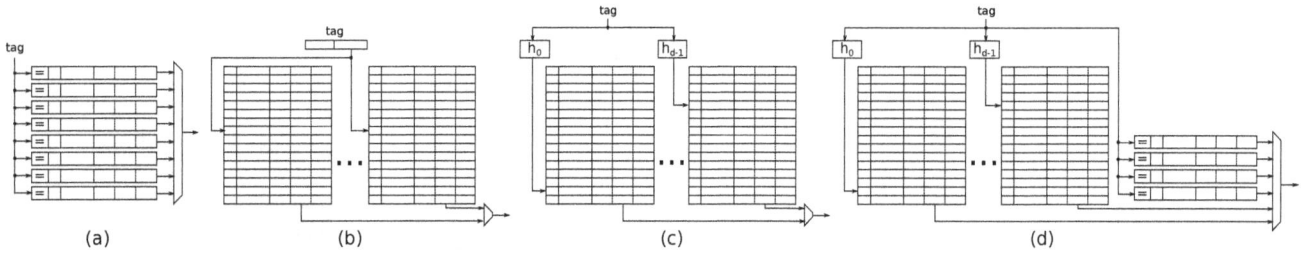

Figure 4: MSHR-rich architectures for FPGAs. Because of the associative lookup, a traditional architecture (a) does not scale beyond a few MSHRs and MSHRs can only be mapped to flip flops. Using a set-associative memory with a single hash function (b) allows MSHRs to be mapped to block RAM but stalling on every collision results in low load factors. Cuckoo hashing (c) reduces the probability of collision and a stash (d) allows collisions to be handled in the background when the unit is idle.

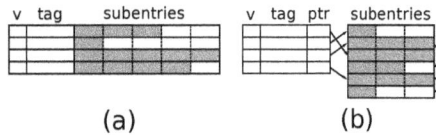

Figure 5: Subentry organization in memory. Allocating a fixed number of subentries to every MSHR (a) results in a difficult tradeoff between a low maximum load factor and a high probability of stall, especially if there is a large variation in the number of secondary misses per cache line. Using a separate buffer to store blocks of subentries organized as linked lists (b) provides greater flexibility at a modest cost.

an increase in area or, in other words, a decrease in load factor due to increased internal fragmentation. To mitigate these drawbacks, we propose a hybrid approach (Figure 5b): we store subentries in a separate buffer and we dynamically allocate blocks of subentries to each MSHR. Specifically, the subentry buffer, mapped to block RAM, contains N_R subentry rows, each comprising n_s slots. Each MSHR is initially assigned one subentry row; whenever a row gets full, an additional row is allocated for that MSHR. Subentry rows are logically organized as a linked list: the head pointer is stored in the MSHR buffer and each subentry row contains a field for the pointer to the next row. We will evaluate the benefits of the linked-list architecture in Section 6.4.

4 DETAILED ARCHITECTURE

Figure 6 shows the top-level view of our memory controller based on an MSHR-rich MHA. To simplify the design and to maximize the scope for memory access optimization, our controller can return responses out of order, which is not unusual among high performance memory systems [14, 15]. Therefore, requests must be tagged with an ID, which will be used to match it with the corresponding response. Requests received from each of the N_i input channels are redistributed across N_b banks by means of a crossbar. We use a multi-banked structure in order to handle multiple requests and responses per cycle. Requests pertaining to consecutive cache lines are served by different banks, an interleaved scheme commonly used in multi-banked caches. Each bank consists of a set-associative cache, an MSHR buffer, and a subentry buffer. Data for requests that hit in the cache are immediately returned to the crossbar, while

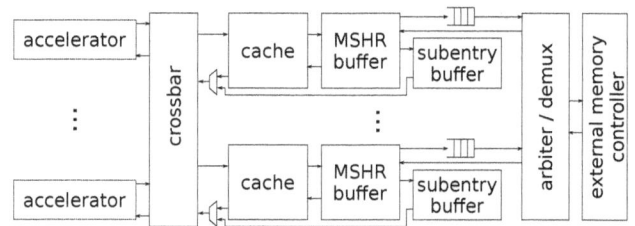

Figure 6: Top-level view of our memory controller. A crossbar steers memory requests from N_i accelerators to N_b banks according to their address. Each bank consists of a cache, an MSHR buffer and a subentry buffer. An arbiter time-multiplexes the input channel(s) of the external memory controller among banks.

misses are handled and stored by the MSHR and subentry buffer. On a primary miss, we also generate a memory request; requests from each bank are forwarded to a round-robin arbiter and then to the external memory controller. Cache lines received from the external memory controller are multicasted both to the cache and to the subentry buffer, which generates the responses to the cache line's pending misses.

4.1 MSHR Buffer

For the MSHR buffer, we use one block RAM per hash table, with the address of the cache line (tag) as key. We use universal hash functions in the form $h_a(x) = (ax \bmod 2^{w_t}) \operatorname{div} 2^{w_t - w_M}$ with w_t being the number of bits of the tag, $w_M = \log_2(M)$ where M is the number of buckets per hash table, and a is a random positive odd integer with $a < 2_t^w$ [29]. Each bucket contains a valid bit, the tag of the missing cache line, and the address of the first subentry row in the subentry buffer as described in Section 3.2. The stash is a content-associative memory made of flip-flops. To integrate the stash in the pipeline, we include the stash entries among the locations that are searched during lookups or that can be deallocated when a response is received.

4.2 Subentry Buffer

Figure 7 shows implementation and operation of the subentry buffer. A subentry consists of an (ID, offset) pair; a subentry row contains a) n_s subentry slots, b) the number of allocated subentries, and c)

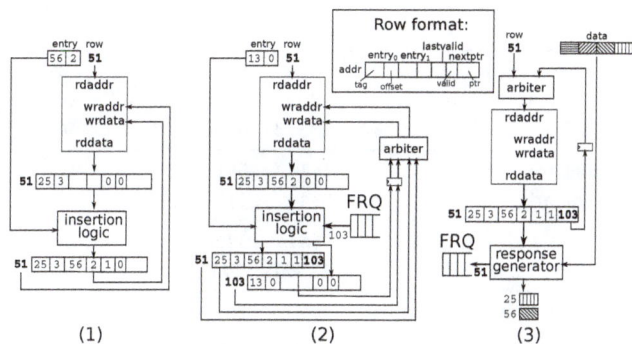

Figure 7: Block diagram and operation of the subentry buffer. For requests, the subentry buffer receives ID, offset, and the address of the first subentry row (head row) from the respective MSHR. The head row is firstly retrieved from the buffer. If it is not full (1), the row is updated with the new entry and written back to the buffer. If the row is full (2), the new entry is inserted in a new row, whose address is stored in the previous row. When a response is received (3), all subentries are retrieved by traversing the subentry row list. After all subentries have been forwarded to the response generator, the row is deallocated by pushing its address to the free row queue.

a pointer to the next subentry row with its valid bit. To allocate a subentry, the first subentry row is retrieved from the buffer. If the row is not full (1), the new entry is appended and the row is written back to the buffer. If the row is full (2), a new row must also be allocated. We use a FIFO (free row queue, FRQ) to store the addresses of the empty rows, and allocating a row simply means extracting the first element of the FRQ. The FRQ is also shared with the MSHR buffer to allow the allocation of the first subentry row for newly allocated MSHRs. When the FRQ gets empty, further allocations are stalled.

When a cache line is received, the corresponding MSHR is deallocated from the MSHR buffer and its subentry rows retrieved from the buffer. The response generator parses the subentry rows and emits one response per allocated subentry. The row is then recycled by inserting its address into the FRQ and the process is repeated for the entire linked list of rows.

4.3 Pipeline Efficiency and Throughput

As long as an MSHR has a single subentry row, the primary and all secondary misses can be handled without stalling the pipeline as they require no more than one read and one write per dual-ported block RAM: lookup in the MSHR buffer, allocation of the MSHR for primary misses, lookup in the subentry buffer for secondary misses, and row update in the subentry buffer. Each block RAM has a data forwarding circuit to ensure that we always read the most up-to-date data despite reads having two-cycle latency. MSHR collisions are handled transparently when the unit is idle, as long as there are free entries in the stash. Allocating an additional subentry row requires stalling the pipeline for one cycle to perform two writes: inserting the pointer of the newly allocated row into the tail of the

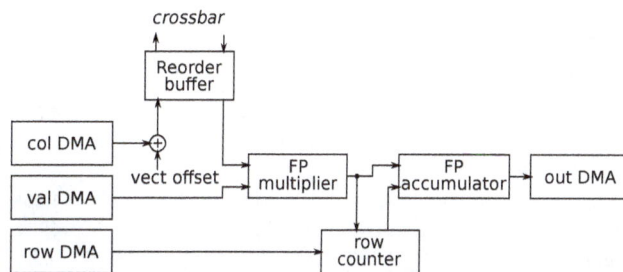

Figure 8: Structure of our benchmark sparse matrix-vector multiplication accelerator. Xilinx AXI DMAs are used to stream all CSR vectors accessed sequentially. The values of the col array are used to compute the addresses of the vector elements that are retrieved through our memory controller.

list, and writing the new subentry into the newly allocated row. Allocating a subentry on an MSHR that has more than one row requires traversing the linked list, which costs an extra read per additional row. The traversal cost can be significant for MSHRs with many subentries: to mitigate it, we use an 8-entry fully-associative cache indexed by the head pointer of the subentry list to jump directly to the tail whenever possible. In our subentry architecture, the tradeoff between internal fragmentation and stall cycles, which depend on the number of subentries per row, remains; however, the cost of a full subentry row is reduced from completely stalling the pipeline until the full MSHR is deallocated to a few bubbles in the pipeline. Responses whose MSHR has a single subentry row can also be handled without stalls; each additional subentry row costs one stall cycle.

Most of the operations are therefore fully pipelined, with the caveat that a single pipeline is shared between accelerator requests and memory responses. However, the more secondary misses we can merge to the same memory request, the fewer memory responses we will have to handle, reducing the cost of pipeline sharing. Ultimately, N_b fully-pipelined banks can supply up to $N_b - 1$ responses per cycle from a single-ported external memory.

5 EXPERIMENTAL SETUP

We wrote our memory controller in Chisel 3, compiled it with Vivado 2017.4 and tested it on a ZC706 board with an XC7Z045 SoC. The board has 1 GB of DDR3 on the processing system side, connected to the dual-core ARM's memory controller, and 1 GB of DDR3 on the programmable logic side which can be accessed directly from the FPGA. The FPGA has 437,200 flip flops, 218,600 LUTs—which could implement up to 4.3 Mib of LUTRAM, if no LUTs were used for logic—and 1090 18 kib block RAM modules (19.2 Mib of block RAM).

As a benchmark, we implemented a simple accelerator for sparse matrix-vector multiplication (SpMV), an important kernel in a broad range of scientific applications [3] and to which many sparse graphs algorithms can be mapped [17]. Moreover, SpMV can easily generate a wide range of access patterns depending on the matrix sparsity pattern. Our accelerator, shown in Figure 8, is an almost direct implementation of Algorithm 1 for SpMV of a CSR-encoded sparse matrix; we do not include any SpMV-specific optimizations as our

matrix	NZ	rows	vect size	st. dist. percentiles		
				75%	90%	95%
dblp-2010	1.62M	326k	1.24 MB	2	348	4.68k
pds-80	928k	129k	1.66 MB	26.3k	26.6k	26.6k
amazon-2008	5.16M	735k	2.81 MB	6	6.63k	19.3k
flickr	9.84M	821k	3.13 MB	3.29k	8.26k	14.5k
eu-2005	19.2M	863k	3.29 MB	5	26	69
webbase_1M	3.10M	1.00M	3.81 MB	2	19	323
rail4284	11.3M	4.28k	4.18 MB	0	13.3k	35.4k
youtube	5.97M	1.13M	4.33 MB	5.8k	20.6k	32.6k
in-2004	16.9M	1.38M	5.28 MB	0	4	11
ljournal	79.0M	5.36M	20.5 MB	19.3k	120k	184k
mawi1234	38M	18.6M	70.8 MB	20.9k	176k	609k
road_usa	57.7M	23.9M	91.4 MB	31	601	158k

Table 1: Properties of the benchmark matrices we used. The number of columns corresponds to the vector size divided by 4 bytes and, except for pds-80 and rail4284, it corresponds to the number of rows.

controller aims for a generic architectural solution for any applications with irregular memory access pattern. Indices are 32-bit unsigned integers while values are single-precision floating point values. All CSR vectors, accessed sequentially, are provided via AXI4-Stream through DMAs; the dense vector, accessed randomly, is read through an AXI4-MM port connected to our memory controller. The 8192-entry reorder buffer provides the vector values to the multiply-accumulation pipeline, which is based on floating-point Xilinx IPs. We use the index vector to clear the accumulator every time a new row begins, and the output vector is streamed to DDR through a DMA. Each accelerator can process one nonzero matrix element (NZ) per cycle; we parallelize the SpMV by interleaving rows across multiple accelerators.

All data structures are stored in DDR3 memory. Access to the programmable logic (PL) memory occurs through the soft MIG controller, which exposes a single AXI-MM port. The only way to possibly exploit the full DDR3 bandwidth (12.8 GB/s) is to use a 512-bit wide interface running at 200 MHz. Therefore, we set the clock frequency of all of our designs to 200 MHz. The processing system (PS) memory can be accessed from the FPGA through five 64 bit-wide ports on the processing system-programmable logic bridge logic. On non burst accesses, we noticed a higher performance degradation on the PS ports compared to the MIG; therefore, we decided to use the PS memory to store the vectors that are accessed sequentially and the PL memory for the vector that is accessed randomly through our controller. By isolating random and sequential accesses, we also prevent any possible influence of the DMA accesses on the performance of the random memory operations.

Algorithm 1 Sparse matrix-vector multiplication (SpMV)

1: **for** $r \leftarrow 0$ to $ROWS - 1$ **do**
2: $\quad out[r] \leftarrow 0$
3: $\quad$ **for** $i \leftarrow idx[r]$ to $idx[r + 1]$ **do**
4: $\quad\quad out[r] \leftarrow out[r] + val[i] \times vect[col[i]]$
5: $\quad$ **end for**
6: **end for**

	LUT	FF	BRAM	DSP
4 accelerators	**4640**	**6472**	**0**	**32**
16 DMAs	**12692**	**17192**	**144**	**0**
MIG	**13373**	**9380**	**2**	**0**
4x4 Crossbar	1644	3412	0	0
Bank arbiter/demux	334	1101	1	0
Cache with assoc. MSHR	9664	14000	0	0
Traditional MHA	**12301**	**19391**	*****	**0**
Cache with cuckoo MSHR	1900	8396	*****	*****
Subentry buffer	7696	4228	*****	0
Proposed MHA	**11186**	**18208**	*****	*****

Table 2: Resource utilization of the entire system. Rows not in bold represent MHA sub-modules. The asterisks denote values that depend on the controller's configuration. The proposed MHA has very similar LUT and FF utilization than the baseline 16 MHSR, 8 subentry associative MHA.

Each iteration of the inner loop of Algorithm 1 consumes three 32-bit words: two provided by the DMAs (`val[i]` and `col[i]`) and one from the vector. Given a measured bandwidth of 3.5 GB/s on all PS ports and 12.0 GB/s on the MIG, the bottleneck will be on the PS memory, which limits the system throughput to ~2.4 NZ/cycle (ignoring, for now, the minor bandwidth requirements for the `idx` and `out` vectors). However, without any memory system on the single-port MIG side, the theoretical throughput would be limited to 1 NZ/cycle instead, and in practice even up to 40% less due to DRAM row conflicts [2]; therefore, there is still at least a 2.4× scope for speedup that relies entirely on the optimization of the random memory accesses. To ensure that neither the accelerators, nor the controller's banks, nor the crossbar become the bottleneck, we instantiate four SpMV accelerators and four banks. We use one of the ARM cores to initialize the data in the DDR memories, to orchestrate the DMAs and the accelerators and to check the correctness of the output vectors.

Table 1 shows the properties of our benchmark matrices, which are essentially the largest benchmarks used in prior work on SpMV [3]. All benchmarks are available on SuiteSparse [8]. We use the stack distance, introduced in Section 1.2, to characterize the regularity of the access pattern to the dense vector. All benchmarks except for dblp-2010 and pds-80 operate on a vector that does not fit in the FPGA memory, which means that they are out of the scope of approaches based on transferring the entire vector to block RAM [9, 13].

6 EXPERIMENTAL RESULTS

6.1 Resource Utilization

Table 2 shows the resource utilization of the entire system, with proposed and baseline MHA. The traditional MHA contains the largest number of associative MSHRs that can be implemented under the 200 MHz clock constraint: 16 MSHRs with 8 subentries each. We do not consider the case of a blocking cache because it performs significantly worse than the non-blocking cache for modest area savings. The values for the proposed MSHR refer to three cuckoo hash tables and a 2-entry stash; four hash tables and a 4-entry

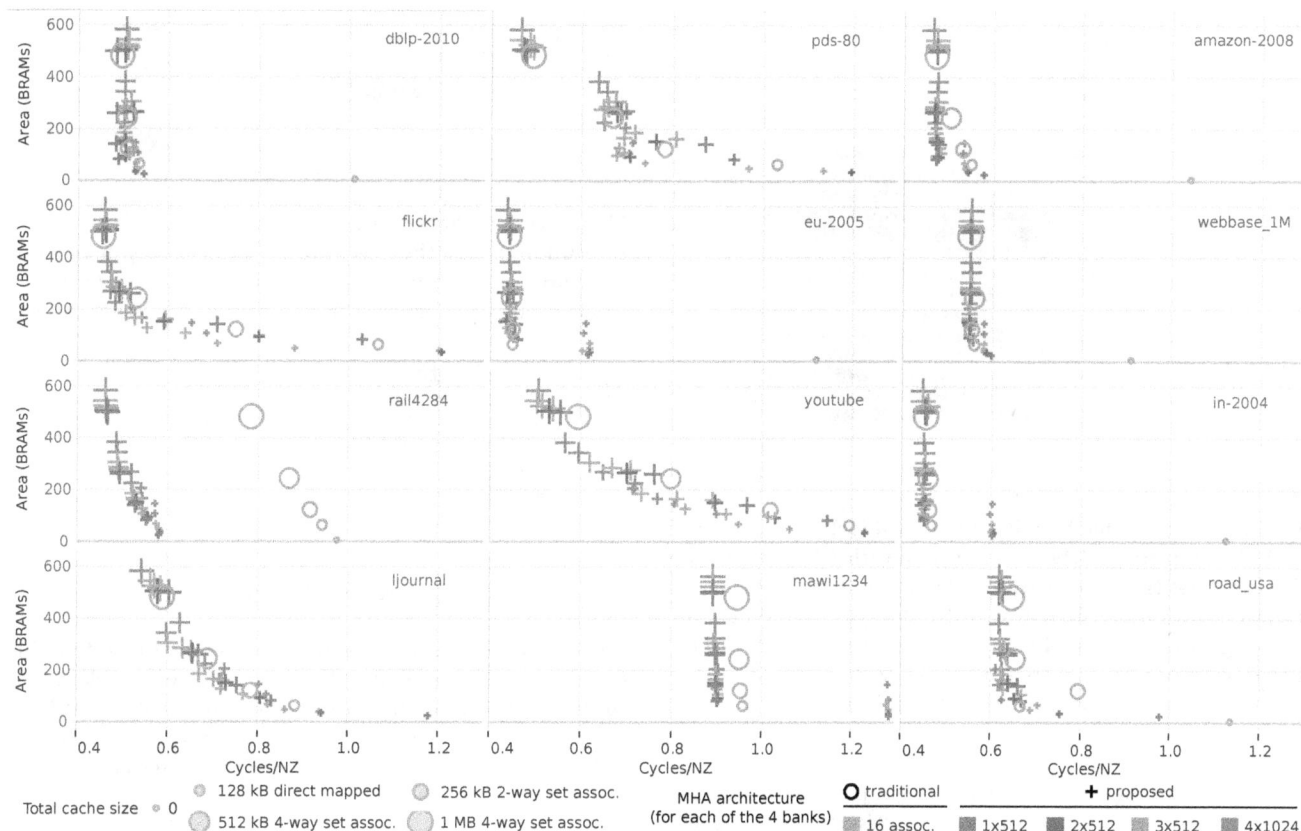

Figure 9: Area of the memory system and normalized execution time for all benchmarks and a broad range of MHA architectures. For the cuckoo architectures, we indicate the number and depth of cuckoo hash tables in each of the four banks, whereas the cache size refers to the entire multi-banked structure. Charts are sorted by increasing vector size and have been truncated at 1.3 cycles/NZ. On half of the benchmarks, all the Pareto-optimal designs are cuckoo MHAs, except for the smallest possible but low-performing design with no cache and associative MSHRs. For the other benchmarks, our MHA provides additional Pareto-optimal designs, especially on the low area side. Designs with no cache nor MSHRs, where the DRAM is time-multiplexed among the accelerators, are 1.9×-7.8× (4.1× geomean) slower than the best performing design. On the other hand, with a 1 MB blocking cache, the slowdown is 1.4×-14.6× (4.5× geomean).

stash costs about 300 LUTs and FFs more. The BRAM utilization of cache, MSHR and subentry buffers depend on their sizing, which will be explored in Section 6. Indicatively, the minimum cache that is worth implementing due to the minimum block RAM depth – a single 32 kB way (512 lines × 512 data bits) – has similar block RAM requirements as 3×512 MSHRs with 3×2048 subentries. In general, the cache requires 15 block RAMs per 32 kB per cache way, the MSHR buffer requires 1 block RAM per 512 MSHRs per cuckoo hash table for storage plus 1 block RAM per 512 MSHRs for the request queue to the external memory arbiter, and the subentry buffer requires 2 block RAMs per 512 subentry rows of up to 3 subentries each, plus 1 block RAM every 1024 subentry rows for the FRQ. Each cuckoo hash function also uses 1 DSP block.

6.2 Performance Evaluation

We ran our benchmarks on a set of different memory controllers, both with associative and cuckoo-based MHAs. We used 4-way set associative caches except in the smallest caches due to the limited

minimum block RAM depth (see Section 6.1). For the associative MHAs, we only consider the best architecture that can run at 200 MHz, with 16 MSHRs with 8 subentries each. For the cuckoo MHAs, we fixed the number of subentries per row to three since, due to the finite choice of block RAM port widths, they occupy the same amount of block RAMs as two and provide a good compromise between utilization and stall cycles (see Section 6.4). We also fixed the stash size to two entries, which provides timing closure in all cases. We explored the number and depth of MSHR hash tables, as well as the depth of the subentry buffer.

Figure 9 summarizes the results. Our MSHR-rich MHAs provide the highest performance benefit to the benchmarks with the highest stack distance percentile (90% and 95%), i.e. the most challenging ones for caches. With rail4284, misses to multiple cache lines are so frequent that even the smallest MHA with no cache at all performs 25% better than the traditional MHA with the largest cache, which has a 24× larger area. On mawi1234, a small cache is enough to capture any existing temporal locality; after that, investing 2% of

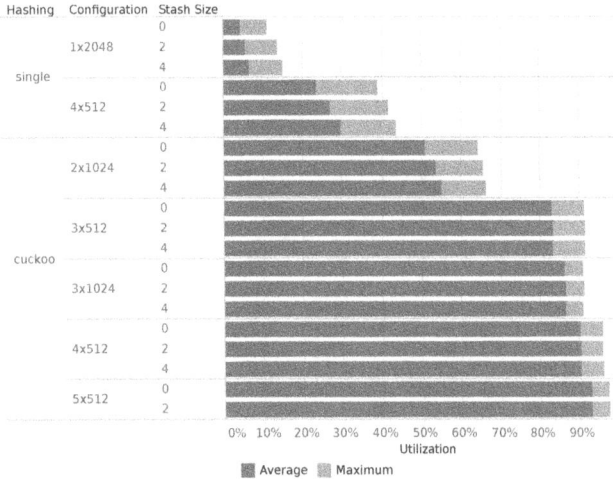

Figure 10: Achievable MSHR storage load factor for several MSHR architectures. The 5×512 system with a 4-entry stash did not meet timing constraints. Single-hash architectures cannot utilize more than 40% of the storage space. Cuckoo hashing can handle collisions more efficiently and three hash tables are enough to achieve more than 80% average and 90% peak load factors, even without stash.

block RAMs for the smallest proposed MHA provides higher returns than any further increase in cache size. Pds-80, flickr, youtube, and ljournal offer a more gradual area-delay tradeoff and can benefit from the largest MSHR solutions, which constitute most of the Pareto-dominant points. On these benchmarks, we achieve 10% to 25% throughput increase with the same area or 35% to 60% area reduction at constant throughput. Dblp-2010, eu-2005, in-2004, and webbase_1M have higher locality and thus benefit more than other benchmarks from larger caches; however, the simplest proposed MHA with no cache, which uses 3× fewer BRAMs than the smallest cache, is enough to saturate the PS DRAM bandwidth only by merging memory requests. On eu-2005 and in-2004, the performance gain provided by the cache-less MHAs is limited by handling the subentry linked lists. Applications with higher temporal locality may thus benefit from an increase of subentries per row. Benchmarks with few non-zero elements per row such as mawi1234 and road_usa have a lower maximum performance due to the higher bandwidth requirements for the sequential vectors; however, they are among the eight benchmarks that do not saturate the PS DRAM bandwidth without an MSHR-rich MHA.

6.3 Number of MSHR Hash Tables and Stash Size

Figure 10 analyzes the performance of the MSHR storage architectures described in Section 2.2. For each architecture, we measure average and peak utilization of the MSHR storage space. To make sure the benchmark always uses all of the available MSHRs, we use a synthetic 1M×1M matrix with 5M uniformly distributed non-zero elements generated with the Python function scipy.sparse.random(1e6, 1e6, 5e-6), no cache, and each bank contains 4096

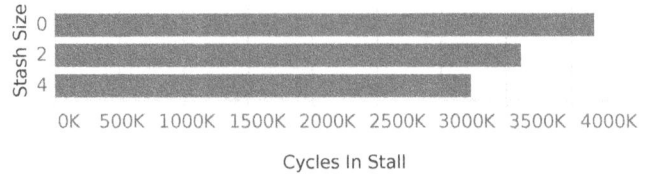

Figure 11: Number of cycles lost due to stalls for collision resolution during the execution of a uniformly distributed benchmark. A 4-entry stash, which occupies less than 0.1% of LUTs and FFs, reduces the number of stall cycles by 30%.

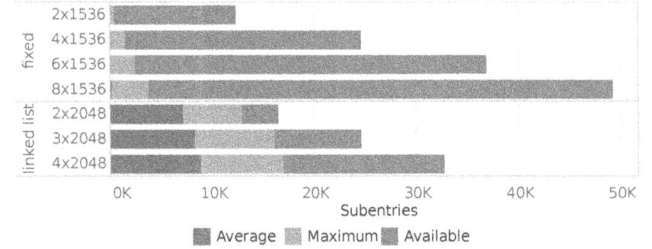

Figure 12: Average and maximum subentry utilization during the execution of ljournal with a 3x512 cuckoo MSHR. Allocating a fixed number of subentries per MSHR results in less than 1% average utilization and resource waste. Linked-list architectures provide a more efficient usage of the subentry memory.

subentry rows with 3 subentries each. All architectures have 2048 MSHRs per bank or the closest possible value.

Because any collisions result in a stall that lasts until one of the colliding MSHRs is deallocated, all of the single-hash architectures achieve poor utilization: even by introducing a stash to tolerate up to four collisions, a 4-way set-associative architecture does not go beyond 30% average and 45% peak load factors. Even a simple 2-way cuckoo hash table achieves 50% average and 70% peak utilization, and three ways enough to reach more than 80% average utilization, which is consistent with prior findings on cuckoo hashing [11]. Interestingly, using a 3-way 512-entry architecture (1536 MHSRs) has higher absolute utilization than a 2-way, 1024-entry organization (2048 MSHRs). For three or more ways, adding a stash does not affect MSHR utilization but decreases the number of stall cycles by up to 30% with a 4-entry stash (Figure 11), which is the largest stash that we could implement within the 200 MHz constraint.

6.4 Subentry Organization

We performed a similar analysis for the memory organization of the subentries, as described in Section 3.2. We use the ljournal benchmark, which has a large number of secondary misses, and an MHA with no cache and a 3×512 cuckoo MSHR buffer per bank. As shown in Figure 12, with a fixed number of subentries per MSHR, stalls are so frequent (Figure 13) that they prevent misses from accumulating in the buffers, resulting in very low utilization but also fewer opportunities for request merging and thus a higher traffic to external memory (Figure 14). We believe this problem is more pronounced in an MSHR-rich architecture than in an associative

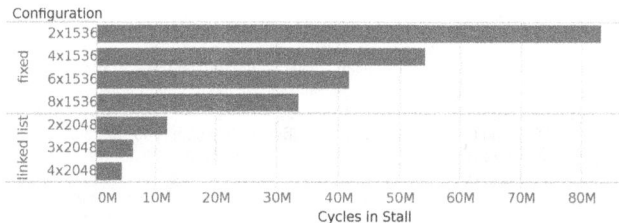

Figure 13: Number of cycles lost due to subentry-related stalls. Stalls occur when (a) filling all subentries of an MSHR for the fixed architectures or (b) handling the linked list or running out of subentry rows for the linked list architectures. The smallest linked list architecture has three times fewer stall cycles than the largest fixed architecture despite having three times fewer subentries.

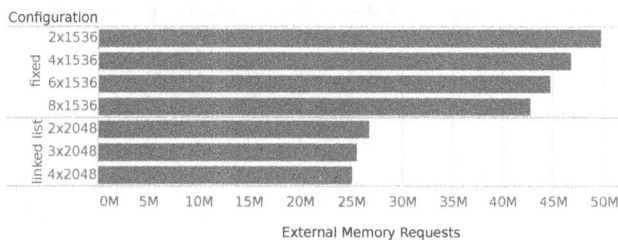

Figure 14: Number of external memory requests during the execution of ljournal with a 3x512 cuckoo MSHR and no cache. By increasing subentry utilization, linked list architectures increase the number of accelerator requests that can be served by the same external memory request, resulting in a 37% decrease of external memory traffic.

MHA because it is far more likely to encounter at least one MSHR that needs more than a given number of subentries when handling thousands of misses rather than a few tens of them. Our linked list-based architectures provide much higher average and maximum buffer utilization, fewer stall cycles and decrease the number of DDR memory requests by a factor 1.3× to 2×, with evident great energy impact.

7 RELATED WORK

7.1 Miss Handling Architectures

The first non-blocking cache was proposed by Kroft in 1981 [20]. Farkas and Jouppi [10] evaluate a number of alternative MHA organizations, including the explicitly-addressed MSHRs that inspired our MHA. They observed that non-blocking caches can reduce the miss stall cycles per instruction by a factor 4 to 10 compared to blocking caches, that the most aggressive architectures (such as explicitly-addressed) are beneficial even for large cache sizes, and that overlapping as many misses as possible allows processors to maximize the benefit provided by non-blocking caches.

Tuck et al. [25] introduced a novel MHA for single processor cores with very large instruction windows. They propose a hierarchical MHA, with a small explicitly-addressed MSHR file for each L1 cache bank and a larger shared MSHR file. MSHRs are explicitly-addressed and shared MSHRs have more subentries than

the dedicated ones. On a number of SPEC2000 benchmarks running on a 512-entry instruction window superscalar single-core processor, dedicated files with 16 MSHRs and 8 subentries and a shared file with 30 MSHRs and 32 subentries achieve speedups that are close to those provided by an unlimited MHA. However, we believe that a set of parallel accelerators is fundamentally different from a single-core processor even with a large instruction window for two reasons: a) parallel accelerators with, for instance, decoupled access/execution architectures [7, 22] could generate even more requests per cycle with no fundamental limitations on the total number of in-flight operations, and b) requests to be merged can come from the same as well as a different accelerator, so it is important to have a shared MHA to maximize the merging opportunities. Our results indeed showed that, for parallel accelerators with massive MLP, small caches with thousands of MSHRs can achieve similar or even better performance of larger caches with few MSHRs.

7.2 Memory Systems for Irregular Memory Accesses

Several pieces of work aimed at improving the efficiency of traditional caches on non-contiguous memory accesses. Impulse [5] introduces an additional address translation stage to remap data that is sparse in the physical/virtual memory space into contiguous locations in a shadow address space. However, it is a processor-centric system which relies on the intervention from the OS to manage the shadow address space. Traversal caches [24] optimize repeated accesses to pointer-based data structures on FPGA. Such approach is however limited to pointer-based data structures that are repeatedly accessed and that can fit entirely in the FPGA block RAM.

Another line of work explored the automatic generation of application-specific memory systems. Bayliss et al. [4] proposed a methodology that automatically generates reuse buffers for affine loop nests, which reduce the amount of memory requests and of DRAM row conflicts. However, the approach is restricted to kernels consisting of an affine loop nest whose bounds are known at compile time. TraceBanking [30] does not rely on static compiler analysis and uses a memory trace to generate a banking scheme that is provably conflict-free. It also supports non-affine loop nests but requires the dataset to fit entirely in the block RAM. ConGen [16] focuses on optimizing DRAM accesses without relying on any local buffering on FPGA. It uses a memory trace to generate a mapping from the addresses generated by the application to DRAM addresses such that the number of row conflicts is minimized. All of these solutions rely on exact information about the application's memory access pattern at hardware compile time. Our approach is application-agnostic, fully dynamic and does not make any assumptions on the access pattern properties.

Coalescing aims at increasing bandwidth utilization between datapath and DRAM by merging multiple narrow memory accesses into fewer, wider ones. Modern GPUs dynamically coalesce accesses from the same instruction executed by different threads [26] in the same warp, and the load-store units instantiated by the Intel FPGA OpenCL compiler can perform both static and dynamic burst coalescing [28]. To increase the opportunities for coalescing and thus the utilization of the bandwidth to the GPU L1 cache, Kloosterman et al. propose an inter-warp coalescer [19]. Wang et al. [27] proposed a dynamic coalescing unit for HMC memories in a multi-core system, implemented on a small RISC-V core. Incoming requests are stored in a binary tree and forwarded to the HMC after a timeout or after receiving 128 bytes of requests. All of these approaches have a very short window where coalescing can occur, at most a few requests wide. We showed that explicitly-addressed MSHRs also perform coalescing, on wider request windows and over multiple bursts at the same time (one per MSHR).

8 CONCLUSION

Conventional wisdom has it that some form of local buffering such as caching is the best way to optimize the access to external memory, hence the vast effort in maximizing the hit rate under all possible scenarios. Non-blocking caches are one of the few architectures for *miss* optimization instead. In this paper, we took the key idea behind non-blocking caches to the extreme: we designed a scheme to handle three orders of magnitude more misses without stalls compared to classic fully-associative MHAs. We presented an efficient FPGA implementation of such MSHR-rich cache, where we map tens of thousands of MSHRs and subentries to the abundant FPGA block RAM and all stages of miss handling are pipelined with minimal stalls. On twelve sparse matrix-vector multiplication benchmarks, most of which cannot fit in the FPGA block RAM, we showed that, under a limited block RAM budget, repurposing some block RAMs from cache to MSHRs can provide higher performance gains when the access pattern is such that a relevant amount of misses cannot be avoided. This is especially true for the benchmarks with the lowest temporal locality, but even on more regular access patterns, MSHRs can complement caches by optimizing long-distance reuse, providing similar performance gains as a larger cache at lower area costs. Therefore, we believe MSHR-rich MHAs open up new opportunities to increase performance of bandwidth-bound, latency-insensitive applications with irregular memory access patterns. Our MHA, as well as the benchmark SpMV accelerators, can be downloaded as an open-source project from https://github.com/m-asiatici/MSHR-rich.

ACKNOWLEDGMENTS

The authors would like to thank Dick Sites, Stephen Neuendorffer, Kristof Denolf, and Kees Vissers for their valuable feedback and suggestions.

REFERENCES

[1] Michael Adler, Kermin E. Fleming, Angshuman Parashar, Michael Pellauer, and Joel Emer. 2011. LEAP scratchpads: automatic memory and cache management for reconfigurable logic. In *Proceedings of the 19th ACM/SIGDA International Symposium on Field Programmable Gate Arrays*. Monterey, Calif., 25–28.

[2] Adrian Cosoroaba. 2013. *White Paper 383 - Achieving High Performance DDR3 Data Rates*. Xilinx Inc.

[3] Arash Ashari, Naser Sedaghati, John Eisenlohr, Srinivasan Parthasarathy, and P. Sadayappan. 2014. Fast sparse matrix-vector multiplication on GPUs for graph applications. In *Proceedings of the international conference for high performance computing, networking, storage and analysis*. New Orleans, La., 781–792.

[4] Samuel Bayliss and George A. Constantinides. 2011. Application specific memory access, reuse and reordering for SDRAM. In *Proceedings of the 7th International Symposium on Applied Reconfigurable Computing*. Belfast, 41–52.

[5] John Carter, Wilson Hsieh, Leigh Stoller, Mark Swanson, Lixin Zhang, Erik Brunvand, Al Davis, Chen-Chi Kuo, Ravindra Kuramkote, Michael Parker, Lambert Schaelicke, and Terry Tateyama. 1999. Impulse: Building a smarter memory controller. In *Proceedings of the 5th International Symposium on High-Performance Computer Architecture*. Orlando, Fla., 70–79.

[6] Calin Cascaval and David A. Padua. 2003. Estimating cache misses and locality using stack distances. In *Proceedings of the 17th annual international conference on Supercomputing*. Phoenix, Az., 150–159.

[7] Tao Chen and G. Edward Suh. 2016. Efficient data supply for hardware accelerators with prefetching and access/execute decoupling. In *The 49th Annual IEEE/ACM International Symposium on Microarchitecture*. Taipei, Taiwan, 46.

[8] Timothy A. Davis and Yifan Hu. 2011. The University of Florida sparse matrix collection. *ACM Transactions on Mathematical Software (TOMS)* 38, 1 (2011), 1.

[9] Richard Dorrance, Fengbo Ren, and Dejan Marković. 2014. A scalable sparse matrix-vector multiplication kernel for energy-efficient sparse-BLAS on FPGAs. In *Proceedings of the 22nd ACM/SIGDA International Symposium on Field Programmable Gate Arrays*. Monterey, Calif., 161–170.

[10] K. I. Farkas and N. P. Jouppi. 1994. Complexity/Performance Tradeoffs with Non-blocking Loads. In *Proceedings of the 21st Annual International Symposium on Computer Architecture*. Chicago, Ill., 211–222.

[11] Dimitris Fotakis, Rasmus Pagh, Peter Sanders, and Paul Spirakis. 2005. Space efficient hash tables with worst case constant access time. *Theory of Computing Systems* 38, 2 (2005), 229–248.

[12] Nithin George, Hyoukjoong Lee, David Novo, Tiark Rompf, Kevin Brown, Arvind Sujeeth, Martin Odersky, Kunle Olukotun, and Paolo Ienne. 2014. Hardware System Synthesis from Domain-Specific Languages. In *Proceedings of the 24th International Conference on Field-Programmable Logic and Applications*. Munich, 1–8.

[13] Song Han, Xingyu Liu, Huizi Mao, Jing Pu, Ardavan Pedram, Mark A. Horowitz, and William J. Dally. 2016. EIE: efficient inference engine on compressed deep neural network. In *Proceedings of the 43rd Annual International Symposium on Computer Architecture*. Seoul, 243–254.

[14] Intel Inc. 2016. *Hybrid Memory Cube Controller IP Core User Guide*. Intel Inc.

[15] Intel Inc. 2018. *Acceleration Stack for Intel Xeon CPU with FPGAs Core Cache Interface (CCI-P) Reference Manual*. Intel Inc.

[16] Matthias Jung, Deepak M. Mathew, Christian Weis, Norbert Wehn, Irene Heinrich, Marco V. Natale, and Sven O. Krumke. 2016. Congen: An application specific dram memory controller generator. In *Proceedings of the 2nd International Symposium on Memory Systems*. Alexandria, Va., 257–267.

[17] Jeremy Kepner and John Gilbert. 2011. *Graph algorithms in the language of linear algebra*. SIAM.

[18] Adam Kirsch and Michael Mitzenmacher. 2007. Using a queue to de-amortize cuckoo hashing in hardware. In *Proceedings of the 45th Annual Allerton Conference on Communication, Control, and Computing*, Vol. 75. Monticello, Ill., 751–758.

[19] John Kloosterman, Jonathan Beaumont, Mick Wollman, Ankit Sethia, Ron Dreslinski, Trevor Mudge, and Scott Mahlke. 2015. WarpPool: sharing requests with inter-warp coalescing for throughput processors. In *Proceedings of the 48th Annual International Symposium on Microarchitecture*. 433–444.

[20] David Kroft. 1981. Lockup-free instruction fetch/prefetch cache organization. In *Proceedings of the 8th Annual International Symposium on Computer Architecture*. Minneapolis, Minn., 81–87.

[21] Sheng Li, Ke Chen, Jay B. Brockman, and Norman P. Jouppi. 2011. *Performance impacts of non-blocking caches in out-of-order processors*. HPL Tech Report.

[22] Feng Liu, Soumyadeep Ghosh, Nick P. Johnson, and David I. August. 2014. CGPA: Coarse-grained pipelined accelerators. In *Proceedings of the 51st Design Automation Conference*. San Francisco, Calif., 1–6.

[23] Mario D. Marino and Kuan-Ching Li. 2017. System implications of LLC MSHRs in scalable memory systems. *Microprocessors and Microsystems* 52 (2017), 355–364.

[24] Greg Stitt, Gaurav Chaudhari, and James Coole. 2008. Traversal caches: A first step towards FPGA acceleration of pointer-based data structures. In *Proceedings of the 6th International Conference on Hardware/Software Codesign and System Synthesis*. Atlanta, Ga., 61–66.

[25] James Tuck, Luis Ceze, and Josep Torrellas. 2006. Scalable cache miss handling for high memory-level parallelism. In *Proceedings of the 39th Annual International Symposium on Microarchitecture*. Orlando, Fla., 409–422.

[26] Vasily Volkov. 2016. *Understanding latency hiding on GPUs*. Ph.D. Dissertation. UC Berkeley.

[27] Xi Wang, John D. Leidel, and Yong Chen. 2016. Concurrent dynamic memory coalescing on GoblinCore-64 architecture. In *Proceedings of the Second International Symposium on Memory Systems*. 177–187.

[28] Felix Winterstein and George Constantinides. 2017. Pass a pointer: Exploring shared virtual memory abstractions in OpenCL tools for FPGAs. In *Proceedings of the 2017 International Conference on Field Programmable Technology*. Melbourne, 104–111.

[29] Philipp Woelfel. 1999. Efficient strongly universal and optimally universal hashing. In *International Symposium on Mathematical Foundations of Computer Science*. Szklarska Poreba, 262–272.

[30] Yuan Zhou, Khalid Musa Al-Hawaj, and Zhiru Zhang. 2017. A New Approach to Automatic Memory Banking Using Trace-Based Address Mining. In *Proceedings of the 25th ACM/SIGDA International Symposium on Field Programmable Gate Arrays*. Monterey, Calif., 179–188.

Improving Performance of Graph Processing on FPGA-DRAM Platform by Two-level Vertex Caching

Zhiyuan Shao
Services Computing Technology and System Lab
Cluster and Grid Computing Lab
School of Computer Science and Technology
Huazhong University of Science and Technology
Wuhan, 430074, China
zyshao@hust.edu.cn

Ruoshi Li
Diqing Hu
Information Storage and Optical Display Division
School of Computer Science and Technology
Huazhong University of Science and Technology
Wuhan, 430074, China
liruoshi@hust.edu.cn,hudq024@hust.edu.cn

Xiaofei Liao
Hai Jin
Services Computing Technology and System Lab
Cluster and Grid Computing Lab
School of Computer Science and Technology
Huazhong University of Science and Technology
Wuhan, 430074, China
xfliao@hust.edu.cn,hjin@hust.edu.cn

ABSTRACT

In recent years, graph processing attracts lots of attention due to its broad applicability in solving real-world problems. With the flexibility and programmability, FPGA platforms provide the opportunity of processing the graph data with high efficiency. On FPGA-DRAM platforms, the state-of-art solution of graph processing (i.e., Fore-Graph) attaches each pipeline with local vertex buffers to cache the source and destination vertices during processing. Such one-level vertex caching mechanism, however, results in excessive amounts of vertex data transmissions that consume the precious DRAM bandwidth, and frequent pipeline stalls that waste the processing power of the FPGA.

In this paper, we propose a two-level vertex caching mechanism to improve the performance of graph processing on FPGA-DRAM platforms by reducing the amounts of vertex data transmissions and pipeline stalls during the execution of graph algorithms. We build a system, named as FabGraph, to implement such two-level vertex caching mechanism by using available on-chip storage resources, including BRAM and UltraRAM. Experimental results show that: FabGraph achieves up to 3.1x and 2.5x speedups over ForeGraph for BFS and PageRank respectively, on the FPGA board with relatively large BRAM; and up to 3.1x and 3.0x speedups over ForeGraph for BFS and PageRank respectively, on the FPGA board with small BRAM but large UltraRAM. Our experience in this paper suggests that the two-level vertex caching design is effective in improving the performance of graph processing on FPGA-DRAM platforms.

CCS CONCEPTS

• **Hardware** → *Reconfigurable logic and FPGAs*; *Hardware accelerators*; • **Theory of computation** → *Graph algorithms analysis*;

KEYWORDS

Hardware Accelerators; Graph Analytics

ACM Reference Format:
Zhiyuan Shao, Ruoshi Li, Diqing Hu, Xiaofei Liao, and Hai Jin. 2019. Improving Performance of Graph Processing on FPGA-DRAM Platform by Two-level Vertex Caching. In *The 2019 ACM/SIGDA International Symposium on Field-Programmable Gate Arrays (FPGA '19), February 24–26, 2019, Seaside, CA, USA.* ACM, New York, NY, USA, 10 pages. https://doi.org/10.1145/3289602.3293900

1 INTRODUCTION

Graph data structure is widely used to organize the data in many scientific research and industry fields, including social networking [16], bio-informatics [1], etc. Solutions to the real-world problems in these fields (e.g., discovering communities in social networks, finding interesting patterns in DNAs) are obtained by conducting graph algorithms in collected graph data. The executions of graph algorithms in the graph data (i.e., graph processing), however, incur high volumes of irregular and random memory accesses, especially when the graph under processing is large. Researches [3, 8] show that general purpose processors (i.e., CPUs) are not well suited for such workloads due to architecture reasons, such as high *Last Level Cache* (LLC) miss rates, severe contentions in *Reorder-Buffer* (RoB). Under such background, FPGA-based graph processing becomes a promising solution, due to its flexibility and programmability, by which customized processing logics can be built.

In the past several years, lots of FPGA based graph processing solutions and systems are proposed, including GraphGen [14], [25], FPGP [5], ForeGraph [6], and those based on the *Hybrid Memory Cube* (HMC) [11, 23, 24]. ForeGraph [6] is the state-of-art system that works on the FPGA-DRAM platform. Its idea is to represent the graph data under processing as a 2-Dimensional (2D) $Q \times Q$ grid [4, 26], and store both the vertex and edge data of the graph in the off-chip DRAM. During processing, ForeGraph processes a portion of the graph at a time, and repeats the process until the entire graph is processed. ForeGraph builds multiple pipelines in the FPGA to exploit its massively parallel processing power and configures each of the pipelines with two vertex buffers in the on-chip Block RAM (BRAM). During processing, the source and destination vertices of the graph portion to be processed are first loaded from the DRAM and stored in the vertex buffers attached to the pipelines, and then the edges are transferred to the pipelines and processed in a stream fashion. When processing switches from one portion of the graph to another, the vertex data residing in the pipeline-attached vertex buffers will be replaced by writing the intermediate results back to, and reading new vertex data from the off-chip DRAM.

Nevertheless, such design of ForeGraph results in excessive amounts of vertex data transmissions via the DRAM bus during graph processing. Even worse, as the pipelines in ForeGraph cannot begin to process the edges until all the vertex data of the graph portion under processing are fully loaded in their buffers, they stall during the vertex data transmission, which wastes the processing power of FPGA. *Our insight to this excessive vertex data transmission problem in ForeGraph is that the design of pipeline-attached vertex buffers is, in essence, an one-level cache architecture, with which the contents of these buffers have to be replaced according to the processing logic during graph processing, even when the BRAM is large enough to store all the vertex data of the graph under processing.*

In this paper, we propose a two-level vertex caching mechanism by using the on-chip storage resources (i.e., BRAM and UltraRAM) to address the limitations of ForeGraph: the L1 cache is the vertex buffers attached to the pipelines, and the L2 cache is a shared vertex buffer that temporarily stores the vertex data of the graph portion under processing. During processing, the L2 cache communicates with the DRAM to read/write the vertex data, while the L1 cache communicates with the L2 cache (not the DRAM) to save DRAM bandwidth. We build a system named as FabGraph to implement such two-level vertex caching mechanism. FabGraph designs dual-set pipelines, to minimize the pipeline stalls incurred by the vertex data transmission by overlapping the computation of one pipeline set with the communication of the other. By leveraging the symmetric nature of the 2D grid graph representation, FabGraph employs an L2 cache replacement algorithm that uses Hilbert order-like scheduling to reduce the amount of vertex data replaced when switching from one graph portion to another.

This paper makes the following contributions:

• proposes a two-level vertex caching mechanism, and its accompanying replacement and computation/communication overlapping techniques, for graph processing on FPGA-DRAM platforms.

• gives the performance model of our proposed two-level vertex caching mechanism by considering various possible configurations.

• builds FabGraph that efficiently uses the on-chip storage resources, including both BRAM and UltraRAM, to implement the two-level vertex cache mechanism.

• extensively evaluates FabGraph to demonstrate the power of the two-level vertex cache mechanism on improving the performance of graph processing on FPGA-DRAM platforms.

The rest of this paper is organized as follows: Section 2 presents the background and related works of this paper. Section 3 gives an overview of FabGraph. Section 4 and 5 elaborate the vertex data replacement and computation-communication overlapping mechanisms of FabGraph. Section 6 gives the performance model of FabGraph. Section 7 evaluates the performance of FabGraph by conducting graph algorithms in the chosen real-world graphs. Section 8 concludes the paper and discusses the future works.

2 BACKGROUND AND RELATED WORKS

In this section, we first review the existing approaches for graph processing on FPGA-DRAM platforms and give a discussion after analyzing the design choices of the state-of-art approach.

2.1 Graph Processing on FPGA-DRAM Platform

A graph, denoted as $G = < V, E >$, consists of a finite set of vertices V, and a set of edges E, where $E = \{(v, u) | v, u \in V\}$. Each edge connects exactly two endpoint vertices and is said to be "directed" if one of its endpoints is the source and the other is the destination, or "undirected" if there is no difference in its endpoints. A graph is directed if it contains only directed edges, or undirected if all its edges are undirected. In order to simplify our discussion in this paper, we consider the processing of directed graphs, as undirected graphs can be converted into directed ones by considering each its edge as two directed edges with opposite directions.

Generally, processing a graph means to conduct various graph algorithms in the given graph to obtain useful results. Two fundamental graph algorithms are *Breadth First Search* (BFS) that computes the distance of the vertices in the graph from a given root vertex, and PageRank that computes the ranking of web pages (vertices) according to their connections (edges). Most graph algorithms are iterative: computations are conducted repeatedly in the input graph by changing the values of the vertices (i.e., the results) till convergence (results do not change further) or for a predefined amount of iterations. As each edge connects two arbitrary vertices in V, conducting graph algorithms generally incurs high volumes of random memory accesses.

In an FPGA-DRAM platform, there are two kinds of storage media: the on-chip BRAM (or UltraRAM) and the off-chip DRAM. The on-chip BRAM (or UltraRAM) is expensive and has small storage capacity, but can handle random accesses with much higher performance than the off-chip DRAM. On the contrary, the off-chip DRAM is relatively cheaper, has much larger storage capacity, but favors only sequential or predictable access patterns. Conducting graph algorithms on such platform needs to take into account these differences in these two types of memories.

There are two widely used graph processing models: the vertex-centric model [13] that conducts graph algorithms by iterating along the vertices, and the edge-centric model [18] that performs graph algorithms by iterating along the edges. FPGA-based approaches that adopt the vertex-centric model, such as GraphStep [7] and GraphGen [14], incur large volume of random accesses to the DRAM, which leads to unpredictable performance. [25] adopts edge-centric processing model, and stores the intermediate results generated while processing the edges in the DRAM before applying them to the vertices. This mechanism, however, introduces extra overheads by reading/writing the intermediate results from/to the DRAM. GraphOps [15] introduces a modular approach of constructing graph accelerators in FPGA.

2.2 State-of-Art Approach

The state-of-art practice on graph processing in the FPGA-DRAM platform (i.e., ForeGraph) represents the graph under processing as a 2D grid, that divides the vertex ID space into multiple (Q)

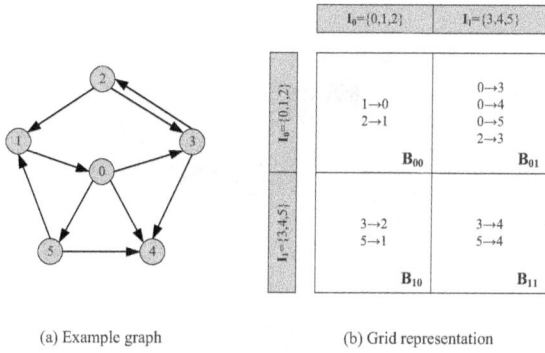

(a) Example graph
(b) Grid representation

Figure 1: An example graph and its grid representation

equal-length *intervals*, and catalogs all edges of the graph into the Q^2 *edge blocks* according to the intervals, to which their source and destination vertices belong respectively. Figure 1 shows an example graph and its grid representation. Graph algorithms are then conducted on the graph by iterating along the edge blocks of the grid. Algorithm 1 and 2 list the pseudo codes of conducting BFS and PageRank in a graph with grid representation. In these algorithms, $B_{i,j}$ denotes the edge block at the ith row and the jth column of the grid, and is "active" if at least one of the vertices in its source vertex interval has message to be sent to other vertices.

Algorithm 1: Conduct BFS in graph $G =< V, E >$.

Input : grid dimension Q; root vertex r; interval length $|I|$.
Output : values associated with the vertices in V.

1 **foreach** $i \in [0, |V| - 1]$ **do**
2 $\quad$ $V[i].value \leftarrow \infty$
3 $V[r] \leftarrow 0$;
4 **foreach** $j \in [0, Q - 1]$ **do**
5 $\quad$ Activate $B_{r/|I|, j}$
6 $Updated \leftarrow Ture$;
7 **while** $Updated$ **do**
8 $\quad$ $Updated \leftarrow False$;
9 $\quad$ **foreach** $i \in [0, Q - 1]$ **do**
10 $\quad\quad$ **foreach** $j \in [0, Q - 1]$ **do**
11 $\quad\quad\quad$ **if** $B_{i,j}$ is active **then**
12 $\quad\quad\quad\quad$ **foreach** $e \in B_{i,j}$ **do**
13 $\quad\quad\quad\quad\quad$ **if** $V[e.dst].value > V[e.src].value + 1$ **then**
14 $\quad\quad\quad\quad\quad\quad$ $V[e.dst].value \leftarrow V[e.src].value + 1$;
15 $\quad\quad\quad\quad\quad\quad$ **foreach** $k \in [0, Q - 1]$ **do**
16 $\quad\quad\quad\quad\quad\quad\quad$ Activate $B_{j,k}$
17 $\quad\quad\quad\quad\quad\quad$ $Updated \leftarrow True$

From Algorithm 1 and 2, we can observe that there are two kinds of iterators: the block iterator and the edge iterator. The block iterator (Line 9-11 in Algorithm 1 and Line 5-6 in Algorithm 2) chooses the edge blocks, in which the computation will be conducted, while

---

Algorithm 2: Conduct PageRank in graph $G =< V, E >$ (d is the damping factor, generally equals to 0.85).

Input : grid dimension Q; iteration count $Iter$.
Output : values associated with the vertices in V.

1 **foreach** $i \in [0, |V| - 1]$ **do**
2 $\quad$ $V[i].value \leftarrow 1$
3 $i \leftarrow 0$;
4 **while** $i < Iter$ **do**
5 $\quad$ **foreach** $i \in [0, Q - 1]$ **do**
6 $\quad\quad$ **foreach** $j \in [0, Q - 1]$ **do**
7 $\quad\quad\quad$ **foreach** $e \in B_{i,j}$ **do**
8 $\quad\quad\quad\quad$ $V[e.dst].value \leftarrow$ $V[e.dst].value + (1 - d) / V[e.dst].deg + d \times V[e.src].value / V[e.src].deg$;
9 $\quad$ i++;

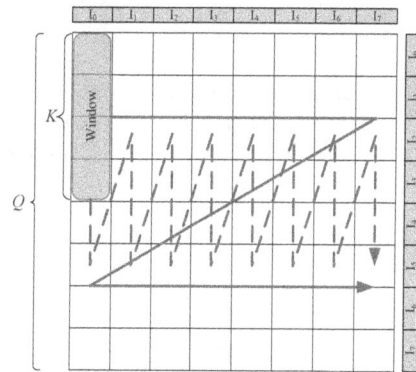

Figure 2: The sliding window mechanism in ForeGraph (assume $Q = 8$, $K = 4$). Dashed arrow denotes the sliding direction of *Source First Replacement* (SFR) algorithm. Solid arrow denotes that of *Destination First Replacement* (DFR) algorithm. ForeGraph chooses DFR when $K > 2$)

the edge iterator (Line 12-17 in Algorithm 1 and Line 7-8 in Algorithm 2) browses all edges of a chosen block, and conducts computation according to the values associated with the endpoint vertices of each edge. Note that in the edge iterator, although edge browsing is sequential, the computation incurs random accesses against the vertices in the block's corresponding intervals.

ForeGraph designs multiple (K) pipelines, and configures each of the pipelines with two vertex buffers by using the BRAM to store the source and destination vertices of an edge block. During processing, the vertex intervals associated with an edge block are first loaded into the vertex buffers, and then, the edges of the block are loaded from the off-chip DRAM to the pipelines in a stream fashion. ForeGraph uses a sliding window (whose size is $K \times 1$) mechanism, as illustrated in Figure 2, to implement the block iterator. With the *Source First Replacement* (SFR) or the *Destination First Replacement* (DFR) algorithm, when graph processing switches from one window to another, the contents of the pipeline-attached vertex buffers that store source or destination vertices, have to be replaced by writing the results to the DRAM, reading new source vertices of the new window from the DRAM, or both.

2.3 Discussion

The design of ForeGraph, however, leads to excessive amounts of vertex data transmissions during graph processing. Such problem manifests itself obviously when the BRAM has enough storage space to store *all* the vertex data of a graph under processing: in such case, at each step of window sliding, the vertex data (source if using SFR, or destination if using DFR) still need to be transferred between DRAM and BRAM. Besides, the design of ForeGraph suffers from the edge inflation problem: as the pipelines are assigned to process the edge blocks falling in the same window in parallel, to balance loads of the pipelines, the edge blocks in the same window need to be normalized to the one with the maximal size by adding empty edges to the blocks with less edges, which leads to an 11% to 34% inflation on the sizes of the edge blocks according to [6].

A two-level vertex caching mechanism can hopefully solve these problems: the vertex data of the graph portion under processing can be stored in a large L2 cache (to reduce the vertex data transmissions between FPGA and DRAM), such that during processing, the vertex data to be used by the pipelines can be transferred between these two cache levels. At the same time, such two-level vertex caching mechanism can effectively use the on-chip storage resources, especially the emerging UltraRAM [21], which is not suitable to be used as the L1 cache due to its coarser granularity (e.g., severe waste will be result, if it were used as the L1 cache), but ideal to be used as the L2 cache with its large storage capacity.

We thus develop FabGraph to implement the two-level vertex caching mechanism, and evaluate its effectiveness in graph processing on FPGA-DRAM platforms in the following sections.

3 SYSTEM OVERVIEW

The on-chip processing logics of FabGraph are shown in Figure 3. FabGraph stores the graph under processing in the off-chip DRAM, and organizes the on-chip storage spaces (BRAM and UltrRAM) into two parts: the local stores (i.e., *Source Vertex Store* and *Destination Vertex Store* in Figure 3) that attached to the pipelines (i.e., *Algorithm Kernel Pipeline* in Figure 3), and the *Shared Vertex Buffer* (SVB for short). The pipeline-attached local stores work as the L1 cache, and the SVB works as the L2 cache. During processing, the SVB first communicates with the off-chip DRAM via the *DRAM Controller* to obtain the vertex data of the graph portion to be processed. The *Shared Vertex Buffer Controller* then transfers the vertex data, chosen by the *Scheduler*, from the SVB to the local stores of the pipelines. Finally, the edges of the selected block are streamed in from the DRAM to the pipelines by the *Edge Dispatcher*.

With this two-level vertex caching design, the vertex data exchanged during graph processing are conducted by transferring the vertex data between the local stores and the SVB. When processing switches from one graph portion to another, the contents of the SVB (i.e., the L2 cache) will be (partially) replaced. In Section 4, we will elaborate on the vertex data replacement mechanism of the SVB. Moreover, FabGraph designs two pipeline sets (PSes), i.e., Pipeline Set1 and Pipeline Set2 as shown in Figure 3, to mask the pipeline stalls by overlapping the computation of one PS with the vertex data transmission of the other PS. We will elaborate on this mechanism in Section 5.

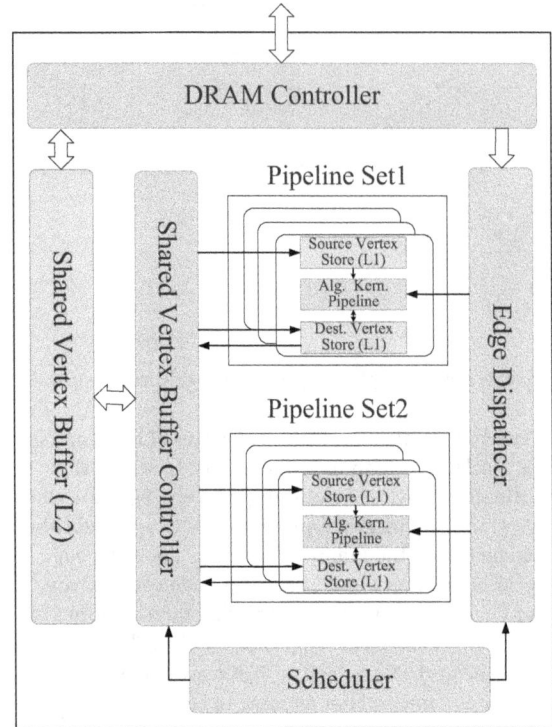

Figure 3: On-chip processing logic of FabGraph

3.1 Graph Representation

Similar as ForeGraph, FabGraph also represents the graph under processing as a grid as shown in Figure 1, and stores the graph data (both vertices and edges) in the off-chip DRAM. FabGraph adopts the techniques that are proven to be successful in Fore-Graph to compress the graph representation. There are two kinds of compressions:

• **Vertex ID Compression.** As the grid representation partitions the graph under processing into Q^2 blocks, considering the alignment factor, the ideal choice for vertex indexing after compression is 16 bits for an interval. FabGraph thus represents each edge by using 32 bits (4 Bytes), i.e., each of its endpoint vertex IDs occupies 16 bits. In the following discussions, we take the storage size of an edge, denoted as S_e, as 32 bits (4Bytes), and each vertex interval has 2^{16} vertices.

• **Vertex Value Compression.** The values of the vertices are the computing results of a graph algorithm. According to the characteristics of a graph algorithm, such results can also be compressed to reduce the storage sizes of the vertex values. For example, for BFS, we can use only 8 bits (1 Byte) to store the vertex value if we know in advance that the diameter, the maximal distance from one vertex to another vertex, of the graph is below $2^8 - 1$. We use this observation to compress the values of the vertices, and in the following discussions, regard the storage size of each vertex, denoted as S_v, as 8 bits when conducting BFS, and as 32 bits when conducting PageRank in the graphs listed in Table 2. The storage size of a *vertex interval*, denoted as $S_{interval}$, which is an important unit of measurement in this paper, is computed as $S_{interval} = 2^{16} \cdot S_v$.

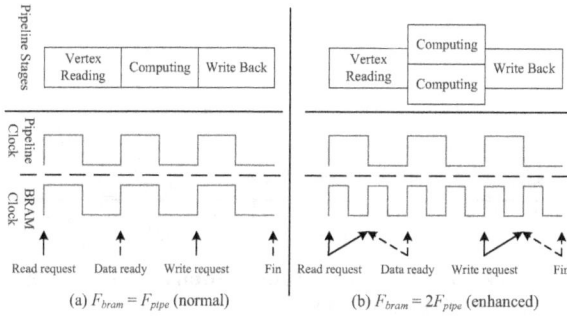

Figure 4: Pipeline enhancing

3.2 Block Cascading and Pipeline Enhancing

FabGraph relies on the communication between the pipeline-attached local stores (i.e., the L1 cache) and the SVB (i.e., the L2 cache) to transfer the vertex data during graph processing. To achieve a high bandwidth between these two cache levels, the blocks of BRAM or UltraRAM that form the local stores or SVB are cascaded in *parallel*.

Generally, the on-chip BRAM or UltraRAM consists of multiple blocks of fixed sizes and configurable output data wires, and when multiple blocks are cascaded in parallel, the resulting circuit will have a large bit-width for communication. For example, when cascading 57 blocks of the BRAM, each of which has 36Kb storage space and is configured with a port width of 512×72 bits, in parallel, we have a memory region of 256KB with the width of 4096 bits (aligned to integer power of 2). When the frequency of BRAM (denoted as F_{bram}) is $200MHz$, the theoretical communication bandwidth of these cascaded blocks will be: $BW_{blocks} = 4096bits \times 200MHz = 100GB/s$, which is much higher than the bandwidth (typically from $17GB/s$ to $25.6GB/s$) of the off-chip DDR4 RAM. More importantly, transferring vertex data between a pipeline-attached local store and the SVB does not consume DRAM bandwidth and does not incur pipeline stalls if it is overlapped with the computation conducted in other pipelines.

The dual pipeline-set design of FabGraph may consume a lot of BRAM space. Based on the observation that with the complex processing logic, the frequency of the pipelines (denoted as F_{pipe}) is generally low (typically around $150MHz$ to $200MHz$) , we can raise the frequency of the BRAM (denoted as F_{bram}) such that $F_{bram} = 2 \cdot F_{pipe}$ to "enhance" a pipeline, such that it can process two edges within one clock cycle. Figure 4 illustrates this technique. With doubled F_{bram}, an enhanced pipeline can read a pair (source and destination) of vertex data from, or write one result back to its local store, at both the rising (posedge) and falling (negedge) edges of its own clock cycle, and thus can processes two edges of the graph in one clock cycle.

4 VERTEX DATA REPLACEMENT IN SVB

FabGraph employs a sliding window mechanism as shown in Figure 5 to choose the blocks during computation (i.e., block iterator) and govern the data replacement in the SVB (i.e., L2 cache). Different from the $K \times 1$ rectangular window mechanism in ForeGraph, the window in FabGraph is square.

One obvious advantage of the square window over the rectangular window in ForeGraph is that when the source and destination

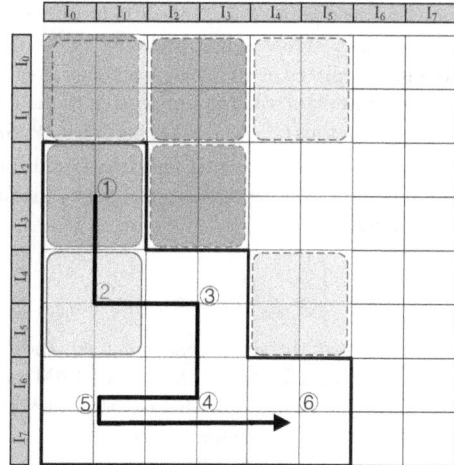

Figure 5: Sliding window mechanism in FabGraph

vertex intervals are loaded to the SVB, the window can cover not only the edge blocks within it, but also the symmetrical edge blocks, and the diagonal edge blocks of the grid. For example, in Figure 5, the solid-line deep-blue window that covers the edge blocks of B_{20}, B_{21}, B_{30}, B_{31}, also covers the other three dash-line deep-blue windows, as the source and destination vertex intervals (i.e., I_0, I_1, I_2, and I_3) are loaded in the SVB. For the same reason, when the solid-line light-orange window is scheduled, the vertex data loaded in the SVB also cover the areas that are marked by dash-line light-orange windows. Note that the edge blocks within the diagonal windows are scheduled (covered) twice. In practice, we use a register to track the scheduling sequences of edge blocks and schedule the diagonal windows only once.

With the advantage of the square window, FabGraph only needs to slide the window to cover the upper-triangular part or lower-triangular part of the grid. FabGraph chooses to slide the window in the lower-triangular part, and uses a Hilbert order [10, 12] like algorithm as shown in Figure 5 to guide the window sliding. Such algorithm minimizes the vertex data replacement in the SVB. For example, when the window slides from the 2×2 area marked by ① to the area marked by ②, only vertex intervals I_2 and I_3 need to be replaced with I_4 and I_5, while I_0 and I_1 remain in the SVB.

Denote the size of the SVB as S_{L2} (in the unit of vertex intervals), the size (height or width) of a window in FabGraph is thus $S_{L2}/2$. We call the vertex intervals that are loaded together into the SVB during window-sliding as *batched intervals* (e.g., $I_0 + I_1$, or $I2 + I3$, in Figure 5). When sliding in a grid with the dimension of Q, there will be $2 \cdot Q/S_{L2}$ sets of such batched intervals. As each window contains two (i.e., source and destination) such batched intervals, there will be $C_{2 \cdot Q/S_{L2}}^2$ possible combinations, which is also the number of square windows required to cover the whole grid. For example, in Figure 5, we have $Q = 8$ and $S_{L2} = 4$, and therefore, we need $C_4^2 = 6$ square windows to cover the whole grid.

Consider an all-active graph algorithm with multiple iterations (e.g., PageRank), when $S_{L2} \geq Q$, i.e., the SVB is big enough to store all vertex intervals, if precluding the data read during the beginning stage and written at the ending stage, there will be no need to replace any vertex data in the SVB during computation.

When $S_{L2} < Q$, as the content of SVB needs to be fully replaced at the beginning of the window sliding, and only half of the vertex data in SVB will be replaced at the window-slidings afterward, the amount of vertex intervals read from or written to the DRAM to cover the whole grid is thus $C_{2 \cdot Q/S_{L2}}^2 \cdot S_{L2}/2 + S_{L2}/2 = Q^2/S_{L2} - (Q - S_{L2})/2$. Therefore, the amount of vertex data transferred during one algorithm iteration in FabGraph can be computed by the following conditional equation:

$$Read = Write = \begin{cases} 0, & S_{L2} \geq Q \\ Q^2/S_{L2} - (Q - S_{L2})/2, & S_{L2} < Q \end{cases} \quad (1)$$

We can observe from the above conditional equation that the amount of vertex data read from or written to the DRAM is inversely proportional to the size of the SVB. That is, the bigger the SVB is, the smaller amount of vertex data transmissions will result. Table 1 compares the amount of vertex data (in the unit of vertex intervals) transferred via the DRAM bus in ForeGraph and FabGraph.

Table 1: The amounts of vertex data (in unit of vertex intervals) transmitted via DRAM bus during one algorithm iteration in ForeGraph and FabGraph (K denotes the number of pipelines in ForeGraph and S_{L2} denote the size, in unit of vertex intervals, of the SVB in FabGraph)

	ForeGraph (DFR)	FabGraph	
		$S_{L2} < Q$	$S_{L2} \geq Q$
Read	$Q + Q^2/K$	$Q^2/S_{L2} - (Q - S_{L2})/2$	0
Write	Q^2/K	$Q^2/S_{L2} - (Q - S_{L2})/2$	0

From Table 1, we can observe that increasing the size of SVB (i.e., S_{L2}) in FabGraph has similar effects as increasing the number of pipelines (i.e., K) in ForeGraph. However, when S_{L2} exceeds the breakpoint of Q, there will be no need to transfer vertex data during graph processing. On the contrary, ForeGraph still needs to read $2 \cdot Q$ and write Q vertex intervals (totally, $3 \cdot Q$), when $K \geq Q$.

5 OVERLAPPING COMPUTATION AND COMMUNICATION

FabGraph processes the edge blocks in a chosen window *sequentially*: suppose there are multiple edge blocks to be processed in the current window, the system will first load the vertex intervals of these edge blocks into the SVB, and then process the edge blocks *one after another*. The advantage of the sequential processing is that it disassociates the correlations between the edge blocks, and thus solves the edge inflation problem, that is incurred by processing K edge blocks of the same window in parallel as in ForeGraph. Nevertheless, such sequential processing mechanism leads to an amount of W^2 vertex interval data transmissions, as there are W^2 edge blocks in a $W \times W$ window.

FabGraph uses the two pipeline sets as shown in Figure 3, to overlap the vertex data transmission (communication) between the local stores and the SVB at one PS, with the processing of streamed edges (i.e., computation) at the other PS. Figure 6 illustrates this idea. We classify the situations of overlapping into two types: *perfect overlapping* and *imperfect overlapping*. In the case of perfect overlapping, the time spent on vertex data transmission at one

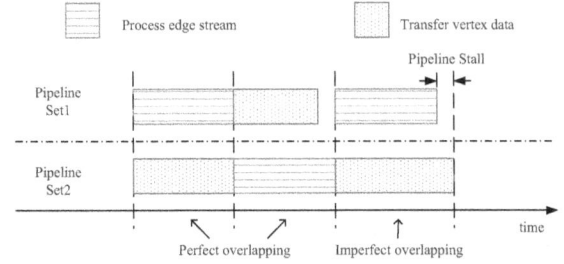

Figure 6: Overlapping the communication of one PS with the computation of the other PS

PS is less than or equals to that spent on the streamed edge processing that happens simultaneously at the other PS. In such case, the speed of graph processing is determined by the speed of edge streaming via the DRAM bus, and thus achieves the highest theoretical performance (as with its relatively low bandwidth, DRAM bus is generally considered as the bottleneck of graph processing). On the other hand, in the case of imperfect overlapping, the time spent on vertex data transmission at one PS is larger than that spent on the streamed edge processing conducted simultaneously at the other PS, which consequently leads to pipeline stalls, and prevents the system from reaching the theoretical performance. In order to achieve perfect overlapping, FabGraph needs to 1) reduce the time spent on vertex data transmission, and 2) balance the edge blocks to make them have (approximately) identical sizes.

FabGraph employs two techniques to reduce the time spent on vertex data transmission: a) schedule the edge blocks in a window with the *Source First Replacement* (SFR) algorithm as shown in Figure 2, and b) improve the communication bandwidth between the L1 and L2 cache. By SFR, the blocks of the same column are scheduled sequentially before switching from one column to another, which results in only one replacement of the (source) vertex interval in most cases. Moreover, FabGraph cascades multiple blocks of the BRAM in parallel to achieve large bit-width to improve the communication bandwidth between the L1 and L2 cache, and doubles the frequency of BRAM (discussed in subsection 3.2) when necessary.

With the power-law degree distribution [9], real-world graphs are hard to be partitioned into equal-sized subgraphs [2]. When representing a graph as a $Q \times Q$ grid, the vertex set of the graph can be considered as being partitioned into Q partitions. We study the *Cumulative Distribution Functions* (CDFs) of the edge block sizes by two widely used partitioning methods: range-based partitioning and hash-based partitioning. Since there are 2^{16} vertices in a vertex interval, the range-based partitioning method group the vertices whose IDs fall in range $[i \times 2^{16}, (i+1) \times 2^{16}]$ to the ith partition, while the hash-based partitioning method groups two vertices into the same partition when the remainders are the same when their IDs are divided by a given number. Figure 7 compares the CDFs of the edge block sizes of LiveJournal listed in Table 2.

From Figure 7, we can observe that compared with the range-based partitioning, the size distribution of the edge blocks by using hash-based partitioning is much evener. FabGraph thus uses hash-based partitioning to construct the grid representations of the graphs under processing.

To describe and measure the effectiveness of the overlapping mechanism, we define a term named *overlapping factor*, denoted as

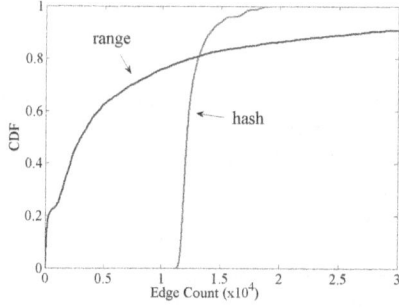

Figure 7: Size (in number of edges) distribution of the edge blocks of LiveJournal when represented as a 74 × 74 grid by range and hash partitioning methods

α, that is computed by $\alpha = T_{actual}/T_{theory}$, where T_{actual} is the time actual paid on processing a set of edge blocks in FabGraph, and T_{theory} is the time paid on processing the edges within the edge blocks. Denote the set of edge blocks as $\mathcal{E} = \{E_1, E_2, ..., E_L,$ where $L > 1\}$, the number of edges in E_i as $|E_i|$, T_{theory} is thus: $T_{theory} = \Sigma_1^L |E_i| \cdot S_e/BW_{dram}$, where S_e is the storage size of an edge, and BW_{dram} is the DRAM bandwidth.

Consider conducting an all-active graph algorithm in Graph G with Q^2 edge blocks, use $AVG(|e_i|)$ to denote the average size (in number of edges) of the edge blocks of G, and denote the bandwidth of communication between L1 and L2 cache as BW_{L1-L2}, the overlapping factor can be computed approximately by using following equation:

$$\alpha \approx \frac{\max(S_{interval}/BW_{L1-L2}, AVG(|e_i|) \cdot S_e/BW_{dram}))}{AVG(|e_i|) \cdot S_e/BW_{dram}} \quad (2)$$

From Equation 2, we can observe that if BW_{L1-L2} is big enough (and thus $S_{interval}/BW_{L1-L2}$ is small enough), the system will "perfectly" overlap the communication and the computation, such that $\alpha = 1$. Nevertheless, when the graph under processing is extremely sparse, and thus $AVG(|e_i|)$ is extremely small, such that $S_{interval}/BW_{L1-L2} > AVG(|e_i|) \cdot S_e/BW_{dram}$, the overlapping will be "imperfect", i.e., $\alpha > 1$.

6 PERFORMANCE MODEL

Consider conducting an iteration of all-active graph algorithm in graph G, the graph processing time in FabGraph consists of two parts: the time paid on vertex transmission between DRAM and SVB, and that paid on processing the streamed edges. Denote the former as $T_{vertex\_transmission}$, and latter as T_{edge_stream}, the time of conducting an all-active algorithm in graph G with Fab-Graph (denoted as $\mathcal{T}$) can thus be computed as:

$$\mathcal{T} = T_{vertex\_transmission} + \alpha \cdot T_{edge\_stream} \quad (3)$$

where $T_{vertex\_transmission}$ can be computed using following conditional equation (derived from Equation 1):

$$T_{vertex\_transmission} = \begin{cases} 0, & S_{L2} \geq Q \\ \dfrac{2 \cdot Q^2/S_{L2} - (Q - S_{L2})}{BW_{dram}}, & S_{L2} < Q \end{cases} \quad (4)$$

Denote the number of pipelines of one PS as P, the number of edges in graph under processing as $|E|$, T_{edge_stream} can be

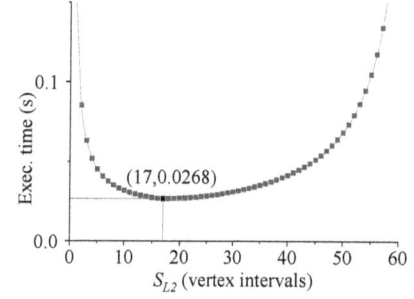

Figure 8: Theoretical execution times of PageRank in Fab-Graph when varying S_{L2} by assuming $Q = 74, M_{bram} = 64, |E| = 69M, \alpha = 1, \beta = 2, BW_{dram} = 19.2GB/s, F_{pipe} = 150MHz$

computed by using the following equation:

$$T_{edge\_stream} = \max(|E| \cdot S_e/BW_{dram}, |E|/(P \cdot F_{pipe})) \quad (5)$$

When there is enough BRAM space for the local stores (L1 cache) of the pipelines and logic resources in FPGA, we have $P = BW_{dram}/S_e$, and thus $T_{edge\_stream} = |E| \cdot S_e/BW_{dram}$. However, when there is not enough BRAM space (e.g., the board has only limited BRAM resource, or part of the BRAM space is occupied by the SVB), we have $P = S_{L1}/4$, where S_{L1} denotes the L1 cache size in unit of vertex intervals if the pipelines are not enhanced, and $P = S_{L1}/2$ when using enhanced pipelines. Therefore, we have:

$$T_{edge\_stream} = \begin{cases} |E| \cdot S_e/BW_{dram}, & S_{L1} \geq \beta \cdot BW_{dram}/S_e \\ \beta \cdot |E|/(S_{L1} \cdot F_{pipe}), & S_{L1} < \beta \cdot BW_{dram}/S_e \end{cases} \quad (6)$$

where $\beta = 4$ if the pipelines are not enhanced, and $\beta = 2$ if the pipelines are enhanced. Use TH_{L1} to denote the threshold of $\beta \cdot BW_{dram}/S_e$, i.e., $TH_{L1} = \beta \cdot BW_{dram}/S_e$, we can further transform Equation 3 into the following conditional equation:

$$\mathcal{T} = T_{vertex\_transmission} + \alpha \cdot T_{edge\_stream} =$$
$$\begin{cases} \dfrac{\alpha \cdot |E| \cdot S_e}{BW_{dram}}, & S_{L1} \geq TH_{L1}, S_{L2} \geq Q \\ \dfrac{\alpha \cdot |E| \cdot S_e}{BW_{dram}} + \dfrac{2Q^2/S_{L2} - (Q - S_{L2})}{BW_{dram}}, & S_{L1} \geq TH_{L1}, S_{L2} < Q \\ \dfrac{\alpha \cdot \beta \cdot |E|}{S_{L1} \cdot F_{pipe}}, & S_{L1} < TH_{L1}, S_{L2} \geq Q \\ \dfrac{\alpha \cdot \beta \cdot |E|}{S_{L1} \cdot F_{pipe}} + \dfrac{2Q^2/S_{L2} - (Q - S_{L2})}{BW_{dram}}, & S_{L1} < TH_{L1}, S_{L2} < Q \end{cases} \quad (7)$$

One of the interesting cases in Equation 7 is when both L1 and L2 cache share the same BRAM (i.e., $S_{L1} + S_{L2} \leq M_{bram}$, where M_{bram} is the storage size of BRAM in the unit of vertex intervals), and there is no enough BRAM space for these two cache levels, i.e., $S_{L1} < TH_{L1}$ and $S_{L2} < Q$. Assume the BRAM resource is efficiently used (i.e., $S_{L1} \approx M_{bram} - S_{L2}$), for this case, we have:

$$\mathcal{T} = \frac{\alpha \cdot \beta \cdot |E|}{(M_{bram} - S_{L2}) \cdot F_{pipe}} + \frac{2Q^2/S_{L2} - (Q - S_{L2})}{BW_{dram}} \quad (8)$$

Assume conducting PageRank algorithm in a graph with $Q = 74$ and $|E| = 69million$ (i.e., LiveJournal in Table 2), on an FPGA board with 16.61MB BRAM (i.e., $M_{bram} = 64$, the VCU110 board to be

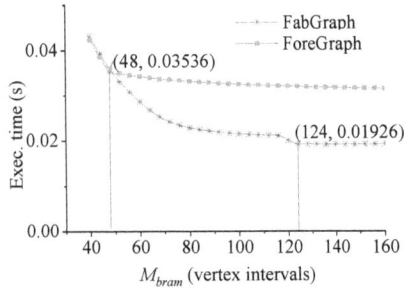

Figure 9: Smallest theoretical execution times of PageRank in FabGraph and ForeGraph, when varying the size of BRAM by assuming $Q = 74, |E| = 69M, \alpha = 1, \beta = 2, BW_{dram} = 19.2GB/s,$ and $F_{pipe} = 150MHz$

used in Section 7), $\alpha = 1, \beta = 2$ (enhanced pipelines), $F_{pipe} = 150MHz, BW_{dram} = 19.2GB/s,$ and varies S_{L2} from 1 to 60 (in unit of vertex intervals), the theoretical execution times of PageRank in FabGraph varies accordingly (governed by Equation 8) as shown in Figure 8. From Figure 8, we can observe that the smallest $\mathcal{T}$ (i.e., 0.0292s) appears when $S_{L2} = 17$. Therefore, by compute the choice of S_{L2} that produces the smallest $\mathcal{T}$ in Equation 8, we have the optimal configurations, that achieve best performance for PageRank in a given graph, for the L1 and L2 cache, when allocating the storage space from a given BRAM.

We further predict the performance of FabGraph with above settings by varying the storage capacity of BRAM, and compare the best performances (the theoretical smallest execution times) that can be achieved in FabGraph when conducing PageRank, with the theoretical performances (execution times) of ForeGraph in Figure 9. From Figure 9, we can observe that with a small BRAM (below 48 vertex intervals, approximately 12MB), ForeGraph outperforms FabGraph, as FabGraph cannot have large L2 cache with such small BRAM. However, when the size of BRAM exceeds this breakpoint (i.e., 48 vertex intervals), PageRank achieves better performance with FabGraph than with ForeGraph, and the performance gains due to the enlarged BRAMs increase with a much faster speed (FabGraph's curve has larger slope) in FabGraph than ForeGraph. When M_{bram} is greater than 124 vertex intervals, FabGraph achieves the best theoretical performance for PageRank (only edges are transmitted during computation).

7 EVALUATIONS

We choose two graph algorithms, i.e., BFS and PageRank, and four real-world graphs taken from [19] and listed in Table 2 to evaluate the performance of FabGraph.

Table 2: Real-world graph data-sets

Graphs	#Vertices	#Edges	Q
com-Youtube (YT)	1.13 million	2.99 million	18
soc-Pokec (PK)	1.63 million	30.62 million	26
wiki-Talk (WK)	2.39 million	5.02 million	38
soc-LiveJournal (LJ)	4.85 million	68.99 million	74

We use two FPGA boards to evaluate FabGraph:

• **VCU110**: Xilinx Virtex UltraScale VCU110 Development Kit, configured with an XCVU190-2FLGC2104E FPGA chip, 16.61MB

$(3780 \times 36Kb)$ on-chip BRAM, 1.07 million LUT (*Look-Up-Table*) slices and 2.15 million FFs (*Flip-Flop*).

• **VCU118**: Xilinx Virtex UltraScale+ VCU118 Development Kit, configured with an XCVU9P-L2FLGA2104E FPGA chip, 9.48MB $(2160 \times 36Kb)$ on-chip BRAM, 33.75MB $(960 \times 288Kb)$ UltraRAM , 1.18 million LUTs and 2.36 million FFs.

VCU110 has much larger BRAM storage space than VCU118, and it is the same board used by ForeGraph in [6]. Compared with VCU110, VCU118 has much smaller (about half of) BRAM storage space, but large UltraRAM. With about half tag price [22], VCU118 is much cheaper than VCU110.

We use Xilinx Vivado 2017.4 to conduct simulations by implementing FabGraph on these two boards, use Block Memory Generator v8.3 [20] to control BRAM cascading, and use DRAMSim2 [17] to simulate the off-chip data accesses against a 2GB DDR4 Micron MTA8ATF51264HZ-2G3 SDRAM, which runs at $1.2GHz$ and provides a peak bandwidth of $19.2GB/s$. We use $S_v = 8$ bits for BFS, $S_v = 32$ bits for PageRank, and compute the storage size of an interval as $S_{interval} = 2^{16} \cdot S_v$ during the following experiments. The storage size of an edge is fixed to $S_e = 32$ bits.

7.1 On VCU110

As VCU110 has only BRAM resource, FabGraph allocates both the L1 cache (i.e., the pipeline-attached local stores) and the L2 cache (i.e., the SVB) in its BRAM.

7.1.1 Resource Utilization and Performance. Table 3 reports the on-chip resource utilization and performances of BFS and PageRank conducted in the chosen graphs with FabGraph on VCU110.

We cascade 29 and 57 blocks of BRAM in parallel to build the individual pipeline-attached local store for BFS and PageRank respectively. The reason of using 29 blocks of BRAM (its storage space is $29 \cdot 36Kb \approx 130KB$) to build a local store is that we want a pipeline-attached local store to have the width of 2048 bits, to promote the communication bandwidth between it and the SVB. However, as the vertex interval in BFS consumes only $64KB$, nearly half of its space is wasted (we trade space for time here).

When conducting BFS, FabGraph configures enough pipeline resources, i.e., 48 pipelines for first three small graphs listed in Table 2, and 32 enhanced pipelines for LiveJournal, to handle all the incoming stream edges (24 edges when $F_{pipe} = 200MHz$, and 32 edges when $F_{pipe} = 150MHz$. Remember, FabGraph has two sets of pipelines) at each clock cycle. At the same time, FabGraph leaves enough BRAM resources to store *all* the vertex data of these graphs during the algorithm's execution. The first condition of Equation 7 (i.e., $S_{L1} \geq TH_{L1}$ and $S_{L2} \geq Q$) thus applies, and there is no need to transfer any vertex data during the algorithm's execution, except for the transmissions at the beginning and ending stages.

When conducting PageRank, due to the large storage requirements of the vertex intervals (57 blocks of BRAM for each), the BRAM resource of VCU110 is not enough to configure enough pipelines to handle all incoming edges at each clock cycle, and leaves enough space to store all the vertex data at the same time for even the smallest graph in Table 2. The fourth condition of Equation 7 (i.e., $S_{L1} < TH_{L1}$ and $S_{L2} < Q$) thus applies. We use the best solutions of Equation 8 to configure both S_{L1} and S_{L2} to achieve the best performances of PageRank in FabGraph.

Table 3: Resource utilization and performances of graph algorithms in FabGraph on VCU110 (α stands for the Overlapping Factor discussed in Section 5)

Algorithm	Graph	BRAM	S_{L1} (MB)	S_{L2} (MB)	#Pipelines	LUT	FF	F_{pipe} (MHz)	F_{bram} (MHz)	Runtimes (Seconds)	MTEPS	Speed up over ForeGraph	α
BFS	YT	88.6%	12	3.25	48	34.71%	19.19%	200	200	0.0032	2801	3.1x	1.0
	PK									0.0253	2768	-	1.0
	WK									0.0154	1628	1.2x	1.80
	LJ	77.4%	8.1	4.77	32 (enhanced)	23.87%	12.79%			0.168	2840	2.7x	1.0
PR	YT	93.4%	11.02	4.53	22 (enhanced)	28.42%	25.45%	150	300	0.0116	2565	2.5x	1.28
	PK	90.48%	12.02	3.01	24 (enhanced)	31.02%	27.67%			0.0971	3150	-	1.0
	WK	86.5%	8.01	6.5	16 (enhanced)	31.02%	27.67%			0.0515	976	1.0x	2.41
	LJ	93.4%	11.02	4.53	22 (enhanced)	28.42%	25.45%			0.276	2494	2.1x	1.0

From Table 3, we can observe that with the two-level vertex caching mechanism, the performances of both BFS and PageRank in FabGraph exceed those of ForeGraph. In the case of BFS, the speedups of FabGraph over ForeGraph are from 1.2x to 3.1x, while in the case of PageRank, the speedups of FabGraph over ForeGraph are from 1.0x to 2.5x. The performances of BFS and PageRank in wiki-Talk are not optimal as the graph is extremely sparse (with an edge factor about only 2), which incurs high overlapping rates and thus brings down the performance in FabGraph.

7.1.2 Data Transmission Amounts. To demonstrate the effectiveness on reducing the amounts of data transmissions with the two-level vertex caching mechanism of FabGraph, we collect the amounts of both vertex and edge data transmissions when conducting PageRank in Figure 10, and compare them with the data amounts in theory (take into account the edge inflations) of ForeGraph.

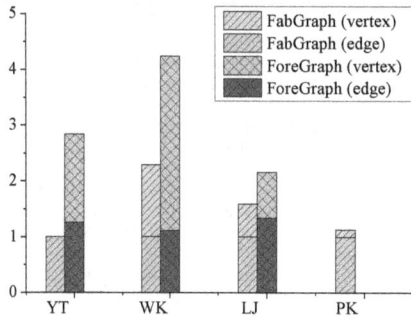

Figure 10: The amounts of data transmissions (all figures are normalized to $|E| \cdot S_e$ for each graph) when conducting PageRank on VCU110

From Figure 10, we can observe that the two-level vertex caching mechanism of FabGraph effectively reduces the amounts of data (especially the vertex data) transmissions during graph processing. However, the ratio of reduction on vertex data transmissions cannot be directly translated to performance improvements. For example, compared with ForeGraph, the amount of vertex data transmissions reduces about 50% when conducting PageRank in LiveJournal with FabGraph, but the speedup is 2.1x over ForeGraph. The reason is that compared with the DRAM-to-BRAM communication in ForeGraph, the efficiency of communications between the L1 and L2 cache is more efficient. On the other hand, in wiki-Talk, although the data transmission amounts reduce by 2x when comparing FabGraph

and ForeGraph, the performance of PageRank with FabGraph is almost the same as that of ForeGraph, due to its high overlapping factor (2.41), resulted by the sparsity nature of the graph.

7.2 On VCU118

VCU118 is configured with both on-chip BRAM and UltraRAM resources. We use the BRAM as the pipeline-attached local stores (L1 cache), and the UltraRAM as the SVB (L2 cache).

7.2.1 Resource Utilization. The resource utilization rates are listed in Table 4. As the UltraRAM is big enough to store all the vertex data of graphs listed in Table 2, we have a large L2 cache on this FPGA board, i.e., $S_{L2} > Q$.

As on VCU110, FabGraph cascades 29 and 57 blocks of the BRAM in parallel to build individual pipeline-attached local store for BFS and PageRank respectively on VCU118. The BRAM of VCU118 thus offers 72 or 36 cascaded blocks, each of which can store a vertex interval, for BFS or PageRank respectively (i.e., $S_{L1} = 72$ for BFS, and $S_{L1} = 36$ for PageRank). With these cascaded blocks, FabGraph can build 36 or 18 pipelines for BFS or PageRank (remember, each pipeline consumes two local stores).

Table 4: Resource utilization in FabGraph on VCU118

Resource	BFS	PageRank
kernels	32 (enhanced)	18 (enhanced)
LUT	22.85%	12.72%
FF	15.48%	14.10%
BRAM	85.92%	95.00%
UltraRAM	11.88%	59.38%
F_{pipe}	150 MHz	150MHz
F_{bram}	300MHz	300MHz

Considering the DRAM bandwidth and the frequency of the pipelines, the FPGA will accept 24 edges when $F_{pipe} = 200MHz$, and 32 edges when $F_{pipe} = 150MHz$. When $F_{pipe} = 200MHz$, FabGraph needs to build 48 (24×2) pipelines to handle all incoming edges, as the system divides the pipelines into two sets with identical number of pipelines. Obviously, in such case, the cascaded blocks offered by the BRAM of VCU118 are not enough. We thus use 32 and 18 *enhanced* pipelines for BFS and PageRank respectively. With these enhanced pipelines, we have $S_{L1} \geq TH_{L1}$, where $TH_{L1} = 2 \times 32 = 64$ for BFS, and $S_{L1} < TH_{L1}$, where $TH_{L1} = 2 \times 28 = 56$ for PageRank.

Table 5: Performance of FabGraph on VCU118 (α stands for the Overlapping Factor discussed in Section 5)

Algorithm	Graph	Runtimes (Seconds)	MTEPS	Speed up over ForeGraph	α	Speed up over VCU110
BFS	YT	0.0032	2801	3.1x	1.0	1.0x
	PK	0.0253	2768	-	1.0	1.0x
	WK	0.0205	1088	1.7x	2.41	0.66x
	LJ	0.168	2840	2.7x	1.0	1.0x
PR	YT	0.0101	2958	3.0x	1.064	1.2x
	PK	0.0972	3150	-	1.0	1.0x
	WK	0.0434	1157	1.2x	2.71	1.2x
	LJ	0.219	3150	2.6x	1.0	1.3x

7.2.2 Performance. The performances of the algorithms conducted in the graphs are listed in Table 5. From Table 5, we can observe that BFS achieves identical performances like those on VCU110 in most of the graphs in Table 2, except for wiki-Talk. The reason is that the UltraRAM works at $150MHz$ as the pipelines, and thus has lower L1-to-L2 communication bandwidth than that on VCU110. This exacerbates the overlapping problem (2.41 > 1.80) due to the extreme sparsity of the graph. Whereas, such degradation of communication bandwidth does not affect the performance in the other three graphs as they are much denser than wiki-Talk.

On the other hand, PageRank achieves even better performances in all chosen graphs than those conducted on VCU110. The reason is that with a large UltraRAM, the L2 cache (SVB) stores all the vertex data of these graphs during the executions, and thus effectively reduces the vertex data transmissions from the off-chip DRAM, and avoids the pipeline stalls. These experimental results imply that the two-level vertex caching mechanism performs well with large L2 caches, and can even help some of the graph algorithms to achieve better performances on FPGA boards with small BRAM but large UltraRAM than on more expensive FPGA boards with large BRAM.

8 CONCLUSIONS AND FUTURE WORKS

In this paper, we proposed a two-level vertex caching mechanism to improve the performance of graph processing on FPGA-DRAM platforms. By building a system based on this idea, and evaluating it on two typical DRAM-based FPGA boards, we demonstrated the effectiveness of the two-level vertex caching mechanism on graph processing. The future works of this paper include further tuning of FabGraph with the objective of decreasing the overlapping factor when processing sparse graphs, and extending the system to distributed (multi-board) settings.

ACKNOWLEDGMENTS

This paper is supported by National Key Research and Development Program of China under grant No.2018YFB1003500, National Natural Science Foundation of China under grant No. 61825202, 61832006, 61732010, and the "Fundamental Research Funds for the Central Universities of China" under grant No. 2017KFYXJJ066.

REFERENCES

[1] Tero Aittokallio and Benno Schwikowski. 2006. Graph-based methods for analysing networks in cell biology. *Briefings in Bioinformatics* 7, 3 (2006), 243–255.
[2] Konstantin Andreev and Harald Räcke. 2004. Balanced Graph Partitioning. In *SPAA*. ACM, 120–124.
[3] Scott Beamer, Krste Asanovic, and David Patterson. 2015. Locality Exists in Graph Processing: Workload Characterization on an Ivy Bridge Server. In *IISWC*. IEEE, 56–65.
[4] Yuze Chi, Guohao Dai, Yu Wang, Guangyu Sun, Guoliang Li, and Huazhong Yang. 2016. NXgraph: An efficient graph processing system on a single machine. In *ICDE*. IEEE, 409–420.
[5] Guohao Dai, Yuze Chi, Yu Wang, and Huazhong Yang. 2016. FPGP: Graph Processing Framework on FPGA A Case Study of Breadth-First Search. In *FPGA*. ACM, 105–110.
[6] Guohao Dai, Tianhao Huang, Yuze Chi, Ningyi Xu, Yu Wang, and Huazhong Yang. 2017. ForeGraph: Exploring Large-scale Graph Processing on Multi-FPGA Architecture. In *FPGA*. ACM, 217–226.
[7] Michael deLorimier, Nachiket Kapre, Nikil Mehta, Dominic Rizzo, Ian Eslick, Raphael Rubin, Tomas E. Uribe, Thomas F. Jr. Knight, and Andre DeHon. 2006. GraphStep: A System Architecture for Sparse-Graph Algorithms. In *FCCM*. IEEE, 143–151.
[8] Assaf Eisenman, Ludmila Cherkasova, Guilherme Magalhaes, Qiong Cai, Paolo Faraboschi, and Sachin Katti. 2016. Parallel Graph Processing: Prejudice and State of the Art. In *ICPE*. ACM, 85–90.
[9] Michalis Faloutsos, Petros Faloutsos, and Christos Faloutsos. 1999. On Power-law Relationships of the Internet Topology. *SIGCOMM Comput. Commun. Rev.* 29, 4 (1999), 251–262.
[10] David Hilbert. 1891. Ueber die stetige Abbildung einer Linie auf ein Flächenstück. *Math. Ann.* 38, 3 (1891), 459–460.
[11] Soroosh Khoram, Jialiang Zhang, Maxwell Strange, and Jing Li. 2018. Accelerating Graph Analytics by Co-Optimizing Storage and Access on an FPGA-HMC Platform. In *FPGA*. ACM, 239–248.
[12] Steffen Maass, Changwoo Min, Sanidhya Kashyap, Woonhak Kang, Mohan Kumar, and Taesoo Kim. 2017. Mosaic: Processing a Trillion-Edge Graph on a Single Machine. In *EuroSys*. ACM, 527–543.
[13] Grzegorz Malewicz, Matthew H. Austern, Aart J.C. Bik, James C. Dehnert, Ilan Horn, Naty Leiser, and Grzegorz Czajkowski. 2010. Pregel: A System for Large-scale Graph Processing. In *SIGMOD*. ACM, 135–146.
[14] Eriko Nurvitadhi, Gabriel Weisz, Yu Wang, Skand Hurkat, Marie Nguyen, James C. Hoe, José F. Martínez, and Carlos Guestrin. 2014. GraphGen: An FPGA Framework for Vertex-Centric Graph Computation. In *FCCM*. IEEE, 25–28.
[15] Tayo Oguntebi and Kunle Olukotun. 2016. GraphOps: A Dataflow Library for Graph Analytics Acceleration. In *FPGA*. ACM, 111–117.
[16] Louise Quick, Paul Wilkinson, and David Hardcastle. 2012. Using Pregel-like Large Scale Graph Processing Frameworks for Social Network Analysis. In *Proceedings of IEEE/ACM International Conference on Advances in Social Networks Analysis and Mining*. 457–463.
[17] Paul Rosenfeld, Elliott Cooper-Balis, and Bruce Jacob. 2011. DRAMSim2: A Cycle Accurate Memory System Simulator. *IEEE Comput. Archit. Lett.* 10, 1 (2011), 16–19.
[18] Amitabha Roy, Ivo Mihailovic, and Willy Zwaenepoel. 2013. X-Stream: Edge-centric Graph Processing Using Streaming Partitions. In *USENIX SOSP*. 472–488.
[19] Stanford. 2018. Stanford large network dataset collection. http://snap.stanford.edu/data/index.html.
[20] Xilinx. 2017. Block Memory Generator v8.4. https://www.xilinx.com/support/documentation/ip_documentation/blk_mem_gen/v8_4/.
[21] Xilinx. 2018. UltraScale Architecture Memory Resources-User Guide. https://www.xilinx.com/support/documentation/user_guides/.
[22] Xilinx. 2018. Xilinx Boards and Kits. https://www.xilinx.com/products/boards-and-kits.html.
[23] Jialiang Zhang, Soroosh Khoram, and Jing Li. 2017. Boosting the Performance of FPGA-based Graph Processor Using Hybrid Memory Cube: A Case for Breadth First Search. In *FPGA*. ACM, 207–216.
[24] Jialiang Zhang and Jing Li. 2018. Degree-aware Hybrid Graph Traversal on FPGA-HMC Platform. In *FPGA*. ACM, 229–238.
[25] Shijie Zhou, Charalampos Chelmis, and Viktor K. Prasanna. 2016. High-Throughput and Energy-Efficient Graph Processing on FPGA. In *FCCM*. IEEE, 103–110.
[26] Xiaowei Zhu, Wentao Han, and Wenguang Chen. 2015. GridGraph: Large-scale Graph Processing on a Single Machine Using 2-level Hierarchical Partitioning. In *USENIX ATC*. 375–386.

FASED: FPGA-Accelerated Simulation and Evaluation of DRAM

David Biancolin[1], Sagar Karandikar[1], Donggyu Kim[1], Jack Koenig[1], Andrew Waterman[2],
Jonathan Bachrach[1], Krste Asanović[1,2]

[1]ADEPT Lab, Department of Electrical Engineering and Computer Sciences, University of California, Berkeley, USA

[2]SiFive Inc., San Mateo, California, USA

{biancolin,sagark,dgkim,jack.koenig3,waterman,jrb,krste}@eecs.berkeley.edu

ABSTRACT

Recent work in FPGA-accelerated simulation of ASICs has shown that much of a simulator can be automatically generated from ASIC RTL. Alas, these works rely on simple models of the outer cache hierarchy and DRAM, as mapping ASIC RTL for these components into an FPGA fabric is too complex and resource intensive. To improve FPGA simulation model accuracy, we present FASED, a parameterized generator of composable, high-fidelity, FPGA-hosted last-level-cache and DRAM models. FASED instances are highly performant, yet they maintain timing faithfulness independently of the behavior of the host-FPGA memory system. For a given scheduling policy, a single FASED instance can model nearly the entire space of realizable single-channel DDR3 memory organizations, without resynthesizing the simulator RTL. We demonstrate FASED by integrating it into a flow that automatically transforms RTL for multicore RISC-V processors into full-system simulators that execute at up to 150 target MHz on cloud-hosted FPGAs.

CCS CONCEPTS

• **Hardware** → **Simulation and emulation**; *Dynamic memory*; Reconfigurable logic applications.

KEYWORDS

emulation; FPGA prototyping; memory systems

ACM Reference Format:
David Biancolin, Sagar Karandikar, Donggyu Kim, Jack Koenig, Andrew Waterman, Jonathan Bachrach, Krste Asanović. 2019. FASED: FPGA-Accelerated Simulation and Evaluation of DRAM. In *The 2019 ACM/SIGDA International Symposium on Field-Programmable Gate Arrays (FPGA '19), Feb. 24–26, 2019, Seaside, CA, USA.* ACM, New York, NY, USA, 10 pages. https://doi.org/10.1145/3289602.3293894

1 INTRODUCTION

With the slowdown in process technology improvements, architects are increasingly turning to specialization to deliver advances in performance and energy efficiency. Modern SoCs contain a collage of fixed-function units and specialized accelerators, with general-purpose application processors consuming a dwindling fraction of the die. Heterogeneous specialized systems add new complexity at all levels of the computing stack, and research into new programming models, runtimes, and operating systems is expanding.

Architects and systems designers will need a comprehensive set of simulation technologies to enable this research. Both architectural and microarchitectural full-system software simulators will remain important sandboxes for prototyping new ideas. In many domains, sampling techniques permit the use of slower but more detailed microarchitectural simulators, providing greater fidelity without loss of simulation throughput. Unfortunately, there are many cases in which existing software-based microarchitectural simulators are too slow, and sampling techniques fail because samples cannot be reused for changes that have large impacts on execution behavior. A few such cases include tuning highly parallel specialized multiprocessors; runtimes that dynamically schedule and optimize code based on performance; and hardware-software co-design flows, where the hardware and software change simultaneously. In such cases, FPGAs are the only technology that can provide high-fidelity full-system simulation with low experimental latency, high throughput, and low cost per simulation cycle.

FPGA-accelerated simulation has been actively studied over the past decade, notably in the multi-university RAMP project [23], but it has seen little adoption for a number of reasons:

(1) FPGA-accelerated simulators are difficult to write or modify, and lengthy compilation times make them onerous to debug.
(2) FPGAs have historically been resource-constrained, limiting the scale of the system under simulation or incurring the great additional complexity of multi-FPGA partitioning.
(3) Purchasing and maintaining an FPGA cluster is prohibitively expensive.

Fortunately, recent technological advances address the latter two challenges: FPGAs have been scaling well, providing greater f_{max} and capacity, and are now widely available as cloud-hosted resources [1]. Alas, design complexity challenges remain.

One promising avenue is to automatically generate the FPGA-hosted components of the simulator from RTL produced by highly configurable generators such as the Rocket Chip RISC-V SoC generator [2]. The biggest limitation of this approach so far has been modeling the main memory system. The DRAM controller RTL, physical interface, and chip models cannot be simply mapped to the FPGA, so prior work used simplistic, handwritten RTL models (e.g., latency pipes) backed by FPGA-attached DRAM [11]. In this paper, we address the challenge of flexibly modeling DRAM memory-systems at greater fidelity. The techniques we propose can be applied to modeling other memory types, such as non-volatile memories, and I/O devices where transformation from ASIC RTL is difficult or impossible. This paper makes the following contributions:

First, we propose separating the concerns of host-platform mapping from target modeling, by writing the timing model of a split-timing-functional model as *target-time* RTL. This approach makes it considerably easier to describe detailed timing-model *generators* and allows new users to add new timing models without a detailed understanding of how the model will be mapped to the FPGA.

Second, we demonstrate the flexibility of this approach by presenting FASED, a last-level-cache and multi-rank DDR3 timing-model generator with fidelity comparable to cycle-accurate software-based simulators like DRAMSim2 [19]. FASED instances can be reconfigured without FPGA recompilation and are instrumented to provide the same performance and power measurements as software-based simulators.

2 ON FPGA-BASED SIMULATION

We first review the use of FPGAs for architecture studies. Throughout this paper, we make a distinction between the *target* and the *host*. The target is the design under study. Combining the target with a model of the environment in which it executes forms a determinate closed system whose behavior is defined independently of the simulation host. The host is the hardware that executes (*hosts*) the simulation. In this paper, a host consists of one or more CPUs connected to one or more FPGAs.

2.1 FPGA Prototyping

FPGAs have long been used to *prototype* ASICs by implementing the ASIC RTL directly in FPGA logic. While FPGA prototypes are both fast (10s to 100s of MHz) and detailed, they require a complete RTL description of the target design. Furthermore, larger designs must be painstakingly partitioned across multiple FPGAs. Since these multi-FPGA prototypes advance in lockstep, cycle by cycle, they are considerably slower (100s of KHz to 1s of MHz). Nonetheless, FPGAs are used widely in industry, as they allow software development and hardware validation to proceed months before silicon is available.

2.2 FPGA-Accelerated Simulation

Prior work has explored techniques to make FPGAs more usable and powerful simulation hosts. Motivated by the dawn of the multicore era, the multi-university RAMP project [23] made large strides in improving FPGA-accelerated simulators by improving resource efficiency, developing FPGA partitioning techniques, and avoiding FPGA recompilation by using reconfigurable models.

ProtoFlex [6] was an architecture-level simulator that demonstrated 16-way host-multithreading of a single FPGA-hosted functional model. ProtoFlex could switch between FPGA-hosted and CPU-hosted modes via *transplantation*. FAST [5], a cycle-accurate simulator, was split into CPU-hosted functional and FPGA-hosted timing models. RAMP Gold [20] used FPGA-hosted timing and functional models with 64-way host-multithreading to model a larger target on a single FPGA. HAsim [17] also used FPGA-hosted timing and functional models, but provided more detailed pipeline and memory hierarchy models.

Other work studied partitioning targets over multiple FPGAs. [8] showed that by partitioning HAsim over two FPGAs, they could model eight times as many cores, due to improved resource sharing between virtual instances. To model a datacenter-scale target,

DIABLO [21] leveraged RAMP Gold's multithreading to simulate 3072 servers on 24 FPGAs.

A unifying theme of FPGA-accelerated simulators is that one clock-cycle of target time is executed over a variable number of FPGA-host cycles. This lets an FPGA-hosted simulator hide variable host latencies to DRAM and CPU-hosted components, enables optimizations that trade host time for host resources, and, crucially, facilitates deterministic simulation. This *host-target decoupling* is what differentiates an FPGA-accelerated simulator from an FPGA prototype. We expand on this property in Section 3.2.1.

2.3 Adoption Challenges

Despite their promise, FPGA-accelerated simulators have only been successfully employed by those who designed them. We attribute their limited appeal to several factors:

(1) **Availability.** Much of the early FPGA-accelerated simulator research relied on boutique FPGA-emulation platforms or custom board designs, whose high cost and limited availability prevented adoption.

(2) **FPGA Capacity.** Common ASIC structures, such as CAMs and multi-ported RAMs, map poorly to FPGA fabrics [24], making it difficult to host large ASIC designs on FPGAs.

(3) **Ease of Use.** To avoid partitioning across multiple FPGAs, previous work focused on efficiently mapping more of the target to a single FPGA. The abstract, multithreaded models these simulators typically employ can be more difficult to implement than the machines they model, greatly undermining their usability. This complexity limits configurability, forcing users to modify a sophisticated piece of RTL to make larger changes. Furthermore, these abstract models must, like their software counterparts, be validated and calibrated, making them even more laborious to use.

2.4 Recent Technological Advances

Even as Moore's law wanes, FPGA capacity continues to scale. The largest FPGAs have over 50 MiB of BRAM and millions of logic cells. As they have scaled, FPGAs have become more heterogeneous, adding features that make them better hosts for full-system simulators. Both Intel and Xilinx sell FPGAs with embedded microprocessors, making it easier to co-simulate tightly coupled hardware and software models. Modern FPGAs include dedicated DRAM controllers that support memory bandwidths rivaling those of ASICs.

Lower cost and increased on-chip integration have also made FPGAs more accessible to researchers. Not only are commercial off-the-shelf development boards cheaper and more full-featured, FPGAs are now available as a cloud service [1]. Where in the past academics would have to purchase their own FPGAs to reproduce published experiments, instead, it is now possible to spin up identical simulations on FPGAs in the cloud. This development promises to foster more collaboration around FPGA-accelerated simulation.

2.5 Usability Through Automation

While the trends described in the previous section solve the *availability* and *FPGA capacity* challenges, usability remains a problem. Previous work [7, 12] has shown that much of an FPGA-accelerated simulator can be automatically generated from source RTL. This